The Italian American Experience:
An Encyclopedia

The Italian American Experience:
An Encyclopedia

Editors
Salvatore J. LaGumina
Frank J. Cavaioli
Salvatore Primeggia
Joseph A. Varacalli

GARLAND PUBLISHING, INC.
A MEMBER OF THE TAYLOR & FRANCIS GROUP
New York & London
2000

Published in 2000 by
Garland Publishing Inc.
A Member of the Taylor & Francis Group
19 Union Square West
New York, NY 10003

10 9 8 7 6 5 4 3 2 1

Library of Congress Cataloging-in-Publication Data
The Italian American experience : an encyclopedia / editors, Salvatore J.
    LaGumina ... [et al.].
        p.   cm. -- (Garland reference library of the humanities; vol. 1535)
    Includes bibliographical references and index.
    ISBN 0-8153-0713-6 (alk paper)
    1. Italian Americans Encyclopedias.   I. LaGumina, Salvatore John,
1928– .   II. Series.
E184.I8I673   1999
973'.0451--dc21   99-38629
                                                                      CIP

Printed on acid-free, 250-year-life paper
Manufactured in the United States of America

Contents

Introduction

The Italian American Experience: An Encyclopedia represents the first attempt to provide a truly comprehensive encyclopedic account of the Italian experience in the United States. Over five years in the making, the more than four hundred entries contain much more than the standard set of biographies; the volume includes substantial analyses of topics relating to the arts, history, religion, Italian organizations and groups, archival depositories, and other resource material, literature, pop culture, social science/politics, sports, wartime military and home front activities, and science and technology. Each area is treated both in general, thematic essays and pieces devoted to specific aspects of a subject. Entries include suggested bibliographic references for further study.

One hundred sixty-six scholars contributed their expertise to the project, many of them members—as are the four main editors—of the American Italian Historical Association (AIHA), the only professional organization devoted solely to studying objectively the Italian American experience. These connections and the general familiarity with the key scholars in the field served the editors well in assembling an outstanding and active advisory board, in soliciting many useful and exciting suggestions, and in recruiting the leading writers in Italian American scholarship.

The major purpose in any encyclopedia is to amass knowledge and information, and this is precisely what the editors have endeavored to do. However, it is also true that all scholarship comes from a distinctive point of view. It is important to point out that the interpretive versions that may be apparent in some essays are the sole responsibility of authors. The policy of the editors in this respect was quite ecumenical; readers will find in this volume intellectual work that is based on quite divergent philosophical perspectives, thereby reflecting prevailing diversity in the field of Italian American studies.

It is not customary for projects of this scope to emanate, even in part, from the community college sector. It is therefore especially important to thank the administration of Nassau Community College—and especially its president, Dr. Sean A. Fanelli—for the support and encouragement provided. It stands as a validation of the college's commitment to an intellectually rigorous and honest understanding of multicultural education. Among the indispensable assistance afforded the editors was the service of Patricia Forte, a tireless and competent administrative aide. Mention should be made of the hospitality, and courtesies extended, by the Nassau Community College Department of History, the Library Department, and the Computer Laboratory.

As a final note, the editors want to make the obvious admission that *The Italian American Experience: An Encyclopedia* is, as is all scholarship, a provisional piece of work. On the one hand, we are proud of the accomplishment that the completed work represents. We hope it contributes to the cause of scholarship in Italian Americana and serves to promote a realistic awareness of the Italian contribution to American civilization. On the other hand, we know that no work is perfect. We both expect and hope that future scholars can further perfect and build upon the information and insight contained within this work.

This encyclopedia is dedicated to all Italian immigrants who came to American shores to build a better life. It is dedicated to their progeny also, who continue to validate the dream of their ancestors.

Salvatore J. LaGumina
Frank J. Cavaioli
Salvatore Primeggia
Joseph A. Varacalli

Contributors

Richard Alba
Department of Sociology
State University of New York, Albany

Carol Bonomo Albright
Department of English
University of Rhode Island

Emelise Aleandri
John J. Calandra Italian American Institute
City University of New York

John Andreozzi
Author
St. Louis Park, Minn.

Diane T. Aquila
Author
Steubenville, Ohio

Dominic A. Aquila
Franciscan University of Steubenville

Mario Aste
Department of Foreign Languages
University of Massachusetts, Lowell

Patrizia Audenino
Universita di Torino, Italy

Carlo Avvisati
Author
Naples, Italy

Alan Balboni
Department of History
Community College of Southern Nevada

Helen Barolini
Author
Hastings-on-the-Hudson, N.Y.

Paul Basile
Editor
Fra Noi, Chicago

Giuseppe Battista
Department of Foreign Languages
Suffolk Community College, N.Y.

Valentine Belfiglio
Department of History
Texas Women's University

Samuel J. Bellardo
Opera International
Princeton, N.J.

Peter L. Belmonte
United States Air Force

Joseph J. Bentivegna
Author
Loreto, Pa.

Joanna Bevacqua
Library Department
Borough of Manhattan Community College

Robert Hoyt Block
Department of History
Nassau Community College, N.Y.

Sando Bologna
Author
Waterbury, Conn.

Mary Jo Bona
Department of English
Gonzaga University
Spokane, Wash.

Carol J. Bradley
University of Florence, Italy

John M. Brindisi
Author
Northport, N.Y.

Mary Elizabeth Brown
Department of History
Marymount College, N.Y.

Geoffrey S. Cahn
Yeshiva High School, N.Y.

Dominic Candeloro
Governors State University
University Park, Ill.

Philip V. Cannistraro
Department of History
City University of New York

Rocco Caporale
Department of Sociology
St. John's University, N.Y.

Sharon DeBartolo Carmack
Author
Sima, Colo.

Betty Boyd Caroli
Department of History
Kingsborough Community College, N.Y.

Nancy N. Cassella
New Haven Colonial Historical Society, Conn.

Camille Cauti
Author
New York, N.Y.

Frank J. Cavaioli
Professor Emeritus
State University of New York, Farmingdale

Teresa Cerasuola
Author
Huntington, N.Y.

Catherine Cerrone
Historical Society of Western Pennsylvania

Rita Ciresi
University of South Florida

William S. Clements
Arkansas State University

Maureen M. Daddona
Department of Biology
Nassau Community College, N.Y.

Peter R. D'Agostino
Stonehill College
North Easton, Mass.

Anthony D'Angelo
Long Island University, N.Y.

William V. D'Antonio
Department of Sociology
Catholic University of America
Washington, D.C.

Angela D. Danzi
Department of Sociology
State University of New York, Farmingdale

Louisa Del Giudice
University of the City of Los Angeles

Donald J. D'Elia
Department of History
State University of New York, New Paltz

Gina Dell'Aquila
National Italian American Foundation
Washington, D.C.

Giovanna P. Del Negro
Indiana University

Judith N. DeSena
Department of Sociology
St. John's University, N.Y.

Paul J. Devendittis
Department of History
Nassau Community College, N.Y.

Denise Mangieri DiCarlo
Washington Irving High School, N.Y.

John Louis DiGaetani
Department of English
Hofstra University
Hempstead, N.Y.

James J. Divita
Department of History
Marian College
Indianapolis, Ind.

William S. Egelman
Department of Sociology
Iona College, N.Y.

Nicholas Joseph Falco
Author
Bronx, N.Y.

Sean A. Fanelli
President
Nassau Community College, N.Y.

William Feigelman
Department of Sociology
Nassau Community College, N.Y.

Marilyn Ferrari
World Bocce Association
Bensenville, Ill.

Philip Ferrari
World Bocce Association
Bensenville, Ill.

Carlo Ferroni
Department of History
Ashland College, Ohio

Joseph Fioravanti
Professor Emertitus
Technical College of Delhi, N.Y.

Mario Fratti
Professor Emeritus
Lehman College, N.Y.

Donna Gabaccia
Department of History
University of North Carolina

Charles Gabriele
Author
Venice, Fla.

Richard Gambino
State University of New York, Stony Brook

Fred Gardaphé
Department of English
State University of New York, Stony Brook

Joseph Giordano
Ethnic and Mental Health Association
Bronxville, N.Y.

Paolo A. Giordano
Loyola University
Chicago, Ill.

Edvige Giunta
Jersey City State College, N.J.

Rose Basile Green
Author
Lafayette, Pa.

George Guida
City University of New York

Deanna Paoli Gumina
Museo Italo Americano
San Francisco, Calif.

Richard Hinshaw
Department of Political Science
Dowling College, N.Y.

Luciano J. Iorizzo
Department of History
State University of New York, Oswego

Irma B. Jaffe
Professor Emerita
Fordham University, N.Y.

Richard Juliani
Department of Sociology
Villanova University, Pa.

Mary C. Kalfatovic
Author
Arlington, Va.

Blossom S. Kirschenbaum
Brown University, R.I.

Jerome Krase
Department of Sociology
Brooklyn College, N.Y.

Suzanne Nicoletti Krase
Brooklyn Hospital, N.Y.

Alan M. Kraut
Department of History
American University
Washington, D.C.

Marisa Labozzetta
Smith College
Northampton, Mass.

Charles La Cerra
Department of History
College of Staten Island, N.Y.

Salvatore J. LaGumina
Professor Emeritus
Nassau Community College, N.Y.

Vincent A. Lapomarda
Department of History
College of the Holy Cross
Worchester, Mass.

John La Puma
North Suburban Clinic
Chicago, Ill.

Michael La Sorte
Professor Emeritus
State University of New York, Brockport

John A. Lent (Zinghini)
Temple University
Philadelphia, Pa.

Stefano Luconi
University of Florence, Italy

Dianne Francesconi Lyon
Montgomery College, Md.

Russell M. Magnaghi
Department of History
Northern Michigan University

Adele Maiello
University of Genoa, Italy

Frances M. Malpezzi
Arkansas State University

Jerre Mangione
Professor Emeritus
University of Pennsylvania

Margherita Marchione
Department of Foreign Languages
Villa Walsh
Morristown, N.J.

Cesare Marino
Smithsonian Institution
Washington, D.C.

Phylis Cancilla Martinelli
Department of History
St. Mary's College, California

Roseanne Martorella
William Paterson College
Wayne, N.J.

Edward Albert Maruggi
Rochester Institute of Technology, N.Y.

Joseph Maselli
American Italian Renaissance Foundation
New Orleans, La.

Dominic R. Massaro
Supreme Court of New York

Mary Nona McGreal
Author
Chicago, Ill.

Elizabeth G. Messina
Psychologist
New York, N.Y.

Mario B. Mignone
Department of Foreign Languages
State University of New York, Stony Brook

Vincenzo Milione
John J. Calandra Italian American Institute
City University of New York

Marie Di Stefano Miller
Opera International
Princeton, N.J.

Philip M. Montesano
San Francisco Community College

Gary R. Mormino
Department of History
University of South Florida

Dan Morrison
Author
New York, N.Y.

Franco Mulas
Department of Literature
University of Sassari
Sardinia, Italy

Julia Volpelletto Nakamura
Author
Nutley, N.J.

Louise Napolitano-Carman
Department of English
State University of New York, Farmingdale

Christopher Newton
University of Singapore

Nina daVinci Nichols
Rutgers University, N.J.

Philip F. Notarianni
Utah State Historical Society

Remigio U. Pane
Department of Foreign Languages
Rutgers University, N.J.

Nishan Parlakian
John Jay College of Criminal Justice, N.Y.

Ciro C. Poppiti, III
Author
New York, N.Y.

Jack Nusan Porter
The Spencer Institute
Newton, Mass.

Salvatore Primeggia
Department of Sociology
Adelphi University
Garden City, N.Y.

Stanislao G. Pugliese
Department of History
Hofstra University
Hempstead, N.Y.

Olga Ragusa
Columbia University, N.Y.

Richard Renoff
Department of Sociology
Nassau Community College, N.Y.

Marco Rimanelli
St. Leo's College, Fla.

Bridget Oteri Robinson
John J. Calandra Italian American Institute
City University of New York

Anne T. Romano
Department of Sociology
Nassau Community College, N.Y.

Vincent S. Romano
Commission for Social Justice
Order Sons of Italy in America

Ernest E. Rossi
Department of Political Science
Western Michigan University

Alfred Rotondaro
National Italian American Foundation
Washington, D.C.

Elissa Ruffino
National Italian American Foundation
Washington, D.C.

John Paul Russo
Department of English
University of Miami, Fla.

Lisa Jo Sagolla
Department of Theater and Dance
Columbia University, N.Y.

Joseph J. Saladino
Supreme Court of New York

Frank A. Salamone
Department of History
Iona College, N.Y.

Aldo E. Salerno
Department of History
Nassau Community College, N.Y.

Betty Santangelo
New York, N.Y.

Patricia Santangelo
New York, N.Y.

Carmela E. Santoro
Rhode Island

Joseph Scafetta, Jr.
Author
Arlington, Va.

Vincenza Scarpaci
Department of History
Sonoma State University, Calif.

Joseph V. Scelsa
John J. Calandra Italian American Institute
City University of New York

Rose D. Scherini
Author
Kensington, Calif.

Frederick J. Simonelli
Mount St. Mary's College
Los Angeles, Calif.

Regina Soria
Art Department
College of Notre Dame
Baltimore, Md.

Frank M. Sorrentino
Department of History
St. Francis College, N.Y.

Nicholas A. Spilotro
Italian American Labor Council, N.Y.

Dennis J. Starr
Rider College
Lawrenceville, N.J.

Frank D. Stella
National Italian American Foundation
Washington, D.C.

Edward C. Stibili
Calumet College of St. Joseph
Whiting, Ind.

William E. Studwell
Department of Music
Northern Illinois University

Mary Louise Sullivan
President Emeritus
Cabrini College
Radnor, Pa.

Linda Santarelli Susman
Communications Department
Nassau Community College, N.Y.

Anthony Julian Tamburri
Foreign Language and Literatures
Purdue University, Ind.

Delfina Tersigni
Hofstra University
Hempstead, N.Y.

Salvatore Testaverde
Author
Georgetown, Md.

Lydio F. Tomasi
Director
Center for Migration Studies, N.Y.

Nancy K. Torrieri
Bureau of the Census

Rosario J. Tosiello
Pine Manor College
Chestnut Hill, Mass.

Donald Tricarico
Department of Sociology
Queensborough Community College, N.Y.

Angelo Tripicchio
Library Department
Kingsborough Community College, N.Y.

Joseph A. Tursi
Department of Foreign Languages
State University of New York, Stony Brook

Joseph A. Varacalli
Department of Sociology
Nassau Community College, N.Y.

Dianne C. Vecchio
Furman University
Greenville, S.C.

Rudolph J. Vecoli
Director, Immigration History Center
University of Minnesota

Gaetano L. Vincitorio
Department of History
St. John's University, N.Y.

David Anthony Witter
Fra Noi, Chicago

Janet Worral
Department of History
University of Northern Colorado

Charles A. Zappia
Department of History
San Diego Mesa College, Calif.

A

Abate, Catherine M.
See LAW ENFORCEMENT

Actors and Actresses
See MOVIE ACTORS AND ACTRESSES

Agriculture
At the beginning of the twentieth century, observers of immigration wondered why so many Italian immigrants from agricultural backgrounds, estimated in 1909 as 67 percent of the total 1.2 million Italian working population in the United States, seemed indifferent to opportunities in rural America. One contemporary suggested that these immigrants chose to work in urban-industrial centers because they could save more money than working as regular farm laborers. Others pointed out that the typical American crops, agricultural methods, and rural residential patterns appeared strange to *contadini* (peasants) unfamiliar with large farm machinery, chemical fertilizers, and scattered settlements.

Because some immigrants supplemented their agricultural income with urban or industrial employment, and official enumerators listed only the "major" occupations, the numbers of Italians working the land was probably larger. For example, although approximately 156 Italians in Occidental, California, in 1900 were listed in the United States census as holding one job, most worked different jobs throughout the year, including lumberman, charcoal maker, tanbark peeler, and agricultural laborer.

Although only a small percentage of Italians farmed in 1909, they had a diverse and significant impact upon American agriculture and society. In 1905 Eliot Lord commented that "[t]here is not a single one of the cities of this country yet reached by the Italians where there is available market land nearby that is not now receiving vegetables and fruits as the produce of Italian labor." Even within urban boundaries immigrants went to the outlying areas in search of cheap land. Transplanted *contadini* patiently cultivated backyards and vacant lots with *basilico* (basil), tomatoes, peppers, and other items important to their diet.

Italian immigrant farmers and farm laborers settled across the United States. They worked as sugarcane harvesters in Louisiana; berry pickers in New Jersey; grape growers in Arkansas and California; cotton growers in Texas and Mississippi; and truck farmers in Minnesota, Colorado, New York, Oregon, and Rhode Island. For many, the transition to farming was gradual. Railroad construction or mining often served as catalysts that transported immigrants into areas they identified as suitable for farming.

In addition to working on the land, many Italian Americans had subsidiary occupations related to agriculture. Italian immigrant workers in fruit-packing houses, canneries, creameries, and wineries, and Italian fruit and vegetable peddlers, wholesalers, and retailers all participated in and extended this infrastructure of ethnic and generic food production. One study suggested that the major collective role of Italians in California agriculture was that of providing a substantial part of the wage labor in the state's commercialized agriculture (vineyards and wineries) and its satellite food-processing industries.

In Italy most agricultural workers toiled

on large estates owned by absentee landowners or traveled throughout Italy picking crops. In the United States this pattern of seasonal labor brought thousands (with estimates of fifteen thousand to twenty thousand) of immigrants each year both from small towns in Sicily and from urban/industrial areas such as Chicago, New Orleans, and St. Louis to Louisiana's sugarcane region for the annual harvest, or *zuccarata*. From 1880 to 1910 sugar planters and state immigration officials encouraged the recruitment of labor to harvest the crop. These immigrants might work on railroad construction or other outdoor labor elsewhere for part of the year and come to Louisiana in October to harvest and process the cane.

Italian agricultural laborers also worked as seasonal workers at canneries and their farms in New York State. Most of the seasonal workers came from northern New York cities each year with their families. The manager of one of the farms owned by a cannery established a system that reinforced immigrant customs. He preferred to hire families rather than individuals so that the entire family would work together. He also appointed a committee of four or five of the men to supervise daily upkeep in the workers' quarters, which the company supplied. Such progressive management attracted Italians to seek positions for the summer months.

In southern New Jersey and Delaware, Italian immigrants from Philadelphia, Trenton, and Camden harvested berries and vegetables, with estimates of six thousand to ten thousand coming to Hammonton and Winslow townships each year to work the land.

Some migrant workers used their earnings to supplement their day laborer jobs in urban areas. While wages in the canning companies were probably higher than on railroad section gangs or construction, agricultural wages did not compare favorably with wages earned from unskilled "pick and shovel" endeavors. Over time, the numbers of Italian agricultural workers declined as they found more permanent employment. However, as late as 1940 an estimated five thousand Italian migrants continued to be employed in New Jersey.

Other seasonal workers applied their savings to purchase small farms for themselves. Depending on the location, some members of the family would continue to work at nonagricultural pursuits to supplement the family income and to pay off mortgages. In Hammonton, New Jersey, 82 percent of the Italian landowners worked on some "outside" employment from one to ten years until a living could be made off the land. Regardless of the location, Italian immigrant farmers earned recognition for their dedication to hard, monotonous labor. Whether they grew cotton in Texas, strawberries in Louisiana and New Jersey, or grapes and vegetables in Arkansas and California, they devoted time and energy far beyond what most native American and older immigrant farmers would endure.

Government officials gave mixed reports on immigrants who overrode American farming customs and practices with their Old World agrarian traditions. For example, farmers in Vineland and Hammonton, New Jersey, tended to use every inch of land for crop cultivation. On the one hand, government reports criticized the lack of amenities such as front lawns and flower beds as evidence of resistance to adopting "typical" American customs; on the other hand, these same observers praised the Italians' intensive style of agriculture that used all available space to produce higher yields per acre than their neighbors.

The Immigration Commission Report of 1911 concluded:

> Unless settled in communities, the Italians have not proved successful pioneer farmers; neither are the most of them engaged in extensive agriculture, where many acres and considerable equipment are necessary. In almost every instance, they seem to succeed best when they live close together, cultivate small farms and raise crops that require hand labor rather than expensive complicated machinery . . . the primary reason for the Italians' choice of trucking and vegetable gardening preference to diversified farming is a social one: [they] can have both land and neighbors.

The commission maintained that Italians had introduced little that was new to American agriculture and that they learned farm methods by observing their neighbors. While observing that some immigrants were slower at adapting to innovations in crops, methods, or machinery, this report also concluded that Italian farmers seemed skilled at developing cooperative marketing and purchasing systems.

Studies by government-employed agents reported that colonies of Italian farmers, without exception in the northern United States and elsewhere, had enriched and improved the land and increased the agricultural wealth of area neighborhoods. Finally, the commission praised Italians on the land for showing more interest and participation in community concerns such as good roads and schools than their urban/industrial conationals. Such civic involvement seemed to bring them closer to mainstream America.

By 1920 approximately thirteen thousand to eighteen thousand foreign-born farm operators (out of a total of 140,667) in the United States were Italians, with the greatest concentrations in California, New York, New Jersey, Louisiana, and Colorado. Italian immigrant populations ranked first numerically in urban areas and fourth in rural areas. Success of farming enterprises depended on a number of factors: the price and availability of land, soil quality, capital outlay required for specific crops, sufficient labor for harvesting, accessibility to markets, and, most often, opportunity for "outside" employment to supplement farm income.

California had the largest numbers of Italian farmers and farm laborers: about half of its sixty thousand Italian immigrant population in 1900 were engaged in agriculture. Northern Italian immigrants arrived at a time when California was newly opened to American settlement with opportunities not available elsewhere in the United States. And, because the expense of travel and the distance involved precluded seasonal migration to California, the majority of immigrants tended to stay for longer periods of time. That the first Italians flocked to California gold fields as miners, then remained as merchants and farmers to "mine the miners," reflects a pattern of ethnic enterprise. Genoese and Piedmontese were prominent in the Mother Lode region as dairymen and truck gardeners.

The largest numbers of Italians in California agriculture were in the packing houses and canneries of San Jose, San Francisco, and Fresno, and in the wineries throughout the San Joaquin and Napa Valleys. The Immigration Commission found that Italians and Greeks combined were the most numerous foreign workers in these facilities. The agents noted that workers were usually supplied by bosses or *padrones* (labor brokers), who also often served as foremen supervising immigrants in the cannery. This pattern also operated in some eastern canneries.

In California, and elsewhere in the United States, most of the Italian farmers began as tenants, accumulating capital until they were able to purchase land. Many used the partnership system to pool or extend resources in the leasing or purchase of land.

Nicola Marini came to California during the gold rush, and, after prospecting in gold country, settled in San Francisco, where he and two friends grew vegetables. In 1855 they resettled out to the Bayshore district, where they cultivated strawberries as well as vegetables. Other Italians joined them and, by the 1860s, Italian truck farming extended from San Francisco southward into San Mateo County.

Along with the more common types of garden vegetables, the Italians grew crops new to California, including artichoke, eggplant, bell pepper, oregano, marjoram, fennel, and rosemary. At first these items supplied Italian and French customers in San Francisco, but they were soon in demand by all segments of the market.

Colonies of Italian farmers established a community life that reinforced immigrant expansion into agriculture. Throughout California, most immigrants engaged in intensive farming that required much hard labor for which they usually employed other Italians, often recent arrivals who came from the same areas of Italy. This network of mutual immigrant employers/laborers channeled workers to Italian-owned farms, where they found a familiar ethnic *ambiente,* receiving board and lodging, as a rule, with the farmer's family, in addition to their wages.

While California agriculture did not use as extensively the *padrone*/labor boss system that pervaded Italian communities in the east, Italians in California experienced another form of compatriot exploitation. Although they usually worked for Italian growers, they were among the lowest paid and worked the longest hours of any immigrant groups.

Italian farmers also developed cooperative marketing techniques that produced profits while creating a strong ethnic cohesiveness. Organized by Italians in 1874, the San Francisco Gardeners and Ranchers' Association maintained the Colombo Market occupied mainly by Italian growers. Members controlled eight thousand acres of land worked by twelve hundred laborers who first supplied produce to storekeepers and commission men,

A

then sold to the public. Genoese dominated the produce market scene early on, but the Lucchese (Tuscans), local peddlers and greengrocers, came to dominate distribution to the consumer.

In the 1920s San Francisco's Italian farmers began to ship their produce to eastern markets. This pattern was maintained until the 1950s, when the rapid southward spread of San Francisco and its suburbs forced land prices so high that the farmers could not afford to stay.

Many prominent Italians in California came from agricultural-related backgrounds or launched their own business careers in such enterprises. Marco Fontana, an Italian immigrant from near Genoa, became co-owner in 1868 of the fourth largest food cannery in San Francisco, which employed mostly Italian workers. By 1916 Fontana's Del Monte brand was produced in canneries throughout the state. The father of Bank of America's (originally Bank of Italy) founder, Amadeo P. Giannini, was a vegetable gardener in San Jose; and Giannini's bank financed many Italian agricultural enterprises.

Others like Joseph Maggio, the Petri (father Raffaleo and son Angelo) and Cella (brothers Giovanni Batista and Lorenzo) families, Joseph Di Giorgio, and the D'Arrigo brothers (Stephano and Andrea) started as retailers or wholesalers of produce and became large producers of agricultural products by vertically integrating production and marketing.

By 1910 the value of Italian-grown crops in California was sixty million dollars, including the production of Fontana's canneries. California Italians also participated in the shift to highly mechanized and large-scale vegetable operations. In 1940 Joseph Maggio, "Carrot King" of California, built a million-dollar operation in the Imperial Valley marketing carrots. He eventually ran an assembly line organization that dug, selected, tied, washed, iced, crated, and loaded up to forty-two railroad carloads of carrots per day.

While northern Italians outnumbered southern Italians in California, some of the larger success stories belong to Italians from southern Italy. Two D'Arrigo brothers from the province of Messina, Sicily, migrated before World War I, first settling in Boston. They invested in the California production of anise (fennel) and broccoli in 1925. Using seed from Italy and land they purchased near San Jose,

they developed the broccoli market. In 1928 they began advertising on Italian language programs and expanded out to English-speaking markets. Broccoli soon lost its designation as an "Italian vegetable."

Another Sicilian, Joseph Di Giorgio, started importing fruit from California for his fruit commission business in New York and Baltimore. In 1910 he purchased the Earl Fruit Company, a large distributor of California fresh fruit, and established extensive operations at Arvin near Bakersfield in 1910.

Di Giorgio increased his acreage into California and Florida. The fruits he produced were canned under the S & W label. In 1919 he purchased lumber mills in Oregon to produce fruit boxes. He also grew and transported grapes for the Italian Swiss Colony in exchange for a 37.5 percent interest in the firm. Later he acquired his own huge winery in Arvin, California. Like the D'Arrigos, much of the Di Giorgio business was family run. The pattern of a vertically integrated, highly diversified agricultural corporation that Di Giorgio established and pioneered came to be the typical one in the production of California fruits and vegetables. His firm became the largest producer of pears, apricots, grapes, and plums in the world.

Italian presence in California's wine industry has been prominent since the founding of the Italian Swiss Colony in 1881. As an observer stated: "One may assert that the present existence of the California wine industry is attributable to the activities of Italians and their descendants" who kept the industry going through Prohibition and the Great Depression by making sacramental wine, shipping fresh grapes, and developing wine by-products.

Elsewhere in the West Italian immigrants engaged in truck farming activities usually on the outskirts of cities. Italian immigrants were attracted to the excellent land around Seattle and Tacoma, which was cheaper than California and received more rainfall. As early as 1875 Genovese and Tuscani were supplying urban markets with vegetables, milk, poultry, and flowers. While some went into farming directly from Italy, most worked their way to Washington State as railroad section hands. By 1915 approximately two hundred Italian gardeners lived in and around Seattle. One truck farmer, Joe Desimone, purchased Pike Place Market, where many Italians operated stalls.

Similar patterns developed in Oregon on the outskirts of Portland and in Nevada along the Truckee Meadows outside Reno and along the Carson River near Dayton. In both states northern Italian immigrants settled in the 1860s or 1870s working as agricultural laborers or in the mines to save enough money to lease or buy small tracts of land.

Choice of crops varied according to region. While Italians in New Jersey, Louisiana, and Texas grew strawberries for the market, Japanese immigrants dominated this industry on the Pacific Coast. Time of arrival, the presence of other sources of ethnic labor, and market niches explain some of these variances.

Agricultural settlements outside Denver, Colorado, followed a different pattern. Both northern and southern Italians settled in separate colonies near this city in the 1890s. Most lived in the area for several years before they went into truck farming. The southern Italians originally came from farming areas in Basilicata. They raised vegetables and most peddled their produce through the streets of the city, each having his own route.

Although Denver offered supplemental work opportunities, these farmers spent all their time on their small properties, from ten to twenty acres. Entire families worked the land, and other Italian immigrants provided additional help as needed. Pleased with the contributions of Italians to the state's economy, the Colorado State Board of Immigration advertised in 1910 for Italian farmers to settle in the state. Many who responded to the call clustered around the farming community of Welby, north of Denver.

In the Midwest, the settlement of Genoa, Wisconsin, near La Crosse was another Italian immigrant success. Farmers from Piedmont arrived in 1860 to take government land that was rough, hilly, and forest covered. Before coming to Wisconsin, these immigrants had worked in South America and in the lead mines of Galena, Illinois. Some settlers took advantage of the homestead law and others paid five to ten dollars an acre. They cleared the land and planted crops of wheat, corn, rye, oats, and barley. After 1880, some added tobacco, clover, and dairy and beef cattle. In fact, many Italians owned stock in the creamery.

The unusual characteristics of the Genoa farm community conformed more closely to the expectations of native-born Americans. Here the immigrants engaged in general agriculture, raised crops typical to the region, used farm machinery, and adopted native rural residency patterns of land use and type of dwellings. This colony, and later the northern Italian settlements at South Glastonbury, Connecticut, and Tontitown, Arkansas, tended to set the standard by which all other Italian agricultural colonies with immigrants from southern Italy were judged.

It was Cumberland, Wisconsin, in 1909, a community of 250 Italian families from Aquilia, Campobasso, Calabria, and Catania, that more closely represented the common type of immigrant settlement where settlers supported their rural lifestyles with nonagricultural labor. In 1881 three large families, a stonecutter and his two brothers-in-law, came from Chicago to this area of wilderness, where they obtained cheap land but little opportunity for work.

Immigrants came to the area when the Omaha Railroad began to construct a line in Cumberland. Once the road was finished some laborers stayed and used railroad shanties as homes. Population increased as other families, mostly from Chicago, where they had worked in various unskilled occupations or in railway construction gangs, moved into the area. They built their houses with lumber from their wooded acres, and most worked on railroad section gangs in order to accumulate money to purchase land.

While the men worked on the railroads, their families cultivated the land and harvested hay, potatoes, peas, barley, and corn. Each family had a garden that provided a year's supply of vegetables. During the winter the men sold firewood cut from their land or worked as lumberjacks. With the establishment of several canneries and processing plants in the area, some immigrant farmers cultivated cash crops. A few families eventually acquired large farms.

Italian truck farming characterized immigrant agriculture in other sections of the Midwest, such as around Cincinnati, Cleveland, and Chicago. Most of these growers came from southern Italy. In Montana and the Dakotas, Italian immigrants rejected the dry farming of the treeless plains; instead, some became truck farmers outside Billings, Missoula, Anaconda, and Great Falls. In Kansas, Italians avoided wheat farming, which demanded substantial capital investment and unfamiliar techniques. Some operated small

A

truck farms outside Topeka and Kansas City as a supplement to other employment. Wherever there was a place to have a garden, Italians raised food for their family.

Although few immigrants from southern and eastern Europe settled in the southern United States, many of the Italians living there earned their livelihood from agriculture. In 1900 Louisiana had 636 Italian farmers and 3,651 Italian farm laborers. Texas had 484 Italian farmers and 322 Italian farm laborers.

Most Italians in Louisiana were Sicilians who came to harvest the sugarcane crop each year. Some stayed, sent for their families, and became tenants on sugar or cotton plantations. Few Italians moved from tenant to independent sugar or cotton planter because of high land prices and large-scale operations, but many immigrants became small local specialty farmers or merchants.

The communities of Independence, Hammond, and Amite City attracted Italians who first came from New Orleans as strawberry pickers each season. In 1890 the first Italian farm laborer settled in Independence and was followed by others who worked as sharecroppers and tenants, saving money to purchase land offered at low prices by local lumber companies. Native-born American farmers considered these cutover and swampy lands worthless. By 1909 some 250 immigrant families grew berries in Tangipahoa Parish on farms of five to thirty acres.

Italians dominated the Independence Farmers Association formed in 1909 as a marketing cooperative. This organization provided financial and marketing services for members, and the organization created the foundation for an overall national Italian identity as individuals from different towns in Italy (both Sicily and the mainland) participated. Italians also became prominent in the banking community. By 1926 they owned a majority of Independence Bank stock, which had a seal embossed "American-Italian Bank."

Sicilian agricultural immigrants also developed a truck farming community in Kenner, ten miles west of New Orleans. They harvested three crops of vegetables a year from the same fields. Here they replicated the residential patterns typical of their *paesi* (fellow townspeople). Starting as renters, they first purchased house lots close together and then bought a few acres of land at some distance from their houses on which they raised their garden crops.

Italian truck farmers in Louisiana were praised for the modern scientific methods they used to produce higher yields, and were regarded as "models in the agricultural art and splendid object lessons in progressive, profitable farming."

Planned immigrant farm communities also settled in the South. In 1893 an Italian Waldensian minister negotiated an agreement with an agent of the Morgantown Land Improvement Company for land, later known as Valdese, in the mountainous area of North Carolina, where he settled with colonists from the province of Torino in northern Italy.

In 1908 Valdese had fifty families with 250 people and although the soil was poor, the Italians proved superior cultivators to the native farmers in the area. The average immigrant farmer maintained from fifteen to twenty acres and produced a good living for his family. In addition, two of the colonists established a hosiery mill, which employed about forty people, giving some supplemental income to the residents.

All the colonists had taken out at least their first naturalization papers within six years. As grape growers, practically all of them took a lively interest in any political activity regarding the "liquor question"—a hotly debated temperance issue.

The liquor question played a strong influence in the welfare of another North Carolina colony. In 1905 Hugh MacRae's company sent an agent to recruit settlers from the province of Venezia near Rovigo to establish a community in Pender County, New York. MacRae sought northern Italians specifically because he believed they were superior to immigrants from southern Italy and also to appease North Carolinians who were suspicious and somewhat prejudiced against newcomers from southern and eastern Europe. His agent, Ernesto Valenti, offered prospects a ten-acre farm from which they would clear the land of trees and drain the swamps. Although the contract required approximately two hundred dollars down payment and allowed 50 percent of the settlers to live on a farm with no down payment at all, fewer than twelve families out of approximately eighty who settled over time received deeds to their land—most remained as tenants or sharecroppers.

Immigrants sold wood cut from their ten acres to the company and also worked at ten cents an hour on company land, digging drainage ditches and cutting trees. By 1908 the colonists had established a cooperative store, a blacksmith shop, and large outdoor ovens for bread making. And, as the company divided the town into city blocks, the immigrants named the streets and christened the town St. Helena.

Although Italian officials in New York had promoted viniculture for St. Helena, this enterprise had no potential in an area that adopted Prohibition in 1909. Prohibition undermined wine production, and the coming of World War I lured Italian families away.

In Arkansas, two examples of organized agricultural settlements, one a failure, the other a success, illustrate the difficulties that were encountered when establishing and maintaining such communities. When Austin Corbin of New York, the owner of Sunnyside Plantation in Chicot County, southeastern Arkansas, decided to employ Italian laborers, he made an agreement with the mayor of Rome to recruit workers. A group of 125 northern Italian families (from Venezia and the Marches) arrived in 1895.

Disappointed in the conditions and the unhealthy climate, which harbored malaria, many families returned to Italy. In 1898 a new management company took control and sent for more immigrants. In 1909 approximately 120 families of 576 persons lived on the plantation. The immigrants rented the land rather than sharecropped. This cash approach en-abled them to select better quality land that produced a higher yield of cotton. They kept their living expenses to a minimum by supplementing their diet with vegetables they grew in their gardens, which aided them in earning a year-end profit.

In 1910 a new company changed the plantation's policy when it eliminated the rental arrangement and insisted that everyone sharecrop. The Italian tenant farmers rejected this idea and slowly deserted Sunnyside, moving to the vicinity of Lake Village and buying their own land.

Some of the disappointed settlers at Sunnyside left the plantation in 1898 with Father Pietro Bandini, an Italian priest who had come to Arkansas to provide spiritual guidance. Searching for a healthier climate, he traveled for two months with a group of thirty-five families to Washington County in the Ozarks of northern Arkansas and arranged to purchase eight hundred acres with money the men had earned from part-time work along their route. The uncleared land had been given by the government to Civil War veterans, who were subsequently unable to develop the area.

Families drew lots for individual parcels of land, which came to about ten acres. The immigrants called the new community Tontitown to honor Enrico de Tonti, an Italian who explored the Mississippi Valley in the 1680s.

Italian farm workers in Vineland, New Jersey. Entire families of Italian immigrants labored on the land on truck farms such as this, where they supplied urban centers with fruits and vegetables. Courtesy Center for Migration Studies.

Most of the men worked in Oklahoma coal mines or nearby railroads to make payments on the land, while the women tended the gardens and cultivated the crops.

Early on, Father Bandini realized that the farmers needed a cash crop to market. Apples were tried first, and then, after disease infected the trees, grapes. Soil analysis showed that Concord grapes were most suitable for the location, and Father Bandini sent back to Italy for grapevines. He also persuaded the Kansas City/Memphis Railroad to connect Tontitown to market destinations.

Besides orchard fruit and grapes, early vegetables were cultivated in the rows between the trees or vines and shipped to northern cities. With the long open seasons, farmers grew two or three crops of the same vegetables. Then they would plant nitrogen-producing crops—such as cow peas—to use as fodder for the cattle and to replenish the soil. By 1921, four years after Bandini's death, Welch's Grape Juice Company opened a plant in nearby Springdale.

In Texas, Italian immigrants developed prosperous farm communities. Italians came to Bryan, located about eighty miles from Houston, as laborers on the Houston and Texas Railroad in 1880. When the road was completed, the company offered incentives for the immigrants to work as sharecroppers in order to eventually buy farm land in Bryan.

Earlier native American, Bohemian (Czech), and German farmers rejected this land because it flooded and was considered too heavy for cotton. This led the way for Sicilian immigrants to purchase land cheaply and increase their holdings to over three thousand acres. Cultivating their crops with their entire families, they kept production costs down and by intensive labor produced yields of cotton production per acre that exceeded that of their neighbors.

Near Dickinson, outside Galveston, about 155 southern Italian families ran truck farms in 1909. Most owned their own farms and raised vegetables and strawberries. The settlers first worked as sharecroppers to earn enough money to purchase land. The majority came directly from Sicily to Dickinson. Other families moved there from Galveston. As native American farmers sold their property, at a profit, to the Italians, the immigrants constituted the largest group in Dickinson. Four Italian stores practically controlled the trade of the town and were patronized by both Italians and Americans.

In some communities store owners initiated settlements by purchasing land and then encouraging friends and family to farm the acreage. An Italian merchant named Bozza who ran a store in Nashville, Tennessee, purchased a large tract of land and then wrote to Italy in 1876 for families to settle. These immigrant farmers came from Udine in northern Italy. On farms ranging from twenty to sixty acres they raised garden truck and small fruits. They sold all their produce at stands in the marketplace in Nashville. By 1909 all the immigrants owned their land and had adopted so many American customs that they were almost indistinguishable from other older farm groups like the Germans.

In 1909 Vineland, New Jersey, had the largest single colony of Italian farmers in the United States with 950 families. In 1873 a land developer, Charles Landis, negotiated with the editor of *L'Echo D'Italia* in New York to advertise for immigrant farmers and sent agents to Italy to recruit settlers who contracted for land at 6 percent interest.

In order to pay off their debt, the immigrants worked for American neighbors, and whole families picked berries on a seasonal basis. Some worked on the railroad or in mills, glass works, and factories. The settlers cleared the swampy land and raised grapes and truck crops. By the second year nearly everyone made a living from the farm and met payments by day labor. Although Italians learned farming methods from their American neighbors, their family workforce produced higher yields per acre through intensive labor.

The immigrants introduced Italian beans and peppers. With farms averaging thirty acres, about three-fourths of which contained orchards, the Italians produced about nine-tenths of the area's strawberries and supplied the local juice factory with 25 percent of their grapes.

Although Italians in Vineland did not participate in a cooperative association, they did own 80 percent of stock in a canning company they incorporated in 1909, and they enjoyed a rich social and cultural life. By 1885 the community had two churches and good public schools.

In nearby Hammonton, Neapolitan and Sicilian immigrants created another farm community. The two groups lived in different parts of town with little dissension between them. (Residential delineation was common, as in Walla Walla, Washington, where Milanese farmers lived separately from the Calabrese, and in Bryan, Texas, where settlers from different Sicilian villages lived on opposite sides of the river.)

In 1867 Matteo Campanella, a native of Gesso, Sicily, came to Hammonton to work for an Italian farmer and purchased five acres. Soon other Gesso farmers followed. Other immigrants came first to Hammonton as seasonal harvesters as early as 1877. Some stayed to buy cheap land, which they cleared of pines. Others purchased land from the native farmers who had died or retired.

Farms in Hammonton averaged twenty acres, about the maximum for one person to cultivate. Berries (strawberries, raspberries) constituted the major crop, but sweet potatoes and white potatoes were also grown. While the Italians modeled their berry cultivation after that of native farmers, the immigrant method of vineyard planting was, in turn, adopted by the Americans. Italians participated in four cooperative marketing associations in the area. Colony of Fruit Growers, founded in 1892, was exclusively Italian and Italians served on the boards of the other cooperatives. Many Italians were shareholders also in building and loan associations.

Further evidence of self-motivation by Italian American farmers occurred in New York, where Sicilian immigrants founded a community in Fredonia. Christenzo Seragosa and a friend first arrived in 1894 to work in Fredonia's cannery. Local hostility toward the Italians made it difficult for them to find housing near the factory. Nevertheless, in a year they gained general acceptance and opened the door for other Sicilian families. The immigrants recognized that the surrounding land was suitable for grapes. By 1909 some twelve hundred Italians lived in Fredonia, and their vineyards set the standard of farming for that vicinity.

At Canastota in central New York, about fifty Italian families transformed uncleared and undrained land into productive acreage. Before arriving in Canastota, most of these immigrants worked as pick and shovel men, railroad section men, and construction laborers in Syracuse, Utica, Cortland, Buffalo, or New York. Some continued to work on the railroads or on other farms while their wives and children cleared the land. They grew onions, celery, beets, carrots, and potatoes. Large families with ten to fourteen children provided ready labor for the fields. At first the immigrants lived in town, going out to the farms each morning and returning in the evening as they had done in Sicily. Later, some built houses on their land, forming a community called Onion Town. Other immigrants maintained shacks on their land, where they lived during the summer.

A group of northern Italians who had worked in nearby lumber camps or in New York City, settled in western Connecticut in South Glastonbury Township in 1892. They purchased abandoned farms and sold the wood as they cleared the land. Some grew tomatoes, potatoes, cabbage, corn, and peppers; others grew berries. Most produce found receptive customers in nearby Hartford. Although peach cultivation predated Italian settlement, the immigrants quickly planted peach trees. In 1909 they formed the North Italy Fruit Growers' Union of Connecticut, a cooperative association to market produce and to buy fertilizers, baskets, and other farm supplies.

In Rhode Island, another Italian community, located close to Providence, engaged in truck farming. Most settlers first came to work in the textile mills. One early settler from Naples arrived penniless in 1875 and worked as a farm laborer for two years, earning seven dollars per week. At the end of the two-year period he purchased ten acres for five hundred dollars, paying cash. By 1909 he owned fifty-seven acres on which he built two houses and made other improvements.

While there was never a mass migration of Italians to farm the land, individuals and groups seemed ready to take advantage of potentially profitable agricultural enterprises wherever they arose. In Hockessin, Delaware, an Italian colony formed in the late 1920s when several coal miners in Pittsburgh heard about opportunities for mushroom cultivation in the Kennett Square area. They sent Corrado Amabili to assess the location. He found the area promising because of its climate, proximity to large markets, and availability of manure from nearby stables.

Giuseppe Iaconi, Domenico Paloni, and Amabili joined with Nazzareno Antonini in Wilmington to purchase a farm in the Hockessin vicinity. While none of these men had prior experience in mushroom cultivation, they applied their hard work ethic and soon gained success. As they expanded production, friends and relatives moved into the Brandywine

A

Valley and established additional mushroom facilities. In the 1920s and 1930s Italian growers responded to the appearance of canned mushrooms and canned soup. Ten families organized to form the Delaware Mushroom Cooperative Association in 1939 to acquire, preserve, can, and sell goods produced by its subscribers. Descendants of these Italian settlers still operate many of the mushroom plants in the Hockessin area.

Throughout America, on the outskirts of cities or in rural areas, Italian agricultural entrepreneurship often created a base for wholesale and retail trade. Immigrant peddlers and storekeepers purchased produce from their farmer *paesani* (fellow countrymen). In some areas these merchants had themselves started out as agricultural workers. In addition, Italians who sold fruit and produce on the streets of Chicago, Philadelphia, and other towns across the country served as marketing agents as they introduced native Americans to "new" produce, such as Italian beans, artichokes, asparagus, *cocozza* (squash), and peppers. Also, by making a variety of fresh produce more easily available to urban populations, Italian agricultural enterprise transformed the eating habits of the native population.

While Italian involvement in agriculture across the country declined as small family farms on the outskirts of large cities fell to the spread of suburbia in the post–World War II period or suffered from the competition of large agribusiness, some Italians continued family traditions of farming and produce distribution.

In Baltimore, Boston, Seattle, Tampa, and countless other places produce markets still reflect a heavy concentration of Italian entrepreneurs. In today's markets Italian greens such as arugula and radicchio create the "designer" salads of the leading chefs. Customers regard garlic not only as a flavor enhancer but also as a "health food" supplement. Menus with healthy heart choices include the traditional Italian peasant diet of vegetable and pasta dishes as beneficial for a healthier America.

Vincenza Scarpaci

Bibliography

Andreozzi, John. "Italian Farmers in Cumberland." *Italian Immigrants in Rural and Small Town America,* edited by Rudolph J. Vecoli, 110–125. New York: American Italian Historical Association, 1987.

Baiamonte, John. "Community Life in the Italian Colonies of Tangipahoa Parish, Louisiana, 1890–1950." *Journal of Louisiana History* 30 (1989): 365–397.

Belfiglio, Valentine J. "Italians in Small Town and Rural Texas." In *Italian Immigrants in Rural and Small Town America,* edited by Rudolph J. Vecoli, 31–49. New York: American Italian Historical Association, 1987.

Calomiris, Ellen. "Conflict, Cooperation and Acceptance: The Italian Experience in Delaware." *Journal of Delaware History* 20 (1983): 269–290.

Lewellen, Jeffrey. "Sheep Amidst Wolves: Father Bandini and the Colony at Tontitown, 1898–1917." *Arkansas Historical Quarterly* 45 (1986): 19–40.

Meade, Emily Fogg. *The Italian on the Land: A Study in Immigration.* Hammonton, NJ: Hammonton Historical Society, 1992.

Scarpaci, Jean Ann (Vicenza). *Italian Immigrants in Louisiana's Sugar Parishes: Recruitment, Labor Conditions, and Community Relations, 1880–1910.* New York: Arno Press, 1980.

U.S. Immigration Commission Reports, Senate Document no. 633, 61st Cong., 2nd sess., vols. 21, 22, Immigrants in Industries: Part 24, Recent Immigrants in Agriculture.

See also BANDINI, PIETRO; BUSINESS AND ENTREPRENEURSHIP; COLONIES IN SMALL TOWNS; FOODWAYS AND FOOD; POPULATION; SAN FRANCISCO

Albanese, Licia (b. 1913)

A soprano from the Italian-European verismo operatic tradition, Licia Albanese debuted at the Metropolitan Opera Company in 1940. Prior to her career of twenty-six years with the Metropolitan, she had sung at the Convent Garden, La Scala, and other major European opera houses. Puccini's operas are associated with her career. A master of *portamento* and *messa di voce,* her artistry has been analogous to superb acting and stylistic interpretation.

Born in Bari, Italy, to Michele and Maria (Rugusa) Albanese, she was admitted at the age of 14 to the conservatory of Pietro a Marella, where she studied with tenor Emmanuele de Rosa. She then went to Milan to study verismo operas with Giuseppina Baldassare-Tedeschi, who was considered the greatest "Butterfly" of her time.

Cio-Cio San in *Madame Butterfly* is synonymous with Mme. Albanese's name. It served as her debut at Milan's Teatro Lirico (1935), in Parma (1937), at the Metropolitan (1940), and San Francisco (1941). She sang the role seventy-two times with the Metropolitan, ranking second in number of performances. Her twenty-fifth anniversary with the Metropolitan was celebrated with an all-Puccini program.

Mme. Albanese's career includes a total of 427 performances of seventeen roles in sixteen operas. Her repertory was the *lirico spinto*. In addition to the Italian roles of Puccini, Verdi, and Mozart, she performed many roles in the French operas of Bizet, Massenet, and Gounod. Her many recordings are available on compact discs. She has also appeared on radio broadcasts and telecasts. The Vatican selected her to sing during the commencement of its radio station in the 1930s. Arturo Toscanini chose her to be Mimi in the fiftieth anniversary of *La Boheme* with his NBC Symphony Orchestra.

Mme. Albanese's post career has been devoted to preserving the Italian operatic tradition. With her late husband, Joseph Gimma, she established the Puccini Foundation, which is dedicated to training the careers of promising operatic singers. She conducts master classes for the Juilliard School of Music, San Francisco Opera Center, Marymount College, and throughout the world. She serves on many opera boards and holds honorary memberships in numerous Italian organizations. She was decorated Lady Grand Cross, Order of the Holy Sepulchre, and received the Order of Merit of Italy. In 1995 President Clinton awarded her the National Medal of the Arts for her contributions in music.

Marie Di Stefano Miller
Samuel J. Bellardo

Bibliography
Hines, Jerome. *Great Singers on Great Singing.* New York: Doubleday, 1982.
Price, Walter. "One of the Great Ones." *Opera News,* 3 February 1990, 9–13.

See also OPERA

Albanians
See ITALIAN AMERICAN ALBANIANS

Amato Opera

Located in lower Manhattan, the Amato Opera is the third repertory opera company in New York to have a permanent home. Although this fact puts it in a league with the more famous Metropolitan and New York City Opera companies, it differs from them in significant ways, especially in size. It has been called the smallest opera house in the world, seating only 107 people and has a stage 18 feet wide by 28 feet deep, and an orchestra pit 20 feet by 10 feet. Yet in this tiny auditorium audiences enjoy a full season of opera performances from September through May.

The founders of this company are Anthony and Sally Amato, who sang professionally between 1940 and 1970 and still fill a tenor or soprano role in an emergency. Anthony Amato's family arrived in the United States from Minori, Italy, in 1927 when he was seven years old. The Amatos met in a 1943 production of *The Vagabond King* and were married two years later. They started their own company in 1948, and in 1962 they moved to their present home at 319 Bowery, where they continue today.

Each year about two hundred singers audition, and the Amatos select fifty. The couple choose five operas, usually well-known works, but occasionally a rarity such as Boito's *Nerone*. The American premieres of such Verdi works as *La Battaglia di Legnano, Oberto,* and *Aroldo* took place at the Amato Opera. Each work is given about ten performances, often with different casts in each show. Works are usually performed in their original operatic language. Some former Amato singers, such as Mignon Dunn and Neil Shicoff, have gone on to sing at the Metropolitan and other famous opera houses throughout the world.

Since the mid-1970s the Amato set designer has been Richard T. Cerullo, who also designs department store windows. He is known for his ability to make the small stage seem larger. Cerullo has also translated Italian librettos into English, such as a 1993 series of *Otello* and a 1996 series of Donizetti's *Don Pasquale*.

It is not unusual for every performance at Amato opera to be sold out. Low ticket prices and excellent sight lines to the stage are contributing factors. However, it is evident that the skills and talent of Anthony and Sally Amato, Richard T. Cerullo, and performers are the main reasons for this company being an Italian American success story.

Robert Hoyt Block

Bibliography
Woyton, Michael. "Bowery Boys." *Opera News,* 18 March 1995, 32–33.

See also OPERA

Ameche, Don
See MOVIE ACTORS AND ACTRESSES

American Committee on Italian Migration
Founded in 1952, this organization's aim is to foster an understanding and implementation of fair immigration laws and to provide information to Italian immigrants in resettling and adapting to American society. Its creation was a response to the immigration crisis resulting from the social and economic chaos occurring in Italy after two world wars.

In its early years the American Committee on Italian Migration (ACIM) lobbied to eliminate the national origins quota system, enacted in the 1920s, and other unjust obstacles to southern European immigration. Italians stood to gain from reform, because Italy's annual quota of 5,666 did little to lessen the pressure of more than 250,000 immigrants waiting to enter the United States.

Judge Juvenal Marchisio of the New York City Family Court served as national chairman through 1968, and the Reverend Caesar Donanzan, a member of the Scalabrinian order, was executive secretary through 1966. Their dedicated leadership helped to establish ACIM as a widely respected and prominent voluntary immigration group.

The Immigration and Nationality Act of 1965, signed into law by President Lyndon B. Johnson on Liberty Island in New York Harbor on October 3, 1965, was the culmination of successful lobbying efforts of ACIM and other interested organizations. This historic document abolished the national origins quota system and placed the immigration selection process on a fairer, more humane foundation; it provided for a new method of selection based on family relationships to American citizens or resident aliens. The new law placed all nations on equal terms concerning immigration. Its immediate effect benefited Italians whose backlog of oversubscribed visa applications was exhausted within a few years.

ACIM has continued to provide assistance to Italians interested in the admission of relatives, helping migrants before their departure from Italy and hastening their adaptation to American life. It also serves as a "watchdog" in the nation's capital to assure fairness in immigration legislation. Accordingly, ACIM officials have provided expert testimony before congressional committees promoting changes to immigration law.

Headquartered in New York City, ACIM publishes *La Nuova Via,* a bimonthly in Italian, and the *ACIM Newsletter,* a bimonthly in English. For a time, it also broadcast on Italian radio. It has a membership of ten thousand and conducts an annual conference highlighting major immigration priorities.

Frank J. Cavaioli

The Reverend Joseph A. Cogo, C.S., National Secretary of the American Committee on Italian Migration during the 1980s. His weekly radio program in the 1980s on WEVD in New York City provided information on ACIM's work regarding immigration legislation and assistance to Italian immigrants. Courtesy Frank J. Cavaioli.

Bibliography
Cavaioli, Frank J. "Chicago's Italian Americans Rally for Immigration Reform." *Italian Americana* 6 (spring/summer 1980): 142–156.
——— . "Italian Americans Slay the Immigration Dragon: The National-Origins Quota System." *Italian Americana* 5 (fall/winter 1979): 71–100.

Juvenal Marchisio, National Secretary of the American Committee on Italian Migration from 1952 to 1968, shakes hands with President John F. Kennedy at the Third ACIM National Symposium in Washington, D.C., June 1963. Marchisio was a New York City judge whose leadership contributed to ACIM's success in reforming immigration policy. Courtesy Immigration History Research Center, Minnesota.

Higham, John. *Strangers in the Land.* New York: Athenaeum, 1971.

See also ORGANIZATIONS

American Italian Historical Association

Over the course of the past century and a half more than five million men, women, and children left their Italian birthplaces to make new lives for themselves in North America. Although much is now known about this folk migration and its impact on American society, more remains to be discovered. Today, under the aegis of the American Italian Historical Association (AIHA), systematic, scientific Italian American studies enjoys institutional support and is sustained by a network of dedicated scholars.

In December of 1966, a group of historians, educators, sociologists, and other interested persons met at the LaGuardia Memorial House in New York City and founded the American Italian Historical Association. The AIHA has grown from a small but distin-

guished group to an inclusive membership of over five hundred individuals.

The first AIHA conference was held in New York City at the Casa Italiana of Columbia University on October 26, 1968. Since then they have been held in Albany, Baltimore, Boston, Chicago, Cleveland, Lowell, Minneapolis, New Brunswick, New Haven, New Orleans, New York City, Philadelphia, Pittsburgh, Providence, San Francisco, South Orange, Toronto, and Washington, D.C.

Each fall AIHA conducts a multidisciplinary meeting where scores of expert participants present and critique their most recent research; this is done in the form of papers, panel discussions, and multimedia. Creative writing has also become a part of the annual conference as an expression of the Italian American experience, as well as an Italian American Studies Book Fair. The best papers are selected through a referee process and are published in AIHA's uninterrupted series of annual *Proceedings,* which have become the most informative objective historical record of the Italian experience in America. The annual meetings and publications have been supported by Italian American groups, universities, and the government and people of Italy through the Italian Consulates and Italian Cultural Institutes.

AIHA fosters the collection and preservation of American Italian historical records including printed materials, private and public papers, photographs, and oral history tapes. Its own archive is located at the Center for Migration Studies in Staten Island, New York, where scholars and other interested persons from all over the world go for research.

The association's endowed Memorial Fund presents two annual prizes: a Scholarship Award to a graduate student in any discipline whose work focuses on the Italian American experience, and the Leonard Covello Award for the best written essay in Italian American studies.

The American Italian Historical Association has promoted American Italian studies and has facilitated multiethnic studies through international, national, regional, and local activities. Over the past three decades, it has sponsored joint conferences and programs with such groups as the American Jewish Historical Society, Balch Institute of Philadelphia, Canadian Italian Historical Association, Casa Italiana of Columbia University, Center for Migration Studies of New York, Multicultural

Historical Association of Ontario, Kosciuszko Foundation, Polish Institute of Arts and Sciences in America, and the Polish American Historical Association. In November 1997, the AIHA joined with the Italian American Foundation of Cleveland in conducting its thirtieth annual conference entitled "Shades of Black and White, Conflict and Collaboration Between Two Communities."

Current chapters of the association include the Western Regional (1974), Long Island (1976), Stella del Nord, Minnesota (1978), Metropolitan New York City (1978), Central New Jersey (1979), Central New York State (1986), and Cleveland (1994).

In addition to the *Proceedings,* the American Italian Historical Association publishes a semiannual newsletter of conference notes, announcements, and book reviews. It also vigorously supports the efforts of publications and organizations that focus on Italian Americans as annual contributing patrons of *Italian Americana* and *VIA (Voices in Italian America)*. The newsletter and meetings provide vehicles for these and other important publications, such as *Altreitalie, Arba Sicula, Differentia, Forum Italicum, Fra Noi, The Italian Journal,* and the *Italian American Review.*

Association members serve in advisory capacities to Italian American civic, fraternal, community, and professional organizations from local community organizations to the Commission for Social Justice of the Order Sons of Italy and the National Italian American Foundation. To further promote outreach, the AIHA maintains an information network with a speakers' bureau and, periodically, publishes a *Directory of Members* listing each member's affiliations, expertise, and interests.

The AIHA has encouraged the formation of other Italian American scholarly and academic groups, as well as Italian American interest sections in other professional organizations. By their participation in groups such as the American Sociological Association, American Historical Association, and Modern Language Association, members informally serve as liaisons to other scholarly organizations. It also seeks to facilitate the furtherance of Italian American studies through the growing networks of telecommunication. In addition to its members in Italy, the association maintains ties with Italian universities and research foundations such as the Giovanni Ag-

nelli Foundation and the Italian Sociological Association.

The members of the American Italian Historical Association seek to create an accurate, complete, and objective understanding of the complex history of Americans of Italian descent through the collection, preservation, study, and popularization of information and materials that illuminate the experience of American Italians in the United States and Canada.

Jerome Krase

Bibliography

Cavaioli, Frank J. "The Rise of Italian American Studies and the American Italian Historical Association." *The Italian American Review* 5, no. 1 (spring 1996): 1–22.

Velikonja, Joseph. "The Scholarship of the AIHA: Past Achievements and Future Perspectives." In *Italian Ethnics and Their Languages, Literature and Lives,* edited by Dominic Candeloro, Fred Gardaphé, and Paolo A. Giordano, 109–124. New York: American Italian Historical Association, 1990.

See also ORGANIZATIONS

American Justinian Society of Jurists

Founded in 1966, this organization has a membership of twelve hundred Italian American judges throughout the United States.

The purpose of the society is to act as a medium for the exchange of ideas in the interest of improving the administration of justice and deepening legal scholarship among society members. This is achieved by conducting workshops, seminars, and other educational functions for judges and by gathering and disseminating informational material for member judges.

Participation in the society's activities provides opportunities to meet other jurists and form lasting friendships. The meetings also afford members the occasion to expand their knowledge of various aspects of the law by attending stimulating educational programs. Seminars and other activities are conducted by fellow members in the host city, including chief judges, governors, and mayors.

In recent years, seminars have been held in Italy, Louisiana, Virginia, Rhode Island, Pennsylvania, Maryland, New Jersey, Illinois, and New York. Among issues discussed were suggested changes in Codes of Civil Procedure Law, bioethics and the law, death with dignity, surrogate mothers' contracts, parental custody of frozen zygotes, in vitro fertilization, and family values and the law.

Joseph J. Saladino

Bibliography
Marchetto, Ezio, ed. *A Directory of Italian American Associations in the Tri-State Area.* Staten Island, NY: Center for Migration Studies, 1989.

See also ORGANIZATIONS

Andretti, Mario (b. 1940)

An internationally renowned auto racing driver, Mario Andretti was born in Montana, Istria (now Motovun, Croatia), and at age five he and his twin, Aldo, were precociously swooping down hills in a wooden cart. After the region came under Yugoslav rule, the family moved to Lucca, Tuscany, in 1948. Soon the boys were avid Grand Prix fans and, unknown to their parents, were racing cars and motorcycles as teenagers. Their hobby made them reluctant to depart for America in 1955, when the family settled in the steelmaking town of Nazareth, Pennsylvania.

Having built their own stock car, they raced in eastern Pennsylvania and on the NASCAR circuit. However, when Aldo was critically injured in 1959, the brothers' activities could no longer be hidden from their father. Mario became estranged from him and continued racing. Marriage in 1961 to Dee Ann Hoch brought unwavering support to his career, as her father provided Andretti with financial aid.

European motor car racing was mainly a sport for wealthy participants, but the Andrettis fit in with young working-class people who were enamored of fast cars and technology. Andretti drove in stock car races in 1961 and 1962 and midget car races in 1963. In 1965 Andretti entered the United States Auto Club (USAC), which is the most prestigious race circuit because it uses Indianapolis-type cars and tracks. That year brought him international attention when he placed third in the Indianapolis 500, was the USAC's top driver, and was voted Rookie of the Year. Some veteran drivers thought his success would be short-lived because he was considered reckless. Their skepticism soon vanished.

Before the 1966 Indianapolis event, *Sports Illustrated* published a laudatory profile in which Andretti was labeled an "unknown." Although having the lowest qualifying speed, he nonetheless won the USAC national championship that season by accumulating eight victories in fifteen championship races he entered. Switching back to stock car competition, he won the 1967 Daytona Beach NASCAR 500 in a Ford Fairlane.

Andretti's finest triumph was placing first in the 1969 Indianapolis 500. In 1981, Bobby Unser beat him in Indianapolis by eight seconds. In 1977 he won the Italian Grand Prix. Unser placed first at the line, but Andretti charged him with violating the rule against failing to maintain position during a yellow flag. Andretti was ruled the winner, but that verdict was later reversed. Mario placed second at Indianapolis in 1987, but he suffered ignition failure and, despite earning the pole position, fell to ninth.

Mario and Dee Ann's sons, Michael and Jeffrey, and Aldo's son, John, race professionally, their sport being one in which bravado and skill have been passed through the generations.

Richard Renoff

Bibliography
Andretti, Mario. *Andretti.* San Francisco: Collins, 1977.
Chapin, Kim. "La Dolce Indy." *Sports Illustrated,* 9 June 1969, 24–29.
Hinton, Ed. "Inherit the Wind." *Sports Illustrated,* 11 May 1992, 78–84f.
La Fontaine, Barbara. "Fastest Hee-ro at Indy." *Sports Illustrated,* 30 May 1966, 37–43.

See also SPORTS

Andriola, Alfred
See CARTOONISTS AND ILLUSTRATORS

Anfuso, Victor L. (1905–1966)

The first Sicilian-born member of the United States House of Representatives, Victor L. Anfuso achieved a distinguished career in public service.

He was born in Gagliano Castelferrato, Sicily, Italy, on March 10, 1905. He immigrated to America with two brothers and two

A

sisters in 1914. They settled in the Little Italy neighborhood of Williamsburg in Brooklyn. He was educated in public schools and attended Columbia University. Anfuso obtained his law degree from Brooklyn Law School and was admitted to the bar in 1928. In 1930 he married Frances Stallone, and they had three sons and two daughters.

Anfuso was active in humanitarian and civic affairs. In 1936 he organized the Citizens Welfare Association, which assisted the needy in obtaining economic relief, aided the unemployed in finding jobs, advanced the cause of amicable resolution of disputes between individuals, and assisted those who came into conflict with the law. His concern with youth motivated him to form the Italian Board of Guardians in 1936 to aid delinquent children and children from broken homes. He also formed the Tolerance Day League in 1943 to promote goodwill and better understanding among people of all races and religious denominations and the Youth Congress in 1948 to combat juvenile delinquency through educational programs for parents and children.

During World War II Anfuso served with the Office of Strategic Services in Sicily, where he assisted in establishing an anti-Fascist government there. In 1946 he was appointed Assistant to the Commissioner of Immigration and Naturalization Service, where he headed a study of the immigration "quota" laws and their discriminatory impact on Italian immigrants. In 1948 he was appointed Consul General for San Marino, where he proposed that Italian Americans with dual citizenship be allowed to vote in the Italian elections to defeat communism. He also organized a massive letter-writing campaign from Italian Americans to their Italian relatives and friends to urge them to vote against the Communist Party.

Anfuso's civic, humanitarian, and political activities catapulted him into a political career in 1950, when he was elected as a Democrat for the House of Representatives in the 8th District in Brooklyn. When Anfuso's district was reapportioned, he did not seek reelection. In 1954 Mayor Wagner appointed him as city magistrate. He resigned less than a year later to run successfully once again for Congress. He served a total of ten years in Congress.

In Congress Anfuso spoke against colonialism and stressed the need for a strong national defense. As a member of the House Agricultural Committee, he proposed a Social Security bill to reduce the retirement age to 62 with full benefits and advocated the free distribution of surplus food to the elderly and needy through the food stamp plan. Anfuso was successful as the author of several bills designed to repeal the McCarran-Walter Immigration and the National Quota System.

Anfuso maintained close relationships with the leaders of the Italian government and on several occasions served as an intermediary between the United States and Italy. He served as chairman of the Italian Centennial Celebration in 1961 and was named chairman of the congressional delegation appointed by President Kennedy to represent the United States at the centennial celebration in Italy on September 30, 1961.

In 1962 he was appointed a New York Supreme Court Justice. Victor L. Anfuso died on December 28, 1966.

Frank M. Sorrentino

Bibliography

Congressional Record of the 87th Congress. Washington, D.C.: Government Printing Office.

Nelli, Humbert S. *The United States and Italy: The First Two Hundred Years.* New York: American Italian Historical Association, 1977.

See also POLITICS

Anti-Italian Discrimination

It was the unfortunate fate of Italian immigrants to be the largest nationality of "new immigrants" at a time of a thriving anti-immigrant sentiment that characterized the late nineteenth and early twentieth centuries. It was during these decades that most of the legislation designed to restrict southeastern and central European immigration reached its peak. The anti-immigrant sentiment once again reflected American ambivalence toward immigration, which oscillated between welcoming newcomers in order to develop the country and harboring suspicions about those who originated from areas other than Anglo-Saxon, northwestern Europe.

Not all Italian Americans experienced the same degree of discrimination. Those who settled in the western part of the United States, such as California, experienced a milder form of bigotry, perhaps because their limited numbers were not perceived as a threat. It was far different, however, for the bulk of Italian immigrants who settled in large cities in the eastern part of the country. In these settings Italian Americans were subjected to some of the most scurrilous campaigns ever directed against any immigrant group. Immigrants encountered the Italian counterparts to the "No Irish need apply" when seeking employment. Other examples include a Milwaukee fraternal organization early in the century specifically prohibiting Italians from membership and a 1916 Queens, New York, real estate advertisement informing prospective buyers that the residential development was committed to an "Italians excluded" policy.

Prior to the 1920s it was evident that Italian Americans earned a low score of acceptability, not only when compared to immigrants from northwestern Europe, but also when evaluated against other participants in the post–Civil War migration. Studies show that they were rated "below even the Portuguese and the Poles," and that "they show the beginnings of a degenerate class." During a congressional hearing they were described as a non-white people and in some work situations were conferred wages substantially lower than whites. Literacy tests and other restrictions on alien immigration, culminating in the rigid quota system, pinpointed Italians as one of the major, if not the principal, targets. The dichotomous picture of how Americans beheld Italians is not new; it was also true of the pre-1880 period when Americans could read popular accounts about Italy that, while describing a land of beautiful scenery and impressive ruins and churches, bewailed a region of ragged beggars, voracious *banditti* (bandits), and violent feuds.

Times of economic hardship usually intensify prejudice as a restive populace seeks scapegoats. Thus, where Italian immigrants were previously welcome to work the mines, build subways, construct dams, manufacture clothing, and perform other menial but necessary tasks, economic reverses in the mid-1890s found them no longer welcome. With the increased flow of Italian immigrants came another workforce: seasonal laborers who, because of rapidly moving steamships, performed outdoor work for part of the year and then returned to Italy with their earnings.

These Italian migrant workers angered old-stock Americans who considered their temporary work status as a sign of weak character and derisively labeled them "birds of passage," thereby exacerbating the problem of anti-Italian discrimination.

Before 1880, during the embryonic stage of Italian immigration, negative images of Italians were based on several perceptions, such as indolence, ignorance, massive illiteracy, overwrought religious superstition, and an inherent criminal mentality. As a consequence, it was not surprising to find opinionated newspaper reporters focusing on newly arrived Italians who supposedly rejected genuine work opportunities and resorted instead to begging on the streets for their livelihood. It was observed that disgraceful Italian *padroni* (bosses) were responsible for the shameful exploitation of their own kind as they herded newcomers into dismal, low-paying work situations.

It was at the turn of the twentieth century, a time of dramatic increase in Italian immigration and a period of economic crisis, that anti-Italian sentiments flourished. Conspicuous illiteracy, ragged dress, and massive ignorance of the niceties practiced by the Anglo-Saxon world rendered the immigrants as an easy target for prejudice. More than in previous decades, newspapers denounced the situation whereby "proper" Americans could no longer safely walk city streets that had become overrun by indolent intruders from sunny Italy replete with the ubiquitous hand organ and monkey. A respectable New York newspaper maintained that never in the city's history had it been subject to "so low and ignorant a class . . . as the southern Italians." It was popular speculation that Italian authorities deliberately emptied their provinces of extraneous riff-raff by sending them to the United States. The belief that unscrupulous *padroni* were inveigling immature Italian youth to emigrate to this country in the form of slave wage earners was so prevalent that Congress passed a bill to prohibit the practice.

Prejudice against Italian Americans rested considerably on their religious identification. From the nativist viewpoint, they were overwhelmingly Catholic and members of an unenlightened creed that succumbed to superstition. A blatant example occurred in 1923 in Patchogue, New York, when a Ku Klux Klan leader, also a college president, maligned Catholics by excoriating these newcomers

A

whose first allegiance was to a "Dago Pope" who resides "on a river in Italy" (*Patchogue Advance,* March 16, 1923). Many a Protestant American leader, while less extreme than the above example, nevertheless averred that Italian immigrants would be more easily assimilated if they were to abandon their peculiar religion in favor of enlightened Protestantism. The pressures exerted upon the newcomers caused an untold number to try to gain acceptance by resorting to such extreme steps as name-changing and converting to Protestantism.

Perhaps the oldest and most damaging stereotype Americans harbored against Italians was a fear of their inherent criminality. Even before large-scale Italian immigration, Americans read fulsome accounts of unlawful activity that permeated the Italian peninsula. This woeful situation was said to have compromised Italian officials who deliberately closed their eyes to extortion, bribery, and thievery in order to achieve national unification. Interestingly, writers on Italy were much kinder to northern Italians, tending instead to concentrate on rings of gangs operating in southern Italy, especially Naples, Calabria, and Sicily. Media preoccupation with this amoral behavior increased with the rise of Italian immigration and persisted throughout the middle and latter part of the twentieth century, resulting in a veritable industry of gangster literature and movies with Italian names playing a central role.

There were some American leaders who were sympathetic to Italian immigrants and who spoke out against anti-Italian discrimination. A case in point is famed social worker Jane Addams, who established her settlement house in the midst of a heavily Italian neighborhood in Chicago and who ministered to the ethnic poor with understanding and compassion.

Diminution of discrimination followed a protracted path through the 1920s and 1930s. The early phase of World War II was especially critical since Italy was an enemy nation and over six hundred thousand Italian aliens resided in this country. The latter were required to register as "enemy aliens," and certain restrictions were placed on their activities. On the West Coast several hundred were forced to abandon their regular means of livelihood, to relocate, and, in some instances, were interned. The highly patriotic era was hostile to activities that seemed to celebrate an adversary nation, and subsequently a number of Italian American enterprises were curtailed,

such as fishing. Fortunately, the "enemy alien" stigma lessened after Columbus Day 1942. In addition, there was a growing realization that Italian Americans were performing their tasks as patriotically as other American citizens. Their unstinting work effort on the home front and their heroic participation in the Allied armed forces, which exceeded their percentage of the population, brought them a degree of respect.

The post–World War II era found Italian Americans participating in the enormous societal changes that were altering the country. Their economic positions improved, their children were beginning to receive better educations, and they joined in demographic shifts with increased movement to the suburbs. They were ready to take positions of equality in society; however, they still had to contend with prejudice and discrimination, only now the slights were more subtle and indirect. Although they continued to be overrepresented in blue-collar jobs, they were gradually moving into more prestigious professional positions. No longer affronted with the blunt, brazen, and direct discrimination experienced earlier in the century, Italian Americans continued to be denied positions in various occupations and professions because of their ethnicity and/or religious background.

During the 1960s and 1970s Italian Americans began to create organizations specifically designed to curb discrimination. Furthermore, members of the ethnic group had attained important public offices where they could affect public policy. For example, by the 1980s over thirty members in Congress were Italian Americans. In 1950 John Pastore became the first of his nationality elected to the United States Senate, while in 1982 Mario Cuomo was elected New York governor. In 1984 Geraldine Ferraro became the first woman and the first of her ethnic background to be nominated as vice president of the United States. While these accomplishments may be regarded as impressive, if of limited success, the cumulative effect was a reduction of discrimination toward Italian Americans.

Yet Italian Americans still faced a variety of stereotypes. Some perceptions refuse to go away. In the 1970s and 1980s television viewers saw a steady portrayal of Italian Americans as ignorant buffoons who could not be taken seriously as citizen models except as transgressors of the law. Indeed, association with criminality persisted as the single most negative characteristic with which Italian Americans had to deal. An old stereotype, the link between Italian Americans and transgression, was reinforced by a genre of "mob" and "Mafia" novels and movies as typified by Mario Puzo's *The Godfather*. Media preoccupation became an industry that continues to dominate the public image. Accordingly, in 1992 the comptroller of New York City, without incontrovertible proof, denied a New York City contract to an Italian American contractor because of his "criminal" associations. Although the decision was later reversed by a higher state court, the incident damaged the individual's reputation. Furthermore, and as incredible as it may seem, a federal judge during the trial process unwittingly joined in the character assassination of the Italian ethnic group by inferring that young Italian Americans are attracted to criminal life. In another recent trial, *Scelsa v. CUNY*, a federal court enjoined the City University of New York from discriminating against Italian Americans with respect to faculty recruitment and promotions, the dismemberment of the Italian American Institute, and the dismissal of Joseph Scelsa.

Anti-Italian discrimination has been a part of the Italian American experience. On the one hand, it was a part of the same discrimination that most minorities underwent to pay the price of becoming an American. On the other hand, although greatly diminished, it has not altogether disappeared. What should be emphasized is the ethnic group's ability to absorb insults and slights and thereby overcome bigotry, albeit not without a cost.

Salvatore J. LaGumina

Bibliography

Gallo, Pat. *Ethnic Alienation: The Italian Americans*. Rutherford, NJ: Fairleigh Dickinson University Press, 1974.

Gambino, Richard. *Blood of My Blood: The Dilemma of the Italian Americans*. Garden City, NY: Doubleday, 1974.

Iorizzo, Luciano J., and Salvatore Mondello. *The Italian Americans*. New York: Twayne, 1980.

LaGumina, Salvatore J. *WOP: A Documentary History of Anti-Italian Discrimination*. Toronto: Guernica, 1999.

Rolle, Andrew. *Troubled Roots: Italian Americans*. New York: Free Press, 1980.

See also CRIME AND ORGANIZED CRIME; DISCRIMINATION AT CITY UNIVERSITY OF NEW YORK (CUNY); FILM DIRECTORS, PRODUCERS, AND ITALIAN AMERICAN IMAGE IN CINEMA; LABELS AND STEREOTYPES

A

Antonini, Luigi (1883–1968)

Labor leader, born in the province of Avellino, Italy, the son of a schoolteacher and mother who was a poet and a member of a prominent family, Luigi Antonini was schooled in Italy, where he also served as a soldier. He was part of the mass immigration in 1908. Settling in New York City, he worked for a time in various occupations as a cigar roller and a piano tuner before entering the garment trades. He forthwith joined the infant International Ladies Garment Workers Union (ILGWU) and quickly became active, emerging as a convincing speaker in rallying Italian Americans in behalf of the union during the 1913 general waistmakers' strike.

In 1916 he became editor of *L'Operaia*, a periodical in which he trumpeted the cause of unionization among fellow Italian immigrants who were then emerging as a substantial segment in the garment industry. The results were rewarding as reflected in the founding of Local 89, which was on its way to becoming the largest Italian local in the ILGWU. He became first vice president of the ILGWU, a position he would hold for the rest of his life.

A fervent orator, Antonini increasingly became a spokesman for Italian Americans within and without the labor community during the 1920s and 1930s. It was during this period that he entered the political arena, becoming a founder of the American Labor Party (ALP) and its New York State chairman. Despite his earlier flirtation with communism, Antonini left the ALP when it moved too far left. Together with other prominent labor leaders such as David Dubinsky and Alex Rose, he helped found the Liberal Party, a political organization that was to have a significant impact in New York politics for years to come.

He become an ardent foe of Fascism and denounced Benito Mussolini in publications such as *L'Operaia* and *Il Progresso Italo-Americano*. Italian American radio listeners also followed his booming fulminations on the airwaves.

The outbreak of World War II found Antonini playing the dual role of rallying Italian Americans in the war effort, while defending their rights as American citizens. The alacrity with which he and other Italian American labor leaders supported the war effort was reflected in their sponsorship of a huge rally of Italian American workers at New York's Madison Square Garden in January 1942. Antonini emerged as one of the main opponents to the government's designation of Italian alien residents as "enemy aliens."

In the post–World War II years, Antonini became a stalwart advocate of aid for Italy. He demonstrated labor's commitment to the cause, becoming instrumental in founding the Franklin D. Roosevelt Vocational School in Mondello, Sicily.

The visual image he proffered was one of flamboyance. A big, warm man with flowing bowtie and a mane of white hair, he resembled an opera singer. He was also known to have a great love for animals, maintaining a private "zoo" in his Yonkers, New York, home. He was married to Jennie Costanza of Italy, who preceded him in death. He died in December 1968, at age 85.

Salvatore J. LaGumina

Bibliography

Fenton, Edwin. *Immigrants and Unions, A Case Study: Italians and American Labor.* New York: Arno, 1975.

Null, Gary, and Carl Stone. *The Italian Americans.* Harrisburg, PA: Stackpole, 1976.

See also LABOR; RADICALISM

Apostolate, Italian

The Italian Apostolate was a religious society established to promote, preserve, and strengthen a normative system of Roman Catholic thought and practice among Italian immigrants and their descendants in the United States. While many of the American Catholic institutions that made up the Italian Apostolate were common to other European immigrants, initiatives taken by the Italian Church and the Vatican also constituted a significant feature of the Italian Apostolate.

The task of the Italian Apostolate was twofold. On the one hand, institutions within the apostolate were vehicles intended to "preserve the faith" of Italian immigrants, presumably Roman Catholics, in the Protestant and increasingly secular environment of the United States. This first task implied that Italian immigrants were a part of the larger American Catholic subculture whose canopy protected insiders from both the acids of American society and secular ideologies among Italian liberals and radicals. Within this Catholic "ghetto," as it came to be called, the American Church, in order to placate the dominant Anglo-Saxon cultural custodians, became an agent of "Americanization," using ecclesial structures to teach English and inculcate American civic values.

On the other hand, the Italian Apostolate sought to harness the premodern religio-cultural system of Italian peasants into Roman Catholic orthodoxy as it evolved in the nineteenth and twentieth centuries. This orthodox system of Roman Catholicism, formulated at the Ecumenical Council of Trent (1545–1564) and elaborated in the following centuries, evinced strong antimodern tendencies in both ecclesiopolitical and social spheres. Its hierarchical authority was grounded in a clerical activism that promoted sacramental regularity and a plethora of devotional practices under the aegis of priests and religious. This second task revealed the cultural diversity of Catholic practice, as the American Church sought to integrate a variety of European religious and cultural traditions into a working unity. This project generated both ethnic conflict and accommodation between groups within the American Catholic subculture with which the Italian Apostolate contended.

A considerable number of Italian priests and members of religious communities (male and female) worked in the Catholic Church in North America in the first six decades of the nineteenth century. Nevertheless, these apostolic endeavors were not part of an Italian Apostolate, which only began to take discernible form with the emergence of Italian colonies in American industrial cities of the Gilded Age. Only with the increased ethnic differentiation of the American Church and society did most, but not all, Italian priests and sisters move into an explicitly Italian Apostolate. Furthermore, there were always American, Irish, and German priests and sisters who worked with Italian immigrants and their descendants in the American Church under the directives of the American hierarchy.

The Italian Apostolate was an international endeavor shaped by contending ideologies of late-nineteenth-century European and North American society. The unification of Italy, culminating in the fall of the Papal States and Rome itself (1870) to the Kingdom of Piedmont, precipitated the Roman Question, which set Italian nationalism and Roman Catholicism at loggerheads. For several decades the Vatican refused to recognize the legitimacy of the new Italian nation-state. As a result, the dominant expressions of Italian liberalism and nationalism took an anticlerical form, quite unlike the liberalism of American society. The Roman Question, not resolved until the signing of the Lateran Pacts of 1929, profoundly conditioned the evolution of private and public emigration assistance in Italy, as well as the efficacy of Italian pastoral care in the United States. Thus, on the one hand, the Vatican sought to mobilize Italian and American bishops in a coordinated migrant assistance effort without links to the modern state, Italian or American. On the other hand, in the United States, clerical uses of Italian national sentiment as a cohesive agent of social organization of Italian immigrants were attacked and often undermined by American Catholics who interpreted such pastoral efforts as expressions of disloyalty to the papacy.

In 1887 Bishop Giovanni Battista Scalabrini of Piacenza organized the Christopher Columbus Institute in Piacenza, lay emigration assistance committees in Italy, and a Pious Society of Missionaries of St. Charles Borromeo to provide Italian Catholic assistance to immigrants in South and North America. Pope Leo XIII sought to promote Scalabrini's missionaries to the American bishops in his encyclical *Quam Aerumnosa* (December 10, 1888) after having received reports of the horrendous state of Italian immigrants in North America. Although their efforts were coordinated, Pope Leo and Bishop Scalabrini did not share identical motivations for their promotion of Italian emigration assistance. The lack of pastoral care for Italians and the fear of Italian "losses" to Protestantism disturbed both pope and bishop, but Scalabrini was motivated by a desire to see the Roman Question resolved so that Italian nationalism and Roman Catholicism might be reconciled in the hearts of his compatriots. Scalabrini hoped his missionaries might work in a coordinated effort with the Italian state for Italian nationals resident in the Americas,

thus contributing to the resolution of Italian church–state conflict. In any case, these international efforts met resistance from some American bishops. The two most important events regarding the development of the Italian Apostolate and its relationship to the American hierarchy were the Third Plenary Council of Baltimore (1884) and the public controversy over what came to be called "Cahenslyism" (1890–1891).

In the last decades of the nineteenth century, internal divisions plagued the American hierarchy in ways that compromised the efforts of the papacy and Italian emigrant priests in the United States to provide pastoral care for Italians. When the American hierarchy met at the Third Plenary Council in 1884, the bishops were well aware of the problems surrounding a Catholic apostolate to Italian immigrants. These issues, dubbed the "Italian Problem," included Protestant proselytizing, anticlericalism, excessive provincialism, poor or scarce Italian clergy, the debilitating effects of the *padrone* (labor broker) system, and Italian indifference toward the Church. In spite of the Vatican's efforts to have the American episcopacy directly address the distinctive problems of Italian immigration at the Plenary Council, the American hierarchy chose not to develop any distinctive pastoral structures for Italian newcomers.

"Cahenslyism" was the ascription given to the efforts of the international St. Raphael Society, which met in Lucerne, Switzerland, in December, 1890, and the groundswell of negative public sentiment the Lucerne Memorial generated in the United States. The St. Raphaelsverein was founded by Peter Paul Cahensly in 1871 to assist German emigrants. With Pope Leo's encouragement, Cahensly internationalized the society, which held its first meeting at Lucerne. The Lucerne Memorial, signed by fifty-one representatives of seven national branches of St. Raphael and presented by Cahensly to Pope Leo, included phrases that exaggerated the losses of Catholic immigrants to Protestantism in America, along with suggestions for national parishes under immigrant clergy, and representatives of all national groups in the American episcopacy. The contents of the Lucerne Memorial were purposely distorted by Denis J. O'Connell, Rector of the North American College in Rome, and Archbishop John Ireland of St. Paul, to suggest that the Memorial reflected a

A

German national effort to interfere in the American Church. Thus, political intrigues within the American hierarchy, motivated by a desire to weaken the conservative German wing of the episcopacy, inadvertently undermined an international Catholic endeavor that would have assisted the evolution of the Italian Apostolate.

The "language" or "national" parish was the principal religious institution created for American Catholic immigrants. The national parish functioned to contain ethnic and religious conflict, aided immigrants in their adjustment to American society, and helped ethnic groups articulate, maintain, and reinvent ethnic identities. National parishes had met with success among German immigrants before they became normative for French-Canadian, Polish, and Italian newcomers. Although the success of Italian national parishes varied widely depending upon such factors as episcopal support, quality of clergy, and the structure of the local community, one can generalize that Italian immigrants were less likely than other Catholics to build and support their own parishes and schools without financial subsidies from American bishops. Italian parishes mirrored Italian communities, which were often divided by *campanilismo* (localism) and ideological cleavages resulting in contested meanings of Italian national identity. Thus, while the normative form of local religious organization in the American Church was based upon the presumption of a shared national identity and language, as a pastoral strategy this was not conducive to success for Italian immigrants whose provincial identities and dialects inhibited the organization of a national institution.

Before World War II the Italian Apostolate exhibited an ironic combination of weaknesses and strengths. In comparison with Irish, German, or Polish Catholics, Italian Catholics rarely developed newspapers, rarely had a priest to represent them in significant diocesan organs of governance in the American Church, had fewer cemeteries, never developed a national association of priests or religious, produced a remarkably small number of vocations, and did not have a bishop in the American Church who worked in a diocese with a significant number of Italians. The three (arch)dioceses of New York, Newark, and Brooklyn, which had large Italian populations, were exceptions to this pattern only in limited ways.

In 1914 Monsignor Gherardo Ferrante, who had served as Archbishop Michael A. Corrigan's secretary, became a Vicar General for Italians in the Archdiocese of New York. He served as a type of liaison between the American Church and the Apostolic Delegation with regard to affairs relating to Italian emigrant clergy. In April 1912 the Archbishop of New York, John Cardinal Farley, established the New York Apostolato Italiano, a mission band of three to four Italian priests under the leadership of Father Roberto Biasotti. From September 1912 to May 1921, when the Apostolato Italiano ceased its labors, the missionaries reported giving over twenty thousand sermons in 361 missions in its efforts to revitalize Italian parishes throughout the eastern United States. In addition, the Italian Catholic newspaper, *L'Italiano in America,* established in 1900 and published by the New York Diocesan Council for Italian Affairs, was a significant presence in New York until 1920. But Italian priests and sisters never attained the influence through organizational cooperation, in comparison to the German Deutsch-Amerikaner Priester-Verein, the Central German Verein and the St. Raphaelsverein, nor the Polish Roman Catholic Union and the Polish National Alliance. A Congress of Italian Clergy met in New York on December 5, 1917, when 260 Italian priests from the eastern United States made plans to organize a Union of Italian Clergy, a Union of Italian Catholics, and a Catholic newspaper for all Italians in North America. But these efforts were short-lived and never culminated in national organizations.

While the institutional development of Italians within American Catholic structures remained weak, the Vatican promoted the Italian Apostolate that in many ways functioned as an organizational extension of the Italian Church. During the Third Plenary Council of Baltimore in 1884, the Vatican pushed the American bishops to confront the distinctive problems of Italian pastoral care. Soon thereafter, Leo XIII published an encyclical for the American bishops on Italian emigration. The Vatican established an Apostolic Delegation in the United States in 1893 that worked closely with Italian clergy in the United States. The Vatican passed legislation to bring order and discipline to Italian emigrant clergy, which eventually evolved into more general structures for Roman Catholic pastoral care for migrants and refugees. The Vatican established a Prelate for Italian Emigration in 1920 who served as a chaplain for Italian emigrant clergy and rector of the Pontifical College for Italian Emigration, created to prepare Italian clergy for work among Italian emigrants. Italian emigrant clergy under the authority of the Prelate for Italian Emigration exercised a considerable influence on the Italian Apostolate in (arch)dioceses such as Providence, Philadelphia, and Nashville during the 1920s and 1930s. Thus, while American diocesan seminaries and the North American College in Rome had a bewildering scarcity of Italian American seminarians, Vatican-controlled institutions, linked to the evolution of the Italian Church, became the source of male religious leadership in the Italian Apostolate.

This distinctive relationship to the Vatican and Italy was a unique feature of the Italian Apostolate. It gave Italian priests an international source of prestige, but at the price of considerable segregation from the American Catholic Church. For example, Italian Servites in the United States separated from their American Province in 1927 and became affiliated with their Roman Province. Italian Augustinians were the only national group within their religious order not under the jurisdiction of their American Province, and they formed their own Italian Vice-Province in 1925; Italian Missionaries of the Most Precious Blood formed an Italo-American Delegation in 1928 and remained isolated from the jurisdiction of their large American Province; the Fathers of Our Lady of Mercy worked directly under their Roman Province; the Fathers of the Most Holy Trinity formed their own Italian vicariate in the United States in 1920; the Society of the Catholic Apostolate (Pallottine Fathers) formed an Italian American Province in 1909, separate from confrères of other nationalities; Italian Capuchins formed an Italian American Custodia recognized in 1918; Italian Franciscans (Minor) had their own Italian American Province after 1901, autonomous from Franciscans of other nationalities. Furthermore, during the period of Italian mass migration to the Americas, there was no Italian or Italian American bishop consecrated to a diocese in the United States. Charles Greco, the son of Italian immigrants, born in Rodney, Mississippi, was consecrated bishop of Alexandria in 1946. It was not until Sicilian-born Joseph Pernicone was consecrated auxiliary bishop in New York in 1954 that the United States had a hierarch of Italian descent in a see where a substantial Italian ethnic community lived.

The Italian Apostolate had been deeply invested in the industrial order of American cities. The social and religious system characterized by the network of Italian national parishes, overwhelmingly an urban industrial creation, has been transformed by the rise of a consumerist suburban Italian American middle class, the deindustrialization of American cities, the crisis of American liberalism, and changing American Catholic attitudes toward national parishes. Italian Americans, aided by the GI Bill of 1944, moved increasingly out of national parishes of Little Italies, into suburban parishes of single-family residences. The loss of unionized industrial labor in the last three decades undermined the social and financial base needed to maintain the national parish system. Federal housing projects and the modernization of transportation networks often contributed to the destruction of Italian neighborhoods.

In response to these sweeping transformations of American society, the Italian Apostolate sought to develop new forms of ministry not dependent upon the integrity of a geographical community. During and immediately after World War II, the Italian Apostolate played a significant role in the efforts of the American Catholic Church to aid refugees in war-torn Italy. In 1952 the American Committee for Italian Migration, under a Scalabrini executive director, became a member of the (American) National Catholic Resettlement Council (now Catholic Relief Services). In Chicago and its suburbs the Scalabrini Fathers established Villa Scalabrini, a home for elders, under the umbrella of Catholic Charities. Furthermore, they founded an Italian Catholic radio show, an Italian American newspaper, and an Italian cultural center. These efforts reflect the extension of the Italian Apostolate toward mobile Italian American ethnics who, although integrated into American society, still nurtured a symbolic ethnicity to which the Roman Catholic Church had become linked.

Since World War II, very few Italian diocesan emigrant clergy have come to the United States to work in an Italian Apostolate as the Pontifical College began to send priests to Latin America and elsewhere. Furthermore, the distinct structures religious orders developed for Italians have been largely eliminated. For example, in 1967 the Italian Servites were reintegrated into their American Provinces and the Italian Augustinian Vice-Province was suppressed in 1995. The decline of the Italian Apostolate in the postwar period has not inhibited Italian Americans from playing an active role in the cultural expression of their faith. Influenced by the legitimation of cultural pluralism occurring during the 1960s and, more recently, multiculturalism within the larger society, there has been a revitalization of traditional Italian *feste* and distinguished efforts to record the history and culture of the Italian American religious experience.

Peter R. D'Agostino

Bibliography

Browne, Henry J. "The 'Italian Problem' in the Catholic Church of the United States, 1880–1900." United States Catholic Historical Society, *Historical Records and Studies* 35 (1946): 46–72.

D'Agostino, Peter R. "The Scalabrini Fathers, the Italian Emigrant Church, and Ethnic Nationalism in America." *Religion and American Culture: A Journal of Interpretation* 7 (winter 1997).

DiGiovanni, Stephen Michael. *Archbishop Corrigan and the Italian Immigrants.* Huntington, IN: Our Sunday Visitor, 1994.

Juliani, Richard N. "L'assistenza religiosa agli italiani in USA e il Prelato per l'Emigrazione Italiana, 1920–1949." *Studi Emigrazione* 19 (June 1982): 167–189.

————. "The Parish as an Urban Institution: Italian Catholics in Philadelphia." *Records of the American Catholic Historical Society of Philadelphia* 96 (March/December 1986): 46–65.

Palmieri, Aurelio. "The Contribution of the Italian Catholic Clergy to the United States." In *Catholic Builders of the Nation,* Vol. 2, edited by C.E. McGuire, 127–149. Boston: Continental, 1923.

Schiavo, Giovanni E. *Italian-American History: The Italian Contribution to the Catholic Church in America.* Vol. 2. New York: Vigo, 1949.

Tomasi, Silvano M. *Piety and Power: The Role of the Italian Parishes in the New York Metropolitan Area, 1880–1930.* New York: Center for Migration Studies, 1975.

————, ed. *The Religious Experience of Italian Americans.* New York: American Italian Historical Association, 1975.

Vecoli, Rudolph J. "Prelates and Peasants: Italian Immigrants and the Catholic Church." *Journal of Social History* 2 (spring 1969): 217–268.

See also CHURCH LEADERS; RELIGION

Arcaro, Eddie (1916–1997)

Possibly the most successful thoroughbred jockey ever, George Edward Arcaro was born in Cincinnati on February 19, 1916, to Pasquale and Josephine (Giancola) Arcaro, weighing only three pounds. While a young boy his family moved across the Ohio River to Kentucky, where at the age of 14 he obtained work as an exercise boy at Latonia Race Track in Covington. He obtained his first mount on May 18, 1931, at Bainbridge Park outside Cleveland, but rode in forty-four more races before his first victory at Caliente, Mexico, on January 14, 1932. In his first Kentucky Derby in 1935 he finished fourth.

Arcaro won five Kentucky Derbies and two Triple Crowns (Derby, Preakness, Belmont Stakes). The first Derby victory was in 1938 aboard the horse Larwin, the second in 1941 on Whirlaway, whom he called the most exciting horse he ever rode, followed by Hoop Jr. in 1945, Citation in 1948, and Hill Gail in 1952. Whirlaway and Citation carried Arcaro to the Triple Crown. He also won seventeen Triple Crown events, the last being on Fabius in the 1956 Preakness.

Although he estimated that he was thrown from his mount more than fifty times, the falls resulted in only two serious injuries. After his horse fell in a race in Chicago in 1933, he was trampled by another horse and hospitalized for three months with a fractured skull and punctured lung. In the 1959 Belmont Stakes he was thrown and suffered a concussion and neck sprain. Yet he was rated a fearless athlete who considered death to be a part of his sport.

Although gracious and a good sportsman in his mature years, the younger Arcaro was suspended several times for alleged deliberate fouls. The most serious occurred at Aqueduct

Raceway in 1942, when he tried to bump Cuban jockey Vincenzo Nodarse, whose mount went over the rail. Although initially suspended for an indefinite period, he was allowed to resume riding one year later.

Arcaro remains the only jockey to have won the Triple Crown twice. He holds the record for total stakes victories (554). All told, he won 4,779 races on 24,092 mounts during his thirty-year career. His drive contributed to the financial success he attained before and after his 1961 retirement. He is a member of the National Horse Racing Hall of Fame. *Sports Illustrated* described him as "the most famous man to ride a horse in America since Paul Revere." Arcaro died in 1997.

Richard Renoff

Bibliography

Frank, Stanley. "A Visit with Eddie Arcaro." *The Saturday Evening Post,* 28 June 1958, 26–27, 125–126.
Leggett, William. "What a Fine Little Man." *Sports Illustrated,* 16 April 1962, 20–21.
Stout, Nancy. *Great American Thoroughbred Racetracks.* Forward by Eddie Arcaro. New York: Rizzoli, 1991.

See also SPORTS

Archives, Italy

There exist in Italy numerous archives that house the documents of emigration that are indispensable when researching the exodus of Italians. Despite the quantity of these archival sources, they were rarely consulted until the mid-1970s; and it is only recently, after both private and public state archival centers began to improve their research facilities, that greater utilization has developed.

Private Archives

Although bank archives that received immigrant remittances should contain vital financial records, most of these institutions have not provided sufficient care of such records. There are important exceptions, however, including, among others, the Banco di Napoli and the Banco di Chiavari. Archives in such institutions render it possible to document a quantitative shape to the wealth that was transferred from the new country to the old one and accordingly show how individual family histories affected national economies. The main problem with bank archives is the life span of these institutions; some either went out of existence, or, more likely, merged with other banks with consequent name changes. One way of dealing with this is to consult the archives of the local Archivo di Stato (State Archives in Bergamo, for example) or the Camera di Commercio (Chambers of Commerce), some of which also have information about local emigration.

Cultural Foundations or Associations

These institutions, standing midpoint between the private and the public, contain useful archival information. Among the more serviceable are the Società Umanitaria (Humanitarian Society) and the Fondazione Brodolini in Milan and the Società Dante Aligheri (Dante Aligheri Society) in Rome. For years these associations focused on Italian culture abroad.

Ecclesiastical Archives

These are among the most important private archives to trace the emigration phenomena. Created by religious orders for the spiritual and material support of prospective emigrants, these archives house documentation that is chronologically structured and can be readily comprehended. One of the most important of these sources in Centro Studi Emigrazione (CSER) in Rome, of the Scalabrini Fathers Missionary Order (La Società di S. Raffaele), founded in 1887 by Monsignor Giovanni Scalabrini. This archival center maintains a systematic archival collection and also catalogs state archives. The most important of the CSER emigration holdings are to be found in the Prelato dell'Emigrazione fund.

The central archives of other religious institutions, such as the Jesuits, the Franciscans, the Salesians, and the Figlie di Maria Ausiliatrice (Salesian nuns), the Augustinians, the Servites, and the Missionarie del Sacro Cuore di Gesù (Missionaries of the Sacred Heart of Jesus, also known as Cabrinians), contain files of life within religious communities, their missionary activity in Italy and abroad, and documents concerning individual missionaries engaged in assisting masses of people at port of embarkation and debarkation. The missionaries' activity usually went beyond their entry into the United States as they were also involved in helping emigrants to assimilate into the receiving society, while simultaneously working to preserve their religion and culture. The Propaganda Fide archives keep documents relating to similar activity from the viewpoint of American bishops. All the above-mentioned archives are located in Rome, with the exception of the Figlie di Maria Ausiliatrice, which are located in Turin.

Public Archives

These may be divided into two main groups. The local state archives and the central archives are present in each Italian province that antecede Italian unification (1861–1871) and that concentrate on provincial matters. Their focus expanded after unification. Given the history and varying background, these records are not easily comparable. Funds devoted to archival work were mainly those of the local Prefettura Italiano, which corresponded to the Ministero degli Interni (Department of the Interior) and commence with the date of unification. Such documents can yield information covering a wide scope of emigration topics and, especially, between emigrants and state offices on the following items: emigrants' physical suitability, assistance, or subvention applications, repatriation (in archives of Padova, Treviso, Catanzaro), sex, profession, age, destination, presumed length of absence from Italy, and the number of people in a single application. They sometimes contain passenger lists of local ports.

Official emigration information, emigration laws, and regulations of sending and receiving countries often shed light on the difficulties encountered. The files frequently contain newspaper articles on specific emigration problems in such locales as Avellino, Chieti, Enna, Como, Varese, Genova, Napoli, and Palermo. In these prefettura (civil officer) files are to be found papers of the local Commissioni arbitrali dell'emigrazione who administered the province. Especially important is the fund of commissione (commission) in Genova, which lasted until 1929 and which focused on the following regions: Piemonte, Lombardia, Veneto, Liguria, Toscana, Emilia, and Sardegna.

The Questura constitutes another important fund in the local state archives. Concerned primarily with problems of public order, police, and passport issuance, it occasionally yields information about specific groups of emigrants; however, its main value revolves around the quantification of passport applications and passports issued. This makes it possible to trace population movements abroad. This fund also supplies data from the liste di leva and ruoli matricolari (conscription lists and regimental rolls) from which it is possible to extract quantitative and qualitative descriptions of those receiving and those who failed to receive passports. Young men abroad were conscripted in the nearest consular missions. These missions contain archives that are helpful in analyzing the background of recruits.

Communal archives are very important for the study of local emigration. They provide information similar to that available from provincial archives. School class registers offer another reliable source of information regarding students' birthplaces. Local state archives may contain private documents pertaining to anti-Fascist individuals who communicated with immigrants in the United States.

The above-mentioned archives render it possible to study Italian emigration until World War II. For a period following the war, emigration was treated as a subject of public relief that tended to look upon emigrants as refugees. Archives dealing with this include the Ufficio Provinciale di Assistenza (Provincial Office for Assistance) or the Enti Communali di Assistenza (Communal Organization for Assistance) (ECA), and International Refugees Organization (IRO) of Padova or L'Aquila.

The archives of the Capitanerie di Porto (harbor office) recorded files of ship departures, listing each emigrant's name, profession, sex, and destination. Some of these documents may be found in the archives of the Consorzi Autonomi del Porto (a kind of port authority) present in most Italian port cities such as Livorno, Trieste, Genova, Napoli, and Venezia. Additionally, such information may be found in the central archives of the Ministero della Marina Mercantile, serie, Direzione Generale Personale (Ministry of Mercantile Marine, General Direction of Personnel). These contain ship captain reports on passengers.

The central state archives form the second major division of public archives, undoubtedly the largest and most important in Italy. Among the most informative are those of the Archivo Storico Diplomatico (Diplomatic History Archive) of the Ministero degli Esteri (Foreign Ministry), which collected the documents of Sardinian and, later, Italian diplomatic missions to the United States. These archives, particularly those of the consulates of Cleveland, Chicago, Denver, New Orleans, and San Francisco, have recently been reorganized by the CSER under the direction of Gianfausto Rosoli and Vicenzo Pellegrini, thus opening to researchers the possibility of studying emigration through largely unexplored sources.

Other central state structures concerned with emigration and that possess organized archives are the Fondazione Brodolini, the Ministero di Agricoltura Industria e Commercio (Ministry of Agriculture, Industry, and Trade), the Commissariato General dell'Emigrazione (General Commissariat of Emigration), and the Commissione Central Arbitrale per l'Emigrazione (Central Arbitration Commission for Emigration). The latter contains data on those emigrants who were refused entry into the United States.

Collectively, Italian archives render it possible to gather information on its emigrants, the relationship between the United States and Italy, defense of Italian immigrants who were victims of prejudice, transportation obstacles, and the process of adaptation into the new society. All these sources are available in Direzione Generale Emigrazione e Affari Sociali (DGEAS) (General Direction for the Emigration and Social Affairs) of the Ministero degli Esteri in Rome, which is publishing a collection of publications on the *Fonti per la storia dell'emigrazione* (Sources for the history of emigration). Central administrative bodies, such as the Istituto di Ricostruzione Industriale (IRI) (Industrial Reconstruction Institute), house archival sources that enable researchers to gain information regarding investments of Italian immigrants.

Documents in the Ministero delgi Interni, Direzione generale della sanita pubblica (Department of Interior, General Direction of Public Health), and the Ministero della Marina Mercantile provide information on food and sanitation on board emigrant passenger ships. They also provide insight into the mental and physical stresses and diseases connected with travel and the trauma of interaction between cultures. Also, the files of the Casellario Giudiziario catalog information on political exiles to the United States during the Fascist period.

Improvements in the organization of archival holdings in recent years has led to the accumulation of detailed information on the subject of Italian emigration to the United States. Further, the availability of such material, together with archival material accessible in the United States, has opened possibilities for new ways of analyzing the Italian immigration experience. Utilization of these archives can lead to a clearer understanding of the economic, political, social, cultural, and religious aspects, along with quality of life issues surrounding Italian American immigrants.

Adele Maiello

Bibliography

Cordasco, Francesco. *The Italian American Experience: An Annotated and Classified Bibliographical Guide.* New York: Burt Franklin & Co., 1974.

D' Ambrosio, Manlio A. *Il Mezzogiorno d' Italia e l'Emigrazione negli Stati Uniti.* Roma: Atheneum, 1924.

Dore, Grazia, *La Democrazione e l'Emigrazione in America.* Brescia: Morcelliana, 1964.

International Migration Review. Vol. 1 (summer 1967).

[Istituto Di Studi Americani] *Gli Italian negli Stati Uniti.* Università degli Studi di Firenzi, 1972.

Rosoli, Gianfausto. *Perspectives on Italian Immigration.* Edited by Silvano Tomasi. Staten Island, NY: Center for Migration Studies, 1977.

Savona, A.V., and M. L. Straniero. *Cauti dell' Enigrazione.* Aldo Garzanti Edit, 1976.

See also ARCHIVES, UNITED STATES

Archives, United States

Archival research of Italian Americans can involve a broad span of resources. Collections began as a historical analysis of Italian culture and its effect on early American life. As more Italians migrated to the United States at the turn of the twentieth century, collecting data became more bureaucratic and systematized through census tabulations and immigration counts recorded at entry ports. Collections have been donated to research organizations by Italian American families, businesses, and private organizations. Although research usually begins at the local library and through electronic retrieval systems such as the Internet, primary sources can be obtained from specialized libraries devoted to migration and ethnicity, private collections, and government records (at the federal, state, and local levels).

The earliest collectors in the United States specifically interested in Italian materials concerned themselves with the impact of Italian culture and history on Euro-American civilization in general and on the United States in particular. During the revolutionary and constitutional periods, Americans read classical Latin and Renaissance Italian political philosophers as resources for developing their new governments. During the Transcendental period, authors such as Nathaniel Hawthorne integrated Italian motifs into their fiction. Italian opera has been incorporated into the American repertoire, Italian architectural forms are part of the American architectural vocabulary, and events in the Catholic Church in Italy, such as Bishop Giovanni Battista Scalabrini's migrant apostolate, have affected the Catholic Church in the United States. Institutions such as the Casa Italiana at Columbia University have extensive holdings illustrating the relationship between the performing arts, literature, and the plastic arts in Italy and the United States.

By the early twentieth century, a second category of collectors had become more prominent. These people did not intend to collect material for scholarship, nor were they collecting in the area of Italian culture. They were the record keepers who generated and maintained information for increasingly bureaucratic local, state, and federal governments. Immigration officials counted Italian migrants passing through American ports. Census takers enumerated Italians settled in the United States. Private philanthropies and government agencies studying urban or industrial conditions collected data on the ethnic origins of tenement dwellers and residents. The Gilded Age (1866–1900) and Progressive Era (c. 1890–1920) needed these statistics for other purposes (the federal census, for example, is constitutionally mandated only to apportion congressional representation), but the facts and figures can be used for research. Most of the government records are still in the hands of the government that created them, albeit moved from the care of active agencies to that of a records-management office. Records collected by private agencies may still be with those agencies; the Catholic Church, for example, keeps records at the parish and diocesan level. The records may also have been do-

nated to a specialized library; the Italian Welfare League's case histories of its work with Italians in New York and Brooklyn, for example, are at the Center for Migration Studies.

Since the 1960s a third category of collectors has become important. Unlike the first group, these collectors do not specialize in high culture; they collect material relevant to the mass migration from Italy to the United States between the 1870s and the 1920s and on the experiences of the Italians and their descendants since that time. Unlike the second group, these collectors do not generate records; they gather them from private sources (i.e., they accept deposits of family papers, the papers of businesses owned by Italians, or the papers of Italian American institutions) and bring them together into larger institutions, which is a more efficient way of preserving and presenting data.

Given that Italian American material has not been collected according to one unified scheme and is not available in any one place, researchers should plan before plunging into work. The first step is to investigate the reference (not necessarily Italian American) resources at the closest and best library. This may be a local public library. Institutions of higher education often have arrangements whereby local residents have access to their collections; so it may also be possible to start one's research at a two-year college, four-year college, or university library.

The most expeditious way to acquire a precise description of a library resource is to consult the reference book *Library of Congress Subject Headings Catalog,* which identifies the terms librarians use to shelve books. Checking this will allow researchers to see if they should be looking under Italians, Italian Americans, Italians in America, Italians in the United States, etc. The subject headings catalog will also help with specialized topics. For example, researchers studying Italian American food might check to see if they should look under food, cooking, cuisine, or some other relevant term.

Once oriented to the possible subject headings, researchers can begin searching the secondary literature to see if anyone has published a book or article on specific information concerning Italian Americans. In most libraries, this is a two-step process. First, one consults the printed bibliographies of books and articles on Italian Americans. Unfortunately, many such bibliographies were published in the 1970s, at the peak of interest in ethnicity, and have not been revised to include more recent publications. Still, bibliographies such as those compiled by Francesco Cordasco and Salvatore LaGumina, *Italians in the United States: A Bibliography of Reports, Texts, Critical Studies and Related Materials* (Oriole Editions) are good guides to the classics in the field. Italian topics are also included in more general bibliographies. One volume of the reference work *Books in Print* lists current book-length publications by subject heading. Another reference work, *America: History and Life,* lists both current books and articles in scholarly journals. A third reference work, *Dissertation Abstracts International* (often referred to as DAI), describes doctoral theses.

The second step is to consult the reference librarian for possible assistance with electronic searches. The exact policies and procedures for electronic searches vary from library to library: some services are free and some charge fees; some let the library patron conduct the search, others require that the librarian access the information. Research materials on Italian Americans are beginning to be listed on the Internet. For a useful and recent article, see Charles A. D'Aniello's "An Internet Sampler for Italian Americans," *Italian Americana* (summer 1987: 211–223), which covers directories, search engines, and search strategies. Electronic searches also consist of checking different catalogs: for example, *America: History and Life* and the DAI are both on-line. Internet search engines narrow down research to a specific topic. For example, instead of asking for all the references to Italian Americans and then sorting through entries for those pertaining to agriculture, researchers can ask for "Italian Americans and agriculture," and, depending on the program, the computer will find all references that combine all three terms.

After exhausting local library references and readily available interlibrary loans, researchers should consult DAI and *America: History and Life* before embarking on their own in-depth research into primary sources. More extensive electronic searches to check the holdings of a more distant university or special collection may be necessary. The two most common searches at present are On-Line Catalog of the Library of Congress (OCLC)

and Research Library Information Network (RLIN, pronounced "Arlynn"). Libraries with electronic search resources may be able to help with these searches.

There are specialized guides to primary source material. The most traditional is the National Union Catalog of Manuscript Collections (known as NUCMC), previously available in print and soon to be available electronically. NUCMC can help track down specific items. For example, papers of the late Ellis Island commissioner Edward Corsi can be traced to the University of Syracuse and those of philosopher and World War II refugee Max Ascoli can be found at the Boston Public Library. However, researchers interested in social history may want to access papers that delineate activities in Italian American everyday life, which are found in specialized libraries devoted to migration and ethnicity or among government documents.

An excellent starting point for primary material on Italian migration to the United States is the Center for Migration Studies (CMS). Founded in 1964 and headquartered on Staten Island, New York, CMS combines three scholarly services. It holds conferences, including conferences on Italian migration; it publishes books and scholarly journals, including an extensive list of books and occasional papers on various aspects of the Italian American experience; and it collects materials. It has one of the most comprehensive collections on Italian American history in the world: books, scholarly journals, magazines, newspapers, newsletters, a clipping file, and unpublished scholarly papers. CMS has nearly ninety processed collections of materials relevant to the Italian American experience, from personal and institutional papers to rare books by Italian American authors.

CMS is especially strong in the area of Italian American Catholicism. It has Italian Catholic parish papers from several cities as well as papers of Italian-born priests who spent their years of active ministry in the American mission field. CMS also has thousands of photographs from the late nineteenth century to the present depicting many aspects of Italian American life.

The Immigration History Research Center was founded in 1965 as the Center for Immigration Studies. It adopted its present name in 1974. It is housed on the campus of the University of Minnesota in Minneapolis. IHRC specializes in collecting material from European and Near Eastern ethnics settled in the United States. Its most recent guide, *The Immigration History Research Center: A Guide to Collections* by Suzanna Moody and Joel Wurl (Greenwood, 1991), lists twenty-three collections, ranging from Albanians to Ukrainians. Researchers have restricted access to some IHRC collections, and other collections are actually copies of papers available elsewhere. The IHRC's Italian American Collection includes an extensive amount of processed papers from private individuals and organizations, such as the American Committee for Italian War Relief. The collection is especially rich in material pertaining to the Sons of Italy. It has papers from lodges and from individuals connected with the organization, and a separate guide to that collection. The IHRC has an extensive collection of Italian American newspapers on microfilm and in the original paper copies. The archival collection is supplemented by microfilm copies of papers available elsewhere, and by a library of over 1,400 monographs.

The third organization, the Balch Institute, is headquartered in Philadelphia. The Balchs were a prominent family in that city until the 1920s. When the last members died without heirs, their estates provided the founding contribution. The Balch Institute was incorporated in 1971. It combines a research library, a museum, and an educational program. It emphasizes ethnic American material independent of migration, and thus includes documents from Native Americans and from African Americans. As of 1992 it had fifty-six collections ranging from African Americans to Wendish. Some of its Italian collections are quite small but very precious, as they consist of rare family documents or photographs. It also has papers and photographs from several organizations and Italian language newspapers.

Scattered throughout the United States are smaller collections of material on particular Italian Americans, or Italian American organizations, and on Italian American life generally. Silvano M. Tomasi edited a survey of these collections in 1980. This finding aid is titled *National Directory of Resource Centers, Repositories and Organizations of Italian Culture in the United States*. A more recent finding aid identifies active Italian American communities: Margaret Hobbie, *Italian American Material Culture: A Directory of Collections, Sites, and Festivals in the United States and Canada*.

In some cities in which Italians settled in large numbers, the public libraries maintain special collections on them. The San Francisco Public Library maintains a special collection on Italians. The Belmont (Bronx) Regional Branch of the New York Public Library performs the same function for that city.

In other cases, researchers need to consider how seemingly unrelated collections may yield material on Italians. The Sacco and Vanzetti legal case is a good example. Material on the case is in the records of individuals who were not themselves Italian and who generally did not involve themselves in Italian American affairs; for example, in the papers of A. A. Lawrence, president of Harvard at the time of the trial.

Primary source materials on Italian American history sometimes appear in the context of documentation of some other subject. One example is religion. Individuals who may have thought of themselves as evangelical Protestants or Roman Catholic missionaries, and whose papers are in the hands of religious organizations, could also be studied as individuals of Italian American descent. A finding guide to archival and published materials on this intersection of topics is *Italian Americans and Religion* by Silvano M. Tomasi and Edward C. Stibili, second edition (Center for Migration Studies, 1992).

Another topic with which Italian American studies frequently intersects is women's studies. *Immigrant Women in the United States: A Selectively Annotated Multidisciplinary Bibliography* by Donna Gabaccia (Greenwood, 1998), is a good example. There is no separate listing for Italians, but Italian women appear in the various sections devoted to women's work, intellectual life, family role, etc. Similarly, the fields of ethnicity and literature intersect to the point that most library card catalogs list drama, fiction, and poetry by the ethnicity of the authors as well as by genre.

For much of America's industrial period, the assumption that many laborers are members of ethnic groups is so prevalent that there are no finding guides arranged by ethnicity and labor. The same is true of the intersection of ethnicity and urban history, especially for the period that coincides with the greatest Italian migration. Researchers interested in Italian American labor or Italian American cities should pinpoint the occupations and urban areas in which Italians were prominent, and consult finding guides for those subjects.

U.S. federal government records touch on a number of topics relevant to Italian American history, from diplomatic relations between the United States and the various governments on the Italian peninsula since 1788 to the number of Italian Americans as of the last decennial census. Two units of the federal government concern themselves with record keeping. The first is the Library of Congress, which is located in several buildings in Washington, D.C. The Library of Congress has a manuscript division that maintains and makes available papers donated by various sources. It also collects nonprint materials, such as sound recordings, prints, photographs, film, videotape, and electronically stored data. Researchers should contact the Library of Congress directly for current information on accessing materials.

The second branch of record keeping is the National Archives and Records Administration, which is responsible for noncurrent federal records. Material comes to the NARA from the judicial branch, the House and Senate, the cabinet departments, and the president's office. The NARA then catalogs the information and makes it available to researchers. Like the Library of Congress, the NARA has material in a variety of formats. It has grown so much since its inception that it maintains its Washington, D.C., building as office space and a museum, and warehouses most of its records in Suitland, Maryland. The NARA publishes a guide to its "processed" collections (material prepared for researchers use), which is available at local research libraries. However, given that some collections have been transferred out of Washington, it might be best to phone the NARA for updated information as to access.

One final piece of information about federal documents is that the federal government has depositories all over the country for its published records. Most of these are in research libraries. The libraries may be part of a private college or university, but the depositories themselves are always open to the public. Data on historical matters (numbers of Italian immigrants, numbers of Italians in the census, reports on working conditions in industries in which Italians are employed) can be found at these depositories.

At the state level, most states have a state library, usually in the same city as the state capital. *Directory of American Libraries with Genealogy or Local History Collections* by P. William Filby (Scholarly Resources, 1988) is the best current source of proper names, addresses, and basic information on collections. These state libraries perform the same functions as the Library of Congress and the NARA, but for the state level.

Below the state level, almost all states are divided into county-level governing units (except Louisiana, which uses the term parishes). However, there are units within counties removed from county jurisdiction and incorporated separately as cities, towns, townships, villages, boroughs, etc., depending on their size and on local nomenclature. There are also listings of cities that sprawl over several counties. Some substate levels of government have their own archives. (For example, there is a New York City Archives that is part of city government.) Others deposit certain records at the state library.

There are several ways to start on the trail of local history records. The aforementioned Filby provides names and addresses of local historical collections on a state-by-state basis. State libraries or state historical commissions might have updated surveys of what is available within their states. Researchers interested in genealogy might find government and state documents useful; city or county vital statistics offices maintain birth and death records, courts keep wills, and some government offices maintain real estate and tax records.

Another avenue for archival research is to use the resources of local Italian American organizations. There is no one national telephone book of Italian American agencies, but there are regional reference books such as *A Directory of Italian American Associations in the Tri-State Area: Connecticut, Eastern New Jersey, and New York* (Center for Migration Studies, 1989). Not all of these organizations are dedicated to promoting scholarship, but they may have research advice, especially on local history. The American Italian Historical Association is another resource. Founded in 1966 and headquartered at 209 Flagg Place, Staten Island, New York, the AIHA has provided the most comprehensive, systematic, and scientific research on Italians in the United States; it conducts an annual conference, the proceedings of which provide an excellent statement on Italian American studies (it is multidisciplinary) as well as creative ideas for

A

finding and using resources. The AIHA has chapters throughout the United States.

One final research guide is available to genealogists. The Church of Jesus Christ of Latter Day Saints gathers and makes available genealogical materials. The Mormon religion calls for such genealogical research, but the Mormons will share their work with non-Mormons. The local Mormon congregation can guide genealogists to the nearest center for Mormon genealogical work.

Mary Elizabeth Brown

Bibliography

Cordasco, Frank, and Salvatore J. LaGumina. *Italians in the United States: A Bibliography of Reports, Texts, Critical Studies and Related Materials.* New York: Oriole Editions, 1972.

Gabaccia, Donna. *Italian American Women in the United States: A Selected Annotated Multi-disciplinary Bibliography.* Westport, CT: Greenwood, 1989.

Moody, Suzanna, and Joel Wurl. *The Immigrant History Research Center: A Guide to Collection.* Westport, CT: Greenwood, 1991.

Tomasi, Silvano. *National Directory of Research Centers, Repositories and Organizations of Italian Culture in the United States.* Torino: Fondazione Giovanni Agnelli, 1980.

Tomasi, Silvano, and Edward Stibili. *Italian Americans and Religion: An Annotated Bibliography.* Staten Island, NY: Center for Migration Studies, 1992.

See also AMERICAN ITALIAN HISTORICAL ASSOCIATION; ARCHIVES, ITALY; GENEALOGY AND FAMILY HISTORY; IMMIGRATION HISTORY RESEARCH CENTER; ITALIAN WELFARE LEAGUE, ORDER SONS OF ITALY IN AMERICA

Armetta, H.

See MOVIE ACTORS AND ACTRESSES

Art

Almost every aspect of image making in the United States has been enriched by the presence of Italian artists. From the fine arts to films, from commemoration to decoration, artists of Italian heritage have contributed significant works in such numbers and variety that a large volume is required to treat the subject fully. For present purposes, this entry will cover painting and sculpture, *le belle arti,* with a few brief excursions into other art forms.

The first Italian artist in North America was Cosmo Medici, about whom we know only that he painted a portrait of Lucy Briggs in Virginia in 1772 and probably served in the Revolutionary War against the British. Even less is known of one Caffieri—not even his first name—who executed the tomb of Revolutionary War General Richard Montgomery in New York in 1777, considered to be the first national monument erected in this country.

The first Italian artist of substantial importance to the development of American art was Giuseppe Ceracchi (1751–1801), an ardent believer in republican government, who in 1791 left Europe, where he had established a substantial reputation as a sculptor, and migrated to the United States, being attracted to the philosophical and political ideas on which it was founded. His hope of creating a colossal equestrian monument to George Washington with many allegorical figures was not fulfilled because of congressional refusal to pay for such a huge undertaking. He did, however, make an over-life-size statue of the president in terra cotta, one of only two sculptured likenesses modeled after the living figure of Washington. The other is by the French sculptor Jean Antoine Houdon.

Ceracchi is credited with introducing the portrait bust into the art of the new nation, which became the most widely practiced form of sculpture in early-nineteenth-century American art. He modeled in terra cotta and translated into marble more than two dozen busts of prominent Americans including Washington, Thomas Jefferson, John Quincy Adams, and the artist John Trumbull, who, in turn, used Ceracchi's marble bust of Alexander Hamilton for his posthumous portrait of the nation's first Secretary of the Treasury, the same image that is on the ten-dollar bill. The busts of Washington and Jefferson, as well as those of Amerigo Vespucci and Christopher Columbus, were lost in the fire set by the British that destroyed most of the Capitol and many other public buildings in the War of 1812. Copies in marble exist in various American public and private collections.

As a European familiar with art academies, Ceracchi collaborated with Charles Willson

Peale in creating the "Columbianum," the first art academy in the United States. The academy was unfortunately short-lived, as it split into deadly political factions: some of the founders wanted to establish their academy on the British model, the Royal Academy, which Ceracchi and his cohorts rejected for its monarchical associations. Ceracchi's passionate embrace of liberty cost him his life. He was executed for anti-Napoleonic activity in France.

The history of art by Italian heritage artists in the United States is closely bound to the history of art manifested in the U.S. Capitol building during the nineteenth century. This began when Giovanni Andrei (ca. 1757–1824) and Giuseppe Franzoni (1777–1815) arrived in America in 1805 at the invitation of Benjamin Latrobe, architect of the Capitol, to carry out sculptural embellishments for the Capitol, then being built. According to Latrobe, they were "the only sculptors in America" at that time. Andrei was commissioned to carve twenty-four Corinthian column capitals in the Hall of the House of Representatives in the south wing, while Franzoni was given the task of carving the frieze above them. Only a few of the columns were completed when the building was torched in 1814 by the British, and Andrei was sent to Italy in 1815 to arrange for the carving of the Corinthian capitals there.

In 1808 Andrei had received a commission from the Union Bank in Baltimore for a tympanum lunette representing Ceres and Neptune; the piece is now in the garden of the Peale Museum in that city. When he returned to the United States in 1816 he carried out other private work in Baltimore.

Franzoni's frieze was completed by 1808, with figures representing Commerce, Agriculture, Art, and Science. An enormous eagle at the center, however, did not please Latrobe because it looked, he said, like an Italian, or Roman, or Greek eagle. He wanted an American bald eagle, which the artist, with the help of a drawing by Charles Willson Peale or one of his sons, achieved to the utter satisfaction of the architect, who found it equal to the greatest of ancient or modern images of eagles. This and all other carvings by Giuseppe Franzoni, except six capitals representing corncobs designed by Latrobe (the earliest example, aside from the marble portrait busts by Ceracchi, of a synthesis of Italian carving and American imagery), fell victim to the fire of 1814.

Despite the loss of most of their work, it must be realized that the presence of these Italian-born artists in the United States in those years, sponsored by the government and working in the heart of the new nation, was of major importance in providing an impetus for the development of American sculpture.

When Andrei returned from Italy in 1816 he brought with him Giuseppe Franzoni's brother, Carlo (ca. 1786–1821), and their cousin, Francesco Iardella (1793–1831). Carlo Franzoni was the creator of the masterful "Car of History" (1819) in Statuary Hall, probably the earliest carved-in-the-round marble statue in the United States. It represents Clio, the muse of History, standing in the winged chariot of Time, recording events. The chariot wheel is a functioning clock. It is said that one of Giuseppe Franzoni's daughters was the model for Clio. Franzoni also produced a plaster relief (1817), which is now in the Law Library of the Supreme Court. It depicts an allegorical figure of Justice seated on a bench at the center; she holds her traditional attributes, scales and the sword, while on her left an American eagle guards four books of the law and on her right, a seated, winged boyish figure representing the young nation holds the Constitution, the rising sun behind him.

Iardella is best remembered for his carving of the tobacco plant motif, also designed by Latrobe, on the sixteen column capitals in the lobby of the small rotunda in the Senate wing. He became sculptor-in-charge of the work at the Capitol when Giovanni Andrei died. Iardella also inherited by marriage the widow of Giuseppe Franzoni.

The art mentioned thus far was executed in the Neoclassical style, which dominated European art in the wake of the rediscovery in 1748 of Pompeii, the Roman resort town buried by the eruption of Vesuvius in 79 A.D. The artists who came to America, born to this stately, quiet aesthetic taste of the ancient classical world, thus helped to introduce Neoclassicism to the United States and established the precedent for the style of embellishment of our public buildings.

The work of three more Italian sculptors active in the Capitol in the early phase is also highly important: Enrico Causici, Antonio Capellano, and Luigi Persico (1791–1859) introduced American mythology into their sculptures and thus contributed to the development of native symbolism in art, called iconography.

Between 1825 and 1827 Causici, who came to the United States in 1815, executed two reliefs in sandstone for the newly completed Rotunda, *The Landing of the Pilgrims* and *Conflict of Daniel Boone and the Indians.* In Statuary Hall his larger-than-life-size figure, mistakenly known as Liberty, more properly, *Genius of the Constitution,* replaced in 1819 a statue by Franzoni destroyed in the fire of 1814. It stands at the center of a niche in Classical drapery, her right hand holding the Constitution, with the American eagle at her right, a serpent (wisdom) twined around a column segment at her left. Capellano was in the United States from 1815 to 1829 (when he returned to Italy) and carved two reliefs for the Rotunda, also in sandstone, *Preservation of Captain Smith by Pocahontas* (1825) and *Fame and Peace Crowning George Washington* (1827). This panel was replaced by a copy in marble in 1960. Causici and Capellano collaborated on four panels for the Rotunda with profile reliefs of Columbus, John Cabot, Sir Walter Raleigh, and Robert Cavelier sieur de LaSalle, all in the Rotunda.

Persico arrived here from Naples in 1818. His first commission in Washington was a group of figures for the pediment at the east front of the Capitol, *Genius of America.* It represents America at the center, flanked by Justice, holding her traditional scales, and Hope, resting her left elbow on her symbolic anchor. Persico's figures, executed in sandstone between 1825 and 1828, were badly deteriorated by the time the east front was extended in 1959, and marble copies were made to replace them. Persico returned to Italy in 1829 to execute his commission for statues representing *War* and *Peace,* which he brought back to America with him in 1834. These also deteriorated—the marble of Italy could not withstand the cold weather—and were copied in 1958 in Vermont marble by George Giannetti from plaster models of Persico's originals. They occupy the same niches of the originals to the left and right of the east central entrance. Persico's final group for the Capitol was an enormous *Discovery of America,* which was placed on the left of the east front steps in 1844; it, too, was ruined by weather and is now in storage.

Among the Italian painters active in the United States in the first half of the nineteenth century, Michele Felice Corne (1752–1845) is known for his New England marine scenes

and is credited with introducing the tomato to the American diet. Nicolino Calyo (1799–1884) painted landscapes and city panoramas. The only Italian-born painter who worked in the Capitol was Pietro Bonanni (1792–1821), who was born in Cararra and arrived in Washington in 1816 or 1817. In 1818 he painted the half-dome of the ceiling in Statuary Hall to look like the ceiling of the Pantheon, creating the illusion of relief. When it was removed to install a fireproof ceiling in 1901, the new decoration was actually executed in relief to make it look like the original illusion. Also by Bonanni in the Capitol is a portrait of Carlo Franzoni (1818). Nicola Monachesi (?–1851) painted a mural in the dome of the Philadelphia Exchange (1834), which is reputedly among the first true frescoes ever painted in this country.

In the second half of the nineteenth century the greatest Italian-born artist in the United States was the painter Constantino Brumidi (1805–1880). He is credited with the extraordinary embellishment of the Capitol Rotunda dome, the frieze that circles its base, and many rooms in the Senate and House wings, work that earned him the epithet "Michelangelo of the United States Capitol." Inspired by the American principles of liberty and justice, Brumidi migrated from Italy in 1852. He was here, fortunately, when Captain Montgomery C. Meigs, appointed superintendent of the new extensions of the Capitol in 1853, had begun the new wings and dome and wanted monumental frescoes for those sections, although he was aware that no American artist was capable of such work. Brumidi's presence gave him the opportunity he needed to carry out his vision. The artist began his mural work in 1855 and continued working unceasingly in the Capitol until his death, which was caused by an accident on his scaffold while working high above the floor on the frieze.

Brumidi's subjects in the House and Senate wings, painted between 1855–1871, included traditional allegories such as the *Four Seasons* on the ceiling of the chamber of the House Committee on Appropriations, and depictions of American history such as the *Boston Massacre* and Revolutionary War battle scenes in the Senate Appropriations Committee Rooms. It is interesting to note his "quotations" from Italian Renaissance masters in these and other works, for example, in his *Four Seasons* where the male figure, "Winter," straddles an icy cloud, his arm outstretched with the finger extended as in Michelangelo's famous image of God creating Adam on the ceiling of the Sistine Chapel, with many *putti* (cupid-like figures) cavorting in the empyrean of this and all the *Seasons,* drawn from similar figures in Donatello's famous *Singing Gallery.* In the *Boston Massacre,* as well as in *The Death of General Wooster* in the same room, a victim is carried away by two fellow fighters in the same grouping and similar poses as seen in Raphael's *Deposition of Christ.*

Over a period of twenty-five years, this artist, with assistants, painted portraits, historical scenes, allegories, and decorations in eight rooms plus corridors and stairways of the Capitol. In addition and literally above all, Brumidi's greatest works are the frescoes that he painted on the canopy of the Rotunda dome and on its frieze. The theme of the former is *The Apotheosis of George Washington,* of the latter, American history visualized by sequential scenes starting with the landing of Columbus to the discovery of gold in California. The canopy is 180 feet above the Rotunda floor and slightly over 62 feet in diameter. The figures are about 50 feet tall. Brumidi's first sketches for the canopy were made in 1859, but his actual painting did not begin until Congress authorized it in 1863. He finished this gigantic task in eleven months.

Characteristic of the great Italian tradition of dome painting initiated by Mantegna in Mantua between 1468–1474, the scene floats illusionistically above in a space that, as one spectator observed, "arrests the gaze as though the sky had opened up." The figures are disposed in two circles, in accordance with the shape of the dome. Washington sits enthroned in the inner circle with the female embodiments of Liberty on his right and Victory and Fame on his left, the circle completed with thirteen female figures symbolizing the thirteen original states. The outer circle on the rim of the canopy is composed of six groupings: War, Art and Sciences, Navigation, Commerce, Manufactures, and Agriculture. The historical narrative on the frieze is painted to give the effect of sculptural relief. Considered together, canopy and frieze constitute an extraordinarily successful synthesis of Italian technique and mythology with American iconography.

Brumidi died before he had finished the frieze. The task of completing it was entrusted to Filippo Costaggini (1837–1904).

Costaggini finished *Penn's Treaty with the Indians* on which Brumidi was working at his death, and continued through the gold discovery. These scenes did not complete the circle, and in 1950 Allyn Cox was commissioned to add *The Civil War, The Spanish-American War,* and *The Birth of Aviation in the United States.* Grime and retouching during the twentieth century hid Brumidi's work, and it was not until a thorough and brilliant conservation was performed by Bernard Rabin, with the consultative help of Laura and Paolo Mora from the Istituto Centrale del Restauro, that Brumidi's achievement was revealed. A marble bust of Brumidi (1967) by Jimilu Mason is located in the Brumidi corridor on the first floor of the Senate wing; a painted portrait (ca. 1973) by Allyn Cox is in the east corridor of the House wing.

Other Italian American artists active here in the second half of the nineteenth century include Giuseppe Fagnani (1819–1873), who became well-known for his *Types of American Beauty,* a series of nine portraits of fashionable women acquired by the Metropolitan Museum of Art in New York City; Eugenio Latilla (1808–1861), who gained a reputation as portraitist of fifty of the most eminent American clergyman of the time; Domenico Togetti (1806–1892), a muralist who fortunately did not live to see his works destroyed in the earthquake of 1906, and his sons, Eduardo and Virgilio, who also became muralists; and Louis Rebisso (1837–1899), who executed the equestrian monuments of President Grant in Chicago's Lincoln Park and General Harrison, in Cincinnati. Luigi Palma Di Cesnola (1832–1904), an archaeologist, not an artist, should nevertheless be recognized as one of the most important Italian Americans in the history of American art: he was the first director of the Metropolitan Museum of Art when the new building was erected at its present site in 1879 and remained in office until his death.

Among Italian American artists of the next generation, Luigi Amateis (1855–?) was the only one to receive an important commission for the Capitol. In 1904 this sculptor designed a bronze door for the west facade. Taking for his model the famous *Doors of Paradise* by Lorenzo Ghiberti, in Florence, Amateis divided his field into eight square panels (the Ghiberti doors have ten) and included a transom panel above extending the full width of the doors within their frames. Instead

A

of composing scenes from the Bible as the Renaissance master did, Amateis once again wedded the Italian tradition to American symbolism: on the transom is figured *Apotheosis of America,* with "America" in a chariot drawn by lions, symbolizing strength; on the eight panels are allegorical scenes representing on the left Jurisprudence, Sciences, Fine Arts, and Mining, on the right Agriculture, Iron and Electricity, Engineering, and Naval Architecture and Commerce. At the side of each panel, instead of the Ghibertian prophets and sybils, Amateis created statuettes of major personages in history associated with the panel: for example, flanking Fine Arts are figures representing Edgar Allan Poe and William Thornton, the first architect of the Capitol. While Ghiberti alternated his prophets and sybils with high-relief heads, Amateis alternated his figures with portrait medallions of distinguished Americans such as, for the Fine Arts, the painter Gilbert Stuart and the sculptor Henry Kirke Brown.

Vincenzo Alfano (1854–1929) executed sculpture for the Pennsylvania Capitol at Harrisburg, the Court House in St. Louis, and reliefs for the Church of St. John the Baptist in New York City. Pasquale Civiletti (1858–1952) created the impressive, beautiful monument to Verdi that dominates the intersection of Broadway and 72nd Street in New York City. Giuseppe Moretti (1859–1935) is remembered for the monuments he created such as the *John Henry Patterson Memorial* in Dayton, Ohio, an equestrian statue flanked by two groups of figures representing Education and Fruits of Labor. But he is known even more for his major contribution to American sculpture: Moretti brought the *cire perdue* method of bronze casting to the United States, and, together with Riccardo Bertelli (1870–1955), in 1897 he founded the highly successful Roman Bronze Works in New York City. Bertelli became sole owner a year later, and his firm is credited with casting the General Ulysses S. Grant Memorial in Washington, D.C., the largest bronze casting of its time. Many distinguished American sculptors of the period had their work cast by the Roman Bronze Works, including Frederic Remington, Daniel Chester French, and Paul Manship.

Working with stone has been an Italian tradition for centuries and often a family tradition. Such was the case with the Piccirilli family. Giuseppe Piccirilli (1843–1910), a sculptor, brought six sons to the United States in 1888, all of whom became sculptors. Giuseppe's principal works are decorations for the new Customs House (1907), the New York Stock Exchange, and other public buildings. Giuseppe Piccirilli's sons belong to the next generation of Italian heritage artists in the United States, those born between 1860 and 1879. Attilio, Ferruccio, Furio, Horatio, Maso, and Orazio, all born in Massa di Carrara, Italy, together established a studio in New York in 1889 that became the largest sculptural studio in the country. The most famous, and probably most gifted, was Attilio (1866–1945), whose name is attached to a number of important monuments, including the great marble *Lincoln* (1916) in Washington, designed by Daniel Chester French but carved by Attilio and his brothers. A landmark in New York City, the many-figured *Maine Monument* (1901) in Columbus Circle, is credited to Attilio but was no doubt executed with the assistance of his brothers. It should be noted that Gaetano Russo designed Columbus Circle.

Among other works by Attilio are those executed for Rockefeller Center: the first bas-relief in the United States cast in glass, *Eternal Youth* (1935), at the main entrance of the Palazzo d'Italia; *Youth Leading Industry* (1936), in the International Building; and *Joy of Life* (1937), on the doorway at 15 West 48th Street. He is also the designer of the pediment at the entrance of the Frick Collection. In addition to his work as a sculptor, Attilio was a cofounder in 1923 (with Onorio Ruotolo) and president of the Leonardo da Vinci Art School in New York.

John Rapetti (1862–1936) worked in Paris with Frédéric Bartholdi on the Statue of Liberty; his name is engraved in the crown as one of its creators. In the United States his most important works were statues of Hamilton and Jefferson at Columbia University and of Grant in Grant Park, Brooklyn. Among the most important works by Leo Lentelli (1879–1961) are the figure of Christ and sixteen angels for the reredos of the Cathedral of St. John the Divine, five figures for the facade of the San Francisco Public Library, and sculptural decorations for Rockefeller Center. The prolific Pompeo Luigi Coppini (1870–1957) settled in Texas, where he executed perhaps twenty-four public monuments including the *Littlefield Memorial Fountain,* University of

Texas at Austin; a statue of George Washington given as a gift from the United States to Mexico; a cenotaph to the heroes of the Alamo, plus numerous portrait statues and busts. He was head of the Art Department, Trinity University, San Antonio, 1942–1947.

Among painters born between 1860 and 1879, Joseph Stella (1877–1946) stands out as the single best-known Italian American artist of the first half of the twentieth century. His subjects ranged widely to include bridges and factories in the United States, peasants in Italy, the industrial landscape in his adopted country, views of his mountainous homeland, lush tropical flowers and fruit, portraits, and still life. He worked in many styles: realistic, semi-abstract, nonobjective, and decorative. His best-known painting, *New York Interpreted* (1918–1923), in the Newark Museum (New Jersey), is a wall-size, five-panel semi-abstract rendering of "The Port," "The White Ways" (the Broadway theatrical district), "The [Brooklyn] Bridge," and "Skyscrapers." Conceived as a "shrine," and composed as an altarpiece, Stella's painting with its bridge cables swooping upward and its skyscrapers reaching the heavens, expresses his perception of technology as the modern world's religion. The work is generally recognized as one of the most important modern American paintings.

Although Stella lived most of his life in the United States, he made several prolonged visits to Italy and spent a few years in France. His feeling of *Italianità* (sense of being Italian) was strong, and in many paintings and drawings he depicted the people and the mountainous, rocky landscape of his *paese* (town) in a realistic style. However, his large, impressive *Tree of My Life* (1919), a fanciful, tapestry-like image filled with flowers and birds and a view of the arched bridge and village of his birthplace, is painted in a decorative style.

Gottardo Piazzoni (1872–1945) was the acknowledged "dean" of San Francisco painters. Principally a muralist, Piazzoni's early wall paintings were destroyed or lost. His masterpiece, however, a suite of fourteen murals in the San Francisco Public Library, survives in perfect condition due to cleaning in 1972. The theme is California, which he called his "religion." The subjects of the first ten panels, installed in 1932, are *The Sea* and *The Land;* four additional panels completed shortly before he died are on related themes: *The Mountain, The Forest, Night, Dawn, The Soil,* and *The City.*

Nicola D'Ascenzo (1871–1954) enhanced many walls with his work in stained glass, mosaic, and paint, including windows for the Folger Library, Washington, D.C.; for the Firestone Library and the Chapel at Princeton University; the Saint Thomas Protestant Episcopal Church and the Chapel of the Intercession, New York City; and the Washington Memorial Church, Valley Forge, Pennsylvania. Among his mosaics is the frieze in Cooper Library in Camden, New Jersey. As a muralist he decorated the municipal buildings in Springfield, Massachusetts. Another outstanding muralist of this age group is Vincent Aderente (1880–1941), whose long list of credits indicates that he was in demand by architects who wanted the walls of their buildings embellished with murals: the United States Mint Building, Denver; the Court House and City Hall, Youngstown, Ohio; the Hudson County Court House, Jersey City, New Jersey, among others.

Although not painters or sculptors in the strict sense, there are four Italian Americans renowned for the innovative quality of their artistic work. Simon Rodia (1879–1965) worked from 1921 to 1954 building his now famous towers in the Watts section of Los Angeles. Encrusted with broken bottles, broken china, shells, machine parts, screwdrivers, and pliers, the brilliantly decorative towers conceived by this miner-logger-construction worker have been declared a Cultural Heritage Monument.

Joseph Maturo (1876–1938) designed more than two hundred posters for some of the most successful movies of the thirties.

Antonio (1875–1941) and Giuseppe Mungo (1881–1965) worked as parchment illuminators. Having learned their craft at the Vatican School in Rome, they created commemorative sheets of jewel-like beauty, sold, not surprisingly, by Tiffany. Their masterwork is *Old Glory* (1916–1926), a composition using various American symbols such as the flag and portraits of Washington, Jefferson, Lincoln, and Wilson. For this tribute to their adopted country and its sesquicentennial celebration, the Mungo brothers joined eight or nine skins of parchment by a method of their own devising to create a virtually seamless surface, its dimensions 43 by 63 inches. It is thought to be the largest illuminated manuscript in the world and the most intrinsically valuable: the borders and interior lettering, and other details, are executed in twenty-four carat gold and it has been estimated that the amount of gold used represented an expenditure of $250,000. The work can be seen at the Fordham University Library on the Bronx campus.

In the group of Italian heritage artists born between 1880 and 1899, more than fifty practicing professionals are recorded in artists' directories, among whom several may be singled out as having won the broadest recognition. Alfeo Faggi (1885–1966) came to the United States when he was 28 years old in rebellion against the prevailing neoclassicism of the Italian school. Here he developed a flowing, elongated figure style. His successful career as a sculptor brought him numerous prizes, and his work is in leading American museums: Whitney Museum of American Art, Art Institute of Chicago, Brooklyn Museum, and Cleveland Museum, among others. Faggi was also a founder and later director of the Woodstock Artists Association.

Onorio Ruotolo (1888–1966) is known for his portrait busts of famous people, especially his *Enrico Caruso* in the Metropolitan Opera House. He was cofounder (with Attilio Piccirilli) of the Leonardo da Vinci Art School that flourished until the mid-1940s.

Sculptures by Oronzio Maldarelli (1892–1963) are in the collections of the Metropolitan Museum, which acquired his female nude *Reclining Figure* in 1941 and his *Bianca No. 2,* also a female nude, in 1953. Additional works appear in other public collections, including the Federal Post Office Building in Washington, D.C. Other sculptors and their particular works include Marcello Rebecchini (birth and death dates unavailable) for his statue *Evangeline,* the heroine of Henry Wadsworth Longfellow's famous poem, which attracted ten thousand people when it was dedicated in St. Martinville, Louisiana, April 19, 1930; Richard H. Recchia, who founded the Boston Society of Sculptors in 1923; and Antonio Salemme (1892– 1995), who created a nude standing statue of Paul Robeson and a portrait bust of General Dwight Eisenhower, both at Columbia University, and a portrait bust of John F. Kennedy in the Kennedy Memorial Library, Boston. Felix Peano (?–1948) was commissioned to execute his *Door of Life* for the Episcopal Church of the Holy Faith in San Francisco, but the work was never installed because parishioners objected to its nude figures, which the artist refused to change. It is now in a private collection. An artist who worked in many media, Peano drew dinosaurs for the first animated cartoons in Hollywood.

Peppino Mangravite (1896–1978) worked as a muralist in the art section of the Works Progress Adminstration. His easel paintings are in the Museum of Modern Art; Whitney Museum of American Art; Corcoran Gallery of Art, Washington, D.C.; De Young Museum in San Francisco; and other American museums. From 1942 to 1965, he was professor of painting at Columbia University. The unusual career of John Castano (1896–1978) deserves mention: he was a muralist as well as a scene designer. Between 1922 and 1929 he designed eighty-six stage sets for the Cincinnati grand opera. Although outside the realm of sculpture and painting, Tina Modotti (1896–1942), a migrant from northern Italy, became renowned for her photography, which she learned from her famous teacher (and lover), Edward Weston, and also for her extravagant life spent largely among the outstanding Mexican artists of the twentieth century such as Diego Rivera, José Clemente Orozco, and Frida Kahlo. Pablo Neruda, her friend after she broke up with Weston, wrote the poem that is inscribed on her tomb in the Pantéon de Dolores, in Mexico City.

The twentieth century has seen a large increase in the number of Italian-born and Italian-descended artists who have enriched American aesthetic culture. Outstanding among those born between 1900 and 1919, Peter Agostini (b. 1913) has been recognized as an important sculptor by the Museum of Modern Art, the Whitney Museum, and many other museums that have acquired his work. Harry Bertoia (b. 1915) became known for his innovative flowers made of metallic rods that created sounds as they moved. Clara Fasano (1900–?) was one of only two Italian American women of her generation to have a distinguished career as a sculptress (see Scaravaglione below). She received a medal from the National Academy of Arts and Letters and made many portrait busts in New York before going to settle in Rome in 1960. Costantino Nivola (1911–1988) cast relief sculptures in concrete that powerfully evoke memories of the ancient Near East with their archaic figures and writing suggestive of cuneiform exemplified by the 35,000-square-foot relief on the facade of the Post Publishing Company in Bridgeport, Connecticut (1957). Winner of many honors, he was elected to the National Academy of Arts and Letters in 1972. Phillip Pavia (b. 1912) was an influential sculptor-member of the first generation of abstract-expressionists. He was the moving force of the now famous "Eighth Street Club," whose members largely shaped the abstract-expressionist movement. Concetta Scaravaglione (1900–1975) was the first woman to win the Rome Prize Fellowship in Fine Arts of the American Academy at Rome. Her sculptures in marble, wood, terra cotta, and other media are in many museums including the Museum of Modern Art, Whitney Museum of American Art, and at Vassar College, where she taught (1952–1967). Salvatore Scarpitta (b. 1919) is a leading artist among those who have taken up unconventional materials. He is known especially for his "sleds," constructed with hockey sticks, skis, chair backs, and other "found" objects, tied together and coated with resins, rubber, tar, coffee, and wax. He was represented in the prestigious Venice Biennale in 1993.

Among painters, Giorgio Cavallon (1904–1989) is important in the history of modern American art as a first-generation abstract-expressionist. He was much admired for the subtle form and lyric color of his compositions, which place him in the Venetian tradition and won him his election to the American Academy and Institute of Arts and Letters. His work can be seen in the permanent collections of major museums of modern art. Jon Corbino (1905–1964), whose works are in the foremost American museums, was elected to the National Academy of Arts and Letters in 1941.

Ralph Fasanella (1914–1997) had no formal training in art. He began to paint in 1945, choosing for his subject matter working-class life and its struggles, scenes derived from his years as a union organizer. He is widely admired for his sense of design, and his paintings have become recognized as the most expressive American works dealing with this subject. His passion for a decent society is visualized in such scenes as *May Day,* a Labor Day parade, and *Garment Factory,* the actual factory where his mother worked. O. Louis Guglielmi (1906–1956) is distinguished in American art for a style that combined realism, precisionism, and surrealism, creating pictorial dramas of the plight of human life. *Terror in Brooklyn* (1941) in the permanent collection of the Whitney Museum is probably the most famous of his enigmatic compositions.

Luigi Lucioni (1900–1988) was said to be the youngest artist ever to be represented in the Metropolitan Museum when his *Pears with Pewter* was acquired in 1934. His super-realist still lifes of fruit made him one of the best-known artists in America during the 1940s and 1950s. Corrado Marca-Relli (b. 1913), a member of the "Eighth Street Club" (see Pavia above), participated in the international triumph of abstract-expressionism during the 1950s. His distinguished career included significant prizes such as the Logan Prize awarded by the Art Institute of Chicago. Gregorio Prestopino (1907–1984) won a number of awards including the Prix de Rome for 1968–1969. He was the subject of a prize-winning film at the Cannes Film Festival in 1961. Critically compared to the sixteenth-century master Peter Breughel, he was widely known at first for his social realist work, but in the 1960s he changed his artistic vision radically, creating lyrical landscapes that sometimes suggested his debt to Venetian masters.

The next two decades saw numerous Italian heritage artists rise to prominence. Mark Di Suvero (b. 1933) triumphed over an accident when he was 27 years old that disabled him for four years to become one of the most prominent of modernist artists. His monumental constructions featuring industrial materials such as huge steel beams, gigantic timbers, and automobile tires contrast massiveness with floating, delicate balance reminiscent of the great Italian Baroque sculptor Gianlorenzo Bernini, whose mammoth Cathedra in St. Peter's, Rome, seemingly hovers in space with only the support of the fingertips of four Fathers of the Church who stand at either side. Robert De Niro (1922–1993), whose work is represented in the Metropolitan Museum, Brooklyn Museum, and other major institutions, was critically admired for an unusual quality of physicality in his paintings. He is the father of the eminent actor and film producer who bears his name. The art of Frank Stella (b. 1936) is practically synonymous with post–abstract-expressionist American art. His solution to the major problem of modernist painting, identifying literal space with pictorial space, came with his black pin-stripe paintings shown in the Museum of Modern Art's *Sixteen Americans* exhibition (1959): they represent nothing, they symbolize nothing; they are literally black rectangular fields articulated by stripes from

A

the white canvas that are parallel to the four sides—a "pictorial absolute," the Italian futurists' term for pure art, which is art that rejects a representational relationship between artists and society. Stella has maintained a pre-eminent position internationally among his contemporaries as his art has gone through many radical changes. He continues to deal with its three basic components, space, color, and medium, always challenging the critical interest of the art world.

The history of Western art since Giotto can be seen as a progressive dialogue between succeeding generations, each generation responding to the previous one with new solutions to the problems of space and color, and adding in the twentieth century the problems of medium, this last element taken up most famously by the Italian futurists. Indeed, art since mid-century, and even earlier, has seen the realization of the futurist manifestos that were published in 1912, which called for intuition over tradition, for new materials, "glass, wood, cardboard, iron, cement, horsehair . . . etc. etc.," over marble and bronze, the shift of the spectator from observer to participant, the space/time merging of the painted, sculpted, or constructed object with its environment.

The new generation of Italian-born or Italian-descended American artists born since 1940 will doubtless continue to contribute to the constant pushing forward of the aesthetic frontier, endlessly finding new ways to move the human imagination.

Cavaliere Professor Irma B. Jaffe

Bibliography

Fairman, Charles E. *Art and Artists of the Capitol of the United States of America.* Washington, D.C.: Government Printing Office, 1927.

Fryd, Vivien Green. "The Italian Presence in the United States Capitol." In *The Italian Presence in American Art, 1760–1860,* edited by Irma B. Jaffe, 132–149. Rome, Italy, and Bronx, NY: L'Istituto della Enciclopedia Italiana and Fordham University Press, 1989.

O'Connor, Francis V. "The Murals of Constantino Brumidi for the United States Capitol: An Iconographic Interpretation." In *The Italian Presence in American Art, 1860–1920,* edited by Irma B. Jaffe, 81–96. Rome, Italy, and Bronx,

NY: L'Istituto della Enciclopedia Italiana and Fordham University Press, 1992.

Soria, Regina. *American Artists of Italian Heritage, 1776–1945.* Rutherford, NJ: Fairleigh Dickinson University Press, 1993.

[White, George M.]. *Art in the United States Capitol.* Washington, D.C.: Government Printing Office, 1976.

Wolanin, Barbara. "Constantion Brumidi's Frescoes in the United States Capitol." In *The Italian Presence in American Art, 1760–1860,* edited by Irma B. Jaffe, 150–164. Rome, Italy, and Bronx, NY: L'Istituto della Enciclopedia Italiana and Fordham University Press, 1989.

See also BRUMIDI, CONSTANTINO; CRIMI, ALFRED D.; FASANELLA, RALPH; MODOTTI, TINA; RODIA, SABATINO; RUOTOLO, ONORIO; SCARAVAGLIONE, CONCETTA MARIA; STELLA, JOSEPH

Ascoli, Max (1898–1978)

Author and teacher, Max Ascoli was born in Ferrara, Italy, in 1898, and received a Ph.D. degree from the University of Rome in 1928. Early in his youth he demonstrated an aversion to Fascism then emerging as the dominant force in the Italy of Benito Mussolini. His outspoken articles attacking Mussolini agitated authorities, who suppressed his writings and arrested him for a brief period. For a short time he taught in Italian universities, always under the surveillance of authorities. Along with other Italian exiles, he left for the United States in 1931.

Ostensibly in the United States to teach, he never returned to the land of his birth and became a U.S. citizen in 1939. For many years he taught in the graduate division of the New School for Social Research in New York City, becoming dean of the Graduate School. He also continued his association with anti-Fascist activities, becoming president of the Mazzini Society, an umbrella group of Italian radicals and liberals.

After divorcing his first wife, he married Marion Rosenwald, daughter and heiress to Julius Rosenwald, chief executive officer of Sears and Roebuck. With her assistance, from 1949 to 1958, he served as the publisher and editor of *The Reporter,* a highly esteemed journal of public opinion. The journal published some of the finest writers of the period: Mary

McCarthy, Eric Sevareid, and Theodore White. Although never a mass periodical—its circulation approximated three hundred thousand—it was read by intellectuals, the influential elite.

An implacable foe of dictatorships, he followed his anti-Fascist beliefs with a strong anti-communist stance. He inveighed against any accommodation with communists, warning that it would be tantamount to a "Munich" type of appeasement in which the Allies acquiesced to Hitler.

Over a long career Ascoli continued to teach and write. Among his published books are *Intelligence in Politics, Fascism for Whom?, The Power of Freedom,* and *The Fall of Mussolini.* Enjoying a position among New York's academic and social elites, Ascoli met many influential people and befriended prominent names, such as Nelson Rockefeller. Accordingly, Ascoli was credited with introducing a young Harvard professor, Henry Kissinger, to Rockefeller, thus helping to launch an important career.

Ascoli died in 1978 at the age of 79, survived by his wife and son. A funeral service was held at Corpus Christi Roman Catholic Church in Manhattan.

Salvatore J. LaGumina

Bibliography

Iorizzo, Luciano J., and Salvatore Mondello. *The Italian Americans.* Revised edition. Boston: Twayne, 1980.

Null, Gary, and Carl Stone. *The Italian Americans.* Harrisburg, PA: Stackpole, 1976.

See also FASCISM

Assimilation

Students of assimilation recognize that it is not an indivisible concept, but is instead composed of several distinct dimensions that need not occur simultaneously. Four of these dimensions are important considerations when discussing changes among Italian Americans and other European-ancestry groups: socioeconomic assimilation, the attainment of parity with the majority population to achieve social goods, such as a college education or a prestigious job; acculturation, the erosion of a distinctive ethnic culture and its replacement by the mainstream culture (which may in turn absorb traits that were originally ethnic); social or structural assimilation, entry into close relationships, such as friendship or marriage, with non-members of the ethnic group; and psychological assimilation, the internal withering and eventual disappearance of ethnic identity.

The evidence for the assimilation of many Italian Americans on the first three of these dimensions is compelling; less so for the fourth characteristic. Several points should be kept in mind in reviewing this evidence. First, assimilation is a gradual process, occurring across generations, and should not be evaluated on an all-or-nothing basis. Second, the claim that assimilation is occurring for many Italian Americans does not mean it is occurring, at least to the same degree, for all; the patterns of assimilation to be reviewed leave room for a substantial group of Italian Americans, albeit a minority, who are still firmly rooted in ethnic social worlds. Third, the occurrence of assimilation need not imply that Italian Americans generally have wanted to assimilate; conversely, that many may not want to do so does not imply that assimilation can be avoided. Advances in assimilation are frequently the unintended by-product of other choices made by individuals and families to improve their social situations, such as a move to the suburbs.

Socioeconomic changes indicative of assimilation are clearly visible in the educational attainment of the group. Since they have unfolded through historical shifts in opportunities, a direct way of viewing these changes is through differences across what demographers call "birth cohorts," or groups of people born in the same period. Different cohorts of the Italian American group have matured under quite different conditions. Older cohorts were substantially disadvantaged by comparison with members of the then core group in the United States, white Americans whose ancestry was from the British Isles or elsewhere in Northern and Western Europe. For instance, among men born in the United States before 1916, those of British ancestry attended college and graduated at rates 50 percent higher than the rates for Italians (according to data collected by the U.S. Census Bureau in 1979). Among women, the discrepancy was even greater: the rates for those of British ancestry were more than 100 percent higher. Yet this disadvantage has been largely erased for those cohorts born after World War II. According to 1990 Census data, nearly

A

Società Politica Italo Americana, 1899. This announcement illustrates immigrant willingness to engage in political activity early in their arrival years. Courtesy Salvatore J. LaGumina.

two-thirds of men of British and Italian ancestry in the 25 to 34 age range had attended college and a third had completed bachelor's degrees; the figures were just slightly lower among women.

Of course, such data does not demonstrate the absence of any ethnic discrepancy in educational opportunity. In all likelihood, some differences remain, such as in the access to elite private schools. Moreover, local variations may exist. Insofar as Italians in some cities are still concentrated in the working class, they may suffer also from educational disadvantages, though probably more due to their social class than to their ethnic backgrounds.

In tandem with improving educational opportunity has come occupational mobility that has dispersed Italians more evenly throughout the American occupational structure. This is demonstrated by the growing parity in the occupational status scores of Italian and British American men. For instance, as of the late 1970s, Italian American men born between 1930 and 1945, who were then at or near the maturity of their careers, had an average occupational prestige that was virtually the same as men of British ancestry of the same ages. Hand in hand with this mobility has come a decline in the strength of Italian occupational niches.

Viewed in historical perspective, Italians have had their share of occupational niches—among them barber, tailor, shoemaker, and opera singer. But these niches, though they still exist to some degree, have become less typical of the group as a whole. Thus, Italian Americans are now much less easily stereotyped according to specific occupational callings.

The power of acculturation is revealed by the changes that are occurring in language. Even in the immigrant generation, linguistic adaptation took place, as immigrants imported words from English for objects that were unfamiliar in the rural Italian areas where their dialects had developed. Thus, *shoppa* (for shop) and *frigidaria* (for refrigerator) made their entry into immigrant speech. But the more important acculturation took place across the generations. Italians are no exception to the principle of three-generation language shift that has been found among most American ethnic groups: by the third generation, ethnics typically speak only English in everyday life, although some may have fragmentary knowledge of the mother tongue from contact with grandparents. Among the Italians, this process was probably accelerated by the absence of linguistic unity among the immigrants, who spoke mostly dialects. Data collected by the U.S. Census Bureau in the late

1970s suggest this process: over 4 million Americans stated that Italian was spoken in their childhood homes, making it one of the most frequently claimed mother tongues; but fewer than 1.4 million then spoke the language in their current homes, testifying to a high rate of language loss. In terms of absolute numbers, Italian has more or less held its own since then. The 1990 Census counted 1.3 million speakers of Italian; however, they now represent less than 10 percent of the ancestry group. Moreover, since the number of the Italian-born, who are very likely to use Italian regularly, is still more than half a million (580,000), it is clear that only a small proportion of the second, third, and fourth generations, who total about 14 million, speak Italian at home.

A marked change is also occurring in the residential settings where the group's members can be found, suggesting the growing importance of one form of structural assimilation. In this respect, a strong contrast exists between the contemporary situations of Italian Americans and the group's image, even among scholars. There is still great attention to inner-city ethnic pockets, such as Belmont and Bensonhurst in New York City. Yet, despite the continuing image of the group as settled in stable urban villages, Italian Americans now reside predominantly in suburbs. As of 1980 about two-thirds were in suburbs throughout the nation, the same proportion as found for other white Americans. The suburban proportion was even higher (nearly three-quarters) among persons who are only partly Italian in ancestry; these individuals can serve as a good tracer for the residential patterns of Italians who have intermarried. Furthermore, suburban Italian Americans reside for the most part in non-Italian neighborhoods, although a notable minority are in suburban communities with a decided Italian flavor, such as New Jersey's Belleville, which is, rather typically for such suburban areas, an extension of a former urban Italian enclave, in Newark.

The ultimate test of assimilation for an ethnic group is intermarriage; by this test, the growing integration of Italians with the American mainstream is beyond question. Intermarriage is a sensitive barometer of the acceptability of an ethnic group to others, a reflection of the state of contacts across ethnic lines, and the ethnic context in which the next generation will be raised. Intermarriage by Italian Americans has surged since World War II, a trend not unique to the group, but one that reflects the broader decline in the role of ethnic and religious backgrounds in determining marriage choices among white Americans. Among young Italian Americans in the 1980s, the rate of marriage to non-Italians reached between two-thirds to three-quarters, the precise figure depending on whether one looked at women or men and on how one defined intermarriage. Consistent also with the broader pattern, these intermarriages were overwhelmingly to other Americans of European ancestry. Also, marriages by Italians are no longer confined mostly to other Catholics. Among members of the group born in the post–World War II era, marriages are almost evenly divided between those with other Catholics and those with non-Catholics, mainly Protestants.

As a result of rising intermarriage, a massive shift is occurring in the composition of the Italian group, as is true also for some other white ethnic groups. In the recent past, most of the adults in these groups were individuals who, by virtue of their undivided ethnic heritage and their families' recency of immigration, had grown up in quite ethnic family and community environments. In the near future, this will no longer be true. Today, the majority of young people entering adulthood come from ethnically mixed families, belong to the third if not the fourth generation, and were raised outside of ethnic communities. Among Italians, more than three-quarters of those born during the late 1960s and the early 1970s, who are entering their early adult years during the last decade of the twentieth century, come from mixed ethnic backgrounds. By contrast, only about a quarter of Italian Americans born before World War II have mixed ethnic ancestry. This contrast implies a profound shift of cardinal importance for ethnicity. On average, persons with mixed ancestry are much less exposed in their upbringing to ethnic traits, from language to values, than are persons of undivided ethnic heritage.

Yet despite the declining significance of ethnic origins in determining life chances among European-ancestry Americans, Italian American ethnic identities remain relatively strong. In this respect, Italians are perhaps an exemplar for many other white ethnics who seek to preserve some subjective attachment to their ethnic origins. Evidence of the relative strength of Italian American identity comes from surveys on ethnic identity. One of them, from a northeastern metropolitan region, found that nearly three-quarters of individuals of Italian ancestry identify, at least to some extent, with their Italian origins. Furthermore, virtually all who do so believe that their ethnic background is important to them, whether because it provides a sense of roots, is a source of their personal values, or for some other personally defined reason. In these ways, Italians stand apart from most other white ethnics, such as the Irish or Germans. Italians are also more likely than other white Americans to manifest their ethnic origins by eating ethnic foods, talking with others about their ethnicity, or teaching their children ethnic tradition.

However, ethnic identity has its own unavoidable dynamics. The greater intensity of Italians' ethnic identity is linked to their demographic distinctiveness as a group, a distinctiveness that is being eroded by rising intermarriage, educational and residential mobility, and generational change. What is, then, to become of the Italian American identity? Can it survive the growing number who have grown up in ethnically mixed families and outside of very ethnic environments? Is psychological assimilation perhaps just the culminating stage in the multigenerational assimilation process? These questions remain unsettled, but one point can be taken for granted: the Italian American experience will be a critical test case for theories about ethnicity and assimilation in the United States.

Richard D. Alba

Bibliography

Alba, Richard. "Assimilation's Quiet Tide." *The Public Interest* 199 (1995): 3–18.
———. *Ethnic Identity: The Transformation of White America.* New Haven: Yale University Press, 1990.
Gans, Herbert. "Symbolic Ethnicity: The Future of Ethnic Groups and Cultures in America." *Ethnic and Racial Studies* 2 (1979): 1–20.
———. *The Urban Villagers: Group and Class in the Life of Italian-Americans.* Updated and expanded. New York: The Free Press, 1982.
Glazer, Nathan, and Daniel Patrick Moynihan. *Beyond the Melting Pot.* 2nd ed. Cambridge: MIT Press, 1970.
Lieberson, Stanley, and Mary Waters. *From Many Strands: Ethnic and Racial Groups in Contemporary America.* New York: Russell Sage Foundation, 1988.
Nelli, Humbert. *From Immigrants to Ethnics: The Italian Americans.* Oxford: Oxford University Press, 1983.
Vecoli, Rudolph J. "The Coming of Age of the Italian Americans: 1945–1974." *Ethnicity* 5 (1978): 119–147.
Waters, Mary. *Ethnic Options: Later Generation Ethnicity in America.* Berkeley: University of California Press, 1990.

See also POPULATION

Atlas, Charles (Angelo Siciliano) (1893–1972)

Body-builder extraordinaire, Charles Atlas (Angelo Siciliano) was born in the Calabrian town of Acri, Italy, in 1893, and immigrated to the United States eleven years later. A sickly lad who was humiliated by defeats in physical fights with other young boys, he was determined to overcome his weaknesses by building himself into a strong physical specimen. He accomplished this by using isometric, nontraditional exercises that he called "dynamic tension" in contrast to the more prevalent weight-lifting exercises that were used in most gymnasiums. Employing his own techniques, he recast himself from a slender youth to a 5 foot, 10 inch barrel-chested man of 180 pounds. Even in middle age his chest measured 47 inches in normal position. By pitting one muscle against the other, he was able to transform his body into an impressive array of muscles that enabled him to win a muscle-building national contest in 1922 when he was named the "World's Most Perfectly Developed Man."

Having won the body-building contest two years in a row, he was now able to move beyond his job as janitor in Coney Island, Brooklyn. In emulation of the Greek god Atlas, he took on the name Charles Atlas and began to earn substantial sums of money posing as a model for artists. In 1929 he began a correspondence course designed to help other men with emaciated or slight bodies develop and maintain muscular physiques.

He promoted his business with the aid of resourceful promotional techniques, such as a 1942 advertisement showing him pulling six cars over the distance of a quarter mile. His pictures appeared in numerous magazines and comic books. Americans became familiar with a 97-pound "weakling" who got sand kicked in his face and lost his girl to the "bully"; however, after taking the Charles Atlas course, the "weakling" with newly developed biceps knocked his rival out and took back his girl.

Atlas demonstrated that athletics was a road in which prejudice against foreigners could be minimized. He lived on Long Island until his death in 1972.

Salvatore J. LaGumina

Bibliography

Null, Gary, and Carl Stone. *The Italian Americans*. Harrisburg, PA: Stackpole, 1976.

See also SPORTS

Autobiography

The writing of autobiographies by Italian Americans is a recent phenomenon in the scheme of American literary history. Louis Kaplan, in *A Bibliography of American Autobiographies* (1961), identified twenty-eight Italian Americans who are responsible for thirty entries out of more than six thousand written prior to 1945. Patricia K. Addis, in *Through a Woman's I* (1983), identified fourteen Italian and Italian American women autobiographers out of more than two thousand between the years 1946 and 1976. While the number of Italian American autobiographies has increased significantly in the past twenty years, critical study of only a few of those produced during this recent period is limited to a handful of articles, two dissertations, and one book.

To any one intimate with Italian American culture, what is surprising about this literature is not how few autobiographies there are, especially in comparison to other major ethnic groups, but that any autobiographies have been produced at all. The small number of self-narratives can be attributed to a number of cultural obstacles within southern Italian culture, which most Americans of Italian descent have had to confront before they could first speak publicly and then write about the self. Identifying these cultural constraints and then examining how writers either work within or against them is important when attempting to understand the self-fashioning that takes place in Italian American autobiography.

The idea of speaking of one's self as independent of the community into which one was born is a recent development in Italian American culture. Telling the story of self in public was not part of any cultural tradition found south of Rome (the region from which came over 80 percent of Italians who migrated to America). In the Italian oral tradition, the self is suppressed and is not used as a subject in storytelling in the communal settings of Italy, where one function of such stories was to create a temporary respite from the harsh realities of everyday peasant life. Traditional stories served both to entertain and to inform the young, while reminding the old of traditions that have endured over the years. Personal information was expected to be kept to one's self.

The caution against speaking publicly of one's self became a strong warning against writing about the self. In southern Italian culture there was a strong distrust of the written word; an Italian proverb warns: *Pensa molto e scrivi meno* (Think much and write even less). The institutions of Italy—the Church as well as the State—maintained power over the peasant of southern Italy by controlling literacy. Hence came the immigrant's distrust of American cultural institutions that represented the ruling classes. There was little or no parental encouragement of American-born children to pursue literary careers, and great pressure was placed on these children to earn money as soon as they were old enough to be employed. In her introduction to *The Dream Book* (1985), Helen Barolini offers an explanation of why few children of Italian immigrants wrote: "When you don't read, you don't write. When your frame of reference is a deep distrust of education because it is an attribute of the very classes who have exploited you and your kind for as long as memory carries, then you do not encourage a reverence for books among your children. You teach them the practical arts not the imaginative ones."

In spite of the low priority given to writing by Italian Americans on the whole, a number of authors have emerged who have documented their experiences as Italian Americans. These writers have created the basis for a distinctive literary tradition that emerges out of a strong oral tradition. In this respect, Italian American writers have much in common with writers from Native American, Mexican American, and African American traditions.

A

While, more often than not, the models for the structure of Italian American autobiographies come from the dominant Anglo-American culture, the content found in those structures is shaped by a home life steeped in an orally maintained culture. Thus, the work produced by these writers should be read with an understanding of the inherited oral traditions as well as the American literary tradition, which contribute to their cultural formation.

The strong storytelling traditions evident in Italian American oral culture are filled with tales that explain the reasons for traditional rituals and provide guidelines on how to live one's life. American writers of Italian descent point to oral tales as the impetus for the creation of their own stories. In retrospect, many of these writers have realized that these stories provide the very keys to their self identity. Much of Jerre Mangione's *Mount Allegro* (1942, 1989 reprint) deals with the stories told by his family; Diane di Prima recalls in her autobiography-in-progress that her grandfather told her stories that have stayed with her. Gay Talese recounts quite a number of stories told by his family in *Unto the Sons*. Examining the role that oral tradition plays in the development of Italian American literature enables us to trace the evolution of the Italian American's conception of self and its progress into public discourse.

Besides a strong connection to oral tradition, Italian American autobiography exhibits a number of characteristics reflective of behavior determined by social codes found in southern Italian culture. The act of writing in any culture is a means of connecting the author to the society that surrounds the self, a means of bridging the public and the private. For any autobiographer, the initial society is the nuclear family, which branches out to the extended family (grandparents, uncles, aunts, cousins, godparents), and then expands to the neighborhood, and the larger society outside the neighborhood. The unwritten rules that govern behavior within, between, and among these levels of interaction can be found manifested in Italian American autobiography.

Though Italians have been part of this country's history since Columbus's voyage, it has only been in recent times that they can now claim a tradition of autobiography that dates back to the accounts of missionaries (such as Father Samuel Mazzuchelli and Sister Blandina), explorers, and statesmen. And while the written tradition of the Italian auto-

biography goes back to Dante and continued developing through Benvenuto Cellini, Giambattista Vico, and Benedetto Croce, it must be remembered that these writers are representatives of an Italian experience that differs greatly from those who left Italy for political or economic reasons. Southern Italians who attempt to tell the story of self are writing against the tradition, doing something that in the minds of most Italian immigrants is considered American. However, to the extent that the Western tradition of autobiography has been informed by these writers, it is inevitable that the work of these writers can be valuable intertexts that will most likely prove influential to Italian American writers.

In his essay, "Autobiography and the Making of America," Robert F. Sayre suggests that "an American seems to have needed to be an American first and then an autobiographer." Bringing this thought to bear on writing by American immigrants implies that there is some process of Americanization that occurs before a writer can become an American autobiographer. For Italian American writers, autobiography seems to be an essential step, perhaps even the process itself, by which the writer creates an American identity.

Essentially, immigrant autobiographies document a remaking of the Italian self into an American self. The foreign born "I" argues for acceptance from the "you" that represents the established American who serves as the autobiographer's model reader. In immigrant autobiographies can be found the sources of an autobiographical tradition that contrasts Italian culture with American culture, creating a tension that drives the narrative. This tension is found in the overriding theme of these immigrant narratives, a flight to a better world or a promised land, a theme found in many immigrant autobiographies and slave narratives. Arrival in America brought the immigrant to a new system of codifying cultural signifiers, a system that often conflicted with a previous way of interpreting life. The resulting conflicts are most obvious in the early language encounters between Italian-speaking immigrants and English-speaking Americans. Arrival in America also required that the immigrant develop a new sense of self in the context of the larger society. Many immigrant *cantastorie* (folk singers) shift from recounting traditional tales to telling personal narratives about the immigrant experience. This is the case with the earliest Italian

American autobiographies of Constantine Panunzio, Pascal D'Angelo, and Rosa Cavalleri.

Panunzio's *The Soul of an Immigrant* (1921) contains two stories of conversions that both relate to his Americanization. The first is his conversion to an "American" religion, the second to American citizenship. His use of English and American poetry before each chapter provided the authenticating evidence that he has understood and accepted "the genius of the Anglo-Saxon mind and character of the soul of America." D'Angelo's *Son of Italy* (1924) tells the story of his rise from "hunger-artist" immigrant to citizen of literary America through his winning of a national poetry contest and can be read as a version of the American success story. *Son of Italy*, as many African American slave narratives, is introduced by an established American personality, who functions as both authenticator and model reader. In D'Angelo's case, the American is Carl Van Doren, former editor of *The Nation*, the magazine that awarded D'Angelo first prize in its 1922 poetry contest. One of the strongest Italian American immigrant autobiographies is the story of Rosa Cavalleri, as told to Marie Hall Ets, a social worker who came to know Rosa through contact at a half-way house in Chicago known as The Chicago Commons. Rosa is the illegitimate daughter of a famous Italian actress whose name Rosa refuses to reveal. Rosa's story of life in an impoverished northern Italian village and her forced immigration to America to join her husband (through a marriage arranged by her stepmother, who would not allow Rosa to marry the man she loved) comes to us through the filter of an American recorder. Though Ets has retained the lilt of Rosa's Italian American dialect and the storytelling immediacy by maintaining Rosa's consistent use of present tense, we must remember that as an illiterate, Rosa (like many of the voices of slave narratives) had little control over the publication of her life's story. The choice of Rosa's material was entirely in the hands of Ets. Through Rosa's story we gain insight into the poor conditions in Italy that forced hundreds of thousands of Italians to migrate. One of the most overwhelming emotions we witness is that of fear. And it is this notion of fear in the native land that becomes a key to understanding the impoverished Italian's worldview and how this fear was overcome and the worldview changed through the process of immigration to America. Rosa's fear in Italy is generated from the Italian class system, which demands that the poor never look into the eyes of the rich; this fear is also present in the traditional man/woman relationship, which turns females into the property of fathers, husbands, bosses, and priests. Rosa's story is filled with fear of men and the Italian authorities who impose their will upon hers. But there is another fear that Rosa experiences: the fear of God, and this fear is not lost in her move to America; in fact, her experiences as an immigrant strengthen her Italian religious convictions. For Rosa, and many of the immigrants like her, leaving Italy meant leaving a time-trapped traditional system of life that could be escaped only by death or migration. This dynamic of Old World sense of destiny and New World sense of freedom from fate, so well portrayed in Rosa's as-told-to autobiography, makes up a dominant theme in Italian American autobiography. However, not every immigrant could escape or would wish to escape that sense of destiny the move to America enabled. Often the decision would be left to their children as a strange sort of inheritance.

Those autobiographies of the children and grandchildren of immigrants, in opposition to immigrant autobiographies, often document the remaking of the American self as Italian American. In these works, the more established and Americanized "I" explains, as it explores, the mystery of its difference from the "you" that is the model reader. Thus, for these Italian American writers, there exists the interesting option of identifying or not identifying with the American model reader. While it is important for the immigrant writer to be accepted as an American, this argument is one that is needed less as the Italian American assimilates into American mainstream culture. However, what does become more important to these later writers is the establishment of a connection with one's Italian ancestry. When reading Italian American writers, such as Gay Talese and Diane di Prima, it is necessary to observe the ways in which traditions both American and Italian, both oral and literary, function in their narrative constructions.

There are a number of social codes found in Italian American culture that generate the signs through which Italian American autobiography can be read. The two selected here are *bella figura/brutta figura*—proper/improper

A

public image and silence. The code of *bella figura* hails back to the writings of Machiavelli and Lorenzo the Magnificent through their use of the word *sprezzatura*, an oxymoron that signifies the concept of both appraising and not appraising something. *Sprezzatura* explains the ironic quality of Italian culture that has informed the writing of Italian Americans. Until now this irony, which plays a major role in the Italian American narrative, has never been examined through its Italian origins. It is a concept that forms the basis of public representation of the Italian self. In *"Che Bella Figura!,"* a recent and fascinating dissertation (University of Illinois at Chicago, 1995), Gloria Nardini suggests that Italian life is not understandable without understanding the importance placed on presenting a *bella figura*. Nardini defines *bella figura* as a "construct which refers to face, looking good, putting on the dog, style, appearance, flair, showing off, ornamentation, etiquette, keeping up with the Joneses, image, illusion, social status—in short performance and display." Understanding the code of silence, literally the rules by which one can speak about family affairs in public, will heighten the reception of the writings of Italian Americans. Silence is generated out of a perceived need to protect the family from outsiders who are capable of using information to harm the family's reputation, and thus their standing in the community. Southern Italian culture is replete with aphorisms and proverbs that advise against revealing information that can be used against the self or the family. *A chi dici il tuo segreto, doni la tua liberta:* To whom you tell a secret, you give your freedom; *Di il fatto tuo, e lascia far il fatto tuo:* Tell everyone your business and the devil will do it; *Odi, vedi e taci se vuoi viver in pace:* Listen, watch, and keep quiet if you wish to live in peace.

The act of writing creates a more permanent record than conversation and is capable of generating unintended interpretations. In this way, silence is tied to *bella figura;* by keeping silent about personal subjects, one does not reveal one's true self and can continue to maintain a self-controlled presence that is less vulnerable to penetration by outsiders. Often, hyperbolic language and actions are used to simultaneously vent pent-up feelings and disguise the impact new knowledge has on one's self. Any one who has observed a conversation between two Italians that seems to be going out of control (evidenced by intense screaming,

threatening gestures, etc.) and then dissipates into a hug or an arm-in-arm stroll toward a bar, has witnessed *bella figura* in communication. Semblances of this behavior carry over into the writing of Italian Americans.

What is often found in the autobiographical work of Italian Americans who are children and grandchildren of the immigrants is an intense politicization of the self. Immigrants from southern Italy and Sicily brought to America a belief in a destiny that humans were powerless to change. Such beliefs were supported through centuries of domination by outside forces. Parents could not expect that their children's lives would ever be better than their own. Proverbs such as *Fesso chi fa il figlio meglio di lui* (Only a fool makes his son better than himself) pointed to the futility of progress through generations.

The tension between the Italian's adherence to such notions of life and to the American's sense of freedom to become whatever one wishes can best be seen in the body of work created by Jerre Mangione. Moving from a rigid class-based system of life in the Old World to a system of life that not only allows social mobility but in many ways assists it, was a change that not all immigrants could handle or trust. Mangione is one of the most celebrated of Italian American writers. His *Mount Allegro* has remained in print nearly every year since its first appearance in 1943. An American-born son of Sicilian immigrants, Mangione grew up in a multiethnic neighborhood of Rochester, New York. *Mount Allegro* is the first of four nonfictional books written by Mangione, all of which can be read as autobiography. Throughout *Mount Allegro* one gets the sense that the narrator is documenting the decline of a people, the end of an era, an era that ends the moment the narrator separates himself from his immigrant relatives. In fact, Mangione can only write this book after he has left his home. By leaving home, he begins the process by which he becomes Americanized. The guiding principle of Mangione's style and dominant theme in his work is that one can challenge destiny and make his or her own destiny. He writes out of a felt need to explain the people who have affected his notions of self; he also writes in order to bridge the gap between the Sicilian and the American. He knows the sophistication and the wit these illiterate immigrants are capable of communicating to each other; a sophistication and wit that is not experienced by outsiders who observe the immigrants stumbling through the English language. As one moves through his writings, a sense develops of a more political person emerging from an Italian enclave. In fact, Mangione's *An Ethnic at Large* (1978) becomes a testament to his politicization during the 1930s and to his role as an informal ambassador of Italian America.

If creating an American identity was difficult for Italian American men, the process for Italian American women would prove even more difficult. As Helen Barolini explains in the introduction to *The Dream Book,* "[T]he displacement from one culture to another has represented a real crisis of identity for the Italian woman, and she has left a heritage of conflict to her children. They, unwilling to give themselves completely to the old ways she transmitted, end up, in their assimilationist hurry, with shame and ambivalence in their behavior and values." Shame and ambivalence often become the very building blocks of Italian American women's writing, which to date, has produced very few autobiographies.

In *Memoirs of a Beatnik* (1969, 1988 reprint), the first major autobiography by an Italian American woman, Diane di Prima opens her narrative with the violation of two traditional taboos based on the two proffered codes: she *talks* about *sex* in public. *Memoirs,* which begins with di Prima recounting the loss of her virginity and closes with her first pregnancy, represents the definitive fracturing of silence that has been the cultural force suppressing the public personae of Italian American women. While *Memoirs* does not constitute a traditional autobiography, it should be considered as a precedent against which one might better read the sexual personae of Italian American women like Madonna and Camille Paglia.

Helen Barolini, though she has not written an autobiography per se, has provided the reader with a sense of one through various personal essays, critical writings, and most recently with *Festa: Recipes and Recollections* (1988). Like Barolini, Marianna DeMarco Torgovnick, has begun to tell stories of her upbringing as a daughter in an Italian American working-class family. Her *Crossing Ocean Parkway: Readings by an Italian American Daughter* (1994) is a collection of personal and critical essays that provide a glimpse into the challenges created by assimilation and issues of class mobility.

More and more Italian Americans are beginning to document their life stories in traditional as well as nontraditional forms of autobiography. Critics, such as Camille Paglia, Louise De Salvo, Frank Lentricchia, Sandra Mortola Gilbert, and Robert Viscusi, and social scientists such as Richard Gambino, have all included personal references in their scholarly writings. Most recently a literary technique, defined by this author as "autofiction," has begun appearing and is most obvious in Lentricchia's *The Edge of Night* (1994) and Viscusi's *Astoria* (1995). In both of these books, the author's lives are imaginatively recollected using all the techniques of fiction writing.

The cultural conditioning that takes place within American families of Italian descent figures strongly in the way the personal saga is presented in public, whether in print or in conversation. Many, if not most, of the earlier autobiographies served as arguments for the acceptance of the Italian as an American; they featured individuals taking on a spokesperson's role as a representative of the immigrant community. Contemporary Italian American writers working in the self-narrative mode refuse such responsibility while maintaining a strong connection to that community; their self-writings demonstrate that the social codes of *bella figura* and silence continue to affect the relationships between the Italian American self and the societies in which that self interacts.

Fred L. Gardaphé

Bibliography

Addis, Patricia K. *Through a Woman's I.* Metuchen, NJ: Scarecrow Press, 1983.

Barolini, Helen, ed. *The Dream Book: An Anthology of Writings by Italian American Women.* New York: Schocken Books, 1985.

Boelhower, William. *Immigrant Autobiography in the United States.* Verona, Italy: Essedue Edizioni, 1982.

D'Angelo, Pascal. *Son of Italy.* New York: Macmillan, 1924.

di Prima, Diane. *Memoirs of a Beatnik.* 1969. Reprint, San Francisco: Last Gasp Press, 1988.

———. *Recollections of My Life as a Woman.* New York: Viking, 1995.

Ets, Marie Hall. *Rosa: The Life of an Italian Immigrant.* Minneapolis: University of Minnesota Press, 1970.

———. "From Oral Tradition to Written Word: Toward an Ethnographically Based Literary Criticism." In *From the Margin: Writings in Italian Americana,* edited by Anthony Julian Tamburri, Paul Giordano, and Fred L. Gardaphé, 294–306. West Lafayette, IN: Purdue University Press, 1991.

Gardaphé, Fred L. "Autobiography as Piecework: The Writings of Helen Barolini." In *Italian Americans Celebrate Life: The Arts and Popular Culture,* 19–27. Staten Island, NY: American Italian Historical Association, 1990.

———. *Italian Signs, American Streets: The Evolution of Italian American Narrative.* Durham, NC: Duke University Press, 1996.

Kaplan, Louis, *A Bibliography of American Autobiographies.* Madison: University of Wisconsin Press, 1962.

Krause, Corrine Azen. *Grandmothers, Mothers, and Daughters: Oral Histories of Three Generations of Ethnic American Women.* Boston: Twayne, 1991.

Lentricchia, Frank. *The Edge of Night.* New York: Random House, 1994.

Lloyd, Susan Caperna. "The Making of Ethnic Autobiography in the United States." *American Autobiography: Retrospect and Prospect,* edited by Paul John Eakin, 123–141. Madison: University of Wisconsin Press, 1991.

———. *No Pictures in My Grave: A Spiritual Journey in Sicily.* San Francisco: Mercury House, 1992.

Mangione, Jerre. *An Ethnic at Large: A Memoir of the Thirties and Forties.* Putnam, 1978. 2nd edition, with an introduction by Bernard Weisberger. Philadelphia: University of Pennsylvania Press, 1983.

———. *Mount Allegro.* 1942, reprint, New York: Harper and Row, 1989.

———. "My House Is Not Your House: Jerre Mangione and Italian American Autobiography." In *American Lives,* edited by James Robert Payne, 139–177. Knoxville: University of Tennessee Press, 1992.

Napoli, Joseph. *A Dying Cadence: Memories of a Sicilian Childhood.* Bethesda, MD: Marna Press, 1986.

Nardini, Gloria. *"Che Bella Figura!"* Ph.D. diss., University of Illinois at Chicago, 1995.

Panella, Vincent. *The Other Side: Growing Up Italian in America.* Garden City, NY: Doubleday, 1979.

Panunzio, Constantine. *The Soul of an Immigrant.* New York: Macmillan, 1921.

Patti, Samuel J. "Autobiography: The Roots of the Italian-American Narrative." *Annali d'Italianistica* 4 (1986): 243–248.

Pellegrini, Angelo. *American Dream: An Immigrant's Quest.* Berkeley, CA: North Point Press, 1986.

Sayre, Robert F. "Autobiography and the Making of America. In *Autobiography: Essays Theoretical and Critical,* edited by James Olney, 146–168. Princeton, NJ: Princeton University Press, 1980.

Segale, Sister Blandina. *At the End of the Santa Fe Trail.* 1912. Milwaukee: Bruce Publishers, 1948.

Siringo, Charles A. *A Texas Cowboy.* Lincoln: University of Nebraska Press, 1979.

Talese, Gay. *Unto the Sons.* New York: Knopf, 1992.

Tamburri, Anthony Julian, Paul Giordano, and Fred L. Gardaphé, eds. *From the Margin: Writings in Italian Americana.* West Lafayette, IN: Purdue University Press, 1990.

Torgovnick, Marianna DeMarco. *Crossing Ocean Parkway: Readings by an Italian American Daughter.* Chicago: University of Chicago Press, 1994.

Viscusi, Robert. *Astoria.* Toronto: Guernica, 1995.

See also LITERATURE; MANGIONE, JERRE; PANUNZIO, CONSTANTINE MARIA; TALESE, GAY

B

Baltimore's Little Italy

This residential and business center for Italian Americans, a short water taxi ride or healthy walk from the restored Inner Harbor, is a treasure covering a twelve-block square area in East Baltimore.

The first Italian immigrants attracted to Baltimore were Genoese sailors, political expatriates, and adventurers who were lured to the West by the California "gold fever," but chose Baltimore instead. A settlement grew around the President Street Station, which was the passenger terminus from north Baltimore. Little Italy became a place to find a job and a secure place to live.

Italians from Naples, Abruzzi, Cefalu, and Palermo followed the earlier immigrants. They helped to build the Columbus Monument in Druid Hill Park; laid bricks; ran fruit and vegetable stands; opened restaurants; unloaded cargoes; became barbers, tailors, lawyers, politicians, doctors, and educators.

In 1880 Bishop James Gibbons dedicated St. Leo's Church, which became the spiritual and social center of Little Italy. When the "Great Fire of 1904" raged in the downtown business section, the parishioners of St. Leo's prayed to St. Anthony of Padua for a miracle to save them; the wind changed direction and Little Italy was spared.

A Society of St. Anthony was established and an annual festival resulted. In 1924 a Saint Gabriel Society was inaugurated by immigrants from Abruzzi in dedication to their patron saint.

Baltimore Italians organized lodges, mutual aid societies, and social clubs as their population increased. L'Italia Club, the

William Paca Democratic Club, the Sons of Italy, and an Italian branch of the War Veterans Association of New York all helped to foster a sense of community.

Little Italy has been the nurturer of the well-known D'Alessandro political dynasty. Thomas D'Alessandro, Jr., was a member of the Maryland House of Delegates in 1926 and subsequently became a city councilman, member of the United States House of Representatives, and mayor of Baltimore. His parents came from Abruzzi. Thomas (Tommy) D'Alessandro III followed the family tradition when he became mayor in 1967.

The stately brick structure of St. Leo's with its parish hall, the town bocce area, restaurants, pastry shops, grocery stores, carefully maintained houses, and, most of all, the Italian people are the reasons why Baltimore's Little Italy remains a vibrant ethnic community. The 1990 census recorded 25,489

Pride remains high in Italian American communities as seen in this directional sign to Little Italy, Baltimore, April 11, 1980. Courtesy Frank J. Cavaioli.

citizens who claim Italian ancestry in this city.

Dianne Francesconi Lyon

Bibliography

Chapelle, Suzane, Jean H. Baker, Dean R. Esslinger, and Whitman H. Ridgway, eds. *Maryland: A History of Its People.* Baltimore: Johns Hopkins University Press, 1986.

Nast, Leonora Heilig, Lawrence N. Krause, and R.C. Monk. *Baltimore: A Living Renaissance.* Baltimore: Historic Baltimore Society, 1982.

Sherwood, John. *Maryland's Vanishing Lives.* Baltimore: Johns Hopkins University Press, 1994.

Warren, Marion E., and Mame Warren. *Baltimore When She Was What She Used to Be: A Pictorial History, 1850–1930.* Baltimore: Johns Hopkins University Press, 1983.

Bambace, Angela and Maria
See LABOR

Bancroft, Anne (b. 1931)

A highly regarded stage, film, and television actress, Anne Bancroft has won all three of American show business's highest accolades: the Oscar, the Tony, and the Emmy. She was born Anna Maria Italiano in the Bronx, New York. She participated in student productions at Christopher Columbus High School and radio station dramas. Bancroft planned to become a laboratory technician upon graduation from high school in 1948, but her mother scraped together enough tuition for Bancroft to attend the American Academy of Dramatic Art in Manhattan.

Using the name Anne Marno, she made her debut as a professional actress in a Studio One production of Turgenev's *The Torrents of Spring* in April 1950. In 1951 she signed a contract with Twentieth Century Fox Pictures and moved to Hollywood. The studio changed her name from Marno to Bancroft. The acquisition of an Anglo-Saxon surname kept the dark-haired, olive-skinned actress from being typecast as an "ethnic." Bancroft's first film appearance was as Richard Widmark's girlfriend in the suspense thriller *Don't Bother to Knock* (1952). Over the next five years she had medium and large parts in a string of undistinguished, low-budget pictures. In 1953 Bancroft married Martin May, a law student from a wealthy Texas family. The couple divorced in 1957.

Unhappy with her professional and personal life in Hollywood, Bancroft returned to New York in 1957 and studied acting at the Actor's Studio and with Herbert Berghof. She quickly won the role of a "beatnik" New Yorker in William Gibson's play *Two for the Seesaw* (1958). Bancroft won the Tony Award for this performance. Greater acclaim was accorded to Bancroft's work as Helen Keller's Irish-born teacher, Annie Sullivan, in *The Miracle Worker* (1962). She earned a second Tony Award for this portrayal and won an Oscar for her recreation of the role in the 1962 film version of the same title. In 1964 Bancroft married comedian/writer/director Mel Brooks, with whom she has a son.

Bancroft has continued to be active in both films and the theater. On Broadway she has starred in *Mother Courage* (1963), *The Devils* (1965), *The Little Foxes* (1967), *A Cry of Players* (1968), *Golda* (1977), and *Duet for One* (1981). Bancroft is known for her most celebrated film role as the philandering middle-class matron Mrs. Robinson in *The Graduate* (1967). Other film appearances include *The Pumpkin Eater* (1964), *Young Winston* (1972), *The Turning Point* (1977), *The Elephant Man* (1980), *Garbo Talks!* (1984), *Agnes of God* (1985), *84 Charing Cross Road* (1987), *Honeymoon in Vegas* (1992), and *How to Make an American Quilt* (1995). Bancroft made an unsuccessful attempt at film directing with *Fatso* (1980). A talented singer who made several appearances on *The Perry Como Show,* Bancroft won an Emmy Award in 1970 for her musical variety special *Annie: The Woman in the Life of a Man.* She has also appeared on television as Mary Magdalene in the mini-series *Jesus of Nazareth* (1977).

Mary C. Kalfatovic

Bibliography

Linfante, Michele. "The Real Anne Bancroft." In *Dream Streets: The Big Book of Italian-American Culture,* edited by Lawrence Di Stasi. New York: Harper and Row, 1989.

Morris, Joe Alex. "Second-Chance Actress." *Saturday Evening Post,* 9 December 1961, 38–42.

Shipman, David. *Great Movie Stars: The International Years.* Boston: Little, Brown, 1995.

See also MOVIE ACTORS AND ACTRESSES

Bandini, Pietro (1852–1917)

One of the most frequently cited Italian Catholic priests in immigration literature, Father Pietro Bandini's life encompassed missionary work among the Indians in Montana, social work on behalf of arriving Italian immigrants in New York City, and leadership of two Italian colonies in Arkansas.

He was born in Forli, Romagna, Italy, on March 31, 1852, of a well-to-do family. He was admitted to the Society of Jesus in 1869. After two years of theological studies, Bandini was ordained a priest in 1877.

Father Bandini was sent to Montana in 1882 as part of the Jesuits' Rocky Mountain Mission. He spent his first year in the American missions at the Sacred Hearts of Jesus and Mary Church in Helena, the territorial capital and the largest city in Montana, where he studied English and Indian languages. A year later Bandini was stationed at St. Ignatius Mission in northeastern Montana. There, Bandini continued the study of the Indian language and was appointed preacher in the church and circuit rider. He also organized a musical band composed of Indian boys.

In early 1887 Bandini, accompanied by Father Peter Prando and Eddie Dillon, established a new mission called St. Xavier's, which worked among the Crows in southeastern Montana. With the aid of the Bureau of Catholic Indian Missions he established a boarding school there.

In 1890 he left the Society of Jesus and was admitted into a new congregation being established by Bishop Giovanni Battista Scalabrini of Piacenza to work among the Italian immigrants in America. Scalabrini sent him to New York in 1891, where he organized the St. Raphael's Italian Benevolent Society to assist the Italian immigrants at the port.

He opened an office, put together a local committee, and drafted a constitution for the society. Bandini and the Society's two agents provided various services to the immigrants, first at the Barge Office and after 1892 at Ellis Island. He opened a labor bureau to help immigrants find jobs. In 1892 Bandini noted that the Society had assisted over twenty thousand immigrants. The chapel of the Society's home at 113 Waverly Place in Greenwich Village, New York City, was dedicated to Our Lady of Pompei.

In 1896 Father Bandini left New York to join an Italian colony being formed at the Sunnyside Plantation in Chicot County in southeastern Arkansas. A shortage of labor led Austin Corbin, a New York financier involved with the Sunnyside Company, to enlist Italian immigrants to grow cotton on his plantation, located between Lake Chicot and the Mississippi River. The first group of Italian immigrants, mostly from the Marches and the Veneto and composed of family groups, arrived at Sunnyside in December 1895. More arrived in early 1897.

Many of the immigrants, unaccustomed to the hot, humid climate and cotton cultivation, fell ill and died of malaria. In early 1898 thirty-five families, led by Bandini, set out for the Ozarks in northwestern Arkansas. Other families moved to Knobview in Missouri, while some remained at Sunnyside.

Bandini's group crossed Arkansas and reached Springdale in Washington County on April 6, 1898. Bandini bought 800 acres, seven miles west of Springdale, and founded Tontitown. The land was cleared and each family received ten acres of land to be paid for from the earnings of their future crops and any other available work. Horses and plows were also bought on credit. Simple cabins, a church, and a school were built. Early on, the colonists faced bad weather and the prejudice of the local inhabitants. Economic survival depended on the cultivation of apples as a cash crop. Eventually, the cultivation of grapes was introduced and made the colony prosper.

A post office was opened at Tontitown in 1900 and the town was incorporated in 1909. The Kansas City and Memphis Railroad reached Tontitown in 1911, linking it to a market area that included Kansas City and St. Louis. Throughout this period, Father Bandini provided the colony with strong leadership. He was elected the town's first mayor, taught in the parish school, and organized a community band. His leadership and the success of the colony were recognized by both the pope and the Italian government. In 1905 the Italian ambassador visited the colony. Bandini continued to provide inspiration and leadership until his death of a stroke on January 2, 1917.

Edward C. Stibili

Bibliography

Francesconi, Mario. *Storia della Congregazione Scalabriniana.* Vol. 2. *Orga-
nizzazione Interna—Prime Missioni negli
Stati Uniti (1888–1895).* Roma: Centro
Studi Emigrazione, 1973.

Lewellen, Jeffrey. "'Sheep Amidst the
Wolves': Father Bandini and the Colony
at Tontitown, 1898–1917." *Arkansas
Historical Quarterly* 45 (spring 1986):
19–40.

Milani, Ernesto R. "Marchigiani and Veneti
on Sunnyside Plantation." In *Italian Immigrants in Rural and Small Town
America,* edited by Rudolph J. Vecoli,
18–30. New York: American Italian Historical Association, 1987.

———. "Peonage at Sunnyside and the Reaction of the Italian Government."
Arkansas Historical Quarterly 50 (spring
1991): 30–39.

Schoenberg, Wilfred P. *Paths to the Northwest:
A Jesuit History of the Oregon Province.*
Chicago: Loyola University Press, 1982.

See also EXPLORERS; RELIGION

Barbera, Joseph. *See* CARTOONISTS AND
ILLUSTRATORS

Barbuti, Raymond J. (1905–1988)

The only American male to win an individual
gold medal in a running event, the 400-meter
race, at the IXth Olympic Games of 1928
(held in Amsterdam), Raymond J. Barbuti
also won a second gold medal by running anchor on the victorious American team that
set a world record in the 1,600-meter relay
race. General Douglas MacArthur, then president of the United States Olympic Committee, persuaded Barbuti to compete in the
relay race.

Born in the Greenpoint section of Brooklyn, Barbuti and his family moved to Long Island, first residing at Rockville Center for two
years, then moving to the Italian American
community of Inwood. His father was employed as Italian court interpreter in Nassau
County. Barbuti often recounted street battles
with other kids in Greenpoint over ethnic differences and how his Tuscan father urged him
to either fight or run. He decided to take up
running.

At Lawrence High School he participated
in all major sports, excelling in baseball, football, and track. After graduating in 1924 he
received a football scholarship to Syracuse
University, where he became an All American
and also starred in track. He graduated in
1928 with academic honors.

Ray Barbuti, two-time gold medal winner in track for the United States in the 1928 Olympics, here wins
the Long Island half-mile championship at the Agricultural School at Farmingdale, Spring, 1924. Courtesy
Frank J. Cavaioli.

Barbuti's spectacular victory in the 400-meter race incited the Italian spectators to yell, *"Barabooti! Barabooti! Barabooti!"* With ten meters to go, and a slight lead, he lunged at the finish line, broke the tape, and defeated his nearest opponent by a head.

From 1928 to 1963 he officiated at over five hundred college football and bowl games. Among his many honors are his elections to both the National Track and Field Hall of Fame in 1967 and the Long Island Sports Hall of Fame in 1986.

During World War II Barbuti enlisted as a private in the Army Air Corps and served in Europe, China, Burma, and India. He received the Air Medal, Bronze Star, and Presidential Unit Citation, and was discharged in 1945 with the rank of major.

After the war he supervised the establishment of the War Veterans Counseling Service of the State Division of Veterans Affairs in New York City, became Nassau County Chief of Civil Defense Intelligence and Warning, and Director of Administration of the New York State Civil Defense Commission. He worked for New York State for thirty years. He moved to Queechy Lake, near Albany, in 1951. Barbuti died on July 8, 1988, at the age of 83.

Frank J. Cavaioli

Bibliography

Carlson, Lewis H., and John J. Fogarty. *Tales of Gold.* Chicago: Contemporary Books, 1987.

Cavaioli, Frank J. "The Italian American Chariot of Fire." In *Italians and Irish in America,* edited by Francis X. Femminella, 35–43. New York: American Italian Historical Association, 1985.

Wallechinsky, David. *The Complete Book of the Olympics.* Boston: Little, Brown, 1992.

See also SPORTS

Barolini, Helen (b. 1925)

Preeminent Italian American woman of letters, Helen Barolini was born in Syracuse, New York, and has worked as a translator and freelance writer since 1948. In 1947 Barolini graduated from Syracuse University magna cum laude; she received a *diploma di profitto* from the University of Florence three years later and received her master's degree in library science from Columbia University in 1959. Her marriage to Italian writer Antonio Barolini in 1950 afforded her further access to Italy. She eventually traveled one summer with her youngest daughter to Calabria to see the village of Castagna, where her maternal grandmother was born. Unable to communicate in Italian dialect when her grandmother was living, Barolini subsequently learned the language and translated several Italian works into English, including her husband's novel, *A Long Madness.*

Though Barolini was engaged in translating for many years, she simultaneously published *Duet,* poems co-authored with Antonio in 1966, wrote a radio play, *Margaret Fuller,* first broadcast in Rome in 1971, and published several essays in journals, including *New Yorker, Ms., Yale Review, Paris Review, Kenyon Review, South Atlantic Quarterly,* and *Prairie Schooner.* Because she lived in Italy with her husband and children for over ten years, much of Barolini's writing reflects the influence of Italian culture in her life. Essays such as "The Birth and Death of a Poet: Lucio Piccolo" and "Neruda vs. Sartre at the

Author Helen Barolini discusses her work on the Italian American novel before the Long Island chapter of the American Italian Historical Association, May 1988. Courtesy Frank J. Cavaioli.

Sea" reflect Barolini's wide-ranging comprehension of the Italian literary tradition and Italian writers themselves. In 1970 Barolini won the Marina-Velca Journalism Prize for her essay "Etruscan Places Today."

After receiving a National Endowment of the Arts grant for fiction writing, Barolini completed *Umbertina* (1979), for which she won the Americans of Italian Heritage award for literature in 1984. Barolini's 1978 essay, "A Circular Journey," is the literary precursor of *Umbertina*. Barolini has described it as "the seminal essay from which *Umbertina* was born." In it Barolini explains that it took her thirty-seven years to return to her grandmother's grave; her novel, *Umbertina,* is named after the grandmother in the novel, a figure of vital importance for each generation of women that follow in the story. In this novel Barolini succeeded in wedding Italian and American characters, themes, and topographies.

Aware of the invisibility of and lack of advocacy for Italian American women's voices, Barolini edited and wrote the introduction to *The Dream Book: An Anthology of Writings by Italian American Women* (1985), for which she won the American Book Award for literary achievement by people of various ethnic backgrounds in 1986. Barolini's collection was instrumental in making accessible and recognizable the names of Italian American women. The introduction to *The Dream Book* remains central to understanding the cultural and social reasons undergirding the Italian American women's perceived lack of visibility.

Barolini's second novel, *Love in the Middle Ages* (1986), moves away from a strict emphasis on Italian American identity and instead focuses on the relationship between a middle-aged couple, who have each experienced loss from either the death or the estrangement of a spouse. In keeping with her fervent passion for things Italian, Barolini next published *Festa: Recipes and Recollections of Italian Holidays* (1988). Engaging, lively, and thoroughly detailed, Barolini's *Festa* takes the reader on a month-by-month excursion through the holidays and saints' days and the recipes associated with the seasons. Combining her interest in rare books with the artistic innovations of printing, Barolini wrote *Aldus and His Dream Book* (1991), a history of the pioneering scholar-publisher Aldus Manutius (1450–1515).

Chiaroscuro: Essays on Italian-American Culture, her most recent work, comprise both personal and critical writings of Barolini's, highlighting the skills of a virtuoso essayist and scholar.

Mary Jo Bona

Bibliography

Barolini, Helen. "Becoming a Literary Person Out of Context." *Massachusetts Review* 27, no. 2 (1986): 262–274.

———. "A Circular Journey." *Texas Quarterly* 21, no. 2 (summer 1978): 109–126.

Gardaphé, Fred L. *Italian Signs, American Streets.* Durham, NC: Duke University Press, 1996.

See also LITERATURE; WOMEN WRITERS

Baroni, Geno C. (1930–1984)

Catholic civil rights priest Geno C. Baroni helped shape American thinking on ethnic pluralism and urban policy through his leadership in the social revolution of the 1960s and 1970s. He was born on October 24, 1930, in Acosta, Pennsylvania, the son of Italian parents, Guido and Josephine (née Tranquillini).

After graduating from Mount St. Mary's College, Emmitsburg, Maryland, in 1952, he entered the seminary there, becoming a priest four years later. He served as assistant pastor of St. Columbia Church in Johnstown and Altoona, Pennsylvania. He taught high school subjects, became active in community affairs, and organized credit unions for the needy.

Father Baroni was next assigned as pastor, 1960 to 1965, to the Washington, D.C., parish of Sts. Paul and Augustine, a merger of black and white parishes. He applied Catholic social doctrine in ministering to the urban poor; his dedication to civil rights propelled him into a national leadership role. Robert Kennedy noticed him and helped him become treasurer of the first Head Start in Washington, D.C. He also served on the city's Human Relations Council and the Mayor's Commission on Economic Development.

From 1965 to 1967 Father Baroni was executive director of the Office of Urban Affairs of the Washington Archdiocese and, from 1967 to 1970, director of the Urban Task Force of the United States Catholic

Monsignor Geno Baroni (right). Born and raised in an Italian enclave in a mining area of Pennsylvania, he became a priest, civil rights advocate, and ethnic activist. He served as undersecretary in the Department of Health, Education, and Welfare during the Carter administration. Courtesy National Urban Ethnic Affairs.

Conference, which helped to create the Campaign for Human Development. In 1970 he prepared the United States Catholic Conference Labor Day statement urging that attention be given to the concerns of white urban ethnic people.

With Ford Foundation aid, he founded the National Center for Urban Ethnic Affairs in 1971, whose aim was to rebuild traditional neighborhood institutions through community organization. He worried about the emerging polarization of American society and believed that Catholicism's future rested upon the development of an intercultural ministry. He visited every major city to convey this message, eventually going to 360 neighborhoods across the nation. Father Baroni was a coordinator for Martin Luther King's 1963 March on Washington. He went to Mississippi in 1964 and marched in the 1965 Selma civil rights demonstration.

In March 1977 President Jimmy Carter appointed him Housing and Urban Develop-ment Assistant Secretary for Neighborhood Development, Consumer Affairs, and Regulatory Functions to work with inner-city groups. In 1978 he lobbied Congress to add fifteen billion dollars to an appropriations bill for self-help in twenty-one cities.

Father Baroni was instrumental in founding the National Italian American Foundation in 1975; he became its first president. NIAF continues to serve as a clearinghouse for an Italian American agenda in the nation's capital.

He lectured extensively and wrote many articles on urban policy and ethnicity. His most widely known work is *Pieces of a Dream* (1972). He was a fellow at Harvard's Kennedy School of Government, a trustee on the Robert F. Kennedy Foundation, and participated in the Miners Legal Defense Fund.

He died on August 26, 1984, after a long struggle with cancer.

Frank J. Cavaioli

Bibliography

Baroni, Geno, Silvano F. Tomasi, and Michael Wenk, eds. *Pieces of a Dream*. Staten Island, NY: Center for Migration Studies, 1972.

Cavaioli, Frank J. "In Memoriam, Geno C. Baroni." In *Italians and Irish in America,* edited by Francis X. Femminella, 12–18. Staten Island, NY: American Italian Historical Association, 1985.

O'Rourke, Lawrence M. *Geno, The Life and Mission of Geno Baroni*. New York: Paulist, 1991.

See also CHURCH LEADERS; RELIGION

Basilone, John
See MEDAL OF HONOR WINNERS

Bellanca, Augusto (1880–1969)

A founder and three times vice president of the Amalgamated Clothing Workers of America, Augusto Bellanca was born in Sciacca, Sicily, and migrated to the United States in 1900. Bellanca helped establish the union in 1914 and served as its vice president from 1916 to 1934, 1946 to 1948, and 1952 to 1966. He was the brother of Giuseppe, aeronautical designer, and Frank, labor leader and businessman.

Bellanca was the head of the Italian section of the Amalgamated Clothing Workers of America, a crucial post for the union because of the tension that had existed between Jewish and Italian tailors and seamstresses at the turn of the century. In 1913 Bellanca was instrumental in bringing sizable numbers of Italian workers into the mass strike of New York men's clothing workers. He made concerted efforts to prevent scabbing by Italian workers and to bring Italian men and women into the ranks of the union. Bellanca sought the support of his close friend, Fiorello LaGuardia, to represent the union. They made a formidable team. Bellanca was a subtle, skilled negotiator adept at keeping various factions within the union in harmony, while LaGuardia, with his Italian and Jewish background, was the ideal figure to heal the distrust between Italian and Jewish workers in the Amalgamated. The strike introduced LaGuardia to New York labor leaders who would one day support him for political office.

In August 1918 Bellanca married Dorothy Jacobs, a leading trade union organizer. Dorothy Jacobs Bellanca was particularly concerned with the condition of women workers in the men's clothing industry and committed herself to the organization of immigrant women. She was a key organizer in the successful Amalgamated Clothing Workers campaign among the shirt workers on the East Coast. Together, she and her husband committed their lives to trade unionism.

A militant anti-Fascist, Bellanca helped found the Mazzini Society, an American group opposed to Mussolini. He was active in organizing aid to Italy after World War II and was twice decorated by the Italian government for his services: in 1957 with the Italian Order of Merit and in 1967 with the Knight of the Grand Cross of the Order of Merit of the Republic of Italy. He died in New York City.

Diane C. Vecchio

Bibliography

Asher, Nina. "Dorothy Jacobs Bellanca: Women Clothing Workers and the Runaway Shops." In *A Needle, A Bobbin, A Strike: Women Needleworkers in America,* edited by Joan Jensen and Sue Davidson, 195–226. Philadelphia: Temple University Press, 1984.

Fraser, Steven. *Labor Will Rule: Sidney Hillman and the Rise of American Labor*. New York: The Free Press, 1991.

Mangione, Jerre, and Ben Morreale. *La Storia, Five Centuries of the Italian American Experience*. New York: HarperCollins, 1992.

See also LABOR; RADICALISM

Bellanca, Giuseppe Mario (1886–1960)

A prominent aeronautical designer, Giuseppe Bellanca was born in Sciacca, Italy, on March 19, 1886. He was the son of Andrew and Concetta (née Merlo) Bellanca and brother of Frank Bellanca, labor leader and businessman, and Augusto, labor leader and founder of the Amalgamated Clothing Workers of America.

Giuseppe Bellanca attended the *Istituto Tecnico* and the *Politecnico* in Milan, Italy, where he received degrees in mathematics and engineering. He began experimenting in aircraft design while still a student and built his first plane in 1907.

In 1911 he came to the United States, learned how to fly, and operated the Bellanca Airplane School in Mineola, New York, where Fiorello LaGuardia served as his attorney and one of his students. From 1917 to 1920 he was associated with the Maryland Pressed Steel Corporation as a consultant engineer in its airplane division. In 1925 he joined the Wright Aeronautical Corporation, airplane engine manufacturers in Paterson, New Jersey, where he subsequently constructed the monoplane *Columbia*. In 1927 he formed Columbia Aircraft Corporation in Staten Island, New York, which was later incorporated as the Bellanca Aircraft Corporation. Bellanca served as president of the company from its inception until 1954.

Bellanca was a leader in formulating trends in aviation design. With the Wright Aeronautical Corporation, Bellanca designed a series of single-motored monoplanes. In 1922 he built the Bellanca CF Monoplane, which won first prize in thirteen races, including the Country Club of Detroit Trophy Race for Speed and Efficiency held in St. Louis, Missouri, in 1923. In 1926 Bellanca founded the Columbia Aircraft Company in partnership with Charles Levine, a Brooklyn millionaire. The company purchased the prototype of an aircraft known as the W-B II, modified, christened it *Columbia,* and in March 1927, established an endurance record of fifty-one hours and thirty minutes. The aircraft's performance sparked the interest of Charles Lindbergh, who sought to acquire it for his proposed transatlantic flight. While Bellanca favored the idea, Levine did not. Instead, *Columbia* was readied for a transatlantic flight with Clarence Chamberlin as pilot. Legal complications prevented the aircraft's departure until after Lindbergh's successful flight. Two weeks late, from June 4 to June 6, 1927, Chamberlin flew *Columbia,* with Levine as passenger, from Roosevelt Field, Long Island, to Eisleben, Germany, a distance of 3,905 miles, 301 miles farther than Lindbergh had flown. In 1931 a Belanca-designed plane, the *Miss Veedol,* made the first nonstop flight across the Pacific from Tokyo to Wenagchee, Washington, making the 4,500-mile trip in forty-one hours.

Bellanca continually experimented with new materials and simpler methods of internal structural configuration to produce stronger, safer aircraft. He also designed a number of military fighters and bombers. In 1951 his company focused almost entirely on defense operations, mainly converting bombers for the United States Air Force and manufacturing aircraft parts and radar antennae under military contracts.

Bellanca was married to Dorothy Brown and had one son, August Thomas. He retired to his home in Galena, Maryland, where he devoted his last years to designing aircraft of fiberglass construction. He died in New York City.

Diane C. Vecchio

Bibliography

Amfitheatrof, Erik. *The Children of Columbus: An Informal History of the Italians in the New World.* Boston: Little, Brown, 1973.

See also PATENTS AND INVENTORS; SABELLI, CESARE

Bennett, Michael (1943–1987)

A musical theater director-choreographer, Michael Bennett created notable and innovative dances for Broadway shows from the 1960s through the early 1980s. He is best known for creating and staging the Pulitzer Prize–winning musical *A Chorus Line.*

Born on April 8, 1943, in Buffalo, New York, Michael Bennett Di Figlia was the son of Helen Ternoff and second-generation Sicilian-American Salvatore Di Figlia. As a child Bennett danced to music played on the radio in his home. His talents for dancing and creating his own steps were soon evident and nurtured by an aunt who took him to dance classes. Bennett quickly began earning money choreographing and performing locally. During his teenage years, he spent summers studying in New York City and danced in professional summer stock theaters. Bennett dropped out of high school in 1960 to dance in the European touring production of *West Side Story.* He next appeared in the Broadway musicals *Subways Are for Sleeping* (1961), *Here's Love* (1963), and *Bajour* (1964) and also danced on numerous episodes of the *Hullabaloo* television series.

Bennett's Broadway choreography career began with the 1966 musical *A Joyful Noise,* followed by *Henry, Sweet Henry* in 1967, and his first hit show, *Promises, Promises,* in 1968. In 1969 he created the musical staging for *Coco* and, in 1970, choreographed *Company,* Broadway's first significant concept musical, a show in which the drama was not structured along a linear plotline, but instead pivoted around a central theme. For the 1971 musical *Follies,* Bennett served as both choreographer and co-director.

In 1975 he conceived, directed, and choreographed *A Chorus Line,* a landmark production in the history of dance in the American musical. The show was a tribute to the lives of Broadway "gypsies," dancers who travel from show to show performing in the ensembles that are often the lifeblood of many musicals. *A Chorus Line* was created from a series of rap sessions and workshops in which Broadway dancers shared stories from their personal and professional lives. The individual true stories offered by the dancers were then shaped by Bennett into the musical's script. In 1976 Bennett married Donna McKechnie, the star of *A Chorus Line.* The couple had no children and were divorced in 1978.

Following the remarkable success of *A Chorus Line,* Bennett went on to direct and choreograph *Ballroom* in 1978 and *Dreamgirls* in 1981. As he had done throughout his career, Bennett found innovative ways to use dance and movement to enhance the dramatic fabric of these Broadway musicals. While working on the London production of the musical *Chess* in 1986, Bennett revealed that he had contracted the AIDS virus and withdrew from the project. He died on July 2, 1987.

Lisa Jo Sagolla

Bibliography

Videotapes of Bennett's choreography can be viewed at New York City's Museum of Television and Radio and in the Theatre on Film and Tape Collection at the Library and Museum of the Performing Arts, the New York Public Library at Lincoln Center.

Kelly, Kevin. *One Singular Sensation: The Michael Bennett Story.* New York: Doubleday, 1990.

Mandelbaum, Ken. *A Chorus Line and the Musicals of Michael Bennett.* New York: St. Martin's Press, 1989.

See also DANCE

Bentivoglio, Mary Magdalen and Mary Constance
See WOMEN AND THE CHURCH

Bernardin, Joseph Cardinal (1928–1996)

A Roman Catholic cardinal and archbishop of Chicago, Joseph Bernardin was a driving force in American Catholicism and liberal reform in issues of peace, racial justice, and economic progress.

Bernardin was born in Charleston, South Carolina, on April 2, 1928, the first son of Joseph (Bepi) and Maria Simion, who came from Tondico in northern Italy. Their new home in America was in a region hostile to Catholics and to Italians. With Bepi's death in 1934, Maria was compelled to support Joseph and his sister by working for the WPA, a New Deal program, and as a seamstress. Joseph learned to prepare Italian dishes, a skill he maintained for the rest of his life. In 1941 his mother moved her family to a garden apartment public housing complex in Charleston, and a decade later, using an inheritance of five thousand dollars, she built a house in the suburbs.

After attending St. Peter's grammar school, Bernardin went to St. Mary's Seminary in Kentucky, then to St. Mary's in Baltimore, Maryland, where he received a bachelor of arts degree, summa cum laude. He spent a year in pre-medical studies at the University of South Carolina before he enrolled in the Catholic University of America in Washington, D.C., to study theology. At the age of 24 he was ordained to the priesthood.

He served as a curate in St. Joseph's Church in Charleston, was assigned to teach at Bishop England High School, then to the chancery office in Charleston, and became a chaplain for five years at the Citadel Military Academy. His rise in the Catholic Church was rapid and due to two mentors, Paul Hallinan, then the first archbishop of Atlanta, and to Archbishop John Deardon of Detroit. He also displayed extraordinary administrative skills. In 1966, at the age of 38, Bernardin became auxiliary bishop to Hallinan and the youngest bishop in the country.

He became the first general secretary of the National Catholic Conference of Catholic

Bishops and in 1974 was elected president of the conference. He played an active role in decisions the bishops made in church life and politically sensitive issues.

As archbishop of Cincinnati, he played a crucial part in the bishops' pastoral, *The Challenge of Peace,* which explained their views on war and peace, as it applied to the threat of nuclear war. Bernardin applied the right-to-life doctrine (the "seamless garment" ethic) to abortion and to other threats to human life.

At the age of 54, on February 2, 1983, Bernardin was made a cardinal by Pope John Paul II. He became the first Italian American to administer a large archdiocese (Chicago), with a Catholic population of 2.3 million—a role long dominated by Irish Americans. Bernardin was at the pinnacle of his influence. His travels to Mexico and Poland drew large crowds. But his influence in Rome declined when the pope curbed some American bishops for straying from Roman directives. Nevertheless, Rome still employed Bernardin to be a troubleshooter and "honest broker." He was the most influential American bishop of his time.

In 1996 Cardinal Bernardin announced that pancreatic and liver cancer would cut short his life, but he continued to inspire what some observers said was the dominant figure among liberal bishops. Bernardin promoted the Catholic Common Ground Project, which strived for a consensus between the orthodox teaching of the pope and the new catechism of the Catholic Church and between theological dissent that flourished in some Catholic universities, in some dioceses, and in a number of religious orders.

President Clinton awarded Bernardin the Medal of Freedom. He died on November 14, 1996, while the American bishops were at their annual meeting in Washington, D.C.

Gaetano L. Vincitorio

Bibliography

Byrnes, Timothy A., *Catholic Bishops in American Politics.* Princeton: Princeton University Press, 1991.

Kennedy, Eugene. *Cardinal Bernardin: Easing Conflicts and Battling for the Soul of American Catholicism.* Chicago: Bonus Book, 1989.

Reese, Thomas J. *A Flock of Shepherds: The National Conference of Catholic Bishops.* New York: Sheed and Ward, 1982.

Woodward, Kenneth L., and John McCormick. "The Art of Dying Well." *Newsweek,* 25 November 1996, 60–63, 66–67.

See also CHURCH LEADERS; RELIGION

Berra, Lawrence Peter "Yogi" (b. 1925)

Son of Pietro and Pauline (née Longsani) Berra, both Italian immigrants, "Yogi" was born in the Italian "Hill" section of St. Louis. He quit school at age 14, took odd jobs, excelled at baseball, and signed with the New York Yankees for five hundred dollars. Yogi stated in his autobiography that his father did not believe "playing baseball or playing anything was good. Work was good. Work was why he came from Italy."

In 1943, at age 18, Berra played for the Yankee farm team in Norfolk, Virginia, joined the Navy, and after his discharge in 1946

Yogi Berra. Pride of the Italian "Hill" section of St. Louis, Missouri, Berra entered the Baseball Hall of Fame because of his accomplishments as a catcher for the New York Yankees. Known for his malapropisms, he also managed the New York Yankees and New York Mets. Courtesy New York Yankees.

played for the Newark Bears. He began his first full year with the New York Yankees in 1947 and continued to play for them until 1964.

Berra was an American League All Star catcher from 1948 through 1962. He played in fourteen World Series, ten on the winning side. After retiring, he managed the Yankees to a pennant but was fired when he lost the World Series. He coached the New York Mets from 1965 to 1972; in 1973 he managed the Mets to the National League pennant, only to lose again in the World Series. From mid-season 1975 through 1983, he coached the Yankees, and the following year he managed the Yankees to an 87–75 record. After a slow start in 1985, the Yankees fired him, and the Houston Astros later hired him as a coach.

He married Carmine Short in 1949; they have three sons. Berra is a member of the Baseball Hall of Fame. In 1972 the Yankees retired his uniform number 8. He was famous for swinging at pitches out of the strike zone, and he has delighted the public with his malapropisms.

Frank J. Cavaioli

Bibliography

Berra, Yogi, with Tim Horton. *Yogi: It Ain't Over.* New York: McGraw-Hill, 1989.

Halberstam, David. *Summer of '49.* New York: Avon, 1989.

See also SPORTS

Bevilacqua, Anthony Cardinal (b. 1923)

Rising from humble immigrant origins to become head of the important Archdiocese of Philadelphia, Cardinal Bevilacqua is noted for his intellectual achievements, mastery of civil and canon law, and pastoral concerns for his parishioners.

Anthony J. Bevilacqua was born in Brooklyn on June 17, 1923, one of eleven children of Luigi Bevilacqua, who came from the province of Bari in Italy, and Maria Codella, who was born in the province of Avellino. In 1910 Luigi immigrated to New Rochelle, New York, and later sent for Maria and a baby son. They lived in Hartford, Connecticut, in Brooklyn, then in Woodhaven, Queens, New York. A stonemason by trade, Luigi opened a hat cleaning and shoe-shine parlor. Although the parents were illiterate,

they instilled a great love of learning in their children.

After graduation from Cathedral Preparatory and College with high honors in 1943, Anthony entered the Immaculate Conception Seminary in Huntington, Long Island, and was ordained on June 11, 1949. He had two parish assignments before returning to Cathedral for three years as instructor in history and social studies. He next turned to the study of canon law in Rome's Gregorian University and in 1956 received a doctorate, summa cum laude.

He enrolled at Columbia University in 1962 and received a master's degree in political science, while he served as assistant chancellor in the Brooklyn Diocesan Tribunal. A decade later, he studied civil law and received a doctorate in law from St. John's University, New York. He was now qualified to practice as a civil lawyer in the courts of New York and Pennsylvania and before the Supreme Court of the United States.

His responsibilities in the Brooklyn Diocese mounted. He became vice-chancellor and was also assigned to teach canon law in the diocesan seminary (1968–1980). He was moderator of the service group known as the Italian Board of Guardians; head of the Catholic Migration and Refugee Office in 1976; and chancellor, a position he held until 1983. Meanwhile, he taught immigration law at St. John's School of Law.

He was made auxiliary bishop of Brooklyn in 1980. Pope John Paul II soon selected Bevilacqua as the tenth bishop of Pittsburgh, and in 1991 he assigned him to replace Cardinal Krol as archbishop of Philadelphia. In 1991 he became a cardinal.

His tenure has been characterized by his devotion to the pope and Catholic traditions, by his frequent visits to clergy and lay people in his jurisdiction, and by his sustained interest in ecumenical meetings with Protestant and Jewish leaders. He streamlined the administration of his archdiocese and undertook his own radio call-in show in Philadelphia ("Live with Cardinal Bevilacqua" on WZZD) to induce former Catholics to return to the Church.

On the national scene, the American bishops chose him to chair their committee on migration. Accordingly, he visited refugee camps in Southeast Asia and Africa. He worked with the Congregation for Religious and Secular Institutes and also the Pontifical Council for Migration and Itinerant People.

Gaetano L. Vincitorio

Bibliography

Archdiocese of Philadelphia, Communications Center. *Biography: His Eminence Anthony J. Bevilacqua.* Archdiocese of Philadelphia, 1996.

Bevilacqua, Anthony Cardinal. "Church and State: Partners in Freedom." *The Catholic Lawyer* 33 (1990): 281–284.

———. "Save the Family." *Columbia* 74 (October 1994): 8–13.

See also CHURCH LEADERS; RELIGION

Biscaccianti, Eliza (Ostinelli) (1824–1896)

The first Italian American recognized as an opera star in Europe, Eliza Biscaccianti was the daughter of (Paul Antonio) Louis Ostinelli (1795–184?), from Como, Italy, and his wife, Sophia Henrietta Hewitt (1799–1845), a native of New York.

Eliza Ostinelli was born in Boston. Her father, who had served as a conductor for the Handel and Haydn Society, was the best violinist in Boston, while her mother, whose father and brother were composers, was an expert organist and pianist. After Eliza reached her eighteenth birthday, she went with her father to Italy in 1843. There, in his native city and elsewhere, she undertook special voice lessons in music. She eventually married Count Biscaccianti. According to an obituary of Eliza published in the *Boston Daily Globe,* Count Biscaccianti, a member of a distinguished Mantuan family, was helpful in launching Eliza's operatic career in Italy, where she made her debut in Milan in May of 1847. The following year she returned to America and made her debuts in New York, Philadelphia, and her native Boston.

Following her return to America, her musical career was marked by both triumphs and tragedies. It soared upward as her fame as a soprano spread, with concerts in San Francisco during 1852 and in Lima, Peru, the following year. Henry Wadsworth Longfellow, a native of Portland, where the Ostinellis had contributed to its musical life, described her as "a fine little woman of genius with large eyes and coquettish ways." Her coloratura voice had enchanted audiences in North and South America as well as in Europe.

Unfortunately, Eliza's successes, including a world tour, were undermined by a failing marriage to Count Biscaccianti. She abandoned Biscaccianti and fell into an abusive relationship that proved destructive to her career as a successful prima donna. She returned to Biscaccianti, who sent her to live with his relatives in Italy while he pursued his own career in opera before his death in Melbourne, Australia, in 1875.

Meanwhile, Eliza had regained respectability and remained devoted to opera by becoming a singing teacher in Milan even after losing her charming voice. Unfortunately, she was taken advantage of by a man who left her penniless. When she died in Paris, July 1896, she was living at a home for artists and musicians that was supported by a foundation in memory of Gioacchino Antonio Rossini (1792–1868).

Vincent A. Lapomarda

Bibliography

Dickson, Samuel. "The Biscaccianti." In *Dream Streets,* edited by Lawrence DeStasi. New York: Harper, 1990.

Johnson, H. Earle. *Musical Interludes in Boston.* New York: Oxford University Press, 1943.

Owen, Barbara. "Sophie Hewitt Ostinelli." *American Organist* 25 (May 1991): 50–52.

Schiavo, Giovanni E. "Dictionary of Musical Biography." *Italian-American History.* Vol. 1. New York: Vigo, 1947, 254–256.

See also OPERA

Bocce

When Italian immigrants came to America, they brought with them the customs of their native country. In Italy, in towns large and small, men gathered together in their clubs to play cards, drink, socialize, and play bocce. They would often gather in the evenings and on Sundays for a few games of bocce. Men traditionally kept bocce to themselves—women, children, and non-Italians were not invited to play. As years went by and as women achieved greater equality, they began to embrace the game. This tradition continued in America, as small clubs were formed in Italian American neighborhoods. Many of these clubs exist to this day in the United States.

Bocce is considered the world's oldest sport; it began around 5200 B.C. in Egypt, was picked up by the Greeks, then passed to the Romans. Bocce, as it is played today, is often a family affair, having moved from the secretive men's clubs to an environment of picnics and backyards. In its simplest form, bocce is played by throwing a *pallino* (little ball) or jack onto the court or grass and rolling larger balls to see how close the players can get to the *pallino*. A point is awarded for each ball that lands closer than any of the opponents' balls. While advanced strategies and skills are used by the more serious player, bocce can be enjoyed by all types of people—men, women, children, and the physically challenged.

Just as Italians brought different dialects to this country, so did they bring regionalized variations on the rules of bocce. These range from strict international rules, in which every ball is marked and each player must indicate when he or she will be "hitting" (trying to knock the opponents' ball out) and the method by which it will be done; by *raffa*, or rolling hard at the ball, or by *volo*, hitting the ball on the fly; to the more free-form open rules in which almost anything goes and all balls remain in play on the court whether rolled or hit. Even when open rules are played, style of play and rules vary from one area to another. More recently there has been a concerted effort to standardize the open rules and bring together the various areas in the country, thereby promoting greater interest in the sport. The World Bocce Association has formed a professional league tour that will hold tournaments all over the world, similar to the PGA golf tour.

Bocce is a game enjoyed by many groups and nationalities throughout the world, including Canada, Europe, South America, and China. When golf and tennis were first introduced in our country, only the privileged few enjoyed these games. Now they are played by the masses, and professional tournaments have huge purses and an abundance of devoted fans. By unifying and promoting organized bocce tournaments, proponents of the game hope that one day the sport will receive the same devotion and attention as other popular sports.

Marilyn Ferrari
Philip Ferrari

Bibliography

Daniele, Rico. *Bocce, A Sport for Everyone.* Springfield, MA: Self-published, 1994.

Eisen, George, and David K. Wiggins, eds. *Ethnicity and Sport in North American History and Culture.* Westport, CT: Greenwood, 1994.

Ferrari, Marilyn, and Philip Ferrari. *Rolling Generation.* The World Bocce Association. Winter, 1994–1995.

Pagoni, Mario. *The Joy of Bocce.* Indianapolis: Masters, 1995.

See also SPORTS

Boehm, Helen Franzolin (b. 1920)

A world-famous entrepreneur and chairperson of the Boehm Porcelain Studio, Helen Franzolin Boehm realized her own potential as a successful business person by bringing her husband's porcelain sculptures to the attention of the world. The sixth of seven children born into an Italian immigrant family in Brooklyn, she married Edward Marshall Boehm in 1944. He was a quiet veterinarian's assistant who yearned to be an artist. In 1950, with her determined support and his talent, they opened the Boehm Porcelain Studio in Trenton, New Jersey. In the years since, Helen has been the driving force behind the company's successful marketing of exquisite sculptures of birds, flowers, and animals. Every American president since the 1950s has used the company's figures as official state gifts. Today Boehm porcelain is on exhibit in over 130 museums throughout the world, including the Metropolitan Museum of Art, the Vatican Museum, the White House, and in the Great Hall in Beijing. Helen Boehm, whose husband died in 1969, continues to travel the world, meeting with heads of state and royalty and sharing the beauty of Boehm porcelain. She is affectionately known as Trenton's "Queen of Porcelain."

Helen grew up in Bensonhurst, Brooklyn. Her father died when she was 13. She helped support her family by sewing dresses for her junior high school classmates. Helen's first job was as a receptionist in an occulist's office; later she went on to become one of the first women in New York to earn a license as a dispensing optician.

The Boehm porcelain-making method involved a technique called hard-paste porcelain which yielded translucence. This made it possible to make fine porcelain sculptures. Helen continued to work at the optical shop on Fifth Avenue in New York City and one day approached a prominent client to ask if he would be interested in financing the establishment of the only hard-paste porcelain studio in America. Her persistence was rewarded when the gentleman finally agreed to invest, and the Boehms moved to Trenton to open a studio in 1950.

Helen's role was to obtain financing and to display the porcelains; by 1951 she had succeeded in getting two of her husband's pieces placed on display in the Metropolitan Museum of Art. A few years later, she was working fourteen hours a day as office manager, bookkeeper, and sales representative. In 1954 she wrote to Mrs. Dwight Eisenhower and received an invitation to lunch at the White House. She arrived with a Boehm sculpture and made a lasting impression. Every American president since Eisenhower has commissioned Boehm for gifts for foreign dignitaries.

Over the next four decades, Helen Franzolin Boehm has brought her husband's works of art to the attention of world leaders, royalty, popes, and patrons of the arts. She still manages to find time to devote to charitable causes. A self-made millionaire, she has lived out the American dream.

Joanna Bevacqua

Bibliography

Boehm, Helen Franzolin. *With a Little Luck . . . An American Odyssey*. New York: Rawson Associates, 1985.

Cateura, Linda Brandi. *Growing Up Italian*. New York: Morrow, 1987.

"On the Boehm." *New York Magazine*, 1 October 1984, 30.

See also ART; BUSINESS AND ENTREPRENEURSHIP

Boiardi, Hector (1898–1985)

A household name, Hector Boiardi achieved success as a restaurateur and mass producer of Italian-style foods. His company, Chef Boyardee Quality Foods, Inc., was the first food processor in the country to receive the Army Navy award of "E" (Excellence) for recognition of its outstanding contribution to the war effort.

Born in Piacenza, Italy, in 1898, Hector, at age 11, became an apprentice chef in a hotel in his native Piacenza. He came to the United States at the age of 17 at the urging of his older brother Paul, who had arrived a few years earlier. The great Italian singer Enrico Caruso, a friend of the Boiardi family, also encouraged them to come to America. He went on to become a famous chef in such renowned hotels as the Plaza, Ritz Carlton, Claridge, and Rector's in New York, then at the Hotel Greenbrier in West Virginia.

In 1929 Boiardi became an independent restaurateur in Cleveland, Ohio. His specialty was spaghetti served with a piquant sauce of his own creation. Since his sauce was so popular, and his clients were buying it for home use, he conceived the idea of packaging his dinners as a complete unit. It was at this time that Hector Boiardi changed the spelling of the product to Boyardee, because customers and salesmen had difficulty pronouncing the Boiardi name. He said he made the change with sorrow, since "everyone is proud of his family name."

His initial operation could no longer keep up with demand and needed larger quarters. During the 1930s, at the height of the Great Depression, Chef Boyardee Quality Foods outgrew three Cleveland plants. In 1938 the company was moved to Milton, Pennsylvania, to a converted old silk mill to be nearer to a supply of tomatoes. This plant supplied grocery stores throughout the country with the Chef's dinners, spaghetti sauces, and canned pastas.

Shortly after the outbreak of World War II, Chef Boyardee Quality Foods, Inc. offered its production facilities to the government for use in manufacturing foodstuff for the armed forces and the Allies. In 1943 the company was recognized for its contribution to the war effort. Chef Boyardee Quality Foods was the first food processor in the country to be awarded the Army Navy "E".

Soon after the war, Boiardi sold the company to American Home Products. He remained a valued advisor and consultant to the company until his death at the age of 87. He died in Parma, Ohio, on June 27, 1985. The Chef's picture is still on every label that bears the Chef Boyardee name.

Delfina Tersigni

Bibliography

DiStasi, Lawrence. "The Face that Made Spaghetti Famous." In *Dream Streets*, edited by Lawrence DiStasi, 72–73. New York: Harper & Row, 1989.

B

Bonacci, Frank (1884–1954)

A central figure in the Carbon County, Utah, coal fields, Frank Bonacci battled as a labor organizer for the United Mine Workers of America (UMWA) and moved from one branded as a "foreigner" and "radical" to the first Italian American elected to the Utah state legislature. Bonacci was born in Decollatura, province of Catanzaro, Calabria, Italy, on November 22, 1884. He migrated to the United States in August 1896, settled in Carbondale, Pennsylvania, moved to Michel, British Columbia, Canada, in 1898 and in 1912 moved with his family to Sunnyside, Utah.

While in British Columbia, Bonacci became a member of the Western Federation of Miners. In 1905 he transferred membership to the UMWA and from then until 1912 served on various committees and local offices for the union. Upon the family's move to Carbon County, he continued his union activity. In 1917 the Bonaccis relocated to Helper, Utah, where Frank labored for the Denver & Rio Grande Railroad. Soon after he became a member of the International Association of Machinists. Bonacci initiated a third move to the coal camp of Hiawatha in 1918, and in 1919 he became financial secretary of the Hiawatha local of the UMWA.

Frank Bonacci labored tirelessly for unionization. Within the union he struggled to curb abuses. In a struggle with District #15 (Colorado and Utah) officials, he sought union reform. In the end, Utah was transferred to District #22 (Wyoming and Utah), and Bonacci demonstrated an unwavering loyalty to union causes. He frequently contributed to the *Wyoming Labor Journal.*

Throughout the 1920s and into the 1930s, Bonacci carried the union banner in conservative Utah. His family, especially his wife, Filomena, suffered incredibly because of Frank's union activity. Frequent evictions left Filomena and their children literally out in the cold. Bonacci was followed by a spy from the Globe Inspection Agency, dismissed, blacklisted, and eventually forced to submit to a "yellow dog contract." Such a contract required miners to denounce the union, swear that they would not join the union, and agree to recognize the company as sole authority, working grievances through official channels only.

With the beginning of Franklin D. Roosevelt's New Deal programs and a coal miners' strike in 1933, recognition of the UMWA finally came in Utah. Thus, Bonacci moved to a more "legitimate" status. He continued to work for the UMWA and later the Congress of Industrial Organizations (CIO). In 1936 he became the first Italian American elected to the Utah State House of Representatives, serving six full terms and four special sessions. He died on January 20, 1954.

Philip F. Notarianni

Bibliography

Notarianni, Philip F. "Rise to Legitimacy: Frank Bonacci as Union Organizer in Carbon County, Utah." *Rendezvous* (Idaho State University Journal of Arts and Letters) 19 (1983): 67–74.

Powell, Allan Kent. *The Next Time We Strike: Labor in Utah's Coal Fields, 1900–1933.* Logan: Utah State University Press, 1985.

See also LABOR; RADICALISM; UTAH

Bonaparte, Charles Joseph (1851–1921)

A civil service reformer and the first Italian American attorney general of the United States, Charles Joseph Bonaparte was born in Baltimore. As attorney general, he was architect of President Theodore Roosevelt's trust-busting policies and was the founder of the Federal Bureau of Investigation.

Charles J. Bonaparte descended from an extraordinary family: he is the son of Jerome Napoleon Bonaparte and Susan May (Williams) Bonaparte. His great-uncle was Napoleon Bonaparte; his aunt was the queen of Naples; and his grandfather, Jerome Bonaparte, was the king of Westphalia.

Educated at a French school near Baltimore and then by private tutors, he entered Harvard in 1869 as a junior and received a bachelor's degree and a law degree in 1871. He married Ellen Channing Day. Her grandfather had been a famous jurist, and her father was the owner and editor of the *Hartford Courant.* The Bonapartes had no children.

Bonaparte was a devout Roman Catholic who was greatly influenced by his mother's puritanical Presbyterianism, which made him unsympathetic to corrupt public servants. As a prominent Baltimore attorney, his clients included major corporations and the wealthy. He also provided legal service to the poor for little or no remuneration.

Bonaparte was a leader of civil service reform and founded the Civil Service Reform Association of Maryland in 1881. That year he helped to establish the National Civil Service Reform League, and from 1901 to 1905 served as its chairman. As a result, several successes followed in Maryland, including the adoption of the Australian ballot, a civil service law, and a corrupt practices act.

His interest in civil service reform brought him into contact with Theodore Roosevelt, who was then civil service commissioner. When Roosevelt became president, he appointed Bonaparte to the Federal Board of Indian Commissioners. In that post he investigated corruption in the Indian Territories, and his published report in 1904 persuaded Congress to revise government policy.

Bonaparte was made secretary of the Navy in 1905 in what President Roosevelt described as a "stopgap" means of keeping Bonaparte in government until the attorney general's job became available. On December 16, 1906, Bonaparte became the forty-sixth attorney general of the United States and the first Italian American to hold this position.

As attorney general, Bonaparte was the chief architect and chief strategist for Roosevelt's trust-busting policies. He continued many actions begun by his predecessor, including a major case against Standard Oil. He initiated twenty antitrust suits and secured eight trust dissolutions. His most successful action was against the American Tobacco Company, although the final decree dissolving the trust was not issued until 1911, many years after he left the attorney general's office. Bonaparte was not opposed to wealth but rather to trusts that denied successful business advancement to other entrepreneurs.

Bonaparte discovered that his work as attorney general was hampered by the lack of a permanent investigative staff. Until then, the Justice Department was restricted to hiring temporary investigators, usually from the Treasury Department's Secret Service. Despite congressional and public opposition Bonaparte issued on July 26, 1908, the order that made this investigative force a permanent subdivision of the Justice Department. It remained for his successor to name the new unit the Bureau of Investigations. In 1935 it was renamed the Federal Bureau of Investigation.

He left the office of attorney general in 1909. He resumed his law practice and maintained his involvement in reform issues. He died after a long illness at age 70 at Bella Vista, his estate near Baltimore.

Frank M. Sorrentino

Bibliography

Bishop, Joseph B. *Charles Joseph Bonaparte: His Life and Public Services.* New York: Scribner, 1922.

Goldman, Eric F. *Charles J. Bonaparte, Patrician Reformer: His Earlier Career.* Baltimore: Johns Hopkins University Press, 1943.

See also LAW ENFORCEMENT

Bonavita, Rose

According to the National Italian American Foundation, the original "Rosie the Riveter" was Rose Bonavita, an Italian American woman who later married James Hickey and resided on Long Island, New York. She became the symbol for women replacing men in the war production industry during World War II.

Although discriminated against during World War II, Italian American men proved their loyalty to the United States by fighting the Axis abroad, while Italian American women contributed to the building of defense industries at home. At that time, Rose Bonavita, a riveter in the aircraft industry, became the prototype for a wartime folklore about women as factory workers. A popular song of 1942, "Rosie the Riveter," with words and music by Rodd Evans and John Jacob Loeb, was written about her. She was featured on the famous cover of the *Saturday Evening Post* painted by Norman Rockwell for the issue published on May 29, 1943. And in 1944 the film *Rosie the Riveter* was released, in which Jane Frazee portrayed the life of the fictitious Rosie Warren in a story based on the life of Bonavita.

During World War II many "Rosies" replaced men as riveters, shipfitters, and welders. The period was a major turning point in the history of the American labor movement: more women were employed than at any other time in U.S. work history, numbering over eighteen million at one time. This reflected a dramatic change in the role of women in society.

Judging from available photographs, there are a number of "Rosies" depending on geography, industry, nationality, and race. Others like Geraldine Hoff Doyle and Charles Etta ("Charlie") Turner have emerged as prototypes who have also contributed to the folklore of "Rosie the Riveter." In Richmond, California, at the Kaiser Shipyard No. 2, Marina Bay, a project was launched on October 5, 1996, for the dedication of a national monument at Rosie the Riveter Park, commemorating all those women who replaced men in the nation's industries during World War II. The project group also publishes the *Rosie the Riveter Newsletter* to help realize that memorial.

Vincent A. Lapomarda

Bibliography

Colman, Penny. *Rosie the Riveter: Women Working on the Home Front in World War II*. New York: Crown, 1995.

Frank, Miriam, and others. *The Life and Times of Rosie the Riveter: The Story of Three Million Working Women During World War II*. Emeryville, CA: Clarity Educational Publications, 1982.

Honey, Maureen. *Creating Rosie the Riveter: Class, Race, Gender, and Propaganda During World War II*. Amherst: University of Massachusetts Press, 1984.

Nichols, Nancy A. "Whatever Happened to Rosie the Riveter?" *Harvard Business Review* 71 (1993): 54–62.

See also WARTIME MILITARY AND HOME FRONT ACTIVITIES; WOMEN IN THE WORKFORCE

Borgatti Jr., Anthony A. ("Spag") (1916–1996)

A retailer and merchandising giant, Anthony A. Borgatti's discount supply store became famous as a tourist attraction in central Massachusetts during the last part of the twentieth century.

He was the son of Antonio and Brigida (Minelli) Borgatti, born in Worcester, Massachusetts, on February 29, 1916. Known as "Spag" (a nickname derived from the association of spaghetti with Italian Americans), he started his merchandise supply business during the Great Depression with thirty-five dollars that his mother had loaned him following his graduation from Shrewsbury High School in 1934. His company, Spag's, eventually brought in close to $100 million a year.

Borgatti attributed his success to his wife, Olive I. (Lutz) Borgatti, who died in 1990 after fifty years of marriage. He mentioned the importance of her role when offering advice on how to succeed in business: "Do what I did, marry a good wife—who can do everything for you." While Mrs. Borgatti played a very significant role as president of the operation, it was "Spag" himself who made the business an exceptional retail supply company. Not only did Borgatti share the store's wealth with its employees (he had 450 of them by the time of his death), he spread it throughout the town of Shrewsbury and the broader Worcester area.

A retail expert, Borgatti taught others how to become successful through humanitarian efforts, which he put into practice by providing the community with good merchandise at low costs. According to one report, he purchased, in 1967, 1.6 million rolls of Life Savers, the largest ever sold to one retailer by Beech Nut Company. He treated his employees as part of his family, bestowing bountiful gifts on special occasions. For his altruism, humility, and service, he was honored with various awards.

At his death, Borgatti's company, which is being carried on by his three daughters, was among the top twenty-five private businesses in central Massachusetts. Borgatti showed his love for Shrewsbury by supporting its businesses and helping its citizens. He died in Shrewsbury on February 23, 1996, and is buried in Mountain View Cemetery.

Vincent A. Lapomarda

Bibliography

Jones-D'Agostino, Steven. "Majority Rules." *Worcester Business Journal,* 24 June–7 July 1996.

Kush, Bronislaus B., and James A.W. Shaw. "Retail Giant 'Spag' Dies: Borgatti Shared Store's Wealth." *Worcester Telegram & Gazette,* 24 February 1996.

Vigue, Doreen Iudica. "Anthony Borgatti, Colorful Retailer, Owned Spag's in Shrewsbury; at 79." *Boston Globe,* 24 February 1996.

Borgnine, Ernest

See MOVIE ACTORS AND ACTRESSES

Boston's North End

Boston's North End became the city's predominant Italian section late in the nineteenth century. Originally settled in the seventeenth century by the Puritans, the North End was the home of such Boston notables as Governor William Phipps and Paul Revere. By the end of the eighteenth century it had become the city's most densely populated section.

The North End was home to successive waves of immigrant and ethnic peoples from the African American settlement on Copps Hill (which gave the nickname of "New Guinea" to that area), to the Irish and German settlers early in the nineteenth century, to the Jews of eastern Europe at mid-century, and finally to the Italians at the end of the nineteenth century.

In 1905, during the period of massive European immigration to the United States, the North End was the principal area for Italian settlement in Boston, although it still contained sizable Irish and Jewish populations. Most of the Italians who migrated to the North End were from the southern Italian regions of Campania and Sicily. Twenty-six provinces from this region of Italy populated the congested streets and alleys of the North End, making it a reservoir from which Italians overflowed to other Italian neighborhoods and cities such as East Boston, the West End (Boston), East Cambridge, Revere, Everett, Somerville, and Medford.

The congestion and the antiquated housing stock (between 1930 and 1940 only eleven structures were built) contributed to the North End's characterization as an "immigrant slum." By 1944 the area had a population density of 924.3 persons per inhabited acre compared to that of its nearest neighbor, the West End, which had 369.7 persons.

North End Italians were isolated geographically and socially from the rest of the city's population. Hemmed in by ever-encroaching commercial development, the North End was described as a "tight little island." This isolation not only contributed to the ethnic identity of the North End and its inhabitants but may have lessened conflict with the city's other ethnic and racial groups. It was this very isolation that differentiates the Italian urban experience in Boston from that of other cities in the United States.

The North End's Italian American identity caused many to view it as "picturesque,"an image that may have spared the North End from the urban renewal bulldozer in the late 1950s.

While outsiders viewed the early North End as distinctly "Italian," there is evidence of residential, religious, and social patterns reflecting the diverse origins of the inhabitants, creating enclaves. These differences produced religious and social organizations that originated the North End's most distinctive activity—the feasts. Among the most popular of these was the Feast of San Rocco, organized by the San Rocco Society.

In recent times the North End's character has undergone change. The process of gentrification and condominium conversion have broken down the social isolation, while the depression of the elevated highway, which geographically isolates the North End, will knit it again into the physical geography of Boston.

Still considered Boston's Little Italy, the North End is no longer exclusively Italian and has become a tourist attraction. It actively attracts those seeking the Old North Church and Paul Revere's house, as well as those yearning for a taste of Italy in America. Consequently, the area has been "sanitized" of its sidewalk stands with their products spilling into the streets and many of the sights and sounds of the original North End Italians living their daily lives. Sensing the danger to their community, the remaining Italian residents are seeking to preserve their identity.

Even the distinctive feasts, commemorating local patron saints, have become such a commercialized tourist staple in the North End that Italians in other sections of the city are competing with them to recreate what they consider to be the original essence of the practice—neighborhood togetherness and celebration. The North End will continue to be regarded as Boston's Little Italy for its past and present ethnic associations, but the human qualities that helped to create the Italian identity of the North End are slowly disappearing.

Rosario J. Tosiello

Bibliography

DeMarco, William. *Ethnics and Enclaves.* Ann Arbor: UMI Research Press, 1981.

Firey, Walter. *Land Use in Central Boston.* Cambridge: Harvard University Press, 1947.

Martellone, Anna Maria. *Una Little Italy Nell'Atene D'America.* Napoli, Italy: Guida Editori, 1973.

Stack, John F. *International Conflict in an American City.* Westport, CT: Greenwood Press, 1979.

Botto House

The house of Pietro Botto (1864–1945), an Italian immigrant weaver from Biella, Italy, became famous during the 1913 Paterson, New Jersey, silk strike. In 1982 the Botto House became the first Italian American site to be designated a national landmark.

When Paterson's mayor refused to allow the strikers, upwards of twenty thousand strong, to assemble in Paterson, radical labor leader William "Big Bill" Haywood (1860–1928) urged the strikers to congregate in the adjacent suburb of Haledon. The socialist mayor of Haledon, William Brueckman, permitted the strikers to assemble in Haledon. The Botto House became the Sunday rallying point from March 3 to the end of the strike in June.

At the time of the strike, Pietro Botto worked as a silk weaver at the Cedar Cliffs mills in Haledon, which were not on strike. The home of an Italian immigrant who had no personal involvement in the strike became the center of mass Sunday rallies and strike strategy sessions. His wife, Maria, kept the house in order and fed the activists on these occasions. Famous labor activists who addressed the crowd, either from the house's balcony or in front of it, included Haywood, Upton Sinclair, Elizabeth Gurley Flynn, Carlo Tresca, Adolph Lessig, and Patrick Quinlan.

Botto had arrived in the United States in 1892, settled in West Hoboken, and moved to Haledon in 1908. He had four daughters. He could not find work after the strike, nor could his daughter Eva, who was blacklisted.

The Botto House features the American Labor Museum, which contains a permanent exhibit.

Dennis J. Starr

Bibliography

Golin, Steve. *The Fragile Brigade: Paterson Silk Strike of 1913*. Philadelphia: Temple University Press, 1988.

Tripp, Anne Huber. *The I.W.W. and the Paterson Silk Strike of 1913*. Urbana: University of Illinois Press, 1987.

See also RADICALISM

Bovasso, Julie

See PLAYS, CONTEMPORARY

Broccoli, Albert Romolo (1909–1996)

A descendant of Italians in Calabria who developed the famous vegetable that bears the family name, Albert R. Broccoli left an impact on the American film industry as one of the nation's leading producers.

The son of Giovanni and Cristina (Vence) Broccoli, he was born in New York City on April 5, 1909. Known from his early days in school as "Cubby" (a nickname derived from a chubby character in newspaper comics), he was educated in the public schools of New York City. He had no formal secondary education, and like his ancestors, he began work selling vegetables before entering a career in film.

Going to work for 20th Century Fox, Broccoli moved from a mail clerk to an assistant director for Howard Hughes, helping to produce the film *The Outlaw* (1943) before entering the United States Navy in 1942 and serving until 1947. He resumed his film career that year with RKO Studios, but branched out with Irving Allen and became the producer, for Warwick Films in England, of approximately twenty films from 1951 to 1960, including *Red Beret* (1952), *Black Knight* (1954), *Safari* (1956), and *Arrivederci Roma* (1957). On June 21, 1959, he married Dana Natol Wilson, and they became the parents of four children.

Assuming leadership of EON Productions, in 1960 Broccoli entered the most productive phase of his career. To these years belong such films as *The Trials of Oscar Wilde* (1960); *Chitty Chitty Bang Bang* (1967), which won the 1968 Family Film Awards; and more than a dozen films about James Bond, superspy 007 of Ian Fleming's novels. The Bond series, worked on in partnership with Harry Saltzman from 1961 to 1976, included such hits as *Dr. No* (1962), *From Russia with Love* (1963), *Thunderball* (1964), *You Only Live Twice* (1966), *On Her Majesty's Secret Service* (1969), *Live and Let Die* (1972), and *The Man with the Golden Gun* (1974). Most of these won awards, and Broccoli himself was decorated by France, Italy, and Spain. In addition to a number of other honors like the Irving G. Thalberg Award (1982), he received the Order of the British Empire (1987) for his film achievements.

Broccoli's achievement as a producer is linked with James Bond just as film director Francis Ford Coppola is linked with *The Godfather*. He was known for sharing his wealth with the needy. He died of heart complications on June 27, 1996, in Beverly Hills, and he is buried in Forest Lawn Memorial Park (Hollywood Hills) in Los Angeles.

Vincent A. Lapomarda

Bibliography

Jackson, Devon. "The Cubby File." *The New York Times Magazine,* 29 December 1996, 40.

Oliver, Myrna. "Albert Broccoli, Bond Movie Producer, Dies." *Los Angeles Times,* 29 June 1996.

Smith, Danitia. "Albert Broccoli, Film Producer Dies at 87." *New York Times,* 29 June 1996.

Westhoff, Jeffrey. "A Tribute to Cubby Broccoli." *Northwest Herald,* 3 July 1996.

See also FILM DIRECTORS, PRODUCERS, AND ITALIAN AMERICAN IMAGE IN CINEMA

Brumidi, Constantino (1805–1880)

An accomplished painter, especially of murals, Constantino Brumidi had a Greek father and a mother who was born in Rome. As a child he studied art formally in Italy and, while a student, proceeded to win a number of distinguished awards. He worked for years as a professional artist in Rome, where he became known for his restorations of classical works, decorations of chapels and church altars, and portraits of popes.

He continued as an artist upon his immigration to the United States in 1852. Among his works in this country are the Altarpiece, Cathedral of Saints Peter and Paul, Philadelphia; *The Immaculate Conception,* ceiling, Saint Ignatius Loyola Church, Baltimore; and *St. Charles Borromeo Giving Holy Communion to Saint Aloysius Gonzaga,* oil canvas, St. Aloysius Church, Washington, D.C.

In 1855 he began his lifetime work in the United States Capitol. He was responsible for the fresco of *Cincinnatus,* located in several congressional rooms and corridors, and George Washington, *Apotheosis,* in the Rotunda cupola. Indeed, the latter, his most acclaimed work, has led art critics to describe Brumidi as the Michelangelo of the Capitol. However, because his style so evidently evoked the works of Raphael, he also could be called the Raphael of the Capitol.

Brumidi died after a fall from the scaffold in the Rotunda in 1880. He was buried in Germon tomb, Glenwood Cemetery, Washington, D.C.

Regina Soria

Bibliography

Ahrens, Kent. "Constantino Brumidi's Apotheosis of Washington in the Rotunda of the United States Capitol." *Records of the Columbia Historical Society of Washington, D.C.* 73 (1976): 187–208.

Cosentino, Andrew J., and Henry H. Glassic. *The Capitol Image: Painters in Washington, 1800–1915.* Washington, D.C.: Smithsonian Institution Press, 1983.

Murdock, Myrtle Cheney. *Constantino Brumidi: Michelangelo of the United States Capitol.* Washington, D.C.: Monumental Press, 1950.

Soria, Regina. *American Artists of Italian Heritage, 1776–1945.* Rutherford, NJ: Fairleigh Dickinson University Press, 1994.

See also ART

Christopher Columbus—Discovery, *mural by Constantino Brumidi on the ceiling of the President's Room of the U.S. Capitol, Washington, D.C., 1859. Note the navigational devices at the bottom of column. Courtesy Library of Congress.*

Buitoni, Giovanni (1891–1979)

An international producer of macaroni products, chocolates, and confections, Giovanni Buitoni achieved international success creating the businesses of Buitoni pasta and Perugina candy. He was born on November 6, 1892, in Perugia, Italy.

It was Giovanni's great-grandmother, Giulia Buitoni, who started a small macaroni business in San Sepolcro, Italy, in 1827. Three generations of Buitonis contributed to the pasta and chocolate dynasty, but it was great-grandson Giovanni who brought the company to the international arena with pasta plants in San Sepolcro, Italy; Rome; Paris; and South Hackensack, New Jersey. He also built a lithography plant in Perugia, Italy, as well as American subsidiary corporations and a multitude of retail stores.

While in high school, Giovanni was an excellent student. After graduation in 1909, his father gave him a trip to Germany, where he studied the German language and observed industrial operations. While in Germany he received news that the Perugina chocolate company was in danger of failing. At age 18 his father granted him permission to become its general manager. With the help of the candy manufacturing Spagnoli family, Giovanni succeeded in increasing the staff from fifteen workers in a basement to hundreds in a large factory. He did this while getting his doctor of law degree from the University of Perugia.

In the 1930s Buitoni was the first Italian in Italy to use a contest to encourage customers to buy Buitoni products. He placed pictures of figurines in his pasta and chocolate products. Prizes could be won by collecting a complete set of these cards. This form of advertising, incorporated during the Great Depression, quickly became very popular and led to extensive bartering. The figurines were exchanged like stocks and bonds on the business pages of the newspapers.

Buitoni married Letizia Cairone, an opera singer, on October 22, 1936. In 1939 he and his wife came to the United States to attend the thirtieth anniversary celebration of the Hershey Chocolate Company in Pennsylvania as representatives of the Italian candy industry. While in the United States they opened a Buitoni restaurant in the Italian building at the New York World's Fair and a Perugina store on Fifth Avenue. Buitoni and his wife were already considering staying in America when Italy entered into World War II. This caused them to be cut off from Italy without funds or merchandise.

Buitoni's wife pawned her jewels as Giulia Buitoni's mother had done previously, and she and her husband established a modest branch of the Buitoni business in Jersey City, New Jersey, followed by two Buitoni restaurants on Broadway.

Buitoni served as mayor of Perugia from 1930 to 1935, where he is remembered for his insistence that cement pipes be installed in aqueducts instead of the previously used iron pipes, which were subject to disintegration. This change ultimately became standard practice by Italian law. He was awarded the Italian Star of Solidarity for his efforts in promoting understanding between the United States and Italy. He also received the Unico national award and the Columbia University Casa Italiana award. He was a *cavaliere* of Sts. Maurizio and Lazzaro and a *cavaliere del lavoro*.

Delfina Tersigni

Bibliography

Null, Gary, and Carl Stone. *The Italian Americans.* Harrisburg, PA: Stackpole, 1976.

See also BUSINESS AND ENTREPRENEURSHIP

Buscaglia, Leo (1924–1998)

A popular educator, author, and lecturer, Leo Buscaglia was world-renowned for improving human relationships through his philosophy of love.

The son of "Tulio" (Rocco Bartolomeo) and Rosa (née Cagna), immigrants from Aosta, in the Italian Alps, (Felice) Leonardo Buscaglia was born in Los Angeles, California, on March 31, 1924. When he began his schooling in Los Angeles at 5 years of age, young Buscaglia, who had already spent most of his early years in the Italian hometown of his parents, was fluent in Italian but deficient in English. Buscaglia's first experience with formal American education was not a pleasant one. Fortunately, he was able to derive from his parents a love of learning and of neighborliness, which compensated for the obstacles he encountered in school, including discrimination.

When he entered Roosevelt High School in Los Angeles, Buscaglia decided on a career in teaching. However, upon graduation, he had to postpone that goal to serve in the United States Navy during World War II. Discharged from military service in 1944, he eventually entered the University of Southern California, where he earned bachelor's (1950), master's (1954), and doctorate (1963) degrees in education. During the next five years, he administered special education programs for the schools of Pasadena City, California.

Subsequently, between 1965 and 1984, Buscaglia was employed as a professor in the Department of Special Education at the University of Southern California in Los Angeles. Having discovered that love was the common key among peoples of different cultures and religions, Buscaglia offered an evening course entitled "Love 1A," the so-called Love Class, which led the students at the university to vote him the most popular teacher during the 1969–1970 academic year. Because he found Buscaglia's ideas so exceptional, Charles B. Slack, a book publisher in the health industry, published a number of the educator's works such as *Love* (1972), a best-seller for a generation, and *The Disabled and Their Parents: A Counseling Challenge* (1975). Buscaglia coauthored with Biba Caggiano a cookbook entitled *Love Cookbook* (1994).

Although some of his contemporaries in psychology and sociology disagreed with Buscaglia's insights, this did not sidetrack him from lecturing on his philosophy of love throughout the world. His popularity was underscored in 1983 when five of his dozen or so books made the the *New York Times* best-seller list. He moved from Los Angeles in 1984 and established the Felice Foundation in Glenbrook, Nevada, with himself as chairman. Since its inception, Buscaglia used this nonprofit enterprise to spread his ideas. Dr. Buscaglia also proved to be a very effective television personality, leading television seminars on love and personal relationships.

Buscaglia received a number of awards, including the Cavaliere of the Order of Merit from the Republic of Italy in 1988 and the Columbian Award from the Federated Italo Americans of Southern California in 1991. Known as "Dr. Hug," he was included in Hershey's Hugs Hall of Fame in 1993. Close to twenty million copies of his works are in circulation and have been translated into more than a dozen languages.

Vincent A. Lapomarda

Bibliography

Albin, Len. "The Long, Loving Arms of Leo Buscaglia." *50 Plus* 25 (June 1985): 59–63.

Buscaglia, Leo F. *Born for Love*. Thorofare, NJ: Slack, 1992.
———. *Bus 9 to Paradise: A Loving Voyage*. Thorofare, NJ: Slack, 1986.
———. *Living, Loving and Learning*. Thorofare, NJ: Slack, 1982.
———. *Love*. Thorofare, NJ: Slack, 1972.
———. *Loving Each Other: The Challenge of Human Relationships*. Thorofare, NJ: Slack, 1984.
———. *Papa, My Father: A Celebration of Dads*. Thorofare, NJ: Slack, 1989.

Business and Entrepreneurship

Italian Americans, a number of whom who have risen to prominence as corporate leaders, are an integral part of America's business and financial world. Their success rests on the foundation set by Italian immigrants in the nineteenth and early twentieth centuries. Though little has been written of these pioneers, their accomplishments are an indispensable part of Italian American heritage and an inspiration to their descendants who play a vital role in America's economic history.

Centuries before the mass migration of Italians to America's shores, citizens of northern city-states on the Italian peninsula played an important role in the formation and development of banking and the capitalist system. Before Italy was unified, Italian migration to the United States was marked by a small but effective number of merchants, mostly from northern Italy. They settled in, but were not limited to, New Orleans, Chicago, St. Louis, San Francisco, and New York. Eventually, the merchant class was represented by Italians from all parts of Italy and could be found wherever Italians colonized. In the second half of the nineteenth century, those who became merchants in the United States were overwhelmingly male and about 38 years old. Mostly married, they generally stayed in business for ten years, though the range ran from one year to fifty-five years. Their average worth was $81,766. Some went bankrupt and others became millionaires, with the majority somewhere in the middle.

Many of these merchants were rated for credit. Most of them, 60 percent, drew favorable comments; 27 percent were mixed; and 13 percent were negative. The credit reports were mostly based on an individual's ability to pay bills on a timely basis, character, business

The bar of Liccione and Pittaro at the corner of Hester and Mulberry Streets, New York City, 1893. Vito Pittaro, second from right, was a successful businessman and importer of wines and liquors. Courtesy Immigration History Research Center, Minnesota.

acumen, industry, attention to detail, and reputation in the trade and in financial circles. Those who scored high in those areas generally found credit easy to come by. Those who were incompetent and/or had vices, such as gambling, drinking, and womanizing, found it difficult to get credit. For some, however, the crucial element was the ability to generate revenue. Talented individuals, no matter how honorable and hard-working, might not warrant much credit if raters thought that their business would be unprofitable with no potential for increase. Less able entrepreneurs, if they came from a rich family known for financial integrity and business success, would continually be looked on favorably because of their lucrative resources.

Italian and Italian American merchants occupied a wide array of vocations in America's business world. A list of some of the more common occupations includes artists and stone painters, barbers, clothiers, confectioners, pharmacists, jewelers, jobbers, lawyers, musicians, peddlers, physicians, publishers, shoemakers, steamship agents, tailors, tobacconists, and watchmakers. They were active primarily in commission houses, general stores, groceries, saloons and as importers and manufacturers of macaroni, chocolate, and chemicals. They were flexible, willing to relocate, or to move from one business to another. They traveled extensively, even abroad, in order to make a success of their operation.

This mobility was seen in the case of E. B. Pasquale, an Italian who started out as a struggling miner in California, switched to selling toys and flags, and invested his profits in real estate. A daredevil individual involved in the complexities of running an American business, he was considered one of the pioneer entrepreneurs of California. Equally mobile was Philip Ronzone of New York. Having trouble with his custom house and European Express business, he took to sailing the Atlantic regularly and became a supplier to dressmakers with stock he purchased on those semiannual excursions. The new business improved both his credit and his reputation. The stories of countless other Italian and Italian American merchants in big and small town America as well as on the frontier in the nineteenth century reveal this drive to attain upward social and economic mobility. These intrepid entrepreneurs often succeeded and contributed to the success story that was America.

In 1850 Louisiana had more Italian-born inhabitants than any other state. Barelli and Company began as a commercial house around 1839 (under the name of Mansoni) in New Orleans led by I. Barelli, son of the Portugal vice counsel of Sicily. By 1853 Barelli had become counsel of Portugal and vice counsel of the Two Sicilies (a poliical entity that existed in preunification Italy). His business thriving, he invested in real estate, had excellent credit, and was said to be worth over one hundred thousand dollars. After he died in 1858, his son, Joseph, took over the firm and continued to operate a large foreign business. In 1860 the firm committed to building a block of iron buildings, which proved to be its undoing. Its major source of revenue cut off by the Civil War, the company went from riches to rags in 1865 and was forced out of business. While it was not unusual for small businesses to fail, it was atypical for larger Italian businesses to fall by the wayside.

Another New Orleans firm, Lanata, Gandolpho, and Company, was among the earliest and most successful of any Italian American nineteenth-century enterprise. It operated in the 1840s and 1850s. Composed of the partners Dominic Lanata, I. Gandolpho, and I. Viosca, it speculated in general commerce, especially with Mexico and Spain; Havana produce; and real estate. The firm also ran a retail grocery. At the height of their business, the partners were worth close to a million dollars and were considered to be honest, reliable, successful businessmen. In 1856 Viosca entered into business with the Piaggio brothers, Enrico and Rinaldo, importing French oils and wines. Hailing from Genoa, Viosca and the Piaggios did a large-scale business with European and South American firms. The Piaggios also owned a mercantile house in Montevideo and invested heavily in real estate. In 1865 Viosca retired, and the company became Piaggio and Brothers. The following year Enrico Piaggio stepped down and left the operation to Rinaldo. Throughout their careers, Viosca and the Piaggios received the highest accolades from the general business community. Collectively worth over a million dollars, they set a high standard for excellence in entrepreneurial activities.

Southern Italians were also found among the business class during the early years of immigration. One of the most successful was Captain Salvatore Pizzati, a Sicilian. He came to New Orleans on the eve of the Civil War and shipped in boatloads of fruit from Central America. In 1880 he sold a flotilla to the company United Fruit for a handsome profit. He then owned or supervised the Columbian Brewery and the Southern Insurance Company. He also operated fourteen thousand acres of citrus trees and invested in banks or other commercial and industrial institutions. Easily one of the wealthiest Italians in the United States, he built and endowed a New Orleans orphanage for Italian children shortly after 1900.

Chicago had a large complement of Ligurian businessmen in the nineteenth century. The most successful of them was Giovanni Garibaldi, a Genoese who worked his way over to America on a sailing vessel at age 13. Lacking a formal education, but possessing the proverbial "native shrewdness" of his homeland, he started out selling fruit from a basket. He eventually married into a pioneer family of Chicago, the Cuneos, and established a fruit commission house with his brother Francesco. The firm of Garibaldi and Cuneo became the largest importer and wholesaler of fruits and nuts in the United States. He became a millionaire and was reputedly the wealthiest Italian in Chicago at the time. Other successful Genoese merchants included Domenico Botto and Francesco Gazzolo. Botto started a confectionery store in 1854, acquired choice real estate, and, at the time of his death in 1896, had holdings valued at a quarter of a million dollars. Gazzolo went from fruit merchant to real estate tycoon and died a millionaire in 1902. Italian merchants tended to invest their profits in real estate. In 1886 it was estimated that Italians in Chicago owned land valued at approximately two and one half million dollars.

Exemplifying the diversity of business interests among Italians was the Piedmontese Dominic Bertoglio of Meaderville, Montana. Staking himself by working mines in Wisconsin and Arizona, he arrived in Butte in 1892. He opened up the Bertoglio Mercantile Company, was one of the founders of the Spokane Telephone Company, owned substantial mining property, and associated himself with the Tivoli Brewing Company and the Patent Plow

Point Company of Detroit, Michigan. Many of his descendants carried on in business in Montana in the twentieth century.

Italian entrepreneurs of the nineteenth century whose businesses remained successful well into the twentieth century and still operate, in one form or another, include Eugene Grasselli, Carlo Barsotti, Domingo Ghirardelli, and E. F. Sanguinetti.

Coming from an Italian family of chemist-druggists and perfumers who moved to Strasbourg, Germany, Eugene Grasselli immigrated to Cincinnati in 1836 and established a small chemical manufacturing plant around 1838. The business failed in 1842. Bolstered by his faith in his knowledge of the chemical business, Grasselli pushed on. By 1870 Grasselli was worth about four hundred thousand dollars and emerged as one of Ohio's success stories. Among his holdings were twenty-two acres of farmland two miles outside Cincinnati, plus building lots and homes in both Cincinnati and Cleveland, where his family had moved to in 1867, attracted by the developing oil industry.

In the 1870s, joined by his son, Caesar Augustine, Grasselli continued his expansion. They held interests in the Titusville Chemical Works of Pennsylvania and, in partnership with others, bought the Pittsburgh Acid Works, which became the Pittsburgh Acid Company. As the years went by, father and son continued to buy other companies outright, such as the Olean Chemical Company of Olean, New York, or acquire interests in other ventures, such as the Union Acid Restoring Company of Cleveland. Headquartered in Cleveland, the Grassellis built an empire that included a branch on Wall Street under the name of Standard Chemical Works. Supplying refiners, they had more orders than they could fill. Their strength was a secret process for the manufacturing of acids used extensively by refiners.

Eugene Grasselli died in 1882. His son, Caesar Augustin, remained strong in the business. He led Grasselli Chemical Company as it expanded its manufacturing and distribution operations and produced new products, such as zinc or spelter, becoming a leader in the field. Caesar Augustin was eventually recognized as a distinguished manufacturer and philanthropist, not only in the United States, but also abroad in Rome and in the Vatican. By the turn of the century, the Grasselli Company was valued at over one million dollars.

Its growth in the twentieth century was phenomenal. By World War I, involved in making explosives, it was worth close to twenty million dollars. In 1936 Grasselli lost its corporate identity when it became part of the giant Du Pont firm.

Charles (Carlo) Barsotti is best known as the founder of *Il Progresso Italo-Americano,* the first Italian daily and the largest Italian newspaper in America. Born in Pisa in 1850, he came to America as an infant and settled in New York City. Starting out as a porter in an Italian grocery store, he soon became a *padrone* (labor broker), supplying contract labor to the city and to private establishments. He made a handsome profit from low-income rentals in the Bowery and in area neighborhoods. By 1880 he was confident enough to establish his newspaper. Three years later he opened the Italian American Bank with Carlo Pavia as his general manager. This freed up Barsotti to take frequent trips to Italy and solidify his exchange business with Italian immigrants. By the mid-1880s his profitable lodging houses spread to other neighborhoods, his bank and foreign exchange business continued to do well, and *Il Progresso*'s circulation grew substantially. In addition, Barsotti had acquired valuable property in nearby Fort Lee, New Jersey. Indicative of his rising good fortune, the Italian government honored him for his charitable deeds toward his countrymen in America in connection with his banking business. This underscored his excellent reputation as a respectable businessman in the general merchant community and added to his stature as a vigorous leader of a widely influential newspaper.

Domingo Ghirardelli was one of California's most successful Italian settlers, best known for establishing the world-famous Ghirardelli Chocolate Company. He prospered early by selling sweets to miners in the gold rush, but suffered through financial difficulties that lasted from the Civil War through the early 1870s. His firm, D. Ghirardelli and Company (his partners, also Italians, were his son-in-law, F. Barbagelata and Carlo Peters), specialized as an importer, jobber, and manufacturer of chocolate. Shrewd and energetic, Ghirardelli provided the capital for the firm, which established two stores in Oakland and others in San Francisco and Nevada. The firm failed in 1870. Though the reasons were never specified, Ghirardelli's excessive speculations in real estate were believed to be major contributing factors. Ghirardelli was forced to mortgage his personal real estate in Oakland in order to obtain an extension from his creditors, who were principally Italian American fishermen. Apparently, they were a major source of merchant capital for Italian immigrants in the nineteenth century.

By late 1874 Ghirardelli was slowly but surely working his way out of receivership by prudent buying and by meeting financial obligations on time. In 1877, helped by the infusion of fresh capital from a new partner, Gustov Danzell, Ghirardelli was able to free himself from receivership. Thereafter, his energy, optimism, and charisma helped pave the way for the successful chocolate company that bears his name today.

E. F. Sanguinetti was born in 1867 in Coulterville, Mariposa County, California, into an Italian American merchant family. His father, Antonio Sanguinetti, operated a general store in Agua Frio, where he dealt chiefly with the Chinese. Later he opened a store in San Diego and taught the trade to his son. A business trip to Europe highlighted their experience. In 1882, at age 15, E. F. went to Yuma, Arizona, a sparsely populated desert trading station on the border of Mexico and California through which railroads hauled mostly precious metals, provisions, and animal skins. He took a job, probably sweeping floors, with the Genoese merchant John Gandolfo, for which he was paid forty dollars a month and board. He roomed in an open air porch above a meat market and barber shop. Living a spartan lifestyle, he was able to save enough to buy into Gandolfo's firm and eventually open his own business.

In the early years mining was a major activity, and Sanguinetti, alert to the needs of the miners and of the industry, expanded his operations. He employed hundreds of people in his stores, which he located throughout the territory. He set up the first undertaker's home "so that the dead would not have to be packed in ice until burial." He operated his own mines, introduced the first wheel plow to the area as farmers began moving in, and helped lead a fight to bring flood control along the Colorado and Gila Rivers flowing to Yuma. Over the years, he built the first packing shed for shipping produce, farmed, ranched, and opened the first and only creamery in the region. An expert assayist, he could identify from which location miners had taken their precious haul. Blessed with a wide vision, he emerged as a leader in community affairs, spearheading moves in education, banking, land development, public utilities, road and bridge building, and in a host of activities designed to transform Yuma into an attractive desert oasis.

Sanguinetti had his share of setbacks due mostly to floods and fires, for which he had no insurance, and an uncharacteristic investment failure occasioned by a disastrous speculation in cotton in the 1920s that almost wiped him out. He pressed ahead, however, and on his death in 1945 left a sizable estate of over $150,000 in solid assets. It included over fifty-five parcels of land in the city and county of Yuma and five hundred shares of E. F. Sanguinetti, Inc. preferred stock valued at fifty thousand dollars. This was a remarkable legacy given his financial troubles in the 1920s and the subsequent worldwide depression. His worth to the community was invaluable. Sanguinetti was formally cited for his distinguished civic service as one of the most influential leaders in Yuma's history. His daughter, Rose Marie S. Gwynn, a successful merchant in her own right, carries on the family tradition today. Owner and operator of an upscale shop in the downtown historic district of Yuma, Gwynn continues a tradition of Italian entrepreneurship that includes community involvement, diversity, and multiculturalism in the late twentieth century.

The success of Italian American merchants in the early twentieth century presaged the group's full blooming by the latter half of the century. Though a few industries stand out, virtually no area of the business world has remained untouched by them.

California provided a number of key examples. There, Italians exercised some significant influence on the economic development of the United States mostly in the fishing industry, agriculture, viniculture and viticulture, food preservation, and banking.

By the 1880s Italians in California, led first by Genoese and then Sicilians, were the dominant ethnic group in the fishing industry. Bringing with them their specialized equipment or introducing their preferred style of fishing boat, they enjoyed great success both in deep-sea operations and freshwater fishing. Moreover, they developed important canneries where the catch could be smoked, cured, and packed for shipment across the country. The Genoese eventually sold out to Sicilians and took up a number of other endeavors, favoring the refuse business where they made their fortunes in reclaiming papers, bottles, and other valuable throw-aways. It was in land and activities connected with it that they put down their sturdiest roots.

Andrea Sbarboro, a Genoese banker who founded early building and loan associations and later the Italian American Bank, helped lead the way for Italian entrepreneurs. Combining with Pietro C. Rossi, his chief winemaker, Sbarboro formed the Italian-Swiss Agricultural Colony in the Sonoma Valley. It eventually went on to gain international fame for its high-quality wines and dominated the wine industry in the United States. In 1953, the Petri family, which had started a small San Joaquin Valley winery in the 1880s, took over the company. To be sure, not all Italian vintners became giants, but even those like the Mondavis with their Napa Valley white wines, the Guastis with their Cucamonga dessert wines, and the Martinis with their Napa Valley Cabernet Sauvignon and Pinot Noir red wines, distinguished themselves by producing high-quality wines.

Spearheaded by the efforts of Marco Giovanni Fontana, Italians pioneered in the large-scale canning operations that were essential to maintaining the phenomenal growth of California's farm production. Having worked with fellow Ligurians in the early days of the Italian-Swiss Colony, Fontana was dedicated to putting out the best possible product, thereby making a difference in molding tastes as consumers demanded an ever-improvimg quality of fruits and vegetables. Fontana, who had come to the United States in 1859, helped form the California Fruit Packing Corporation (Calpac) in 1889. Better known by its Del Monte label, it became the largest fruit and canning operation in the world. By the time he died in 1922, he had also served as the president of the California Wine Association, amassed a fortune, and founded the town of Fontana, San Bernardino County, where he had extensive vineyard holdings.

Friends and colleagues of Fontana were the Sicilian immigrant brothers Joseph and Rosario Di Giorgio. Joseph started working in a warehouse specializing in wholesale fruits, then jobbed on his own, and at 19 years of age began importing fruit from Jamaica. By age 36, he established the Atlantic Fruit Company in Baltimore, Maryland, said to be worth $12 million. In 1911 he went to California and aided in the development of the San Joaquin Valley as a grape and wine center. With his brother, Rosario, he established the Di Giorgio Fruit Corporation. Known as the largest shippers of fresh fruit in the world, they also sold a wide distribution of canned fruits and vegetables under the respected S & W label. The Di Giorgios controlled more than forty thousand acres of land, mostly in California. The balance was in other states, Latin America, and Mexico. Beyond these specific accomplishments in agriculture, Italians are generally credited with bringing bell peppers, artichokes, eggplants, and broccoli to California as well as producing the tomato puree desired for pasta dishes.

Italians in California made substantial contributions in other areas of manufacturing, though less crucial to the overall economic development of the state. The Jacuzzi family established a name in water pumps and hydraulic machinery, and Gabriel Giannini (no relation to A. P.) staked a position in the production of electronics.

In California, one of the better-known and well-respected steamship agents was J. F. Fugazy. While running a barbershop in Sacramento, he started selling tickets on commission in 1872 for White Star Line and did so well that he was appointed its bona fide agent. He also acted as an agent for several other steamship lines and marketed a "medicinal" preparation called the Bloom of Youth that brought him a handsome profit.

Yet it was in the field of banking and finance that Italians made their most dramatic impact on the American economic scene. There were countless immigrants and their progeny who opened up banks, large and small, throughout the land. However, none was the peer of Amadeo Peter Giannini. Standing out above all the others, he had the most far-reaching influence on both the Italian American and American business scene, where he made an indelible mark.

The son of modest immigrant parents, Giannini started to work at age 12 for his stepfather's produce firm, became a full partner at 19, and retired in 1901 at age 31. Living off his real estate investments and the proceeds from the sale of his 50 percent interest in the produce business, he entered banking when a legacy from his wealthy father-in-law,

Joseph Cuneo, who put him on the board of a savings and loan association. He soon decided to strike out on his own and formed the Bank of Italy in San Francisco in 1904. Giannini did nothing less than revolutionize the banking business. He was a prime mover in changing it from an elitist institution to a democratic one. He set the example for an industry that would transform itself from an inflexible, conservative operation that was slow to respond to the needs of an incipient industrial society to one that would activate unparalleled economic opportunity for many individuals in America. Not content with the customary banking system that acted as a wholesaler for those few who had the right social status and nationality, he succeeded in making a retail bank for the masses. He made loans to merchants, farmers, and laborers often with no tangible collateral outside his faith in their character. He encouraged self-employment by furnishing money for small businesses. He provided advice concerning best business location, how much inventory to carry, and how much return on capital the business could expect. He expanded his business of mostly Italian clientele by going door to door with a message that extolled the virtues of interest-bearing accounts, actively soliciting the wider marketplace at a time when bankers thought it unethical to do so. In many ways, the Bank of Italy was a misnomer, for it served not only Italians, but Americans, Greeks, Russians, Chinese, Spanish, Portuguese, any immigrant community that needed capital. His foresight, daring, and willingness to act decisively enabled him to come through the disastrous earthquake of 1906, the subsequent fire, and the Panic of 1907 in sound financial condition, while still serving those in need. He soon saw his confidence in his customers come back many-fold as more and more turned to him as a symbol of ability and integrity at a time when bank failures could mean ruin to depositors. Convinced by the Panic of 1907 that big banks were the key to safety, and following the English example, he embarked on the nation's first significant attempt at branch banking by buying up small banks and making them arms of the Bank of Italy. To facilitate the process he established, in 1919, the Bancitaly Corporation and then the Transamerica Corporation that acted as a holding company for Giannini's banking, insurance, real estate, and industrial organizations. Branch banking enabled Giannini to shift funds from one bank to another in a timely fashion and in response to farmers' needs. This was no small accomplishment given the enormity and importance of agriculture in California.

In 1929 he bought the Bank of America and emerged with the world's biggest commercial bank. Yet Giannini continued to lend money to workers on their signatures alone. He entered a field where other bankers feared to tread: the financing of motion-picture films. Giannini's example of readiness to respond to the changing needs of modern society helped place the banking business on solid ground and in a proper mode to react promptly and effectively to the needs of businesses and consumers in the age of electronics, computers, and telecommunications. In what seems to be a reprise in the 1990s of early-twentieth-century banking, while many banks seem to be resisting the advent of a cashless society, Bank of America is anticipating the future, closing traditional branches and, in typical Giannini fashion, sending out its loan officers on the street with their laptop computers to find potential borrowers to whom they can give a loan decision within a few minutes. In essence, Giannini did more than just make money. He recognized the value of hard work and the inevitability of change. He knew the importance of incentive and believed that big business would best be served by employee participation and ownership. Accordingly, his employees could take advantage of a profit-sharing program. At one point, the vast majority of holders of Transamerica stock were small investors, most of whom had no more than one hundred shares. These were the principles that guided him as he pioneered banking changes in the twentieth century, expanding into national and international financial waters. They proved to be a positive force for America in general. Italian Americans in California were especially grateful to him. He gave them material support, and his success made it easy for them to find acceptance in the wider American community. As the twentieth century progressed, Giannini's legacy was carried on by his son, Lawrence Mario, who served in various high-ranking executive capacities for a number of American corporations.

Among the other early-twentieth-century success stories is that of Amedeo Obici, the "Peanut King." After arriving in the United States in 1888 at age 11, Obici's experience amounted to three months of school and a number of odd jobs around Scranton and Wilkes-Barre, Pennsylvania, in a tailor shop, a cigar factory, a fruit stand, and a bar. Eventually he found work at a peanut stand. He quickly learned various aspects of the business and discovered a process for roasting peanuts so that they could be easily blanched before salting without breaking in half. He joined with M. Peruzzi to establish Planters Peanut Company and became its president and manager. They incorporated in 1908 and changed the name to Planters Nut and Chocolate Company of Wilkes-Barre. The company soon spread its operations throughout the United States and into Canada. Retail stores scattered throughout those countries marketed the various peanut products. Like so many before him who succeeded, Obici remained an ethnic while becoming Americanized. A member of Wilkes-Barre's Italo American Club, he also joined the Elks, the Moose, and Rotary and was a thirty-two-degree Mason.

Though participation by Italian Americans in corporate America was noteworthy in the earlier half of the twentieth century, by century's end it has become commonplace. A perusal of companies' annual reports, business magazines, and standard reference works of successful Americans reveals a full participation by Italian Americans in the business life of America. Lee Iacocca, John Riccardo, and Eugene A. Cafiero have become well known for their accomplishments in the automobile industry. Another, Jeno Paulucci, is highly regarded in the food business. Cafiero served as president when Riccardo was chairman and chief executive officer of Chrysler Corporation. But it was Lee (Lido) A. Iacocca who made the greatest impact. Coming from immigrant parents who saw their modest success in business come crashing down in the Great Depression, he graduated from Lehigh University with a degree in industrial engineering and went on to earn a master's degree in mechanical engineering from Princeton. Taking a job with the Ford Motor Company, he quickly worked his way up the ladder in sales and marketing. Called to Detroit, he assumed the mantle of director of vehicle marketing and got a vice-presidency at the age of 36. Using market research to a profitable advantage, he created an automobile that appealed to the young: the Mustang. It had styling, performance, and low pricing that made it an instant

success. In time, Iacocca became president of Ford. His success at Ford landed him the job of president and chief executive officer at the heavily troubled Chrysler Corporation. Saddled with a debt exceeding five billion dollars, the company was on the verge of bankruptcy. Respected for his knowledge and integrity, Iacocca was able to rally labor, union leaders, suppliers, bankers, and eventually the support of the U.S. government, which extended loan guarantees up to 1.5 billion dollars. He appealed persuasively to customers via television. He turned out the first American-made small cars that could sit six passengers comfortably and still achieve fuel efficiency. In sum, Iacocca turned the company's fortunes around. The U.S. government made 800 million dollars on the deal, Chrysler was once again a major force in the automotive industry, and Iacocca emerged with few peers, if any, in the upper echelons of the automobile industry. A Gallup poll on respect in 1985 placed him behind only two people, President Ronald Reagan and Pope John Paul II.

The son of an Italian immigrant miner in Minnesota's Iron Range, Jeno Paulucci made a fortune packaging chop suey and eventually establishing Chun King, which he brought boldly into the homes of Americans via television. In 1966 he sold the company to the R. J. Reynolds Tobacco Company for 63 million dollars. He repeated this successful formula when he founded Jeno's Pizza in 1967 and sold it in 1981 to the Pillsbury Corporation for 150 million dollars. Showing no signs of slowing up at age 72, he started a new company selling frozen Italian entrees, which he named after his mother, Michelina. Despite losing millions on *Attenzione,* a magazine he started for Italian Americans, he was worth one half billion dollars in 1990, according to *Forbes* magazine. His success is attributed to his restless energy, business acumen, personal attention to detail, and willingness to work seven days a week around the clock if necessary.

Like many successful entrepreneurs, Paulucci and Iacocca also make their presence felt in the wider community. Among their civic work, Paulucci is a leading force in the National Italian American Foundation, an organization that, among other things, fosters research and writing on the Italian American experience. Iacocca established the foundation named after him that supports diabetes research and offers scholarships to children of

Chrysler employees. He also served as chairman of the Statue of Liberty–Ellis Island Foundation that raised money to restore the Statue of Liberty.

Other Italian Americans, male and female, though not household names, have made worthwhile contributions to the American economy. A few include Benjamin F. Biaggini, chairman of the Southern Pacific Railroad; Ross D. Siragusa, a pioneer in television with Admiral Corporation; Joseph F. Alibrandi, an industrial company executive in a diversity of positions, including engineering and missiles, who also served as a director of the Federal Reserve Bank of San Francisco; Joseph Iannicelli, Ph.D., founder and chief executive officer of Aquafine Corporation of Macon, Georgia; Michael J. Critelli, vice chairman and chief executive officer of Pitney Bowes; Joseph V. Vittoria, who was president of both the number one and number two companies in automobile rentals, Hertz and Avis, respectively; Emil J. "Buzzie" Bavasi, executive vice president of the California Angels baseball team; Frank Biondi, president of Home Box Office; and Daniel J. Terra, founder of Lawter Chemicals International (Terra revolutionized the magazine publishing industry in the 1930s).

It is difficult to read about any business news without learning of Italian Americans obtaining important corporate positions. More than a few are becoming company presidents, board chairs, and chief executive officers. Italian American women are also making strides in the business world. In keeping with the disproportionately small number of women at the top of companies in the United States, however, they are still poorly represented there. For example, in 1996, women accounted for 10 percent of the corporate officers at the nation's five hundred largest companies and 2 percent of the top earners. Both figures were up slightly from prior years, giving hope that women are moving in the right direction. Among the Italian American women who have made it as successful business entrepreneurs are Olga Scoppa Amendola, Bernadette Castro, Marcella Vecchione Innocenzi, Helen Franzolin Boehm, and Jane Iorio Hirsch. Driven by ambition, intelligence, talent, and common sense, Amendola used an ad hoc education and a competent, low-keyed, self-assured demeanor to propel her career in the financial field. Starting in 1972 as a bookkeeper for Comprehensive Capital Cor-

poration, a small investment banking concern headquartered in Westbury, New York, and having branches in Boca Raton, Florida, and Knoxville, Tennessee, she became its president in 1991.

Castro took a different route. Bernard Castro, a Sicilian immigrant furniture maker and upholsterer, noticed that many post–World War II Americans were living in cramped quarters. His answer to the space crunch was to create a convertible sofa. He advertised on television the practicality of his sofa. This was before the age of the slick, sophisticated television commercials. Castro filmed his own advertisement with his sixteen-millimeter camera. He cast his daughter, Bernadette, age four, as the star. The response was overwhelming. When viewers saw how easily a 4-year-old could open the Castro Convertible, people flocked to buy it. The Castro Convertible became a household name, and Bernard Castro was considered a genius at creating and marketing furniture. When he died in 1991, Bernadette, a University of Florida graduate who was an executive in the company for fourteen years, took over as president and chief executive officer. Facing increased competition especially from lesser-priced models and sensing her children were gravitating to other professional interests, Castro sold the company and its trademark to devote all her efforts to managing the family land and real estate holdings in central Florida, while pursuing other interests.

Innocenzi's success combines elements of the paths taken by Amendola and Castro. Upon graduating from high school, she immediately went into her father's business, United Canning Corporation. It was John Vecchione who started this small mushroom cannery in North Lima, Ohio, in 1962. He served as chairman of the board until he died in 1992. At that time, Marcella, who had learned the entire canning operation and had moved into the front office, took over as president. She maintains the operation that cans under its own brand names, Snotop and Masterbrand, and packs under private labels for customer orders.

Hard work and creativity helped Boehm become a millionaire. Her porcelain figurines have been given as standard official gifts by presidents of the United States from Eisenhower on. Hirsch, who is chief executive officer and chair of Copley Pharmaceutical, is acclaimed internationally in business circles

B

for her financial and scientific expertise, management skills, and ability to turn out high-quality drugs.

Attracted to the field of fashion as a child, Rose Marie Bravo, whose father owned and operated a beauty shop, also learned how to run a successful business. After graduating from Fordham University in 1971, she accepted a position with Abraham and Strauss, then went on to become chairwoman and chief executive officer of I. Magnin, a specialty division of Macy's. Innovative and industrious, Bravo became president of the prestigious Saks Fifth Avenue in 1992.

Grace Mirabella became one of the most successful Italian American women entrepreneurs in the 1970s, 1980s, and 1990s. As the editor (1973–1989) of *Vogue,* the nation's foremost fashion magazine, she was the doyenne of American fashion. So respected was she in her field that after she left *Vogue,* she was financed to establish the competing fashion magazine *Mirabella.*

The list of entrepreneurs, while impressive, does not begin to tell the story of Italian Americans who have succeeded with little fanfare. The heyday of the concentration of Italian Americans in the barber shop, shoe repair, music store, and grocery businesses has long since passed. In the 1990s Italian Americans have taken their places beside the countless individuals who fortify the economy with their businesses, which include manufacturing, factoring, financing, selling, insuring, transporting, building, and retailing. The latter two areas, building and retailing, are truly hotbeds of activity for Italian Americans. In many communities throughout the United States, they can be found erecting houses, putting up developments (commercial, industrial, or residential), and running restaurants, clothing stores, dress shops, and the like. And in contrast with earlier times, when they depended upon an ethnic clientele to jump-start and sustain their businesses, in modern times they deal with the entire population. Many of these small business entrepreneurs have helped to save more than a few inner-city neighborhoods. Italian Americans, men and women alike, have become integral parts of the American economic scene. Most of them make a comfortable living. Some, even in very small communities of America, have become millionaires. As the twentieth century comes to a close, an Italian American, Richard A. Grasso, is capping a distinguished career in management and finance by serving as chairman and chief executive officer of the New York Stock Exchange. Never attending college, he spent his entire twenty-seven-year career at the exchange and was elected to the post in 1994 by the board of the New York Stock Exchange, whose members recognized his expertise and ability to lead the exchange in its attempt to attract more companies to its listings, especially from the area of technology and the foreign market. From the beginning of the twentieth century, when Giannini opened up banking to serve an ever-growing grass-roots public demand as well as to satisfy the enormous capital needs of America's burgeoning businesses and industries, to the end of the century, with Grasso leading the equities market to face the challenges brought on by lightning-quick changes in the high-technology age of computers and telecommunications that make possible instant world-wide communication and information dissemination, Italian Americans have played a significant role as merchants and entrepreneurs. This truly befits a people who had no small role in the birth of capitalism hundreds of years ago when Italy was a collection of city-states.

Luciano J. Iorizzo

Bibliography

Bonadio, Felice A. *Amadeo P. Giannini Banker, Philanthropist Entrepreneur.* Washington, D.C.: The National Italian American Foundation, 1983.

Iorizzo, Luciano J. "Dun and Bradstreet's Assessments of Merchants, A Neglected Source for Italian American Studies." In *New Explorations in Italian American Studies. Proceedings of the 25th Annual Conference of the American Italian Historical Association,* edited by Richard N. Juliani and Sandra P. Juliani. New York, 1994.

——— . "The R. G. Dun Collection's Assessments of Merchants: A Neglected Source for Italian American Studies." In *The Columbus People Perspectives in Italian Immigration to the Americas and Australia,* edited by Lydio F. Tomasi, Piero Gastaldo, and Thomas Row. New York: Center for Migration Studies, 1994.

Standard and Poor's Register of Corporations, Directors and Executives. New York: McGraw-Hill, 1996.

Vecoli, Rudolph John. "Chicago's Italians Prior to World War I: A Study of Their Social and Economic Adjustment." Ann Arbor, MI: University Microfilms, 1967.

Who's Who in America. New Providence, NJ: Reed References Publishing Company, 1995.

Ligurian Entrepreneurs in the United States

Although comparatively small in number compared to the masses of Italians who emigrated in the late nineteenth century, the sailors, merchants, and peasants who came from the Republic of Genoa and Liguria were especially unique. They were, in fact, among the first Italians to migrate to the Americas, prompted, not by driving poverty, but by the stimulus of adventure and opportunity against a backdrop of political uneasiness that accompanied the post-Napoleonic submission of the Republic of Genoa to the Piedmont Region. Accordingly, many Ligurian political exiles settled in the coastal areas of North and South America, where they utilized their capital to engage in various trades and businesses.

This background enabled them to integrate rapidly into the new society. Francis B. Spinola, a descendant of a noble Ligurian family that came to America, is an example. Born in New York in 1821, he became a state legislator, a general during the Civil War, and was elected to Congress in 1887—long before Italian Americans constituted a meaningful electoral bloc. Other signs of their integration was their early presence as a merchant community in Greenwich Village in New York City in the mid-nineteenth century. However, at the beginning of the twentieth century, a time of massive Italian immigration from southern Italy, the New York Ligurian colony disappeared as a recognizable community.

Meanwhile, on the Pacific coast Ligurian sailors and merchants, who had previously settled in South America, where they had developed many rich communities, began to migrate to California. Coming before 1850, an embryonic time for that West Coast state, they seemed to be regarded as settlers rather than as immigrants. Thus, the environment was much more favorable for them to pursue entrepreneurial risk and organization in their congenial fields, namely trades basic to a growing state such as sailing or fishing; and with the arrival of Ligurian peasants they also went into agriculture.

Ligurian peasants were attracted to California by the 1849 gold rush, the mild climate, and the possibilities for cultivating a land very similar to the Mediterranean environment. They found it advantageous to settle in an open society in which no single ethnic group predominated. To some of them, California offered new chances to create a successful trade frequently dissimilar from their original work. This is the case, for example, of the mountain villagers from Lorsica, where they used to produce silk; in California, after a difficult beginning, they succeeded in establishing important scavenging firms.

Periodically, during slack times, Ligurians engaged in fishing and agriculture to earn the money necessary to support themselves and their small businesses—money, a commodity that would be supplied by Genoese and Milanese merchants. Indeed it was this practice that gave birth to the first group of Italian banks in the United States, among them the Bank of Italy, founded by Amadeo P. Giannini, who was of Ligurian ancestry.

Simultaneously, some agricultural firms transformed themselves into important and extant allied fields. Ligurian names like Ghirardelli Chocolates and Del Monte Fruit Canning, founded by the Genoese Marco Fontana, are cases in point. At the outset these industries and banks operated with Italian workers for the Italian American market. However, the unprecedented growth of American society that transformed the industrial system by the second half of the nineteenth century opened up the entire American market to Ligurian entrepreneurs. Furthermore, the interests of these Ligurian capitalists had undergone change, leaving some of their trades in the hands of new Italian and non-Italian immigrants.

Accordingly, the enterprises now found an integration with immigrants from the regions of Tuscany and Sicily as well as with ethnic Mexican and Chinese. The entrepreneurs of Ligurian origin no longer employed workers belonging exclusively to their region or nationality, especially after Italian unification in 1861 led to the assimilation of Liguria. After a successful start among primarily Italian customers, these banks had evolved to become institutions for the general American public, so much so that Giannini's bank changed its name to the Bank of America.

With the onset of the twentieth century, the business community of Ligurian entrepreneurs faded out as an enclave, thereby emphasizing its homogeneity with the ethics and organization of American society.

Adele Maiello

Bibliography

Cinel, Dino. *From Italy to San Francisco: The Immigrant Experience in Italian American Communities in the United States.* Stanford: Stanford University Press, 1982.

Gumina, Deanna P. *The Italians of San Francisco.* New York: Center for Migration Studies, 1985.

LaGumina, Salvatore J. "Gli Italo-Americani a Long Island: gli anni della fodazione." *Euroamericani.* Vol. 1. Torino: Fondazione Agnelli, 1987.

Maiello, Adele, ed. *L' emigrazione nelle Americhe dalla provincia di Genova.* Bologna: Patron, 1992.

Rolle, Andrew F. *The Immigrant Upraised: Italian Adventurers and Colonists in an Expanding America.* Norman: University of Oklahoma Press, 1968.

Vecoli, Rudolph John. *Chicago's Italians Prior to World War I: A Study of Their Social and Economic Adjustment.* Ann Arbor: University Microfilms, 1967.

Ware, Caroline. *Greenwich Village, 1920–1930.* New York: Harper, 1965.

See also BOEHM, HELEN FRANZOLIN; BOIARDI, HECTOR; BUITONI, GIOVANNI; D'AGOSTINO SR., NICHOLAS; DEBARTOLO, EDWARD J.; DI GIORGIO, JOSEPH; FUGAZI, GIOVANNI F.; GIANNINI, AMADEO P.; IACOCCA, LEE; LEONE, LUISA; MARCIONI, ITALO; OBICI, AMEDEO; PAULUCCI, JENO F.; PERINI, LOUIS R.; REGGIO, NICHOLAS; SBARBORO, ANDREA; SPERANZA, GINO CARLO; TERRA, DANIEL J.

Business Interrelations with Italy

Since the founding of the American Republic, commercial and business ties with Italy have been strong. In fact, the very discovery of the New World was the result of a commercial enterprise by Christopher Columbus. Other Italians, such as Giovanni Caboto (John Cabot) and Amerigo Vespucci, made their way to America. Ironically, these Italians were usually in the service of Spain, Portugal, or England, rather than the Italian cities or regions from which they came. But as early as 1610 Italian wine growers came to America with Captain John Smith, while eleven years later Venetian glassmakers settled in Virginia. These were the earliest attempts to establish commercial ties between the new colony and Italian cities. During the era of the American Revolutionary War, Filippo Mazzei influenced Thomas Jefferson's political thinking while experimenting with various types of plants, fruits, and vegetables in America. In 1800 Paolo Busti, an entrepreneur from Milan, arrived to manage the Holland Land Company, which developed five million acres of land into villages and towns in northern New York State; he eventually became known as "the father of Buffalo, New York."

Once Italy was unified as a nation-state in 1861, commercial ties were expanded. Citrus fruits and wine were major exports from southern Italy, especially Sicily. Silk and textiles were imported from northern Italy. But by the 1880s Italian American settlers had reached California and began their own citrus and wine industries that severely curtailed imports from Italy. Discovery of sulfur in Texas in the 1890s effectively destroyed the sulfur mining industry in Sicily, acting as a catalyst for migration to the United States. The great migration of Italian immigrants between 1880 and 1920 created a strong market for Italian products and, accordingly, trade increased. The Italy-America Chamber of Commerce was established in 1887 to foster trade between Italy and the United States. In 1904 Amadeo Giannini founded the Bank of Italy in California, later changing its name to the Bank of America.

During World War I, many exports were prohibited by Italian law. Trade began to increase again under the Fascist regime (1922–1943). During the 1920s, trade restrictions were relaxed, but by 1930 Italy was forced to deal with the worldwide effects of the Great Depression. When Italy invaded Ethiopia in 1935, the League of Nations applied limited sanctions, further reducing trade with the United States. In response to the sanctions, Mussolini declared an economic policy of "autarky" or self-sufficiency, which was eventually abandoned after defeat in World War II.

In the wake of the economic devastation caused by the war, America took the initiative in rebuilding the Italian economy with the

	American Exports to Italy	Italian Imports to America
1965	$891,000,000	$620,000,000
1970	$1,353,000,000	$1,316,000,000
1975	$2,867,000,000	$2,397,000,000
1980	$5,511,000,000	$4,313,000,000
1985	$4,625,000,000	$9,673,000,000
1990	$7,987,000,000	$12,723,000,000
1991	$8,578,000,000	$11,787,000,000

U.S. Department of Commerce

Marshall Plan. The import and export of goods increased rapidly in Italy in the early 1950s. The demand for Italian goods skyrocketed as the label "Made in Italy" came to symbolize quality and sophisticated products. The above United States Department of Commerce table represents trade between Italy and the United States over the last thirty years.

By 1992 the United States was the third largest market for Italian exports (fifteen trillion lire [approximately ten billion dollars] or 7 percent of total Italian exports) and Italy was the fifth largest market for American goods (twelve trillion lire [approximately eight billion dollars] or 2 percent of total American trade). In 1993 exports rose to twenty trillion lire. One aspect of the growing trade between Italy and the United States is the increasing sophistication of technology. Italy continues to import from America components vital for the increased development of its products, such as computers, semiconductors, scientific and medical instruments, and aircraft. U.S. trade focuses on Italian consumer goods, especially jewelry, which comprises nearly one-third of Italian exports to the United States. In addition to the traditional goods of leather, textiles, foodstuff, and ceramics, Italy has increased its exports of technological equipment. Although recent developments such as the North American Free Trade Agreement (NAFTA) and the evolution of the European Union point to larger, transnational economic forces, it seems that the special trade relationship forged between Italy and the United States will continue to prosper in the future.

Stanislao G. Pugliese

Bibliography

Banca d'Italia. *Annual Report.* Banca d'Italia, 1994.

Doing Business in Italy. New York: Price, Waterhouse, 1976–current.

Kurzweil, Edith. *Italian Entrepreneurs.* New York: Praeger, 1983.

OECD Economic Surveys, 1994–1995 Italy. Paris: OECD, 1995.

Trade With Italy. New York: Italy-America Chamber of Commerce, 1945–current.

See also COLD WAR: U. S. FOREIGN POLICY TOWARD ITALY; MAZZEI, PHILIP; UNITED STATES–ITALIAN DIPLOMATIC RELATIONS, 1776–1945

C

Caboto, Giovanni (c. 1450–1498?)

Genoese explorer on whose voyages of discovery to North America in 1497 and 1498 England based its later claim to the continent. The exact details of Caboto's life and career are still a matter of controversy among historians.

Born in Genoa around 1450, Giovanni Caboto (commonly known as John Cabot) migrated with his family to Venice in 1461. Historical records indicate that he became a citizen of the republic fifteen years later. By 1484 Caboto was married and had at least two sons, the youngest being Sebastian, who also achieved fame as an explorer. In Venice he engaged in the spice trade and gained a reputation as a skilled mariner and navigator. Caboto, after learning that spices originated from the Far East, soon formulated a plan to reach Asia by sailing across the North Atlantic.

From 1491 to 1493 Caboto was in Valencia, Spain, trying in vain to promote the construction of a harbor improvement project. During this period he became aware of the voyages of Columbus, who by 1493 had returned to Spain in triumph. Caboto, however, remained unconvinced that Columbus had sailed far enough westward across the Atlantic to reach China. For the next two years, Caboto traveled to Lisbon and Seville in a futile effort to obtain financial support for his plan to sail to Asia by a more northwesterly and supposedly shorter route.

In 1495 Caboto had arrived in England determined to gain sponsorship from Henry VII for a transatlantic voyage. The king, lured by the promise of exotic Asian riches, issued letters patent on March 5, 1496, that authorized Caboto to sail in his name.

Financed by English merchants, he attempted one voyage in 1496, but it failed due to a shortage of pro-visions and foul weather. Caboto soon arranged another voyage on a tiny seagoing caravel, the *Matthew,* named after his wife, Mattea. The ship departed from Bristol harbor on or about May 22, 1497, with a crew of eighteen, including Caboto's fifteen-year old son, Sebastian. After passing the coast of Ireland near Dursey Head, the *Matthew* sailed westward for almost a month. Landfall occurred at 5:00 A.M. on June 24, 1497, most likely on Cape Breton Island, Nova Scotia, which Caboto mistook for the northeastern coast of Asia. He and his crew disembarked, took possession of the land for England, and erected a cross and the banners of Henry VII, the pope, and St. Mark of Venice. The landing party found numerous signs of life but saw no people. Fearful of an at-tack, Caboto decided not to explore any further and promptly disembarked. For the next twenty-six days, the *Matthew* cruised for about 300 leagues (954 miles), presumably surveying the east coast of Newfoundland. On about July 20, 1497, the ship headed for the open sea and home. The *Matthew* arrived in Bristol sometime between August 6 and 10.

Upon his return, Caboto received a hero's welcome from the people of England. On August 11, 1497, he met with Henry VII and proposed another voyage to sail south and west from his original landfall to Japan and China. Letters patent were reissued and preparations made for a second expedition. The small fleet of five ships set sail from Bristol in May of 1498, only to meet with tragedy. Caboto disappeared without a trace, presumably lost at sea, although one or more of his ships may have returned to England after exploring the Atlantic.

Aldo E. Salerno

Bibliography

Quinn, David B. *England and the Discovery of America, 1481–1620.* New York: Alfred A. Knopf, 1974.

Williamson, J.A., ed. *The Cabot Voyages and Bristol Discovery Under Henry VII.* Cambridge, England: Cambridge University, 1962.

See also COLUMBUS, CHRISTOPHER; EXPLORERS

Cabrini, Mother Frances Xavier (1850–1917)

An immigrant who dedicated herself to assist other Italian immigrants, Mother Cabrini established schools, hospitals, orphanages, educational, health care, and social service outreach programs across America.

She was born in Sant'Angelo Lodigiano, Lombardy, Italy, in 1850. She first arrived in New York in 1889 and followed with eight subsequent journeys during which she witnessed the saga of human migration at its peak as she crisscrossed the country seeking to respond to the socioreligious needs of Italian immigrants. Mother Cabrini died in Chicago in 1917. Having been naturalized in Washington State in 1909, her canonization in 1946 rendered her the first American citizen to be proclaimed a saint by the Roman Catholic Church—Saint Frances Xavier Cabrini.

The prodigious work accomplished by Mother Cabrini was performed in conjunction with the religious community she founded in Italy in 1880—the Missionary Sisters of the Sacred Heart of Jesus. As new recruits came from Italy, and young women in the United States, predominantly of Italian heritage, joined the community, Mother Cabrini and her Missionary Sisters were able to establish foundations in New York, New Jersey, Pennsylvania, Illinois, Louisiana, Colorado, California, and Washington State. She also personally visited Italian immigrants in Buffalo, Pittsburgh, and Cincinnati, as well as the mining camps located in the western part of the United States and the plantations and other rural areas of the South. She sent the sisters to assess the immigrants' needs in Connecticut, Delaware, Kansas, Maryland, Nevada, New Mexico, and Wisconsin.

Frances Xavier Cabrini, a licensed schoolteacher, developed a pedagogy that she called "education of the heart." She wanted the children in her care to sense that they were loved. She sought a synthesis of culture, faith, and life based upon individual dignity and concern for others. Mother Cabrini advocated a gradual assimilation process for immigrants rather than the rapid "Americanization" promoted in her day. It was her aim to preserve cultural identity, so, while providing students with strong English skills, daily instruction was also given in Italian language and heritage. In her Columbus Hospitals, newly arrived immigrants found places where their language, customs, and nutritional preferences were catered to with understanding.

Mother Cabrini saw to it that the immigrant poor were tended to in their homes, children and adults were given religious instruction in parishes, and both the sick and

Mother Frances Xavier Cabrini, a naturalized citizen from Italy, was the first American officially proclaimed a saint of the Catholic Church. She was tireless in her efforts to assist Italian immigrants, making numerous visits to Italian American centers throughout America and establishing schools, orphanages, and hospitals. Courtesy Center for Migration Studies.

the incarcerated were visited in city hospitals and area prisons. Cabrini and her sisters helped the unemployed find work, provided training in practical arts for young women, expanded outpatient departments for needy sick immigrants, and brought disaster relief to those affected by floods, earthquakes, and yellow fever epidemics. Religious societies and oratories were started for boys and girls, spiritual retreats for women, and civic lessons for men. In addition, assistance was given to those wishing to repatriate.

Despite these multifaceted services, Mother Cabrini's primary focus was on growth in personal holiness for herself and for her sisters. Faithful to a rule of life that prescribed long hours of meditation and prayer, Cabrini and her sister companions ministered assiduously to immigrants.

Mother Cabrini developed in her person a profound spiritual life by blending the contemplation of a mystic with the dynamism of a twentieth-century social activist. While remembered primarily as the "Saint of the Immigrants" for her efforts in the United States, her zeal impelled her to undertake missionary work in her native Italy, Nicaragua, Panama, Argentina, France, Spain, and Brazil. As a religious leader, business administrator, and spokesperson for the downtrodden, Mother Cabrini became an international figure in ecclesiastical and civic circles, where women of her day were notably absent. Mother Cabrini's loving trust in God was the source that enabled her to accomplish so much despite her lifelong struggle with frail health.

Mary Louise Sullivan

Bibliography

Green, Rose Basile, ed. and trans. *Mother Frances Xavier Cabrini.* Chicago: Missionary Sisters of the Sacred Heart, 1984.
———. "Mother Cabrini: Missionary to Italian Immigrants." *U.S. Catholic Historian* 6 (fall 1987): 265–279.
Sullivan, Mary Louise. *Mother Cabrini.* New York: Center for Migration Studies, 1992.

See also RELIGION; WOMEN AND THE CHURCH

Caliandro, Bruno L. (1931–1996)

A member of a family of Italian Americans noted for its Methodist ministers, Bruno L. Caliandro was an award-winning producer of religious and educational television programs in this country. The son of Tommaso M. (1901–1965) and Frances (née Alauria) Caliandro, Bruno was born on July 24, 1931, in Portland, Maine. His parents were immigrants from Italy (his father came from Ceglie, near Brindisi in Apulia, and his mother from Sicily) and Catholic in family background, but they were drawn to Protestantism. Bruno's father became the leader of the Italian Methodist Church in Portland (1928–1950) during the Great Depression, World War II, and in the opening years of the Cold War.

Ordained an elder in the United Methodist Church, New York Conference, Bruno was put in charge of developing programs for United Methodist Communications and for the Faith and Values channel. In this work, he was responsible for "Catch the Spirit," a weekly series for the United Methodist Church that included about one hundred episodes, and "Guideposts," a series of three hundred programs for Norman Vincent Peale, a good friend of Caliandro and his family. Bruno's expertise in creating and producing television programs for children, including *Animals, Animals, Animals* and *Kids Are People Too,* reflected such talent and experience that his advice was sought for the production of popular programs such as *Afterschool Specials, Captain Kangaroo,* and *Mr. Rogers' Neighborhood.*

Caliandro won Emmy Awards for two of his productions: ABC's *The Halloween That Almost Wasn't* and PBS's *Heroes of Conscience.* Some of his other achievements include NBC's *The Fourth King,* an animated special, and *Reading Incentives,* a film series featuring such celebrities as Harry Belafonte, Bill Cosby, and James Garner, among others.

At the time of his death, on June 11, 1996, Bruno was a resident of Somers, New York, and had been a member of the faculty of the graduate school at Bank Street College of Education for more than twenty years.

Vincent A. Lapomarda

Bibliography

Caliandro, Arthur P. "Pastor Marble Collegiate Church: A Methodist Boyhood." In *Growing Up Italian: How Being Brought Up as an Italian-American Helped Shaped the Characters, Lives, and Fortunes of Twenty-four Celebrated Americans,*

C

edited by Linda Brandi Cateura, 202–211. New York: Morrow, 1987.

See also RELIGION

Califano, Joseph A. (b. 1931)

Serving in influential positions in two presidential cabinets, Joseph A. Califano was only the fourth Italian American to achieve such political status. Born in Brooklyn, New York, of a father of Italian descent and a mother of Irish heritage, Califano's formal tutelage was steeped in the tradition of Jesuit education, which included matriculation at Brooklyn Prep and graduation from Holy Cross College. He also graduated from Harvard Law School. Califano's schooling was supplemented by several years of professional legal experience for major law firms in New York City and Washington, D.C., during which time he also wrote impressive articles on law and contemporary public issues.

Califano's attraction to politics, which was gleaned from his wife who was a Democrat, was rewarded with a position as a White House aide and a domestic policy specialist in the Lyndon B. Johnson administration. The caliber of his work in domestic policy was deemed so noteworthy that the *New York Times* referred to him "as the man who next to the President, has contributed more than any other individual to the concept, formulation and implementation of the program of the Great Society."

In 1976 President Jimmy Carter nominated Joseph A. Califano Secretary of Health, Education and Welfare (HEW), a move that was resoundingly supported by 95 votes in the Senate. At 45 years of age, Califano presided over the second largest budget in government, exceeded only by the Department of Defense.

Regarded as a corporate lawyer with a conscience, Califano was able to make a major dent in the mountains of red tape that regularly beleaguered the bureaucratic system. Political analysts also attributed his appointment to President Carter's awareness that there was a lack of Catholics in the cabinet. It was said that his selection to the cabinet also rested on ethnic grounds in that Italian Americans needed reassurance of inclusion. In other words it provided "recognition to the ethnic group whose doubts about Mr. Carter probably cost him the electoral support of Connecticut and New Jersey."

Califano went about his task of dealing with Washington labyrinthine bureaucracy with the same energy he displayed as a successful high-priced lawyer, working twelve-hour days, six days a week. He acquired an admirable expertise interacting with Washington insiders, lawyers, lobbyists, journalists, politicians, and socialites. Notwithstanding his expertise with the innards of government, it was also said that he "knew government, but he didn't know politics." Having never run for public office, he was unfamiliar with the needs and requirements that politics ascertained by working the local streets and precincts. Nevertheless, Califano was determined to make his department manageable and effective. He strove diligently to restore dignity to civil rights programs by taking a series of administrative steps aimed at monitoring laws against sex and race discrimination. Consequently, school districts were pressured to comply with court-mandated decisions or face a cutoff of federal funds.

He moved to request that the State Department work out an agreement with the Mexican government to cease spraying the herbicide paraquat on marijuana fields. In pursuit of providing quality medical care for all Americans, he advocated a national health insurance plan. He took positions on controversial public issues that elicited their share of praise and criticism, for example, his opposition to tuition tax credits and his antiabortion stand that led to a prohibition of abortion under federal health programs unless the courts ruled otherwise. He was also a strong presence in campaigns against smoking and alcohol abuse. The intensity of his positions earned for him the dubious sobriquet as the "most Napoleonic" of Carter's aides.

Califano remained Secretary of Health, Education and Welfare until July 19, 1979, when he was ousted by Carter. The prevailing view was that he was dismissed not because of incompetence—indeed, he was considered the best head of HEW since its inception in terms of rendering the monster department workable. Rather, his departure was attributed to his failure in playing the game of politics. Known for his connection to the Washington "establishment," he was also known for his feistiness and abrasiveness, which were not acceptable to the Georgia cohorts who advised the president to fire the pushy Brooklyn Italian American Catholic official. Califano maintained that his dismissal was generated by his antismoking campaign and by his decision to withhold federal funds to segregated schools.

After his departure from the cabinet, Califano resumed his dual career as a lawyer and a keen observer of the public arena. In 1982 he published a widely reviewed book on the impact of drug abuse and alcoholism, and in 1986 he was the author of a profound study on America's health care system. He was also the founding chairman of the board and president of the center on Addiction and Substance Abuse at Columbia University. Throughout his career, Califano has remained an active commentator on contemporary critical issues.

Salvatore J. LaGumina

Bibliography
Califano, Joseph A. *American Health Care Revolution: Who Lives? Who Dies? Who Pays?* New York: Touchstone, 1986.
———. "Fictions and Facts About Drug Legislation," *America*, 16 March 1996, 7–9.
———. *Jimmy Carter.* New York: Scribners, 1987.
———. "Memories of a Jesuit Education." *America*, 25 May 1996, 10–17.

See also POLITICS

Califano, Michael (1889–1979)

Born in Naples, Michael Califano became an internationally famous portrait and landscape artist. Considered a poet with a paintbrush, he handled his craft with restraint and refinement, displaying an impressionistic style.

He served in the Italian army during World War I, when he suffered partial deafness because of ear-shattering on the battlefield while under commission from the king of Italy to paint war scenes. Califano was appointed court painter for Queen Elena of Italy after the war. However, in 1922, he became restless and migrated to America—a move that led to his becoming a cause celebre. Skeptical immigration authorities, dismissing his claims of being an artist, detained him at Ellis Island since Italy's immigration quota for the year was filled. While waiting at the depot, he painted a remarkable portrait of a Dutch immigrant girl in the island's great hall, causing such a stir among officials that newspapers carried front-page accounts of the detainment

and Califano's artistic genius. As a consequence, immigration officials admitted him into his new country.

Having already achieved fame for his portraits of King Victor Emmanuel III, other family members of the House of Savoy, and Guglielmo Marconi, Califano continued his painting during the 1920s. Among his noted portraits of world-famous personalities were those of Franklin D. Roosevelt, Wendell Willkie, Rudolph Valentino, Charles Lindbergh, and the wife and son of President Calvin Coolidge. His portrait of Judge John Freschi hangs in the Casa Italiana at Columbia University.

Califano underwent a traumatic experience in 1935 when he incurred the wrath of American Nazis who were angered at his negative depiction of Adolf Hitler and the Nazi Party. Specifically, his critics were displeased with *The Ignominy of the Twentieth Century,* a life-size painting in which he portrayed his moral outrage at the persecution of Albert Einstein and Hitler's increasing reign of terror against Jews in Germany. Califano produced postcards of the painting, which were sold to raise funds to assist German Jewish refugees. The angered Nazis reacted by entering his studio, beating him unconscious, and destroying thirty of his canvases. Einstein was so touched by the humanitarian act of a non-Jew that he wrote to Califano and later visited him. The terrifying event caused irreparable damage, leading the disillusioned Califano to remain a recluse in Lattingtown, Long Island, for the rest of his life.

Salvatore J. LaGumina

Bibliography
Daily Mirror (New York), 13 December 1926.
Newsday, 27 December, 1979.

See also ART

Cambria, Frank (1883–1966)

Scenic director, theatrical art director, and manager, Frank Cambria was one of the first Italian Americans to enter the field. Born in Barcellona in the Province of Messina, he migrated to New York with his parents.

Upon completion of high school, he entered the National Academy of Design in New York for specialized studies. He earned a diploma in both painting and sculpture, and won the prestigous Suydan Award for sculpture. He also studied under the famous theatrical producer David Belasco. While still in school, he sought work with theatrical companies and gravitated toward the painting of stage scenery that was being used with greater frequency by the many companies located in New York City's Broadway and theatrical districts.

Because the motion picture was also making greater inroads as a vehicle for entertainment and learning, Cambria began to move toward this relatively new art form, relocating with his family to Chicago in the 1920s. He acquired work with the Balaban & Katz chain of motion pictures in that city.

His next move was to Rochester, New York, where he became a scenic designer for the Jessie Bonstelle Repertory Theater. He soon returned to the theater in New York, and in a few years advanced to the positions of director of the New York Studio of Scenic Design, artistic director of Paramount Theaters, and later of Capitol Theater, companies that were all leading producers in the entertainment industry.

Cambria's greatest achievement was his appointment in the early 1930s as general manager of the newly established Roxy Theater (built in 1927), called by some "the motion picture cathedral," and considered by many historians the most luxurious of New York theaters, and, indeed, of the country. A huge structure that could seat some six thousand individuals, it doubled as a play theater and motion picture theater showing the latest Hollywood production on its huge screen. It also had the largest music library of any theater and could accommodate three hundred people on its stage. Some seventy musicians comprised the orchestra, and about thirty-two "Roxyettes" performed on stage. It was Cambria's responsibility to ensure that the elegant Roxy ran smoothly and well.

The Roxy Theater, though considered a landmark, was eventually demolished in 1961 to make way for office buildings along a renewed Broadway and Sixth Avenue district. Cambria died at his summer residence in Westport, Connecticut.

Nicholas Joseph Falco

Bibliography

Jackson, Kenneth T., ed. *The Encyclopedia of New York City.* New York: The New York Historical Society, 1995.

Obituary, *New York Times,* 18 September 1966.

See also THEATER HISTORY

Capone, Al
See CRIME AND ORGANIZED CRIME

Capra, Frank (1897–1991)
An Academy Award–winning filmmaker whose productions espoused optimism and portrayed faith in common people, Frank Capra endeared himself to generations of Americans. He was born Francesco Capra into a family of peasant farmers in Bisacquino, Sicily, on May 18, 1897.

His family departed for America on May 10, 1903, in steerage class, and made their way to Los Angeles to join his eldest brother Benedetto. Determined both to get an education and to rise from poverty, Capra worked at numerous jobs, beginning while in elementary school. Unique among his six siblings, he attended college, graduating from the California Institute of Technology in 1918. He subsequently taught mathematics in the Army during World War I. Upon returning to civilian life, he found it difficult to secure work in engineering. In his autobiography Capra constructed the myth that he had bluffed his way into the film industry knowing nothing about it, but he actually had some early studio experience.

His first official production was the 1922 one-reeler *Fultah Fisher's Boarding House.* Following this, he studied his craft diligently and rose through the studio hierarchy at Columbia Pictures, working as prop assistant, film cutter, and gag writer for "Our Gang" and the Keystone Comedies. After directing several adventure movies during the 1920s, his breakthrough came with his 1933 comedic success *Lady for a Day.* The following year, his *It Happened One Night,* starring Claudette Colbert and Clark Gable, swept the Academy Awards, becoming the first picture to win all five major commendations: best actor, actress, screenplay, director, and film.

A string of popular and critically acclaimed films followed, including *Mr. Deeds Goes to Town* (1936, Academy Award–winner for best director), *Lost Horizon* (1937), *You Can't Take It With You* (1938, best director, best picture), *Mr. Smith Goes to Washington* (1939), and *Meet John Doe*

(1941), in which he typically depicted idealistic crusaders fighting corrupt powerful forces. Capra helped launch the careers of Jean Harlow and Barbara Stanwyck, and coaxed archetypal performances from James Stewart. *Arsenic and Old Lace* (1944) is also memorable. After the attack on Pearl Harbor, Capra reenlisted in the Army and produced propaganda films, one of which, *Prelude to War,* won a 1943 Oscar for best documentary. Colonel Capra also was awarded the Distinguished Service Medal, the Order of the British Empire, and France's Legion of Merit.

After the war Capra formed his own independent production company, Liberty Films. Through Liberty, he released the film most frequently associated with his name and his personal favorite, the Christmas classic *It's a Wonderful Life* (1946). It failed to attain critical favor at the time of its release, however; many reviewers disliked its unabashed sentimentality, its trademark "Capra-corn." Capra had served as president for both the Director's Guild and the Motion Picture Academy. The widely panned *Lady for a Day* (1961) was Capra's last film; he left Hollywood and the film industry in 1967, and died in La Quinta, California, on September 3, 1991.

Camille Cauti

Bibliography

Capra, Frank. *The Name Above the Title: An Autobiography.* New York: Macmillan, 1971.

Lourdeaux, Lee. *Italian and Irish Filmmakers in America: Ford, Capra, Coppola, and Scorsese.* Philadelphia: Temple University Press, 1990.

McBride, Joseph. *Frank Capra: The Catastrophe of Success.* New York: Simon & Schuster, 1992.

See also FILM DIRECTORS, PRODUCERS, AND ITALIAN AMERICAN IMAGE IN CINEMA

Carlino, Lewis J.

See PLAYS, CONTEMPORARY

Cartoonists and Illustrators

Italian Americans have been part of United States cartooning and illustration for a century and a half, either as the stereotyped butt of cartoons or caricatures or as the creators of comic art.

Italian Americans experienced their share of ridicule in the early days of cartooning. Stereotyped images of Italian Americans began appearing in cartoons by the mid-1800s, a time when ethnic groups in general were associated with recognizable peculiarities such as their native foods, dress, or pastimes. For example, the Italian American was included in famous cartoonist Thomas Nast's "Nick-Nax of All Creation," an 1851 stereotypical depiction of youth from twelve nations.

By the late 1800s, as cartoonists (no Italian Americans identifiable among them) narrowed the identity cues down to one or two for each ethnic group, the Italian American was identified as a male with a hand-cranked street organ and a monkey on a leash or as a stiletto-wielding maniac with vengeance on his mind. In at least one case, a derisive moniker for Italian Americans was used in the title of a comic strip. Called "The Dago, the Monkey and the Cable Slot," and, featuring "Signor Organetto," the cartoon was published by the sensationalist *New York Journal and Advertiser* on October 10, 1897. The *Journal* was the flagship daily of William Randolph Hearst, the major promoter of newspaper funnies, many of which initially poked fun at ethnic groups. In the same paper there appeared in early episodes of the "Katzenjammer Kids" an Italian American character, who was drawn with a threatening scowl, a hook nose, and a mustache; he wore patched trousers, a huge earring, and spoke broken English.

Over the years, other Italian Americans have appeared in cartoons and comics (notably Rocky in Mort Walker's "Beetle Bailey" and a number in some of Will Eisner's graphic novels), but without the harsh and negative characteristics. Campaigns by minority pressure groups, culminating in the political correctness binge of the 1990s, were responsible for the removal of ethnic and gender stereotypes.

Italian Americans entered the United States comic art professions in the early twentieth century, first in animation and later in gag cartoons, comic strips, and comic books. The imprints left by some of them were indelible: Gregory La Cava helped establish the first animation studios in the United States and trained other pioneers; Walter Lantz (Lanza) developed some of animation's most durable characters, including "Woody Woodpecker";

Joe Barbera invented limited animation; Alfred Andriola helped develop five different newspaper comic strips; Giovanni Fischetti initiated change in the nature of political cartoons in the early 1960s.

Animation studios emerged in the 1910s as some enterprising publishers and budding filmmakers realized the potential of cashing in on the popularity of newspaper comic strips. The three main studios were operated by Raoul Barre, Hearst, and J.R. Bray. Gregory La Cava worked for Barre and Hearst.

After studying at the Chicago Art Institute and the Art Students League, La Cava took odd jobs as illustrator and cartoonist before being picked up by Barre in 1913. When Barre established his studio in the Bronx, La Cava was one of the two young cartoonists he hired. Their first series was "Animated Grouch Characters," produced and released by Edison in 1915–1916. The episodes opened with live action that evolved into animation.

When Hearst opened International Film Service (IFS) in 1916 to put on the screen the successful comic strips that he had previously syndicated, he lured animators from other studios with doubled salaries. La Cava was his prized catch, and at age 24 he was made supervisor of the Hearst studio.

La Cava was proficient as a studio head, producing weekly releases of series such as "Krazy Kat," "Happy Hooligan," "Bringing Up Father," "Silk Hat Harry," and the "Katzenjammer Kids." His work abounded with witty gags. La Cava knew how to motivate his animators, establishing each character series as a semiautonomous production, so that the "Krazy Kat" crew would compete with that of "Bringing Up Father." He also introduced some of the most talented animators to the profession, including Grim Natwick, Isadore Klein, and Walter Lantz. His career in cartooning was short lived, however, for in 1918 Hearst closed the studio in order to focus on establishing the live action film career of his mistress, Marion Davies. La Cava then worked at the Greenwich Village studio of John Terry for a brief time before moving to live action comedy, where he became one of Hollywood's foremost directors, with such films as *My Man Godfrey* (1936), *Stage Door* (1937), and *Unfinished Business* (1941) among his credits.

One of those trained by La Cava at IFS was Walter Lantz (Lanza), an Italian American born in New Rochelle, New York, in 1900.

Lantz, who studied cartooning through a correspondence course, landed a job as copy boy on Hearst's *New York American*. Shortly after, his editor, Morrill Goddard, recommended him to La Cava, who hired him as cel washer (who scraped drawings off celluloid for reuse) and gofer at IFS. Lantz was with the studio two years and when it closed, he worked briefly for Barre. From there he moved to Bray Productions, where he became director general, responsible for reviving the "Colonel Heeza Liar" series. Lantz also directed the "Dinky Doodles" and "Unnatural Histories" series before quitting animation altogether in 1927 and moving to Hollywood to write for Mack Sennett. He found employment at Universal Studios, where he was asked to return to animation and take over Walt Disney's "Oswald the Lucky Rabbit." In the late 1920s he was one of the pioneers who experimented with adding sound to cartoons.

By 1934 Lantz had attracted a number of animators to his studio, prompting him to explore the possibility of establishing his own company. He did that in 1936, informing Universal he no longer wanted to work for them, but, instead, wished to be his own producer and sell distribution rights to Universal on a contractual basis. Universal agreed to the terms, and, until he found separate quarters in the 1940s, Lantz operated his studio on the Universal lot. His most successful characters were created at the dawn of the 1940s, when, always on the lookout for animals that had not been used as cartoon stars, he came up with "Andy Panda." In one of the "Andy Panda" episodes called "Knock Knock," his pesky "Woody Woodpecker" appeared for the first time.

A third Italian American among the giants of animation is Joe Barbera. With Bill Hanna, he was largely responsible for reviving the industry from the 1940s through the 1960s, creating a slew of new characters, including "Tom and Jerry," "The Flintstones," "Huckleberry Hound," "Josie and the Pussycats," and "Scooby-Doo." He opened up television as a venue for cartoons and invented the cost-effective limited animation process.

When asked at age 82 to name the person he most admired, Barbera cited his grandmother, Francesca Calvacca, who came to New York's Lower East Side from the little town of Sciacca in Sicily in 1898. He said her most endearing quality was her sense of humor. As was the case with many children of Italian immigrants, Barbera was not always willing to discuss his family background. In his autobiography, *My Life in 'Toons,* he said:

> Among the many stupid and ridiculous things I've done in my life, the stupidest was generally to scorn my Italian heritage. I deliberately refused to pick up any of the language. I looked down my nose at all the wonderful food.

Barbera's sixty-five years in animation started at the Van Beuren studio in New York in 1932, where, admitting he knew nothing about the field, he was taken under the tutelage of Carlo Vinci. He quickly advanced to a director's slot, making, among others, a series about a mismatched couple of humans called "Tom and Jerry." After five years at Van Beuren, Barbera moved to California to establish a new animation unit for Metro-Goldwyn-Mayer. Initially, his hopes for MGM animation did not materialize, and at about the time the studio was to be closed, he met Hanna. Their first cartoon, "Puss Gets the Boot," won an Academy Award nomination in 1940. It was the start of a series of "Tom and Jerry" cartoons that eventually captured seven Academy Awards, as well as the beginning of the Hanna-Barbera partnership. They created more than two hundred cartoons at MGM before the animation unit was closed in 1957. Hundreds more were produced when they established their own company, Hanna-Barbera Productions, which specialized in television animation. Even after Hanna-Barbera was sold to Taft Communications and later to Turner, Barbera remained active in the field.

There have been other Italian Americans who played key roles in animation, one of the more recent being John Canemaker (Cannizzaro), who has won awards for his freelance animated short subjects. He has also compiled and documented the work of eminent animators from the past, many of whom had remained anonymous until he wrote about them.

The United States in the early twentieth century saw very few Italian Americans drawing comic strips. Although this was the time of mass migration for Italians (five million between 1880 and 1924), very few artists of any type were among them. Most of the immigrants were common laborers and farmhands from the south and Sicily.

Prominent among those few Italian American comic strip creators were Alfred Andriola and Dick Cavelli. Andriola, born in New York City in 1912, was tied to five newspaper strips, the most famous of which was "Kerry Drake." Lasting from 1943 until Andriola's death in 1983, this detective story won the coveted National Cartoonists Society Reuben Award. Andriola started his career in an unusual way. In 1935 he wrote a fan letter to cartoonist Milton Caniff, expressing admiration for his "Terry and the Pirates" strip, at the same time sending one of his own sketches. Caniff hired him as an assistant. The Caniff style was incorporated in Andriola's first strip, "Charlie Chan" (1938), which lasted until 1942. After that, he did "Yankee Rangers," a wartime adventure strip, for six weeks, followed by "Dan Dunn," for nine months in 1943. His fifth strip was "It's Me, Dilly!," a comedy about a blonde model, which ran between 1958 and 1959, under the pseudonym of Alfred James.

Andriola usually took full credit for his strips, even when they were ghosted by others, and earlier, he had balked at the suggestion that he not use his birth name. Writing in Jerry Robinson's *The Comics,* Andriola cited as one of his major disappointments "the day a syndicate head, looking at my samples, suggested that I change my name, because an Italian by-line would not help sales (this, after Mussolini started making the sounds of a jackal abroad)." Andriola's drawing style mixed illustration and caricature for a realistic, but nonphotographic, effect, while his innovative stories emphasized the emotional development of characters.

Cavelli, also a New Yorker, was one of the most successful gag cartoonists of the 1940s and 1950s, prompting *Writers' Digest* to comment that he had "risen to the top faster than any other cartoonist in the business." However, by the mid-1950s, Cavelli recognized the unstable nature of the magazine business and decided to seek a more secure outlet for his drawing talents. The result was the newspaper strip "Morty Meekle," bought in 1955 by Newspaper Enterprise Association. The strip's name was changed to "Winthrop" in 1966, as Cavelli realized that the precocious kid character by that name was outshining the previously featured meek office worker.

Other Italian American comic strip artists were Tony Di Preta, who did "Rex Morgan,

C

M.D." and "Joe Palooka," the latter from 1959 until its demise in the 1980s; Dan De Carlo, chief artist for "Archie," who, earlier in the 1940s, drew and set the style for "Millie the Model"; and a few others who switched to doing comic books after they came on the scene in the early 1930s. In fact, of all comic art genres, the comic book has been the one favored most often by Italian American cartoonists. This may be attributable to the existence of an unplanned, inconspicuous network of Italian American comic book artists, originally located in New York City's boroughs, that accommodated other Italian Americans; a more comfortable atmosphere, generally freer of the prejudices that were prevalent earlier; and the prestige and importance accorded comic books back in Italy. It may have resulted, too, from the fact that the Italian American came of age in the post–World War II period when comic books themselves were experiencing their heyday.

Some Italian Americans have risen to the top echelons of the comic book industry in recent decades. The current president of the Marvel Comics Group is Gerard Calabrese, while other comic book executives include Carmine Infantino, publisher at National (later, Detective Comics or DC); Joe Orlando, DC editor; Dick Giordano, DC vice president and editorial director; and John Romita, Sr., Marvel Comics art director. The largest comic book distributor, Diamond, was started by Steve Geppi when he left his Baltimore mail carrier job in 1974 and opened Geppi's Comic World. The business, which brings in $200 million in revenues yearly, has twenty-two regional centers. Since 1976 an Italian American, Joe D'Angelo, has been president of King Features, the largest syndicate for comic strips.

Born in Brooklyn, Infantino began his career at National, where, in collaboration with Frank Giacoia, he illustrated a number of comic book titles, including "Flash," "Johnny Thunder," and "Green Lantern." Later, he was responsible for revamping "Batman," giving the strip a new look that reversed a decade-long decline. He left drawing in 1967 to become National's editorial director and advanced to publisher four years later.

One of the first of the new wave artist-editors that Infantino hired when he moved into administration was Joe Orlando. Born in Bari, Italy, Orlando and his family migrated to the United States in 1929, when he was 2 years old. He attended New York's High School of Art and Design, where his classmates were comic book artist Rocco Mastroserio and singer Tony Bennett. His debut into comics was with the educational *Treasure Chest* comic book, but soon after, he found his niche with science fiction and horror stories, working in conjunction with cartoonist Wally Wood in their own studio, before moving to the innovative EC comic books of the 1950s. After EC, Orlando contributed to *Atlas Comics* titles, *Classics Illustrated, Mad,* and *Creepy;* in 1966, he joined National (DC) as an editor and has risen to vice president and head of special projects.

Like Infantino and Orlando, both of whom he worked with, Dick Giordano is also known for his skills both as an editor and as an artist. Born in New York City, he started working in Jerry Iger's comics shop in 1951 drawing the "Sheena" adventure strip. In 1952 he moved to Charlton, where he inked an assortment of war, crime, western, romance, horror, and science fiction comics, before becoming an editor in 1966. When Charlton folded two years later, he was employed by National as an editor, working alongside Infantino and Orlando. In a 1981 interview, Giordano talked about his association with the latter:

> Joe [Orlando] and I . . . first started at DC and we had a lot of fun together. . . . We were the first two editors hired under the new regime there and we were both artists . . . and we were both Italian, and so was Carmine Infantino. God! I mean, in a Jewish community we were really the outcasts. We sort of stood back-to-back in the middle of the room!

Before becoming vice president and executive editor at DC, Giordano was best known for his artwork on the classic "Green Lantern/Green Arrow" series. He was one of DC's most artistically successful editors, advancing the notion that a superior editorial approach can shape and enhance the work of artists and writers. Books he edited or drew for were lively, fresh, and original. In the early 1990s Giordano left DC to become a freelance cartoonist.

John Romita's fame was achieved when he penciled, inked, and co-plotted "Amazing Spider-Man" (1966–1973), helping the character to achieve its huge popularity. From

1977 to 1981 he also drew the "Spider-Man" comic strip. Born in Brooklyn, Romita began working in comics with *Famous Funnies* in 1949, when he was 19. He drew "Captain America" and many other characters of every imaginable genre for Marvel through the early 1950s, moved on to DC in 1957, and later switched back to Marvel, where he is now art director. His son, John Jr., is also a well-known comic book artist, working exclusively for Marvel. His credits include work on "Uncanny X-Men," "Daredevil," and "Iron Man."

Perhaps the most noted Italian American comic book artist is Frank Frazetta, even though his career in the genre lasted less than a decade. He earned much respect for his fantasy artwork, exquisitely drawn with many violent and sexual images that were later recaptured in posters, illustrations, and cover paintings. Brooklyn-born Frazetta possessed innate artistic and athletic talents; while in high school, he was offered a baseball contract with the New York Giants, but instead chose art. His first job was as a 16-year-old assistant to science fiction artist John Giunta at Baily Comics. For the rest of the 1940s and part of the 1950s, he drew many comics, such as "Thunda," "Conan," and "Tarzan," for Fawcett, Toby, Pines, Prize, Fiction House, Avon, and others. Some originals of this work today bring auction bids of one hundred thousand dollars. Like Romita and others, he also drew newspaper strips: "Johnny Comet" (1952), about a muscular race car driver, and "Li'l Abner," which he ghosted for Al Capp for nine years in the 1950s. Frazetta regarded his Sicilian background as important to his work.

Contemporaries of Frazetta, John Giunta, the Buscema brothers, and John Belfi, all had an artistic hand in the development of many post–World War II superhero and adventure comics. Giunta, whose inventive and unique style influenced Frazetta, had his glory in the 1940s, drawing *Spook Comics* in 1945, and later, "Airboy," "Deacon and Mickey," "Flamingo," "The Fly," "Golden Arrow," and others under the pen name of John Gee. His nephew, Aldo, wrote for *True Crime Comics* in 1949.

The Buscemas of Brooklyn, occasionally as a team, but usually individually, drew almost every Marvel Comics book published. The older John broke into comics in 1948 with the Marvel/Timely/Atlas group, and for the next two years, worked on a variety of strips of the love, crime, and western genres. After his Marvel stint, he worked at other companies such as Orbit, Charlton, Western–Gold Key, and the ACG Group; he returned to Marvel in 1966, where he has stayed for thirty years. Along with John Romita and Jack Kirby, Buscema established the Marvel way to draw comics, emphasizing straightforward storytelling and superheroes, complete with blemishes. He has drawn such popular titles as "Conan," "Silver Surfer," "The Avengers," "The Incredible Hulk," "Sub-Mariner," "Roy Rogers," "Captain Marvel," and "Fantastic Four." Buscema is known for his excellent penciling, storytelling, and artwork.

His brother, Silvio (Sal), worked as a commercial artist in advertising for thirteen years before joining Marvel in 1968. He has had exceptionally long runs as artist for "Captain America," "The Incredible Hulk," and "Spectacular Spider-Man," at the same time he had some role in creating most other Marvel hero books. Sal's work is more stylized, cartoony, and less realistic than that of his brother.

Upon moving to the Bronx at age 14, John Belfi began assisting Frank Frollo, who was drawing westerns. He attended the New York School of Industrial Arts, where his classmates were other future comics artists Infantino, Frank Gidcosa, and Mike Roy. He worked primarily as an illustrator and inker on more than five hundred comics in a relatively short time before switching to advertising in 1955. At various times, he teamed up with Will Eisner and Joe Certa, the latter on "The Durango Kid" and "Straight Arrow." In 1977 he began teaching at the Joe Kubert School of Cartoon and Graphic Arts.

The comic book field has been inundated with Italian American artists in more recent times. Unusual among them is Don Rosa, a university-educated civil engineer with a passion for drawing Carl Barks' ducks, especially "Uncle Scrooge." A full partner in his father's Louisville, Kentucky, terrazzo business, Rosa found time in between running the business to do a strip, "Captain Kentucky"; a comic book, *Don Rosa's Comics and Stories;* and a regular column on collecting comics, which printed in a fan magazine (fanzine). He did all of this as a hobby. When Gladstone Comics started in 1985, he became employed as an animator of duck stories for them and his first "Uncle Scrooge" story appeared two years later. He thinks of himself as custodian of Carl Barks' works, drawing and writing "Donald Duck" and "Uncle Scrooge" exactly the way they were done by their creator.

Another Italian American cartoonist who went a different way is Paul Celli (b. 1935), who has spent considerable time furthering artistic elements of the comic strip. He has attempted to do this with his self-published *Ink Comics,* an aesthetic and amusing look at how an artist thinks about a picture.

Among contemporary comic book artists with an Italian American heritage are David Mazzucchelli and John Constanza. Mazzucchelli, who has held positions as writer, penciler, inker, letterer, colorist, editor, and publisher, is part of a team that set the foundation for the past decade of superhero comics. He worked on the revamping of "Batman," as well as on "Daredevil," and then converted to alternative comics, self publishing *Rubber Blanket*. In recent years, he has done *New Yorker* illustrations and other forms of animation.

John Constanza is a noted letterer, having done "Conan," "Swamp Thing," "Ronin," "The Omega Man," and many other DC and Marvel titles, but he has also written and drawn comics such as "Tweety and Sylvester," "Bugs Bunny," and "Yosemite Sam," and illustrated a number of children's books. He was encouraged in his youth by his grandfather who used to hang his drawings in his barber shop. His brother Pete is also in the comics field.

Still others working in the superhero genre are Mike De Carlo, an inker since 1977; Mike Mignola, a penciler, inker, and painter known for his comics covers; Marc Silvestri, a penciler, inker, and co-plotter who has done work for both DC and Marvel; and Rick Leonardi and Tom De Falco, both of whom were heavily involved with the "Spider-Man" series.

While they have not permeated the comic book genre on a grand scale, Italian Americans have become prominent in caricature, gag, political, and sports cartoons and illustration.

The artistic process of exaggerating facial features was born in Italy, and Italian Americans have continued that tradition as caricature artists. In the late sixteenth century the painter Annibale Carracci, along with his brother Agostino, invented portrait caricature, and the word "caricature" itself was imported from Venice, where artists who practiced anthropomorphism called their art *caricatura*.

In the United States, caricaturists such as Sam Viviano, Joe Ciardello, and Anthony Russo have plied their art in recent years. Viviano, born in Detroit in 1953, has been a *Mad* staff member and a regular contributor to *Reader's Digest, Rolling Stone,* and *Family Weekly*. He has also done many cartoons for corporate and advertising clients. Anthony Russo's work has appeared in many places, including *Vanity Fair* and *Esquire*. Joe Ciardello is widely published. His caricatures are praised for capturing the essence of his subjects with a minimum of distortion.

The most famous Italian American political cartoonist was Giovanni Fischetti, born in Brooklyn in 1916. In fact, as editorial cartoonist for the National Enterprise Association (NEA) from 1951 to 1962, he was probably the most famous member (certainly the most published in terms of newspaper clients) of any ethnic group in the United States. He left NEA because of editorial strictures and accepted an offer at the New York *Herald-Tribune* under the condition that he be given complete editorial freedom. Fischetti changed the format and presentation of his cartoons while at the *Herald-Tribune,* abandoning vertical cartoons for horizontal ones and substituting wry humor for the usual word clusters. Because his work was often reprinted and emulated, he helped revolutionize political cartooning a few years before Pat Oliphant and others were credited with doing so. One of the nation's most prestigious cartooning awards has been established in his name.

Gag cartoons, usually meant for a magazine audience, have existed longer than about any other genre. Yet not many gag cartoonists are easily recognizable by the public because they usually work freelance and publish in a variety of places; thus, their identity and fame are elusive. Significant Italian American gag cartoonists include Orlando Busino, John LaGatta, and Gregory D'Alessio.

Busino's gag cartoons have graced the pages of all types of magazines, from the general interest *Saturday Evening Post,* where he made his first sale in 1954, to gender-specific ones such as *Ladies' Home Journal* and *Argosy*. His family humor panels have been especially popular with the major women's magazines, and, steadily, they have found their way into King Features Laugh-a-Day and McNaught Syndicate's Funny World, syndicated gag-a-day features. Additionally, Busino for years drew a monthly panel, "Gus," for *Boy's Life* magazine.

Born in Naples, Italy, in 1894, John La-Gatta grew up in New York City. His first sales were of "fadeaway" cartoons, some of which were for *Life* in the early 1910s. La-Gatta became a major fiction and advertising illustrator in the 1930s and 1940s.

D'Alessio, born in New York City in 1904, hit specialized audiences with his gag cartoons, which often employed a sophisticated sense of humor. A deviation from that occurred in 1940 with his daily panel, "These Women," syndicated by Publishers Syndicate. During World War II D'Alessio chaired a committee on war cartoons for the American Society of Magazine Cartoonists, where he determined ways to use cartooning for the war effort.

Illustrators can be found in advertising, book and other publishing, newspaper and magazine formats, industrial, and other design, as well as a myriad of other professions. Because illustration and cartooning are closely aligned at times, some previously mentioned cartoonists—particularly Frank Frazetta—have been equally well known as illustrators. Three Italian Americans that can be singled out here as pure illustrators are Vincent Di Fate, Sandra Filippucci, and Giancarlo Impiglia.

Di Fate, born in Yonkers, New York, in 1945, is a noted science-fiction illustrator, drawing covers for novels and magazines. In 1975 he worked as the Smithsonian artist for NASA's Apollo-Soyuz launch. His artwork has been displayed in a number of group and one-man shows and acquired for permanent collections, notably at the Smithsonian's National Air and Space Museum.

Filippucci, a Brooklynite born in 1953, has had a far-ranging career as a songwriter and singer; television, film, and stage actress; and design consultant, in addition to scientific illustrator. Her pictures have been self-described as mysterious, humorous, and insightful.

Born in Rome, Italy, in 1940, Impiglia came to the United States in 1974, where he has worked as a graphic artist, illustrator, and muralist. His illustrations have been featured in dozens of shows. Impiglia said his work is an example of "society's preoccupation with appearance. Costume and posture are epito-

mized to the exclusion of content, communication, and emotion."

Italian Americans in the fields of cartooning and illustration have made their presence felt in recent years. Although some Italian Americans helped pioneer different genres of comic art, most did not enter the field until the post–World War II period, exemplifying the general upward social and economic mobility and the greater ethnic consciousness that began to occur at that time.

John A. Lent (Zinghini)

Bibliography
Barbera, Joe. *My Life in 'Toons*. Atlanta: Turner, 1994.

Crafton, Donald. *Before Mickey*. Cambridge: MIT Press, 1982.

Groth, Gary. "Brushes and Blue Pencils." *Comics Journal* (March 1981): 44–79.

———. "Frazetta." *Comics Journal* (February 1995): 53–95.

Lent, John A. *Animation, Caricature, and Gag and Political Cartoons in the United States and Canada: An International Bibliography*. Westport, CT: Greenwood, 1994.

Robinson, Jerry. *The Comics*. New York: Putnam, 1974.

Smith, Kenneth R. "Fantasy's Michelangelo." *Comics Journal* (February 1995): 91–95.

Caruso, Enrico (1873–1921)

This great operatic tenor's relatively short life was filled with irony, controversy, and triumph. Although he was the eighteenth child born on February 27, 1873, of a poor machinist in Naples, he was the first to survive. Though he studied with Guglielmo Vergine from 1891 to 1894 and with Vincenzo Lombardi from 1894 to 1897, his musical training was irregular and far from complete. As a youth he sang in churches and tried unsuccessfully for a role in Ambroise Thomas's opera *Mignon*; he was eventually replaced because he could not follow the orchestra. His first significant success was on November 16, 1894, when he made his operatic debut in Mario Morelli's *L'Amico Francesco* at the Teatro Nuovo in Naples. Composer Morelli was as much an amateur as Caruso was at this time.

After a few more years of mixed success in opera, he had his first real triumph in Milan on November 17, 1898, in the first performances of Umberto Giordano's *Fedora*. This was followed by appearances in Buenos Aires, Rome, St. Petersburg, and Moscow in 1899 and 1900, all of which added to his rapidly blossoming reputation. In 1900 and 1901 he sang again with mixed success at the famed La Scala opera house in Milan. Perhaps his biggest success at La Scala was in Gaetano Donizetti's *L'Elisir d'Amore*. He performed the same work at the Teatro San Carlo in Naples in 1901, but the audience's reaction made Caruso resolve never to sing in that city again. During 1902 and 1903 he made debuts in Monte Carlo and Covent Garden in London, and sang in Rome and Lisbon, but the most important appearance of all was on November 23, 1903, when he made his debut at the Metropolitan Opera in New York, in Giuseppe Verdi's 1851 masterpiece *Rigoletto*.

Although he did appear elsewhere after 1903, he was associated mostly with the Metropolitan between 1903 and his final public appearance at the New York opera house on December 24, 1920. He received great acclaim throughout the world for his live performances and his recordings, which began being released in the United States around 1902. Recording technology during his lifetime was primitive compared to the compact discs of the late twentieth century, yet the power, richness, and drama of his voice on these early recordings, which were numerous, is evident. During his younger days his lack of mastery of higher tones make it appear that he was a baritone rather than a tenor. However, Caruso used this fault and others to his best advantage with the result being a combination of the smoothness of a tenor and the fullness of a baritone. Brilliant, sensuous, alternatively caressing and fiery in mood, Caruso knew how to please audiences with his warm, sumptuous voice and his vivid characterizations. One of his most impressive effects was the dramatic "Caruso sob."

Widely considered to be the best tenor of the twentieth century, he was an enormous legend on the stage and somewhat of one in his personal life. Away from the opera houses, Caruso had a life that was controversial. His overactive lifestyle contributed to his early death. In 1906 he was accused of behaving inappropriately toward a woman at a New York zoo, and in 1912 he had to appear in court concerning his affair with a woman, which had resulted in the birth of two sons. Other legal actions brought further negative

publicity. He brought some stability into his life by marrying Dorothy Park Benjamin of New York on August 20, 1918. But by late 1920 his excessive activity had turned his robust state of health into a fragile one, causing him to retire. He died of pleurisy in Naples on August 2, 1921.

Caruso was the standout male singer of his era, receiving various official honors in Italy, France, and Prussia. In the United States, his achievements were honored by a fictional 1951 film biography with the most appropriate of titles: *The Great Caruso*.

William E. Studwell

Bibliography

Bolig, John Richard. *The Recordings of Enrico Caruso*. Dover: Delaware State Museum, 1973.

Caruso, Dorothy Park Benjamin. *Enrico Caruso: His Life and Death*. New York: Simon and Schuster, 1945.

Caruso, Dorothy Park Benjamin, and Torrence Goddard. *Wings of Song: The Story of Caruso*. New York: Minton, Balch, 1928.

Freestone, John, and Harold John Drummond. *Enrico Caruso: His Recorded Legacy*. London: Sidgwick and Jackson, 1960.

Greenfield, Howard. *Caruso*. New York: Putnam, 1983.

Robinson, Francis. *Caruso: His Life in Pictures*. New York: Bramhall House, 1957.

Scott, Michael. *The Great Caruso: A Biography*. New York: Knopf, 1988.

See also OPERA

Casa Italiana of Columbia University

The first, and for many years the only, academic "Casa Italiana" in the United States, is not to be confused with similarly named institutions in different countries that were created by and administered under Italian government sponsorship. It was a gift of the Italian American community to Columbia University, built on ground donated by the trustees and administered by directors chosen from departments with links to Italian studies, not only language and literature, but history, art, and government. Located at 1161 Amsterdam Avenue in New York, the seven-story building in Florentine Renaissance style (McKim, Mead, and White Architects) was inaugurated October 12, 1927, the anniversary of Columbus's discovery of America, at a ceremony that received international press coverage. The Italian government was represented by Guglielmo Marconi (1874–1937), inventor of wireless telegraphy, Nobel Prize–winner for physics in 1909, Italian senator, and at the time the best-known Italian in the world.

The brain child of students of Italian descent from New York's Little Italies (especially in East Harlem, not far from the Columbia campus), who between 1910 and 1914 were the first of their respective immigrant families to go to college in preparation for careers in medicine, law, and public service, Casa Italiana was intended to complement the already existing French and German language houses. Peter M. Riccio (1898–1990), in 1920 vice-president of the Columbia College Italian Club, wrote the letter to President Nicholas Murray Butler (1862–1947) that sparked a series of fund-raising campaigns under the leadership of Judge John J. Freschi (1887–1944); Professor John L. Gerig (1878–1957), chairman of the Department of Romance Languages (of which Italian was at that time a part); and others, winning the support of thousands of contributors directly and through organizations such as the Order of the Sons of Italy, the Dante Alighieri Society, the Italy-America Society, and countless Italian American associations of businessmen, professionals, artisans, and laborers. At the culmination of Riccio's career at Columbia, he became director of the Casa Italiana (1957–1966) and brought back members of the original group of sponsors and their families, who again took up efforts to create an endowment fund, thus underlining the recognition and continuity of Italian American interest in the support of Casa activities.

Outside the United States, the Casa owes its fame to the presence during its formative years of Giuseppe Prezzolini (1882–1982), well-known Italian man of letters and cultural animator, who was its director (1930–1940) and professor of Italian at Columbia (summers of 1923 and 1927, and 1929–1950). He put forth the many initiatives that made it not only the center of Italian studies at Columbia but the headquarters at various times of local and national groups, such as the American Federation of Italian Clubs, the Educational Bureau under the direction of Leonard Covello (1887–1982), the Italian Teachers Association, the Italian Historical Society, and the Italian Inter-University Bureau. Fellowships and scholarships were instituted and awarded to students both in Italy and in America, publications undertaken (*Casa Italiana Bulletin,* 1930–1933, 1936–1938; *Il giornalino,* 1933–1941, for high school students of Italian), visitors from Italy hosted, lectures sponsored, and requests for information answered from every part of America and abroad. The "Heart of the Casa" was the Paterno library, gift of Charles V. Paterno (1878–1946), brother of the important New York builders and real estate developers, Joseph and Michael, and brother-in-law of Anthony Campagna, all of them at the forefront of support for the Casa in its building and endowment campaigns. A first-rate collection devoted to contemporary Italian literature and history, rich in reference works, periodicals, and bibliographical tools, the Paterno Library attracted users from other institutions and served Prezzolini and his students in research projects that resulted in theses and dissertations, and in significant publications, such as the four-volume *Repertorio bibliografico della storia e della critica della Letteratura italiana dal 1902 al 1942* (1937–1948) and the Italian contributions to *Columbia Dictionary of Modern European Literature* (1947). Prezzolini's forceful personality, his tireless industry, and his vision guided the activities of the Casa for many years after his retirement from its directorship, which occurred on the eve of the outbreak of war between the United States and Italy in 1941.

Among more recent directors of the Casa Italiana have been Professors John A. B. Faggi (history), Maristella Lorch (Italian), Luciano Rebay (Italian), Joan Ferrante (English), Giovanni Sartori (political science), and James Beck (art history).

In 1990 an agreement was signed between the president of Columbia and the Italian government whereby the latter acquired the building to become the home of the Italian Academy for Advanced Studies in America, a multidisciplinary research institute. With the advent of the Italian Academy in 1991 (sponsored by the Italian government), the original functions of the Casa Italiana came to an end. In 1993 the building was closed for internal restructuring, the facade being under the protection of the Landmarks Preservation Commission.

Olga Ragusa

Bibliography

Betocchi, Silvia, ed. *Giuseppe Prezzolini: The American Years 1929–1962.* Florence/New York: S.F. Vanni, 1994.

Prezzolini, Giuseppe. *L'Italiano inutile.* Milan: Longanesi, 1953. Reprint, Milan: Rusconi, 1994.

Ragusa, Olga. "Italian Department and Casa Italiana at Columbia University: The Prezzolini Years." *Italian Americana* 13 (1995): 60–74.

See also PREZZOLINI, GIUSEPPE

Casa Italiana Zerilli-Marimò of New York University

The institutional articulation of Italian culture through academic structures reflects different aspects of the cultural dialogue between Italy and the United States. The promotion of Italian studies has been the goal of various academic institutions. Thus, for example, the Casa Italiana of Columbia University was established in 1927, restructured in 1978 as the Center for Italian Studies, and recreated in 1991 as the Italian Academy for Advanced Studies in America through a $17.5 million endowment from the Italian government. The Casa Italiana at Stanford University was established in 1976 and in 1978 the Casa Italiana at the University of California at Berkeley. Similar initiatives are endowed chairs at American universities. For example, the Emiliana Pasca Noether Chair in Modern Italian History created in 1990 at the University of Connecticut, Storrs, is the first endowed university chair dedicated exclusively to promoting the study of modern Italian history in the United States.

Among the most recent organized channels of cultural contacts between the United States and Italy is Casa Italiana Zerilli-Marimò of New York University, which was inaugurated in November 1990. Located in the Greenwich Village Historic District in a renovated national landmark, once the five-story townhouse of General Winfield Scott, Casa Italiana Zerilli-Marimò is dedicated to the study of Italian language, institutions, art, and heritage, and to the strengthening of ties between Italy and the United States. This center of Italian studies at New York University encompasses a wide range of courses and seminars leading to an M.A. and Ph.D. in Italian, as well as an M.A. in Italian studies with a concentration in Italian language and civilization or Italian life and institutions. It also includes exchange agreements with Italian universities as well as with the Italian Ministry for Foreign Affairs that networks visiting professors. The Casa was created through a gift of $4.8 million presented by the Baroness Mariuccia Zerilli-Marimò in memory of her husband Guido Zerilli-Marimò (1903–1981), industrialist, journalist, writer, and diplomat. He was president, chairman of the board, and chief executive officer for more than forty years at the international pharmaceutical manufacturing company of Lepetit, headquartered in Milan, Italy, with factories, offices, or active participations in 104 countries.

Under the donor's precepts, the Casa must reflect the spirit of the person whose memory is honored. Guido Zerilli-Marimò, whose father was Professor Baron Vito Zerilli-Melilli, naturalist and biologist, and whose mother was Carolina Marimò, professor of pedagogy and ethics, was a successful businessman and a renaissance man. Also, in 1965, ever interested in international relations, he founded the Italo-American Association in Milan, Rome, Genoa, Florence, and Venice to promote cultural and social connections between Italy and the United States.

Lydio F. Tomasi

Bibliography

Tomasi, Silvano M., ed. *National Directory of Research Centers, Repositories and Organizations of Italian Culture in the United States.* Torino, Italy: Fondazione Giovanni Agnelli, 1980.

Zerilli-Marimò, Mariuccia. *Casa Italiana Zerilli-Marimò.* New York University, 1990.

Casamento, Anthony
See MEDAL OF HONOR WINNERS

Cascieri, Arcangelo (1902–1997)

An architect and sculptor who achieved renown as dean of the Boston Architectural Center for half a century, Arcangelo Cascieri, the son of Corrado and Marie (Trabucco) Cascieri, was born in Civitaquana, Italy, and died in Lexington, Massachusetts. Coming to the United States with his parents at the age of 5 in 1907, Arcangelo was educated in East Boston, where Italian immigrants had settled. By the time he was 13, he went to work in the shipping room of a shoe factory to help support his family because his father thought that he had enough formal education. Fortunately, at the age of 16, Arcangelo was able to pursue his interest in wood sculpturing as an apprentice under John Kirchmayer, a leading sculptor in the Boston area.

Consequently, when Arcangelo reached 21, he realized that education was very important and continued his study at the Boston Architectural School from 1922 to 1926 and at the School of Fine Arts at Boston University from 1932 to 1936. While at the university, he was so adjusted to his adopted country that he became a naturalized American citizen in 1934. Following his graduation from Boston University, he taught for a time in both Connecticut and Massachusetts before he was called upon to head the Boston Architectural School in 1937. Later, on September 19, 1943, he married Eda Di Biccari.

His appointment to the leadership of the Boston Architectural School became the defining moment of Cascieri's life. Even though he became a partner with Adio Di Biccari and was associated with various sculpturing studios in the Boston area, what Cascieri did for the Boston Architectural Center remained central throughout his long career. During his tenure there, he brought the institution from obscurity as a local evening school into cultural status as a nationally recognized academic institution. By 1995 he was able to keep costs down by gathering a faculty of more than 125 teachers who, on a volunteer basis, worked with at least 700 students.

Yet Cascieri's artistic creations have also fixed his name in history. In Europe he designed the World War I Memorial for the United States at Belleau Wood, France, and the World War II Memorial at Margraten, Holland. In North America his work can be seen in several cathedrals, including the Most Holy Redeemer, Cornerbrook, Newfoundland, and St. John the Evangelist, Spokane, Washington.

Cascieri's sculptured works can also be seen in a number of other places in the United States, including Washington, D.C., in the National Basilica of the Immaculate Conception and in the National Cathedral; New York City, in the Cathedral of St. John the Divine, St. Patrick's Cathedral, and Riverside Baptist Church; and the Boston area, in the Parkman Plaza on the Common, in the chapel at Boston University, and in St. Ignatius Church on Chestnut Hill. His work also appears in the Mary Chapel at the College of the Holy Cross in Worcester.

Arcangelo Cascieri's skill in creating statues out of wood was extraordinary. He was honored with a silver medal by the General Alumni Association of Boston University as "a poet with a mallet" in 1976. Other honors include a gold medal from the National Sculpture Society and Italy's Order of Merit. His genius is memorialized in his art and his legacy continues in the Boston Architectural Center, where a hall and an annual lecture have been named for him.

Vincent A. Lapomarda

Bibliography:

Architectural Education and Boston: Centennial Publication of the Boston Architectural Center, 1889–1989. Boston: Boston Architectural Center, 1989.

Biemiller, Lawrence. "An Architecture School Develops Environmentally Friendly and Affordable Starter Houses." *The Chronicle of Higher Education,* 26 January 1994, 51.

Valentine, Eve, ed. *Arcangelo Cascieri: Teacher, Sculptor, Architect, Poet, Philosopher.* Boston: Boston Architectural Center, 1982.

See also ART; HIGHER EDUCATION

Castro, Bernard
See BUSINESS AND ENTREPRENEURSHIP; PATENTS AND INVENTORS

Cataldo, Joseph Mary (1837–1928)
The Italian Jesuit who founded Gonzaga University, Joseph M. Cataldo "fathered" the city of Spokane, Washington, and evangelized Native American and white populations of the Pacific Northwest and Alaska in the late nineteenth and early twentieth centuries. He was born Giuseppe Maria, the son of Antonio and Sebastiana Borusso Cataldo, at Terrasini, province of Palermo. After preliminary studies

at home and in Castellamare del Golfo, he entered the novitiate of the Society of Jesus at Palermo in late December 1852. During his second year as a novice, he was dismissed because he was consumptive; when doctors observed no further development of the disease, he was readmitted after six months.

When Giuseppe Garibaldi and his "Thousand" invaded Sicily (1860), it was demanded that Cataldo and other Jesuits forsake the Society or be expelled from their homeland. Although the young Cataldo retained his affiliation with the Jesuits' Sicily Province, he decided on missionary work and resumed theological studies at Louvain, Belgium. He was ordained a priest in Liège on September 8, 1862, and left shortly thereafter for the United States.

From 1854 to 1909 the Rocky Mountain missions in the Pacific Northwest were affiliated with the Jesuits' Turin Province. Some Italians who ministered there were Urban Grassi, Paschal Tosi, Anthony Ravalli, and Peter Paul Prando. After finishing his studies in Boston and in Santa Clara, California, Cataldo was assigned to Coeur d'Alene in present-day Idaho (October 1865). He founded St. Michael's mission on Peone Prairie near Spokane Falls in present-day Washington (1866). In the next decade he founded two missions among the Nez Percé: near Lapwai (1867) and St. Joseph's mission near Culdesac, Idaho (1876). Once his horse stumbled and threw him against a tree. He retained a limp and thereafter the Nez Percé called him Kaoushin (Broken Leg). When the Nez Percé, evicted after Chief Joseph's War (1877), were asked their religion, they responded: "We believe in Cataldo's teaching and that is the only teaching we wish to have."

Cataldo was superior-general of the Rocky Mountain missions from 1877 to 1893. After attending the Third Plenary Council of Baltimore (1884), he sailed for Europe to recruit missionaries. The Jesuit traveled in Italy for three months, "casting his nets" in Rome, Naples, and his native Sicily. After visiting France, the Low Countries, and Britain, Cataldo returned to the missions with thirty-one recruits, eight of whom were Italian.

The missionary Cataldo resided in Lewiston, Idaho, until 1883, then at St. Michael's mission until 1886, and thereafter at the newly founded Gonzaga College, Spokane. For two years (1901–1903) he labored in Alaska. He mastered twenty European and Native American languages. Then in 1915 Cataldo returned to the mission he had founded near Culdesac.

Exhausted after giving a spiritual retreat for the Nez Percé and Umatilla Indians, Cataldo died at age 91 in Pendleton, Oregon, and was buried at Mount St. Michael's outside Spokane. A town along Interstate Highway 90 near Idaho's Sacred Heart mission, as well as a dining hall on the campus of Gonzaga University, is named after him.

James J. Divita

Bibliography

Bischoff, William N. *The Jesuits in Old Oregon 1840–1940.* Caldwell, ID: Caxton, 1945.

McKevitt, Gerald. "'The Jump That Saved the Rocky Mountain Mission': Jesuit Recruitment and the Pacific Northwest." *Pacific Historical Review* (August 1986).

Schoenberg, Wilfred P. *Gonzaga University, Seventy-five Years, 1887–1962.* Spokane: Lawton, 1963.

See also HIGHER EDUCATION

Center for Italian Studies at State University of New York at Stony Brook

Affiliated with the University at Stony Brook in New York State as a nonprofit, tax-exempt organization, the Center for Italian Studies fosters a better understanding of Italian and Italian American cultures through a variety of activities funded mainly by private contributions.

When the center was founded in 1985, it aimed to help people of Italian descent appreciate their cultural heritage and preserve their ethnic identity. Such an objective was to be achieved through a program of cultural activities that focused on the contributions made by Italians and Italian Americans. After the first few years of activities, however, it became clear that Italian and Italian American culture had a wider public appeal and that the general public, as well as Italian Americans, were attracted to cultural events that engaged in a process of understanding and appreciation of cultural diversity. By the mid-1990s, the center had expanded its objectives and the methods to achieve them through a rich program of activities sponsored with the support and the cooperation of local political and civic leaders, other cultural and fraternal organizations, and the Italian government.

Housed in a research university, the center saw as one of its most important responsibilities the development of a research program to assess Italian and Italian American heritage through artistic, political, economic, and social manifestations, and to deliver the latest scholarly findings to the attention of the general public. To that end, it organizes and sponsors conferences, symposia, lectures, seminars, and meetings. Scholars from various disciplines engage in a common effort to assess Italy's standing as a nation, analyze Italian Americans as an ethnic group, and provide directions to enhance their image and true role as a people. The intent of these activities is not to be polemical but constructive, not cynically intellectual but rationally curious, to compare and contest conceptions and hypotheses. The present purpose of the center is to interface diverse disciplines and cultures, thus creating the opportunity for an original synthesis or integration. In addition to a yearly conference on "Italy Today" that deals with Italy's social institutions (political, economic, educational, religious) and an annual symposium on Italian Americans in a multicultural society, the center sponsors a yearly one-week seminar and a workshop on the most recent changes and problems facing the Italian political scene (retracing them, where possible, to their causes), and an annual one-week seminar and a workshop on the Italian American experience. Each seminar consists of one main speaker, two or three discussants, and several more respondents.

Another important activity of the center is the visiting fellows program that enables the center to bring scholars of international reputation to Stony Brook for intensive interaction with faculty, students, and the local community. As part of his/her residency, each fellow gives public lectures, conducts faculty seminars, teaches graduate and undergraduate courses, and holds an informal seminar with graduate students. In addition, the fellow is available for informal interactions with faculty and students and to give lectures at local public gatherings. The research and papers presented at the conferences, symposia, seminars, and workshop organized by the center are published in books, pamphlets, professional journals, the center's annual report, and the center's newsletter. The center also considers for publication in the *Filibrary Book Series,* published under the auspices of *Forum Italicum,* a literary journal of Italian studies housed in the center, relevant material submitted by individual scholars or organizations (e.g., the American Italian Historical Association) focusing on topics within the realm of the center's interests.

To engage the younger generation in the activities of the center and/or assist in their interest in Italy and the Italian American experience, the center sponsors two different types of contests for students in secondary schools: an Italian poetry contest and an essay contest on the "Italian American Experience." These contests have the objective of raising the awareness and appreciation in junior and high school students of the accomplishments of Italian poets and the contribution Italian Americans have made to this country.

However, in its purpose to reach the general public as a source of public cultural enrichment, the center has become a regional resource center. Through its collection of cultural material (books, feature films, travelogues, documentaries, etc.) on Italy and Italian Americans, made available to the public free of charge, the center is a forum of intellectual exchange and a source of general cultural information.

Through the enthusiastic support on the part of many local constituencies and the large number of Italian Americans who reside on Long Island and the nearby metropolitan region, the center has also been able to establish scholarship and fellowship programs for qualified students seeking degrees in Italian studies at Stony Brook. The Pope Foundation is the largest supporter of this program through an annual generous contribution.

The success of the center is due to the strong support given by the community. This support takes on many forms and includes contributions to the academic program by visiting lecturers and colloquium speakers, participation in the growing number of research projects, and assistance in organizing the outreach programs that strengthen the center's links with the community. The center for Italian Studies at Stony Brook is an example of what can be achieved by cooperative efforts between a university and the wider community.

Mario B. Mignone

Bibliography

Marchetto, Enzo, ed. *A Directory of Italian American Associations in the Tri-State Area.* Staten Island, NY: Center for Migration Studies, 1989.

C

See also CASA ITALIANA OF COLUMBIA
UNIVERSITY; CASA ITALIANA ZERILLI-
MARIMÒ OF NEW YORK UNIVERSITY

Cesnola, Luigi Palma di (1832–1904)

A professional soldier, diplomat, and archaeologist who became the first director of the
Metropolitan Museum of Art, Luigi Palma
di Cesnola was born on June 29, 1832, in
Rivarola, Piedmont, in the Kingdom of Sardinia, Italy. He was the second son of a
nobleman and military officer. At age 15, he
volunteered for the Sardinian Army of Revolution when war broke out between Austria
and Sardinia. During the battle of Novaro in
March 1849, Cesnola was decorated for bravery and promoted to second lieutenant, making him the youngest officer in the army. He
graduated from the Royal Military Academy
at Cherasco in 1851, and subsequently became a staff officer in the Crimean War.

He migrated to New York City in 1858
and for the next few years struggled to support himself, taking jobs as a translator, music
composer, and language teacher. Early in
1861 he married his student, Mary Isabel
Reid, an American heiress. Soon afterwards
he opened a private military officer training
school. For a $100 fee, payable in advance,
young men received a crash course in the rudi-
ments of warfare. Within six months he
trained over seven hundred students, many of
whom later served in the Union Army.

At the start of the American Civil War,
Cesnola closed his academy and volunteered as
a Union Army cavalry officer, in which he rose
to the rank of colonel. Although well respected
by his troops, he often antagonized his superiors with brash and egotistical behavior. In June
1863, during the Battle of Aldie, Virginia, a superior officer placed the volatile Italian under
arrest for challenging a subordinate to a duel.
When his troops refused to charge without
their commander, Cesnola ignored his arrest
and led his men in four gallant cavalry charges
against enemy lines. On the final advance, he
was badly wounded and captured. After being
released in a prisoner exchange in March 1864,
he served again with distinction.

As the war drew to a close, President
Abraham Lincoln granted Cesnola the honorary rank of brigadier general and appointed
him consul to Cyprus, where he remained
from 1865 to 1877. On the island he prac-

ticed amateur archaeology, supervising the excavation of dozens of ancient sites. Cesnola,
assisted by native diggers, unearthed the historic Golgoi temple and the ancient city of
Curium, from which were extracted over
35,000 artifacts. Most of the objects were
eventually sold to the newly opened Metropolitan Museum of Art in New York City. In
1877 Cesnola returned to New York and two
years later became the first director of the
Metropolitan Museum of Art, a position he
held for a quarter of a century. Under his direction the museum evolved into a world-class
institution. He received honorary degrees
from Columbia and Princeton universities and
a special knightly order from the king of
Italy. In 1897 he received the Congressional
Medal of Honor for his bravery during the
Civil War.

Aldo E. Salerno

Bibliography

Cesnola, Luigi Palma di. *Cyprus: Its Ancient
  Cities, Tombs, and Temples*. New York:
  Harper, 1878.
Marinacci, Barbara. *They Came From Italy:
  The Stories of Famous Italian-Americans*.
  New York: Dodd, Mead, 1967.
McFadden, Elizabeth. *The Glitter and the
  Gold: A Spirited Account of the Metro-
  politan Museum of Art's First Director,
  the Audacious and High-handed Luigi
  Palma di Cesnola*. New York: Dial,
  1971.
Pane, Remigio U. "Italian Expatriates and the
  American Civil War." In *The Italian
  Americans Through the Generations*,
  edited by Rocco Caporale, 35–47. New
  York: American Italian Historical Associ-
  ation, 1986.

Chicago

Italians have been in Chicago since the 1850s.
Until 1880 they consisted of a handful of enterprising Genoese fruit sellers, restaurateurs,
and merchants with a sprinkling of Lucchese
plasterworkers. Most Chicago Italians, however, trace their ancestry to the central and
southern parts of Italy. They were part of intricate chains of migration that reestablished
villages and towns in Chicago's neighborhoods and suburbs.

As a rail center and America's fastest
growing major city, Chicago (1870–1920)

offered opportunities for immigrants from all nations. Being part of the complex interaction of ethnic groups, and outnumbered by the Germans, Irish, Poles, African Americans, and Hispanics, Italian aspirations for power and prestige have often been thwarted. While Italians have played a significant role, they have never been as important in Chicago's mix of ethnics as they have been in New York, for instance. Their major colonies, as outlined by Rudolph J. Vecoli, centered on a variety of enclaves. The original Genoese/Lucchese neighborhood in the shadow of today's Merchandise Mart established the first Italian Catholic Church of the Assumption in 1881. Toward the south end of the Loop, near the Polk Street Station, the Riciglianesi (Salerno) lived. Men and boys from Ricigliano eventually monopolized the Loop area news vending stands. Over the years the colony moved farther south into what is now known as Chinatown, where they were joined by Sicilians from Nicosia. The Scalabrinian Church of Santa Maria Incoronata (patron saint of Ricigliano) remained the focal point for this community.

On the West Side, near Jane Addams' Hull House, the largest Italian colony developed and included a mixture of people from Naples, Salerno, Bari, Messina, Palermo, Abruzzo, Calabria, Basilicata, the Marche, and Lucca. A multiethnic zone, the neighborhood included Russian Jews to the south and Greeks to the north. Tina De Rosa's novel, *Paper Fish,* is a superb account of family life there in the 1950s.

On the near Northwest Side a varied community of Baresi, Sicilians, and others grew up around still another Scalabrinian church, Santa Maria Addolorata.

Perhaps the most colorful Italian sector was on the city's near North Side. Known alternately as "Little Sicily" and "Little Hell," this neighborhood became home to some twenty thousand native-born Italians and Italian Americans by 1920. Most originated from the small towns surrounding Palermo and from Catania, Vizzini, and Sambuca-Zabat. The neighborhood was the focus of Harvey Zorbaugh's classic sociological study of life in 1929, *Gold Coast and Slum.*

In addition to these major inner-city Italian enclaves, a number of outlying and suburban colonies formed in the pre-1920 period. A settlement of Tuscany grew up a few miles southwest of the Loop at 24th Street and Oakley Avenue. Major towns of Italy contributing to this zone were Ponte Buggianese, Bagni di Lucca, and Montecatini. Sociologist Peter Venturelli has written a dissertation and several articles about this neighborhood.

At 69th Street and Hermitage and in the Grand Crossing area were two minor settlements of immigrants from Salerno and Calabria, respectively. St. Mary Mount Carmel served the former. Also to the south in Pullman there was a colony of Italian brickmakers and others from the Altopiano Asiago area of the Veneto region. The nearby Roseland neighborhood was also home to a contingent of Piedmontese and Sicilians. The Scalabrinian Church of St. Anthony of Padua served this group.

The town of Blue Island at the southwest border of the city was heavily settled by railroad workers from Rippacandida (Basilicata). Chicago Heights, thirty miles to the south of the Loop, had a population that was 50 percent Italian stock by 1920, most of which came from San Benedetto del Tronto (Marche), Caccamo (Sicily), Amaseno (Lazio), and Castel di Sangro. Melrose Park, sixteen miles to the west of the central city, was a place of second settlement attracting Riciglianesi, Trivignesi, and others from the inner city to the wide open spaces of the western suburbs. As the feast of Our Lady of Mount Carmel (established in 1894) grew to a major festival, more Italians were attracted to the area, and Melrose Park eventually became identified as the quintessential Italian suburb in the Chicago area.

The Highwood community, twenty-eight miles north of the Loop, developed after the turn of the century when immigrants from the Modenese towns of Sant'Anna Peligo and Pievepeligo settled there after venturing into the coal mining towns of downstate Illinois. As explained by Adria Bernardi in her *Houses with Names,* they made their way in the world "working for some rich people."

The proudest moment in the history of the Chicago colony came in July 1933, when Italo Balbo's squadron of planes completed their transatlantic flight, landing in Lake Michigan as part of the World's Fair activities. The event and the hoopla surrounding it put Italians on the front pages of the *Tribune*—in a positive light for a change.

The second generation emerged in the period 1920–1940. Born in Chicago, educated according to American and/or Catholic standards, influenced by Prohibition in the twenties,

Two proud Italian Americans in traditional Sicilian dress with Italian flag during the Columbus Day Parade, Chicago, 1978. It is the most important event organized by the area's Italian Americans. Courtesy Frank J. Cavaioli.

tempered by the Great Depression, and tested by service in World War II, this group was often ambivalent about ethnicity. Though they had experienced the joys of Italian family life, they internalized the feeling that middle-class America would always frown on their parents' language and customs.

World War II Americanized the second generation. Military experience exposed Italian Americans in Chicago to a wider range of life's possibilities. The G.I. Bill opened up the first opportunities for a college education or suburban housing. Yet other governmental policies, such as urban renewal, public housing projects, and the creation of interstate highways and urban expressways, destroyed Chicago's Italian neighborhoods. Location of the new Chicago branch of the University of Illinois in the Taylor Street neighborhood virtually eliminated the near west side Italian enclave. The overall result was that Chicago's old Little Italies were destroyed. Any community identity that survived had to be based in-

stead on a unified body of interest that developed almost entirely from voluntary associations and self-conscious identification with Italianness. The focus of this movement was the founding of the Villa Scalabrini Home for the Italian Aged. The campaign to support the Villa also resulted in the establishment of L'Ora Cattolica in the late 1940s (an Italian language radio program), and in 1960, *Fra Noi,* a bilingual Italian-English–language monthly.

A brief demographic analysis of the Italians in the city in recent times yields some varied conclusions. Illinois in 1980, with a total population of 640,304, ranked sixth among the states in the number of residents of Italian ancestry, which amounted to 5.3 percent of the state's population. The 1980 census also showed 44,756 Italian-born persons in the Chicago area and classified 12,618 of them as noncitizens. The census figures for 1970 and 1980 show Italian Americans in the city to have above average incomes, but to be slightly underrepresented in the professions. Andrew Greeley's survey of 1975 showed Italians in third place, behind Jews and Irish Catholics, in income. Other studies have shown Chicago Italians, along with African Americans, Poles, and Hispanics, to be woefully underrepresented on the boards of directors of corporations. Though recent trends have shown that Italian Americans are beginning to attain educational levels in proportion to their percentage in the population, small business rather than education has been the traditional means of social and economic mobility for Italians in Chicago.

Statistics show the highest concentration of people of Italian ancestry in the Dunning, Montclare, and Belmont-Cragin areas located in the northwest corner of the city; approximately twenty thousand of the 138,000 Italian Americans in the city live there. This forty-block area is shared with second- and third-generation Poles but contains few African Americans.

There has never been an Italian American candidate for mayor of Chicago. Until 1978 no Italian American had ever been slated for a statewide elective office. In that year Jerome Cosentino was the first to break the barrier when he ran successfully as the Democratic candidate for state treasurer. Italians have been more fortunate getting elected as state legislators, county judges, and suburban mayors. In the mid-1980s there were Italian

American mayors in Chicago Heights, Blue Island, Evergreen Park, Stone Park, Melrose Park, Elmwood Park, Lincolnwood, and Highwood, among others.

The dominant political figure among Chicago Italians for the past thirty years has been Democratic Representative Frank Annunzio. He allied himself with the Joint Civic Committee of Italian Americans' campaign to support the Villa Scalabrini, bringing together the two most dynamic groups in the city. The personal alliance between Annunzio and church leader Fr. Armando Pierini was a powerful and a lasting one. In 1964 Annunzio was elected to Congress and fashioned for himself an image as the "nation's leading Italian American congressman." He was a major protagonist in having Columbus Day proclaimed a national holiday and was a founder of the National Italian American Foundation in Washington, D.C. In 1992 old age and redistricting prompted Annunzio's retirement and the loss of his district for Italian Americans. In that same year, Representative Marty Russo lost the primary for his redistricted seat, leaving the Illinois congressional delegation with no Italian Americans.

The litany of Italian American achievers in Chicago is headed by Mother Cabrini, Cardinal Bernardin, and Enrico Fermi. Less well known are Serafina Ferrara, who helped plan thousands of Italian American weddings in the back room of her Taylor Street bakery; Dominick De Matteo, who parlayed a small North Side grocery into the supermarket chain that bears his first name; Anthony Scariano, who served in the Office of Strategic Services in Italy, became a popular liberal Democratic state legislator, and eventually joined the Illinois Appellate Court; and Dino D'Angelo, who created a real estate empire that included the Civic Opera House. The list continues with former federal judge Nicholas Bua, whose courageous decisions outlawed political coercion of city and county employees; Virginio Ferrari, a Veronese minimalist sculptor, who created *Being Born,* which is located at the Ohio Street approach to River North; Theresa Petrone, a member of the State Board of Elections; Professor Robert Remini of the University of Illinois at Chicago, the winner of the American Book Award for nonfiction for his three-volume biography of Andrew Jackson; Dominick Bufalino, who is the former chair of the Board of Governors of State Universities; Leonard Amari, the former executive director of the Illinois Bar Association; Professor Fred Gardaphè, of Columbia College, who has written a definitive work on Italian American literature; and the late Harry Caray, baseball announcer for the Cubs.

Dominic Candeloro

Bibliography

Bernardi, Adria. *Houses with Names.* Urbana: University of Illinois Press, 1990.

Candeloro, Dominic. "Chicago's Italians: A Survey of the Ethnic Factor." In *Ethnic Chicago: A Multicultural Portrait* edited by Melvin G. Holli and Peter d'A. Jones. Grand Rapids, MI, 1995.

Nelli, Humbert. *Italians in Chicago: 1880–1930.* New York: Oxford University Press, 1970.

Vecoli, Rudolph J. "Contadini in Chicago: A Critique of *The Uprooted.*" *Journal of American History* 51 (December 1964): 404–417.

Chicago Area Organizations

The Italian American community in the Chicago area is endowed with an extraordinarily rich and diverse organizational milieu. More than 120 independent chartered Italian American clubs, societies, and associations are located in the metropolitan area, with the total number approaching two hundred if the posts, branches, lodges, and chapters of national groups are taken into account. Ranging in size from two dozen members to nearly five thousand, these groups are organized around religious, professional, recreational, charitable, social, educational, and cultural themes.

The oldest of these groups, the Italo American National Union (IANU), was founded in 1895 and has nineteen chapters in northeast Illinois and northwest Indiana. A charitable and fraternal organization offering insurance benefits to its members, the IANU merged in 1991 with the Italian Sons and Daughters of America (ISDA), at which time the ISDA took over the IANU's financial programs, with the charitable work being carried on by the IANU Foundation.

The largest of Chicago's Italian American organizations, the National Italian American Sports Hall of Fame (NIASHF), also boasts the area's most impressive edifice. With nearly five thousand members in eighteen chapters across the country, the NIASHF is housed on seven and one half acres in Arlington Heights in a building that contains a sports museum, eleven educational video monitors, a sixty-seat theater, and a gift shop.

Other national organizations with Chicago area outposts are the American Chamber of Commerce in Italy, Italian American War Veterans, Italian Catholic Federation, Italic Studies Institute, National Italian American Foundation, Order Sons of Italy in America, Pursuing Our Italian Names Together, and UNICO National.

Of the local organizations, many trace their roots to specific towns, provinces, and regions in Italy. These include the Associazione Regionale Campania, Calabresi in America Organization, Campobello di Mazzara Social Club, Lucchesi Nel Mondo, Marchegiani Society of Chicago Heights, Mola Foundation of Chicago, Molisani Nel Mondo, Piemontesi Nel Mondo, Società Alleanza Riciglianese, Società Modenesi di Mutuo Soccorso, Trentino Alpine Club, Veneti Nel Mondo, and Veneti Del Nordamerica. More than a dozen local Sicilian organizations come under the umbrella of the Associazione Regionale Siciliana in America, and local Pugliese groups have a counterpart in the Associazione Regionale Pugliese in America.

Nearly three dozen Chicago area societies are dedicated to honoring the patron saints of Italy, including Beato Giovanni Liccio (Caccamo, Palermo), Maria Santissima Incornata (Ricigliano, Salerno), Maria Santissima Della Croce (Triggiano, Bari), Maria Santissima Lauretana (Altavilla Milicia, Palermo), San Biagio Platani (San Biagio, Agrigento), San Francesco di Paolo (Calabria), San Gennaro (Napoli), San Giuseppe (Casteldaccia, Sicily, and Sannicandro, Bari), San Leoluca (Corleone, Palermo), San Rocco (Modugno, Bari; Simbario, Catanzaro; Potenza, Luciani; and Valenzano, Bari), Sant' Amatore (Cellamare, Bari), Santa Fara (Cinisi, Palermo), Santa Rosalia (Campofelice di Roccella), and Santissimo Crocifisso (Rutigliano, Bari). In addition, five Chicago area parishes hold Italian patron saint festivals annually. These celebrations range in scope from a simple Mass to a large outdoor Mass in Italian, followed by a solemn procession with *festa* band and fireworks, and preceded for several days by a street festival and a novena. Among the largest are the feasts of Maria Santissima Lauretana in Berwyn and San Francesco di Paola in Stone Park, both sponsored by societies, and the feasts of Our Lady of Mount Carmel in Melrose Park and Saint Donatus in Blue Island, both parish-based festivals.

On the secular side, major Italian summer festivals—complete with food booths, live performances, cultural exhibits, and entertainment for children—are sponsored by the Heart of Italy Association (Heart of Italy Festival), the Greater Rockford Area Columbus Day Committee (Festa Italiana), and the American Italian Society (La Festa).

The Chicago area has several noteworthy sports-oriented clubs. The Highwood Bocce Court hosted the 1996 World Cup bocce championships; the Lakeview Betterment Club is home to some of the best bocce players in the country; the World Bocce Association is dedicated to making the sport a part of mainstream American life; and the Italo American Soccer Club team, the "Maroons," dominates the local soccer scene.

Chief among local business and professional organizations are the Italian American Chamber of Commerce (IACC) and the Justinian Society of Lawyers. The IACC is among the most progressive Italian chambers in the world, sponsoring frequent trade missions to Italy, building bridges between Italian and United States firms, working closely with scores of Italian chambers worldwide, and serving as Midwest representative to the Milan Chamber of Commerce and Fiero Milano, one of Europe's largest exposition centers. The Justinian Society of Lawyers and the DuPage County Justinians have a combined membership of more than one thousand Chicago-area lawyers and judges, with chapters in three local law schools.

Other business and professional groups include the Arcolian Dental Arts Society, Columbian Club of Chicago, Gregorians (an association of educators), Harlem Avenue Italian and American Business Association, Heart of Italy Association, Italian American Executives of Transportation, Italian American Labor Council, Italian American Medical Association, Italian American Police Association, and the Italian Midwest Exchange.

Twenty-five of these organizations have clubhouses at which they gather to meet, socialize, relax, celebrate, and worship. Amenities can include a meeting area, card tables, bocce courts, a restaurant-grade kitchen, and even a chapel. The Old Neighborhood Italian American Club stands two stories tall, contains fifteen thousand square feet, and houses a banquet hall, a library, a racquetball court, a steam room, a boxing gym, a workout room, and a pool. The lodge of the Congregazione di Maria Santissima Lauretana of Altavilla Milicia in Chicago contains a faithful re-creation of the original chapel in the members' hometown.

The Italian Cultural Center (ICC) in Stone Park is also an asset to the Italian American community. Run by the Missionary Order of Saint Charles, better known locally as the Scalabrinian fathers, the ICC houses an "Italians in Chicago" photographic exhibit, an art gallery, oral history archives, a research library, and a recording studio. It also hosts several patron saint celebrations and serves as a meeting place for several local organizations throughout the year. The Scalabrinians have created an impressive legacy in the Chicago area since their arrival in 1903, building eleven parishes, Villa Scalabrini Home for the Aged, Casa San Carlo Retirement Community, a provincial house, a house of theology, a seminary, and a mission center for the Missionary Sisters of St. Charles.

Every year, new groups are woven into this complex and vibrant tapestry. Among the most recent additions are the Italian American Political Coalition, a political action group; the Italians at Fermilab, a scientific and cultural endeavor; and the Società Italiana di Cultura, a group dedicated to uniting Italian Americans on the far Southeast Side of Chicago.

The umbrella organization for these groups is the Joint Civic Committee of Italian Americans (JCCIA). Founded in 1952 in response to strong anti-Italian sentiment at the time, the JCCIA has developed into a coordinating body for local groups, and the sponsor of some of the highest profile events in the community. The JCCIA sponsors Chicago's annual Columbus Day festivities, an opulent Humanitarian of the Year gala named for Chicago Archbishop Joseph Cardinal Bernardin, and the coveted Dante Award, given each year to members of the local media who best exemplify Dante's warning against being a "timid friend to truth." Its Human Relations Committee responds to defamation and discrimination on the local and national levels, and its Women's Division sponsors an annual Impresa awards ceremony, which honors local Italian American women, and the Italian Heritage Board and Cotillion. A West Suburban Women's Division and Youth Division round out the opportunities for involvement offered by the JCCIA.

Paul Basile

Bibliography

Fra Noi Italian American Directory. Elmhurst, Il: Fra Noi, 1994.
Sorrentino, Anthony. *Organizing the Ethnic Community: An Account of the Origin, History, and Development of the Joint Civic Committee of Italian Americans (1952–1995).* New York: Center for Migration Studies, 1995.

See also BERNARDIN, JOSEPH CARDINAL; CABRINI, MOTHER FRANCES XAVIER; CRIME AND ORGANIZED CRIME; FERMI, ENRICO; PIERINI, ARMANDO

Church Leaders

Italian American Roman Catholic leaders have come from a variety of backgrounds and exercised different leadership roles throughout American history. During the period of colonization and the early years of the United States, Italian Catholic missionaries were the first to travel to the Americas. When migration from Italy increased, laymen emerged to maintain community religious traditions. The presence of so many Italian immigrants and the rush to assimilate them into American Catholicism produced religious leaders outside the experience of Italian culture. Non-Italians concerned about "the Italian problem" worked to organize parishes and educational institutions for the new immigrants. The Italian community also produced several important leaders: diocesan clergy, clergy from religious institutes, and women from religious orders who shaped community organizations. As Italian Catholicism became part of American Catholicism, Italian American Catholic clergy exercised leadership within the ethnic group and also on behalf of all Catholics, and Italian American Catholic laity emerged as intelligent and articulate representatives of their faith.

The Genoan-born Christopher Columbus sailed from Spain as a missionary intending not only to explore new trade routes but also to open up new ways for missionaries to get to Asia. He was part of a tradition of spreading

Francis Cardinal Spellman, Archbishop of New York (1939–1967), enjoys a light moment at St. Patrick's Cathedral with a group of Italian priests who recently came to the United States to work with Italian people in Italian parishes in New York. He received the priests in the Chancery Office on August 2, 1949. Courtesy National Archives.

the gospel that continued during the period of American colonization.

The first documented case of an Italian Catholic missionary in what is now the United States is that of Pedro Linares, S.J. His real name was Mengozzi (which the Spanish spelled Mencoci); Linares was an alias enabling him to penetrate in an area claimed by Spanish Catholics, English Protestants, and Native Americans. Linares was one of eight missionaries traveling under Spanish Catholic auspices. They ventured into Virginia, guided by a Native American convert to Catholicism, whom they called Don Luis Velasco. Their guide led them into a trap. Between February 4 and 9, 1571, members of his tribe killed the missionaries.

Several Italians participated in Spanish missions in the western region of the United States. Eusebio Francisco Kino, S.J. (1645–1711) was an Italian member of the Spanish Jesuit mission to Mexico. He worked in what is now Arizona. Other Italians operated under the French flag. Between 1642 and 1650, Francesco Giuseppe Bressani, S.J. (1612–1672) worked among French Catholics in Quebec, Algonquins in Three Rivers, and Hurons along the Canadian–New York border. He was captured by the Iroquois, tor-

tured, then sold to a Native American, who in turn sold him to the Dutch at Fort Orange, present-day Albany. When he returned to Europe, he described his years in "New France" in *Breve Relatione d' alcune Missioni dei PP. della Compagnia di Gesu nella Nuova France* (1535). This work was later included in the English-language *Jesuit Relations,* which delineates the story of French Jesuit martyrs in North America.

Most English colonies were established under English Protestant auspices. Italian Catholic missionaries became important when the United States became independent and adopted a constitution that promoted religious freedom. Then, several missionaries worked on the frontier, performing the delicate balancing act of ministering both to the native tribes and to the settlers displacing these tribes. Joseph Rosati, C.M. (1789–1843), a Neapolitan Vincentian, eventually becoming the first bishop of Saint Louis. Samuel Mazzuchelli, O.P. (1806–1864), a Milanese Dominican, came to the United States in 1828 and worked in the upper Mississippi. Paul Maria Ponziglione, S.J. (1817–1900), a Piedmontese Jesuit, ministered to Osages and whites in southeastern Kansas.

Anthony Ravalli, S.J. (1827–1884), originally of Ferrara, became so thoroughly identified with Montana that the state named a county after him.

Italian Catholic missionaries figured prominently in the development of American Catholic higher education. John Anthony Grassi, S.J. (1775–1849) is a pioneer educator. Grassi was at Georgetown from 1810 to 1817 and guided the institution through the difficult period during the War of 1812. As the United States extended westward, so did Italian Catholic Jesuit educational missionaries. John Nobili (1812–1856), originally from Rome, was the founder of the University of Santa Clara. Anthony Maraschi (1820–1897), a Piedmontese, was the force behind the development of the University of San Francisco. Giuseppe Maria Cataldo (1837–1928) founded what is now Gonzaga University.

Italian Catholics from other institutions also participated in higher education. The Diocese of Philadelphia depended on Italian Lazarists to organize its Saint Charles Borromeo Seminary. Italian Franciscans, facing government hostility in their native peninsula, followed through on a plan for a Catholic college in the Diocese of Buffalo and founded Saint Bonaventure University. The Missionaries of the Sacred Heart founded Cabrini College in Radford, Pennsylvania.

There were a few antebellum Italian American Catholic vocations. The most notable was Charles Constantine Pise (1801–1866), son of an Italian-born father and an American-born mother. A respected public speaker and writer, Pise was the first Catholic priest to serve as chaplain of the U.S. Senate, a post he held for the 1832–1833 session. During the early 1850s, when anti-immigrant, anti-Catholic Know Nothings were a powerful political force, Father Pise defended the Catholic faith and American patriotism.

These early Italian Catholic leaders had a particular constituency. They were leaders in American Catholicism, working in the elite, assimilated institutions of higher education or on the American frontier. As the nineteenth century progressed, their language skills became useful in parish work. Toward the end of his life, the aforementioned Ponziglione ministered to Italian immigrants in Chicago, gathering together the nucleus of the congregation of Holy Guardian Angel parish.

Nicholas Russo, S.J. (1845–1902) migrated from Foggia to America in 1875 and spent over fifteen years in academe. In 1891 he entered an entirely different field and spent the rest of his life working with the Sicilians at Our Lady of Loreto, New York.

When mass Italian migration began, the participants in it were unable to transplant complete religious institutions from Italy to the United States. Many migrants were transient males who planned on earning enough money to return home and restore the family's economic position. Among those who brought their families, many were uneducated, impoverished, and generally unable to re-create a religious system complete with parishes and clergy. Among the better-off were political exiles who had become alienated from Catholicism.

The immigrants re-created religious institutions that they could organize and lead without clergy assistance, specifically mutual-benefit societies. Some mutual-benefit societies provided health insurance and death benefits. All provided spiritual care. They were named in honor of the patron saint of the organizers' hometown in Italy and attempted to perpetuate veneration of that saint in the new setting. The people turned to their patron saint in times of trouble. Women in Italian families maintained the relationship between the saint and the family by lighting candles at the saint's shrine, participating in novenas, and, when the patron was the Blessed Mother, praying the rosary. The mutual-benefit society's men arranged an annual celebration of the patron's feast day, or *festa*. A *festa* was an elaborate event. A Mass was celebrated and a procession carried the patron saint's statue through the streets. Recreational activities were held, such as gambling, musical bands, and fireworks. Non-Italians viewing an Italian *festa* considered it an example of Italian ignorance and superstition; even northern Italians considered this southern Italian behavior as unseemly. Recent scholars, such as Michael Eula, have interpreted southern Italian religious practices as part of a complex cultural transaction in which workers defended themselves against exploitation via rituals under the protection of a supernatural patron.

The task of connecting mutual-benefit societies to parishes fell to another kind of Italian lay leader, usually a male entrepreneur or professional. Victor Greene provides an example in Luigi Fugazy (1839–1930), who migrated to the United States in 1868. When larger numbers of Italian immigrants followed, he sold them services: employment, banking, transatlantic shipping and traveling. In short, he was a mediator between them and the New World. Fugazy was a mediator in another way: he encouraged his compatriots' associational life in order to stabilize their community and thus provide a platform for socioeconomic advancement. He was a trustee at the time of the incorporation of Our Lady of Pompei in New York City's Greenwich Village and was buried from another Italian parish in the neighborhood, Saint Anthony of Padua. He helped his compatriots to develop social institutions that were more effective in their American environment.

Mass migration from Italy presented both an opportunity and a threat to Italian Catholic clergy already in the country. Immigrants needed assistance with settling in the new country, and who better to supply it than Italians already familiar with America. However, their association with numerous uneducated, impoverished southern Italians and Sicilians with distinctive religious customs could tarnish the reputation of Italian clergy in America. This dilemma gave rise to a particular form of leadership: clergy spokespersons who tried to explain and defend their compatriots. Gennaro De Concilio was the earliest champion for immigrants. In 1888, while pastor of Saint Michael's in Jersey City, the Neapolitan-born De Concilio published a pamphlet, *Su lo Stato Religioso degl' Italiani negli Stati Uniti d' America* (On the State of Religion of the Italians in the United States). De Concilio recounted the most common complaints against Italians and gave explanations that made Italian behavior seem reasonable. For example, the American hierarchy complained that the Italians did not contribute financially to the church; De Concilio attributed this to Italian custom in which the government supported the church. He suggested that the Italians might respond better to clergy who spoke their language. Aurelio Palmieri, an Augustinian in Philadelphia, published a number of articles and pamphlets in the same vein in the late 1910s and early 1920s, including *Il Grave Problema Religioso Italiano negli Stati Uniti* (The Grave Religious Problem of the Italians in the United States, 1921). John Zarrilli, a diocesan priest from the Diocese of Duluth, published similar pieces in the 1920s, notably *A Prayerful Appeal to the American Hierarchy* (1924).

In the early years of Italian migration, many Catholic sees tried to find Italian-speaking (but not necessarily Italian ethnic) clergy to work in the immigrant apostolate. Edward M. Dunne is an example. An Irish American, he was ordained in 1887 for service in the Archdiocese of Chicago and was pastor of the predominantly Italian American church, Holy Guardian Angel, from 1899 to 1905. In the Bronx, Irish-American, Italian-speaking Daniel Burke founded Saint Philip Neri in 1898. Until his death in 1931, Burke served as the liaison between Bronx Italians and the Archdiocese of New York. He traveled to Italy to recruit seminarians and ordained clergy for the archdiocese, and his parish acted as a kind of training ground where Italian priests served as assistants before assuming the responsibilities of pastors.

American ordinaries occasionally used immigrant Italian diocesan clergy as pastors for Italian immigrants. Nicholas DeCarlo's career is a case in point. Born and ordained in Naples, DeCarlo migrated to the United States in 1908. From 1910 to 1929 he was a member of the Augustinians. His longest commitment, however, was to Holy Rosary in Washington, D.C., the Italian parish he founded in 1913 and presided over until his retirement in 1960. Despite their efforts, though, Italian diocesan priests were generally regarded with suspicion. Some were indeed escaping misadventures in Italy or were ill-prepared for the American environment. And there were scandals, such as the 1903 alleged kidnapping of the Reverend Giuseppe Cirringione by a New York loan shark who claimed that Cirringione had borrowed money for the renovation of his church basement. Religious orders provided a more predictable supply of clergy.

The first religious order to work with Italian immigrants was the Franciscans. In 1866 John McCluskey, then archbishop of New York, recruited the Italian Franciscans at Saint Bonaventure's to tend the Irish-Italian parish of Saint Anthony of Padua. The Franciscans also pioneered Italian pastoral care in Boston, opening Saint Leonard of Port Maurice in 1876. The Servites, a group that also left Italy due to government hostilities, opened Our Lady of Sorrows in Chicago in 1875, and from there began ministering to Italians in that city. The Salesians of Don Bosco were founded in Turin in 1859 mostly to work with youth, but its members became involved in the Italian apostolate as well. The first Salesians came to the United States in 1898. The institute provided the leaders of Italian Catholics in the large colony of San Francisco.

The first institute to develop a pastoral theology of Italian migrant care was the Missionaries of Saint Charles, later known as the Scalabrinians. Their founder, Bishop Giovanni Battista Scalabrini (1839–1905), developed an interest in migrants as part of his concern for his flock in Piacenza, where he was bishop from 1876 to his death. In 1887 he gathered his first missionaries and the next year sent them to New York with instructions to help Italians preserve their language and culture as a way of protecting their faith.

These male religious institutes served as conduits through which Italian clergy could get to the United States and then establish themselves independently of their institute. Francesco Beccherini is a case in point. At the time of his ordination, May 23, 1891, Beccherini was a Barnabite; he was released from that institute and joined the Scalabrinians on October 2, 1891. At that time, the Scalabrinians required only five-year commitments from their members. From October 31, 1897, to January 15, 1943, Beccherini was pastor of Saint Francis in Detroit. He died July 4, 1949, a priest of the archdiocese of Detroit.

Italian women also took on leadership roles in Italian religious and community life. The Missionaries of the Sacred Heart are an example. Frances Xavier Cabrini (1850–1917) envisioned her institute's members as true missionaries, not only working in parochial schools but establishing their own academies, orphanages, and hospitals. In New Orleans the Missionaries' convent was a kind of substitute for an Italian parish. In New York their Columbus Hospital positioned the Italian community within the broader spectrum of Catholic New York.

The church leaders of the mass migration had a different constituency than earlier leaders. Some worked in urban areas, where their followers held various jobs and hailed from various parts of Italy. Others worked in one-company mining towns, where the entire congregation could be wiped out by a single accident, as in the case of Our Lady of Pompeii of Monongah, West Virginia, whose parish was devastated by a mine explosion in 1907. However, they were all specifically ethnic leaders rather than leaders in the universal Catholic Church.

During the period of mass migration, Italian-speaking clergy were generally tied closely to the Italian ethnic community. Even Italian clergy who were assigned to administrative rather than pastoral work became involved in Italian ministry. Gherardo Ferrante (1853–1921) was born in Frosinone and was recruited by Archbishop Michael Augustine Corrigan of New York to work as Corrigan's Italian secretary, translating correspondence with the Vatican and Italian bishops. He became a liaison between the archbishops of New York and the Italian-speaking members of their congregations. He handled the business affairs of Italian Pallottine sisters in the city and served on a chancery board that coordinated Italian American ecclesiastical affairs. After World War II Italian or Italian American clergy who had served in the Italian immigrant apostolate advanced to episcopal ranks. Joseph M. Pernicone was born in Sicily and ordained in the Archdiocese of New York; he was the first Sicilian American promoted to auxiliary bishop. Francis Mugavero was the first postmigration Italian American to became the ordinary of a see, serving as bishop of Brooklyn from 1968 to 1990. The first Italian American to become a cardinal was Archbishop Joseph Bernardin of Chicago, who was elevated to that position in 1983.

Italian American clergy have also progressed from their migration-period role as ethnic leaders. Luigi Ligutti (1894–1983), although born in Friuli, was known not as an Italian American leader but as a rural leader, serving as executive director of the National Catholic Rural Life Conference and as permanent observer of the Holy See to the Food and Agricultural Organization of the United Nations. Geno Baroni (1930–1984), the son of immigrants from northern Italy, became an assistant secretary of Housing and Urban Development during the Carter Administration (1979–1981). The Missionaries of Saint Charles have become advocates for all migrants, refugees, and people in transit, regardless of ethnic background.

Mary Elizabeth Brown

Bibliography

Eula, Michael James. "Between Contadino and Urban Villager: Italian-Americans of New Jersey and New York, 1880–1980. A Comparative Exploration into the Limits of Bourgeois Hegemony." Ph.D. diss., University of California at Irvine, 1987.

Gillette, Howard Jr., and Alan M. Kraut. "The Evolution of Washington's Italian-American Community, 1890–World War II." *Journal of American Ethnic History* 6 (fall 1986): 7–27.

Greene, Victor R. *American Immigrant Leaders, 1800–1910: Marginality and Identity.* Baltimore: Johns Hopkins University Press, 1987, 122–137.

Schiavo, Giovanni E. *The Italian Contribution to the Catholic Church in America.* New York: Vigo Press, 1949.

Severino, Robert. "Father John Anthony Grassi: Co-Founder of Georgetown University." In *Support and Struggle: Italians and Italian Americans in Comparative Perspective,* edited by Joseph L. Tropea, James E. Miller, and Cheryl Beattie-Repetti, 23–32. New York: American Italian Historical Association, 1986.

See also RELIGION; WOMEN AND THE CHURCH

Ciampi, Anthony F. (1816–1893)

Jesuit priest and college president, Anthony F. Ciampi, like other outstanding Italian Jesuits (Joseph M. Cataldo, John A. Grassi, Anthony Maraschi, Victor R. Yanitelli), was a major contributor to American higher education.

He was born in Rome on January 29, 1816, and died in Washington, D.C., on November 24, 1893. Coming from a prominent family (Giuseppe Cardinal Sala was his uncle), he was educated by the Jesuits at the Roman College before he entered their novitiate at San Andrea in his native city on September 7, 1832. After completing his philosophical studies at the Roman College, he taught grammar in the Jesuit school at Piacenza (1839–1840) and grammar and humanities in Ferrara (1840–1844) in Italy. Return-

ing to Rome, he completed a year of theological studies in 1845. He then responded to an invitation made by James Ryder, Jesuit president of the College of the Holy Cross, to join the Jesuits in the United States.

After further studies, Ciampi was ordained a priest at Georgetown University on July 23, 1848, and his talents were quickly used by the religious order to which he had pledged his life. At age 35, he was chosen to serve as president of the College of the Holy Cross in Worcester, Massachusetts. He held that position for three separate terms (1851–1854, 1857–1861, and 1869–1873). Today the Jesuit residence there is named after him because he kept Holy Cross open after a destructive fire had threatened to close down the college in 1852. That Holy Cross stands today as the oldest Catholic college in New England and one of the best undergraduate colleges in the nation testifies to his courage and the vision.

Ciampi's administrative and priestly skills were so highly regarded that his name was submitted to Rome as a possible choice for first bishop of the newly created Diocese of Portland in Maine. When he learned of this development from the pope's representative in February of 1854, Ciampi pleaded with his provincial superior to have Rome stop the appointment. After his first term at Holy Cross, Ciampi served the poor Irish Catholics of Maine for two years, returning to Holy Cross in 1857.

Later, Ciampi held administrative positions outside New England. In Maryland, he was appointed president of both Loyola College (1863–1866) in Baltimore and the Jesuit House of Studies (1883–1887) in Frederick. Returning to the District of Columbia, he served as parish priest and pastor at Holy Trinity Church (1856–1857, 1867–1868, and 1878–1881) and at St. Aloysius Church (1876–1878).

A cultured, holy, and kind priest, Ciampi was genuinely outgoing to non-Catholics as well as to Catholics in a society that was predominantly Protestant. His relationships with Americans of different religious, social, political, and economic backgrounds reflected a person of refinement and vision. This was evident in raising funds for a Catholic college while in Worcester, in heightening the value of religious music while in Baltimore, and in ministering to the spiritual needs of others everywhere. Appropriately, this Italian American religious leader is buried in the Jesuit Cemetery at Georgetown University, where he began his career in this country and where his papers can be found in the Jesuit Archives.

Vincent A. Lapomarda

Bibliography

Earls, Michael. *Manuscripts and Memories: Chapters in Our Literary Tradition.* Milwaukee: Bruce, 1935.

Lucey, William Leo. *The Catholic Church in Maine.* Francestown, NH: Marshall Jones, 1957.

Meagher, Walter J., and William Grattan. *The Spires of Fenwick: A History of the College of the Holy Cross, 1843–1963.* New York: Vantage, 1966.

Varga, Nicholas. *Baltimore's Loyola, Loyola's Baltimore, 1851–1986.* Baltimore: Maryland Historical Society, 1990.

See also HIGHER EDUCATION

Cianelli, Edwardo

See MOVIE ACTORS AND ACTRESSES

Ciardi, John (1916–1986)

An influential and beloved poet, essayist, translator, editor, and teacher, John Ciardi created evocative poetry that draws on his experience as an Italian American but is not limited by it. His translation of Dante's *Divine Comedy* (1977), praised by numerous critics, retains both the spirit and beauty of the original.

The only son of immigrant parents from near Avellino in the Campania region of Italy, he was born on June 24, 1916, in Boston. Ciardi's father was killed in an automobile accident in 1919; two years later his family moved to Medford, Massachusetts, where Ciardi graduated from public high school. After working for a year to earn money for higher education, he enrolled in Bates College, Lewiston, Maine, to begin pre-law studies. In the second half of his sophomore year, he transferred to Tufts University, where he studied with the poet John Holmes, who was to have a profound influence on his choice to follow a literary career. Ciardi received a bachelor's degree, magna cum laude, in 1938. The following year he earned a master's degree from the University of Michigan, where he also won the first of many awards for his poetry. Ciardi's first book of poems, *Homeward to America,* was published in 1940.

Following his first teaching position at the University of Kansas City, Ciardi enlisted in the Army Air Force in 1942. He experienced combat as a B-29 gunner during air offensives against Japan and was honored with the Air Medal and Oak Leaf Cluster. After the war, he returned to Kansas City for another semester, married Myra Judith Hostetter, and fathered three children. Ciardi served a popular tenure as Briggs-Copeland Instructor in English at Harvard University, beginning in 1946. His close association with the Bread Loaf Writers Conference at Middlebury College began in 1947 and lasted thirty years. Ciardi left Harvard for Rutgers University, where he taught until 1961, leaving to devote himself entirely to literary pursuits.

As poetry editor of the *Saturday Review* from 1956 to 1972, Ciardi earned a reputation as a sharp but witty curmudgeon through his often brutally honest criticism. He served as president of the National Institute of Arts and Letters and won numerous awards for his work, including the Prix de Rome from the American Academy of Arts and Letters (1956) and the National Council of Teachers of English award for excellence in children's poetry (1982). Starting in 1980, Ciardi produced a weekly radio program on etymology, "Word in Your Ear," for National Public Radio.

He published some forty diverse books of poetry, etymology, essays, and criticism, including *Other Skies* (wartime poems, 1947), *Mid-Century American Poets* (ed., 1950), *From Time to Time* (poems, 1951), *How Does a Poem Mean?* (1959, rev. 1975), *The Reason for the Pelican* (children's poetry, 1959), *Lives of X* (poems, 1971), and *A Browser's Dictionary* (etymology, 1980). Ciardi died on Easter Sunday, March 30, 1986, in Edison, New Jersey.

Camille Cauti

Bibliography

Cifelli, Edward, ed. *Selected Letters of John Ciardi.* Fayetteville: University of Arkansas Press, 1991.

Clemente, Vince, ed. *John Ciardi: Measure of the Man.* Fayetteville: University of Arkansas Press, 1987.

Krickel, Edward. *John Ciardi*. Boston: Twayne, 1980.

White, William. *John Ciardi: A Bibliography*. Detroit: Wayne State University Press, 1959.

Williams, Miller. *The Achievement of John Ciardi*. Glenview: Scott, Foresman, 1969.

See also POETRY

Cleveland

The 1870 census accounted for only thirty-five Italians in Cleveland. One of these, Eugene Grasselli, established a chemical works that later merged with Du Pont. The fifty years that followed saw Cleveland become a magnet drawing more than twenty thousand Italians hoping to find bread and work. Most of those who emigrated were *contadini* (peasants) from the Mezzogiorno (southern Italy), where conditions of extreme poverty and governmental neglect brought unbearable hardship to the family. The history of Cleveland's Italians begins in the poverty of the Mezzogiorno and is made up of three separate stages: formation, 1870–1929; transformation, 1930–1945; and realization, 1945 to the present.

By the late 1920s, the formative period was complete; the foundations of Italian ethnicity were set. Demographic patterns were established and in each community the Italians transplanted their institutions, including nationality parishes, hometown societies, mutual aid organizations, a foreign language press, and a multiplicity of family-owned businesses. The Italians eked out a living, saved money, bought property, and maintained a respected distance from other nationality groups. Their American-born children inherited thriftiness, respect for property, a sense of piety, family discipline, and distrust of political bureaucracy.

Cleveland's Italians found work on bridges, sewers, and streetcar tracks. They also provided much of the labor for the city's shops, factories, and railroads. "Big Italy," the oldest colony located in the Hay-Market district, became the center of the city's produce industry. Frank Catalano, a pioneer settler of this community, introduced to the Cleveland area oranges, olive oil, figs, anchovies, garlic, bananas, nuts, mushrooms, rice, canned fish, and other delicacies. Catalano, with his Italian competitors, made Cleveland the center of the produce industry in Ohio.

In Little Italy, located in the Murray Hill area, the chief occupations included tailoring, stone monument work, and gardening. The pioneers in stonecutting were James Broggini and Joseph Carabelli. Before his death in 1912, Carabelli's reputation had reached beyond the borders of Cleveland's Little Italy. In 1908 he became the first Italian American elected to the Ohio legislature.

Cleveland's Italians were also active in manufacturing during the formative period. For example, the Ohio Macaroni Company, established in 1910 by Joseph Russo, became the largest macaroni company in Ohio by 1920. The Roma Cigar Company, started in 1913 by Albert Pucciani, was producing twenty thousand cigars weekly by 1920. In banking, Nicola and Salvatore Gugliotta opened an office in Big Italy, while the leading banker in Little Italy was Vincent Campanella. By the end of the formative period, Cleveland's Italians made up 80 percent of the city's barbers and 70 percent of the city's cooks. Although only four of the city's restaurants were owned by Italians in 1920, one of these, the New Roma, was reputedly the largest and most attractive restaurant in Ohio.

In the medical and dental professions, Cleveland's Italians increased progressively in number. Twenty professionals were serving the community by 1920. Medical prescriptions could be obtained from Italian pharmacist Angelo Serra, who owned the Italian Drug Company in Little Italy.

Unlike the medical profession, Italian-born attorneys did not follow the immigrants to Cleveland. Consequently, the community had to wait for the children of fishermen and *contadini* to fill this void. The first attorney of Italian descent in Cleveland was Benedetto D. Nicola, who practiced law between 1904 and 1964. He was the most prominent among Cleveland's twelve Italian attorneys during the formative period. It was not until the late 1920s that Cleveland's Italians took an active interest in politics as certain events stimulated the community to act. Political leadership became dependent on the small nucleus of Italian American attorneys who, like Nicola and Alexander De-Mairoribus, had already established their reputations by the end of the formative period.

One of the most effective means of ethnic expression that emerged from Cleveland's early community was the Italian American press. In 1903 *La Voce de Popola Italiano* was founded by Olendo Melaragno; it was the first Italian newspaper in Ohio. By 1920 it claimed a circulation of fifteen thousand in the city and another thirty thousand throughout Ohio and other states.

The nationality church was a natural outgrowth of the ethnicity that expressed itself during the formative period. The bishop of Cleveland, responding to the requests of some five thousand Italians in the Hay-Market district, sent for an Italian priest. Father Pacifico Capitani arrived from Rome in July 1886, and on May 8, 1887, the first Italian nationality church in Ohio was dedicated to St. Anthony. By the late 1920s, Cleveland's Italian-born exceeded twenty-three thousand. As the population increased, so did the nationality churches. Those established during the formative period include St. Marian, Holy Rosary, St. Rocco, Holy Redeemer, and Our Lady of Mount Carmel West.

The transformation stage was set in the late 1920s when events within the American experience challenged Cleveland's Italian community. The burdens created by Prohibition, the Great Depression, and the passage of restrictive immigration legislation were temporarily lightened as the rise of "Young Italy" gained respect on the international scene.

On October 3, 1935, when Mussolini ordered the invasion of Ethiopia, Cleveland's Italians, basking in the glory of a rejuvenated Italy, responded with patriotic spontaneity. At the height of hostilities with Ethiopia, more than one thousand Cleveland Italians sent their wedding rings to Italy. In return they received steel rings from Mussolini, who asked that they be worn as symbols of their faith in Italy.

Ethnic momentum continued unabated until June 10, 1940, when it was announced that Il Duce had declared war on France and England. In the months that followed, Cleveland's Italians were eager to prove that they were loyal Americans, and when Germany and Italy declared war on the United States, they were "struck at the heart."

Ethnicity underwent a transformation as the Italian community redirected its energy toward the war effort. When the public schools dropped the Italian language, the order of the Sons of Italy did not complain. Lodges that had been named after Italian royalty were renamed Abraham Lincoln, Betsy Ross, etc. Membership in the order of the Sons of Italy declined.

The junior lodges were closed, and in 1945 a temple that had been dedicated by Italian Ambassador Rosso was up for sale.

World War II was a watershed in the history of Cleveland's Italians. Many had relatives fighting on both sides. Still, they supported the American war effort with enthusiasm, leading the city in scrap drives and bond drives. By 1942 Italian Americans had sent 2,500 of their sons to the United States' armed forces. One of these, Pfc. Frank Petrarca, was the first Ohioan awarded the Medal of Honor.

Cleveland's Italians emerged from the war with a clear understanding of their place within the framework of American pluralism. Ethnic identity had survived the war, but it had been transformed. Italian Americans entered the postwar years with the realization that they were Americans of Italian descent. Their history was neither Italian nor American, but Italian American. Their heroes were the immigrants who built Italian American communities and established institutions with ethnic values that prevented them from becoming plastic persons. They had inherited a bicultural way of life that offered a choice, and there were more opportunities to choose from as the postwar years brought many changes to the community.

Much of the impetus for change after 1945 came from the returning veterans. Having been exposed to experiences outside the community, they sought advanced educational opportunities, more space, higher income, and contact with non-Italians. What followed was an increase in intermarriage and a movement to the suburbs for better housing and educational facilities.

Cleveland's Italians have learned that to be rooted is important, but to be able to live beyond one's roots is part of the American experience. The Italian community had come of age. Anthony Celebrezze exemplifies this spirit during this period of realization. The first Italian American to serve as Secretary of the Department of Health, Education, and Welfare of the United States, he directed the department's 85,000 employees from 1962 until 1965. Celebrezze helped enact the Elementary and Secondary Education Act of 1965, the Economic Opportunity Act of 1964, the Civil Rights Act of 1964, the Appalachian Regional Development Act of 1964, the Urban Mass Transportation Act, and the Medicare Bill.

C

President Lyndon B. Johnson congratulates Anthony Celebrezze, Secretary of the Department of Health, Education, and Welfare, on the passage of the Saline Water Conservation Act in 1965. Senator Robert F. Kennedy, left, looks on. Photo by Yoichi Okam. Courtesy Lyndon Baines Johnson Library.

In naming Celebrezze to the Sixth Circuit United States Court of Appeals, President Johnson said, "Cleveland's Anthony Celebrezze had presided over the greatest thrust for the future of American education and health that this nation has ever known. I have both a feeling of pride in Secretary Celebrezze's accession to this high court and a reluctance in seeing him depart the department he has guided so skillfully. There is something powerful and remarkable in the American legend that directs a young immigrant of Italian birth who as a baby came to this country with his parents and as a man widens the dimensions of his adopted land."

Carlo Ferroni

Bibliography
Alesci, Frank. *It Is Never Too Late: A True Life Story of an Immigrant.* Cleveland: St. Francis Publishing House, 1963.
Andrica, Theodore, and Anthony J. Suster, eds. *All Nationalities Directory.* Cleveland: Cleveland Press and Nationalities Services Center, 1961.
Bisceglia, John B. *Italian Evangelical Pioneers.* Kansas City: Brown, White and Lowell Press, 1948.
Coulter, Charles W. *The Italians of Cleveland.* Cleveland: Cleveland Americanization Committee, 1919.
Hynes, Michael J. *The History of the Diocese of Cleveland: Origin and Growth.* Cleveland: World Publishing, 1953.
The Peoples of Cleveland. Cleveland: Works Projects Administration, 1942.

Clinical Medicine
See MEDICINE, CLINICAL MEDICINE

Cold War: Italian Americans and Italy
During the Cold War period in America, from 1946 to 1989, the level of interest and range of political activity of the Italian American community concerning Italy passed through several phases. In the early periods, the United States government and most Italian Americans saw Italy as an arena within which the struggle between democracy and communism played an important part. As the Cold War evolved, however, interest in Italian affairs declined, for Italian Americans noted that the Italian economy had recovered from the effects of the war and the threat to Italian democracy had declined.

Except for anti-Fascist Italian exiles in the United States and Italian American labor leaders, many Italian Americans and the Italian American press had looked with favor on Italian Fascism. This support wavered when Benito Mussolini's government pursued aggressive foreign policies in the late 1930s. When Italy entered World War II in 1940 by attacking France, major opinion shifted within the Italian American community, with its press loudly proclaiming its loyalty to the United States. Strong support of the United States war effort and a complete rejection of Fascism followed in 1941, when the United States entered the war.

During the course of the war, politically active Italian Americans differed on issues pertaining to the postwar political reconstruction of Italy. Fascism was fully rejected, but the community became divided over the "institutional question," that is, whether the Italian monarchy, which had collaborated with Fascism, should be retained. Conservatives and the conservative Italian American press supported keeping the monarchy as a constitutional head of state, while anti-Fascists, leftists, and some labor leaders favored a republic. Popular elections in Italy resulted in a multiparty system dominated by the Christian Democrats, Communists, and Socialists. In 1947 a constituent assembly adopted a parliamentary system of government and the monarchy question was resolved in a plebiscite vote in favor of a republic.

At the conclusion of the war, conservative Italian American leaders pressured the United States government to grant economic relief assistance to Italy, and all political factions took an interest in issues concerning the Italian peace treaty. The Italian American press, led by *Il Progresso Italo-Americano* (New York), and most Italian American groups agitating for a "just peace" for Italy, supported the position of the Italian government on treaty questions. Leaders in these efforts included former New York governor Charles A. Poletti, former New York mayor Fiorello H. LaGuardia, and Luigi Antonini, president of the Italian American Labor Council and vice president of the International Ladies Garment Workers Union (ILGWU). Buttressed with political support from non-Italian American political leaders, such as New York governor Thomas E. Dewey, these groups supported a nonpunitive treaty for Italy. They pushed for Italy's retaining of its prewar territory in the Istrian peninsula, its border with Austria, and its pre-Fascist

colonies, and for Italian membership in the United Nations. Except for the boundary with Austria, the Italian position on these questions did not prevail in the treaty negotiations.

When it became clear that the United States and the Soviet Union could not resolve their differences on the broader questions regarding postwar political settlement, especially those concerning Germany and Eastern Europe, the divisions within the Italian American community soon resolved themselves into anticommunist and much smaller leftist groups. In Italy the government was reorganized by Christian Democrats and the democratic center, and the Marxist left was excluded from power. The country prepared for the critical elections of April 1948, in which the Communists and Socialists were allied against a conservative-centrist coalition. During this time, the Italian American press, reinforcing the views of the United States government, portrayed Italy on the verge of a civil war and in great danger of a communist takeover.

The April 1948 election was a watershed in postwar Italian politics and was considered as such by the U.S. government and Italian Americans. Throughout the United States, a massive campaign was conducted to enlist Italian Americans and others to participate in an effort to save democracy in Italy by asking Italians to vote against communism. National, state, and local political leaders, prominent citizens and newspaper columnists, major newspapers, the Italian language press, the Catholic Church, labor and business leaders, Italian American politicians, and entertainment industry celebrities led the effort. Largely uncoordinated, with many local committees and individual efforts, the campaign included letter-writing, shortwave radio broadcasts, cablegrams, and the like.

Although the idea of a letter campaign arose independently in several locales, the project was much publicized by Generoso Pope, publisher of *Il Progresso Italo-Americano*. The proposal rapidly spread throughout the Italian American community and received overwhelming support. Many prominent Italian American leaders and personalities called for participation, including Toledo mayor Michael V. DiSalle and Francesca Braggiotti Lodge, wife of Representative John Davis Lodge. Hundreds of thousands of form letters and postcards were

C

printed in Italian and distributed in churches, clubs, and newspapers, and thousands were sent to Italy in bulk for distribution there. Local clubs of the Sons of Italy (SOI) and the Italian Sons and Daughters of America (ISDA) distributed thousands of form letters. A sender needed only to sign the letter and send it to relatives in Italy, sometimes with postage paid. New York Italian American radio stations WHOM and WOV recorded appeals from citizens that were sent to Italy or broadcast to Italy by Boston shortwave radio station WRUL. Italian-language newspapers participating in the campaign included *L'Italia* (Chicago), *La Voce del Popolo* (Detroit), *La Tribuna Italiana* (Milwaukee), and *La Voce Italiana* (Paterson). *OSIA NEWS,* the national publication of the Sons of Italy, whose copies were sent to Italy, appealed to Italian people to vote against communism. Well-known Catholic diocesan newspapers that also published appeals included the Brooklyn *Tablet,* the Boston *Pilot,* and the Davenport *Catholic Messenger.* Among labor organizations, Local 89 of the ILGWU, whose forty thousand members were mostly Italian Americans, and the Italian American Labor Council (IALC), representing three hundred thousand members of the AFL-CIO, were active in denouncing communism and sending funds to a social democratic party in Italy. Along with the parent AFL-CIO, the IALC earlier had encouraged free labor unions to break away from the communist-dominated national labor confederation.

The letter campaign gave strong, tangible support to the statements and actions of the American government toward Italy, especially those that threatened to stop Marshall Plan aid if Italy voted communists into power and that called for a return of Trieste to Italy. The messages in letters, radio broadcasts, and statements were clear: if Italy voted for a communist government, the U.S. government would cut off economic assistance, no longer support Italian foreign policy goals, and ties with Italian Americans would be broken. Church leaders and the conservative press specifically called for the election of the Christian Democrats. The letters produced a great impact, but so did the large increase of aid (food, clothing, and money) sent to Italy by Italian Americans.

This grassroots campaign of intervention in a foreign election was unmatched in American or Italian history. Many letters were received in Italy, estimated at over one million by both supporters and critics of the campaign. Many were published in the Italian conservative press along with photographs showing heaps of private aid packages just arrived from America that served as both an admonishment and encouragement to Italian voters. Unable to ignore the letters and unwilling to attack the Italian American relatives of Italian voters, the communist and socialist press condemned the letters as an initiative of the "Fascist" Generoso Pope, the "greatest friend of Mussolini in America." Since the election campaign in Italy often turned on the issue of whether a party was for or against America, the participation of Italian Americans became an important factor for many Italian voters, particularly in southern Italy.

A few voices in the United States raised up against the interventions of the American government and those of private citizens. Communists, leftists, and others, including New York Representative Vito Marcantonio of the American Labor Party, criticized the interventions roundly. Some former Italian exiles and American intellectuals, such as Gaetano Salvemini, protested against the unwarranted interference in a free election. In the end, the center-right government, led by Christian Democrats, won a substantial victory, which was received with much joy and relief by the Italian American press.

In subsequent years during the Cold War period, the interest of Italian Americans in Italian politics declined steadily as the locale of Cold War confrontations shifted to other regions of the world. Despite its loss in 1948 and the subsequent splitting away of the Socialist Party, the Communist Party of Italy maintained strong support from Italian voters, second only to the Christian Democrats. In the United States, *Il Progresso Italo-Americano* continued to report on Italian politics and, along with some Italian American politicians, attempted to rekindle interest when Italian national elections took place. For the 1952 Italian elections, New York mayor Vincent R. Impellitteri, other Italian American leaders, and Catholic clergy attempted to refashion a repetition of the 1948 letter campaign, but the effort received little support from the people. Italian American politicians seemed to be interested in Italian politics as a way to generate support for themselves in their intramural struggles in American politics.

Thoughout the next two decades, reportage on Italian politics in the Italian American press declined significantly and Italian Americans were not mobilized to intervene. The Communist Party of Italy continued to maintain its popular support, however, and, having asserted a nonrevolutionary route to power, it tried to forge a "historic compromise" with the dominant Christian Democrats in a coalition government. Alarmed by the Communist hold on one-third of the Italian electorate, the United States government revitalized its interventions in Italian politics, especially in the election of 1976. Communist voting strength peaked in that election, but the party was still excluded from power and its popular support declined in later years. U.S. warnings to keep communists out of power were heeded by the majority parties in Italy; and while most Italian Americans felt relieved, they had also, by this time, lost much interest in Italian politics.

Italian Americans provided a strong source of support for American foreign policies during the Cold War, especially those affecting Italy. Based on principles established at the end of World War II, these policies provided postwar relief and economic reconstruction assistance, support for democratic political parties, opposition to communists and the Marxist left, and the inclusion of Italy into the United Nations and the North Atlantic Treaty Organization. In the early period, Italian Americans contributed substantial funds and a significant number of aid packages to relatives, and, often following leads from secular and church leaders, they intervened directly into Italian politics. Their goals overlapped with those of U.S. officials in helping to build a free, democratic, and economically healthy political system in Italy, fully incorporated into the Western alliance. The early period saw a remarkable show of interest, unity, and mobilized action by the Italian American community. This declined significantly once their goals were firmly achieved. Italian Americans took less interest in Italian politics, but they continued to support American Cold War foreign policies in other regions of the world.

Ernest E. Rossi

Bibliography

Hughes, H. Stuart, *The United States and Italy.* 3rd ed. Cambridge: Harvard University Press, 1979.

Rossi, Ernest E. "Italian Americans and U.S. Relations with Italy in the Cold War." In *The United States and Italy: The First Two Hundred Years,* edited by Humbert S. Nelli, 108–129. New York: American Italian Historical Association, 1977.

———. "NSC-1 and United States Foreign Policy Towards Italy." In *Italian Ethnics: Their Languages, Literature and Lives,* edited by Dominic Candeloro, Fred L. Gardaphé, and Paolo A. Giordano, 147–168. New York: American Italian Historical Association, 1990.

See also COLD WAR: U.S. FOREIGN POLICY TOWARD ITALY; MARCANTONIO, VITO; POPE, GENEROSO

C

Cold War: U.S. Foreign Policy toward Italy
American foreign policy toward Italy during the Cold War period, from 1946 to 1989, was based in part on principles that informed its wartime policies and especially by the new international power configurations and economic conditions of the period after World War II. Lacking a historical policy and vital interests in Italy, the United States followed a policy of noninvolvement in Italian affairs during the prewar period, and early in the war it recognized that Great Britain had superior interests in the Mediterranean area and Italy. The U.S. government's primary concerns were that Fascism be defeated, that a lasting peace be established in Europe, and that economic reconstruction and prosperity provide the foundation for a democratic and stable Italian government. By 1944 specific American objectives concerning the peace settlement and postwar Italian politics differed from those of Britain. Recognizing that Britain could not maintain the peace or provide economic relief assistance for captured territory, the United States assumed an increasingly interventionist role in Italian affairs.

The United States favored a nonpunitive peace treaty for Italy and a postwar plebiscite on the question of whether Italy should retain the monarchy. It also supported some Italian claims to retain national territorial boundaries.

It forced French troops to leave Italy and Yugoslav troops out of Trieste, and it assumed the burden of providing relief assistance for a destitute country. American policy toward Italy in the mid-1940s under President Harry Truman slowly faced the consequences of Soviet Union expansion in Eastern Europe and its threats to American interests and objectives elsewhere. The United States became increasingly concerned over the rise of communist and radical leftist forces in Europe, which were sympathetic to and assisted by the Soviet Union. The Truman Doctrine was adopted, which provided economic and military assistance to Greece and Turkey to resist communist forces there.

In 1947 the United States proposed the Marshall Plan, a massive program of economic assistance to Europe. It was adopted in 1948 as the European Recovery Program (ERP), ultimately providing over thirteen billion dollars in grants and loans to the sixteen noncommunist states in Western Europe; one and a half billion dollars went to Italy. The North Atlantic Treaty Organization (NATO) was established in 1949, a mutual security pact of the United States and Western European members of the Atlantic Alliance. Of particular concern was the protection of West Germany and the maintenance of a Western presence in West Berlin. The Soviet blockade of ground access to West Berlin in 1948–1949 and the communist takeover of Czechoslovakia in February 1948 intensified the belief that strong interventionist measures needed to be taken to defend Western territory.

United States policy toward Italy in this period was thus framed in the wider context of its broader program to promote democracy, rebuild the European economy, prevent any communist takeover of Western European nations, and defend Western Europe from Soviet aggression. Anticommunism and the containment policy to forestall any further Soviet expansion became a justification of particular actions in Italy. The economy of Italy at the close of the war—ravaged, unproductive, and on the verge of collapsing—needed emergency relief supplies of food, fuel, and other necessities, and it required massive economic aid for reconstruction.

Italian politics was heavily split among communist, socialist, reformist, conservative, liberal, monarchist, and neo-fascist forces. Three mass parties dominated the scene,

Christian Democrat, Communist, and Socialist, but the multiparty system required coalitions of parties to form majority governments. The Italian Communist Party became the largest communist party in Western Europe and second largest party in Italy. It defended Soviet actions, received Soviet aid, and followed the Soviet line on international events. Most organized workers in Italy were members of a single large labor confederation, which had politicized "currents" that were linked to the mass parties. The largest group of workers were members of the communist current, and its leaders supported the political objectives of the Communist Party. Reformist leaders and movements, some of which provided governmental leadership at the conclusion of the war, had little mass backing, and Italian politics came to be a contest of the radical left, dominated by the Communist Party and its occasional Socialist ally, and the conservatives, led by the Christian Democrats, who rallied centrist forces to its side.

In this political context, American policy was decidedly anticommunist and interventionist. It moved from a wartime period of ad hoc decisions to a comprehensive program of diplomatic, economic, political, and military actions whose objectives were to keep the communists out of power, strengthen the conservative and moderate political forces, and rebuild the Italian economy along the lines of U.S. policy. Strongly supporting the American government in its objectives and actions was the Italian American community, which launched a widespread program of its own. It sent funds and aid packages and strongly communicated its anticommunist views to relatives in Italy, thus reinforcing the policies of the U.S. government.

In 1946 American diplomats influenced the political composition of the Italian government, the powers and functions of the elected Italian assembly, features of the Italian constitution that emerged from the assembly, and the establishment of local elections. Regarding Sicily, it supported the Italian government's opposition to a separatist movement, but it pushed for the calling of local elections before the constitution was adopted and the creation of a system of quasi-federal regional governments. As Communist Party opposition to American policies grew and the party reversed itself by supporting Soviet opposition to the Marshall Plan, the United States became more interventionist. It strongly supported Christian Democratic governments, the breakaway of a social democratic wing of the Socialist Party, the establishment of a center-right coalition government, and the creation of non-communist labor confederations.

These actions increased Communist propaganda, demonstrations, and strikes; American intelligence and diplomatic analysts feared that the Italian government might well fall to communists either through violent or by constitutional means. Government officials and Italian Americans thus intervened strongly in the critical election of 1948, in which a joint Communist-Socialist front opposed the center-left coalition led by Christian Democrats. A comprehensive plan of action was proposed, including propaganda, economic assistance, financial and political support for anticommunist forces, and the possible use of military intervention. The United States granted economic assistance as an interim stopgap measure before the Marshall Plan was finally approved by Congress and stepped up deliveries of food and fuel. It sent funds to conservative and centrist political groups, proposed Italy for membership in the United Nations, announced that it would reconsider withholding Marshall Plan aid if Italy voted communist, and proposed that Trieste be returned to Italy. The Italian conservative coalition won a substantial victory in the election, which set the pattern for subsequent governments, later including the Socialists.

As the Cold War proceeded with increasing or decreasing intensity in other geographical areas, American foreign policy objectives toward Italy continued as before, but with much less concern, for Italy became clearly locked in the Western camp. Italy joined the Atlantic Alliance, agreed to American military bases on its soil, became a founding member of the European Economic Community, joined the United Nations, and generally supported American foreign policies in other regions of the world. Italian politics were marked by a high degree of cabinet instability and the continuing popular strength of the Communist Party, which, however, often distanced itself from the Soviet Union. In 1976, with Italian politics in shambles, United States officials and Italian Americans again tried to influence Italian voters with another campaign of intervention, but given the Italian "economic miracle" and a renewed sense of independence within the country, their efforts were of little use. Although the Communist Party received its highest vote totals in the postwar period, it remained out of government. Its claim of a constitutionalist route to power, acceptance of European integration and the Western alliance, and efforts to make a "historical compromise" to share power with the Christian Democrats did not prevent its steady decline in popular support in subsequent elections.

In the early decades of the Cold War, the U.S. government, supported by Italian Americans, took a great interest in Italian affairs, but the interest and interventions declined as Italy became prosperous and integrated with Western Europe. American economic aid and political interventions had supported those Italian forces that were willing to take a junior partnership role to ensure that the Italian political system would be refashioned along democratic lines, become economically viable, and be tied to the Western nations. The two partners often disagreed on a number of specifics, as in the use of Marshall Plan funds, but the overlapping goals of the U.S. government and those of Italian conservative elites provided the incentives for their successful policies.

Ernest E. Rossi

Bibliography

Harper, John Lamberton. *America and the Reconstruction of Italy.* Cambridge: Cambridge University Press, 1986.

Hughes, H. Stuart, *The United States and Italy.* 3rd ed. Cambridge: Harvard University Press, 1979.

Kogan, Norman. *A Political History of Postwar Italy.* New York: Praeger, 1981.

Miller, James Edward. *The United States and Italy, 1940–1950.* Chapel Hill: University of North Carolina Press, 1986.

Rossi, Ernest E. "NSC-1 and United States Foreign Policy Towards Italy." In *Italian Ethnics: Their Languages, Literature and Lives,* edited by Dominic Candeloro, Fred L. Gardaphé, and Paolo A. Giordano, 147–168. New York: American Italian Historical Association, 1990.

See also AMERICAN COMMITTEE ON ITALIAN MIGRATION; COLD WAR: ITALIAN AMERICANS AND ITALY

Colombo, Joseph

See ITALIAN AMERICAN CIVIL RIGHTS LEAGUE

Colonies in Small Towns

As historian Rudolph J. Vecoli has observed, "[T]he big city did not exhaust the categories of environments in which the Italians lived and worked. We know that many families settled in small factory towns, others in mining villages, and not a few on farms. Collectively they amounted to a sizable percentage of the total Italian immigration, and numerically to several hundred thousand." The first discernible waves of Italians coming to the United States began in the 1870s, with ever-increasing numbers up to World War I. The bulk of jobs available to this mainly male migration was as laborers in factories, construction, on railroads, and in the primary sectors of lumbering, mining, and gardening/farming. Most of the initial waves of immigrants settled in the ports of entry such as New York, Boston, and Philadelphia.

From the 1890s onward, once these large-city colonies had expanded and consolidated, a growing number of Italians responded to employment opportunities in the small cities and towns of the northeast, and to the west. By the time large-scale migration ceased in the early 1920s, Italians settled in colonies—large and small, temporary and permanent—located throughout most states of the Union.

There were at least three typical patterns of migration, work, and settlement that characterized town settlement in the decades before 1914. In the first, Italians went directly from the processing centers to the *paesani* (fellow townsfolk) neighborhoods in the cities. After a period of residence some then moved on to other employment in the interior of the country, in response to an appeal either from friends or relatives or from employers recruiting immigrant labor.

The first pattern of direct settlement was most effective and accounted for much of town colony growth. *Paesani* communication networks, both between the native village and the United States and from one colony to another, operated in intricate ways. One example of a *paesani* network that remained effective for several decades can be represented by the Alberobellesi. A few families from Alberobello initially established a small colony in New York City's South Bronx in 1900. Once the South Bronx colony was established, it became a stepping-stone to the founding of satellite colonies in Scranton, Pennsylvania; Paterson, New Jersey; and Utica and Endicott in upstate New York. By 1914 the Utica colony, with over one thousand persons, had the largest concentration of Alberobellesi in the country. The Alberobellesi found a variety of employment, including work as piano factory laborers (South Bronx), shoeworkers (Endicott), Paterson silk workers, miners in Scranton, and Utica textile workers. There were also outside laborers and a scattering of farmers who sold produce to their *paesani*.

In the founding of a town colony, the immigrant pioneers were mostly unattached males and a few family units. Once roots were laid down, work acquired, and general conditions found amenable, word of the "discovery" would be relayed by post or person to other colonies as well as to Italy. This passing along of colony information initiated the second pattern. In the early stages roots were shallow. Many of the unattached males would move easily from colony to colony in search of a more accommodating environment. Others, women and children especially, arrived from Italy to be reunited with family members. The completed family units formed the colony core and a basis for a permanent immigrant settlement.

The third pattern involved the mobile immigrant workforce of outside laborers, composed primarily of railroad workers and small construction gangs headed by Italian foremen. These transient workers came and went from job to job, and scores were sojourners who had little or no intention of long-term residence in the host country. However, there were those who settled in more or less makeshift communities (of workers) along railroad lines or in towns where their work had sent them. The small Italian colony in Manchester, New York, was one that was formed exclusively by railroad hands and their families, as were many other colonies as the lines westward were laid and maintained by Italians.

An outstanding characteristic of the town immigrant as compared to his city counterpart was his geographic mobility. Some of the men changed jobs with such regularity that the term *mille mestieri* (thousand jobs) was used to describe the phenomenon. Reasons for this were several and obvious, including seasonal or temporary employment, inadequate pay, and intolerable working conditions. Losing a job in the city did not require a change of residence to find new employment as often as losing work in a construction gang or a company town, when employment usually had to be sought in another town. Therefore, at least in the early stages of the history of the colony, the turnover in population was often very high. The economies of these towns were not predictable. Salt mining, for example, was seasonal work that relied on supply and demand. In Retsof, New York, where, by the late 1890s, the salt miners were predominantly Italian, all those who were there in 1900 had been replaced, at least once over, by 1910. In instances of industry shutdown the colony was subject to drastic reduction or complete relocation. The latter occurred in Geneseo, New York, where a substantial colony of Sicilians moved on after the town's factory closed its doors. An Italian worker camp in the Adirondacks is now a ghost town.

The town colony canvas is a complex weave of occupation and location. The subject stretches from the logging camps of Maine and Washington State, to the mines of Minnesota, Texas, Illinois, and Colorado, to the coal fields of the Appalachians. Italian quarry workers were found in the most unlikely hamlets. The quarrymen of Vermont have been well documented. Hamlets such as Holley, New York, have not. The Italian gardeners and caretakers of Port Chester, New York, cannot be lumped with the Italian farmworkers who toiled in the fields and vineyards of California, nor with those of western New York and New Jersey or with the sugarcane workers of the parishes of Louisiana. Separate consideration must be given to the rural communal experiments, such as that at Sunnyside, Arkansas. The colonies of Italian railroad or factory workers often defined the communities where they settled, like Solvay, New York, where Italians became the majority in the immigrant population. On the other hand, in railroad towns in states like Montana, Italians were indeed rare and their assimilation rapid.

Thus, no simple set of descriptions would suffice to define town colonies or the Italian American experience as a whole. Town colony statistics have most likely been derived from studies made in Chicago or New York. A broad application of such findings would be problematic at best, especially if regional and demographic differences are ignored. Questions concerning the process of assimilation, intermarriage, patterns of discrimination and prejudice, and economic and educational mobility of both the immigrants and the succeeding generation remain a function of place of residence.

Michael LaSorte

Bibliography

Belfiglio, Valentine J. *The Italian Experience in Texas.* Austin: Eskin, 1985.

Bohme, Frederick G. *A History of Italians in New Mexico.* New York: Arno, 1958.

———, ed. *Italian Immigrants in Rural and Small Town America.* Staten Island, NY: American Italian Historical Association, 1987.

LaGumina, Salvatore J. *From Steerage to Suburb: Long Island Italians.* New York: Center for Migration Studies, 1988.

Marchello, Maurice R. *Black Coal for White Bread: Up from the Prairie Mines.* New York: Vantage, 1972.

Scarpaci, Jean A. *Italian Immigrants in Louisiana's Sugar Parishes, 1880–1910.* New York: Arno, 1990.

Schiavo, Giovanni. *The Italians in Missouri.* New York: Arno, 1929.

Schiro, George. *Americans by Choice: History of Italians in Utica, New York.* New York: Arno, 1940.

Starr, Dennis J. *The Italians of New Jersey.* Newark: New Jersey Historical Society, 1985.

Vecoli, Rudolph J., ed. *Italian Immigrants in Rural and Small Town America.* New York: American Italian Historical Association, 1987.

Zahavi, Gerald. *Workers, Managers, and Welfare Capitalism: The Shoeworkers and the Tanners of Endicott Johnson.* Urbana: University of Illinois, 1988.

See also POPULATION

Columbia

Americans devised the name "Columbia" from Christopher Columbus to convey the poetic and political personification of the

Patriotic float with Italian and American colors and flags at the Columbus Day Parade in Chicago, 1978, the most important event expressive of Italian American pride. Courtesy Frank J. Cavaioli.

lyrical term Columbia in their verses, from early American poets such as Phillis Wheatley, Philip Freneau, Joel Barlow, and Benjamin Young Prime to the later poets Walt Whitman, Sidney Lanier, Paul Laurence Dunbar, Joseph Tusiani, and Rose Basile Green. The Columbus image, Columbia, has served as an inspirational and unifying force in a pluralistic society.

Frank J. Cavaioli

Bibliography

Cavaioli, Frank J. "Columbus and the Name Columbia." *Italian Americana* 11 (fall/winter 1992): 6–17.

———. "Columbus and the Rise of American Literature." In *New Explorations in Italian American Studies,* edited by Richard N. Juliani and Sandra P. Juliani, 3–17. Staten Island, NY: American Italian Historical Association, 1994.

———. "Columbus and the Whitman Connection." *The Long Island Historical Journal* 6 (spring 1994): 233–244.

See also COLUMBUS, CHRISTOPHER

Columbia Associations

This group of Italian American associations was founded to safeguard the interests of its members in civil service jobs on the local, state, and national levels.

Columbia associations have been very active in New York City, where they were organized among the Italian Americans involved in most areas of municipal services, especially education, fire, police, and sanitation. Extending beyond the local to state workers, the group has attracted workers in such areas as the customs service, the post office, and the port authority so that the umbrella organization, the National Council of Columbia Associations in Civil Service, has a membership today in excess of ten thousand, with most of its twenty-three associations, except for the police officers in New Jersey, anchored in New York.

Under the influence of the association established by the police department in New York City in 1932, the local focus of the Columbia Associations broadened into a national one when Mario Biaggi, who had risen to leadership in that same police association, founded the grand council of the

United States. Original reference to the image of Columbus suggested a link between the discovery of America and the foundation years of nationhood. Colonists, searching for a heroic reference point and in expressing their gratitude, turned frequently to the man who opened up the New World and made the American experiment possible.

Attempting self-definition, especially at the time of the American Revolution, the name Columbia attained wide popularity as its use demonstrated the beginning of nationhood and historical continuity. The use of the name Columbia emerged in the early years of the republic as its leaders searched for an appropriate title to signify a distinct nationality quite separate from the rest of the world.

Americans have honored Columbus with the name Columbia through the construction of countless monuments and statues, formation of various societies, and composition of songs and poems. Names with Columbia have been applied to towns, cities, counties, and other entities such as rivers, colleges, and institutions.

Poets, in particular, have included the

Columbia Associations and was elected its president at the start of 1958. The police association had gained such recognition that Mario Cuomo in 1982 and Rudolph W. Giuliani in 1993, during their campaigns for public office, addressed the Columbia Association of the New York Police Department, whose membership has since grown to more than six thousand after the city's police force combined with the city's housing and transit police in 1996.

The Columbia Associations have been engaged in a number of activities. Their scholarship program provides educational opportunities for the younger generation of Italian Americans. Their members participate in the Columbus Day Parade, frequently with the largest representation. They have contributed to the landscape of New York City in Lower Manhattan by dedicating a park in memory of Joseph Petrosino, the first Italian American in New York to rise to the rank of police lieutenant and whose life was dramatized by Ernest Borgnine in the movie *Pay or Die* (1960). While most of the associations have their own means of communication, the firefighters and the police officers, who make up the largest contingency in the Columbia Associations, publish their own newspapers, both entitled *Columbia News*.

Although such associations are vanishing among established ethnic groups in today's multicultural society of the United States, the associations within the National Council of Columbia Associations in Civil Service remain effective in defending the interests of Italian Americans.

Vincent A. Lapomarda

Bibliography

Brizzolara, Andrew. *A Directory of Italian and Italian-American Organizations and Community Services in the Metropolitan Area of Greater New York.* New York: Center for Migration Studies, 1976.

Rolle, Andrew. *The Italian Americans: Troubled Roots.* Norman: University of Oklahoma Press, 1984.

Sayre, Wallace S., and Herbert Kaufman. *Governing New York City: Politics in the Metropolis.* New York: Russell Sage, 1960.

See also ORGANIZATIONS; POLITICS

A modern Christopher Columbus monument, sculpted in bronze by Enzo Gallo, was placed at Port Everglades, Fort Lauderdale, Florida, in preparation for the quincentennial celebration of the discovery of America. From a souvenir journal, October 1989. Courtesy Frank J. Cavaioli.

Columbus, Christopher (1451–1506)

An Italian explorer who discovered America, Christopher Columbus was born in Genoa, the major port and trade center. The Italian form of his name is Cristoforo Colombo, and the Spanish form is Cristóbal Colón. His father was a wool weaver, and he was the oldest of five children.

Columbus went to sea at an early age and settled in Lisbon, Portugal, where he married and had a son. He had little formal education, but he learned Latin, Portuguese, and Spanish, and he acquired the necessary geographical knowledge to conceive a plan to prove the earth was round. Most of all, he believed that Asia could be reached by sailing due west. He offered his plan to the king of Portugal, who rejected it. He next offered his plan to the Spanish rulers Ferdinand and Isabella, who were successfully solidifying their control over

Spain. After long delays, they agreed to support the enterprise. The belief that the earth was round was not new. Part of Columbus's genius was his total commitment and divine vision to carry out his plan to prove the theory as true.

Ferdinand and Isabella agreed to fit out three caravels, *Santa Maria, Nina,* and *Pinta,* and to grant Columbus material and political rights to any lands he might discover, as well as the titles of admiral of the ocean sea, viceroy, and governor. The expedition set sail from Palos on September 6, 1492. On October 12, land was sighted, called Guanahani by the natives, but named San Salvador by Columbus, now Watling Island in the Bahamas. He thought he had reached Asia (calling the natives Indians) but had actually discovered Cuba, Haiti, the Dominican Republic (Hispaniola), and other lands. He returned to Spain triumphantly in March 1493, with two ships—the *Santa Maria* had been lost.

Columbus made three more voyages to the New World to discover and explore more lands: 1493–1496, 1498–1500, and 1502–1504. He returned from his fourth voyage a sick man, out of favor with the Spanish monarchs. His last days were spent fighting to reclaim his political and economic rights due him and his crew. He died on May 20, 1506, at Valladolid, Spain, still believing he had reached the Indies. If there had been voyages to the New World before 1492, as some have speculated, no records exist.

His discovery accelerated the transition into modern history, ushering in revolutionary social, political, and economic changes. Columbus, a man of the Renaissance, opened the gates to a vast new world. As a man of science, and deeply religious, he was unswerving in his search for truth. His adventurous spirit matched his courage in the face of seemingly impossible odds. Columbus's discovery shifted power to the nation-states of Europe, and then to America. He brought together the agricultures of the Old and New Worlds, thereby increasing the number and kinds of useful plants. New wealth, coupled with the rise of capitalism, laid the foundation for a vastly different and challenging world. Columbus initiated the process of colonization, which resulted in the settlement of the original thirteen American colonies, paving the way for the growth of the United States

and a democratic society that has served as a beacon to the oppressed.

It is no wonder, then, that Americans have traditionally regarded Columbus as a hero in their history. Also, Italian Americans have made Columbus, an Italian by birth, their unifying hero. Scholar Christopher J. Kauffman has stated: "Italian Americans grounded legitimacy in a pluralistic society by focusing on the Genoese explorer as a central figure in the formation of their sense of peoplehood."

A century ago there was a serious attempt to canonize Columbus. Today, however, some historians have questioned the idealistic view of Columbus and the discovery of America. They have portrayed Columbus and those who followed him as aggressors who conquered and exploited innocent people. The result was disease, destruction, and slavery. Despite this criticism, Italian Americans have continued to revere Columbus.

Frank J. Cavaioli

Bibliography

Granzotto, Gianni. *Christopher Columbus, The Dream and the Obsession.* London: Grafton, 1988.

Lunenfeld, Marvin. *Discovery, Invasion, Encounter.* Lexington, MA: Heath, 1991.

Mignone, Mario B. *Columbus: Meeting of Cultures.* Stony Brook, NY: Forum Italieum, 1993.

Sammartino, Peter. *Columbus.* Rome: ITALY ITALY, 1988.

Taviani, Paolo Emilio. *Columbus: The Great Adventure. His Life, His Times, and His Voyages.* New York: Orion, 1991.

See also COLUMBIA; EXPLORERS

Comedy

The years spanning 1920 to the present have been enhanced by many comedians of Italian American descent who have gotten laughs for performances that reflect little or no Italian American humor. From Lou Costello (Louis Francis Costillo), whose 1940s and 1950s comedy incorporated a few references to a Mr. Baccigalup; to Jimmy Durante, who, from the 1930s through the 1970s, occasionally sang *"Imbriago"* and flecked his banter with sporadic Italian phrases; to Jerry Colonna's singular Italian American offering of the humorous

"Rosie Rocula" song in the 1940s; to Charlie Manna, whose 1950s Italian American humor was limited to one impression of Gabby Hayes singing *"Vicin 'O Mare"*; to the currently popular Jay Leno, whose material and delivery are devoid of any Italian American flavor, many Italian American comedians have opted for mass appeal to a mainstream audience rather than a smaller Italian American crowd.

At the same time, however, a long line of successful comedy performers, who can trace their backgrounds to Italian or Italian American roots, have consciously chosen to identify with and play to a primarily Italian American audience. Through the decades, these performers have shone a humorous spotlight on the experiences of newly arrived Italian immigrants and subsequently, on those of the following generations who continued to interact with American society from their unique ethnic perspective.

Italian-style entertainment was one of the numerous aspects of Italian culture that were transplanted to American shores as a result of mass migration. Almost immediately, comedy, in the form of entertainment, became a voice for Italian expression in the New World. Whether in the Italian American popular ethnic theater, Italian American vaudeville, amateur clubs, cafés (coffeehouses), feasts, or later, through modern media, comedy provided (and continues to serve as) an essential vehicle of emotional release for the immigrants and their descendants.

The first Italian American theater companies presented customary entertainment fare from the Old World, which always included a farce (perhaps an offering in the Neapolitan dialect by Pasquale Rapone). Most often, familiar figures performing in the commedia dell'arte tradition served as the agents of laughter. Italian American theater provided all-too-brief respites from the rigors of surviving in the New World, during which the immigrants were afforded opportunities to enjoy a chuckle on an elusive level of comfort, courtesy of *Pulcinella, Scaramuccia,* and *Pasquino.* However, as the immigrants and their humor began to adapt and evolve, the early, homegrown favorites were rapidly replaced by more germane comedic interpretations of an immigrant society adjusting to American life both in and out of the Little Italys.

One especially noteworthy figure, who helped to shape the stock character of the Americanized Italian, was the Neapolitan Eduardo Migliaccio (1892–1946), better known by his stage name, *Farfariello* (Little Butterfly). His comedy sketches (*macchiette*) were brilliant satires of social stereotypes, featuring a parade of clownish figures, modeled in exaggerated forms after denizens found in Little Italy. A quick-change artist of the highest caliber, Farfariello would sing and present a hilarious bit as one character—the undertaker, for example—then rush backstage and reappear, almost instantly, in another costume, perhaps as the anxious bride. He would then continue his performance in the new persona, repeating his skillful transformations as many as six times per show.

Farfariello's *macchiette* captured the essence of life in the Italian enclave, enabling his audiences to recognize and laugh at their own assimilation foibles and setbacks. His one-man cast of characters—from Pasquale Passaguai (Full of Troubles), singing *"Iammo a Cunnialando"* ("Let's Go To Coney Island"), to the iceman and his hapless antics—spoke directly to individual and collective spirits of the Italian American colonists. The relevant impact of his burlesquing was further heightened by crafty plays on words in Italian dialects, in the immigrant Italglish, and in the improper use of English by second-generation Italian Americans.

Another comedian who enjoyed great popularity among the immigrant community was Giovanni DeRosalia, creator of the character DeNofrio. A Sicilian caricature on the order of *Pulcinella* (without mask), DeNofrio was a *cafone* (half-wit) in shabby clothes and with large false nose. Through his farces such as "Millionaire Nofrio Marries Beautiful Peaches," "Nofrio Arrives en L'America," and "Nofrio at the Dentist," DeRosalia made wry observations and comical asides concerning the situations at hand, overturning the American world-taken-for-granted attitudes of those on stage and in the audience.

Other important comedians of the immigrant era were Aristide Sigismundi (father of pop singer Alan Dale), Giuseppe DeLaurentis, and Gennaro Amato, whose big hits "U Shoemaker" and "Glad to Meet You Paisan" were sung in the immigrants' broken English. Like Farfariello, Sigismundi was a *macchiettista,* who presented humorous sketches, such as the much-requested *"ll Morte Di Festa al Mulberry Street"* ("The Death of the

Mulberry Street Feast"), which parodied the harsh realities of life in Little Italy. He created the comic characters Frichino (a *buffo* type) and Don Peppe Rusacatore, and he sang such numbers as the 1920s hit "No Beer, No Work."

In the 1930s, along with Pasquale C.O.D. and the comedy team of Luigi Aguaglia and Angela DeAngelis (*I Cipudduzze*), Allesandro "Sandrino" Giglio, son of impresario Commandetore Clemente Giglio, performed in Italian for an Italian American audience. Because of his facial resemblance and attire (large eyeglasses, bow tie, wide pants, and short jacket), he became known as the "Italian Harold Lloyd." His routines were improvisational, employing ad-libbed plays on words and confusing misunderstandings between English and Italian sayings. Often working with his sister Adelina (called Perzechella in their skits), he performed at their own Giglio Theater, on the Italian American entertainment circuit, and on tour in Montreal, playing to Italian Canadian audiences. Among Giglio's best-known comedy songs were "Tony the Shoeshine Boy," "*Marito Sfortunato*" ("Unfortunate Husband"), "*Pasca O'mbbriacone*" ("Pasquale the Drunkard"), and "*L Avevo e L'Ho Perduta*" ("I Had Her and I Lost Her").

The period spanning the 1920s through the 1940s represented overlapping and transitional phases for comedians who appealed to the immigrant generation and those who were able to entertain more acculturated Italian American audiences. Spearheading the transition were such performers as Nicola Paone, Matteo Cannizzaro, and the team of Rocco DiRusso and Ria Sampieri (whose bits featured the Italian greenhorn and the Irish wife). Their group success stemmed from an ability to adapt—beyond catering to changing Italian American tastes and frames of reference—to evolving entertainment venues.

Throughout the 1930s and 1940s, the Italian American comedic tradition was carried on via Italian-language radio airways. New York's radio stations (WBNX, WEVD, WHOM, and WOV) presented daily offerings of humor as well as dramatic enactments that appealed to the ears of ethnic theatergoers and lovers of Italian American vaudeville. The proliferation of Italian-language radio stations—and ethnic programming in general—was not restricted to New York. Once its commercial advantages were substantiated,

the paradigm quickly mushroomed in every American city with a sizable Italian American population.

Humor, in any language, had always translated well on radio, and the Italian American brand of comedy was no exception. Boston's Biagio Farese, for example, kept listeners in stitches with episodes based on Italian folkloric tales and stories by Boccaccio concerning the age-old battle of the sexes. Updated story lines chronicled a modernized woman's struggle to win her reluctant immigrant husband over to contemporary American ways. Farese's characters spoke in various Italian dialects, increasing the possibilities for droll innuendo and comical misunderstandings, as each derived different meanings from the same words. By the 1950s, however, waning immigration and the advent of television made Italian-language programs and radio personalties like Farese obsolete.

Another avenue of expression for the new breed of Italian American comedians was the record industry. Victrolas and record collections were already part and parcel of the standard trappings in Italian American households. Artists cut records in Italian dialect or that switched between Italian and English. Recordings often made use of double entendre, confusion and misuse of language, male and female confrontations, and Old versus New World culture and value standards. In the vaudeville tradition, the songs and dialogues not only poked fun at the Americans and their foreign ways, they also satirized Italian newcomers who dealt with the immigrant experience by rejecting their roots and putting on airs that they were better than their *paesani* (fellow townsfolk).

In the 1940s Nicola Paone (b. 1915) stepped into the Italian American entertainment arena and, on stage, radio, and records, enriched its legacy with his monumental contributions. The composer and singer of many serious ballads—"*Uei Paesano*" ("Hey Townsman"), the Italian immigrants' anthem, and "*U Sciccaredu*" ("The Little Donkey")—he is the originator of countless novelty sings. Still performing on occasion today, and regardless of whether he is inspiring tears or laughter, Paone's appeal lies in his ability to speak to the hearts and souls of transplanted Italians with sensitive reflections on immigrant and ethnic life. His music dispels any need for Italian Americans to measure themselves against Anglo-Saxon standards of acceptability. Instead, a Paone audience receives emotional sustenance from its unique heritage and, in turn, revels in it.

Paone's voluminous songbook is filled with titles, such as "Betty, She Eat the Spaghetti," "Viola No Likea the *Bracciola*," and "Giuseppe Runs for President," that use humor to make pointed commentary. His comedic songs, sung in English, Italglish, Italian, and the Sicilian dialect, deal with the dual challenge of adjusting to an alien society while maintaining one's ethnic identity. "The Telephone Song," for example, typifies the exasperation of newly arrived (and even second-generation) Italians dealing with non-sympathetic Americans who are unable or unwilling to bridge language and cultural gaps. The much-requested "Tony the Iceman" lists Italian delicacies (in Italian American food-song tradition) and offers the immigrants' descendants a light-hearted glimpse at bygone days in the Little Italy of the 1930s. "The Bigga Professor" is yet another example of Paone's gentle satire in which a self-proclaimed *professore* is invited to teach broken English at an American university to those who wish to secure jobs (largely held by Italian Americans) as barbers or waiters.

An important contemporary of Paone, Matteo "Matty" Cannizzaro (1913–1998) began freelancing in the Italian variety theater circuit *(varietà)* during the early 1930s. By the mid-1930s, he was a *capo-comico* ("top banana"), performing throughout the New York metropolitan region. His career included shared billings with Italian performers like Domenico Modugno and Claudio Villa (on American tours) as well as Italian American headliners like Sal "Tuddi" Ferrara and Alan Dale. Cannizzaro continued in his vocation as a classic Italian American clown, joking around in three languages: Italian dialect, English, and pantomime. For the last twenty-five years, he traveled with an entertainment troupe that performed for East Coast Italian American audiences in theaters, at clubs and feasts, and most recently, at colleges, where young third- and fourth-generation Italian Americans, eager to reconnect with their roots, responded positively to the shows.

While Cannizzaro had updated some material to accommodate contemporary issues and sensibilities, he was the last comedian to perform Italian American comedy that dates back to the immigrant era. He worked in the *macchiettista* tradition, but with an American vaudeville flair. Dressed in a checkered jacket, with a large bow tie, ostentatious handkerchief, and constantly pummeled fedora, he incorporated hints of Pinky Lee, Milton Berle, and Red Skelton into his distinctly Italian American presentation. Cannizzaro alternated between humorous songs and stand-up bits, often ad-libbing with band members, the emcee, and the audience. On stage, his broad, slapstick comedy was highly visual, as he came to an abrupt, mid-song halt and then began to strut in a large circle, rolling his saucer eyes and smirking mischievously. At the clank of the drummer's cowbell, Cannizzaro executed a skidding stop, accentuated by a pelvic thrust and leg kick, before beginning his next round of stories, gags, and songs.

The musical component figures significantly in Cannizzaro's repertoire, which included such crowd-pleasers as *"T'e Piacuta?"* ("Did You Like It?") and *"Torna Pulcinella"* ("Pulcinella Returns"). Allegiance to the *macchiettista* format, which relies extensively on double entendre, is nicely illustrated in his song *"Margari Fammi Trasi"* ("Margari, Let Me In"), in which Mama's rule that no one can enter her daughter's bedchamber when the girl is in her bedclothes is circumvented by removal of the nightgown. In terms of content, Cannizzaro's comedy covered traditional Italian American themes of food, marriage, family, neighborhood, and the immigrant's perspective on the American dream. In one routine, Cannizzaro asked directions to the rest room in a large department store. A clerk pointed distractedly and muttered "escalator" to an agitated Matty, who cried, "Ask-a-later? I have to go now!" In another classic story, a man is decapitated in a serious auto accident. Upon discovering the head, aghast patrons of a local pastry shop are determined to identify it. "Could it be Don Vincenzo?" asks one. Another suggests consulting the barber, who would be familiar with the faces he shaves daily. The barber ends their speculation when he declares, "I don't think so; Don Vincenzo is much taller!"

While most of the earlier Italian American comedians were known primarily to Italian Americans, their successors began to incorporate nonethnic material into their acts in order to broaden their audience bases. Such was the case for Lou Monte (1917–1989), born Louis Scaglione to parents who had migrated from Calabria. His popular novelty songs were always replete with Italian sayings, images, and dialect, but many of his serious ballads featured English lyrics. Monte's career skyrocketed after he recorded an Italian and English version of "Darktown Strutter's Ball" in 1953. As he became more famous, he was invited to perform in many prominent nightclubs and, unlike the vast majority of his Italian American comedy contemporaries, he often appeared on national television. At the height of his popularity, Monte was promoted in various press releases as "The Godfather of Italian Humor" and "The King of Italian American Music." He is probably best remembered for his comedic songs, such as "Dominic the Donkey," "*Peppino U Suriciello*" ("The Italian Mouse"), "Italian Jingle Bells," and "Lazy Mary" *("C' Era Luna Mezza Mare"),* although his act included a good deal of stand-up comedy, usually performed in English with a liberal interspersion of Neapolitan and Calabrian dialects.

A crucial underpinning of Monte's Italian American humor, and its sociological impact, was his Italian Americanization of American history. His preposterous infusion of Italian Americans into their adopted country's early history actually served to make this marginal group feel more connected to the American psyche. Monte's malapropos layering of Italian American themes and stories onto concrete Anglo-Saxon domains, although comically absurd, strengthened Italian Americans' social footholds, from both internal and external standpoints. For example, according to the lyrics of one Monte song, when Washington crossed the Delaware he commented to his Indian guide, "*Fa Fridd*!" (It's cold!). To which the guide responded, "*Uei, puro tu sei italiano?*" ("Hey, are you Italian too?"). In yet another song, an Italian sailor aboard Columbus's ship pleads, "Turn the ship around." When the ship reaches land, the sailor is greeted by an Indian who asks, "*Hai portato un pezz' di pane?*" ("Did you bring a piece of bread?"). Again, the punch line is "*Uei, puro tu sei italiano?*"

Running concurrently with Monte's show business career was that of Louie Prima. Born in New Orleans, his humorous songs were heavily spiced with Italian dialect, Cajun slang, Creole colloquialism, and his own form of Italglish, southern style. Prima was the first Italian American musical clown to become popular in mainstream America. Many of the songs popularized by Prima captured the flavor of Italian American life and were embraced by members of both the Italian American and American audiences. Representative titles are "Josefina Please No Leana on the Bell," "Mari Yooch, She Walk the Pooch," "*Felicia No Capisca*" ("Felicia Doesn't Understand"), "My *Cuccuzza*" (squash), "Please No Squeeza the Banana," and "Baccigalup, He Makes Love on the Stoop."

Prima became a well-known entertainer (jazz performer, trumpet player, singer, and comedian), first throughout New Orleans and then later on a national level. With his trumpet playing and throaty vocalizing, reminiscent of Louis Armstrong (an entertainment idol of Prima's youth), almost immediately Prima's style found an eager audience. His combination of scat vocals, trumpet playing, innovative and fun arrangements, and madcap stage mayhem kept Prima in the entertainment spotlight for most of his fifty-year career.

In the 1950s Prima was a featured headliner throughout many Las Vegas casino nightclubs. Louie Prima's stage shows involved wild interaction with his fellow performers—band leader Sam Butera and band members—as well as with his audience. When he teamed with singer Keely Smith in the 1950s, their incongruous deliveries provided increased opportunities for outrageous exchanges. She played the deadpan recipient of Prima's onstage exuberance and comical mayhem. Their individual songs and duets were constantly interrupted by crazy, tangential dialogues, peppered with Italian dialect and phrases.

Prima was able to build upon his Italian American entertainment roots and succeeded in America's entertainment mainstream. He performed in movies, made numerous recordings, and was a regular television guest on the Ed Sullivan show. Prima's talents went beyond comedy. This is evident when, in 1938, Benny Goodman recorded Prima's composition of "Sing, Sing, Sing," securing Prima's preeminence as a jazzman. Yet Prima is best known for his contributions as a performer who had the ability to make people laugh at his humorous lyrics and comedy routines.

In the 1950s Pat Cooper (Pasquale Caputo) became a popular performer among Italian American as well as mainstream audiences, and his comedic style continues to hold strong. Cooper's stand-up comedy routines consist of recounting nostalgic and contemporary situations or stories of Italian American life. Cooper can always be counted on to include Italian dialect words, such as substituting the word *scarol* (escarole) for dollars and *schiafatoni* (smackers) for money. Or Cooper will get a laugh, especially with his Italian American audience, when he relates that Mafia spelled backwards is *afam* (hunger) and donuts spelled backwards is *stunard* (dunce). The foreign phrases, play on words, and one-liners sound funny to any receptive audience member, but they become especially meaningful "in-jokes" for Italian Americans.

Cooper's Italian American audiences recognize words, references, and characters that revive pleasant memories of former neighbors and erstwhile neighborhoods. His humorous narrations, such as "The Italian Wedding" and "My Genuine Italian Mother," accurately chronicle the intergenerational progression of Italians in America. For example, Italian regionalism, carried over to this country, is reflected in Cooper's story of his mother's reaction when he dated a Jewish girl. "Respect her for her beliefs and treat her like your sister," Mamma advises. When he goes out with a Polish girl, Mamma offers the same response. "Finally I'm seeing an Italian girl," exclaims Cooper, "and I can't wait to tell my mother because I know she'll be in ecstasy." When he introduces the two, Mamma's first question is, "What part of Italy are you from?"

Cooper's vignettes, with their special Italian American twist, strike a harmonious and a happy chord among those who share a common ethnic background. In one of Cooper's best-known illustrative examples, his father imparts a folkloric belief that if a man wishes to sire a male child, he should eat broccoli. "I ate broccoli for five years," grouses Cooper, "and finally had a son. He was green! We named him Andy Boy." While an at-large audience understands the punch lines, Italian Americans attach even deeper significance to the name of an Italian-owned produce company.

From the 1960s onward a fair number of Italian American comedians, like Cooper, have pointed out the humor in the everyday lives of their predominantly Italian American fans. Comics such as Lou "Baccala" Carey, Dom DeLuise, Joy Behar (Josephine Occhiuto), and Uncle Floyd (Floyd Vivino), for instance, continue, to varying degrees, in the tradition of Italian American humor as established by their immigrant forebears. However, these Italian American comics have up-dated their material so as to reflect more accurately the present state of Italian American life, taking into account changing generational and gender perspectives. While the trend for Italian American comedians is to entertain increasingly in non-Italian American venues, certain above-mentioned performers still incorporate many Italian American comedic references in their work, while others (such as Carey and Vivino) still perform to specifically Italian American audiences on a regular basis.

One important and distinctly modern Italian American comedian is Dom DeLuise. Early in his career, Dom DeLuise introduced his pantomime routine of the character "Dominic the Great" (a bungling Italian American magician), and to the present, Italian American subject matter runs consistently through his comedy, with its uniquely Italian American perspective on language, neighborhood, family, religion, and—the centerpiece of his comedic format—food. As a regular on television's popular *Dean Martin Show* of the 1970s, DeLuise engaged in a weekly banter with Dean Martin. The two Italian American entertainers featured, in dialect, double entendre about certain edibles—*cetriolo* (cucumber), *bracciola* (meat roll), and *cuccuzza* (squash)—that to Italian Americans have phallic connotations. Other bits by DeLuise discuss the merits of *polenta* for home repairs ("Patch the cracks, and later if you get hungry, you can lick the wall!"), wearing garlic necklaces to repel vampires, and how eating *pasta fagiole* (with beans) could come between a man and a woman.

A representative joke from Dom DeLuise's popular comedy cookbook (and follow-up videocassette series), *Eat This: It Will Make You Feel Better* (1988), demonstrates his use of Italian American tradition to make people laugh. He states: "Eggplant is to an Italian what sex is to a nymphomaniac. You can exist, but without it, what is the use of living?"

Dom DeLuise is not primarily a stand-up comedian; rather, he is a comedic character actor. He is at his best when he has a loosely knit story or script within which he is free to improvise and ad-lib. This format has served DeLuise well in his many comedic movie roles, television, and theater appearances.

Since the 1970s Floyd Vivino, and his Uncle Floyd television show and nightclub act, has been able to reach a substantial non-ethnic audience with material largely based on Italian American topics and themes. His, at times, anachronistic style of humor parallels the southern Italian commedia dell'arte, with its slapstick *lazzi* (improvised bits), and pays homage to the traditions of vaudeville and Italian puppetry. In addition to a pantomime segment of his act entitled *"Senza Parole"* ("Without Words"), Vivino's comedic repertoire includes a catalog of stock characters and hand puppets that are easily recognizable as Italian or Italian American, such as "Senator Stunata," a toga-wearing citizen of ancient Rome; "Don Goomba," a godfather type with unlimited money-making schemes; "Rocky Rock 'n' Roll," an Italian American greaser lost in the 1950s; "Pasquale the Pizzeria Man," who fights an ongoing battle of wits with an Irish beat cop; and "Mr. Tony," an Italian immigrant store owner who scolds, "Go wanna! Go wanna," as he chases the neighborhood kids.

Like the other comedians mentioned in this article, Vivino's delivery includes interjecting random Italian words and phrases throughout his act. A talented pianist and singer, his musical selections include a variety of Italian American titles, such as "Josefina Please No Leana on the Bell," "Angelina," "My *Cuccuzza*," and *"Felicia No Capisca"* ("Felicia Doesn't Understand"). Like Lou Monte, he has also been known to Italian Americanize classic songs such as his version of "The Twelve Days of Christmas," in which Vivino substitutes Italian foods (ziti, meatballs, mozzarella, sheep heads, and so forth) for the items delivered by "my true love" in the original song. According to Vivino, there was a thirteenth gift that, not surprisingly, was a bottle of Brioschi—the Italian American Alka Seltzer.

The significance of Uncle Floyd Vivino's success is the integration of the best of Italian American and American components in his comedy. Yet, as long as contemporary Italian American comics follow Vivino's lead of combining the two perspectives in their work, there is a future for Italian American humor. Future Italian American comedians will continue to draw, at least in part, upon those "insider" comedic references that are solely understood by their Italian American audiences. As long as a distinctive Italian American lifestyle continues, there will always be those Italian American comedians who will draw their inspiration, themes, and vignettes from this rich background and make their *paesani* laugh.

Salvatore Primeggia

Bibliography

Aleandri, Emelise, and Maxine Schwartz Seller. "Italian American Theatre." In *Ethnic Theatre in the United States,* edited by Maxine Schwartz Seller, 237–276. Westport, CT: Greenwood, 1983.

Gumina, Deanna Paoli. "Connazionali, Stentorello and Farfariello: Italian Variety Theatre in San Francisco." *California Historical Quarterly* 54 (1975): 29–36.

Primeggia, Salvatore, and Joseph A. Varacalli. "Pulcinella to Farfariello to Paone to Uncle Floyd: A Socio-Historical Perspective on Southern Italian and Italian American Comedy." *Eastern Community College Social Science Association Journal* 5 (1990): 45–54.

———. "Southern Italian Comedy: Old to New World." In *Italian Americans in Transition,* edited by Joseph V. Scelsa, Salvatore J. LaGumina, and Lydio Tomasi, 241–252. Staten Island: American Italian Historical Association, 1990.

Primeggia, Salvatore, Pamela Primeggia, and Joseph Bentivegna. "Nicola Paone: Narrator of the Italian American Experience." In *Italian Americans in a Multicultural Society,* edited by Jerome Krase and Judith N. DeSena, 89–106. Stony Brook: Forum Italicum, 1994.

Primeggia, Salvatore, Pamela Primeggia, and Joseph A. Varacalli. "Uncle Floyd Vivino: A Modern Italian American Comic." *New Jersey History* 2 (1989): 1–20.

Primeggia, Salvatore, Joseph A. Varacalli, and Floyd Vivino. "Southern Italian American Comedy: The Cases of Matteo Cannizzaro, Lou Monte, Louie Prima, and Dom DeLuise." In *Italian Americans and Their Public and Private Life,* edited by Frank J. Cavaioli, Angela Danzi, and Salvatore J. LaGumina, 194–211. Staten Island: American Italian Historical Association, 1993.

Sogliuzzo, Richard A. "Notes from the History of Italian American Theatre." *Theatre Survey* 14, no. 2 (1973): 59–75.

See also MIGLIACCIO, EDUARDO (FARFARIELLO); THEATER HISTORY

Community Issues

As southern Italians settled in the United States, they attempted to transplant their villages from Italy to America. In America many community organizations were formed, such as mutual-aid societies, social and athletic clubs, associations in honor of the patron saint of a particular town in Italy, and nonprofit corporations offering services to the community. Traditionally, these organizations assisted Italian immigrants in adjusting to life in a new country and offered a way to gather with one's *paesani* (fellow townsfolk). They also served as informal social service agencies, aiding neighbors who encountered the loss of a loved one and/or financial disaster. Even as Italian Americans become suburbanized, community organizations have remained the loci of communication among Italian Americans. Through them, traditions such as *la festa* (the feast) are displayed and transmitted to younger generations. Often Italian language courses are offered, and social services are provided. These organizations serve as a way for Italian Americans to connect with the community, to preserve the neighborhood, and to invent and maintain ethnicity. The ethnic village and neighborhood preservation continue to be of great importance to Italian Americans.

Because of the existence of numerous local institutions and community organizations, residents of older, usually inner-city, Italian American neighborhoods have been able to mobilize themselves against perceived threats to community well-being and diminished municipal services. It is typically women who organize community efforts, participate in local struggles, and attend meetings of church groups, block associations, and rallies related to neighborhood issues. Women usually set up meetings, mobilize resources, and alert elected officials and members of government agencies to local problems and development plans.

On an informal level, Italian American women are the "gatekeepers" of the neighborhood. They act as local surveillants or block watchers and take responsibility for the ongoing observation of street life. Women also maintain a local network in which they serve as informal brokers in the local housing market, renting available apartments and recruiting potential tenants. In the Italian American community, women are the rank and file of neighborhood activism and community preservation.

Traditional Italian American neighborhoods are very important to its members, creating camaraderie and a sense of belonging. Community members participate in local networks, organizations, and institutions and frequently speak Italian, or the regional dialects of their ancestors. The tightly knit, cohesive, and largely homogeneous neighborhoods have a positive influence on the society at large. Italian American neighborhoods are very important to the viability of cities. Italian American neighborhoods provide the local governments with employed taxpayers and lower crime and abandonment rates relative to other city neighborhoods. These neighborhoods tend to be stable over time and usually do not experience large shifts in population.

Yet a paradox exists regarding neighborhood preservation. In Italian American communities, a dilemma exists between preserving neighborhood stability and using exclusionary practices. For example, Italian American residents attempt to maintain a low crime rate, relative to other areas, in the neighborhoods in which they live. This is viewed as a positive characteristic and is done through active citizen participation, such as civilian patrols and block watchers. Another example is the maintenance of stable housing. Italian American neighborhoods are admired for their well-kept appearances, their quality of life, and their attempt to keep out criminals. A complication ensues when exclusionary practices, such as discrimination and vigilantism, are employed by Italian Americans as part of their strategies to achieve low crime rates and stable housing.

While most Italian Americans resided in ethnic neighborhoods during most of the twentieth century, this is no longer the case. Indeed, the stereotypical Italian neighborhood is now home to a distinct minority of the ethnic group.

Judith N. DeSena

Bibliography

DeSena, Judith N. "Community Co-operation and Activism: Italian and African Americans." In *Italian Americans: Their Public and Private Lives,* edited by Frank J. Cavaioli, Angela Danzi, and Salvatore J. LaGumina, 116–124. Staten Island: American Italian Historical Association, 1993.

———. "Defending One's Neighborhood At Any Cost?: The Case of Bensonhurst." In *A Century of Italian Immigration: The Lesson of the Past and Future of Ethnicity,* edited by Harral Landry, 177–190. Staten Island: American Italian Historical Association, 1994.

Reider, Jonathan. *Canarsie: The Jews and the Italians of Brooklyn Against Liberalism.* Cambridge: Harvard University Press, 1985.

———. "Women: The Gatekeepers of Urban Neighborhoods." *Journal of Urban Affairs* 16 (1994).

See also INTERGROUP RELATIONS: ITALIAN AMERICANS AND AFRICAN AMERICANS

Perry Como and Nancy Sinatra. The son of Italian immigrants, Como left his trade as a barber in Canonsburg, Pennsylvania, to become a ballad singer. A pleasant, likeable man with an endearing voice, his records were at the top of the popular charts for many years and continue to sell. His NBC television shows were among the most watched in the nation. Courtesy NBC.

Como, Perry (b. 1912)

This Italian American crooner with the deceptively relaxed manner wound up being "King of the Jukes" and a singing star of radio and television. Perry Como was born in Canonsburg, Pennsylvania, May 18, 1912. His parents migrated from Italy in the early 1900s. His father worked as a mill hand.

Baptized Pierino, Perry was one of thirteen children. He began working after school in a barber shop and, at age 21, owned his own shop. After six years he was hired as a singer by Freddy Carlone. He and his bride, the former Roselle Belline, toured with the band through the Midwest for three years.

Several years of singing for Ted Weems was followed by a CBS radio program offer. Ever the family man, Como accepted the latter only after being assured that he would be permitted to live in New York for the duration of the program.

He made his nightclub circuit debut at the highly popular Copacabana in New York City. Harriet Van Horne, radio critic for New York's *World Telegram,* considered him a refreshing improvement because he was "darkly handsome, pleasantly wholesome and mercifully unaffected. His voice is a clear, full-throated baritone and, when he sings, he appears to be suffering no pain at all."

In 1943 RCA Victor launched Como on what was to become another very successful facet of his career—recording. By the fall of 1946 he had become the first popular singer to achieve the two-million sales mark on two of his releases at the same time. His popularity in nightclubs, on radio, and on disc jockeys' play lists led to a Twentieth Century Fox seven-year contract.

Como became the idol of "bobby-soxers" in the post–World War II era and a leading record and television star in the Big Ballad era of the 1950s. After years as a band vocalist, he became a bigger star on television, hosting a weekly variety show from 1955 until 1963.

Between 1944 and 1958 Como had forty-two top hits on the *Billboard* charts. He continued to record, occasionally doing specials, guest spots, or commercials on television, and remained on the pop-music charts through 1973. He was inducted into the Hall of Fame, Academy of Television Arts and Sciences in 1990.

Margherita Marchione

Bibliography
Ebert, Alan. "Perry Como: His Song Goes On." *Good Housekeeping* 212 (January 1991): 70–75.

See also POP SINGERS; TELEVISION

Composers, Classical

The diverse styles of Italian American composers have enriched America's musical landscape with numerous influential and critically acclaimed works. If the range of composition methods makes their music hard to classify, their ethnicity, in some instances, enables us to distinguish their music from other American composers. Italy's long and rich musical tradition has had a significant impact on a selection of their work. Italian operas and other vocal music constitute their finest contributions to musical composition. Sacred works and religious themes are also outgrowths of some of these composers' closer ethnic influences.

A number of Italian composers settled in the United States during the nineteenth century. Filippo Trajetta (1777–1854), whose name was changed to Philip Traetta when he arrived in Boston in 1799, established American musical conservatories in Boston and Philadelphia. Predominantly a composer for the voice, Traetta wrote several oratorios and cantatas and distinguished himself by being the first Italian American composer in the new nation to write an opera, *The Venetian Maskers* (n.d.). The first opera to be based on an American text (James Fenimore Cooper's novel, *The Spy*), was *La Spia* (1856), which came from the pen of Luigi Arditi (1822–1903), who spent a good part of his life in the United States conducting operas. Another composer who based some of his operas on American themes was Francesco Fanciulli (1850–1915), who actually composed *The Voyage of Columbus* during his own journey to the United States in 1876. Better known for his marches, he succeeded John Philip Sousa in 1892 as the conductor of the U.S. Marine Band in Washington, D.C.

Two immigrant composers continued the grand opera tradition into the twentieth century. They were Pietro Floridia (1860–1932), who composed the first city-commissioned opera, *Paoletta,* which was successfully produced in Cincinnati in 1910, and Alberto Bimboni, who effectively incorporated Native American music into his own opera, *Winona* (1926); he later taught at the Opera Department of the Juilliard School of Music. A second-generation Italian American, Vittorio Giannini (1903–1966), carried on the tradition of Italian opera with twelve of his own, emphasizing fine melodic lines, which endeared him to both American singers and audiences. *The Taming of the Shrew* (1952), his most successful opera, reached a sizable audience when it was produced by NBC Opera Theater for national television in 1954. Though critics praised the insouciant score for its "poignant Italianate melodies" and spright ensemble numbers written in the fashion of opera buffa and Verdi's *Falstaff* (1893), Giannini's music, which also includes instrumental works, avoids contemporary usages of dissonance and other modernistic traits.

Gian Carlo Menotti, who was born in Italy in 1911 but at age 17 took up residence in the United States, was the first composer to write American operas that gained permanent repertoire status. In fact, his music has reached a larger audience than any opera composer of the twentieth century. Very much influenced by the great operas of Verdi and Puccini, Menotti continued to emphasize the expressive vocal line. At the same time he also incorporated atonality and polytonality, thereby propelling Italian American opera into the twentieth-century musical styles.

Writing his own librettos, Menotti chose eternal themes of human conflict and placed them in topical settings. Considered by many to be his greatest work, *The Consul* effectively deals with a repressive police state. This Pulitzer Prize winner for music in 1950 was successfully produced for the Broadway stage for eight months, a run that exceeded the first opera productions ever presented for an extended Broadway run—Menotti's own earlier double bill of *The Medium* and *The Telephone* (1947). *The Saint of Bleecker Street,* which won another Pulitzer for its Broadway run in 1955, was Menotti's first opera set in a classic Little Italy of contemporary America. The high tension of the drama, which deals with the conflict between the physical and spiritual worlds, is captured in a gripping score. No opera has been seen by more people than the composer's religious fable, *Amahl and the Night Visitors,* which was commissioned for television by NBC and first presented on Christmas Eve in 1951.

Menotti amassed an impressive list of some twenty opera premieres. Though his nontheatrical works, most notably the *Piano Concerto* (1945) and *Violin Concerto* (1952), have received less recognition, they include passages of rare melodic and harmonic richness. A man of broad talents, Menotti founded the Festival of Two Worlds at Spoleto, Italy, in 1958 and its American companion at Charleston, South Carolina, in 1977, attracting visitors from all over the world each summer to performances of contemporary music and new productions of established works.

No Italian American composer could rival Menotti's operatic successes, but other composers of his generation were writing orchestral, chamber, instrumental, and choral music that was both inventive and critically acclaimed. Mario Castelnuovo-Tedesco (1895–1968) wrote his most evocative compositions while he was living in his native Italy during and immediately after World War I, and his guitar concertos and solos stemming from his settlement in America in 1939 are among the most beautifully rhapsodic and frequently performed works. Like other political refugee composers and filmmakers at the time, Castelnuovo-Tedesco moved to the West Coast. There he composed many first-rate film scores for Hollywood studios.

Among the major composers who embraced more modern methods of composition in this country were Italian Americans Walter Piston (1894–1976), Paul Creston (1906–1985), Norman Dello Joio (b. 1913), Peter Mennin (1923–1983), and Vincent Persichetti (1915–1987).

Piston, whose family name was originally Pistone, wrote music that spanned a wide realm of moods—from the furiously energetic to the ruminatively introspective. His most popular work was the sprightly suite to his ballet, *The Incredible Flutist* (1938), but his greatest achievements were his eight symphonies (1937–1965). Though much of his work shows an affinity for neoclassicism and the enormous impact Igor Stravinsky (1882–1971) had on many American composers, toward the end of his life, he was also influenced by Arnold Schoenberg's (1874–1951) cacophonic twelve-tone music.

Creston's Sicilian parentage (his birth name was Giuseppe Guttiveigi) instilled in him a love for Italian folk songs, and through-out his one hundred symphonic compositions, the composer never waivered in his commitment to lyricism. Though he was never considered a revolutionary, Creston composed in a harmonic and rhythmic idiom that was quite complex. He showed his affinity to Catholicism in several of his works. His *Symphony No. 3* (1950), for example, is subtitled *The Three Mysteries;* in this composition Creston uses Gregorian chants to describe the Nativity, Crucifixion, and Resurrection.

As a descendant of three generations of Italian organists and an organist and choir director himself at the early age of 14, Dello Joio wrote compositions that were heavily influenced by church music. Among these are his *Magnificat* (1942) and Pulitzer Prize–winning *Meditations on Ecclesiastes* (1957). This highly effective composer's handling of the Joan of Arc story took several operatic and symphonic forms, all of which contain liturgical music and some of the lyrical and dramatic elements influenced by Verdi and Puccini. Initially successful as a neoclassicist very much influenced by the craftsmanship and modern style of Paul Hindemith (1895–1963), Dello Joio later composed music that is extroverted, colorful, and of vast lyrical beauty.

Peter Mennin (who dropped the *i* from the family name, unlike his lesser-known composer brother, Louis) followed neither the more conservative trends of twentieth-century American music nor the progressive methods of the post–World War II period. Predominately a symphonist (although he did write some choral and chamber music), Mennin's nine symphonies (1941–1981) are marked by a nervous energy that attenuates into periods of solemn reflection. In 1962 he was appointed to the prestigious post of president of the Juilliard School of Music, where he established its Theater Center, American Opera Center, and Contemporary Music Festival.

Another composer who began his career as a church organist was Vincent Persichetti. A prolific composer of almost all genres, his works for wind band are often overlooked. His compositions have given musicians a contemporary yet accessible repertoire to perform. Like Piston, Creston, and Mennin, Persichetti clearly emerges at mid-century as one of America's chief symphonists. His aesthetic is for the most part conservative; yet he successfully fuses the seemingly incompatible idioms of classicism, romanticism, and austere modernism into his compositions. In some of his works Persichetti uses melodic lines that maintain a kind of Italianate lyricism set against a complex atonal polyphony. During the last year of his life, while he was dying from lung cancer, Persichetti returned to liturgical music. His last opus is *Hymns and Responses for the Church Year,* Vol. II (1987).

The next generation of Italian American composers, who emerged after World War II, were influenced by the predominant trends in composition. Salvatore Martirano (b. 1927) followed dodecaphonic principles until the late 1950s, a style represented by his *Mass for Double Chorus* (1952–1955). By 1958, like many other composers of his generation, he began to fuse elements of jazz and popular music into his works. During the 1960s, while at the University of Illinois, Martirano became one of the first to employ computers in his music. His later works use a wide variety of media, placing him firmly in the avant-garde.

Donald Martino (b. 1931) is one of the most highly acclaimed postwar twelve-tone composers. Not to be restricted by the astringent methods of serialism, his modified use of the twelve-tone row has produced music of dramatic imagination and expressive lyricism. His Pulitzer Prize–winning composition, *Notturno* (1974), a chamber piece written for flute, clarinet, violin, cello, and piano, is a truly romantic work, which, according to one critic, projects "nocturnal theater of the soul." Not straying far from his Italian roots, Martino was equally effective in writing choral music. The *Paradiso Choruses* (1974), which uses texts from *The Divine Comedy,* is a static hymn of praise. The music is lush, dense, and complex.

In the last three decades, many composers have recoiled from some of the modern trends of the postwar era and have returned to conservative styles like neoromanticism. Italian American composers have played an important role in these movements, and a number of their works have been acclaimed by critics and audiences alike.

Domenick Argento (b. 1927) has displayed an unusual songfulness in his writing for the voice and a Verdian respect for the demands of good theater in composing opera. "The voice is our representative of humanity," observes the composer, and all his vocal writing echoes his belief that instruments are essen-tially imitators of the voice. As founder of the Center Opera in Minnesota, later renamed the Minnesota Opera, Argento was able to supervise the production of his own operas, which now number nine. Both *The Voyage of Edgar Allan Poe* (1976) and *Casanova's Homecoming* (1985) have been hailed as major American operatic achievements. Argento's intrinsic lyricism extends to his orchestral works as well, but it is his vocal compositions that have earned him the greatest acclaim. He was awarded the Pulitzer Prize in 1975 for his song cycle, *From the Diary of Virginia Woolf,* which combines eight excerpts from Woolf's diaries with a variety of musical styles that follow her life to the brink of suicide.

Thomas Pasatieri (b. 1945), who had written fifteen operas by age 33, is perhaps the most prolific purveyor of Italian American opera today. Like Italian bel canto composers of the nineteenth century, Pasatieri writes operas tailored for specific singers, indulging his pieces with soaring lyrical passages. With libretti often drawn from literary masterpieces, his operas all deal with heartrending characters caught up in strong theatrical situations. These works include *Black Widow* (1972), *The Seagull* (1974), *Washington Square* (1976), and *Three Sisters* (1979).

Another composer whose specialty is writing for the voice (particularly for soprano) is David Del Tredici (b. 1937). Almost all of his music prior to 1968 employs post-Webernian serialism, which includes *I Hear an Army,* for soprano and string quartet (1964) and *Night Conjure* (1966), for soprano, mezzo-soprano, woodwind septet, and string quartet. Both works use the novel language of James Joyce as texts. Del Tredici's style changed radically when he turned his attention to Lewis Carroll's *Alice's Adventures in Wonderland* and *Through the Looking Glass.* In utter defiance of all modernistic practices, the "Alice" pieces return to unabashed romanticism, becoming more melodic and harmonic with each consequent portrait of Alice. *Final Alice,* commissioned for the American bicentennial and performed by eight major orchestras, has become a bona fide contemporary warhorse. A recording of the piece went straight to the top of the classical charts in 1981 and still remains a consistent seller. The eighth portrait of "Alice," *Child Alice (In Memory of a Summer Day),* won the Pulitzer Prize in 1980.

C

Another composer who writes in an accessible style and is currently regarded as one of America's finest creators is John Corigliano (b. 1938). Most of his scores, which mix avant-garde effects and neoromanticism, contain strong theatrical elements. His *Symphony No. 1,* which memorializes the victims of AIDS, moved listeners to tears when it was first performed in Chicago in 1990. A recording of the piece was met with both critical and popular acclaim and rose near to the top of best-selling classical CDs. Corigliano's concertos, especially the *Oboe Concerto* (1975) and *Clarinet Concerto* (1977), had already gained earlier recognition for their virtuosity and polished craftsmanship. The score for the film *Altered States* (1981) and a composition written for the internationally renowned flutist James Galway, *Pied Piper Fantasy* (1982), made this composer even more renowned.

Corigliano's greatest success came with the Metropolitan Opera premiere of his grand opera buffa, *The Ghosts of Versailles* (1991). Based on the third play of Beaumarchais's trilogy, it follows the fortunes of Figaro some twenty years after the events of Mozart's *Le nozze di Figaro* (*The Marriage of Figaro,* 1786). This musical evocation of a lost world (Mozart's earlier masterpiece and Rossini's most popular opera, *Il barbieri di Siviglia* [*The Barber of Seville,* 1816], are quoted throughout) became an immediate hit and quickly sold out its remaining performances.

The Ghosts of Versailles was the first new work performed by the Metropolitan Opera in nearly twenty-five years (especially commissioned for the company's centennial celebration), and it came from the pen of an Italian American. These composers have been successfully writing different styles of music for all types of ensembles for two centuries. Their most splendid selections of music incorporate the diverse musical influences from America with the rich musical traditions from Italy.

Geoffrey S. Cahn

Bibliography

Chase, Gilbert. *America's Music: From the Pilgrims to the Present.* Urbana: University of Illinois Press, 1987.

Gruen, John. *Menotti: A Biography.* New York: Macmillan, 1978.

Tawa, Nicholas. *A Sound of Strangers: Musical Culture, Acculturation, and the Post–Civil War Ethnic American.* Metuchen, NJ: Scarecrow, 1982.

See also COMPOSERS, POPULAR MUSIC; MENOTTI, GIAN CARLO; OPERA; PISTON JR., WALTER (HAMOR)

Composers, Popular Music

Prominent Italian American composers of popular songs have not been numerous, but their works constitute some of the most recognized tunes and theme songs in the twentieth century. For example, Vince Guaraldi, born Vincent Anthony Guaraldi in San Francisco in 1928, is hardly a household name to the average American, although his music has been hummed by generations. The nephew of bandleader Muzzy Marcellino and an accomplished jazz pianist, Guaraldi wrote original jazz themes for the various "Peanuts" television specials and feature films, including Christmas tunes that have become an integral part of holiday celebrations. America's most beloved cartoon characters have several times danced and cavorted to Guaraldi's lively and attractive melodies before mass audiences.

On the other hand, Henry Mancini (1924–1994), born in Cleveland, Ohio, is quite familiar to the American public. Like Guaraldi, he effectively composed in the medium of jazz, creating the dramatic and rugged theme for the television series *Peter Gunn* (1958–1961) and the pseudo-mysterious theme for the 1964 film *The Pink Panther* and its sequels. Mancini also wrote the more reflective theme for the television series *Mr. Lucky* (1959–1960) and the theme for the 1983 television serial *The Thorn Birds.* Although a number of his film and television theme songs have become popular classics, it was in other songwriting genres that Mancini became the most successful and the best connected. He wrote three outstanding songs with lyricist Johnny Mercer (1909–1976). Mancini and Mercer's "Moon River," introduced in the 1961 movie *Breakfast at Tiffany's,* has become a frequently recorded romantic classic and won an Academy Award and two Grammys. "Days of Wine and Roses," which Mancini and Mercer wrote for the 1960 movie of the same name, also won an Academy Award and two Grammys. Mercer and Mancini also collaborated on "Moment to Moment" (1966), "The Sweetheart

Tree" (1965), and "Charade," written for the 1963 film of that name. In addition, Mancini wrote some other noteworthy songs, including the playfully instrumental "Baby Elephant Walk" (1962), plus "Wait Until Dark" (1968) and "Dear Heart" (1964), both with Ray Evans and Jay Livingston. He also created over seventy film scores, including *The Glenn Miller Story* (1954), which honored the legendary bandleader.

Other Italian American musical connections with Glenn Miller were Glen Gray and Frankie Carle. Gray (1915–1976), born Generoso Graziano in Boston, was a top arranger with Miller and helped lead the Glenn Miller Orchestra after Miller's untimely death in December 1944. He wrote the melodies for two of the more famous numbers in the Miller repertory, "A String of Pearls" (1942, lyricist Eddie DeLange) and "Pennsylvania 6-5000" (1939, lyricist Carl Sigman). Another Miller favorite, "Sunrise Serenade" (1939), was written by lyricist Jack Lawrence and composer Frankie Carle. Born in Providence, Rhode Island, under the name Francisco Nunzio Carlone, Carle (b. 1903) was a notable bandleader. He composed "Falling Leaves" (1940, lyricist Mack David) and "Carle Boogie" (1945).

Another popular big band tune, "You Made Me Love You," was composed by Italian American musician James V. Monaco (1885–1945), who created it in 1913 with accomplished lyricist Joseph McCarthy (1885–1943) (not the infamous Communist-hunting senator from Wisconsin). Monaco, also known as Jimmy Monaco, was born in Genoa, Italy, and came to the United States at age 6. After working as a pianist in nightclubs, he started on a career in composition. In addition to the 1913 classic, Monaco and McCarthy created the 1914 novelty "Shave and a Haircut, Bay Rum," which was revived in 1939 and provided the melody for the advertising jingle "You'll Get a Kick Out of Kix." With a later collaborator, lyricist Johnny Burke (1908–1964), Monaco wrote a number of other songs including "An Apple for the Teacher" (1939), "April Played the Fiddle" (1940), "East Side of Heaven" (1939), "Go Fly a Kite (1939), "Hang Your Heart on a Hickory Limb" (1939), "My Heart Is Taking Lessons" (1937), "On the Sentimental Side" (1937), "Only Forever" (1940), "(I've Got a) Pocketful of Dreams" (1938), "Rhythm on the River" (1940),

"Sweet Potato Piper" (1940), "That's for Me" (1941), and "Too Romantic" (1940). "Pocketful of Dreams" was one of the top numbers of notable bandleader Russ Morgan.

Another famous bandleader, trumpet player Ray Anthony, took the 1950s by storm. Born Raymond Antonini in Bentleyville, Pennsylvania, in 1922, Anthony's orchestra had smash hits in 1951 with "The Bunny Hop" and in 1953 with "The Hokey Pokey," two big dance crazes. "Bunny" was written in 1951 by Anthony and Leonard Auletti, and "Hokey" around 1948 by Larry LaPrise, Charles P. Macak, and Tafft Baker.

Famous bandleader Guy Lombardo (1902–1977) was born Gaetano Alberto Lombardo in London, Ontario. Legendary Lombardo led his Royal Canadians for many years, primarily in the United States. Helping to make the Lombardo ensemble the most influential of the sweet bands was Guy's brother, Carmen Lombardo (1902–1971). Carmen was a notable composer of the big band era, creating one of the theme songs for his brother's orchestra, "Coquette" (1928), with co-composer Johnny Green and lyricist Gus Kahn. Carmen also created "Boo Hoo" (1937) with Edward Heyman and John Jacob Loeb; "Get Out Those Old Records" (1951), "Seems Like Old Times" (1945), the longtime theme of radio and television personality Arthur Godfrey, and "Sailboat in the Moonlight" (1937), all three with Loeb; "The Sweetest Music This Side of Heaven" (1934) with Cliff Friend; "Sweethearts on Parade" (1928), lyrics by Charles Newman; "Return to Me" (1958), lyrics by Danny DiNinno; "Snuggled on Your Shoulder, Cuddled in Your Arms" (1932), lyrics by Joe Young; and "Powder Your Face with Sunshine" (1949) with Stanley Rochinski.

Almost as famous as Henry Mancini, and also connected with Johnny Mercer and Glenn Miller, was the outstanding big band and film score composer Harry Warren (1893–1981). Born Salvatore Guaragna in Brooklyn, New York, Warren played piano and accordion, joined a touring carnival while in his teens, and served in the United States Navy in World War I before turning to composition. He wrote standards and classics with four noted lyricists: Mort Dixon (1892–1956), Al Dubin (1881–1945), Mack Gordon (1904–1959), and Mercer. With Dixon he wrote "Would You Like to Take a Walk?" (1930), co-lyricist Billy Rose;

"I Found a Million Dollar Baby" (1931), co-lyricist Rose; and "You're My Everything" (1931), co-lyricist Joe Young. With Dubin he wrote "You're Getting to Be a Habit with Me" (1932), "Shuffle Off to Buffalo" (1932), the enduring "We're in the Money" (1933), "I Only Have Eyes for You" (1934), "Lulu's Back in Town" (1935), the classic "Lullaby of Broadway" (1935), which won an Academy Award for its appearance in the film *Gold Diggers of Broadway,* and "Love Is Where You Find It" (1938), with co-lyricist Mercer. With Gordon he wrote the classics "Chattanooga Choo Choo" (1941), "I've Got a Gal in Kalamazoo" (1942), and "Serenade in Blue" (1942), all three favorites of the Glenn Miller Orchestra, plus "You'll Never Know" (1943). With Mercer he wrote "Jeepers Creepers" (1938), "You Must Have Been a Beautiful Baby" (1938), and another Academy Award winner, "On the Atchison, Topeka, and the Santa Fe." The last song was magnificently rendered by Judy Garland in the 1946 film *The Harvey Girls.* Garland's daughter, Liza Minnelli, born in Hollywood that same year, has often performed the same old-fashioned songs as her famous mother, showing that the hit tunes of old, many composed by Italian Americans, still have an audience.

William E. Studwell

Bibliography

Lax, Roger, and Frederick Smith. *The Great Song Thesaurus.* 2nd ed., updated and expanded. New York: Oxford University Press, 1989.

Studwell, William E., and Mark Baldin. *The Big Band Reader.* New York: Haworth, 1998.

———. "The Complex Web of Composition: American Popular Songwriting Teams of the 20th Century." *Music Reference Services Quarterly* 5, no. 2 (1996): 1–24.

———. *The Popular Song Reader.* New York: Haworth, 1994.

See also COMO, PERRY; JAZZ; POP SINGERS; SINATRA, FRANCIS ALBERT

Consolazio, William V.
See SCIENCE

Conte, Richard
See MOVIE ACTORS AND ACTRESSES

Conte, Silvio O. (1921–1991)

United States representative from Massachusetts and a liberal voice in the Republican Party, Silvio Ottavio Conte was a defender of the nation's neediest. The son of Ottavio and Lucia (Lora) Conte, immigrants from northern Italy, Silvio was born in Pittsfield, Massachusetts. Growing up in Lakewood, the Italian area of his native city, Conte went to public schools and graduated from Pittsfield Vocational High School in 1940. He was employed by the General Electric Company and, later, by the *Berkshire Eagle* before he enlisted in the Seabees and served in the Pacific between 1942 and 1944. Qualifying for the G.I. Bill of Rights, he attended Boston College, graduating from its law school in 1949. Meanwhile, he married Corinne L. Duval in 1947, and together they had three daughters and one son.

Denied a job as a census taker by the Democrats, thereby experiencing the saying in Massachusetts politics that "Gaelic (Irish) and Garlic (Italian) don't mix," Conte became a Republican and was elected to the Massachusetts State Senate in 1950, serving there for four terms until 1958. His record reflected a concern for the blue as well as the white collar worker. He was responsible for the state law granting accident and health insurance coverage to government employees. Conte defeated Professor James MacGregor Burns of Williams College, a close friend of then Senator John F. Kennedy, for the seat of the First Congressional District of Massachusetts in 1958.

For the next thirty-two years, Conte forged a legislative record that was the product of his hard work in committees and on the floor of the United States Congress as he became the ranking Republican on the important House Committee on Appropriations. He is remembered for writing the 1970 legislation preserving passenger rail service (Amtrak) and for co-sponsoring the original law providing massive funds for AIDS research. His voting record on agriculture, defense, energy, labor, trade, and welfare won approval from the Americans for Democratic Action, a liberal group. While he fought tirelessly against wasting federal funds by repre-

sentatives in their districts, Conte construc-
tively and generously aided his own constituency, especially in education, the environment, and health and human services,
including developmental disabilities. In foreign affairs Conte proved a loyal assistant to
eight presidents. A World War II veteran,
Conte had the integrity to confess that he
was wrong in supporting the Gulf of Tonkin
Resolution in 1964, and he refused to support a Republican president in waging the
Gulf War against Iraq in 1991.

Conte died February 8, 1991, in Bethesda,
Maryland. He is buried in St. Joseph's Cemetery
in Pittsfield. An Italian American who made a
difference, he is memorialized in the Conte
Forum at Boston College, the Silvio O. Conte
National Archives and Records Center in Pitts-
field, and the Silvio O. Conte National Fish and
Wildlife Refuge on the Connecticut River.

Vincent A. Lapomarda

Bibliography

Lynch, Peter E. *Silvio: Congressman for Every-
one.* Sante Fe: Sunstone Press, 1997.
Ralph Nader Congress Project. *Silvio O.
Conte, Republican Representative from
Massachusetts.* Washington, D.C.:
Grossman, 1972.
United States Congress. *Memorial Tributes
and Services, Silvio O. Conte,
1921–1991.* Washington, D.C.: United
States Government Printing Office, 1993.
University of Massachusetts, *The Guide to
the Silvio O. Conte Congressional Pa-
pers, 1950–1991.* Amherst: W.E.B. Du
Bois Library, 1995.

See also POLITICS

Cooper, Pat
See COMEDY

Coppini, Pompeo (1870–1957)
Noted Texan sculptor, Pompeo Coppini was
born in Tuscany, graduated from the Accademia di Belle Arti in Florence, migrated to New
York in 1896, and opened a studio there. He
relocated to Texas in 1901 and settled permanently in San Antonio. His monuments
throughout Texas are remnants of his creative
work that spanned over more than four
decades.

C

His works include the following: the five
statues comprising the Confederate monument at Austin; an equestrian statue honoring
Terry's Texas Rangers; the monument of President Rufus S. Burleson of Baylor; the Governor Sul Ross memorial on the campus of
Texas A&M; the monument at Sam Houston's Tomb in Huntsville; the Texas Heroes'
memorial at Gonzales; a series of statues at
the Hall of Heroes in Dallas; and the remarkable Alamo Cenotaph in San Antonio. He also
executed the James P. Clarke marble statue in
the Hall of Columns in the United States
Capitol building.

Coppini's Alamo Cenotaph has received
considerable praise and attention thoughout
the world. This memorial to the dead (but not
containing the remains) is constructed of
Georgia gray marble and rests on a Texas
pink granite slab base. The shaft is 60 feet
high, with a base 40 feet long and 12 feet
wide. The monument's theme reflects the sacrifice made for Texan independence, which is
specifically depicted in the heroic statues of
Jim Bowie, James Bonham, Davy Crockett,
and William Travis.

From 1942 to 1945, Coppini was chairman of the art department at Trinity University. He died in 1957 and is buried in San
Antonio.

Frank J. Cavaioli

Bibliography

Belfiglio, Valentine. *The Italian Experience in
Texas.* Austin: Eakin, 1983.
Soria, Regina. "Early Italian Sculptors in the
United States." *Italian Americana* 2
(spring 1976): 171–189.

See also ART; TEXAS

Coppola, Francis Ford (b. 1939)
Director, producer, screenwriter, and winemaker, Francis Ford Coppola has provided
motion picture audiences with almost every
conceivable cinematic genre, and his reputation is firmly established as one of Hollywood's most famous and controversial filmmakers. Coppola was born on April 7, 1939,
in Detroit, Michigan. His mother, Italia, had
been an actress, and his father, Carmine, a
musician and composer; both were the children of southern Italian immigrants. When he
was nine years old, Coppola contracted polio

and remained partially paralyzed for almost a year, during which time he entertained himself with a film projector and tape recorder, trying to create his first "soundtrack." Coppola received a bachelor's degree in theater arts from Hofstra University in Hempstead, Long Island, 1959, and a master's degree in fine arts from UCLA, 1967, becoming one of the first Hollywood directors to have graduated from film school.

Coppola got his professional start making nudie comedies and worked as a production assistant to Roger Corman in the early 1960s. *Dementia 13* (1963), a horror film about an ax murderer, was Coppola's first feature-length film. He followed this project with the romance *You're a Big Boy Now* (1967), which he submitted as his master's thesis. He next directed the unsuccessful musical *Finian's Rainbow* (1968), starring Fred Astaire, and the drama *The Rain People* (1969). Also in 1969 Coppola founded American Zoetrope Studios in San Francisco. Coppola unexpectedly won his first Academy Award in 1970 for screenwriting *Patton,* but *The Godfather* (1972), based on the novel by Mario Puzo, established him as a major directorial figure, winning Oscars for best picture, actor (Marlon Brando), and screenplay, and a nomination for best director.

Continued success followed: his next film, *The Conversation* (1974), took the Palme d'Or at Cannes. *The Godfather, Part II* (1974) won six Academy Awards, including best picture and director; *Apocalypse Now* (1979), legendary for its extreme working conditions on location in the Philippines, received three Oscars and the Palme d'Or. Coppola's more recent work has not matched the positive critical reception granted him during the 1970s. His many later projects include *The Outsiders* (1983), *The Cotton Club* (1984), *Peggy Sue Got Married* (1986), *Tucker: The Man and His Dream* (1988), *The Godfather, Part III* (1990), *Bram Stoker's Dracula* (1992), and *Jack* (1996).

Throughout his career, Coppola has enthusiastically experimented with new developments in filmmaking technology with varying degrees of success. His films have also helped to launch the careers of many acclaimed actors, including Robert De Niro, Al Pacino, Nicolas Cage, and Tom Cruise. Members of Coppola's family have frequently participated in his projects; footage shot by his wife Eleanor became *Hearts of Darkness* (1991), a documentary about the making of *Apocalypse Now.* Screenwriting *The Great Gatsby* (1974), producing *American Graffiti* (1973), and serving as international producer for Akira Kurosawa's *Kagemusha* all figure among Coppola's many other credits. American Zoetrope distributed such experimental films as *Koyaanisqatsi* (1982) and originally rereleased Abel Gance's restored 1927 classic *Napoleon.* In 1985 Niebaum-Coppola wineries introduced their California Rubicon to favorable reviews.

Camille Cauti

Bibliography

Cowie, Peter. *Coppola.* London: Andre Deutsch, 1989.

Lewis, Jon. *Whom God Wishes to Destroy—: Francis Coppola and the New Hollywood.* Durham, NC: Duke University Press, 1995.

Lourdeaux, Lee. *Italian and Irish Filmmakers in America: Ford, Capra, Coppola, and Scorsese.* Philadelphia: Temple University Press, 1990.

See also FILM DIRECTORS, PRODUCERS, AND ITALIAN AMERICAN IMAGE IN CINEMA

Cordiferro, Riccardo (Alessandro Sisca) (1875–1940)

Poet, lyricist, journalist, editor, satirist, lecturer, and political activist, Riccardo Cordiferro was born Alessandro Sisca on October 27, 1875, in San Pietro, Guarano, in the province of Cosenza. In 1886 Alessandro entered the Franciscan seminary San Raffaele a Materdei in Naples, but left the religious life for a career in letters. In Naples his early poetry was published under the pen name of Riccardo Cordiferro. Although in later years he briefly used other pseudonyms (Corazon de hierro, Ironheart, Eisenberg, Sandro, Ida Florenza) for political and personal reasons, Cordiferro (which means "heart of iron") all but supplanted his real name in the literature and politics of this period.

In 1892 he immigrated to Pittsburgh and later settled permanently in New York City. In January 1893, together with his father, Francesco, and brother, Marziale, he founded a weekly literary newspaper, *La Follia,* at 202 Grand Street. The paper was widely read not only in New York City, but by the *literati* of the Italian colonies in the major cities of the East. His literary articles, editorials, and political commentary usually expounded socialist doctrine. He gave speeches to labor organizations and at political rallies, a practice that sometimes landed him in jail. Threats and persecutions led to his resignation from *La Follia*'s editorial board, although under various pseudonyms he continued to publish in the paper and in other publications, such as *La Notizia,* the *Haarlemite,* and *La Sedia Elettrica,* the weekly paper of which he later became editor. His three-act comedy in martellian verse, *Chi ha la testa di vetro non vade a battaglia di sassi* (If you can't take the heat, stay out of the kitchen), published in 1900 in *La Sedia Elettrica,* satirizes the tendency on the part of the amateur theater groups to undertake productions of plays beyond their capabilities. A professional theater company, the Maiori-Rapone-Ricciardi troupe, produced Cordiferro's first plays in the nineteenth century: *Mbruoglie 'e femme* (Feminine intrigues, 1893), a one-act comedy in the Neapolitan dialect, staged in 1894, and *Il genio incompreso* (The misunderstood genius), a one-act satirical comedy in verse portraying immigrant theater companies, staged in 1894. Dramatic social monologues were recited in 1895: "*Per la Patria e per l'onore*" (For the Fatherland and for honor), and "*Il Pezzente*" (The beggar). Cordiferro produced in 1896 a one-act satirical comedy in martellian verse, *Dio Dollaro* (Mammon) and the one-act comedy *Il matrimonio in trappola* (The marriage trap) in 1897. In the same year, Codiferro wrote a three-act social drama, *Da volontario a disertore* (From volunteer to deserter).

In 1897 and 1898 Cordiferro's first wife, Annina Belli, and their two children, Emilia and Franchino, died. He married Lucia Fazio in 1899. A full-length three-act social drama followed: *La vittima* (The victim). Another social drama in four acts, *L'onore perduto* (Lost honor) was adapted from his poem of the same name and depicts the exploitation of Italian immigrants in Little Italy, New York. The play premiered in 1901 and was produced by many other companies until 1933. Its sequel, another four-act social drama entitled *Giuseppina Terranova ovvero l'onore venvendicato* (*Giuseppina Terranova or Honor* avenged), premiered in 1906 and was later translated into the Sicilian dialect by Filippo Catalfo and into English by Annie Leitch. In 1906 Cordiferro worked on the third part of a potential trilogy that never materialized into production: *L'onore conquistato* (Honor conquered).

Cordiferro also wrote *macchiette* or character sketches: "*Il prominente coloniale*" (The prominent colonist), "*Io me 'u fatto monaco*" (I became a monk), "*Don Vicienzo 'o purtugallero*" (Don Vicienzo the Portuguese), "*O guappo*" (The dandy), "*Muglierema m'ha Passato*" (She passed as my wife), and "*Il Cavaliere*" (The knight), all in 1898; "*Il Falsi Monetari*" (The false coins) and "*Don Vincenzo o Cammorista*" (Don Vincenzo the grafter), both in 1899; and "*Il poliziotto italo-americano*" (The Italian-American detective) in 1902.

A prolific poet, his odes and poems were published in *La Follia* and elsewhere. His lyrics in the Neapolitan dialect for songs such as "*Nun 'o credere Luci,*" "*Abbrile,*" "*Nu Riccio 'e Capille,*" "*Strazio d'O Core,*" "*Si a Capa Femmene 'e Sta Citta,*" and "*Luntano 'a Te,*" some of which were performed by Farfariello (Eduardo Migliaccio) and Enrico Caruso, who made famous Cordiferro's song "*Cor 'Ngrata.*"

A frequent lecturer at political meetings and labor rallies, Cordiferro's many lectures and speeches dealt with social issues: "*Il destino della Russia*" (The destiny of Russia) and "*La donnoa del passato, la donna d'oggi e la donna dell'avvenire*" (The woman of yesterday, the woman of today, and the woman of the future). He also became active in the Sacco and Vanzetti controversy. Cordiferro, "The Singer of the Red Muse," died August 24, 1940.

Emelise Aleandri

Bibliography
Aleandri, Emelise. "The History of the Italian-American Theater in New York City: 1900–1905." Ph.D. diss., City University of New York, 1983.
———. "Riccardo Cordiferro." In *Italian-Americans: The Search for a Usable Past,* edited by Richard N. Juliani and Philip V. Cannistraro, 165–178. New York: American Italian Historical Association, 1986.
Sisca, Alessandro (Riccardo Cordiferro). L'Onore Perduto *and Other Plays,*

Poems, Memoirs. St. Paul: Alessandro Sisca Collection, Immigration History Research Center, University of Minnesota, 1965.

See also POETRY; SACCO AND VANZETTI; THEATER HISTORY

Corona

The Italian American community of Corona represents the classic example of urban-ethnic loyalty at the close of the twentieth century. Located in the north central section of Queens County, New York City, Corona is surrounded by Shea Stadium, the old World's Fair site, Long Island Expressway, and Lefrak City. According to 1990 census data, the largest white ethnic group in the central area of Corona remained Italian American.

Italians began to move to Corona along Corona Avenue and its side streets after 1890. In October 1903 St. Leo's Roman Catholic Church was organized as a mission church for the Italian population of five hundred, which grew to approximately two thousand by 1913. More arrived after 1917 upon completion of the elevated rail line and trolley that made it a short commute to Manhattan.

These Italian immigrants had arrived from southern Italy, were poor, and lacked formal education. Men worked in the booming construction industry, on railroads, in farming, and at reclaiming meadows. Most women remained at home, although some young women worked at nearby shirtwaist factories along Corona Avenue and its side streets.

Those who settled in Corona came from an agricultural background. They harvested vegetables and fruits on their small plots of land. Many kept chickens and goats. Some trained pigeons on their roofs. Winemaking continued as an important custom, the consumption of which was vital to maintaining their Old World culture.

Architecturally, one- and two-family structures have been built to accommodate gardens, arbors, and other amenities that do not encroach on the residents' living space, but allow for enough human contact within the context of city life. Ethnic cultural support services remain evident in language, food, religion, family, *comparaggio* (godparenthood), games, and social clubs. The local VFW hall reveals many names of Italian Americans who lost their lives in wars of the twentieth century.

On either side of the main thoroughfare, Corona Avenue, there are Italian restaurants and delicatessens, pastry shops, pizza parlors, and red, white, and green flags. The Parkside Restaurant, the Lemon Ice King, Baldi's Bakery, and the bocce court are some of the neighborhood's long-standing institutions. Corona residents spend their leisure time at the little park on Corona Avenue and 108th Street, where the annual Italian *festa* is held.

The viability of this community was tested when New York City attempted to condemn sixty-nine Corona homes and seize twelve and one-half acres of land to build a high school and athletic field. The Italian American community secured the legal services of Mario Cuomo and fought New York City from 1966 to 1972, when a compromise was reached: the high school was built, but the field was relocated elsewhere, thus saving the homes.

Frank J. Cavaioli

Bocce court in the park at Corona Avenue and 108th Street, Corona, Queens, New York, 1995. Bocce remains a popular game for Italian Americans. Courtesy Frank J. Cavaioli.

Bibliography

Cavaioli, Frank J. "Corona's Little Italy." In *Through the Looking Glass,* edited by Mary Jo Bona and Anthony Julian Tamburri, 194–214. Staten Island, NY: American Italian Historical Association, 1996.

Cuomo, Mario Matthew. *Forest Hills Diary.* New York: Vintage, 1974.

Harney, Robert F., and J. Vincenza Scarpaci, eds. *Little Italies in North America.*

Toronto: Multicultural History Society of Ontario, 1981.

Seyfried, Vincent F. *The Story of Corona.* Garden City, NY: Queens Community Series, 1986.

See also CUOMO, MARIO M.; ETHNIC NEIGHBORHOODS

Cosenza, Mario E. (1880–1966)

A classical scholar and for more than ten years academic dean at Brooklyn College, Mario E. Cosenza was born in Naples, Italy, and arrived in this country in 1889. His began his education in Italy and completed it in the United States. He was an excellent student and graduated from City College of New York, where he was elected to Phi Beta Kappa. In 1905 he received a doctorate in classical studies from Columbia University. A year of his graduate work for Columbia was at the American School in Rome.

While serving as a director of Townsend Harris Hall, City College's high school preparatory school (1919–1926), Dr. Cosenza became interested in the life of Townsend Harris, the first United States General Consul to Japan. He edited the journal Harris kept during his Japanese years. Dr. Cosenza maintained his interest in the Far East throughout his life. In 1922 Dr. Cosenza wrote in the *New York Times:* "The new theater of human activity is in the far-east—Japan, strong alert and rightly anxious of her future; China, weak at present but confident in her coming strength."

Dr. Cosenza spent most of his career at New York City University, starting at Townsend Harris Hall, going on to City College Center in Brooklyn, and finally, at Brooklyn College, where he was a member of the founding group that worked diligently to establish a quality institution of higher education. While at Brooklyn College Dr. Cosenza was appointed professor of classical languages. Later he headed the department, and, after two years, became dean of men. He became acting president while a search for a new president was conducted. His influence pervaded such areas as academic infrastructure, student behavior in the local community, and helping to design the university seal.

Dr. Cosenza published early in his career and continued into his retirement. In 1905 he translated a work by Ettore Pais, *Ancient Legends of Roman History.* Many of the chapters were prepared as lectures for the Lowell Institute of Boston, while others were read at the Universities of Wisconsin and Chicago. He wrote a five-volume set, *Biographical and Bibliographical Dictionary of Italian Humanists* (1962). Among his other works was, most prominently, *The Four Voyages of Amerigo Vespucci.* Widely respected for his scholarship, Dr. Cosenza was invited to lead or join many organizations, such as the Council on Immigration, Italian Board of Guardians, American Classical League, New York Educational League, Japan Society, and the Italian Teachers Association.

He represented the best that Italy gave to America. His work benefited all immigrants and others searching for an education.

John Brindisi

Bibliography

Cosenza, Mario E. *Biographical and Bibliographical Dictionary of Italian Humanists.* 5 vols. Boston: G.K. Hall, 1967

———. *Francesco Petrarca and the Revolution of Cola di Rienzo.* Chicago: University of Chicago Press, 1913.

Horowitz, Murray H. *Brooklyn College, The First Half-Century.* New York: Brooklyn College Press, 1981.

See also HIGHER EDUCATION

Costello, Lou

See COMEDY

Covello, Leonard (1887–1982)

Born Leonardo Coviello, his name was changed by an American teacher. It was one form of discrimination Covello would spend his career trying to abolish. Born in Avigliano, Italy, on November 26, 1887, his father had migrated to the United States previously; the rest of the family followed in 1906. They settled in East Harlem, New York.

Covello attended Anna C. Ruddy's Home School and then New York City public schools; however, he found his studies irrelevant and his surroundings hostile. His father's admonitions and brief experience as a laborer led him to complete his education. He received a Pulitzer scholarship, which he used to attend Columbia University. He received a bachelor's degree in 1911. That fall, he began teaching Spanish and French in De Witt Clinton School for Boys, a public high school, where he successfully championed (in 1922) the addition of Italian to the curriculum. In 1934 he was appointed principal of the proposed Benjamin Franklin High School in Italian East Harlem. Plans called for a vocational-technical institution for Italian American boys, but Covello argued for an academic high school and got his way. Fiorello LaGuardia dedicated the high school in 1942.

The school reflected Covello's holistic educational philosophy. Before the building was completed, he led students in renovating empty storefronts for extracurricular activities. His community-centered system invited the boys' parents, many of whom had limited educational experience, to visit the school so the students could show them the value of education. He also had the students study neighborhood issues such as slum clearance.

The entrance into the school of black students from central Harlem and of Puerto Ricans moving into Italian East Harlem led to Covello's interest in racial tolerance and equal opportunity. He worked to calm tempers after a September 29, 1945, riot between black and white students.

Upon his 1956 retirement he became educational consultant of the Puerto Rican Migration Division. In 1962 he left that post to become executive for health and physical education of the Greater New York YMCA. In 1964 he became director of the Puerto Rican–sponsored East Harlem Youth Career Information Conference. Along with his interracial work, he remained interested in his Italian roots. His New York University Ed.D. dissertation was published in 1967 as *The Social Background of the Italo-American Schoolchild* and is a standard in the field. He was part of the group that founded the American Italian Historical Association in 1966.

In 1972 Covello again "retired" but continued working; this time he relocated to Italy and cooperated with Danilo Dolci, the Italian radical reformer. He died August 19, 1982, and was buried in Italy. His papers were donated to Philadelphia's Balch Center.

Mary Elizabeth Brown

Bibliography

Cordasco, Francesco, ed. *Studies in Italian-American Social History: Essays in Honor of Leonard Covello*. Totowa, NJ: Rowman Littlefield, 1975.

Covello, Leonard, with Guido D'Agostino. *The Heart Is the Teacher*. New York: McGraw-Hill, 1956.

Cozza, Carmen (Louis) (b. 1930)

Yale's most successful and legendary football coach, Carmen (Louis) Cozza was born in Parma, a suburb of Cleveland, Ohio, on June 10, 1930, the son of James and Carbita (DeLuca) Cozza. He grew up in his native town and graduated from its high school with varsity letters in baseball, basketball, football, and track. He entered Miami University in Oxford, Ohio, where he earned a bachelor's degree in science (1952), in addition to proving himself outstanding in both football and baseball. Cozza married Jean Adele Annable on June 28, 1952, a marriage that produced three daughters.

After college Cozza played minor league baseball for the Cleveland Indians and the Chicago White Sox and coached at Gilmour Academy and Collinwood High School before he took a job as coach of freshman football at Miami University in Ohio from 1956 to 1963. During that period, he continued his graduate education at Miami by earning a master's degree (1959) before he joined the coaching staff at Yale, where, starting as assistant coach in 1963–1964, he moved up to head coach in January 1965.

Coaching at Yale until the end of the 1996 football season when he retired, on November 23, 1996, Cozza had led the Bulldogs through nineteen winning seasons to ten Ivy League championships. His career of slightly more than three hundred games tallied to a record of 179 wins, 118 losses, and 5 ties. Cozza has been the recipient of many awards including a Gold Medal from the Connecticut Sports Writers Alliance, the Distinguished American Award by the Walter Camp Foundation, the Eastern Coach of the Year Award, and the New England Coach of the Year Award. He also coached the all-stars of the Ivy League to victory over the college all-stars of Japan in the Epson Ivy Bowl first held in Tokyo in 1989.

When Italian Americans think of Yale, they tend to remember A. Bartlett Giamatti and Carmen Cozza. While the former reflected the best in the classroom at Yale, the latter reflected the best on the playing field. "For thirty-two years," Yale president Richard C. Levin declared, when reflecting on Cozza's career, "Yale has been lucky enough to have a football coach who has embodied all of its highest ideals." Not only did Cozza's players become most valuable players in the Ivy League, but there were among them National College Athletic Association postgraduate scholarship winners, academic All-Americans, Hall of Fame scholar-athletes, and at least five Rhodes scholars, not to mention about twenty who have gone on to play professional football. Thus, in many ways, he was "the winningest coach" in the history of Yale.

Vincent A. Lapomarda

Bibliography

Bergin, Thomas G. "Forza, Ragazzi! Hold 'em, Yale!" *Italian Americana* 3 (spring/summer 1977): 193–203.

Keith, D. "Carmen L. Cozza, Yale University." *Coach & Athlete* 43 (May/June 1981): 8–9.

Montville, Leigh. "Early Retirement." *Sports Illustrated*, 9 September 1996, p. 14.

See also SPORTS

Crime and Organized Crime

Italian immigrants and their children have contributed no more and no less to crime in America than any other people. They have had and continue to have their fair share of criminals. Yet the criminal history of the United States would have remained essentially the same had Italians not migrated to America. They have not introduced any new crime, though they have made a difference of degree in some areas, organized crime for example, where their approach has had greater intensity and/or hastened an inevitable innovation.

Almost overlooked in their criminal history is the enduring negative impact that these few stereotyped criminals have had on the Italian American community as a whole. For the most part, this was not done knowingly. Rather, the stumbling block came from circumstances of birth, or country of origin, which continues to carry a burden of criminality. This stigma emanates from two criminal groups in Italy: one from the mainland known as the Camorra, which is now relegated to history; the other, Mafia, from western Sicily, which is still very much alive in the hearts and minds of people on both sides of the Atlantic. To comprehend Italian American crime, one must understand what is Italian and what is American about it.

From colonial days on, immigration and crime have gone hand in hand. "Americans," mostly Anglo-Saxon Protestants, often blamed "foreigners" for the problems, criminal and otherwise, that occurred on their shores and generally viewed immigrants as threats to their society whose "social average" would be lowered by the influx of "rejects" from other nations. These fears were fed by academic and popular writers who, since the middle of the nineteenth century, were pushing for the exclusion of foreigners as the answer to America's ills. Nativist attacks on immigrants were especially strident and effective as one group after the other suffered through the stings of bias and discrimination, both open and subtle. The Irish, Jews, Poles, Chinese, Japanese, and Italians were not exempt.

From the start of migration from the Italian peninsula in the mid-nineteenth century with first the northern migration and later that from the south, Italians were characterized as inferior people, morally deficient, and prone to criminal activity. In time, most immigrant groups outlived such negative stereotypes. What makes Italian American history different from other immigrant sagas is the permanent nature of the criminal label bestowed on them and the crushing effect it has had on their development in America.

Propagating this stereotype was the blanket judgment that Italians in America were, if not innately criminal, certainly a Mafia-ridden people. Feeding this label was the association in the popular and academic mind of Italian Americans with organized crime to such an extent that the two became one in the eyes of many, if not most, Americans. Even the U.S. government came to take the official position that organized crime and Mafia, that is the Italian American criminal, were one and the same. Despite the government's recent retreat from that position, many Americans still believe that Italian Americans are the be-all and end-all of organized crime.

C

Is it myth or reality that Italian Americans and organized crime are synonymous? Would organized crime not exist in the United States but for Italian Americans? It is first necessary to look at the general record of Italian Americans in crime and then examine organized crime and their role in it.

In the early days of Italian migration to America, Italians seldom stood out as criminals. The data show that in a number of instances—for example, crimes of stealth and white collar types—Italians committed fewer crimes, proportionately, than other groups. In other cases, usually dealing with violence, they were greater offenders, proportionately. Prior to World War I, Italian immigrants were often cited for brawls stemming from drunkenness. Family feuds also brought out the worst in them as they resorted to mayhem, maiming, and murder to settle disputes. Italians made police blotters for vagrancy, disturbing the peace, boarding house thefts, wife-stealing, and game-law violations. Avid hunters, they paid little heed to laws in their new land that established certain boundaries on such activities. *Padroni* (labor brokers) skipping town with people's money, and fraternal presidents and treasurers doing likewise, were noted in many Italian American communities. These were intra-ethnic episodes. Gambling and vice crimes were a minor part of the general Italian American population.

Confrontations with the Irish were another occasion for criminal behavior. Living in close proximity, the Irish often made work situations or certain neighborhoods, which were considered Irish "turf," off-limits to Italians. Too often, the resolution was through violence. In this period Italians carried knives and guns and were not reluctant to use them to settle disputes. For a time, then, their proclivity to violence stood out in American history. However, given America's history of violence on the frontier and elsewhere, Italian American behavior was hardly unique. With the inception of Prohibition, rank-and-file Italians began making and selling wine and assorted home brews for neighborhood consumption. Cut-throat competition, which included driving beer trucks, hijacking, and informing on rivals, was an outgrowth of legislation prohibiting the sale of alcohol. These bootlegging activities were commonplace in a land where the general population

was unwilling to live by the letter of the law.

With the end of Prohibition, calmer times prevailed. Italian immigrants found themselves better accepted in America. Many had fought and died for their new country in World War I. Neighbors who were once likely to be enemies now turned friendly, or at least more accepting of Italian immigrants. Most Italian Americans no longer felt the need to carry knives and guns. Parents, anxious to settle in as Americans, advised their children to shun weapons. The younger generation heeded this advice. At the same time, a tremendous opportunity presented itself in the field of organized crime.

The other side of Italian criminality in the pre–World War II period had to do with Mafia, Camorra, and Black Hand, elements that were associated with a larger and deeply rooted phenomenon in American history, organized crime. The foundation of organized crime, with its emphasis on satisfying "consumer" needs, rests on centuries of interactions between people who would circumvent the law to satisfy their desires. Unlike the criminal who forces victims to give in to his or her demands, organized crime figures usually find willing participants eager to avail themselves of the illegal services. This system developed from the colonists' wish to justify actions against what they considered an irrelevant or oppressive rule from a distant mother country. In time, American society allowed for a dual existence, one that set ideal social and moral values, and another that permitted, unofficially, deviation from the code.

In colonial times, there was a profitable illegal trade in Spanish and French wines and other products restricted by England's trade laws. Piracy was often encouraged by and for the enrichment of the colonies, their officials, and their entrepreneurs, all of whom vied for economic superiority. As the United States pushed west, the rough life on the frontier held little recognition for law. Debts to older communities in the east were lightly regarded, but horse stealing was punishable by shooting on sight. Vigilante action, persecution of immigrants and blacks, race riots, lynchings, and popular opposition to many wars in the 1800s all point to a society that claimed the right to decide for itself which laws were to be obeyed and which were to be flaunted.

The American habit of trying to bring an ideal society into existence through legislation presented enormous problems for officials. Inasmuch as it was nearly impossible to have the real world coincide with the ideal one, officials had to decide which laws to take seriously and which ones to overlook but occasionally enforce.

What came about was a mechanism to control but not eliminate the illicit activities conducted by early Americans. In the nineteenth century, activities kept under check by the law were gambling, prostitution, and bootleg liquor. Yet early on, politicians and police were the first large-scale criminal entrepreneurs, owning and operating gambling halls and brothels that were often combined under one roof. Having control over the police, politicians were the senior partners in such ventures. Later, they began "licensing" their illegal operations to gang leaders. By the 1890s Americans had a hard time distinguishing between politicians and criminals, between lawmen and thugs.

Early immigrant gangs, such as the Irish, were the forerunners of modern urban gangs. They were allowed to operate because they could deliver the vote and paid for the privilege of furnishing illicit services. They did not corrupt the city, but willingly played the venal game run by the politicians and police who were responding to and taking advantage of the public's wishes. Michael Cassius McDonald in Chicago provided an early model for gang leadership. Financed by profits from roulette, dice, and cards, McDonald's support was crucial to the careers of many aldermen, mayors, senators, and congressmen. His counterpart in New York City was John Morrissey. Irish immigrant and former heavyweight champion, Morrissey operated luxurious gambling houses in New York City and Saratoga Springs and became a prominent figure in New York's politics, serving two terms in Congress.

The American public was aware of the collusion between politicians and police and the criminal element and, along with law-abiding officials, initiated reform movements in the nineteenth and twentieth centuries. It was into this society that the masses of Italian immigration came. The criminally ambitious few among them had stepped into a ready-made criminal world. But, it was an event in 1890, the murder of New Orleans' police chief David C. Hennessy, that pushed the American character of crime to the background and spotlighted the foreign danger of crime in America: the Mafia.

Despite the fact that New Orleans was infamous for its political and police corruption and that Hennessy's credentials were less than sterling, the allegation that he was gunned down by *mafiosi* stuck. Fourteen Italians were indicted, nine were tried, six were acquitted, and a mistrial was declared on the remaining three. Certain of the Italians' guilt and spurred by talk of witness intimidation and jury fixing, a citizens' group lynched eleven Italians. A grand jury justified the action, and the press around the country generally applauded the outrage. In a typical response, the *New York Times* held that the vigilantes took the only course available to stop the Mafia and its bloody practices. Elsewhere, Americans were warned of an international conspiracy designed to assassinate public officials who dared oppose the Mafia. The possibility that Hennessy was a victim of an internal department feud or of warring factions for the control of New Orleans' docks, facts that were well known at the time, was essentially ignored.

What was this so-called Mafia that Americans were being warned about? It was basically a rural phenomenon of western Sicily. It drew its strength from the effective use of violence and corruption by men who were often related by blood and sworn to secrecy about their activities. Over the centuries, *mafiosi* were able to enlist as members people from all walks of life. Essentially, they could commit crime with impunity because they were able to curry favor from all sorts in officialdom. They garnered the support of local citizens by instilling fear or by establishing a kind of personal justice. This was preferable to a system that was forced upon Italians by centuries of foreign rule that was often out of sync with the peasants' concept of right. Few cared or dared to oppose the local Mafia head who ruled supreme over his group called *cosca* (a Mafia clique). The system was highly decentralized. There was no national or international organization that made up a monolithic Mafia geared to take over Italy, let alone other foreign nations. The Camorra, a Neapolitan criminal group leaning more toward the urban aspects of crime, was also deeply rooted in corruption.

However efficient this system was in parts of Italy, it was doomed to failure in America. Mafia developed a justice system based on local mores free from the oppressive constraints of foreign rule. Set in small communities, it had a solid family foundation. Members were blood relatives who represented all strata of society. They followed a code of behavior, identified generally as *omertà,* which demanded unfailing loyalty, dedication, secrecy, and respect for authority in the group's hierarchy. It was a system that fostered honor among thieves. Operating in a nascent capitalist atmosphere, the emphasis was more on power derived from favors owed than on the amassing of wealth. Saving face was all important to these people. To be taken for a fool was a grievous offense. The higher up in society a *cosca* could place its members, the more effective the *cosca* became. And the more power these individual Mafia groups attained, they more corrupt they were.

Basically, Mafia were low-profile, rigidly structured, closed groups who stood independently in various towns designed to function in tight-knit situations where their members could go about their business. They could move easily and unobtrusively in and out of societal structures as the need arose. The system was not designed for nor could it be used by a large society of immigrants. It could not be transplanted.

By the late 1800s, the masses from southern Italy began seeking economic betterment in America. Virtually none of them could speak the language. They were conspicuous. They had few connections to American institutions. Indeed, they found it hard to join any group on an equal member basis. Even the American Catholic Church often relegated Italian Americans to religious services in the basement. Under these conditions the few who were criminally inclined were best suited to, if not limited to, taking advantage of their own kind. Black Hand extortionists in the early 1900s were an example of this sort of criminal activity. (The Black Hand was a group of unorganized criminals who used the fear of the *mano nera* [Black Hand] in Italy to terrorize immigrants in America.) The masses suffered these indignities until they learned that local police and federal forces could protect them against criminal intimidation. Soon, many respectable Italians cooperated with law enforcement. Before Prohibition

came about, the Black Hand had been eliminated. By then, talk of Mafia had died out. In fact, Mafia virtually disappeared from the lexicon throughout the entire Prohibition period. It was not until after World War II that it burst forth on the scene, despite the rise during Prohibition of the one man most connected with Italian American crime, Al Capone. But Capone was no *mafioso.* Descended from mainland Italians, he was the leader of a multiethnic American gang. Later and erroneously, Americans caught up in Mafia hysteria associated him with Mafia.

In essence, despite the talk of an imminent threat of a Mafia takeover in the 1890s, Mafia did not manifest itself in America. In all probability, some *mafiosi* migrated, but they had no societal connections to which they could attach themselves. Nor would they trust any Americans to take into their confidence. They were on the outside looking in. They found that a deep-rooted centuries-old institution could not be easily, if at all, transplanted into a different and hostile environment. Neither would Americans welcome *mafiosi* with open arms. The United States was a burgeoning capitalist nation in which politicians, businessmen, and the like jealously guarded their turf. They were not about to let in alien interlopers. Many old country-minded Italian criminals had to be content to ply their trade in a narrow range in their neighborhoods and surrounding areas. Others who were beginning to Americanize soon became aware of the greater opportunities available in the larger society. This was especially true during Prohibition, which provided a booming atmosphere for illicit activities and opened the eyes of criminals intent on expanding their operations. This meant joining up with non-Italians both in the criminal world and in straight society.

In this way, Italian Americans would plug into the system on the bottom rungs, usually through politicians, and make their way up the ladder of crime. Some would do so as "independents." The more sophisticated among them would combine efforts and link together people throughout regions in the nation or even throughout the nation. They engaged in what came to be called organized crime. Their criminal activity matched their moneymaking interests. In the 1920s liquor was a primary concern. Prior to, and after Prohibition, gambling was the major focus. Other areas included, but were not restricted to, prostitution, labor racketeering, loan sharking, and drugs, which has become a major moneymaker today, both for independents and for various organized crime groups.

Prime among the "independents" was Al Capone. Born in Brooklyn of Neapolitan parentage, Capone was a young tough who was called to Chicago to help John Torrio, a friend who had gone earlier to assist his uncle, Jim Colosimo. Following the example of McDonald, Colosimo, with the help of political regulars, built an empire on vice and gambling in downtown Chicago. Enjoying success, he sought respect and downplayed the new opportunities presented by Prohibition. Eager to expand and make their fortunes, Torrio and others were not about to let the moneymaking possibilities within Prohibition pass them by. Colosimo was assassinated. Torrio and Capone began to build a multiethnic gang, mainly Italian, Slavic, Jewish, and Irish. Torrio then laid out a blueprint for crime that encouraged cooperation and spheres of influence among the various ethnic gangs. There would be ample profit for all. Capone emerged as sole leader when Torrio, surviving an attempt on his life by dissidents, opted to leave Chicago. The warfare that followed became legendary, as did Capone.

Capone became famous for selling "good" liquor and infamous for violently eliminating those who opposed him and the integration of Chicago's mobs. The infamous St. Valentine's Day massacre of 1929 has been attributed to him. Capone had a dichotomous reputation. He gambled recklessly, especially on racehorses, while he also fed the hungry during the Great Depression years. He was a model for the axiom "Easy come, easy go." His criminal career came to an end when he was convicted and imprisoned for income tax evasion. He did not have to cope with how to make a living when Prohibition ended. His followers, Frank Nitti, Tony Accardo, Sam Giancana, and others, turned mainly to gambling and, secondarily, to a budding illicit enterprise: drugs. In the process, they cooperated more with gangs from other cities, especially when their interests crossed in Las Vegas. Originally financed by old American stock, Nevada's gaming industry attracted organized crime money from the 1940s on. Bugsy Siegel, Meyer Lansky, and their Italian American partners, mainly from New York, were the major forces of organized crime as Las Vegas outstripped Reno as the gambling mecca of the United States.

New York City had its counterpart to Chicago's McDonald, Colosimo, and Capone with Morrissey, Arnold Rothstein, and a host of criminals led by Lucky Luciano, Frank Costello, Meyer Lansky, and Bugsy Siegel. They participated in the most consistent thread running through organized crime's historical fabric: gambling. These were the men responsible for a giant move toward its consolidation. Eventually, organized crime would provide Americans with the opportunity to bet, legally or illegally, on just about any sporting event in the world. The New York mobsters also involved themselves in prostitution, drugs, racketeering, loan-sharking, scamming of legitimate businesses, black marketing, and a host of other illegalities. Crime business was mostly enforced by muscle and sometimes by murder. Victims were usually those from their own ranks who stepped outside the lines. Force was not an end in itself, but was used to protect business interests of which gambling was prime.

By 1916 Arnold Rothstein, having won the gambling concession from Jimmy Hine's Monongahela Democratic Club, was the most important gambler in New York City and on his way to being the most influential and powerful figure in gangland. He backed many illicit activities, among which were large-scale drug operations. But, more importantly, he is credited with establishing a lay-off system whereby bookmakers (those who determine odds and receive and pay off bets) across the nation could safely take any bet knowing they could give part or all of it to a bookmaker's bookie if the risk of the wager became too great. Rothstein tutored the up-and-coming gangsters of the day, people like Lansky, Luciano, Costello, and Siegel.

Rothstein was gunned down by unknown forces in 1928. Soon after, Lucky Luciano emerged as one of the major underworld forces in New York. Born in Sicily but raised in New York, he realized the limitations of Italo-centered gangs. Unfettered by Old World criminal ways, he stressed the American aspects of crime. Charting new waters, he encouraged integration, especially between Italians and Jews, and broadened horizons across America. Unable or unwilling to break with Old World ways, Italian gangsters like Joe

"The Boss" Masseria and Salvatore Maranzano were reluctant to branch out beyond the Italian American community. With help from Lansky and Siegel, Luciano is generally credited with eliminating those Italian leaders and putting together a national crime commission. It was a multiethnic organization that enriched all members. In effect, these individuals implemented the scheme of Rothstein and Torrio to put crime on a solid business foundation across the land. "Murder, Inc.," a hit man group established within the ranks, was often used as the chief enforcement agency to ensure that members would comply with the group's decisions. Lepke Buchalter and Albert Anastasia were the prime muscle men. In time, observers narrowed their focus and viewed Luciano's combination as "La Cosa Nostra," a term popularized by Joseph Valachi, one of the early informers who revealed inside information about Italian American criminal organizations.

Valachi described La Cosa Nostra as a national syndicate composed of twenty-six families headed by a commission on which sat New York City's five families. He claimed that only Italian Americans were allowed to join. In time, La Cosa Nostra was interpreted to mean Mafia, and Mafia became synonymous with organized crime. Thus, Italian Americans came to mean organized crime and vice versa. This scenario ignored Luciano's history of mobbing up with non-Italian Americans and left influential criminals like Lansky, Siegel, and the like out of the formal picture. The inconsistencies were explained away by relegating the other ethnic criminal participants to subservient or consulting roles.

Luciano's plan to integrate and consolidate organized crime members had its drawbacks. It meant greater opportunities and profits. But it left the combine open to infiltration by the authorities. Expansion meant taking in gang members who were greater security risks, because they were either not blood relatives or not well known in the community. Keeping a tighter rein on membership could not stop an insider like Valachi from cooperating with the authorities. Nor could it stop an Abe Reles from turning on his Jewish compatriots in "Murder, Inc.," and, it could not guarantee that there would be no Federal Bureau of Investigation infiltration. Eventually, the dream of Luciano and Lansky would be shattered by internal informants and FBI infil-

trators, but organized crime would remain, powerful as ever, a major force in the national and international drug trade. Before that, Luciano and Lansky were to taste success as they put their plans into operation.

Though the La Cosa Nostra commission would last into the 1990s, Luciano's crime career, unlike that of Lansky, was cut short when he was convicted on prostitution charges. Sentenced to thirty-five years in prison in 1936, he was released after World War II and deported to Italy. The reason for his release at that time was unclear. But, with the uncovering of relevant documents, most scholars believe it came about because, from his cell and with Lansky's help, Luciano contributed to the allied war cause both on the home front and in Italy by working with federal agents, his union leadership, and members of the Italian underground and mafiosi in Italy. His role in organized crime in America then diminished, though he was thought to continue to draw a share of organized crime's profits in the United States. After his efforts to operate out of Cuba were thwarted, he resigned himself to living in exile in Italy. When Fidel Castro came to power and drove out Lansky and the other organized crime figures who ran the casinos in Havana, Luciano's income took a decided drop. This suggested that gambling had continued to provide him with a sizable income and that his drug activities, which authorities had claimed were substantial, were minor, if not nonexistent.

With Luciano in Italy, Frank Costello took over and won the title "Prime Minister" of crime. Terms such as *capo* (the ruler or boss of a family) and "godfather" came later when the works of Peter Maas (*The Valachi Papers,* 1968) and Mario Puzo (*The Godfather,* 1969) popularized them. Luciano had lived a high-profile life and was well known as an underworld figure. Costello went about his business in relative obscurity until the Kefauver Committee put him in the spotlight through broadcasts on the newly emerging medium of television. Estes Kefauver, chairman of a Senate committee investigating crime, was empowered to look into illegal gambling in America. His committee uncovered a smorgasbord of gambling rings across the nation, reflecting its diverse criminal involvement. But, encouraged by an aggressive Federal Bureau of Narcotics hot on the heels of Italian American drug operators, the committee reported that a Mafia conspiracy led by two crime families threatened the United States. One was in Chicago: the old Capone gang now known as the Accardo-Guzik-Fischetti combination. The other was in New York, called the Costello-Adonis-Lansky syndicate. Behind the scenes, Luciano was allegedly masterminding the processing and shipping of heroin from Turkey through Italy and France to New York. This conclusion was a long stretch from the evidence Kefauver had uncovered. In fact, Kefauver himself, shortly after the release of the committee report, never mentioned Mafia in a speech to the American Bar Association on the threat of organized crime. Though the evidence pointed to gambling rings representing America's diverse population, the bottom line in the discoveries made by the Kefauver Committee was an alien conspiracy. The second coming of the Mafia was upon America.

The McClellan hearings featured the testimony of Joseph Valachi in 1963. They were followed by President Johnson's Task Force Report on Organized Crime in 1967. Given full support by the media, they presented a powerful statement to the American public that painted organized crime as a monolithic, alien conspiracy. Though Valachi had testified to La Cosa Nostra, most officials called it Mafia. In 1967 the task force equated "Mafia" and "organized crime." They were now officially one and the same.

The fact that it was possible to have Italian Americans involved in organized crime without a Mafia was never considered. Nor could people envision organized crime existing without Italian Americans despite the considerable evidence the task force gathered on multiethnic involvement but rejected.

One result of the government's official conclusion was that law enforcement efforts against organized crime were totally focused on Italian Americans. Thus, from the 1930s on, Luciano, Costello, Bonanno, Genovese, Gambino, and others became household names. As these leaders passed on, sometimes due to natural causes, the new generation of younger gangsters paid little heed to the lessons of their elders. Energized by the enormous fortunes to be had by concentrating on the burgeoning drug market, criminals like John Gotti burst forth on the scene. A throwback to the 1920s, they captured the public's eye. Violence prone, their high-profile lifestyle brought forth condemnation from public officials. With few exceptions, the media had a field day in selling the government's message that Italian Americans and organized crime were one and the same. This was bad news for Italian American gangsters, but good news for non-Italian American criminals who essentially were given a free hand in organized crime.

Believing traditional law enforcement efforts to be inadequate in combating organized crime, experts and legislators combined to push for special legislation to root out the problem. Most effective were the Witness Protection Program and the Racketeer Influenced and Corrupt Organizations statute (RICO). In addition, the FBI began to infiltrate mob gangs. The end of Italian American hegemony in organized crime was near. Seeking to save their hides, make money, or avenge some real or imagined wrong, organized crime members flocked into the arms of federal agents and willingly testified against their bosses and cohorts.

The results were phenomenal. Under the relentless onslaught of federal agents, virtually all of the bosses of the leading Italian American crime families were convicted and jailed. When put to the test, the centuries-old code of *omertà,* thought to be unshakable, crumbled. The idea that gang members would unflinchingly embrace the ideals of secrecy, loyalty, honor, obedience, manliness, and respect proved to be a myth. Today, the back of Italian American organized crime has been broken. What remains is a shell of its former self. And yet, organized crime thrives as always. No longer do Italian Americans and gambling rings pose the most serious threat. (Legalization of gambling has turned most customers away from that organized crime activity.) Now the major players are Latinos, Asians, Russians, Jamaicans, African Americans, and a polyglot membership of motorcycle gangs. For decades, they have enjoyed virtual immunity from prosecution while federal authorities concentrated only on Italian Americans.

The new organized crime's central focus is on narcotics, especially cocaine and heroin. Despite the "war on drugs," narcotics have become a more intensive and widespread problem, even as the influence of Italian American organized crime has progressively lessened. When federal agents began to vigorously prosecute Italian American drug activity, drug arrests were about thirty thousand a year. Now that La Cosa Nostra has all but been eliminated, such arrests have soared to one million a year. The low correlation between drug arrests and La Cosa Nostra activity confirmed a mid-1980s study that centered on the fifty leading Italian American organized crime bosses. Sixty percent got their income from gambling. Union business accounted for 38 percent; loan-sharking, 34 percent; the construction business, 24 percent; at the bottom was narcotics at 12 percent. Most criminals were involved in more than one area. Simply put, Italian American organized crime has had little participation in the volatile area of narcotics, which is the source of major problems in American society in the 1990s.

Italian Americans excelled in organized crime in the 1940s through the 1960s, when they held dominant positions in many cities in the United States. Paradoxically, as the mythic power of Mafia and godfathers grew by leaps and bounds, Italian American criminals lost control to other ethnics and fell victim to the enforcement efforts of federal officials. The television show *The Untouchables,* focusing on Capone, Nitti, and Prohibition, was pure fantasy, yet it was taken seriously even by some crime reporters. But it was Mario Puzo who opened the floodgates to the stream of Mafia-consciousness. *The Godfather* and the spate of books, movies, articles, and media events it spawned "immortalized" Mafia and the idea of an alien conspiracy threatening Americans. They were warned that *mafiosi* could exploit them from cradle to grave and advised to take extra-legal measures to rid the country of this foreign cancer. In fairness to Puzo, he did not write all that. In fact, his novel was about Italian American crime. But the effect was the same. Few people saw it as fiction; fewer still recognized the American side of corruption and the crime it had originated. Ironically, Italian American figures in organized crime began to lose out when the romanticizing of "godfather" and "Mafia" touted their invincibilty.

Today, most of the crime family heads are retired, dead, or in prison. Their decline has been lamented by some law enforcement officials who credited them with bringing some order and control to the criminal community. Barring that, the murder and mayhem of Italian American organized crime were kept "in house." Respect was shown to honest public officials who were seen as

doing their duty. Now, young Italian Americans vie for power in a different world. No longer are the values of family and respect dominant in building Italian American criminal organizations. This change is reflected in the acceptance of Italian American criminals of American ways who have brought into question the role in society of family, authority, and elders. These values were the heart and soul of what has become known as "traditional (Italian American) organized crime."

Compounding the problem are the narrowing opportunities available to organized crime. Over the years, illegal gambling presented the most consistent field for economic success. Combined with a willing political or law enforcement nexus, either by corrupting those in legitimate power or by responding to their invitation, Italian American gambling networks worked with Americans and other ethnics to furnish customers with the chance to wager on racehorses, baseball, football, boxing, and other sporting events across the country. By the 1960s these opportunites began to shrink. The proliferation of nationwide legalized betting began with "numbers" and spread to all varieties of that game such as Lotto, Keno, Quick Draw, Pick Three, Pick Four, Pick Five, and Powerball. In addition, many state governments allowed legal intrastate and interstate off-track and on-track wagering on horses. Initially, states did that for a dual purpose: to raise revenue and to fight organized crime. They have succeeded to the point that many former operators who specialized in such gambling have had to move into other illegal areas, sports betting for example, or find employment in legitimate areas. Illegal casino businesses, once a fruitful field for organized crime, was dealt a severe blow by the revelations of the Kefauver Committee and then given a mortal wound by the spread of legalized casinos from Nevada to New Jersey and numerous other states where casinos run by American Indians have exploded onto the scene. Further, offshore gambling ships and the return of riverboat gambling took advantage of Americans' need to bet. The boom in legal casinos has done little to swell the coffers of organized crime. Once thought to be under the control of criminals, large-scale legal casinos today are mostly public corporations being run under strict regulations that effectively prevent crime figures from exerting any direct influence or control.

Italian American crime figures are also a casualty of their own success and that of the wider Italian American community. Upward mobility and the exodus of Italian Americans out of the inner cities where criminals found their most fertile ground have reduced the base of "recruits" for their criminal organizations and thinned the ranks of customers. Italian Americans hoping to emerge as leaders of organized crime will have to find a new way to do so. The old route that proved fruitful in the past is no longer operative.

If organized crime was a successfully "queer ladder of mobility" for numerous Italian American criminals, it was anathema for many honest, hardworking men and women trying to make it in America. It will never be known how many Italian Americans failed to attain their potential because of the "Mafia" stereotype. Anecdotal evidence suggests the number of victims is considerable. Given the history of Italian American criminality and its inflated threat due to the myth of the Mafia conspiracy, too many Italian Americans have suffered unduly.

Though many have fatalistically accepted the notion and nonsense of Mafia, others continue to see it as an ongoing threat. They believe that no one is free from suspicion: politicians, educators, businessmen and women (especially successful ones), and even clergy all fall under scrutiny. If you are an Italian American, you are expected to know at least some of the inner workings of the Mafia and its members. Upward mobility is often attributed to Mafia membership or connections.

Too many Italian Americans have come to believe the media's decades-long onslaught of Mafia and are beaten down by it. They either think of themselves as inferior or feel it is useless to combat the criminal/inferior stereotype. Fearful of pushing their luck, many who are able and talented are content with a position far short of their potential. This is especially true in politics, where many likely and able candidates have failed to come forth for fear of having to defend against a bogus Mafia charge. To her credit, Geraldine Ferraro ran as the Democratic vice-presidential candidate and bore the brunt of such reckless charges. She continues to be a respected politician and public servant. Even education is thought to have its *mafiosi*. When Verrazzano College was being established in Saratoga Springs, New York, it was believed by some to be a Mafia-connected school.

Italian Americans have been tagged with stereotypic labels when they innocently use words such as "family," "godfather," "friend," and "respect." Their children have been known to shy away from taking violin lessons so as to avoid the merciless teasing they might have to endure when carrying a violin case, the symbol of "Godfather" crime.

Future generations of Italian Americans might not have to face these generalizations as the role of Italian Americans in organized crime becomes demythologized. Italian criminals were quick to adapt to American ways. They made their alliances with police, politicians, and non-Italian gangsters. They emerged as leaders during Prohibition. When it ended they made their way to the top ranks of organized crime, consolidating their gains, bringing together gangs from across the nation, and setting up a national gambling mechanism. They covered a wide area of activities that included prostitution, drugs, racketeering, loan-sharking, unions, pornography, and a host of other illegitimate businesses. They paid off authorities when they had to and used force when necessary to discipline members or to intimidate reluctant participants. And they often moved into legitimate businesses: some they ran properly, others they drove into illegal activity. In sum, Italian Americans took part in "a series of endlessly shifting alliances" that have been "inherently American and fundamentally linked to a market economy." They were once a big part of organized crime. But their star is fading, their role in it diminishing. They are not, nor have they ever been, the whole of organized crime.

Luciano J. Iorizzo

Bibliography

Albini, Joseph L. *The American Mafia: Genesis of a Legend.* New York: Appleton-Century-Crofts, 1971.

Haller, Mark H. "Bootleggers and American Gambling 1920–1950." In *Second Interim Report of the Commission on the Review of the National Policy Toward Gambling.* Washington, DC: GPO, 1976.

Ianni, Francis A. J., with Elizabeth Reuss-Ianni. *A Family Business, Kinship and Social Control in Organized Crime.* New York: Russell Sage Foundation, 1972.

Iorizzo, Luciano J., and Salvatore Mondello. *The Italian Americans*. Rev. ed. Boston: Twayne, 1980.

Kenney, Dennis J., and James O. Finckenauer. *Organized Crime in America*. Belmont, CA: Wadsworth, 1995.

Lacey, Robert. *Little Man, Meyer Lansky and the Gangster Life*. Boston: Little, Brown, 1991.

Landesco, John. *Organized Crime in Chicago*. Part 3 of the *Illinois Crime Survey 1929*, with a new introduction by Mark H. Haller. Chicago: University of Chicago Press, 1968.

Moore, William H. *The Kefauver Committee and the Politics of Crime, 1950–1952*. Columbia: University of Missouri Press, 1974.

Nelli, Humbert S. *The Business of Crime, Italians and Syndicate Crime in the United States*. New York: Oxford, 1976.

Smith, Dwight C. *The Mafia Mystique*. New York: Basic Books, 1975.

See also LABOR; LAW ENFORCEMENT

Crimi, Alfred D. (b. 1900)

An internationally recognized architectural consultant, easel and mural painter, teacher, and writer, Alfred D. Crimi was born in eastern Sicily and came to America in 1910. He returned to Europe in 1929 to study fresco painting.

Crimi attended public school in the teeming Little Italy of East Harlem, New York City. He earned a living by doing manual work, such as painting, and by teaching formal painting classes.

Over the course of his career, he taught at Pratt Institute and City University of New York. His major works include a mural and ornamental design at the Polish Roman Catholic Church, Bayonne, New Jersey; the Public Works of Art Project, Key West, Florida; fresco work on Relief Organization Building, Key West, Florida; five fresco panels, Medical Board Conference Room, Harlem Hospital; Workroom of a Great Post Office, Post Office Building, Washington, D.C.; and portrait paintings below the wing of the main lobby, Breakers Hotel, Palm Beach, Florida.

Crimi is the recipient of more than forty awards. He has had exhibitions at the Metropolitan Museum of Art, Whitney Museum of American Art, Academy of

Arts and Letters, Chicago Art Museum, Museum of Modern Art, and in Paris, Rome, Bologna, and Trieste.

Regina Soria

Bibliography

Crimi, Alfred D. *Crimi, My Life Story*. Staten Island, NY: Center for Migration Studies, 1987.

Soria, Regina. *American Artists of Italian Heritage, 1776–1945*. Rutherford, NJ: Fairleigh Dickinson University Press, 1994.

See also ART

Cuomo, Mario M. (b. 1932)

A three-time Democratic governor of New York, Cuomo is the most successful and esteemed Italian American politician of his generation. His ability to inspire people and his impressive skills as an intellectual and orator have enabled him to overcome numerous obstacles grounded in anti-Italian bias.

Cuomo was born of Italian immigrants in Queens, New York, on June 15, 1932, attended St. John's Preparatory School, and graduated from St. John's University Law School in 1956. After Manhattan's Waspish law firms refused to hire him because of his Italian last name, he clerked for a New York State Court of Appeals judge, practiced law in Brooklyn, and taught at his alma mater.

In 1972 his effective defense of a group of Italian Americans fighting against the demolition of their houses in Corona, Queens, New York, and his authoritative mediation in a controversy over a Forest Hills public housing project brought Cuomo enough public recognition to launch him into politics. After making an unsuccessful bid in the 1974 Democratic primary for lieutenant governor, he waged a fruitless campaign for the Democratic nomination as mayor of New York in 1977. Although Edward Koch had defeated him in a Democratic run-off election in September, Cuomo stayed in the mayoral contest as the candidate of the Liberal Party but lost again to Koch in the November election.

After serving as secretary of state to Governor Hugh Carey from 1975 through 1978, Cuomo was eventually elected lieutenant governor as Carey's running mate in 1978 and succeeded him after defeating Republican Lewis Lehrman in the 1982 gubernatorial race. Cuomo was reelected governor in 1986 and 1990.

His political philosophy combined a populist version of New Deal liberalism with the social thought of Catholicism and the family values of his Italian ancestry. The son of a ditchdigger who rose to unexpected heights, he cherished a vision of the United States as a land of opportunity guaranteed by a democratic government. In his view, the rewards of government-stimulated growth in the private sector should be used to benefit the socially disadvantaged. Indeed, Governor Cuomo increased social security and medical benefits and was a pre-Clinton supporter of national health insurance. He also brought family values to the center of the political debate in his 1982 campaign, but later refused to discontinue Medicaid funding of abortions. Moreover, he vetoed capital punishment legislation, but built more prisons than any other governor in the history of New York and proposed life sentences without parole for three-time felons.

His galvanizing keynote address at the 1984 Democratic convention and a 1986 landslide reelection made Cuomo a potentially serious contender for the Democratic presidential nomination. Indeed, the mass media, rather than the leaders of the Democratic Party, long regarded Cuomo as the Democrats' best chance of recapturing the White House in the aftermath of the Reagan presidency. Cuomo might have been able to forge a Roosevelt-type coalition of middle-class whites, progressive intellectuals, Catholic ethnic minorities, unionized workers, and African Americans that had enabled the Democratic Party to control the White House between 1933 and 1953. Yet he chose not to run for president in both 1988 and 1992. Although he argued that the constraints of the party primary schedule conflicted with the responsibilities of the governorship, the wish to protect his family from the Mafia-related innuendos that had long plagued Italian Americans seeking elective offices may also have deterred Cuomo from contesting his party's nomination. He also faced an increasingly conservative trend.

Unlike the late 1980s, the 1990s needed a Democratic candidate who was less idealistic and more pragmatic than Cuomo. His social policies had expanded welfare rolls

Governor Mario Cuomo of New York and his wife, Matilda. Known for his intellectual leadership, Cuomo has gained wide respect as an influential politician. Courtesy of the National Italian American Foundation (NIAF), Washington, D.C.

by 32 percent between 1989 and 1993, granting 9 percent of the state's population some form of benefit and making the tax burden of New York State the second heaviest in the country. Cuomo lost public approval as the electorate grew weary of government spending on social programs for the poor. When he sought a fourth consecutive term in 1994, he lost to Republican George Pataki.

Although Pataki capitalized on his conservative pledge to cut taxes, the 1994 defeat did not necessarily imply public rejection of Cuomo's liberal stands. His Republican challenger also profited from the anti-incumbent mood of the electorate and cashed in on the state's economic recession. Cuomo retained his role as the critical conscience of the Democratic Party. He endorsed President Bill Clinton at the 1996 Democratic convention but censured him for signing a centrist welfare reform that some thought threatened the children of the poor.

Stefano Luconi

Bibliography

Cuomo, Mario M. *Diaries of Mario M. Cuomo: The Campaign for Governor.* New York: Random House, 1984.

———. *Forest Hills Diary: The Crisis of Low-Income Housing.* New York: Random House, 1974.

———. *The New York Idea: An Experiment in Democracy.* New York: Crown, 1994.

McElvaine, Robert S. *Mario Cuomo: A Biography.* New York: Charles Scribner's Sons, 1988.

See also CORONA; GOVERNORS; POLITICS

D'Agostino Sr., Nicholas (1910–1996)

An innovator in the grocery business, Nicholas D'Agostino Sr., was instrumental in developing a chain of supermarkets out of a family business. He was born in Bugnara, Italy, on June 8, 1910, the son of Ignazio and Loretta D'Agostino. In 1924, at the age of 14, Nicholas came with his parents from their native village, not very far from Rome, to New York City and, with his brother Pasquale, helped his father in the sale of groceries. Trained as a butcher, he became an expert on the quality of beef, lamb, and veal available in the city's main meat market, which he then visited daily. In 1932 he and his brother opened their own grocery store on East 83rd Street and Lexington Avenue in an exclusive area of Manhattan, where they attracted a prosperous clientele. That same year Nicholas married Josephine Tucciarone, and they had three children.

After six years in their own business and in need of more space to expand from groceries and dry goods to meats, the D'Agostino brothers opened up the Yorkville Food Market on Third Avenue and 77th Street. The supermarket for which the family became famous, where shoppers could make most of their grocery purchases all under one roof, was developed here. Having prospered through the Great Depression and World War II, their business expanded into the area of the East River and Peter Cooper Village by the 1950s with more supermarkets equipped with such innovations as shopping carts and freezers to store meats and vegetables.

After Pasquale, who had been president of the family business of eight stores, died in 1960, Nicholas bought out his brother's share and further improved the supermarkets. Eventually, the stores expanded from the East to the West Side of New York City into a chain of twenty-six extending into Westchester County. Though Nicholas withdrew from the daily operation of the chain in 1964 and passed responsibilities over to his two sons, Nicholas Jr., and Stephen, graduates of the College of the Holy Cross, he remained in the business as a consultant for the next twenty years during which he turned more of his attention to charities, family, and retirement.

Nicholas included among his charities the Catholic Church in the Archdiocese of New York and institutions in his native Italy that cared for abandoned and orphaned children. These and his other humanitarian and philanthropic works flowed from his pioneering efforts as a founder of the supermarket chain that bears his family name. The recipient of the Horatio Alger Award, Nicholas Sr., was honored with the B'nai B'rith Anti-Defamation Award, and, at the time of his death, the Horticultural Society of New York recognized his generous support. He died in Manhasset, Long Island, New York, on June 23, 1996.

Vincent A. Lapomarda

Bibliography

"D'Agostino Founder Dies." *Crain's New York Business* 12, no. 27 (1996): 54.

Horowitz, Shel. "D'Agostino: Be a Steam Engine, Not a Boat Anchor." *UMass Family Business Center Newsletter* (fall 1995).

See also BUSINESS AND ENTREPRENEURSHIP

D'Alessandro, Thomas
See POLITICS

Dance

When Italian dancers migrated to America, they introduced a virtuoso ballet technique and, in subsequent generations, made unique individual contributions to the development of new American dance styles.

While the earliest dance artists in America were largely French, as early as 1774 the celebrated Italian ballet master Pietro Sodi (1716–1775) arrived in New York and began to teach the fashionable social dances of the day. Soon after, the Italian Lorenzo Papanti (1799–?) settled in Boston, where he became a respected dance instructor and, in 1823, was appointed master of dancing and deportment at the United States Military Academy at West Point. By the mid-1800s, the French influence on dance in America began to wane as Italian dancers trained by the great Carlo Blasis introduced American audiences to the dazzling Italian ballet technique characterized by intricate footwork, jumps, and turns. One of Blasis' first pupils to appear in the United States was Giovanna Ciocca (c. 1825–?), who made her American debut in 1847. The following year the Italian technical virtuoso Gaetano Neri (1821–1852) arrived and toured with Ciocca, who had become a favorite of American audiences. In 1857 the great Italian ballet mime and choreographer Domenico Ronzani (1800–1868) was asked to form an Italian ballet company to perform at the opening of Philadelphia's Academy of Music. While contemporary critics cited Ronzani's troupe as the finest ballet company ever to have come to the United States, American audiences began to lose interest in classical ballet in favor of popular musicals, such as the 1866 production of *The Black Crook*. This show's unprecedented success spurred on more productions of these spectacular musicals that included hordes of dancing girls in tights and often featured imported Italian ballerinas who then chose to remain in the United States. They organized their own ballet companies and made transcontinental tours that brought classical ballet to American cities, mining camps, and frontier towns. Since it became too costly to import large dancing ensembles for these productions and the available American performers had no tradition of ballet schooling, the Italians began to teach, introduc-

ing American dancers to their style of ballet technique. This technique eventually dominated virtually all formal dance training in the United States for almost the next fifty years.

The most well-known ballerina of this period was the Italian Maria Bonfanti (1845–1921), who came to the United States to star in *The Black Crook* and continued to perform throughout the country until 1891. She then started a ballet school in New York, where she taught the strict Blasis method until her death. The Italian ballerina Rita Sangalli (1849–1909) was also imported to dance in *The Black Crook* and remained until 1870, touring the American West, performing bits of the La Scala ballet repertory mixed with burlesque and minstrelsy. In 1867 the Italian ballerina Giuseppina Morlacchi (1843–1886) arrived to perform in the theatrical spectacle *The Devil's Auction*. Morlacchi married "Buffalo Bill" Cody's sidekick, "Texas Jack" [John Omohundro], and toured as a dancing Indian in their Western dramas as well as with her own ballet company. In 1880 she retired to Lowell, Massachusetts, where she taught ballet to underprivileged mill girls.

From its inception in 1883, New York's Metropolitan Opera company has maintained its own ballet troupe, though the dancers were, initially, imported from abroad. Programs and reviews from the first few decades of the Metropolitan Opera Ballet contain numerous Italian names in the listings of soloists and ballet masters who brought their La Scala training and experience to the New York opera stage. The Metropolitan Opera's first prima ballerina and choreographer was the Italian dancer and mime Malvina Cavallazzi (1852–1924). In 1909 Cavallazzi was chosen to found and direct the Metropolitan Opera Ballet School to train an American ballet troupe for the opera company. Though Cavallazzi retired in 1913, her rigorous Italian exercises were still taught and considered invaluable for building strength and quickness long after her departure.

In 1895 the Italian Luigi Albertieri (1869–1930) made his Metropolitan Opera debut and became its first male ballet star. Noted for his spectacular pirouettes, he continued to dance and act as ballet master for the company intermittently for the next fourteen years. Albertieri had been a pupil of the Italian Enrico Cecchetti, probably the most revered ballet teacher of all time and, in 1915, founded a school in New York, where he taught the strict Cecchetti method to many American dancers. A generous man, Albertieri was known to teach any student in whom he recognized talent even if the pupil could not pay for the lessons. Albertieri spoke very little English, accompanied his classes on the violin, and is remembered for his strict adherence to ballet traditions, never allowing the girls to do big jumps and permitting only waist-high kicks.

The most important dancer at the Metropolitan Opera during this period was the Italian Rosina Galli (1896–1940). A prima ballerina at La Scala, she left Italy in 1911 to become the star of the Chicago Grand Opera Ballet. When the company disbanded in 1914 Galli was immediately engaged by the Metropolitan Opera. A tiny elf-like dancer, she was acclaimed for her strong pirouettes and powerful Italian technique. In 1919 Galli was appointed ballet mistress, but continued to dance lead roles through 1931. As supervisor of the ballet school, Galli taught in the traditional nineteenth-century Italian manner, pounding the floor with an old curtain pole and hurling insults at unsatisfactory performers. Her outbursts, however, were always followed by embraces for the crying dancers. She deserves much credit for maintaining a reputable ballet company at the Metropolitan Opera during the economic hardships of the early 1930s when dancers continuously left the opera for more lucrative jobs in Broadway musicals.

From 1938 to 1941 the prima ballerina at the Metropolitan Opera was Maria Gambarelli (1900–1990). Though born in Spezia, Gambarelli was raised and trained in the United States and is considered one of the first American ballerinas in that her dancing reflected multicultural training. Gambarelli began her studies at the Metropolitan Opera, performed with Anna Pavlova's company and in vaudeville, and in 1920 headed the bill at the Capitol Theatre, a New York movie house that presented live stage shows along with feature films. Gambarelli became a popular success with movie-going audiences, dancing more than four thousand performances at the Capitol, where, by 1923, she had become ballet mistress. Her popularity continued to grow when she became a featured performer on "Roxy's Gang," a 1920s radio program directed by the theatrical impresario Samuel "Roxy" Rothafel. The ballerina became known as "Gamby" to radio audiences, who delighted in her singing of Italian patter songs. In 1927, when Gambarelli became prima ballerina and ballet mistress at the newly opened Roxy Theatre, she organized a precision dancing troupe called the "Roxyettes," the precursor of the famous Rockettes of Radio City Music Hall. When the Music Hall opened in 1932, Gambarelli directed its ballet corps and performed as prima ballerina. Gambarelli also appeared in Hollywood films and made guest appearances throughout the United States, striving to teach the American public about ballet.

While the opera and popular ballet stages of early-twentieth-century America were dominated by Italian dancers, the prominent dance studios of the time were run by Italian teachers who laid the foundation of Italian ballet technique on a new generation of American dancers. One of the most influential teachers of the time was Vincenzo Celli (1900–1988) [Vincenzo Yacullo]. Though born in Salerno, Celli and his family moved to Chicago when he was two years old. In 1919, however, he returned to Italy, studied with Cecchetti, and became ballet master at La Scala, where he grew to resent Mussolini's control. Moreover, as he had spent his boyhood in Chicago, Celli felt he was more American than Italian and returned to the United States and set up his New York studio in 1941, where he taught the Cecchetti technique for forty years. Celli always maintained that the Italians created their style of ballet technique "out of their genius"; that is, their dance movements did not exist previously, whereas the Russians simply evolved and changed what the Italians had taught them.

When Russian dancers began appearing in the United States, a new Russian-based style of American ballet developed. However, while Italian immigrants lost their controlling position in ballet performance and training, new generations of Italian Americans emerged who continued to play major roles in shaping American dance. For example, while it was the Russian choreographer George Balanchine who invented a new American ballet style, one of his first American prima ballerinas was the Italian American Gisella Caccialanza (b. 1914). Sent to Italy at a young age to study with Cecchetti, Caccialanza was the last important dancer to have trained directly under

D

the Italian master. During the 1930s and 1940s Caccialanza was a prima ballerina with the American ballet companies that showcased Balanchine's work prior to the founding of his New York City Ballet. In 1944, as a guest artist with the San Francisco Ballet, Caccialanza starred in what was the first complete performance of *The Nutcracker* in the United States. One of the first male dancers to work extensively with Balanchine was the Italian American Fred Danieli (b. 1917) [Alfredo Carlo Danieli], who performed the choreographer's work on the ballet stage as well as in Broadway musicals. In 1949 Danieli established New Jersey's first professional ballet school and, in 1961, founded the Garden State Ballet.

Unquestionably, the most popular American male ballet dancer of all time is the Italian American Edward Villella (b. 1936), who became a principal with New York City Ballet in 1960. Balanchine was inspired to create many ballets for Villella including *Tarantella,* a furiously fast, exhausting dance tailor-made to Villella's personality and technical strengths. Villella has stated that his inherited southern Italian temperament was a valuable theatrical force in his performing, infusing his dancing with passion and the ability to be operatic in his interpretations. Villella's dancing was characterized by an athletic virility that did much to popularize the role of the male dancer among the general public. Injuries forced Villella to stop dancing in the late 1970s, but in 1986 he became the founding artistic director of the Miami City Ballet, which has achieved worldwide fame under his leadership. In the tradition of Gambarelli and the nineteenth-century ballerinas, Villella worked to increase Americans' awareness of ballet by dancing on television programs and making guest appearances across the country, frequently partnering the Italian ballerina Anna Aragno (b. 1945). Another Italian-American male dancer, Robert Maiorano (b. 1946), was a soloist with New York City Ballet from 1969 to 1984 but made his most unique contributions to dance when he retired from performing and wrote *Balanchine's Mozartiana,* a book that gives an insider's perspective on the choreographer's working methods. He also authored award-winning children's books about his life and the ballet world.

Unlike most dancers of Italian heritage, the Italian American Kay Mazzo (b. 1947) was a serene, lyrical dancer, technically brilliant but not dramatic. She joined the New York City Ballet in 1962 and was a principal by 1969, when Balanchine's then-favorite ballerina, Suzanne Farrell, left the company after many of her roles were given to Mazzo. In addition, Balanchine created roles for Mazzo in almost a dozen ballets. One of New York City Ballet's recent stars is the Italian-American ballerina Maria Calegari (b. 1957), who became a principal in 1983. While critics have marveled at her versatility and technical skill, she has also been described as the most romantic and mysterious ballerina of her generation.

Though many Italian Americans contributed their talents to the development of Balanchine's work at New York City Ballet, others chose to dance the eclectic repertoire of American Ballet Theatre. The company's most famous Italian American dancer was Eleanor D'Antuono (b. 1939) [Eleanor Jacobs], who, as a child, lived with her maternal Italian immigrant grandparents and chose to use their name when she began performing at the age of fourteen with the Ballet Russe de Monte Carlo. In 1961 D'Antuono joined American Ballet Theatre as a soloist and was a principal by 1963. In 1979 she became the first American star invited to perform with Russia's Kirov Ballet on a Russian stage. While American Ballet Theatre has frequently presented Italian stars such as Carla Fracci (b. 1936) and Paolo Bortoluzzi (b. 1938) as guest artists, the Italian ballerina Alessandra Ferri (b. 1963) joined the company as a principal dancer in 1985. A supple, willowy dancer, Ferri brings a bigger and more passionate acting style to her roles than do her American colleagues. In 1987 Ferri co-starred with Mikhail Baryshnikov in the film *Dancers* and, in 1988, was chosen to dance *Giselle* with Rudolf Nureyev at his fiftieth-birthday celebration in Los Angeles.

New York City Ballet and American Ballet Theatre are generally considered America's leading ballet troupes, while the third-ranked company is often thought to be the Joffrey Ballet. Named after its founder, Robert Joffrey (1930–1988) [Abdullah Jaffa Bey Khan], who was born in Seattle of an Italian mother and an Afghan father, the company is currently headed by the Italian American Gerald Arpino (b. 1928). The Italian mothers of Arpino and Joffrey had been personal friends, so when Arpino was sent to Seattle with the Coast

Guard, his mother asked him to contact Joffrey, who convinced Arpino to join him in his dance studies. Joffrey relocated to New York City, where he founded a ballet school in 1953 and invited Arpino to serve on its faculty. Three years later Joffrey began choreographing and formed a company to showcase his work. Arpino, one of Joffrey's original company members, made his choreographic debut with the company in 1961 and remained with the company until Joffrey's death, at which time he assumed artistic directorship.

In addition to their work in New York companies, Italian Americans have played major roles in the development of regional ballet. For example, the Italian American Val Caniparoli (b. 1951) is a principal character dancer and one of the resident choreographers of San Francisco Ballet. Since he began choreographing in 1979, Caniparoli has been recognized for the inventiveness of his musical selections and for the implicit drama in his movement. Caniparoli dedicated his 1989 ballet *Connotations* to the memory of *Dance Magazine's* late editor-in-chief, the Italian American William Como (1925–1989). Other Italian Americans who have influenced regional ballet include Ronn Guidi (b. 1936), the founder and artistic director of California's Oakland Ballet; Salvatore Aiello (1944–1995), formerly the artistic director of Charlotte's North Carolina Dance Theatre; and Tony Catanzaro (b. 1946), who was a principal with the Boston Ballet before he founded the Ballet Academy of Miami in 1984 and became artistic director for Tampa Bay's Ballet Theatre in 1994.

In addition to their ballet work, Italian Americans have made remarkable contributions to American popular dance forms in vaudeville, burlesque, nightclubs, Broadway musicals, Hollywood films, and television. Many first-generation Italian Americans discovered popular dancing to be a lucrative profession whereby they could call forth and combine their exceptional athletic skills with the innate musicality and artistic sensibilities often nurtured in their Italian homes. For example, two of the most extraordinary American vaudeville dancers were the Mosconi Brothers, who amazed viewers with their acrobatic hoofing routines. Their grandfather, who had been a ballet master in Genoa, migrated to Philadelphia, where, in 1908, his son, Charles Mosconi (c. 1867–1942), opened a successful dancing school and fathered the famous brothers, Charles (c. 1891–1975) and Louis Mosconi (1895–1969). The duo set a vaudeville record by playing the Palace fifty-two weeks out of a seven-year period. They performed as vaudeville headliners throughout the country and at London's Palladium Theatre, where they were billed as "The 8th Wonder of the World."

One of the greatest stars of burlesque was the Italian American stripper Ann Corio (1916–1999). Described as the most beautiful and highest-paid of all striptease artists, Corio was never vulgar onstage and did not perform the traditional bumps and grinds. Instead, she was known as a dignified "walker" who moved back and forth across the stage with an undulating glide. Corio's performances at Boston's Old Howard Theatre became legendary, inspiring the popular saying among Harvard men: "You can't graduate until you've seen Ann Corio."

The Broadway musical, America's unique contribution to the theater arts, has been strongly influenced by the work of Italian American choreographers and dancers. One of the most acclaimed Broadway shows of all time is the 1957 musical *West Side Story* and, while it is well known that the show was directed and choreographed by Jerome Robbins, many viewers never realized that it was Robbins' assistant, the Italian American dancer Peter Gennaro (b. 1924), who created the show's fiery Latin-American choreography. Critics have called Gennaro "the greatest white jazz dancer in America." In addition to choreographing *Fiorello!* (1959), *The Unsinkable Molly Brown* (1960), and *Annie*, for which he won a 1977 Tony Award, during the 1950s and 1960s Gennaro was the leading choreographer of television variety programs. One of Gennaro's early performing jobs in New York was as a member of a dance troupe directed by the Italian American Danny Daniels (b. 1924) [Daniel Giagni, Jr.]. An acclaimed Broadway dancer, Daniels choreographed Hollywood films, staged nightclub and television shows for numerous celebrities, and won a 1983 Tony Award for choreographing Broadway's *The Tap Dance Kid*.

A Chorus Line, the longest-running Broadway musical of all time, won the Pulitzer Prize in 1976. The show was conceived, directed, and choreographed by the Italian American Michael Bennett (1943–

1987) [Michael Bennett Di Figlia]. Bennett's first Broadway hit was *Promises, Promises* (1968), followed by *Company* (1970) and *Follies* (1971), which he co-directed. Bennett was also director-choreographer of *Ballroom* (1978) and *Dreamgirls* (1981). One of the original cast members of Bennett's *A Chorus Line* was the Italian American dancer Wayne Cilento (b. 1949), who won a 1993 Tony Award for choreographing Broadway's *The Who's Tommy* and recently choreographed the 1995 Broadway revival of *How to Succeed in Business Without Really Trying*. Another Italian American who has figured prominently on Broadway in recent years is Dan Siretta (b. 1940). His specialty is recreating dances of the past for Broadway revivals of musicals from the 1920s and 1930s.

Other Italian American dancers worked extensively on Broadway but made greater contributions in other dance arenas. Lou Conte (b. 1942), for example, performed in Broadway musicals during the 1960s then, in 1977, founded the Chicago-based, nationally recognized jazz dance company Hubbard Street Dance Chicago. Though Tony Stevens (b. 1948) [Anthony Edward Pusateri] danced and choreographed on Broadway, he is best known as choreographer of the Hollywood films *The Great Gatsby* (1974) and *The Best Little Whorehouse in Texas* (1982).

One of Hollywood's most prolific choreographers was the Italian American Nick Castle (1910–1968) [Nicola Casaccio], who choreographed dozens of films and worked with virtually every dancing film star. He devised the patterns for Sonja Henie's skating sequences and created tap numbers for Shirley Temple. For the film *Royal Wedding* (1951), Castle helped Fred Astaire choreograph his duet with the hat rack as well as the amazing number in which Astaire dances on the walls and ceiling. For the acrobatic tap dance duo, the Nicholas Brothers, Castle invented what became their most famous trick—climbing up a wall and back flipping into a split—a variation of a stunt invented by the Mosconi Brothers. Castle's son, the film director Nick Castle, Jr. (b. 1947), honored the memory of the Hollywood musicals his father worked on by making the 1989 film *Tap*, starring dancer Gregory Hines. The film celebrates the history of tap dance and includes Hines' performance of a contemporary electronic tap number inspired by the work of the Italian-American

dancer Al Desio (b. 1932), who was a consultant on the film. Desio built electronic transmitters into Hines' tap shoes that connected to synthesizers, giving the dancer the ability to create a variety of different sounds while dancing. As a child Desio recalled his Italian cobbler grandfather proudly showing him a special pair of shoes he had made and, as an adult, came to value that memory when he achieved recognition as the inventor of electronic tap shoes.

During the heyday of exhibition ballroom dance, the 1930s and 1940s, the two most popular teams, Veloz and Yolanda and The Dancing De Marcos, each featured an Italian-American dancer. Yolanda Veloz (c. 1911–1995) [Yolanda Casazza], in a dancing partnership with her husband, Frank Veloz, did much to elevate ballroom dance to a concert form and performed the first recital of ballroom dance ever given at Carnegie Hall. Tony De Marco (1898–1965), who became one of the world's most famous ballroom dancers, performed for four decades, with ten different partners. De Marco's father, a farmer, was vehemently opposed to his son's interest in dance because his own father had lost the family's mill near Palermo due to his penchant for sneaking off to dance in folk festivals around Italy and neglecting his work at home. Unlike his grandfather, De Marco became a millionaire as a dancer and brought innovations such as comic patter and classical-music accompaniment to the exhibition ballroom dance stage. One of the most prominent figures in social ballroom dance was the Italian American Frank "Killer Joe" Piro (1921–1989), the first non–African American to win the National Jitterbug Championship at the Harvest Moon Ball. During World War II, Piro danced regularly at New York's Stage Door Canteen, where he earned the nickname "Killer Joe" as his nonstop dancing left numerous exhausted partners "dead" on the floor. In 1947 Piro opened a studio in New York and became the city's most fashionable social dance instructor.

Italian Americans have distinguished themselves as important educators in all fields of dance. One of the world's most beloved jazz dance teachers is Luigi (b. 1925) [Luigino Facciuto], who went to Hollywood in 1946 to pursue film work and was injured in a car accident, paralyzed, and severely disfigured. Though doctors predicted he would not walk again, Luigi worked religiously reteaching his body how to balance on his legs and gradually regained his ability to move. During his rehabilitation period he developed an innovative method of dance training based on a personally discovered understanding of how the body learns to move. After relocating to New York in 1956, Luigi opened his own studio and developed an international reputation as the world's most respected jazz dance teacher. Another world renowned figure in the field of jazz dance education is the Italian American Gus Giordano (b. 1930). After a brief performing career, in 1956 Giordano founded a dance school, and later a company, in Chicago. In 1990 he organized the first Jazz Dance World Congress, an international conference held biannually in Chicago to promote the continued development of jazz dance. One of the most famous names in children's dance education is Al Gilbert (b. 1921) [Allesandro Zicari], who opened his Hollywood Theatrical Dance School in 1947 and developed the first spoken dance records, with music and vocal instruction, to teach dance to children.

In addition to their work as artists and educators in ballet and popular dance forms, Italian immigrants and their descendants also contributed to American modern dance, beginning with the Braggiotti sisters, who were born in Italy and moved to Boston in 1919. Berthe de Pourtales Braggiotti (1901–1928) and Francesca Braggiotti (b. 1903) gave what was probably the first barefoot dancing performance on a Boston stage and were criticized for wearing gold earrings that the Bostonians felt made them look like Italian peasants. Their performance sparked interest in this new free style of dancing, however, which they began to teach to the children of Boston's wealthy families in a studio that became one of the most successful modern dance schools in the country. Francesca also dubbed Greta Garbo's earliest sound films into Italian. When the dancer later appeared in Italian films, another actress had to speak her lines because Italian audiences had come to associate her voice with Garbo.

One of the first Italian Americans to figure prominently in modern dance was the noted choreographer Paul Sanasardo (b. 1928). He has referred to his Sicilian blood when explaining why he lost interest in ballet in favor of modern dance, which he felt better encompassed a sense of anguish and accommodated his expressionistic choreography that often conveyed pain and despair.

The most influential figure in American modern dance was, unquestionably, Martha Graham (1895–1991), who developed her technique and much of her choreography on her own body. When she could no longer perform, she carefully chose the dancers who would inherit the great dramatic roles she had created. During the 1970s, 1980s, and 1990s, Graham's works have been danced by three remarkable Italian-American women. Elisa Monte (b. 1946) joined the Martha Graham Dance Company in 1974 and, as a principal dancer, was noted for her intense dramatic presence and keenness of attack. Another acclaimed Graham interpreter, Jacqulyn Buglisi (b. 1950), danced with the Martha Graham Dance Company from 1977 to 1990 and founded the first dance company in Italy based on the Graham technique. In the mid-1980s Terese Capucilli (b. 1956) was considered the foremost interpreter of Graham's dramatic roles. For a new work, *The Rite of Spring* (1984), Graham created the role of "The Chosen One" for Capucilli.

In contrast to Graham's expressive choreography, the inventive work of Italian Simone Forti (b. 1935) exemplifies the postmodern intellectual approach to dance. Forti was born in Florence but raised in California, where, from 1956 to 1960, she worked with Ann Halprin's Dance Workshop making collectively choreographed dances. Forti's esoteric works have been counted among the most influential avant-garde works of the 1960s and 1970s and played a major role in shaping the postmodern dance aesthetic.

A more popular-style modern dancer, the Italian American Louis Falco (1942–1993), was first noticed by critics when he was a principal dancer with the José Limon Dance Company in the 1960s and formed his own company in 1968. Falco attributed his explosive dance style to the robust Neapolitan gaiety of his Italian heritage, a quality that permeates Falco's most well-known choreography, the dances he created for the 1980 film *Fame*.

One of the 1990s most provocative postmodern choreographers is the Italian American Stephen Petronio (b. 1956). The first male dancer in the Trisha Brown Company, Petronio was recognized as a charismatic, technically brilliant performer and, in 1984, formed his own company. Petronio's work induces shock and rapture and often wrestles with questions of sexual identity.

As unlikely as it may seem, the leading performer and popularizer of Spanish dance in the United States, Jose Greco (b. 1918) [Costanzo Greco], was born in Italy and raised in Brooklyn. In 1948 he founded his own company that brought Spanish dance performances to numerous venues across America and made many television appearances. The fact that Greco was Italian, and not Spanish, was held against him by purists, but the critics conceded that Greco was the undisputed American Spanish dance star. Perhaps the most prominent expert in the field of ethnic dance is the Italian American performer, choreographer, teacher, and author Matteo [Matteo Vittucci]. In 1961 Matteo started the Foundation for Ethnic Dance, a research and advisory organization, and introduced the study of ethnic dance into the curriculum at New York City's High School for the Performing Arts.

The contributions of Italian Americans to dance go beyond the performers and choreographers. For example, the presentation of dance on television in recent years represents a major advance in the preservation of American dance history and is best exemplified by the public television series "Dance in America," which was created by the Italian American producer Jac Venza (b. 1926). Furthermore, the series' director was the Italian American filmmaker Emile Ardolino (1943–1993). It is also important to recognize the contributions of a nineteenth-century Italian immigrant who has had an unusually far-reaching impact on dance in that virtually every American dancer has at some point in his or her career worn a dance shoe manufactured by the Capezio company. Salvatore Capezio (1871–1940) came to the United States in 1887 and opened his cobbler's shop across the street from the Metropolitan Opera House. Capezio made friends with the Italian immigrants who worked in the company's wardrobe department and who, in turn, suggested that the ballet dancers bring their shoes to him for repair. Capezio soon began constructing dance shoes for all kinds of dancers, including the ballerina Anna Pavlova as well as Eleanor Powell and Broadway chorus girls. His company grew into a large corporation that is still run by descendants of the Capezio family.

Taken together, the Italian contributions to dance in America exhibit some illuminating common characteristics. Virtually all of the great performers of Italian descent were recognized for their technical and dramatic abilities. They excelled in the performance of extraordinarily difficult physical movements and were often noted for their passionate dancing. Philosophically, the dancers of Italian descent were not elitist and seem to have been committed to educating the American public about dance, both as distinguished, innovative teachers and as performers who unselfishly toured the country to dance in whatever venues or media the public enjoyed. In reviewing the history of American dance, it becomes clear that the Italian influence permeated all forms of dance—classical, modern, popular, and ethnic—and that many Italian Americans found dance to be an important arena in which to exercise their artistic talents.

Lisa Jo Sagolla

Bibliography

Bailey, Sally, ed. "Letters from the Maestro: Enrico Cecchetti to Gisella Caccialanza." *Dance Perspectives* 4 (1971): 1–56.

Barker, Barbara. *Ballet or Ballyhoo: The American Careers of Maria Bonfanti, Rita Sangalli, and Giuseppina Morlacchi.* New York: Dance Horizons, 1984.

Braggiotti, Gloria. *Born in a Crowd.* New York: Thomas Y. Crowell, 1957.

Greco, Jose, and Harvey Ardman. *The Gypsy in My Soul.* Garden City, NY: Doubleday, 1977.

Kelly, Kevin. *One Singular Sensation: The Michael Bennett Story.* New York: Doubleday, 1990.

Limarzi, Tullia. "She Trills With Her Toes: The Metropolitan Opera Ballet Career of Rosina Galli." *Proceedings of the Society of Dance History Scholars Ninth Annual Conference,* 1986.

Maiorano, Robert. *Worlds Apart: The Autobiography of a Dancer from Brooklyn.* New York: Coward, McCann & Geoghegan, 1980.

Mandelbaum, Ken. *A Chorus Line and the Musicals of Michael Bennett.* New York: St. Martin's, 1989.

Villella, Edward, and Larry Kaplan. *Prodigal Son: Dancing for Balanchine in a World of Pain and Magic.* New York: Simon & Schuster, 1992.

See also BENNETT, MICHAEL; GENNARO, PETER; THEATER HISTORY

Danza, Tony
See TELEVISION

Da Ponte, Lorenzo (1749–1838)

Opera librettist and poet, Lorenzo Da Ponte was born on March 10, 1749, in Ceneda (now Vittorio Veneto), near Venice. He and his two brothers converted from Judaism to Christianity at age fourteen when his father, Geronimo, converted to marry Catholic Orsola Pasqua Paietta. At the same time, the family name was changed from Conegliano to Da Ponte in honor of the bishop of Ceneda.

His life remained unorthodox. He studied at the Ceneda Seminary and the Portogruaro Seminary, where he taught from 1770 to 1773. He then taught at the seminary in Treviso (1774–1776), from which he was dismissed because of his beliefs on natural laws. In 1773 he was ordained a priest but was banned from the republic of Venice in 1779 because of adultery. He then went to Gorizia, where he wrote occasional poems to earn a living. He had begun dabbling in poetry (Italian and Latin) while teaching literature at Portogruaro. After visiting Vienna in late 1780, he settled in that fabled city in 1781, where he became the librettist at the new Imperial Theater.

For the next decade he wrote librettos for Antonio Salieri (1750–1825) and Vicente Martin y Soler (1754–1806), two lesser operatic lights, and the great Wolfgang Amadeus Mozart (1756–1791). Da Ponte and Mozart became friends and Da Ponte wrote the librettos for three of the master's greatest operas, *Le nozze di Figaro* (The Marriage of Figaro) (1786), *Don Giovanni* (Don Juan) (1787), and *Cosi fan tutte* (All Women Are Like That) (1790). By 1790 he was in trouble again, antagonizing the artistic section of Vienna by his haughty attitude. He left that city in 1792. Behind him he left three of the finest librettos of the eighteenth century. Although not always original, his texts were inventive and utilized ideas and styles from others very well.

From 1792 to 1805 he resided mostly in London, where he was librettist to the Italian Opera from 1793 to around 1798, when he again lost his position because of his personal traits. He tried several business enterprises, including a bookstore and a print shop, but they were not successful partly due to Da Ponte's tendencies for intrigue and unpopular business practices.

In 1805, he and his longtime mate, Nancy Grahl, together with their children, migrated to New York. Grahl had lived with Da Ponte until 1832, but they never married. In the new land, Da Ponte taught Italian language and literature at institutions such as Columbia University, in between more business failures. He published his memoirs in 1823 and produced his *Don Giovanni* in 1825 in New York. He died in that city on August 17, 1838.

William E. Studwell

Bibliography

Da Ponte, Lorenzo. *Memoirs of Lorenzo Da Ponte*. Edited by Arthur Livingston. New York: Orion Press, 1929.

Fitzlyon, April. *The Libertine Librettist: A Biography of Mozart's Librettist Lorenzo Da Ponte*. London: J. Calder, 1955.

Hodges, Sheila. *Lorenzo Da Ponte: The Life and Times of Mozart's Librettist*. London: Grafton, 1985.

Russo, Joseph Louis. *Lorenzo Da Ponte: Poet and Adventurer*. New York: Columbia University Press, 1922.

Steptoe, Andrew. *The Mozart–Da Ponte Operas: The Cultural and Musical Background to Le nozze di Figaro, Don Giovanni and Cosi fan tutte*. Oxford: Clarendon Press, 1988.

See also OPERA

DeBartolo, Edward J. (1909–1994)

Starting from the bottom and reaching the top of the business world, Edward DeBartolo combined ingenuity and hard work to become the leading builder of shopping malls in the United States. He also operated a lucrative road and motel building business and constructed an empire in sports, which now has a multimillion-dollar investment in racetracks, hockey, baseball, and a football team (the San Francisco '49ers).

DeBartolo was born in Youngstown, Ohio, in 1909 and was the oldest of three sons and three daughters of Michael and Rose DeBartolo. He grew up in a disciplined Italian household and became an assistant to his father, who was a master mason and later a general contractor. DeBartolo earned a bachelor of science degree in civil engineering, graduating from Notre Dame University. After college, he joined his father as partner in the family business and immediately expanded into commercial building. In 1940 he made his first real estate deal, buying a corner in Boardman, Ohio. He entered the Army Corps of Engineers in 1941 during World War II. In 1948, after the war, he started his own company. Two years later he developed Boardman Plaza, and his success story began. He served as chairman of the board and chief executive officer of the Edward J. DeBartolo Corporation in Youngstown, where he remained a lifelong resident until his death in 1994.

In 1980 DeBartolo actively pursued the purchase of the Chicago White Sox baseball team, but was ultimately rejected by Baseball Commissioner Bowie K. Kuhn because he owned several racetracks and was not a resident of Chicago. Kuhn's rejection of DeBartolo's offer outraged Italian Americans. Many concluded that the real reason was DeBartolo's Italian American heritage and its association with gangster stereotypes. Several newspaper reports, as well as a letter released by the National Italian American Foundation, pointed out that a number of owners were absentee owners and did not live in the cities in which they owned and controlled baseball franchises, such as Edward Bennett, owner of the Baltimore Orioles. Also, DeBartolo indicated that he would be willing to divest himself of gambling interests in order to obtain the approval. George Steinbrenner, managing partner and principal owner of the New York Yankees, also had an interest in racetracks.

DeBartolo married Marie Patricia and had two children, Edward Jr., and Marie Denise, who are both officers and stockholders in the company. He has been recognized as the "shopping center king of the world." At one time, he was opening a shopping center on the average of one every ten days in the United States. The Edward J. DeBartolo Corporation continues to be an active real estate firm in many parts of the country, and DeBartolo is remembered nationally as an innovative business leader and one of the largest developers of shopping malls in America.

Gina Dell'Aquila

Bibliography

Carney, Charles J. "An American Success Story." *Congressional Record.* Vol. 119. May 2, 1973.

Lear, Martha Weinman. "A Master Builder Sites a Shopping Mall." *New York Times Magazine,* Section 6, 12 August 1973.

Rothman, Seymour. "Ohio's Empire Builder." *Toledo Magazine, The Blade,* 8 January 1978.

See also BUSINESS AND ENTREPRENEURSHIP

De Biasi, Agostino (1875–1964)

A writer, editor, and journalist, Agostino De Biasi was born in the town of Santo Angelo dei Lombardi in the province of Avellino, Italy. A legal and religious strain ran through the family's background: some of his forebears had been in religious orders, and both his grandfather and father were lawyers. During the period 1892 to 1898 he worked in Milan as a writer and, more especially, as an editor for such newspapers as *La Tribuna* and *Del Popolo Irpino*.

In 1900 he migrated to the United States, settling in New York City. He soon became associated with *Il Progresso Italo-Americano,* a popular and prestigious newspaper. Within a few months he achieved the rank of editor-in-chief, and four years later in 1904 he served as editor of the newspaper *Il Telegrafo* for a two-year period. In 1905 he also became founder of a Philadelphia paper, *L' Opinione,* and six years later De Biasi severed his relationship with *Il Progresso Italo-Americano* to become editor-in-chief of another New York City newspaper, *L'Araldo Italiano.*

In 1915 De Biasi fulfilled his ambition of establishing a magazine devoted to political and literary aspects when he became the chief founder of *Il Carroccio.* This magazine continued with a brief lapse until 1935. Considered a leading monthly periodical, it served at times as a vehicle for Fascist propaganda during the early rise of Mussolini and Italian nationalism after World War I. De Biasi equated Fascism with his strong Italian nationalism, and he saw its philosophy as the best way to enable Italy to gain more political power in Europe and to aid the country economically.

During 1923 and 1924 he was secretary general of the *Consiglio Centrale Fascista del Nord America,* an organization that sought to implement Fascist propaganda among Italians in North America. De Biasi, however, soon became disillusioned with Fascism, fell out of favor with its leaders, and in 1927 *Il Carroccio* was banned in Italy. For a three-year period (1928 to 1931) publication had to be suspended due to a decline in readership. As his interest in journalism and writing remained strong, De Biasi, at the age of 60, began to write occasional articles for the Brooklyn, New York, Catholic weekly, *Il Crociato,* with which his brother Carlo, also a journalist, was very closely associated. At the same time, he wrote a syndicated column carried by many Italian American newspapers in the United States.

De Biasi wrote several books, including *La Tradizione Musicale Italiana* (1911), *Kara-Kiri* (1922), and *La Battaglia dell'Italia negli Stati Uniti* (1927). He was well known for his participation in Italian American affairs in New York City and was one of the moving forces behind the establishment of the Italy-America Society, a cultural organization, and the Dante Alighieri Society of New York.

Nicholas Joseph Falco

Bibliography
Della Cava, Ohla. *Guide to the Archives of the Center for Migration Studies.* Vol. II. Staten Island, NY: Center for Migration Studies, 1977.
Flamma, Ario. *Italiani Di America—Enciclopedia Biografica Completa Da Ario Flamma.* New York: Cocce Press, 1949.
LaGumina, Salvatore J. *The Immigrants Speak: Italian Americans Tell Their Story.* Staten Island, NY: Center for Migration Studies, 1979.
Salvemini, Gaetano. *Italian Fascist Activities in the United States.* Staten Island, NY: Center for Migration Studies, 1977.

DeCarlo, Nicholas (1879–1961)
A pioneer Roman Catholic priest in the mid-south area of the United States, Father Nicholas DeCarlo was born in Avigliano near Potenza Italy, and attended Our Lady of Good Counsel Seminary in Naples. He was ordained in 1902, and most of his earlier years as a priest were spent as a member of the Augustinian Order. He petitioned Church authorities to release him from his monastic vows so that he could join the ranks of the diocesan clergy.

After serving as a parish priest in Naples for six years, he was commissioned to assist in the newly established parish of Saint Rita in Philadelphia, and from 1908 to 1912 was a curate there. The next year, at the suggestion of Archbishop Bonzano, the Apostolic Delegate, he was asked by the archbishop of Baltimore, Cardinal James Gibbons, to try to establish a parish for the growing Italian American population in the nation's capital, Washington, D.C., which up to that time had not had a parish of its own. Father DeCarlo accepted the challenge and opened a small chapel called the Holy Rosary. He then gradually made a more refined analysis of the area's demographics, which guided his plans to build a larger church. By 1919 enough funds had been collected so that in September of that year a foundation for the church could be laid. By 1923, a magnificent edifice, the Church of the Holy Rosary, was built and dedicated at Third and F Streets, Northwest, just about a mile from the United States Capitol.

Known for his administrative skills, Father DeCarlo early in his pastorate formed several church groups including a boys' marching band and a Union of Italian Catholic Women, a group that provided health and death benefits to its members. Holy Rosary Parish attracted not only the Italian American population of the District itself, but also suburbanites who were not numerically concentrated to establish ethnic parishes in their own areas. Italian communities were not as strong in the South as they were farther north along the Atlantic seaboard. Hence, Holy Rosary became a symbol of Italian presence, and Father DeCarlo, with his interest in every detail of his parishioners' lives and abiding concern for their welfare, often served as their spokesman.

In the early 1950s, moved by the needs of senior citizens, he purchased land for a nursing and rest home to be called the Villa Rosa Rest Home in the nearby Washington suburb of Mitchellville, Maryland. He did not live long enough to see his dream reach fruition. Father DeCarlo remained pastor of the Holy Rosary until his retirement in 1960 at the age of 81.

Nicholas Joseph Falco

Bibliography
Della Cava, Olha. *A Guide to the Archives of the Center for Migration Studies.* Vol. II. Staten Island, NY: Center for Migration Studies, 1977.

45th Anniversary Celebration. Holy Rosary
    Church, Washington, D.C., 18 April
    1959.
50th Golden Jubilee. Holy Rosary Church,
    Washington, D.C., 1913–1963.
*The Parish of Holy Rosary in Washington,
    D.C.: Twenty–five Years of Mission
    Work, 1913–1938.*

See also RELIGION

Delaware

One of the most successful, yet rarely examined, regions of Italian settlement occurred in the state of Delaware. Italian presence in the nation's first state dates back to the colonial period. In 1656, the Waldensians, a group of Italian Protestants who had fled from Piedmont, set sail from Holland to the New World. Scholars have long asserted that Waldensians established a colony in New Castle, Delaware; however, while Waldensians did pass through the area, no evidence proves conclusively that they stayed.

Caesar Rodney (1728–1784), a signer of the Declaration of Independence, was of Italian descent, with his lineage tracing back to an Italian doctor who migrated from the city of Treviso to England in 1550. During his lifetime, Rodney served in nearly every official capacity for Delaware, including president of the state and major general during the Revolutionary War. On July 2, 1776, though sick with cancer and detained by inclement weather, he rode to Philadelphia to cast his vote for independence.

Paralleling the national trend in immigration, Italians began arriving in Delaware in the late nineteenth century. The majority were laborers who found work with the Du Pont Company and the Baltimore & Ohio Railroad. The immigrants settled predominantly in northern Delaware, forming colonies in the greater Wilmington area, New Castle, Claymont, Montchanin, and Hockessin. Migrant farm laborers also worked throughout the state's southern counties, but they generally rotated their time between Delaware, Pennsylvania, and New Jersey.

One distinguishing characteristic of the Italian immigrants in Delaware was their desire to assimilate. The immigrants wanted to be contributing Americans; they studied English, became citizens, and worked diligently for victory in World War I. Indeed, the oldest-

known club formed by the immigrants was the Italian Republican League, a forum through which they participated in local political affairs. Also of note is the West End Neighborhood House in Wilmington, which provided assimilation classes and programs for Italians.

St. Anthony's Church, located in the heart of Wilmington's Little Italy, has served as a unifying force for Italians. Chartered in 1924 as an explicitly Italian parish, St. Anthony's became a community power through its talented stewards, Father Francis Tucker (1889–1972) and Father Roberto Balducelli (b. 1913). The church, along with its schools, summer camp, annual festival, and outreach programs, continues to serve as a marker by which the Italian Americans define their heritage.

In 1880 there were forty-three Italian-born residents in Delaware. According to a 1990 census, there are today over 63,000 residents of Italian descent. Along with the professional fields, Italian Americans have evinced themselves in land development and construction. Since 1950 Italian Americans have played a role in nearly every parcel of land developed in northern Delaware. Indeed, rather than diminishing over time, Italian American influence continues to flourish within the confines of this small but noteworthy state.

Ciro C. Poppiti, III

Bibliography

Benson, Barbara. *Arriving in Delaware: The Italian American Experience.* Wilmington: Italo-Americans United, 1989.

Frank, William P. *Caesar Rodney Patriot: Delaware's Hero for All Times and Seasons.* Wilmington: Delaware Heritage Commission and Italo-Americans United, 1992.

Thompson, Priscilla M. *Pockets of Settlement: The Italian American Experience in Delaware.* Wilmington: Italo-Americans United, 1979.

DeLillo, Don
See LITERATURE; PLAYS, CONTEMPORARY

Della Chiesa, Vivian (b. 1914)
A major Italian American opera star, Vivian Della Chiesa was born in Chicago, the daughter of Ettore from Varese and Olivia Morelli of

Lucca. She made her operatic debut in the Chicago Opera on November 15, 1936, after winning a contest the year before in which 3,800 women competed. She is a lyric soprano and became a protege of Arturo Toscanini after he heard her singing in a Mozart festival in the early 1940s. At the age of 20 she launched a meteoric rise to fame when she sang three different operas in one week.

Della Chiesa sang opposite all the leading tenors and baritones of the golden age of opera. She was Marguerite in *Faust* with Ezio Pinza, appearing also with him in *Don Giovanni;* in *L'Elisir d'Amore, La Boheme,* and *La Juive,* with Tito Schipa; with Giovanni Martinelli in *Cavalleria Rusticana, Pagliacci,* and *Otello;* as Donna Alicia in *Falstaff,* opposite the basso Salvatore Baccaloni; and as Desdemona with Lawrence Tibbet in *Otello.* Leonard Warren, Robert Merrill, Jan Peerce, Richard Tucker, and Robert Weede played and sang the male leads with her in many operatic and classical musical productions. Her repertoire also included roles in *Andrea Chenier, La Traviata, Madama Butterfly,* and *Tosca.*

She has sung in all the leading opera houses in the United States and throughout the world. During a performance in Grant Park, Chicago, before an audience of two hundred thousand people, she broke the encore record as Henry Weber conducted the Chicago Symphony Orchestra.

Conductors with whom she sang were Arturo Toscanini, Pierre Monteux, Alfred Wallerstein, and Laszlo Halasz (who founded the New York City Opera).

Della Chiesa was the star of her own network radio shows during the period 1935–1960 and appeared in a television weekly network vehicle entitled *Vivian* during the 1960s. She was also a cabaret singer.

During the 1950s and 1960s she made guest appearances in such major television variety shows as *Milton Berle, Bell Telephone Hour,* and the *Ed Sullivan Show.*

Married and widowed twice and presently living in Greenlawn, New York, she continues to teach operatic voice and participates in concerts for charitable causes.

Teresa Cerasuola

Bibliography

Dizikes, John. *Opera in America: A Cultural History.* New Haven, Yale University Press, l993.

New York Times, 3 August 1997.

See also OPERA

Dell Isola, Salvatore (1901-1989)

An outstanding musical director and conductor, Salvatore Dell Isola was born in the province of Salerno, Italy, where as a youngster he gained recognition as a musical prodigy. He migrated with his family to New York in 1907. Displaying musical brilliance while studying the violin, his father returned him to Italy to study at the music conservatory in Salerno. By the time he was 12 he played at the Giuseppe Verdi Opera House and virtually all other theaters in that city.

Upon his return to the United States, he worked as a union musician in a variety of mediums including opera, vaudeville, silent movies, and hotels. Always ready for a challenge, he became a scorer for foreign films in the RKO Studio stock. During his twenties he began a career as the orchestra conductor and musical scorer for a live radio program that engaged prominent singers of the day including Licia Albanese, Mario Del Monaco, Salvatore Baccaloni, and Giovanni Martinelli. Simultaneously, he served as assistant conductor for another orchestra that supplied music for such outstanding show people as Sophie Tucker and Bill "Bojangles" Robinson.

During a ten-year stint, he played violin for the Metropolitan Opera House, where he worked with stars like Ezio Pinza, for whom in 1949 he conducted the Broadway production of *South Pacific.* Dell Isola conducted most of the over 1,900 performances, including the tour, of that Rodgers and Hammerstein musical masterpiece, which also starred Mary Martin. He was also engaged by the United States State Department to conduct for the European touring company of *Oklahoma.*

Dell Isola conducted a number of Broadway hits by Rodgers and Hammerstein including *Allegro, Carousel, The Sound of Music, Me and Juliet,* and *The Flower Drum Song,* for which he won a Tony Award in 1959. For sixteen years he conducted the New York Philharmonic Orchestra in its annual Rodgers and Hammerstein concerts, which consistently attracted audiences of over twenty thousand people.

Dell Isola conducted a television program called *Opera Cameos*. In addition, he conducted at various opera houses in New York and New Jersey. Through a long and active career this versatile musician found a variety of outlets for his talent: opera, symphony, chamber music, string quartets, popular musicals, movie music, radio, television, and vaudeville.

He came out of retirement in 1981 to conduct a benefit performance for victims of the devastating 1980 earthquake in Italy. Although in failing health, he continued to conduct until a year before his death in Babylon, Long Island, in 1989.

Salvatore J. LaGumina

Bibliography
Newsday, 15 March 1989.
New York Times, 16 March 1989.

Dello Joio, Norman (b. 1913)

Member of the Academy of Arts and Letters; recipient of fellowships, awards, and honorary doctorates; educator; and retired dean of Boston University's School of the Arts, Norman Dello Joio ranks among the nation's leading composers. He has written in all traditional genres of serious music and for television and film. Encompassing the Italian legacy, his music is inclusively, multiculturally American.

Casimiro, the composer's father, migrated from Gragnano, near Naples. As band flutist on a naval flagship he gained United States citizenship. Later, organist at a New York church, he married a piano student of Italian parentage. Their only child, Norman, trained early at the keyboard, soon played duets daily with his father and, at 12, became organist and choirmaster at Star of the Sea Church on City Island. In 1940 Norman broke a long family tradition and left his position as church organist. But the organ remained his favorite instrument, and Gregorian themes occur in his compositions. He also kept strong ties to Italian opera.

Dello Joio went on to graduate work at Juilliard, married Grayce Baumgold in 1942, and won the Town Hall Composition Award with an orchestral *Magnificat*. He succeeded William Schuman in teaching composition at Sarah Lawrence College. In 1946, the Polish consul general, having heard Dello Joio perform, invited him to tour Poland. Jazz clarinetist Artie Shaw heard his work at Carnegie Hall, went backstage, and commissioned the *Concertante* for clarinet and orchestra. Other premieres followed nationwide. Universities were hospitable to *A Song of Affirmation* (1953) and the one-act opera *The Ruby* (1955).

Television debuts came in 1956: *The Trial at Rouen* on NBC and *Air Power* on CBS. While composing *Meditations on Ecclesiastes,* which earned him a 1957 Pulitzer Prize, he also wrote a ballet score for José Limon and background music for over twenty CBS films. In 1959 he received the New York Music Critics Circle Award for *The Triumph of St. Joan.*

His internationally performed works include tributes to predecessors (*Homage to Haydn,* 1969; *Salute to Scarlatti,* 1979); arrangements for biblical themes (*Meditations on Ecclesiastes,* 1956; *The Psalmist's Meditation,* 1979); Masses, fantasies, concerti, Christmas music, love songs, satiric dances, vocal, keyboard, chamber, band, orchestral works, operas, and incidental pieces.

Thematically, Dello Joio's American music includes *Ballad of Thomas Jefferson* (1937); Whitman-inspired *Song of the Open Road* (1952), *Songs of Walt Whitman* (1966), and *As of a Dream* (1979); the mixed-chorus *Notes from Tom Paine* (1975); *Colonial Ballads* (1976); and the full-length opera *Blood Moon* (1961), a love story not unlike *La Traviata* derived from the life of Ada Isaacs Mencken, a famous young mid-nineteenth-century octoroon actress.

Dello Joio chaired the Project Policy Committee for the Contemporary Music Project; hosted Soviet and American composers (1959); toured Russia, Romania, and Bulgaria for the State Department (1964); was appointed to the Office of Education's Research Advisory Council (1965); and represented the United States at an arts festival in Hawaii (1966). Other awards followed.

In 1972, divorced, he joined the Boston University faculty and assumed the dean's duties. Even as an administrator, he continued composing. After retirement in 1978, he moved to East Hampton, New York, with actress Barbara Bolton, whom he had married in 1974.

As conventional melody gave way to dodecaphony, serial music, and more avantgarde styles, Dello Joio's repertoire seemed old-fashioned. Yet he endures as a "people's composer," concerned with supporting younger artists and with educating new audiences. Accessibility, lyricism, pleasurable rhythms, master craftsmanship, humor, and boldness keep his music in current performance. His son Justin (b. 1954), one of three children from the first marriage, is also a composer.

Blossom S. Kirschenbaum

Bibliography

The New Grove Dictionary of American Music. New York: Macmillan, 1986, 596–598.

Null, Gary, and Carl Stone. *The Italian Americans.* Harrisburg, PA: Stackpole Books, 1976.

See also COMPOSERS, CLASSICAL

DeLuise, Dom

See COMEDY; MOVIE ACTORS AND ACTRESSES

Demo, Antonio (1870–1936)

A pastor of one of the leading Italian American churches in New York City, Father Antonio Demo was born at Lazzaretto di Bassano in the province of Vicenza. He was a member of the Congregation of the Pious Society of Missionaries of St. Charles (popularly called the Scalabrini Fathers) and ordained a priest in 1896 at the hands of Bishop Giovanni Battista Scalabrini, founder of the order. He enrolled in the diocesan seminary of his area but soon transferred to a newly established Scalabrinian seminary after a brief mandatory duty with the army (1891–1892). Father Demo was one of the most active Scalabrini priests during the first half of the twentieth century. After ordination, he departed for the United States to his first assignment, a brief one, at the Church of the Sacred Heart in Boston's North End. This church was the first parish established by the order in New England and served a congregation largely composed of immigrants from Genoa.

On July 19, 1899, he was assigned as pastor of the parish of Our Lady of Pompeii, established by the pioneer Father Pietro Bandini in 1892 in New York City's Greenwich Village. The church was one of two parishes in the city that the Scalabrini Order had founded up to that time, the other being the mother church of the order, the Church of Saint Joachim. Father Demo would be intimately connected with Our Lady of Pompeii for the rest of his life as pastor (pastor emeritus for his last two years), the longest tenured pastor in the parish's history. From 1905 to 1919, with the exception of one year, he simultaneously served in the demanding position as provincial of the order's Province of Saint Charles Borromeo. By the time of Our Lady of Pompeii's Silver Jubilee in 1914, the parish had a congregation of some twenty thousand, one of the largest in the New York Archdiocese. It drew most of its congregants from the then thriving Little Italy, which comprised so much of the area south of 14th Street.

A crucial turning point in the parish's history occurred in the following decade when, in 1925, city authorities ordered the demolition of the church so that Sixth Avenue, a major thoroughfare, could be extended and widened. Undaunted, Father Demo was able to construct a new church with the help of a leading Italian American architect, Matthew Del Gaudio. By October of the following year, the cornerstone was blessed, and in May 1927 the new structure was partially available for the congregation. In late summer 1931, Father Demo realized another ambition: the opening of a parochial school. Though Christian Brothers and the Missionary Sisters of the Sacred Heart, founded by Mother Frances Xavier Cabrini, had taught Sunday school since the early days of the parish, a formal elementary school had been lacking.

Father Demo's work as provincial brought him into contact with many priests, religious leaders, and government officials, with whom he carried on a voluminous correspondence. He was also active with and helped to strengthen the Saint Raphael Society, an organization that had been specifically formed to help newly arrived immigrants in New York City. He was known for his work with charitable organizations, for his work with children (as early as 1908 he had founded what would be considered today a day care center), for his concern with the plight of the Italian immigrants, and for his pastoral work in general. In 1940, not long after his death, by order of a New York City local law, a small park and square near the Church of Our Lady of Pompeii was named in his honor. Today the church is a well-known landmark in the Greenwich Village area of New York City, and it is there that the provincial of the Scalabrini Order resides.

Nicholas Joseph Falco

Bibliography

Brown, Mary Elizabeth. *Churches, Communities and Children: Italian Immigrants in the Archdiocese of New York, 1880–1945.* Staten Island, NY: Center for Migration Studies, 1995.

———. *From Italian Villages to Greenwich Village: Our Lady of Pompeii, 1892–1992.* Staten Island, NY: Center for Migration Studies, 1992.

Tomasi, Lydio F., ed. *Italian Americans: New Perspectives in Italian Immigration and Ethnicity.* Staten Island, NY: Center for Migration Studies, 1985.

Tomasi, Silvano. *Piety and Power: The Role of Italian Parishes in the New York Metropolitan Area, 1880–1930.* Staten Island, NY: Center for Migration Studies, 1975.

See also CHURCH LEADERS; RELIGION

De Niro, Robert (b. 1943)

Regarded by many as one of the greatest actors working in film today, Robert De Niro was born in New York City. He trained for the stage with Stella Adler and Lee Strasberg. Early in his career he appeared in a number of Off-Broadway productions and performed with touring companies. Also a distinguished producer and director, De Niro is today considered to be one of the quintessential "actor's actors." His immersions into roles seem effortless when compared to similar work done by his contemporaries, a quality which suggests that he is able to accomplish the purist form of method acting by practically replacing his inner self with that of any given character.

In the late 1960s De Niro entered the film world when he worked in a number of low-budget Brian De Palma films, including the *Wedding Party* (1969), a hilarious black-and-white look at wedding day "cold feet." By 1973 he had twice won the New York Film Critics' Award for best supporting actor in recognition of his acclaimed performances of a simple-minded baseball player dying of cancer in *Bang the Drum Slowly* (1973), and that of a young violent hood, Johnny Boy, in Martin Scorsese's *Mean Streets* (1972). De Niro's performance in *Mean Streets* began an ongoing relationship with Scorsese that has lasted to this day. This working relationship has brought the seamier side of Italian American life to the screen, much to the anguish of Italian American groups.

In 1974 De Niro received the Academy Award for best supporting actor for his portrayal of the young Vito Corleone in *The Godfather, Part II.* In 1980 he won his second Oscar, this time for best actor, for his extraordinary portrayal of boxer Jake La Motta in Scorsese's *Raging Bull* (1989). Unlike earlier boxing dramas such as *Somebody Up There Likes Me,* where the main characters undergo a transformation from evil to good, *Raging Bull* does nothing to purify its subject; De Niro played La Motta as a nasty character with few redeeming qualities, who surrendered to his instincts and disintegrated as a human being. As usual, Robert De Niro completely submerged himself in the role, to the point of gaining sixty pounds for the final scenes in which the bloated, washed-up Jake tries his luck as a strip-joint emcee.

De Niro has earned Academy Award nominations for four additional roles. In *Taxi Driver* (1976) he plays Travis Bickel, an on-the-edge loner who takes a job as a late-shift taxi driver in the worst sections of New York. As Bickel's hatred toward all that he considers abhorrent consumes him, he withdraws from reality and becomes obsessed with the well-being of a 12-year-old prostitute (Jodie Foster). As the film races to its violent end, Bickel vents his rage by killing the child hooker's pimp (Harvey Keitel) and his gangster cohorts. The irony of this movie resides in the fact that instead of being considered a murderer, society (with the help of the press) makes Bickel into a hero. Two years later De Niro was nominated for his role as a Vietnam vet in Michael Cimino's *The Deer Hunter* (1978), the first Vietnam movie to become a hit with the public. *Deer Hunter* is the story of a group of friends from a Pennsylvania mill town whose lives are changed forever, as was the case with millions of American citizens and with America itself, by the war in Vietnam. In 1990 he was nominated for his role as a catatonic patient brought to life in Penny Marshall's *Awakenings.* He awakes as an adult having gone into a coma in his early teens. The film then examines the lives of the patients and the reactions of their relatives to the changes in the newly awakened. His last nomination came for his portrayal as the vengeful ex-con Max Cady in Scorsese's 1991 remake of the 1962 classic *Cape Fear*.

Based on Chazz Palminteri's play, *A Bronx Tale* (1997) marked De Niro's directorial debut and was released out of De Niro's own Tribeca Productions. The film is about a young man, Calogero (Francis Capra), who grows up during the 1960s under the twin influences of a neighborhood wiseguy, Sonny (Palminteri), and his bus driver father, Lorenzo (De Niro). Calogero is attracted to Sonny and to his lifestyle, while Lorenzo does what he can to keep his son from falling under mob influence and make him understand the importance of honesty and hard work. Both men want Calogero to succeed in life and try to steer him away from what they are, a mobster and a bus driver. The movie ends with Sonny's violent death while Calogero is still a teenager. Despite the "mean streets" setting, the audience sees a tender side of De Niro. Other Tribeca features include *Cape Fear* and *Night and the City* (1992).

In 1995 De Niro starred in Scorsese's *Casino* and in Michael Mann's *Heat*. *Casino* is a drama about three people whose passions bring down an empire. In this story of greed and betrayal, De Niro plays "Ace" Rothstein, the consummate bookie who could change the odds merely by placing a bet. "Ace" has been picked by the mob to front for them in Las Vegas and run their casinos. *Heat* examines the characters of two driven men whose actions tear through the fabric of Los Angeles. De Niro plays Neil McCauley, a cool, hardened professional criminal who has spent many years behind bars and is determined never to go back.

A review of some of De Niro's best movies demonstrates that, contrary to what many believe, De Niro, the consummate actor, does not only do gangster movies or portray Italian American wiseguys. The totality of his roles show an ability to interpret a wide range of roles, from the gangster to the sensitive policeman in *Mad Dog and Glory* (1992); from the decadent Jake La Motta to the compassionate Lorenzo in *A Bronx Tale*; from the delusional Rupert Pupkin in *King of Comedy*

(1983) to the psychotic Travis Bickel of *Taxi Driver*.

Paolo A. Giordano

Bibliography
Flatley, Guy. "Look—Bobby's Slipping into Brandon's Shoes." *New York Times* Section 2, 4 November 1973, pp. 13, 26.
Maltby, Richard. *Hollywood Cinema*. Oxford (UK) and Cambridge (USA), 1995.
Maltin, Leonard, ed. *Movie Encyclopedia*, New York: Plume, 1994.

See also FILM DIRECTORS, PRODUCERS, AND ITALIAN AMERICAN IMAGE IN CINEMA; MOVIE ACTORS AND ACTRESSES

DeNonno, Anthony (b. 1947)

In Anthony (Tony) DeNonno's short film, *Part of Your Loving* (1997), Brooklyn baker Ben Togati talks about his work as a man might talk about his religion. "The bread is you," he says. "It's part of your intelligence. It's part of your dedication. It's part of your loving also, because you gotta feel a little love in order to do good things." The filmmaker, born in Brooklyn, January 12, 1947, follows the same philosophy in his own work. DeNonno has been the subject of retrospectives at both the Museum of Modern Art in New York and the Los Angeles County Museum of Art. His heart and lens are planted firmly in the neighborhoods of New York City and take their strength from the Italian spirit of *umanità* (humanity).

Several strains are evident in his work. One focuses on the arts of the city's working people, and the ways with which they are passed from old generation to new. *It's One Family Knock on Wood* (1981) portrays the marionette-building Manteo family, who carry on a Sicilian folk tradition dating to the sixteenth century. In *It's All in My Hands* (1972) shoemaker John Prince narrates his occupation for eight minutes, after which it is hard to imagine how anyone could not want to devote his or her life to the repair of shoes. *One Generation Is Not Enough* (1981) illuminates the relationship between immigrant master violin maker Max Frirsz and his America-born son and protege, Nicholas, as the latter sets out for the first time to build a viola without his father's help. Through DeNonno's eye, the shoemaker and the violin maker are equals, artisans contributing to society through dedication of hand and spirit.

Flowing naturally from his views on the dignity of the working family comes a concern for the social fabric of New York City. DeNonno's long catalog of documentary films for city school children includes such topics as racism, sexism, and classism. DeNonno's educational works stress the common traits, concerns, and pastimes that bind people of different cultures to a single fate and a single humanity.

The third distinctive leg of the DeNonno repertoire seeks to celebrate the lives of Italian Americans and to rehabilitate their image in a country often prone to "Goodfella" stereotypes. He aspires to do this via films like *Heaven Touches Brooklyn in July* (forthcoming), *Italian American Visions* (1994), and *A Crack in the Bell* (forthcoming), a planned docudrama for the large screen based on the life of Antonio Meucci, a Florentine immigrant believed by many to be the true inventor of the telephone.

Dan Morrison

Bibliography

"Un Documentario Su Antonio Meucci," *Oggi,* 24 February 1996, p. 9.

Lanning, Rebecca, and Pamela Dell. "Tony DeNonno: Celebrating the Diversity of America." *Fast Times* (January 1993): 16.

Morrison, Dan. "Artist Takes Pride in His Work." Part 2, "Brooklyn Neighborhoods." *Newsday,* 17 March 1995, Part 2, NYB.

Poppiti, Ciro C. "Ringing Meucci's Bell." *Fra Noi* 34 (December 1995): 47, 69.

De Rosa, Tina (b. 1944)

Born in Chicago, October 20, 1944, of Italian and Lithuanian parents, Tina De Rosa's paternal grandparents came from Boscoreale near Naples at the beginning of the twentieth century. She spent her childhood in the Taylor Street area of Chicago, the Italian ghetto she would celebrate in her novel *Paper Fish.* At 17 she moved out of the old neighborhood that was destroyed to make space for the University of Illinois. After receiving a B.A. from Mundelein College of Loyola in Chicago, where she majored in sociology, she took a master's degree in English at the University of Illinois. Michael Anania, one of her teachers,

recognized her talent as a writer and encouraged her to begin writing stories about her childhood. She later turned these stories into *Paper Fish.*

Published in 1980 by a small local press, the Wine Press, De Rosa's story is the first novel about Italian Americans in Chicago. In poetical language and through evocative images, the author depicts the joys and tribulations of an Italian American family living in Chicago in the 1940s and early 1950s. The protagonists of this bildungsroman are a third-generation Italian American child, Carmolina, and her family, composed of her parents, Marco and Sarah; her astonishingly beautiful but mentally retarded older sister, Doriana; and her paternal grandmother, Doria, who through her storytelling empowers Carmolina to embark upon her journey toward self-definition. Although the events are filtered primarily through Carmolina's intelligence and sensitivity, *Paper Fish* unfolds as a choral narrative that gives voices to the disenfranchised Italian American working-class community of the west side of Chicago. Through her protagonist, the author creates a compelling, yet unobtrusive, attack on anti-Italian sentiments pervasive in the United States: as she wanders away from home and gets lost in hostile areas of Chicago, the young Carmolina is labeled as a "Dago kid."

That *Paper Fish* is set in Al Capone's neighborhood makes the novel all the more powerful, especially in light of the absence of references to Mafia. Although the novel was praised by critics Jerre Mangione, Fred Gardaphé, and Mary Jo Bona, it soon went out of print. Over the years, De Rosa's novel, defined by Louise DeSalvo as a work of "genius," acquired a somewhat mythological status among Italian American scholars, due to its lyrical beauty and its unavailability.

De Rosa has also published a few essays, mostly in the Italian American Chicago newspaper *Fra Noi,* poetry, and a biography of Bishop Giovanni Battista Scalabrini. After struggling for years with enormous economic difficulties and not receiving any recognition, De Rosa has emerged again onto the literary scene. In 1995 she received an award from the Rona Jaffe Foundation. The Feminist Press reprinted *Paper Fish* in 1996.

Edvige Giunta

Bibliography

Bona, Mary Jo. "Broken Images, Broken

Lives: Carmolina's Journey in Tina De Rosa's *Paper Fish*." *MELUS* 14, no. 3–4 (fall/winter 1987): 87–106.

De Rosa, Tina. *Bishop John Baptist Scalabrini, Father to the Migrants*. Darien: Insider, 1987.

Gardaphé, Fred L. *Italian Signs, American Streets, the Evolution of Italian American Narrative*. Durham: Duke University Press, l996.

———. "Jerome," "Mary of Magdala," "Therese," "The Poet." *VIA: Voices in Italian Americana*. Special Issue on Women. Guest editor Edvige Giunta. 7, no. 2 (fall 1996).

———. "Psalm to the Eucharist." In *From the Margin: Writings in Italian Americana,* edited by Anthony J. Tamburri, Paolo Giordano, and Fred L. Gardaphé, 193–201. West Lafayette, IN: Purdue University Press, 1991.

See also CHICAGO; LITERATURE; NOVELS AND NOVELISTS

Desmond, Humphrey J. (1858–1932)

An Irish Catholic Progressive, born on a farm in Mequon, Ozaukee County, Wisconsin, Humphrey J. Desmond used his political and journalistic skills to tend to the religious needs of Italian immigrants.

In 1866 the Desmond family moved to Milwaukee, where Humphrey's father held a variety of jobs and was active in both church and public affairs. The elder Desmond taught his children to defend and stand up for their Catholic faith.

Humphrey Desmond attended the University of Wisconsin from 1877 to 1880, where he was active in campus affairs. While in Madison, he befriended the future Progressive leader Robert M. La Follette, whose views he shared. After graduation, he returned to Milwaukee, where he established a law firm. Several successful real estate investments gave him some financial independence and allowed him to turn his attention to politics and journalism, his major interests. A lifelong Democrat like his father, Desmond was elected to the Milwaukee School Board in 1883 and the state legislature in 1890, where he served one term.

In 1891 Desmond bought *The Catholic Citizen,* Wisconsin's leading Catholic weekly, and spent the next twenty years professionalizing it and expanding its scope. A Progressive and an Americanizer, he wrote on current topics such as anti-Catholicism, temperance, socialism, economic injustice, and the problems created for American society and Catholicism by the millions of "new" immigrants coming to the United States at the time. A significant number of these immigrants were Italian.

Italians began to arrive in Milwaukee in large numbers after 1880, when a small colony developed near the yards of the Chicago and Northwestern Railroad in the third ward. Soon others settled in Bay View and the seventeenth ward. By 1910, Italians, mostly from Sicily, constituted the fourth largest ethnic group in the city, after the Germans, Poles, and Bohemians. They worked on railroads, coal docks, electric street car lines, tanneries, and as garbage collectors. Many peddled fruit or ran saloons and grocery stores.

The Catholic Citizen followed developments among Italians in Milwaukee and elsewhere. The paper emphasized the religious indifference of the Italian immigrants, their general deficiency in religious instruction, lack of Italian clergy, and fear that Italians would convert to Protestantism. In a September 30, 1899, front page memorial addressed to the Italian hierarchy, Desmond argued that not enough Italian priests were migrating with the Italian immigrants. He blamed the Vatican's Propaganda Fide for this neglect and recommended that Italian priests be encouraged to migrate with their countrymen. Desmond also published the memorial in pamphlet form, titled *The Neglected Italians, A Memorial to the Italian Hierarchy,* and sent copies to Italian church officials.

In a series of five editorials from September 6 to October 4, 1913, the paper claimed that of the three million Italians who had come to this country in the past fifteen years, nearly a million were lost to the faith, due to indifference or Protestant proselytism. The paper concluded that "this situation constitutes our biggest Catholic question." The claim received national attention when it was reported in the *Literary Digest* on October 11 of that year.

In highlighting the "Italian Problem" in *The Catholic Citizen,* Desmond joined a national debate on this question. As a muckraker in the best tradition of Progressivism, he wrote many books and articles on topical and controversial issues. The "Italian Problem" was just another one of these. A devout Catholic and ardent Americanizer, he wanted to see the "new" immigrants, including the Italians, remain active within Catholicism and eventually adapt to American culture. Desmond's concern for the "neglected" Italians helped stimulate a more aggressive response on the part of church authorities to the "Italian Problem." However, his fear that, if neglected, Italian immigrants would turn in large numbers to Protestantism proved to be groundless.

Edward C. Stibili

Bibliography

Andreozzi, John A. "Converting the Italians: Protestant and Catholic Proselytizers in Milwaukee." In *Italian Ethnics: Their Languages, Literature and Lives,* edited by Dominic Candeloro, Fred L. Gardaphé, and Paolo A. Giordano, 245–269. New York: The American Italian Historical Association, 1990.

Meloni, Alberto C. "Italy Invades the Bloody Third: The Early History of Milwaukee's Italians." *Milwaukee History* 10 (summer 1987): 47–60.

Orsi, Richard J. "The Laity and the Americanization of the Catholic Church: The Career of Humphrey J. Desmond, 1880–1915." In *An American Church: Essays on the Americanization of the Catholic Church,* edited by David E. Alvarez, 73–86. Moraga, CA: Saint Mary's College of California, 1979.

Shaughnessy, Gerald. *Has the Immigrant Kept the Faith? A Study of Immigration and Catholic Growth in the United States, 1790–1920.* New York: Macmillan, 1925. Reprint, New York: Arno, 1969.

See also APOSTOLATE, ITALIAN; RELIGION

DeVito, Danny
See MOVIE ACTORS AND ACTRESSES; TELEVISION

di Donato, Pietro (1911-1992)

An anomaly in American literature and an eccentric in the true sense of being off-center, Pietro di Donato burst like a meteor on the literary scene of the late 1930s. This mainly self-taught son of Italian immigrants immortalized his worker-father as a veritable Christ figure in his classic novel, *Christ in Concrete,* published in 1939 to extraordinary critical acclaim.

It was, perhaps, the right moment for this novel to be acclaimed: the portrayal of exploited workers fit the social protest sympathies of the period; and the unique language, which expresses in English the Italian rhythms and thought patterns of di Donato's immigrant characters, appealed to critics newly receptive to the linguistic innovations of modernism.

Christ in Concrete remains the classic expression of the Italian American experience. It delineates a young boy's search for identity in a new and alien world that is as rejecting as his father's old one is off-limits. *Christ in Concrete* remains the most searing and thorough representation of the emarginated human condition of an immigrant suspended between two worlds and held in the thrall of work and the job.

Christ in Concrete, which began as a short story in *Esquire,* is an autobiographical

Pietro di Donato, 1979, author of the powerful autobiographical novel Christ in Concrete, *which relates the dramatic story of the Italian immigrant in America. Courtesy Frank J. Cavaioli.*

rendering of the most haunting, ineluctable event of di Donato's life—the tragic accident that killed his father on a construction job just days before his own twelfth birthday. The incident cast the young boy into his father's role as bricklayer and supporter of the destitute family. When, during the Great Depression of the 1930s, di Donato was laid off the job, the circumstance brought about his Golden Age: "With unemployment and Home Relief I was permitted the leisure to think. . . . That sent me to the Northport Library (Long Island) and the discovery of the immortal minds of all countries. They gave me freedom. . . ."

He put words to paper, "not . . . with logic and outlined structure, but with each and all of my senses: feel, sight, sound, tempo, color, dream, prayer, dance, elegy, violence, comedy, bawdiness, paganism, catholicism, spiritualism, the charisma of the Great God Job, sin, virtue, faith, love, and finally, the critical question of the existence of the supposed Deity . . . when I could go no further, I scribbled 'The End.' And mailed the story."

When it appeared in 1939, *Christ in Concrete* was hailed as "the epithet of the 20th century." It was chosen over John Steinbeck's *The Grapes of Wrath* for the Book-of-the-Month Club, and di Donato, the working man, was transformed into a literary lion only to have the too-instant celebrity status and financial affluence render him silent for the next two decades.

From 1942 Pietro di Donato spent time in a Cooperstown, New York, camp as a conscientious objector during World War II, and it was there that he met the widowed Helen Dean, a former showgirl. They were married in 1943, became the parents of two sons, and subsequently moved to Long Island, where di Donato continued to work on his unfinished manuscript, *The American Gospels.*

The searing energy and the raw idealism behind di Donato's literary debut was not again achieved in his later work. Some of his internal conflict—the contradictory pull between sensual hedonism and idealism, between the attraction to the woman he married and the insane jealousy harbored toward the dead husband who preceded him, between his feeling of having betrayed his Italian American identity and his unsure place in American society—found expression in his second autobiographical novel, *This Woman.*

Critics were not impressed with this work, which has also been dramatized, nor his next novel, *Three Circles of Light,* which was called "a loose collection of episodes rather than a sustained narrative. . . . The novel's descent into sentimentality, bathos, and just plain scurrility is rapid."

Subsequently, di Donato secured his identity by reclaiming the religious faith of his people, and he went on to write two religious biographies: *Immigrant Saint: The Life of Mother Cabrini* and *The Penitent,* which is the life of Maria Goretti.

Di Donato's short pieces, articles, and stories have been collected in *Naked Author.* In 1978 his reportage on the kidnapping and murder of Aldo Moro, "Christ in Plastic," which appeared in *Penthouse,* won the Overseas Press Club Award.

At his best, as in *Christ in Concrete,* di Donato's narrative patterns form, in their diversity, one of the richest linguistic textures to be found in the twentieth-century novel and make the bridge, for him and for his characters, between a lost and mythical Italy and a real but never realized America.

Helen Barolini

Bibliography

Beranger, Jean F. "Italian-American Identity: The Masks of Religious Differences in the Novels of John Fante and Pietro di Donato." In *The Columbus People,* edited by Lydio F. Tomasi, Piero Gastaldo, and Thomas Row, 58–78. New York: Center for Migration Studies, 1994.

Gardaphé, Fred L. *Italian Signs, American Streets: The Evolution of Italian American Narrative.* Durham: Duke University Press, 1996.

Napolitano, Louise. *An American Story: Pietro di Donato's* Christ in Concrete. New York: Peter Lang, 1995.

See also LITERATURE

DiFranco, Anthony (b. 1945)

Manhattan born, of Sicilian heritage, Anthony DiFranco is a prominent Long Island–based writer and professor. Educated in the graduate programs of the Union Institute, St. John's University, and Fordham University, he has taught writing and literature at Hofstra

University, St. Joseph's College, State University of New York at Stony Brook and, for over twenty years, Suffolk Community College.

DiFranco is the author of the O. Henry Prize–winning short story, *The Garden of Redemption,* which was the result of the author's travels in Italy and research into the military history of World War II. The story was inspired by the reckless courage of young Italian partisans during the violent last stages of the war in Europe. *The Garden of Redemption* was adapted to the screen, produced by Paramount Pictures, and aired on cable network Showtime in May of 1997.

He has published two novels for Bantam Books. *The Streets of Paradise* (1984) takes as its point of departure the turn-of-the-century mass migration from Italy to America, while *Ardent Spring* (1987) portrays the political turmoil that accompanied the rise of Fascism in Italy. DiFranco has also authored nonfiction books for Dillon Press, and many short stories and essays. Besides the O. Henry Prize, his publications have won awards from the Catholic Press Association and the New York Foundation for the Arts. His third novel is a crime thriller titled *The Girl in the Trunk.*

A longtime film buff, DiFranco is currently involved in graduate film studies. He has authored one screenplay, *Blue Moon,* and co-authored another, *A Silent War.*

Giuseppe Battista

Bibliography

DiFranco, Anthony. "Choosing to Remember." *Newsday,* 18 November 1984, pp. 54–55.

———. *The Streets of Paradise.* New York: Bantam Books, 1984.

Gardaphé, Fred. *Italian Signs, American Streets.* Durham: Duke University Press, 1996.

See also NOVELS AND NOVELISTS, LESSER-KNOWN NOVELISTS

Di Giorgio, Joseph (1874–1951)

Within seven years after arriving in Baltimore in 1888 at age 14, Joseph Di Giorgio transformed a small shipment of lemons into one of the most important immigrant-owned businesses in the United States. He introduced a new system for distributing fruit and produce, and built a vertically integrated business to import, grow, and market citrus and other fruits and vegetables.

Di Giorgio was born June 10, 1874, in Cefalu, Sicily, where his land-owning father grew lemons and directed a local packers' cooperative that exported fruit to the United States. Conflicting reports surround the circumstances on Di Giorgio's migration. Di Giorgio himself claimed to have run away from home, while his nephews reported that Di Giorgio's father, unhappy with the marketing of his produce in New York, sent his son to handle the sale of a load of lemons.

Di Giorgio first worked with *paesani* (compatriots) in Baltimore and Washington, alternating work as a "jobber" (wholesaler) and a small retailer of fruit. In 1893, with five thousand dollars borrowed from a Baltimore bank, he successfully imported his first shipment of Jamaican oranges and became a major figure in Baltimore's fruit and vegetable trade. In 1899, already a millionaire and working in collaboration with his recently arrived brother, Salvatore, he began importing bananas. (The brothers' Atlantic Fruit Company was later bought by United Fruit.) Rather than work through commission agents or jobbers, Di Giorgio created a series of auctions to sell his bananas directly to retailers in large East Coast and Midwestern cities.

Di Giorgio's network of auctions for imported fruits revolutionized the fruit trade in the United States, and within ten years allowed Di Giorgio to build a large family-owned and managed company in California. Auctions were the most common way of marketing fruit in Europe, but they were unknown in the United States, where many small middlemen, agents, and jobbers connected small-scale producers and importers and small-scale urban retailers. Before 1910, when the Interstate Commerce Commission (ICC) prohibited auctions as a monopolistic restraint on trade, most fruit packed in California or Florida traveled to eastern jobbers in small shipments on the refrigerated cars owned by major meatpackers. The Armour Company had purchased orchards to increase business on the trains that delivered packaged, refrigerated meats to the West. In 1910 Di Giorgio purchased the Earl Fruit Company from Armour; the money came from the Erie Railroad after Di Giorgio guaranteed the company eight hundred cars of business, shipping fruit to the eastern auctions he had developed.

By 1920 the Earl (later the Di Giorgio) Fruit Company was the largest private distributor of deciduous and citrus fruits in the United States; it owned its own southern and West Coast orchards, its own packing facilities, and its own lumber (to build crates). It also owned the Baltimore fruit exchange and held stocks in the many fruit auctions Di Giorgio had initiated in Chicago, New York, Cincinnati, and Pittsburgh. Later Di Giorgio would also acquire part interest in the vineyards and wine-making facilities of the Italian Swiss Colony.

Although married, Di Giorgio had no children. His brothers and their sons were his most important business associates until his death in 1951, when a nephew assumed leadership of the company. Only in 1962, after a period of selling orchards and farms, and diversification through purchase of other food corporations, did a Di Giorgio CEO come from outside the family group.

Donna Gabaccia

Bibliography

Iorizzo, Luciano J., "The R. G. Dun Collection's Assessment of Merchants: A Neglected Source for Italian American Studies." In *The Columbus People, Perspectives on Italian Immigration to the United States and Australia,* edited by Lydio F. Tomasi, Piero Gastaldo, and Thomas Row. New York: Center for Migration Studies, 1994.

Iorizzo, Luciano J., and Salvatore Mondello. *The Italian Americans.* New York: Twayne Publishers, 1971.

Rolle, Andrew F. *The Immigrant Upraised.* Norman: University of Oklahoma Press, 1968.

See also BUSINESS AND ENTREPRENEURSHIP

DiMaggio, Joseph Paul (1914–1999)

The greatest representative of Italian descent in America's most popular American sport, baseball, Joe DiMaggio was born in Martinez, California, in 1914. His parents had migrated from Isola delle Femmine, Sicily. Descended from generations of hard-working Sicilian fishermen, his father worked at the

same trade in his new country, as his family expanded to four girls and five boys. Three, including next-to-the-youngest Joe, would become major league baseball players.

During the 1932 season, Joe replaced the retiring shortstop for the San Francisco Seals. When outfielder brother Vince injured himself, Joe was chosen to replace him and from the very first day "covered the outfield like a tent." In the space of one year, the 20-year-old rookie was acknowledged as the greatest player the Coast League had ever produced.

The New York Yankees signed him up in 1935, but despite accidents and injuries that would bedevil him during his whole career, he ended his first season (1936) with a batting average of .323, which earned him a World Series bonus.

In 1939 he won the *Sporting News'* annual award as Most Valuable Player in the American League. In his fifth season he had distinguished himself in batting, fielding, and throwing, and also for being one of only three players in the American League to hit two home runs in a single inning. His greatest

Joe DiMaggio. This best known and most respected Italian American baseball player and Hall of Famer was the "pride" of the New York Yankees and of Italian Americans for many years. Courtesy New York Yankees.

D

season came in the summer of 1941 when he set a new record by hitting successfully in fifty-six consecutive games, a record still unequaled.

With the attack on Pearl Harbor on December 7, 1941, DiMaggio enlisted in the Army Air Force, never asking for preferential treatment. When the war ended, DiMaggio returned to the Yankees for the final phase of his baseball career. In 1947 he earned his third award as Most Valuable Player in the American League.

DiMaggio's last big season came in 1948 when he batted .320 and led the American League with 155 runs batted in, 39 home runs, and 110 runs scored. The record won him his first one hundred thousand dollar contract but, unfortunately, that summer his right heel began aching. He never played again without pain. In his last turn at bat in the 1951 World Series, he doubled to right center field, a fitting farewell performance.

His first marriage ended in divorce, as did his marriage to movie star Marilyn Monroe. For a short period after his active days as a player, he functioned in administrative and coaching positions. He served as batting coach for the Yankees and became vice-president of the Oakland Athletics team. For years he appeared at Yankee Stadium during "Oldtimers Day." The esteem with which he was regarded in the sports world is evidenced by the award he received in 1969 at the White House on the commemoration of the one hundredth anniversary of baseball. On that occasion, DiMaggio was named the Greatest Living Baseball Player.

Margherita Marchione

Bibliography

Allen, Maury. *Where Have You Gone, Joe DiMaggio?* New York: Dutton, 1975.

De Gregorio, George. *Joe DiMaggio: An Informal Biography.* New York: Stein and Day, 1981.

DiMaggio, Joe. *Lucky to Be a Yankee.* New York: Grosset & Dunlap, 1947.

Kahn, Roger. *Joe and Marilyn.* New York: William Morrow, 1986.

See also SPORTS

DiMaggio, Margaret

See LABOR

di Prima, Diane

See AUTOBIOGRAPHY; LITERATURE; POETRY; WOMEN WRITERS

Discrimination at City University of New York (CUNY)

The Italian American community's struggle to obtain its civil rights in academia was successfully achieved when a federal court approved a settlement in the case of *Scelsa v. City University of New York* on January 7, 1994. The case involved an attempt by the CUNY administration to remove Dr. Joseph V. Scelsa from the directorship of the John D. Calandra Italian American Institute and move the Institute to CUNY's college on Staten Island, a move that some felt would have stripped the institute of its leadership and diminished its presence in the community, thereby making it possible to eventually phase it out.

Scelsa, with the support of the Italian American Legal Defense and Higher Education Fund, had filed a civil rights suit in September 1992, alleging retaliation and discrimination. Federal judge Constance Baker Motley of the Southern District of New York issued a temporary restraining order barring CUNY from preventing implementation of the institute's original 1978 mission to serve students, faculty, and community, a mission that had been designed by New York State's Italian American legislators. One of the political leaders responsible for the creation of the institute (and for whom it was named) was State Senator John D. Calandra. The hearings he held led to a report, *A History of Italian American Discrimination at CUNY.* In the lawsuit, Judge Motley enjoined CUNY from discriminating against Italian Americans with respect to faculty recruitment and promotions, the dismemberment of the institute, and the removal of Dr. Scelsa as its director.

Judge Motley's opinion has had far-reaching importance for the Italian American community because she recognized Dr. Scelsa in his official capacity to represent the interests of New York City's Italian Americans, traditionally the manner in which civil rights cases have been processed. She also invoked Section 1981 of the first national law of its kind, the Civil Rights Act of 1866. In doing so, she recognized Italian Americans

Joseph V. Scelsa, left, director of the City University of New York Calandra Italian American Institute, meets in New Orleans with Joseph Maselli of the American Italian Renaissance Center in 1990 over the status of Italian Americans in higher education. Courtesy Frank J. Cavaioli.

as a "cognizable group." Section 1981 was "designed to protect identifiable classes of persons, such as Italian Americans, who are subjected to intentional discrimination solely because of their ancestry or ethnic characteristics."

The settlement agreement has done much to protect the rights of Italian Americans in academia. First, it provided full university recognition of the Calandra Institute within CUNY for service and research on the Italian American experience with an academic affiliation with Queens College, while physically remaining at its headquarters at the CUNY Graduate Center in Manhattan. Second, the settlement also provided for the creation of the new position of a Distinguished Professor of Italian American Studies at Queens College who would work with the Calandra Institute. Third, it extended the principle of affirmative action to Italian Americans for at least ten more years. Italian Americans had originally been designated as a distinct class worthy of affirmative action protection in December 1976 by then CUNY Chancellor Robert Kibbee, and reaffirmed ten years later by Chancellor Joseph Murphy. Finally, CUNY agreed to enter into binding arbitra-tion in resolving class action complaints of discrimination against Italian Americans.

The landmark case of *Scelsa v. CUNY* is the first time that the existence of illegal Italian American discrimination in academia has been officially recognized and remedies have been provided to safeguard and protect against its occurring again.

Joseph V. Scelsa

Bibliography

Foglia, Philip. "The Calandra Institute at the Bar of Justice." *Italian American Review* 2, no. 1 (17 April 1993): 89–92.

LaRusso, Maria-Grace. "The Calandra Institute." *Ambassador* no. 29/30 (1996): 11–13.

Massaro, Dominic R. "Italian Americans As a Cognizable Racial Group." *Italian American Review* 3, no. 1 (17 April 1994): 5–15.

Scelsa, Joseph. "Italian Americans and Civil Rights: A Case Study at the City University of New York." *Italian American Review* 3, no. 2 (12 October 1994): 21–32.

See also ANTI-ITALIAN DISCRIMINATION

Di Stefano, Emmanuella

See WOMEN AND THE CHURCH

Dorothea's House

Serving as a volunteer social worker, Dorothea van Dyke assisted the newly arrived Italian immigrants living in Princeton, New Jersey. The Dorothea House was built there in her honor by the Dorothea van Dyke McLane Association, which was incorporated in 1913 as a nonprofit organization by her husband and father after she and her infant daughter died in childbirth the year before. She was the daughter of Dr. Henry van Dyke, a Princeton professor, poet, and diplomat, and her husband, Guy Richards McLane, a New York City stockbroker.

Dorothea's House was officially opened October 7, 1914. Over three hundred Italians attended the opening ceremonies of Dorothea's House whose purpose was "to originate, foster, develop, promote, carry on and engage in charitable and benevolent work for the welfare of the inhabitants of Princeton . . . primarily those of the Italian race." It was built on land donated by her father, and an endowment was established by her husband to provide for future expenses.

Dorothea's House, located at 120 John Street, is a two-story Italianate structure. Soon after it opened, a full-time employee was assisted by Princeton University students and other volunteers to conduct instructional and recreational programs for Princeton's Italians. The 1923 report stated the average monthly attendance was 529, with winter months increasing to over six hundred. Clubs for boys and girls and fraternal lodges were organized and met there regularly. Classes in such disciplines as English, citizenship, sewing, summer camp, and athletics were central to the program; a library and playground were built.

The Italian government honored Guy Richard McLane in 1919 with the Order of the Crown of Italy for his gift to Princeton's Italians. McLane died in 1921 and left three-fifths of his estate to finance the work of Dorothea's House.

The dispersal of Italian Americans following World War II and the construction of the Princeton Italian American Sports Club shifted the center of Italian American activities from Dorothea's House, although many Italian American lodges continued to meet there. In 1986 the board of trustees encouraged wider use of the building by arranging cultural, educational, and social programs to be conducted by an active Italian American committee. Dorothea's House has enriched the lives of all Princetonians, especially Italian Americans, and continues to play an important role in the community.

Frank J. Cavaioli

Bibliography

A Directory of Italian and Italian American Organizations and Community Services in the Metropolitan Area of Greater New York. Staten Island, NY: Center for Migration Studies, 1980.

Starr, Dennis J. *The Italians of New Jersey.* Newark: New Jersey Historical Society, 1985.

Tomasi, Lydio F., ed. *National Directory of Research Centers, Repositories and Organizations of Italian Culture in the United States.* Torino: Fondazione Giovanni Agnelli, 1980.

Dulbecco, Renato (b. 1914)

An Italian-born American virologist, Renato Dulbecco is a distinguished scientific researcher who won the Nobel Prize in medicine or physiology in 1975. His plaque assay technique has enabled a number of discoveries in cancer and virology research.

Dulbecco was born in Catanzaro on February 22, 1914, to Maria (Virdia) and Leonardo Dulbecco. The family moved several times, first to Turin, then to Cuneo, and, finally, to Imperia, where Renato received his primary and secondary education. His initial interests, not unlike Enrico Fermi, were in the basic sciences. But in 1930, at age 16, he entered the University of Turin to study medicine. His interests in biology led him to study with Giuseppe Levi, the well-known anatomist who specialized in the study of nerve tissue. It was here that he met and was influenced by Salvador Luria and Rita Levi-Montalcini who would also win Nobel prizes. He received his doctorate in medicine in 1936.

Dulbecco, like Luria, served in the Italian army and was wounded in 1942 in Russia. He was returned to Italy and was reunited with his wife, Giuseppina (Salvo). They had two children, Peter Leonard and Maria Vittoria. He served the partisans who were resisting German occupation. At the conclusion of the war he briefly served as a city councilor in Turin, but eventually returned to scientific research at the University of Turin. In 1947, at the request of Salvador Luria, he migrated to the United States to teach and do research at the University of Indiana at Bloomington. Rita Levi-Montalcini came to the United States in the same year.

Dulbecco experimented extensively with bacteriophages, a form of virus that infects and destroys bacteria. He discovered that white light could reactivate bacteriophages that had been inactivated by ultraviolet light. Max Delbrück invited Dulbecco to come to the California Institute of Technology to work with him in 1949. Dulbecco remained at Caltech until 1963. It was during this period that he began his studies of animal viruses and devised a method of counting the number of viruses in a cell culture. This plaque assay technique became invaluable in the future studies of viruses. His work also included the study of cancer-causing viruses and the mechanism that induced the cancer in the host cell.

Following a divorce and remarriage to Maureen Muir, Dulbecco left Caltech to join Jonas Salk at his newly formed institute in La Jolla, California. Here he continued his studies of tumor-inducing viruses in animals.

In 1972 he moved to the Imperial Cancer Research Fund in London, where he engaged in studies involving breast cancer. In 1975, he and two others, David Baltimore and Howard Temin, were awarded the Nobel Prize in medicine or physiology for their work on tumors and virology. Dulbecco returned to the Salk Institute in 1977 as a distinguished research professor. He served as its president from 1982 to 1992.

Renato Dulbecco discovered an assay technique that has led to a number of medical discoveries that have saved countless lives. His decision to pursue a career in research rather than medicine has earned him a special place in the halls of science as an Italian American innovator.

Sean A. Fanelli

Bibliography

Dulbecco, Renato. *The Design of Life*. New Haven: Yale University Press, 1987.

See also MEDICINE; SCIENCE

Durante, Jimmy (1893–1980)

A top-billed and much beloved comedian, actor, singer, and song writer, Jimmy Durante was one of the first Italian American popular entertainers to achieve worldwide recognition. He was born in New York City's Little Italy. His parents had migrated from Salerno, Italy. As a child, Jimmy displayed an early interest in music and was given classical training on the piano, and as a young man he formed a five-piece jazz band and played razzmatazz piano at Coney Island and in New York's Bowery, Chinatown, and Harlem.

In 1921 he married the singer Jeanne Olson. By the late 1920s Jimmy Durante had met vaudevillians Eddie Jackson and Lou Clayton, and they formed the nightclub act billed as "Clayton, Jackson, and Durante." The team enjoyed great success on the New York City nightclub circuit. Durante was the star of the act with a brand of comedy that was unique for the period. It avoided off-color material and acerbic commentary. Instead, their act concentrated on extemporaneous clowning with physical humor and large doses of self-parody, much of it directed at Durante's soon-to-be-famous exceptionally large nose. In time, this physical attribute was developed into a signature that was instantly recognized everywhere. He was soon dubbed "Schnozzola," "Schnozzle," or simply "The Nose." This was coupled with his innate split-second sense of timing and a feel for a particular audience.

A characteristic and often imitated feature of this self-parody was Durante's penchant (some say unconsciously) for distorting and fracturing polysyllabic words and using malapropisms, all delivered in a raspy New York accent that was his natural speech. Durante also wrote dozens of comic songs that were popular in their own right and became his musical trademarks such as "Inka Dinka Doo" and *"Umbriago."* Critics have traced the origins of Jimmy Durante's freewheeling humor to the traditional Italian comedy of Pulcinella and the commedia dell'arte.

After a brief and successful stint in vaudeville during its declining years, Durante appeared in a number of high-profile musicals such as Ziegfeld's *Show Girls* (1929), Cole Porter's *The New Yorkers* (1930), and Billy Rose's *Jumbo* (1933). Around 1930, the trio broke up and Clayton became Durante's business manager. During this period he also appeared in twenty-one motion pictures, most of which were considered second-rate. According to critics, many of his films were disappointing because they used material that merely emphasized his physical buffoonery. Although Durante continued to enjoy success performing live in Broadway musicals and musical comedy reviews, his career was in a decline by the early 1940s according to Hollywood standards.

Durante's "comeback" occurred in 1943 with his return to the Copacabana nightclub in New York City after an absence of twelve years from this venue, followed by a series of radio programs that were very popular. Hollywood eventually "rediscovered" Durante, and he appeared in a few more pictures, such as *Two Girls and a Sailor* (1945), in which Durante was praised by Bosley Crowther of the *New York Times* as possessing "a sort of undertone of sadness which all great comedians have." In the mid-1940s he introduced his famous sign-off, "Good night, Mrs. Calabash, wherever you are," which has intrigued his audiences ever since. At this time he also introduced his popular character *Umbriago* ("The Drunkard" in dialect Italian), in a song by the same name. In 1950 Durante launched his career into television and won the industry's Peabody Award for Entertainment. Here again, as in radio, he was an immediate success because of the cabaret-like format of the program. In 1952, he won television's Emmy Award for "Best Comedian." He ended his regular television show in 1956 fearing overexposure would damage his professional standing. Henceforth, he appeared occasionally as a guest on television and in nightclubs in New York, Las Vegas, and other big cities until the early 1970s. In 1962 he reprised his role in the early Rodgers and Hart musical comedy *Jumbo,* in a movie version which was well received.

In 1960 Jimmy Durante married Marjorie Little, and they adopted an infant daughter in 1961. His last public appearance of note was in April 1974, when he was the guest of honor at a luncheon attended by sixteen hundred newspaper executives and guests in New York City. Apart from his artistry, Durante was known for his generosity to needy friends and destitute strangers, as well as for his many benefit appearances to entertain American servicemen and to raise funds for medical research. As proof of his enduring popularity, recordings of his vocal renditions are used repeatedly on television, especially for children's programs. In 1989, a failed musical comedy, *Durante,* opened and closed. In 1993, one hundred years after his birth, recordings of his singing were used in a popular movie, *Sleepless in Seattle,* as background music, and they were reissued on compact discs.

Angelo Tripicchio

Bibliography

Fowler, Gene. *Schnozzola, The Life of Jimmy Durante.* New York: Viking, 1951.

Robbins, Jhan. *Inka Dinka Doo: The Life of Jimmy Durante.* New York: Paragon House, 1991.

See also COMEDY; TELEVISION

Duse, Eleonora (1859–1924)

At the very time that Italy was fighting for unification, Eleonora Duse, who was to revolutionize the art of acting during her lifetime, was born in a hotel in Vigevano near Venice, on October 3, 1859. Both her parents were players in a large family troupe of actors that had been founded by grandfather Luigi Duse, famous for his roles in the Italian theater style commedia dell'arte.

Poorly paid, traveling from city to city, barely having enough to eat, Eleonora's childhood formed a personality described as one of sadness, passion, arrogance, tenacity, ferocity, and in later years, despondency. Her wildly applauded debut as Juliet at age 14 in the city of Verona was overshadowed shortly after by the death of her mother, Angelica, who was buried in a pauper's grave in Bologna.

Struggling with one little company after another, at 20, Duse won over Naples with her rendition of Ophelia, Desdemona, Nana, and Electra, moving the audience to such an extent that one critic described it as "to have seized its heart and squeezed like a handkerchief." Her liaison with Martino Cafiero resulted in the birth of a son, in 1879, who died soon after birth.

During the years 1881 and 1882, when she married Teobaldo Checchi and gave birth to her daughter Enrichetta, she was diagnosed with tuberculosis, the disease that had killed her mother. It would afflict Duse for the rest of her life.

Duse's talent was acclaimed throughout Italy, inspiring great authors such as Dumas to write roles especially for her. Her fame earned her an invitation to tour South America in 1885, starring in *Feodora,* one of her best-known roles. It was here that her marriage ended.

As manager and star of her own drama company, Duse won the admiration of royalty and those famous in the world of art and literature. Arrigo Boito, Verdi's librettist, entered her life in 1887 in a loving relationship that lasted eight years.

In 1890 her tour of Russia (whose climate exacerbated her illness) so moved Stanislavsky that he conferred upon her the nickname "Her Holiness"; while Chekhov, who had not understood one word of her Italian performance, claimed "to have not ever seen anything like her."

America beckoned next in 1893, again to great applause, although she was stunned by the American press and its inane curiosity with her ability to cook spaghetti and meatballs. Duse, who was considered rather plain, with large dark eyes and a mass of black hair, never wore makeup on or off stage. In 1895 she competed with Sarah Bernhardt in London. George Bernard Shaw praised Eleonora by saying, "Bernhardt is a babe in arms compared to Duse."

In the last years of the nineteenth century, Gabriele d'Annunzio (1863–1938), poet and playwright, began an artistic and a romantic association with the actress, which proved to be both rapturous and disastrous for Duse. Her repertoire in her next American tour included *La Giaconda* and *Francesca da Rimini,* written by him. D'Annunzio's novel *Il Fuoco,* denounced by most critics because it so resembled the intimate life he shared with Duse, is said to have precipitated their separation. In 1909, at age 50, she announced her retirement with the words: "I carry autumn with me."

Her dream to establish a home for young actresses finally came to fruition in 1914, but World War I forced its termination. She worked tirelessly during the war, ministering to the wounded and dying, who never knew her true identity.

Twelve years into retirement, Duse, ill and in need of money, returned to the Metropolitan Opera House in New York, acting to a packed house at every performance. She died in Pittsburgh, April 21, 1924, while on this triumphant American tour.

Teresa Cerasuola

Bibliography
Rheinhardt, E. A. *The Life of Eleonora Duse.* London: Martin Seckler, 1930.
Weaver, William. *Duse: A Biography.* New York: Harcourt Brace Jovanovich, 1984.

See also THEATER HISTORY

D

E

Education: Sociohistorical Background

Italian Americans constitute a group that has experienced extraordinary change in levels of educational achievement. During the early stages of immigration, that period between 1880 and 1929, most Italian immigrants experienced very little, if any, formal schooling. In more recent years, they have shown dramatic increases in formal schooling, especially in the area of higher education.

Most immigrants arriving from southern Italy and Sicily came from small village backgrounds as peasant farmers or simple artisans. They brought with them a folk-peasant culture that was formed over hundreds of years as the result of a long and dramatic period of political domination and economic exploitation. These peasants constituted approximately 80 percent of all the immigrants from Italy.

The southern region of Italy is referred to as the *Mezzogiorno*. It is an area that has served as a battleground for a number of European powers. At one time or another the area has been dominated by the Romans, Arabs, Normans, and Spanish. The history of the *Mezzogiorno* differs from that of northern Italy. Italians continue to perceive their country as being two Italys.

During the period of heaviest emigration, parts of the south were still living under an antiquated feudal system. Because of this oppressive system, landowners in the south had great difficulty developing modern programs. The landowners did not have a tradition of business or trade. Typical of a feudal system, the landed aristocracy exploited the peasant labor and did not seek to develop new or innovative business enterprises. The local government officials were no better in their treatment of the peasants, and they were guided by self-interest. Patronage was common. Private projects, such as the building of private roads, were supported at the public's expense.

After the *Risorgimento* or reunification of Italy in 1870, it was believed by many that the problems of the south, or the "southern question," would soon be alleviated. Northerners believed that the south had great potential wealth, especially in the area of agriculture. This was not the case. The north had better land and climate, besides having a stronger economic base to work with, and a more enlightened ruling class.

The *Risorgimento* did not eliminate the problems of the *Mezzogiorno*. Politically, the north replaced foreign powers as the dominant force in the south. At the turn of the twentieth century, the south still had no real middle class, no foreign capital investment, and few skilled technicians. The political and economic conditions had a direct impact on education. In general, the south failed to develop any type of modern educational system. Funding for education was inadequate. In addition, many citizens in the rural areas of the south resisted formal education. Also, the political leadership was, at best, indifferent toward educational programs. Another factor contributing to the lack of education was the fact that local taxes were to pay for education. If the government built a school, the local village was charged with the costs. Needless to say most overtaxed villages had no desire to pay increased taxes. These conditions contributed to the very high illiteracy rates that existed in the south. In 1871 the illiteracy rate was 90 percent. By the year 1900 it had dropped to 70 percent, a figure still significantly higher than the rate of illiteracy in the north. In sum, the experience of southern Italians with respect to education was influenced by such factors as exploitative control by landed aristocracy, discriminatory practices from the northern power bloc, the lack of appropriate facilities, and the overwhelming condition of poverty.

The historical antecedents of foreign rule led to a particular set of values developed by the southern Italian culture that were central to the social and cultural life of the people. These core values included the primacy of personal relationships, the importance of reciprocal obligations, a strong respect for authority, and the overriding importance of home and family. The last value, strong allegiance to domesticity, became the central value of the traditional southern Italian folk society. The folk culture was somewhat synonymous with the institution of the family.

The term "amoral familism" has been used when describing the ethos of the family life in southern Italy. According to this concept, family members are to be treated in one fashion, while those outside the family are to be treated in an entirely different manner. In a society that had been ruled by foreigners for so long a period, and when even fellow Italians in positions of power and authority exploited their own people, the family became the last refuge in a socially hostile environment.

At the center of this kin network was the nuclear family. But the importance of kin relationships would extend beyond the nuclear group. The Italian family was not only the married couple and their children. It included grandparents, aunts, uncles, and even in-laws. They cooperated with one another in all areas, especially in the area of finances. They were closely knit in both emotions and family structure. The oldest male held the position of authority. He made all the decisions affecting the family. His word was accepted as law by the other members of the group. Each member of the family had a sense of duty toward one another. There was a strict order of authority and obedience. The individual was totally entwined in the family structure; self and family were intimately linked.

As they migrated to the United States, Italians brought with them their skills, foods, customs, values, and traditions. These traditions included the emphasis on family, which, in turn, influenced their attitudes toward education. The immigrants brought with them a long history of antipathy toward formal education. This antipathy was based upon a complex interweaving of the historical antecedents noted above.

The antieducation position had a number of additional root causes. School was seen as an upper-class institution, and those with too much learning were not to be trusted. Italian peasants were exploited by the nobility; therefore, anything associated with the nobility was treated with disdain. And, as in all peasant societies, children's labor was highly valued. The idea that children in their early teens should attend school was anathema to the adult members of the Italian immigrant community. Children by the age 13 or 14 were expected to make a meaningful contribution to the family income.

The economic value of immigrant children stems from the Old World tradition that dictated the child should share in the economic upkeep of the family regardless of the child's age and capacity. The need for the child's labor was made even more immediate given the economic position of early Italian immigrants. Many of the immigrants were unskilled or semiskilled workers. Upon their arrival in the United States, they would find jobs with meager earnings. Thus, a child's wages, however meager they were, was still seen as significant for the family's economic well-being.

The children of these immigrants faced the problem of trying to live in two worlds: the world of southern Italian rural peasantry transplanted to the United States and the world of modern urban America. It became a classic instance of value conflict, whereby one individual participates in two distinctive value systems. An added dimension to this problem was that the two worlds were both critical and suspicious of each other, an opposition brought about by reciprocal ignorance. The immigrant child, in turn, was caught in the midst of this dilemma. While the family was emphasizing values of the Old World, the school was promoting independent, American patterns of behavior.

From the point of view of the family, the ideas and experiences the children received in the educational system was seen as constituting a direct attack on their traditional way of life. This holds true for all immigrant groups, not only Italian immigrants. The educational system of any society is charged with creating new generations of citizens: individuals who will participate in the social, political, and economic life of the society. Schools thus become major acculturating institutions that help convert "foreigners" into American citizens.

For a large part of each day, the children of Italian immigrants attended public school classes. Here they were immersed in the mainstream of American life. Old World traits were looked upon as being "foreign" or "alien." A certain number of children developed contempt for their parents. They viewed their parents as being "stupid" or "greenhorns." The less assimilated world of the parents shared the same space with the more assimilated world of their children. This sharing of space was not always peaceful and contributed to the conflict between first and second generations.

The immigrants found a value system in the United States dramatically different from the value system of southern Italian folk society. Americans have faith in education; it is a central institution of American society providing a major mechanism for social mobility. Americans believe that through education, one is given the opportunity to achieve greater status in life. Education fulfills certain basic functions such as preparing people for occupational roles, improving personal adjustment, preserving the common culture, and producing patriotic citizens. The propagandizing function of schools had an important role in American society: America was a land of immigrants, so it was essential for some institution to indoctrinate and incorporate the new arrivals into the American cultural system. The American public school was the institution selected to perform this task. It was a major institutional setting through which large numbers of immigrants and their children would pass. The public schools, night schools, and parochial schools were given the responsibility of resocializing the immigrants. In this resocialization process, Old World traits were to be eliminated, values of the New World were to be inculcated. It is not surprising that the extensive development of public education coincided with the first large wave of immigration during the mid-nineteenth century.

If assimilation is to proceed smoothly, members of the incoming group should see education as desirable. They should be motivated to attend school, and thus willing to pass through the Americanization process. If, on the other hand, they find school unappealing, value conflict ensues, and the assimilation process is impeded. The idea of compulsory schooling, which developed during the early part of the nineteenth century, was rather firmly entrenched in the ideological system of the United States by the time the Italians arrived in the 1880s. However, simultaneous to the arrival of large numbers of Italian immigrants, the question arose whether these immigrants, and others, were in fact assimilable. Could the United States truly absorb and Americanize all these newcomers?

The issue of a free and open immigration policy came under popular scrutiny. Popular opinion and opinions expressed in the intellectual community began to challenge this policy. Calls for restrictive immigration began to circulate. The ideology of social Darwinism was invoked to support these restrictions. Darwin's theory of evolution was transferred to the study of human behavior and by invoking the name of Darwin, the ranking of human groups obtained scientific legitimacy. Notions of racial superiority were given scientific substantiation and respectability. The "newer" immigrants, those people from southern and eastern Europe, were cited for their differences, and these differences, in turn, were interpreted as barriers to their absorption into American society. Italian immigrants were one of the groups specifically targeted in this anti-immigrant rhetoric.

The anti-Italian perception was heightened by the fact that Italians migrated to the United States in large numbers, and the pace of immigration was very rapid. Americans seemed overwhelmed by these newcomers, and many saw immigration as an invasion. This hostile view led to physical attacks on Italian Americans, and even to lynchings. Yet as Italians began to participate in the schooling process, the negative stereotypic perceptions began to wane.

In order to understand the structural set or opportunity structure of society at the time of the mass immigration, it is important to remember that most of the Italian immigrants settled in urban areas, especially in the Northeast. Many urban areas were experiencing rapid economic growth. For example, in New York City, between the years 1860 and 1890, textile firms grew from 600 to 10,000, and the number of employees in the industry went from 30,000 to 236,000. Most of these employees were drawn from the pool of new immigrants.

Yet the American Dream was not an easy acquisition for immigrants. There were a number of jobs available to these newcomers, but they were on the lowest rung of the occupational ladder. In 1880 over one-half of Italian household heads were labeled as unskilled, and only 2 percent were in the highest category of "high white collar." By 1905 Italian Americans had shifted out of the unskilled category and into the semi-skilled category. While this change was small, it still was an indication of some upward movement.

The fact that opportunities did exist, but only at the lowest levels of employment, was to have a direct impact on immigrant attitudes toward education. For the older generation, the bulk of the unskilled Italian male immigration was drawn to backbreaking physical work, much of it in new construction. For the children of these immigrants, many worked at the most menial level of the job market. They worked as common laborers, often as "gofers," newspaper boys, and shoe shiners. While their pay was at the lowest end of the wage scale, it did supply an important contribution to family income.

Because of financial obligations, it is estimated that at the beginning of the twentieth century 10 percent of Italian children in New York avoided school entirely, and other children of Italian ancestry did not stay in school long. In part, this was due to the belief that occupational skills could be learned on the job rather than in the classroom. And this training, in turn, would lead to more skilled positions in the future.

Thus, faced by an economic opportunity structure that was open at the bottom, but to a large extent closed at the top, Italian immigrants entered the job market where they could. The immediate challenge of meeting day-to-day needs was the focus of all their energy. Schooling was something of a luxury, not undesirable, but, given the conditions of the times, unattainable.

Immigrants often withdrew from their economically depressed situations. In the Italian case, return migration was seen as a real alternative to building a new life in a foreign society. For example, between 1892 and 1896, twenty thousand Italians per year returned to Italy. For those immigrants looking to Italy as their even-tual resting place, education in the United States held little value. These immigrants were much more concerned with accumulating capital than gaining an education.

Most scholars hold the view that Italian immigrants were not quick to take advantage of the educational process. Weisz (1976), in his study of Irish and Italian immigrants during the period 1870–1900, found evidence of much resistance to schooling. He also discussed the attempt to establish Italian day schools, and afternoon sessions and evening schools. Most of these efforts did not meet with great success. Even an attempt to stimulate interest in the parochial school system was not warmly received by the immigrant.

While the lack of interest appears to have existed during the very early stages of Italian immigration, change was on the horizon. Once the decision to remain in America was made, Italian immigrant attitudes toward education changed. As new generations came on the scene, the old ways within the group began to face challenges from the young. Separation from the old country had a great deal to do with this change. Attitudes toward women's work began to undergo change. The effect of neighborhood clubs and settlement houses impacted the lives of the immigrants, especially their children. Pressures to Americanize were prevalent.

In addition to changes within the group, there were changes in the general cultural environment. Cohen (1978) reported that by the 1930s there was a dramatic upsurge in Italian American school attendance. She attributes this upswing to three factors: a decrease in the birthrate, government efforts to put a halt to child labor, and the growing availability of more white-collar jobs for high school graduates. As new occupational opportunities emerged, they influenced the Italian American community.

It is not that Italian Americans instantly developed a favorable attitude toward education. Instead, education began to be viewed in a more pragmatic manner. Realistically, education could provided better employment opportunities. There was a realization that education could be a means for achieving social mobility. Once external conditions allowed for it, appreciation for education blossomed.

During the mid-1960s, larger numbers of young Americans entered colleges and universities. Italian Americans became part of this educational revolution. Analyses from a number of different data sources indicate that Italian Americans have made substantial gains in their overall level of educational attainment. For example, in 1950 less than 3 percent of all Italian Americans had graduated from college. By 1970 the figure was closer to 6 percent.

Andrew Greeley examined changes in 1977 in educational attainment for Italian Americans and found that Italian Americans, with respect to educational achievement, have been among the most upwardly mobile groups. According to Greeley's data, during the World War I period, 7 percent of all Italian Americans were attending college. By the early 1970s, or the Vietnam War era, the figure had increased to 45 percent, which was 2 percentage points higher than that for the total sample studied.

Other studies do not appear to support Greeley's findings. For example, a 1979 study by the Bureau of the Census found that single-ancestry Italian Americans, those Americans who claim only one ethnic ancestry, were the second lowest group out of eight ethnic groups analyzed in the category Percent College, One Year or More. The figure for Italian American males was 28.6 percent; for females the figure was 16.5 percent. Italian Americans of mixed ancestry, Italian American and Others, fared better with 50.2 percent of the males and 34.3 percent of the females counted in the Percent College, One Year or More category, according to data studied by William E. Egelman in 1985.

A closer examination of more recent data reveals a more complex picture. On the one hand, educational attainment levels have increased. At the same time there are substantial numbers of Italian American males and females who have not completed high school. This bipolar pattern may be observed by examining recent data on Italian Americans in New York City. While New York City Italian Americans are not necessarily representative of all Italian Americans, they do constitute the single largest community in the United States and number some 837,730 persons in 1990. This is approximately 6 percent of the total Italian American population.

In 1980, 14 percent of all Italian American males were college graduates. For females, the graduation rate was 7.1 percent. In 1990 the figure for males had increased to 22 percent, and for females 15.2 percent. Another way of stating this is to say that for males the number graduating from college went from one out of fourteen to one out of five. By any standard, this is a dramatic increase in a ten-year period. The change for females is no less dramatic, going from one out of fourteen to one out of six. Female educational attainment as measured by percent of college graduates is increasing at a faster rate than it is for males.

This, however, is only part of the story. According to 1990 census data for New York City, almost one-third of all Italian Americans in the city have not completed high school. The figures are 31.2 percent for males and 32.6 percent for females, constituting a decrease from the 1980 figures when almost one-half of all Italian American females did not complete high school, and 45 percent of the males did not complete high school.

All these data taken together indicate diverse educational patterns. Over time and between the generations Italian American educational attainment has increased. There are a greater number and a greater proportion of Italian Americans attending and graduating from college today than in the past. At the same time, there is a sizable proportion of Italian American adults who have not graduated from high school.

Changes in educational attainment often have an impact on other areas of Italian American life. Education influences marital patterns, fertility, migration, and a host of other behavioral patterns including values, beliefs, and self-perceptions. The manifestation of the effects of educational change are likely to emerge in the not too distant future.

While the early immigrants may have faced many serious problems of adjustment, there is growing evidence that their children and grandchildren are having less difficulty taking advantage of the educational process. This could have a major impact on the Italian American community. There is an assumption in sociological literature that can be stated as follows: the higher the level of educational attainment, the greater the degree of assimilation. Stated another way, the greater the level of educational achievement, the more tenuous the connection with one's ethnic traditions. Educational mobility, along with occupational and income mobility, is seen as a major indicator of assimilation. As second- and third-generation ethnics move into the white-collar professional middle class, some feel that ethnic diversity will disappear and what will be left is a highly homogeneous mass culture.

Following from this, one may suggest that Italian American identity is on the wane, and may eventually disappear. However, such a conclusion is premature. A number of factors, other than education, affect the continuity of ethnic identification. For example, family structure, geographical mobility patterns, religious beliefs, and economic status all have an effect on ethnicity. It is even possible to hypothesize that higher educational attainment may strengthen ethnic ties. Education can heighten an individual's awareness of his or her own ethnic past.

William S. Egelman

Bibliography

Barzini, Luigi. *The Italians.* New York: Atheneum, 1964.

Battistella, Graziano, ed. *Italian Americans in the 1980s: A Social Demographic Profile.* New York: Center for Migration Studies, 1989.

Briggs, John W. *An Italian Passage: Immigrants to Three American Cities, 1890–1930.* New Haven: Yale University Press, 1978.

Cohen, Miriam Judith. "From Workshop to Office: Italian Women and Families in New York City, 1900–1950." Ph.D. diss., University of Michigan, 1978.

Egelman, William. "Italian American Women: Changes in Educational Attainment." In *Italian Americans: The Search For a Usable Past,* edited by Richard N. Juliani and Philip V. Cannistraro, 244–57. New York: American Italian Historical Association, 1989.

Egelman, William S., and Joseph Salvo. "Italian Americans in New York City, 1990: A Demographic Overview." In *Italian Americans in a Multicultural Society,* edited by Jerome Krase and Judith N. DeSena, 114–26. New York: Forum Italicum, 1994.

Greeley, Andrew. *The American Catholic: A Social Portrait.* New York: Basic Books, 1977.

———. "Italian and Irish Americans in Education: A Sociohistorical Analysis." In *Italians and Irish Americans in Education,* edited by Francis X. Femminella, 163-76. New York: American Italian Historical Association, 1985.

Kessner, Thomas. *The Golden Door: Italian and Jewish Immigrant Mobility in New York City, 1880–1915.* New York: Oxford University Press, 1977.

Smith, Denis. *Italy: A Modern History.* Ann Arbor: University of Michigan Press, 1959.

U.S. Bureau of the Census. *Current Population Reports,* P-23, No. 116. Ancestry and Language in the United States. Washington, DC: Bureau of the Census, November 1979, 1982.

Weisz, Harold R. *Irish-American and Italian-American Educational Views and Activities 1870–1900: A Comparison.* New York: Arno Press, 1976.

See also ANTI-ITALIAN DISCRIMINATION

Ethnic Neighborhoods

For many, Italian America and the Italian American neighborhood are virtually synonymous. Ethnic neighborhoods have existed from ancient times. When, for example, ancient Egyptians built their pyramids, the various peoples who contributed the labor lived together in temporary urban settlements until their work was completed. The cosmopolitan character of medieval cities was accounted for by commercial ethnic ghettos. Industrialization and modernization produced mass migrations that resulted in the current version of urban ethnic neighborhoods. It is therefore unlikely that a postmodern world will see the elimination of this versatile and resilient urban residential form.

At the abstract level, the evolution, dynamics, and functions of ethnic neighborhoods are no different than for any other kind of residential community. The neighborhood is a spatially bound local institution that serves the needs of its residents and mediates between them and the greater society. More concretely, the local community is a place in which ordinary lives are lived and recounted as history. The many transformations that have taken place in the world have affected ethnic neighborhoods in much the same way that they have affected other institutions. As populations have moved from a traditional to a modern and now a postmodern society, most crucial have been the technologically driven changes that have reduced the efficacy of local institutions.

Ethnic urban villages, initially established to provide mutual assistance and support among immigrants, have survived despite upward social mobility, suburban migration, urban renewal, and invasions by subsequent groups. Interestingly, the local Italian community (as an aggregation of families) has been better suited than many other ethnic groups to survive the transformations, having inherited a tenacity from Old World Italy that evolved over centuries within a variety of oppressive social, political, and economic structures.

Until recently, most social scientists predicted the imminent disappearance of Italian ethnic neighborhoods, thus producing a large collection of studies on the birth and death of one or another Little Italy. The dominant models for these rather pessimistic analyses have been based on various assimilationist and/or ecological theories. Contemporary studies of where Italian Americans are going and staying present a complex picture, one that does not easily fit the social scientists' models that projected their total eclipse. Although one must concede the disappearance of many, both new and old Italian American neighborhoods continue to appear on the urban, and increasingly suburban, scenes. A few of these "new" enclaves are products of Italian immigration, but most are the result of central city Italian Americans migrating to local and distant suburbs.

For historians, the major rubric under which Italian residential communities are discussed is that of Little Italy. For other social scientists it is the "urban village." Although most of these, almost stereotypical, enclaves are still found in the central areas of large metropolises, many others can be found in smaller cities, and virtually every location where heavy industry, construction, sewer, road, or canal work, or major railroad or seaport connections required immigrant labor. Also, a sizable percentage of Italians have lived and worked in small factory towns, mining villages, and in rural America.

Although these Italian American neighborhoods have many variations based on such elements as size, concentration, and immigrant generation, from tiny California fishing villages to the huge concentration of Italians in New York City's East Harlem, it is possible to speculate about similarities by asking questions such as What are the regularities in the physical and social structures and functions of Italian American communities? How does Italian culture influence the physical environment in which Italian Americans reside? What are the reciprocal influences of American culture and environment on Italian patterns?

Not all of the neighborhoods in which Americans of Italian descent reside are regarded as Little Italys. Ironically, it is possible that an area in which all of the residents are Italian might not be called a Little Italy while another locale at which there is not a single Italian resident will be regarded as such. The taken-for-granted ethno-territorial label "Little Italy" is generally applied in ordinary, as well as academic, parlance only to those urban neighborhoods whose appearances (physical structure and observable social life) are easily recognized by passersby and social researchers alike, as meeting particular sensory criteria. Adding to the sociological mystique of the territory, however, is the fact that, for example, although Little Italys are frequently described as having *Old World Italian* airs, in most cases what is defined as *Old World,* or even *Italian* is arbitrarily ill-defined, if defined at all. People just seem to know when they are in a *real* Italian neighborhood.

What do these neighborhoods have in common? To varying degrees, most Italian American neighborhoods have been produced and maintained by practices inherited from the historical experiences of the vast majority of Italians in America: (1) Italian American communities endorse the supremacy of private (family) over public (nonfamily) values and interests in regard to territory and activities related to local spaces. (2) Italian American residential communities tend to be small scale and arranged so they facilitate intrafamily and interpersonal relations. (3) Italian Americans seem to have a great tolerance, if not a preference, for high human density. (4) Among Italian Americans, individuality and competitiveness are emphasized over conformity and cooperation in spatial interactions. (5) Where feasible, Italian Americans have introduced traditional architectural and other aesthetics in new construction, maintenance, and renovation. (6) Toleration for the mixing of commercial and industrial activities with residence is common in Italian American neighborhoods. (7) Italian American communities provide a wide range of different types of places for various age and sex groups. (8) The physical and symbolic defense of the

E

individual, family, and neighborhood is the most important feature of the community.

The evolution of Italian American ethnic neighborhoods is presented most often as a series of stages roughly corresponding to periods of immigration: 1880–1930, 1930–1960, and post-1960, or to their thematic equivalent of immigrant generations: first-generation Italian-born (Italians), second-generation American-born of Italian parents (Italian Americans), and third, or subsequent generations (American Italians). This provides a range of settings; from those of first-generation Italians in teeming ports of entry in 1880, for example, to those of the third-generation residents living in "idyllic" suburbs of the 1990s.

Between 1880 and 1930 over four million Italian immigrants flooded America. The general pattern of settlement was for Italian immigrants to gravitate to large industrial and manufacturing cities in the East in search of employment. Initially, these Italian immigrants, most of whom were male, formed enclaves of first settlement near their work in multiethnic neighborhoods sharing streets and buildings with other groups. Others later followed these pioneers using patterns of informal networks to attract fellow workers, relatives, and family members from their hometowns or regions, settling in the same areas. This chain migration led to the building of tight little "islands" of varying sizes with regional and smaller divisions such as Little Calabrias and Little Sicilys.

Intellectuals and higher-class Italians were often embarrassed by their fellow countrymen and therefore claimed that the first enclaves were aberrant, temporary, marginal, and anachronistic. Simultaneously, many American critics of immigration saw these settlements as colonies that served the interests of an increasingly imperial Italy's foreign policies. Referred to initially as "birds of passage," many, if not most, Italians in America were sojourners who came to earn money and return home to Italy. This attitude toward their American residence also had a profound affect on the structure of their local communities, which were weak and vulnerable to exploitation. In 1911 the widely accepted, but severely flawed, "scientific" results of the Dillingham Commission not only led to restrictions on immigration, but also labeled Italian enclaves as pathogenic environments.

Incidents such as the raids against Communists and other leftist "subversives" conducted under Attorney General A. Mitchell Palmer as part of the anti-immigrant, anti-Left hysterias of the 1920s made Italians more defensive toward outsiders, isolating them even further.

Despite the intense hostility toward them, the colonies grew and multiplied. The vast majority of the four million Italian immigrants were from the rural Italian south, the Mezzogiorno, whose traditions contrasted and conflicted with American norms. The development of each enclave varied as each city drew a different type of immigrant from Italy or elsewhere. This resulted in a wide range of dominant occupational structures and degrees in the extent and intensity of Italian ambience.

As the local populations grew and the length of tenure in the United States increased, so did the communal associations that helped create a fuller community life: mutual-aid societies, fraternal organizations, Roman Catholic churches (and Protestant missions), political and/or *paese* clubs, Italian-speaking local unions, and other related entities, parochial schools, sodalities, sports teams, and credit unions. These community centers in turn attracted businesses, ethnic newspapers, and restaurants, and produced a wide range of ethnic density and material culture.

Within the dominant framework of the "melting pot" and amid periodic nativist xenophobia, Little Italys were seen by the most generous commentators as places in which newcomers prepared for eventual entrance into the dominant society. As the flood of immigrants slowed to a trickle, nativists expected, and hoped for, a gradual process of increasingly successful individuals moving outward from central city slums to newer and better areas. However, as conditions for the group improved, conditions in the enclaves also improved, and they were not abandoned wholesale. Other factors, such as the onset of the Great Depression, also made it increasingly unlikely that Italians would easily improve their occupational or residential status in a general stagnating economy.

World War I in Europe had already effectively cut off large-scale immigration a decade before the radical immigration law changes in the 1920s. The cutoff also meant that cultural replenishment would depend more on impersonal forms (foreign language newspapers, radio, touring Italian officials) of contact with a rapidly changing Italy. By 1930 most Italian residents in America had already made a commitment to stay. The severe limitations on the number of Italians who could legally enter meant the end of rapid growth and expansion into new areas, such as the fringe and near-suburban areas where a few more successful Italian communities had already emerged.

In many places the non-Italian (German and Irish) Roman Catholic hierarchy received the different brand of Catholicism practiced by southern Italians with apprehension. As the enclaves matured, the occasional demands for Italian-speaking pastors and Italian parishes caused considerable friction, and fertile ground for Protestant missions, as well. Only begrudgingly did the hierarchy recognize the critical value of town and regional *feste* which many in the American clergy saw as pagan rituals. The Italian Roman Catholic institutions became integral in the development and maintenance of ethnic enclaves.

The change in the neighborhood to domination by native-born residents was concomitant with transformations in the traditional family system, especially the roles of women and children. The process of Americanization was greatly enhanced by compulsory education and the public school system. The intrusion of other American institutions into the locality produced strain, and eventual adjustments. Ironically, one of the most powerful of these outside American "intrusions" was Prohibition, which brought together the police and organized crime whose enterprises frequently found a home in Italian neighborhoods.

Once Italians made a commitment to stay, and the second-generation population of native-born citizens reached majority age, participation in electoral and party politics increased and Italian ethnic neighborhoods became an integral part of the urban political machine system.

At first the deprivations of the Great Depression was a counterforce of Americanization as it made people rely on coethnics. By the end of the 1930s the distributive programs of the New Deal brought government into the community but did not totally eliminate ethnic centeredness as local distribution of assistance was funneled through ethnically sensitive machine politicians.

The greatest shift in neighborhood patterns came with the onset of World War II.

The L'Unione Italiana Building, as it stands today, was dedicated in Ybor City, Tampa, Florida, in 1918. The Italian Club was a mutual aid society that assisted its members in time of need. Courtesy Frank J. Cavaioli.

Although both world wars greatly increased the rate of cultural assimilation, in the Second World War, Italy was an enemy, and for a short time foreign-born Italians were enemy aliens. Prior to the war, large Italian American neighborhoods in major cities were staging areas for Fascist outreach to the Italian community. Italian American leadership was split between left and right, and the outbreak of the war forced both groups into oppressed states.

Government-sponsored efforts at increasing solidarity and fears of a subversive "fifth column" led to a lessening of ethnic divisions among Americans, as indicated by the decrease in foreign language newspapers and radio stations. In multiethnic cities all immigrant neighborhoods became more American and visible signs of Italian ethnicity were muted, as was the Italian language. Isolated areas in the suburbs, small towns, and rural areas became even less Italian in operation and appearance.

During the war, direct contact between Italy and the community was virtually nonexistent. The end of the war brought thousands of Italian American servicemen back home, many of whom had served in Italy. Films from and about Italy and other contact with postwar Italy increased, but the Italian American community had been irreversibly changed. Like other Americans they saw Italy as foreign and, except for older generations, they lacked an understanding of their own ethnic connection.

After World War II, Italian immigration surged again for a short time. As economic conditions in Italy gradually improved, however, the impetus to emigrate lessened. Since then much smaller numbers have come to America and wide fluctuations of immigration can be easily correlated with the variations in the two economies.

Other factors that affected the evolution of Italian American neighborhoods were domestic. Federal housing policies encouraged the rapid growth of suburbs and mass exodus of the white population from the central city. Being less geographically mobile then other white ethnics of the same immigrant generation, Italian Americans were more likely than others to resist the trend. In the first Little Italys, before transportation technology made commuting easier, poor immigrants had to live near the availability of work. But in later years Italian Americans preferred to stay close to home, not only because of economics but because of cultural propensities. Those who stayed behind were faced with many other problems such as assaults on their neighborhoods by programs such as urban renewal and highway construction which began in the 1950s and continued into the next decade. These factors set the stage for later decades when urban Italian Americans, as the last of the white ethnics, occupied a diminishing number of variously "defended" neighborhoods.

During World War II, large numbers of African Americans had migrated from the South to industrial cities in pursuit of job opportunities previously denied them. The 1950s witnessed further large-scale migration of African Americans and Hispanics. By the 1960s most Italian American neighborhoods in the central city uneasily coexisted with substantial minority populations. Mandated integration of public schools and government efforts to end discrimination in employment and housing made relations between Italian Americans and nonwhites more problematic.

Italian immigration is no longer a major demographic factor in the dynamics of Italian America. Although changes in the 1965 immigration law eliminated the old discriminatory preference system, since then the yearly numbers vary only in the thousands. Except for a small number of first-generation communities, and those dominated by post–World War II immigrants, Italian American neighborhoods are affected more by America than by Italy.

Since the 1960s many Italians did come to Italian American neighborhoods, but they did not necessarily mix easily with the local population, and cultural divisions (especially based on language use, which persist) occurred between the two groups. There are also a considerable number of upper-class, cosmopolitan Italians who live in America but not in ethnic neighborhoods per se. The post-1965 Italian American enclaves, whether in the central city, fringe, or suburbs, are much more Italian in appearance and maintain a greater connection to Italy. These Italian Americans also come from a different modern Italy than did early Italian American generations. These two varieties of Italian neighborhood are possible because the ease of air travel makes it possible for Italians to maintain residences in two countries.

The New York region, as the most important center of Italian ethnic population, can be used as a model. Recent studies show that Italian American neighborhoods continue as visible features of the center and fringe of the city. Concentrations of Italian American population (neighborhoods) are, however, rapidly increasing in the near and far suburbs as the population in general disperses from the Northeast.

These postmodern Italian American neighborhoods have many varieties, but whether urban or suburban, Italian Italian, Italian American, or American Italian, they still share a few elements of appearance and traditions, such as interest in ethnic foods, which result in the opening of Italian groceries and delicatessens. Except for the touristy Little Italy theme parks maintained in large cities, these constantly evolving neighborhoods are not like the enclaves of the past. They remain, however, as somewhat distinct variants of American and Italian residential cultures.

Most social scientists employ structural-functional theories and view ethnic neighborhoods as transitional. For example, according to assimilation theory, they argue, at least in part, when Italian Americans are no more likely to live and work with one another than with non-Italian Americans, they have taken another step toward becoming another dissolved ingredient in the melting pot or a tasty tidbit bit in the "stew pot." Thus, random dispersal of the ethnic population is an indicator of assimilation.

As do nonethnic neighborhoods, ethnic enclaves, or urban villages, come into being and persist because they serve the reciprocal needs and functions of individuals, the groups to which they belong, and the greater societal structures of which they are a part. Ethnic neighborhoods are studied using many perspectives: classical ecology, cultural ecology, socio-spatial, symbolic interactionist, and phenomenological. All theories look at those factors that directly or indirectly increase or decrease ethnic concentration and integrity.

Social scientists, following the classical tradition of the Chicago School of Urban Ecology, for example, posited that poor Italian immigrants would first concentrate in slums, move to second-generation working-class ethnic areas, and then assimilate in the fringe and suburbs. Cultural ecologists such as Firey (1966) used the Italian North End of Boston to show that space is imbued with sentimental as well as economic values. Relatedly, Wirth (1943) argued that as the ghetto disintegrates, ethnics assimilate due to contact with outsiders. Other classic studies by Whyte and Gans (1962) captured both the complexity of local life and the connections between the neighborhood and society-wide structures and institutions such as politics, achievement, and urban development.

For the individual Italian immigrant, the neighborhood continues to lessen the shock of adjustment. It is a place where he or she can more easily find a job, housing, and familiar foods to eat. On the negative side villagers can avoid learning how to operate in the world, perhaps explaining why recent data show that residents of central city Italian American enclaves are more likely to be members of the working class. Some of these "defended" working-class areas engage in spatial competition with nonwhite groups in the central city.

For the most part, Italian ethnic communities were voluntary as opposed to involuntary ghettoes with varying degrees of exclusivity.

The concentration of members facilitates ethnic socialization and makes it easier for families and kin to exercise social control. Ethnic agglomeration (and gerrymandering) facilitated ethnic machine politics. In the system, population concentration is a group power base. Conversely, it makes it easier for them to be controlled by ethnic leaders. Concentration and proximity not only maintain *campanilismo* (provincialism), they also support mutual-benefit societies and then provide a base for other local institutions that support ethnic vitality.

Society as a whole can benefit from ethnic concentration. Ethnic neighborhoods serve functions for a city, for example, as staging areas of poor first immigrant workers for low-cost industry, household workers, and day laborers. In the postmodern society, neighborhoods are less important to individuals, but new functions evolve, such as people returning to their own and other's old neighborhoods to visit, shop, and recharge their ethnicity at *la festa*. Italian American neighborhoods can also provide real estate with saleable ambience. For example, Italian American neighborhoods in generally dangerous center city areas are often described as safe. Today's Italian immigrants and ethnic villagers still have a need for ethnic concentration, which can increasingly be found in the urban fringe and suburbs. Finally, in the postmodern world that allows for voluntary ethnicity, if people wish to be ethnic they can choose to live, or not to live, in an ethnic enclave.

Since they are seen by scholar, and common-sensically, by the average person-in-the-street alike as "typical" of Italian America, understanding enclaves of all sorts is critical in the emerging discipline of Italian American studies. Public opinion and academic examination of Italian Americans is greatly influenced by their place of residence.

Little Italys, ghettos, ethnic enclaves, or simply good old-fashioned Italian American neighborhoods are important places to study because they are venues for assimilation and acculturation. The idea of the Italian American local community is a powerful force in Italian, Italian American, and American culture and society. It is important to consider not only the places where Italians demographically dominate(d), but where Italians live as minorities, where they once lived, and where they never lived at all.

Today's immigrant neighborhoods can be created almost overnight. Inexpensive regular air transportation, telephone, fax, modem, and electronic access to funds make it possible for Italian extended families, clans, and virtually whole villages to alternate the continents on which they live. Because of this mobility, small but thriving enclaves can even remain unseen. The appearances of more recent Italian neighborhoods reflect the continuities and changes of residential life in Italy about which most students of Italian America are unaware. All these spaces (real or actual and imagined or virtual) help to understand Italian American past, present, and future.

Jerome Krase

Bibliography

Alba, Richard D., John R. Logan, and Kyle Crowder. *White Ethnic Neighborhoods in an Immigration Metropolis: The Greater New York Region, 1980–1990.* Albany: State University of New York at Albany, 1995.

Firey, Walter, *Land Use in Central Boston.* Cambridge: Harvard University Press, 1966.

Gans, Herbert. *The Urban Villagers.* New York: The Free Press, 1962.

Harney, Robert F., and J. Vincenza Scarpaci, eds. *Little Italies in North America.* Toronto: Multicultural Historical Society of Ontario, 1981.

Krase, Jerome. "Traces of Home." *Places: A Quarterly Journal of Environmental Design* 8, no. 4 (1993): 46–55.

Krase, Jerome, and Charles LaCerra. *Ethnicity and Machine Politics.* Lanham, MD: University Press of America, 1991.

Lofland, Lyn H. *A World of Strangers: Order and Action in Urban Public Space.* Prospect Heights, IL: Waveland Press, 1985.

Suttles, Gerald. *The Social Order of the Slum: Ethnicity and Territory in the Inner City.* Chicago: University of Chicago Press, 1968.

Whyte, William F. *Street Corner Society.* Chicago: University of Chicago Press, 1943.

Wirth, Louis. *The Ghetto.* Chicago: University of Chicago Press, 1928.

See also POPULATION

Ettor, Joseph

See LABOR

Explorers

Beginning in the fifteenth century, several natives of Italy expanded European knowledge about the Americas. They continued in the tradition of earlier Italians, who broadened Europe's geographical perspective by exploring unknown Eurasian lands. Giovanni da Pian del Carpini (1180?–1252), Marco Polo (1254?–1324), Odoric of Pordenone (1286?–1331), and Niccolò de Conti (1395?–1469) explored land routes from the Mideast to Mongolia and China in order to secure and maintain economic, political, or religious contacts with the Orient. Although at the time ships from Venice and Genoa carried most of Europe's Mediterranean trade with the Orient, the Florentine mathematician and geographer Paolo Toscanelli (1397–1482) was a leading proponent of the notion that the Orient lay conveniently westward across the Atlantic Ocean from Europe. Italian Renaissance rulers were uninterested in finding any new trade routes, but individual Italians, among the most skilled seamen of Europe, were employed by the Spanish, Portuguese, English, and French to traverse the Atlantic in search of the alternate, all-water route to the Orient.

The premier explorer to seek this elusive route was the Genoese navigator Cristoforo Colombo (1451–1506), better known as Christopher Columbus. Very familiar with Polo's account of travel in China and the cartography of Toscanelli, he set sail from Palos, Spain, on August 3, 1492. On October 12 he sighted San Salvador island in the Bahamas and then proceeded to map Cuba and Hispaniola. Returning three more times (1493, 1498, 1502), he charted Jamaica, Puerto Rico, and other Caribbean islands as well as the American mainland from Honduras to Trinidad. He not only firmly established a Spanish claim to this vast territory but, more importantly, he made the world one by linking Eurasia and Africa permanently to the Americas.

Giovanni Caboto (1455?–1499?), also a Genoese but naturalized in Venice (1476), resided in England as John Cabot. Departing from Bristol to explore a route directly west of the British Isles, he sighted Cape Bauld, the northern tip of Newfoundland, on July 24,

1497, and unfurled the English and Venetian flags. (Sebastiano Caboto, who accompanied his father, believed that they landed near Cape North on Cape Breton Island. Plaques in English, French, and Italian mark that presumed spot today.) Whatever his exact location, Caboto established an English claim to North America. Wishing to learn more about the area and the extent of the great fishing banks south of Newfoundland, he launched a second expedition from which he never returned.

Following Caboto, the Florentine Amerigo Vespucci (1454–1512) explored Brazil and the northeastern coast of South America during two voyages for Spain and Portugal between 1499 and 1502. He confirmed Columbus's suspicion that the unknown region across the Atlantic was not the Orient, and appears to be the first to call these lands *Mundus novus* (the New World). Vespucci soon published such an illuminating description of his travels that the German cartographer Martin Waldseemueller named *Mundus novus* "America" after him (1507).

News of the explorations made by these three Italians aroused interest in what lay between and beyond their landfalls. Sebastiano Caboto (1476?–1557), born in Chioggia, sailed to America in 1508. He traced the Atlantic coast from Baffin Island to Florida and inspired others to continue the search for a northwest passage to the Pacific Ocean. He entered Spanish service in 1512 and explored the basin of the Rio de la Plata (1526). Returning to England in 1548, he worked with the Merchants Adventurers (Muscovy) Company of London, an early trading group, to discover a possible northeast passage and establish a profitable trade with Russia.

The French employed Giovanni da Verrazano (1485?–1528), born at Greve in Tuscany, to find the passage to China and obtain a supply of spices. In 1524 he charted the coastline from South Carolina to Nova Scotia. Verrazano was the first European to see New York harbor (a bridge there memorializes him) and to explore Narragansett Bay and Cape Cod. He later sailed the coast of Brazil and noted Guanabara Bay (Rio de Janeiro); but while cruising the Caribbean, he was killed and eaten by natives on the island of Guadeloupe. Verrazano established a French claim to both Americas overlapping those of Spain, Portugal, and England.

Italians also accompanied other great explorers on their expeditions. Antonio Pigafetta (1491–1534), a gentleman of Vicenza, traveled with the Portuguese explorer Ferdinand Magellan on his 1519 expedition and became its chief chronicler. He was gossipy and amusing, but provided large amounts of information on flora, manners, customs, and languages hitherto unknown to Europeans. One of eighteen survivors who returned to Spain in 1522, he was therefore the first Italian to circumnavigate the globe. After the publication of Pigafetta's chronicle, Europeans concluded that the Americas were continents separate—and distant—from Asia.

Helping to clarify the shadowy image of the New World, Italians explored the continental interior and provided accurate geographical descriptions. Some of these observers were missionaries whose reports and maps increased geographical knowledge. The first Catholic bishop in the New World, the Umbrian Alessandro Geraldini (1455–1525), arrived as bishop of Santo Domingo in 1516. His published travel experiences were widely read in Europe. Franciscan friar Marco da Nizza (1495?–1558) arrived in Santo Domingo (1531), ministered in Guatemala, Peru, and Ecuador, and eventually landed in Mexico (1537). He explored Arizona and claimed to have sighted the legendary "Seven Golden Cities of Cíbola" (1539). Fra Marco accompanied the Coronado expedition until Cíbola was found to be a cluster of humble pueblos in western New Mexico. Yet his inaccurate report of a rich kingdom inspired this expedition that discovered the Grand Canyon, penetrated to central Kansas, and provided accurate information on the indigenous population over a large portion of the American Southwest (1540–1542). Jesuit Father Eusebio Kino (1645–1711), born at Segno near Trento, explored much of Sonora and Arizona as far north and west as the Gila and Colorado Rivers, and concluded that California was not an island as shown on earlier maps.

Other Italians contributed to cementing economic and political ties between Europe and America. In 1678 Enrico Tonti (1649?–1704), born at Gaeta, accompanied the great French explorer René-Robert La Salle into the American Midwest. They were the first Europeans to canoe the Mississippi from the Illinois River to its delta (1682). To develop the trade in furs and buffalo hides, Tonti constructed Fort Crèvecoeur (near Peoria), Fort St. Louis (at Starved Rock) along the Illinois River (1682–1683), and Arkansas Post near the confluence of the Arkansas and Mississippi Rivers (1686). He explored internal waterways, describing the lands and peoples along Lake Superior (1695) and from eastern Texas to southern Alabama. After La Salle's murder (1687), Tonti became the most important entrepreneur in the Mississippi River basin and along the Gulf of Mexico. He maintained the French presence in this region despite Spanish and English encroachments. Tonti's brother Alfonso followed him to America in 1687 and served as French governor of Detroit for twelve years.

As Italians charted the Atlantic shores of the Americas, an Italian also helped chart the Pacific coastline. Alessandro Malaspina (1754–1810) was born at Mulazzo near La Spezia, studied in Parma, and entered Spanish service. He proposed to launch the most comprehensive scientific survey of the plants and animals of the "most remote regions of America" while preparing detailed hydrographic charts of the southern Atlantic and Pacific coasts. A naval captain at age 35, Malaspina spent three years (1789–1792) studying the coastal lands from Brazil south to Cape Horn and then from Chile north to Russian America. The glacier which he discovered along the southern base of Mount St. Elias in Alaska (1791) bears his name. (The first to reach the summit of Mount St. Elias was Luigi Amadeo di Savoia, Duke of the Abruzzi, member of the Italian royal family, in 1897.) Malaspina then sailed west to the Philippines and the southwestern Pacific (1792–1794). Upon his return to Spain, he was jailed for six years because he supported colonial independence. His reports and maps gathered dust for thirty years until geographers learned to appreciate his fascinating, astute observations without reference to his political views.

In the late eighteenth and early nineteenth centuries, Count Paolo Andreani and Giacomo Costantino Beltrami explored the Upper Midwest. Andreani (1763–1832) was a Milanese naturalist and physicist, and the first Italian to ascend in a balloon (1783). He arrived in the United States, led a scientific expedition to study the shape of the earth, described the extent of the fur trade in the Lake Superior region (summer 1791), and recorded his daily scientific observations. Andreani was the first man to circumnavigate Lake Superior during a single expedition.

Beltrami (1779–1855) was a lawyer born in Bergamo, a commissary inspector and judge under Napoleon, and a strong supporter of a united Italy. Out of favor in Italy after the fall of the French emperor, he went into self-imposed exile in the United States (1822). He became interested in locating the source of the Mississippi River, and joined the military expedition that traced the Minnesota and Red Rivers north to the 49th parallel. Then, outfitted as a frontiersman, carrying a large red umbrella, and accompanied by Chippewas, he plunged into the wilds of northwestern Minnesota. Following the course of rivers into Red Lake (near present Bemidji), he then pushed southward through woods and marshes until he reached Lake Julia (named after his late friend Contessa Giulia Spada de Medici) on August 31, 1823. Here he stood on the Mississippi's northernmost watershed with Hudson Bay and the Arctic Ocean. Although the Chippewas advised him that Lac la Biche (now Lake Itasca) was the Mississippi's primary source, he concluded that Lac la Biche, thirty-five miles to the southwest of Lake Julia, was really a secondary source. In the following year, Beltrami published an account of his adventures and discovery of Lake Julia. Others almost immediately attacked and denied his claim. Beltrami returned to Europe in 1826 and to Italy in 1837. Years later a Minnesota historical commission decided that the primary source of the "Father of Waters" was Lake Itasca, a name explorer Henry Rowe Schoolcraft invented when he visited this lake in 1832. Yet the state legislature acknowledged the exploration of the proud and romantic traveler from Bergamo when it named the region around Red Lake and Lake Julia Beltrami County (1866).

By the late nineteenth century, only the Arctic region and Antarctica remained as areas for exploration. Umberto Nobile (1885–1978), born at Lauro di Nola, was an aeronautical engineer who pioneered Arctic aviation. He designed the airship *Norge,* which could reach a speed of 50 mph in windless conditions. In 1926 *Norge,* with Nobile as pilot, became the first airship to reach the North Pole and to fly from Europe to Amer-ica (Spitsbergen to Alaska) over the Pole. The flight proved that, unlike at the South Pole, no continent existed at the North Pole, only a frozen ocean. Nobile then de-

A bronze plaque at the Italian Mausoleum in San Francisco honoring the Italian pioneers who helped settle and build California. Courtesy of Augusto Troiani.

signed and commanded a new dirigible, *Italia,* to explore other unknown Arctic regions. He began to chart Siberian islands and the north end of Greenland, and during his third flight, on May 24, 1928, he circled the Pole; but *Italia* crashed in a heavy fog during its return to base. Although he and a few others were rescued, most of his crew perished. When an Italian Fascist inquiry commission held him personally responsible for this national dishonor, he resigned his rank of general in the Italian Air Force. In 1931 he participated in a Soviet voyage to the Arctic. After the fall of the Fascist government, the commission's report was discredited, and Nobile was reinstated in the Air Force and resumed teaching aeronautical engineering at the University of Naples.

Historically, Italians are recognized for their role in and contributions to culture (art, architecture, music, literature), politics, religion and philosophy, fashion, and culinary arts. Equally important are their contributions to geographical exploration from the 1400s to the 1900s. Our view of the very world we inhabit, especially the Americas, is shaped by their discoveries.

James J. Divita

Bibliography

Bolton, Herbert E. *Coronado, Knight of Pueblos and Plains.* Albuquerque: University of New Mexico Press, 1964.

McKee, Alexander. *Ice Crash, Disaster in the Arctic, 1928.* New York: St. Martin's, 1979.

Miceli, Augusto P. *The Man with the Red Umbrella: Giacomo Costantino Beltrami in America.* Baton Rouge: Claitor's, 1974.

Morison, Samuel Eliot. *The European Discovery of America: The Northern Voyages,* A.D. *500–1600.* New York: Oxford University Press, 1971.

Murphy, Edmund Robert. *Henry de Tonty, Fur Trader of the Mississippi.* Baltimore: Johns Hopkins Press, 1941.

Smith, G. Hubert. "Count Andreani, a Forgotten Traveler." *Minnesota History* 19 (March 1938): 34–42.

———. *The European Discovery of America: The Southern Voyages,* A.D. *1492–1616.* New York: Oxford University Press, 1974.

See also CABOTO, GIOVANNI; CATALDO, JOSEPH MARY; COLUMBUS, CHRISTOPHER; KINO, EUSEBIO FRANCISCO; MAZZUCHELLI, SAMUEL; VERRAZZANO, GIOVANNI DA; VIGO, FRANCIS

F

Family Life

Arguably the most central and important institution in their lives, the family has often been presented in popular films, stage dramas, television programs, novels, and studies by historians and social scientists as the principal means of understanding Italian Americans. In the mass media, while frequently depicted as a contentious experience for its members, the Italian American family is also projected as a warm and supportive sanctuary of individual life and group experience that provides the final and dependable refuge against everything that is external and threatening to its members. This simple stereotype of popular culture stands sharply in contrast to how scholarly research has presented the complex realities of family life among Italian Americans.

From the first serious studies on Italian immigrants in the United States, the family has been recognized as an important factor in explaining individual motives and social mechanisms for departure from the homeland as well as the subsequent adjustment to American conditions. Although the initial period of mass migration from southern Italy in the final decades of the nineteenth century was dominated by unattached younger males, who sought employment in American industries, it was later augmented by the arrival of women and children, particularly in the years preceding World War I, who completed family units and normalized the structure of the community. Family and kinship ties provided chains of migration that contributed greatly to the demographic growth of Italian immigration to the United States and to the structural development of Italian communities in American cities.

One outstanding element of early immigrant study has been the contrast between the cultural values and social organization of the traditional Italian family and other immigrant groups as well as with the dominant American society. Derived from regions of southern Italy, and carried to American society by immigration, "familism" provided the principal element in interpreting the experience of Italian Americans. This concept meant that group cohesion subordinated individualism and the extended family dominated the nuclear unit. The division of labor ostensibly reflected a pattern of patriarchal power, while it also allowed wives and mothers a subtler, but vital, role in certain matters of family decision making.

The family provided the most salient institutional context for the conflict between traditional culture and folkways of Italian immigrants and the newer values and aspirations of their American-born children. The result of this conflict was sometimes characterized as "the dilemma of the second generation," that is, the particular personal difficulties encountered by the children of foreign-born parents. The synonymous idea of "marginality" described the situation of an individual, caught between two social worlds, who had chosen to abandon his or her original culture by the act of migration, but who had neither learned all the ways of, nor had been fully accepted by, the new society. The implications of this concept for understanding the adjustment of individuals to new situations in general made it a valuable tool of the social sciences, with applications that extended into other areas far beyond immigration.

Another dimension in the study of Italian American life has been the degree of rigidity,

Italian immigrant workers and their families. These workers constructed roads in Roslyn, New York, in the late 1800s. The family was the most important institution for Italians. Courtesy Suffolk County Historical Society.

and conversely flexibility, in the family as an institution. The adages passed down by older generations also transmitted the wisdom of folk culture that urged children to respect and preserve the ways of the past, often at the cost of their own aspirations. While early analysis depicted a relatively intractable system, more recent research has emphasized the adaptability of the family's values and behavior. Family members often made great sacrifices that overcame barriers of immigrant status and contributed to upward mobility for the next generation. In the latter interpretation, rather than being another obstacle for the individual, the family became a useful instrument in taking advantage of economic opportunities presented by the new society.

A closely related issue has been the role of the family in the acculturation and assimilation of individuals. This concern has often focused upon the degree of compatibility of traditional parental values and material needs of the family with the educational and occupational aspirations of American-born children. The question is whether family culture

and structure served more as a deterrent and restraint or as a resource and instrument for the motivation, achievement, and mobility of later generations.

In its adjustment to American society, it has become customary for scholars to describe the Italian American family system as it has evolved through a series of stages that represent different patterns of values, behavior, and relationships of members with one another. Each stage also represents an attempt to locate the position of Italian Americans in terms of acculturation, assimilation, and social mobility. For a long time, it was believed that this sequence was inevitably moving toward the complete absorption of Italian Americans. In the late 1960s, however, a newer view argued that some form of the enduring persistence of ethnicity in a culturally pluralistic society was a more accurate interpretation of American ethnicity. The family provided an obvious milieu for the examination of these issues.

With the current debate over the "twilight of ethnicity," the lingering possibility

Italian American wedding party. Ethnic neighborhoods like this one in the Little Italy of downtown New York City frequently witnessed celebrations of marriage. Courtesy Center for Migration Studies.

of the imminent dissolution of a distinctive Italian American family also directs attention to the conditions which challenge its continuation. The extinction of the final vestiges of the immigrant population, the continuing demise of older ethnic neighborhoods in the cities, and the redistribution of later generations of Italian Americans into middle-class lifestyles and suburban communities has again placed the changing character of the family at the center of concern. In recent generations, fertility patterns have become comparable to other groups and average family size has decreased. While intermarriage rates have remained lower than for other groups, exogamy among Italian Americans has greatly increased. Divorce rates, even for the most recent generation, remain very low compared to all other ethnic groups. Italian Americans still maintain a pattern of relatively frequent family contacts, with some studies actually indicating an increase in visiting among relatives for later generations. The strength of family ties has been identified as a deterrent to residential mobility and as a factor in the maintenance of Italian American neighborhoods.

With social change, newer issues have emerged that reflect even more recent dimensions of family experience among Italian Americans. With variations in personal mobility, different class positions and lifestyles have

separated members of the same family. Holidays and ceremonial events become occasions that bring together family members who must reconcile themselves with one another, at least for the moment. Similarly, the interpretation of meaning and function behind family stories has become an issue. As the family past continues to fade, the awareness that power is also shifting to the young encourages older members to relate, and sometimes to invent, tales of the past whose function is to restore the balance of power to what it once was. As American society increasingly directs attention to the aging of its population, the role of the Italian American family as a support system in the care of its elderly members has also become the subject of research in recent years.

While the study of family life has produced a plethora of valuable knowledge, complex differences that have distinguished the experiences of Italian Americans have been ignored. Despite the tendency to develop a uniform interpretation of immigrant and ethnic life, some research has emphasized the internal variation that has distinguished individuals and families within the Italian American population. Whether by the stage of assimilation at which they are found, or by the region of American society in which they reside, or by differences of personal achievement and mobility, as individuals and as family units, Italian Americans reflect a wide range of patterns. As a result of such differences, some scholars have concluded that Italian Americans behave more like members of similar class levels than they do to the rest of their own ethnic category. Similarly, as for other ethnic groups, rather than a singular Italian American family type, it is far more likely that there are, and perhaps have always been, several Italian American family systems that are primarily based upon differences in the degree of assimilation and class position.

Many issues remain to be more adequately examined by students of Italian American life: the techniques of child rearing and early socialization; the patterns of family life at different stages of the life cycle; the experience of individuals at particular periods of their lives (such as adolescence); mate selection and marital compatibility in ethnic intermarriages; the personal identities and behavior of individuals with mixed ethnic antecedents; patterns of sexuality and gender relations; the future of original immigrant residences and older neighborhoods within urban areas; and the persistence of ethnic identity and distinctive lifestyles in the suburbs. These questions, along with many others, are not only directly or indirectly related to the study of family life, but also provide a challenging agenda for the future of Italian American studies.

In their family life in particular, Italian Americans display a broad spectrum of beliefs and values, overt behaviors, and interpersonal relations. Through the accumulation of a massive amount of empirical data, as well as the development of research techniques and conceptual analysis, the study of Italian American family life continues to provide opportunities for a greater understanding of the experience and position of Italian Americans within society. With the great attenuation of communal institutions that once organized their lives, family life may be more significant now than at any previous period for their personal identity and group cohesion as Italian Americans.

Richard N. Juliani

Bibliography

Campisi, Paul. "Ethnic Family Patterns: The Italian Family in the United States." *American Journal of Sociology* 53 (1948): 443–449.

Child, Irwin L. *Italian or American: The Second Generation in Conflict.* New Haven: Yale University Press, 1943.

Covello, Leonard. *The Social Background of the Italo-American School Child.* Leiden, The Netherlands: E. J. Brill, 1967.

Feminella, Francis X. "Changing Perspectives on Italian American Family Life." In *Italian Americans in the '80s: A Sociodemographic Profile,* edited by Graziano Battistella. New York: Center for Migration Studies and Fondazione Giovanni Agnelli, 1989.

Ianni, Francis A. J. "The Italo-American Teen-Ager." *The Annals of the American Academy of Political and Social Science* 338 (1961): 70–78.

Johnson, Colleen Leahy. *Growing Up and Old in Italian-American Families.* New Brunswick, NJ: Rutgers University Press, 1985.

Orsi, Robert. "The Fault of Memory: 'Southern Italy' in the Imagination of Immigrants and the Lives of Their Children in Italian Harlem, 1920–1945." *Journal of Family History* 15 (1990): 133–147.

Squier, D. Ann, and Jill S. Quadagno. "The Italian American Family." In *Ethnic Families in America,* 3rd ed., edited by Charles H. Mindel, Robert W. Habenstein, and Roosevelt Wright Jr., 109–137. New York: Elsevier, 1988.

Tomasi, Lydio F. *The Italian American Family: The Southern Italian Family's Process of Adjustment to an Urban America.* New York: Center for Migration Studies, 1972.

Tricarico, Donald. *The Italians of Greenwich Village.* New York: Center for Migration Studies, 1984.

See also ASSIMILATION; EDUCATION: SOCIOHISTORICAL BACKGROUND; FOLKLORE, FOLKLIFE; HOSPITALITY

Fante, John (1909–1983)

Novelist, short-story writer, and screenwriter, John Fante was born in Denver, Colorado. His father had migrated from Abruzzi, Italy, and his mother (née Capolungo) was born in Chicago. He attended Catholic primary and secondary schools and attended Regis College, the University of Colorado at Denver, and Long Beach Junior College. In 1930 he moved to Los Angeles.

His mother and siblings, whom he subsequently supported, followed him there after his father had left the family for another woman. Later his father rejoined the family to settle with them in Roseville, California. Fante remained in Los Angeles and continued his writing as he worked at odd jobs in hotels, grocery stores, and fish canneries. He later supported himself by selling his stories to various magazines and by screenwriting for Hollywood.

As an aspiring writer in the early thirties, Fante wrote many letters to H. L. Mencken, then editor of the *American Mercury,* who eventually published Fante's first two stories in 1932: "Altar Boy" and "Home Sweet Home." Thereafter Mencken became his mentor, published more of his stories in the *American Mercury,* found a publisher for his first novel, and suggested he try screenwriting as a means of supporting himself as he wrote novels and short stories, many of which were published in the *Saturday Evening Post,* the *Atlantic Monthly, Collier's, Esquire,* and *Harper's Bazaar.* Although Fante eventually made his living mostly by writing for Hollywood, he preferred writing novels and short stories. Hollywood attracted and repulsed him: he was lured by the money and movie stars, but repelled by the general mediocrity of Hollywood productions and the ultimate cost to his own creativity. Writing for Hollywood was a compromise with which he never felt fully comfortable.

In 1937 Fante married Joyce Smart, a Stanford graduate and poet, with whom he had four children. After achieving a degree of financial security through his writing, he moved his family in 1952 to Malibu, where he lived for the remainder of his life. Toward the end of his life, Fante became blind (1978) due to diabetes and glaucoma, and his legs were amputated (one in 1977, the other in 1981). In spite of his condition, Fante continued to write, dictating the novels to his ever-supportive wife Joyce. Fante died on May 8, 1983, in Motion Picture Hospital, Los Angeles.

Fante's life became the source material for his art. His writing is autobiographical: each piece concentrates on a specific period in his life. *Wait Until Spring Bandini* (1938) describes the adolescence of Arturo Bandini. It focuses on the dynamics of an Italian American family living in Colorado, particularly their hardships, and on Arturo's developing understanding of his family and of himself. An older Arturo Bandini appears as narrator in *Ask the Dust* (1939) and *Dreams From Bunker Hill* (1982), both about Arturo's (Fante's) struggling years as a young writer living in a rooming house in Bunker Hill, Los Angeles. Both novels reveal the underbelly of American society: the uprooted, directionless, broken people with shattered lives and shattered dreams; the poor; and the deformed, both physically and spiritually. In *Dreams From Bunker Hill,* more than in other works, Fante reveals his contempt for Hollywood's treatment of talented writers. *Dago Red* (1940) and *The Wine of Youth* (1985) (in which *Dago Red* is included) are collections of short stories dealing with specific events in Fante's parents' life and in Fante's youth. The collections also include two poignant stories about Filipino men who work in the fish canneries in Los Angeles and pursue the golden-haired women of their American Dream.

Other works include the following: *Full of Life* (1952), a novel about the birth of Fante's first child and his wife's conversion to Catholicism; *The Brotherhood of the Grape* (1977), about the final days of Fante's father's life, where the protagonist Henry Molise recollects earlier times at home and bemoans the destruction of the Italian immigrant community, all of which cause him to ponder his own Italian American identity; *1933 Was a Bad Year* (1985), set during the height of the Great Depression, about the hopes, dreams, and despair of the Molise family—their very life a parody of the Horatio Alger myth; and *West of Rome* (1986), which consists of two novellas, *My Dog Stupid,* a candid view of Fante's relationship with his wife and children, and *Orgy,* about a 10-year-old boy catapulted into the duplicitous world of adults when he witnesses his father participating in an orgy.

Fante's screenplays include the following: *Dinky* (1935), *East of the River* (1940), *The Golden Fleecing* (1940), *Youth Runs Wild* (1944), *My Man and I* (1952), *Full of Life* (1956), *Jeanne Eagels* (1957), *Walk on the Wild Side* (1962), *The Reluctant Saint* (1962), *My Six Loves* (1963), and *Maya* (1966).

Fante's fiction, in varying degrees, renders the following issues through a self-conscious, insecure narrator/protagonist who is at times not unlike Huck Finn, at other readings similar to T. S. Eliot's Prufrock, and at other times he seems to be a cross between Huck Finn and Prufrock: ambivalence concerning

F

God, Catholicism, his Italian American identity, women, sex, writing, and the American Dream, particularly the Horatio Alger equation between hard work and success. In many works the narrator/protagonist embarks on a Walter Mitty–like flight of fancy—imagining life as he wishes it to be or simply superimposing an alternate reality on the current one. All the works contain naturalistic elements, reminiscent of Stephen Crane, though the determinism and resulting despair are often mitigated by hope, faith, and humor. The forces of nature and society appear to work against the individual—be it the snow in *Wait Until Spring Bandini* that prevents Bandini from working, or the hostile sun, dust, and indifferent urban environment and society in *Ask the Dust.*

Fante uses simple, lucid, uncomplicated language to describe situations that are anything but simple. Some works are more lyrical than others, as in *Wait Until Spring Bandini;* some more somber, as in *Ask the Dust.* In all his works, Fante manages to elicit from the reader a complex knot of emotions while keeping the reader sympathetic, angry, laughing, and crying simultaneously. His works gracefully combine pathos and humor, tragedy and comedy.

Louise Napolitano-Carman

Bibliography

Cooney, Seamus, ed. *John Fante: Selected Letters 1932–1981.* Santa Rosa: Black Sparrow Press, 1991.

Gardaphé, Fred. *Italian Streets, American Signs: The Evolution of the Italian American Narrative.* Durham, NC: Duke University Press, 1996.

Green, Rose Basile. *The Italian American Novel: A Document of the Interaction of Two Cultures.* Rutherford, NJ: Fairleigh Dickinson University Press, 1974.

Mulas, Francesco. *Studies on Italian American Literature.* New York: Center for Migration Studies, 1995.

Napolitano, Louise. "The Bittersweet Promise of America in Selected Works of Italian American Fiction." In *Italian Americans in a Multicultural Society,* edited by Jerome Krase and Judith DeSena, 254–262. Stony Brook, NY: Forum Italicum, 1994.

Patti, Samuel. "Recent Italian American Literature: The Case of John Fante." In *From the Margin: Writings in Italian Americana,* edited by Anthony Tamburri, Paolo Giordano, and Fred Gardaphé. West Lafayette, IN: Purdue University Press, 1991.

See also AUTOBIOGRAPHY; LITERATURE; NOVELS AND NOVELISTS

Farming
See AGRICULTURE

Fasanella, Ralph (1914–1998)

Born to a working-class family, Ralph Fasanella was deeply influenced by the hardship of his father, an iceman, and his mother, a buttonhole maker. He was part of the proletarian class in his early years in Greenwich Village, New York. Passionately interested in the plight of exploited workers, he became active in the labor movement as an organizer for the United Electrical Workers of the Congress of Industrial Organization. He was also attracted to left-wing politics and at one point ran unsuccessfully for the New York City Council on the American Labor Party ballot headed by Vito Marcantonio.

Notwithstanding his frenetic activity in labor and political movements, he turned to painting at age 30 because he felt he was losing touch with his ethnic roots and his fingers were itching to paint. Supporting his family by working at his brothers' Bronx gas station in the evenings, he reserved his daylight hours for painting. Despite his lack of formal training, he produced a corpus of work that finally, at age 58, elicited recognition, including a cover story in *New York* magazine in 1972 that hailed his "primitive" canvases as treasures.

Many of his paintings reflect a love-hate relationship he had with the Catholic Church, much of which was rooted in his childhood experience of being placed in a church-run reformatory for boys. Thus, numerous Fasanella paintings depict church scenes. Even family scenes show an interplay with the religious; for example, *The Iceman Crucified* portrays his father's body as a Christ-like figure on the cross. Indeed, the religion of his childhood permeates virtually all his works, which serve as social statements of his working-class Italian background.

Salvatore J. LaGumina

Bibliography

"Portrait of the Artist as a Garage Attendant in the Bronx," *New York 5*, no. 44 (1972, Oct. 30): 37–45.

Soria, Regina. *American Artists of Italian Heritage, 1776-1945*. Rutherford, NJ: Fairleigh Dickinson University Press, 1994.

Watson, Patrick. *Fasanella's City: The Paintings of Ralph Fasanella, With the Story of His Life and Art*. New York: Alfred A. Knopf, 1973.

See also ART

Fascism

When Benito Mussolini became prime minister of Italy in 1922, amid general turmoil that included strikes, violence, local insurrections, and killings by Communists, Socialists, and Fascists, Italians seemed unaware of the great changes that were taking place among them. Americans showed even less concern, though some U.S. newspapers regularly carried stories that criticized the rise of Fascism. Americans, in general, and Italian Americans, in particular, gave Benito Mussolini and his Fascist dictatorship greater support than did the people of any other Western nation.

Many Americans, rejecting Wilsonian internationalism that had led them into a seemingly senseless war, welcomed Mussolini's commitment to patriotic virtues and his contempt for the League of Nations. Much of the sympathy for Mussolini came from former Progressive reformers and from American fundamentalists who had upheld William Jennings Bryan's anti-evolutionist crusade and extolled Mussolini's polemics against materialism and anticlericalism in Italy. Americans who followed the rise of Mussolini saw Fascism as a fit foe blocking the advance of Bolshevism. American businessmen, especially, saw him as the savior of capitalism. Patriots at home and abroad hailed his reinforcement of Italy's nationalist movement. American officials in Italy reported favorably on Il Duce, citing the restoration of order, discipline, and stability in that country. Americans who visited Italy commented warmly on Mussolini's intelligence, common sense, and charm. More perceptive observers warned of the dangers of a developing brutal dictatorship, but little heed was paid to those caveats. While Mussolini renounced democracy as a way of life, he carefully exempted the United States from his attacks. Most Americans viewed his diatribes as rhetoric for home consumption. They viewed his militarism and imperialism neither as a threat nor as a danger to America. Except for Mussolini's seizure of Corfu and his threatening posture, he did not seem to be an international menace. However, though American liberals had become anti-Fascist by 1930, most others continued to view him benevolently.

Even so, from the start, a vocal minority, mostly Italian American labor leaders and liberal intellectuals, warned of the rising Fascist regime. They were joined by Italian political refugees (the *fuorusciti* or *emigranti*) and editors and publishers of radical Italian language newspapers. Whenever Italian Americans got together the topic usually turned to Mussolini and the merits of his Fascist dictatorship. Family gatherings often grew heated on the subject. And battles were sure to break out on holidays when large numbers of Italian Americans came together to celebrate Columbus Day or some other event such as a local saint's day which evoked their ties to Italy. The anti-Fascists were in the minority and at a disadvantage. Most Italian Americans and their media, some subsidized with Fascist funds, praised the accomplishments of Mussolini. Among other things, they claimed, he kept the beggars off the streets, made the trains run on time, and restored the glories of ancient Rome. To be against Mussolini would make an Italian American appear "un-Italian." But, in truth, what the anti-Fascists deplored most was the denial of personal liberties in Italy as attested to by such luminaries as Arturo Toscanini and Count Carlo Sforza, to name two.

In an age when immigrants were expected to "Americanize," Italian Americans acted much like Americans in championing Mussolini in the twenties and thirties. Constantine Panunzio, a minister of truly progressive leanings, wrote that during the 1920s his anti-Fascist views "encountered far more stubborn opposition . . . among native Americans descended from other racial stocks especially those of legitimist bent, than among Italian Americans."

Within the Italian American community Fascism did not have a uniform effect. The young, born in the United States and educated in American public schools, viewed Italy with indifference and Fascism as a European ideology. Many naturalized Italian immigrants and their American-born children had served in the

American armed forces during World War I and were grateful to the United States for entering the holocaust on the side of Italy against Austria. Following years of discrimination, these soldiers used the war as a vehicle to demonstrate their loyalty to their adopted country. Once despised, they emerged from the conflict with acceptance, if not complete equality, and an exaggerated sense of American nationalism. Most Italian Americans during the 1920s and 1930s were too busy earning a living to take any interest in the Fascist regime of Mussolini.

Nevertheless, during the twenties, pro-*Fascisti* and anti-*Fascisti* groups emerged in the Italian communities of America, and some Italian immigrants became rabid disciples of Il Duce. Some ethnic leaders saw an opportunity to pose as the American exponents of an ideology that appeared destined to replace the seemingly moribund liberal thought of the prewar era. Other Italian Americans, sensitive to former racial slurs, saw in Fascism a movement that would give them the prestige that had eluded them in the past.

Italian American support for Mussolini increased in 1929 when he established cordial relations with the Catholic Church, a move that endeared him to non-Italian American Catholics as well. In this manner, Il Duce unwittingly accelerated the process by which a Catholic identity partially replaced the ethnic label in the Italian Americans' quest for acceptance by the larger society in general and the Irish American community in particular. Little wonder that some saw in Mussolini a new Messiah. For instance, the pro-Fascist and anti-Semite Domenico Trombetta founded the New York weekly *Il Grido della Stirpe* (The Cry of the Race). John Di Silvestro of the Sons of Italy went to Rome and dramatically presented Il Duce with the support of that Italian American organization. Not welcomed by all members of the Sons of Italy, his actions caused a split in the society. Still Panunzio could write in the 1920s that the messianic anti-Communist and pro-capitalist bent of Fascism and the flamboyance with which it was carried out swept many Americans off their feet. The enthusiasm caused many an Italian American chest to swell and to join the bandwagon of singing Il Duce's praises.

The conservative decade of the twenties marked the high point in America's flirtation with Mussolini's Fascist state. Indeed, Washington did its best to please Il Duce. It sought to deny Gaetano Salvemini, the brilliant historian and anti-Fascist, asylum in the United States. But an investigation into his activities did not show him to be an anarchist or a Communist, and he was not denied political asylum. The Coolidge administration negotiated a lenient debt settlement with Italy that was in no small way due to Richard W. Child's (the American ambassador to Italy) exuberant praise of Mussolini's administration.

Though not all Italian officials thought it wise for the Fascists to proselytize vigorously overseas, those in favor of doing so won Mussolini's support. With the help of some Italian Americans, for example, Domenico Trombetta's *Grido* and Macaluso's *Giovinezza,* a monthly published in Boston, the Fascist League of North America (FLNA) was set in motion. Uniting the Italian American *Fasci* into a national organization, it would perform functions similar to those of the YMCA and the Knights of Columbus, two organizations from which Italian Americans were estranged by virtue of their Roman Catholicism and their Italian roots, respectively. The FLNA would encourage cultural and athletic activities among Italian Americans in accordance with their ethnic preferences. When Italian ambassador Giacomo de Martino, an opponent of the American *Fasci,* offered to curb their activities if the State Department would declare them illegal or even troublesome, his suggestions were dismissed by American government officials who viewed the *Fasci* as anticommunist and therefore dedicated to upholding law and order. Nonetheless, de Martino warned his government to avoid any meddling in America's internal affairs. He believed that Mussolini and his "great domestic reforms" were the best proponents of Fascism in America. The American government saw no need to make an issue of the FLNA unless driven to do so.

Opposition to the American *Fasci* came initially from Italian American labor leaders, radical partisans, and a few liberal intellectuals who unleashed one of the first anti-Fascist campaigns in the Western world. In 1923 the Anti-Fascist Alliance of North America (AFANA) was organized with Arturo Giovannitti, the "poet of the proletariat," as its secretary. First endorsed by Italian American communists, socialists, and anarchists, AFANA also won the support of the New York Federation of Labor (NYFL), the Amalgamated Clothing Workers (ACW), and the International Ladies

Garment Workers Union (ILGWU). During the 1920s AFANA denounced the American government for financially assisting Mussolini and reaffirmed the necessity of a continuing revolutionary war against Fascism. The organization contended that it was not sufficient to defeat Mussolini; the capitalist system that supported him had to be destroyed, too. It argued the Italian Fascists were arriving in great numbers in the United States to conquer Italian Americans in the name of Fascism. *Il Lavoratore* (The Worker), the official Italian-language newspaper of the Communist Workers Party of America, warned that the Fascists sought to control American hospitals, orphanages, schools, and the Sons of Italy. Mussolini, it argued, intended to conquer America by making extensive use of Italian American priests and his ambassadors and consuls. The newspaper even played upon America's fear of an Italian criminal conspiracy and linked Fascism to the myth of the Black Hand, a label for Italian American crime that had not been used since the early twentieth century. In 1927, objecting to the fact that AFANA seemed communist controlled and that it advocated violence, the NYFL, the ACW, and the ILGWU left the organization. AFANA then joined with the Italian Socialist Party of America and formed the Anti-Fascist Federation of North America for the Freedom of Italy.

One of the earliest and most unequivocal foes of Fascism, Communism, and man's inhumanity to man was Carlo Tresca, founder of the anarchist newspaper *Il Martello* (The Hammer). Believing that America had to take steps to correct socioeconomic injustices, Tresca spoke out against both Fascism and communism. The Italian government prevailed upon the United States' government to harass Tresca because he had written an editorial entitled "Down with the Italian Monarch." Incarcerated over other writings in his paper, Tresca was released after four months when the government's action was attacked by the media and Congressman Fiorello LaGuardia. In 1931 there were unconfirmed reports that the Fascists marked him for death. And, indeed, he did die at the hands of an unknown assailant in 1943.

The FLNA survived all these attacks. What led to its dissolution in 1929 was the public and official clamor that attended the publication in *Harper's* magazine of Marcus Duffield's article "Mussolini's American Em-

pire." A journalist with slight regard for accuracy, Duffield declared that "part of Mussolini's empire, from his point of view, lies within the United States." He detailed nefarious schemes whereby Mussolini would conquer the United States. *Fascisti* in America would pressure Italian Americans to accept Mussolini's suzerainty under threats of boycotts and intimidation. In a sensational statement Duffield argued that Mussolini "sees no reason why perhaps a half million potential soldiers of Fascism should slip from his grasp by becoming Americanized." Duffield charged that all but two Italian American newspapers had been brought under the influence of Fascism and all but one Sons of Italy lodge suffered the same fate. Despite the fact that a subsequent State Department inquiry proved the inaccuracy of what Duffield was claiming, the Italian government concluded that the American *Fasci* did Italy more harm than good. Ambassador de Martino was instructed by Mussolini to dissolve the Fascist League of North America.

Still, the anti-Fascists carried their crusade against Fascist influence in America into the 1930s. But Fascism was not abandoned by its Italian American supporters until it became clear that Italian diplomacy was venturing upon a collision course with the United States. As long as there was a tendency among America's non-Italian population to admire Mussolini's Fascist dictatorship, which lasted until the mid-1930s, some Italian Americans could, without fear of reprisals, demonstrate their loyalty to America by expressing their admiration for Mussolini. If forced to choose, however, between loyalty to Italy or to the United States, the pick was simple: America. The case of Generoso Pope is illustrative. Pope, the wealthy president of the largest construction materials company in the world, a supporter of the Democratic Party, and a Fascist sympathizer, was the owner of *Il Progresso Italo-Americano*, the most influential Italian language newspaper in America. Despite his defense of Italy's invasion of Ethiopia, Pope remained an admirer of Mussolini only as long as the American government did. It was not long before Mussolini's reckless foreign policy changed his course of support. By the time of Pearl Harbor, Mussolini had lost his backers among Italian Americans and other ethnic groups. Pope, as chairman of a committee for Italian Americans of New York State, sold more than $49 million worth of United

States war bonds in the Third War Loan Drive and his newspaper publicly repudiated "past errors and past illusions."

What can best summarize the Italian American participation in the events dealing with Fascism in America? Despite the countless Americans who came to believe the anti-Fascist hysteria taking place in the United States and who held Italian Americans as a subversive or potentially subversive people, many Italian Americans turned against Mussolini even before Pearl Harbor. And the Italian American press followed suit. Italian Americans served courageously in America's armed forces and/or contributed unselfishly on the homefront. Equally noteworthy, fewer than two hundred Italian aliens were placed in internment camps when the United States entered World War II. Professor Alexander De Conde most likely said it best when noting that Italian American Fascists "made a lot of noise and attracted considerable attention. But, there were few genuine Fascists among them."

Luciano J. Iorizzo

Bibliography

De Conde, Alexander. *Half Bitter, Half Sweet: An Excursion into Italian American History.* New York: Charles Scribner's Sons, 1971.

Diggins, John P. "Flirtation with Fascism: American Pragmatic Liberals and Mussolini's Italy." *The American Historical Review* 71 (January 1966): 487–506.

Iorizzo, Luciano J., and Salvatore Mondello. *The Italian Americans.* Rev. ed. Boston: Twayne, 1981.

———. "The Italo-American Anti-Fascist Opposition." *The Journal of American History* 54 (December 1967): 589–598.

See also POPE, GENEROSO; RADICALISM; SALVEMINI, GAETANO; WORLD WAR II, INTERNMENT, AND PRISONERS OF WAR

Fauci, Anthony Stephen (b. 1940)

Born in Brooklyn and raised in the borough's Bensonhurst section, Anthony Stephen Fauci, son of Stephen A. and Eugenia A. Fauci, has achieved success as a health facility administrator and physician, and is a leader in AIDS research.

He graduated from Regis High School in Manhattan in 1958, which he considered "the defining experience" in his educational career because "there was a combination of open-mindedness and inquisitiveness with an incredible amount of intellectual discipline." He received a bachelor's degree from Holy Cross four years later and a medical degree from Cornell University in 1966. He moved into hospital work and researched allergic, infectious, and immunologic diseases, earning wide respect among his colleagues and receiving numerous honorary awards. He has been at the center of AIDS research since the epidemic began and the most visible spokesman on nearly all aspects of the disease.

In 1980 he became director of the National Institute of Allergy and Infectious Disease in Bethesda, Maryland, which conducts and supports broadly based research and research training on the cause, treatment, and prevention of infectious, allergic, and immunologic diseases. Special attention is given to AIDS, sexually transmitted diseases, hepatitis, influenza, tuberculosis, and vaccine development. From 1984 to 1994 he also served as director of the Government's Office of AIDS Research. At the Bethesda campus he directs basic research on how the human immunodeficiency virus destroys the immune system; such research has produced significant insights on AIDS.

Dr. Fauci is committed to fighting infectious diseases and is known for working sixteen hours a day all year long, except on Saturday evenings and Sundays, when he devotes time to his wife and three daughters. He has lectured and written extensively on his research findings. Despite the lack of a major breakthrough in AIDS research, he has continued to be optimistic in his dedication to solving the riddle of the AIDS disease.

Frank J. Cavaioli

Bibliography

Fauci, Anthony S., and Eugene Braunwald. *Harrison's Principles of Internal Medicine.* 14th ed. New York: McGraw-Hill, 1997.

See also MEDICINE; SCIENCE

Favalora, John C. (b. 1935)

Installed as third archbishop of Miami on December 20, 1994, at St. Mary Cathedral, a Roman Catholic diocese, Archbishop John C. Favalora administers to over one million

Catholics in south Florida. He was also named metropolitan (an honorific title within the hierarchy of the metropolitan Miami area) of the Province of Miami, which includes all of Florida.

He was born in 1935 in New Orleans to an Italian American father and a Cajun mother. Archbishop Favalora began his education at Mater Dolorosa grade school, attended New Orleans Jesuit High School, and received a bachelor's degree in theology from the Pontifical Gregorian University in Rome. He earned a master's degree in education from Tulane University, and has also studied at Xavier University and the Catholic University of America.

He began studying for the priesthood at Notre Dame Seminary in 1956. Following his ordination in Rome, December 20, 1961, he served as secretary to the archbishop in New Orleans, as pastor of St. Angela Merici Church in Metairie, Louisiana, and as director of vocations and permanent deaconate for the archdiocese. He took a leadership role as rector and president at his alma mater, Notre Dame, in New Orleans.

In 1986 he was ordained bishop for the Diocese of Alexandria, Louisiana, and three years later became bishop of the Diocese of St. Petersburg, Florida, a position that lasted through 1994.

As a church leader, his priorities have included vocations in the priesthood, education, multicultural ministries, and immigration. He has promoted interfaith dialogue, especially among Catholics and Jews.

Frank J. Cavaioli

Bibliography

Saunders, Kathy. "He Was Always a Leader." *The Florida Catholic* 6 (16 December 1994): 1–17.

See also RELIGION

Ferlinghetti, Lawrence (b. 1919)

A prominent voice of the Beat poetry movement of the 1950s whose primary aim was to bring poetry back to the people, Lawrence Ferlinghetti has fulfilled that goal in his prolific career as editor and publisher of the renowned City Lights Books Press in San Francisco. His literary production has embraced many areas: translation, fiction writing, travelogues, playwriting, film narration, and essays. Yet his impact and importance remain as a poet and as a voice of dissent, which is reflected in his political self-description as "an enemy of the State."

Ferlinghetti was born "Lawrence Ferling," probably in Yonkers, New York. He assumed the original family name of Ferlinghetti in 1954. Following service in World War II, Ferlinghetti received a master's degree from Columbia University in 1948 and a doctorate from the Sorbonne in 1951. From 1951–1953, when he settled in San Francisco, he taught French in an adult education program. In 1953 he became co-owner of the City Lights Bookshop, the first bookstore featuring paperbounds in the country, and by 1955 he had founded and become editor of the City Lights Books Publishing House. City Lights served as a meeting place for Beat writers while his press published and promoted Beat writings, and he himself encouraged them as, in the case of Diane di Prima, writing the introduction for her first collection, *This Kind of Bird Flies Backward*.

Ferlinghetti's publication of Allen Ginsberg's *Howl* in 1956 led to his arrest on obscenity charges, and the trial that followed (during which he was acquitted) drew national attention to the Beat movement and established him as its prominent voice. In fact, Ferlinghetti's own *A Coney Island of the Mind* (1958) was, along with *Howl,* the most popular poetry book of the 1950s. Often focusing on political or social issues, Ferlinghetti's poetry set out to dispute the literary elite's definition of art and the artist's role in the world. Though imbued with the commonplace, his poetry cannot be dismissed as polemic or personal protest, for it stands on his craftsmanship, thematics, and grounding in tradition.

Ferlinghetti's one novel, *Her* (1960), has been described by him as "a surreal semiautobiographical blackbook" and deals with a young man's search for his identity, although its free-association experimental language proved baffling to critics.

Known for his political poetry, he explained his commitment in art as well as life by saying "Only the dead are disengaged." Well aware of the incongruity of his social dissent with his success as a publisher, Ferlinghetti, in an interview for the Los Angeles *Times,* remarked on "the enormous capacity of society to ingest its own most dissident elements. . . . It

F

happens to everyone successful within the system. I'm ingested myself."

Helen Barolini

Bibliography

Ferlinghetti, Lawrence. *A Coney Island of the Mind.* San Francisco: City Lights, 1958.

———. *Her.* San Francisco: City Lights, 1960.

———. *Literary San Francisco.* San Francisco: City Lights, 1980.

———. *The Mexican Night:.* San Francisco: City Lights, 1970.

———. *Over All the Obscene Boundaries.* San Francisco: City Lights, 1984.

———. *Pictures of the Gone World.* San Francisco: City Lights, 1955, 1973.

———. *The Secret Meaning of Things.* San Francisco: City Lights, 1969.

———. *Starting from San Francisco.* San Francisco: City Lights, 1961, 1967.

———. *Who Are We Now?* San Francisco: City Lights, 1976.

See also LITERATURE; POETRY

Fermi, Enrico (1901–1954)

Considered the "Columbus of Nuclear Physics," Enrico Fermi pioneered work in nuclear physics that won him a Nobel Prize. He is credited with conducting the first self-sustaining, fission reaction in which the controlled splitting of uranium atoms released atomic energy. His work contributed to the development of the atomic bomb.

Enrico Fermi was born in Castro Pretorio district of Rome on September 29, 1901. He was the third of three children born to Ida (de Gattis), a schoolteacher, and Alberto Fermi, a department head of the railroad. Enrico's older brother, Giulio, with whom he was very close, died unexpectedly at age 15, during a minor operation. Enrico sought solace in studying scientific books and technical publications.

In 1918, at age 17, he enrolled in the renowned Reale Scuola Normale Superior in Pisa, where he excelled in his studies while making a name for himself as a prankster. In 1922 he graduated with the title doctor of physical science, magna cum laude. Upon his graduation, he returned to Rome, where he began writing scientific papers on a variety of topics in physics, including relativity. To broaden his knowledge of physics he went to study in the laboratory of Max Born in Göttingen, Germany. He returned to Rome in 1923 to lecture in elementary mathematics in the university, where, in 1924, he met the woman he would eventually marry, Laura Capon. In 1924 he researched physics in a laboratory in Leyden, Holland. After his return to Italy from Leyden, Fermi was given an appointment in mechanics and mathematics in the University of Florence. It was here that he entered the world of particle physics when he published a widely received paper on "a perfect mono-atomic gas."

By 1925 Fermi had brought Italian physics into the world arena. A chair for the Institute of Physics was created in the University of Rome, and Fermi was appointed to the post.

In 1928, Laura Capon and Enrico Fermi were married, an event that was inextricably entwined with the history of the times. Benito Mussolini was gaining power and, in ten short years, he would introduce a manifesto that all but eliminated the rights of Jewish people. The Capon family was Jewish. Anti-Semitic laws and restrictions would later force Enrico and his young family to flee the Fascist tyranny against Jews.

A Royal Academy was founded by Mussolini in 1929, and Fermi, at age 27, was chosen to represent physics in this august body. In 1930 he visited the United States for the first time to deliver lectures at the University of Michigan.

When he returned to Italy, Fermi published his first papers on artificial radioactivity in 1934 and during this period began to experiment with the effects of modulated neutron bombardment of various elements. The element uranium yielded strikingly different results that included the creation of a new element and the release of energy.

Unfortunately, politics, especially anti-Semitic laws, and personal circumstances led to the breakup of the Fermi research team. The Fermis now had two children, Nella, born on January 31, 1931, and Giulio, named after Enrico's brother, born on February 16, 1936. With the publication of the anti-Semitic laws in September 1936, Fermi made a secret decision to accept a position at Columbia University.

In December 1938 he was awarded the Nobel Prize in physics. Instead of returning to Rome, the family went from Sweden to London and then on to the United States. As he sailed past the Statue of Liberty, Fermi announced that the American branch of the Fermi family had now begun.

At Columbia University, he quickly became a principal investigator in a research project involving the nuclear fission of uranium. After the United States' entry into World War II, the efforts of the research team were accelerated and the project moved to the University of Chicago. The first controlled nuclear reactor was constructed beneath the grandstand of Stagg Field on a squash court. On December 2, 1942, the first self-sustaining nuclear chain reaction occurred under the supervision of Enrico Fermi.

With the United States engaged in war, nuclear energy was quickly seen as a source of tremendous power for a weapon of destruction. Fermi and his family moved to Los Alamos, where he became an important part of the Manhattan Project, a research endeavor to construct a nuclear bomb.

The first explosion of an atomic bomb took place in the Alamogordo Desert in "Trinity Terrain" on July 16, 1945, with Fermi and his associates looking on from a distance of ten miles away. A few short months later, in August 1945, two separate atomic bombs were dropped on the Japanese cities of Hiroshima and Nagasaki with never-before-seen devastating results. For his efforts in helping to develop the atomic bomb Fermi received the Congressional Medal of Merit.

Shortly after the detonation of these devices, the University of Chicago established the Institute of Nuclear Studies. Fermi returned to Chicago with his family, where he lectured and conducted research using nuclear accelerators at the newly established Institute. He traveled throughout the world lecturing on the subatomic particles he had helped discover in his research projects.

In the fall of 1954, Fermi was diagnosed with advanced stomach cancer. On November 29, 1954, he died at age 53.

The scientific legacy of Enrico Fermi was celebrated by naming the atomic element 100 fermium and by the renaming of the University of Chicago Institute of Nuclear Studies as the Fermi Lab. Fermi's pioneering work in nuclear physics brought world recognition to Italian physics, while his work in the United States placed him among the best of its scientific minds. His exploration of the atom has enhanced future study in nuclear physics.

Sean A. Fanelli

Bibliography

de Latil, Pierre. *Enrico Fermi, The Man and His Theories.* New York: Paul S. Eriksson, 1966.

Fermi, Laura. *Atoms in the Family.* Chicago: University of Chicago Press, 1954.

Segrè, Emilio. *Enrico Fermi, Physicist.* Chicago: University of Chicago Press, 1970.

See also SCIENCE

Ferraro, Geraldine Anne (b. 1935)

The first woman to be nominated by a major political party as candidate for vice president of the United States (1984), Geraldine Anne Ferraro is the first Italian American woman to achieve this high political status. She was born in Newburgh, New York, August 26, 1935, the fourth child and only daughter of Dominick Ferraro, an Italian immigrant who owned a restaurant and five-and-dime store, and Antoinette L. (née Corrieri) Ferraro. When her father died in 1943, her mother moved the family to New York City. Subsequent poor investments left Antoinette Ferraro with little money. She was forced to move the family to a small apartment in the Bronx and later to Queens, where she earned a meager living crocheting beads on dresses to support her family. Geraldine first attended a Catholic school for girls, Marymount School in Tarrytown, New York, then received a scholarship to Marymount College in Manhattan, where she majored in English and received a bachelor's degree in 1956.

From 1956 to 1960 she taught grade school in public school in Queens, New York, while attending night classes at Fordham University Law School. She earned a J.D. degree in 1960. Just after her graduation from law school, she married John Zaccaro, a fourth-generation Italian American and New York real estate developer. She and her husband have three children.

While raising a family, she practiced civil law in private practice. She began her career in government service in 1974, when she served as assistant district attorney in Queens County. There she headed the Special Victims Bureau, which she helped create to handle cases of child abuse, domestic violence, and rape. Ferraro was admitted to practice before the United States Supreme Court in 1978. When the U. S.

F

Geraldine Ferraro, former congresswoman from New York, was the first woman to run for vice president (1984) on a national political party ticket. Courtesy of the National Italian American Foundation (NIAF), Washington, D.C.

Since 1988 she has been a fellow at the Harvard Institute of Politics in Cambridge, Massachusetts. In 1993 she was appointed to the United States delegation to the United Nations Human Rights Commission. She has been a commentator on a nationally broadcast television show, *Crossfire,* and author of two books. She relinquished her television commentator role in order to return to the public political arena, entering the race for the Democratic Senate seat in New York City in 1998, but she was defeated in the primary.

Anne T. Romano

Bibliography

Ferraro, Geraldine. *Ferraro, My Story.* New York: Bantam, 1985.

———. *Geraldine Ferraro: Changing History, Women, Power, and Politics.* Wakefield, RI: Moyer Bell, 1993.

See also POLITICS

representative of her Queens district retired in 1978, Ferraro swept aside two challengers in a three-way congressional primary and won the general election to become Queens' first female congressperson. She was reelected in 1980 and 1982. Ferraro was known for her political sophistication and intelligence, quickly gaining respect and influence in the house. Generally liberal, she opposed many of the policies put forth by President Ronald Reagan.

In 1981 she became a member of the Democratic Steering and Policy Committee, which controls committee assignments for Democratic House members. She regularly voted for bills to benefit workers, women, and the elderly, and she opposed efforts to ban abortion. In 1984 Ferraro became the first woman to be named chair of the National Platform Committee of the Democratic Party. A few months later, the party's presidential candidate Walter F. Mondale, surprised most political observers when he announced he had selected her as his vice presidential running mate. Ferraro proved to be a lively campaigner with a solid grasp of the issues.

After her nomination, however, questions were raised about her and her husband's business activities and about whether she had violated the Ethics in Government Act. In 1992 Ferraro narrowly lost her bid for the New York Democratic Senate nomination after a bitter primary campaign in which she was once again forced to respond to questions about her family's finances.

Festa

The present-day *festa* demonstrates ethnic pride in Italian neighborhoods, funded by an Italian American association in conjunction with an Italian parish church. However, feast day celebrations have also become largely commercial endeavors that have lost their original religious and ritualistic tone; they were at one time strictly religious observances of Roman Catholic saints' feasts. They still present scenographic environments of food, game stalls and rides, decorated with strings of lights, as well as a procession and a Solemn Mass in honor of the saint. The feast often ends with firework displays.

Feast day celebrations of patron saints are conducted essentially in the same manner as they were in Italy, with church services followed by processions through the streets of the district. These feasts are held in areas with large Italian immigrant populations and take place from the spring through the fall seasons.

The Italian American *festa* documents the role of ritual performance and active construction of ethnicity. The *festa* in the United States gradually transformed from an event that expressed a village's or particular enclave's identity into a depiction of southern Italian national ethnicity. Development of this form of ethnicity embodied the *festa* as a rit-

Feast of St. Liberata, Patchogue, New York. Immigrant Carmen Bianco's strong devotion to the patron saint of his hometown in Italy provided for decades the inspiration for the annual feast in honor of St. Liberata. Photo by Marie Contino. Courtesy Salvatore J. LaGumina.

ual performance that mediated the immigrant relationship to both Italian and American cultural ethnic forms of experience. The *festa* must be seen as a creative response to the immigrant experience that transformed the *festa* from a particularist, communal performance to an associational ritual reflecting civic and nationalist values.

A typical program of the feast at the turn of the twentieth century in New York can be exemplified by the annual festival in honor of San Gandofo, protector of Polizzi Generosa, Sicily. On Saturday September 14 (the actual feast day), at ten in the morning, the feast began with a musical performance by a well-known band, led by the renowned Maestro Domenico Angelino. The "flight of angels," the most outstanding feature of this celebration in New York as in Polizzi Generosa, was achieved by stretching ropes across the street from one fire escape to another and then lowering on pulleys two young girls dressed as angels until they were suspended over the saint's statue as it passed. The procession halted, and the "angels" recited verses in honor of the patron. Although this act lasted only ten minutes, the children were under considerable physical strain; they received twenty-five dollars each for their efforts. This feast represents the sacrifices made by Italians to worship a particular saint.

During the New York feast celebrations of the Madonna del Carmine, in recognition of the Madonna's healing powers, wax offerings in the shape of human limbs and parts of the body were brought and laid on the altar at each of the several Masses celebrated throughout the morning. Each supplicant received a scapular. In the procession, celebrants carried the statue, followed by a band and a crowd of worshipers and spectators. After Mass, people gathered at the stalls and purchased traditional food. Other stall owners catered to those dreading the "evil eye" and announced the availability of amulets: "Roba di Napoli, per il mal'occhi! Our Lord Jesus Christ and preserved in a silver casket by the Most Holy and Christian Emperors and Empresses."

Ritual practices assumed distinct prominence in the lives of Italian immigrants, thereby gaining a power emanating from long established traditions in southern Italy. Black magic forms, traced to pre-Christian customs, were so important to the emotional life of the people that they could not be treated indifferently by the American Catholic Church hierarchy, which, however, refused to recognize them officially. As evident in the above, one of the enduring examples of superstition was the "evil eye," thought to be an inborn trait in certain men and women, who by a mere glance could cause physical injury, business reversals, sickness, and even death. To ward off these evils, the people wore many kinds of amulets.

The Italians' belief in such powers ascribed to an evil eye is a characteristic example. This ritual is essentially a performance, an enactment. The traditions "frame" the ritual process, but the ritual process transcends its frame. These rituals nearly always "accompany transitions from one situation to another and from one cosmic or social world to another." The order in which the ritual events follow one another is an important religious process. The ritual components of the festa find varied expression, in both substance and sequential events, such as the Mass and procession, as well as the carrying of the saint, and the pinning of money or requests upon the robes of the saint, which is an appeal from one social world to a higher but intangible one that can be reached only through rituals.

The Italian festa demonstrates the ritual performed in prescribed formal behaviors, in specific religious acts of the Mass. While displaying beliefs in invisible beings, the festa also typically illustrated cherished values through the procession. There is also a self-transcending flow of ritual events in many performative genres such as dance, music, games, contest, role playing, and festive food preparations and visual symbols such as statues of saints, flags, banners, lights, and fireworks.

The discussion of ritual, though distinct, can be considered in broader terms against the general background of the festa; it can also be tied specifically to religious institutions in Italy at the turn of the century and then to America in the same time period. For an ethnic group threatened with loss of local regional identity, the church served to organize the group as a community more than any other institution. When Italian immigrants left their villages, they turned to a new Italian ethnicity and to local American and religious organizations, which became the central point of their communal life. The church structure served to maintain the cultural persona by organizing parishioners around religious and cultural symbols or the behavioral modes of the country of origin. The immigrants conceived their identity in terms of concrete and particular symbols. They envisioned religion as combining all the social and institutional mores of society. Religion was more a way of life than a prescribed set of beliefs and practices. In America, they needed to rework the peasant way of life to fit the conditions of their environment. The ethnic parish was not only an efficient instrument of social control; it became the dominant force in the cultural change in the ethnic community. If ethnic stratification is viewed as an ongoing process rather than as a structure, then the ethnic parish should be considered as the chief force presiding over the change from a communal to an associational society. This transition was necessary not only for social mobility and integration, but also for maintaining the ethnicity of the immigrants.

Religion was an integral part of the life of southern Italians. Each locality had its periodic church festivals; participants carried on devotions even in the midst of business activities; and Italians displayed churches, shrines, and crosses in every small town. However, the same continuity with the past, colorful ceremonies, and stability in local Italian towns was not to be found in festas in the United States. The folk quality of southern Italian religion corresponded to its social environment. In America, instead, this quality became an immediate source of conflict with the more urbanized, law-and-organization-oriented Irish Catholics who frequently interpreted the peasant religious behavior of Latin and Slavic immigrants as an eclectic survival of pre-Christian and medieval beliefs and traditions. But often unlettered Italian immigrants were neither in a position nor of a mind to speculate philosophically on their religious experiences with the same formal reparation of the bishops and priests they met in the new society.

The cultural problem of adjusting to new living patterns, the result of moving from a rural to an urban environment, constituted a key factor responsible for immigrant difficulties in urban America. Contemporaries failed to recognize that the same type of adjustment would have been necessary had the southern villagers migrated to a northern city in Italy or to some other European city rather than across the Atlantic.

Critics who saw an irreligious attitude in immigrant superstition and idolatry ignored the fact that image-worship, especially of the Virgin, and an anthropomorphic view of nature and religion made Catholicism real for the newly arrived immigrant. In the same way, critics considered Italians' addiction to festivals, processions, and feasts as a perversion of religion, although to participants these celebrations formed an integral part of worship. In their new churches, Italian immigrants who celebrated these functions in America did so in an effort to re-establish those elements of religion that had strongly appealed to them in Italy, but also to counteract Irish influences. Thus, what seemed to the American as a falling away from religion was, in the least, an adaptation of old habits to new conditions.

Identification with the colony and the use of institutions signified a growth away from homeland outlooks, but also, for many newcomers, a vital step in assimilation. This group of first-generation arrivals gradually absorbed or consciously adopted American habits and speech in the outside community, in politics, schools, settlement houses, work, and streets.

One can conclude that the ethnic parishes, with their saints and festivals, novenas, and processions, bound together the Italians in America, embodying the ideals in which the people believed, and uniting them structurally through strong group ritual and social functions. The network of ethnic parishes became the basis for religious fulfillment. An understanding of the Italian *festa* embodies the mores of the Italian American immigrant and demonstrates how religion was not traditionally in compliance with the rules of the Catholic religion, as well as a social identification with peasant life in Italy. The Italian American *festa* can claim a significant place in the study of ethnic traditions because it examines the qualities of religious rituals in a social and cultural relationship with the Americanization of an immigrant people.

Denise Mangieri DiCarlo

Bibliography

Banfield, Edward C. *The Moral Basis of a Backward Society.* New York: The Free Press, 1958.

Brown, Peter. *The Cult of Saints. Its Rise and Function in Latin Christianity.* Chicago: University of Chicago Press, 1981.

Foerster, Robert. *The Italian Emigrant of Our Time.* New York: Russell & Russell, 1968.

Turner, Victor. *From Ritual to Theatre.* New York: Performing Arts Journal Publications, 1982.

Williams, Phyllis H. *Southern Italian Folkways in Europe and America.* New Haven: Yale University Press, 1938.

See also FOLKLORE, FOLKLIFE; RELIGION

Fiaschetti, Frank
See CARTOONISTS AND ILLUSTRATORS

Filippini Sisters
See WOMEN AND THE CHURCH

Film Directors, Producers, and Italian American Image in Cinema

Italian Americans have a long history of image and influence in American cinema. The topic embraces the representation of Italian America by non-Italian American directors (the largest category of Italian-image film production by far) as well as by Italian Americans (e.g., Frank Capra, Gregory La Cava, Vincente Minnelli, Ida Lupino, Francis Ford Coppola, Martin Scorsese, Michael Cimino, Brian De Palma, Quentin Tarantino, Stanley Tucci, Nancy Savoca, and Michael Corrente). Italian image has also been shaped by a number of renowned actors and actresses, such as Ernest Borgnine, Robert De Niro, John Travolta, Sylvester Stallone, Anne Bancroft, Al Pacino, Danny DeVito, and Marissa Tomei (to name a few). A dichotomous representation occurs when comparing the film works by non-Italian American directors and movies made by Italian Americans. From the silent film era to the latter half of the twentieth century, stereotypes of gangsters and romanticized versions of Italian lifestyle have dominated subject matter in mainstream movies on Italian American life. Only as more Italian American directors and producers concerned with ethnic identity enter the Hollywood flow of image making does the cinematic story of Italian America become infused with life and reality.

Italian American film production (and American film work in general) owes a debt to the contributions made by the Italian cinema. The long epic-spectacle films like Guazzoni's enormously successful nine-reel *Quo Vadis?* (1912), *Caserini's Gli Ultimi Giorni di Pompei* (1913), and Pastrone's *Cabiria* (1914), which influenced D. W. Griffith and Cecil B. DeMille, kept middle-class audiences entertained for over two hours and thereby justified high ticket prices, which in turn enabled entrepreneurs to invest in big movie "palaces." When *Quo Vadis?* charged a dollar per person (twenty times the price of the nickelodeon) and drew large crowds in New York, American movie producers took immediate note. Later there was the influence of Italian neorealism in the 1940s and early 1950s, and of Italian directors including Roberto Rossellini, Vittorio DeSica, Luchino Visconti, Federico Fellini, and Michelangelo Antonioni. Italian actors and actresses have also helped shape the American image of Italy: Rudolph Valentino, Anna Magnani, Gina Lollobrigida, Sophia Loren, and Marcello Mastroianni.

Above all, Italian American image in cinema concerns a century-long history of interconnected themes (passion, excess, violence, family, food, love of spectacle) and stereotypes (lover, playboy, gangster, betrayer, boxer, mother, madonna, grandmother, entertainer, buffoon). Though American film has produced a substantial body of work on Italian American life, its reliance upon labels and stereotypes (and their "slow transformation" [Brunetta]) has severely compromised its chronicle that is, at best, incomplete and unreliable, and, at worst, complicit in shaping, purveying, and promoting the stereotypes. At the same time, Hollywood has left an important record of mainstream perspectives on Italian America.

Dozens of silent films treat the subject of Italian American life, beginning with such works as D. W. Griffith's *At the Altar* (1909), *In Little Italy* (1909), and *The Avenging Conscience* (1914). *At the Altar* presents an idealized image of an Italian family and a young couple about to be married. A rejected suitor lays a trap with a loaded pistol set to go off when the couple kneels at the wedding ceremony, but a police officer arrives in time to find the gun. The film plays on nativist fears of sexual fertility, love, and violence among Italians, while prizing the Italian sense of family and community. In *The Avenging Conscious,* the Italian character (played by George Siegmann) is a scoundrel and a blackmailer. One of the gems of the silent era, Thomas Ince

and Reginald Baker's *The Italian* (1914), attempts to chart the parabola of immigrant life: the homeland in the Abruzzi, lyrically shot in the hills of California (similar to the Sicilian scenes in Coppola's *Godfather I* and *II* that capture idealized family memories); the steamer's departure; and the slums of New York presented with gritty naturalism. The central character, Beppo Donnetti, played by George Beban, emigrates to America and makes enough money to send for his *fidanzata* (betrothed). Then the fates turn against him. Pent up in the ghetto during the torrid summer, he loses his baby son to disease. Though tempted, he resists avenging himself on the child of the Irish politician who had refused to help him. In the final scene he lies inconsolable on his son's grave. The promise of the New World has proven false.

Other silent films characterize Italian American stereotypes, oscillating between violence and sentimentality. An Italian American woman is a radical terrorist in *Dangerous Hours* (1919), which manages at once to be xenophobic, antifeminist, and antilabor (Cortes, 1987). In *Little Italy* (1921, director George Terwilliger) explores a family crisis in which a father banishes his daughter for refusing to marry the man he has chosen for her. Two brothers portray opposite sides of the so-called Italian character, honest worker and criminal, in *The Beautiful City* (1925, director Kenneth Webb), a film that looks forward to Robert Siodmak's *Cry of the City* (1948). In *Rose of the Tenements* (1926, director Phil Rosen) a flower-girl named Rose Rosetti is the orphaned daughter of an Italian gangster. *The Secret Hour* (1928, director Rowland V. Lee) tells the story of a California fruit grower named Tony who woos a waitress by sending her a picture of his handsome foreman; the waitress and foreman fall in love and marry, but Tony forgives her and eventually wins her heart. The plot of Henry King's *The White Sister* (1923, director Henry King), starring Lillian Gish, was taken from the novel by Francis Marion Crawford, the late-nineteenth-century American writer who, having spent much of his life in Italy, created a richly textured tapestry of Italian characters in his fiction. Set in Italy, this film shows the sublimation of passion in religious devotion and self-sacrifice. It was remade in 1933 by Victor Fleming, with Helen Hayes in the title role.

The major representation of the Italian

in 1920s cinema is unquestionably Rudolph Valentino. He migrated to America from Puglia when he was 18, fell into trouble with the law, became a dancer, and drifted to Hollywood. *The Four Horsemen of the Apocalypse* (1921) and *The Sheik* (1921) made him an overnight sensation, and, as Hollywood's quintessential matinee idol, he never lost his grip on the public down through *Cobra* (1925) and *Son of the Sheik* (1926). Though he did not play an Italian in his major roles, he was always seen by the public as an Italian; yet he did not embody a mere "stage Italian," but often acted with a fine sense of humor and irony. One of the first international screen celebrities, he was the symbol of sexual passion, exoticism, and the outlaw: in other words, he encapsulated the archetypal Italian in the mainstream psyche. It seemed as if the entire world went into mourning when he died prematurely at age 31 in 1926, some inconsolable fans reportedly going so far as committing suicide.

In the 1930s the gangster came to dominate the Italian American film image. Mervyn LeRoy's *Little Caesar* (1930) features non-Italian Edward G. Robinson in the role of the dapper Caesare "Rico" Bandello, an ambitious underworld thug who rises to great wealth only to lose all. This was the second of Robinson's twelve roles that portrayed an Italian American, more than any other screen actor of his stature. He endowed each of these roles with power, sensitivity, and pathos. Perhaps his most memorable portrayal is that of Johnny Rocco in John Huston's *Key Largo* (1948), a low-life megalomaniac who can't pinpoint what he wants except that he wants "more." The Italian American woman in *Little Caesar* was represented by the "*strega*-like" Ma Magdalena, the "female gangster," who first hides Rico but ends up betraying him: "[T]he very paradox of her name suggests the perennial American infatuation with an exotic mixture of maternalism and moral corruption." Howard Hawks's *Scarface* (1932), starring Paul Muni as the Sicilian immigrant Tony Camonte, is loosely based on the life of Al Capone in gangland Chicago, including its own St. Valentine's Day Massacre. The film was successfully remade by Brian De Palma in 1983. Set in contemporary Miami among Cuban Americans, Al Pacino delivers a mesmerizing performance in the leading role. Other early gangster films with Italian Americans include *Night Ride* (1931), *Manhattan Merry-Go-Round* (1938), *They Knew What They Wanted* (1940, director Garson Kanin), *Lady of the Lake* (1946, director Robert Montgomery), *Kiss of Death* (1947, director Henry Hathaway), and *Force of Evil* (1948, director Abraham Polonsky). Sometimes the gangster and Italian themes were mixed with boxing, as in Michael Curtiz's *Kid Galahad* (1937) and Rouben Mamoulian's *Golden Boy* (1939), *Somebody Up There Likes Me* (1956)—and, much later, in Martin Scorsese's *Raging Bull* (1980). Sometimes the gangster theme was parodied, as in Billy Wilder's *Some Like It Hot* (1959).

Unlike the gangster genre or crime drama, film noir does not frequently represent Italian America. A notable exception is *Cry of the City* (1948), in which Richard Conte and Victor Mature portray the good and bad Italian Americans rising out of the same ghetto, one becoming a criminal, the other a policeman hunting him down. Edward Dmytryk's *Christ in Concrete* (also known as *Give Us This Day*, 1949) is based on the novel by Pietro di Donato and is influenced by Italian neorealism. Its story of the life struggles experienced by bricklayer Geremio and his death on the construction site is powerfully rendered, though Peter Bondanella rightly speaks of the film's "grave defect" of employing a false "ghetto Italian" speech that amounts to unintentional parody (the novel has the same implacable flaw). More successful films in genres outside the gangster motif are Daniel Mann's *The Rose Tattoo* (1955, screenplay by Tennessee Williams) and Delbert Mann's *Marty* (1955, screenplay by Paddy Chayefsky). In the former, Anna Magnani won an Academy Award for best actress for her brilliant portrayal of an Italian American widow. The latter is mediocre in its representation of Italian America (as seen by outsiders), but there is an unforgettable performance by Ernest Borgnine as a great-hearted small-time hero and a fine study of the Italian American mother by Esther Minciotti. The film won Academy Awards for best picture, and Borgnine won as best actor.

One of Hollywood's greatest directors of the century, Frank Capra, was born in Sicily, but left at the age of 5 and grew up in Los Angeles. His rise to the director's chair was sure and rapid; the first film he could wholly call his own, the comedy *The Strong Man*, appeared in 1926. Although he depicted Italian Americans in only one film at the very end of his career (Mario and Tony Manetta, played by Edward G. Robinson and Frank Sinatra in *A Hole in the Head* [1959]), his works are permeated by Italian values wedded to American populism. *It Happened One Night* (1934), *Mr. Deeds Goes to Town* (1936), *Mr. Smith Goes to Washington* (1939), *Meet John Doe* (1941), and *It's A Wonderful Life* (1946) articulated a capacious vision of individualism, family, and community, which reassured America of its fundamental values in a period stretching from the Great Depression to the Cold War.

Other directors of Italian heritage whose careers overlapped Capra's include Gregory La Cava (1892–1952), Vincente Minnelli (1910–1986), and Ida Lupino (1917–1995). La Cava's career straddled both the silent and the sound screen era. Known mostly for his screwball comedies of the 1930s, in reality La Cava's films evoked the many-faceted ills of the Great Depression and ranged in tone from the sublime to the ridiculous. These depictions were evident in his *My Man Godfrey* (1936), starring William Powell and Carole Lombard, and *Primrose Path* (1940), with Ginger Rogers and Joel McCrea. Drunkenness played a large role in La Cava's characters, as in *Unfinished Business* (1941) with Irene Dunne and Robert Montgomery. La Cava tried to balance the absurdities of social extremes in comic and dramatic contexts.

His name synonymous with Hollywood musicals, Vincente Minnelli was the director for some of the most cherished films of that genre in the 1940s and 1950s. Moviegoers looked to his films more for sheer beauty and entertainment than for social analysis. Among his most famous works were *Meet Me in St. Louis* (1944), *Ziegfield Follies* (1946), *An American in Paris* (1951), and *Gigi* (1958). In the course of a long movie director career Minnelli worked with some of the greatest stars such as Judy Garland, whom he married, Fred Astaire, and Gene Kelly.

Of English and Italian descent, Ida Lupino became not only a leading actress but also a noted screenplay writer and director. She wrote the screenplay for *Not Wanted* (1949), a daring exposé of the plight of an unwed mother. Lupino took over direction of the film after the death of the original director. *The Hitch Hiker* (1953) was considered the best of the films she directed. This thriller concerned two men on a Mexican vacation who are menaced by a psychopathic killer.

From the 1940s through the 1970s, Albert R. Broccoli (1909–1996) enjoyed an outstanding career as a director and producer. Some of the more notable productions attributed to him are *Chitty Chitty Bang Bang* (1967) and a successful series of James Bond adventures, including *From Russia with Love* (1963) and *Live and Let Die* (1972).

With the new ethnicity of the 1960s, Italian Americans played an ever-increasing role in both Hollywood and independent cinema. The stereotypes did not change, even if perspectives on those stereotypes did undergo occasional reevaluation. The difference between the old and new Hollywood is immediately apparent when contrasting Sidney Lumet's stilted *A View from the Bridge* (1962) (despite a fine performance by Raf Vallone) with the early work of Coppola and Scorsese.

The career of Francis Ford Coppola is unlike that of any other director of his quality in American film history. He made two early masterpieces, *The Godfather* (1972) and *The Godfather, Part II* (1974) (drawn from Mario Puzo's *The Godfather*), both of which won Academy Awards for best picture, the second of which won the award for best director. He then went into seemingly irreversible decline. But his achievement in these films, both for their style and content, is undeniable. One of the principal sources of that achievement was an unswerving desire to represent Italian America. Coppola said that he had "almost never seen a movie that gave any real sense of what it was like to be an Italian American" (1972). Taking the genre that had stereotyped the Italian American image, Coppola gave new life to the gangster film by portraying not only the mob boss from the inside (which had been done also by LeRoy and Hawks), but his whole family and culture. This involved an accurate depiction of religious rituals (from baptism, First Communion, and saint's day, to wedding and funeral), street life, and private life: the *cucina* (cuisine), the decor, the music, the daily tone, gesture, habit, conversational rhythms, and atmosphere. Coppola captured the entire visual reality of the "godfather's" heyday and the first two-thirds of Italian American twentieth century—that is, up to the moment of Coppola's own career. His complex treatment of the Corleone family over some seventy years and four generations, from Sicily to New York, to Nevada, uncovers the underlying assumptions concerning one segment of Italian American culture, from which he generalizes, rather disingenuously, to project a "metaphor for America." Marlon Brando and Al Pacino play the godfathers, father and son, in what amounts to twin monuments of American screen acting.

The strongest impression made by both *Godfathers I and II* is of the enormous gulf between the (sometimes false) plenitude of family life and the corrosive, death-dealing Mafia business: two codes of behavior and their systems of metaphor that confront each other in inexorable opposition. Gradually, the Mafia business wins out, destroying every vestige of real family life. The films created a sensation and set off an avalanche of imitation both on film and television for almost two decades.

Coppola has never equaled his success in *The Godfather, Parts I and II,* though moments of fine movie-making punctuate his later work, specifically in *Apocalypse Now* (1979) (e.g., the Las Vegas show in the Vietnam jungle) and in *Peggy Sue Got Married* (1986). *Godfather III* (1989) did not receive the same high acclaim as *Godfathers I and II.* Still, in the leading role, Al Pacino performs with great distinction.

Martin Scorsese has maintained a high level of achievement throughout his career. By the 1990s he had reached the pinnacle of American cinema and was regarded as the greatest director of his generation. Even more than Coppola's, his best work has been inspired by his social and cultural heritage. *Mean Streets* (1973), the first film that brought him wide attention, is set in New York's Little Italy, where he grew up. The film portrays the lives of two cousins, played by Harvey Keitel and Robert De Niro, with great depth of feeling, but at the same time with objectivity and moral judgment. In his masterpiece *Raging Bull* (1980) Scorsese examines the rise and fall of the prize fighter Jake La Motta (played by De Niro), who through his violence, guilt, and suffering earns a measure of self-discovery and redemption. The gangster element, in the background of this film, comes to the fore in *Goodfellas* (1990) and *Casino* (1995). Our introduction to the various "goodfellas," as the camera follows Henry on a walk through the local nightclub,

is a model of cinematic economy—each face that nods a greeting is clearly etched in memory. Scorsese has also shown a continuing interest in Italian American religious life and religion generally, a concern that developed in the biblicalism of *The Last Temptation of Christ* (1986), in the pentecostalism revealed in his remake of *Cape Fear* (1991), and in the spiritual destiny manifested in *Kundun* (1998), his work on Eastern mysticism and the Dalai Lama. He has also directed *The King of Comedy* (1982), with De Niro and Jerry Lewis; the film, explores the nature of celebrity, publicity, and scandal.

Scorsese has produced major works in five genres: gangster film, satiric comedy, thriller, urban melodrama, and documentary (*Italianamerican, The Last Waltz*). Though he is still in mid-career, already his artistic achievement is "unparalleled in the history of Italian Americans."

Michael Cimino won an Academy Award for directing *The Deer Hunter* (1978), which was also voted best picture. The film is set in western Pennsylvania among a Ukranian American community and tells the story of three friends who do a tour of duty in Vietnam. In the starring role, De Niro delivers a spellbinding performance: the scene in which, as a captive, he plays Russian roulette on a river barge is among the finest of his career. But the film suffers from the excessive length of certain scenes and some contrived allegorizing, visual and otherwise. *Heaven's Gate* (1980), underrated because publicity concentrated on its notorious cost overruns, is a beautiful film, pitting cattle ranchers against immigrants in late-nineteenth-century Wyoming.

Brian De Palma (b. 1940) in 1983 made a remake of *Scarface*. In this depiction, however, Chicago's Italian American mobster Antonio Camonte (Al Capone) is transformed into a contemporary Miami Cuban American drug dealer, Antonio Montana (played by Al Pacino). De Palma returned to a film portrayal of Italian Americans in 1987 with *The Untouchables* (a portrayal of Al Capone). Based upon the book, by the same title and co-authored by crime-buster Eliot Ness, this is yet another depiction of the confrontation between Prohibition mobster Capone and federal agents.

Michael Corrente's film *Federal Hill* (1994) is a tale about five Italian American friends in the Federal Hill section of Providence, Rhode Island. This film focuses on the

Mafia, crime, and violence as well as love of family, friendship, loyalty, and honor and on the sense of community in an inner-city Italian American neighborhood.

Nancy Savoca's (b. 1959) two strongest portrayals of Italian Americans are *True Love* (1990) and *Household Saints* (1993). *True Love* looks in on a young Italian American working-class couple in the Bronx as they prepare for a big wedding with all of the trimmings. The film deals with the issues of how marriage is viewed by the different generations of males and females in this Italian American neighborhood. *Household Saints* is a magical-realistic tale, based upon the novel by Francine Prose, of the marriage of a sausage maker and a neighborhood woman. The story, spanning from the 1940s to the 1970s, is set in one of New York's Little Italies (Greenwich Village). The story ultimately focuses on their daughter, who possesses a mystical faith that places stress on all of the film's protagonists.

Stanley Tucci's (b. 1961) film *Big Night* was co-written and directed by himself and Joseph Tropiano. Set in the 1950s, the film tells the story of two brothers, Primo (first) and Secondo (second), who wish to achieve the immigrants' American dream by having their restaurant become a flourishing and successful concern. The film works on many levels, from the conflicts embodied by the two brothers concerning the art of fine cooking versus the bottom-line accountability of the business as well as the personal costs involved in gaining financial success. One of the strengths of the film is the bond between the brothers that often needs no words to convey their love and concern for each other.

Winner of the Academy Award for the best screenplay of *Pulp Fiction* (1994), which he also directed, Quentin Tarantino (b. 1963) took Hollywood by storm after directing only two films. He soon became a cult figure and was frequently compared with another cinematic genius, Orson Welles.

During the 1970s and 1980s, Italian American actors and actresses made large contributions to the cinema and garnered numerous awards. They were led by De Niro, who possesses matchless intensity and such a capacity to become his characters that for many years he looked entirely different from film to film. Indeed, to play the older Jake La Motta in *Raging Bull* he gained fifty pounds, which

he promptly lost for his next film. His artistic collaboration with Scorsese has been one of the two most fruitful of any actor–director team in American film history, the other being that of John Wayne and John Ford. Commercially, one of the most successful stars of the period has been Sylvester Stallone, who wrote his first film, *Rocky* (1976), and who subsequently became the premier action hero in his *Rambo* series and other films. Already a teen idol as a television actor, John Travolta launched an important film career in *Saturday Night Fever* (1977) with the role of Tony Manero, a teenager on the brink of adulthood who has not yet broken with Little Italy.

There were only sixty-eight films between 1918 and 1971 with an Italian American setting or principal character, though there were numerous other films with minor Italian American characters. By contrast, in the post-1960s era a great many films by non-Italian American directors on Italian and Italian American themes have appeared. This resulted from two powerful factors: the prominence of ethnic, even during what Richard Alba aptly describes as "the twilight of ethnicity" in his book of that title; and the popularity and marketability of the Italian as a cultural sign for sex, luxury, consumerism, carnival, and idleness, as well as the edge given these themes by the Italian stereotype of violence and virtuoso crime. Italy has also pervaded the world of advertising (e.g., the large number of automobiles with Italian or Italian-sounding names). Film and advertising are mutually permeable worlds and attract the same audiences.

Notwithstanding that the Italian image in film is extremely complex, its various themes can dovetail and cluster, all too neatly, around such polarities as sex and violence, feral instinct and high-fashion sophistication, the loner and family values, cunning and sincerity, tough guy and mama's boy. The common denominator is that each quality is usually portrayed in an intense extreme—Italians do not abide in the middle ground. As in magnetism, the positive and negative charges on these values can jump poles. Yet the many directors who structure films about these polarities generally treat them in a rigid, nondialectical way that replicate certain familiar stereotypes, for example, Peter Yates's *Breaking Away* (1979), John Huston's *Prizzi's Honor* (1985), and Norman Jewison's *Moonstruck* (1987).

Yates's film capitalized on the Italian vogue beginning in the 1970s as well as on a "new" sport, cycling; it was nominated for best picture, won an Oscar for best original screenplay, and led to a TV series. The film tells of middle-class Midwestern teenagers, just out of high school and facing an uncertain future. The main focus is on Dave, who becomes "Italian," an illusion that insulates him from reality and change. Dave is an amateur speed cyclist—a Rossini soundtrack accompanies training runs—and the Italians are in town for a race. Sleek, predatory, elegant in their designer outfits, they play dirty, gang up on Dave, and throw a wrench into his wheel, sending him flying. With the crash ends the Italian fantasy. Dave works long hours at his father's used-car dealership but continues to train at night. Dave refuses to make a dishonest sale, further exacerbating their differences and precipitating his father's mild heart episode. When Dave admits his true identity to his girlfriend, she drops him; she too had been in the grip of an Italian illusion. Humbled physically and emotionally, both father and son are reunited before the final race, which Dave predictably wins, and the spiritual uplift rings false. Because only the fluffy stereotypes attracted him, nothing breakaway attaches to his "Italian" experience, emotionally, sexually, or culturally. Breaking away applies rather to speed cycling, a form of play that looks suspiciously like work, the extrovert American solution that merely sublimates his problems.

A mob family in crisis is the starting point of *Prizzi's Honor*: an aged don, his son's murder, attacks from without, betrayal from within, the troubles of the non-Italian wife of the heir apparent—a reprise of *The Godfather*. Yet Huston's film cannot bear comparison with Coppola's: it does not adequately render the iconicity and body language of Italian Americans, their habitat and cultural decor. *Moonstruck* never rises above the commonplace, and sometimes slips below it, though its three Oscars prove that the movie industry applauds the Italian stereotype. In this film Italians are all the same—obsessed by love, emotionally supercharged, "moonstruck." But lest they spin out of kilter, they are controlled by family, which they betray when the advantage lies the other way. These qualities are reinforced by the fact that the Italians have similar sounding names:

Castorini, Cammareri, Cappomaggi. As with *Prizzi's Honor,* Italian American stereotypes are reinforced.

Because "Italy" is a world cultural marker, the image of the Italian is likely to remain in service to technological society, usable everywhere as advertising becomes global. Since non-Italian American directors have largely failed to capture the iconic authenticity and ethos of Italian America, it remains for Italian American directors to record and interpret, in the ethnic twilight, both the long and continuing process of assimilation and also the counter-tendencies to assimilation.

John Paul Russo

Bibliography

Affron, Mirella Jona. "The Italian-American in American Film." *Italian Americana* 3 (1977): 233–55.

Bonadella, Peter. "*Christ in Concrete* di Edward Dmytryk e il neorealismo italiano." *Cinema & Cinema* 38 (1984): 9–16.

Brunetta, Gian Piero. "Breve Viaggio con l'emigrato cinematografico." *Cinema & Cinema* 38 (1984): 5–8.

Buss, Robin. *Italian Films*. London: Holmes & Meier, 1989.

Casillo, Robert. "Moments in Italian-American Cinema: From *Little Caesar* to Coppola and Scorsese." In *From the Margin: Writings in Italian Americana,* edited by Anthony J. Tamburri, Paolo Giordano, and Fred Gardaphé. West Lafayette, IN: Purdue University Press, 1991.

———, guest ed. "Italian American Filmmakers." *Italian Americana* 13, no. 1 (1995): 5–23.

Cortes, Carlos E. "Hollywood e gli italo-americani: evoluzione di un'icona dell'etnicita." *Altreitalie* 10 (1993): 52–72.

———. "Italian-Americans in Film: From Immigrants to Icon." *Melus* 14, nos. 3–4 (1987): 107–26.

Everson, William K. *American Silent Film.* New York, 1978.

Friedman, Lester, ed. *Unspeakable Images: Ethnicity and the American Cinema.* Urbana: University of Illinois Press 1991.

Golden, Daniel S. "The Fate of La Famiglia: Italian Images in American Film." In *The Kaleidoscopic Lens: How Hollywood Views Ethnic Groups,* edited by Randall M. Miller. Englewood, NJ: Jerome Ozer, 1980.

F

———. "Pasta or Paradigm: The Place of Italian-American Omen in Popular Film." *Explorations in Ethnic Studies* 2, no. 1 (1979): 3–10.

Lourdeaux, Lee. *Italian and Irish Filmmakers in America: Ford, Capra, Coppola, and Scorsese.* Philadelphia: Temple University Press, 1990.

Papeleo, Joseph. "Ethnic Pictures and Ethnic Fate: The Media Image of Italian-Americans." In *Ethnic Images in American Film and Televison,* edited by Randall M. Miller. Philadelphia, 1978.

Russo, John Paul. "The End Is Everything." Review of *Godfather III. Italian Americana* 9, no. 2 (1991): 290–302.

———. "The Hidden Godfather: Plenitude and Absence in Francis Ford Coppola's *The Godfather I-II.*" In *Support and Struggle: Italians and Italian Americans in a Comparative Perspective,* edited by Joseph L. Tropea et al., *Il Padrino nascosto: la pienezza e l'assenza nel Padrino I-II,* revised ed. Gela, 1987.

Woll, Allen L, and Randall M. Miller. *Ethnic and Racial Images in American Film and Television: Historical Essays and Bibliography.* New York: Garland Publishing, 1987.

Zagarrio, Vito. "F.C.-F.C. Ovvero: Italian-American Dream dal film muto alla televisione." *Cinema & Cinema* 38 (1984): 36–40.

See also COPPOLA, FRANCIS FORD; CAPRA, FRANK; DeNONNO, ANTHONY; MOVIE ACTORS AND ACTRESSES; SCORSESE, MARTIN

Fireworks Industry

Each year, millions of Americans gather to be entertained by fireworks, an industry dominated by Italian Americans throughout the entire Western Hemisphere.

In the United States, for instance, the Gruccis of Bellport, New York; the Zambellis of New Castle, Pennsylvania; the Rozzis of Loveland, Ohio; the Cartianos of Kingsbury, Indiana; and the Souzas of Rialto, California, are the dominant companies in firework production and displays.

Today all of these companies use sophisticated electronic firing systems, computer design and choreography, and musical synchronization that combine pyrotechnical beauty with state-of-the-art technology. This high-tech artistry stems from a tradition that began well before the sixteenth century.

Fireworks were developed by the Chinese during the Mongol Yuan dynasty, which lasted from 1206 to 1368. Legend has it that gunpowder was invented by a cook who accidently started a kitchen fire and noticed that three of the elements causing the conflagration—sulfur for the stove, saltpeter (potassium nitrate) as a salt substitute, and charcoal from charred wood—burned with intense power and heat. It was later discovered that when compressed or put in a closed area, the combination exploded. Soon it was used at New Year's festivals and other celebrations to frighten away evil spirits.

It was the Europeans, specifically the Jesuit missionaries, who converted gunpowder into cannon balls and other military purposes. Yet while many Europeans used gunpowder and cannons to conquer continents, the Italians, with their love of beauty, advanced the Western tradition as an artistic endeavor.

The great explorer Marco Polo is credited with bringing fireworks to the New World in the 1400s. Polo wrote in his journal that a fireworks display "made such a dreadful noise that it can be heard for ten miles at night, and anyone who is not used to it could easily go into a swoon and even die."

In 1532 Emperor Charles V, ruler of the Holy Roman Empire, had his army use fireworks in their victory displays. Among his great artistic and scientific inventions, Leonardo da Vinci used fireworks to create a great lion that was designed to walk a few steps, roar, and then burst its chest in a display of flowers and birds. But the first historical figure to harness fireworks as a viable, stand-alone art form was an Italian named Virgarini, who amazed Louis XIII with his pyrotechnical displays and was hired by the king as the permanent pyrotechnist at Versailles. He was later replaced by Claude Fortune Ruggieri, who hailed from Bologna. To this day the Ruggieri family dominates the French fireworks industry.

In Italy fireworks are used to celebrate Easter in Florence. On saints' days and religious feasts, firecrackers announce the presence of the statue of the saint as it travels through the streets of the village. After the parade and feast, it is customary to end festivities with a giant fireworks display in the town square.

It was through these types of celebrations that many of the great Italian American fireworks moguls, such as the Zambellis of Pennsylvania, gained their experience in the trade. Known as the "first family of fireworks," the Zambellis have provided pyrotechnical exhibitions for such events as the Statue of Liberty Anniversary Gala, the inaugurations of Presidents Kennedy, Johnson, Carter, and Reagan, and over eighteen hundred annual Fourth of July celebrations.

The company was founded by Antonio Zambelli, who migrated to New Castle, Pennsylvania, in 1893. Once in America, he began displaying fireworks at feasts but quickly began performing at Fourth of July celebrations, bank openings, ball games, and other events. In 1957 his son, George Sr., took over the company, and it was his dream to make fireworks more than just a sideshow, but a major entertainment spectacular. To this end he pioneered such features as electronic firings, synchronized fireworks and music, blazing displays of emblems, and laser light shows.

Today the Zambellis produce events such as the annual "Thunder in the Sky," which opens the Kentucky Derby and is known as the largest annual fireworks display in the world. For this event they use more than 20,000 pounds of explosives, 5,000 tons of sand, 250,000 pounds of iron mortar, 100 miles of wire, and dozens of technicians who work mainly by computer to process over 5,400 pyrotechnic cues.

The Zambelli's largest rival in the fireworks business is the Gruccis of Bellport, New York. The Grucci family originally came from the town of Apulia, Bari. Felix Sr., who began the company in America, learned the fireworks business from his mother, who fired shows on feast days and won a prize from the king of Italy for a fireworks spectacle carried up in a balloon. After moving to Long Island, New York, young Felix began what is now a multimillion-dollar, multinational business.

Some of the effects and different types of shells and displays manufactured by companies like the Gruccis and Zambellis are described in the Zambelli's Press Guide, published in 1995. These include *Battles in the Clouds,* a number of salutes timed to sound like a fusillade of musketry; *Weeping Willows,* colors that fall, outlining the dropping branches of a weeping willow; *Chrysanthemums,* which bloom before onlookers' eyes in the sky like flowers; and *Strobes,* a regular part of all finales, which are clusters of glistening silvery lights that appear to float slowly to the ground.

These fireworks displays highlight grand celebrations that are enjoyed throughout America. Italian Americans watch them with pride knowing that they are a special part of their culture.

David Anthony Witter

Bibliography

Conkling, John A. "Pyrotechnics." *Scientific American* 263 (1 July 1990): 96–102.
Plimpton, George. *Fireworks.* Garden City: Doubleday, 1984.

See also BUSINESS AND ENTREPRENEURSHIP

Fishing

In his classic 1924 study, *The Italian Emigration of Our Times,* Princeton economist Robert F. Foerster notes the central role of the fishing industry in the lives of Italian immigrants and their descendants in America. That Italian fishermen were and are to be found widely scattered across the United States is a direct result of their heritage: "Italy is bordered by fish-abounding seas, supplying in a country where meat is expensive, one of the most valued of foods." Foerster documents, for example, that immigrants from Tuscany and Sicily founded a fishing industry in Tampa, Florida and those from the isle of Elba did so in Galveston, Texas. He also notes concentrations of Italian fishermen in Oregon and Alaska. The largest and most significant impact that Italian Americans have made in the fishing industry has been on the East Coast, in the Boston/Gloucester area by Sicilian immigrants, and on the West Coast, in San Francisco by immigrants from Genoa, Naples, Calabria, and Sicily.

East Coast Fishing

The East Coast commercial fishing industry is one of America's oldest industry. Fish, especially salted cod, provided the New World colonists with their first export commodity throughout the Western world. For almost three hundred years, vast numbers of sailing vessels thrived and fished along the entire eastern seaboard. The new nation's commercial fishermen, representing many nationalities, expressed their resourcefulness and became an integrated part of American history.

During the last two decades of the nineteenth century millions of immigrants who experienced poor conditions in the south of Italy, particularly Sicily, migrated en masse to the industrial centers of the United States. The fishing industry provided a strong means to work in an active and consolidated industry. Since fishing was a traditional trade throughout Italy, Boston, the largest fishing port of the nation, attracted many Italian fishermen to its shores. It was there in Boston Harbor, in the shadows of the tall sailing masts of the "Yankee" schooners, that Sicilian dory hook-fishermen attained a toehold into the oldest industry in America.

These early Sicilian dorymen rowed and sailed their small wooden boats to the fishing grounds in and around Boston Harbor. In 1908 the first fuel-powered "motor fishing boat" in Boston was a Sicilian-owned Swampscott dory fitted with a gasoline motor. The evolution of fueled fishing vessels began with a four-horse-power, two-cycle motor. The overwhelming fishing success that followed induced the Italian fleet to grow in number, size, and fishing capability. Within a few years, a portion of this fleet moved to the fishing port of Gloucester to become a major component of that fishing area. This expanded flotilla was known as the "guinea" fleet. It is said that there was no offense taken at their description; indeed, it hardly seemed important as the Italian fishermen struggled to survive, planting the seeds of a new ethnic tradition among the Nova Scotian, Newfoundlander, and Portuguese fishermen who were already established in the area.

Almost concurrently with the appearance of the Boston Sicilian fishermen, a North Sea technological improvement spurred an enormous innovation in commercial fishing that changed the course of the industry. Otter trawling or drag nets were introduced. These conical-shaped "bag" nets are dragged along the ocean bottom catching vast amounts of bottom fish species. The vessels first using these drag nets came to be known as "Boston Beam Trawlers." They were large, steel vessels, initially steam driven, that perfected the use of this drag gear within ten years. The accomplishment of this fishing gear persuaded many fishermen, including the small hook-vessel fleet, to abandon their hooks to drag trawls.

With greater opportunities and financial success came a desire to build and own larger, more versatile vessels. Soon many of the "guinea" fleet fishermen converted to more effective otter draggers fishing wooden draggers, especially from the port of Gloucester.

With the end of World War I, an abundance of larger and surplus ex-Navy vessels became available to fishermen. Fishermen, eager to own larger vessels, purchased sub-chasers to convert into Atlantic mackerel purse seiners and drag vessels. Purse seining was a form of fishing that encircled great, surface schools of fish, especially the abundant mackerel stocks. Mackerel had become an important food fishery along the coast since the mid-1800s. From 1920 to the 1950s a prosperous mackerel fishery flourished, an industry composed primarily of Gloucester Italian fishermen. At its peak, about one hundred vessels and one thousand fishermen landed up to 35 million pounds a year.

The converted sub-chasers, with their long sterns (which once housed the depth-charge racks) and their tall masts crowned with lookout towers nicknamed "crow's nests," cruised the entire East Coast in search of fish. These Italian American vessels and their crews were the embodiment of a determination to triumph.

The last thirty years has witnessed a serious decline in the industry due to the expansion of the number and size of fishing vessels along the entire East Coast, the increase of fishing gear types, and increased fishing competition. Especially devastating were the foreign fleets that fished off the East Coast from the early 1960s to the mid-1970s. One after another, targeted finfish stocks fell to insignificant levels only to have fishermen springboard to another type of fish until that species also fell to low levels. In 1976 Congress implemented the two-hundred-mile limit law that mandated all fishing be regulated within these boundaries. Today, federal government regulations are designed to contain the way fishermen capture fish with the intent to rebuild fish stocks to their former levels.

Salvatore A. Testaverde

Bibliography
Testaverde, R. Salve. *Memoirs of a Gloucester Fisherman*. Rockport, MA: Rockport, 1987.

White, Donald J. "The New England Fishing Industry: American's Oldest Industry Faces Crisis." *Monthly Review Federal Reserve Bank of Boston* 32 (1950): 1–12.

West Coast Fishing

Fishing was one of the two main industries of early Italians in San Francisco. Between 1850 and 1870 these Italians were described as monopolistic fishermen and fish merchants in San Francisco Bay waters. Their domination continued until World War II.

The economics of the fishing market system were simple. The fishermen brought their fish to wholesale dealers or fish brokers, who sold and distributed the fish to retailers for a fee. The brokers became the central figures who controlled the market prices and provided immigrant fishermen with loan services, extending credit when needed.

Initially, the efficiency and effectiveness of Italian immigrant fishermen were due to the use of the *paranzella,* a tightly knitted, meshed trawling net that was dragged along the floor of the bay, and the felucca, a lateen-rigged shallow vessel built to withstand high winds and rough waters. With these, Italians had the advantage over other ethnic and native fishermen.

The spirit of *campanilismo* (localism) bonded fishermen to their fellow provincials. Initially, the majority of the Italian fishermen were from Genoa or the Camogli district; they then became the fish brokers intent on developing a market system. They left the actual fishing to incoming immigrants. As Italian immigration intensified in the 1890s, more fishermen from the southern provinces of Naples, Calabria, and Sicily arrived to develop the inshore fishing industry and eventually led the state in salmon and sardine fishing. Other Italian fishermen worked in the coastal fishing communities of Monterey, Martinez, San Pedro, Santa Cruz, and Pittsburg, California, following the runs of seasonal fish. Those in San Diego concentrated on tuna-albacore fishing.

The fishing community was located at the base of several wharf areas that became known as "Italy Harbor." Here fishermen unloaded their catches, cleaned nets, and repaired boats. Monday through Friday, after midnight, the fishermen sold their catches to the fish brokers. Fishermen were charged dock fees according to the number of men working in a boat. These fees became the basis for protective or benevolent associations that served as bargaining agents with the fish brokers as well as the state fish and game commission, and provided for rudimentary donations in case of an accident or the death of a fisherman.

The growth of the San Francisco Bay fishing industry prompted the state of California to create a permanent commercial fishing area between Taylor and Leavenworth Streets in what has become known as Fisherman's Wharf. A wharfinger, berths, and an outdoor market were established to benefit the fishermen. Large wholesale houses were established by independent fish brokers who bought and sold fish and controlled the market prices. The success of the fishing industry saw the creation of a state market director who oversaw the wholesalers and threatened to revoke licenses of those wholesalers who under- or oversold fish. "Crab wars" and "fish trusts" were common terms spoken by the fishermen who found themselves at the mercy of a controlling wholesaler who attempted to "fix" the market price of a fish species.

F

Feluccas berthed at the wharf of San Francisco at the turn of the twentieth century. These boats were popular with Genoese and Sicilian fishermen. Courtesy of Augusto Troiani and the National Maritime Museum.

There were other innovations that accompanied the growth of the bay fishing industry. The introduction of a single-cylinder engine easily installed in feluccas and small half-decked vessels increased the efficiency and speed of the fishing process. This allowed fishermen to stay out on the waters longer without the fear that the hoped-for breeze might fail to bring them home. These gas engines were hand started, with minimum upkeep and low operating costs, handled safely, and promoted the construction of larger fishing boats known as the "Monterey" fishing boats. With their clipper-beaked bows and gas engines the Montereys replaced the feluccas. They were also equipped with long poles towering high above the decks that were lowered for salmon fishing, and a gurdy, a power-reeled pulley, that lifted the strained fishing lines. Purse-seiners (nets), easily tossed over the sides, remained open until the ends were tightened, catching the fish in the same fashion as a lady's purse opened and closed.

The attractiveness of the wharf area promoted the growth of tourism. Small stand-up coffee stands and chowder stands that catered to the appetites of hungry fishermen gave way to restaurants that served "walk-away" seafood cocktails and fried fish. Cauldrons boiled crabs and the highly seasoned fish stew, cioppino, lured local San Franciscans. By the end of World War II, San Francisco's Fisherman's Wharf became a popular tourist spot. With the advent of radar- and sonar-equipped vessels and the depletion of sardine schools, the fishing industry of San Francisco Bay has diminished.

Deanna Paoli Gumina

Bibliography

Foerster, Robert F. *The Italian Emigration of Our Times.* Cambridge, MA: Harvard University Press, 1924.

Gumina, Deanna Paoli. "The Fishermen of San Francisco Bay: The Men of Italy Harbor." *The Pacific Historian* 20, no. 1 (spring 1976): 8–21.

——— . "Fishermen and Trunk Farmers." In *The Italians of San Francisco, 1850–1930,* 80–98. New York: Center for Migration Studies, 1976.

——— . *The Italians of San Francisco, 1850–1930.* New York: Center for Migration Studies, 1976.

See also OCCUPATIONS OF ITALIAN IMMIGRANTS IN TURN-OF-THE-CENTURY AMERICA

Florio, James J. (b. 1937)

The first Italian American governor of New Jersey, James J. Florio was born in Brooklyn, August 9, 1937, the son of an immigrant from Bari, Italy, and a Protestant mother who was of Scottish and German descent. He was named for his father, Vincenzo "Jim" Florio, and his grandfather, Giuseppe (Joseph) Florio. He dropped out of Erasmus Hall High School in his senior year, enlisting in the United States Navy. He served from 1955 to 1958 as an aviation weatherman and remained in the Naval Reserves until 1975, retiring with the rank of lieutenant commander. He was a boxer throughout his active naval career.

After earning his high school equivalency diploma in the Navy, Florio received a bachelor's degree in 1962 from Trenton State College, where he was elected student body president and graduated magna cum laude. He was the first member of his family to receive a college degree. He won a Woodrow Wilson Fellowship to Columbia University, where he studied public law and government, 1962–1963. While at Columbia, he took courses with presidential scholar Richard Neustadt, and this experience drew him to government service.

During this period he married Maryanne Spaeth, and they became the parents of two sons and a daughter. He moved to Camden, where he worked at odd jobs, studied law at night, and received a doctor of law degree in 1967 from Rutgers University. He practiced law and became active in the Democratic Party, winning elections to the New Jersey General Assembly, 1966 to 1974, and to Congress from New Jersey's First Congressional district, 1975 to 1989.

Florio's success in Democratic Party politics earned him the nomination for governor in 1981. He lost by 1,797 votes, the closest election in New Jersey's history. Nominated a second time, in 1989, he was elected governor by a margin of 538,180 votes, defeating conservative congressman Jim Courter. Four years later, he was defeated for reelection by Republican Christine Todd Whitman. The voters blamed him for the increase in taxes during his term as governor.

After divorcing his first wife, Florio married Lucinda Coleman in February 1988.

Frank J. Cavaioli

Bibliography
Cavaioli, Frank J. "Charles Poletti and Fourteen Other Italian American Governors." In *Italian Americans in Transition,* edited by Joseph V. Scelsa, Salvatore J. LaGumina, and Lydio Tomasi, 137–152. New York: American Italian Historical Association, 1990.

See also GOVERNORS; POLITICS

Fo, Dario
See PLAYS, CONTEMPORARY

Folklore, Folklife
Folklorists study forms of knowledge and expressions of culture that are transmitted from one generation to the next by word of mouth or by example, such as lace-making, stonecutting, or family narratives, recipes, games, songs, or proverbs. *Folkways, folklife, traditional culture, oral traditions, folk art,* and *material culture* are terms associable with the discipline of "folkloristics."

Today's folklorists are no longer only interested in the lore and behavior of people from the backwoods or mountaintops—remote, rural, and isolated—but in all aspects of the traditional culture of the "folk"—urban and rural. Popular misconceptions of what folklore is—frequently taken to mean something quaint and colorful, antiquated, false, or relevant only to the poor, uneducated classes—prevent many from recognizing folklore as a more encompassing discipline, as much concerned with popular culture in the present as in the past. Tales, myths, jokes, handcrafts, even "superstitions" (which equals beliefs) persist because they continue to be meaningful to us. Were they mere archaic survivals of a more "primitive" way of thinking, they would have been long forgotten. As Italo Calvino, for instance, discovered, in the course of compiling his collection of Italian folktales in 1956, *le fiabe sono vere* (fables are true).

Folk or traditional cultural expressions tend to be associated with specific groups whose identity is either defined ethnically, by religion, gender, geography, occupation, and so forth, so that we most often speak of Sicilian puppet theater or fishermen's festivals, Molisano shepherds' *zampogne* tunes, Toronto Italian vernacular architecture, Burano women's needlework patterns, Argentine Italian stereotypes, Colorado Italian cowboys, or Lombard narrative songs.

Italians have known diversity throughout the centuries: from the patchwork of individual city states and republics within the peninsula, to foreign occupations, overlaying pre-Latin and Latin tribes. Italian Americans therefore, have inherited this cultural complexity. Today we divide Italy roughly into North, Central (following the La Spezia-Rimini line) and South regions, although at the micro-level many more regional and dialectal Italies exist, including ethnic minorities (Albanian, German, Greek, Slovene, Provençal, and so forth). Finally, where large Italian diaspora populations scattered to the four corners of the world (but most numerously in North and South America and Australia), cultural contact and successive waves of immigrants further contributed to the diversification of Italian culture, as regional location once did on American soil (e.g., East vs. West Coast). Thus, Italian Americans are differentiated according to immigration dates as well: from the earliest eighteenth-century immigrants to the thirteen colonies to the mass migrations of the late nineteenth century and early twentieth century, to the more modest influx after World War II, up to the arrivals of the 1980s and 1990s, part of the latest Italian "brain drain."

The majority of Italian Americans were of peasant origin and many were bearers of an archaic European folk culture, which they imported directly to the New World. Here the old (their regional and national Italian identities) sometimes interacted dynamically with the local and national American realities to create new forms of cultural expression. Some examples are Northern Italian vernacular architecture as it was adapted in the Western ranch environment of Colorado or in the wineries of California and the Sicilian St. Joseph's Day altar/table as it interacted with the New Orleans Mardi Gras celebrations (later to be adopted by African American Spiritualist churches). But the harsh anti-peasant bias running through much of Italian history, and producing a hierarchic society, contributed to the immigrant's often ambivalent attitude toward his or her own folk culture. Southern Italians, who experienced the feudal system and foreign domination longest, were especially marked by this oppression, in some instances making their culture more insulated and resistant to change. Add to this psychological mix the initial prejudice experienced by the vast wave of southern Italians, the social reform programs designed to help alter everything from immigrant diet to their medical and religious practices, the negative stereotypes linking Italians to Prohibition-era organized crime, and Fascist-era despotism, and the reasons for this cultural ambivalence become even more apparent. Media stereotypes are compounded by the nationalist and internally adopted stereotype of the red, white, and green flag-waving ethnic-prider. Although the experiences of, for instance, San Francisco and New Orleans Italians may have differed from those of the largest and most compact communities of the Northeast, such as New York and Chicago, negativity and prejudice from without, reinforced by regional and class prejudice from within, confused Italian immigrants landing in any location. Finally, the devaluing of Italian folk culture has often been reinforced by representatives of "official" Italian culture to the New World, as well, such as government officials and functionaries, media representatives, Italian cultural offices, Italian departments at universities, and even the Catholic Church. The "boom" of Italian culture in the last decades has frequently represented a continuation of this antipeasant bias, since contemporary Italian commercial and high-end cultural interests derive little benefit from Italian folk culture—except for, perhaps, on the labels of food products. Concurrent factors such as these conspire against an appreciation of Italian folklife and have been offset only moderately by recent trends of ethnic revivalism and cultural ecology.

A prime requisite to the study of Italian American folklore, therefore, is an understanding of the complex intersection of local, regional, and national Italian cultures with sociocultural forces that shaped and transformed the emigrants' culture in diaspora contexts, for example, factors such as the attitudes of Italians toward their folk culture, intergenerational dynamics, biculturalism, commercial and professional pressures, the role of the media, the alternate effects of affluence and penury, the dynamics between "old" and "new" immigrants, local geography, and history, as well as religion, occupation, class, and gender.

Few aspects of Italian American folklife have resisted change. While the making of home altars, the celebration of a saint's day, or the practice of traditional foodways, appear more or less to be direct carryovers from the Old World, other usages are outright borrowings (e.g., the beauty queen crowned at so many Italian festivals, or nationalistic flag-waving). Others still are newly "invented traditions." The eighteenth-century "Yankee" commemoration of Columbus, for example, celebrated rugged American individualism, conquest, and civic virtues. In its subsequent "reinvention," the historic figure of Columbus was restored to his ethnicity and religion of origin. Indeed, the contemporary celebration of Columbus Day (October 12)—the primary, institutionalized pan-Italian American festivity—has now become a self-celebration of this group's accomplishments and contributions to American society.

Fieldwork in Italian American communities has been shared among ethnomusicologists, oral historians, sociologists, linguists, and others, and many archives serve as depositories for these precious materials. Folklorists, although relatively new participants in the "Italian American experience" dialogue, bring a valuable interdisciplinary perspective to the field. The most successful folkloristic work engages in a geo-historical dialogue, which involves a direct knowledge of Italy as well as of America—often the fruit of fieldwork on both continents. Such studies seek not merely to record the *what* (tales, songs, proverbs, etc.), but to answer the *how, why,* and *when* of Italian folklife. That is, while earlier folklorists collected *texts,* today's folklife specialist seeks to place texts in *contexts* in order to derive meaning from the larger picture. Folklife studies are holistic rather than item-based. A pioneer example of a researcher working in the folklife tradition was Phyllis Williams' 1938 monograph, *South Italian Folkways in Europe and America,* which treats employment, diet, housing, dress, marriage, family, recreation, education, beliefs, folk medicine, death, and funerary practices.

Many internal processes and external forces are at play in the evolution and transmission of folk culture. An internal "natural" law indicates that metrically bounded oral expressions, such as songs, nursery rhymes, proverbs and rhymed riddles, change less over time, than do, say, prose narratives. The paradox in the Italian American context, however, is that such bounded expressions require the maintenance of Italian dialect and where there is language loss, such oral expressions become extinct since they cannot be "translated" as can more freely structured narratives. Another principle is that in oral cultures, oral expressions depend on memory and transmission for survival. Elements of culture that survive, therefore, are those that continue to have meaning and are therefore "popular"; those that cease to be relevant obsolesce or are refunctionalized (children's nursery rhymes, many of which were never meant for children but began as vendors' cries, tavern songs, and political satire). Further, because many components of folklore exist and derive meaning from the functions they served in specific social contexts, once these social parameters are changed so does that aspect of folklife. Take, for instance, the social institution of the nightly *filò* (recounting, storytelling) in the stable; once this practice ended, a major occasion for storytelling disappeared. The occupational songs of Sicilian fishermen (the *Cialoma*), of Romagnol dike builders (*scariolanti*), or of women grape- or olive-harvesters or rice-workers (*mondine*) have experienced the same demise. When occupational techniques are industrialized or certain occupations cease to exist (itinerant vendors such as the water seller, the umbrella repairman, the bargeman, the carter), the "natural" social settings for the songs cease to exist and the songs obsolesce as well, surviving at best only as part of memorial culture, not living tradition, or refunctionalized (vendors' cries → nursery rhymes).

External factors also have important effects on the evolution of folklore: the impact of mass media in determining the relative prestige and accessibility of certain types of music over others (e.g., contemporary Italian popular music or opera over traditional song) is the most conspicuous of these forces today. Yet in the recent past, government policies (the squelching of minority languages during Fascism, the closing or opening of immigration quotas), Church policy (the desanctifying or conversely, the sponsorship, of saints' feast days, the "outlawing" of specific folk beliefs, or the creation of national Italian parishes), and social change (from urbanization, upward mobility and acculturation, or exogamy) were equally powerful.

The phenomenon known in linguistics as a koiné (a common language that emerges when two different languages converge), was practiced by regional Italians in America who had come in contact with one another and with English, drew on mutually understood terms, and formed a "hybridized" and "leveled" language (alternatively referred to as "Americanized Italian," "Itagliese," or "Engliano"). Cultural koinés have developed as well. Italian Americans have established shared cultural expressions that depend on several factors: the demographic weight of one regional group over another, the role of pan-Italian associations, the need to represent a unified Italian heritage at public display events (Columbus Day), and the host culture's values and aesthetics that may favor one Italian expression over another.

For any one of these reasons, koinés have evolved in all areas of Italian American folklife: the "generic" tarantella, the Italian costume of red, white, and green, wine-stomping at harvest festivals. A common food "parlance" that cuts across Italian regional lines (but finds its main sources in southern Italian cuisine) has arisen as well: the sausage and pepper sandwich, now-dated spaghetti and meatballs, pizza, pasta with red sauce, are found at most Italian public events such as street festivals, for instance. As for rituals, most religious feast days follow the canonical procession, Mass, and dinner with very little variation among them, and most associations largely organize events around "the dinner dance." Frank Sinatra, Tony Bennett, and other crooners have formed the koiné in their musical repertoire, especially when "folksong" is on the program. Italian folksongs that seem to belong to no specific region but are shared up and down the Italian peninsula (*Mazzolin di fiori*) are called upon by northerner and southerner alike.

Another linguistic principle that can be usefully adapted is that of the *area seriore,* meaning simply that the periphery is often more conservative than the center. In Italian linguistic terms, subdialects of outlying, remote areas have characteristically retained more archaic, conservative features than that of a *capoluogo* (provincial capital). By exten-

F

sion, it has been presumed that immigrant dialects are more conservative than the language spoken in the mother country. So, too, Carla Bianco (*The Two Rosetos,* 1974) discovered, by way of analogy, that elements of folk culture were more intact in Roseto, Pennsylvania, than they were in Roseto, Puglia. The paradox she attempted to answer was why third- and fourth-generation immigrants still retained this folklore.

Various aspects of Italian American folklore have been alternatively suppressed, exploited, misinterpreted, even "folklorized," by the popular media but rarely presented with sensitivity and accuracy. There are many uses (and "users") of folklore still in practice in the private and community lives of Italian Americans. There are features of "oral" culture surviving at the local level, in the family, church basements, and town clubs. Indeed, many aspects of folklife may never go beyond family foyer: celebrations, home altars, a backyard garden, stories, songs, and rhymes shared between grandmother and grandchild. Family narratives may preserve oral family and community history; immigrant stories often focus on or create mythic characters and give epic dimensions to personal narratives (e.g., Jerre Mangione's *Mount Allegro,* 1942). Group customs shared among *paesani* (fellow townspeople) such as neighborhood mumming or caroling, singing of local dialect songs, affirm local cohesion within the network of regional and national identities in which the participants interact. Coregionalists, such as Sicilians, may commemorate a time of want and oppression as well as celebrate present well-being through a St. Joseph's Day table while adapting this village custom to contemporary urban social needs, such as helping to feed the American poor. Calabrians may sing their *villanella* (village/country songs) as a regional "anthem" thereby reinforcing regional identity in an urban American setting. In certain instances the American neighborhood may actually replace the Italian *paese* (village), such as the custom of serenading in South Philadelphia.

Foodways may serve a wide variety of functions. Seasonal specialties such as Christmas *ciambelle* (a hard ring-shaped cookie), New Year's *zeppole* (leavened fritters), and Carnival *cenci* (fried and sugared egg dough), if prepared only once a year, help mark ritual moments in the nature or life cycles and maintain family traditions through reenactment; other culinary events may even perpetuate accompanying Old World technical knowledge, such as the slaughtering of a pig and the preparation of cured meats or the home-distilling of spirits. An Italian market may actually function as a surrogate piazza for the community, where information is exchanged, informal associations with coethnics fostered, and Italian specialties made possible. Foodways may even serve as an ethnic "display event" at common *feste italiane* (Italian feasts) or in Italian American restaurants—readily assimilable or consumable by the out-group.

"Folklorismus" generally refers to staged, decontextualized representations of folk culture. Folk dance is a frequent candidate for this phenomenon (such as the *tarantella* dancers in red white and green so much in evidence at Italian American "folklore" events). Invariably these events convey a contented, problem-free, and simplistic perspective on a culture, portraying "Merry Olde Italy" (or "Sunny Italy") for the public's enjoyment. "Applied folklore" takes many forms and seeks consciously to employ folklore to affect some ulterior goal. Along with the folk pageants staged under Mussolini, another early example of "applied" folkore may be inferred from the subtitle of Phyllis Williams' monograph *South Italian Folkways in Europe and America: A Handbook for Social Workers, Visiting Nurses, School Teachers, and Physicians,* that is, ethnic comprehension to serve social reform. Current applications of folklore may introduce "folk artists" in the classroom in order to promote intercultural understanding and tolerance across ethnic boundaries, or in a heritage program to build self-esteem through positive cultural identification. Folklore has therapeutic applications as well: folksong singing in a senior citizens' home, personalization of folktales, and myth in psychotherapy.

"Public sector" folklore, on the other hand, refers to state- or institution-sponsored events in which community groups are presented in public forums such as folklife festivals, museums, and cultural and civic centers. Notable examples of public folklore forums presenting "authentic" Italian folklore in naturalized contexts (without folk costumes and painted backdrops) have been promoted by agencies such as the Smithsonian's Festival of American Folklife. Mike Manteo, Sicilian

American marionettist in the *opera dei pupi* Sicilian puppet theater tradition in New York and Calabrian *villanella* singers Raffaella and Giuseppe De Franco received the prestigious National Heritage Fellow Award in 1991, through the National Endowment for the Arts (Folk and Traditional Arts Program), which recognizes traditional arts and life in America. Some folklife agencies at the state government level may also make similar awards. Furthermore, there are a number of professional folk revival performers who engage in fieldwork and perform traditional song, music, and theater with varying degrees of success; currently, the most commendable among these are I Giullari di Piazza of New York and the recently formed Musicàntica of Los Angeles.

Several contemporary social trends may be contributing to a rediscovery of Italian folklore, trends that frequently go beyond the specific experience of Italian Americans. The positive effects of the ethnic revival in the 1970s now form a permanent record. The "roots" experience has prompted many Italians to search for their personal history and reconstruct their ethnic identities: family genealogies, revival of festival and family traditions, return trips to the ancestral town, enrollment in language classes, and the creation of new regional associations (Arba Sicula, Fameja Veneta, Piemontesi nel Mondo) have all contributed to this search for past. Several other current trends are also favoring this renewed interest: women's spirituality movements may be reviving Marian cults as the Madonna/goddess sites of the Mediterranean are revisited and popular forms of folk Catholicism (from mystic healers such as Natuzza di Paravati to matriarchal wisdom embodied in vernacular natural medicine) are reexamined; cultural ecology has rekindled appreciation for indigenous music (known as "world music")—including Italian regional folk music and song styles—as engaging and meaningful; *cucina rustica* (peasant cuisine), now widely fashionable in America (aided by commercial concerns in Italy and the United States), is helping to redefine Italian food sources as regional and local (*polenta, bruschetta, pecorino, rucola arugula, radicchio rosso,* etc.) and has spawned a plethora of Italian regional cookbooks, not to mention the newly aligned regional (often spuriously "northern") Italian restaurants. While the promoters of ethnic diversity programs may often be perceived as striving to overcome a Eurocentric bias, renewed interest in Third World folk civilizations could potentially foster heightened esteem for Italy's folk cultures, which are shaped by many of the same forces. On the other end of the political spectrum may be found a nostalgic reaffirmation of conservative family and community traditions.

National culture and Italian government programs are also having their impact on folk culture. The current vogue of Italian commercial culture (the marketing prestige of the "Made in Italy" label) and a renewed interest in Italian travel and high culture (an interest that has never waned among the elite) have been actively promoted by Italy. Establishing Italian cultural institutes, Italian trade commissions, branches of Italian banks, and study and cultural exchange programs has helped to bridge the distance and to blur the boundaries between the Old and New Worlds. Recent Italian government policy is also helping to bring about change that will translate culturally. Italy has, for a variety of political and economic reasons, become interested in its immigrants and in reestablishing active links with these communities. It has even considered granting the vote to Italian residents abroad. At the regional level as well, governments in Italy are becoming increasingly aggressive about forging direct links with their coregionalists abroad. (The Regione Friuli—in conjunction with the Foglars Furlans—is sponsoring a Friulian language and culture program, soon to be followed by the Regione Molise, at the University of Toronto, although it is not certain to what degree these regions' folk cultures will be represented.) These larger cultural movements may all contribute to a future folk revival in this country as even third- and fourth-generation Italian Americans recover their peasant, dialectal, cultural patrimony and "return home."

With *folklife* we include the holistic, everyday life of a group rather than the isolated, "framed" expressions of the group (e.g., songs, tales, proverbs), suggested by the term *folklore*. "Italian Americans" represent all phases along a continuum that incorporates fourth- and fifth-generation acculturated "old immigrants," post–Word War II or "new immigrants," and the latest influx of Italians in the 1980s and 1990s who maintain strong and ongoing ties with Italy. While the vast majority of Italian Americans are of peasant stock, post–economic boom Italians (1960s)

F

instead have often arrived as middle-class professionals. The cultural expressions of these distinct groups vary widely and so do their attitudes vis-à-vis Italian traditional culture; they alternatively scorn Italian American culture in favor of a more contemporary view of Italian culture or, conversely, if influenced by the leftist Italian politics of the 1960s and 1970s, appreciate Italian folk culture in more "authentic" (less hybridized) versions—that is, not the tricolored *tarantella* dancers, but real Sicilian fishermen singing their own songs. Some, however, see Italian Americans as a more innocent and nostalgic backwater yearning after Italian values long superseded in the homeland.

The most direct link to that pre-boom Italy is the first-generation Italian immigrants of the 1950s and early 1960s who predate contemporary, technocratic Italy and hence maintain a direct memory and practice of life in rural Italy. Large communities of this sort may be found, for example, in Canada and Australia, but many urban neighborhoods in the United States have received such recent immigrants as well, although in fewer numbers.

Italian American folklife studies encompass all aspects of the traditional life of Italians in America, although not all traditions are equally vital or diffused. Yet because Italian traditional life has not been fully documented in all areas of the continent, it would be unwise not to recognize that a patchy "atlas" of Italian folklife reflects this state of fieldwork and scholarship. A major field collecting campaign among rural and urban

Italians from all regions of America would create a more accurate picture of the current folklife of Italian Americans. The following list of categories or "genres" therefore is meant only to provide some general orientation in the field and to focus on the most salient features.

Food has a primary role in Italian culture, and it has become a truism that traditional culinary folkways show a tenacity and longevity unmatched by any other area of Italian immigrant folklife. Foodways may include family eating habits, ethnic foods consumed on a daily basis, Sunday *pranzo* or dinner; ritual or festival foods made exclusively for holidays (Sicilian braided breads, egg-based pasta specialties, Jordan almonds or *confetti*); food exchange; food preservation (from pickling *giardiniera*, canning tomatoes, curing olives, wine making, to the slaughtering of pigs and making of sausage, *prosciutti*, and other cured meats); gardening (kitchen, truck, and commercial) and hothouses for special fruits such as figs and lemons; gathering of wild foods (mushrooms, snails, rapini, etc.); and food-related occupations, such as agriculture, fishing, and related industries (including food processing, importing and distribution), markets, bakeries, and restaurants. The popularity of Italian food has contributed, in part, to the de-ethnicization of Italian foods as they enter the mainstream's culinary vocabulary. Old-style Italian American restaurants, further, are evolving away from the red-and-white-checkered tablecloth and wicker Chianti wine flasks.

Folk belief encompasses a vast area of traditional life, from the creation of sacred space (home altars and backyard shrines to public devotional sites) to forms of worship and ritual celebration (patron feast days), to medicine, oral expressions (orations, novenas, incantations), music, drama, and material culture (*presepi* or crèche manger scenes, the modeling of figurines for shrines, palm-weaving), devotional practices and individual beliefs ("superstitions" when stated unsympathetically). Folk medicine, using a pharmacopia of herbs and ingredients largely from the kitchen (such as camomile, garlic, oil, wine), treats everything from physical to spiritual ailments (colds and headaches to *malocchio* ["evil eye" or "worms"]); amulets such as gold, coral, or plastic horns, saints'

Madonna and child in the window of a home in Little Italy, Baltimore, April 1980. Such representation exhibits a traditional religious practice of Italian Americans. Courtesy Frank J. Cavaioli.

medallions, and crucifixes are also used for physical and spiritual well-being.

Ritual practices and festivals involve those that have been formulated around the life cycle (birth, marriage, death) and the nature cycle (vernal and autumnal equinoxes), and are moments punctuated by private and collective traditional expressions of both Christian and pre-Christian origins. Italian forms of folk Catholicism are tenaciously preserved in the images, processions, feasts, and festivals of Italian Americans both with and without the support of the Church. Italian national parishes have alleviated some of the conflicts in worship styles encountered between the early Italian immigrants and the Hibernian Church hierarchy. Yet the Italian clergy has also shown resistance toward forms of folk devotion, along with the Irish.

Festivals include religious feast days (following almost invariably the Mass, procession, communal dinner framework) that are frequently promoted by town clubs in celebration of their patron saint, to ethnic street festivals (often named *Festa Italiana* or *Heritage Days* or variants thereof), which tend to be food and song fests or full-blown commercially promoted events with concessionaires and mechanical rides; civic celebrations such as Columbus Day; and the most recent *Festa della Repubblica,* promoted primarily by the Consular office.

From the domestic handicrafts to *mestieri* (skills, crafts, occupations) in the Italian artisan tradition to the organization and use of space, material traditions that still may be found (although many dwindling) among Americans of Italian descent include stone carving, fresco and mural painting, mosaics, wrought iron work, plaster casting, bread and pastry making, tailoring, and the domestic arts (which include needlework, palm weaving, braided breads, and so forth). Because Italians went into the building trades in large numbers and settled wherever the work happened to be, their handiwork and artisanship may be found in many private and public structures across the country. Stone masons have built villas and civic monuments, and Italian stone carvers contributed significantly to the National Cathedral in Washington.

These artisan traditions have contributed to what may be considered a positive ethnic stereotype, namely that "Italians are artistic," just as famous operatic tenors helped contribute to the cliché that "Italians are musical." In the case of the "artistic Italian," the presence of skilled Italian craftsmen coinciding with the large public building projects of the 1910s and 1920s, meant that a New World niche had been found for Old World Italian traditions. The association of Italians with Michelangelo, Leonardo, and high art, furthermore, conferred prestige and therefore provided economic and status incentives to the addition of this element to the construction of "Italian" identity. The adoption of a "high" art aesthetic may be reflected in the painting of Raphael Madonnas in home basements, Mario Lanza making a career out of being a South Philadelphian Caruso, or Toronto Italians putting columns and arches in their architecture. The artisan appropriated the (often) Baroque art aesthetic as his own, replicating its forms in American churches, movie palaces, and public buildings, but also in "folk" contexts of home decoration and religious imagery, long after elite artists had abandoned it.

Vernacular architecture embraces the use of domestic and public, sacred and secular, and symbolic spaces, the (ethnic) personalization of these spaces, and their architectural styles. Italian Americans have created public shrines (e.g., Rosebank Grotto in Brooklyn) and pilgrimage sites; they have sought to replicate the "piazza" by relocating it to other functional spaces (e.g., malls, street corners, markets, church) or to the urban neighborhood (e.g., the "urban village" or "street corner society"); in their domestic landscapes they have included gardens, pizza ovens, cantinas, fountains, arbors, and other idealized or "symbolic" features with roots in agrarian life.

From family singing, folksong choirs, and dance ensembles to professional and semiprofessional bands and disc jockeys, to Italian media programming, the Italian musical idiom among Italian Americans is a mixed bag. In that bag is found the ever-popular Neapolitan song tradition (the Mario Lanza Museum in South Philadelphia) and the Italian operatic tenors (heightened by the careers of such masters as Caruso), or popular music sung by Claudio Villa; it also includes a smattering of an immigrant repertoire that is, in part, homegrown (Enrico Farina in Toronto), the "crooners" in the Sinatra and Bennett vein, and the more recent pop tunes of the annual Italian San Remo Festivals. On the other

F

Bouquets of roses are being presented to members of the folk dance group Il Quartiere Italiano made up of students from California State University at Hayward. This group has just finished performing dances from different regions of Italy at Golden Gate Park, San Francisco. The event was conceived and organized by Augusto Troiani in 1982 to honor the memory of Giuseppe Garibaldi on the centennial of his death. The event is now called Italian Day at the Park and takes place the first Sunday in June. Courtesy Augusto Troiani.

hand, a variety of traditional song styles (sometimes referred to as *musica paesana*) still survives among clearly defined and relatively small groups (*villanella* singing among the Calabrians from Acri, or *zampogna* playing among Molisano mountain folk). Precious little survives of these orally transmitted family repertoires.

Early immigrant music halls provided venues for predominantly popular (rather than traditional) music forms as well as a stage for vaudeville (Farfariello and the immigrant theater of New York). The music halls also popularized performances of opera arias and other forms of theater such as puppet and marionette shows (*see* Manteo family and the Sicilian *opera dei pupi* in New York, inspired by the deeds of Charlemagne and Roland [Orlando]). Traditional dramatic forms of carnival mumming and all male dramatizations in the "mock wedding" tradition, and religious dramatization or pageants have now become extremely limited (the reenactment of the Holy Family seeking lodging is one aspect of St. Joseph's celebrations, Christmas pageants, and tableaux). The recitation of traditional narratives or songs, such as *novena* cycles leading up to a saint's day, also form part of this patrimony. Italian Carnival is experiencing a revival of sorts—not necessarily in the folk vein, but rather in the aristocratic Venetian tradition recently revived in Venice itself. The *cuccagna* or greased pole (a remnant of an ancient topos known as the *Paese di Cuccagna*—a "poor man's paradise") still survives at many festivals, while the beauty pageant (with the selection of a Miss Italia) has been borrowed from American tradition.

As far as games are concerned, soccer has come to be the Italian sport of choice among the younger generations rediscovering contemporary Italy. Yet by far the most popular traditional game for Italian immigrants is *bocce,* a variant of *boules* or *pétanque*: lawn bowling on hard ground. Among the games associated with earlier immigrants are the finger-counting game *morra*, the drinking games *passatella*, and *padrone e sottopadrone* (boss and underboss). Games using an Italian deck of forty cards (with its regional variations: *piemontesi, napoletane, triestine, modenesi*) still played are *scopa* (or *scopone*), *tresette, briscola,* and also lesser-known local and regional games such as *coteccio* for the Veneti.

From their earliest arrival to the present, Italian Americans have spawned a plethora of associations and clubs. Some were primarily mutual-aid and benevolent societies created for sustaining newly arrived immigrants, arranging relief for victims of the Depression, and so forth. Many of these societies formed around a hometown's patron saint's name, making the celebration of the banner saint a focus of their activities, along with the express purpose of raising funds for charities at home in Italy (an orphanage or hospital). Italian associations were largely a New World necessity by which many normally factious Italians learned to band together to effect change, maintain cohesion, and protect themselves from natural disasters and the human environment while celebrating the values and traditions they held most dear. Although in large urban centers with significant numbers of post–World War II Italians, a splintering of groups persists (for example, approximately twenty-five Abruzzese clubs in Toronto alone in the mid-1980s, with similar proliferation for Calabrians, Friulians, Sicilians); in older communities pan-Italian associations have evolved both from necessity and from fraternal idealism. Associations organize the major and minor social, religious, and civic events of the Italian community with a strong propensity toward the dinner dance.

In addition to such national organizations as the Order Sons of Italy and the National Italian American Foundation, the abundance of associations include professional associations (American Educators of Italian Origin United, American Italian Dental Association), sports clubs, philanthropic and cultural associations, associations devoted to Italian folk culture (Italian Folk Art Federation of America), and one dedicated to the study of the Italian experience in North America (American Italian Historical Association).

Luisa Del Giudice

Bibliography

Bianco, Carla. *The Two Rosetos.* Bloomington: Indiana University Press, 1974.

Del Giudice, Luisa, ed. *Studies in Italian American Folklore.* Logan: Utah State University Press, 1993.

Hobbie, Margaret, ed. *Italian American Material Culture: A Directory of Collections, Sites, and Festivals in the United States and Canada.* Westport, CT: Greenwood Press, 1992.

Malpezzi, Frances M., and William M. Clements. *Italian-American Folklore.* Little Rock: August House, 1992.

Mathias, Elizabeth L., and Richard Raspa. *Italian Folktales in America, The Verbal Art of an Immigrant Woman.* Detroit: Wayne State University Press, 1985.

Noyes, Dorothy. *Uses of Tradition: Arts of Italian Americans in Philadelphia.* Philadelphia: Philadelphia Folklore Project, 1989.

Taylor, David A., and John A. Williams, eds. *Old Ties, New Attachments: Italian-American Folklife in the West.* Washington, DC: Library of Congress, 1992.

Williams, Phyllis H. *South Italian Folkways in Europe and America: A Handbook for Social Workers, Visiting Nurses, School Teachers, and Physicians.* New Haven: Yale University Press, 1938. Reprint, New York: Russell and Russell, 1969.

See also FAMILY LIFE; FESTA; FOODWAYS AND FOOD; FUNERAL CUSTOMS; HOSPITALITY; PASSEGGIATA; RELIGION

Fontana, Marco Giovanni

See BUSINESS AND ENTREPRENEURSHIP

Foodways and Food

Italian American foodways may be viewed from three perspectives: (1) its core traditional foodways largely linked to Italian regional peasant culture (from earliest immigration to the 1950s), transmitted in various domestic and festive contexts; (2) "Italian American" cuisine that evolved in this country, with central-southern Italian cooking as its source and shared by mainstream America (e.g., pizza, spaghetti with meatballs); (3) the recent

Italian food revolution combining direct contact with Italian cuisine as evolved in the nouvelle era, with particular attention to the "Mediterranean diet," to regional Italian cuisines, and the rediscovery of Italian peasant food.

"Foodways" spans topics that range from what foods are eaten (their production, preparation, and preservation) to the various contexts in which food is found (domestic, ritual, commercial), food discourse, mythology, its symbolic value and its role as a marker of ethnic identity, and how food determines the use of domestic space (the place of kitchen, garden, and cantina within that space). Food discourse is a particularly rich area to explore. Food memory, family history, and immigrant narratives do much to help understand the perceived place of food in Italian American culture. Consider, for example, recurring food-centered narratives (in private discourse as well as in Italian American literature and film): the transmission of a secret family recipe (e.g., "wedding soup," Aunt Rosalia's tomato sauce), stowaway food from a journey to Italy (the "salami in the suitcase"), the power of memorable family gatherings and holiday celebrations, stories of hunger and poverty in the old country, encounters with American food and food habits (first-generation immigrants' school-lunch "trauma"), and so forth. How food figures in belief systems (food taboos, e.g., avoiding meat on Fridays and ritual foods, e.g., Sicilian braided breads on St. Joseph's tables) and in folk medicine (the traditional pharmocopeia, for example, consists essentially of common kitchen and garden ingredients: chamomile, oil, wine, garlic) are other worthy areas to examine in order to understand the Italian American food "system." There is perhaps no one other single factor that touches so many aspects of Italian American culture as does food.

The vast majority of the earliest to the immediate post–World War II immigrants maintained peasant diets and personally experienced hunger. The peasant diet, largely unaltered throughout the past three or four centuries until the 1960s, consisted of large quantities of greens, legumes, bread, and to a lesser degree pasta (in the center-south) or polenta and to a lesser degree rice (in the north). America, familiarly known as a *Paese di Cuccagna* (the mythic land of abundance where rivers ran with wine and mountains were made of cheese), became a mecca where *miseria di pane*—the most basic sort of hunger—practically disappeared overnight. It was in America that many "found, first of all, the meaning, the consumable, edible meaning, of a simple word, lost in the dictionary among thousands of others—the meaning of the word *abundance*." Yet the scars or "incarnate" memory of hunger—and *fear* of want—persisted in the immigrant psyche as did the countervailing desire to create abundance; jointly they continued to animate Italian American foodways long after hunger was defeated. Italian immigrants maintained their own vegetable garden, prepared and stocked the cantina (wine cellar) and later the freezer with all kinds of food, kept chickens, rabbits, pigeons, cured their own meat, made cheeses, produced wine, etc., in a semi-defensive, "cottage industry" sort of self-sufficiency.

Due to their peasant background, many Italians (particularly first-generation immigrants) still maintain an archaic relationship to land, perceiving it as capable of yielding wealth. Shade trees are replaced with fruit trees, flower beds with rows of vegetables. Even though gardens may have become greatly reduced (no longer featuring vegetables but now only herbs such as basil, Italian parsley, oregano, and rosemary), gardens continue to be an important part of Italian home life. Cultivating and harvesting Italian gardens nourishes both body and soul and literally reconnects Italian American to his or her roots, just as returning to Italy does. Many schedule return trips to Italy to coincide with various harvests and town feast days and often bring back prized edible "souvenirs." Garden, kitchen, and cantina hold—symbolically and practically—the key to realizing dreams of abundance.

This newfound abundance allowed Italians to add new items to their diet, items (such as meat and sweets) once exclusively used in the domain of the wealthy or reserved for festive occasions only. Additionally, this abundance undoubtedly contributed to the oversaucing, overspicing, and overcheesing of Italian American dishes. Angelo M. Pellegrino best describes the new Italian American gastronomy as the "naturalization of Italian cuisine" created out of food variety and abundance: Italians brought the grammatical structure to America, from America they adopted an expanded vocabulary. But traditional dishes, once associated with festive occasions,

Macaroni factory. The immigration of millions of Italians served as a catalyst for business enterprises that catered to the immigrants' desire for familiar food products. Courtesy Center for Migration Studies.

survived in their original state, evolving with only slight variations. Every family conserved their special egg-noodle dish and traditional sweet (e.g., Sicilian *cudureddi, cannoli, sfingi,* and *cassadini* or Neapolitan *sfogliatelle*) for Christmas or Easter, even though the home-made *fettuccine* or *lasagne* with meat sauce might well be followed by a traditional American turkey.

Early Italians contributed pasta (reduced to spaghetti/macaroni) and pizza to the American diet through family-style restaurants. Such restaurants purveyed a standard menu, among which featured prominently such items as: spaghetti with meatballs, chicken cacciatore, eggplant parmesan, and pepper and sausage sandwich. In time, a reduced Italian "haute" cuisine—lumped together with French—could be found at upscale "continental" restaurants as well.

The late 1970s and 1980s have witnessed an Italian food revolution due to a combination of factors. New health concerns brought greater attention to the "Mediterranean diet" and has given new currency to (largely southern) Italian food staples and to simple "country" cooking: fresh tomatoes, herbs, bread, pasta, olive oil, and cheese. The nouvelle trend featured fresh ingredients, quickly cooked with a minimum of elaboration, and the elimination of heavy ingredients such as butter and flour roux, *besciamella* (béchamel), and sauces. Further, the flow of Italian master chefs to America, along with food and wine products promoted by the Italian Chamber of Commerce, helped make this traditional cuisine and its ingredients known to a wider American audience. Professional restaurateurs, such as Piero Selvaggio in Los Angeles, have been instrumental in this redefinition of Italian food in America. Some of the items that have gained wide currency in the last ten years are: risotto (with arborio rice); polenta; fresh pasta; fresh herbs such as basil, rosemary, and Italian parsley; radicchio and arugula *(rucola)*; porcini mushrooms *(boletus edulis)*; balsamic vinegar; signature olive oils; prosciutto; parmigiano Reggiano; *mozzarella di bufala;* biscotti; panettone; rustic breads such as *ciabatta* or *pagnotta;* and espresso coffee. Markets ranging from large supermarkets and farmer's markets, to specialized catalogues and elite food "boutiques" catering to affluent clients with gourmet tendencies, have become the prime channels for the distribution of these foods.

Italian American family restaurants, characterized by heavy and rich red sauces and Chianti reds, have been complemented visually by dim lighting from candles in wine flasks, red-and-white-checkered tablecloths, murals of the Bay of Naples, statuary (Colosseum, leaning tower of Pisa, or Michelangelo's David), and family memorabilia (photos, passports, etc.). The food has been enhanced aurally by opera; by crooners such as Tony Bennett, Frank Sinatra, and Dean Martin; or with Neapolitan classics (such as *O Sole Mio, Torn'a Sorrento*). The elements of decor and music have been reciprocally affected by the new food revolution and are either going under or are undergoing varying degrees of "re-Italianization." Italian American foodways are in an ongoing state of flux.

As the tide turns away from spaghetti with red sauce, and toward elite "northern Italian" cuisine (a term often erroneously applied to central-southern dishes, betraying a disturbing and persistent anti-southern Italian and anti-immigrant bias), and finally toward Italian regional cuisine, which consists of, paradoxically, foods that were once exclusively in the domain of the Italian *contadino* or peasant—such as *panzanella, bruschetta, polenta, focaccia* (and even *pizza bianca* with nothing more than rosemary, for that matter), traditional Italian foodways are gaining gourmet status, just as Italian Americans were largely forgetting their own "country" cooking. In part, therefore, a food trend that goes beyond the ethnic community has helped reconnect Italian Americans to their Italian gastronomic heritage.

Luisa Del Giudice

Bibliography

Camporesi, Piero. *Il paese della fame.* Bologna, 1978.

Del Giudice, Luisa, ed. *Studies in Italian American Folklore.* Logan: Utah State University Press, 1993.

Malpezzi, Frances M., and William M. Clements. *Italian American Folklore.* Little Rock: August House, 1992.

Pellegrino, Angelo M. *The Unprejudiced Palate.* New York: Macmillan, 1952.

Sorcinelli, P. *Gli italiani e il cibo. appetti, digiuni e rinunce dalla realtà contadina alla societa del benessere.* Bologna, 1992.

See also FOLKWAYS, FOLKLIFE; HOSPITALITY

Francis, Connie (b. 1938)

The most popular female recording artist in America during the late 1950s and early 1960s, Connie Francis possessed a mellow and powerful voice that set her apart from other pop singers of the early rock music era. She was born Concetta Maria Franconero in Newark, New Jersey, the daughter of George Franconero, a dockworker at the Brooklyn Navy Yard, and Aida Ferrari. Her grandparents were from Calabria and Naples.

Francis, who grew up in Newark and in Belleville, New Jersey, commenced her musical career at age 4 with accordion lessons and was singing professionally by age 10. As a teenager, she made demonstration records for music publishers and sang on several New York–area television programs. She also made an appearance on the nationally televised *Arthur Godfrey's Talent Scouts.* It was Godfrey who suggested she change her name from Franconero to Francis.

In 1955, just before she graduated from Belleville High School, Francis signed a contract with Metro-Goldwyn-Mayer (MGM) Records. Her first notable recording was "Majesty of Love," a duet with Marvin Rainwater in 1957. The following year, Francis's up-tempo rendition of the old standard "Who's Sorry Now?" went to the top of the charts and established her as a major recording star. She bolstered her popularity with regular appearances on television's *American Bandstand.*

Although Francis, a petite, brown-eyed brunette, had great success with peppy, teen-oriented novelty tunes such as "Stupid Cupid" (1958) and "Lipstick on Your Collar" (1959), she was at her best with lush, romantic songs that showcased her vocal range. Her reworkings of the standards "My Happiness" (1958) and "Among My Souvenirs" (1959) sold millions of copies. She also recorded Italian songs, most notably "Jealous of You" *("Tango della Gelosia")* in 1960. Sung half in English, half in Italian, the song was a hit in Italy.

Francis made her film debut in *Where the Boys Are* (1960), a comedy about college students on spring break in Florida. Her recording of the film's title song was another million seller. Francis's popularity continued into the early 1960s with "Don't Break the Heart that Loves You" (1962) and "Follow the Boys" (1963). Francis's appeal to young record buyers waned in the mid-1960s. Turning to older audiences, she performed in nightclubs and recorded albums in Italian, French, German, and Japanese for the international market. A rape and robbery attack in 1974 sent Francis into an emotional tailspin, and she temporarily abandoned her career. In the 1980s she returned to performing and published her autobiography. Francis has been married four times and has one child.

Mary C. Kalfatovic

Bibliography

Francis, Connie. *Who's Sorry Now?*. New York: St. Martin's Press, 1984.

Jennings, Dean. "Girl on the Glamour-Go-Round." *Saturday Evening Post*, 23 September 1961, 38–44.

See also POP SINGERS

Franzoni, Carlo and Giuseppe
See ART

Fratti, Mario (b. 1927)

The prolific, prize-winning playwright Mario Fratti, born in L'Aquila, Italy, earned his doctorate in languages and literature from the University of Ca'Foscari, completed his military service in the Italian army, and settled into teaching and writing—a novel, two volumes of poetry, and a mass of criticism—before completing his first full-length play, *The Third Daughter* (1959).

He came to America in 1963 as theater correspondent for the Italian press and has remained to earn the most prestigious drama awards for his more than seventy plays. Among these are *The Cage* (1977); *Suicide* (1986); *Return* (1986); *Refusal* (1972); *Refrigerators* (1977); *The Academy* (1977); *Seducers* (1972); *Victim* (1978); *Che Guevara* (1970); *Young Wife* (1983); *Birthday* (1974); *Mothers and Daughters* (1972 & 1975); *Eleonora Duse* (1967, 1980); *Mafia* (1971); *Gift* (1963, 1972); *Bridge* (1972); *Lovers* (1990); *Friends* (1972, 1995); *Encounter* (1991); *A.I.D.S.* (1987); *Porno* (1987); *Two Centuries* (1990); *Dolls No More* (1973); *Family* (1972, 1995); *Sister* (1972); and *Leningrad* (1996). His works have been performed to critical acclaim in eighteen languages in more than six hundred theaters around the world. His adaptation of the musical *Nine*, based on Fellini's *8½*, won the O'Neill

Connie Francis. An ever popular performer from New Jersey, she recorded major hits that attracted a wide general audience. She was especially popular among Italian Americans. *Courtesy Joseph Fioravanti.*

Selection Award, the Richard Rodgers Award, The Outer Critics Circle Award, the Leone di San Marco Literary Award, the Heritage and Culture Award, eight Drama Desk Awards, and five Tony Awards.

Fratti has two children from his first wife, Lina Fedrigo: Mirko and Barbara. In 1964 he married the concert pianist Laura Dubman; their daughter, Valentina, was born in 1965. From 1967 to 1995 Fratti served as professor of Italian at Hunter College of the City University of New York. Although now retired from teaching, he continues to write and participate actively in all aspects of theater production and criticism.

While Fratti has experimented with differing dramatic forms, above all he is a satirist whose cool, cerebral wit penetrates to the secret agendas driving people into chicanery, dishonesty, and deceit. Typically, his inventive and concise plots compel characters and audiences to confront the reality beneath everyday experiences and events. Apparently commonplace situations—a telephone call, a chance meeting of acquaintances—grow increasingly complex as he probes into miscommunications that eventually explode into grotesque revelations and unwelcome truths. Simple dialogue echoes with

Prize-winning playwright, novelist, poet, and critic Mario Fratti, 1989. Courtesy Frank J. Cavaioli.

the evasions, small treacheries, and betrayals out of which Fratti makes dramatic capital. These characteristics have led some critics to associate him with Absurdists, though he shares none of their nihilistic view of a basically meaningless world. Nor do his plays "develop" from early to late; from the first they demonstrate the competence of a "born playwright," in the words of Erich Maria Remarque.

Several of his longer plays written in Italian during the 1960s examine the psychosis of postwar life and the twisted rationalizations of individuals struggling to survive. Among these, the best known is *The Cage* (1961), a drama about an idealist unable to cope with the horrors of working class life in Milan; he isolates himself from all human contact by literally locking himself in a cage, which serves as the play's central conceit. Equally celebrated is the later *The Academy* (1972), a one-act farce about a Roman school of gigolos learning how to prey on lonely American women. Differing in genre and tone, both nonetheless reveal Fratti's egalitarian and socialist principles, as well as the dry incisiveness that distinguishes his style.

In more recent plays written in English and often set in New York City, Fratti casts his ironic eye on American social habits, values, and relationships, from sexual to familial to political. His ethical consciousness remains acute

and his imagination vivid; but the satire is darker and its targets—hatred, humiliation, lovelessness—describe a civilization in crisis. Several one-act plays in the collection *Races* (1972) dramatize desire between interracial couples locked either in disguised aggression or violent warfare. Four newer plays in the Italian collection *Teatro italiano contemporaneo* (1995) express desperate desires for communion among friends, lovers, and relations who either fail to connect or destroy those who do. The optimistic psychiatrist in *Family* (1992), for instance, presides over a bizarre family of patients who rape, murder, and brutalize as a result of his permissive approach to treatment. Fratti implies that the doctor's abdication of responsibility is endemic among institutions and professions.

In the European tradition of theater as a forum for critical ideas, Fratti's mission as a playwright is to communicate a vision of humanity not as it wishes to be, but as it is. He shares this aim with all satirists, who dramatize vice in an effort to awaken a social conscience.

Nina daVinci Nichols

Bibliography

Bonin, Jane F. *Mario Fratti.* Twayne Authors Series. Boston: G. K. Hall, 1982.

Corrigan, Robert W. "The Disavowal of Identity in the Contemporary Theatre." In *The New Theatre of Europe,* 15–27. New York: Dell, 1964.

Mignone, Mario. "It teatro de Mario Fratti e la lotta per la sopravvivenza." *La Parola del Popolo* 27, no. 134 (1976): 183–289.

Nichols, Nina daVinci. "The Way of the World According to Mario Fratti." *Modern Drama* 36, no. 4 (1993): 519–529.

See also PLAYS, CONTEMPORARY; THEATER HISTORY

Frazetta, Frank
See CARTOONISTS AND ILLUSTRATORS

Freeh, Louis
See LAW ENFORCEMENT

Fugazi, Giovanni F. (1838–1916)
Businessman, banker, and philanthropist Gio-

vanni F. Fugazi was born on February 12, 1838, in Santo Stefano della Badia, province of Milan, Italy, and spent his boyhood there before coming to America in 1855. He traveled the American South and Midwest, married, and had four children before going west to California.

He arrived in San Francisco (the exact date uncertain) and established two short-lived, relatively unsuccessful businesses: hair products, Tintura di Capelli Orientale, and a newspaper, *La Scintille Italiana*. By the late 1870s, however, he had achieved success in the travel business as John F. Fugazi and Co., agency Casa Italo-Svizzera-Americana (C. Palmieri partner), selling tickets for several steamship lines, including the White Star Line and Compagnie Générale Transatlantique. By the turn of the twentieth century, his two sons, James and Samuel, were working with the Fugazi firm.

Although Fugazi retired in 1911 from the travel business, he continued his other businesses. In January 1893 he had established the Columbus Savings and Loan Society. Called Banca Colombo, the bank had twenty subscribers and a capital stock of some three hundred thousand dollars. It prospered, and by 1900 its resources exceeded a million dollars. Around 1905 Fugazi relinquished his position as bank president. In 1923 Banca Colombo merged with Andrea Sbarboro's Italian American Bank, and, in 1927, the combined Banca Colombo–Italian American Bank merged with A. P. Giannini's Bank of Italy.

When an earthquake and fire destroyed much of San Francisco in 1906, Fugazi provided rebuilding capital by opening a new bank, Banca Popolare Operaia Italiana. Incorporated in 1906, he opened the bank with $250,000 in capital. Its board of directors included men and women from the Italian community. The second Fugazi bank did well, and, by the time of Fugazi's death in 1916, the bank's resources reached $7 million. In 1928 Fugazi's bank merged with the United Bank & Trust Company of San Francisco, a bank later absorbed by Giannini's Bank of America National Trust and Savings Association.

With the money he made in banking and the travel agency, Fugazi turned to philanthropy. He supported a number of Italian community organizations, such as the Garibaldi Guards (a quasi-military and social organization) and the Società Italiana di Mutua Beneficenza and its Italian Cemetery in Colma, California. Before Fugazi's second wife's death, the

Fugazis built a multistoried edifice called Casa Coloniale Fugazi at 678 Green Street and endowed it with a twenty thousand dollar maintenance fund. Formally opened on February 12, 1913, Casa Fugazi stands as one of Fugazi's most important contributions to the Italian American community and to the city of San Francisco. Today, Italian American organizations use the building, and Beach Blanket Babylon, a cabaret show, remains its most famous resident.

When Fugazi died on June 4, 1916, the phrase *Il papa della colonia* (the father of the colony) truly described his importance to the Italians of San Francisco and, even in death, his mausoleum at the Italian Cemetery towers over those around him. In recognition of his philanthropy and community activities, the Italian Government conferred on this Italian immigrant the title of Cavaliere Ufficiale, a title that Fugazi proudly appended to his name until his death.

Philip M. Montesano

Bibliography

Canepa, Andrew M. "Seventy Five Years of Fugazi Hall: The Story of a Building, a Man and a Community." In *Casa Coloniale Italiana John F. Fugazi*. 21–28. San Francisco: Italian Welfare Agency, 1988.

Cross, Ira B. *Financing an Empire: History of Banking in California*. 4 vols. San Francisco: S. J. Clarke, 1927.

Gumina, Deanna. *The Italians of San Francisco, 1850–1930*. New York: Center for Migration Studies, 1978.

Montesano, Philip M. "John F. Fugazi: Businessman, Banker, Community Leader and Philanthropist." In *Casa Coloniale Italiana John F. Fugazi*, 30–34. San Francisco: Italian Welfare Agency, 1988.

See also BUSINESS AND ENTREPRENEURSHIP

Fugazy Family

The Fugazy family clan, which has had a place of prominence in the business world on the East Coast since 1870, can trace its roots to a small private bank founded in Greenwich Village by Louis V. Fugazy. When Fugazy died, the law required that the family sell the bank's charter. However, it retained the travel department, which functioned as the Fugazy Travel Bureau. Fugazy's grandson Louis, along with William, his younger brother, built the travel bureau into an international agency. They promoted Italian American tourism to Italy, and in 1951, in recognition of this, the Italian government made grandson Louis a Commander of the Order of St. George.

Louis, a Columbia University graduate, was a boxing enthusiast who became the 1935 Flyweight New York City Golden Gloves champion. Later, he also became a United States Navy boxing champion. In these prewar years, Louis was active in resettling Jewish refugees. He retired from Fugazy International in 1980.

Louis's younger brother, William, a graduate of Cornell University, built Fugazy International into a multimillion-dollar enterprise. He served as an intelligence officer in the United States Naval Reserve during World War II. This family-owned business included a variety of corporate transportation services, such as fleet buses and limousines, and a nationwide network of franchised travel agencies. By 1960 William had nursed this small family business into a 150-branch Fugazy Travel business. He believed that the best business contacts were made on the golf course, turning personal associations into business deals. Some of Fugazy's friends included Frank Sinatra, Bob Hope, Roy Cohn, Jackie Gleason, Gerald R. Ford, and Terence Cardinal Cooke. Through his friends in the sports world, for example, and as president of Feature Sports, Inc., he and Roy Cohn promoted championship fights such as the Floyd Patterson–Ingemar Johansson fight in 1964. In tandem with another friend, Lee Iacocca, of the Ford Motor Company, Fugazy pulled Lincoln Continental into the transportation business. Iacocca contracted with Fugazy, and Fugazy Continental Corporation became the first of seven subsidiaries of what is now Fugazy International.

In the 1990s Fugazy International faced many financial difficulties. It fell behind in payments to its vendors and banks. Unhappy franchisees have sued, and the company also owes back taxes to New York State.

Despite financial strains, William Fugazy, a prominent Roman Catholic layman, remains active in church and charitable affairs.

Charles La Cerra

Bibliography

Iorizzo, Luciano J. "The R. G. Dun Collection's Assessment of Merchants: A Neglected Source of Italian-American Studies." In *The Columbus People*, edited by Lydio F. Tomasi, Piero Gastaldo, and Thomas Row, 509–521. New York: Center for Migration Studies, 1994.

Morgenson, Gretchen. "The Lovable Rogue." *Forbes* (October 1990): 80–82.

See also BUSINESS AND ENTREPRENEURSHIP

Funeral Customs

Italian American funeral customs have reflected a heritage traceable to Old World roots, but have also responded to the expectations and demands of life in a new sociocultural environment. Italian immigrants brought beliefs and practices associated with death—including omens presaging its occurrence, funeral and burial procedures, and conventions regarding mourning. Immigrants also influenced their customs with desires to improve their economic circumstances and to emulate mainstream American ways. In addition, Catholic Church regulations brought about changes. People from peasant backgrounds often adopted practices similar to those of the Italian gentry, particularly elaborate floral decorations, funeral bands, and sometimes even paid mourners.

Early in the twentieth century, funeral Masses occurred only after a wake, which ideally lasted forty-eight hours. Wreaths in such shapes as the throne in heaven awaiting the deceased or a clock with hands stopped at the time of death surrounded the body, dressed in its best finery, as family members maintained a round-the-clock vigil. While the wake lacked the festive spirit associated with similar customs in other ethnic communities, it did provide an opportunity for socializing and for sampling an array of foods. (Minestrone was recommended as a way of restoring fluids lost in weeping.) While food might be provided by friends of the family, the deceased might have joined a burial society in anticipation of other expenses associated with the wake, Mass, and burial. Sometimes the custom of *poste,* or burial debt, assisted with expenses: someone would collect contributions from those who came to the wake, keeping a record so that the bereaved family could reciprocate when the need arose.

Traditionally, wakes took place at home, funeral homes being considered too impersonal a place to leave the remains of a dead family member. But many funeral homes came to have distinct regional identities so that a family could use the services of a *paesano* (fellow townsfolk). Undertakers came to be central figures in Italian American communities. Moreover, family members staying with the body throughout the night mitigated the impersonality of a commercial establishment.

Mourners might offer to the body objects representative of the deceased's interests. Typically, these included jewelry, religious medals, and favorite clothing, but bocce balls and wine bottles also found their way into the casket to accompany the deceased into the grave.

Once the body had been taken to the funeral home or to the church from where it was to be buried, folk custom required that arrangements be made at home to ward off the contaminating influences of death. Turning mirrors to the wall, draping them in black for a week after the funeral, not doing any cleaning for the same period, and sprinkling salt in the corners were among the prophylactics against the contagion of death practiced by some Italian Americans. It was also inadvisable to return directly home after attending a wake or funeral. Stopping at a public place lessened the chances that death would follow one home. Nor should a funeral attendant pay a visit on the way home, since doing so might cause someone in that household to become sick.

Perpetual care cemeteries have eliminated the practical need for family gatherings at the burial site of a loved one in order to maintain the physical appearance of the grave location. Yet family assemblies allow an opportunity for the living to regain a sense of community with those who have died. On occasions such as the anniversary of the death, the deceased's saint's day, or Memorial Day (referred to as "Decoration Day"), families might bring a picnic lunch to eat among the tombstones of their loved ones. While Italian American tombstones may still be imposing monuments, few are now adorned with the porcelain photographs of the deceased that once characterized these ethnic burial sites. But the graves of Italian Americans may still be identified on Palm Sunday when they are decorated with palms woven into elaborate symbolic shapes and affixed to cardboard crosses and hearts.

Frances M. Malpezzi
William M. Clements

Bibliography
Cowell, Daniel David. "Funerals, Family, and Forefathers: A View of Italian-American Funeral Practices." *Omega* 16, no. 1 (1985–86): 69–85.
Malpezzi, Frances M., and William M. Clements. *Italian-American Folklore.* Little Rock: August House, 1992.
Mathias, Elizabeth. "The Italian-American Funeral: Persistence Through Change." *Western Folklore* 33 (1974): 35–50.
Williams, Phyllis A. *South Italian Folkways in Europe and America: A Handbook for Social Workers, Visiting Nurses, School Teachers, and Physicians.* New York: Russell and Russell, 1969.

See also FOLKLORE, FOLKLIFE

F

G

Gabriele, Charles (b. 1921)

An internationally noted composer of classical music, best known in America for patriotic marches, Charles Gabriele was born on May 31, 1921, in New York City. His father was an electrical engineer and his mother an accomplished pianist. He began his study of music at age 12 after seeing Giuseppi Creatore conduct *Il Guarany* Overture and vowed that he would one day compose a stirring overture. His *Lilia Craig* Overture accomplished this goal. As a youth he played flute in the Stuyvesant High School Band and in the orchestra of the historic Henry Street Settlement. At age 16, he directed a wind ensemble at the Verdi monument, New York City, in commemoration of *Aida*.

Gabriele majored in music at New York University, where his mentor was Charles Haubiel, professor of composition. He also attended other schools and holds a B.A., M.A., Ph.D., and an honorary degree of doctor of music. He served in the military as a Navy public information officer and composer-in-residence of the United States Naval Academy Band, Annapolis. As an educator he was on the faculty of Rutgers Uni-versity, the University of Maryland, and other schools.

Gabriele's awards and honors include the Patrick Henry Patriotic Achievement Award, Cavaliere in the Order of Merit of the Republic of Italy, and United States Congressional Commendation. On August 10, 1988, at the Vatican, he presented Pope John Paul II a copy of his *Ave Maria for Band and Chorus*. His *Christopher Columbus* Suite was designated the Official Music of the Christopher Columbus Quincentenary Celebration, and on October 8, 1989, at 3:00 p.m., EST, it pre-miered on radio and television stations simultaneously around the world as a kickoff to the start of the Quincentenary Jubilee. He guest conducted at Genoa Expo '92 and an "All Gabriele" concert was presented June 16, 1992, in his honor at the Verdi Theatre, Genoa. Gabriele was project officer for the Genoa Philarmonica American Tour, which included a performance at the White House.

Gabriele is a member of the American Society of Composers, Authors and Publishers (ASCAP); Phi Mu Alpha Music Fraternity; and the United States Naval Academy Band Alumni Association. His other major compositions include *Concertino for Clarinet* (1992); *Pinocchio* (1993); *Il Gallo Lirico, Retaggio* (1994); *Espana Nuestra* (1990); *Queen Isabella* (1987); *John Paul Jones March* (1989); *Vietnam Veterans March* (1984); *Korea Veterans March* (1984); *Armed Forces Medley* (1996) (arr.); and *Pass in Review and National Guardians March* (1990). Dr. Gabriele resides with his wife, Marion, in Venice, Florida.

Charles Gabriele

Bibliography

Camp, Amos T., "Composer of March Made Honorary Member." *The Graybeards* 10, no. 2: 21.

Encyclopedia of Band Music. Vol. 1, 267.

Gleason, Pamela, "Meet Columbus' Ambassador of Music." *The Italic Way* 5, no. 1 (spring-summer 1992): 3.

The Korean War Veterans Association (November–December 1995).

Mancini, John L., "Columbus Set to Music." *The Italic Way* 2, no. 3 (summer 1989): 26.

See also COMPOSERS, CLASSICAL

Gallo, Robert Charles (b. 1937)

Known for having discovered and isolated the virus that is linked to leukemia, Dr. Robert C. Gallo is also a co-discoverer, with Frenchman Dr. Luc Montagnier, of the AIDS virus. He was born on March 23, 1937, in Waterbury, Connecticut.

His parents migrated from northern Italy. His father, a self-made metallurgist, owned his own welding company. Tragedy struck unexpectedly when Robert was 13 years old: his younger sister, Judith, contracted leukemia. The family was devastated by her death. Also, Robert broke his back playing basketball during his senior year at high school.

The family friend and pathologist, Dr. Marcus Cox, who had diagnosed his sister's ailment, guided Robert during his long convalescence, deftly neutralizing the boy's acquired negativism toward medicine and science. Indeed, as soon as he was able, young Robert began spending his Saturdays following Dr. Cox on his rounds at St. Mary's Hospital. As his admiration for the doctor grew, Robert resolved to become a researcher and a doctor.

Gallo graduated from Providence College in Rhode Island in 1959 and entered Thomas Jefferson Medical College in Philadelphia. While still a student, he conducted experiments involving the growth of red blood cells. Officials at the National Cancer Institute in Bethesda, Maryland, were impressed by his published account of that research and hired him in 1965 as a clinical associate. In three short years he advanced to the post of senior investigator in the laboratory of human tumor-cell biology. Inevitably, his research focused on studying leukocytes.

In 1978 the research pursued by Gallo and his staff bore fruit. One of the variants of his HTL (human T-cell leukemia) virus was identified as a cause of leukemia. This marked the first time that a cancer-causing virus had been found in humans. For that achievement, Gallo was honored with the Albert Lasker Award, and he was invited to lecture at the most prestigious organizations.

His next research culminated in May of 1984 when Gallo and his team identified the human T-cell leukemia virus (HTLV-III B) as responsible for AIDS; they had also developed a blood test to screen for the disease. However, controversy soon vitiated the great satisfaction initially enjoyed. For a team of scientists at the Pasteur Institute in Paris, led by Professor Luc Montagnier, claimed prior discovery of the AIDS virus. Their virus, LAV, was proven virtually identical to Gallo's HTLV-III.

In 1986 Gallo and Montagnier and their respective teams were the co-recipients of the Albert and Mary Lasker Foundation Award that honored "their unique contributions to the understanding of AIDS." In the fall of 1990 the American team and the French team acknowledged each other's crucial contributions and concluded that both III B and LAV cause AIDS. The American team of thirty-odd researchers continues work at the National Cancer Institute. The ultimate goal is a vaccine to prevent AIDS and halt its transmission.

Gallo is married to Mary Jane Hayes, and they have three sons. His book, *Virus Hunting,* was published in 1991.

Margherita Marchione

Bibliography

Marchione, Margherita. *Americans of Italian Heritage.* New York: University Press of America, 1995.

Who's Who Among Italian Americans. Ed. Serena V. Cantoni. Washington, DC: The National Italian American Foundation, n.d.

See also MEDICINE; SCIENCE

Gambera, Giacomo (1856–1934)

Born September 17, 1856, in Lumezzane Piave, Brescia, to Benedetto Gambera, a landowner and town official, and his wife, Teresa Falconi, Giacomo Gambera decided to become a priest at age 12. He received his education at the local seminary and was ordained May 31, 1879. He served briefly as an assistant to his uncle, and for almost ten years he was pastor of Saint Zenone, Brione. He became acquainted with Bishop Giovanni Battista Scalabrini and his community of clergy, the Society of Saint Charles, which included Scalabrinians, who ministered to Italian immigrants, and the Saint Raphael Society for the Protection of Italian Immigrants. From May to November 1889 Gambera was at the Scalabrinians' Christopher Columbus Institute in Piacenza. He embarked for the United States on November 20, 1889.

Gambera spent the rest of his long life among American Italians. From December 1889 to October 1893 Gambera worked in

New Orleans; he was there during the 1891 lynching, and it was he who called Frances Xavier Cabrini to the Crescent City. From 1893 to 1895 he was at Saint Peter's in Pittsburgh. From 1895 to 1901 he served as pastor of the Scalabrinians' second-oldest mission, Sacred Heart, Boston; from 1897 to 1901 he was also provincial superior. He resigned both positions in 1901 and became director of the New York branch of the Saint Raphael Society. In 1905 he became the first Scalabrinian pastor of Santa Maria Addolorata, Chicago.

In 1921 he returned to Italy to recuperate from illness. He hoped to retire there, but he had no pension and the Scalabrinians wanted him in the mission field. On January 21, 1926, he returned to Chicago as chaplain of Columbus (now Cabrini) Hospital in Chicago. On May 5, 1928, he entered semiretirement at Our Lady of Pompeii in New York City. He died there on August 13, 1934, and is buried in the Scalabrinian plot at Calvary Cemetery, Queens. It was in retirement that Gambera made his lasting contribution to Italian American studies when he wrote his memoirs. They are a valuable source of information on urban Little Italies, Italian American Catholicism, the development of the Scalabrinians, and the ethnic perspective during the Roaring Twenties. His papers are at the Center for Migration Studies, Staten Island, New York.

Mary Elizabeth Brown

Bibliography

Gambera, Giacomo. *A Migrant Missionary Story: The Autobiography of Giacomo Gambera.* New York: Center for Migration Studies, 1994.

See also RELIGION

Garibaldi, Giuseppe (1807–1882)

Italian nationalist revolutionary, once resident on Staten Island, New York, who was offered a Union army generalship during the American Civil War, Giuseppe Garibaldi was born on July 4, 1907, at Nizza (Nice) along the Ligurian coast in Napoleonic France. His father was the pious Catholic merchant captain Domenico Garibaldi, and his mother was Rosa Raimondi; they wanted him to become a lawyer or priest, two professions he grew to detest.

Garibaldi saw Rome for the first time in 1825; its ancient buildings recalled Italy's former glories and stirred him to associate with revolutionary groups struggling for the country's independence, unity, and liberty. Convicted of treason, Garibaldi departed for South America, where he lived for twelve years (1836–1848). There he led guerrillas against Brazil and commanded an Italian Legion of Redshirts (a force for national unification) during Uruguayan resistance to Argentina. When revolutions and war broke out in Italy, he returned home and led an ill-fated defense of the Roman Republic (1849).

Again forced to leave his homeland, the revolutionary arrived in the United States (July 1850). He filed for citizenship, began to learn English, and was issued a passport. Although he did not complete the formalities of naturalization, he later claimed to be an American. He joined a Masonic lodge, applied for work at the post office, and tried to sign up as an ordinary seaman. The Florentine Antonio Meucci employed him as a candlewick maker on Staten Island for several months. After sailing to Latin America and the Orient, Garibaldi returned to the United States (September 1853), where he visited Boston, New York, and Baltimore.

In May 1854 Garibaldi returned to his native country and bought a homestead on Caprera, an island between Corsica and Sardinia. By the end of the decade, Sardinia-Piedmont united all of Italy, except Venice, Rome, and the south. Learning of a revolt in Sicily (1860), Garibaldi gathered one thousand Redshirts and departed from Liguria for western Sicily. Sardinia-Piedmont annexed the south after his volunteers captured Palermo (June) and Naples (September).

Soon after the attack on Fort Sumter, the Lincoln administration offered Garibaldi a major general's commission in the Union army (June 1861). The "Soldier of Freedom" agreed to serve the Union cause on condition that Abraham Lincoln assure him that the war was not a political conflict but really a struggle against slavery; and secondly, that Lincoln appoint him commander-in-chief of all Union forces. The president's concern about the preservation of the federal union, as well as

The Garibaldi Guard was a multiethnic regiment containing Italian Americans who fought for the Union cause during the American Civil War. It upheld the principles of Italian patriot Giuseppe Garibaldi. This certificate indicates acceptance of C. Boero into membership of the Garibaldi Guard of San Francisco on February 14, 1885. Courtesy Augusto Troiani.

the constitutional provision that only the president could be commander-in-chief, precluded Garibaldi's receiving the necessary assurances. Yet he regarded the United States as his "second country." On August 6, 1863, after Union victories at Gettysburg and Vicksburg, Garibaldi addressed Lincoln as the "great emancipator" and "a true heir of the teaching given us by Christ and [John] Brown."

The "hero of two worlds" last appeared on the battlefield during his unsuccessful revolutionary attack on papal Rome (1867). Dislike for political factionalism after unification (1870) led to his retirement as a semirecluse on Caprera, where he died at age 75, June 2, 1882.

James J. Divita

Bibliography

Hibbert, Christopher. *Garibaldi and His Enemies.* New York: New American Library, 1970.

Mack Smith, Denis, ed. *Garibaldi.* Englewood Cliffs, NJ: Prentice-Hall, 1969.

See also WARTIME MILITARY AND HOME FRONT ACTIVITIES

Gatti-Casazza, Giulio (1869–1940)

This world-renowned opera impresario was born in Udine, February 3, 1869, attended the Universities of Bologna and Ferrara, and graduated as an engineer from the Naval Engineering School at Genoa. Abandoning engineering, he succeeded his father as director of the Teatro Comunale in Ferrara in 1893. His success at this community opera company secured him a position as director, in 1898, of La Scala in Milan, which became the most prestigious opera house in Italy under his leadership. In 1908 he was invited to become manager and director of the Metropolitan Opera in New York, remaining there until 1935, the longest managerial tenure in the history of this prestigious company.

While at the Metropolitan he made a number of improvements and innovations, and his administration was the most successful period ever, financially and artistically, for the Metropolitan. He brought with him from La Scala the soon-to-be legendary conductor Arturo Toscanini, who stayed at the Metropolitan until 1915. He also had as supporting talents the noted Italian choral conductor Giulio Setti, the prominent American theatrical set designer Joseph Urban, and the best singers, such as Italy's Enrico Caruso and Norway's Kirsten Flagstad. He introduced a number of American operas and ballets, and even offered a ten thousand dollar prize to encourage American composers. Also, about 110 foreign operas had their premieres at the Metropolitan, including well-known works such as Engelbert Humperdinck's *Die Königskinder* (The king's children) (1910), Umberto Giordano's *Madame Sans-Gêne* (1915), Enrique Granados' *Goyescas* (1916), and even one of the great Giacomo Puccini's best, *La Fanciulla del West* (The girl of the golden West) (1910). In addition, he revived a number of older European operas, for example, one of the finest works of Christoph von Gluck, *Iphigénie en Tauride* (1779).

Gatti's best period at the Metropolitan was his early years, and in time his concepts started to become stale. The Great Depression, which started in 1929, exacerbated the already vulnerable and shaky policies of Gatti, and in 1935, two years after he finished his memoirs, he resigned. He returned to Italy to retire with his second wife, Rosina Galli, the prima ballerina at the Metropolitan, whom he married in 1930. (In 1929 he had divorced his first wife, New Zealand soprano Frances Alda, whom he had married in 1910.) Gatti died in Ferrara, September 2, 1940, the locale of his first artistic successes.

Despite his less than ideal later years at the Metropolitan Opera, Gatti was a key innovator in making the New York company one of the premiere opera houses in the world. He was also notable for bringing together top talents from both Europe and America and making available to American audiences some of the better contemporary operas of Europe. Thus, he was not just a successful impresario but also a man of international vision.

William E. Studwell

Bibliography

Gatti-Casazza, Giulio. *Memories of the Opera*. New York: Scribner, 1941.
Kolodin, Irving. *The Metropolitan Opera, 1883–1966*. 4th ed. New York: Alfred A. Knopf, 1966.

See also OPERA

Genealogy and Family History

Many ethnic groups are in danger of losing their unique customs and traditions through the ongoing assimilation process into American culture. One way of keeping the ethnic culture alive is to research and record a family's history. The field of genealogy and family history offers guidance for Italian Americans who wish to pursue an interest in their heritage and their ancestors.

Genealogy (tracing one's ancestral lineage) and family history (in-depth research emphasizing whole families) are branches of history and the social sciences. Scholarly genealogical and family history research requires an inquisitive and analytical mind. There is great emphasis on presenting evidence of genealogical connections and documenting all facts.

A family history project begins with basic information: names, dates, and places. In order to research Italian immigrants and continue the search in Italian records, it is necessary to learn the ancestor's full original name,

the date, and place of birth. This information is usually obtained through oral family history interviews or by looking at such documents as passports; citizenship papers; alien registration cards; and birth, marriage, or death certificates, which may be found among family papers.

All this statistical information should be recorded on pedigree charts and family group sheets, noting from where each piece of information came. These forms may be purchased from organizations such as the National Genealogical Society, 4527 17th St. North, Arlington, VA 22207-2399.

General genealogical research methods and sources can be gleaned from a basic how-to book, such as Ralph Crandall's *Shaking Your Family Tree* (1987) or Val Greenwood's *The Researchers Guide to American Genealogy* (1990). After obtaining and researching such basic historical documents as vital records, censuses, and passenger arrival lists, researchers can move on to study a specialized guidebook, such as *Finding Italian Roots* (1993) by John Philip Colletta. More detailed information on family records in Italy can be found in Trafford Cole's *Italian Genealogical Records* (1995).

Many American and Italian records can be obtained through mail request, or they may have been microfilmed by the Church of Jesus Christ of Latter Day Saints (LDS). These microfilmed records are available at the LDS Family History Library in Salt Lake City, Utah, or through one of their many Family History Centers located throughout the country. The only charge is the rental fee for ordering microfilm through their loan service at their centers.

Two of the most common mistakes some genealogical researchers make when tracking their Italian origins are isolating research on one ancestor or family and "jumping the ocean" to start research in Italy before thoroughly exhausting American records.

It is entirely possible to trace the wrong ancestors if each generation in America has not been thoroughly researched and documented. While investigating particular ancestors, researchers should also take note of friends, relatives, and possible acquaintances who lived near immigrant family members. Problems in finding records on a particular ancestor are often overcome when the research is expanded to include members from the same community of the ancestors in question; these neighbors may have generated documents that will aid in the genealogical search.

The trend in scholarly genealogy is shifting; no longer are sophisticated genealogists satisfied with just names, dates, and places. They want to go beyond the skeletal pedigree chart and family group sheet—the who, where, and when—to uncover the person behind the name—the why, how, and what was it like? Why did an ancestor come to America? How did the ancestor cope upon arrival? What was it like to be a stranger in a strange land? Genealogical records do not ordinarily reveal this information, leaving gaps in the details needed to write the family history. In order to supplement the information found in records, genealogical scholars now study Italian American social history: the broader, common experiences and trends, the day-to-day activities, and the folkways of Italian Americans to blend with a specific family history.

Researching Italian American genealogy and family history is a fun and challenging way to learn about those who have preceded us. By supplementing with social history, the names on a chart become flesh and blood people. In the latter half of the twentieth century when Italian families are often split by distance and there may be a loss of culture and tradition, researching and recording a family's history is imperative to maintaining a sense of heritage.

Sharon DeBartolo Carmack

Bibliography

Cole, Trafford R. *Italian Genealogical Records: How to Use Italian Civil, Ecclesiastical, and Other Records in Family History Research.* Salt Lake City: Ancestry, 1995.

Colletta, John P. *Finding Italian Roots: The Complete Guide for Americans.* Baltimore: Genealogical Publishing, 1993.

Crandall, Ralph. *Shaking Your Family Tree.* Dublin, NH: Yankee Publishing, 1987.

Glazier, Ira A., and P. William Filby, eds. *Italians to America: Lists of Passengers Arriving at U.S. Ports 1880–1899.* 12 vols. projected. Wilmington, DE: Scholarly Resources, 1993– .

Greenwood, Val D. *The Researcher's Guide to American Genealogy.* 2d ed. rev. Baltimore: Genealogical Publishing, 1990.

Author's note: For more information, contact the Italian Genealogical Society of America, P.O. Box 8571, Cranston, RI 02920-8571.

See also ASSIMILATION

Gennaro, Peter (b. 1924)

One of America's finest jazz dancers and a leading choreographer of television variety programs and Broadway musicals, Peter Gennaro was born in Metaire, Louisiana, the son of Italian immigrant parents, Charles Gennaro and Conchetta (née Sabello). He studied dance as a child and, after serving in World War II, used the GI Bill to further his dance training.

Gennaro's first professional performing job was with Chicago's San Carlo Opera Company, where he met ballet dancer Margaret Jean Kinsella, whom he married. In 1954, after dancing in the ensembles of several Broadway musicals, Gennaro achieved acclaim as one of the original trio who performed "Steam Heat," the dance in *The Pajama Game* that introduced Broadway audiences to Bob Fosse's innovative choreographic style. In 1956 Gennaro appeared as a featured dancer in *Bells Are Ringing*.

In 1957 he was the co-choreographer for *West Side Story,* one of the most successful Broadway shows of all time. While it is generally known that the show was directed and choreographed by Jerome Robbins, little credit is given to Gennaro, who choreographed most of the Latin dancing in the show, most notably the "America" sequence.

Following *West Side Story,* Gennaro continued to choreograph Broadway musicals, including *Fiorello!* (1959), the musical based on the life of New York City's Italian American mayor Fiorello H. LaGuardia; *The Unsinkable Molly Brown* (1960); *Mr. President* (1962); *Bajour* (1964); *Jimmy* (1969); and *Annie* (1977), for which he won a Tony Award. Though Gennaro went to Hollywood and choreographed the film version of *The Unsinkable Molly Brown,* he chose not to continue working in the film industry and returned to the East Coast to be with his wife, son, and daughter. He worked, instead, on television shows taped in New York. During the 1960s and 1970s Gennaro created numerous dances for television variety programs and was extensively involved in dance education, teaching professional dancers as well as training dance instructors. Gennaro has also donated funding to the Stage Directors and Choreographers Foundation to support a new training program for emerging choreographers.

As a child Gennaro had contracted an ear infection that led to a significant loss of hearing, a condition that has afflicted him throughout his life. He developed a compensating sense of rhythm and a feeling for vibrations in music. In 1974 the New York League for the Hard of Hearing granted him the Eleanor Roosevelt Humanitarian Award for overcoming his hearing loss in a field dependent on sound and movement. As a dancer, choreographer, educator, and philanthropist, Gennaro has made many varied and significant contributions to the development of American popular dance.

Lisa Jo Sagolla

Bibliography

Fields, Sidney. "Annie's Dance Master." *New York Daily News,* 1 December 1977, 96.

"Peter Gennaro." *Current Biography* (June 1964): 16–17.

Stern, Harold. "The Master of the Jazz Forms Turns to TV." *Dance Magazine* (June 1970): 44–47.

Terry, Walter. "The Choreographer's Job." *New York Herald Tribune,* 8 January 1961, 5.

See also DANCE

Gentile, Charles (Carlo) (1835–1893)

A pioneer photographer of American Indians and benefactor, explorer, "accidental prospector," and magazine and newspaper editor, Charles (Carlo) Gentile was born in Naples, Italy, in 1835.

He migrated to San Francisco in the late 1850s and subsequently to the commercial town of Victoria, Vancouver Island, in 1862 in the wake of the Fraser River gold rush. During his four-year stay in Victoria, Gentile acquired an excellent reputation as a professional studio and field photographer. An inquisitive and energetic character, and a lover of adventure, Gentile divided his time between his studio in Victoria and the field, bringing his camera to the remote Nootka villages on Vancouver Island and to the gold mining towns and Interior Salish settlements on mainland British Columbia. He assembled an impressive collection of landscape photographs of the Pacific Northwest and *cartes de visite,* small photographic portraits of Native and non-Native subjects.

Gentile intended to travel to Europe in 1866, but the loss (or possibly theft) of his "square deal box" containing many of his photographs and negatives forced him to change his plans. He sold his business in Victoria, returned briefly to San Francisco, went to southern California, and then to the Arizona Territory. He photographed the Indians of the region, including the Yuma (Quechan), Cocopa, Mohave, Maricopa, Pima, and Yavapai, and took photographic views of picturesque mission churches and prehistoric ruins.

In 1871 Gentile joined a large gold and silver mining expedition headed by Arizona governor Anson P. K. Safford; it was during this expedition that, according to Gentile's own recollections later published in the *Chicago Daily Tribune* (March 21, 1875), he came across three Pima warriors who had captured a little Yavapai boy named Wassaja during a raid on his camp. Indian servitude was still common practice in the Southwest, and Gentile, pitying the little boy, ransomed him from his captors for thirty silver dollars, cleaned and dressed him, had him baptized as Carlos Montezuma in the Catholic Church, and legally adopted him.

With little Carlos, Gentile toured the Southwest experimenting with color photography. The two eventually traveled to Chicago, where in late 1872 they joined an early Wild West show created by Edward Z. C. Judson, alias the "great rascal" Ned Buntline, featuring renowned scouts Buffalo Bill Cody and Texas Jack (J. B. Omohundro), and Italian ballerina Giuseppina Morlacchi, who played the part of an exotic Indian maiden and later married Texas Jack. The *sodalizio* (sodality) did not last, and Gentile and Montezuma proceeded to New York. There Gentile opened a photography and art studio, receiving two important professional awards in 1877 and 1878; soon thereafter, a fire destroyed much of his business and forced him to settle finally in Chicago. Gentile placed 13-year-old Carlos Montezuma in the care of two Protestant ministers, who secured the young Indian's education. Montezuma eventually enrolled at Chicago Medical College and became a respected Chicago physician, a critic of the Bureau of Indian Affairs, and an advocate of American Indian assimilation through education.

In Chicago, Gentile operated two photographic studios and was appointed director of the prestigious Photographers' Association of America. In 1884 he began publication of his own professional magazine *The Eye*, which he soon renamed *The Photographic Eye and The Eye*. The weekly magazine sold for ten cents an issue and gained a large readership. Gentile's association with journalistic circles (he was one of the founders of the Chicago Press Club) led him and fellow Neapolitan Oscar Durante in 1886 to publish *L'Italia*, which became one the most popular Italian-language newspapers of the period. Two years later, while still managing his studio, Gentile and Giuseppe Ronga published *Il Messaggiere Italo-Americano*, a short-lived bilingual newspaper in Chicago. In 1889 Gentile tried yet another journalistic venture, *La Colonia*, which did not succeed. Gentile's investments in photographic ventures connected with the 1893 Chicago World's Columbian Exposition also failed. These professional setbacks were compounded by health problems and personal tragedies, including the death in 1891 of his (third?) wife and a daughter in early 1893. Gentile died that same year, on October 27, 1893, at age 58, an apparent suicide. He is buried in Chicago.

Gentile made important contributions to early Canadian and American photography, to the history of Italian American journalism, and to Indian-white relations. Gentile's pioneering photographs can be found in repositories throughout the United States, Canada, England, and New Zealand.

Cesare Marino

Bibliography

Arnold, Oren. *Savage Son*. Albuquerque: University of New Mexico Press, 1951.

Marino, Cesare. *The Remarkable Story of Carlo Gentile: Pioneer Photographer of American Indians, Benefactor, and Entrepreneur*. Typescript copy in the Center for Migration Studies, Staten Island, NY, n.d.

Mattison, David. *Camera Workers: The British Columbia Photographer Directory, 1858–1900*. Victoria, BC: Camera Workers Press, 1985.

Nelli, Humbert S. *Italians in Chicago, 1880–1930: A Study in Ethnic Mobility*. New York: Oxford University Press.

Geppi, Stephen

See CARTOONISTS AND ILLUSTRATORS

Gherardi, (Aaron) Bancroft (1832–1903)

The first Italian American to become an admiral in the United States Navy, (Aaron) Bancroft Gherardi was born in Jackson, Louisiana, November 10, 1832, to Donato Gherardi (c. 1800–1851) and Jane Putnam Bancroft (1798–1843), sister of renowned historian George Bancroft (1800–1891). His father, who had arrived in Boston as a political refugee from Italy at age 22 in 1822, met his mother while teaching at the Round Hill School in Northampton, Massachusetts, which Jane's brother had established to educate young boys. The Gherardis were married in Worcester, Massachusetts, in 1825 and named their son after his maternal grandfather, Aaron Bancroft (1755–1839), a minister in that city.

By the time Gherardi was 11, his mother had died of yellow fever in New Orleans and his father, who had been teaching school in Louisiana, ended up in a mental institution in Massachusetts. According to the probate records for Worcester County, in Massachusetts, Bancroft and his sister, Clara Jane, came under the guardianship of foster parents. Fortunately for Gherardi, his famous uncle (George Bancroft), who became Secretary of the Navy for President James Knox Polk, appointed the young man to the United States Naval Academy, which Gherardi entered after first serving in the Mexican War at age 14.

Graduating from the Naval Academy on June 8, 1852, Gherardi was prepared for a long career of military service. In the Civil War he had participated in a number of conflicts, including the decisive Battle of Mobile Bay. Here Gherardi distinguished himself by serving in the fleet under Admiral David G. Farragut, who won fame for that victory on August 5, 1864. In charge of the steamer *Port Royal*, Gherardi's calm demeanor during the heat of battle helped to defeat the Confederate fleet.

Becoming a full commander on July 26, 1866, Gherardi witnessed a revolution in the role of the navy as the United States armed forces began to rely more on sea power. Promoted to captain by 1874 and to commodore by 1884, Gherardi was a rear admiral by 1887. In command of the North Atlantic Squadron (1889–1892), Admiral Gherardi moved his fleet into Haitian waters in 1889 and restored peace there without waging war. Similarly, when relations between the United States and Chile reached a critical point in 1891, Gherardi moved his flagship towards Montevideo and the crisis subsided. Later, as an Italian American, it was appropriate for him to hold the top command in reviewing the international fleets marking the fourth centennial of America's discovery by Christopher Columbus. His career in the navy spanned a half century, and he became an articulate spokesman for naval power and development of the ironclad battleship.

Gherardi married Anna Talbot Rockwell in 1872, and they became the parents of Bancroft Gherardi (1873–1941), a pioneer in the communications industry, and of Walter R. Gherardi (1875–1939), another rear admiral. He died in Stratford, Connecticut, December 10, 1903. The bodies of Admiral Bancroft Gherardi and his wife rest in the cemetery of the United States Naval Academy at Annapolis.

Vincent A. Lapomarda

Bibliography

Buckley, Oliver E. *Bancroft Gherardi, 1873–1941: Biographical Memoir.* New York: Columbia University Press, 1957.

Hanlin, Lilian. *George Bancroft: The Intellectual as Democrat.* New York: Harper & Row, 1984.

Nye, Russell B. *George Bancroft: Brahmin Rebel.* New York: Alfred A. Knopf, 1944.

United States Navy Department. *Official Records of the Union and Confederate Navies in the War of the Rebellion.* 30 vols. Washington, DC: Government Printing Office, 1894–1922.

See also WARTIME MILITARY AND HOME FRONT ACTIVITIES

Ghirardelli, Domingo
See BUSINESS AND ENTREPRENEURSHIP

Giacalone, Diane
See LAW ENFORCEMENT

Giacconi, Riccardo (b. 1931)
This Italian-born American astrophysicist headed a team whose work was instrumental in the development of X-ray astronomy. Riccardo Giacconi received a doctorate in physics from the University of Milan in 1954 and migrated to the United States two years later. He began his career as a research associate, first at the University of Indiana in Bloomington and then at Princeton University. In 1960 Giacconi joined American Scientific and Engineering, Inc., and two years later he and his group sent up a rocket to search for X-rays emitted by florescence from the moon's surface. Much to everyone's surprise, it detected strong X-rays from a source located outside the solar system. Giacconi and his team went on to build the first orbiting X-ray detector, *Uhuru*, a small astronomy satellite. This was launched and led to the discovery of a host of X-ray stars. In 1971 Giacconi and his team reported the discovery of a "possible black hole."

The team went on to develop a telescope capable of producing X-ray images. Giacconi later worked on a Cherenkov detector, a device he helped develop to observe the existence and velocity of high-speed particles. Giacconi's work on the Cherenkov detector has advanced the study of cosmic radiation and experimental nuclear physics. In 1992 he became director of the European Southern Observatory in Germany.

Joanna Bevacqua

Bibliography
Porter, Roy, ed. *Biographical Dictionary of Scientists.* 2nd ed. New York: Oxford University Press, 1994.

See also SCIENCE

Giamatti, A. Bartlett (1938–1989)
Scholar, educator, college president, and baseball commissioner—such was the gamut of professions and careers brilliantly practiced by Angelo Bartlett Giamatti in the course of an all-too-brief life span of fifty-one years. The broad and variegated scope of his interests and pursuits was greatly influenced by his heritage.

G

One grandfather, Angelo Giamattei (the original surname), landed at Ellis Island about 1900; in the same period, the other grandfather—Bartlett Walton—was entering Harvard College. Valentine Giamatti, A. Bartlett's father, won a four-year scholarship to Yale and subsequently earned a Ph.D. from Harvard. He married Mary Clayburgh Walton, a Smith College junior studying abroad.

"Bart" and his sister Elvira, the children of Valentine and Mary, grew up near Mount Holyoke College, where their father was teaching Italian. The Giamatti family spent a couple of years in Italy. In later years Bartlett was to credit those years abroad for imparting on him an Italian fatalism, a sense of history, and a concern for the fragility of institutions.

Young Giamatti attended Phillips Academy and became a devoted fan of the Boston Red Sox. This love of baseball enhanced his passion for learning and culture. He received his bachelor's degree in 1960 and, four years later, was awarded a Ph.D. in comparative literature from Yale University.

Professor Giamatti devoted much time and unlimited energy to student interests, concerns, and potential. Students responded enthusiastically to Giamatti's approach and high standards. His teaching was enriched by the research he continued to do on classical, medieval, and Renaissance literature.

Against a background of deteriorating economic conditions, he became Yale's nineteenth president on July 1, 1978. At 40, Bartlett Giamatti was the youngest Yale president in two hundred years. He was also the first of its presidents not entirely of Anglo-Saxon heritage.

Giamatti's approach to fund-raising elicited unprecedented contributions from alumni, corporations, and foundations. He traveled the country promoting a $370 million fund-raising campaign—a goal that would be exceeded by more than $3 million during his tenure. Within two years, Yale University boasted its first balanced budget in a decade. Giamatti did not neglect academic matters. He maintained that the goal of Yale University traditionally had been and should continue to be liberal education. Seven years at Yale took their toll on him physically. In February 1985 Giamatti announced his resignation, which went into effect in June 1986. He then was chosen to be the president of baseball's National League.

Ever the idealist, Giamatti hoped to purify the game of baseball and clean up the national pastime. In January 1989 Giamatti was chosen Commissioner of Baseball—the consummation of his childhood dream. In a press conference, after he had announced that Pete Rose was banished forever from the game, Commissioner Giamatti stated: "I will be told that I am an idealist . . . I hope so." On September 1, 1989, Giamatti died of a heart attack.

Regarding assimilation, Giamatti stated that it is a two-way process: it is giving and receiving, of becoming American while adding to America what is enduring in the energy, history, and devotion to life in being Italian.

Giamatti contributed a fresh voice to the debate over higher education in America. He stressed that the university's greatest strength is its pluralism, its lack of a narrow academic mission other than the search for truth. "The university serves the country best," he wrote in *A Free and Ordered Space: The Real World of the University* (1988), "when it is a caldron of competing ideas, and not a neatly arranged platter of received opinions."

Margherita Marchione

Bibliography
Giamatti, A. Bartlett. *A Free and Ordered Space: The Real World of the University.* New York: W.W. Norton, 1988.

Reston, James. *Collision at Home Plate: The Lives of Pete Rose and Bart Giamatti.* New York: Harper Perrenial, 1992.

Valerio, Anthony, comp. *Bart: A Life of A. Barlett Giamatti, by Him and About Him.* New York: Harcourt Brace Jovanovich, 1991.

See also HIGHER EDUCATION; SPORTS

Giannini, Amadeo P. (1870–1949)

A banker extraordinaire, Amadeo P. Giannini ranks as one the great pioneers in the branch banking system. Born May 6, 1870, Giannini lived in San Jose, California, but his parents came from Chavari, Genoa, Italy. After the murder of his father in 1876, his mother, Virginia, married Lorenzo Scatena. Under Scatena's guidance, Amadeo quickly and successfully learned the produce business in San Francisco. He married Clorinda Cuneo on September 12, 1892, and soon his family included

Amadeo, Jr., Lloyd Thomas, Lawrence Mario, Agnes Rose, Virgil David, and Claire Evelyn.

Giannini's marriage introduced him to banking. When Clorinda's father, Joseph Cuneo, died in June 1902, Giannini replaced him as a director of Banca Colombo, but philosophical differences with other directors prompted Giannini to establish his own bank. On October 17, 1904, he opened Banca d'Italia and began canvassing Italian North Beach for depositors. He shocked customers and bankers alike by lending money without collateral. To him "a character loan" backed by a handshake sufficed.

The earthquake and fire of 1906 made Banca d'Italia a household name. Before the bank building burned, Giannini gathered money and records in a produce wagon and drove them to safety. Reopening a makeshift bank on the Washington Street wharf, he lent money to help rebuild San Francisco. The bank's post-earthquake success encouraged him to expand to San Jose, Stockton, Fresno, Bakersfield, and Los Angeles. Giannini encouraged people of all backgrounds to deposit money in Banca d'Italia through school savings programs; the Women's Bank (1921); and Italian, Chinese, Greek, French, Portuguese, Slovenian, Hispanic, and Russian divisions.

Within California, Giannini undertook large-scale expansion by establishing the Liberty Bank of San Francisco (1921) and acquiring the Bank of America Los Angeles (1924). He consolidated Liberty Bank, Bank of America Los Angeles, Commercial National Trust and Savings Bank (Los Angeles), and Southern Trust and Commerce Bank (San Diego) into Liberty Bank of America. In 1927 he transferred control of Liberty Bank of America to Banca d'Italia and named the amalgam the Bank of Italy National Trust and Savings Association. He purchased several more banks, including the Bank of America, San Pedro, and merged them to form Bank of America of California in 1928.

In 1930 Giannini's banks underwent further consolidation when the Bank of America of California and the Bank of Italy National Trust and Savings Association joined to form the Bank of America National Trust and Savings Association. To facilitate his bank purchases, Giannini created holding companies such as Stockholders Auxiliary (1917), Bancitaly Corporation (1919), and Americommercial Corporation (1923).

Outside California, Giannini's acquisitions expanded into New York when he purchased the New York East River National Bank (1919) and the Bowery National Bank (1925), which he joined to form the Bowery East River National Bank (BERNB). In 1928 Bancitaly Corporation purchased almost half of the shares of the New York Bank of America (NYBA). Giannini merged BERNB, one other bank, and NYBA into the Bank of America N.A. His son, L. Mario Giannini, conceived the idea of creating a new holding company to include Bank of Italy, Bancitaly Corporation, the Bank of America N.A., and Bank of America of California. In 1928 the Transamerica Corporation emerged from this conglomeration. With his banking system coordinated under Transamerica, Giannini decided to retire in 1930. Wall Street banker Elisha P. Walker assumed the chairmanship and Mario the presidency.

When the Great Depression and Walker's inconsistent leadership caused fiscal and internal problems for Transamerica, Giannini decided to save his collapsing system. Giannini solicited votes from about 200,000 Transamerica stockholders that reinstated him as chairman in 1932. With restructuring, layoffs, reduced salaries, and loans from the Reconstruction Finance Corporation, financial stability returned to Transamerica and Bank of America National Trust and Savings Association. Giannini then confounded the banking establishment by lending money to customers for automobiles, homes, farms, and movie making, such as $1.7 million that funded the production of Walt Disney's *Snow White*.

The reinvigoration of the Giannini banking system troubled Franklin Delano Roosevelt's administration. It saw a monopoly in Giannini's banking organization, but World War II sidetracked the investigation. Monopoly or not, World War II and its aftermath brought growth to Giannini's bank. Statistics show that resources exceeded $2.7 billion in 1942 and $5.7 billion in 1946.

On May 5, 1945, Amadeo resigned as chairman of the Bank of America. That same year, with an endowment of $509,235, he established the Bank of America–Giannini Foundation for employee scholarships and medical research. This donation complemented $1.5 million given to the University of California for agricultural research through the Bancitaly Corporation in 1928.

During Giannini's last years, Bank of America opened new branches, expanded its international operations, and pushed its capital above $6.2 billion. Giannini died on June 3, 1949. His mausoleum is at Holy Cross Cemetery, Colma, California.

Philip M. Montesano

Bibliography

Bonadio, Felice A. *A.P. Giannini, Banker of America.* Berkeley: University of California Press, 1994

Cross, Ira B. *Financing an Empire: History of Banking in California.* 4 vols. San Francisco: S. J. Clarke, 1927.

Dana, Julian. *A.P. Giannini, Giant in the West, A Biography.* New York: Prentice-Hall, 1947.

James, Marquis, and Bessie Rowland James. *Biography of a Bank: The Story of Bank of America N.T. & S.A.* New York: Harper, 1954.

Nash, Gerald D. *A.P. Giannini and the Bank of America.* Norman: University of Oklahoma Press, 1992.

See also BUSINESS AND ENTREPRENEURSHIP; SAN FRANCISCO

Giannini, Margaret J.

Known for her outstanding work and research in the field of medicine and for the treatment of the handicapped, Dr. Margaret J. Giannini's initial specialty after graduating from Hahnemann Medical College (1945) was in pediatrics. As associate professor at the New York Medical College (1948–1967) and professor of pediatrics since 1967, she began to concentrate on the problems of mentally retarded and physically handicapped children.

This soon led to Dr. Giannini's Mental Retardation Institute, which she founded and started directing in 1950. Beginning as a clinic in New York City's Spanish Harlem, it was the first facility for the handicapped in the world. Since then, it has become the largest.

President Jimmy Carter appointed Dr. Giannini as director of the National Institute on Handicapped Research in the Department of Health, Education, and Welfare. As director, she was charged with coordinating the many facets of research on the handicapped undertaken by the various federal agencies.

Dr. Giannini's invaluable contribution to the project has been widely recognized. She has been made chairperson of the International Seminar on Mental Retardation and of the Mental Retardation Task Force State-Wide, which plans vocational rehabilitation programs for the New York State Department of Education Services.

Her original focus on handicapped children was extended to adults, veterans or otherwise, and to the mentally and physically handicapped. Also, her speeches and articles have advanced progress in the field of rehabilitation.

Margherita Marchione

Bibliography

Marchione, Margherita. *Americans of Italian Heritage.* New York: University Press of America, Inc., 1995.

See also MEDICINE; SCIENCE

Gioia, Dana (b. 1950)

Poet and essayist Dana Gioia was born in Los Angeles in 1950. He received a B.A. and an M.B.A. from Stanford University and an M.A. in comparative literature from Harvard University. Of his nearly twenty years as an executive with a major American corporation, Gioia has said, "Whatever the other burdens my employment put on my literary aspirations, the job allowed me to write about whatever interested me most—however odd or unfashionable. It also freed me from the necessity of adopting an academic style."

Gioia's first collection of poetry, *Daily Horoscope* (1986), is characterized by his stating the obvious in unusual ways and in various types of nostalgic tones. In the section entitled "Journeys in Sunlight," Gioia subtly meshes an old world with a new in such poems as "An Emigre in Autumn" and "The Garden in the *Campagna.*" More obvious and powerful images emerge in his second book, *The God's of Winter* (1991). In "Planting a Sequoia," from this collection, the narrator likens the planting of the "native giant" to ceremonialize a son's birth and death to the planting of an olive or fig tree in Sicily. The British edition of *The God's of Winter* became the chief selection for the London-based Poetry Book Society, an honor rarely given to American authors.

Gioia's critical collection, *Can Poetry Matter?: Essays on Poetry and American*

Culture (1992), was written to appeal to a broad audience of "the intelligent, engaged non-specialist." Gioia writes of poets past and present who are popular or might be popular if better known. He proposes that it is time to "restore a vulgar vitality to poetry and unleash the energy now trapped in the subculture."

Gioia co-edited *Poems from Italy* (1985), a comprehensive bilingual anthology of Italian poetry from the Middle Ages to the present, and *New Italian Poets* (1991). *Motetti: Poems of Love* (1990) is Gioia's translation of Eugenio Montale's *Motetti*. Gioia, hailed by critics from the *New York Times* as a refined and unusually gifted writer, was chosen by *Esquire* in 1984 for their first register of "Men and Women under 40 Who Are Changing the Nation." He serves as poetry editor for *Italian Americana,* a cultural and historical review of the Italian American experience.

Marisa Labozzetta

Bibliography

Gioia, Dana. *Can Poetry Matter?: Essays on Poetry and American Culture.* St. Paul: Graywolf Press, 1992.

———. *Daily Horoscope.* St. Paul: Graywolf Press, 1986.

———. *The God's of Winter.* St. Paul: Graywolf Press, 1991.

Swiss, Thomas. "Daily Horoscope: Poems by Dana Gioia." *New York Times Book Review,* 30 November 1986, 17.

See also POETRY

Gioseffi, Daniela (b. 1941)

Pioneer Italian American woman writer and social activist, Daniela Gioseffi has occupied an important place in American culture since the early 1970s. A renowned poet of the Italian American and woman's experience, Gioseffi has also achieved notable success as a novelist, playwright, editor, lecturer, educator, broadcast journalist, actress, and singer.

Born to an Italian immigrant father and a mother of mixed heritage, Gioseffi has crusaded for social justice in America and around the world. At 21 she went to work as a journalist and activist in Selma, Alabama, at the height of the civil rights movement. There she helped integrate Southern television. Her activism led to her arrest and subsequent abuse at the hands of Alabama authorities, an experience she reconstructs in the story, later a stage play, *The Bleeding Mimosa* (1991).

Upon her return from the South, Gioseffi moved to New York City, where she began her career as a poet. Since the late 1960s she has been published in numerous anthologies and journals such as *Antaeus, Italian Americana, The Nation, Paris Review,* and *Voices in Italian Americana.* Her first collection, *Eggs in the Lake,* appeared in 1979; her second, *Word Wounds and Water Flowers,* in 1995. The poems of both volumes, while lyrical, address a host of complex social and political issues—from racism to sexism to the ravages of war to the threat of global nuclear destruction—with unfailing "poetic vision."

A number of her best poems express the frustrations and joys of being Italian American. Several merit mention here: "Bicentennial Anti-Poem for Italian-American Women" from *Eggs in the Lake;* and "Unfinished Autobiography," "For Grandma Lucia La Rosa, 'Light the Rose,'" and "American Sonnets for My Father" from *Word Wounds and Water Flowers.* All but the last of these poems explore the connections and effects of anti-Italian American prejudice and the repression of women in the traditional Italian American family.

Gioseffi has also published a satirical novel, *The Great American Belly* (1979), and a collection of short stories, *In Bed with the Exotic Enemy* (1997), and has had two award-winning poetic plays—*Care of the Body* and *The Golden Daffodil Dwarf*—produced in New York. In addition, she has edited two prose anthologies: *Women on War: Global Voices for Survival* (1990), which won an American Book Award, and *On Prejudice: A Global Perspective* (1993), which won a Ploughshares World Peace Award.

Gioseffi's other endeavors have complemented her copious literary output. She has presented her work on National Public Radio, BBC, and CBC; taught creative writing and intercultural communications; and lectured throughout the United States and Europe on world peace and disarmament. While continuing to champion these causes, Gioseffi has taken a leading role in the ongoing Italian American literary and cultural renaissance. Her work and presence have inspired writers of all backgrounds to strive for cross-cultural understanding.

George Guida

Bibliography

Alfonsi, Ferdinando. *Dictionary of Italian American Poets.* New York: Peter Lang, 1989.

Barolini, Helen, ed. *The Dream Book: An Anthology of Writings by Italian American Women.* New York: Schocken, 1985.

Bona, Mary Jo, ed. *The Voices We Carry.* Montreal: Guernica, 1994.

Mangione, Jerre, and Ben Morreale. *La Storia: Five Centuries of the Italian American Experience.* New York: Harper Collins, 1992.

Reed, Ishmael. *Cultural Wars, Cultural Peace.* New York: Viking Press, 1996.

See also LITERATURE; POETRY; WOMEN WRITERS

Giovannitti, Arturo (1884–1959)

Early in the twentieth century, poet and political activist Arturo Giovannitti migrated to Canada, where he studied for the Protestant ministry and worked on a railroad gang. He then moved to the United States, where he took odd jobs and attended Columbia University. He was born in the Italian town of Ripabottoni, near Campobasso in the Molise region, a town that "continued to live in misery." His father was a doctor who survived by bartering his services for food.

Giovannitti watched his fellow immigrants' illusions about America evaporate in the misery of hard work and discrimination. His studies at McGill University in Montreal prepared him for evangelical ministry. He eventually turned away from religion and toward socialism with all the fury of an angry poet.

Giovannitti's early years in the United States included considerable hardship, resulting in great compassion for his fellow sufferers. He worked as a coal miner in Pennsylvania. He experienced unemployment and cold, homeless nights. His hatred toward wealthy industrialists, government officials, and clergy hypocrisy transformed him from poor immigrant to passionate socialist.

In his adopted city of New York, he joined the Italian Socialist Federation. His eloquence gained him the position as journalist-editor of *Il Proletario.* He became a close friend and associate of labor organizer Joseph Ettor. They participated in the textile strike of 1912 in Lawrence, Massachusetts, where they were jailed, charged falsely, brought to trial, and found innocent. Giovannitti wrote the poem "The Walker," in which he describes himself lying in his cell at night, awake, listening to the pacing footsteps of the prisoners in the cell above. This poem and others written while in jail were published under the title *Arrows in the Gale* (1914), which many consider a masterpiece and a condemnation of the prison system.

Giovannitti traveled around the United States urging workers to join the Industrial Workers of the World, which was an amalgamated union consisting of workers regardless of race and nationality. His advocacy brought many Italian Americans into the radical labor movement.

After the Lawrence strike, he became editor of *Il Fuoco,* an Italian American leftist political-literary journal. He wrote an antiwar play, *As It Was in the Beginning,* which had a successful run on Broadway in 1917. He wrote for *The Masses,* a radical magazine that was edited by Max Eastman and John Reed. When this publication was replaced by *The Liberator* in 1918, Giovannitti served as a contributing editor. In 1923 he led the fight against the fascist movement in the United States by organizing the Anti-Fascist Alliance in North America. This "poet of the proletariat" became the Alliance's secretary.

Giovannitti was the most extroverted of Italian immigrant poets. He wore flowing cravats and velvet vests. His oratorical skills, in Italian and English, set him apart from other labor leaders. Toward the end of his life, suffering from paralysis in his legs, he published a collection of his Italian poems, *Quando canta il gallo* (1957), and was editing a collection of his English poems at his death in 1959.

Frank J. Cavaioli
Jerre Mangione

Bibliography

Fenton, Edwin. *Immigrants and Unions, A Case Study: Italians and American Labor, 1870–1920.* New York: Arno Press, 1975.

Giovannitti, Arturo. *The Collected Poems of Arturo Giovannitti.* Chicago: E. Clemente and Sons, 1962.

Pozzetta, George, ed. *Pane e Lavoro: The Italian American Working Class.* Toronto: American Italian Historical Association and Multicultural History Society of Ontario, 1980.

Sillanpoa, Wallace P. "The Poetry and Politics of Arturo Giovannitti." In *The Melting Pot and Beyond: Italian Americans in the Year 2000,* edited by Jerome Krase and William Egelman, 175–189. Staten Island, NY: American Italian Historical Association, 1987.

Vecoli, Rudolph J., ed. *Italian American Radicalism: Old World Origins and New World Developments.* Staten Island, NY: American Italian Historical Association, 1972.

See also LABOR; POETRY; RADICALISM

Giuliani, Rudolph W. (b. 1944)

The third Italian American to become mayor of New York City, his election epitomized the consolidation of a shift in Italian American political leadership toward the right, which had witnessed the rise of conservatives such as John Volpe, Frank Rizzo, and Alphonse D'Amato since the 1960s.

Rudolph W. Giuliani was born on May 28, 1944, in Brooklyn. He studied at Catholic schools, attended Manhattan College, and graduated from New York University's Law School in 1968. After working for a federal district judge, Giuliani alternated prosecutorial positions with offices in the Justice Department. He served as assistant United States attorney in New York's Southern District from 1970 to 1975. He was then appointed assistant to the deputy attorney general under the Gerald Ford administration, practiced law following the Republican defeat in 1976, and returned to Washington as associate attorney general in 1981 after the Republican Party recaptured the White House.

Although he was the third-ranking official in the Justice Department, Giuliani resigned his position in 1983 and returned to New York to head the United States attorney's office in the city's Southern District.

Giuliani had already established a creditable record as a tough and effective prosecutor during his previous tenure, but the subsequent four years brought him into the limelight. He won national fame for directing high-profile prosecutions of racketeers, Wall Street securities dealers, and corrupt politicians. His office secured the conviction of prominent members from the Colombo, Genovese, and Bonanno crime families for drug dealing and racketeering. He successfully prosecuted leading investment bankers for inside trading and cracked down on bribery rings in which famous politicians were involved. Giuliani made a point of fighting organized crime and the few Italian American mobsters who had besmirched the reputation of his own ethnic group.

Giuliani's successful record placed him in a position to enter politics in the late 1980s. In those years he capitalized on citizen outrage toward the savings and loan scandal as well as the cost of the ensuing bailout: he fought white-collar crimes of Wall Street and banking executives. In addition, the indictments of Bronx Democratic leader Stanley Friedman and United States Representative Mario Biaggi attuned Giuliani to the voters' growing distrust of politicians. His national prominence as a racket buster also shielded Giuliani from the stigma of the Mafia, which had affected the election campaigns of a number of other Italian Americans.

After declining to run for the United States Senate in 1988, Giuliani received the nomination of the Republican and the Liberal parties for mayor of New York the following year. He became the front-runner when he announced his candidacy in February. Eventually, however, Giuliani was beaten by David Dinkins, an African American Democrat, possibly because his own inexperienced staff of lawyers and former prosecutors relied too much on negative commercials: Giuliani's campaign as a law and order candidate supporting the death penalty lost its initial momentum.

He challenged Dinkins again in 1993 and defeated him, though by a narrow 2 percent plurality. He benefited from the escalating crime rates and increasing racial animosities in New York during the previous four years. The election outcome revealed a growing polarization of voters along racial lines. While Dinkins carried the African American community by 95 percent, Giuliani received 77 percent of the white vote. In particular, between 1989 and 1993, the political following of Giuliani increased from 63 to 68 percent among the Jews, from 69 to 78 percent among the Irish, and from 76 to 88 percent among the Italian Americans.

A former liberal Democrat who had turned Republican because of dissatisfaction with the foreign policy of the Democratic

Party in the 1960s, Giuliani displayed the traditional unpredictable independence that New York mayors had become famous for in the past. For instance, he endorsed incumbent Democratic governor Mario M. Cuomo in 1994 for fear that the tax cuts proposed by his Republican challenger would reduce the appropriation of state funds to New York City. Similarly, Giuliani supported Democratic President Bill Clinton's 1994 Crime Bill, including its ban on assault weapons, which many Republicans opposed. Giuliani was overwhelmingly reelected to a second term as mayor in 1997.

Stefano Luconi

Bibliography

Cateura, Linda Brandi. *Growing Up Italian: How Being Brought Up as an Italian American Helped Shape the Character, Lives, and Fortunes of Twenty-Four Celebrated Americans.* New York: Morrow, 1987.

Litwak, Mark. *Courtroom Crusaders.* New York: Morrow, 1989.

Logan, Andy. "Two-Per-Cent Solutions." *New Yorker,* 15 November 1993, 52–59.

See also CRIME AND ORGANIZED CRIME; LAGUARDIA, FIORELLO H.; LAW ENFORCEMENT; POLITICS

Governors

Nineteen Americans of Italian descent have served in the office of governor in the United States. The first was William Paca, who was born 1740 in Abington, Harford County, Maryland, and died 1799 at his country home, Wye Hall. Paca's forebears had left Italy for England and from there migrated to Maryland in the middle of the seventeenth century. A successful lawyer, he served in the provincial legislature, supported the revolutionary cause, and was a member of the First and Second Continental Congresses and signer of the Declaration of Independence. In 1782 the Maryland legislature elected him governor, and he was unanimously reelected the next two years.

Andrew Houston Longino served as governor of Mississippi from 1900 to 1904. He had a distinguished career as lawyer, legislator, and jurist. Born in Lawrence County, 1854, he received a bachelor's degree from Mississippi College, a law degree from the University of Virginia, and was admitted to the Mississippi bar. He clerked in the Lawrence County circuit and chancery courts from 1876 to 1880.

From 1880 to 1884 Longino served in the Mississippi State Senate. Other positions held by him were United States District Attorney for the Southern District of Mississippi, judge of the Mississippi Court of Chancery, and chairman of the 1900 Mississippi delegation to the Democratic National Convention. In 1899 he decisively defeated his Populist Party opponent for governor: 42,273 (87.6 percent) to 6,007 (12.4 percent). He ran again for governor in 1919 but was defeated. He served as judge for Hinds County until his death in 1942. He was a Baptist and married Marion Buckley in 1889, with whom he parented five children.

Alfred Emanuel Smith's multiethnic ancestry of Irish, English, German, and Italian qualifies him as an Italian American governor. A Democrat and Catholic, he served as New York State governor for four two-year terms: 1919–1921 and 1923–1929. The future governor was born on New York City's Lower East Side in 1873. Smith's maternal grandfather (Thomas Mulvihill) was Irish; his maternal grandmother (Maria Marsh) was English. His paternal grandfather (Emanuel) was born in Genoa, Italy; his paternal grandmother (Magdalena) was born in Germany. Two years after the governor's father's first wife died, the father married Catherine Mulvihill.

Smith left parochial school in the eighth grade to support his sister and widowed mother. He married Catherine Dunn, and they had five children. He joined the Tammany Hall political organization, was elected state assemblyman, and rose to the powerful positions of majority leader and speaker.

The first governor with full Italian ancestry was Charles Poletti. He served as New York State's chief executive for a brief twenty-nine days from December 2, 1942, to January 1, 1943. Poletti had been lieutenant governor; he filled out the last days of Governor Herbert Lehman's term when Lehman resigned to assume the post of United States Director of Foreign Relief in World War II.

Poletti was born in Barre, Vermont, 1903, to Dino, a stonecutter, and Carolina (née Gervasi), both of whom were immigrants and Presbyterians. His father came from Piedmont and his mother came from Lombardy,

Italy. He excelled academically in public school and worked to contribute financially to the family. He received a scholarship to Harvard College and supported himself by waiting on tables, washing dishes, delivering newspapers, and tutoring students. He was elected to Phi Beta Kappa and graduated in 1924 with a B.A. in history and political science. He won an Eleanora Duse Scholarship to study at the University of Rome, 1924–1925. He also studied at the University of Madrid in 1928. In both instances he perfected his fluency of Italian and Spanish. He completed his studies at Harvard Law School in 1928.

Poletti joined the New York law firm headed by John W. Davis, 1924 Democratic presidential candidate, and became legal assistant to the St. Lawrence Power Development Commission. In 1932 he became counsel to the Democratic Party National Committee. The following year he assumed the position of counsel to Governor Lehman. Poletti wrote speeches, drafted legislation, recommended patronage appointments, lobbied for New Deal legislation, and became Lehman's confidant.

Poletti chaired a commission that produced a twelve-volume report in preparation for the 1938 New York State Constitutional Convention, in which he was a delegate. He was elected justice of the State Supreme Court in 1937. The following year he won a four-year term for lieutenant governor with Governor Lehman. It was from this position that he succeeded to the governorship in 1942. After leaving office, Poletti became Special Assistant to United States Secretary of War Henry L. Stimson, receiving a commission of lieutenant colonel. From 1943 to 1945 he was appointed commissioner of the Allied Military Government in Sicily, Naples, Rome, Milan, and Lombardy. After the war he resumed law practice in New York City.

John Orlando Pastore, a Catholic, is the first Italian American governor from a Little Italy, the Federal Hill section of Providence, Rhode Island, where he was born in 1907. His parents had migrated there from Italy eight years earlier. His father died in 1916, and at age 9 he helped to support his mother, brother, and sisters. He completed high school and, unable to afford tuition to either of the two Ivy League colleges that accepted him, became a night student at Northeastern University, where he completed a law degree in

1931. He passed the bar examination and began law practice a year later in Providence. In 1933 he won the election for Democratic state assemblyman, serving from 1935 to 1937. From this point on he became the most popular Italian American politician in Rhode Island. His district had been controlled by Yankee elites, but a political transformation was taking place as the children of the new immigration battled for power.

Pastore was appointed state assistant attorney and held that position from 1937 to 1938 and 1940 to 1944. In 1941 he married Elena Caito, and they had three children. In 1944 he became the first Rhode Island Italian American to win a statewide elective office as lieutenant governor. On October 6, 1945, he assumed the governorship at age 38 when Governor Howard J. McGrath resigned to become United States Solicitor General. He was elected on his own in 1946 and again in 1948.

Pastore next won a United States Senate seat in a 1950 landslide to become the first Italian American senator. His first election was for two years to complete an unexpired term, but he was reelected in 1952, 1958, 1964, and 1970. The Limited Nuclear Test Ban Treaty of 1963, Nuclear Non-Proliferation Treaty of 1969, Public Broadcasting Act of 1967, Communications Satellite Act of 1962, and Civil Rights Act of 1964 are some of Pastore's legislative achievements. He keynoted the 1964 Democratic National Convention.

He helped to establish, in 1975, the National Italian American Foundation, an umbrella group that provided an Italian agenda in Washington, D.C. He retired in 1976 to spend more time with his family.

The sixth governor, and first from Massachusetts, was Foster J. Furcolo, a Catholic and Democrat who served from 1957 to 1961. Born in New Haven, Connecticut, 1911, son of Dr. Charles L. Furcolo and Alberta Foster Furcolo, he married Kathryn Foran, with whom he parented five children. He earned a bachelor's degree and a law degree (1936) from Yale. During World War II he served in the Navy. Afterwards he moved to Massachusetts, where he became active in politics.

Furcolo was elected to the United States House of Representatives in 1948 and was reelected two years later. He resigned in 1952 to accept an appointment as Massachusetts state treasurer. After being defeated in a bid for

G

United States senator in 1954, he won election to the governorship in 1956 and again in 1958. His attempt to win the Democratic nomination for United States Senate in 1960 failed, and he left office in January 1961 to return to private practice.

A second Italian American to win a gubernatorial election in 1956 was Democrat Albert Dean Rossellini of Washington state. Four years later he was reelected. Born in Tacoma in 1910, a Catholic, to John and Annunziata Pagni Rossellini, he married Ethel K. McNeil, and this marriage produced five children. He received a bachelor's and law degrees from the University of Washington. He established a successful law practice, 1933–1935 and 1938–1956, and continued it after he returned to private life. Other public positions held by Rossellini were assistant prosecuting attorney for King County, state assistant attorney general, and state senator.

Michael V. Di Salle, Ohio Democrat and a Catholic, became the eighth Italian American governor, serving from 1959 to 1963. Born in 1908 in New York City to Anthony and Assunta (née Arcangelo) Di Salle, he graduated from Toledo Public School, Central Catholic High School, and received a law degree from Georgetown University in 1931. A year later, he was admitted to the Ohio bar, beginning practice in Toledo. He married Myrtle Eugene England, and they had five children. In 1933 he took a position as assistant district counsel of the Home Owners Corporation.

Di Salle's political career began in 1936 when he was elected to a term in the Ohio House of Representatives. He served as Toledo City law director, city counsel member, vice mayor, and mayor (city manager). He moved to Washington, D.C., to become director of Price Stabilization and then director of Economic Stabilization. In 1956 he won the Democratic primary for governor but was defeated in the regular election by his Republican opponent. Two years later he won the gubernatorial election, now a four-year term, and was defeated for reelection in 1962.

Christopher Del Sesto ranks as the ninth Italian American governor. Born in Providence in 1907, a Catholic, to Eraclio and Rose Giremia Del Sesto, both immigrants, he later married Lola Elda Farone, and this marriage produced three sons. Del Sesto received a B.B.A. from Boston University in 1928 and a law degree from Georgetown University, 1938. Admitted to the bar in Washington, D.C., and Rhode Island, he held the following positions in his formative years: chief accountant in the state treasury, Rhode Island budget director, chief accountant of the Securities Exchange Commission, special assistant to the United States Attorney General, and director of the Rhode Island division of the Office of Price Administration.

When the Democrats refused to support his candidacy for lieutenant governor in the mid-1940s, Del Sesto switched to the Republican Party. In 1952 he ran unsuccessfully for mayor of Providence on a Republican-Fusion-Independent ticket. Four years later, in 1956, Del Sesto lost the election for governor when the Rhode Island Supreme Court rejected all civilian absentee votes.

In 1958, however, he achieved victory by defeating the Democratic incumbent for governor. During his term, Del Sesto vetoed ninety-eight bills passed by the Democratic-controlled legislature. In 1960 he lost his bid for reelection to John A. Notte. He returned to private practice and later was appointed associate justice of the State Superior Court, a position he held until his death in 1973.

John A. Notte, a Democrat, became the tenth Italian American governor. He was born in 1909, a Catholic, to John A. and Eva (née Rondina) Notte. He married Marie Herth in 1934, and they had two children. A graduate of Providence College, Notte attended Cornell but received a law degree from Boston University in 1935. During World War II he served in the Navy, achieving the rank of lieutenant. He became town solicitor in North Providence in 1937 and was secretary to United States Senator Theodore Francis Green from 1946 to 1958.

Notte was elected Rhode Island secretary of state, 1957–1959, and lieutenant governor, 1959–1961. In 1960 he defeated Christopher Del Sesto for governor in a landslide, but lost two years later by only 398 votes to Republican John H. Chafee. Notte returned to private practice. He failed to win a primary nomination for a congressional seat in 1967.

John A. Volpe, the eleventh Italian American governor, was born in Wakefield, Massachusetts, in 1908 to Vito and Filemeno Benedetto Volpe, both of whom had migrated from Abruzzi. His father, a hod carrier and plasterer, began a construction company that his son successfully expanded. Volpe's marriage to Jennie Benedetto in 1934 produced three children. A graduate of Wentworth Institute, he was unable to attend college because his father needed him to work for the company. During World War II he served in the Navy Civil Engineering Corps.

Volpe entered public life as a Republican, became chairman of the Republican state committee and served as public works commissioner. He became the first federal highway administrator for the interstate highway program. He was a delegate to the Republican National Conventions of 1960, 1964, 1968, and 1972.

Volpe won the 1960 Massachusetts gubernatorial election. He lost a disputed election in 1962 to Endicott Peabody by a vote of 1,053,322 to 1,047,891. Running again in 1964, he defeated Francis X. Bellotti in another close election. In 1966 he won a landslide victory, this time to a four-year term. On January 12, 1969, Volpe resigned from the governorship to become President Richard M. Nixon's secretary of transportation. Four years later President Nixon appointed him ambassador to Italy.

Philip William Noel, son of Seraphim Joseph Noel and Emma B. Crudeli, became the twelfth Italian American governor, serving two terms from 1973 to 1977 in Rhode Island. He was born in Warwick on June 6, 1931. His father, a mechanic, was born in Quebec, Canada; his maternal grandmother, Nilda, came from Carrara, Italy. Philip's mother was the daughter of an immigrant Italian sculptor.

Noel attended public schools in Warwick, where he excelled as a student and athlete. He received a bachelor's degree in economics and finance from Brown University (1954) and a law degree from Georgetown University (1957). He was admitted to the Rhode Island bar in 1957 and began a law practice in Warwick and Providence.

A Democrat, Noel began his political career as an intern in the Washington office of Senator John O. Pastore. He served as a city councilman (1960–1966) and mayor (1967–1972) in Warwick. During his six years as mayor, Warwick became the fastest-growing city in Rhode Island.

In 1972, Noel defeated Herbert F. DeSimone for governor by 22,638 votes. As Rhode Island's chief executive, Noel advanced the state's economy through a coalition of business, industry, labor, and government leaders and through a modernization of the tax system. In 1974 he was reelected to a second term with nearly 80 percent of the vote. Noel served as a member of the executive committee of the National Conference of Governors (1973–1974) and vice chairman of the Democratic National Convention Party Platform (1976). President Richard M. Nixon appointed Governor Noel to serve with a distinguished group of government leaders on a mission to the People's Republic of China as part of the process of normalization of relations with that country. In 1976, Noel decided to run for the United States Senate seat vacated by Senator Pastore, but he was defeated by wealthy automobile dealer Richard P. Lorber in the Democratic party primary by 100 votes.

Noel married Joyce Ann Sandberg in 1956, and they had three daughters and two sons. He is a Roman Catholic. After leaving the governorship, he returned to practice law as principal, chairman of the board of directors, and managing officer of McGovern, Noel & Benik.

Ella Tambussi Grasso became the thirteenth Italian American governor, serving as chief executive of Connecticut from 1975 to 1980. She was born in Windsor Locks in 1919, a Catholic, daughter of Giacomo, a baker, and Maria Olivia Tambussi. She attended St. Mary's School, the Chaffee School, and received a B.A. in 1940 and an M.A. in 1942 from Mount Holyoke, where she earned a Phi Beta Kappa key. She married Thomas Grasso, a school principal, and they had two children.

As a Democrat, Grasso's career included two elected terms to the Connecticut legislature, twelve years as secretary of state, and two terms in the United States House of Representatives. In 1974 Grasso won the gubernatorial election. She was reelected in 1978. Her successful political career earned her serious consideration for the Democratic Party vice presidential nomination. However, she became ill with cancer, which forced her to resign from the governorship on December 31, 1980, and she died in early 1981.

Three Americans of Italian descent were elected governor in the 1980s: Richard F. Celeste, Democrat, Ohio, 1983–1990; Mario M. Cuomo, Democrat, New York, 1983–1994;

G

and Edward D. Di Prete, Republican, Rhode Island, 1985–1989.

Celeste, a Methodist, was born in Cleveland in 1937, to Frank P. Celeste and Margaret Lewis Celeste. His marriage to Dagmar Ingrid Braun produced six children. A recipient of a Phi Beta Kappa key, he graduated from Yale with a B.A. in history and was a Rhodes scholar and an Oxford graduate with a Ph.D. in politics. He was executive assistant to Ambassador Chester Bowles in India, 1963–1967; a member of the Ohio legislature, 1971–1975; lieutenant governor, 1975–1979; and Peace Corps director, 1979–1981. Elected governor in 1982, he was reelected four years later.

Cuomo, the fifteenth Italian American governor, a Catholic, was born in Queens County, New York City, to Andrea Cuomo, who had migrated from Nocera Inferiore, and Immaculata Giordano, who had migrated from Messina. He attended public school in Queens and St. John's Prep School in Brooklyn. After graduating from St. John's College in 1953 and St. John's University Law School in 1956, he became confidential legal secretary to Judge Adrian P. Burke of the New York State Court of Appeals from 1956 to 1959. He practiced law in Brooklyn until 1974 and taught law at St. John's University for seventeen years.

Cuomo became immersed in community affairs when New York City Mayor John Lindsay appointed him to mediate the Forest Hills housing conflict and when he helped to save sixty-nine houses from being demolished in the Little Italy neighborhood of Corona. He chronicled these events in his book, *Forest Hills Diary: The Crisis of Low-Income Housing* (1974).

Governor Hugh Carey appointed Cuomo secretary of state, a position he served in from 1975 to 1978. In 1978 he was elected to a four-year term as lieutenant governor with incumbent Governor Carey. In 1982 Cuomo won a four-year term as governor, and he was reelected in 1986 and 1990 but was defeated for a fourth term in 1994. For a time Cuomo was considered a front-runner for the Democratic Party presidential nomination, the only Italian American to receive that recognition. He is married to Matilda Raffa Cuomo, and they have five children.

The sixteenth Italian American governor, and fourth from Rhode Island, is Edward D. Di Prete. A Republican and Catholic, he was born in Cranston in 1934 to Frank A.

and Maria Grossi Di Prete. He married Patricia Hines, and they had seven children. After receiving a B.S. in 1955 from Holy Cross College, he became a successful businessman. He served in the Navy and rose to the rank of lieutenant commander.

Di Prete worked his way up the political ladder by becoming Republican committeeman, Cranston school committee member, Cranston city councilman, mayor of Cranston (1979–1984), and member of the State Republican Executive Committee. In 1984 he was elected governor and two years later was reelected, this time to a four-year term. He suffered a defeat in a 1990 bid for a third term.

James Joseph Florio is the seventeenth Italian American governor. A Democrat and Catholic, born in Brooklyn in 1937, he later relocated to New Jersey. His marriage to Maryanne Spaeth produced three children, but resulted in a divorce and a second marriage. A graduate of Trenton State College, he continued his studies at Columbia and Rutgers, where he received a J.D. degree in 1967. He practiced law until 1974, when he was elected to the House of Representatives to serve from 1975 to 1989.

Florio served in the Navy from 1955 to 1958, and in the Naval Reserve as lieutenant commander from 1958 to 1975. He held various local public offices in Camden and was a member of the New Jersey General Assembly from 1969 to 1974. Florio lost one of the closest gubernatorial elections to Thomas Kean in 1981. He again received the Democratic nomination for governor in 1989 and won a four-year term, 1990–1993. He was defeated for reelection.

George Elmer Pataki, a Catholic, the eighteenth Italian American governor, defeated Mario M. Cuomo in 1994 and became New York State's chief executive on January 1, 1995. He was reelected in 1998. Part of Pataki's heritage is Italian. His maternal grandfather, Matteo Lagana, who migrated in 1908 from Reggio Calabria, Italy, married Agnes Lynch, who came from Ireland. His paternal grandparents, John Pataki and Elizabeth Szunich, migrated from Hungary in 1910. He was born to Margaret Lagana and Louie Pataki in 1945.

Pataki graduated from Yale University in 1967 and three years later received a law degree from Columbia University. As a Republican, he was elected mayor of his hometown-city, Peekskill, New York, in 1982 and was re-elected the following year. In 1984 he was elected to the New York Assembly until 1992, when he won a seat in the New York State Senate representing all of Putnam County, parts of Westchester County, and eastern Dutchess County. He is married to Elizabeth Rowland; they have four children.

Upon the resignation of Governor William F. Weld of Massachusetts on July 29, 1997, Lieutenant Governor Argeo Paul Cellucci became the nineteenth Italian American governor. Cellucci was born in Hudson, Massachusetts, April 24, 1948, to Argeo R. and Priscilla Rose Cellucci. His grandfather was born in Anzio, Italy, and his grandparents immigrated to America from the village of Velletri, in the province of Abruzzi.

Cellucci graduated from Boston College's School of Management in 1970, where he served in the Reserve Officers Training Corps. He also served in the United States Army Reserve from 1970 to 1978, when he was honorably discharged with the rank of captain. He graduated from Boston College Law School in 1973. Cellucci began his political career at an early age in the blue-collar town of Hudson, where he served as a member of the town charter commission (1970–1971) and as a selectman (1971–1977). In 1976 he was elected to the first of four terms in the Massachusetts House of Representatives from the Third Middlesex District (1977–1984). In 1984, Cellucci was elected to the Massachusetts Senate from the Middlesex and Worcester District (1985–1990), and during his third senate term became Assistant Republican Leader.

On November 6, 1990, Cellucci was elected lieutenant governor of Massachusetts on a ticket with William F. Weld. Four years later, Cellucci and Weld were reelected by a wide margin, winning 71 percent of the vote.

Governor Cellucci is a strong advocate of smaller government, lower taxes, and fiscal responsibility. He has been a leader in educational reform, access to health care, and the fight against domestic violence. He is a hands-on public official who has a reputation for seeking political consensus.

Cellucci married Janet Garnett in 1971, and they had two daughters. He is a Roman Catholic, a member of the Sons of Italy, and a partner in the law firm of Kittredge, Cellucci, and Moreira. He is an avid sports fan, runs two miles each morning, and plays bocce on weekends. In 1998 he was elected to a full term on his own merits.

Frank J. Cavaioli

Bibliography

Cavaioli, Frank J. "Charles Poletti and Fourteen Other Italian American Governors." In *Italians in Transition,* edited by Joseph V. Scelsa, Salvatore J. LaGumina, and Lydio F. Tomasi, 137–152. Staten Island, NY: American Italian Historical Association, 1990.

DiLeo, Joseph Marc. "Governor Alfred Emanuel Smith, Multi-Ethnic Politician." In *Italians and Irish in America,* edited by Francis X. Femminella, 241–258. Staten Island, NY: American Italian Historical Association, 1985.

Glasman, Roy R., comp. *American Governors and Gubernatorial Elections, 1775–1978.* Westport, CT: Merkler, 1978.

LaGumina, Salvatore J. "John Pastore, Italian American Political Pioneer." In *The Melting Pot and Beyond: Italian Americans in the Year 2000,* edited by Jerome Krase and William Egelman, 1–14. Staten Island, NY: American Italian Historical Association, 1987.

Sobel, Robert, and John Raimo, eds. *Biographical Directory of the Governors of the United States 1889–1978.* 4 vols. Westport, CT: Merkler, 1978.

See also CUOMO, MARIO M.; GRASSO, ELLA T.; LONGINO, ANDREW HOUSTON; PACA, WILLIAM; PASTORE, JOHN ORLANDO; POLITICS; VOLPE, JOHN A.

Grasso, Ella T. (1919–1981)

The first Italian American woman to rise to prominence in national politics, Ella Grasso, wife of a school principal, Thomas Grasso, was also the first woman to become a state governor in her own right and not as a widow or wife of a previous incumbent.

She was born Ella Tambussi to Italian immigrants in Windsor Locks, Connecticut, on May 10, 1919. She attended Mount Holyoke College and received a B.A. in 1940 and an M.A. in economics two years later. While working as assistant director of research in

G

Connecticut for the Federal Manpower Commission during World War II, Grasso joined the League of Women Voters and started a successful political career. She served in the Connecticut House of Representatives from 1951 to 1956, held the post of Connecticut's secretary of state between 1959 and 1970, and was elected to the United States House of Representatives in 1970 and in 1972. An effective vote getter, Grasso was slated for governor of Connecticut in 1974 by the political organization of Democratic Party boss John Bailey, who had been her mentor since her early days in politics. She defeated her Republican opponent, Robert H. Steele, with almost 59 percent of the vote, profiting in part by the fact that Italian Americans were the largest ethnic group in the state.

Grasso's election to the governorship marked a major turning point in her political stance. As a liberal congresswoman, Grasso advocated the appropriation of federal funds to expand social programs and to stimulate the economy, especially in the deindustrializing cities of her own district. For this reason, Steele nicknamed Grasso "Spender-Ella" during the 1974 campaign and forced her to promise that she would not introduce a state income tax if she was elected. In order to stick to her pledge and to keep her administration solvent at the same time, Governor Grasso lowered spending on welfare, held increases in benefits below the inflation rate, and dismissed a number of state workers. Furthermore, she displeased feminist voters by denying state funds for abortion under Medicaid. Yet Grasso also cut her own salary and replaced the governor's limousine with a compact car.

Although she had become a fiscal conservative, her frugality, her availability to citizens with any personal problem, her adherence to Roman Catholic principles in a state in which over half the voters shared her religious faith, and her prompt intervention to relieve the hardships of the population during a 1978 blizzard made Grasso quite popular in Connecticut. When she ran for reelection in 1978, she carried the state again with 59 percent of the vote.

In national politics, Grasso opposed the Vietnam War, walking out of the 1968 Democratic convention in sympathy with antiwar protesters who had been beaten by Chicago's police, and endorsed President Jimmy Carter against Senator Edward Kennedy in the 1980 primaries. She was also rumored to be under consideration as a potential vice-presidential nominee of the Democratic Party. Grasso fell ill with cancer during her second term. As a result, she resigned on December 31, 1980, and died on February 5, 1981.

Stefano Luconi

Bibliography

Cavaioli, Frank J. "Charles Poletti and 14 Other Italian American Governors." In *Italian Americans in Transition,* edited by Joseph V. Scelsa, Salvatore J. LaGumina, and Lydio F. Tomasi, 137–152. Staten Island, NY: American Italian Historical Association, 1990.

Chamberlin, Hope. *A Minority of Members: Women in the U.S. Congress.* New York: Praeger, 1973.

D'Andrea, Vaneeta. "The Ethnic Factor and Role Choices of Women: Ella Grasso and Midge Costanza—Two Firsts for American Politics." In *Italian Americans in the Professions,* edited by Remigio U. Pane, 253–264. Staten Island, NY: American Italian Historical Association, 1983.

Purmont, Jon E. "Ella Grasso." In *Italian Americans and Their Public and Private Life,* edited by Frank J. Cavaioli, Angela Danzi, and Salvatore J. LaGumina, 9–19. Staten Island, NY: American Italian Historical Association, 1993.

See also GOVERNORS; POLITICS

Green, Rose Basile (b. 1914)

Writer, scholar, poet, professor, and education administrator, Rose Basile Green has had a distinguished career in the academic fields of American and English civilization and literature. Her pride and interest in her Italian origins are reflected in creative writing, research, and organizational activities.

Her paternal grandfather, Giovanni Basile, migrated with his family from Calitri, Avellino, Italy, to the United States. Her father, Salvatore, and her mother, Carolina Galgano Basile, prospered in New Rochelle, New York, as a result of their business enterprises. However, they moved to Connecticut because of Salvatore's illness. They bought a large farm in Harwinton, where Rose and her siblings attended a one-room schoolhouse, opposite their home, on property that Salvatore had donated to the town.

Green earned a B.A. in English at the College of New Rochelle, an M.A. in Italian studies at Columbia University, and a Ph.D. in American civilization at the University of Pennsylvania. She worked one year in Torrington, Connecticut, with the Works Projects Administration Writers Project. Subsequently, she taught English and Italian for six years in the Torrington High School and dramatics in the evening adult education program. In her prose and poetry, she has lauded Italians for enriching all phases of American life. She has distinguished herself as an Italian American woman in the academic and literary world.

After one year (1942–1943) as registrar and associate professor of English at the University of Tampa in Florida, Green—who by then had married Raymond Silvernail Green—worked with the National Broadcasting Company in New York as a freelance writer of radio scripts (1943–1953). The Greens' two children were born within that decade.

Green's university-teaching career began in 1953 at Temple University and culminated at Cabrini College in Radnor, Pennsylvania (1957–1970). She was one of the college's founders, and she served as associate professor and chairman of the English department. Her major scholarly work is *The Italian American Novel: A Document of the Interaction of Two Cultures* (1974). In this book, she examines seventy writers of Italian descent and demonstrates their importance, both for their aesthetic value and their social implications, critically evaluating them within the framework of American literature.

Rose Basile Green has also been a major Italian American poet, producing the following: *To Reason Why* (sonnets 1971); *The Violet and the Flame* (poems 1968); *Primo Vino* (sonnets 1974); *Seventy-six for Philadelphia* (sonnets 1975); *Woman: The Second Coming* (sonnets 1977); and *Songs of Ourselves* (sonnets 1982).

Since her academic retirement in 1970, Dr. Green has remained active writing and contributing to Italian American cultural and educational affairs. Throughout her highly productive careers she has been motivated by her dedication and loyalty to her ancestry.

Margherita Marchione

Bibliography

Green, Rose Basile. *The Italian American Novel: A Document of Interaction of*

Two Cultures. Rutherford, NJ: Fairleigh Dickinson University Press, 1974.

Marchione, Margherita. *Americans of Italian Heritage.* New York: University Press of America, 1995.

Who's Who Among Authors and Journalists 1988.

See also LITERATURE; POETRY

Greenwich Village

Although renowned for its literary bohemia, Greenwich Village has supported an ethnic Italian community since the middle of the nineteenth century. In the 1850s the exiled Giuseppe Garibaldi worked as a candle maker in a shop on Bleecker Street. In 1866 the first Italian national parish in the city was established on Sullivan Street, although its first official act was a baptism of an Irish infant.

There were some fifty thousand Italians living in the south section of Greenwich Village by World War I. They were representative of the mass immigration from Italy, although the Village was also a second settlement for more prosperous families. Typical housing stocks were the five- and six-story tenements with small railroad flats (most of the buildings still stand and, in some cases, apartments have bathtubs in the kitchen and toilets in the hallway). Housing was in proximity to employment opportunities in small manufacturing, notably the garment industry.

While many Italian neighborhoods were breaking up after the war, especially following the immigrant quotas introduced in 1924, enough families remained in the Village to sustain a vibrant ethnic community. In the process, community life was restructured around the generations born or raised in the Village. They transcended the narrow *paesani* (fellow townsfolk) loyalties and dialect communities that were the basis for immigrant social organizations. The second generation articulated a broader ethnic identification within the context of the urban neighborhood. The Italian neighborhood was a further adaptation of traditional ethnic culture within urban America at a particular historical juncture. With the eclipse of immigrant aid societies, a restructured ethnic community featured an active parish and district politics, in both cases institutional frameworks shaped by the

G

Irish. An Americanized Mafia also acquired communal significance.

The core of community life was the Italian American family and kinship network; in 1955, one localized kinship group consisted of thirteen related households spanning four generations, with the oldest member migrating to the Village in 1882. Ethnic familism supplied a value system, or ethos, that was the basis of ethnic communal solidarity, evidenced in the exchange of respects occasioned by family life-crises. A family neighborhood articulated with a social neighborhood based on peer relationships, including the classic urban "cornerboy" group. These localized relationships made the Italian neighborhood a safe moral world, promoting cultural conformity and monitoring the movement of "strangers."

Presently, the historic Italian community in Greenwich Village is imperiled by the gentrification of lower Manhattan, in particular by the expansion of SoHo. Ethnic community institutions are withering, although family-centered social networks are buttressed by relocated relatives and friends. History and nostalgia keep the "old neighborhood" relevant for the ethnicity of those who have moved further into the mainstream; the urban Italian neighborhood is an American *paese* (village) that symbolizes the family's connection to a meaningful ethnic past. To an extent, the image, if not substance, of an Italian community in the Village is fostered by thriving Italian restaurants, food stores, and annual street festivals. The commercialized residue of Italian ethnic culture is in keeping with the cosmopolitan character of the new neighborhood.

Donald Tricarico

Bibliography

Tricarico, Donald. *The Italians of Greenwich Village*. New York: Center for Migration Studies, 1984.

Ware, Caroline. *Greenwich Village, 1930–1935*. New York: Harper, 1965.

See also COLONIES IN SMALL TOWNS

Grocers

See OCCUPATIONS OF ITALIAN IMMIGRANTS IN TURN-OF-THE-CENTURY AMERICA

Groppi, James Edward (1930–1985)

Civil rights activist James Groppi was born on November 16, 1930, in "Guinea Hill," the Italian neighborhood on the south side of Milwaukee, Wisconsin. His parents, Giacondo and Girgina, migrated from Italy to Wisconsin. After attending the Immaculate Conception School, he went to Bay View High School, where he captained the basketball team. He keenly felt the persecution of Italians and resented all kinds of ethnic humor. The shame felt because his parents spoke broken English caused Groppi to remark, "It hurt."

Groppi studied for the priesthood at Mount Calvary Seminary in Fond du Lac and during vacations assisted poor black children in the ghetto. Later, he attended St. Francis Seminary, where he boycotted the minstrel show produced by his classmates.

After his ordination in June 1959, he was assigned to a parish on the south side of Milwaukee, St. Veronica's, and later to St. Boniface, then an almost all-black parish and the scene of his fervent civil rights struggle. In 1963 he took part in the civil rights march on Washington, and in the following year, with some Protestant and Catholic clergy, he drove to Selma, Alabama, to support the Reverend Martin Luther King Jr. Unlike Dr. King, he advocated direct and violent response. On his return home he wanted to make Milwaukee the "Selma of the North." Within a short time he had been arrested a dozen times and was considered, nationally, to be a radical priest.

By now Groppi was totally committed to fighting injustice close to home. His first protest in June 1965 was aimed at blocking access to a school. Two brief arrests preceded his participation in a big riot in that city at the end of July 1967.

When an NAACP office in Milwaukee was bombed, Groppi recruited some young blacks to guard it, furnished them with a carbine, and organized a commando unit. All this occurred during a period of social activism in the wake of Vatican Council II, when the dominant white majority in Milwaukee became embittered. One commentator remarked that Groppi was "the sandpaper who rubbed the white majority raw." The attacks on him grew sharper, and he was labeled the "white nigger."

In September 1967 commandos trashed Mayor Henry W. Maier's office. When some twenty-three thousand local and national protestors convened, political leaders feared widespread violence. Some clergy denounced Groppi and demanded that his religious superiors muzzle him. However, his archbishop, William Cousins, while denouncing Groppi's methods, approved of his goals.

Groppi criticized not only white domination but some aspects of the Catholic faith as well. He believed in salvation through agitation. He rejected the "pietistic sweet gospel of wait after death" for solving problems, and would substitute drastic rhetoric and action. In the fall of 1969, for instance, he led some 600 welfare mothers on a ninety-mile march to the Wisconsin Assembly in Madison and forced his way into the chamber, for which he was arrested and jailed. He was also imprisoned for burning draft board records.

After the tumultuous years of the 1960s, Groppi fell into relative obscurity. But his niche as a violent agitator was secure. More than six hundred admirers, led by the comedian and activist Dick Gregory, honored him at a testimonial dinner in the last year of his life.

Groppi broke with the Catholic Church in April 1976 and married Margaret Rozga, like him, a militant agitator. They had two daughters. In December 1984 he underwent brain surgery that left him partially paralyzed and confined to a wheelchair. Despite his desire to be reconciled with his church, he died on November 4, 1985, before achieving this end.

Gaetano L. Vincitorio

Bibliography

Adams, James Truslow. *The March of Democracy: A History of the United States,* continued by Gaetano L. Vincitorio, as *The Record of 1969.* New York: Charles Scribner's Sons, 1970.

Aukofer, Frank A. *City With a Chance.* Milwaukee: Bruce, 1968.

Tracy, Phil. "Groppi." *The Critic* 29 (March–April 1971): 12–24.

James Groppi, radical civil rights priest, discusses social issues at the University of Wisconsin at La Crosse, April 29, 1976. Courtesy Frank J. Cavaioli.

Zahn, Gordon. "Father Groppi: An Evaluation." *U.S. Catholic* 33 (January 1968): 19–22.

See also RADICALISM; RELIGION

Grosso, Sonny
See LAW ENFORCEMENT

Grucci Family
See FIREWORKS INDUSTRY

H

Health and Italian Americans

Immigrants bring with them predispositions, based on genetics and lifestyle, from their native countries that impact on their health in their new environment. Italian Americans, and others who were raised in ethnic collectives, acquired from that experience concepts and attitudes toward health and illness and also fundamental styles of interpersonal behavior and concerns about society as a whole. The influence of this enculturation carries over into health care situations and influences personal activities vis-à-vis health maintenance and disease prevention, often irrespective of socioeconomic class and acculturation, regional origins, or urban–suburban residence.

Epidemiological data that compared the health status of Italians and Americans in the early decades of this century, and for the contemporary era, found that the leading causes of death for adults at both times were similar in Italy and in the United States. During the peak periods of immigration, from 1900 to 1930, adults and their children were more likely to be ill and die from diseases of bacterial origin. For the past thirty years the leading causes of death for the adult populations in both countries have been the degenerative diseases, particularly cardiovascular disease and cancer.

Studies of Italian-born immigrants in New York and Pennsylvania at the turn of the century showed that they had relatively low death rates when compared to other recently arrived groups. From 1928 to 1932 Italian males had the lowest death rate from all causes of any foreign-born group (except for Polish Jews in New York City), even lower than the native-born population. The rates for Italian females were slightly higher than for the native born. Studies also determined lower mortality from heart disease and from nephritis among Italian males and from cancer for both sexes. Moreover, the mortality from tuberculosis among Italians was also lower than for the native born. On the other hand, there was a high mortality from pneumonia for both sexes and from diabetes for females, which contrasted to lower figures for southern Italy. Studies of data collected during the 1950s and 1960s showed similar results.

As late as 1980, Italian immigrants were reported to have lower mortality rates when compared to the Irish. Similarities in health status were found between Jewish and Italian foreign-born residents in New York City. Both groups showed a low proportional mortality ratio for cerebral vascular disease, pneumonia and influenza, cirrhosis, and accidents when contrasted to the Irish immigrants.

Italian immigrants, especially those from southern Italy, arrived in the United States with a lower risk for heart disease and certain cancers than the general population. However, incidence of disease and mortality rates change with succeeding generations when compared to those of the general population in the host country. This is related to the learning of new health behaviors and/or exposure to new environmental risks.

In a landmark community study and analysis of ethnic health and disease patterns, the Italian American community of Roseto, Pennsylvania, was compared with Bangor, an immediately adjacent town, and three other nearby communities. Researchers discovered an unusually low rate of incidence and mortality from myocardial infarction (heart attack) in

Roseto from 1955 to 1961. It was also noted at the time that Roseto, which had been settled by immigrants from a town in southern Italy in 1882, displayed a high level of ethnic and social homogeneity, close family ties, and cohesive community relationships.

Research in Roseto indicated that variations in the incidence of coronary heart disease existed between different ethnic groups and also among ethnically similar groups in different localities. After the initial period of study, investigators predicted that the eventual loosening of social ties as immigrants assimilated in Roseto would decrease their apparent protection from deaths due to myocardial infarction. By the late 1960s and early 1970s, social change was evident in the community and the predicted increase in the incidence and mortality was recorded.

Data on cancer rates and immigrants focus on the risk of disease upon arrival in the host country and the subsequent changes in that risk over time. Reports on cancer risk in Italy show that rates are lower for most cancers when compared to the United States rates, and immigrants arriving in the United States from southern Italy are reported to have the lowest cancer risk of all.

Looking at data on Italians who migrated to the United States, Australia, and England, it was established that Italians arrived in the United States with a low mortality rate of colon, breast, lung, prostate, and rectal cancer. Stomach and esophageal cancer rates were the only two that were higher in Italian immigrants than in the general population of United States.

Many researchers have noted that the risk of cancer for Italians changes with the duration of stay in the host country. People who migrate from countries, such as Italy, with low rates of particular cancers show rapid increases for colon and rectal cancers that are ascribed to a new diet rich in animal products. In recent U.S. studies, the lack of a significant difference between breast cancer rates for Italian immigrant women, who arrived with lower risk than the local population, was attributed to the longer duration of women's stay in this country.

Ethnic groups have been studied to determine how culture influences illness behavior—how symptoms are perceived, evaluated, and influence the seeking of appropriate and timely health care. Zabrowski's pioneering study (1952) on the cultural perception of pain among Italians, Irish, Jewish, and "Old American" stock showed that Italian American and Jewish American patients exhibited more emotional responses to pain than did the other two groups. Time orientation was also noted to have a bearing on people's attitudes toward pain. Italian Americans were the most present-oriented since they appeared more concerned with pain relief than with the implications of their pain on future conditions.

Another important study of culture and symptoms by Zola (1966) paid particular attention to the way Italian and Irish patients reacted to and perceived their illnesses. The Irish were more likely than Italians to deny that pain was a feature of their illness and this difference held true even when the patients were diagnosed with the same problem. The Italians also presented more symptoms than the Irish, and unlike Irish patients, who denied that their symptoms interfered with their relationships with people, Italians reported the disruption in interpersonal relationships as a major part of their complaint. Reliance on interpersonal relationships is said to influence the use of medical consultants. In seeking medical advice, Italian Americans exhibited a greater use of lay consultations within family and kinship networks than other ethnic Americans.

When Italian Catholics, Protestants, and Jews were surveyed for their response to symptoms, "feeling state" changes, such as pain and weakness, were listed as the most important cues to seeking health care. The Italian respondents, however, were the only ethnic group to list *only* feeling states as symptoms of illness. Reliance on the presence of pain and weakness among Italian Americans negatively affected the early detection and treatment of degenerative diseases.

Ethnicity continues to be a significant factor in perception of pain. A 1984 study (Koopman, Eisenthal, and Stoeckle) found that female Italian American patients over sixty years of age reported pain more frequently than their Anglo-American counterparts. Older Italian immigrant women's freedom to react to pain was attributed to their maintenance of Italian traditions. On the other hand, increases in formal education, and ongoing interactions with people from other ethnic groups were given as explanations for the lack of significant ethnic difference in response to pain for people under the age of 60.

Suzanne Nicoletti Krase

Bibliography

Calabresi, Massimo. "The Relation of Country of Origin to Mortality for Various Causes in New York State." *Human Biology* 17 (1945): 340.

Egolf, Brenda, et al. "The Roseto Effect: A 50 Year Comparison of Mortality Rates." *American Journal of Public Health* 82, no. 8 (1992): 1089–1092.

Facchini, Ugo, et. al. "Geographical Variation of Cancer Mortality in Italy." *International Journal of Epidemiology* 14 (1985): 538–548.

Geddes, Marco, et al. "Cancer in Italian Migrants." *Cancer Causes and Control* 2 (1991): 133–140.

Koopman, Cheryl, Sherman Eisenthal, and John D. Stoeckle. "Ethnicity in Reported Pain, Emotional Distress and Requests of Medical Outpatients." *Social Science and Medicine* 18, no. 6 (1984): 487–490.

Ragucci, Antoinette T. "Italian Americans." *Ethnicity and Medical Care,* edited by A. Harwood. Cambridge: Harvard University Press, 1981.

Rosenwaike, Ira, and Katherine Hempstead. "Differential Mortality by Ethnicity: Foreign-born Irish, Italians and Jews in New York City, 1979–1981." *Social Science and Medicine* 29, no. 7 (1989): 885–889.

Stout, Clarke, et al. "Unusually Low Incidence of Death from Myocardial Infarction—Study of an Italian American Community in Pennsylvania." *Journal of the American Medical Association* 188, no. 10 (1964): 845–849.

Zabrowski, Mark. "Cultural Components of Response to Pain." *Journal of Social Issues* 8 (1952): 16–20.

Zola, Irving Kenneth. "Culture and Symptoms: An Analysis of Patients Presenting Complaints." *American Sociological Review* 31 (1966): 615–630.

See also ASSIMILATION; MEDICINE

Health Menace and the Italian Immigrant

The concept of equating disease with outsiders is a historical perennial. Throughout history, communities have often regulated who could enter their society by the fear that strangers often brought disease in the form of deadly epidemics. Traditionally, the best defense against foreign sickness was quarantine, a procedure inaugurated in the Middle Ages by the Venetians. In July 1377 the municipal council of Ragusa on the Dalmatian coast had mandated a thirty-day period of isolation from those coming from places known to have experienced the plague. Extension of the isolation period to forty days gave rise to the term "quarantine," which was derived from *quarantenaria.* Five centuries later, emigrants from Venice and other locations on the Italian peninsula would be suspected of endangering the public health of other lands by their very arrival.

During the era of mass migration to America at the end of the nineteenth century, fear of diseases from abroad persisted. The discovery of germ theory in the 1880s enhanced and refocused preexisting apprehensions that newcomers presented a health menace to host populations. In the United States, some American nativists medicalized their prejudice, advocating curbing immigration in the name of public health. However, even Americans who did not oppose immigration often feared that immigrants posed a public health threat for which quarantine was inadequate.

Between 1880 and 1921, 23.5 million immigrants arrived in the United States, most from Southern and Eastern Europe, including 4.5 million Italians, the largest number of any national group. Faced with a migration unprecedented in its size and diversity, the federal government established procedures to interrogate and inspect newcomers. At federal immigration depots such as New York's Ellis Island, uniformed physicians of the United States Marine Hospital Service conducted line inspections of newcomers traveling third class and steerage. Those with higher priced tickets were seen by health inspectors in their passenger cabins prior to landing. The purpose of these inspections was twofold: to ensure that newcomers were not arriving with harmful, contagious diseases that might endanger Americans and to determine whether immigrants were sufficiently healthy and robust to support themselves and become economically productive members in their adopted country. Only 2 to 3 percent of newcomers inspected annually were ever rejected at immigration depots; most of those who were rejected were halted for health reasons.

Although there was no evidence that any single immigrant group was a health menace or that there was a direct relationship between

H

any immigrant group and a particular disease, nativists often sought to blame a specific ethnic group for the presence of a particular disease. The Italians were an especially popular target of such stigmatization. During a virulent polio epidemic along the eastern seaboard in the summer of 1916, the Italians were blamed for the presence of the paralyzing disease that often struck children. In New York the polio death rate per one thousand estimated population of children under ten years of age was 1.63 for Italian children, well below the 3.42 for the native-born in 1916. However, the 1,348 polio cases contracted by those of Italian nativity in New York City was the highest for any immigrant group, second only to the 3,825 cases among native-born. What did polio have to do with being Italian? Nothing, according to public health officials. Still, because there were so many Italian immigrants living in tightly concentrated neighborhoods, and because immigrants were viewed by many as a marginal and potentially subversive influence upon society, the incidence of Italian polio made a dramatic impact on the imagination of a public shaken by the virulence of the epidemic.

Italians who were impoverished workers from the southern provinces were frequently denigrated by critics as unclean and unhealthy. Columbia University political economist and ardent nativist Richmond Mayo-Smith offered an unflattering Italian depiction of immigrants in New York's tenements: "Huddled together in miserable apartments in filth and rags, without the slightest regard to decency or health, they present a picture of squalid existence degrading to any civilization and a menace to the health of the whole community."

Also troubling to many critics was the synthesis of Christian and pagan beliefs that influenced southern Italian views of what caused disease and what cured it. Among newcomers' cultural baggage was often the belief that illness was the result of *il malocchio,* the "evil eye" of envy and jealousy. The person who had the evil eye, it was believed, could cause physical injury, sickness, or even death with a glance. Prayer was one response, amulets and incantations another. Coral, silver, gold, or bone amulets representing animals' claws or teeth could ward off the evil eye. Amulets were placed in the home or worn on the body. Back in their native villages, southern Italians had coped with illness by ap-

plying folk remedies derived from a reservoir of folk traditions and customs, and by consulting "specialists" such as witches, barbers, midwives, and herbalists. Physicians were expensive and often held in suspicion as overeducated outsiders. Such preferences and practices found their way into Italian immigrant enclaves in the United States.

Anti-Italian nativists seeking to portray Italian immigrants as health menaces resistant to Western physicians and their therapies met vocal opposition from Italian physicians who had also migrated to the United States. Antonio Stella, M.D., was born in Muro, Lucania, in 1868. Educated in medicine at the Royal University in Naples, he migrated to the United States in 1909. He specialized in internal medicine, becoming a prominent physician with such famous patients as opera star Enrico Caruso. Stella and other Italian physicians argued that any health problems suffered by Italians were the results of their American experience rather than an unhealthy predeparture life or innate biological inferiority. He refuted charges that Italians were especially slovenly or weak of moral fiber. He reminded the public that "the Italians, together with the Slavs more than any other foreign group, engage in hazardous occupations, in mines, steel mills, blasting, excavations, besides all sorts of dusty and unhealthy trades—thus many times they pay with their health and life, while adding to the prosperity of the United States."

Stella, long interested in tuberculosis among the Italians, often wandered the streets of Little Italy on New York's Lower East Side. He blamed congested housing and dark unventilated sweatshops for weakening the bodies of robust Italian laborers, making them fertile soil for the "Koch bacillus." He wrote,

> Six months of life in the tenements are sufficient to turn the sturdy youth from Calabria, the brawny fisherman of Sicily, the robust women from Abruzzi and Basilicata, into the pale, flabby, undersized creatures we see dragging along the streets of New York and Chicago, such a painful contrast to the native population! Six months more of this gradual deterioration, and the soil for the bacillus tuberculosis is amply prepared.

Stella's observations were confirmed by Italian immigration officials, who watched as their "birds of passage" flocked home to Italy wilted and sick. Ship physicians reported that the rate of illness was higher among those returning to Italy than among the America-bound and that tuberculosis was the most frequently diagnosed ailment. In 1904 a list of the most common diseases treated on ocean voyages back to Italy showed that the 278 cases of tuberculosis detected were greater than all the others combined; malaria, contracted by Italians in rural migrant labor, was a distant second place with forty-nine cases.

The relationship of Italian immigrants and their descendants to disease and medicine did not remain stagnant. As Italians climbed the ladder of economic success, they improved the physical and material conditions of their lives, including health conditions. Moreover, customs, traditions, and beliefs about health and disease altered as Italians became incorporated into American middle-class life. With each succeeding generation raised in the United States, physicians increasingly replaced folk healers as the health care providers of choice. Italian immigrants and their children embraced American standards of public health and hygiene. By World War II few nativists sought to stigmatize Italians in America as health menaces. However, the Italian immigrant experience shows how readily nativists incorporated the double-helix of health and fear in their anti-immigrant diatribes aimed at persuading the native-born that immigrants from the southern provinces of Italy were unfit for America.

Alan M. Kraut

Bibliography

Brindisi, Rocco. "The Italian and Public Health. " *Charities* 12 (1904): 483–486.

Caroli, Betty Boyd. *Italian Repatriation from the United States, 1900–1914*. New York: Center for Migration Studies, 1973.

Kraut, Alan. *Silent Travelers: Germs, Genes, and the "Immigrant Menace."* New York: Basic Books, 1994.

Mayo-Smith, Richmond. *Emigration and Immigration: A Study in Social Science*. New York: Scribner's, 1890.

Orsi, Robert Anthony. *The Madonna of 115th Street: Faith and Community in Italian Harlem, 1880–1950*. New Haven: Yale University Press, 1985.

Rogers, Naomi. *Dirt and Disease: Polio Before FDR*. New Brunswick, NJ: Rutgers, 1992.

———— . *Some Aspects of Italian Immigration to the United States, Statistical Data and General Consideration Based Chiefly Upon the United States Census and Other Official Publications*. 1924. Reprint, New York: Arno Press, 1975.

Stella, Antonio. "The Effect of Urban Congestion on Italian Women and Children." *Medical Record* 74 (2 May 1908): 722–732.

Williams, Phyllis H. *South Italian Folkways in Europe and America: A Handbook for Social Workers, Visiting Nurses, School Teachers, and Physicians*. New Haven: Yale University Press, 1938.

See also HEALTH AND ITALIAN AMERICANS

Higher Education

Initially, the role of Italians in American education had been dominated by the priests (mainly Jesuits) and religious leaders who have helped to found many Catholic colleges and universities. This was particularly true in the western part of the country in the development of such colleges and universities as Gonzaga University in Spokane (Joseph Cataldo and Lawrence Palladino), Regis University in Denver (John B. Guida, Joseph M. Marra, Dominic Pantanella, and Salvatore Personé), University of Santa Clara (Aloysius Brunengo, Nicholas Congiato, Felix Cicaterri, Aloysius Masnata, John Nobili, John Pinasco, and Aloysius Varsi), and the University of San Francisco (Joseph Bayma, Nicholas Congiato, Camillus Imoda, Anthony Maraschi, Aloysius Masnata, John Pinasco, and Joseph Sasia).

In the eastern part of the country in the nineteenth century, Catholic higher education emerged with Jesuit priests such as Anthony F. Ciampi at the College of the Holy Cross (Worcester) and at Loyola College (Baltimore), John A. Grassi at Georgetown University, and Nicholas Russo at Boston College. Grassi became the first president of a Catholic university in the United States when, on March 1, 1815, President James Madison signed a bill recognizing Georgetown as a university.

Understandably, the founders and presidents of seminaries also played a key role in the development of higher education. They included priests Angelo Paresce, a Jesuit at Woodstock College, Maryland, Anthony Penco, a Vincentian at St. Joseph's (Fordham), Bronx, New York, and Joseph Rosati, also a Vincentian, from St. Mary's (Perryville, Missouri). Other leading Jesuit educators include Jesuit educators Leonard Nota of St. Xavier's in Cincinnati, Nicholas Congiato of St. Joseph's College in Bardstown, and John Cambiaso of Immaculate Conception College, now Loyola University in New Orleans.

The work of the Italian Franciscans in higher education during the last century is best illustrated with the founding of St. Bonaventure's College in Allegheny, New York. The high academic standards at this college were established by such Franciscan educators as Pamphilius da Magliano, its founder, and his successors, namely, Augustine da San Damiano, Diomede Falconio, Maximus Cassini, Charles Vissani, and Leo Rizzo da Saracena.

A selection of Italian American educators of the nineteenth century had a special expertise in administering institutions of higher learning; they differ from those outstanding educators who were famous as teachers. Among these were Francesco DeVico, Giambattista Pianciani, and Angelo Secchi, who taught at Georgetown University; Charles Constantine Pise, who taught at Mount St. Mary's College in Emmitsburg; and Emilio DeAugustinis, Camillus Mazzella, and Aloysius Sabetti, who taught Jesuit seminarians at Woodstock. There were also educators who taught Italian at other important institutions of the nineteenth century. Following in the footsteps of Carlo Bellini who had been appointed professor on the faculty of William and Mary before the United States won its independence, there were, during the nineteenth century, teachers such as Pietro Bachi at Harvard, Vincenzo Botta and Eleuterio Foresti at New York University, Lorenzo Da Ponte at Columbia, Luigi Monti at Vassar, and Tullio S. Verdi at Brown.

More recent educators of Italian heritage in the upper echelons of university administration include the late A. Bartlett Giamatti, the former president of Yale University and expert teacher of comparative literature, and Neil L. Rudenstine, the president of Harvard University, whose mother (Mae Esperito) is Italian. Also worthy of note are the deans of law schools such as Guido Calabresi at Yale University, Antonio R. Papale at Loyola University (New Orleans), and Frank J. Macchiarola at Yeshiva University (and now president at St. Francis College in Brooklyn).

Other Italian Americans who have become established as outstanding educators include Max Ascoli, a political scientist at New York School for Social Research; John A. Baldessari, an artist and educator at California Institute of Arts; Pietro Belluschi, an architect at School of Architecture and Planning at the Massachusetts Institute of Technology; Luciano Berio, a composer at Juilliard School of Music; the late F. Leo Buscaglia, an expert in special education who taught at University of California at Los Angeles; Arcangelo Cascieri, a celebrated sculptor at the Boston Architectural Center; Edward Chiera, a distinguished Orientalist at the University of Chicago; John A. Ciardi, a poet and literary critic at Rutgers University; John Paul Corigliano, a composer at Manhattan School of Music; the late Jan DeGaetani, a singer at Eastman School of Music at the University of Rochester; Amitai W. Etzioni, a sociologist at the Center for Policy Research at Columbia University; Giuseppe Fagnani, an Old Testament scholar at Union Theological Seminary; the late Enrico Fermi, a Nobel Prize physicist at University of Chicago; Alfred Ferretti, an engineering professor at Northeastern University; Gaetano Lanza, a pioneering engineer at Massachusetts Institute of Technology; Salvador E. Luria, a Nobel Prize biologist at Massachusetts Institute of Technology; A. J. Montanari, an expert in child behavior at the Montanari Clinical School; Camille Paglia, cultural critic and professor of humanities at University of the Arts in Philadelphia; Joseph V. Paterno, the football coach at Pennsylvania State University; Mario A. Pei, a philologist of the Casa Italiana at Columbia University; Floyd Zulli, Jr., an arts and literature professor at New York University; Gaetano Salvemini, a historian at Harvard University; Emilio G. Segrè, a Nobel Prize physicist at University of California; and William A. Vacchiano, an expert on the trumpet at the Juilliard School of Music.

While American history reveals a number of Italian Americans on the administrations and the faculties of the nation's colleges and universities, the number of Italian Americans among the students of these institutions has also grown in the major cities of the Northeast. In New York City, for example, during the last three decades, the percentage of Italian Americans attending college has been estimated to be as low as 25 percent and as high as 50 percent among students at institutions such as the City University and Fordham University.

Simultaneously, that same period has witnessed a growing consciousness among Italian Americans in academia as evidenced by the birth in recent years of such organizations as the John D. Calandra Institute, which defends the civil rights of Italian American faculty members and provides educational services to Italian American students, and Fieri National, which attempts to foster among Italian American college and university students a deeper appreciation of higher education. The library at Harvard University is the leader in the country among graduate institutions for the largest collection of works on Italian Americans; the College of the Holy Cross leads undergraduate institutions in this area.

Finally, in striving for reliability, any study of Italian Americans in higher education is necessarily elusive. While daughters and sons of Italian American fathers are easy to recognize through their family names, this is not true of an equal number of others with Italian mothers who have been administrators, students, or teachers. Their ethnic identity as Italian Americans, as illustrated already in the case of the president of Harvard University, cannot be so readily deciphered because their Italian American mothers had married men of a different ethnic background. That some Spanish family names can easily pass for Italian ones further complicates the problem.

Vincent A. Lapomarda

Bibliography

Angelo, Marl V. *The History of St. Bonaventure University*. St. Bonaventure, NY: Franciscan Institute, 1961.

Battistella, Graziano, ed. *Italian Americans in the '80s: A Socio-Demographic Profile*. New York: Center for Migration Studies, 1989.

Gambino, Richard. *Italian-American Studies and Italian-Americans at CUNY: Report and Recommendations*. New York: CUNY, 1987.

Garraghan, Gilbert J. "John Anthony Grassi, S.J." *Catholic Historical Review* 23 (1937): 273–293.

McGloin, John B. *Jesuits by the Golden Gate: The Society of Jesus in San Francisco, 1849–1969*. San Francisco: University of San Francisco, 1972.

McKevitt, Gerald. *The University of Santa Clara: A History, 1851–1977*. Stanford: Stanford University Press, 1979.

National Italian American Foundation. "Dr. Peter Sammartino Releases Study on Italian American Presidents of U.S. Universities." *Washington Newsletter* 3 (March 1979): 6, 8.

Schiavo, Giovanni E. *Four Centuries of Italian-American History*. Reprint of 4th ed. New York: Center for Migration Studies, 1992.

Stansell, Harold L. *Regis: On the Crest of the West*. Denver: Regis Educational, 1977.

See also BUSCAGLIA, LEO; CIAMPI, ANTHONY F.; GIAMATTI, A. BARTLETT; PAGLIA, CAMILLE; SAMMARTINO, PETER

Hill of St. Louis

By the end of the twentieth century the Hill in St. Louis, Missouri, had become one of America's most celebrated and enduring Little Italys. At the beginning of the twentieth century few would have predicted the extraordinary success of this ethnic enclave; indeed, few would have even noticed this obscure colony.

The origins of the Hill as an Italian immigrant colony date to the 1880s, when a handful of Lombard emigrants arrived in the area of southwest St. Louis, then known as Cheltenham. Nature had endowed the locale with rich clay deposits suitable for fire brick and terra cotta pipe. Underneath the terrain hundreds of miners extracted the valuable clay, and Cheltenham quickly became a flourishing hive of brick and pipe factories.

Why and how Lombard emigrants found their way to this isolated enclave in St. Louis in the early 1880s is unclear. Part of a much larger emigration, Lombards from a cluster of villages west of Milan—most notably Cuggiono, Inveruno, · and Robbechetto—for decades, had trekked throughout Europe and other continents in search of work.

Once a St. Louis beachhead had been established, a vigorous chain migration followed. An 1888 inventory counted ten dilapidated wooden shacks, several dozen workers, and three women. By 1907 the St. Ambrose parish census recorded an Italian population of 2,264 and almost three thousand second-generation Italian Americans. Sicilians constituted a minority on the Hill. Relationships between northern and southern Italians reflected Old World stereotypes, but in time the tensions faded. The economic maturation of the locale, especially the coming of several factories and foundries, secured the economic fortunes of immigrants and their children.

Journalists lyricized "Dago Hill" as "provincial" and "old world," but no phrase captured the neighborhood ethos better than "blue collar." From 1900 through World War II, the Hill persisted as the most working-class district in St. Louis. Hill Italians were drastically overrepresented in jobs at the bottom of the occupation ladder.

The Hill community that evolved after 1900 boasted a near exclusive Italian population, which was the result of cultural independence, geographic isolation, and ethnic solidarity. One of its residents recalled, "The Hill is strictly an Italian neighborhood, except I can remember one German family that lived on the same block with us."

The Catholic church played a critical role in negotiating a sense of solidarity and brokering ethnic tensions on the Hill. Until the 1920s the residents of the Hill seemed indifferent to efforts luring them to St. Ambrose parish. The 1925 dedication of a new St. Ambrose church, built in Lombard Romanesque style, rallied residents to the parish. Some extraordinarily talented priests worked to bring young people into the church, especailly through athletic enterprises. The athletic fame of Joe Garagiola and Lawrence "Yogi" Berra burnished the colony's reputation. Parish priests worked hard to keep the community together during World War II, as hundreds of men and women left the neighborhood.

By the 1950s the Hill faced a crisis shared by many other Italian neighborhoods. A litany of problems confronted the Hill: increasing numbers of impoverished African Americans flooded into south St. Louis, housing stock deteriorated, the industrial base declined, and a large number of elderly residents populated the area. By the late 1960s many urban planners were already writing the Hill's obituary. To add urban insult to ethnic injury, the federal government announced plans to build an interstate highway through a section of the Hill.

The interstate highway crisis spurred action. A dynamic priest, Father Salvatore Palumbo, rallied residents to fight and mobilize. Residents organized Hill 2000, a watchdog organization that monitored communal needs and helped find housing for young Italian Americans. Newly revived *feste* drew large crowds in the late 1960s and 1970s. Urban planners lauded the Hill as a model community, albeit one that made no sense—modest homes sandwiched by trendy restaurants and small factories—but worked nevertheless. The Hill attracted streams of writers and television crews. Young families abound. The future of the Hill augurs well for the twenty-first century.

Gary R. Mormino

Bibliography

Ets, Marie Hall. *Rosa: The Life of an Italian Immigrant.* Minneapolis: University of Minnesota Press, 1970.

Mormino, Gary Ross. *Immigrants on the Hill: Italian Americans in St. Louis, 1882–1982.* Urbana: University of Illinois Press, 1986.

Wood, Elmer Shorb. "Fairmount Heights: An Italian Colony in St. Louis." Master's thesis, Washington University, St. Louis, 1936.

Hospitality

The widely celebrated personal warmth and generosity of Italian American hospitality (*buon costume*) flows from the Italian spirit of abundance, *abbondanza*, which is based on southern Italian lifestyle with its interchanges of want and plenty, division and unity, and, in general, a life lived in close sympathy with the rhythms of the seasons. Although the practice of hospitality is predominantly something private and familial, it has been deeply informed and energized by Italy's long tradition of public festivals, which are the preeminent expressions of the contrasting Italian life cycles. Their origins extend back to premodern times to the civic, agrarian, and religious festivals (*feste*), which were not merely days free of labor, but times of civic communion and public joy when even the otherwise strict social distinctions among Italians were relaxed. During Italian festivals, then as now, epic amounts of meats with polenta or pasta accompaniments are prepared and served in the public square; and barrels provide a never-ending supply of wine, the epitome of *abbondanza*.

The feast as the public expression of Italians' "legendary hospitality" persists among Italian Americans in their many religious feasts: *Festa Dei Gigli, San Gennaro, San Donato, Santa Lucia,* among others. Over the years these celebrations have become gradually more commercial and have lost the intensity and totality of the earlier *feste*.

In the private sphere of Italian American life, the spirit of the *festa* and *abbondanza* persists down to the third and fourth generations. Italian American writer Suzanne M. Rini states: "One always empties the larder for dinner for guests, makes way too much of everything, and especially exhausts oneself making complicated dishes from complete scratch (not to mention the hunting and gathering of specialty shopping). Afterward . . . the spirit is not dampened by Herculean effort. No, the first irrational desire that springs to mind is to make *all* of the desserts in the Italian cookbook on the next auspicious occasion."

Italian American hospitality at its best is spontaneous and graceful; its subtlety is reflected in the Italian habit of referring to good manners (*buon costume*) rather than hospitality (*ospitalità*). During a visit, as the polite preliminaries of conversation progress, a table (*una tavola*) gradually fills up with fresh coffee, cannoli, and biscotti, or perhaps fruit, wine, bread, cheese, and prosciutto. All of the food and drink appear without frenzy or pretention.

Such automatic generosity reflects how essential hospitality was to the Italian ethos, and still is to many Italian Americans today. There is nothing incidental or adventitious about it. For to be inhospitable, or even to offer hospitality disingenuously, is to be somehow inhuman, *non cristiano*. (Since the Middles Ages southern Italians, who make up the greater part of the Italian American community, have referred to human beings as *cristiani*.) It is precisely the unaffected quality of Italian American hospitality that other Americans have always found highly attractive. Richard Gambino in *Blood of My Blood* (1974) underscores the attractiveness and primacy of Italian American hospitality by way of an episode from the career of a New York City social worker. Intimately familiar with the family life of the various ethnic groups who had immigrated to New York, this social worker was impressed deeply by her first visits to the homes of Italian American families during the Great Depression. She quickly recognized that nothing substantial could be discussed before some food or drink was shared in common. Thus, as Gambino points out, even the intrusive and distrusted "agents of the state" were introduced into the communion of the family by way of the table before they could have anything to do with the family's concerns.

The appeal of Italian American hospitality is perhaps even greater today than it was earlier in this century because person-to-person hospitality in the mainstream American culture has given way to a "hospitality industry" dominated by large hotel chains and fast-food restaurants for the masses and bed-and-breakfasts and specialty restaurants for the more discriminating.

The tradition of Italian hospitality had developed historically as a response to the ever-vexing social and political problem of how to treat the "other," foreigners, the ones who Italians refer to as *stranieri*, strangers. It was by way of hospitality, a hospitality of the table, that southern Italians dissolved a person's "otherness" and brought the stranger in closer. Italians, and first- and second-generation Italian Americans, held fast to a strictly ordered hierarchy of social relations (*l'ordine della famiglia*) that strongly discouraged relations with strangers. The family occupied the center of one's social existence. Next came *compari* and *padrini* and their female equivalents, *commare* and *madrine*, who were not simply godparents in the religious sense, but "intimate friends" and "venerated elders." Then there were *amici* and *amici di cappelo*, those whose standing in the community demanded deference. Last were *stranieri*, all those who one encountered in daily living: coworkers, tradesmen, shopkeepers. "It is an iron rule," writes Gambino, "that one has nothing to do with *stranieri*. One had to go up the hierarchy from the class of 'stranger' to 'friendly acquaintance' before one could even have human discourse."

One may rightly ask how such a tightly regulated social order, with its deep suspicion of strangers, produced a "legendary hospitality." The answer lies in what Gambino calls "a curious psychological twist of logic" that transforms *stranieri* into *amici* "through the rite of sharing a meal (or just coffee), a symbolic entering into the ceremony of family communion." For centuries southern Italians sustained themselves and absorbed wave after wave of invaders by means of this hospitality of the table. As was seen in the example of the New York social worker, it was the way in which Italian immigrants engaged the dominant American culture. Today, hospitality is no longer driven by such fundamental social necessities; where it persists it does so either as a natural and unself-conscious mannerism, or as part of a deliberate (but emphatically unpretentious) strategy to cultivate a distinctive Italian American identity. In the latter case, hospitality of the table, animated by the spirit of *abbondanza,* compels Italian Americans to be closely attentive to food and mealtime as "elusive subtleties" of their Italian heritage. According to Piero Camporesi, food, and especially its careful preparation and presentation, is a "voyage in time in search of roots, of irremediably lost origins; an attempt to recuperate through the mediation of the dinner table . . . a universe of lost smells and flavors that restores the ghost of a lost culture."

Dominic A. Aquila
Diane T. Aquila

Bibliography

Calvino, Italo, ed. *Italian Folktales.* New York: Pantheon, 1981.

Camporesi, Piero. *Bread of Dreams: Food and Fantasy in Early Modern Europe.* Cambridge, UK: Polity Press, 1989.

Field, Carol. *Celebrating Italy.* New York: William Morrow, 1990.

Gambino, Richard. *Blood of My Blood: The Dilemma of the Italian-Americans.* New York: Doubleday, 1974.

Rini, Suzanne M. "Food for Thought." *Fidelity* (February 1991): 37–41.

See also FOLKLORE, FOLKLIFE; FOODWAYS AND FOOD

Howard Beach and Bensonhurst

Two separate incidents that took place in the 1980s in a space of several years in boroughs of New York City helped perpetuate defamatory stereotypes of Italian Americans. The first occurred in the Howard Beach section of Queens, the other in the Bensonhurst section of Brooklyn.

On December 19, 1986, an African American man was killed in Howard Beach, a community populated by white ethnic groups among whom were Jews and Italian Americans. On that day, three African American men from the East New York section of Brooklyn experienced car trouble in Howard Beach. They walked down Cross Bay Boulevard in search of a telephone, which they found at the New Park Pizzeria. They also found grave danger in the form of a gang of white youths, some of whom were Italian Americans, who challenged their presence. One of the black men, Cedric Sanford, was beaten viciously. Another, Michael Griffiths, ran on to Belt Parkway, a nearby superhighway, and was hit by a car and killed. Within days, the Rev. Al Sharpton, a minister and civil right activist, led a group made up mainly of African Americans on a protest march through the streets of Howard Beach. The incident and the march received extensive media coverage, and racial tensions in the community and in the city overall grew. Although many Howard Beach residents held prayer services for the victims under the auspices of local churches and civic groups, these activities were mostly unreported by the media.

A special prosecutor, Charles J. Hynes, was appointed by Governor Mario Cuomo to investigate the matter. Hynes brought charges against Jason Ladone, Michael Pirone, John Lester, and Scott Kern, who were the alleged ringleaders of the gang. Pirone was acquitted, while the other three defendants were convicted. The prosecution convinced the jury that there was criminal liability because the white youths had, by their actions, paved the way for the unintentional death of Michael Griffiths. The convictions upset some white residents of Howard Beach, who felt their community was unfairly stigmatized.

On August 23, 1989, in Bensonhurst, Brooklyn, Yusuf Hawkins, a young African American man on his way to purchase a used car, was killed in a school yard. Seven young white men were arrested in connection with the murder, which, according to police statements, was racially motivated. The media picked up on this theme and suggested that Hawkins was killed because the Italian American community saw the African American as a dangerous and unwanted outsider. Many residents of Bensonhurst, a neat working-class neighborhood of tree-shaded streets, expressed shock at the killing, but as was the case three years earlier in Howard Beach, this fact was largely ignored. Instead, the predominant images on TV were of young Italian American youths carrying watermelons and shouting at marchers who had come to Bensonhurst to protest the murder. Efforts by religious and community leaders to hold vigil and prayer meetings to decry the killing and to bring calm to the area went unreported. Thus, the role of the media in creating an unflattering stereotype of young Italian males as bigots was significant. A serious examination of underlying issues and attitudes gave way to imagery that left Italian Americans looking like violence-prone racists.

Vincent S. Romano

Bibliography

DeSantis, John. *For the Color of His Skin.* New York: Pharos Books, 1991.

Richter, Robert, and Linda Richter. *Italian American Characters in Television Entertainment.* New York: The Commission for Social Justice, Grand Lodge of the State of New York, Order Sons of Italy in America, 1982.

Rieder, Jonathan. *Canarsie: The Jews and Italians Against Liberalism.* Cambridge: Harvard University Press, 1985.

See also ANTI-ITALIAN DISCRIMINATION; DISCRIMINATION AT CITY UNIVERSITY OF NEW YORK

H

I

Iacocca, Lee (b. 1924)

Automotive executive, captain of industry, persuasive spokesman, and marketing genius are just a few of the monikers used to describe Lee Anthony Iacocca. His father, Nicola, came to America at the age of twelve in 1902 from San Marco, twenty-five miles northeast of Naples. Lee (Lido) was born in Allentown, Pennsylvania, where the family settled.

For thirty-two years at the Ford Motor Company, Iacocca made his name as a marketing master. He rocketed through the Ford ranks as management trainee and into the higher echelons, eventually becoming president and chief operating officer. His career was highlighted by the marketing successes of the Mustang in 1964 and later the Mercury Cougar and the Lincoln Mark III.

He resigned from the Ford Motor Company in 1978 and assumed leadership of the Chrysler Corporation, where he fought for Chrysler's financial survival. As president, chief operating officer, and chairman of the board of directors, he doted over the company's ledgers and corporate finances. Iacocca required his staff to set goals on a quarterly basis. He then put together a package required by the congressional bill that gave the ailing corporation $1.5 billion in loan guarantees. He paid the loan back in full, years before it fell due. He initiated Chrysler's highly successful new front-wheel drive compact "K" cars and the minivan, thus assuring that Chrysler competed effectively with foreign carmakers.

Iacocca tried to enlist in the United States Army during World War II, but was classified 4F because of impairments from rheumatic fever. He attended college and earned a bachelor of science degree in industrial engineering from Lehigh University and a master's degree in mechanical engineering from Princeton University.

Lee Iacocca. One of the best known and most successful members of the business community, Iacocca was highly regarded as president of the Ford Motor Company. He is credited with rescuing the business fortunes of the Chrysler Motor Company. Courtesy Ford Motor Company.

Iacocca is active in many charitable and civic organizations and is chairman of the Statue of Liberty–Ellis Island Centennial Commission.

Elissa Ruffino

Bibliography
Abodaher, David. *Iacocca.* New York: Macmillan, 1982
Iacocca, Lee. *Iacocca.* New York: Bantam, 1984.
————. *Talking Straight.* New York: Bantam, 1988.
Wyden, Paul. *The Unknown Iacocca.* New York: Morrow, 1987.

See also BUSINESS AND ENTREPRENEURSHIP

Immigration History Research Center

The Immigration History Research Center (IHRC) of the University of Minnesota was established in 1965 with the objective of collecting and studying immigration documents from eastern, central, and southern Europe and the Near East. The center's scope was based on the observation that the second wave of immigration (1890–1930) had been neglected by scholarship; little had been done to preserve the primary sources that record this chapter of American immigration history. Influenced by the research agenda of the "new social history" with its concerns for the inner history of ethnic communities, the bulk of these materials was created by the immigrants (and their descendants) themselves.

Today the center's Italian American collection constitutes the most extensive body of source material in the country for the study of Italian immigration and ethnicity. Including over two hundred manuscript collections, a library of over 1,500 volumes, and files of some 450 newspapers and periodicals, it is one of the IHRC's largest and richest ethnic collections. The newspapers run from *L'Eco d'Italia* (1862–1894) to contemporary publications that span the political, religious, and cultural spectrum. Italian American imprints include autobiographies, plays, poetry, novels, and political and religious works. Many of these are rare items such as Camillo Cianfarra, *Il diario di un emigrante* (1904).

While the center holds materials relating to Italians in the Midwest, Far West, and South, the largest number of collections originated in the New York metropolitan area and New England, reflecting the residential patterns of Italian Americans. With respect to religion, in addition to a large collection of jubilee and commemorative albums of Italian parishes, the center holds the papers of Monsignor Luigi Pioletti and Father Nicola Carlo Odone, including the latter's diary covering almost a half century. Protestant evangelism among Italians is represented by a small number of manuscripts and several autobiographies and commentaries, while publications, such as *L'Asino,* reflect widespread anticlericalism among the immigrants. Italian American women are represented by the memoir of Rosa Cassettari (published as *Rosa: The Life of an Italian Immigrant* [1970]) and the papers of Angela Bambace, Clara Grillo, and Rose Ciresi.

Manuscript collections and publications documenting the participation of Italian Americans in labor and radical movements include works by Luigi Galleani, Arturo Giovannitti, Carlo Tresca, and Flavio Venanzi, which complement the center's labor press holdings and the papers of labor organizers, socialists, and anarchists, such as Emilio Grandinetti, Nino Capraro, and Fred Celli. The opposition to Fascism is documented in the manuscripts of George Quilici, Alberto Cupelli, Domenico Saudino, and Max Ascoli.

The center's holdings of Italian American professional and business persons include the papers of Charles Anzalone, a politician and leader in the strawberry industry in Louisiana; the correspondence of physician Diego Delfino; manuscripts of attorneys and authors Robert Ferrari and Maurice Marchello; and the papers of Vito Pittaro, prominent business and civic leader from Stamford, Connecticut. In addition, the IHRC holds the personal papers of a number of journalists, such as James Donnaruma, editor and publisher of *La Gazzetta del Massachusetts;* Vincent Massari, editor and publisher of *L'Unione* of Pueblo, Colorado; and Pasquale Mario De Ciampis, editor of the syndicalist publication *Il Proletario.*

Theater and music are richly recorded in the papers of Eduardo Migliaccio ("Farfariello"), Rocco de Russo, Fortunato Gallo, and Nicola Berardinelli. Italian Americans have been prolific writers of autobiographies, novels, and especially poetry. In addition to the papers of Alessandro Sisca ("Riccardo Cordiferro"), the center holds manuscript collections of Nino

Caradonna, Michelangelo Crisafi, Antonino Crivello, and Onorio Ruotolo.

The keystone of the Italian American Collection is the archives of the Order Sons of Italy in America (OSIA), which entails approximately 800 linear feet of documentation. The collection includes records of local as well as state and national lodges. Extensive insurance records provide data for demographic analyses. Membership applications and death claims provide place and date of birth, father's name, place of residence, occupation, spouse, children, citizenship, and medical information. The OSIA archives also include collections of papers from officers such as Giovanni Di Silvestro and George Spatuzza. The archives document the OSIA's response to political and natural disasters in Italy as well as its lobbying on foreign policy issues, United States immigration policy, and defamation.

The IHRC's Italian American Collection has been used extensively by American and foreign scholars, particularly from Italy. Their findings have been incorporated in books, articles, dissertations, and family and community histories, as well as films, television programs, and exhibits. In addition, the center has held a number of conferences dealing with aspects of Italian American history. In 1981 it sponsored the American Italian Historical Association's annual conference devoted to the theme of Italians in rural and small town America. On the occasion of its thirtieth anniversary (1996), the center's conference and variety show featuring immigrant cultures and the performing arts included a wide range of Italian American material.

External funding from the National Endowment for the Humanities and the National Historical Publications and Records Commission, supplemented by grants from the Northwest Area Foundation and the Rockefeller Foundation, has underwritten many of the center's activities. The Italian American Collection has been particularly supported by the Giovanni Agnelli Foundation and the Ministry of Foreign Affairs of Italy. OSIA has contributed generously to the gathering and processing of the Order's archives. Additional financial aid has come in the form of gifts from Italian American organizations and individuals.

Rudolph J. Vecoli

Bibliography
Andreozzi, John, comp. *Guide to the Records of the Order Sons of Italy in America.* St. Paul, MN: Immigration History Research Center, 1989.

Moody, Suzanna, and Joel Wurl, comps. and eds. *The Immigration History Research Center. A Guide to Collections.* New York: Greenwood, 1991.

Vecoli, Rudolph J. "Saving the Past for the Future: A Minnesota Library Contains 150 Years of Italian American History." *Ambassador: National Italian American Quarterly* 24 (winter 1994–1995): 18–21.

Wurl, Joel. "The Immigration History Research Center: a Historical Profile and Prospective Glimpse." *Ethnic Forum* 6 (fall 1988): 73–85.

See also ARCHIVES, ITALY; ARCHIVES, UNITED STATES

Impellitteri, Vincent
See COLD WAR: ITALIAN AMERICANS AND ITALY; POLITICS

Independent Order Sons of Italy (Ordine Indipendente Figli d'Italia)

In 1907 Vincenzo Sellaro, founder and first Supreme Venerable of the Order Sons of Italy in America (OSIA), clashed with other leaders of the Order and led a group of lodges in seceding from the organization. On April 29, 1907, articles of incorporation were filed in Manhattan for the "Independent Order Sons of Italy," and signed by the first directors: Giuseppe Mattina, Stefano Cognata, Accursio Azzara, Francesco Bongiorno, and Giuseppe Navarra.

The stated goal of the Order was "to give voluntary aid and protection to its members, and establish the relationship of fraternal brotherhood among them; and to voluntarily further the practices of Christian charity, benevolence and aid towards all who are in need (and) deserving of assistance." The Independent Order Sons of Italy (IOSI) used the same nomenclature as OSIA, and also adopted it's symbol, the lion, and it's motto, "Liberty, Equality, and Fraternity." IOSI began to form lodges in New York City and continued its growth despite the return of

Sellaro and several of the original lodges to OSIA in 1910.

In 1915 the Order amended its Articles of Incorporation. The expanded goals called for adoption of a constitution and bylaws, the establishment of a Supreme (national) lodge, and a system of Grand (state) lodges, the acquisition of property, and the provision of financial aid to unemployed or ill members and to the families of deceased members. ISOI quickly moved beyond New York State and by 1926 had organized 400 local lodges throughout the United States and several in Canada. At least five grand lodges were founded: in New York, Pennsylvania, Massachusetts, New Jersey, and Ohio. By 1940 there were lodges in twenty-three states. ISOI lodges sponsored a variety of social events, fostered activities that centered on the cultural achievements of Italians in Europe and America, and actively defended the good name of the ethnic group. Many lodges celebrated Columbus Day, and during the 1920s the Roma Band of the Massachusetts Grand Lodge actively participated in parades throughout the Boston area.

As ISOI grew, a national organ for communication became a necessity. In 1924 Rosario Ingargiola, Assistant Grand Venerable in New York State, began the publication of ISOI's monthly magazine, *L'Indipendente.* The first issue included articles on Luigi Pirandello and Christopher Columbus, news from local lodges, and a critique of the "hundred percent American" nativists who ignored the accomplishments of Italian Americans.

In 1924 the offices of *L'Indipendente,* the New York Grand Lodge, and the Supreme Lodge were all at 194 Bowery in New York City. Early Supreme Venerables (national presidents), such as attorney Jerome Licari, Francesco Trapani, M.D., and Peter Giambalvo, were regular residents of New York City, as the majority of the lodges were located in New York and other northeastern states. However, this pattern changed when Charles Giffoniello of New Jersey was elected to the highest national office of the Order in the 1940s, followed by Frank Ramacorti of Massachusetts a decade later. More lodges were formed in the Midwest, such as Freedom Lodge #557 in Youngstown, Ohio, which was chartered during the early 1950s.

At the biennial Supreme Convention held in Youngstown in 1958, the delegates passed a resolution decrying the media for placing "undue and unfair emphasis upon Americans of Italian ancestry" who appeared before the McClellan Senate Committee on organized crime. Another resolution called on the federal government to use its discretionary powers under the McCarran-Walters Act to expand the number of immigrants allowed into the United States. The Order attempted to attract new members by changing its name to the Knights of Italy in America. Frank Ramacorti of Massachusetts was re-elected as national president, Ralph Stabile of Pennsylvania as assistant national president, Mary Mattinat of Ohio as national treasurer, Anthony Costa of New Jersey as national secretary, and Joseph Ferrara of Pennsylvania as national orator.

The absence of New Yorkers among the national officers elected in 1958 suggested that the Order was inactive in that state. Despite the active national agenda in the 1950s, the Knights of Italy in America faltered in most other states in the years following the Youngstown convention. The national lodge was moved to Massachusetts, and by the 1970s only the Ohio and Massachusetts state organizations were functioning. In the following decade both the national lodge and the Massachusetts state lodge folded. Finally, in 1994, the Ohio state lodge was disbanded and the seventy-seven year history of the Knights of Italy in America came to an end.

John Andreozzi

Bibliography

Andreozzi, John. *Guide to the Records of the Order Sons of Italy in America.* St. Paul: Immigration History Research Center, 1989.

Aquilano, Baldo. *L'Ordine Figli d'Italia in America.* New York: Società Tipografica Italiana, 1925.

Directory of Italian American Organizations, 1988–89. Washington, D.C.: National Italian American Foundation, 1988.

See also ORGANIZATIONS

Indianapolis

Italians are the largest demographic element of southern and eastern European heritage in the Hoosier capital, estimated in the 1990 federal census at 18,589 (2.3 percent) of the total population.

The city, founded in 1821, counted nineteen Italian-born residents out of 18,600 at the outbreak of the Civil War. Then in 1882 Frank Mascari of Termini Imerese, province of Palermo, opened a fruit store near Virginia Avenue and East Washington Street. His brothers and other family members soon followed, confident of success in an expanding market. Italian-born citizens numbered 1,137 of the 234,000 city residents in 1910. The largest element among them were Sicilians, who operated fruit stands on street corners and in City Market and reputedly introduced the banana to the city. After World War I Calabrese tailors, gas and rubber company employees, shoemakers, Neapolitan barbers, and Friulian terrazzo and marble workers settled on the southeast, east, and near north sides. Successful businessmen and professionals resided on the fashionable north side. By 1930 the Italian community numbered over two thousand immigrants and their children.

Various organizations united the diverse elements of the community. A mutual aid society for men, Umberto Primo, organized around 1891; its female counterpart, Regina Margherita, organized in 1908. Several cultural and political clubs subsequently formed, the most important of which was the Francesco Crispi Society for Sicilian Men (1918). These groups helped raise money among Italians throughout the state to erect the Christopher Columbus monument on the Indiana state house grounds (1920).

Nominally Catholic, Italians attended German and Irish parishes until Nicolo Accomando and others operated a Methodist mission (1908–1920). Father Marino Priori organized Holy Rosary national parish among the Sicilians on the southeast side (1909), opened a school (1911), and built the present brick and stone church (1923–1925).

Italians advanced economically both before and after World War II. Hardworking and ambitious, some invested in the deflated real estate market during the Great Depression, amassed considerable fortunes, and began to send their sons to college. Several joined together to build the Indianapolis Produce Terminal (1954). Fred Iozzo and Pietro Iaria operated two early popular Italian restaurants in the city. A few Italian Americans became county officials and city legislators. The death of immigrant parents and social mobility, however, affected the cohesiveness of the Italian neighborhood. Many moved to the far south or far northeast sides, and the number of Holy Rosary parishioners (1,011 in 1950) declined to 160 in 1977.

Today the Italian community includes the old-line families who still dominate the city's produce industry, businessmen transferred here by their companies, doctors, lawyers, college teachers, Italian-born World War II war brides, and middle-class employees. This combination of traditional families, professionals, and new immigrants recreated ethnic consciousness. Holy Rosary Church has experienced a revival (411 parishioners in 1993) and sponsors a highly successful spring St. Joseph Table, summer street festival, and fall spaghetti dinner. The Columbus '92 Commission sponsored a Mass, a gala dinner-dance, and the rededication of the Discoverer's monument, the city's only events marking the Columbus Quincentenary. The Commission has subsequently reorganized as the Italian Heritage Society of Indiana.

James J. Divita

Bibliography

Divita, James J. *The Italians of Indianapolis: The Story of Holy Rosary Catholic Parish 1909–1984.* Indianapolis: Holy Rosary Parish, 1984.
———. *L'Italia on the White River: Introducing the Italian Presence in Indianapolis by Tracing Its History and Describing Its Material Culture.* Indianapolis: Holy Rosary Pastoral Council and Italian Heritage Society of Indiana, 1995.

Innaurato, Albert
See PLAYS, CONTEMPORARY

Intergroup Relations: Italian Americans and African Americans
The study of urban neighborhoods has focused primarily on competition and conflict among various ethnic, racial, and economic groups. Accordingly, conflict and competition among diverse groups who share a neighborhood has, for the most part, been over "turf" and other limited resources, such as housing, jobs, institutions, and municipal services. Behavior patterns reveal that some groups

attempt to preserve and maintain resources, while other groups attempt to obtain those same resources. The outcome is often conflict because resources are limited.

Conflict and competition between groups have taken a variety of forms, including violent attacks; restrictive covenants and zones; and informal, exclusionary strategies. Jonthan Rieder's 1985 study of Canarsie, Brooklyn, illustrates how local residents resist neighborhood change through violence toward newcomers. Canarsie is made up of mainly middle-class Jews and Italians. During the 1960s Canarsie experienced both an increase in the number of black residents and an exodus of white population. Canarsie's white residents resisted change by fire-bombing houses owned by blacks, boycotting local schools to express their opposition to busing, and actively recruiting "other races and ethnics" to replace whites who were leaving Canarsie.

Jerome Krase's analysis (1982) of Lefferts Manor in Brooklyn points out how social class is maintained by a restrictive 1893 covenant that prohibited owners from using Manor homes for anything other than single-family dwellings. In 1960 New York City's Planning Commission also zoned Lefferts Manor as "one-family only," thereby supporting the original covenant.

Research on Greenpoint, Brooklyn, by Judith N. DeSena (1990) describes the informal strategies used by white ethnic residents in their attempt to resist the growth of minority dwellers: an informal housing network in which information about available housing is not advertised publicly, but passed on by word of mouth; informal surveillance in which residents observe street life and often confront strangers; and formal surveillance in which a community organization was formed to serve as additional security to the police.

Another study by Gerald Suttles (1968) has developed the concept of a "defended neighborhood." The defended neighborhood is an attempt by a residential group to isolate itself. This is illustrated by a study of the Addams area in Chicago, which is made up of Italians, Mexicans, Puerto Ricans, and African Americans, who reside in segregated territories and are separated by location and local institutional arrangements. Street corner gangs maintain the boundaries of each group's "turf."

In 1972 a commission of residents in the South Shore of Chicago attempted "managed integration" by developing strategies to maintain a balance between black and white residents, and to prevent white flight. Ultimately, these tactics did not work and the South Shore became a black community.

In the case of Italian Americans and African Americans, there are some recent examples of intergroup conflict. An incident that received great publicity took place in Bensonhurst, Brooklyn, and involved the murder of a young, black youth, Yusuf Hawkins. On August 23, 1989, Yusuf Hawkins and a couple of friends left their Brooklyn neighborhood, East New York, and made their way to Bensonhurst to look at a used car. On that same evening, a young Bensonhurst woman named Gina Feliciano had invited African American and Hispanic youths to her home that evening to celebrate her eighteenth birthday. Gina's invitation angered a number of white Bensonhurst residents, especially Keith Mondello, who believed that Gina's plan was to have her African American and Hispanic friends assault him. As a result of Gina's invitation and Keith's interpretation of it, he organized other young white men from the neighborhood and gathered weapons in defense. Yusuf Hawkins and his friends were sighted by the Bensonhurst group and mistaken for Gina's friends. In the attack that followed, Hawkins was killed. After the first group of trials, a jury convicted Joseph Fama of second-degree murder, believing he had pulled the trigger that killed Hawkins. Keith Mondello, however, was acquitted on the murder count but was found guilty of lesser charges.

Bensonhurst's inhabitants clearly maintain an interest in preserving their community, and in this vein, Bensonhurst can be described as a "defended neighborhood." As previously discussed, this concept focuses on an attempt by residents of a particular area or community to isolate themselves and to exclude others who are different from them. And, as the white working class experiences difficulty maintaining its economic position and standard of living, it often blames African Americans for its problems.

Seldom discussed, however, is community cooperation among Italian Americans and African Americans. Another community in

Brooklyn, Central Williamsburg, illustrates community cooperation: Italian and African Americans worked together on neighborhood issues in which they held common goals and shared interests. In Central Williamsburg, Italian Americans and African Americans have distinct residential patterns. The Italian community owns and rents many smaller, multiple-dwelling homes, which are mostly wood framed. In contrast, the African American community resides primarily in a New York City housing project called Cooper Park Houses. Until the mid-1970s, there was little interaction between Cooper Park and the Italian American community. The numerically larger white community treated Cooper Park like an island and left it alone, while also warning their children not to enter its borders. Through the years, Cooper Park had developed an active tenants association and youth recreation center (Greenpoint-Williamsburg Coalition of Community Organizations [GWCOCO]). With the emergence of this coalition, a forum was available to bring together the white and black communities to work on local issues that affected both groups.

In Central Williamsburg it was Italian Americans and African Americans who gradually learned to talk to each other and who worked together for a common goal: the preservation of neighborhood and community. A resident of the Italian community, who also served as president of the GW-COCO coalition, stated, "We could have built a wall to Cooper Park. The Coalition didn't. Whatever the issue was, we all went out and worked on it." Consequently, their focus was on their shared interests and similarities rather than on their differences.

Judith N. DeSena

Bibliography

DeSena, Judith N. *Protecting One's Turf: Social Strategies for Maintaining Urban Neighborhoods.* Lanham, MD: University Press of America, 1990.

———. "Community Co-operation and Activism: Italian and African Americans." In *Italian Americans: Their Public and Private Lives,* edited by Frank J. Cavaioli, Angela Danzi, and Salvatore LaGumina. Staten Island: American Italian Historical Association, 1993.

———. "Defending One's Neighborhood At Any Cost?: The Case of Bensonhurst." In *A Century of Italian Immigration: The Lesson of the Past and Future of Ethnicity,* edited by Harral Landry. Staten Island: American Italian Historical Association, 1994.

Haywoode, Terry L. "Working Class Women and Neighborhood Politics." In *Contemporary Readings in Sociology,* edited by Judith N. DeSena. Dubuque, IA: Kendall-Hunt, 1989.

Krase, Jerome. *Self and Community in the City.* Washington, D.C.: University Press of America, 1982.

Molotch, Harvey. *Managed Integration.* Berkeley: University of California Press, 1982.

Reider, Jonathan. *Canarsie: The Jews and Italians Against Liberalism.* Cambridge: Harvard University Press, 1985.

Susser, Ida. *Norman Street.* New York: Oxford University Press, 1982.

Suttles, Gerald. *The Social Order of the Slum.* Chicago: University of Chicago Press, 1968.

See also COMMUNITY ISSUES

I

Italian American Albanians

Italian Albanians in Italy trace their origins to an exodus of Albanian Christians from their homeland to Basilicata, Calabria, and northwestern Sicily commencing in the mid-1400s. Most migrants were Eastern rite Catholics united with Rome. Albanian villages in Italy were established in areas of difficult terrain that were vastly separated from the Italian mainstream. Distinctive Albanian characteristics were expressed in the foods, language, and religion. The Greek Catholic Church represents the most influential factor in the survival of the Albanian identity within the community. By the time of the mass migration to America (1890–1914), many younger persons had become linguistically Italian, while retaining some Albanian influences. By then, many villages had become Latin rite.

Cultural and social institutions developed in America early in the twentieth century, notably in Manhattan's Little Italy. Father Ciro Pinnola (1867–1946) of the Palermo diocese founded a Greek rite chapel, Our Lady of Grace, in 1906. Jesuit priest Gerard B.

Donnelly wrote in 1936 that "Our Lady's is undoubtedly the poorest among Gotham's Churches." The chapel closed following Pinnola's death. Baltimore, Chicago, New Orleans, and Philadelphia also contained sizable settlements. A Latin rite parish in Inwood, Long Island, (still heavily Italian Albanian) was named after the miraculous icon of Our Lady of Good Counsel in Genazzano.

While the geographic isolation of the Italian Albanian villages contributed to the maintenance of their ancestral characteristics in Italy, immigrants to the United States experienced a rapid assimilation into the larger Italian Roman Catholic population. Presently, there exists a scarcity of vital, identifiable organizations to keep the Albanian heritage an active part of community life. In the absence of schools with an Italian Albanian base to educate the young and sustain an awareness of their culture and language, the home has remained the most significant source of ethnic identity. An Italian Albanian background may be noted in the family name, the region in Italy from which one's ancestors came, or a few "Arberesh" words casually passed from parent to child. The remnants of one's Albanian heritage are usually captured in the traditional holiday foods that are seasoned more similarly to Greek dishes than southern Italian cuisine.

Over the years, several societies have endeavored to generate an Italian Albanian awakening in America through sporadic liturgical celebrations, feasts, and newsletters. The most active of these has been Our Lady of Grace Italian Byzantine Rite Society, headquartered on Staten Island, New York.

With the dormancy of the official Italian Albanian Church in the United States and the post–World War II migration to the suburbs, the ability of this ancient tradition to maintain its presence in America and pass its rich heritage onto succeeding generations may be in danger.

Maureen M. Daddona
Richard Renoff

Bibliography

Attwater, Donald. "Byzantine Catholics in Italy." *Eastern Churches Quarterly* 5 (1944): 325–330.

Donnelly, Gerard B. "Manhattan's Eastern Catholics: The Italo-Greek Albanians." *America* 28 (March 1936): 589–590.

Nasse, George Nicholas. *The Italo-Albanian Villages of Southern Italy.* Washington, D.C.: National Academy of Sciences, 1964.

Renoff, Richard, Angela Danzi, and Joseph Varacalli. "The Albanese and Italian Community in Inwood, Long Island." In *Italian Americans: The Search for a Usable Past,* edited by Richard N. Juliani and Philip V. Cannistraro, 106–132. New York: American Italian Historical Association, 1989.

Shipman, Andrew J. "Our Italian Greek Catholics." *A Memorial of Andrew J. Shipman: His Life and Writings,* edited by B. Pallen. New York: Encyclopedia Press, 1916.

Skendi, Stavro. *The Albanian National Awakening: 1878–1912.* Princeton, NJ: Princeton University Press, 1967.

Swire, J. Albania: *The Rise of a Kingdom.* London: Williams and Norgate, 1929.

Italian American Civil Rights League

During the late 1960s the hitherto quiet Italian American community learned some lessons from the African American civil rights movement. They began to turn to tactics of confrontation and protest in a manner that surprised "establishment" politicians and media. The somewhat staid Order Sons of Italy in America (OSIA) organized the Italian American Anti-Defamation League, later changed to Americans of Italian Descent (AID), and still later to the Committee on Social Justice.

Chief among the more radical organizations that formed was the Italian American Civil Rights League. Although plagued with charges of ties to organized crime from its inception, the league focused the anger felt by most Italian Americans regarding their portrayal in the media as either lovable buffoons or dastardly criminals.

On April 30, 1970, Joseph Colombo Jr., was arrested on federal charges of melting down coins to more valuable ingots. At that time dimes, quarters, and half-dollars contained more silver than the face value of the coins. Joseph Colombo Sr., began protest marches each night, usually from St. Patrick's Cathedral to the FBI building, denouncing his son's arrest as a clear sign of anti-Italian discrimination. By August 1970 Colombo's powerful message helped inaugurate the Italian American Civil Rights League.

In November 1970 Frank Sinatra headed a stellar cast of Italian American performers who raised money for the league at the Felt Forum. Soon forty-five thousand members joined the league, comprised mostly of neglected blue-collar workers who lived in New York's City's ethnic Italian neighborhoods and who refused to flee to the nearby suburbs.

In October 1970 the league ignored the mainline Columbus Day festivities and sponsored its own Italian Unity demonstration at Columbus Circle. Police estimated the crowd to be forty thousand people; Colombo stated it was two hundred thousand. Many Italian-owned businesses closed for the day and Italian longshoremen and other union members took the day off in a sign of unity.

During the next year, Colombo dominated the Italian American stories in the New York newspapers. He joined with Meir Kahane and prominent African American leaders in a show of unity. Honorary members of the league included Mayor John Lindsay, Governor Nelson Rockefeller, William Kunstler, and other luminaries. Colombo managed to get the movie *The Godfather* to drop references to the Mafia and *La Cosa Nostra*. Offensive commercials, such as Alka Seltzer's "the spiccy meatball," were dropped. Even Attorney General John Mitchell promised to omit the terms "Mafia" and "Cosa Nostra" from official FBI releases and substitute "the syndicate" and "organized crime" for them.

Unfortunately for Colombo, he also drew ridicule and attention to members of organized crime. The FBI found names and phone numbers of reputed *mafiosi* in Colombo's possession. He was ordered to keep a low profile and tone down his protests. Moreover, mob bosses put out the word to people not to participate in the second Annual Unity Day in 1971. Attendance dropped off appreciably.

The attempted murder of Joseph Colombo, Sr., the head of the Italian American Civil Rights League, in Columbus Circle during the second Italian American Unity Day lent credibility to the charges of mob influence in the league. Colombo's assassin, a black man by the name of J. A. Johnson, was killed immediately after the shooting. The question of whether he was killed by members of Colombo's body guard or by others who hired him has never been satisfactorily resolved.

Continual denials of mob influence only led to greater suspicion among the members of more established Italian civic associations. When Frank Cimino, a board member of the Italian American Civil Rights League, stated that the league "may have held hand with the Mafia when it was founded" but that the link was broken when Frank J. Valenti was jailed in 1973, most other Italian American leaders remained skeptical.

Established leaders practiced more subtle ways of displaying their distrust of the league. Rarely did they make their case public or make accusations in the press. Rather, they would exclude the league from major events involving joint efforts of Italian groups. The objectives of the league, however, were not ignored. They deterred the use of Italian stereotyping in advertisements, movies, and television. And the league convinced the FBI and the *New York Times* to stop using the terms "Mafia" and "Cosa Nostra" when describing organized crime.

Historian Salvatore Mondello pointed out that much of the power of the Italian American Civil Rights League came from Italian anger about being left behind during the black revolution. Rochester, New York, for example, had over one hundred thousand Italian Americans in a population of about three hundred thousand in the 1970s, yet there were no Italian American Studies programs nor affirmative action plans for these citizens. That lack of support for a major ethnic group fueled the formation of groups such as the Italian American Civil Rights League.

The league and other organizations that grew up in the 1960s and 1970s focused their attention on a neglected portion of the Italian American population, namely, those blue-collar and other lower-middle-class workers who felt their needs were unmet by established organizations for too long. They had been known as "basement Catholics" in the Catholic Church, mocked by the mass media as mobsters or buffoons, and shunted to the rear of the Democratic Party as new minorities rushed to the front. While very few league members were *mafiosi*, the league did tap a sore spot in the Italian American psyche. Fortunately, it woke up the more "respectable" organizations to address the legitimate issues that concerned Italian Americans.

Frank A. Salamone

Bibliography

Cuomo, Mario. "The American Dream and the Politics of Inclusion." *Psychology Today* 20 (1986): 54–56.

Gambino, Richard. "Italian Americans, Today's Immigrants and the Mark of Cain." *Italian Americana* 12 (summer 1994): 226–234.

Martinelli, Phylis, and Leonard Gordon. "Italian Americans: Images Across Half a Century." *Ethnic and Racial Studies* 11 (1988): 319–331.

Rieder, Jonathan. *Canarsie: The Jews and Italians Against Liberalism.* Cambridge: Harvard University Press, 1985.

Tomasi, Lydio F., ed. *Italian Americans: New Perspectives in Italian Immigration and Ethnicity.* New York: Center for Migration Studies, 1985.

Tricarico, Donald. "The 'New Italian' American Ethnicity." *Journal of Ethnic Studies* 12 (1984): 75–93.

Weed, Percy. *The White Ethnic Movement and Ethnic Politics.* New York: Praeger, 1973.

See also ANTI-ITALIAN DISCRIMINATION; HOWARD BEACH AND BENSONHURST

Italian American Jews

Regardless of social taboos, intermarriage between Americans of Jewish background and those of Italian descent has taken place and is on the increase. Ethnically, these two groups are quite close. They share similar attitudes toward family and children and an indefinable esprit toward life. However, since the vast majority of Italians are Catholics, religion is a barrier. According to Stephen Steinberg (1981), historically the level of ethnic intermarriage has been considerably higher than that of religious intermarriage, a fact that has given rise in sociology to the "triple melting pot" thesis, which states that Protestants, Catholics, and Jews tend to marry across ethnic lines but within religious categories. This means that Italian Catholics will "intermarry" with Irish, Polish, or German Catholics, but not with Jews or Protestants.

However, in recent decades, this pattern has changed and religious intermarriage has been on the upswing. This means that Italian-Catholic Jewish marriages have also increased, especially along the eastern seaboard states of New York (including Long Island), Rhode Island, Connecticut, and New Jersey. The determinants of intermarriage include relative availability of suitable marriage partners, shared family values, and diminished religiosity. Intermarriage of Italians with others in Buffalo, New York, for example, has grown from 12 percent in 1930 to 27 percent in 1950 to 50 percent in 1960 to even higher figures today. Of course, most of these intermarriages were with non-Jews. There are no figures for intermarriage rates between Jews and Italians, but they have increased as general Catholic and Italian population rates have increased. For example, in 1968, 75 percent of Catholics took a Catholic spouse, but this figure stands at 50 percent today, which means that one out of every two Catholics "intermarries" with a non-Catholic. This figure is even higher today.

Jewish intermarriage has also grown, from 17 percent to over 50 percent in two generations. A 1973 study, based on a national sample of over seven thousand Jewish households, showed overall intermarriage at about 9 percent. However, among the youngest generation studied, those marrying between 1966–1972, the rate of intermarriage climbed to 32 percent, and, according to a 1990 National Jewish Population Survey, a staggering figure emerged: 52 percent of all Jews were intermarrying with non-Jews, and the number is growing yearly. Some scholars believe it is as high as 65 to 70 percent today, a definite threat to Jewish continuity.

A number of renowned individuals have a mixed Italian Jewish heritage. Former mayor of New York City Fiorello H. LaGuardia, is a good example. His mother was Jewish, and at the time a Jewish-Italian match was rare. At the other end of the spectrum is radio personality Howard Stern, whose mother is an Italian American. Italian American Jews, despite their small numbers, have made an enormous impact on American life: in academia, science, business, and the arts.

Recent interest in the Holocaust has seen an upsurge of curiosity about the tiny Jewish community of Italy, the Italian-occupied areas of World War II, and the courageous role of Italians (especially of some priests and nuns) who tried to save that community. Such books and movies as *The Garden of the Fitzi-Continis* (1990) and *The*

Righteous Enemy (1982) depict this traumatic period of time. Several prominent Jewish families who endured the Nazi occupation of Italy and came to America after the war include the Almuly and Alcalay families of the greater Boston area.

While Italy has only forty thousand Jews out of sixty million people, they frequently achieved positions of prominence. Such Jewish luminaries include writers Giorgio Bassani (*The Garden of the Fitzi-Continis*, 1970), Carlo Levi (*Christ Stopped at Eboli*, 1969), and Primo Levi (*Survival in Auschwitz; The Drowned and the Saved*, 1959). Other Italian Jews who have risen to prominence include Nobel Prize winner (1985) and Massachusetts Institute of Technology economist Franco Modigliani; physicist and Nobelist (1959) Emilio Segrè of Tivoli, Italy, for his work on anti-protons; Nobelist (1969, medicine and physiology) Salvadore Luria from Turin, Italy, for his work that laid the basis for modern molecular biology; communication specialist Andrew Viterbi; and journalist/writer Ken Auletta.

There are no figures regarding the number of Italian American Jews because defining an Italian American Jew is complex. It can include Jews who came from Italy to America or Italians who converted to Judaism or those who married Jews. In fact, one of the disproportionate ethnic concentrations of Nobel Prize winners in the world are Sephardic Italian Jews (Modigliani, Segrè, and Luria) teaching at Massachusetts Institute of Technology in Cambridge, Massachusetts.

Jack Nusan Porter

Bibliography

Alba, Richard. *Italian Americans, Into the Twilight of Ethnicity.* Englewood Cliffs: Prentice-Hall, 1985.

Battistella, Graziano, ed. *Italian Americans in the '80s: A Sociodemographic Profile.* New York: Center for Migration Studies, 1989.

Glazer, Nathan, and Daniel Patrick Moynihan. *Beyond the Melting Pot: The Negroes, Puerto Ricans, Jews, Italians, and Irish of New York City.* Cambridge, MA: MIT Press and Harvard University Press, 1964.

Gordon, Milton. *Assimilation in American Life.* New York: Oxford University Press, 1964.

Heer, David M. "Intermarriage." In *The Harvard Encyclopedia of American Ethnic Groups,* edited by Stephen Thernstrom and Ann Orlov, 513–521. Cambridge: Harvard University Press, 1980.

Porter, Jack Nusan, ed. *The Sociology of American Jews.* Lanham, MD: University Press of America, 1980.

Rieder, Jonathan. *Canarsie: The Jews and Italians of Brooklyn Against Liberalism.* Cambridge: Harvard University Press, 1985.

Staples, Robert. "Intermarriage." In *Encyclopedia of Sociology.* Vol. 2. New York: Macmillan, 1992.

Steinberg, Stephen. *The Ethnic Myth: Race, Ethnicity, and Class in America.* New York: Atheneum, 1981.

Zuccotti, Susan. *The Italians and the Holocaust.* New York: Basic Books, 1987.

See also ASSIMILATION

Italian American Labor Council

Founded in New York City on October 20, 1941, just before America's entry into World War II, under the dynamic leadership of its president, Luigi Antonini, and the rest of the executive council, which included August Bellanca, E. Howard Molisani, Joseph Catalanotti, and Emil Lucchi, the Italian American Labor Council defended the Italian American community at a time when Italian residents of the United States and Italian Americans were seen by some as a threat to the well-being of the nation. The position of the council in this regard is best illustrated by its aims, which were enunciated at its inception. These aims referred to the duty of helping America morally and materially against World War II enemies; and to the necessity of defending Italian Americans from the psychological effects of the war.

In keeping with these aims, the leadership of the council was deeply involved in removing the stigma of "enemy alien" from Italians and Italian Americans. Finally, after a struggle that reached the White House, Attorney General Francis Biddle announced on October 12, 1942, that Italian Americans were no longer considered enemy aliens.

In addition to raising huge sums of money in war bond rallies and victory meetings, the Italian American Labor Council became actively involved in determining United States policy toward a free and democratic Italy. Several times during the course of the conflict the American government dispatched representatives of the council, most notably Antonini and Molisani, as well as Vanni Montana, to Italy on fact-finding missions. Their recommendations, especially concerning labor, were often incorporated into American policy toward Italy.

With the end of World War II, the Italian American Labor Council continued its deep interest in American foreign policy, especially with regard to Europe and Italy.

From the very early days of the first Italian Republic, the council backed the American policy of providing support for democratic forces in Italy, and, toward this end, helped create and support free and democratic Italian trade unions, Confederazione Italian Sindicati Lavoratori (CISL), and Unione Italiana del Lavoro (UIL). Both unions were formed when democratic elements within the Confederazione Generale Italiana del Lavoro (CGIL) seceded after the leadership of the CGIL was taken over by Communists.

During the Cold War, beginning with the crucial Italian elections of 1948, the Italian American Labor Council supported the policies of the American government that were aimed at keeping Italy out of the Soviet orbit. With the fall of the Berlin Wall in 1989 and the demise of the Italian Communist Party, the council extended its umbrella of friendship to the CGIL.

Following the death of Luigi Antonini, the mantle of leadership of the council was passed to E. Howard Molisani, who, in turn, was succeeded by Thomas Rumore, Salvatore Giardina, and George Altomare.

Nicholas A. Spilotro

Bibliography

Crawford, John. S. *Luigi Antonini, His Influence on Italian American Relations.* New York: International Ladies' Garment Workers' Union, 1950.

Rossi, Ernest E. "NSC 1 and United States Foreign Policy Towards Italy." In *Italian Ethnics: Their Languages, Literature and Lives,* edited by Dominic Candeloro, Fred L. Gardaphé, and Paolo A. Giordano, 147–168. New York: American Italian Historical Association, 1990.

See also COLD WAR: ITALIAN AMERICANS AND ITALY; COLD WAR: UNITED STATES FOREIGN POLICY TOWARD ITALY

Italian American War Veterans of the United States (ITAM)

Founded in Hartford, Connecticut, in 1932, the Italian American War Veterans of the United States (ITAM) was at that time open to men of Italian ancestry who had served in the United States armed forces during World War I. The purpose of ITAM was then, as it is now, to work for the care of fellow veterans and their families, to foster patriotism in the community, and to strengthen the ideals of God and country. At the same time, but independent of the Hartford organization, Italian American war veterans in other states were forming groups with similar interests and goals.

Italian American war veterans groups flourished in cities scattered throughout New York, Massachusetts, and New Jersey as early as 1930. None of these groups were affiliated with the national group that was based in Connecticut, although some groups had obtained state charters. Throughout the 1930s, the national group campaigned aggressively to incorporate all these disparate local groups into the national structure of the Hartford-based organization. By September 1940 the group included posts in Connecticut, Massachusetts, New York, New Jersey, Pennsylvania, and California.

The end of World War II witnessed the return of millions of veterans to civilian life, and among these were as many as one million Italian Americans. These veterans formed the bulk of the new members joining the organization during the last half of the 1940s. More veterans joined ITAM at the end of the Korean War in 1953 and during the Vietnam War from 1961 to 1975. By the 1970s members had formed additional chartered posts in Ohio, Rhode Island, Florida, and Illinois.

Throughout the post–World War II era, the organization tried but failed to obtain federal recognition. Finally, the group's petition for a national charter passed both houses of Congress and was signed into law by President Ronald Reagan on November 20, 1981. With the granting of a national charter, the group's membership was now open to any American citizen, without regard to sex, race, or national origin, who honorably served in the United States armed forces during time of war. The periods of national conflict recognized by ITAM for qualification of membership range from the Spanish-American War in 1898 to the Persian Gulf War in 1991.

With a current membership of approximately ten thousand, the Italian American War Veterans of the United States volunteers thousands of man-hours annually to help hospitalized veterans. Politically nonpartisan, the posts participate in local celebrations of Memorial Day, the Fourth of July, Veterans Day, and other patriotic celebrations. The organization publishes *The Torch,* a quarterly newsletter.

Peter L. Belmonte

Bibliography

Cavaioli, Frank J. "Group Politics, Ethnicity and Italian Americans." In *Immigration and Ethnicity,* edited by Michael D'Innocenzo and Joseph Sirefman, 61–74. Westport, CT: Greenwood Press, 1992.

See also ORGANIZATIONS

Italian Language in America

Though the teaching of Italian in the United States was formally introduced at the beginning of the nineteenth century, it actually began almost one century earlier. Professor Joseph Fucilla, author of *The Teaching of Italian in the United States* (1967), notes that the first distinguished colonist with an intimate knowledge of Italian was George Sandys, who came to America in 1621 as colonial treasurer of the Virginia Company. Several of Sandys' colleagues from England had also studied Italian prior to coming to America. Perhaps the most famous American with a formidable knowledge of Italian was Benjamin Franklin, who studied the language in 1733 and who seemed to enjoy speaking it with other colonists. The earliest known advertisement seeking a teacher of Italian was placed by Augustus Vaughan in the *New York Post Bay,* October 26, 1747, who was opening a school of languages. Several language schools sprang up soon after, and most of these offered Italian. Private teachers became quite numerous at this time, and it appears that many took private lessons in Italian. The greatest number of these private teachers is to be found between 1775 and 1861.

The most celebrated teacher of Italian was Lorenzo Da Ponte, who had come to the United States via England in 1805. Da Ponte, noted librettist for some of Mozart's operas, founded one of the largest private institutes, the Manhattan Academy for Gentlemen, in 1808, with twenty-four students. In 1825 he became the first professor of Italian at Columbia University. Da Ponte also established a private school in Philadelphia in 1832. Soon after, similar schools appeared in Baltimore; Washington, D.C.; Boston; Cambridge; New Haven; Springfield; Providence; Lowell; and Hartford. Language institutes that included Italian were also introduced in southern cities such as Richmond, Raleigh, Charleston, Savannah, Natchez, and Lexington. Italian was taught in Cleveland, Columbus, and San Francisco.

The study of Italian, beginning in the mid-eighteenth century, was also influenced by noted Italophiles, among them Thomas Jefferson, John Adams, John Quincy Adams, Ralph Waldo Emerson, Nathaniel Hawthorne, William Prescott, George Bancroft, Margaret Fuller, Harriet Beecher Stowe, Julia Ward Howe, Washington Irving, William Cullen Bryant, and Edgar Allan Poe.

The first college or university to offer Italian on a formal basis was William and Mary in 1778, when Carlo Bellini was appointed to teach modern languages, among them Italian. Dickinson College followed in 1780, the University of Pittsburgh in 1787, Transylvania College in 1783, and Harvard University in 1816. In 1834 noted poet Henry Wadsworth Longfellow became a professor of Italian at Harvard University and proceeded to attract many to his courses, all of which were highly successful.

Other major institutions, beginning in 1822, introduced the study of Italian into their curriculum. Among the most noted, through 1900, were the following, in chronological order: Middlebury College, University of Virginia, University of Maryland, Bowdoin College, University of Pennsylvania, Princeton, Miami University (Oxford, Ohio), Wesleyan, University of Alabama, New York University, Trinity College (Hartford, Conn.), Brown, Yale, University of Michigan, Amherst College, University of Santa Clara, University of Iowa, University of Wisconsin, University of California, Cornell, Boston University, Syracuse University, Johns Hopkins,

I

University of Illinois, Northwestern, Stanford University, University of Chicago, University of Minnesota, Vassar, Wellesley, Bryn Mawr, Radcliffe, and Barnard College.

Statistics are not available concerning the total number of students studying Italian at institutions of higher learning from 1800 until 1960. However, a survey conducted by Professor A. Michael De Luca of C. W. Post College in 1965 showed that approximately twenty thousand students were enrolled in Italian language courses at the college and university levels by that year.

The next formal surveys were conducted by Professor Edoardo Lebano of Indiana University, the first in 1986, the second in 1990. The survey ending in spring 1986 shows that Italian was taught in colleges and universities in forty-six states, the District of Columbia, and Puerto Rico. There were 40,300 students enrolled in Italian classes at 398 institutions. The most recent survey conducted by Professor Lebano in 1990 showed that Italian was taught at 470 institutions for a total of 49,726 students, from B.A. to Ph.D.

The study of Italian at the secondary level did not begin as early as studies established at the college/university level, although private academies had introduced Italian as early as 1825. Miss Degan, a native Italian, was hired by Catherine Beecher to teach that language in her Hartford Female Academy. Many other academies followed suit, and Italian was offered in Virginia, Delaware, Pennsylvania, New York, Connecticut, Maine, Massachusetts, New Hampshire, Vermont, Maryland, New Jersey, Alabama, Arkansas, Georgia, Kentucky, Louisiana, North Carolina, South Carolina, Tennessee, Illinois, Indiana, Michigan, Missouri, Ohio, Wisconsin, California, and the District of Columbia, all between 1825 and 1860.

The Italian Teachers Association (ITA) of New York City had been established before 1917 but did not become a force until 1921, when it was reorganized. Through the efforts of its president, Dean Mario Cosenza, and its vice president, Leonard Covello, high school enrollment in Italian increased from 898 in seven schools in 1921–1922 to about sixteen thousand in fifty-five schools by 1937–1938. According to Fucilla, junior high school Italian offerings began in 1937–1938. Inspired by the work of the ITA in New York City, several professors of Italian met at the Modern Language Association meeting in Philadelphia in 1922 and organized the American Association of the Teachers of Italian, which became chartered in 1923. With this new organization on the national level, Italian at the secondary level did not limit itself to New York City. A survey by the ITA at the end of 1938 showed that seventy-five thousand students studied Italian at 257 schools in seventeen states. This was considered by many as the peak year of Italian study at the secondary level. Combined with twenty-two thousand at the college/university level, Italian enjoyed its best period of success in the United States. With World War II, however, the study of Italian, at all levels, suffered dramatically. A survey done in 1962–1963 revealed that only 25,771 students studied Italian at the secondary level, mostly in New England, New Jersey, New York, Pennsylvania, and California. At the college level, enrollments were at nine thousand for the same period. However, in the twenty-year span between 1963–1983, Italian studies increased significantly, as did the study of other languages following the launching of *Sputnik* by the Russians in 1959. By 1980–1981, Italian language enrollments in the public schools again climbed to eighty thousand, of which thirty-eight thousand were from New York State. The remainder was divided among New Jersey, Pennsylvania, Connecticut, Rhode Island, Massachusetts, Illinois, Michigan, Wisconsin, Ohio, and California. During this period in New York State, Italian replaced the study of German in third place, behind Spanish and French. Added to the eighty thousand were fifteen thousand from elementary and private schools.

During the decade 1981–1991, Italian at the secondary level had increased by about 4 percent, resulting in eighty-four thousand students of Italian. *The 1992–1993 Report of the New York State Education Department* showed that 33,475 students were enrolled in Italian in public secondary schools while an additional 8,934 students were enrolled in private and parochial secondary schools. No figures are available for this period regarding secondary schools in other states.

Immigrant schools, first begun in New York and Boston in 1842, were also established soon after throughout several states, most of these sponsored by mutual benefit societies. Other organizations, such as local Republican and Democratic Party clubs, particularly in the period 1930–1941, also sponsored Italian classes, free of charge, to children of all ages. The rise of Mussolini to power in Italy had aroused a sense of nationalism among Italians abroad, and the Fascist government encouraged the study of Italian by offering incentives in the form of medals, books, and certificates. When the United States entered the war in 1941, the teaching of Italian in these clubs was discontinued but returned on a smaller scale after 1946. However, enrollments never again reached the heights of the pre–World War II period.

The formal teaching of Italian in elementary schools began in parochial schools, specifically in 1930–1931, when the language was taught in 263 Catholic and Protestant religious schools. A survey conducted by Marjorie Breuning for the Modern Language Association in 1959–1960 revealed that 4,075 children were enrolled in Italian in Catholic schools.

Foreign Language in the Elementary Schools (FLES) was introduced in public schools in 1952–1953, and seven years later figures show that 1,188 students were enrolled in Italian classes, mostly in California, Colorado, Connecticut, Illinois, Michigan, New York, and Washington. In New York City, Italian was taught in seven of 123 public schools. By 1980, because of the bilingual programs funded by U.S. grants, Italian increased to about thirty-five schools. FLES programs, however, because of financial constraints, have been virtually eliminated in most states.

The language of music has been, and continues to be, Italian, and among the first independent music institutions to introduce the language was the New England Conservatory in Boston. Italian was first taught there by M. B. Berlitz, founder of the Berlitz School. Other prominent music schools that have introduced Italian early in their history are Boston Conservatory of Music, the California Institute of the Fine Arts (Los Angeles), the Eastman School of Music (Rochester, N.Y.), the Juilliard School of Music, the Manhattan School of Music, the Peabody Conservatory of Music (Baltimore), and the San Francisco Conservatory of Music. Many major colleges and universities with programs in music studies strongly recommend the study of Italian.

Although the unification was completed by 1870, Italy still remained a very divided north-versus-south nation; Italians considered themselves first Sicilians, Neapolitans, Piemontesi, etc., before admitting that they were Italian. Italian, as a national language, was spoken in government offices, at universities, in industry, and commerce. In 1860 only 2.5 percent spoke Italian (in all of Italy); the rest spoke the dialects of the region. There was no unifying language. In fact, in many, if not most, schools, primarily in the south, the local dialect was often the language of instruction. This persisted until the rise of Fascism and Mussolini, who mandated that Italian be used exclusively in all classes at all levels, with the exception of foreign languages. Although Italians had migrated to the United States since colonial times to 1880, most of those who had come during that period were primarily northern and most spoke Italian. Exiles, such as Giuseppe Garibaldi, Antonio Meucci, and Filippo Mazzei, all spoke Italian. Genoese immigrants who had come during the 1850s and 1860s were mostly artists, musicians, and teachers, and all spoke Italian as well as their dialect. They settled in Philadelphia, Boston, and Baltimore. However, between 1880 and 1920, the vast majority of those who migrated to the United States from Italy, came from the regions of Lazio, Abruzzo, Molise, Sicily, Campania, Basilicata, Calabria, and Puglia. Among these were large numbers from urban areas such as Naples, Rome, Palermo, Bari, and Campobasso.

By 1910 the federal census counted 1,343,000 Italians, mostly poor, ill-educated, unable to speak English, and lacking in technical skills. With native-born children, they numbered well over two million. In the following decade another 1,109,524 had arrived in the United States. Six million persons of Italian origin would ultimately forge a living link between their homeland and America.

Because most of these six million spoke no English, but rather a dialect from their region, they tended to settle in regional ethnic spheres. It was not unusual, for example, to see Calabresi residing in one area of Mulberry Bend, in New York City, Neapolitans in another, Sicilians in another. According to one source, "It was only natural that an Italian would prefer to live where people spoke his own dialect, where he could buy the kind of food he had always eaten, where the storekeeper was someone he had known in Italy and from whom he could expect to receive fair change. These ethnic quarters were not unique to Italians. Irish, Jews, Germans had done this previously. Nowadays it's blacks, Puerto Ricans, and Haitians who inhabit similar ethnic quarters."

Italians settled together primarily because of their inability to speak fluent English. Their clannishness was reinforced by the prejudice they experienced outside their neighborhoods. As a result, the first generation of Italian immigrants found their ethnic identity by living together in Little Italys. The *campanilismo* (provincialism) that the Italians were used to in their hometowns prevailed in the United States. As people in small towns had clustered about their church or piazza, they tended to do the same in large urban centers in the United States. They protected themselves against outsiders and sometimes even separated from Italians from parts other than their own town or region.

Though Italians clung to their dialects, the unifying forces among all these immigrants who had come from so many towns and regions, particularly southern Italy, were the Italian newspapers and radio shows. Among the first newspapers to appear was *Il Progresso Italo-Americano,* published in 1880. Many others then followed in a steady flow: *La Sentinella, L'Italia, Il Risveglio Coloniale, La Stampa Unita, La Montagna, Il Vesuvio, Il Corriere del Connecticut, Il Messagero, L'Avvenire, L'Unione, Secolo Nuovo, Corriere di Rochester, La Luce, L'Eco del Rhode Island, La Gazzetta del Banchiere, La Frusta, La Questione Sociale, La Tribuna Italiana, Il Proletario, Cronaca Sovversiva, L'Italiano in America, La Nuova Napoli, L'Indipendente, Eco d'Italia, Europeo-America, Il Grido della Stirpe, Corriere della Sera, Il Martello, La Plebe, Sicilia, L'Unità del Popolo.* These newspapers, written in Italian and not in the dialect, allowed Italians to seek information not only of the Italy they had left behind, but news about their communities and other Italian American communities.

Radio stations such as WEVD, WHOM, and WBNX broadcast many hours of Italian soap operas, comedy skits, music, and advertising. These programs were mostly in Italian, though several, especially the comedy skits, were broadcast in dialects, particularly Sicilian and Neapolitan. Newspapers and radio opened new vistas for these Italian Americans. Though still clinging to their enclave, they were undergoing a subtle evolution. "Slowly the Italians were beginning to adjust to the communal needs of their new environment. They were obliged to reach out to mutual aid societies, which paid such benefits as funeral expenses; these societies provided a sense of community as well as nostalgia, since each was made up of members from the same village or province."

The number of Italian American newspapers diminished significantly after 1950 as second- and third-generation Italian Americans reached adulthood, many of whom did not read or speak either Italian or a dialect. The new generations were moving to the suburbs and were being assimilated into the "American" culture. It appeared that by the third and fourth generations the succession of assimilation had been complete.

Dialects spoken by the first and, in some situations, the second generation began to disappear to a large degree. In an effort to preserve some dialects, several organizations focusing on specific enclaves have been formed. Most prominent among these is the society Arba Sicula, which publishes *Arba Sicula, Sicilian Dawn, a Journal of Sicilian Folklore and Literature,* established by Professor Gaetano Cipolla of St. John's University (Queens, New York) with other colleagues from Brooklyn. There are also similar organizations founded to preserve the Neapolitan, the Calabrian, the Abruzzese, and the Ticinese (Switzerland) languages, literatures, and traditions.

Since most immigrants did not attend American schools or learn English from their children, they never really grasped the language, and so their English became an amalgam of fractured English and native dialect. Quite often, people spent a lifetime in one of their enclaves, learning very little English. This was especially true of the women, who often did not work and who spent their time speaking to shopkeepers who spoke their dialect. Slowly American words came into their dialects and a new language appeared, a language that would never have been understood in Italy. Very often an English word with a vowel added to it would become part of the lexicon: *ticchetta* (ticket), *giobba* (job), *grosseria* (grocery), *carro* (car), *cecca* (check), *checca* (cake), *stritto* (street), *storo* (store), *cotto* (coat), *giumpiare* (to jump), *assainare* (to sign), *bricchelieri* (bricklayer), *ruffo* (roof), *bascia sterse* (downstairs), *ngoppa sterse* (upstairs), *fattoria* (factory), *lu omme riliv* (home relief), *marchetta* (market), *bacause* (backhouse, toilet), *uascia mascina* (wash machine), *boccasa* (box), *ise boccasa* (ice box), etc. By bringing such words into the dialects, many Italians felt that they had bridged the gap between themselves and other Americans. Many elderly, to this day, will still use these or similar words or expressions since these have become part of their "American dialect."

Joseph A. Tursi

Bibliography

Amfitheatrof, Erik. *The Children of Columbus.* Boston: Little, Brown, 1973.

Candeloro, Dominic, Fred L. Gardaphé, and Paolo A. Giordano, eds. *Italian Ethnics: Their Languages, Literature and Lives.* New York: American Italian Historical Association, 1990.

Conforti, Joseph. "Italian Americans as 'Ethnics': Description or Derogation." In *Italian Americans in a Multicultural Society,* edited by Jerome Krase and Judith N. DeSena. Stony Brook, NY: Forum Italicum, 1994.

Cordasco, Francesco, and Eugene Bucchoni. *The Italians: Social Backgrounds of an American Group.* Clifton: Augustus Kelley, 1974.

Fucilla, Joseph. *The Teaching of Italian in the United States.* New Brunswick, NJ: American Association of Teachers of Italian, 1967.

Lebano, Edoardo. "Enrollments in U.S. Institutions of Higher Learning Offering Instruction in Italian." *Italica* 64, no. 1 (spring 1987).

———. "Report on the Teaching of Italian in American Institutions of Higher Learning (1981–1990)." *Italica* 70, no. 4 (winter 1993).

Nelli, Humbert. *From Immigrants to Ethnics: The Italian Americans.* Oxford: Oxford University Press, 1983.

Rolle, Andrew. *The Italian Americans: Troubled Roots.* London: The Free Press, 1980.

See also ASSIMILATION; COLONIES IN SMALL TOWNS; LINGUISTIC HISTORY OF ITALIAN DIALECTS IN THE UNITED STATES; POPULATION; RADIO

Italian Welfare League

Formally organized in 1920 and incorporated two years later by Italian American women, the Italian Welfare League was established "to promote the interest of, and to look after the needy Italians in New York." Its principal founders were Lionello Perera and Margherita De Vecchi, who had been active in social work. The league initially served Italian war veterans, but later evolved to serve the needs of Italian newcomers in the areas of immigration, Americanization, family case work, actual distress, employment, and medical care.

After World War I a group of Italian American women formed the Italian Committee of the American Red Cross. They soon acknowledged that many Italian men who had either been called to the armed services of the Italian Army or had volunteered were now returning to their homes and families in the United States. The *riservisti,* as they were called, had been away from their families for a number of years and found it difficult to adjust to family life and to American society. The Italian Committee was asked to assist the *riservisti* in reacclimation. The committee found employment for many and, for those unable to work, gave financial assistance in the form of food, clothing, and medical care.

The league maintained locations in Manhattan, Brooklyn, and on Ellis Island. In the latter location it served as consultants to Italians experiencing immigration problems and was licensed to represent clients before the Immigration Service. During World War II the league was the only organization permitted to work with the Italian "detainees" on Ellis Island, who numbered almost 1,000.

After World War II the league organized the Godparents Committee for Italian War Orphans and in three years sent to Italy approximately $250,000 in money, food, clothing, and medical supplies. The league cooperated with the American Red Cross and the Travelers Aid Society in assisting to reunite the families who had been separated by the war. The league has continued to meet the needs of Italian immigrants by offering to serve as interpreters at the immigration desk, to assist them with customs, and to arrange transportation for them to their final destination.

The work of the league is divided into two areas. The first was social work for those who needed aid in economic, social, or medical emergencies. The second was immigration and naturalization case work, which assisted those immigrants who sought entry in the United States. The leading figure in the

Newly arrived Italian immigrant families seek assistance at St. Raphael Society headquarters in Boston in the early twentieth century. This society, along with other similar organizations, was of immense help to newcomers who were totally unfamiliar with the American language, customs, and laws. Courtesy Center for Migration Studies.

organization was Angela Carlozzi Rossi, whose tenure at the league was from 1934 to 1973. She was a professional social worker as well as executive secretary of the league. Rossi handled many of the cases herself and was assisted by Frank Traverso, also a professional social worker, in the area of immigration problems.

As the need for assisting Italian immigrants has greatly declined in recent years, the Italian Welfare League has become active in raising funds for charitable purposes. Donations provide funding for medical research on such sicknesses as Cooley's anemia and blindness, hospitals and nursing homes, and scholarships to students pursuing advanced degrees in social service. Their present headquarters is at 8 East 69th Street in the Columbus Club, New York City.

Frank M. Sorrentino

Bibliography

The Italian Welfare League, Inc. Archives. New York: Center for Migration Studies, 1916–1987.

Testa, Barbara Ann. *A Study of the Italian Welfare League, Inc.* Master's thesis, sociology, Marymount College, New York City, 1959.

See also ORGANIZATIONS

Italian Workers in the Construction of Roosevelt Dam

The history of the Roosevelt Dam is linked to the Italian workers credited with building it. Roosevelt Dam remains the world's largest masonry dam, a 280-foot-tall cyclopean-gravity-arch structure holding back one of the largest artificial lakes in the world. It was designed to bring irrigation water to 250,000 acres in central Arizona. Italian laborers served as both skilled masons and quarrymen and as unskilled laborers. They came in groups from the East Coast and as independent workers from nearby towns. In 1911 former President Theodore Roosevelt dedicated the dam named after him.

The importance of this massive project is linked to the critical role of water policy in shaping the final transformation of the American West from a lightly populated land claimed by Native American populations to an integral part of a modern nation. Its height alone marked Roosevelt Dam as an example of modern dam structure, since the need for large storage dams was related to the unquenchable demands of emerging twentieth-century cities.

Italian workers were critical in solving the labor problems that plagued this influential project located in the rugged Sierra Ancha and Mazatzal mountains of Arizona. The workforce included men from many nationalities, yet two ethnic groups were identified with the effort. One is the Apache workers who constructed the Apache Trail needed to bring supplies from Phoenix. The other group was the Italians.

These Italian laborers came from a variety of locations and occupations. Experts in stonecutting and masonry were recruited by the chief engineer and the contractor from New York and Pennsylvania. Records show they contacted individual *padroni* (labor brokers) and the Labor Information Office for Italians, formed in 1906 in New York City under the auspices of the Italian government. Others came from towns in Arizona; for example, a number were Piedmontese working in the copper mines of Globe, Arizona. However, none were recruited directly from Italy as some accounts have claimed, since the Foran Act at that time forbade this type of labor recruitment.

Italian stonecutters and stone masons were prized at the dam site; their transportation costs were subsidized and they received high wages. However, most of the Italian laborers were used for their brawn, not their skills. Italian *braccianti* (laborers), along with Mexican, African American, and Apache workers, formed the basis of the workforce doing the heavy semi-skilled and unskilled labor that was also required to make Roosevelt Dam a reality.

Italians from the East ventured to this remote and dangerous work site because wages were competitive. In New York City, Italian laborers were paid $2.00 for a ten-hour day and skilled rock men received $2.48 for a nine-hour day. Masons at Roosevelt Dam received about $5.00 per day and laborers earned $3.00 a day. Also, building the dam was a multiyear project that meant job security and consistent wages.

The Italian workers who were single lived together in bunkhouses; families lived in tent houses. Archaeological evidence of their presence has included the concentration of wine and bitters bottles from Italy found in two areas. Since the dam was a United States government project, alcohol was forbidden on or near the work site, a rule enforced rigorously. However, to keep the Italian workers, especially given the harsh working conditions with extreme temperatures from below freezing in the winter to up to 120 degrees in the summer, Italian saloon owners from Globe and Phoenix were allowed to bring liquor to the living quarters.

In 1910, as the work on the Roosevelt Dam neared completion, census takers enumerated the local population in the Tonto Basin area. The majority of Italians, 53 percent, listed their occupations as laborers, while 19 percent were skilled workers, such as masons and stonecutters. At one site they made up 50 percent of the immigrant population. While other ethnic groups labored on Roosevelt Dam, the skill level and the concentration of Italians made an indelible mark. As in other parts of the nation, Italian laborers deserve credit for building a modern America.

Upon completion of the project, some workers remained in the state. Tomaso Quarelli, for example, worked as a mason at the dam, and his earnings allowed him to bring his family from Italy to join him in 1908. In 1911 they moved to Winkleman, Arizona, establishing a successful mercantile business. The family grew and contributed to the town, so much so that almost seventy years after their arrival a street was renamed Quarelli Street.

Phylis Cancilla Martinelli

Bibliography
Martinelli, Phylis Cancilla. "Italian workers on the Roosevelt Dam." In *Historical Archaeological Investigations at Dam Construction Camps in Central Arizona,* edited by A. E. Rogge and Cindy L. Myers. Springfield, VA: National Technical Information Service, 1988.
Smith, Karen L. *The Magnificent Experiment, Building the Salt River Reclamation Project, 1890-1917.* Tucson: University of Arizona Press, 1986.
Zarbin, Earl. *Roosevelt Dam: A History to 1911.* Phoenix: Salt River Project, 1984.

See also OCCUPATIONS OF ITALIAN IMMIGRANTS IN TURN-OF-THE-CENTURY AMERICA

J

Jacuzzi, Candido (1903–1986)

An inventor and pump manufacturing executive, Candido Jacuzzi was born in Casarsa deila Delizia in the Friuli region of northeastern Italy, the son of Giovanni Jacuzzi and Teresa Arman, farmers. In March 1920 he migrated with his two oldest sisters to join five of his six older brothers already in the United States. His parents and other siblings migrated in 1921. They settled in Berkeley, California, where the brothers operated a machine shop. In 1925 he married Inez Ranieri; they had four children.

Jacuzzi's youngest son, born in 1941, developed rheumatoid arthritis as a toddler, and when the boy was seven his doctor recommended hydrotherapy. Unfortunately, facilities for such treatment were located only in distant spas and in communal tubs in large hospitals, neither of which was accessible or particularly appropriate for a young boy with severe arthritis. Jacuzzi, already an experienced inventor with four United States patents credited to him, attacked the problem, and in 1949 he developed a unique type of pump that created a swirling whirlpool in a bathtub. When his son's suffering was temporarily relieved by the treatment, Jacuzzi patented this invention and assigned it to the family business, which, in turn, assigned 1 percent of the royalties to Candido's son to provide for his care. After Jacuzzi further modified the invention to make it suitable for mass production and to meet state safety requirements (which had delayed its introduction), the company began commercial marketing of the finished product in the early 1950s as a hydromassage unit for bathtubs of conventional sizes. Jacuzzi later evolved the product into a whirlpool pump system for spas and incorporated it into specially designed large baths, now known as hot tubs.

Primarily because of his series of inventions that related to submersible pumps and whirlpool baths, Jacuzzi's company continued to expand in the late 1960s and early 1970s. Jacuzzi established manufacturing facilities in Mexico, Canada, Italy, Brazil, and Chile to meet growing demand abroad.

During his tenure as president, the company's sales emphasis for Jacuzzi whirlpool baths changed from solely health treatment to recreational use, both indoors and outdoors, at public spas and in private residences. In the prosperous consumer-oriented business world that expanded rapidly after World War II, Jacuzzi foresaw success for the hot tub, if it was marketed properly. Moreover, he responded quickly to the evolving demand for whirlpool baths, and, as its principal developer, stayed technologically ahead of competitors. The baths were so popular that the family name became the generic term for a hot tub. "Jacuzzi" now appears in most English dictionaries.

Candido Jacuzzi remained president until 1971, at which time he retired but nevertheless remained active on the board of directors until he became paralyzed in 1975. Resigning from the board, he died a decade later at his home in Scottsdale, Arizona.

Joseph Scafetta Jr.

Bibliography

Scafetta, Joseph Jr. "The Jacuzzi Brothers: Pioneering Inventors." *The Italian American Review* 3, no. 1 (17 April 1994): 29–33.

See also BUSINESS AND ENTREPRENEURSHIP; PATENTS AND INVENTORS

Jazz

One of the earliest and most persistent attributes of Italian immigrants in America has been their artistic achievement. From colonial days on, Italian musicians and their descendants have made major contributions to the development of original American music as it progressed from a primitive stage to a highly refined art. Be it classical music, opera, stage plays, bands (civilian and military), or popular music, Italian Americans pioneered and set high standards for aspiring artists through their teaching and performing. Italian American musicians were not only present at the birth of jazz in the United States, they also contributed significantly to its growth and development. Originally an extemporaneous blend of African American folk music and drumbeats, jazz was played by African Americans principally in Kansas City, Chicago, and New Orleans (in the red light district called Storyville) on European instruments, such as cornets and clarinets. African Americans continued to nurture and improve the art and are due most of the credit for modern American jazz. But a number of Italian Americans played a key role, especially in its formative years. Among the most important are Dominic James (Nick) LaRocca, Eddie Lang (Salvatore Massaro), Giuseppe (Joe) Venuti, Frank Signorelli, Joe Tarto (Vincent Joseph Tortoriello), Adrian Rollini, and Leon Joseph Rappola (Leon Rapps).

Early Italian American jazz performers found themselves in a world where polite society scorned them and expected them to observe a rigid color line. One of the first to gain acceptance and popularize jazz was Nick LaRocca (1889–1961), a self-taught cornetist who ranks highly among the first generation of jazz cornet/trumpet players. Born in New Orleans into an Italian immigrant family, he was the moving force behind the first jazz band, the all-white Original Dixieland Jass Band (ODJB). In 1915 Henry James, a nightclub owner, engaged the ODJB to play at the Shiller Cafe in Chicago. After some initial resistance, the band managed to prevail, and their booking lasted for three months. In 1917, largely due to the recommendation of Al Jolson, the ODJB went east to New York to play at the famed Paradise Club. The same year, for the Victor Studios in New York, the LaRocca band made the first jazz recording. It is said to be "the single most significant event in the history of jazz." Featured on the record's B side was *Livery Stable Blues,* sometimes called *Barnyard Blues.* The clarinet produced rooster crows; the trombone, cow moos; LaRocca's trumpet, horse whinnies. Though considered raucous, crude, and offensive to some serious jazz musicians, the recording grossed over a million dollars, outselling Caruso and Sousa. Special effects soon became a feature of jazz. Side A, *The Original Dixieland One Step,* written by LaRocca, had a deeper, more enduring influence on the development of jazz. In 1919 the ODJB went to London for an eighteen-month engagement. Jazz had crossed continental and transcontinental borders.

The ODJB, beset with personnel problems, disbanded in 1925. Thereafter, LaRocca formed a swing band and led revivals of the ODJB until 1938, when he returned to New Orleans and performed sporadically. As well as being the prime force behind the ODJB, LaRocca's playing and writing single him out as a prominent figure in jazz. His driving, rhythmic performances greatly influenced many players, among them Bix Beiderbecke, who went on to gain fame as one of America's premier horn talents. And many of LaRocca's original compositions, written in the early part of this century, have become standards. Even today, these tunes (e.g., *Tiger Rag* and *At the Jazz Band Ball*) sound fresh and challenging to both musicians and the listening public.

LaRocca's career began to fade as improvisation yielded to European techniques and principles of harmonization. About that time Eddie Lang (1904–1932) and a fellow Philadelphian, Joe Venuti (1903–1978), both classically trained musicians, happened on the scene and did more than fill the gap. Lang became the first well-known solo jazz guitarist and from the mid-1920s on was widely influential. He studied violin for eleven years and learned guitar from his father, who both played and made instruments. Lang's career coincided with the development of recording techniques suited to the acoustic guitar, which partly through his influence supplanted the banjo as a jazz instrument. He was highly regarded for his single-string solos and his accompaniments, which usually interspersed chords and single-string lines in the middle register. Although some contemporary African American guitarists were better soloists, Lang's accompaniments resulted in interesting textures. A good rhythm guitarist with a fine technique who attained a consistently high level of performance, he was cited by one music critic as the "Father of Jazz Guitar."

Lang played with some of the finest musicians of the day, both white and black. He teamed up with Joe Venuti in the early 1920s and made a series of duet recordings with him from 1926 to 1928, including the noteworthy *Stringing the Blues* and a recomposition of *Tiger Rag*. Their *Stringing the Blues* album featured Adrian Rollini on bass sax, and two famed African Americans, Lonnie Johnson on guitar and vocals and King Oliver on cornet. He also recorded some duos in 1928 and 1929 with Johnson. Under the name of Blind Willie Dunn, he again recorded with Johnson and Oliver, who were part of the Gin Bottle Four. Lang was always working in the 1920s, performing and recording frequently with, among others, Red Nichols, Jean Goldkette, Frankie Trumbauer, the Dorsey Brothers, and Paul Whiteman. After playing with Whiteman, Lang became Bing Crosby's accompanist. Lang's acceptance by African American performers speaks volumes about his talent and character. He was in the forefront of integrating musicians, preceding Benny Goodman, who took giant strides in that direction. At the time of his death in 1932, he was under contract with Paramount for five films at fifteen thousand dollars a picture.

Joe Venuti, born in Lucca, Italy, was raised in Philadelphia. A classically trained violinist, he was able to give jazz the stability and continuity it lacked. His ability to integrate the staid violin into the flamboyant jazz band earned him accolades as "one of the greatest jazz violinists of all time." Since Venuti and Lang were often a team, he played with many of the giants of jazz as did Lang, including Benny Goodman and Jack Teagarden. The Venuti-Lang records were highly influential in Europe and served as a model for Django Reinhardt and Stephane Grappelli in Paris. After a period of relative obscurity, Venuti's performance at the Newport Jazz Festival in 1968 brought him new respect among musicians. He recorded often in the 1970s with the likes of Zoot Sims, Marian McPartland, and Earl Hines. Considered the most important early jazz violinist, he had a full tone, a jocular style, and a strong sense of rhythm.

Frank Signorelli (1901–1975) was a New York–born pianist and composer who worked with the best. After starting the Original Memphis Five in 1917, he played with the ODJB, Joe Venuti, Eddie Lang, Bix Beiderbecke, Paul Whiteman, Phil Napoleon, and Bobby Hackett. A number of his songs were recorded by top African American artists such as Billie Holiday, Teddy Wilson, Ella Fitzgerald, and Johnny Hodges.

Joe Tarto (1902–1986) came from Newark, New Jersey, and enjoyed a sterling reputation as a string bass/tuba player and arranger. Before enlisting in the United States Army at age fifteen, Tarto had played with an "Italian" band. While in the army, he started a jazz group. After his discharge, he played Dixieland in New Jersey for two years, then went to New York City, where he kept busy performing and arranging jazz numbers for various bands including the highly respected African American aggregations of Chick Webb and Fletcher Henderson. Tarto was also in demand by the film industry and for radio shows. An integral part of the New York jazz scene, he was the last surviving member of Red Nichols and His Five Pennies. Tarto can also be heard on some 78 rpm recordings of the Joe Venuti band and the Eddie Lang orchestra. Like his contemporary Eddie Lang, Tarto performed with Paul Whiteman intermittently for twenty-five years and was one of the first whites to fit in with black jazz artists.

Adrian Rollini (1904–1956), born in New York, was a brilliant jazz bass sax/vibes man who came out of the California Ramblers, a ten-piece band that included Tommy and Jimmy Dorsey and Red Nichols. In 1926 he put together an all-star eleven-piece group far more jazz oriented than any band Paul Whiteman had ever worked with. It included Beiderbecke, Venuti, Lang, and Signorelli. Musicians loved it. But the general public, though they had come to accept Dixieland, was not ready for that straight-ahead style. It was not until the next decade that Benny Goodman provided the breakthrough. Rollini's outfit disbanded when the Club New Yorker, in which they were booked, folded in 1927. Rollini continued working in the 1930s producing jazz recordings with another fine saxophonist, Bud Freeman.

What Venuti did for jazz with the violin, and Lang did with the guitar, Leon Rappola (1902–1943) accomplished with the clarinet. A violinist by training, he switched to the clarinet and jazz. In 1919, at the age of seventeen, he joined the Friars' Society Orchestra, which later became the New Orleans Rhythm Kings (NORK), organized in Chicago. He "played with soul," a quality that comes through in his recording *She's Crying for Me Blues* (1923). Musicians claim that white jazz clarinet begins with Rappola, who was known for his subtle dynamics and tonal variety. But his influence reached the African American music world also. He used Jelly Roll Morton on some of his later recording sessions in 1925, and he had a strong influence on Barney Bigard, another premier clarinetist who had a distinguished career with Duke Ellington and Louis Armstrong.

By the World War II era, jazz had become an accepted art form in the United States and around the world. Italian American names became commonplace to aficionados: Charlie Ventura, Boots Mussuli, Johnny Guarnieri, Flip Philips (Joseph E. Filipelli), Buddy Greco, Buddy De Franco, and, literally, too many to list. Many today are trained in colleges and universities where jazz is taken as a serious course of study. They follow in the tradition of their ancestors who brought a love for music to America and nurtured it as an integral dimension of American culture.

Luciano J. Iorizzo
Julia Volpelleto Nakamura

Bibliography

Coffin, Robert. *Jazz from the Congo to the Metropolitan.* Garden City, NY: Doubleday, 1944.

Deffaa, Chip. *Voices of the Jazz Age.* Urbana: University of Illinois Press, 1990.

Feather, Leonard. *The Jazz Years: Witness to an Era.* New York: De Capo, 1987.

Nakamura, Julia V. "The Italian American Contribution to Jazz." *Italian Americana* 8 (fall/winter 1986): 22–35.

See also OPERA; POP SINGERS

K

Kefauver Committee
See CRIME AND ORGANIZED CRIME

Kino, Eusebio Francisco (1645–1711)

Catholic missionary, explorer, and cartographer of the southwestern United States and northwestern Mexico, Eusebio Francisco Kino was born August 10, 1645, at Segno in the Val di Non, province of Trento, Italy, son of Francesco and Margherita Luchi Chino. During a "mortal illness" in 1663, Kino promised St. Francis Xavier, the great sixteenth-century missionary to the Orient, that, if he recovered through the saint's intercession, he would enter the Society of Jesus (Jesuits), become a missionary, and add the saint's name to his own. In 1665 he became a Jesuit and was educated in Austria and Germany.

Kino studied mathematics, which was highly prized in China, but he accepted an assignment to Mexico (1678). He sailed from Genoa to Cadiz, Spain, but, delayed there by shipwreck and lack of available passage, landed at Vera Cruz, Mexico, in 1681. He accompanied the Atondo expedition to chart lower California (1683) and reached the Pacific Ocean (1685). Then the Jesuit was sent to the "Rim of Christendom" (present Sonora and Arizona), a region which the Spanish believed contained precious metals. Mining interests soon became concerned with his efforts to end exploitation of native labor. He introduced cattle and sheep as well as new agricultural products, but Native American discontent with the discipline of the new agricultural settlements resulted in an uprising and the martyrdom of Kino's co-worker, the Sicilian Jesuit Francesco Saverio Saeta, at Caborca

(1695). Yet he baptized over four thousand natives, and evangelized the Pimas and their neighbors, who sought Spanish protection from the marauding Apaches to the north and east, to such an extent that he alarmed local "medicine men." His missionary centers were Dolores in Sonora (1687) and San Xavier del Bac near present Tucson, Arizona (1700). He founded missions at Remedios, Cocóspora, Tubutama, Caborca, and Santa Maria Suamca in Sonora and at Tumaca Cori in Arizona. Other Italian Jesuits working with Kino were the Milanese Giovanni Maria Salvatierra (organizer of the Lower California missions), Francesco Piccolo, and Girólamo Minutuli.

In a quarter century Kino undertook fifty journeys, established many mission stations along his routes, discovered the pre-Columbian Casa Grande ruins (1694) near present Coolidge, Arizona, explored as far north as the Gila River (1697), and crossed to the west bank of the Colorado River near present Yuma, Arizona (1701). From his explorations, he concluded that California was a peninsula and not an island, as previously thought. His maps were frequently included in European atlases without attribution.

While at Magdalena in Sonora to dedicate a chapel to his patron saint, Francis Xavier, Kino died (March 15, 1711) and was buried in the new structure. His grave was discovered in 1966. Arizona contributed his statue to the Hall of Statuary in the United States Capitol (1965), and a suitable memorial was built over his grave in the town renamed Magdalena de Kino in his memory (1971).

James J. Divita

Bibliography

Bolton, Herbert Eugene. *Rim of Christen-dom: A Biography of Eusebio Francisco Kino, Pacific Coast Pioneer.* New York: Russell & Russell, 1960.

Polzer, Charles. *A Kino Guide: A Life of Eusebio Francisco Kino, Arizona's First Pioneer and a Guide to His Missions and Monuments.* Tucson: Southwestern Mission Research Center, 1976.

See also EXPLORERS

L

Labels and Stereotypes

Italians who settled in the United States during the period of mass immigration faced extreme ethnic prejudice. This prejudice established their subordinate status in American society and shaped the expression of Italian ethnicity for succeeding generations.

One of the more insidious forms of prejudice directed at Italians was the use of labels, actually defamatory epithets, in lieu of the name that symbolized their ethnic identity. A related practice was the Anglicization of individual and family names by American authorities. The most infamous epithets hurled at Italians were "WOP," "dago," and "guinea." "WOP" stands for "Without Papers"; the label attributed illegal immigrant status to Italians. "Dago" is believed to be a corruption of the common Spanish name "Diego," applied to Italians because they were initially mistaken as Spaniards (reflecting an indifference to ethnic distinctions among immigrant minorities). "Guinea" is a reference to inhabitants of a coastal area in Western Africa as the "Guinea Negro."

The terms "WOP," "dago," and "guinea" stigmatized Italian immigrants as despised foreign intruders. They were used interchangeably, as meanings became confounded by effect; *Webster's Unabridged New Twentieth Century Dictionary,* for example, defines "WOP" and "dago" in terms of racial characteristics but not "guinea." Usage was blatantly public and acceptable. An article in *Popular Science Monthly,* in December 1890, was entitled "What Shall We Do with the Dago?"

Ethnic labels, or epithets, are primarily intended to insult rather than explicate content. The meanings attached to ethnic labels are elaborated by stereotypes. Stereotypes are cognitive categories that emphasize conspicuous attributes and allow them, and the individuals who possess them, to stand for the group.

Stereotypes of Italians imposed a distorted narrative to a system of ethnic stratification. At its core was the view that Italians were not only different from, but inferior to, the Anglo-Saxon race stock of the American majority. This racial stereotype was especially signified by the epithet "guinea" and was underlined in characterizations of Italians as "dark" and "swarthy" in complexion. Racial inferiority, moreover, determined degraded cultural patterns like ignorance and poverty. As a result, it was inferred that Italians would not assimilate "naturally or readily" and would infect the American population and culture in the process. It should be noted that immigrants from northern Italy were often exempted from this scenario as "Teutonic Italians" compatible in race and culture.

The stereotype of biological inferiority was reinforced by images of bodily pollution. Italians were portrayed as dirty and diseased, posing a health threat to Americans; perhaps the greatest fear of bodily pollution was represented by ethnic intermarriage. Italians were likened to animals in their living habits and hygiene ("slimy like eels"). Themes of physical revulsion were expressed in "greaser" imagery ("garlic eating greasers").

Another prominent stereotype accentuated the Italian's reputed criminal and specifically violent nature. The stereotype discerned an inveterate "hotheadedness" marked by "crimes of passion" and the stealthy use of the stiletto. So ingrained was this stereotype that even a supporter of immigrants conceded that "an Italian will stab," even "shoot," disdaining "crimes necessitating subtle and careful planning." Nevertheless, Italians were tainted by conspiratorial violence, sensationalized by the "alien radicalism" of Sacco and Vanzetti. Within American Catholicism, Italians were portrayed as enemies of the church as well as state. After Prohibition, organized crime became the focal point of Italian American lawlessness. A Mafia myth identified a ruthless secret society as an expression of Italian ethnicity.

Ethnic labels and stereotypes are affected by changes in status and power relations. Processes of assimilation and upward mobility contradict insulting ethnic epithets, especially for the generations born after World War II. Stereotypes of degenerate immigrant proletariat are irreconcilable with the record of Italian American cultural adaptation and socioeconomic achievement. (The *New York Times* (May 15, 1983, VI, p. 28), credited the "spectacular rise of Italian Americans in the United States" to "hard work" and "talent" in combination with ethnic family values.) Ethnic stigma was also under assault from Italian American organizations responding to politics based on group identity.

The old epithets and stereotypes are characteristically resilient ("stereo" comes from the Greek and means "hard," or "solid"). Richard Nixon used an ethnic epithet for an Italian American political nemesis on the infamous White House tapes. Into the 1980s, the Verrazano-Narrows Bridge was called "The Guinea Gangplank" in CB radio jargon, which referred to the migration of Italian Americans from Brooklyn to Staten Island facilitated by the span. A sign protesting a decision of Governor Mario Cuomo pertaining to the death penalty read KILL A COP, GET PAROLED BY THE WOP. While public use may be rare, invoking these epithets serves as a status put-down, reducing higher status Italians to a disparaged ethnic category.

Popular stereotypes of Italian Americans also lag behind socioeconomic changes. Although Italian Americans are represented in the cultural mainstream, television and film images portray claustrophobic urban villagers with working-class lifestyles. A salient persona is the streetwise "greaser," with trun-

cated social possibilities and dubious morality; the "greaser" is shaded in the gangster (John Gotti has been labeled "the greaser Don"). The mass media preoccupation with Italian American mobsters sustains the illusions that the Mafia myth can be extrapolated to all Italian Americans.

A recent addition to the lexicon of prejudice against Italian Americans is the label "guido." A conspicuously Italian name, "guido" has given ethnic distinction to an Italian American youth style in New York City in the 1990s. The label probably originated outside the scene, although likely bestowed by more assimilated Italian American youth. Nevertheless, "guido" was embraced by Italian American youth within the scene and used interchangeably with "cugine," derived from the Italian word for "cousin." An underground rap song that became a subcultural anthem referred to the "guido" as a "guinea," perhaps to defiantly appropriate its meaning for a cool, masculine pose (in the manner of "gangsta niggas").

Although "guido" was perceived in the local youth scene in ethnic and style terms ("an Italian who likes disco"), a broader ethnic stereotype was coalescing. Since "guidos" and "guidettes" were perceived as Italian, style became confounded with ethnicity; "guido" meant "looking" or acting Italian as was defined by the prevalent stereotypes. The stereotypes became increasingly negative, transcending the usual style put-downs; a local college newspaper published a satire mixing ethnic prejudice with class snobbery in which "guidos" ("cugines") were ridiculed for linguistic shortcomings such as "axe" in place of "ask."

The "guido" label entered the larger public discourse when an African American teenager was killed in 1989 in Bensonhurst in an altercation with a group of predominantly Italian American youths. Columnists in the major newspapers and the host of a television talk show identified the Bensonhurst youths as "guidos" and identified "guidos" as Italian Americans even though the Bensonhurst contingent included an African American. Furthermore, the stereotype was dramatically altered, as press accounts portrayed "guidos" as criminally deviant ("violent," "depraved," "snarling imbeciles"). "Feral" metaphors envisioned Italian American youths forming "wilding" gangs that were preying on the middle class, although this scenario was not as compelling as the view that "guidos" were incipient Mafiosi. (Columnist Pete Hamill provided a link when he referred to John Gotti Jr. as a "guido.")

In the ensuing moral panic, deviance was attributed to a wider ethnic population. The *New York Times* reported that the Bensonhurst community was characterized by "an insularity with fear and hostility toward the outside." Essays in the *Village Voice* and *Partisan Review* called attention to an even broader "culturally institutionalized neurosis," the "dark side" of family and neighborhood solidarity conducive to "prejudice and racism."

This moral entrepreneurship in local and national news media did not succeed in framing Italian Americans as a front-line social problem. However, the Bensonhurst episode does indicate the persistence of ethnic prejudice against Italian Americans, both in the popular culture and among institutional elites. There remains a repository of disparaging ethnic stereotypes ("guido" as menacing "dago," the "Mafia myth," "amoral familism").

Transcending ethnic stereotypes may be more than a matter of eliminating prejudice. In an information society, conceptualizing multiethnic reality may be constrained by the need for terse communication. Labels and stereotypes are the sound bites and surfaces that simplify ethnicity into facile symbols ("Little Italy," "la via vecchia") for the postmodern consumption and impression management on both sides of the ethnic boundary.

Donald Tricarico

Bibliography

Hall, S. H. "The Italian Americans: Coming Into Their Own." *New York Times Magazine,* 15 May 1983.

Lord, J., et al. *The Italians in America.* New York: B. F. Buck, 1905.

Royce, A.P. *Ethnic Identity: Strategies for Diversity.* Bloomington: Indiana University Press, 1982.

Tricarico, D. "Guido: Fashioning an Italian American Youth Style." *Journal of Ethnic Studies* 19, no. 1 (spring 1991): 41–66.

See also ANTI-ITALIAN DISCRIMINATION; CRIME AND ORGANIZED CRIME; HOWARD BEACH AND BENSONHURST

Labor

Nearly five million people left Italy for the United States between 1880 and 1930, most of whom found jobs as unskilled manual laborers in the nation's burgeoning factories. The history of Italian Americans is bound inextricably with the history of the industrial working class in the United States.

As the American national economy grew in the second half of the nineteenth century, Italian immigration increased so rapidly that Italians dominated United States entry statistics between 1890 and 1930. During the first decade of this century, 23.26 percent of all those arriving came from Italy, primarily from the south and Sicily. Few of the new arrivals had any industrial experience before they migrated. Only 13.3 percent of all southern Italians reported that they had been engaged in manufacturing. Between 1899 and 1910, 77 percent of all southern Italians who entered the United States were classified as agricultural workers by American immigration officials.

Life in America for most Italians was harsh: they had to work under hard and dangerous conditions for meager wages; they had to live poorly among a people who often despised them. While opinion molders from the ranks of the cultural and social elite demeaned Italian immigrants as threats to the purity of American culture, leaders of the nascent American labor movement also condemned them as being unorganizable threats to the American wage standard. The experiences of some American trade unionists, at least since the 1870s, had taught them that immigrants from "backward" countries were most often used by employers to depress wages, break strikes, and smash labor organization. Some pointed to employers' use of Italian strikebreakers in the Pennsylvania coal fields in the mid-1870s and on the New York City docks in 1882. Thus, some American unionists viewed the rising tide of Italian immigrants with great suspicion as they worked with restrictionist legislators to curtail immigration drastically or, at the very least, to outlaw certain employment practices, like contract labor.

Contract labor was a problem that plagued many immigrant communities, including the Italian. *Padroni,* usually Italian-born employment agents, recruited workers with vague promises of jobs. The agent would advance them money to cover the expenses of their transportation, food, work-site housing,

The estate of James Marino, Port Washington, New York. Marino, a padrone *and sand mine operator, ran a boardinghouse for his Italian immigrant workers. As he prospered, he had them build this impressive home that reflected the skill of Italian craftsmanship. Courtesy Nassau County History Museum.*

tools, etc. Of course, the workers would have to repay the *padrone,* over time and usually with interest, out of their future wages. More often than not, the wages were not sufficient to meet the inflated expenses charged by the *padrone;* many Italian immigrants soon found themselves living and working as virtual peons. After Congress outlawed contract labor in the Foran Act of 1885, the contractors simply went underground. The practice of contract labor continued into the early years of the twentieth century, shrinking into insignificance by about 1910. Although some historians have pointed out that the *padrone* often played an important intermediary role for the most recent immigrants, all too often the relationship between worker and *padrone* was an extremely exploitative one.

In the case of the "new" immigrants of the early twentieth century, many old-stock Americans agreed that they were exploited, but argued that the immigrants themselves were at least partly responsible, particularly since they were unwilling to do anything to help themselves. The leadership of the American Federation of Labor also seemed to feel that Italian immigrants were instinctively resistant to unionization: Samuel Gompers, himself foreign-born, once called them "the wrong kind of immigrants." Governmental investigations resulted in conclusions that supported the viewpoints of both the social elite and the "aristocracy of labor." For example, the *Report of the United States Immigration Commission,* published in 1911, filled forty-two volumes with data, charts, and analyses that supported the contention that newcomers like the Italians were not and never could be either real Americans or unionists. The commissioners authoritatively concluded that Italians were not assimilable into the American mainstream and claimed that they were not only reluctant unionists but were virtually unorganizable, implicitly because of the low rung they occupied on Darwin's social ladder, and explicitly because of their lack of industrial experience.

Thankfully, social Darwinism lost its credibility long ago. But for an extended period of time, many scholars did accept as fact the assertion that Italian immigrants brought only "pre-industrial" experiences to industrial America, and thus were ill equipped to understand industrial institutions like unions. Most migration scholars and specialists working today in related areas understand that the southern Italian peasantry, during the great age of emigration, was neither homogeneous nor untouched by the industrialization and other attendant phenomena that were transforming Europe during that era. By the 1890s a process of agricultural proletarianization was transforming the Italian Mezzogiorno. Peasants, while still relying upon the ancient traditions of familism for support and comfort, began to build voluntary organizations to conserve whatever privileges and stability traditional life had granted and to advance family interests in a changing world where human relations were becoming more commodified. Mutual-aid societies, labor unions, and *fascii* (leagues, coalitions) in the Italian south advanced political solutions for peasant problems that were rooted in a nineteenth-century socialist analysis of social relations. Many of those who left Italy between 1880 and 1930 carried with them worldviews already affected by both proletarianization and radicalization.

Between 1880 and 1930, sons and daughters of Italy found employment in virtually every sector of American industry, including construction, textile production, clothing manufacturing, railroad construction and maintenance, mining, and food processing. In addition, Italians continued to work in trades like stonecutting, barbering, shoemaking, tailoring, and fishing, and in service fields, particularly in restaurants, stores, and bakeries. Before World War I, most Italian males, over one-third in 1910, were listed on census records as "laborers," assumedly unskilled workers in a variety of industries, particularly construction. The largest single concentration of men in any particular industry was to be found in coal mining (just under 10 percent), while the largest cohort of Italian women labored in the needle trades (over 35 percent in 1910).

Relatively few Italian immigrant workers, male or female, were members of unions prior to 1930: only 10.6 percent of all southern Italian workers held union cards in 1910. Still, we must remember that before the 1930s, union members made up less than 9 percent of the entire American labor force. In the context of that particular comparison, Italian American unionization rates do not look distinctively low. Moreover, though few joined unions and even fewer maintained their

Italian Americans construct a road in Patchogue, New York, early in the twentieth century. The Romeo Construction Co., started by Frank Romeo, employed almost entirely Italian immigrants for this and other projects. Courtesy Salvatore J. LaGumina.

membership, Italian immigrant workers joined many strikes and supported effective labor organization to the extent that they were able. Some Italian American workers even built their own unions in some industries prior to 1930. Italian craftsmen with needed skills, like granite cutters, were very active unionists between 1870 and 1920. Italians were involved in the Bricklayers and Masons' Union in several East Coast cities in the 1890s, and there was a short-lived Italian Tailor's Society in Philadelphia during the same decade. Italian construction workers participated in strikes on many occasions, and some workers attempted to build an Italian National Union, headquartered at Mt. Vernon, New York, just prior to World War I. In and around Tampa, Florida, Italian cigar makers joined Cuban immigrants in a series of fierce struggles with employers between 1908 and 1921. Italian activists helped to build the precursor of today's Laborers' International Union of America, and two Italians, Domenico D'Alessandro and Joseph Moreschi, held the union's presidency for more than a generation after 1908. But the most dramatic strikes and significant unionization drives in which Italians participated took place in those industries where they were most heavily represented: mining, textiles, and the needle trades.

When owner recalcitrance greeted a United Mine Workers (UMW) organizing drive in 1903, strikes inevitably exploded around the country. In some areas, as in the coal districts of southern Colorado, Italians constituted the largest foreign-born element of the labor force. Many of the Italian miners also lived in company-owned housing throughout the Colorado coalfields. Once strikers were evicted from these houses, strike violence escalated to the point that National Guardsmen was sent to the area. Italian strikers were prevented from holding any open meetings, including those of their local mutual-aid society. A number of prominent Italian strikers were forcibly deported from the region, especially after their local newspaper, *Il Lavoratore Italiano,* excoriated the mine owners and their political supporters. After several months of military occupation and repression, the UMW informed Colorado unionists that it could no longer sustain the strike. Italian delegates to Colorado's District 15 of the UMW agitated for continued resistance; but, by the fall of 1904, the strike was utterly broken.

Violence, strikes, and, at times, near insurrections raged through mining areas of the country between the 1870s and the 1930s, at times moving with the speed and heat of a tunnel fire. From the "Molly Maguire" disturbances in Pennsylvania's anthracite fields in the 1870s, to the "Mingo County War" in West Virginia in the 1920s, American miners learned bitter lessons about the power of capital and its domination of the state in the land that some Italians now called *la terra del dollaro e del dolore* (the land of the dollar and pain). And it was not just bullets that killed Italian immigrant and other workers in America's unregulated and anarchic mines. Seventy-five Italians were among the 250 who died underground at Cherry, Illinois, in 1909 as they tried to escape a mine fire, only to find that long-established emergency routes had been changed by the company. No one told the miners.

Many of the increasing number of Italians passing through Boston moved into the textile factory towns surrounding that New England city after 1900. By 1910 the American Woolen Company, situated in Lawrence, about thirty-five miles north of Boston, employed more than seven thousand Italians among its multicultural workforce of roughly thirty thousand. The owners of the company were growing increasingly peevish toward what they considered the unwarranted intervention of the state in their private affairs. Massachusetts, one of the leading states in terms of progressive factory legislation, already had lowered the hours of the maximum regular work from fifty-eight to fifty-six. Moreover, the state's legislature clearly intended that employers would accept this hours reduction without cutting wages accordingly. In late 1911 the state assembly again passed a workweek reduction act, this time lowering the maximum regular work week to fifty-four hours. Again, it was intended that employers were to accept the reduction without lowering wages; however, rumors circulated throughout the commonwealth that, this time, employers were going to teach "intrusive" legislators a lesson.

The law went into effect on a Thursday, which also was a payday. Some Polish women mill workers ripped open their pay envelopes, confirmed their suspicions that their pay had been cut, and immediately left their work stations, shouting, "Short pay!" Many of the workers, mostly immigrants, of the various textile mills joined them in a spontaneous walkout. That evening, a meeting of nine hundred Italian mill workers voted to strike, effective the following day.

At precisely 9:00 A.M. on Friday, after several hours of work, the Italians left their machines at the Wood Mill of the American Woolen Company, the city's largest employer. They ran through the complex, demanding a walkout and gathering other workers as they proceeded. To make certain the mill would not operate without them, they disassembled machines, cut electrical wires and pulley belts, and intimidated those reportedly few workers who were reluctant to join them. By the end of the day, ten thousand men, women, and children were on strike.

Lawrence's mill workers were highly divided by skill, ethnicity, race, and gender, making the role of unifying leadership very important. Although much of the direction of the strike was undertaken by local workers, many of whom were Italian, the most prominent leaders were drawn from the national ranks of the Industrial Workers of the World (IWW), or the "Wobblies," as they were commonly known. The IWW had been founded in 1905 by a diverse group of labor radicals with the intention of bringing together the unorganized, regardless of race, nationality, sex, or level of skill. By 1912 the IWW was organized around the doctrine of *revolutionary syndicalism,* a theory of trade unionism which held that all workers should be organized industrially, should agitate to control the means of production through general strikes, and would ultimately gain control of their societies by controlling industry, not politics. The Italians were among the strongest IWW partisans in Lawrence. As soon as the strike began, Angelo Rocco, a local Wobbly, sent out a request for national IWW help. The first two strike leaders to arrive were Italians, Joseph Ettor and Arturo Giovannitti.

Ettor was born in Brooklyn of Italian-born, working-class parents in 1886. He joined the Socialist Party in 1901 and was a charter member of the IWW. Ettor was a particularly effective organizer of immigrant workers, as he spoke Italian, Yiddish, Polish, and Hungarian, in addition to English. He was in the process of building a union of Italian shoemakers in Brooklyn when he received the call from Lawrence. Ettor, though a seasoned radical and labor organizer by the time he got to Lawrence, was only 26 years old. He was a short, stocky man, who radiated optimism. Most described him as a "sharp" dresser, partial to fashionable blue suits, which he modified with the floppy hat and flowing tie that identified anarchists in much of Europe.

Giovannitti was born into an upper-middle-class family in Campobasso, Abruzzi, in 1884. He left Italy for the United States at age 16. After arriving in New York City, he moved from job to job and from Catholicism to Marxism. He also became an accomplished poet, a leader of the Italian Socialist Federation, and the publisher of *Il Proletario.* By 1912 Giovannitti was already well known in Italian immigrant circles, and was also invited to Lawrence by the strikers. He had a strong emotional speaking voice that exuded an incisive intellectualism that never alienated his working-class audiences, to which he spoke in Italian, English, and French. His dress was even more bohemian than Ettor's, as he generally wore a cape, rather than a topcoat, along with the floppy hat and anarchist's loose tie.

The strike demands were hardly radical: the workers wanted a 15 percent wage increase based on the new fifty-four-hour week, double-pay for overtime, elimination of the bonus system, and a promise of non-discrimination against strikers. The strikers were also moderate with tactics: although there was mass picketing and some intimidation of scabs, there was no organized use of violence or sabotage. In addition, the strikers held regular, lively parades, in which local Italian bands usually marched and played. These celebrations of solidarity kept worker spirits high; by late January, it was obvious that the strike was holding.

The mill owners, directed by William Wood of the American Woolen Company, moved quickly to subvert the strike. Wood was quoted every day on the front page of local newspapers he controlled, calling the immigrant strikers "ignorant dupes" of radicals like Ettor and Giovannitti. A local businessman, possibly under Wood's direction, even fabricated a bomb hoax in a failed attempt to discredit the strikers. Local politicians continued to insist that revolution was afoot in Lawrence, despite the fact that there had been relatively little strike violence. Still, the peace would not hold indefinitely. Despite attempts by strike leaders to maintain a nonviolent

L

posture, a full-scale riot broke out after a confrontation between police and paraders on the evening of January 29, 1912; one policeman and one striker—Annie LoPezzi—were killed in the melee. Although there was no evidence revealing the perpetrator(s) of either killing, the police immediately arrested the two most important strike leaders, Ettor and Giovannitti, accusing them of the nebulous crime of inciting an unknown person to commit murder. The accused were denied bail and sat in jail through their trial in the fall of 1912. Three months after the first arrests, the police charged an Italian striker, Joseph Caruso, with the murder of LoPezzi. All three men were eventually acquitted.

With Ettor and Giovannitti in jail, even more prominent Wobblies like "Big Bill" Haywood and Elizabeth Gurley Flynn assumed roles in strike management. After a combination of brilliant tactical moves by the strikers and brutal blunders by the police, the owners finally offered a reasonable settlement. On March 14, 1912, the strikers accepted the terms, even though they did not include employer recognition of workers' collective bargaining rights. Eventually, though, American textile workers would win a permanent industrial union, and Italians would play a significant role. After the Textile Workers of America was born in March of 1937, George Baldanzi, a longtime activist, served as first vice president, and later as president of the union.

As the clothing industry expanded and changed in the United States between the 1860s and the 1890s, many Italian laborers, first women and then men, took jobs in the needle trades. Women worked since the late 1880s as home finishers, and by the mid-1890s Italian men found work as machine operators and pressers, both in inside shops and for subcontractors. The Italians followed an earlier influx of Eastern European Jewish workers into the industry. Many observers agreed that the garment bosses opened their arms to the Italians because the employers perceived them not only as cheaper labor, but also as much less susceptible than their Jewish co-workers to the virus of unionism. But those who owned the garment factories and sweatshops soon learned that the desire to unionize was not primarily cultural; it was a natural, transcultural response to conditions of discrimination and exploitation in the needle trades.

Italians, like other workers, found the conditions of labor in the garment trades deplorable. Also, like other workers, Italian cloak makers and dressmakers turned to unionization as the most effective way of ameliorating the exploitative conditions of their trades. In fact, prior to 1910, southern Italians who worked in the garment industry were unionized in a percentage exceeding the overall ratio of labor force organization within garment trades. But compared to the far more organized and more numerous Jewish garment workers, Italians seemed somewhat resistant to unionization throughout the first decade of the twentieth century. Many Italian workers of this period considered themselves to be temporary American workers and, hence, focused on sustaining employment under any conditions, saving, and planning for futures in Italy. Jewish workers, many of whom were refugees from the anti-Semitic violence of the collapsing Russian tsarist empire, were in the United States to stay, and thus focused on building organizations that could win permanent improvements in the American industrial context.

A dozen or so American cities had substantial garment industries; but the largest and most economically significant were to be found in Chicago and, particularly, New York City. In Chicago, a seminal strike against manufacturers of men's clothing was led largely by Anzuino Marimpietri, Emilio Grandinetti, and Giuseppe Bertelli. The strike failed, but it strengthened the Amalgamated Clothing Workers of America (ACWA), the union that would soon represent many workers in the men's trades, including those organized in Rochester by Antonio Capraro and in New York City by Augusto Bellanca. The ACWA would significantly improve wages and working conditions and would produce a leader, Sidney Hillman, who would play a major role in the shaping of New Deal labor policy.

A year before the Chicago struggle, Jewish workers in New York's women's garment trades had launched an even more dramatic strike, virtually a rebellion, against dress manufacturers in that metropolis. By 1909 Italian women constituted over 36 percent of the female labor force in New York's garment industry. During the 1909 dressmakers' strike, one of the most famous in the annals of United States labor history, many young Italian women were constrained from striking by their dependent positions within their families. Still, the generally favorable outcome of that strike convinced many Italian workers, particularly those who were acquiring some permanence in this country, that unionizing was critical to their future prospects of economic and social well-being. In the case of Italian male cloak makers during a general strike of 1910, there seem to have been no cultural or familial restraints, even on the youngest workers. Ultimately, common sense suggested that women, who constituted the majority of needle trades' workers, especially in the rapidly growing sectors like dressmaking, would have to be organized as well. In addition, it became painfully clear that women suffered the travails of American industrialism along with male workers. On March 25, 1911, one of the worst industrial tragedies in United States history occurred: a fire at the Triangle Shirtwaist Company killed 154 men, women, and children, most of them Jewish and Italian. Consequently, more Italian workers, male and female, embraced unionization, most of whom were attracted to the International Ladies' Garment Workers' Union (ILGWU).

Once a sizable number of Italian garment trades workers became union activists and organizers, they turned their attention to a problem internal to the fledgling ILGWU: the formidable language and cultural barriers between Jewish union leaders and Italian needle trades' workers. After 1910 Italian activists argued that Jewish cultural and language domination of the ILGWU was so complete that Italians were being excluded from union business, despite their professed dedication to the goals of the international organization. The carrying out of union business, especially through the operations of elected business agents, was very important to the mostly male Italian cloak makers, led by Eduardo Molisani and Salvatore Ninfo, among others. As late as 1912 there were few Italian business agents. Since business agents were elected within locals, Italians initiated demands for their own locals as a means of ensuring the hiring of business agents who would watch out for the Italian members' particular interests.

There were several other reasons for the Italian demands for nationality locals as well. A posture of relative autonomy within the ILGWU would improve the community-wide reputation of Italian unionists. This seems to have been at least one of the motivating factors behind the work of dressmakers' Luigi Antonini, the man who would become the most powerful Italian American garment trades unionist by the early 1930s and perhaps the most influential Italian American labor movement figure of any generation. Antonini realized the potential for broader political power that leadership of a large labor union local could bestow. The personal ambitions of certain leaders like Antonini were important determinants in the direction of trade union development among the Italian garment workers. On a less self-serving level, Antonini believed that raising the class consciousness of the Italian dressmakers, who were mostly women, was a critical imperative. He argued that this task could be carried out most effectively by Italians within their own organizations. Italians were able finally to win their own locals in 1916 (Local 48, Cloak makers) and in 1919 (Local 89, Dressmakers).

Despite the fact that most dressmakers were women, the leadership of Local 89 was and would remain largely male. Yet some women, such as Margaret DiMaggio and Angela and Maria Bambace, rose into the leadership cadre, while dozens of others served on the local's executive council and as organizers.

Sicilian-born Margaret DiMaggio went to work in the garment shops of Manhattan as a dress operator while still in her teens. She soon gravitated toward a crowd of labor militants, one of whom was Arturo Giovannitti. Despite strong objections from her family, DiMaggio became an organizer and an accomplished strike orator. She devoted most of her life's energy to Local 89 and the ILGWU. DiMaggio did not marry until her mid-forties and never had children, but she did raise a generation of women garment trade organizers and activists. Those women remember Margaret DiMaggio fondly, recalling that she was a very strong person who feared neither the bosses nor the gangsters they employed frequently from the 1920s onward. In fact, DiMaggio was imprisoned several times for her organizing activities. Later in life she would become an ardent New Dealer, work on several issues with Eleanor Roosevelt, and even make a speech in her presence at the White House. Most importantly, DiMaggio had the gift of being able to convince large numbers of Italian American women to join the union. By the time of her retirement from the ILGWU, DiMaggio had risen to the

L

position of assistant manager of the Organization Department. She died in 1962, leaving very few records except for the warm memories of her comrades.

The lives and union careers of Angela and Maria Bambace also are illustrative of the kinds of contributions Italian American women made to building the labor movement. By the time they were in their late teens, both Angela and Maria held jobs as operators in an East Harlem shirtwaist factory. They both attempted to organize workers in the garment shops around 1917, and both were drawn to the more radical activists. Unlike so many parents who responded negatively to female union activism, their mother accompanied them, armed with a rolling pin for protection. Maria, in the course of her union work, met and soon married Antonio Capraro, an anarchist, IWW organizer, and, later, official of the Amalgamated Clothing Workers. After her marriage, Maria's activism took a backseat to her family responsibilities, even though her husband rejected the idea that women should focus on hearth and home. Angela married also but her husband was neither a union activist nor accepting of nontraditional roles for women; he insisted that Angela become a homemaker.

Domestic chores held few attractions for Angela, who chafed at being limited only to concerns about "tomato sauce and handmade gnocchi." In 1925 Angela returned to garment factory work, again became active as an organizer, and moved politically toward the activists of Locals 2, 9, and 22, most of whom were Jewish and communists. Angela soon supported a communist insurgency within the ILGWU, and in so doing, alienated Luigi Antonini and other Italian unionists, most of whom opposed communism for pragmatic rather than ideological reasons. Though leaving the ranks of the Italian dressmakers, Angela worked for the ILGWU for the rest of her life and eventually retired as a member of the International's general executive board. She was the first Italian American woman to hold so high a position in the ILGWU.

Even though a significant number of women, in addition to DiMaggio and the Bambaces, became active in organizing, most of them served in voluntary rather than paid positions, and few of them forged stable careers in the union, especially prior to the 1930s. Since their working-class activism was often episodic, many male unionists sup-

ported the broadly held view that Italian women always put family before politics, as though the two were unrelated. But the women who took active roles in Local 89's administration did not fuel the stereotype of being conservative, religious, and dutifully obedient to husbands and fathers. Their experience as workers convinced them that organization was in their class interests. As to the significance of their gender interests, this perspective seems to have come into play much less in their relationships with male union leaders than in their organizing efforts with women garment workers.

The Italian dressmakers of Local 89 made significant organizational gains during the 1920s, remained committed to a socialist political agenda, and generally improved the conditions of work for Italian Americans in the ladies' garment trades. Throughout the era, Luigi Antonini remained a popular and effective leader of the Italian dressmakers. As the decade reached its midpoint, the leaders of the Italian garment trades locals cultivated broader influence with a rising generation of New York Italian American politicians, many of whom were staking positions with the political left. But when the communists within the ILGWU tried to capture its central administration, Antonini, the cloak makers' Salvatore Ninfo, and most other Italian union activists supported the moderate International administration. By 1926 the Italians were a mainstay of the "anticommunist" camp in the ILGWU. But their anticommunist position was crafted mainly to protect their own nationality organizations and to preserve the political base they had struggled so long to secure. The Italians opposed the communists mostly from the posture of pragmatism, not because they were tradition-bound peasants or because they had embraced a comprehensively anticommunist ideology. Nevertheless, their pragmatic political opposition to the communists within the ILGWU, along with the changing domestic and international political climate after 1929, began to move the Italian unionists rightward on the political spectrum. Organizationally, the policy paid off: by the mid-1930s, New York's Italian dressmakers constituted the largest local union in the United States, with over forty thousand members.

The cultural values of those Italian Americans who built labor organizations in the coalfields of Colorado, the textile mills of New

England, and in the sweatshops of New York City's garment districts stressed the primary nature of familial relationships, the importance of honor and loyalty to one's family, friends, and community, and the efficacy of voluntary associations intended to sustain the stability of the family circle. These values strengthened Italian workers in their struggles to organize. More significant than culture, however, in molding the drive toward unionization among the Italian workers were the conditions Italian immigrants faced in their everyday work lives and the discrimination and exploitation they faced in all other areas of American life as well. The motivations of the Italian workers to unionize, then, were based mainly on class interests. Most of the engaged Italian unionists, at least prior to the 1930s, conceived of the purposes of union activity in broad sociopolitical terms. Belief in class struggle was strong, as was an unintellectualized conviction that alienated labor characterized the conditions under which most workers toiled. To improve their lives in *all* areas, Italian workers joined or organized unions and engaged in union and community politics. The political values articulated by the founding generation of Italian American union activists were influenced as strongly by theories of class struggle as by the older traditions of southern Italian peasant culture. Consequently, their politics were as "radical" in terms of the American society of their era as they were "traditional." But the post–World War I Red Scare, the nativism and conservatism of the 1920s, and pragmatic anticommunism like that molded in the crucible of the ILGWU's internecine political struggles nearly destroyed the generally progressive and often socialist dreams of the immigrant activists.

Since the end of the World War II, Italian unionists have become far less visible as a distinctive group of organized workers. Revealingly, the one Italian American labor leader, newly prominent in the postwar era, who was most often identified as "Italian" was Anthony Scotto, president of a New York City local of the International Longshoremen's Association (ILA). Scotto's name was in the press, not because he was an effective labor leader nor because he was in any way a militant advocate for the ethnic working class, but rather because he had married into the Anastasia "crime family," and had a number of run-ins himself with police and federal authorities. Luigi Antonini, for a brief time in his youth a communist, spent his postwar years supporting the Dean Acheson perspective on the dangers of communism, and even visited Italy on several occasions, under State Department sponsorship, to encourage Italians to reject communists in nationwide elections. There is a younger generation of Italian Americans active today in dozens of unions; however, unlike Luigi Antonini or Anzuino Marimpietri, unionists of Italian extraction are rarely distinguished from their comrades by their ethnicity. At least a dozen Italian Americans hold presidencies of both major industrial organizations and smaller craft unions. Arthur A. Coia heads the large Laborers' International Union, having succeeded Angelo Fosco in 1993. Vincent Sombrotto serves as president of the 311,000-member National Association of Letter Carriers and as vice-president of the National Italian American Federation. Other Italian Americans holding top offices in large industrial unions are Mark Tully Massagli (president, American Federation of Musicians), John DeConcini (president emeritus, Bakery, Confectionery and Tobacco Workers), Jim LaSala (president, Amalgamated Transit Union), Michael Sacca (president, Seafarers International Union), and Paul Policicchio (one of three executive vice-presidents of the giant Service Employees International Union). Italian Americans are well represented in leadership positions of smaller craft unions as well: presidential authority is exercised by Frank D. Martino (Chemical Workers Union), George J. Orlando (Distillery, Wine and Allied Workers), Dominic A. Martell (Plasterers and Cement Masons), and Alfred W. DiTolla (Theatrical Stage Employees and Moving Picture Machine Operators). There are also many union activists of Italian extraction who operate on the rank-and-file level of the labor movement. A prominent example is that of Tony Mazzocchi, former official of the Oil, Chemical and Atomic Workers and one of the principal organizers of Labor Party advocates, a group of labor militants attempting to build an independent Labor Party in the United States.

In several major cities, most notably New York and Chicago, umbrella organizations of Italian American unionists still function, but these are largely fraternal and/or civic in their orientation. Italian Americans in greater urban areas like New York City still hold blue-collar occupations in percentages greater than those of the general population. But as unionization has fallen to record post–New Deal lows in the private manufacturing sector, and as third-generation and now fourth-generation Italian Americans have moved far away from the class perspective shared by many of their immigrant ancestors, the Italian American labor movement is receding rapidly into the as yet unwritten pages of American history.

Charles A. Zappia

Bibliography

DiFranco, Philip. *The Italian American Experience.* New York: Tom Doherty, 1988.

Fenton, Edwin. *Immigrants and Unions, A Case Study: Italians and American Labor, 1870–1920.* New York: Arno, 1975.

Gabaccia, Donna Rae. *Militants and Migrants: Rural Sicilians Become American Workers.* New Brunswick, NJ: Rutgers University Press, 1988.

Iorizzo, Luciano J., and Salvadore Mondello. *The Italian Americans.* Boston: Twayne, 1980.

Pozzetta, George E., ed. *Pane e Lavoro: The Italian American Working Class.* Toronto: Multicultural History Society of Ontario, 1980.

Pozzetta, George E., and Gary Mormino. *The Immigrant World of Ybor City.* Urbana: University of Illinois Press, 1986.

Vecoli, Rudolph J., ed. *Italian American Radicalism: Old World Origins and New World Developments.* New York: American Italian Historical Association, 1972.

See also ANTONINI, LUIGI; GIOVANNITTI, ARTURO; RADICALISM

La Cava, Gregory

See CARTOONISTS AND ILLUSTRATORS; FILM DIRECTORS, PRODUCERS, AND ITALIAN AMERICAN IMAGE IN CINEMA

LaCorte, John N. (1910–1991)

The founder of the Italian Historical Society of America and the Better World John LaCorte (JL) Institute, John N. LaCorte was born in Jersey City, New Jersey. He was a prominent leader of Italian Americans who was instrumental in educating the Italian American community and the larger American society regarding the significant contributions made by Italians and Italian Americans to Western civilization. In addition, he engaged in philanthropic work and promoted a new generation of moral responsibility in America.

At age 3, LaCorte returned to his parents' native town of San Giovanni Gemini in the province of Agrigento in Sicily, where he remained until his 19th birthday. He returned to the United States to sign up for the military draft and to retain his American citizenship. LaCorte arrived in America with only nineteen cents in his pocket to live with family members. He took several jobs including stevedore on a tanker and clarinet player in a band. After moving to Brooklyn, he sold refrigerators and vacuum cleaners. LaCorte later began to sell life insurance and eventually became associated with New York Life Insurance Company, where he became one of their highest volume salesmen. He established the LaCorte Agency, which served the general insurance needs of his mostly Italian American clients.

LaCorte became acutely aware of the defamation suffered by the Italian American community. He first formed an organization called AMERITO in the 1940s. In 1949 he established the Italian Historical Society of America, which continues to carry on the work of its founder. LaCorte, working through the society, was successful in having the Verrazano-Narrows Bridge named after the discoverer of New York, the Florentine navigator Giovanni da Verrazzano. Later, the society worked to have the following recognized for their achievements: Antonio Meucci, as the true inventor of the telephone; Charles J. Bonaparte, as the first Italian American attorney general and the founder of the Federal Bureau of Investigation; Peter Caesar Alberti, as the first Italian immigrant to America; and many others. Through LaCorte's leadership the society's achievements became significant in promoting Italian American achievements.

In his later years LaCorte broadened his altruistic interests by establishing the Better World JL Institute, which is devoted to the universal advancement of humanity. The Model Student's Program was established by LaCorte to inspire today's youth to become the responsible citizens of tomorrow. The organization continues its philanthropic mission. John N. LaCorte worked tirelessly for the two organizations and for the ideals upon which they were founded.

Frank M. Sorrentino

Bibliography
Cavaioli, Frank J. "Group Politics, Ethnicity and Italian Americans." In *Immigration and Ethnicity,* edited by Michael D. Innocenzo and Joseph P. Sirefman, 62–74. Westport, CT: Greenwood Press, 1992.
"John N. LaCorte Fame." *New Yorker Magazine,* 11 February 1980, pp. 26–28.

See also BONAPARTE, CHARLES JOSEPH; MEUCCI, ANTONIO; ORGANIZATIONS; VERRAZZANO, GIOVANNI DA

LaGuardia, Fiorello H. (1882–1947)

LaGuardia was New York's most legendary mayor (1934–1945), although recent historiography suggests that he was a product of his times rather than the mastermind who determined events in the city. His political rise marked the coming of age of Italian Americans in United States politics. However, unlike most of his fellow ethnic politicians in the prewar years, LaGuardia extended his appeal well beyond the boundaries of his own nationality group.

LaGuardia's mixed parentage and the experiences of his younger years endowed him with the means for his career. He was born in New York on December 11, 1882. His Catholic father was Italian. His Jewish mother came from Trieste, an Italian enclave in the Austrian Empire and a crossroad between Central Europe and the Balkans, where LaGuardia himself spent some time before holding lesser positions in the U.S. consular service in Budapest and Fiume. He returned to New York in 1906.

After his years abroad, LaGuardia, fluent in five languages, worked as an interpreter at Ellis Island to pay for his tuition fees at the New York University School of Law and graduated in 1910. His law practice boosted his political ambitions.

LaGuardia sided with the Republican Party to speed up his career because the Irish-controlled Democratic machine usually discriminated against members of other ethnic minorities. He also stood by President William H. Taft in 1912, refusing to bolt to the Progressive Party of Theodore Roosevelt, and gained the 1916 Republican nomination for the U.S. House of Representatives as a reward for his loyalty. LaGuardia ran successfully in 1916 and became the third Italian American in U.S. history to enter Congress. He managed to win reelection two years later notwithstanding protests against his leave of absence to fight in Italy during World War I. However, he resigned in 1919 to serve one term as president of the New York City Board of Aldermen. He regained a seat in Congress in 1922 and retained it until the 1932 Democratic landslide swept him out of office.

In the meantime, LaGuardia had become a maverick politician. In 1918 he exploited Democratic boss Charlie Murphy's pledge to back patriotic Republican candidates against Socialist challengers in order to run on a Republican-Democratic fusion ticket. Three years later, LaGuardia defied the leadership of his own party by waging an independent but fruitless campaign for the Republican nomination for mayor of New York. Once he was back to Congress, he shifted to the left and supported a number of progressive bills, including the Anti-Injunction Act that he cosponsored with Senator George Norris. LaGuardia also established his own organization, the Fiorello H. LaGuardia Political Association, which provided his destitute East Harlem constituents with legal and other services. This organization was instrumental in securing his reelection to Congress in 1924 after he had gone over to Robert La Follette's Progressive Party and decided to run as a Socialist.

It was not, however, the working class that elected LaGuardia as mayor of New York on a fusion Republican ticket in 1933 after another unsuccessful bid in 1929. With the leading exception of the Italian American community and Jewish garment workers, the bulk of LaGuardia's supporters were middle-class New Yorkers who embraced his fight against the corrupt admininistration of Tammany Hall Democrats.

Mayor LaGuardia worked hard to obtain federal funds for New York under the New Deal and used the funds to promote an imposing array of public works that created new jobs and helped modernize the city. He added to the forces that shaped the development of the metropolis, which had been at work for a long time preceding his tenure. LaGuardia reformed the municipal administration and reduced mismanagement in the public service. Yet he also exploited the New Deal patronage and his appointive powers to strengthen his political organization, which contributed to his reelection in both 1937 and 1941 on another fusion ticket that included the Republican Party and the American Labor Party.

LaGuardia was also involved in Italian American disputes. When the Order Sons of Italy in America took a pro-Fascist stand in the 1920s, he led a secession from that organization. Yet he did not stigmatize Mussolini's 1935 invasion of Ethiopia for fear of losing Italian American votes.

LaGuardia did not run for a fourth term in 1945 in the hope of a cabinet appointment in the Democratic administration; however, the highest post he obtained was that of director general of the United Nations Relief and Rehabilitation Commission. He died on September 21, 1947.

Stefano Luconi

Bibliography

Elliott, Lawrence. *"Little Flower": The Life and Times of Fiorello LaGuardia*. New York: Morrow, 1983.

Garrett, Charles. *The LaGuardia Years: Machine and Reform Politics in New York City*. New Brunswick: Rutgers University Press, 1961.

Hecksher, August, with Phyllis Robinson. *When LaGuardia Was Mayor: New York's Legendary Years*. New York: Norton, 1978.

Kessner, Thomas. *Fiorello H. LaGuardia and the Making of Modern New York*. New York: McGraw-Hill, 1989.

Mann, Arthur. *LaGuardia Comes to Power, 1933*. Philadelphia: Lippincott, 1965.

Speroni, Gigi. *Fiorello LaGuardia: Il piu' grande italiano d'America*. Milan: Rusconi, 1993.

Zinn, Howard. *LaGuardia in Congress*. Ithaca: Cornell University Press, 1959.

See also POLITICS

Lantz (Lanza), Walter
See CARTOONISTS AND ILLUSTRATORS

Lanza, Gaetano
See SCIENCE

Lanza, Mario (1921–1959)
An outstanding tenor and film actor, born Alfredo Arnold Cocozza in Philadelphia, January 31, 1921, Mario Lanza was the son of a disabled veteran and a seamstress. Early in life he displayed a talent for singing and took lessons after he quit high school to work. After Lanza worked as a piano mover, or truck driver, or in his grandfather's wholesale grocery business (depending on the source consulted), the distinguished conductor Serge Koussevitzky auditioned Lanza in 1942. Because of this audition, Lanza received a scholarship to the New England Conservatory of Music and appeared at the Berkshire Summer Festival in Tanglewood, the Boston Symphony's summer music camp in western Massachusetts. He was also signed for a concert tour by Columbia records, but World War II forced him to alter his plans. Yet the war may have helped his career, for he was assigned to the Special Services section of the United States Armed Forces and sang on radio for American troops on a regular basis.

After being discharged, he went on a concert tour and appeared in the Hollywood Bowl in 1946. He signed a movie contract with MGM Studios and for about a decade was a very popular entertainer: a combination of actor with a muscular appearance and a singer with a powerful voice and great range. Despite the strength of his voice, he was not a disciplined vocalist. He had operatic potential yet appeared in only one opera, Giacomo Puccini's *Madame Butterfly* (1904), with the New Orleans Opera in 1948.

He had starring or major roles in eight movies. The first was *That Midnight Kiss* (1949), followed by *The Toast of New Orleans* (1950), *The Great Caruso* (1951), *Because You're Mine* (1952), *The Student Prince* (1954), *Serenade* (1956), *The Seven Hills of Rome* (1958), and *For the First Time* (1959). Of these films, the most important were *The Toast of New Orleans,* in which he sang his greatest hit, the two million record–selling *Be My Love* (words by the lyricist Sammy Cahn, music by Nicholas Brodszky); *The Great Caruso*, probably his best film, in which he played the title role; and *The Student Prince,* based on the 1924 operetta by composer Sigmund Romberg and lyricist Dorothy Donnelly, in which he worked as a voice-over for the young and slim actor Edmond Purdom, singing such operetta classics as "Serenade" ("Overhead the Moon Is Beaming") and the rollicking "Drinking Song" (or "Drink, Drink, Drink"). In addition to films, he had his own radio show in the early 1950s.

By the end of the 1950s his popularity waned, and he only worked in minor films in his last years. A lifelong struggle with obesity and problems with alcohol and barbiturates, exacerbated by his volatile personality, all possibly contributed to his death from a heart attack in a Rome clinic, October 7, 1959, at the early age of 38.

William E. Studwell

Bibliography

Bernard, Matt. *Mario Lanza*. New York: Macfadden-Bartel, 1971.

Mannering, Derek. *Mario Lanza: A Biography*. London: Hale, 1991.

Strait, Raymond, and Terry Robinson. *Lanza: His Tragic Life*. Englewood Cliffs, NJ: Prentice-Hall, 1980.

See also MOVIE ACTORS AND ACTRESSES; OPERA; POP SINGERS

La Puma, Salvatore J. (b. 1929)

A novelist and short story writer, La Puma received the 1987 Flannery O'Connor Award for Short Fiction and 1988 American Book Award for his first story collection, *The Boys of Bensonhurst*. It was followed in 1991 by *A Time for Wedding Cake*, a novel, and in 1992 by a second story collection, *Teaching Angels to Fly*.

Most of La Puma's fiction takes place in Bensonhurst, Brooklyn, his own neighborhood until 1959. His father, Giovanni, and his mother, Rose, had settled in Bensonhurst in 1928. He had about one hundred boyhood jobs and claimed that each one had been like reading a book. In 1950 he earned a college degree in English literature.

The following year he was drafted by the United States Army, trained as a medic, and served in Korea and Japan. In 1959 La Puma moved his family to Westchester County, thirty miles north of New York City. He commuted daily to his advertising copywriter job on Madison Avenue.

In 1967 he moved his family to Santa Barbara, California. La Puma tried his hand at selling real estate and came to know countless seekers who became the heartbeats of his fictional characters.

La Puma planted fig trees and clementines alongside Haas avocados and Meyer lemons and inspired in his now Californian children a love for the land, as the Mediterranean had once heartened previous La Puma generations. His writing embraces an Italian American insight.

La Puma was married to Linda Ferrara in 1955 and divorced in 1977. Three years later he married Joan Dewberry. He has six children with his first wife, and a stepdaughter with his second.

John La Puma

Bibliography

La Puma, Salvatore J. *The Boys of Bensonhurst*. Athens: University of Georgia Press, 1987.

———. *Teaching Angels to Fly*. New York: Norton, 1992.

———. *A Time for Wedding Cake*. New York: Norton, 1991.

See also NOVELS AND NOVELISTS

Las Vegas

Italian Americans brought talents and interests that contributed to the development of Las Vegas from a dusty Mojave Desert railroad stop to the entertainment capital of the world. They played key roles in the establishment, staffing, and growth of the Strip and Glitter Gulch hotels. They have had a significant representation among entertainers. Of the headline performers in the 1950s and 1960s, one-fourth were men and women of Italian background. They were also well represented among the lounge performers, musicians, architects, contractors, and developers who transformed Las Vegas into a major city of the American Southwest.

A handful of Italian-born individuals were among the founders of Las Vegas in the first decade of the twentieth century. One, Dominic Pecetto, built a small hotel and bar next to the railroad station, where the Union Plaza Hotel is now located. A few years later, his brother-in-law, John Vinassa, built and operated the National Hotel on Fremont

Street, then the main thoroughfare of Las Vegas, and now the central pedestrian entertainment area among the Glitter Gulch hotels and casinos. Several others owned bars and restaurants during and after Prohibition.

The re-legalization of gambling by the Nevada legislature in 1931 brought a few more Italian Americans to Las Vegas, then a city of less than six thousand. Tony Cornero, a successful California bootlegger, opened the city's first plush casino just a few months after the legislation was signed by the governor. Pietro Orlando Silvagni, a Utah contractor, was so impressed by the potential of Las Vegas that he invested all of his and his associates' capital to build a hotel and casino on Fremont Street.

As Las Vegas gambling expanded immediately after World War I, the mostly Jewish owners of the Strip hotels—Flamingo, Sands, Desert Inn, Sahara, Caesars, Tropicana—recruited Italian Americans with experience in gambling and entertainment management to serve as casino managers, shift bosses, floormen, entertainment directors, and showroom maitres d'. Visitors could not spend more than a few minutes in a Las Vegas casino without hearing a variety of distinctively Italian names being paged. Often Frank Sinatra was featured on the Caesars marquee, Louis Prima was drawing overflow crowds in the lounge at the Sahara, and Antonio Morelli was leading the orchestra at the Sands.

Organized crime interests were active in Las Vegas gambling from the 1940s through the mid-1980s. As men of Italian and Jewish background dominated the casino industry during this period, so too were men of these backgrounds overrepresented among the alleged organizers of the many skims (siphoning of casino profits to East Coast and Midwest organized crime elements) in Las Vegas casinos. Yet they also were represented among the state and federal law enforcement officials who investigated the skimming.

Neither the lack of ethnic neighborhoods in Las Vegas nor the rapid assimilation of Italian Americans precluded a sense of community among Italian Americans. In the early 1960s members of the rapidly expanding Las Vegas Italian American population formed two organizations that have remained viable: the Italian American Club of Southern Nevada and a lodge of the Sons of Italy. Subsequently, other Italian Americans established chapters of the Italian Catholic Federation at several Las Vegas parishes. More recently, Dominic Gentile, a prominent Las Vegas attorney, organized the Nevada Society of Italian American Lawyers, and he and several successful business leaders and professionals formed the Augustus Society to both enhance the image of Italian Americans and provide college and university scholarships to young men and women of Italian heritage.

Alan Balboni

Bibliography

Balboni, Alan. *Beyond the Mafia: Italian Americans and the Development of Las Vegas.* Las Vegas: University of Nevada Press, 1996.

Farrell, Ronald, and Carole Case. *The Black Book and the Mob: The Untold Story of the Control of Nevada's Casino.* Madison: University of Wisconsin Press, 1995.

Moehring, Eugene. *Resort City in the Sunbelt: Las Vegas, 1930–1970.* Las Vegas: University of Nevada Press, 1989.

Law Enforcement

Italian Americans have a long and diverse history of major contributions to law enforcement. They have served as prosecutors who do battle in the courtroom and as criminal justice officers who practice law on the battlefield. The establishment of the first Bureau of Investigation for the detection and prosecution of crimes against the United States, forerunner of the current Federal Bureau of Investigation (FBI), is credited to an Italian American, Charles Joseph Bonaparte (1851–1921), son of Jerome Bonaparte and Elizabeth Bonaparte. First a U.S. secretary of the navy and later attorney general under President Theodore Roosevelt, Bonaparte was the first American of Italian descent to sit in the U.S. Cabinet. At President Roosevelt's request in 1908, Attorney General Bonaparte organized a small force of twelve accountants who came from the Justice Department and began to investigate embezzlement, forgery, and other white-collar crimes.

In July 1993 President Bill Clinton nominated another Italian American to be director of the Federal Bureau of Investigation, Judge Louis J. Freeh, a man he called "a law enforcement legend." Freeh was born in Jersey City, New Jersey, in 1950, to William Freeh, Sr., a real estate broker, and Bernice (Chinchiolo) Freeh, a former bookkeeper. He has spent his entire career in the federal justice system.

After becoming an FBI agent in 1975, Freeh spent five years investigating the activities of organized crime on New York City's waterfront docks. His undercover and surveillance work led to the prosecution of approximately 125 criminals. In 1981 he was hired as an assistant U.S. attorney in the Southern District of New York and became one of the leading prosecutors in the notorious "Pizza Connection" case, which resulted in guilty verdicts for eighteen defendants involved in a heroin operation that used pizza parlors as fronts. In 1990 Freeh received further notoriety for bringing about the successful resolution of a federal investigation into a series of mail bombings that had killed an Alabama judge and a Georgia lawyer.

Another Italian American, one of Freeh's agents, Carmine Russo (b. 1937), is the FBI's leading investigator into organized crime. Russo left Sicily, Italy, and moved to Brooklyn when he was nine years old. In 1997 he returned to Sicily as an agent for the FBI to investigate multinational criminal mob connections to the United States.

John J. Sirica (1904–1992), chief federal judge, United States District Court for the District of Columbia, presided over the Watergate trials. He was named *Time* magazine's "Man of the Year" in 1973.

Antonin Scalia (b. 1936) became the first Italian American to sit on the United States Supreme Court when he was appointed associate justice in 1986. Born in Trenton, New Jersey, Scalia was one of seven children born to Eugene Scalia, a professor of Romance languages who had migrated from Italy, and Catherine, a schoolteacher whose parents had also migrated from Italy. Scalia grew up in Queens, New York, where he attended Jesuit schools. He graduated from Georgetown University in 1957 and Harvard Law School in 1960, after which he practiced law for seven years in Cleveland. Scalia held a series of positions in the administrations of Richard Nixon and Gerald Ford. President Ronald Reagan appointed him to the United States Court of Appeals for the District of Columbia Circuit in 1982, and four years later nominated him to the Supreme Court seat left vacant by William H. Rehnquist's promotion to chief justice.

Prior to being elected mayor of New York City in 1993, Rudolph W. Giuliani (b. 1944) had devoted many years to prosecuting criminals. He was born in Brooklyn to Harold A. Giuliani and Helen Davanzo. Four of his uncles were police officers. Giuliani received his law degree from New York University Law School in 1968. Immediately thereafter, be began serving as law clerk to United States District Judge Lloyd F. MacMahon, Southern District of New York. In 1968, he was appointed assistant attorney, and, from 1970 to 1973, he served as chief of Special Prosecutions. The following two years he served as chief of Narcotics. In 1975 he was appointed U.S. attorney and, from 1983 to 1989, associate deputy attorney, Department of Justice. From 1975 to 1977, as associate attorney general, he continued waging war against organized crime and public corruption. After an admirable career of prosecuting major federal crimes in the courts he was elected mayor of New York City, promising to make the streets of New York safe from crime. He succeeded in reducing crime so sharply that New York City is considered to be one of America's safest cities, and the New York City Police Department's new tactics are being copied around the country.

In the New York City Police Department the first Italian American to be awarded the detective shield was Joseph Petrosino (1860–1909), an immigrant from Salerno, Italy. He migrated to the United States with his family as a child. Joining the police department in 1883, he was promoted to detective in 1895. He was assigned to the Lower East Side, where he began his nonstop battle against the Black Hand, a loosely knit criminal organization of Italian American criminals that extorted money from Italian immigrants. He founded the Bomb Squad, the first unit of its kind in the United States, to counter the Black Hand's use of explosives in carrying out its extortion threats. Petrosino was assigned to protect the great Italian tenor Enrico Caruso whenever he appeared at the Metropolitan Opera in New York and was responsible for arresting several members of the Black Hand who had been harassing Caruso. In 1905 Petrosino was promoted to the rank of lieutenant and placed in charge of the Italian Squad, an elite corps of Italian American undercover cops. The Italian Squad was responsible for arresting thousands of members of the Black Hand, deporting five hundred of them, and reducing crime against Italian Americans by half. Petrosino singlehandedly arrested Enrico Alfano, a notorious member of the Camorra and a Black Hander. During the investigation, Petrosino learned that Alfano had murdered a couple in his native

Naples before migrating to the United States. After learning from the police in Naples that Alfano was a wanted man, Petrosino arranged to have the murderer returned to Italy to be imprisoned. The Alfano case gave Petrosino the idea of traveling to Palermo, Sicily, where he intended to search the files of the local police identifying many fugitives who had committed serious crimes before fleeing to New York. In February 1909 he sailed for Sicily. He spent several weeks going through police files and reportedly identified dozens of criminals whom he knew in New York. He sent this information by mail to New York, where the Italian Squad arrested the men and held them for deportation back to Sicily and imprisonment.

On the night of March 12, 1909, Petrosino, who had arranged to meet an informer who promised to reveal the names of Mafia leaders in Sicily, went to the Piazza Marina. The so-called informer was a Mafia executioner, who with several others murdered Petrosino. His body was found the next morning and was shipped back to the United States, where two hundred thousand people lined the streets of Little Italy in a vast funeral procession that lasted five and a half hours. The policeman's widow was given ten thousand dollars in cash that had been collected from the people of Little Italy, the poor immigrants Joseph Petrosino had spent his lifetime protecting, and in the end, for whom he sacrificed his life. He is the only New York Police Department officer killed in the line of duty outside the United States.

Following in the tradition of Petrosino, other Italian American crime fighters who have excelled in policing America's streets include Frank Serpico and Sonny Grosso. Serpico was the son of Vincenzo, a Neapolitan shoemaker, and his wife, Maria Giovanna, both from a village not far from Naples. Serpico was a New York City undercover cop whose nonconformism and exposure of department corruption led to the formation of the Knapp Commission. His life and police work were documented in a book written by Peter Maas and later made into a Hollywood movie. Sonny Grosso is credited with stopping an attempted heroin smuggle into New York City. His actions became the subject of a Hollywood movie titled *The French Connection*. Now a television producer, Grosso has been named one of the 1997 Ellis Island Medal of Honor winners.

This humanitarian award, given by the National Ethnic Coalition of Organizations, also went to another Italian American crime fighter, former New York State Attorney General Dennis Vacco, who was born in Buffalo in 1952 to Carmen and Mildred Vacco. He received his J.D. degree at State University at Buffalo in 1978. From 1982 to 1988, he served as an assistant district attorney and became chief of the Grand Jury Bureau in 1982. In 1988 he was appointed by President Ronald Reagan to be U.S. attorney of the Western District, the youngest such attorney in the nation. During his service from 1988 to 1993, he made fighting environmental crimes and white-collar crimes a priority and pioneered cases using the RICO statutes (Racketeer Influenced and Corrupt Organizations Act) of 1970 to convict drug organizations.

As women gained the right to join the male-dominated fields of law, police, and corrections, they too made outstanding contributions to crime fighting. Geraldine Ferraro (b. 1935), the New York congresswoman who was the first woman to be nominated for vice-president by a major political party, was born in Newburgh, New York, the only daughter of Dominick Ferraro, an Italian immigrant and Antonetta L. (Corrieri) Ferraro. She received her J.D. degree in 1960 from Fordham University Law School and began a career in government service in 1974, when she served as assistant district attorney in the district attorney's office in Queens. In 1978 she transferred to the Supreme Court to head the Special Victims Bureau for victims of violent crimes, which she helped create to prosecute cases of child abuse, domestic violence, and rape.

Before her election to the New York State Senate, Catherine M. Abate (b. 1947) had been New York State Commissioner of Corrections, overseeing a prison system of fifty-one correctional institutions serving approximately seventy thousand inmates. Abate, born in Atlantic City, New Jersey, to Joseph and Carolyn (Fiore), received her J.D. degree from Boston University School of Law in 1972. From 1973 to 1979 she was a criminal trial attorney for the Legal Aid Society in New York City. In 1982 she was chosen to be acting chairwoman for Governor Mario Cuomo's Task Force on Criminal Justice. In 1984 Abate was chairwoman for the New York State Platform on Criminal Justice.

Abate served on the board of directors for the New York State Crime Victim's Compensation Board from 1989 to 1991. The New York Bar Association presented her with the Outstanding Contribution in the Field of Correctional Service Award in 1994. In 1998 she sought the Democratic nomination for New York attorney general but was defeated in the primary.

In 1987, another Italian American woman made history when she was the lead prosecutor for the government's case against notorious crime boss John Gotti, who was charged with federal racketeering, taking part in a criminal enterprise that involved armed hijacking, illegal gambling, loan sharking, and murder. Assistant U.S. Attorney Diane Giacalone, the prosecutor, presented a strong case for the government during the six-and-a-half-month trial in Brooklyn. Giacalone, who grew up in Ozone Park, Queens, home of one of Gotti's private clubs—The Bergen Hunt and Fish Club—recalled that she would often wonder what went on inside the club, which she passed on the way to the Gate of Heaven Parochial School she attended. Although Gotti was acquitted of racketeering charges in this trial, ten years later Gotti's associate, Sammy "The Bull" Gravano, revealed in his published memoirs that he had fixed the jury.

Anne T. Romano

Bibliography

Ferraro, Geraldine. *Ferraro. My Story.* New York: Bantam, 1985.

Iorizzo, Luciano J., ed. *An Inquiry into Organized Crime.* New York: American Italian Historical Association, 1970.

Maas, Peter. *Serpico.* New York: Viking, 1973.

Wirth, Elder, ed. *The Supreme Court A to Z.* Washington, DC: Congressional Quarterly, 1994.

See also BONAPARTE, CHARLES JOSEPH; CRIME AND ORGANIZED CRIME; PETROSINO, JOSEPH; RODINO JR., PETER W.; SCALIA, ANTONIN; SIRICA, JOHN JOSEPH

Leone, Luisa (Mamma) (1873–1944)

Founder of one of the best-known Italian restaurants in New York City, Luisa Leone was born November 2, 1873, in Italy, married Gerolamo Leone, and migrated to the United States. During the early years of their marriage, Luisa raised the Leone's four sons—Joseph, Gino, Celestine, and Frank—and catered the large dinners to which Gerolamo brought his business contacts and his friends. On November 2, 1905, Gerolamo threw a birthday party for his wife, bringing some fifty friends, including Enrico Caruso, from the New York Metropolitan Opera. Luisa herself cooked for this crowd. During the banquet, Caruso asked if Gerolamo would permit Luisa to open her own restaurant.

The restaurant opened as Leone's on April 27, 1905, in a building at 39th and Broadway where Gerolamo also had his wine shop. Husband and wife continued their separate businesses side by side until 1914, when Gerolamo died. Luisa's eldest son, Joe, became the public head of the family, but Luisa retained leadership in the kitchen, where she took Gino as an apprentice. During World War I the restaurant moved to larger quarters on the same block at 39th and Broadway. In 1919 it moved to 239 West 48th Street, where it continued to expand and was furnished with art Gino purchased on various trips to Italy.

Luisa died May 2, 1944, at which point her sons renamed the restaurant Mamma Leone's in her honor. In 1937 Joe relocated to California, where he opened his own restaurant. Gino's wife, the former Mary Sullivan, and their two daughters, Luisa and Eileen, all worked in the restaurant. His two sons-in-law worked there until they established their own restaurant in Englewood Cliffs, New Jersey. In 1952 Gino bought out his brother Celestine and became sole owner of the restaurant. On June 9, 1959, Gino retired, selling Mamma Leone's to Restaurant Associates for $2.5 million.

In 1988 the Milford Plaza Hotel brought Mamma Leone's to its building at 261 West 44th Street, where it re-created the facade and interior of the West 48th Street establishment. Shifts in the theater business and tourist trade affected patronage, and in 1994, the owners closed the restaurant.

Mary Elizabeth Brown

Bibliography

Iorizzo, Luciano J. "The R.G. Dun Collection's Assessments of Merchants: A Neglected Source for Italian American Studies." In *The Columbus People Perspectives in Italian Immigration to the United States and Australia,* edited by Lydio F. Tomasi, Piero Gastaldo, and Thomas Row. New York: Center for Migration Studies, 1994.

L

Levi-Montalcini, Rita (b. 1909)

A distinguished neurobiologist, Rita Levi-Montalcini's research on nerve growth factor (NGF), a protein that promotes nerve growth, has enabled a better understanding of a number of neurological diseases, including Alzheimer's disease, birth defects, and some forms of cancer. She collaborated with Stanley Cohen at Washington University, and they were both awarded the 1986 Nobel Prize for physiology or medicine.

In 1909 Rita Levi-Montalcini was born with her twin sister, in Turin, Italy, to Adamo Levi and Adele Montalcini. In following Jewish traditions, Rita was sent to an all-girls school to prepare for marriage. The illness of her governess prompted her to choose medicine as a career. In 1930 she enrolled in the Turin School of Medicine, where she studied the nervous system with Dr. Giuseppe Levi, a histologist and embryologist. When she graduated in 1936, she continued her research with Dr. Levi. Because of the Fascist laws of 1938, she was forced to relinquish her medical and research positions.

She went to the Neurological Institute in Brussels for a short period, but the German invasion forced her to return to Turin. She was unable to find a position when she returned but privately continued her research using chick embryos. In 1942 Turin was bombed. She and her family fled to the countryside, but in 1943 the German invasion of northern Italy forced a further relocation to Florence. She and her family hid by using a different family name. Throughout this period she continued her nervous tissue research and published a paper on her findings in 1944.

In 1946, Viktor Hamburger, another neuroresearcher, invited her to come to the United States and work with him at Washington University in St. Louis. At Washington University she continued to study nervous tissue growth in chicken embryos. She observed the differentiation of nerve cells in these embryos. In a brief stay in Rio de Janeiro she documented the presence of an unknown substance that promoted nerve growth.

When she returned to Washington University, she collaborated with Dr. Stanley Cohen. Together they identified the structure of the nerve growth factor, NGF. In 1961 she returned to Italy to establish the Higher Institute of Health in Rome. She continued to do joint research with her colleagues in Washington University, working six months in Rome and six months in St. Louis. In 1977 she retired from Washington University and returned to Italy as a full-time resident, where she continued research on nervous tissue and on various degenerative nervous tissue diseases.

Since becoming a citizen in 1956, she has received numerous awards including her induction in 1968 into the National Academy of Sciences. In 1986 she and Stanley Cohen received the Nobel Prize in physiology or medicine for their pioneering work on NGF. She was recognized by the Vatican when she became the first woman to be given membership in the Pontifical Academy of Sciences in Rome. In 1987 she was awarded the highest honor to an American scientist, the National Medal of Science.

Sean A. Fanelli

Bibliography

Levi-Montalcini, Rita. *In Praise of Imperfection: My Life and Work.* New York: Basic Books, 1988.
———. "Reflections on a Scientific Adventure." In *Women Scientists: The Road to Liberation,* edited by Derek Richter, 99–117. New York: Macmillan 1982.

See also MEDICINE; SCIENCE

Liberace (1919–1987)

Pianist and immensely popular entertainer known for his flamboyant and self-satirizing stage manner and lifestyle, Liberace was born Wladziu Valentino Liberace in West Allis, Wisconsin. His father, Salvatore Liberace, was an Italian-born grocer and a sometime professional musician. His mother, Frances Zuchowski, was the daughter of Polish immigrants. Liberace's father was a French horn player who had appeared with the Sousa Concert Band and the Milwaukee Symphony Orchestra. At age 4 Liberace began piano lessons and, according to an often repeated story, at age 8 he was introduced to the great Ignacy Paderewski, who reportedly predicted a stellar career for the child pianist after hearing him play. At age 7 he won a tuition-free music scholarship that lasted for the next 17 years. During his latter teen years he played mostly with dance bands and in local nightclubs, although by age 17 he had performed with the

Milwaukee Symphony and had soloed with the Chicago Symphony.

By 1940 he had established a career as a pianist in cafe society clubs in Milwaukee, New York, and Los Angeles. During this time he started to develop his unique musical style with its emphasis on popular romantic standards and abridged versions of classical music concert hall favorites highlighting the works of Beethoven, Chopin, Liszt, and Tchaikovsky. These works were presented in a highly sentimental and florid style and were often accompanied by his vocal renditions. Liberace's performances always included playing on an exotic "show" piano on which stood an ornate candelabrum while he was attired in outrageously foppish and costly costumes.

His greatest successes were on television (two Emmys), in concert, and in recordings (six gold albums). Although Liberace repeatedly played to sellout audiences at Carnegie Hall and set box office records at the Hollywood Bowl and Madison Square Garden, he was the object of adverse criticism for his popularization and "bastardization" of classical music. By the early 1950s his syndicated television program was so popular it was carried by more stations than *I Love Lucy*. He is attributed with being television's first matinee idol, and at various times he was rated to be the highest paid popular entertainer. By the late 1980s his career enjoyed a resurgence with more record-breaking concerts in huge theaters such as Radio City Music Hall. Although Liberace had a huge middle-aged female following, his sexual orientation was frequently headlined in the media, and he often alluded to it in an ambiguous and facetious manner during his performances in his last years. Liberace died of AIDS in 1987.

Angelo Tripicchio

Bibliography

Mungo, Ray. *Liberace*. New York: Chelsea House, 1995.
Thomas, Bob. *Liberace: The True Story*. New York: St. Martin's Press, 1987.

See also POP SINGERS; TELEVISION

Ligutti, Luigi Gino (1895–1983)

"The Pope's county agent" was born Aloysius Domenico Ligutti; Luigi was a variant of Aloysius and Gino and a nickname from his infancy. Ligutti was born March 21, 1895, in Udine, Italy, the fifth child and third son of Speridioni Ligutti and Teresa Ciriani. He entered the diocesan seminary in 1909 at age 14 but left two years later to accompany his widowed mother to the United States, where he completed his education. Ligutti received a bachelor's degree from Saint Ambrose College, Davenport, Iowa, in 1914; his seminary education at Saint Mary's, Baltimore; and an M.A. from the Catholic University of America in 1918. He had additional training at summer school at Columbia University and at the University of Chicago from 1918 to 1920. He was ordained in the Diocese of Des Moines September 22, 1917, with a dispensation to accommodate his youth. He became a U.S. citizen in 1918.

Ligutti taught classics at a diocesan high school from 1918 to 1920. Thereafter, he held overlapping jobs: pastor of Sacred Heart, Woodbine, with missions at Saint Bridget of Erin in Magnolia, and Saint Ann in Logan (1921–1925); promoter of the National Catholic Rural Life Conference (NCRLC) (beginning in 1924); pastor of Assumption in Granger (1925–1941); NCRLC president (1937–1939); NCRLC executive secretary (1939–1960); informal contact between the Vatican and the Food and Agricultural Organization (FAO) (1945–1949); Vatican permanent observer to the FAO (1949–1974); and director of Agrimissio (1971–1981).

Ligutti was also involved in international migration. In 1947 he became a founding member of the U.S. National Catholic Resettlement Council. He attended the organizational meeting of the American Committee on Italian Migration on March 29, 1951, and the International Catholic Migration Commission, May 25–June 7, 1951.

Ligutti taught that salvation required social justice as well as spirituality. He promoted independently owned farms that enabled families to avoid the exploitation of wage labor or tenancy. Such farms could join together in cooperative action on issues affecting them. Ligutti communicated this philosophy in a variety of ways. In 1934 he received New Deal money to build fifty homes in Granger and extend long-term, low-interest mortgages to families. The Homestead Cooperative Association dissolved in 1951, having demonstrated the feasibility of Ligutti's methods.

In 1939 Ligutti began traveling to investigate agricultural conditions worldwide; his trips resulted in travelogues mingling local color with rural-life philosophy. In 1951 he helped organize the first International Catholic Rural Life Conference; these conferences became another forum for his views. Accordingly, his long career was devoted to promoting his belief in small, self-supporting, and self-governing agricultural communities guided by Catholic social justice ethics.

Ligutti died December 28, 1983. He is buried in a grave of his own design, in Granger, beneath a stone inscribed AT REST WITH THE PEOPLE I LOVE. His papers are at Marquette University.

Mary Elizabeth Brown

Bibliography

Miller, Raymond W. *Monsignor Ligutti: The Pope's County Agent*. Lanham, MD: University Press of America, 1981.

Yzermans, Vincent A. *The People I Love: A Biography of Luigi G. Ligutti*. Collegeville, MN: The Liturgical Press, 1976.

See also RELIGION

Linguistic History of Italian Dialects in the United States

When the Italian national state was created in 1861, the illiteracy rate was 76 percent and nearly the entire population spoke dialects. Dialects, language variations descended from a common parent language, differ from the parent language and from each other in vocabulary, grammar, and pronunciation. Within ninety years of Italian unification, the number of dialect speakers had sharply decreased as a result of two factors. First, a successful educational initiative by the new central Italian government reduced illiteracy to 14 percent. Second, Italy lost nearly one-third of its poor and uneducated population through emigration.

Between 1880 and 1920 a major exodus to the United States drew Italians from the rural, mountainous, and southern areas. Over 80 percent of the immigrants came from the Mezzogiorno—Abruzzo, Molise, Campania, Basilicata, Apulia, Calabria, and Sicily. In general, these southerners failed to identify with the central government and the standard (northern) version of Italian. Their adherence to their respective dialects symbolized their allegiance to specific Italian regions. While southern dialects have much in common, their distinctive features enable speakers to identify members of their own group.

Each Italian dialect variety exemplifies a cultural or social adaptation that directly reflects the internal structure of the speech community it served and the place of that community in the larger society. The dialects are not crude renditions of the standard form, but individual developments whose characteristics are shaped by their environment. Some dialects are close enough to each other that mutual comprehension is not a problem, but others are as different as if they were separate languages. The new Italian Americans never knew standard Italian, a language unintelligible to a good number of them. Their language contributed to the repository of dialects in the United States.

An immigrant propensity to settle in neighborhoods with others from home was so powerfully expressed that particular city blocks housed transplanted populations from single Italian regions or even towns. For example, Little Italy in Manhattan contained streets whose residents were primarily from one area: Elizabeth Street was Sicilian and Mulberry Street was Neapolitan. Likewise, a Chicago neighborhood was known as Little Sicily. While the newcomers were aware that speaking English was the key to joining the American mainstream, dialects remained the language of family, home, and the immigrant community. At least at the beginning, acceptance and survival in the new land depended more on immigrant connections than assimilation. Fitting into the dialect speech community was essential; therefore, social and linguistic circumstances guaranteed the survival of these languages for at least two generations.

When adult speakers learn a second language the result is rarely an equal use of both languages. The first language inevitably remains the automatic method of communicating, the language in which contextual indications of how and when one should speak are clear, and the one in which strong emotions are expressed. Additionally, songs, stories, and descriptions of the homeland must be repeated in the first language in order to preserve nuances of meaning. In short, the cultural continuity so critically important to immigrants requires the use of their native language.

All languages change in time as a result of contact with and influence by other languages. Although natural forces favor linguistic change, these changes can be slowed through social engineering. Despite their overall reliance on the native dialect, Italian immigrants acquired English vocabulary basic to their functioning. They incorporated this lexicon into their first language with phonological adaptations. The results were words such as *aiscrima* (ice cream), *ticchetto* (ticket), *gioba* (job), *marchetta* (market), and *bacausu* (outhouse), all of which sound more Italian than English. Vocabulary is the language segment most vulnerable to foreign influence precisely because it allows this adoption without changing grammatical form. As the speakers became more assimilated, they followed the usual pattern of second language acquisition and inserted English phrases into their speech. This produced a mixture of two languages within sentences that characterized some stages of bilingualism.

The immigrants' children were true bilinguals who participated in two speech communities and frequently served as translators for their parents. They learned dialects modified by creolization features, such as those noted above, and by predictable generational variation. As the languages passed from one generation to the next, the likelihood of preserving dialects weakened. In addition, many speakers were conscious of the low linguistic status of their language varieties and understood that theirs was not the language of educated twentieth-century Italians. Further, the decreasing dependence of second- and third-generation Italians on the immigrant community for social and economic support lessened their motive for maintaining the dialect. Third-generation Italians who wished to reestablish their ethnicity by speaking the language usually applied for formal instruction in standard Italian.

In 1970, 55 percent of four generations of Italian Americans professed to believe that dialects are not less refined than standard Italian, but less than 18 percent said they would encourage their children to speak dialect. Despite the presence of a substantial number of Italian Americans and the fact that nearly 1.5 million people claimed Italian as their second language in 1975, the dialects are experiencing language death in the United States. Linguistic proofs are depleted vocabularies and a loss of distinction in grammatical aspects among the various dialects. The average age of those who speak primarily dialect is 65 or older, and only 5 percent are under 17; of all foreign speaking populations in the United States, Italian speakers are the oldest. There is no replacement pool of dialect speakers because recent Italian immigrants to the United States are likely to speak standard Italian, the resident dialect speakers are aging, and the third and fourth generations of Italian Americans have not learned dialect. Social and political environmental changes in Italy and the United States have activated an extinction process, but fossils remain in the forms of names, personal correspondence, songs, and rhymes.

This evidence will eventually erode unless purposeful steps are taken toward conservation. Languages die when there are no speakers and no records of how the language was used. The dialects are a valuable piece of cultural, social, and linguistic history that provide proof of cultural contact and, by comparison with the standard, a picture of social stratification.

Analysis of the immigrant languages also provides insight into their status in the Italy they left. Examination of dialect changes in the United States indicates the times and extent to which the speakers were assimilated. In Italy the dialects were overwhelmed by the successful dissemination of standard Italian. In the United States the loss of dialects is testimony to the successful integration of Italian Americans.

Linda Santarelli Susman

Bibliography

Bettoni, Camilla, ed. *Altro Polo*. Sydney, Australia: University of Sydney Frederick May Foundation for Italian Studies, 1986.

DeVoto, Giacomo. *The Languages of Italy*. Translated by V. L. Katainen. Chicago: University of Chicago Press, 1974.

Grandgent, C. H. *From Latin to Italian*. New York: Russell and Russell, 1971.

Haller, Hermann W. "Between Standard Italian and Creole: An Interim Report of Language Patterns in an Italian-American Community." *Word* 32 (December 1981): 181–191.

Pei, Mario. *The Italian Language*. New York: Columbia University Press, 1941.

Pulgram, Ernst. *The Tongues of Italy.* Cambridge: Harvard University Press, 1958.

See also ITALIAN LANGUAGE IN AMERICA; PEI, MARIO ANDREW

Literature

It is the inherent nature of intellectuals to reflect on both the general state of society and the existential situation of the individual. There exists a sizable body of writings that deal with the Italian American experience ranging from systematic historical and social scientific inquiries to more humanistic literary expressions such as letters, poems, novels, and autobiographical and biographical accountings. The writings in Italian Americana—most of which is underacknowledged by the gatekeepers of elite culture—typically provide analytical accounts of the dialectical relationship between individuals of Italian ancestry and the surrounding American environment. This dialectic started, naturally enough, with a focus on the Old World and the immigrant experience in America, moving on to the issue of the second generation caught between competing moralities, then evolving into a pluralism of topics endemic to the situation of writers more fully assimilated into a secular American context. For centuries, conditions across Italy reduced its population to poverty and ignorance. About the year 1880, the suffering *contadini* (peasants, farmers), finding themselves reduced to working as lease holders and day laborers, and fettered by feudal residues of a backward economic system, began to emigrate to the Americas. Their experiences of poverty and survival, loss and abandonment, struggle and triumph, and family solidarity and Christianity are reflected throughout their literature from the very first autobiographical authors, such as Rocco Corresca and Antonio A. Arrighi (*The Story of Antonio, the Galley Slave,* 1911) to the fiction writers of today, such as Helen Barolini (*Umbertina,* 1979) and Salvatore La Puma (*The Boys of Bensonhurst,* 1987; *Teaching Angels to Fly,* 1992; *A Time for Wedding Cake,* 1991).

The early writings show the force of Christianity on the lives of the characters—a triumphant *via dolorosa,* as it were, in which archetypal readings abound. However, later writings often reflect the greater secularization of American society.

None of the early Italian American writers gathered together as a group or formed any discernible literary movement. Despite this isolation, these authors, all born before the 1890s, were nonetheless driven to write about various aspects of the lives of Italian Americans. One such author, Luigi Donato Ventura, published his novel, *Peppino,* in 1886 with Tichnor and Co., after its initial publication in French a year earlier by W. R. Jenkins Co. in its *contes choisis* series. The publication of this novel marked the beginning of Italian American literature. According to critic Frank Lentricchia, this novel's tone both distances the narrator from the masses of immigrants and, at the same time, makes an apologia for them. The novel demonstrates the tension felt between being an educated Italian among mainly poor, uneducated ones and the stereotyping of those lives by an American public cut off from an authentic knowledge and understanding of immigrants.

Other authors of this period were Bernardino Ciambelli, who wrote in Italian; Giuseppe Cautela; Silvio Villa; Italo Stanco; and John Moroso, all of whom wrote in English and made the transition from autobiography to fiction. Of this group, Giuseppe Cautela is the most interesting and subtle. In his only published novel, *Moon Harvest* (1925), Cautela the protagonist attempts to strike out beyond his group and forge his identity through art—similar to some Italian American writers today who identify themselves first as authors and second as Italian Americans, while using (or not using) their Old World cultural background in their work. Cautela's story of a love affair can be read as a metaphor for the tensions associated with emigration. He writes, ". . . his future called him back to this land [America] where his past had been buried."

Italian American autobiographers of the early twentieth century described life in Italy, as well as their experiences of being uprooted, their impressions of the new country, and how the process of assimilation began. Needless to say, they all endured poverty. Excellent examples of these writers are Constantine M. Panunzio's autobiography *Soul of an Immigrant* (1924); Angelo M. Pellegrini's *Americans by Choice* (1956), which describes six immigrants' experiences; and Pascal D'Angelo's *Son of Italy* (1924), the most moving and well-crafted autobiography of this period. It is both a heart-rending account of D'Angelo's "pick and shovel" life and a testimony to the human spirit's aspiration to leave a legacy in writing. Of D'Angelo's autobiography, Carl Van Doren writes, "*Son of Italy* unquestionably belongs with the precious documents of literature of Pascal D'Angelo's adopted country. That literature excels all others in the type of which his book is an example."

Another poet of this early period who achieved some recognition was Emanuel Carnevali, whose friends included the literary establishment of his day, such as Waldo Frank, Kay Boyle, and Ezra Pound. Although Arturo Giovannitti wrote poetry, he is best known for the role he played in the Lawrence Strike of 1912. The letters of Sacco and Vanzetti, also better known for their politics, were considered to have elements of poetry in them. Upton Sinclair judged their letters to contain some of the greatest English prose of the era. Poets publishing in the late twenties and thirties were Anita Petrucci, Hilda Perini, Elda Tanasso, and dialect poet Domenico Adamo.

The broadening of one's perspective through education is recorded by Panunzio as well as immigrant Grace Spinelli in *Italian American Autobiographies* (edited by Maria Parrino in 1993). At a time when few Italian women were able to become educated, Spinelli succeeded in obtaining a college degree. Although nearly all of the early works are by men, the publication of Spinelli's autobiography, well after her death, testifies to the fact that women immigrants were equally interested in expressing themselves and recording their experiences. Though the women did not publish their work, they nonetheless were writing. In one instance, the illiterate Rosa Cassitteri's unforgettable story of resilience and initiative (within the confines of her culture) was recorded for her by Marie Hall Ets, who published in 1974 *Rosa: The Life of an Italian Immigrant.*

One woman who wrote a journal of her activities, begun in 1872, was Rosa Maria Segale (1850–1948). Atypical in her experiences, she spent many years on the western frontier recording her missionary work as a nun among the Indians. Her journal of correspondence, *At the End of the Santa Fe Trail,* was recently translated into Italian and published in Italy.

Generally speaking, four stages of development, usually mirroring generational changes, occur in Italian American literature: first, the immigrant stage of trust and hope for a better life in a material sense; the second-generation stage, which gives way to shame and doubt about one's heritage, personal goals, and vague desire for new goals in life; the third stage of role confusion, in which the goals of a new culture all seem irrevocably at odds; and ideally the final stage of integrated autonomy, in which all three forces are resolved in a personal manner, satisfactory to the specific individual. This emphasis on the individual characterizes much of Italian American fiction published in the last two decades.

Louis Forgione's last novel, *The River Between* (1928), uses numerous symbols and introduces a brooding Gothic atmosphere. He pushes themes of family relationships and assimilation beyond Giuseppe Cautela. Demetrio, a troubling character in a disturbing and uneven book, is sexually attracted to his daughter-in-law, whom he wants to be a traditional wife and mother, despite her own vague longing for other experience. The characters, however, can only view their choices as being between bipolar cultures. Issues of individuation and autonomy, which appear in later novels, such as Helen Barolini's *Umbertina* (1979), do not arise in any meaningful way. Garibaldi Marto Lapolla's *The Grand Gennaro* (1935) focuses on the ruthlessness with which its main character "makes America" in an American frontier style with no behavioral restrictions. But in "making America" and forgetting Italy's humanistic culture, Gennaro dies.

Illustrator and author Valenti Angelo may be best known for his illustrations of *Leaves of Grass.* His novel, *Golden Gate* (1939), aimed at children, deals with problems of assimilation and uses Christian symbols. As Rose Basile Green points out, his approach is positive, optimistic, and more ethnically inclusive.

A new complexity in the Italian American novel is seen in Pietro di Donato's *Christ in Concrete* (1939) and in the novels and short stories of John Fante, both born in America in the early 1900s to immigrant parents. Di Donato's book is one of the few proletarian novels written by a member of the proletariat. A bricklayer, he describes the death of his father—a "Christ" in concrete—a foreman of a construction gang of Italian immigrants. The "job," which heretofore often served as an important backdrop in Italian American novels, now almost takes on the role of antagonist. His innovative style of dialogue captures the cultural values of the immigrants, raising them to the level of mythical characters and, among the women, of a Greek chorus. A later novel, *Three Circles of Light* (1950), reworks the material of the earlier novel. Di Donato brings to it a mature understanding of his father that is absent from his first novel. He questions the father's adultery and whether a wife must endure such actions in silence.

Testifying to the growing importance of John Fante's work is the fact that it has been reissued by Black Sparrow Press and was offered as a selection in the Quality Paperback Book Club. In addition, a conference solely devoted to Fante was held in California in 1994. Two of Fante's books, *Wait Until Spring, Bandini* (1938) and *The Brotherhood of the Grape* (1977), both deal with issues relating to his father and to assimilation, but, like di Donato before, each in very different ways, given that Fante's later novel was published in his maturity.

Fante published nine novels, a collection of short stories, and a collection of correspondence with H. L. Mencken, who published Fante's first stories in *American Mercury,* just as Mencken had done for Giuseppe Cautela. Fante also wrote screenplays. Of the three authors who were born and publishing all within a few years of each other—di Donato, Fante, and Jerre Mangione, it is Fante who is most directly interested in understanding himself in a personal and psychological way.

Jerre Mangione's *Mount Allegro,* published first as a novel (1942) and later as autobiography, records the stories and lives of his immigrant family in Rochester, New York. William Boelhower finds, in his analysis of Mangione's work, a critique of American society as the protagonist deals with issues of assimilation.

Another contemporary of these novelists was John Ciardi (1916–1986). He became the first Italian American poet to gain national recognition not only as a poet but as a critic and a translator of Dante. Born a year after Ciardi, Joseph Tuccio received positive notice from Mark Van Doren for his collection of poetry, *My Own People.*

Around the 1940s, another group of writers of the second generation emerges: authors such as Mari Tomasi, Guido D'Agostino, Joe Pagano, George Panetta, and Jimmy Savo who look back at the immigrant generation from their individual perspective. Tomasi's first novel, *Deep Grow the Roots,* was selected by the *New York Herald Tribune* and the American Booksellers' Associations as one of the ten most outstanding novels of 1940. Her novel, *Like Lesser Gods* (1949), about the granite workers of Barre, Vermont, adds local color and regionalism to her compelling immigrant story of assimilation within continuity.

Guido D'Agostino's *Olives on the Apple Tree* (1940) pits Emile, who wishes to separate himself from everything Italian, against Marco, who looks to farm, family, and communal friendships as the way to be American. The book suggests a gradual mode of acculturation. It is Marco at the end of the novel who attempts to initiate a golden age of bucolic communalism, and in so doing, represents a medieval Christ-hero figure, which is found in the folklore of southern Italy.

Michael De Capite in *Maria* (1943) more subtly explored similar issues in an attempt to resolve the question as to what extent American-born offspring should acculturate. *Bright Banner* (1944) is about Paul Barone's coming-of-age at a time when America is also coming-of-age.

In the 1950s and 1960s, a new group of writers with a new level of sophistication began to publish: Joseph Petrarca, Lawrence Madalena, Charles Calitri, Joseph Caruso, Marion Benasutti, Joe Vergara, Lucas Longo, Marie Chay, Raymond DeCapite, and Rocco Fumento. Of these, the last three are the most important. The cover of Raymond DeCapite's novel, *The Coming of Fabrizze* (1960), describes it as a "tale" and it is exactly that: an exuberant folktale about Fabrizze and his feats in America. Fabrizze's characterization combines the American Paul Bunyan tradition with that of the Sicilian puppet folk theater and the Christ-hero figure seen in D'Agostino's novel. Marie Chay published numerous short stories in the "little" magazines from 1951 to 1979.

Rocco Fumento's *The Tree of Dark Reflection* (1962) is a powerful novel in which a son finds himself only through discovering what his father is all about. The narration is suffused with Christian overtones. The narrator says that "the story of Christ is the only story I can write." Basile Green states that Fumento

creates a conclusive, comprehensive symbol for the Italian American novelists who have integrated their two cultures. Their plots may vary, but the novels they write are architectural structurings along the lines of struggle, sacrifice, isolation (or temporary defeat), compassion (or compromise), and eventual moral victory. In general, then, these works reflect what Fumento reveals, a tradition deep-seated in the Italian ancestry, an optimism for which the writer finds some symbol related to spirituality. . . .

It was Mario Puzo in *The Godfather* (1969) who, according to Robert Viscusi, brought "the Christ-hero fully into the arena of American life" as opposed to such earlier novelists as DeCapite and di Donato, who wrote on an Italian stage. Two other important novels by Puzo are *The Dark Arena* (1953), set in occupied Germany immediately after World War II, and *The Fortunate Pilgrim* (1964), in which he creates a powerful portrait of Lucia Santa and her family. In this novel, one can trace the generational development outlined earlier.

Other novelists of the 1960s are Joseph Papaleo, Ben Morreale, Robert Cenedella, Robert Canzoneri, Frank Miceli, Joseph Arleo, Francis Pollini, Ben Piazza, and Eugene Mirabelli. These authors are a new breed. They move more fully in the American arena than previous authors and concern themselves with more complex and subtle issues regarding assimilation. Unlike the novels published before 1960, job situations are less visible. Rarely present are graphic descriptions of manual labor. Their novels reflect the greater economic ease that Italian Americans were experiencing in real life. These descendants of immigrants were not only attending college, but some were attending Ivy league universities, receiving Ph.D.'s and teaching creative writing and literature on the college level. From the 4.5 million Italian Americans reporting in the 1940 census, only 750,000 claimed English as their mother tongue. From the 1960s on, more Italian Americans designated English as their first language or that they had been brought up bilingually. This change may be responsible for the increasing number of Italian Americans who were publishing.

Eugene Mirabelli is at his best when writing about his Italian roots in such novels as *The Way In* (1968) and *The World at Noon* (1994). In his latter novel there are sections in which Mirabelli writes about his ancestors in a marvelously surrealistic mythic way. Some authors of this period extend their subject matter to Vietnam, just as Phil Caputo will do more than a decade later.

The title of Joseph Papaleo's second novel, *Out of Place* (1970), serves as a good description of the theme he and Robert Cenedella explore in their works. Although Richard Gambino has written mainly in the field of Italian American studies, his novel *Bread and Roses* (1981), about the Lawrence strikes of 1912, is worthy of note.

With the publication of Helen Barolini's novel, *Umbertina,* in 1979, the contemporary Italian American woman was given a voice in literature. Her novel recounts the lives of four generations of Italian American women, beginning with protagonist Marguerite's grandmother, Umbertina, and moves on to the early adult life of Umbertina's great-granddaughter. In presenting these four generations, Barolini's novel demonstrates the generational differences already noted. The specific issues Marguerite explores center on her family's valuing only money, her struggle for autonomy, and her inability to focus on her own artistic desires instead of her husband's and her lover's. References to work concern issues of upward mobility and, later, of individuation. The most significant difference in the way she grapples with such issues is determined by the different expectations for Italian American women and men. Unlike Rose of Forgione's novel, Marguerite and Tina make choices in keeping with the new culture.

Another book of note by Barolini is an anthology she edited, *The Dream Book: Writings by Italian American Women,* which includes excerpts by women novelists, such as Antonia Pola, Julia Saverese, Diana Cavallo, Octavia C. W. Locke, Nancy Maniscalco, and Tina De Rosa, whose novel, *Paper Fish* (1981), is a beautiful impressionistic story about a girl growing up in one of Chicago's Little Italys; it ruminates on memory, imagination, and the function of art.

Other writers represented are Sandra Gilbert, Mary Gordon, Barbara Grizzuti Harrison, poet and novelist Daniela Gioseffi, and poets Diane di Prima, Anne Paolucci,

L

Kathryn Nocerino, Maria Mazziotti Gillan, Anna Bart, and Rina Ferrarelli. Other contemporary women poets are Mary Jo Salter, Peggy Rizza Ellsberg, Kim Addonizio, Cynthia Tedesco, Gabriella Mirollo, Rose Basile Green, Linda Ann Loschiavo, Rose Romano, A. B. Hough, Vittoria Repetto, Diane Raptosh, and Toni Conley, who, like the male poets noted, do not all write on issues of Italian American identity.

In the case of fiction, however, Barolini marked the beginning of Italian American women publishing in increasing numbers: women like Josephine Gattuso Henden, who wrote *The Right Thing to Do* (1988), and Anna Monardo in *The Courtyard of Dreams* (1993), both of whom have female protagonists who echo the struggles of earlier male authors who need to free themselves from their fathers. Since the women's struggle for freedom is from the opposite sex parent, their struggle inevitably deals with the ability to form an adult love relationship. The Christian imagery that permeates many of the early works by male authors is absent in the writings of the women and possibly reflects the more secular times in which they write. With the increasing technocracy of America, a new generation is seen in Monardo's novel and other contemporary authors: a deeper appreciation of the humanistic Italian culture from which Italian Americans draw their roots, as well as a lessening interest in assimilation and an increasing interest in rediscovering the culture of their ancestors.

Of the women authors currently writing, a few stand out: Carole Maso for her avantgarde novels; Mary Caponegro, also avantgarde and who, though not overtly writing about Italian Americans, incorporates themes common to Italian American literature; Mary Bush for her novel *Drowning* (1995), set in the American South in 1905, about Italians and African Americans; Rita Ciresi for her novel and collection of short stories, *Mother Rocket* (1993) (which does not focus entirely on Italian American themes), that captures her incisive irony and wit; the women in an anthology edited by Mary Jo Bono, *The Voices We Carry* (1994); Marianna De Marco Turgovnick for her memoir, *Crossing Ocean Parkway* (1994); and Denise Giardina, who, while only occasionally introducing an Italian American character, concerns herself with the issue of social justice for the miners of her native West Virginia. In her second novel, *Storming Heaven* (1987), she uses biblical allusions.

Like men writing today, the women are a new breed. Often, they too teach creative writing and literature at universities. When both female and male authors create an immigrant character, their depiction is often based on intuition and research, rather than direct experience. When it is direct experience, it is just as often as not through silent observation, as when Barolini writes of Umbertina, with whom her granddaughter could not converse due to the language barrier. Nonetheless, these writers capture the mythic truths about their characters with a force equal to and moving well beyond the earlier authors. When not writing of immigrants, they often explore their own search for identity. Other current women authors include Louisa Ermolino, Agnes Rossi, Renee Manfredi, Anna Quindlen, Christine Palamidessi Moore, Rachel Guido DeVries, playwright Donna DeMatteo, and cultural critic Camille Paglia.

Some of the modern male poets, such as Gregory Corso and Lawrence Ferlinghetti, came out of the Beat generation, as did female poet Diane di Prima. Ferlinghetti's later poetry incorporates references to Italians. Dana Gioia is the most distinguished of the current male poets. His collection of poems, *The Gods of Winter* (1991), was chosen by the London Poetry Society Book Club as its main selection, an honor rarely given to American authors. He also has earned a reputation as one of the country's most perceptive cultural and literary critics with the publication of *Can Poetry Matter?* (1992). Other male poets are Felix Stefanile, Lewis Turco, Frank Polite, Stephen Saratelli, Jay Parini, David Citino, Gerald Costanzo, Michael Palma, Jonathan Galassi, Anthony Lombardy, Michael Bugeja, Ned Condini, Samuel Maio, Emanuel di Pasquale, Joseph Tusiani, Art Casciato, Peter Fortunato, Michael Carrino, and Joseph Ditta; most of whom, like Ferlinghetti, do not reflect the Italian American experience in the majority of their poems. Some only begin to incorporate that aspect of themselves into their writing in their later years, once they have established themselves in the literary mainstream. Tusiani, however, expresses the dual nature of his experience when he writes, "Two languages, two lands, perhaps two souls . . . or two strange halves of one."

The male authors writing today—Gay Talese in *Unto the Sons*; Kenny Marotta; Albert Di Bartolomeo; George Cuomo; Jay Parini; novelist and playwright Joseph Pintauro; Brian D'Amato; playwright Albert Innaurato, the well-known author of *Gemini* (1980); Frank Lentricchia; Robert Viscusi—also write from the same distance as the women and on some of the same themes. On the other hand, Rick DeMarinis, Ralph Lombreglia, Philip Gambone, and Edward Falco have only occasionally included Italian American references in their writings. Giose Rimanelli in *Benedetta in Guysterland* (1993) strikes out in a postmodern vein. Of particular note is Gilbert Sorrentino, about whose literary modernism (as it overlays his Italian American background) critic John Paul Russo has so ably written; and Tony Ardizzone whose short stories in *The Evening News* (1986) deal with other ethnics as well as Italian Americans. His novel, *The Heart of the Order* (1986), has a brilliant passage in which he turns a stereotyped Italian name on its head. Also noteworthy are Anthony Giardina, whose two novels each represent a decade, beginning with the 1950s, in the lives of Italian Americans; and especially Salvatore La Puma, whose distinctive richness of language and surrealistic bent border on and reinvent the Gothic for his own purposes.

The code of silence about family matters, often alluded to as the reason more Italian Americans do not write, has not inhibited this group of authors. There is no way of knowing, however, how many others have been inhibited, or have been selective in their subject matter, due to concern for the reactions of their families. Some of the writers noted above, such as Mary Bush, Joe Pintauro, Rita Ciresi, Philip Gambone, and Albert Innaurato, however, expand their range of subject matter. They write about relations with African Americans and about Italian Americans who are homosexual. Others talk less about geographic migrations and more about class migrations, such as transformations out of the working class and into the intelligentsia. Freer to be Italian American than any of their forebears, many of these authors demonstrate an increasing interest in the culture of their ancestors (including working-class mores) and a decreasing interest in acculturating along prescribed lines.

The two most well-known contemporary authors, Richard Russo and Don DeLillo, do not write about specifically Italian American themes. The former deals with the working-class inhabitants of New York's Mohawk Valley, and the latter follows a postmodernist style. DeLillo is considered to be one of the foremost novelists writing today. Instead of embracing memory, a technique that infiltrates the stories of the authors noted above, it seems—at least in his first novel, *Americana* (1971)—that DeLillo's main character runs from memory. We read, "If you were offended by such [ethnic] jokes [of shock and insult] in general, or sensitive to particular ones which slurred your own race or ancestry, you were not ready to be accepted into the mainstream."

In this passage DeLillo, perhaps unwittingly, touches on an issue related to the lack of high visibility of Italian American authors. The passage suggests that in order to be "mainstream," the Italian American needs to forget his or her ethnic identity. Whether this concept was intuitively grasped by Italian American authors who never wrote about the ethnic aspect of themselves, such as Bernard DeVoto, Paul Gallico (except in *The Small Miracle*), and Frances Winwar (Vinciguerra), there is no way of knowing—although Ciardi is quite specific about his understanding of marginalization and mainstreaming, and Carole Maso's *Ghost Dance* reflects on similar issues. Certainly, just because one is Italian American does not demand that issues of identity be treated; every author deals with his or her own muse.

Whether it is a case of the publishing world not being ready for Italian American authors, or of Italian American authors and readers not being ready for the publishing world, the reading public can expect to see in the next century a flowering of Italian American literature because never before have so many Italian Americans been writing. While it is true that Italian Americans have been assimilated (see the stories of Tom Perrotta and Agnes Rossi, and the plays of Michael Cristofer), the immigrant experience and issues of identity still capture the imagination of many Italian American authors, who feel that the story of the Italians in America has yet to be fully told.

Carol Bonomo Albright

Bibliography
Barolini, Helen, ed. *The Dream Book:*

L

Writings by Italian American Women. New York: Schocken, 1985.

Boelhower, William. *Immigrant Autobiography in the United States: Four Versions of the America Self.* Verona: Essedue Edizioni, 1982.

Cautela, Giuseppe. *Moon Harvest.* New York: The Dial Press, 1925.

Cocchi, Raffaele. "Selected Bibliography of Italian American Poetry." *Italian Americana* 10 (spring/summer 1992): 242–261.

Ferraro, Thomas. *Ethnic Passages: Literary Immigrants in Twentieth Century American Literature.* Chicago: University of Chicago Press, 1993.

Gardaphé, Fred L. *Italian Signs, American Streets.* Durham, NC: Duke University Press, 1996.

Green, Rose Basile. *The Italian American Novel: A Document of the Interaction of Two Cultures.* Rutherford, NJ: Fairleigh Dickinson University Press, 1974.

Lentricchia, Frank. "Luigi Ventura and the Origins of Italian-American Fiction." *Italian Americana* 1 (spring 1975): 189–195.

Parrino, Maria. *Italian American Autobiographies.* Providence: Italian Americana Publications, 1993.

Porcari, Serafino. "Italian American Fiction: A Selected Bibliography of Novels, Short Stories and Juvenile Fiction, 1950–1993." *Italian Americana* 12 (fall/winter 1993): 146–173.

Sollors, Werner. *Beyond Ethnicity: Consent and Descent in American Culture.* New York: Oxford University Press, 1986.

Tamburri, Anthony, Paolo Giordano, and Fred Gardaphé, eds. *From the Margin: Writings in Italian Americana.* West Lafayette, IN: Purdue University Press, 1991.

See also AUTOBIOGRAPHY; NOVELS AND NOVELISTS; POETRY; WOMEN WRITERS

Lombardi, Vincent Thomas (1913–1970)

One of the most successful coaches in the National Football League, Vince Lombardi led the Green Bay Packers between 1959 and 1967 to six Western Conference Championships, five league titles, and two Super Bowl championships. He finished his career as coach of the Washington Redskins in 1969, guiding them to their first winning season in fourteen years.

Lombardi was the eldest of five children born to an Italian-born meat merchant, Henry, and American born Matilda (née Izzo) Lombardi in Sheepshead Bay, Brooklyn, on June 11, 1913. After studying for the Roman Catholic priesthood at Brooklyn's Cathedral Preparatory, he transferred to St. Francis Preparatory, where he played football. He worked hard on studies and sports and earned a scholarship to Fordham University in 1933. From 1934 through 1936 he was part of the Rams' "Seven Blocks of Granite" line, while he majored in business and made the dean's list. He then studied law at night, worked as an insurance investigator, and played minor league football for the Brooklyn Eagles. For eight years, from 1939 to 1947, he was assistant football coach and later head football coach at St. Cecilia's High School in Englewood, New Jersey, where he also taught algebra, chemistry, physics, and Latin. In 1947 he was appointed freshman football coach at Fordham and remained there for two years.

Colonel Earl "Red" Blaik, coach of the United States Military Academy at West Point, became his mentor in 1949 when Lombardi became assistant coach and helped perfect Army's T-formation. Lombardi credited Blaik with molding his approach to the game and considered him the greatest coach of all time. Signed as offensive coach to the New York Giants in 1954, he was a significant influence in their winning the 1956 NFL Championship.

Lombardi's career flourished as head coach and general manager of the Green Bay Packers. His rigorous discipline and call for dedication turned the team from a dismal 1-10-1 record in 1958 to a 7-5 mark during his first season. For this, he was voted Coach of the Year. Lombardi's Packers won the NFL championship in 1962, 1965, 1966, and 1967, plus the first two Super Bowls in 1966 and 1967 by defeating AFL champions Kansas City and Oakland.

Lombardi was an extremely religious man who tried to attend Mass daily. The quotation frequently attributed to him, "Winning isn't everything; it is the only thing," was probably never spoken. He did not condone immoral pragmatism such as deliberately injuring an opponent. Rather, he fostered hard work during the 1960s when hedonism and selfishness flourished. Following his death on September 3, 1970, with his wife, Marie, and son Vincent at his bedside, Father Michael Walsh, S.J., president of Fordham, described Vince Lombardi as "a gentle compassionate family man with deep religious convictions and steadfast loyalty to his alma mater and to his friends."

Richard Renoff

Bibliography

Klein, Dave. *The Vince Lombardi Story.* New York: Lion, 1971.

Lipsyte, Robert, and Peter Levine. *Idols of the Game: A Sporting History of the American Century.* Atlanta: Turner, 1995.

See also SPORTS

Longino, Andrew Houston (1854–1942)

The election of Andrew Houston Longino as the thirty-fifth governor (1900–1904) of the state of Mississippi is unique because of his acceptance into a regional culture not noted for its ethnic pluralism and devoid of a substantial Italian American population. He is the only Italian American to be elected governor in a southern state. Longino had a distinguished career in public service as chief executive, legislator, judge, lawyer, and Democratic Party leader.

Too young to fight for the Confederacy, he joined a new generation of post-Reconstruction leaders in Mississippi that attempted to alter a depressed, outmoded economic system based on agriculture and white supremacy without completely alienating the power structure.

Longino's formal education began in the public schools of Lawrence County, where he was born. He graduated from Mississippi College with a bachelor of science degree. From 1876 to 1880 he clerked in the Lawrence County circuit and chancery courts. After receiving a law degree from the University of Virginia in 1880, he immediately established a law practice. He became an active Democrat and was elected to the Mississippi state senate, where he served from 1880 to 1884, then returned to law practice, after which President Grover Cleveland appointed him United States attorney for the Southern District of Mississippi (1888–1890). Four years later he became judge of the Chancery Court at Greenwood

and held that office until 1899, when he resigned to campaign for governor. He served as delegate to the Democratic Party's national presidential convention throughout his adult life.

Longino captured the party nomination for governor in 1899 and easily defeated the Populist Party candidate. His leadership ability and moderate views prevailed over his opponent's openly racist positions. He also promised a progressive social and economic platform.

As governor from 1900 to 1904, Longino chaired the commission that guided the construction of the new state capitol. Other accomplishments during his administration were creation of the Mississippi Department of Archives, revision of insurance laws and creation of a new insurance department, a road improvement system, and passage of the Primary Law of 1902. He tried but failed to have legislation enacted that would make a county in which a lynching occurred financially responsible to the family of the person lynched. The Longino administration also encouraged extensive railroad construction, capital growth, and increased tax evaluation of property.

In the last year of his term, 1903, he failed to win the United States Senate nomination. In 1919 he ran again for governor but was defeated. From 1927 until his death in 1942, he served as Hinds County judge.

Longino was for several years a deacon and Sunday school superintendent of the First Baptist Church of Jackson. He also was a member of the Masonic Order and the Independent Order of Odd Fellows.

As an Italian American, he overcame obstacles to assimilation because his roots were well established in the South, the first Longino having arrived in 1752 from northern Italy. His Baptist faith fit well with religious practice in Mississippi. Though he lived in a period of mass Italian immigration, he had no ethnic base and was not shaped by it, as others had been in urban northern states.

Frank J. Cavaioli

Bibliography

Cavaioli, Frank J. "Charles Poletti and Fourteen Other Italian American Governors." In *Italian Americans in Transition,* edited by Joseph V. Scelsa, Salvatore J. LaGumina, and Lydio Tomasi, 137–152. New

York: American Italian Historical Association, 1990.

Dunbar, Rowland. *History of Mississippi.* Vol. 2. Chicago: Clarke, 1925.

Sydnor, Charles S., and Claude Bennett. *Mississippi History.* New York: Johnson, 1939.

See also GOVERNORS; POLITICS

Luciano, Lucky

See CRIME AND ORGANIZED CRIME

Luisetti, Angelo Joseph (Hank) (b. 1916)

A Stanford University three-time All American basketball player and two-time College Player of the Year, he was the most heralded player of his era. An only child, Luisetti grew up in the Italian section of San Francisco's Telegraph Hill; his father was a dishwasher who eventually owned his own restaurant. He graduated from Galileo High School in 1934 and enrolled at Stanford on a scholarship.

Luisetti was a skilled passer and dribbler, but was famous for his one-handed shooting style, unique in an era of the two-handed set shot. He led the Stanford freshman team to an 18-0 record. In each of his next three years, he led Stanford to consecutive Pacific Coast championships. He began his career as a center, moved to guard, and later played forward, perfecting the one-handed shot, a move that has revolutionized the game of basketball.

As a handsome 6-foot, 3-inch star on the West Coast, Luisetti achieved greater fame when he played at Madison Square Garden before a crowd of 17,623, when Stanford ended Long Island University's forty-three game winning streak, 45 to 35, on December 30, 1936; he scored fifteen points. During the 1937–1938 season, he scored fifty points (still a Stanford record) against Duquesne University. Despite his offensive ability, he was a respected team player. He set a college season scoring record with 1,596 points, an average of sixteen and one-half points per game. He never played in an NCAA tournament nor as a professional.

After graduating from Stanford in 1938 with a business degree, Luisetti played and coached club and AAU basketball teams, and presented clinics. He became the sales manager of an auto dealership and in 1958 served as president of a West Coast travel agency, from which he retired in 1981. His marriage to Jane Rossiter in 1941 produced a daughter and a son. During World War II he served in the Navy.

Luisetti is a member of Stanford University's Sports Hall of Fame and the Naismith Memorial Basketball Hall of Fame.

Frank J. Cavaioli

Bibliography

Eisen, George, and David K. Wiggins, eds. *Ethnicity and Sport in North American History and Culture.* Westport, CT: Greenwood, 1994.

McCallum, John D. *College Basketball, U.S.A., Since 1892.* New York: Stein and Day, 1980.

Padwe, Sandy. *Basketball's Hall of Fame.* Englewood Cliffs, NJ: Prentice-Hall, 1970.

See also SPORTS

Luria, Salvador Edward (1912–1991)

Considered one of the founders of molecular biology, Salvador Edward Luria was awarded the Nobel Prize in 1969 for his work with bacteriophages or bacterial viruses. He had a distinguished career as a research scientist in the field of molecular biology. His work paved the way to a better understanding of molecular biology and genetics.

Salvador was born on August 13, 1912, in Turin, Italy. His father was the manager of a printing company and a member of an influential Jewish family. Salvador attended high school at the Liceo d'Azeglio and in 1929 he attended the medical school at the University of Turin. In 1935 he graduated with an M.D., earning highest honors. He was mentored by Giuseppe Levi, a renowned histologist and an anti-Fascist activist. He rejected the discipline of his mentor in favor of mathematics and physics, subjects he was first introduced to by Ugo Fano, an astronomist, at the University of Turin. He believed that radiology would be the medical field of his future pursuit.

He was drafted in 1935 and served in the Italian army, where he turned his attention to the study of physics and mathematics. His experiences as an army doctor convinced him that he was not well suited, nor well trained, to be a physician. Upon his discharge in 1937 he studied radiology at the University of Rome's Physics Institute. It was here that he met another future Nobel laureate, Enrico Fermi. During his studies he became interested in radiation biology and the work of Max Delbrück, which described the gene as a distinct molecule. This served as an epiphany for Luria, who changed his area of study and research to molecular genetics.

Two events in 1938 greatly affected his life. The first event was a chance meeting with Geo Rita, a microbiologist, who introduced him to the virus-like bacteriophages that infect bacteria. Since bacteriophages multiply quickly and can be easily observed, he began using them to prove Delbrück's theory. Shortly after, he learned that Delbrück was doing exactly the same thing.

The second event in 1938 involved Mussolini's issuance of the *Racial Manifesto,* which denied civil rights to Jews. Wanting to leave Italy, he sought and was awarded a fellowship to study with Delbrück at the University of California at Berkeley. This was withdrawn with no explanation, and so he left Italy for Paris to study at the Radium Institute.

In 1940, with the Germans approaching Paris, he fled Paris, obtained an American visa, and migrated to the United States. Enrico Fermi helped him to obtain a position at Columbia University. In the summer of 1941, at Columbia's Cold Spring Harbor lab, Luria and Delbrück worked together for the first time. By chance, his mentor and friend, Ugo Fano, was also there at the same time.

Luria was awarded a Guggenheim fellowship in 1942–43 that allowed him to work once again with Delbrück at Vanderbilt University. In 1943 he accepted a teaching position at Indiana University in Bloomington, where he taught bacteriology and virology while conducting experiments on bacteriophages. Luria theorized that bacteria develop resistance to viruses as the result of spontaneous mutations, that is, changes in the genes of bacteria. He studied the ability of radiation to cause these mutations in bacteria.

While observing a man playing a slot machine, Luria realized that bacterial mutations occurred in a similar manner with clusters of small and large mutations occurring spontaneously. He shared his findings with Delbrück, who did the mathematical analysis to confirm this "fluctuation test." The two published what was to become a major work in the field. Soon after, Luria discovered that bacteriophages also undergo spontaneous mutations following the fluctuation-test model.

Luria began working with Alfred Day Hershey, who was studying bacteriophages at Washington University in St. Louis. Luria, Delbrück, and Hershey formed the American Phage Group.

In 1945 Luria married Zella Horowitz, a psychologist. A son, Daniel, was born in 1948. In 1950 Luria accepted a position as professor of bacteriology in the University of Illinois at Champaign-Urbana, where he continued his research on bacteriophages. It was here that he discovered that bits of DNA, the genetic information for cells and viruses, can break apart into pieces that can be identified. This restriction and modification led to a number of discoveries about the genetics of bacteria and bacteriophages by other researchers.

Unfortunately, once again, in 1953, politics intruded on the professional life of Salvador Luria. Because of his political beliefs, as a result of McCarthyism, he was denied a visa to speak at Oxford, despite the fact that in 1947 he had become a naturalized citizen. James Watson, a former student of Luria and a future Nobel laureate, delivered his paper instead.

Luria became chair of the Department of Microbiology at the Massachusetts Institute of Technology in 1959. Throughout his career at MIT he assumed a succession of administrative posts while continuing his research and writings.

In 1969 he, Delbrück, and Hershey were awarded the Nobel Prize for physiology or medicine for their work with the replication and the genetic-molecular structure of viruses. Luria received a number of awards, authored numerous papers, and wrote several books, including an autobiography. He died of a heart attack on February 6, 1991, in Lexington, Massachusetts.

Sean A. Fanelli

Bibliography

Luria, Salvador. *A Slot Machine, a Broken Test Tube: An Autobiography.* New York: Harper & Row, 1984

See also MEDICINE; SCIENCE

L

M

Madonna (b. 1958)

Born in a suburb of Detroit, Madonna Veronica Louise Ciccone was encouraged early on to study dance and music. She was raised in a conservative Catholic family with seven siblings and a stepmother from age 6, when her mother, also named Madonna, died of breast cancer.

Of the numerous things Madonna—and, for that matter, any of her performances—calls to the fore is how little society tends to tolerate that which pushes the envelope, especially when pushed by a woman. Madonna's videos seem to have always caused a stir for one reason or another: too sexual, too provocative, too much skin, provocative clothing, undergarments as outerwear, little boys in peep shows, women in submissive positions.

Most successful as rock singer of numerous albums and videos, a goodly amount of Madonna's music and videos are based on working class, ethnic/racial, and sexual thematics. "Like a Virgin," "Papa Don't Preach," "Isla Bonita," "Open Your Heart," "Like a Prayer," "Justify My Love," "Express Yourself," and "Vogue," in both songs and videos, exhibit to a significant degree some combination of these three major themes. Some videos—"Papa Don't Preach," "Open Your Heart," and "Like a Prayer"—exhibit some degree of Italian American culture, be it the religiosity of the first and third or the actual Italian subtitles of the second. Similarly, a general sense of Latino influence emanates from "Isla Bonita"; and sexual individuality lies at the base of the early "Like a Virgin" or the later "Justify My Love," "Express Yourself," and "Vogue."

Madonna has had less success as a film actor. Whereas her role as Susan (*Desperately Seeking Susan* [1985]) literally stole the limelight from Rosanna Arquette's character, Madonna did not find similar success in later film roles, except for her roles in the blockbusters *Dick Tracy* (1990) and *A League of Their Own* (1991). Other roles proved to be less compatible with her acting style. Her *Evita* (1996), predominantly a musical, is a radical departure from her previous films.

Madonna. World famous, successful, and controversial, Madonna came from an Italian American family in Detroit. She is one of the most popular contemporary entertainers and has had a major impact on American culture. Courtesy Joseph Fioravanti.

But Madonna is not just a singer and actor. Equally significant to her success is her entrepreneurial ability to read the cultural signs around her and benefit from them both commercially and artistically. If there was one stumble in her career, it was her book *Sex* (1991), a veritable aesthetic flop in the United States. Madonna has changed her image from the brassy, smart-mouthed woman to the sure-speaking femme fatale. In addition, her video "Justify My Love," too racy even for MTV, was first shown on national TV during an ABC *Nightline* broadcast and released as a single, grossing millions of dollars.

Whereas early in her career Madonna was very much a pop singer, her later albums, *Erotica* (1992), *Bedtime Stories* (1994), and *Something to Remember* (1995), combine, to a large degree, many of her previous love songs with other, newer sensual ballads. A certain maturity in her music and film performances now seems to accompany her own maturation as a middle-aged artist.

Anthony Julian Tamburri

Bibliography

Freccero, Carla. "Our Lady of MTV: Madonna's 'Like a Prayer'." *Boundary* 2 (1992): 163–83.

Schwichtenberg, Cathy. *The Madonna Connection. Representational Politics, Subcultural Identities, and Cultural Theories.* Boulder: Westview, 1993.

Tamburri, Anthony Julian. "The Madonna Complex: The Justification of a Prayer." *Semiotic Spectrum* 17 (April 1992): 1–2.

See also MOVIE ACTORS AND ACTRESSES; POP SINGERS

Maine's Little Italys

Maine, a state generally overlooked in the broader history of Italian Americans in the United States, has a number of Little Italys. Although the first recorded Italian to visit Maine was Giovanni da Verrazzano, the explorer, in 1524, there was not a significant migration of Italians into that state until after the Civil War. At the end of the nineteenth century and at the beginning of the twentieth century, Italians came as laborers to Maine's cities and towns, where their presence developed enclaves in places like Millinocket, Portland, Rumford, and elsewhere. Due to the efficiency of the controversial *padrone* (labor broker) system at that time, these immigrants, mostly from the towns and villages of the southern part of Italy, were brought into Maine to help build dams, mills, quarries, railroads, and water works. For example, near the end of the nineteenth century, at least six hundred Italians were involved in the construction of railroads in the Waterville area alone.

Historically, the presence of Italians in Maine had grown from about twenty in the census of 1850 to slightly more than 4,500 by 1910. In fact, the same census ranks the job profile of these laborers as mostly railroad workers, stone masons, construction workers, and pulp and paper processors. These Italians constructed the railroads throughout the state, set up dams on its rivers, and built paper mills in Millinocket and Rumford. Hundreds of others were cutting stone from the quarries in Frankfort, Hallowell, Hurricane Island, Mount Desert Island, and Stonington. Still others constructed the water works in Houlton, Norway, Old Orchard, Portland, and elsewhere. And there were those who settled in areas where they engaged in farming, opened grocery stores, or pursued other forms of productive employment.

While one can find enclaves of Italians in a number of cities and towns in Maine, Portland's Little Italy was the major one. The heart of this Italian settlement was centered around what became St. Peter's Parish on Federal Street in 1929. Among its parishioners were barbers, carpenters, fishermen, longshoremen, and masons, in addition to railroad workers and other employees. Not unlike other parishes within Italian communities, St. Peter's has declined to about a fourth of its peak membership.

As the next generation entered into more professional careers and moved up economically and socially, parishioners moved to the suburbs and the population of the city parish declined. The annual bazaar at St. Peter's, held in mid-August, which honors St. Rocco and celebrates the Feast of the Assumption, still brings the generations together. This is also true of the Italian Heritage Center, chartered in 1953, which strives to perpetuate the legacy of the Little Italys in Maine. According to the 1990 census, Italian Americans constitute 4 percent or at least fifty thousand of the state's population.

Vincent A. Lapomarda

Bibliography

Banfield, Alfred T. "The Padrone, the Sojourners, and the Settlers: A Preface to the 'Little Italies' of Maine." *Maine Historical Society Quarterly* 31 (1972): 114–141.

Barry, William David, and Randolph Dominic. "The Italian-Americans." *The Maine Sunday Telegram.* Special Series on Maine. 11, 18, 25 October 1981 and 1, 8 November 1981.

Iamurri, Gabriel A. *The True Story of an Immigrant.* Boston: Christopher, 1945.

Lacognata, Angelo A. *We the Italians of Maine.* Portland: University of Maine, 1975.

Lancia, Peter J. "Coming Home to Mother: Community, Church, and Celebration Among Italian-Americans of Portland, Maine." A.B. thesis, Bowdoin College, Brunswick, ME, 1989.

Mancini, Henry

See COMPOSERS, POPULAR MUSIC

Mangione, Jerre (1909–1998)

Born in the United States to Sicilian immigrants, Jerre Mangione was one of the most celebrated Italian American writers. In 1992 the Library of Congress honored his career with a special exhibit; among his many awards were a 1989 Pennsylvania Governor's Award for Excellence in the Arts; Guggenheim (1946) and Fulbright fellowships (1965); two National Endowment for the Arts grants (1980 and 1984); and the prestigious Italian "Empedocles" prize (1984). In 1971 Italy named Mangione *Commendatore* and awarded him the "Star of Italian Solidarity." He also received two honorary degrees: Doctor of Letters from the University of Pennsylvania, 1980; Doctor of Humane Letters from the State University of New York at Brockport, 1986.

His first book, *Mount Allegro,* has remained in print most of the years since its first appearance in 1943, a feat accomplished by six publishers to date. Its publication prompted Malcolm Cowley to write in a personal letter to Mangione: "*Mount Allegro* has had more lives than any other book of our time." *Mount Allegro* is the first of four nonfiction books written by Mangione that can be read as autobiography. Each book represents a progressive stage in the evolution of an identity, from Sicilian, to American, and eventually to Sicilian-American. The solution to the Sicilian versus American identity conflict dramatized in *Mount Allegro* would be pursued in Mangione's second book, *Reunion in Sicily.*

Writer Jerre Mangione, left, chats with artist Ralph Fasanella at the Nineteenth Annual Conference of the American Italian Historical Association, in Philadelphia, November 1986. Courtesy Frank J. Cavaioli.

Structured as a personal travelogue and political report, *Reunion in Sicily* (1950) opens with a confession: in spite of receiving a Guggenheim fellowship, Mangione is in no mood to go to Sicily. Ten years after his first visit, Mangione states that the goal of this project is to look at postwar life in Italy and to document the transition from dictatorship to self-government. *A Passion for Sicilians: The World Around Danilo Dolci* (1968) is undoubtedly Mangione's least autobiographical work of the four listed here. As a social history written in first person, this book is more an ethnography, an account of a neglected region's fight for progress against the Mafia and a stubborn, slow-moving Italian government, than it is a continuation of the narrative progression of Mangione's life toward an Italian American identity.

An Ethnic at Large (1978) contains the type of material that one expects to find in a traditional "success story" autobiography. In it the son of immigrants emerges out of the neighborhood and into the world. Structured chronologically, *An Ethnic at Large* charts the development of Mangione's career as a writer and civil servant and dramatizes the cross-cultural experiences he encounters in America. The writing becomes an account of the narrator's coming-of-age during America's Roaring Twenties, the Great Depression, through World War II (including visits to the White House) and the McCarthy era.

In the years following the publication of *An Ethnic at Large,* Mangione continued to serve as an ambassador and interpreter of Italian American culture. He reviewed books, presented talks, encouraged younger writers, and continued to examine and chronicle the Italian American experience. His last publication, *La Storia: Five Centuries of the Italian American Experience,* co-written with Ben Morreale, is a monumental social history of Italian Americans that established Jerre Mangione as a true diplomat of Italian American culture at home in America.

Fred L. Gardaphé

Bibliography

Mangione, Jerre. *America Is Also Italian.* New York: Putnam, 1969.
———. *The Dream and the Deal: The Federal Writers' Project 1935–1943.* 3rd ed. Philadelphia: University of Pennsylvania Press, 1983.
———. *An Ethnic at Large: A Memoir of the Thirties and Forties.* 2nd ed. Philadelphia: University of Pennsylvania Press, 1983.
———, with Ben Morreale. *La Storia: Five Centuries of the Italian American Experience.* New York: Harper-Collins, 1992.
———. *Life Sentences for Everybody.* New York: Abelard, 1965.
———. *Mount Allegro.* 5th ed., with a new concluding chapter by the author and introduction by Herbert J. Gans, published as *Mount Allegro: A Memoir of Italian American Life.* New York: Columbia University Press, 1981.
———. *Mussolini's March on Rome.* New York: Franklin Watts, 1975.
———. *Night Search.* New York: Crown, 1965. (Published in England as *To Walk the Night.* London: Muller, 1967.) (Published in Italy as *Ricerca nella notte.* Palermo, Italy: Sellerio, 1987.)
———. *A Passion for Sicilians: The World Around Danilo Dolci.* 3rd ed., with a new concluding chapter by the author. New Brunswick, NJ: Transaction Books, 1985.
———. *Reunion in Sicily.* Boston: Houghton Mifflin, 1950. Reprint: New York: Columbia University Press, 1984.
———. *The Ship and the Flame.* New York: A. A. Wyn, 1948.

See also AUTOBIOGRAPHY; LITERATURE; NOVELS AND NOVELISTS

Marcantonio, Vito (1902–1954)

Lawyer, politician, and public servant, Vito Marcantonio was born in New York City's East Harlem, an enclave that emerged as the largest concentration of Italian Americans in the country. A brilliant polemicist, he attracted the attention of Fiorello H. LaGuardia who named him his congressional campaign manager and his "eyes and ears" in East Harlem. After LaGuardia's election as New York City mayor in 1933, Marcantonio won election to Congress as an unlikely Republican who displayed a tendency toward radical politics from the outset and who emerged as the most controversial congressman of his era—a period that spanned two decades. In time, he eschewed identification with the Republican Party and became a stalwart member of the

Cooperation between African Americans and Italian Americans is evident at a meeting of civil right leaders Paul Robeson, W.E.B. Dubois, and Vito Marcantonio (left to right) in New York City. Courtesy Salvatore J. LaGumina.

American Labor Party, running under the latter label for New York City mayor in 1949.

Denounced as an unregenerate left-winger, he consistently espoused the cause of working people, relentlessly calling for improvements in minimum wages, the right to organize, and protection against occupational hazards. Thus, he fought long and hard to inform Americans of the deleterious effects of inhaling silicosis, which shortened the life of numerous miners and marble workers. He was ahead of his time in speaking out in behalf of the rights of minority peoples, communists, and socialists, and he regularly denounced conservative policies. His service to his community became legendary as he personally met with more constituents on a yearly basis than any other congressional member. He was also a champion of Italian American rights as is evident in his condemnation of stricter immigration policies, his defense of alien rights, and his demands for humane treatment of Italy once that nation became a co-belligerent power in 1943 during World War II.

His left-wing philosophy during the anti-communist milieu of the post–World War II period drew such rigid opposition that virtually all the city newspapers and major political figures reproved him. The *New York Times* went to the extraordinary length of using extended editorial comments against him for three consecutive days as it fought to defeat him for reelection. Even the New York State legislature felt constrained to enact an electoral law designed to prevent him from gaining official nomination from the major political parties in his district. Political observers concluded that Richard Nixon's victory over his Democratic challenger for the United States Senate in California rested in large part on the circulation of a "pink" sheet that indicated the number of times his opponent voted with Marcantonio, which, according to Nixon, measured how "Red" she was.

Finally defeated for reelection in 1950, he broke with the communists and was preparing to run for the congressional seat in 1954 when he suffered a fatal heart attack. The decades following his death have witnessed a revision in the evaluation of Marcantonio: he is now acknowledged as a man of compassion who fearlessly served the needs of the poor and oppressed.

Salvatore J. LaGumina

Bibliography

LaGumina, Salvatore. J. *Vito Marcantonio, The People's Politician.* Dubuque, IA: Kendall/Hunt, 1969.

Meyer, Gerald. *Vito Marcantonio, Radical Politician, 1902–1954*. Albany: State University of New York Press, 1989.

Schaeffer, Alan. *Vito Marcantonio: Radical in Congress*. Syracuse, NY: Syracuse University Press, 1966.

See also POLITICS; RADICALISM

Marchione, Margherita Frances (b. 1922)

Educator, editor, author, and translator, Sister Marchione was born in Little Ferry, New Jersey. Interested in education and attracted to the religious life, she entered the Order of the Religious Teachers Filippini, a congregation that had been founded in Italy in 1692 and later established in the United States in 1910.

Sister Marchione earned her Ph.D. from Columbia University in 1960. It was here that she met Giuseppe Prezzolini, professor of Italian literature and director of the Casa Italiana, who was instrumental in influencing her to undertake the study of Italian literature and culture. Her teaching career has been mainly in the field of Italian language. She has occupied such posts as chairperson of the Department of Foreign Languages at Fairleigh Dickinson University in Madison, New Jersey, and director of the Italian Institute of the University of Salerno. She has served in the capacities of vocation promotion directress, secretary, and treasurer for her religious order.

Her writing and editing career has been concentrated in studying Italian literature and in researching the life and writings of the eighteenth-century Italian political thinker Philip (Filippo) Mazzei (1730–1816). Mazzei's philosophy influenced eighteenth-century political movements in France, Italy, and Poland. He also inspired his friend Thomas Jefferson, especially when writing the Declaration of Independence. In 1978 she was appointed director of the newly formed Center for Mazzei Studies at Fairleigh Dickinson University. Sister Marchione's research on Mazzei has resulted in publishing such works as *Philip Mazzei: Jefferson's Zealous Whig* (1975) and in editing the multivolume work *Philip Mazzei: Selected Writings and Correspondence* (1983). She has also written or edited several other literary works including *L'Imagine Tesa; La Vita e L'Opera Di Clemente Rebora* (1974); *Twentieth Century Italian Poetry: A Bilingual Anthology* (1974); *Carteggio di Clemente Rebora, 1900–1930* (1975); with S. Eugene Scalia, the multivolume *Carteggio di Giovanni Boine, 1905–1917* (1977); and *Incontriamo Prezzolini* (1985). Later works include *Peter and Sally Sammartino* (1994), *Americans of Italian Heritage* (1995), and *Yours Is a Precious Witness: An Oral History of Jews and Catholics in Wartime Italy* (1996). Among her many awards, she was the recipient in 1977 of the Cavaliere dell'Ordine della Stella della Solidarieta Italiana, the highest award conferred by the president of Italy.

Nicholas Joseph Falco

Bibliography

"Religious Teachers Filippini in the United States." *U.S. Catholic Historian* 6, no. 4 (fall 1987).

Women's Project of New Jersey, Inc. *Past and Promise: Lives of New Jersey Women*. Metuchen, NJ: Scarecrow Press, 1990.

See also MAZZEI, PHILIP

Marciano, Rocky (1923–1969)

Rocco Francis Marciano is the only undisputed heavyweight boxing champion to have retired undefeated. He was born in Brockton, Massachusetts, September 1, 1923, to Pierrino and Pasquelena (née Piccento) Marchegiano. His father migrated from Abruzzi and became a shoe factory worker; his mother was born in the Naples region.

Rocky aspired to a baseball and football career, but he was turned down following a baseball tryout with the Chicago Cubs. After dropping out of high school, he worked at odd jobs. His interest in boxing began after he was drafted into the army in March 1943. He boxed at forts in Massachusetts and Washington and later in England and Wales. Marciano became a professional boxer on March 17, 1947.

Most of his early bouts were held in Providence, where the ring announcer had trouble pronouncing "Marchegiano." When it was suggested to Rocky that he change his name to Marciano, he hesitated, not wanting to be disrespectful to his father. But Mr. Marchegiano simply shrugged and said, "At least, it sounds Italian."

Out of Marciano's first twenty-four fights, only two went to a decision. The twenty-fifth, on December 30, 1949, at Madison Square Garden, resulted in the near-death of his opponent, Bronx heavyweight Carmine Vingo, after a sixth-round knockout. A controversial split decision over another rising Bronx Italian American, Roland LaStarza, in March 1950, marked a turning point in his career. After several minor bouts, he knocked out Rex Layne in six rounds in July 1951, and the stage was set for him to box the aging former champion, Joe Louis. The legendary Louis was experiencing a comeback following his 1949 retirement, attempting to settle financial debts, a plight Marciano was determined to avoid for himself. Marciano knocked out Louis.

His next opponent was "Jersey Joe" Walcott, who won the heavyweight title in the summer of 1952. On September 23, 1952, Marciano knocked out Walcott in the thirteenth round of a brutal fight to become heavyweight champion of the world. He subsequently knocked out Walcott in round one of the rematch.

Marciano claimed that his toughest fight was a fifteen-round defense in June 1954 against courageous Ezzard Charles. Following the Charles bout, he fought men of lesser ability, including LaStarza. By 1955 only light-heavyweight champion Archie Moore, although losing by a ninth-round knockout, fully tested Marciano. With no outstanding matches in sight, disgusted with his manager, and pressured by his mother and other relatives, Marciano retired in April 1956, with his health and wealth intact.

At 5 feet, 8 inches and 185 pounds, Marciano won all forty-nine of his professional fights, forty-three by knockouts. Marciano was a well-conditioned athlete whose loyalty to family and friends was congruent with Italian American values. He is a member of *Ring* magazine's Boxing Hall of Fame and the International Boxing Hall of Fame. Marciano died in a plane crash near Newton, Iowa, on August 31, 1969.

Richard Renoff

Bibliography

Libby, Bill. *Rocky: The Story of a Champion.* New York: Messner, 1971.

Nack, William. "The Rock." *Sports Illustrated* 79 (23 August 1993): 52–68.

Skehan, Everett M. *Rocky Marciano: Biography of a First Son.* Boston: Houghton Mifflin, 1977.

See also SPORTS

Marcioni, Italo

Though others have claimed credit for inventing the ice cream cone, the first to actually receive a patent on the idea was an Italian American in the nineteenth century.

Italo Marcioni (or Marchiony), an Italian immigrant who settled in Hoboken, New Jersey, made his claim to the original ice cream cone in 1896. In favor of his claim is a patent that was granted to him in December 1903 for the mold he had invented to produce the cones. His invention was so unique that Hoboken is still heralded as the home of the first ice cream cone.

Later, at the St. Louis World's Fair in 1904, Ernest A. Hamwi, an immigrant from Damascus, Syria, rolled a waffle into the

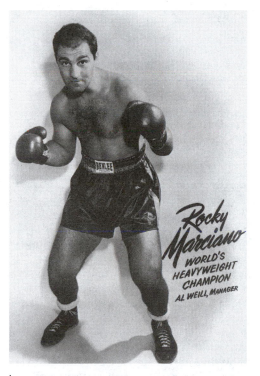

Rocky Marciano. Considered one of the greatest heavyweight boxers, he retired as an undefeated champion. He came from the Italian section of Brockton, Massachusetts. Courtesy Richard Renoff.

shape of a cone when an ice cream man had run out of paper dishes to serve his product. He called it the "World's Fair Cornucopia." A dispute eventually arose over the origin of the ice cream cone.

Marcioni's and Hamwi's claims were further disputed by David Avayou and Abe Doumar, who were at the same World's Fair. Avayou claimed that the cone originated from the paper cone used in France to hold ice cream, while Doumar, another native of Damascus, created a waffle-cone version not unlike that of Hamwi. He later produced his own cone machine, which made him famous in Norfolk, Virginia.

To Marcioni, who holds the patent to the first ice cream cone mold, belongs the credit for the first ice cream cone, while others, in addition to him, spread the idea of the ice cream cone.

Vincent A. Lapomarda

Bibliography

Barone, Arturo. *Italian Firsts: A to Z.* New York: Talman, 1994.

David, Elizabeth. *Harvest of the Cold Months: The Social History of Ice and Ices.* New York: Viking, 1995.

Kroll, Steven. *The Hokey-Pokey Man.* New York: Holiday House, 1989.

Willard, Mildred Wilds. *The Ice Cream Cone.* Chicago: Follett, 1973.

Marconi, Guglielmo
See PATENTS AND INVENTORS; SCIENCE

Martin, Dean (1917–1995)
Popular singer, actor, television star Dean Martin, son of an Italian immigrant barber, was born Dino Paul Crocetti in Steubenville, Ohio, on June 7, 1917. He dropped out of high school after the tenth grade, became an amateur boxer, worked in a steel mill, and as a clerk and croupier. He changed his name to Dean Martin when he began a singing career in clubs and gambling houses. In 1946 he teamed with comedian Jerry Lewis during an Atlantic City engagement, and they soon moved to the Copacabana in New York City for a six-week engagement that was extended to twelve weeks. It was an ideal combination: Martin's soothing singing style and casual manner complemented Lewis's comedic antics. They became an instant success.

From 1950 to 1955 Martin and Lewis hosted and starred in the *Colgate Comedy Hour* on television. They ranked first among the leading stars in show business in 1952. Producer Hal Wallis of Paramount signed them to a movie contract. They made sixteen hit comedies. To the dismay of their millions of fans, the team of Martin and Lewis broke up in 1956 over personal differences. They each went their separate way as performers. Martin said that meeting Jerry Lewis and leaving him were the two pivotal events in his career.

Critics believed that Martin could not make it on his own; he proved them wrong. In a style similar to Bing Crosby and Perry Como, he recorded popular songs that drew a devoted audience: "That's Amore," "Memories Are Made of This," "Everybody Loves Somebody," "Return to Me," and "Volare" each sold more than a million copies. He made eleven albums from 1964 to 1969 under the Reprise label, which was founded by Frank Sinatra; they were all best sellers. His television variety show, *The Dean Martin Show,* enjoyed a successful run from 1965 to 1974. He followed this show with *The Dean Martin Comedy World* and with a series of comedy roasts. His geniality and carefree demeanor added to his star status. He also became a major attraction at Las Vegas and Atlantic City.

Martin performed in fifty-five films that included both comedies and dramas. He worked with Frank Sinatra in *Ocean's Eleven* (1960), *Sergeant's 3* (1962), and *Robin and the Seven Hoods* (1964), earning him membership in the "Rat Pack" that included Sammy Davis Jr., Peter Lawford, and President John F. Kennedy as an honorary member. In four films, beginning with *The Silencers* (1966), Martin spoofed the popular James Bond character. His performances in *The Young Lions* (1958) and *Some Came Running* (1959) revealed his talent as a serious actor. But it was his role as the reforming drunk in the Howard Hawks film *Rio Bravo* (1959) that critics believe was his best.

He was married three times. With his first wife, Elizabeth Anne McDonald, to whom he was married from 1940 to 1949, he had four children. His second marriage, to Jeanne Riegger, lasted twenty-three years and produced three children. A son from this marriage, Dean Paul, was a captain in the California Air National Guard and was killed in an air crash during a training mission. His third marriage, to Catherine Mae Hawn, ended in divorce in 1976.

Dean Martin died of acute respiratory failure at his home in Beverly Hills, California, on December 25, 1995.

Frank J. Cavaioli

Bibliography

Maltby, Richard. *Hollywood Cinema*. Cambridge, MA: Blackwell, 1995.

Parish, James Robert, and William T. Leonard. *The Funsters*. New Rochelle, NY: 1979.

Tosches, Nick. *Dino: Living High in the Dirty Business of Dreams*. New York: Doubleday, 1992.

Wallis, Hal, and Charles Higham. *Starmaker*. New York: Macmillan, 1980.

See also MOVIE ACTORS AND ACTRESSES; POP SINGERS; TELEVISION

Mazzei, Philip (1730–1816)

Philip Mazzei ranks in the company of America's founding fathers and to the group of Italian immigrants who, not being able to achieve the dream of liberty within their own country, sowed its seeds throughout the world.

With his immigration to the colonies in 1773, Mazzei began a forty-three-year fascination with America, wherein he befriended and influenced the founding fathers, contributed to the commerce of the colonies, and added a fiery voice to Virginia's political stage. His intellectual and philosophical ideas—especially concerning the separation of church and state, and the recognition of equality between all men—were as much a part of the American Revolution as was any sea battle or military campaign.

A compelling figure of the Enlightenment, Mazzei was born December 25, 1730, in Poggio a Caiano, near Florence, Italy. He was an enterprising, articulate, and perceptive man who traveled on three continents, lived in ten countries, and participated in such world-shaking events as the American and French revolutions and the short-lived Polish constitutional reform of 1791. He was a surgeon, merchant, language teacher, writer, and diplomat, a royal chamberlain, privy councillor, and an agriculturist and zealous Whig in Virginia.

When Mazzei moved to London in 1756, he met Thomas Adams and Benjamin Frank-lin, who urged him to introduce his Italian products and culture to the Colonies. He set sail for Virginia in 1773 and settled on land in Charlottesville adjoining that of Thomas Jefferson. But farming was soon put aside as he became caught up in the growing political tensions of his adopted country.

Mazzei strengthened the Virginians in their ideas of rebellion based on natural rights. He was warmly welcomed by George Washington and others in Williamsburg, and shared with them the vital information he had acquired during eighteen years in England.

The 1776 Declaration of Rights, adopted by the Virginia Convention, emphasized the priority of individual rights over powers of the state. And, about the same time, Philip Mazzei referred to this document as the Bill of Rights in his forty-two-page "Instructions of the Freeholders of Albemarle County to their Delegates in Convention." He advocated not only independence, but "one and the same Constitution for all the united Colonies." These "Instructions" link him to the group of Virginian statesmen whose ideas on the theory and form of government were incorporated into the major political writings of the period.

Mazzei's correspondence with American revolutionary leaders led to his appointment in 1779 as Virginia's agent in Europe. This gave him a rare chance to support the Colonies overseas. Before joining Jefferson in Paris, he was one of the founders of the Constitutional Society of 1784, whose members were to debate public issues and instruct voters. Its purpose was to preserve the "pure and sacred principles of Liberty" by organizing discussions of important issues before legislative decisions were made.

In 1937 A. Valta Parma, curator of the Rare Book Collection of the Library of Congress, came across a folded-in leaflet among the bound political pamphlets from Thomas Jefferson's library. It consisted of eight pages of the minutes and the declaration of the Constitutional Society. Convinced of the importance of these documents, the curator stated: "There was no other group of men anywhere in the country with the prestige and power of that group of Virginians. There is no question but that the thought of the necessity of a Constitution received its first impulse from them and that here was a definite organization to set about solving many of the problems that would come up in framing a federal

M

constitution." In 1788 Mazzei published a four-volume history of the United States.

The scope of Mazzei's interests and the range of his correspondence provide unusual insights into the tumultuous early years of the French Revolution. Mazzei was a daily witness of, and participant in, many of the epochal events of those years. Hundreds of letters were exchanged between Mazzei and King Stanislaus of Poland, a man who, at that time, was himself creating a revolution with his famed Polish Constitution of May 3, 1791.

In 1792 Mazzei was in Warsaw as a confidant of King Stanislaus during the Polish struggle against a Russian invasion. He then returned to Tuscany and to his new home in Pisa, and his marriage in 1796.

In 1805 Mazzei was pleased to implement Jefferson's request to find Italian sculptors who would help enrich the new capitol of his beloved America. Shortly after the arrival of Giovanni Andrei and Giuseppe Franzoni, Jefferson informed Mazzei that the two sculptors were "greatly esteemed."

At the age of eighty, Mazzei began his memoirs—*My Life and Wanderings*—a rich source book for the life and mores of the eighteenth century. He speaks of his many friends, among whom were the first five presidents of the United States: George Washington, John Adams, Thomas Jefferson, James Madison, and James Monroe.

Both a transmitter of European ideas to the Americans and a bearer of American ideas across the Atlantic, Mazzei was in contact with the most prominent figures of the day in Europe and America. He promoted American ideals and defended the American cause with pen and voice as he befriended and collaborated with the Virginia leaders in their struggle for independence.

Philip Mazzei was a thinker before his time: supporting the environment, he advised Jefferson to enact laws to protect forests; promoting equal rights for all people, he advocated education of slaves before their emancipation, and he opposed the idea of men as the stronger sex and held that women have rights, too; and advocating financial stability, he wrote a pamphlet showing the dangers of monetary inflation.

Philip Mazzei, "a citizen of the world," may also be considered the first Italian immigrant to promote economic and political relations between Italy and the United States. He played an integral part in America's fight for democracy.

Margherita Marchione

Bibliography

Garlick, Richard C. *Philip Mazzei—Friend of Jefferson.* Baltimore: Johns Hopkins Press, 1933.

Marchione, Margherita, ed. and trans. *Philip Mazzei: Jefferson's Zealous Whig.* New York: American Institute of Italian Studies, 1975.

———. *Philip Mazzei: World Citizen.* Lanham, MD: University Press of America, 1994.

———. *The Adventurous Life of Philip Mazzei—La vita avventurosa di Filippo Mazzei.* Lanham, MD: University Press of America, 1995.

Mazzei, Philip. *My Life and Wanderings.* Translated by S. Eugene Scalia and edited by Margherita Marchione. New York: American Institute of Italian Studies, 1980.

Schiavo, Giovanni. *Four Centuries of Italian American History.* New York: Vigo Press, 1951.

Mazzini Society

Founded in 1939, the Mazzini Society was the most important anti-Fascist organization in America. Centered in New York, the new home of many Italian anti-Fascist exiles, it published its own newspaper, *Nazione Unite.* The Mazzini Society attracted the most prominent non-Marxist and non-Stalinist intellectuals of the exiled Italian Left in America.

Inspired by the ideals and moral example of Giuseppe Mazzini, the nineteenth-century Italian patriot, the society counted on the support of historian Gaetano Salvemini (who taught at Harvard), art historian Lionello Venturi, journalist Max Ascoli (who became its president), Alberto Tarchiani (secretary), G. A. Borgese (professor of literature and aesthetics), and conductor Arturo Toscanini. These *fuorusciti* (exiled intellectuals) attempted to synthesize classical nineteenth-century liberalism's concern over the rights of the individual with the goal of social justice derived from twentieth-century democratic socialism. The constitution of the society stated the following objectives: (1) to inform the American public about the real conditions in Fascist Italy, (2) to combat Fascist propaganda in the United States, (3) to defend American democratic institutions against totalitarianism, (4) to assist Italian political refugees who sought asylum in America, (5) to establish contact between anti-Fascist intellectuals and American liberals, (6) to cooperate with the organizations of other nations in the struggle against dictatorship, and (7) to undertake cultural and educational activities in Italian American communities.

The Mazzini Society grew to over forty branches with more than a thousand members in the United States in the early 1940s, and was instrumental in shaping public opinion about Italy and Italians, especially after Pearl Harbor. While many Americans and Italian Americans had looked favorably on Mussolini and the Fascist regime in the 1920s and 1930s, the Ethiopian invasion, the Spanish Civil War, and the emerging alliance with Hitler all worked to discredit Fascism in the minds of Americans and Italian Americans. The Mazzini Society was divided over whether or not to support those who had previously looked with favor on the Fascist regime; in fact, the society suffered a serious blow when Salvemini, Toscanini, Venturi, and others broke with the society over its support of Roosevelt's decision to work with the Badoglio government that replaced Mussolini in 1943. Badoglio was not considered a clear enough break with the Fascist past. Salvemini had insisted on distinguishing between the Fascist regime and the Italian people, and the Mazzini Society adopted this as a central idea in its relationship with the U.S. State Department. Internally, the society was weakened by ideological disputes originating in Italy: anarchists distrusted communists, liberals were suspicious of anarchists and communists, and communists felt betrayed by democratic socialists. By the summer of 1942 communists were banished from the society, but this did little to end the ideological struggles. As Italian intellectuals returned to Italy after 1943, the society became more of an Italian American organization without the bitter ideological dimension, but it also became less effective in political issues.

Stanislao G. Pugliese

Bibliography

Delzell, Charles. *Mussolini's Enemies: The Italian Anti-Fascist Resistance*. Princeton: Princeton University Press, 1961.

Diggins, John Patrick. *Mussolini and Fascism: The View From America*. Princeton: Princeton University Press, 1972.

Salvemini, Gaetano. *Italian Fascist Activities in the United States*. Edited with an introduction by Philip V. Cannistraro. New York: Center for Migration Studies, 1977.

See also ORGANIZATIONS; SALVEMINI, GAETANO

Mazzuchelli, Samuel (1806–1864)

Samuel Mazzuchelli was an eminent Italian American missionary of the nineteenth century. When he reached the port of New York in 1828, he was one of the few immigrants (about two hundred) from Italy, who came to the United States in the entire decade of the 1820s. From a Milanese family of merchants, bankers, artists, and scholars, his background seemed to promise him success in any career. When Samuel chose to become a mendicant friar of the Order of Preachers, or Dominicans, his family was predictably disappointed.

At the age of 17 he became a Dominican novice in Faenza, and in 1825 began his studies in Rome. After three years, the youth answered an urgent call from America. The pioneer bishop of Ohio and Michigan, Edward Fenwick, needed help in his far-flung ministry to natives and new settlers on the frontier. In response, the young Milanese traveled alone to Cincinnati, where he began to learn English and adapt to American culture.

In 1830 at age 23, Mazzuchelli was ordained and sent to be the only missionary in an area larger than the whole of Italy. Extending south from the Canadian border through the Great Lakes region (later the states of Michigan and Wisconsin), the territory contained a wilderness defended by forts.

Mazzuchelli adopted the life and culture of many different people: natives of the woodland tribes; French Canadian fur traders and trappers; and Irish and German immigrants in the Mississippi Valley, who came to mine the rich lead ore and remained to farm the land and build the first towns.

Keeping in touch with Italians at home, Mazzuchelli empathized with their political problems and desire for a united nation, while missing their rich culture. Among the Americans, the priest never heard his own tongue.

Nevertheless, he cherished the writings of his contemporary Alessandro Manzoni, shared the beauties of Italy with frontiersmen, and introduced students to the literature, music, and history of Italy.

Among the Menominee and Winnebago natives, Mazzuchelli was the first resident missionary since the Jesuits, who had been withdrawn fifty years earlier. He traveled on snowshoes or by canoe to their homes, shared their frugal meals, and joined them in ice fishing and gathering maple sugar. He understood their religion, their love of children, and their respect for aging members. As the government pursued its Indian removal policies, he protested the injustices to his congressman and to President Andrew Jackson. The priest also defended the rights of American citizens and deplored the enslavement of African Americans.

In meeting the needs of various people, Father Mazzuchelli displayed his own remarkable talents. In 1833 he published a Winnebago prayer book, and in 1834, a liturgical almanac in Chippewa, the first printed item in Wisconsin. In 1836 he addressed, at their request, the first legislature of Wisconsin Territory. He designed and built more than twenty-five churches in the upper Mississippi Valley. He founded a college for men at Sinsinawa, Wisconsin, in 1846. He also gathered in Sinsinawa the first members of a community of Dominican Sisters who, enrolling more than 3,000 members in subsequent years, have conducted schools and served in various ministries throughout the United States. With the sisters, he founded the St. Clara Academy for young women in Benton, Wisconsin. Through its charter, granted in 1848 by the state of Wisconsin, this frontier prototype of secondary schools became the forerunner of two colleges for women: Rosary College in River Forest, Illinois, and Edgewood College in Madison, Wisconsin.

On his brief return to Italy in 1844, Mazzuchelli wrote and published his *Memorie . . . d'un Missionario Apostolico,* to acquaint the Italians with the people, government, religion, and culture of the United States. In a chapter on freedom of religion the priest explained to his countrymen how Americans had instituted by law "that straight line which separates civil power from conscience," so that "the independence of the civil from the religious official is due to the independence of worship from the civil power. . . ."

Mazzuchelli became a devoted citizen of the United States and admired its democratic principles, but was not blind to its weaknesses such as slavery and the ravages of the Civil War.

Both Catholics and Protestants loved this priest, whom the Irish and others called "Father Kelly," for his zeal, courage, and selfless generosity, especially in tending to the sick.

He died suddenly on February 23, 1864, as a result of exposure in bitter cold weather when he was summoned to visit the sick. After his death, there appeared accounts of his life and ministry in newspapers from California to New York. One writer stated:

Another efficient servant of God is gone to receive the reward of eternal life, and he who was once the only priest west of Lake Michigan has left the people of that vast region in mourning! He was a good man; faithful to his vocation, prompt and zealous in the performance of every duty, inflexible in principle, but so mild, affable and obliging that in him seemed to have been centered for a time all the reverence and respect of a heterogeneous and frontier people.

Descendants of those served by Samuel Mazzuchelli have kept alive their memory of him and their conviction that he was a saint. In 1993 he was given the title Venerable by Pope John Paul II as a first step toward possible canonization.

Mary Nona McGreal

Bibliography

Armato, Maria Michele, and Mary Jeremy Finnegan. *The Memoirs of Father Samuel Mazzuchelli.* Chicago: Priory Press, 1967.

Bridenbach, Flora. "Samuel Mazzuchelli, Gifted Pioneer of the Midwest." In *Italian Americans and Their Public and Private Life,* edited by Frank J. Cavaioli, Angela Danzi, and Salvatore J. LaGumina, 67–75. New York: American Italian Historical Association, 1993.

McGreal, Mary Nona. *Samuel Mazzuchelli, O.P.: A Kaleidoscope of Scenes from His Life.* Sinsinawa, WI: Mazzuchelli Guild, 1973. Reprint, 1994.

———. "Samuel Mazzuchelli, Participant in

Frontier Democracy." *Records of the American Catholic Historical Society of Philadelphia* (March–December 1976): 99–114.

———. "Wherever God Calls." In *Portraits in American Sanctity,* edited by Joseph Tylenda. Chicago: St. Anthony Press, 1982.

See also EXPLORERS; RELIGION

Medal of Honor Winners

Throughout much of American history, Italian immigrants and their children have fought and died on the battlefields of the nation's wars. Upwards of forty Italian Americans have received the Congressional Medal of Honor since its establishment during the Civil War as the military's highest award for combat valor.

When the Civil War broke out, Italian Americans joined both the Union and Confederate armies. In the North an Italian Legion was formed, which later merged into the multiethnic Garibaldi Guard. The first Italian-born recipient of the Medal of Honor was Private Orlando E. Caruana of the 51st Infantry, who risked his life under heavy fire to rescue the color sergeant and the company colors during a battle at Newburn, North Carolina, in March of 1862. Later that same year, he volunteered for a dangerous scouting mission, in which three of his comrades were killed, at the battle of South Mountain, Maryland.

The most famous recipient of the medal was Colonel Luigi Palma Di Cesnola of the Fourth New York Cavalry. Cesnola had fought for the Sardinian Army in the Crimean War and had joined the Union Army in 1861. During the battle of Aldie, Virginia, in June 1863, Cesnola, while technically under arrest for insubordination, led his troops on four gallant cavalry charges against enemy lines. On the final advance, he was shot from his horse and captured.

The Indian Wars, which lasted over thirty years, found Italian Americans engaged in fierce combat on the Great Plains. Only one, Corporal George Ferrari, originally from New York City, obtained the Medal of Honor for gallantry in action against Apache hostiles at Red Creek, Arizona, in 1869, while attached to the Eighth United States Cavalry.

When war was declared against Spain in April of 1898, Italian Americans joined the thousands of citizens who volunteered for military service. Born and raised in upstate New York, Private Frank O. Fournia of the 21st Infantry garnered the sole Medal of Honor for rescuing wounded men in the front lines during the attack on the El Caney blockhouse at Santiago, Cuba, on July 1, 1898.

During World War I Italian Americans like many other immigrants and their children found their allegiance to America divided by emotional ties to the old country. Italians also faced a serious challenge to their loyalty as native-born Americans began to question the patriotism of ethnic groups on the home front. Despite such attitudes, over three hundred thousand Italian Americans served loyally in the armed forces during the war. One of them, New York Army Private Michael Valente of the 107th Infantry, was awarded the Medal of Honor. When his company was pinned down by German machine guns during the assault on the Hindenburg Line in September 1918, the Italian-born infantryman crawled out of his trench while under intense fire, destroyed three enemy machine-gun emplacements, and captured over forty prisoners. A Sons of Italy lodge in Long Beach, New York, is named after him.

On Sunday morning, December 7, 1941, Japanese torpedo planes attacked Pearl Harbor and plunged the United States into World War II. Although Italy was fighting on the enemy side, Italian Americans remained steadfastly loyal and fully supported the war effort. Over five hundred thousand served in both the Pacific and European theaters. Among the twelve Italian Americans who received the Medal of Honor, the most celebrated winner was Marine Gunnery Sergeant John Basilone. Born in 1916 in Buffalo, New York, Basilone grew up in Raritan, New Jersey, where his immigrant tailor father struggled to support a family of ten children during the Great Depression.

On October 24, 1942, Basilone and other soldiers of the First Marine Division landed on Guadalcanal. As the enemy hammered at the Marines' defensive position, Basilone, manning several heavy machine guns, mowed down wave after wave of Japanese infiltrators, virtually annihilating an entire regiment. So spectacular were his actions that General Douglas MacArthur called him a "one-man army." The immigrant's son returned home a hero. The city of Raritan held a "Basilone Day" complete with a brass band and a parade. He spent several months touring the country on a war-bond drive before he voluntarily returned to combat duty in the fall of 1944. On February 19, 1945, Basilone landed on the black, sandy beaches of Iwo Jima with the Fifth Marine Division. While he assaulted a machine-gun pillbox, a mortar shell exploded nearby and killed him instantly. This final demonstration of courage gained Basilone a posthumous Navy Cross.

Corporal Anthony Casamento of East Harlem, New York, also took part in the invasion of Guadalcanal as part of the First Marine Division. On November 1, 1942, Casamento commanded a machine-gun section during a ferocious engagement with Japanese troops. Every member of his unit was either killed or wounded, and Casamento suffered fourteen severe wounds. Nevertheless, the Marine corporal managed single-handedly to hold off the enemy forces until the main attacking force arrived. Despite his obvious show of valor, Casamento did not win the Medal of Honor because no eyewitness supposedly existed to corroborate his heroics. He was forced to wage a thirty-eight-year battle to receive the decoration, a campaign that proved almost as arduous as his struggles on the bloody island beachhead. With the help of Italian American organizations, which exerted pressure on important political figures, Casamento finally secured the Medal of Honor in 1980.

The Korean War was one of the least popular and most frustrating wars in American history. Classified only as a police action, the war inspired little enthusiasm at home. Yet the American soldier exhibited great courage despite the lack of public support. Of the 131 members of the armed forces who received the Medal of Honor during the Korean conflict, four were Italian Americans. The exploits of one winner, Army Captain Reginald B. Desiderio, commanding officer of Company E, Twenty-seventh Infantry Regiment, were among the most extraordinary. Although wounded six times, the Pennsylvania native rallied his troops to halt an onslaught of thousands of Chinese infantrymen near the Yalu River in the early morning hours of November 27, 1950. During the subsequent fighting, Desiderio personally charged into the enemy attackers, driving them back with a rifle and grenades. As the Chinese finally withdrew, a mortar round mortally wounded Desiderio in his command post.

The war in Vietnam produced tremendous conflict within American society. Italian American communities were not immune to the feelings of discord generated by the war. Faced with these painful divisions, most American combatants still fought bravely in the isolated hamlets and jungles of Southeast Asia. Two hundred and thirty-nine servicemen received the Medal of Honor, eleven of whom were Italian Americans. Yet the award brought them little acclaim or publicity. Being a hero during the Vietnam conflict proved more a burden than a badge of honor since the war was so unpopular. Lewis Albanese was the first Italian American to win the Medal of Honor in Vietnam. Born in Venice, Italy, in 1946, Albanese had migrated to Seattle, Washington, as a young child. In 1965 he was drafted and one year later arrived in Vietnam as a private first class attached to the Seventh Cavalry Regiment. On December 1, 1966, enemy fire ambushed his platoon near the tiny hamlet of Phu Huu. When automatic weapon fire erupted from a nearby ditch, Private Albanese crawled into the trench and silenced six Vietcong snipers with rifle fire and grenades. His ammunition exhausted, Albanese was slain as he killed two more enemy soldiers in hand-to-hand combat. The citation for the Medal of Honor, presented to Albanese's parents, bore testament to one immigrant's heroism, a stellar example of Italian Americans serving their country in wartime.

Aldo E. Salerno

Bibliography
Hardy, Gordon, et al. *Above and Beyond: A History of the Medal of Honor from the Civil War to Vietnam.* Boston: Boston Publishing, 1985.
Murphy, Edward F. *Heroes of World War II.* Novato, CA: Presidio, 1990.
———. *Vietnam Medal of Honor Heroes.* New York: Ballantine, 1987.
Schott, Joseph L. *Above and Beyond: The Story of the Congressional Medal of Honor.* New York: G. P. Putnam's Sons, 1963.

See also WARTIME MILITARY AND HOME FRONT ACTIVITIES

Medical Ethics in Modern America

Modern American medical ethics has emerged as "clinical ethics" over the last third of the twentieth century. Two Italian American physician-ethicists have helped to lead the way: Edmund Pellegrino in patient care and Louis Lasagna in public policy.

Edmund Daniel Pellegrino was born in 1920 to Michael J. and Marie Catone Pellegrino in Newark, New Jersey. Pellegrino's ethics are based on the medical details of the patient's case, his or her values, and the importance of tradition, character, and virtue in the process of healing. Infused with a strong faith in a physician's obligation to help patients, Pellegrino advocates teaching ethical principles to medical students early, supporting ethical behavior by example, and modeling that example in his own work. Practical, case-based, bedside instruction by clinicians, Pellegrino believes, carries the preeminent message: Doing good is the soul of medicine.

Regarded as the foremost physician-ethicist in America, Dr. Pellegrino practices, teaches, ministers, and writes with an unrivaled passion. He draws upon a personal and theological understanding of medicine and envisions medical practice as a calling. He offers humility and kindness to his students, colleagues, and friends, many of whom have visited him as their personal internist.

He has been president and chancellor of universities and medical centers, has received the National Italian American Lifetime Achievement Award, and has been honored with more than forty doctorates worldwide. He has authored or co-authored more than four hundred publications, and authored, co-authored, or edited twelve books. He founded the *Journal of Medicine and Philosophy* in 1976 and wrote *Humanism and the Physician* three years later. He has joined with Professor David Thomasma of Chicago's Loyola University to write *The Philosophical Basis of Medical Practice* (1981), *For the Patient's Good* (1988), and *The Virtues in Medical Practice* (1994).

Dr. Pellegrino has trained a cadre of morally dedicated clinicians and scholars who work in disciplines ranging from anthropology to metaethics to nephrology. As leaders themselves, they carry forth Dr. Pellegrino's rich descriptive nature of how people live, what they value, and why.

Dr. Pellegrino has eight children and lives with Clem, his wife of more than fifty years. He is currently the John Carroll Professor of Medicine and Medical Ethics at Georgetown University in Washington, D.C.

Louis Lasagna, born in 1923, has devoted his career to medical education and the discipline of clinical pharmacology, which he helped to pioneer. Currently dean of the Sackler School of Graduate Biomedical Sciences at Tufts University and distinguished professor at the School of Medicine, he held positions of long tenure at both the University of Rochester and Johns Hopkins University. He is a senior member of the Institute of Medicine and received the American Association for the Advancement of Science Lifetime Mentorship Award in 1995.

Dr. Lasagna has studied medical ethics from the perspective of a clinical researcher and taught it by example, both in the laboratory and in public policy arenas. In 1962, for example, he demonstrated the necessity of placebo-controlled clinical trials and promoted an effectiveness requirement for drugs in the Food, Drug and Cosmetic Act before the United States Congress. His work on the government's Lasagna Committee urged speedy AIDS drug approval in the 1980s, at the height of the epidemic.

Lasagna has been a role model and champion for indigent and minority students. He is lauded by colleagues for his quiet, intuitive sense. He is also the generous, caring father of a handicapped child.

Other Italian Americans have contributed to American medical ethics. In the 1960s Joseph Califano served as secretary of the Department of Health, Education and Welfare and began the war on smoking. Califano sought to protect the rights of nonsmokers, citing the shared costs of illness that result from smoking.

In the late 1960s Guido Calabresi, who rose from immigrant to dean of Yale Law School, wrote "Tragic Choices," which advocated compensation of injured victims of clinical research and elimination of such abuses.

In the 1980s John La Puma became the first postgraduate physician fellow in clinical ethics in the country and published the first empiric study of hospital ethics consultation.

John La Puma

Bibliography

La Puma, John. "Consultation Clinical Ethics: Issues and Questions in 27 Cases." *Western Journal of Medicine* 149 (1987): 633–637.

La Puma, John, and David Schiedermayer. *Ethics Consultation: A Practical Guide.* Boston: Jones and Bartlett, 1994.

M

Pellegrino, Edmund. "Toward a Reconstruction of Medical Morality: The Primacy of the Fact of Profession and the Fact of Illness." *Journal of Medicine and Philosophy* 4 (1979): 32–56.

Pellegrino Edmund, and David Thomasma. *For the Patient's Good.* New York: Oxford University Press, 1988.

See also MEDICINE; PELLEGRINO, EDMUND D.; SCIENCE

Medicine

Italy and its people have long been innovators in the field of medical science. Throughout the history of the Western world, research centers and educational institutions in Italy, Catholic hospitals in America, and individuals of Italian descent have all contributed to the advancement of medicine.

Although medicine was not considered as a profession of high prestige in ancient Rome, medical knowledge found a home in the medieval monastery, beginning with the monastic schools of the Benedictine order at the end of the sixteenth century. The School of Salerno and later Bologna acquired outstanding reputations. Salerno, in assimilating the translations from Arabic medical authors in the eleventh century, became a renowned center for medical theory and practice. By the late thirteenth century, the school at Bologna achieved high status as its masters introduced sophisticated Aristotelian natural science and philosophy. The works of a famous physician and lecturer of ancient Rome, Galen, were reinterpreted along with the Canon of Avicenna (980–1037). Surgical works, anatomical dissection of the human cadaver, and case analysis were all introduced at this early time in medical history.

Sicily was the site of some of the first attempts at licensure. Similarly, colleges of physicians, distinct from the university medical faculties and the guilds and vested with licensing authority, emerged in the university towns of northern Italy beginning with Pisa, Bologna, and Milan in the fourteenth century. In fact, the Italian cities of this modern period often had between five and ten medical doctors per ten thousand inhabitants, and even rural areas in Tuscany had university-trained doctors supported by public funds. By contrast, other European urban centers, such as Paris and London, had only two physicians per ten thousand inhabitants and virtually none in the countryside.

Medical professionalization shifted to the centers of London and Paris during the Enlightenment, and to Germany and finally the United States by the late nineteenth century. Beginning in the 1870s and extending until the outbreak of World War I, as many as fifteen thousand American physicians pursued postgraduate studies in the German-speaking world—the foremost center for science and medicine. After World War II Italy (especially Bologna) became the site in which thousands of American students studied for their medical degrees, returning to the United States to get clinical training and certification in hospitals and cities of their choice. This trend ceased by 1980.

Italian American Physicians

Prior to the Civil War, several Italian names are found within the recorded history of medicine in the United States. In New York City, the most famous is Philip Mazzei (1730–1816), who became better known as a philosopher who influenced colonial America. By training, however, he was a surgeon after studying in Florence, and practiced surgery in Smyrna, Delaware, and in Albemarle County, Virginia. He impressed Benjamin Franklin with his philosophy and scientific knowledge, and in 1771, George Washington and Thomas Jefferson commissioned Mazzei to conduct experiments to develop such crops as grapes and olives on their plantations.

The first Italian American physician in the United States was probably Dr. Francis Bertody who graduated from the University of Padua, married an American, and became a citizen in 1788. Records show that Dr. George Alberti lived on Mulberry Street in 1791. The first sons of Italian immigrants to graduate as physicians from an American college were Drs. Joseph Mauran and Charles Grahl Da Ponte (son of the famous librettist).

Dr. Felix Formento (1837–1907) was born in New Orleans and became one of the most prominent surgeons in the South, serving as chief surgeon of the Louisiana Hospital in Richard. During the Civil War, Dr. Tullio Suzzara Verdi was personal physician to Secretary of State William Seward, a member of Lincoln's cabinet.

Several other Italian Americans became prominent during the late nineteenth century, including Drs. Remondino, Ravogli, Masi, Festorazzi, and Mazzuri. Dr. Charles Imperatori, born in New York City in 1878, was professor of laryngology at Columbia University and president of the American Laryngological Association.

Hospitals

The first hospitals in the United States were charity or "almshouses"; among them, Catholic hospitals were widespread. By the midtwentieth century almost a thousand Catholic hospitals were handling some 16 million patients a year.

There were two Italian hospitals in New York City alone by the turn of the twentieth century. In 1889 Mother Frances Xavier Cabrini and six missionary sisters were sent to New York to help immigrants settle in America. She established an orphanage for sick children and the Columbus Hospital in 1892 to care for sick immigrants denied adequate health care. The hospital had insufficient beds, running water, and supplies. Patients received meals from local restaurants, and physicians contributed their time and equipment. The hospital treated thousands of Italians injured in industrial accidents or suffering from other occupational injuries that were common at the time. She also built a Catholic hospital in Chicago in 1899, treating thousands of patients and educating thousands of nurses in subsequent years. The Cabrini Medical Center celebrated its one hundredth anniversary in 1992.

The Catholic archdioceses and dioceses in the United States run over two hundred hospitals and hundreds of nursing homes. This vast and significant network of hospitals has led the way in providing advanced technological research and procedures. These hospitals have also been recognized for their resources in providing quality geriatric and long-term care services to patients denied the necessary services by other cost-driven health providers.

Progress of Italian Americans in Medicine

Modern medicine became more viable with discoveries in experimental physiology, pathology, and bacteriology. More recent advances in genetic and pharmacological research, immunology, cardiology, oncology, and X-ray procedures helped establish the technological age in medicine. Americans, including countless Italian Americans, have been at the forefront of these developments. But it was not until barriers of discrimination were broken, and Italian Americans received postgraduate and professional degrees, that their contributions could be possible.

Despite a long history of medical knowledge and scholarly developments in Italy, American medical professionalization (particularly the academic elite, implanted in the modern medical school and in the university research and teaching hospitals) did not include Italian Americans. Discrimination against ethnic and religious minorities took the form of quotas restricting their entry into medical schools, exclusion from medical societies, and denial of hospital privileges even to the few who managed to qualify. The few Italian Americans before 1960 who managed to open private practices were affiliated primarily with the Catholic hospitals in major cities or practiced in their own ethnic communities. (These institutions of Catholic affiliation had lower prestige at that time and were open to minorities of all faiths.)

Research on discrimination of Italian Americans in medicine addresses the nature of the profession: its elite status, closed network, rigid academic requirements, and early age recruitment are all reasons for the exclusion of Italian Americans to the profession. Italian American physicians are still underrepresented in the Northeast region. Data has revealed that as the prestige of the medical school increases, the number of Italian Americans attending decreases. This is due more to the structure of the profession, in which major medical schools recruit from specific undergraduate schools exclusively, rarely taking into account the personal attributes of the student. So far, Italian Americans, even to date, are highly underrepresented in the academic elite institutions.

Women in medicine have traditionally served as nurses and midwives. However, since the 1970s women in general and Italian American women in particular have gained access to more medical schools across the nation. Currently, more Italian American women than their male counterparts are attending prestigious institutions. Today, most schools boast over 50 percent female candidates.

It was not intellectual curiosity alone that motivated Italian American physicians to organize a professional society. On May 11, 1899, the first Italian Medical Society of the city of New York was formed for "good fellowship and brotherly feeling." The medical directors of the corporation were David A. Casella, Antonio Pisani, Marco Luzzato, John Aquaro, and John B. Corsiglia. This society became the Italian Physicians' Society of America on September 20, 1921, and the Italian Medical Society of New York on February 13, 1942. Today it is known as the Morgagni Society after the famous Italian anatomist and the father of pathology, Giovanni Battista Morgagni (1682–1771).

Graduates of Italian Medical Schools (GIMS) is also located in New York and, along with the Morgagni Society, services all physicians. Meetings promote social and professional interests including lectures, seminars, trips, and dinners. Members generally support each other in their careers, in gaining hospital privileges, referrals, advancement in their fields, and general networking. These organizations have served its members well in the all too exclusionary environment of the medical establishment. A review of several medical, science, and hospital directories reveals that Italian Americans are located in every subspecialty of medicine, engaged as private physicians, researchers and scholars, professors at teaching hospitals, health administrators, and government officials.

Rosanne Martorella

Clinical Medicine

The progression of the Italian American physician from small community doctor to laboratory scientist-clinical specialist back to primary care physician is remarkable for its rapidity and for the odds against professional advancement from the start.

A small percentage of Italian Americans, in proportion to the number who have resided in the United States, are or have been physicians. In the eighteenth, nineteenth, and early twentieth centuries the absence of a tradition of achievement and the presence of language and cultural barriers combined to keep many immigrants away from medical school and medical practice. By the mid-1950s, there were still not more than five thousand Italian American physicians.

Yet as prejudice slowly gave way to tolerance, Italian Americans' scientific achievement took the place of their physical work

and neighborhood storefront businesses. By the late twentieth century, second- and third-generation Italian American physicians had earned international public acclaim.

The history of Italian Americans in medicine is made up of Italian Americans who struggled against numerous obstacles to become physicians and who were imbued with an inexorable work ethic.

Francis Bertody, who lived in the eighteenth century, is reported to have been the first Italian American physician. He trained in Padua before becoming an American citizen in 1788.

A Dr. De Angelis, who emigrated in 1798 and settled in New York, like many practitioners of his time mixed pharmacy and medicine. He advertised in the May 18, 1816, *New York Evening Post* for "anti-rheumatic and anti-syphilitic syrups" to "correct the altered humours, and in consequence, prevent[ing] the consumption."

Joseph Maruan (17??–1873) is reported to have been the first son of Italian immigrants to graduate from an American college of medicine. Dr. Maruan graduated from the New York College of Physicians and Surgeons in 1819 and took a prominent role in Rhode Island in organized medicine and public health.

Tullio Verdi (1829–1902) emigrated from Sardinia and rose from poverty to become the first Italian immigrant to graduate from an American college of medicine. He eventually became the personal physician of Secretary of State William Seward. After the Civil War he helped organize the Homeopathic Hospital in Washington, D.C.

In the nineteenth century Felix Formento (1837–1907) was born in New Orleans but trained in Piedmont at the University of Turin and in Paris, where he studied surgery. He returned to New Orleans in 1860, where he served during the Civil War and practiced for more than forty years.

Antonio Lagorio (1857–1944) attended Rush Medical College and founded the Chicago Pasteur Institute in 1890. He also earned a doctorate of laws from Loyola University in Chicago, becoming one of the first Italian Americans to earn both medical and legal degrees.

Annina Carmilla Rondinella (1865–1949) graduated from the Women's Medical College in Philadelphia in 1899 and is considered to be the first Italian American woman to receive an American medical degree. She achieved considerable advancement in academic medicine at the Women's Medical College and, on her death, was a consulting ophthalmologist emeritus at Wellesley College.

Paolo de Vecchi migrated to the United States to study orthopedic surgery after the Franco-Prussian war. He settled in San Francisco until a 1905 move to New York, where he lived until his death in 1931.

Late in the twentieth century, Leonard Cerullo, a Chicago neurosurgeon, developed the use of lasers in clinical neurosurgical work and, in the 1980s, founded the Chicago Institute of Neurosurgery and Neuroresearch.

Renato Dulbecco, a classmate of Rita Levi-Montalcini, won the Nobel Prize for his work on the carcinogenic effects of viruses. He migrated to the University of Indiana at Bloomington and completed his career there.

Anthony Fauci, born in 1940 in Brooklyn, grew up in Bensonhurst. He is currently director of the National Institute of Allergy and Infectious Diseases and formerly director of the Office of AIDS Research. In the 1970s and 1980s he helped develop effective immunosuppressive therapies against connective tissue diseases such as polyarteritis nodosa. Dr. Fauci works the thin line between the desperation of AIDS patients and the inadequacy of science to answer political and moral questions.

Robert Gallo, born in 1937, identified the human T-cell viral cause of leukemia in 1978, and co-discovered the AIDS virus, with Dr. Luc Montagnier of France, in 1984. The public controversy surrounding the AIDS virus identification and an initial blood test for the virus were not resolved until the 1990s, when the two men agreed to share credit. Gallo is now at the University of Maryland's Institute for Human Virology in Baltimore.

Margaret Giannini surmounted the barriers of gender and culture to become one of the most beloved pediatricians in America. She founded and directed the Mental Retardation Institute in Harlem in 1950, and her work with handicapped children broadened into adult rehabilitation in later decades.

Antonio Gotto, born in 1935, is among the world's leaders in lipid research. Co-chairman of the United States–Italian Cardiovascular Working Group of the National Heart, Lung, and Blood Institute, and chair-

man of medicine at Baylor, he has lectured in Milan on the training of Italian physicians in the United States. His *Chez Eddy Living Heart Cookbook* won a James Beard Foundation Award of Excellence in 1992.

Louis Lasagna, born in 1923, is currently dean of the Sackler School of Graduate Biomechanical Sciences at Tufts University School of Medicine in Boston. He has been keenly interested in the drug regulatory and development process and started the first academic group devoted solely to clinical pharmacology at Johns Hopkins University, Baltimore, in the 1950s.

Rita Levi-Montalcini, born in 1909 in Turin, Italy, shared the 1986 Nobel Prize in physiology or medicine for identifying nerve growth factor and describing how tumors can change the way nerves grow. Her singular passion for research surmounted extremely poor lab conditions, World War I Italian anti-Semitism, and the war itself. She traveled regularly between Italy and the United States until her retirement from Washington University in St. Louis in 1977 and her laboratory in Rome in 1979. She became a United States citizen in 1956.

Cesare Lombroso was professor of forensic medicine and pathology at Harvard. He sustained a continued, scholarly interest in the medical home remedy traditions of the Italian family.

Salvador Luria (1912–1991), also a classmate of Levi-Montalcini's, won the 1969 Nobel Prize for work detailing the microbial aspects of infection. Like Dulbecco, he immigrated to the United States, taking a post at the University of Indiana at Bloomington.

George Mora earned his medical degree in Italy in the 1940s and trained in psychiatry. He has done scholarly work in the history of psychiatry and on the life of Vincenzo Chiarugi, the famous Italian psychiatrist.

Giuseppi Moruzzi, like Luria and colleagues, migrated to the United States in the 1940s and took a position at Northwestern University after 1942. His studies of wakefulness and sleep focused attention on the reticular apparatus of the brainstem.

Edmund Pellegrino, born in 1920, is currently the John Carroll Professor of Medicine and Medical Ethics at Georgetown University in Washington, D.C. During Dr. Pellegrino's fifty years in medicine and university administration, he has been departmental chairman, dean, and university president. A master of

M

the American College of Physicians and a member of the Institute of Medicine, Pellegrino has trained both physicians and philosophers in medical and graduate programs, fostering a virtues-centered approach to medical practice. Centered in professional ethics and the physician-patient relationship, Pellegrino's model of the good doctor is one who takes personal care of the patient.

John La Puma

Bibliography

Bordley, James. *Two Centuries of American Medicine, 1776–1976.* Philadelphia: Saunders, 1976.

Duffy, John. *From Humor to Medical Science: A History of American Medicine,* 2nd edition. Urbana: University of Illinois Press, 1993.

Krase, Suzanne. "An Ounce of Prevention: Community Health and Italian American Women." *Italian Americans and Their Public and Private Life,* edited by Frank J. Cavaioli, Angela Danzi, and Salvatore J. LaGumina, 107–115. New York: American Italian Historical Association, 1993.

Kraut, Alan M. *Silent Travelers: Germs, Genes, and the "Immigrant Menace."* New York: Basic Books, 1995.

Kristeller, Paul O. "The School of Salerno: Its Development and Its Contribution to the History of Learning," *Bulletin of the History of Medicine* 17 (1945): 138–194.

Martorella, Rosanne, and Patricia Perri Rieker. "A Sociological Profile of Italian Americans in Medical Education." In *The Melting Pot and Beyond: Italian-Americans in the Year 2000,* edited by Jerome Krase and William Egelman, 151–165. New York: American Italian Historical Association, 1987.

Pane, Remigio U., ed. *Italian Americans in the Professions.* New York: American Italian Historical Association, 1983.

Schiavo, Giovanni. *Four Centuries of Italian American History,* 3rd ed. New York: Vigo Press, 1954.

Siraisi, Nancy. *Taddeo Alderotti and His Pupils.* Princeton: Princeton University Press, 1981.

Starr, Paul. *The Social Transformation of American Medicine.* New York: Basic Books, 1983.

See also DULBECCO, RENATO; FAUCI, ANTHONY STEPHEN; GALLO, ROBERT CHARLES; GIANNINI, MARGARET; LEVI-MONTALCINI, RITA; LURIA, SALVADOR EDWARD; MEDICAL ETHICS IN MODERN AMERICA; PELLEGRINO, EDMUND DANIEL; SCIENCE

Melfi, Leonard
See PLAYS, CONTEMPORARY

Menotti, Gian Carlo (b. 1911)

Renowned composer, born in Cadegliano, Italy, the sixth of ten children of a well-to-do businessman, Gian Carlo Menotti learned the basics of music from his mother, an amateur musician. After attempting to compose an opera at age 10, he was sent to further his obvious talents at the Milan Conservatory (1924–1927). In 1928 he moved to the United States and studied at the Curtis Institute in Philadelphia. It was there he met fellow student and future distinguished composer Samuel Barber (1910–1981), who became a close friend for many years.

Though he resided in America, he also traveled extensively in Europe. While in Vienna, he started his first serious opera, *Amelia al Ballo* (Amelia Goes to the Ball), which was successfully performed in Philadelphia in 1937 and later at the Metropolitan Opera in New York. This soon led to a commissioned opera, *The Old Maid and the Thief,* broadcast on NBC radio in 1939 and later (1941) staged in Philadelphia. A number of operas followed, including *The Island God* (1942), *The Medium* (1946), *The Telephone* (1947), *The Consul* (1950), *Amahl and the Night Visitors* (1951), *The Saint of Bleecker Street* (1954), *Maria Golovin* (1958), *Le dernier sauvage* (1963), *Help, Help the Gobolinks!* (1968), and *The Most Important Man* (1971). Of these works the most outstanding were *Amelia, The Medium,* and *Amahl,* a charming annual Christmas television favorite, and the more powerful and substantial *Consul* and *Bleecker Street,* both of which won the Pulitzer Prize in music as well as other honors.

Menotti also wrote orchestral works, ballets, cantatas, and other pieces. His ballets include *Errand into the Maze* (1947), *The Unicorn, the Gorgon, and the Manticore* (1956), and best of all, *Sebastian* (1944). One lively and melodic theme from *Sebastian* caught on with audiences and led to Menotti's creation of a 1947 orchestral suite derived from the ballet. Menotti also was a librettist, writing the stories for his own operas and for two of Barber's, *Vanessa* (1958) and *A Hand of Bridge* (1959). Like Barber, his music is traditional, melodic, tonal, and conservative. It is sometimes criticized as sentimental and dull. But his works, most notably the opera medium which he favored and in which he excelled, were accessible, humane, and when staged possess a true sense of the theater. He has continued to compose into the 1990s, though moving to Scotland in 1974 after almost a half century of artistic success in the United States.

William E. Studwell

Bibliography

Ardoin, John. *The Stages of Menotti.* Garden City, NY: Doubleday, 1985.

Grieb, Lyndal. *The Operas of Gian Carlo Menotti, 1937–1972: A Selective Bibliography.* Metuchen, NJ: Scarecrow, 1974.

Gruen, John. *Menotti: A Biography.* New York: Macmillan, 1978.

Studwell, William E., and David A. Hamilton. *Opera Plot Index: A Guide to Locating Plots and Descriptions of Operas, Operettas, and Other Works of the Musical Theater and Associated Material.* New York: Garland, 1990.

Tricoire, Robert. *Gian Carlo Menotti, l'homme et son oeuvre.* Paris: Seghers, 1966.

See also COMPOSERS, CLASSICAL; OPERA

Mental Health

Many young professionals express discomfort with their Italian American identity and feel unaccepted in the outside world. Yet, compared with other ethnic groups, Italian Americans, who have acculturated more slowly, have a stronger sense of who they are. It has taken most Italian American families three to four generations to have "made it"; for Jewish Americans, it often took one generation to go from poor immigrant parents to college graduates. Despite their rise into the middle class and the professions, Italian Americans often feel inferior, in part because of historical prejudice, internalization of stereotypes ("not being smart"), continued influence of a working-class lifestyle, and lack of familial support for their aspirations.

When a group of young professionals was asked about their negative associations with being Italian American, they replied, "not intellectual, not educated or cultured, crude, woman always home cooking, physical and manual, inarticulate." Positive included "emotional, warm, good provider, hard worker, family-oriented, hospitable, giving." Today many young Italian Americans are carrying those values of tradition and family identity into the workplace. As one professional stated, "I can't work in a place where I can't create the feeling of family."

For many, ethnic ambivalence is expressed via relationships with the opposite sex. In ethnotherapy groups, members of each gender attribute negative stereotypes to the other. Men's perception of women still reflects a wish for the traditional role ("women as mothers, cooks") and anger at both old behaviors ("smothering or controlling") and the new, more assertive roles as educated professionals. While intellectually acknowledging domination is no longer an acceptable way to relate to women, they generally have been unable to modify their behavior. Women verbalize a greater resentment and anger toward the traditional male role of domination and assumed superiority, and are indignant about their unequal status in the family. Women no longer want to be subjected to an unequal status.

Italian Americans today seek out relationships with non-Italians in greater numbers than ever before. Research by Richard Alba (1985) has shown that over 80 percent are marrying someone of a different ethnicity.

For Italians, family is an all-consuming ideal as is expressed by Luigi Barzini, among many others. For Italian Americans, "families" usually include grandparents, whose influence on family life can be great. As repositories of traditional values, they are often involved in family conflicts, sometimes actively taking sides or reinforcing "traditional values."

L'ordine della familia, which connotes precise boundaries, role expectations, and clear values for right and wrong behavior, is taught at a very early age and includes:

M

Always respecting parents and grandparents;

Placing family needs first, staying physically and psychologically close to other members;

Not talking about the family to outsiders;

Sometimes maintaining secrets between family members to maintain personal boundaries; other family members do not need to know everything, particularly if it will cause harm;

Showing respect for authority outside of the family, but not trusting it; and

Working hard, but also enjoying life; living well is sharing food, music, and companionship with those one loves.

For most first- and second-generation Italian Americans, this concept provides a strong sense of security and identity; for others, it stifles their individual needs and delays their assimilation with American values. Still, even some third- and fourth-generation Italian Americans return home at a time of a personal crisis—divorce, separation, loss of job, illness—to live with their parents for extended periods of time.

Italian American children are taught early about the importance of familial ties and loyalty. A 75-year-old second-generation woman notes: "I have always taught my children the most important thing is [to] love each other. If I gave them nothing else, that is one thing I drummed into their heads—family." When this woman's sister became a widow, her oldest nephew bought a two-family house so that mother and son could live close to each other. When the mother's own husband died, she went to live with each son for six months a year.

Today, however, most couples need to work to raise a family; parents live longer and sometimes need custodial and nursing home care when they become ill. Non-Italian American spouses also may not share their partners' values ("taking care of your own"). Thus, for today's Italian Americans, decreased physical access to extended family may cause great stress. While taking pride in their children's mobility, traditional Italian Americans still send strong messages that they want their children to "stay close."

Therapists should see positive impulses in negative family dynamics, sometimes by reframing and relabeling dysfunctional patterns.

Labeling intense involvement between Italian American family members as "intrusive and inappropriate" and quickly intervening to change it may only increase the family's anxiety and resistance. Rather, therapists might first note that such behavior is a positive expression of mutual caring within the family.

Traditionally, Italian Americans have avoided seeking mental health services. If a serious problem arises, they try to handle it themselves, often attempting to manipulate or modify the situation. If that is ineffective, they usually turn to the nuclear family, then the extended family, and finally "approved" outsiders connected with it (a family physician, priest, or civic leader). Professional help is often only used following a referral for a child-centered problem.

When obtaining professional help, Italian Americans often do not complete treatment. Once the pain that brought them into therapy is relieved, they see no reason to continue. Also, there often is a cultural incompatibility between the Italian American patient and therapist. The patient may feel misunderstood or inadequate in what the therapist expects of him or her.

First- and second-generation Italians sometimes feel that the needs of others are self-evident, so there is little need to explain everything. What Barzini describes as "the importance of spectacle where everything is displayed everywhere in dramatic and artistic disorder," remains integral to the Italian American character. Some families, achieve "operatic" heights with emotive displays (loudness, shouting, arguing, gesturing melodramatically) that "signal" to the therapist the need to relieve emotional pain. The clinician may have trouble determining whether he or she is actually facing a crisis that needs immediate attention or acting out an expressive style around a less serious problem.

Particularly in working-class families, violent expressions—"I'll break your legs or I'll kill you if you ever do that again"—are not meant literally, but are used as expressions of anger or displeasure. Warm feelings are often expressed in nonverbal ways, for example, touching or hugging. Anger may be expressed physically, as in hitting or slapping children. Sometimes, emotionality becomes a way to control others' behavior by "smothering with affection" or "instilling fear."

Yet Italian Americans can often be quite vague in giving overly detailed narratives of how a problem began and describing the emotional and physical sensations (somatization) they are experiencing. While Anglo-Americans in physical or emotional pain emphasize their inability to function and Jewish Americans articulate their fear of pain's implications for longevity, Italians emphasize their pain experience and wish for immediate relief.

Particularly challenging for third- and fourth-generation families is the need to renegotiate individuals' boundaries to gain greater self-differentiation, without causing harm to others or cutting off relationships. Therapists do well to encourage Italian Americans to negotiate their individuality within the family, even though this is usually a complicated, painful process, for they can pay a high price for emotional disconnection.

Yet even a suggestion of separation may be a "red flag." Indeed, normal separations related to life-cycle changes—a job promotion, acceptance by an out-of-town college, or getting married—can become a source of conflict, leading parents often to "hold back" feelings of pride in their children's accomplishments. Conversely, offspring may become angry at their parents' lack of "shared joy" over their success. The therapist often must help the Italian American family avoid "enmeshment," which can be difficult because some families "team up" to resist the child's efforts.

For example, an Italian American family may reject a discharge plan for a young psychiatric patient that involves his or her separating from parents. Arranging for the patient to live on a separate floor within a house, or establishing some other territorial and emotional boundaries, may be a necessary first step in patiently working with family desires and values.

Caring for terminally ill members in a hospice is culturally compatible for Italian American families. While they may initially resist bringing a "stranger" into the house, the way a hospice functions is congruous with traditional value of "taking care of our own and not placing them in an institution to die."

The Italian American family can also become extremely preoccupied about ill members, ruminating daily about the state of affairs. Underlying this is a real fear of loss and separation, as well as feelings of guilt, self-blame, and anxiety. The family will also frequently make many demands that the therapist relieve its discomforts and mobilize it to take concrete action, thus lending family members a greater sense of control.

As an "outsider," the therapist must expect mistrust. While the client is generally polite, verbally engaging, and deferential, he or she can also be suspicious and cautious, watchful for clues that indicate the therapist is trustworthy. The therapist may experience "a wall of resistance" when families referred by a school or court feel that treatment is "punishment" and that they must "tolerate it." They may sabotage treatment by never actually participating.

Therapists do well to curtail probing before trust is established. Some families interpret extensive questioning as an implication that they are "not smart enough," rather than a way to "get at the truth" or "gain insight." Because parents are more receptive to assistance for their children, joining the family around a child-focused problem may help break through family resistance.

Yet Italian Americans ultimately expect relationships to be open, friendly, and reciprocal, even with authority figures. In early sessions, the therapist sometimes can build trust by being authentically self-disclosing about common values. Therapists who do not respond in this way may appear to patients as being "cold and distant."

Families may also ask therapists to demonstrate loyalty by helping them deal with a bureaucracy. Rather than view this request as "inappropriate," they can show concern by exploring with the family how its needs can be met. Similarly, a client or family that seems to be acting "seductively" by bringing the therapist a home-cooked meal or other gift may be trying to "connect" or show appreciation in a personal way.

Characteristically, "hot issues" are not openly discussed among Italians. It is particularly important for therapists to attend to what is *not* being said. Italian families often "sidestep" key issues early in therapy, which reflects their unwillingness to expose private matters to outsiders.

The therapist should reinforce the idea that the individual or family has the means to solve its own problems. He or she might acknowledge and appreciate traditional values of protection, loyalty, respect, authority, hierarchy, and spirituality, as well as its attributes of hard work, warmth, and spontaneity.

M

Even among pathological individuals and dysfunctional families, these values may be integral to members' personal and group identity. Through alliances and kept secrets, family subgroups set boundaries, thus providing needed "breathing space," so that two or more individuals can remain close while keeping a distance from the rest of the family. This neutralizing of a family's engulfing nature may seem "dysfunctional" to therapists unfamiliar with Italian American culture.

Secrets may persist, although a family seems to talk openly about many intimate issues, including sex and bodily functions as well as feelings of hostility. Italian American families may feel a sense of betrayal if their boundaries are crossed.

When it becomes evident that parents are going to maintain basic family secrets, the therapist's strategy shifts to helping each of them take firm parental control of their own children so as not to let them "act out" anger toward one parent or the other, thus relieving pressure on the family system.

The Italian American therapist can over-identify with Italian patients or become ensnared in his or her own unresolved ethnic issues. One therapist shares her experience of getting "lured" back into a system she thought she left behind many years ago:

> When I told her [the patient] in the beginning that we had similar backgrounds, she moved away from me saying that her Italian background was "unusual" and never inquiring about mine. *Her family system and her secretiveness were so close to my own ethnic identity, that it was acceptable to me and I could barely see it.* I recognized so many things from my own early childhood—speech inflections, words, foods, primitive ideas such as the "evil eye" *(malocchio)* and the horn *(cornuto)* for protection against it— that I shared with her a delicious sense of "our thing" *(cosa nostra).* To some extent, I never went into this ethnic core with my patient.

When an individual or family is "in crisis," the therapist should respond to the problem and avoid lengthy discussions or evaluations. Even a seemingly insignificant suggestion might "hold" a family until more subtle and enduring interventions can be de-termined. However, it is essential not to offer advice that undercuts a family's authority.

The idea of "resolving" a problem in an Italian American household often consists of relieving stress without changing the equilibrium within an individual's family; therapy often means "getting things back to normal." However, many in the third and fourth generation are willing to be more introspective and take greater risks in therapy.

Joseph Giordano

Bibliography

Alba, Richard. *Italian Americans into the Twilight of Ethnicity.* Englewood Cliffs, NJ: Prentice Hall, 1985.

Barzini, Luigi. *The Italians.* New York: Atheneum, 1964.

Crohn, Joel. *Mixed Matches—How to Create Successful Interracial Interethnic and Interfaith Marriages.* New York: Fawcett, 1995.

Giordano, Joe, Monica McGoldrick, and Marie Rotond. "Italian Families." In *Ethnicity and Family Therapy,* 2nd ed., edited by Monica McGoldrick, Joe Giordano, and John Pearce. New York: Guilford Press, 1996.

Papajohn, John, and John Spiegel. *Transactions in Families.* San Francisco: Jossey-Bass, 1975.

Rolle, Andrew. *The Italian American: Troubled Roots.* New York: The Free Press, 1980.

Selvini Palazzoli, Mara, Stefano Cirillo, Matteo Selvini, and Anna Maria Sorrentino. *Family Games.* New York: Norton, 1989.

Sirey, Aileen, Anthony Patti, and Lisa Mann. *Ethnotherapy—An Exploration of Italian-American Identity.* New York: National Institute for the Psychotherapies, 1985.

See also FAMILY LIFE

Mercante, Arthur L. (b. 1920)

An internationally renowned professional boxing referee, Arthur L. Mercante had worked over one hundred world championship bouts by 1966. Several of them are considered to have major historical and sociological significance. He has refereed thousands of other fights in the United States and abroad. Mercante was born in Brockton, Massachusetts, on January 20, 1920. His uncle, Joe Monte, was a professional boxer and brought Arthur to training camps, where he conversed with and watched outstanding boxers, such as world heavyweight champions Max Schmeling and Jack Sharkey. Several pugilists trained in Bedford-Stuyvesant, Brooklyn, where his family moved during his childhood. These role models were emulated when he entered the Golden Gloves as a welterweight during the late 1930s. He graduated from New York University in June 1942 with a B.S. degree.

He served in the United States Navy as a physical education instructor at Norfolk, Virginia, under the command of former heavyweight champion Gene Tunney, attaining the rank of chief specialist. Italian American former middleweight champion Fred Apostoli was a Navy contemporary whom he admired and with whom he trained. After the war, he earned an M.A. in health and physical education from New York University. He became boxing coach at the United States Merchant Marine Academy. His refereeing career began at a time when a number of Italian Americans were prominent as judges, managers, trainers, and attending physicians.

Mercante officiated his first professional contest in a preliminary bout at Brooklyn's Eastern Parkway Arena in 1953 on a card headlined by future heavyweight champion Floyd Patterson. When Patterson regained that title from Sweden's Ingemar Johansson in 1960, Mercante was the referee. Another of his milestones was "Sugar Ray" Robinson's final appearance at Madison Square Garden when young Denny Moyer earned a unanimous decision over the aging master.

Heavyweight championship fights are among the greatest spectacles in sports. Mercante refereed the first Muhammad Ali–Joe Frazier fight (1971), the second Ali–Patterson contest (1972), the third Ali–Norton fight (1976), and the bout between Mike Tyson and Tony Tubbs (1988). He considers the Frazier–Ali unification title fight the most socially significant because each man had been both an Olympic and a professional champion, and it epitomized a classic boxer versus slugger confrontation. Mercante maintains that the referee should be the ultimate judge in fights because of his proximity to the action.

Mercante married Gloria Oggiano in 1955, and the couple has four sons. He serves as Deputy Commissioner of Parks and Recreation, Town of Hempstead, Long Island, New York. In 1995, he was inducted into the International Boxing Hall of Fame in Canastota, New York.

Richard Renoff

Bibliography

Matthews, Wallace. "Call Him King Arthur." *New York Post,* 18 January 1995.

Roberts, James B., and Alexander G. Skutt, comp. *The Boxing Register: International Boxing Hall of Fame Official Record Book.* Ithaca, NY: McBooks Press, 1997.

See also SPORTS

Meucci, Antonio (1808–1889)

Italian American mechanical electrician considered by some to be the inventor of the telephone, Antonio Meucci was born at San Frediano near Florence, the son of Amatis and Domenica Pepe Meucci. He majored in drawing and mechanical engineering at the Florentine Academy of Fine Arts. Employed by various theaters in Italy, he became superintendent of mechanism and scenic designer at the Tacon Theater in Havana, Cuba (1835). Interested in electricity, he opened an electroplating business, used electric shock therapy to treat the ill, and began working on the "speaking telegraph" or *teletrofono.*

In 1850, after the Tacon Theater burned, Meucci departed for New York. He settled on Staten Island, then a thinly populated summer resort, and engaged in various businesses from candle making (he briefly employed Giuseppe Garibaldi) to brewing. All profits were spent on continuing experimentation with an instrument that could convey the human voice by electric wire over considerable distances. He improvised a line between his partially paralyzed wife's bedroom and his laboratory (1855), publicly demonstrated his apparatus when a young man sang over the line (1860), and published a description of his instrument in the New York newspaper *L'Eco d'Italia.*

For the next decade, the Florentine was plagued by a dishonest partner, fires, injury in an explosion, and an inability to find financial backers. Fearing that someone would

M

copy his invention, he wanted to apply for a patent. Unable to pay the attorney's fee, he settled for a caveat: a one-year notice of impending patent, on December 28, 1871. He hurriedly approached a Western Union affiliate to test his instrument in its laboratory, but the company did nothing. Two years later, it informed him that his models and papers were lost. Discouraged and unable to afford the ten dollar renewal fee, Meucci let the caveat lapse in 1874.

On February 14, 1876, Alexander Graham Bell, who had conducted experiments in the same Western Union laboratory where Meucci's materials had been stored, applied for a telephone patent. A startled Meucci inquired at the patent office about his caveat, but all papers related to the "speaking telegraph" had mysteriously disappeared. Knowing that millions of dollars were at stake, Meucci and his newfound supporters, including the U.S. government, initiated action to contest the validity of Bell's patent and the consequent monopoly of the American Bell Telephone Company. Meucci testified and presented extant documentation to verify his experiments but the court decided in Bell's favor on July 19, 1887.

When he died destitute two years later, the *New York World* called Meucci "one of the most important figures in the scientific world of the times." Throughout his lifetime he had taken out thirty caveats and patents, among them preparation of hydrocarbons for paint, treatment of vegetable fiber for paper pulp, manufacture of effervescent drinks, and development of a hygrometer. Although he was an American citizen, the Italian government paid for his funeral and cremation. The ashes were deposited in a monument made of marble, offered by the city of Rome, and bronze from captured Austrian cannon. It was erected near his modest Staten Island house (1923). The house became the Garibaldi-Meucci Memorial Museum in 1956.

James J. Divita

Bibliography

Schiavo, Giovanni E. *Antonio Meucci, Inventor of the Telephone.* New York: Vigo Press, 1958.

Winwar, Frances. "Meucci, Garibaldi, and the Telephone." *La Parola del Popolo* (September/October 1976): 170–178.

See also PATENTS AND INVENTORS

Midwives and Childbirth

The midwife was one of the most integral and familiar figures in Italian American communities, and despite a determined campaign by medical specialists to discredit the foreign-born or foreign-ancestry midwife, many Italian American women maintained a preference for her services well into the 1930s.

Midwives have been used throughout European history, but the tradition of midwifery endured much longer in Italy, probably because the Catholic Church and later the state, in varying degrees, sanctioned and regulated her role, and because of the longstanding aversion of the populace to the involvement of men in obstetrics.

Mario Scipione, author of *La Comare o Ricoglitrice,* published in 1596, one of the earliest midwifery manuals written in the Italian vernacular, describes the midwife as gentle, kind, and nurturing; she was called *comare,* or *mammana,* words derived from *mater* or mother. From at least the Council of Trent (1546) the Catholic Church granted the midwife official status as having the right to baptize. A widely used manual for midwives, written in 1746 by a Catholic priest, combined scientific and religious instruction, emphasizing midwives' solemn responsibility for the soul of the child.

Midwives were held in high esteem because they performed important functions. The midwife was an expert in illnesses affecting women and infants, and was totally in charge at birth. She brought many babies to baptism and removed illegitimate or unwanted children to foundling homes. As witness and confidante in intimate family matters and female sexuality, she provided a way for the male clergy to reform and control the local populace.

Midwives routinely used a birthing chair, which was comfortable and safer for the woman and baby but very uncomfortable for the midwife, who had to crouch on the floor to "catch" the baby. Midwives had knowledge of a variety of remedies and treatments designed to bring on contractions and alleviate pain, as well as knowledge of lifesaving practices including manipulation of breech births and cesarean sections.

After 1800 and the influence of French ideas about social welfare, and later developments in medicine, obstetrical practice, and public health, state-sponsored schools were established to provide formal training, licensing, and supervision for qualified midwives. The educated midwife (or *levatrice*) gradually lost her community and religious prominence as she came more firmly under the supervision of physicians and obstetricians. Unauthorized midwives continued to practice, especially in the south and the rural areas of the north, into the late nineteenth century, mostly because local populations resisted innovations in traditional birth practices.

Undoubtedly, both types of midwives—trained and lay—became part of the turn-of-the-century migration to the United States, and most took up practice among their own people. Unlike other entrepreneurial, professional, or quasi-professional occupations, midwifery generally did not require a capital investment, or a postmigration adjustment of language and technical skills.

The typical Italian midwife in the United States was a married woman with children of her own. Many had been apprenticed to older midwives, perhaps a mother or aunt, and so learned by assisting at many births. Others had formal training from medical schools in Italy, or in New York City at the short-lived Bellevue School for Midwives, the only municipal hospital-based program that from 1911 to 1930 trained many Italian American women who subsequently practiced in their own neighborhoods of the city.

Most Italian women of the first generation, and some of the second, preferred to employ a midwife rather than a male physician for childbirth. Italian American women's intergenerational networks supported the value of homebirth and provided the personal connections needed to locate a suitable midwife. Mothers and other older women were the repositories of advice and knowledge about childbirth for young married women whose levels of education and occupational attainment before and after marriage remained low.

As in Italy, midwives were generally respected and valued members of the community. Local midwives usually spoke the same dialect, shared regional and cultural practices and values, and usually charged far less than the medical practitioner. She did more, providing care for mother and infant and tending to other children and doing routine household tasks for several days after the birth. Mid-wives also routinely applied the *fasce,* the bindings or swaddling used nearly universally by first-generation women following the custom in Italy, which were believed to give strength and protection to newborns. Midwives also pierced the earlobes of infant girls for golden earrings. Following the custom in Italy, families would refer to their midwife as *comare,* in acknowledgment of a deeper relationship formed through her participation in an intimate family event.

While some Italian women and even Italian midwives would occasionally call in a male physician for a difficult birth at home, Italian American women and families nearly always avoided using a hospital for childbirth. Hospitals were feared as places where people died, where hospital personnel routinely inflicted more harm than good, and where babies' identities were often "mixed up." Generally, women who were giving birth believed that the hospital was for the sick, "for something bad," but childbirth was a routine and natural occurrence best conducted at home in one's own bed.

The need for culturally similar, inexpensive assistance in childbirth was greatest among first-generation women whose fertility levels were quite high. Pregnancy and childbirth dominated the lives of adult immigrant women, and the foreign born generally had twice as many children as native women. Italians considered numerous children to be a blessing and a potential source of good fortune. In Buffalo's Italian community, for example, half of all adult women had a child within two years of their arrival in the United States. Frequent births often subjected women to severe health risks, among them, maternal infection, a major cause of death for adult Italian women, whose rate of mortality exceeded that of Italian men.

Birth narratives by Italian American women are rare. Undoubtedly some women had to manage the experience totally alone and without assistance or comfort, as did Rosa Cavalleri in the isolation of a western mining town. But for most Italian American women, birth was a social and communal event that included the midwife, the birthing women's mother, aunts, and other mature female relatives. Often the midwife would receive assistance from female relatives in peripheral tasks, or more directly in some stage of the birth itself. Women were often obliged to render assistance as a part of family or neighborhood reciprocity. For some, assistance from neighbors and relatives was welcome, but in other instances, birthing women experienced a loss of control over the household and the intrusion of perhaps well-meaning but unhelpful relatives overstaying their welcome.

Modern medical specialists sought to eliminate irregular practitioners as a way to achieve professional dominance. One aspect of this campaign that attempted to eliminate the midwife from medical practice, gained impetus with the mass migration of southern and eastern Europeans. Immigrant midwives became special targets, and while some Italian midwives certainly deserved the criticism leveled at them for their unsanitary practices, research well into the 1930s demonstrated that midwives—both lay and professional, native and ethnic—had better records at maintaining the life and health of the mother and infant than did medical specialists, who often used dangerous and intrusive measures. Midwives, more willing to watch and wait while nature took its course, consistently had safer outcomes.

The eclipse and elimination of midwives at childbirth was realized through developments occurring both within and outside the Italian American community. The Johnson Acts of 1921 and 1924 severely reduced immigration and at one stroke eliminated the influx of Italian midwives and women who would prefer her services. Localities enacted public health measures, including the licensing and supervision of remaining midwives and the provision of low-cost maternity clinics in neighborhood hospitals. Gradually, the numbers of Italian American physicians with hospital affiliations increased; women and families who had a social link to an Italian American physician were very likely to use his services. Medical innovations including the use of drugs, as well as a ten-day period of bed rest and recuperation, became powerful incentives to seek out hospital birth.

Within the Italian community, midwives gradually became associated with old-fashioned, traditional ways. Young Italian women who were moving to new levels of education and employment increasingly identified the midwife with their mother's generation. For them, the preference for a physician and hospital birth was another way of demonstrating that they were "modern, Americanized women."

Additionally, second-generation Italian American women, who grew up in the tumult and deprivation of large families with numerous siblings, and whose lives spanned the transition from immigrant to urban values and ideas about appropriate family size, had far fewer children than their mothers. Their fertility rates were in fact even lower than those of native-born white women. Thus, childbirth became a common event, and women's family roles moved from an emphasis on producing children to an emphasis on rearing children.

Angela D. Danzi

Bibliography

Danzi, Angela D. *From Home to Hospital.* Lanham, MD: University Press of America, 1997.

Ets, Marie Hall. *Rosa: The Life of an Italian Immigrant.* Minneapolis: University of Minnesota Press, 1970.

Livi-Bacci, Massimo. *L'Immigrazione e l'Assimilazione Degli Italiani Neglie Stati Uniti.* Milan: Dott A. Giuffre, 1961.

Pancino, Claudia. *Il bambino e l'aqua sporca. Storia dell' assistenza al parto dalle mammane alle ostetriche.* Milan: Franco Angeli, 1984.

Wertz, Richard. W., and Dorothy C. Wertz. *Lying-in: A History of Childbirth in America.* New York: The Free Press, 1989.

See also FOLKWAYS AND FOLKLIFE; RELIGION

Migliaccio, Eduardo (Farfariello) (1882–1946)

One of the most popular entertainers of the Italian American music hall arena, Eduardo Migliaccio was born April 15, 1882, in Salerno and attended the Institute of Fine Arts in Naples. In 1897 he migrated to the United States and worked in the Banca Sandolo in Hazleton, Pennsylvania, writing letters to Italy for the bank's clients. He relocated to New York City, where he secured a similar position at the bank of Don Pasquale Avallone on Mulberry Street. In 1900, he lived at 57 Kenmare Street and began a stage career playing small roles in Shakespearean productions in dialect with the Antonio Maiori Company.

He also sang at intermissions of performances in the Sicilian marionette theater. But the arena in which he produced his greatest work, creating a singular new art form and enjoying enormous popular success, was the Italian American music hall, or *caffe concerto*. Migliaccio launched his career in the Caffe Concerto Pennachio on Mulberry Street in 1900, singing the latest Neapolitan hits for four dollars a week. In this hall, later called the Villa Vittorio Emmanuele III, he performed the song *"Femmene-Fe"* every night, from which his nickname "Farfariello," in the refrain, was derived. This became his signatory stage name with which his identity became indelibly associated and carries the double meaning of "Little Butterfly" and womanizer.

He began his show by performing the Neapolitan comedy skit called *macchietta*, a musical sketch combining sung verses and spoken prose passages. Farfariello's original creation was the *macchietta coloniale* or colonial skit, meaning the Italian immigrant community skit. In this type of skit he impersonated and satirized community figures recognizable to his audiences: Enrico Caruso, the band leader, the president of the social organization, the Irish American, the greenhorn or hick, the wet nurse, the opera diva, the schoolgirl, the soldier boy, the bride, the street cleaner, the iceman, the fireman, the singer, the dancer, the soubrette, the policeman, the gangster, the bootlegger, the undertaker, the street vendor, the Irish cop, and many, many more comprising the entire panoply of Italian immigrant society. These characterizations of Italian American life demonstrated the bewilderment of the Italian immigrant in a foreign country. They earned their creator the title "King of Impersonators" and "King of New York Vaudeville Entertainers" and "King of the Colonial Character Sketch."

Migliaccio used the newly evolving language of the Italian American community: Italo-Americanese, a linguistic "soup" of Italian, English, American, slang, and various dialect distortions. Migliaccio wrote both the lyrics and monologues for all his skits, and frequently the music as well. He directed and choreographed all his own routines, rehearsing in front of a mirror and constructing his own wigs and masks. He performed a dozen routines in a half-hour set with quick costume changes. By 1914 he had a repertoire of 150 skits, and by the time of his death in 1946 he had about six hundred.

Eduardo Migliaccio, known as "Farfariello" (Little Butterfly), was a satirical singer and comedian who was idolized by the Italian Americans. His character sketches (macchiette) were based on immigrants he observed in the United States. Courtesy Immigration History Research Center, Minnesota.

Many were recorded by the Victor Company in 1916, and published by the Italian Book Company in 1917 and the Italian language newspaper *La Follia*.

Farfariello was well known to communities along the East Coast, but he also toured in Chicago and California in 1919, appearing at the theater of Antonietta Pisanelli Alessandro in San Francisco. He formed his own operetta company and developed his art form into longer genres, such as one-act and full-length plays. During the heyday of Italian radio, he performed on many radio programs including the "Donna Vicenza Company," on WAAM, WAAT, and WEVD. In 1936 he toured Italy, and he was knighted a Cavaliere del Ordine della Corona by King Victor Emanuel four years later. He died in Brooklyn of cancer March 27, 1946.

Emelise Aleandri

Bibliography

Aleandri, Emelise. *The History of Italian-American Theatre in New York City: 1900–1905*. Ph.D. diss., City University of New York, 1983.

Seller, Maxine, ed. *Ethnic Theatre in the United States*. Westport, CT: Greenwood, 1983.

See also COMEDY; THEATER HISTORY

Mignonette, Gilda (1890–1953)

Born in the popular "Duchessa" neighborhood of Naples on April 1, 1890, Gilda Mignonette's birth name was Griselda Andreatini; her stage name, which remained with her for the rest of her life, was chosen to commemorate Mistiguett, a star of the Moulin Rouge. Daughter of a humanities high school teacher, Francesco, and of the Marchesa Matilde Ruffo, Griselda used to listen with fascination to the Neapolitan tunes that her father pounded out on an out-of-tune grand piano. One afternoon, while Francesco Andreatini was playing "Santa Lucia," a thin, perfectly pitched voice raised high above the music: it was the very young Griselda singing for the first time. Her real debut on stage took place just a few years later in 1908 at the Umberto Theatre.

Turn-of-the-century Naples was, along with Paris and Vienna, a city alive with artistic, literary, and poetic figures, among them philosopher Benedetto Croce; poets Ferdinando Russo, Salvatore di Giacomo, and Gabriele D'Annunzio; and tenor Enrico Caruso. In this fertile ground of artists and songs, such as "O sole mio," "Torna Surriento," and "Santa Lucia lontana," Mignonette's art and passion for music was born and developed. From the day of her debut at the Umberto as "an unusual star and singer," she performed continuously at the most important theaters and *cafés chantant* for the next eight years. She also appeared with Raffaele Viviani, one of the greatest poets and authors of Neapolitan theater.

Gilda then signed a contract with Cavaliere Feliciano Acierno, head of the most famous Italian theater company in America. Upon her arrival in New York in April 1926, she met Frank Acierno, the producer's son; they were married within two months. Her debut at Brooklyn's Werbas Theater was an immediate success, and at the end of her performance she was carried in triumph through the streets of Brooklyn. In 1927 Gilda launched what later became the "song of Italians in America": "A cartulina é Napule."

In the years before and during World War II, Mignonette and her husband were the targets of investigations by the FBI and other American authorities for performing songs associated with Fascist Italy and for her refusal to ask her Italian American audiences to buy United States war bonds. Her supporters claimed that her preferences in music were merely "patriotic," and that her aversion to selling bonds related to her fear that they might be used to build airplanes "intended for bombing Italy." In any case, she was forbidden to record her music, and her radio broadcasts and shows were censored. During these years she organized numerous recitals for the benefit of Italian prisoners of war.

By the end of the war, Gilda's health was beginning to fail, and although she was rich and respected and had friends and family in America, Naples was in her heart, and she dreamed of going back for good. She was finally able to persuade her husband to make the journey. Her farewell performance was organized at the Brooklyn Academy of Music for March 22, 1953. Reservations for that evening were numerous, but illness prevented her from giving more than a few performances, and these were given from a wheelchair. At last, on May 27, 1953, she embarked on the S.S. *Homeland* with her husband and sister-in-law. During her crossing, she was very sick and the trip was very difficult. A specialist brought on board in Lisbon confirmed the diagnosis: cirrhosis of the liver. Her health deteriorated rapidly, and on June 8, 1953, twenty-four hours before their scheduled arrival in Italy, Gilda Mignonette died silently in her cabin. At the moment of her death, she was looking at a postcard with a panorama of Naples that her husband had glued at her request to an opposite wall, the very image from the song that had brought her so much success.

Carlo Avvisati

Bibliography

"In Memory of a Great Artist." *The Italian Tribune*, Newark, 13 November 1981.

Pantano, Nino. "Gilda Mignonette." *The Phoenix, The Newspaper of Brownsville, Brooklyn* 13, no. 13 (4 October 1984).

Sicignano, John C., "Opera Highlights: A Repeat Performance by a Great Singer." *The Italian Tribune,* 24 June 1982.

See also THEATER HISTORY

Mining

See OCCUPATIONS OF ITALIAN IMMIGRANTS IN TURN-OF-THE-CENTURY AMERICA

Minnesota

Of the millions of Italian immigrants who migrated to the United States, only a very small percentage chose to settle in Minnesota. The state's Italian-born population, which peaked in 1910 at 9,668, totaled only 1,208 in 1990. Yet in 1990 almost ninety thousand persons residing in Minnesota declared themselves to be of Italian ancestry. This figure clearly included many American born immigrants from other states.

Despite their relatively small numbers, Italian Americans have played significant roles in various chapters of Minnesota history. While many Italian immigrants to the North Star state clustered in St. Paul and Minneapolis, a significant portion settled in the port city of Duluth and the towns of the iron ranges. From the 1880s on, initial settlers, artisans, and merchants from northern Italy were joined by Sicilian fruit vendors. Although Minnesota has been primarily an agricultural state, few immigrants became farmers, although some engaged in market gardening.

After 1900 a wave of newcomers from southern Italy inundated the established Italian community. Mostly unskilled laborers, they were responding to the demands by the railroad companies for labor to build and maintain their lines. St. Paul, in particular, became a major center for recruiting and housing these migrant workers. *Padrones* (labor brokers) became wealthy and influential in this traffic in labor. As Italians sent for women from their villages, ethnic neighborhoods in St. Paul, Minneapolis, and Duluth emerged. For the most part, these families were from Abruzzi-Molise, Puglia, Campania, and Calabria. Two other settlements of railroad workers were in Dilworth in western Minnesota, and Cumberland, Wisconsin. The largest concentration of Italians by 1910, however, was in the towns and mining locations of the iron ranges in northern Minnesota. Despite low wages and dangerous work, immigrants from both northern and southern Italy came to work in the expanding mining operations. In addition to settlements in the larger towns, such as Hibbing, Eveleth, and Virginia, many lived in "locations," often in shanties, adjacent to the mines. Although the rate of turnover was high, some settled permanently in the harsh environment of northern Minnesota.

As "the lowest paid, the worst housed, and the most abused by the mine bosses," Italians participated in efforts to organize the mining industry, particularly the two major strikes of 1907 and 1916. Some were members of the Industrial Workers of the World (IWW). During the 1916 conflict, Carlo Tresca, along with others, was charged with murder following a shootout between strikers and company police, provoking an international protest (charges against Tresca were dropped). The 1916 strike ended in defeat for the workers, and not until 1943 did the Oliver Iron Mining Company finally sign a contract with the United Steel Workers of America. Italian Americans were prominent in the drive for union organization in the thirties. John T. Bernard, born in Corsica of Italian parents, was director of the Steel Workers Organizing Committee on the iron range and elected to Congress on the Farmer-Labor ticket in 1936.

A professional and business class of grocers, saloon keepers, tradesmen, doctors, lawyers, and pharmacists emerged to provide for the needs of the growing Italian communities. A number of merchants specialized in grapes for wine making; among them was Cesare Mondavi, whose family became proprietors of the Charles Krug Winery as well as one bearing the family name. Food and liquor provided distinctive fields for Italian American enterprises catering to an American clientele. Spaghetti houses, pizza parlors, and cocktail lounges proliferated. From such modest beginnings grew big businesses like Totino's Pizza, which eventually sold out to the Pillsbury Company. Jeno Paulucci, son of a miner, began his meteoric career producing Chinese food in Duluth.

In their attempts to establish churches, Italian priests encountered widespread apathy and factionalism—and anticlericalism on the part of some. After several failed efforts, the Holy Redeemer Parish in St. Paul was established in 1906. Over time, Italian churches were established in Minneapolis, Duluth, and several towns on the iron ranges. Despite their alleged indifference, the Italians in several communities celebrated the feast days of the patron saints of their *paesi* (villages). In Dilworth, for example, the feast of Our Lady of Mount Carmel was zealously observed from 1912 to 1942, when it was permanently discontinued because of the war.

Like the churches, Italian organizations were bedeviled by conflicts stemming from regional jealousies, personality conflicts, and political differences. In 1883 the Società Dante Allighieri was formed in St. Paul; it was the first of many mutual-aid societies that, in addition to sick and death benefits, sponsored social events. While some organizations bore the names of patron saints, others were of a nationalist and anticlerical character. Following World War I, a younger generation established organizations that sought to unite Italian Americans and to encourage their political participation. The Minnesota State Federation of Italian American Clubs promoted Americanization and citizenship. Columbus Day became the most important observance for Italian Americans because it provided an opportunity to celebrate their dual identities. In 1931 a statue of Columbus on the grounds of the state capitol was dedicated before a crowd of over twenty-five thousand. And in 1945, due to lobbying by Italian American organizations, Columbus Day became a legal holiday in Minnesota.

By 1940 the American born outnumbered the foreign born by a ratio of two to one. Products of American schools and culture, this new generation of Italian Americans aspired to a better life both for themselves and for their ethnic group. William C. Davini, for example, a St. Paul native and educator who was active in many civic and fraternal organizations, was elected national president of UNICO National in 1946. World War II marked a dramatic turning point in the history of Minnesota's Italian Americans. Since their country of origin was at war with the United States, many Italian organizations were disbanded and community functions suspended. Young men and women left for service in the armed forces and war industries, and many did not return to the old neighborhoods. The Little Italys were also disrupted by urban renewal, highway construction, and rezoning.

As more Italian Americans achieved higher education and made their way into business and education, the ethnic group's sta-

tus rose. A growing number served in state government, and in 1976 Bruce F. Vento of St. Paul was elected to Congress. A conspicuous minority in the midst of a Nordic population, Italian Americans were often the recipients of prejudice and discrimination. Although the Twin Cities press flagrantly exploited the Mafia stereotype, there was no organized protest from the Italian American community. Nor has there been a concerted effort to maintain Italian language and culture in the state. The surviving organizations have served primarily as the purveyors of social functions.

Although the Italian presence has contributed flavor and color to the state's composite culture, little outstanding remains of Italian immigrant folk cultures. However, a consciousness of being Italian American persists among many Minnesotans.

Rudolph J. Vecoli

Bibliography

Castigliano, Attilio, and Fred A. Ossanna, eds. *Columbus: A Collection of Historical Facts.* St. Paul: Columbus Memorial Association of Minnesota, 1931.

Vecoli, Rudolph J. "The Italians." In *They Chose Minnesota,* edited by June Holmquist, 449–471. St. Paul: Minnesota Historical Society, 1981.

———. *Italian Immigrants in Rural and Small Town America.* New York: American Italian Historical Association, 1987.

———. "Italian Religious Organizations in Minnesota." *Studi Emigrazione* 19 (June 1982): 191–201.

Missionaries of St. Charles—Scalabrinians

Giovanni Battista Scalabrini (1839–1905), Bishop of Piacenza, founded this Catholic religious congregation on November 18, 1887, with the approval of Pope Leo XIII, as an apostolic institute of missionaries for the purpose of "providing for the care, especially the spiritual care, of the Italians who had emigrated, primarily to the Americas." Subsequently, the congregation extended its mission to Europe and into other countries where the care of migrants was urgently needed. As a result of pastoral needs and under the guidance of Bishop Scalabrini, who conceived a plan of action for the care of all migrants, the congregation began to work among migrants of different nationalities, for internal migrations, and for people of the sea: that is, all those who are living outside their country or outside their social and cultural place of origin and, "because of real necessity," require a specific assistance.

Approximately eight hundred Scalabrinians are now working in nineteen countries in Europe, North and South America, Australia, and Asia. They staff parishes, seminaries, seamen centers, diocesan offices for the pastoral care of migrants, and nursing homes. Since 1963 the Scalabrinian Congregation's commitment to research, study, and strategy in the care of migrants helped to establish a network of Centers for Migration Studies. The centers are located in Rome, New York, Paris, Sydney, Manila, São Paulo, Buenos Aires, and Caracas, and form the Federation of the Centers for Migration Studies J.B. Scalabrini. The centers work toward the total human promotion of migrants through documentation, research projects, symposia, and publications. For example, the *International Migration Review,* the quarterly journal that has developed into the leading scholarly journal in the field, is published by the Center for Migration Studies of New York. This center has also published over thirty books on the Italian experience in North America.

Documentation on the presence of the Scalabrinians in North America can be found at the Archives of the Center for Migration Studies of New York and at the General Archives in Rome.

Lydio F. Tomasi

Bibliography

Brown, Mary Elizabeth. *The Scalabrinians in North America, 1887–1934.* New York: Center for Migration Studies, 1996.

———, ed. *A Migrant Missionary Story: The Autobiography of Giacomo Gambera.* New York: Center for Migration Studies, 1995.

DePaolis, Velasio. *Evolution of the Mission of the Scalabrinian Congregation.* New York: Center for Migration Studies, 1985.

Tomasi, Silvano M. *The Pastoral Action of Bishop John Baptist Scalabrini and His Missionaries Among Immigrants in the Americas, 1887–1987.* New York: Center for Migration Studies, 1984.

———. *A Scalabrinian Mission Among Polish Immigrants in Boston, 1893–1909.* New York: Center for Migration Studies, 1985.

Zizzamia, Alba. *A Vision Unfolding: the Scalabrinians in North America (1888–1988).* New York: Center for Migration Studies, 1989.

See also CHURCH LEADERS; RELIGION; SCALABRINI, GIOVANNI BATTISTA

Modotti, Tina (1896–1942)

A photographer and revolutionary, Tina Modotti was born in the Friulian town of Udine in the Italian province of Venezia Giulia, migrated to the United States in 1913, and settled in San Francisco, where she became a star in the local Italian theater. She married painter Roubaix de l'Abrie Richey. She moved to Los Angeles and began a film career in Hollywood that she gave up to learn photography from American painter and her eventual lover Edward Weston (1886–1958).

Her husband died in 1922, and when she went to Mexico to bury him there, she came into contact and was impressed with the work of the Mexican muralists. While living in Mexico City, she associated with artists, writers, and radicals, and she had an affair with Diego Rivera.

Modotti's brilliant photographic career lasted only seven years: 1923–1930. She captured scenes during a vibrant period of Mexican culture and became a major artist in the modernistic idiom.

Her radical politics led to trouble. In 1929 she was charged with the murder of her Cuban lover. She claimed it was a frame-up. Nevertheless, she was acquitted and the following year was expelled from Mexico.

She gave up photography, went to live in Berlin for a while, then to the Soviet Union, where she became politically active and conducted Comintern activities in fascist countries. She also participated in the Spanish Civil War. In 1939 she returned to Mexico, where she died three years later.

Modotti's photographs are greatly valued and have sold for high prices. In 1991 her original print of *Roses* (1925) sold for $165,000 at Sotheby's, the highest price up to that time paid for a photograph sold at auction.

Frank J. Cavaioli

Bibliography
Caronia, Maria, and Vittorio Vivaldi. *Tina Modotti: fotografa e revoluzionaria.* Milan: Idea Editions, 1979.
Hooks, Margaret. *Tina Modotti.* London: Pandora, 1993.
Lowe, Sarah M. *Tina Modotti, Photographs.* New York: Harry N. Abrams, 1995.

See also ART

Molinari Family
See POLITICS

Mosconi, William Joseph (Willie) (1913–1993)

The last officially recognized world champion of pocket billiards (pool), Willie Mosconi was a native of South Philadelphia, son of Joseph and Helen (Reilly) Mosconi. Willie learned to play in the billiards parlor owned by his father. He secretly practiced with a broomstick and tiny potatoes because his father had forbidden him to play.

He was considered a child prodigy before 1920, when he made a competitive showing in exhibitions against reigning champion Ralph Greenleaf and another child star, Ruth McGinnis. Only Greenleaf rivals Mosconi as the greatest player ever, but Mosconi's record in head-to-head matches and tournament play was better. He won the world championship thirteen times between 1941 and 1956, scored the record high run of 526 in a 1954 exhibition, and holds the record of 18.34 for grand high average in tournaments.

Mosconi helped to popularize pocket billiards as a viable sport. Drafted in the latter part of World War II, he gave exhibitions at Army bases while a member of the Special Services. A 1956 stroke, from which he fully recovered, prompted his semiretirement. He was a technical advisor for the movie *The Hustler* (1961) and made a cameo appearance. Some years later, he was a consultant during the filming of *The Color of Money* (1986). Employed by the Brunswick Corporation, he did much to improve the somewhat sordid image of billiards and aided its popularity on college campuses and as a family activity. His own dapper appearance contributed to this positive image. In his mid-sixties, he easily defeated Rudolf Walter

"Minnesota Fats" Wanderone Jr., on ABC television's *Wide World of Sports.* He subsequently appeared on cable TV. During the era when Muhammad Ali was creating interest in boxing, Willie Mosconi was doing something similar for billiards.

Richard Renoff

Bibliography
Mosconi, Willie. *Willie Mosconi on Pocket Billiards.* New York: Crown, 1959.
Mosconi, Willie, and Stanley Cohen. *Willie's Game: An Autobiography.* New York: Macmillan, 1963.

See also SPORTS

Mount Washington Hotel

The Mount Washington Hotel, an opulent resort in the White Mountains of New Hampshire, was constructed mainly with the help of Italian craftsmen.

Although the census of 1900 recorded slightly less than one thousand Italian immigrants in that state, 250 Italian immigrants, mostly skilled carpenters and masons, took part in the construction of the Mount Washington Hotel. Having arrived in Boston from Italy, these laborers were first shipped to Portland, Maine, then transported in cattle cars by railroad to Bretton Woods, where they went to work building the massive foundation and huge superstructure of the hotel.

Living on the grounds of the resort during their employment, the Italians were foreigners in a country where they faced language barriers and strange customs. They clustered together in enclaves and sent their earnings back to their families in Italy by lining up at the telegraph office on pay day. *Among the Clouds,* the area's newspaper, stated in its issue of August 13, 1901: "The 250 Italian laborers who are employed in connection with the building of the great hotel near the Mount Pleasant House, have made a record for good conduct and thrift which will do credit to men of any nationality." After the hotel opened on July 28, 1902, about twenty Italians were asked to remain at the resort to maintain the grounds.

The Mount Washington Hotel had been subsidized by Joseph Stickney (1840–1903), a native of the state who made his money by mining coal in New Hampshire. An architectural wonder, it was designed by Charles A. Gifford of New York in the revival style of the Spanish Renaissance. The building, standing five stories high, was originally regarded as "a white elephant" until Stickney's wife was able to persuade a number of her friends in high society to visit the place. Thereafter, it became a popular summer resort for the Astors, the Rockefellers, and the Vanderbilts.

For long the state's most imposing structure, the Mount Washington Hotel has attracted not only the wealthy of America but also many everyday tourists who have been impressed by its beauty as they pass the white hotel with its stucco exterior standing out like a gem within the mountains. One of the larger convention areas, this cherished landmark was the site of the international monetary conference that made the dollar the standard for the world's currency in July of 1944 when the world's nations established the International Monetary Fund and the World Bank.

Recognized as a National Historic Site, the Mount Washington Hotel, which today stands as a memorial to its architect and owner, is also a monument that recalls the skilled Italian craftsmen who contributed to the building of America.

Vincent A. Lapomarda

Bibliography

McAvoy, George E. *And Then There Was One: A History of the Hotels of the Summit and the West Side of Mt. Washington.* Littleton, NH: Crawford Press, 1988.

Tolles, Bryant F. Jr., ed. "The Great Resort Hotels and Tourism in the White Mountains." *Historical New Hampshire* 50 (1995): 1–142.

See also OCCUPATIONS OF ITALIAN IMMIGRANTS IN TURN-OF-THE-CENTURY AMERICA

Movie Actors and Actresses

Stereotyping became the lot of Italian immigrants at the outset of mass immigration. Like most newcomers, Italians elicited conspicuous delight from an American public that viewed them as virtually unidimensional beings, synonymous with the excitable, the nonserious, and the humorous. They were buffoons, objects to laugh at and to caricature. However, even before the end of the nineteenth century

the image of Italians as rogues began to replace the jester image. Because the early phase of American moviemaking coincided with the era of mass Italian immigration, a number of these stereotypes made their way into moving pictures. During the era of silent films, moviegoers could see more than a few such screen representations, usually by non-Italian actors. By the 1920s the gangster image had emerged to a point where it became a veritable genre. Again, most of the roles were played by non-Italian actors. Edward G. Robinson and Paul Muni, for example, began illustrious careers in which they frequently impersonated Italian American criminals.

What was missing in this early phase was a sense of multidimensional characterizations that Italian actors and actresses were capable of and which was skillfully evident in the movie industry in Italy. Italian American actors and actresses of outstanding talent who worked in the ethnic theater were also absent from the screen. It would be decades before Hollywood employed some of these individuals who descended from veteran acting family dynasties. For instance, Esther Minciotti, acclaimed for her role as Ernest Borgnine's mother in the Oscar-winning film *Marty* (1955), and Vincent Gardenia, who was praised for playing Cher's father in *Moonstruck* (1987), were already veteran performers from distinguished Italian acting families before Hollywood used their talents in these films. Ironically, there was a foremost Hollywood actor of Italian descent during the golden age of American movies—Henry Fonda. However, neither the actor nor Hollywood made the ethnic association, and it was not until near the end of his career that it became known that the Fonda family had Italian roots, albeit dating from the Middle Ages.

One of the first genuinely recognizable Italian American actors to emerge was Eduardo Cianelli, born August 30, 1897, on the island of Ischia. After his arrival in the United States he made his Broadway debut in *Rose Marie* in 1933. He was a versatile actor of many roles. However, given his craggy face and suave manners, he increasingly played criminal figures and gang leaders and soon developed into one of the most menacing Hollywood actors. From the 1950s on he worked mostly in Italy. Among his memorable films were *Reunion in Vienna* (1933), *Winter Set* (1936), *Gunga Din* (1939), *For Whom the*

Bell Tolls (1943), A Bell for Adano (1945), Dillinger (1945), The Brotherhood (1968), and The Secret of Santa Vittoria (1969). He died in Naples in 1969.

The two Taliaferro sisters, Edith (1894–1958) and Mabel (1887–1979), grew up in New York City. Mabel, who usually played youthful, innocent roles and became the "sweetheart of American movies," was especially acknowledged for her performance in Cinderella (1911).

The Taliaferro sisters were cousins of Bessie Barriscale (1884–1965), star of early silent films that were typically romantic, who reached her peak between 1914 and 1920. Roy D'Arcy, born Ray Francis Giusti in 1894 in San Francisco, made his screen debut in 1919 with Oh Boy. He then performed for a number of years in vaudeville before returning to filmmaking. In 1925 he played the role of a leering, lecherous crown prince in The Merry Widow and continued to play the villainous genre until his retirement in the 1930s.

At the turn of the twentieth century Italian-born Rudolph Valentino began a celebrated career as a leading man and legend for the silent screen by acting the persona of the Latin lover. He was born in Castellaneta, Italy, in 1885 and died of a perforated ulcer at age 31 in New York in 1926. Having tried and failed at becoming an officer in the Italian Army, he worked as a gardener, waiter, and exhibition dancer before going to Hollywood. His first film was Alimony in 1918. He reached stardom with The Four Horsemen of the Apocalypse (1921), and sixteen films later he became the sexual fantasy of many American women of the 1920s who had a penchant for the Mediterranean male. Following his success, he secured his position as a star with The Sheikh (1921); Blood and Sand (1922); Monsieur Beaucare (1924); and Son of the Sheikh (1926), his last film. Thousands of women flocked to his funeral amid reports of mass hysteria and several suicides.

Jimmy Durante, nicknamed the "Schnozzola," was born in New York in 1883 and remained there until his death in 1986. A leading actor both on stage and screen, he began his long show business career at age 16 playing ragtime piano in Bowery nightclubs. Teaming up with Lou Clayton and Eddie Jackson, he became a big success in vaudeville. In 1929 he was featured in the Broadway production of Ziegfeld's Show Girl. He made his film debut in 1930 in the MGM movie Road House, which led to a five-year studio contract. Throughout the 1930s he commuted between Hollywood and Broadway and continued to gain popularity in films and musical theater. Durante was a successful opposite to George M. Cohan in Phantom President (1932) and provided deft comedic relief in the drama The West Parade (1934) and Hell Below (1933). In Joe Palooka (1934) he introduced his signature tune "Inka, Dinka, Doo." In the 1941 film On an Island he played "Banjo," a character modeled after Groucho Marx. His durable career extended into the 1970s, when he could be seen in Las Vegas shows and on television specials. Durante's last film was It's a Mad Mad Mad Mad World (1963), in which he plays yet another comic role. Durante's fame was rekindled posthumously when his recordings "As Time Goes By" and "Make Someone Happy" were used on the soundtrack of Sleepless in Seattle (1993).

Another actor of Italian descent who became a Hollywood fixture in the 1920s and 1930s was Henry Armetta (1888–1945). Born in Palermo, Sicily, Armetta worked as a barber's helper and a pants presser before he started work in theater. He entered Hollywood in the 1920s, playing numerous character roles, mostly comic, and exhibiting an excitable character, as for example in The Big Store (1941), featuring the Marx Brothers.

The comic actor Jerry Colonna was born Gerardo Luigi Colonna in Boston in 1904. He began his show business career as a trombone player but soon discovered the comic value of his rolling eyes, walrus mustache, and bellowing voice. After a successful stint as a nightclub comedian and in musical reviews, he became a radio actor on the Bob Hope Show and made comic appearances in light films such as 52nd Street (1937) and The Bob Hope Christmas Show (1966).

Another Bostonian of Italian descent was Ruth Roman, born in 1924 and educated at Bishop Lee Dramatic School. She became a Hollywood leading lady in the 1940s portraying determined, strong-willed characters. In 1945 she won the title role on the serial The Jungle Queen, in which she played a mythical goddess against the Nazis. She is remembered also as a survivor of the sinking of the passenger ship Andrea Doria in 1956. She starred in her first feature film as the title character in Belle

Starr's Daughter (1948), followed by another leading role in *Colt* (1950). That same year she was featured in *Three Sisters* as an anxious mother waiting to hear if her children had survived an airplane crash. Roman fared well in film noir, especially when she was cast as a femme fatale, as in *The Killing Kind* (1973) and *Impulse* (1976). In the 1970s she surfaced in episodic television roles such as *Knots Landing*.

Born Domenic Felix Amici, in Kenosha, Wisconsin, in 1908, Don Ameche established a long and distinguished acting career. One of eight children of a bartender, he made his stage debut while studying law at the University of Wisconsin. Already a well-known radio personality, he first emerged in films in 1935, becoming one of 20th Century Fox's busiest actors by performing leading roles in more than forty films. Although he seems indelibly associated with *The Story of Alexander Graham Bell* (1939), the film that best capitalized on his dexterity was *Heaven Can Wait* (1943). After a long absence, he made a sentimental appearance on the big screen in *Cocoon* (1985), for which he received the Oscar for best supporting actor. In 1988 he shared the best actor prize at the Venice film festival for his performance in *Things Change*. He starred also on Broadway in Cole Porter's *Silk Stockings* (1955), *Goldie Locks* (1952), and *Thirteen Daughters* (1960). Ameche also had two supporting roles in *Coming to America* (1988) and *Oscar* (1991), and before he died on December 6, 1993, he completed his scenes in *Corrina, Corrina* (1994).

Born in Jersey City, New Jersey, as Nicholas Peter Conte, the actor Richard Conte began a career on Broadway in the mid-1930s. In 1943 he signed a contract with 20th Century Fox, where he became one of the most dependable leading men for many years. The most frequent roles he played were those of a world-weary hero or gangster. Among the many films in which he starred were *The Purple Heart* (1944), *A Walk in the Sun* (1946), and *House of Strangers* (1949).

Robert Alda, born Alfonso Giuseppe Giovanni Roberto D'Abruzzo, in 1914 in New York, was educated at New York University. He worked for a time as an architectural draftsman before entering show business as a vaudevillian singer-entertainer in burlesque and radio. His highly successful film debut in 1945 as George Gershwin in *Rhapsody in Blue* ushered in a period of quality filmmaking including *Cloak and Dagger* (1946) and *Nora Prentiss* (1947). Despite such a promising beginning his later films were low-grade products such as *Tarzan and the Slave Girl* (1950). He was more successful on Broadway, where he received a Tony Award for *Guys and Dolls*. In the 1960s he settled in Rome, where for the next two decades he appeared in Italian and European co-productions including *Toto e Peppino divisi a Berlino* (1962). In 1984 he suffered a stroke from which he did not recover and died two years later. He was the father of actor Alan Alda.

Ernest Borgnine was born Ermes Elforon Borgnino of Italian parents in Hamden, Connecticut, in 1917. After several childhood years living in Milan, Italy, he returned to Connecticut, where he was formally educated, and then spent a few years in the Navy in the 1930s. The latter experience proved to be serviceable when he played the leading role in the popular television series *McHale's Navy* (1962–1966). Upon his return from wartime duty Borgnine studied acting under the G.I. Bill at the Randall School of Dramatics in Hartford. After a short-lived experience with a theatrical group in Virginia, he made his film debut in *China Corsair* (1951). He was very forceful in his portrayal of sadistic Sergeant Fatso Judson in *From Here to Eternity* (1953), in which he was pitted against Frank Sinatra, who won an Oscar Award as supporting actor for his role as Private Angelo Maggio. In 1955 Borgnine received the best actor Oscar for his characterization of Marty Piletti in Paddy Chayevsky's *Marty*. Credible in the role of a beefy, lonely, and sympathetic Italian American butcher trying to reconcile his own personal yearnings with the values of an older Italian ethic, he also won best actor honors at the Cannes festival, the New York Critics Award, and the National Board of Review Award. Performing as an actor in Italy as well as in the United States, his films include *Bad Day at Black Rock* (1955), *McHale's Navy* (1964), *The Oscar* (1966), *Ice Station Zebra* (1968), and *Hannie Caulder* (1971). Borgnine's later film roles lacked the multidimension of his earlier ones.

A character actor of the American stage, screen, and television, Vincent Gardenia was born Vincenzo Sconamiglio in Naples, Italy, in 1922. Gardenia came to the United States as a child, was educated in public schools, and

M

began performing as an amateur at age 5. Coming from a family of actors, he started acting professionally in the mid-1930s. He received a Tony Award for his performance in the 1971–1972 Broadway production of *The Prisoner of 2nd Ave.* In 1973 he obtained an Oscar nomination for his role in *Bang the Drum Slowly,* in which he played the role of baseball manager. Another Oscar nomination came in 1987 for his performance in *Moonstruck.* He had recurring roles in such television series as *L.A. Law,* and he received an Emmy Award for his part in the television film *Age Old Friends* (1989). His ethnicity seemed to be the basis for casting in many other films, as, for example *Murder Inc.* (1960), *Mad Dog Coll* (1961), *The Hustler* (1961), *Lucky Luciano* (1974), and *Death Wish* (1974). He died in 1992.

A New Yorker from Brooklyn, Harry Guardino, born in 1925, became a tough-talking leading man and character actor. He was successful on stage, television, and film, demonstrating his proficiency to play comic as well as dramatic roles. His films include *King of Kings* (1961), *The Pigeon That Took Rome* (1962), *Operation San Gennaro* (1966), *Lovers and Other Strangers* (1970), *Dirty Harry* (1971), *Capone* (1975), and *The Enforcer* (1976).

Tony Franciosa was born Anthony Pappaleo in 1928 in East Harlem, New York. An intense performer, he worked his way up from bit parts off Broadway to a Broadway debut in 1953 with *End as Man.* His success came in 1955 with the Broadway production of *A Hat Full of Rain* that led to a Hollywood invitation to repeat the role on the screen, a portrayal that won him an Oscar nomination and a subsequent role in the film *A Face in the Crowd* (1957). He appeared in many films in a variety of lead roles. He starred on television in the series *Valentine Day* (1965–1965) and *The Name of the Game* (1975–1976) and was featured in the made-for-television film *Stage Coach* (1986). Among his American and Italian films are *Wild Is the Wind* (1987), *Long Hot Summer* (1958), *Naked Maja* (1954), *La cicala* (1980), and *Aiutami a sognare* (1981).

Anne Bancroft was born Anna Maria Louise Italiano in the Bronx, New York, in 1931. She began her career in motion pictures in *Don't Bother to Knock* (1952). Over the next five years she appeared in a number of low-budget pictures. The following year she won the New York Drama Critics Award and another Tony for her performance in *The Miracle Worker.* A turning point for Bancroft occurred when she played the lead role in the film rendition *The Miracle Worker* (1962), for which she received the Oscar Award for best actress. In 1964 she received the award for best actress at the Cannes Festival for the British film *Pumpkin Eater* (1964) and the Golden Globe Award for *The Graduate* (1967). In 1977 and in 1985, she was nominated for an Oscar for her acting in *Turning Point* and *Agnes of God,* respectively. The British Film Academy named her best actress for *84 Charing Cross Road* in 1987. Bancroft has also worked as a director, enjoying modest success with *Fatso* (1980), starring Dom DeLuise. She married comic genius, producer, and director Mel Brooks in 1964. Among her films are *Tonight We Sing* (1953), *Demetrius and the Gladiators* (1954), and *Young Winston* (1972). She has had interesting character cameo roles in such films as *Honeymoon in Las Vegas* (1992), as Nicolas Cage's dying mother.

The son of a Sicilian immigrant laborer, Ben Gazzara was born in 1930 as Biagio Gazzara, and grew up in New York's tough Lower East Side. Although he studied engineering at City University of New York, he quit college and joined the Actors Studio. He soon achieved acting success on Broadway with his performances in *Cat on a Hot Tin Roof* (1954) and *A Hatful of Rain* (1955). His first two films demonstrated intensity and forcefulness in such roles as a sadistic cadet in *Strange One* (1957) and an enigmatic rape suspect in *Anatomy of Murder* (1959). He enjoyed further success in television series *Arrest and Trial* (1963–1964) and *Run for Your Life* (1965–1968). He was also noted for performing sympathetic roles in three films by John Cassavetes *Husbands* (1970), *The Killing of a Chinese Bookie* (1976), and *Opening Night* (1977). He was effective as a scurrilous crime lord in *Road House* (1989). He wrote and directed *Beyond the Ocean* (1990). Among his Italian- and American-made films are *Thief* (1960), *The Young Doctors* (1961), *The Conquered City* (1962), *The Bridge to Remagen* (1969), and *Don Bosco* (1990).

Robert Loggia, of Sicilian descent, was born in 1930 in Staten Island, New York. He was an occasional leading man and character actor on American stage, television, and films, often in lovable, fluff roles. He studied journalism at the University of Missouri and acting with Stella Adler at the Actors Studio. In 1955 he made his Broadway acting debut in *Man With the Golden Arm*. His first screen appearance, *Somebody Up There Likes Me* (1956), was followed by a starring role in the bleak science-fiction saga *The Last Minute*. In television he starred in *T.H.E. Cat* (1961–1963). He was nominated for an Academy Award for his supporting role as a seedy detective in *Jagged Edge* (1985), which elevated him to the top rank of character actors. Loggia's better feature roles include *Che* (1969), *The 9th Configuration* (1980), *S.O.B.* (1981), *An Officer and a Gentleman* (1982), and *Psycho* (1983) as well as three *Pink Panther* films. He was memorably nasty in *Scarface* (1983) and *Prizzi's Honor* (1985). He even nabbed such comedy roles as a boozy priest in *That's Life* (1988). Between 1989 and 1990 he starred in the series *Mancuso F.B.I.* and subsequently *Favorite Sons* and *Sunday Times*. His comic talents were showcased in *Opportunity Knocks* (1990), *The Marrying Kind* (1991), and as mobster turned vampire in *I Love Trouble* (1994).

Dom DeLuise, born in Brooklyn in 1933 and educated at Tufts University, became familiar to moviegoers as a rotund comic character player. He began his acting career in Cleveland as Dominic the Great, a fumbling magician featured on the *Garry Moore Show*. By the mid-1970s he had a number of films to his credit, such as *Fail Safe* (1964), *Every Little Crook and Nanny* (1972), *Blazing Saddles* (1974), *Silent Movie* (1976), and *The World's Greatest Lover* (1977). In 1980 he played the starring role in *Fatso* and also directed himself in *Hot Stuff*. Other films include *Cannonball Run* and *History of the World Part I* (1981), *The Best Little Whorehouse in Texas* (1982), and *Loose Cannon* (1990). He has also provided voice-overs for animated pictures, such as *An American Tale* (1986), *Oliver and Company* (1988), and *An American Tale: Fievel Goes West* (1991).

Danny Aiello, born in New York in 1935, was in his thirties when he made his film debut in *Bang the Drum Slowly* (1973). During the 1970s and 1980s, he frequently played a versatile selection of beefy characters that ranged from sympathetic to menacing. He received an Emmy Award in 1981. Although his characters often appear to be violent and vulgar, he also portrays sensitive, kindly men with an earthy sense of humor. His roles frequently reflect his ethnic background, as in *29th Street* (1991), in which he played the dominant but lovable father of an Italian American clan. His Italian ethnicity came forth with a splendid performance in *Moonstruck* (1987) and in *Do the Right Thing* (1989), for which he wrote some of the script and which won him a nomination for best supporting actor.

Alan Alda, son of Robert Alda, was born in 1936 in New York and educated at Fordham University, and is recognized as an accomplished actor in films and television. Usually playing light, sarcastic roles, often as a restrained and mannered leading man, he enjoyed huge acclaim for his part in the long-running television series *M.A.S.H.* (1972–1983), for which he received several Emmy Awards as best actor, best director, and best writer. Since the 1960s he has made Hollywood films and in 1981 made his directorial debut in *Four Seasons,* a bittersweet romantic comedy. He has been active on the stage both in London and on Broadway with revivals of *Our Town* and *Jake's Women*. Among his more noteworthy films are *California Suite* (1978), *The Seduction of Joe Tynan* (1979), and *Crimes and Misdemeanors* (1989).

Paul Sorvino, born in 1939 in Brooklyn, is a tall, heavyset character lead on stage, television, and film. He took vocal lessons for many years and attempted a career in opera before becoming an actor in the 1960s. The father of acclaimed actress Mira Sorvino, Paul made his film debut in *Where's Poppa* (1970). He is often seen on television in roles both jovial and sinister. He is at his best playing tough urban characters, as in the case of his excellent portrayal of the mobster "Capo" in *Goodfellas* (1990). Among his films are *Blood Brothers* (1978) and *The Champion Season* (1982), in which he reprised his stage role. He was a television fixture on *Law and Order* in the early 1990s.

Brenda Vaccaro, born in Brooklyn in 1939, became a leading lady of the American stage, television, and silver screen. Beginning to act in high school, she continued to study acting at New York's Neighborhood Playhouse and launched her professional acting career in the 1960s. In 1985 she was nominated for an Oscar Award as best supporting actress in *Once Is Not Enough*. She received an Emmy Award for her performance in the television serial *The Shape of Things* in 1976.

Al (Alfred) Pacino, born in 1940 in the Bronx of Sicilian parents, was raised by his mother and grandparents after his father left the family. Not caring for traditional academic subjects, he quit high school and took an assortment of menial jobs while studying acting. One of his mentors was the fabled English actor Charles Laughton, who helped him obtain small supporting roles off Broadway. Following acceptance into Lee Strasberg's Actors Studio, he received an Obie Award for his performance in *The Italian Wants the Bronx*. His qualities as an actor, especially his intensity and brooding manner, led him to anti-hero roles. In 1969 he received a Tony Award for his Broadway performance in *Does a Tiger Wear a Necktie*. His first major film role, that of a junkie in *The Panic in Needle Park* (1971), attracted the attention of Francis Ford Coppola, who chose him to play the complex role of Michael Corleone in *The Godfather* trilogy. His convincing characterization was rewarded with Oscar nominations as best supporting actor in *The Godfather* (1972) and best actor in *The Godfather II* (1974). He also received best actor nominations for *Serpico* (1975), *Dog Day Afternoon* (1979), and *And Justice for All* (1970). He received the elusive Oscar Award in 1992 for his role in *Scent of a Woman* (1992). He continued to act on Broadway and won a Tony Award for *The Basic Training of Pavlo Hummel* (1977).

Born in 1944 in Neptune, New Jersey, Danny DeVito was educated at Oratory Prep School. Although working for a time as a hairdresser, he was determined to act and attended New York's American Academy of Dramatic Arts, his diminutive five-foot stature notwithstanding. His first stage appearance occurred in 1969 and his first film in 1970. His acting career accelerated after he reprised the role he played on stage in the film *One Flew Over the Cuckoo's Nest* (1975). For a number of years he co-starred with Tony Danza in the television series *Taxi,* for which he won an Emmy. His scene-stealing performances in *Romancing the Stone* (1984) and *Jewel of the Nile* (1985) brought more praise and more roles. In 1987 he made his directorial debut in *Throw Mama from the Train,* which was followed by *Twins* (1987), *Other People's Money* (1991), *Batman Returns* (1992), and *Hoffa* (1992). His production

company produced the award-winning film *Pulp Fiction* (1994). He is married to actress Rhea Pearlman.

Joe Pesci, a brash, diminutive character player with a penchant for portraying tough gangsters, was born in 1943 in Newark, New Jersey. The son of a blue-collar worker, he began to act as a child and enjoyed a modicum of success for several years. His first impressive film performance came with his rendition of Robert De Niro's boorish brother-in-law in Jake La Motta's biography, *Raging Bull* (1980), which earned him a nomination for best supporting actor. He won an Oscar in another Martin Scorsese film, *Goodfellas* (1990). He turned to comedy in the popular *Home Alone* (1990) and *My Cousin Vinny* (1992). He teamed again with Scorsese and De Niro in *Casino* (1995).

Bernadette Peters, born Bernadette Lazzaro in 1944 in Queens, New York, became a leading lady on stage and in nightclubs, television, and films by the 1960s. The daughter of an immigrant truck driver, she achieved her first success in an off-Broadway show, *Dames at Sea* (1967). Other Broadway musicals in which she starred include *Sunday in the Park with George* and *Song and Dance,* for which she won a Tony Award in 1985. Her film career has been uneven, with perhaps her best showcase performance in *Pennies from Heaven* (1981).

Robert De Niro, the son of New York artists, was born in 1943. Trained by professional actors Stella Adler and Lee Strasberg, De Niro began appearing in off-Broadway theaters before working in films in 1960. Following a few low-budget films, he received a truly important role in *Bang the Drum Slowly* (1973). This was the precursor to his major commercial success in Scorsese's film *Mean Streets* (1973), and it ushered in an ongoing relationship in which he highlighted the portrayal of Italian Americans. In 1973 he received the Oscar Award for best supporting actor in *The Godfather*. His brilliant acting in *Taxi Driver* (1976) earned him a nomination for best actor. He was nominated again for his performance in *The Deer Hunter* (1978). He also appeared in Bernardo Bertolucci's ambitious epic *1900* (1975). He received the Academy Award for best actor for his role in *Raging Bull* (1980), and won a similar award at the Venice Film Festival for his acting in *True Confessions* (1981). A versatile actor, he has attempted a demanding variety of roles that have elicited much praise. De Niro also directed and starred in the film *A Bronx Tale* (1993).

Sylvester Stallone, actor, director, and screenwriter, was born Michael Sylvester Stallone in 1946 in New York City. A product of a broken home, he grew up in the city's tough Hell's Kitchen section and for a time in the home of foster parents. He held a number of menial jobs but was always determined to become a professional actor—a goal he first achieved in some unremarkable films in the 1970s. Frustrated with his acting career, he wrote the script for and was the lead actor in *Rocky* (1976), a low-budget film that won an Oscar Award. There were several *Rocky* sequels. Stallone's continued success in movies revolved around other tough characters such as *Rambo: First Blood* (1983) and *Cliff Hanger* (1993).

Chicago-born Joe Mantegna (b. 1947) studied drama and toured Europe with the Chicago Organic Theater before benefiting under the tutelage of playwright-director David Mamet. Mantegna subsequently won a Tony Award in Mamet's Pulitzer Prize–winning play *Glengarry Glen Ross* (1984) and began a career in filmmaking. He began to receive attention for his magnetic portrayal of the seductive con man in *House of Cards* (1987) and as Don Ameche's co-star in *Things Change* (1988), for which he won best actor honors at the Venice Film Festival. He played the lead role in Francis Ford Coppola's film adaptation of John Fante's novel of psychological realism and ethnic isolation, *Wait Until Spring Bandini* (1989), that was released as a video.

Ralph Macchio, born in 1962 in Huntington, New York, began his acting career in television commercials and series episodes, the most notable being *Eight Is Enough*. He began to make movies in 1980, gaining huge recognition for *Karate Kid* (1984) and its sequels. He made an impressive Broadway debut opposite Robert De Niro in *Gabe and His Teddy Bear* (1986) and played a feature part in *My Cousin Vinny* (1992).

Born in Columbus, Ohio, in 1954, Beverly D'Angelo is a talented actress who has worked in film and television. She studied art in Italy and worked as a cartoonist before becoming a performer, first as a singer, then as an actress. Her first important role was in *Hair* (1979), a vehicle that allowed her to display her impressive talent.

Of Irish Italian descent, John Travolta was born in 1954 in Englewood, New Jersey. Disdaining formal education for acting, he became a popular young star of television in the *Welcome Back Kotter* series in which he played the dim-witted, lovable Vinnie Barbarino. He also performed on Broadway in such plays as *Grease* (1972). With *Saturday Night Fever* (1977), in which he played Tony Manero, the young King of the Disco beat, he reached film stardom, winning an Academy Award nomination. Although this early success was followed by other popular films—*Grease* (1978) and *Urban Cowboy* (1980), his career sagged for a number of years. However, his career was revived in 1989 after he received rave reviews for his part in *Look Who's Talking*. In 1994 he received his second Oscar nomination for his role in *Pulp Fiction*. He has continued to elicit positive reviews for later films, including *Get Shorty* (1995) and *Phenomenon* (1996).

Madonna was born Madonna Veronica Louise Ciccone in Bay City, Michigan, in 1958. She is a bold, controversial, self-promoting video and pop music superstar who, until recently, has encountered only moderate success in films. Raised by a strict father, she took piano and ballet lessons and did well in academic subjects, eschewing the latter for an acting career. She proved herself to be quite creative in the emerging world of music videos, becoming one of the most energetic performers with her provocative extravaganzas. Critics maintain that Madonna's early acting left much room for improvement, as evidenced in *Desperately Seeking Susan* (1985) and *Shanghai Surprise* (1986). She received more praise for her roles in *Dick Tracy* (1990) and *A League of Their Own* (1992). A more recent film, *Evita* (1996), is regarded as her best acting performance.

Nicolas Cage, born in 1964 as Nicholas Coppola in Long Beach, California, and a nephew of director Francis Ford Coppola, dropped out of high school to become an actor. He began to appear in a number of films in the early 1980s, and attracted much attention for his performances in *Raising Arizona* (1987) and *Moonstruck* (1987). His latest films include *Kiss of Death* (1995), *Leaving Las Vegas* (1996), *Face Off* (1997), and *Con Air* (1997).

M

Vincent D'Onofrio was born in 1959 in Brooklyn. This tall, brooding supporting actor caught the public's eye when he emulated De Niro as an underachiever in *Full Metal Jacket* (1987). He has also played in popular movies such as *Mystic Pizza* (1988) and *Fire Within* (1991). He starred in Nancy Savoca's film *Household Saints* (1993), in which three generations of Italian American women are confronted with issues of religion and assimilation in contemporary American culture.

Born in 1964 in Brooklyn and educated at Boston University, Marissa Tomei acted in daytime television serials (1987–1988) before her debut in films. She showed flair in *Oscar* (1991) and *Chaplin* (1992) and received an Academy Award for her role as Joe Pesci's wise-cracking girlfriend in *My Cousin Vinny* (1992). Recent films include *The Paper* (1994) and *The Perez Family* (1995).

Annabelle Sciorra, born in Connecticut in 1964 and raised in New York City, studied acting at the American Academy of Dramatic Arts. Her pleasant and warm personality won her supporting roles in several films. Her role in Nancy Savoca's *True Love* (1989) attracted the critics' attention and led to other choice roles. She played the lead part as the Italian American woman from Brooklyn in Spike Lee's controversial *Jungle Fever* (1991) and has appeared frequently on the screen since then.

One of the more promising Italian Americans currently making movies is Stanley Tucci (b. 1960), of Westchester, New York, whose grandparents migrated from Calabria. Especially conscious of his ethnic roots, Tucci spent a number of years in routine-like movies in which he played, in his own words, "the heavy—if not a goombah then some other kind of ethnic thug." His 1996 film *Big Night*, which he co-directed, co-produced, and co-starred in, was hailed by international critics. Unlike so many films that feature Italian American actors, *Big Night* eschews violence and conflict in preference for a simple story of two Italian brothers who run a restaurant in New Jersey in the 1950s. It is described as whimsical, sentimental, and appealing, a refreshing passage into the warm, supportive, and sympathetic dimension of Italian American life.

Philip Bosco (b. 1930) of Jersey City, New Jersey, is considered one of the finest actors of the era. He was attracted to theater as a child when he assisted his large Italian family in producing carnival shows. He studied acting at Catholic University and began to perform on the stage in the 1950s; however, it was not until the 1980s that enough serious critics became mesmerized by his theatrical performances in Shakespearean plays and other fine drama such as Robert Bolt's *A Man for All Seasons*. He also won a Tony for his comedic talent in *Lend Me a Tenor*. Although most of his acting has been for the stage format, he has had important roles in numerous television shows and some Hollywood films such as *Children of a Lesser God* (1986).

Other outstanding acting talents of Italian ancestry who have embellished television, stage, and Hollywood formats include Frank Langella and Tony LoBianco. Born in 1941, Langella enjoys taking risks in challenging roles. His thespian talents have elicited winning praise and awards, including a Tony for his Broadway debut in *Seascape*. His work in the movie *Diary of a Mad Housewife* (1970) won the National Society of Film Critics Award. He made a strong impact with his Broadway rendition of a sexy Count Dracula, which was also made into a movie.

Tony LoBianco (b. 1936), a Brooklyn product, is a veteran actor with numerous credits in the varying acting genres, including important roles in movies such as *The French Connection* (1971), *Nixon* (1995), and *F.I.S.T.* (1978). Although he showed athletic promise, LoBianco was captivated by acting as a child and studied at the Dramatic Workshop and Actor's Repertory Theater in New York City. He has played Italian American roles on stage such as Mayor Fiorello LaGuardia in *Fiorello!* and Eddie Carbone in *A View from the Bridge*, and has won his share of acting awards. Proud of his ethnicity, LoBianco has participated in Italian American activities and is currently a spokesman for the Order Sons of Italy in America.

Toward the end of the twentieth century Italian American actors and actresses were common coin on the screen as names like De Niro, Pacino, and Tomei vied with the likes of Hanks, Stone, and Gibson for popularity. It is interesting to note that the more widespread use of Italian Americans in the acting profession corresponded with the ethnic group's emergence in other important phases of movie production such as writers, directors, and producers. Inevitably this accounted for an increase in scripts that dealt with various aspects of Italian American life, which is still often tilted toward criminality. Whereas in the early decades of the movie industry the only Italian American director to make a significant impact in Hollywood was Frank Capra, recent years have seen an impressive growth as reflected by the likes of Alan Alda, Francis Ford Coppola, Michael Cimino, Brian De Palma, Danny DeVito, Martin Scorsese, Sylvester Stallone, Stanley Tucci, and Nancy Savoca. In addition, Coppola, DeVito, and Tucci have produced a number of films.

Whether as directors or producers, these Italian Americans have brought to the screen many depictions that capture the nuances of Italian American life, granted that not all films made by these Italian American directors and producers deal with Italian American themes or subject matter. In the latter half of the twentieth century, however, their films that do depict Italian American protagonists, enclaves, story lines, or themes tend to capture a more realistic range of interpretations rather than stereotypes. Hence, the audience is presented with a multidimensional depiction of Italian Americans unlike the negative one-dimension portrayals seen in the early years of filmmaking. As the list of Italian American Hollywood directors and producers continues to grow, future moviegoers are assured that their films will increasingly address themes derived from their Italian American roots and point to a fuller picture of ethnic life in America.

Mario Aste

Bibliography

Cook, Daniel. *A History of Narrative Film.* New York: W. W. Norton, 1996.

Ebert, Roger. *Videos Companion.* Kansas City: Andrews and McNeel, 1996.

Hollows, Joann, and Mark Jancovich, eds. *Approaches to Popular Film.* Manchester, NY: Manchester University Press, 1995.

Jameson, Richard T. *They Went That Way.* San Francisco: Mercury House, 1994.

Keal, Pauline. *For Keeps.* New York: Plume, 1995.

Maltby, Richard. *Hollywood Cinema.* Cambridge, MA: Blackwell, 1995.

Miller, Randall M. *Ethnic Images in American Film and Television.* Philadelphia: Balch Institute, 1978.

See also BANCROFT, ANNE; DE NIRO, ROBERT; FILM DIRECTORS, PRODUCERS, AND ITALIAN AMERICAN IMAGE IN CINEMA; PACINO, ALFRED JAMES; SINATRA, FRANCIS ALBERT; TELEVISION; THEATER HISTORY

Mugavero, Francis J. (1914–1991)

Roman Catholic bishop of Brooklyn for twenty-two years and a leading social reformer in the American Catholic Church, Francis J. Mugavero was born on June 8, 1914, on DeKalb Avenue in the Bedford-Stuyvesant section of Brooklyn. He was the son of Sicilian immigrants Angelo and Rose Pernice, who lived in the rear of their barber shop with their six children. After attending St. Ambrose Parish School, he enrolled in Cathedral Preparatory School, then in the Immaculate Conception Seminary, Huntington, Long Island, to prepare for the priesthood. Bishop Thomas E. Molloy ordained him on May 18, 1940.

After some parish assignments, he studied social work at Fordham University (1942–1944) and received a master's degree. This led to his appointment to Catholic Charities in Brooklyn, then as director of Catholic Charities in Queens, part of the Brooklyn Diocese, from 1948 to 1961. He was promoted to secretary of Charities (1961–1968).

Pope John XXIII made him a monsignor in 1962, and Pope Paul VI designated him fifth bishop of Brooklyn in 1968. Brooklyn was the smallest diocese in the territory but had the largest population (1.5 million Catholics). It also contained one of the largest concentrations of Italian Americans. He was the first bishop of Brooklyn to be born in his diocese and the first Italian American to fill the position. He quickly established himself as a popular bishop in his diocese with a diverse ethnic population. Considered a "liberal" in church and social matters, he was very popular in New York's progressive circles, as he was with his 850 priests, who regarded him as a compassionate and beloved shepherd of his flock.

Despite his liberal credentials, Bishop Mugavero did not confront Vatican officials. When the latter frowned on his allowing Dignity and other homosexual groups to have their own Masses, he complied and ordered diocesan priests to withdraw support from Dignity. When Brooklyn College changed its mind about granting the bishop an honorary degree, Mayor Edward I. Koch awarded him the La Guardia Medal, New York City's highest honor. While opposing abortion, Bishop Mugavero refrained from attacking Catholic politicians like the governor of New York, Mario M. Cuomo, who approved legalizing abortion.

Mugavero reached his people by broadcasting on commercial radio a weekly "Morning Reflections" on radio station WOR. During his tenure he promoted low-income housing, cared for the elderly, tended to the special needs of Italian and other ethnic minorities, and improved Catholic-Jewish relations. He was one of the architects of the Nehemiah plan, a project sponsored by fifty-two churches intent on constructing five thousand one-family homes in East New York and Brownsville in Brooklyn.

The American bishops designated him as the head of their national Campaign for Human Development, which spent millions to assist the poor, support projects for ethnic minorities, and enroll voters. Many Catholics objected to the use of their funds to underwrite what they viewed not as charity but as a radical political agenda.

Bishop Mugavero retired in 1990 and was succeeded by Bishop Thomas V. Daily. He died on July 17, 1991, while vacationing on Long Island.

Gaetano L. Vincitorio

Bibliography

Culkin, Harry M., ed. *Priests and Parishes of the Diocese of Brooklyn 1820 to 1990*, 3rd ed. Vol. 2. Brooklyn, NY: William Charles Printing, 1990.

"Diocese Mourns Its Loss: Bishop J. Mugavero." *The Tablet* (Brooklyn Diocesan Weekly) 84, no. 16 (20 July 1991): 3–7 and 13.

See also RELIGION

Musmanno, Michael A. (1897–1968)

A flamboyant and outspoken champion of the Italian American ethnic minority, Michael Musmanno served as a dedicated legislator and a zealous jurist. Yet his individualism and dramatic temperament prevented him from rising to national prominence.

Musmanno was born the son of Italian immigrants in Stowe Township, six miles from Pittsburgh, on April 7, 1897. He began working as a coal loader when he was fourteen but managed to earn a law degree from Georgetown University and was admitted to the Pennsylvania bar in 1923. As a lawyer in Stowe Township, he became concerned with labor disputes and served primarily a large clientele of Italian American miners. These blue-collar laborers were his prospective electorate when he ran unsuccessfully for the Pennsylvania House of Representatives on the Republican ticket in 1926. After his defeat, Musmanno moved to Boston to volunteer his services for the defense committee that endeavored to save Italian anarchists Nicola Sacco and Bartolomeo Vanzetti from the electric chair.

Although Musmanno's efforts were to no avail and his role in the committee was marginal, he enjoyed the fame of that notorious case and, after returning to the Pittsburgh area, easily defeated his Democratic opponent in the 1928 election for the Pennsylvania House of Representatives. Two years later he won a second term.

As a state representative, Musmanno pursued a liberal agenda promoting labor legislation. In particular, he introduced a bill to abolish the coal and iron police, a body of private police officers that employers used to fight industrial unionism. When Pennsylvania's Republican governor vetoed his bill, Musmanno distanced himself from his political party. He resigned from the House and won a seat in Allegheny County Court in 1931 after gaining both the Republican and the Democratic nomination with the strong endorsement of the Italian American press and labor organizations. One year later, Musmanno supported Franklin D. Roosevelt for president and, in 1933, became a judge of the Court of Common Pleas of Allegheny County, running on both the Democratic and the Republican ticket.

Musmanno's endorsement by the Democrats came to a temporary halt in 1935 when the state committee refused to endorse him for Pennsylvania's Supreme Court and caused his defeat at the polls. Yet, after Musmanno had campaigned for Roosevelt among Italian Americans in 1940, the Democratic Party slated him for the Superior Court in 1941 and 1942. As Pennsylvania had been a Republican stronghold in state elections since 1938, however, Musmanno suffered more devastating defeats.

The judiciary career did not offer Musmanno opportunities for mobility. So he took leave in 1943 to serve as an officer on the Italian front during World War II and as military governor of Sorrento. In 1946 President Truman appointed him as a judge at the Nuremberg Trials, and Musmanno presided over the case involving the Nazi execution squads in Russia.

Musmanno resumed his duties as a Pittsburgh judge in 1948 and soon joined the Cold War crusade against communism. Besides reflecting the growing conservatism of Italian Americans in the postwar years, his anticommunist stand provided him with a platform to run, though unsuccessfully, as lieutenant governor in 1950 and to win election to Pennsylvania's Supreme Court the following year. Justice Musmanno built a reputation as "the Great Dissenter" for his minority opinions in favor of the underprivileged and the underrepresented. In 1964 he made his last bid for elective office as a candidate for the Democratic nomination for the U.S. Senate. He became embroiled in an internecine struggle within the Democratic Party that brought about his defeat in the primaries despite the backing of former governor David Lawrence and the support of Italian American voters throughout Pennsylvania.

Musmanno was also an effective advocate of the most disparate Italian American causes. In 1962 he petitioned President Kennedy for recognition of Columbus Day as a national holiday. He protested against the publication of Joseph Valachi's memoirs on charges that the volume defamed the Italian American community. He wrote a book, *The Story of Italians in America* (1965), to defend the valuable contributions of his own fellow ethnics to the development of the United States. In *Columbus Was First* (1966), Musmanno made the case for Columbus' discovery of America against the thesis of Yale University specialists that Leif Eriksson had landed there centuries before him. Musmanno died on October 12, 1968.

Stefano Luconi

Bibliography

Falco, Maria J. *"Bigotry!" Ethnic, Machine, and Sexual Politics in a Senatorial Election.* Westport, CT: Greenwood, 1980.

Musmanno, Michael A. *Verdict! The Adventures of a Young Lawyer in the Brown Suit.* Garden City, NY: Doubleday, 1958.

Tuttle, Cliff. "Christopher Columbus' American Lawyer: Michael A. Musmanno and the Vinland Map." *Pittsburgh History* 78 (1994): 130–141.

See also POLITICS

M

N

National Association of the Wolves

An Italian American service and fraternal organization made up of about five hundred members organized in about fifteen local clubs, called "Dens," that are located in Pennsylvania and Ohio, the National Association of the Wolves, popularly known as the Wolves Club, was established in 1951 in New Castle, Pennsylvania, where its national office is located. The organization takes its name and symbol from the legendary founding of Rome, a she-wolf suckling two infants, Romulus and Remus. The symbol represents an act of charity and service to those in need, principles that inspire the club's primary purpose. The club's motto, "Pro Bono Publico," meaning "For the public good," also reflects the goals and membership requirements of the organization.

The origins of the Wolves Club are traced to 1929, when a small group of Italian American professional and businessmen founded a civic club that was patterned after service organizations such as the Rotary, Kiwanis, and Lions. The first club was established in New Castle, and, after several other local clubs were created, the national organization was established in 1951. The organization holds an annual national convention at different sites.

Membership in the Wolves was originally composed of professional and businessmen of Italian descent who would be devoted to raising funds for nonbinding loans to assist worthy and needy Italian American male students to finish their college education. Later, membership in the Wolves was extended to Italian American men from all walks of life, and very recently Dens were permitted to admit women and other "outstanding citizens" not of Italian origin. Current membership includes lawyers, businessmen, government officials, union officials, workingmen, teachers, retirees, and others. Dens are located in cities and towns in western Pennsylvania and eastern Ohio, with local membership ranging from about twenty to seventy.

In 1953 a formal scholarship program was established whereby each Den was required to help maintain at least one student in college. The awards are made to deserving and needy high school students regardless of race, color, creed, national origin, or gender. Dens are not permitted to grant scholarships to children or wards of club members. Some clubs are committed to grant $2,000 each year in college scholarships.

The achievements of the Wolves in raising funds for college scholarships and other community projects is remarkable. Most Dens raise far in excess of the minimal amount. Since its origins, the Wolves have granted over $2.5 million in college scholarships. Other community projects sponsored by local clubs include making contributions to the United Way and to food banks, organizing regional high school athletic contests, and purchasing equipment or furnishings for local hospitals and charitable organizations. Some clubs have contributed funds or books to local libraries for their Italian and Italian American collections.

Ernest E. Rossi

Bibliography

National Italian American Foundation. *Directory of Italian American Organizations, 1988–89*. Washington, DC: National Italian American Foundation, 1988.

Rossi, Ernest E., "The National Association of Wolves." *The National Italian American Foundation* (March/April 1984): 7.

See also ORGANIZATIONS

National Italian American Coordinating Association (NIACA): The Conference of Presidents of Major Italian American Organizations

The National Italian American Foundation (NIAF) and the Order Sons of Italy in America (OSIA), hosted on June 21, 1991, twenty-seven presidents representing the Italian American community throughout the United States. They convened in Washington, D.C., to consider a score of resolutions covering the gamut of Italian American concerns; those approved served as recommendations for implementation by each constituent entity. Thus, the National Italian American Coordinating Association (NIACA), then in its seventeenth year, bifurcated itself into the Conference of Presidents of Major Italian American Organizations.

It was at the urging of John N. LaCorte, president of the Italian Historical Society of America (IHSA), that OSIA, UNICO National, Italian American Labor Council, Grand Council of Columbia Associations in Civil Service, Americans of Italian Descent, and American Justinian Society of Jurists gathered in 1974, in Brooklyn, to form the Coordinating Committee of National Italian American Organizations, the established name until 1978.

The initial purpose of NIACA, to provide "a coordinative role for the national Italian American community," has since given way to consultative direction, using the competence of its constituent member organizations and seeking consensus on matters presented. A highly structured format, allowing for delegates from each affiliated organization vis-à-vis membership strength, and for dues likewise assessed, would guide NIACA through the 1980s.

When members of Congress of Italian background were gathered to establish an affiliate congressional caucus, the latter group, once organized in 1975, gave impetus to the establishment of a separate Washington entity, NIAF. Early enmity between the often con-fused NIACA and NIAF has given way to present-day cooperation.

NIACA was first acknowledged by President Ford in 1976; supportive of cultural pluralism, it expressed concern about "reverse discrimination detrimental to the Italian American community." In 1989 it identified the National Commission for Social Justice as its antidefamation referral agency. In 1990 the IHSA assigned the *Italian American Journal* to NIACA, which has since published it semi-annually as a scholarly journal. In 1991 it named the Italian American Institute at City University of New York (CUNY) as its research and technical assistance subsidiary. In 1992 it was afforded nongovernment observer status at the United Nations on behalf of Italians in America. More recently NIACA has focused attention on the Italian political scene, welcoming new ambassadors and voicing long-standing Italian American concern with communist participation in the Italian government. In 1996 it urged Clinton White House acceptance of an Italian plan guaranteeing Rome a rotating seat on the U.N. Security Council.

Current president is Martin Picillo, Esq., of New Jersey, past president of UNICO National. Constituent organizations include American Committee on Italian Migration, American Italian Federation of the Southeast, Arba Sicula, Coalition of Italo-American Associations of New York, Cooley's Anemia Foundation, Federated Italo-Americans of Southern California, FIERI National, Florida Federation of Italian American Clubs, Italian American Legal Defense and Higher Education Fund, Italian American War Veterans of the United States, Italian Apostolate of the Catholic Bishops Conference, Italian Sons and Daughters of America, Italian Symposium of Texas, Italo-American National Union, Joint Civic Committee of Italian Americans of Chicago, National Council of Columbia Associations, National Italian American Bar Association, National Italian American Hall of Fame, National Organization of Italian American Women, New Jersey Alliance of Italian American Organizations, Tri-State Italian American Congress of New York, New Jersey and Connecticut, and Verrazzano Institute at Mercy College. The American Italian Historical Association enjoys observer status.

Dominic R. Massaro

Bibliography
Maselli, Joseph, ed. *Year 2000: Where Will Italian-American Organizations Be in the Year 2000?* Washington, DC: National Italian American Foundation, 1990.

See also NATIONAL ITALIAN AMERICAN FOUNDATION; ORDER SONS OF ITALY IN AMERICA; ORGANIZATIONS; UNICO NATIONAL

National Italian American Foundation

Organized in 1976 by a coalition of business, political, educational, labor, and community leaders, the National Italian American Foundation (NIAF) has been described by ethnic scholar Dr. John Kromkowski as a perfect example of "the new type of organization." NIAF is "new" in that, while conducting numerous types of ethnic heritage programs, it also has achieved unparalleled success in networking within the Italian American community and in reaching out to spread its message to the public.

The first three major leaders of NIAF exemplify this approach. Businessman Jeno Paulucci was the first NIAF chairman in 1975; Monsignor Geno Baroni, a national community activist and later an assistant secretary of HUD during the Carter administration, was the first president; and Congressman Frank Annunzio of Chicago organized key elements of the Italian American political community to promote the NIAF.

NIAF held its first major event in Washington in 1976, and over two thousand people attended from all over the United States, including President Gerald Ford, his opponent Jimmy Carter, and Carter's running mate, Walter Mondale. All four candidates for national office (President Ronald Reagan, Vice President George Bush, presidential candidate Walter Mondale, and vice-presidential candidate Geraldine Ferraro) attended the annual dinner in 1984, an unprecedented event in American history.

The NIAF gala was at first a biennial event but in 1985 became an annual dinner capping an international convention that now regularly brings in more than three thousand persons from over forty states, Italy, and North and South America.

The first few years of NIAF's existence were spent developing a base of support throughout the country. One of its early executive directors, Joseph Ventura, a onetime staff director for Congressman Annunzio, was instrumental in this effort. Once the base was developed, NIAF began to expand its activities from its biennial dinner and early concerns with discrimination issues into education. Educational issues were important at an early stage, as NIAF organized conferences on such themes as the Italian rescue efforts of the Jews during the Holocaust and the early Italian contributions to America. The NIAF's annual budget for scholarships and grants reached five hundred thousand dollars in 1997, and its goal is to reach $1 million by the year 2000.

NIAF currently has full-time departments for education, dealing largely with scholarship opportunities; youth assistance, aimed at helping young people appreciate their heritage and also compete in the highly competitive job market; and culture and communications, which conduct Italian heritage programs with such institutions as Johns Hopkins University, the Smithsonian Institution, and the Library of Congress.

NIAF also decided at the outset to promote Italian and United States relations and has through the years held international conferences and seminars in New York City, Australia, Argentina, and Italy.

Another major activity has been the development of specific institutes to work on key

Frank Sinatra greets Ambassador John Volpe at the NIAF Gala in Washington, D.C., 1985. Jeno Paulucci, the fast-food king, is center. Courtesy of the National Italian American Foundation (NIAF), Washington, D.C.

areas of American life. NIAF Institutes are coordinated by NIAF vice chairman Frank Guarini, a former congressman. The NIAF Institutes now include interethnic affairs, professional, Italian language and culture, labor and management, media, public policy, and youth.

The growth of NIAF has come about largely because of the leadership of the NIAF board of directors. Detroit businessman Frank D. Stella was elected president, then vice chairman in 1988 and chair in 1992, a post he still held in 1997. United States Court Judge Arthur Gajarsa assumed the presidency in 1988 and was succeeded by Frank Guarini, who in turn was succeeded by Vermont neurologist A. Kenneth Ciongoli in 1996. Ciongoli, who is co-editor of a book on Italian American intellectuals, has concentrated his efforts on promoting the Italian American cause through conferences and seminars at such educational institutions as Princeton University, Harvard University, the University of Pennsylvania, and the University of Virginia.

Other current board members include such Italian American leaders as former Congresswoman Geraldine A. Ferraro, Ambassador Peter F. Secchia, New York Stock Exchange Chairman Richard A. Grasso, Saks Fifth Avenue President Rose Marie Bravo, Senator Pete V. Domenici, Congresswomen Nancy Pelosi and Connie Morella, Conair chairman Lee Rizzuto, and labor leader Robert Georgine, among others.

Alfred Rotondaro

Bibliography

Cavaioli, Frank J. "The National Italian American Foundation: 1975–1985." In *Amadeo P. Giannini,* edited by Felice A. Bonadio. Washington, DC: National Italian American Foundation, 1985.

Maselli, Joseph, ed. *Year 2000, Where Will Italian American Organizations Be in the Year 2000?* Washington, DC: National Italian American Foundation, 1990.

See also ORGANIZATIONS

National Organization of Italian American Women (NOIAW)

Founded in 1980, this organization is the only national membership organization for women of Italian ancestry. NOIAW is dedicated to fostering the interest and concerns of Italian American women by forming a national network to serve as a resource and support for the professional, political, and social advancement of its members; by promoting the accomplishments, history, and heritage of Italian American women; by fostering greater ethnic pride and educational opportunities for young people of Italian American origin; and by helping to serve the health and welfare interests of the national Italian American communities.

Members, all of whom have at least one parent of Italian heritage, serve together as a resource in achieving the following goals: acting as role models for younger Italian Americans and thereby fostering ethnic pride; identifying and encouraging greater unity with other Italian American organizations; networking with other women's ethnic groups; promoting community work; and raising the level of aspiration for other Italian Americans through programs and other related activities. Its structure is governed by a policy-making national board consisting of women throughout the country. Regions are established geographically. Program development, membership recruitment, and the mentor program are developed in the regions and in subdivisions called networks. Regions and networks are governed by steering committees headed by regional directors.

Committees offer an opportunity to contribute to the goals and programs of NOIAW, and include mentor, program, public relations, membership, fundraising, and conference/luncheon. Each region plans programs that address cultural, social, educational, business, and professional interests of members.

The aim of the mentor program is to connect many of the extraordinary women in the organization with undergraduate and graduate students in all fields and with members reentering the workforce. The NOIAW member serves as role model, guide, supporter, and contact to enhance the multidimensional development of these women.

Each year several scholarships are given to outstanding Italian American women who are advancing their education. Monthly networking meetings include book readings, financial seminars, and lectures by its members or other prominent women in the field of advertising, education, law, arts, music, and medicine. International conferences have taken place in Argentina, Australia, and Italy.

Each year distinguished men and women are honored. Past honorees have included the Honorable Susanna Agnelli, Mother Angelica, Gerald Arpino, Kaye Ballard, Joseph Bologna, Dr. Constance Battle, Helen Boehm, Matilda Cuomo, Jo Ann Falletta, Geraldine Ferraro, Sister Irene Fugazy, Concetta Lassavo Hassan, Jeno F. Paulucci, Anna Quindlen, Mary Ann Restivo, Rosanna Scotto, Renee Taylor, Marlo Thomas, and Lina Wertmuller.

On July 12, 1980, at the home of Dr. Aileen Riotto Sirey, a group of prominent women met, including Matilda Cuomo, Geraldine Ferraro, Jackie Biaggi, Donna Di-Matteo, Rosemarie Galinna, Clara Graziani Bronson, Bonnie Mandina, Rosanne Martorella, and Rosemarie Stigliano. Common concerns facing Italian American women at the time were discussed, with the group sharing the belief that neither Italian American clubs nor the American feminist movement represented them.

Italian American women come from a unique background and experience a conflict in roles with regard to their ethnicity, gender, and education. Professional women encounter competing demands and experience an alienation uncommon to other women. From this sense of frustration, and in search of a common identity, the National Organization of Italian American Women was founded to provide the significant role models lacking in contemporary American society.

Rosanne Martorella

Bibliography

Caroli, Betty Boyd, Robert F. Harney, and Lydio F. Tomasi, eds. *The Italian Immigrant Women in North America.* Toronto: Multicultural History Society of Ontario, 1978.

Gabaccia, Donna. "Women and Ethnicity: A Review Essay." *Italian Americana* 12 (fall/winter 1993): 38–61.

Messina, Elizabeth. "Life Span Development and Italian-American Women: A Review." In *Italian Americans in a Multicultural Society,* edited by Jerome Krase and Judith N. DeSena, 74–88. New York: American Italian Historical Association, 1994.

See also ORGANIZATIONS

New Haven

While records show that Italians lived in New Haven, Connecticut, as early as 1715, their numbers grew to a significant amount with the great migrations of Europeans to the United States after the American Civil War. Political turmoil, repression, and poverty in the rural, agricultural areas of southern Italy, as in other parts of Eastern and Central Europe, combined with rapid expansion of both the industrial and rural sectors of the United States to create the great wave of migration that brought 25 million people here between 1870 and 1930, including more than 5 million Italians.

New Haven experienced the beginnings of the migration wave with the arrival of immigrants from the village of Gioia Sannitica, in the province of Benevento, not far from Naples. By 1890 New Haven counted 2,330 Italians among its rapidly expanding population. The rapid growth continued as the Italian population tripled to 7,780 in 1900, including 2,518 native-born children. Italians then constituted some 7.2 percent of the city's population of 108,000.

As was common elsewhere, many early arrivals were men eager to earn money in the great land of opportunity, then return to Italy to live. This pattern was common throughout the East Coast. Yet more and more Italians stayed on in New Haven and brought wives and raised children. In 1884 a delegation went to Hartford to urge the bishop to provide a priest for their needs. The bishop granted their wish in 1885, and, in 1889, the New Haven Italians bought a small Lutheran church near Wooster Square and named it in honor of St. Michael the Archangel, the patron saint of Gioia Sannitica, from which many of its early parishioners had come. Later, the Italians bought a larger Baptist church on Wooster Square, again dedicating it to St. Michael. To this day it stands as the focal point for the Italian community in New Haven.

By 1900 the city was beginning another surge of migration, as thousands of immigrants arrived from the southwestern seaport town of Amalfi and its neighbor, Atrani. Now, almost one hundred years later, the New Haven area counts more descendants from Amalfi (10,000 in the city and 27,000 in the metropolitan area) than actually live in Amalfi itself. There are also several thousand Atranese.

By the mid-twentieth century, New Haven's Italians were the dominant ethnic group in the city. They faced and slowly overcame the discrimination that had confronted Italians in most parts of the United States. The struggle was nowhere better illustrated than in the political arena. Irish Americans had controlled the Democratic Party since the turn of the century. By 1940 Italian Americans outnumbered Irish Americans by more than two to one, but the Irish Americans controlled almost half the jobs in city government. Italian Americans and other ethnic groups had been restricted to minor posts like city sheriff and justices of the peace. Slowly, Italian Americans in both political parties won seats on the board of aldermen. While they tended to identify more with the Democratic Party, the first Italian to run for mayor was a Republican, William Celentano, a funeral home owner from outside the heavily Democratic Wooster Square area. After losing in his first effort, he ran again in 1945 and with the help of a large crossover vote became the first Italian American mayor of New Haven. Shortly thereafter, Republican Albert W. Cretella Sr. won the Third District House seat, while Democrat Anthony S. Avallone was elected to the state senate.

In the fifty years since Celentano's breakthrough, three other Italians, all Democrats, have been elected mayor, including Bartholemew Guida, Biaggio DiLieto, and John DeStefano. Congresswoman Rosa DeLauro, herself a daughter of Wooster Square, a Democrat and the first woman to serve from the Third District, continued to reflect the strong Italian ties in the city, even though African Americans are the largest single ethnic group in the city, constituting about 47,000 of the city's total population of 137,261. As of the late 1990s, 32,000 Italians reside in the central city, accounting for some 25 percent of the New Haven Standard Metropolitan Statistical Area population of 530,000.

The continued vitality of the Italian presence in New Haven can be attributed to two major factors: Wooster Square and the almost mythical quality of the ties that bind the people to the towns of Amalfi and Atrani. Wooster Square is the Little Italy of New Haven. And while the population is no longer overwhelmingly Italian, the character of the neighborhood continues to be heavily Italian. There is a bit of irony in that Wooster Square

In Bridgeport, Connecticut, Italian Americans contributed to the purchase of an ambulance for the Italian Red Cross during the First World War. The fact that Italy was fighting on the Allied side, as was the United States, rendered assistance to the land of their forebears most acceptable. Courtesy Center for Migration Studies.

had been the home to New Haven's "Yankee" elite in the period of rapid industrialization following the Civil War. But the elites abandoned Wooster Square in the face of industrial pollution and flood of European immigrants. By 1940 the Wooster Square area was more than 90 percent Italian. But it was also labeled as one of the city's most blighted areas, and it continued to struggle to survive through the 1950s. It was rescued as one of the few city sections of New Haven's Urban Renewal Program to come close to actual renewal.

Wooster Square's life is enriched also by the presence of the St. Andrew's and Santa Maria Maddalena Societies, the former honoring the patron saint of Amalfi and the latter of Atrani. Their friendly rivalry in the sponsorship of *festas* to honor their saints and their continued ties to their native cities in Italy suggest that the twilight of Italian ethnicity in New Haven will be a lingering and pleasant one for the third-, fourth-, and fifth-generation Italians who work to revitalize a city.

The election of A. Bartlett Giamatti (a native son) to the presidency of Yale University in 1978 marked the final coming-of-age of Italian Americans in New Haven and also a new era in town-grown relations, with Mayor DiLieto and President Giamatti working together to confront the many problems posed for the city and the area by the failure of urban renewal, the collapse of the nineteenth-century industrial system, and the influx of African Americans and Latinos into a suddenly depressed area.

In the late 1990s, Mayor John DeStefano and the board of aldermen have worked their way into the dynamic phase of a partnership with Yale to build a new New Haven for the twenty-first century. They are fortunate in having Wooster Square as a vital link to the past as well as a comfortable gentrified residential area. And for the thousands of Italians who have "made it" and now live in the city's affluent neighborhoods, as well as for the Yale students and alumni, there is still Wooster Street with some of the country's best and oldest pizza houses, pastry shops, and restaurants.

Nancy N. Cassella
William V. D'Antonio

Bibliography

Dahl, Robert A. *Who Governs? Democracy and Power in an American City.* New Haven: Yale University Press, 1961.

D'Antonio, William V. "Facing the Twilight of Our Ethnicity." In *The Columbus People,* edited by Lydio F. Tomasi, Piero Gastaldo, and Thomas Row, 49–53. New York: Center for Migration Studies, 1994.

Kennedy, Ruby Jo Reeves. "Single or Triple Melting Pot, Intermarriage Trends in New Haven 1870–1940." *American Journal of Sociology* 49 (1949): 335–339.

Psathas, George. "Ethnicity, Social Class, and Adolescent Independence from Parental Control." *American Sociological Review* 22 (August 1957): 415–423.

Taeuber, Irene B., and Conrad Taeuber. *Peoples of the United States in the Twentieth Century.* Washington, DC: Bureau of the Census, 1971.

"Wooster Square: Understanding the Neighborhood." *Inside New Haven's Neighborhoods.* New Haven: New Haven Colony Historical Society, 1982, 35–46.

New Orleans

Although this southern city was settled first by the French and then the Spanish, by the nineteenth century it had become a mecca for Italian immigrants. Between 1850 and 1870 the United States Census Bureau estimated that there were more Italians in New Orleans than in any other United States city. By 1910 the population of the city's French Quarter, known as Little Palermo, was 80 percent Italian. Today, there are two hundred thousand Americans of Italian descent living in New Orleans and its suburbs, making Italian Americans the largest ethnic group in the city.

The history and culture of local Italian Americans, the largest percentage being of Sicilian heritage, are preserved in a museum and research center in the heart of New Orleans. The American Italian Renaissance Foundation Museum and Research Library was founded in 1984 with a mission to gather artifacts and memorabilia concerning local Italian American history. To establish the research center, the foundation raised one million dollars in contributions from the city's large Italian American community.

Today, the center's library holds the collected works of Giovanni Schiavo, one of the first historians to document Italian American contributions to the United States. Other holdings include over 250 oral histories and more than two thousand histories of prominent local and national Italian Americans.

The museum and research center also houses a large conference room; a Hall of Honor; and the Louisiana American Italian Sports Hall of Fame, which honors national and local Italian sports personalities. Among them are baseball's Tommy Lasorda, former manager of the Los Angeles Dodgers; boxing/trainer Angelo Dundee; and billiard champion Willie Mosconi.

The museum records Italy's troubled history following unification in 1870 and the closing decades of the nineteenth century, when the country's severe economic and social problems forced millions of Italians to migrate to the United States.

Most of the Italian immigrants who came from Naples settled in New York and other cities along the eastern seaboard. Many of the Sicilians, however, sailed from Palermo and landed in New Orleans. During their month-long voyage, they suffered from dysentery and even death. Once they arrived in New Orleans, the survivors had to struggle with the language barrier, homesickness, and discrimination. The largest mass lynching in United States history took place in New Orleans in 1891 when a mob of over five hundred "upright citizens" hanged or shot eleven Italian immigrants who had been accused, tried, and found innocent of murdering the local police chief.

The Sicilians brought their culture, music, and food to their new country. They also brought a traditional St. Joseph's Day

N

altar, which becomes laden with the specialties Sicilian women prepare to feed the homeless and poor on March 19 every year.

Italian Americans hold places of honor in the city's history. New Orleans has had two Italian mayors: Robert Maestri, who served from 1936 to 1945, and Victor Schiro, whose tenure ran from 1961 to 1970. Italian Americans have served in the city council, the state supreme court, and on the local police force. In Louisiana today, there are more than thirty Italian American judges. Among them are Chief Judge of the United States Fifth Circuit Court of Appeals Henry (Pugliese) Politz, Chief Justice of the Louisiana Supreme Court Pascal Calogero, Chief Judge of the State Criminal Court Frank Marullo, and Criminal Sheriff of Orleans Parish Charles Foti.

The Italians of Louisiana have excelled in business and have dominated the food industry. Immigrants soon opened grocery shops that evolved from the push carts that used to crisscross the city daily, bearing fresh fruits and vegetables. Other immigrants opened fine restaurants like Tortorici's on Royal Street and food processing factories, such as the Progresso Food Company founded by the Uddo and Taormina families.

Italian Americans helped to build New Orleans, putting up more than 50 percent of the city's high-rise buildings and constructing shopping centers and hotels. Local Italian Americans contributed to the city's music: Nick LaRocca wrote "Tiger Rag" and, as leader of the Original Dixieland Jass Band, made the first jazz recording in 1917. He was followed by the Dukes of Dixieland: Frank, Freddie, and Papa Assunto, and by Louis Prima and Sam Butera.

As Italians entered the business and artistic communities of New Orleans they gained visibility and status. In 1971 the Italian American Marching Club was organized to parade annually on March 19, St. Joseph's Day. Today the club has more than fifteen hundred members.

Most Sicilian immigrants were able to build better lives for themselves and their families in New Orleans, where they found land they could afford, a familiar religious community, and a natural climate similar to the one they left behind in Sicily.

Joseph Maselli

Bibliography

Gambino, Richard. *Vendetta*. New York: Doubleday, 1977.

Schiavo, Giovanni. *Four Centuries of Italian American History*. New York: Vigo Press, 1957.

See also SOUTH, THE

Ninfo, Salvatore
See LABOR

Nolcini, (Peter) Charles (1802–1844)

A musician and composer, Charles Nolcini was organist for the Beethoven Musical Society of Portland, Maine, and for King's Chapel in Boston, Massachusetts. Nolcini was born in Moscow of an Italian family, and he died in Boston. Leaving Russia as Peter Charles Nolcini, he arrived in Boston in 1820 and began his American career as a musician. Thereafter, except in legal documents, he rarely used his first name. On November 10, 1821, in an advertisement in *The Euterpeiad*, a musical publication, he offered his services as Charles Nolcini, an expert on the piano. Subsequently, in 1824, he became the organist for the Beethoven Musical Society of Portland, Maine. On February 8, 1826, Nolcini composed *Dedication Anthem* for Portland's First Parish Church, thereby adding to his other compositions, *A Military Waltz* (1821) and *A March Dedicated to New Beginners* (1826).

While in Portland, Nolcini also served as the organist for the Second Parish Church. The city's directories for the 1820s and 1830s list him as a resident and as a teacher, while the newspapers of that period have occasional advertisements about his expertise in music and modern languages. Married to Mary A. Murray, their first child died at nine weeks of age, but their second child, Charles A. Nolcini (1829–1895), became a prominent pharmacist.

Some of those years in Maine saw the couple living in Augusta and Bangor, where they engaged in teaching. Then, when Bangor's Hammond Street Congregational Church constructed a new brick church, Nolcini became organist for its Unitarian Church (1832–1834). As with the dedication of the First Parish Church in Portland, Nolcini composed an anthem that he played for the ceremony on July 23, 1834. He added to his musical compositions with *The Thanksgiving Anthem* (1834), *The Grasshopper's Waltz*

(1839), *Les San Soucis* (1839), and *The Tear of Gratitude Waltz* (1840).

Nolcini's music contributed to those inroads that other Italians had already made into the cultural life of New England. Before Nolcini's arrival in Boston, for example, the first conservatory of music was established there by Filippo Traetta in 1801. Also, as early as 1815, (Paul Antonio) Louis Ostinelli had became a conductor of Boston's Handel and Haydn Society. And, by 1822, when Ostinelli was on a concert tour of New England, his reputation had spread to Portland, where an advertisement in *The Eastern Argus* (October 29, 1822) announced that the conductor and his wife would be presenting a concert with Nolcini that evening. These connections with Ostinelli, who was a witness for Nolcini's naturalization as an American citizen, obviously helped the latter in Massachusetts, where he became organist for Boston's King Chapel (1826–1832) and for Newburyport's First Unitarian Church (1834–1837). Nolcini was buried in the area of Copp's Hill Burial Ground in Boston's North End, a part of the city now known for its Italian traditions.

Vincent A. Lapomarda

Bibliography

Edwards, George Thornton. *Music and Musicians of Maine*. Portland, ME: Southworth, 1928.

Johnson, H. Earle. *Musical Interludes in Boston, 1795–1830*. New York: Oxford, 1943.

Lapomarda, Vincent A. *Charles Nolcini: The Life and Music of an Italian American in the Age of Jackson*. Worcester: Vincent A. Lapomarda, 1997.

Owen, Barbara. *The Organs and Music of King's Chapel, 1713–1964*. Boston: King's Chapel, 1966.

See also COMPOSERS, CLASSICAL

Novels and Novelists

Many literary scholars and critics maintain that there has been a disparity between life as portrayed in the traditionally accepted American novel and the actual experiences, for example, of ethnic minorities. In the volume *The Italian American Novel* by Rose Basile Green (1974), which presents a chronological analysis of the fictional writings of Americans of Italian ancestry, there is a record of interaction between two cultures, immigrant and established, within the composition of American civilization. In order to focus on the stages and evolution of the Italian American novel, the authors of Italian ancestry must be evaluated according to their responses to national movements. Their writings are critically evaluated within the framework of the established literature.

The first writings by Italian Americans were chiefly autobiographical accounts of entering a new world and adjusting to a pluralistic society. An analysis of these early works is useful to evaluate the problems and to judge the verisimilitude of Italian American fiction. Such an analysis authenticates certain consistencies in the various stages of Italian migration to America as to their background, exodus, and arrival. Examples of background conditions in the mother country are *The Story of Antonio, the Galley Slave* (1911) by Antonio A. Arrighi; *The Soul of an Immigrant* (1924) by Constantine M. Panunzio; *Americans by Choice* (1956) by Angelo M. Pellegrini; *The Autobiography of a Bootblack* (1902) by Rocco Corresca; and *I Zappatori* (1953) by Bernard J. Ficarra. The arrival in America is well typified in *Son of Italy* (1924) by Pascal D'Angelo.

Through the filter of their real experiences, these writers composed their own stories to project a more truthful image representing them in American fiction. The autobiographers' stories articulate that the American experience changes the Italians by a gradual process. With this process came the emergence of the Italian American novel, a development that would alter the knowledge of their ethnic experience about which Bernard De Voto wrote in *The Literary Fallacy* (1944), "Never in any country or age had writers so misrepresented their culture, or been so unanimously wrong."

The first stage, then, for Italian American fiction was in the great flux of immigration as presented by Luigi Donato Ventura in *Peppino* (1913), whose protagonist is a shoe shiner who takes great pride in his work and who strives to win the friendship of his customers. Likewise, the work symbol imbues writings by Silvio Villa and is illustrated in Giuseppe Cautela's *Moon Harvest* (1925) and in Garibaldi Marto Lapolla's *The Grand Gennaro* (1935). Novelists of lesser stature, such as John Antonio

Moroso, who produced exemplary works such as *The Stumbling Herd* (1923), also structured themes on the struggle of the underprivileged individual who attempts to achieve success while the will to survive is in conflict with the environment.

In general, the first Italian American novelists wrote stories on the cultural dualism and social conflict surrounding the immigrants' encounter with American civilization. This dualism was a bridge to amalgamation, and the conflict had visible constructive elements.

Though nostalgic reminiscences hindered immigrants from giving up the old tunes of their native villages, they had to establish a home of some permanence for themselves in their new environment. For the most part, writers chose two directions of structure: aggressive violence or lyrical optimism, as exemplified by Louis Forgione and Prosper Buranelli. Forgione's *The Men of Silence* (1928) deals with the repercussions of organized crime in America, while his *The River Between* (1928) removes the locale to a Sicilian colony on the edge of the Palisades, New York. However, as the New World became more receptive to newcomers, Italian American writers approached this compromise with grace and optimism, as expressed in the stories of Valenti Angelo in his books, *Golden Gate* (1939), *Hill of Little Miracles* (1942), and *The Rooster Club* (1944).

In their effort to make homes for themselves in a new environment, Italian Americans, like other pioneers attempting to achieve identity, experienced an immediate revulsion from the erudites of their environment. During the first phase of this revulsion, immigrant writers included Bernard De Voto, Paul William Gallico, Frances Winwar (Francesca Vinciguerra), and Hamilton Basso. Bernard De Voto's works include five novels: *The Crooked Mile* (1924), *The Chariot of Fire* (1926), *The House of Sun-Goes-Down* (1928), *We Accept with Pleasure* (1934), and *Mountain Time* (1947); he also wrote four other novels under the pseudonym of John Austen, many volumes of history, and books of essays. Orlan Sawey stated that De Voto's novels "have not received the place in history that they deserve."

As literary history gained popularity, so did the works of Frances Winwar, who succeeded in writing historical novels that have garnered acclaim from both the popular reading audience and the academicians. A recognized literary editor, her books of fiction include *The Ardent Flame* (1927), *The Golden Round* (1928), *Pagan Interval* (1929), *Gallows Hill* (1937), *The Sentimentalist* (1943), *The Eagle and the Rock* (1953), and *The Last Love of Camille* (1955). Among other things, Winwar relates to the reader that women have levels of virtue that can overcome predicaments caused by gender bias in their historical environments.

Paul William Gallico is one of the most representative Italian American fiction writers who does not treat the immediate problems of adjustment confronting the immigrant; rather, he transforms the themes to recognizable and already familiar American materials. After years of experience as a sports writer and as editor of the *New York Daily News,* Gallico turned to writing numerous works of fiction, such as *The Small Miracle* (1952), in which the author lifts the Italian American subject away from Little Italy to the level of a universal theme. Hence, Italian themes within the literary structure of the American scene are more easily understood when bestowed with universal traits by authors such as Gallico.

In the *Mainstream* (1943), Hamilton Basso wrote that the men who played a prominent part in our political and economic patterns are "tributaries" that swell the mainstream of today's America. To make an adequate analysis of the stream, other springs must be explored. Therefore, in *Days Before Lent* (1939) Basso explores those springs that flow into our general cultural stream. Since the extension of one's life to that of others as part of the "life of his time" is an important concept to Basso's work, his novels contain the struggles of the immigrant as an exclusive area of life that the individual rejects in favor of the broader environment of humanity. Basso rejects the structure he calls "Shintoism" in his novel *The View From Pompey's Head* (1934), in which he is more specific in delineating an established culture as a form of ancestor worship. The writer illustrates the struggle of the individual who seeks his own identity while struggling with the fixed ideas in an established society dedicated to ancestor worship.

When they discovered both the inadequacy and the distortion of themes that represented them in the national literature,

American writers of Italian ancestry returned to Italian American subjects for their fictional materials. Because they were for the most part second- and third-generation Americans, the writers were able to look backward with the advantage of a more firmly established cultural integration than that of their ancestors. Born at the beginning of the twentieth century, they identified their views with those who were not only of a different age, but also of a more advanced technological period. Among others, the group includes Guido D'Agostino, Jo Pagano, Mari Tomasi, Jerre Mangione, George Panetta, Jimmy Savo, Pietro di Donato, and John Fante.

The attempt to overcome isolation is treated by Guido D'Agostino in *Olives on the Apple Tree* (1940) and *Hills Beyond Manhattan* (1942). A variation of the profile he portrays is structured in his other books: *My Enemy the World* (1947) and *The Barking of a Lonely Fox* (1952).

Dramatizing the typical events of Italian American life led Jo Pagano from writing scenarios for Warner Brothers Studio to composing full-length novels: *The Paesanos* (1940) and *Golden Wedding* (1943). Then, with the novel *The Condemned* (1947), Pagano confirmed his concern with various types of nonconformists and misfits who try to adjust to a society whose fixed standards inevitably convict them.

Gradually the themes of Italian American writers of the second generation progressed to deal with a firmer implantation in the native soil, as in the case of Mari Tomasi, who encapsulates the earth and granite of Vermont in *Like Lesser Gods* (1949). The recipient of many awards, Tomasi demonstrates in her books a firm interaction between the cultural concepts of her Piedmontese parents and the established labor society of Vermont. She uses both themes and events to demonstrate that the Italian American laborer is a model of honesty and integrity, parched with a thirst for beauty and driven by a passion for artistic perfectionism. As a novel, *Like Lesser Gods* is a celebration of life and an affirmation of the individual's capacity to resist hostile forces. Her symbols are obvious. She makes Pietro the rock upon which Mr. Tiff, the transcendental figure, builds the intangible monument to Italian character in America; but she also lauds all women as she depicts the Mona Lisa wisdom of Maria as the amalgam of family unity.

The theme of social fragmentation persists in the novels of Jerre Mangione, especially in *Mount Allegro* (1942), a significant example of the return to Italian American life as an autobiographical literary subject in material and presentation. With *The Ship and the Flame* (1948) Mangione proceeds from anecdotal autobiography to more imaginative and progressive action: he creates a day-by-day report of a ship of refugees from Nazi concentration camps who hope to settle in America. His other works include *Reunion in Sicily* (1950), *Life Sentence for Everybody* (1965), *Night Search* (1965), *A Passion for Sicilians* (1968), and *America Is Also Italian* (1969).

Writing more to the tune of immigrant language, George Panetta has crafted novels with his ear keyed to the voice of Italian dialect in America. His novels with Calabrian idiom include *We Ride a White Donkey* (1944), *Jimmy Potts Gets a Haircut* (1947), *Viva Madison Avenue* (1957), and *Sea Beach Express* (1960). With authentic idiom, Panetta has created a veritable sound track for the stories of an enclave.

Meanwhile, Italian American integration has been tested by writers who return to the soil of their ancestors, as exemplified by Jimmy Savo who, after sojourning to Italy, wrote *Little World "Hello!"* (1947). The story relates his first visit to Italy, sixty miles from Rome, where his parents had been born.

The return to original sources, however, was opened to writers only through a more complete cultural integration with the American scene, as is evident in *Christ in Concrete* (1939), the autobiographical novel by Pietro di Donato. With this book, di Donato became the first Italian American writer to stir the American reading public into fully recognizing the Italian American experience, specifically in the world of construction workers in New York City before the 1940s. In the novel *This Woman* (1958), di Donato explores a man's obsession with three things: brickwork, women, and his soul. In *Three Circles of Light* (1960), he shows that many Italians in America eventually returned to their own people, cleared of superstition and betrayal.

As di Donato rediscovered his identity by developing his religious faith, other writers sought to find themselves in different ways. John Fante, for example, became absorbed in a Freudian search for the ideal American existence in *Wait Until Spring, Bandini* (1938).

Representative of his search-for-identity theme, his other books include *Ask the Dust* (1939), *Dago Red* (1940), and *Full of Life* (1952). With the reaffirmation of his religious convictions, Fante "backtracks" to traditional subjects through psychological probings.

Second-generation Italian American writers anticipated the integration of the hyphenated Italian American into a distinctive American in literature, and this optimism is revealed in the books of recent Italian American novelists who may be properly included in the anthologized national literature. Additional members up to 1965 include Michael De Capite, Luigi Creatore, Joseph Petrarca, Lawrence Madalena, Raymond DeCapite, Charles Calitri, Joseph Caruso, and Rocco Fumento.

Revealed in the early novels, in which the writers depicted community fragmentation, were conflicts between two alien cultures that directed the immigrant's withdrawal into isolation. As assimilation increased and gradually dispelled this isolation, the Italian American novelists contributed a new and valid maturity to American fiction.

During the years between 1960 and 1970 the Italian American novel made a great leap into the stronghold of American letters with the works of George Cuomo, Eugene Mirabelli, Robert Canzoneri, Frank Miceli, Robert Cenedella, Joseph Papaleo, Francis Pollini, and Mario Puzo. Representative of particular aesthetic value include Marion Benasutti, Ralph Corsel, Joseph R. Vergara, and Lucas Longo. Significantly, Marion Benasutti exemplifies the trend to recognize the current artist, whether man or woman, who still faces and conquers the problem of national distinction. In her book *No Steady Job for Papa* (1966), Benasutti presents a member of a closely knit family in Philadelphia during World War I. The point of her book is that people should celebrate the spirit that seeks some kind of fortune "beneath the dust of the mythical golden pavements." Her simple objectives of "a steady job for Papa and a nice home" motivate her instinctive insight into current events.

With *Up There the Stars* (1968) Ralph Corsel tells an honest story of crime-breeding factors that are intrinsic to a fragmented and economically limited section within the American population from which a growing boy must make an effort to view some light beyond his sordid surroundings. Joseph R. Vergara cre-

ates in *Love e Pasta* (1968) the father's actions as a galvanizing factor on a value system relating his activities to the family and their environment. With characters who act with warm impulses and human sympathy, the writing of Vergara is unpretentious and persuasive, making optimism a human responsibility.

On the other hand, Lucas Longo recalls in *The Family on Vendetta Street* (1968) a troubling neighborhood situation familiar to Italian Americans. The novel is an analysis of the emotional and economic pressures that dominate personal, familial, and societal areas and lead to the inevitable violence that erupts from unrelieved tension.

Recent Italian immigrant writers continue to supply fresh cultural attitudes to the American literary scene. These writers are generally notable, not for purely ethnic documentation or regional American treatment, but for their distinctive aesthetic concepts of organic control, undisguised good taste, and unashamed propriety. These fiction writers are exemplified by Arturo Vivante, Niccolo Tucci, and Pier M. Pasinetti. The novels of Vivante include *A Goodly Babe* (1966) and *Doctor Giovanni* (1969). Niccolo Tucci's first novel, *Before My Time* (1962), offers a wide scope that leads to more specification in *Unfinished Funeral* (1964). Pier M. Pasinetti sets his two novels in Venice: *Venetian Red* (1960) and *The Smile on the Face of the Lion* (1965). These books are the source settings of *From the Academy Bridge* (1970), whose view extends from Europe to Southern California. With the form and treatment of a well-made nineteenth-century novel, he presents ideas in human forms that live and change with their differences and their mobility in the twentieth century.

With their increased social and economic solidity, writers of Italian ancestry have to a greater degree integrated their endemic concepts with those of a culture now native to them. However, although advanced in assimilation, they have retained certain basic attitudes toward human relations, social structures, and individual resolutions. Representatives of affirmative assimilation are Ben Piazza, Eugene Mirabelli, Robert Canzoneri, and Frank Miceli. Some, like Mario Andrew Pei, have written superbly literate fiction. Others assert dominant themes in response to popular tastes, as evident in the works by Francis Pollini and Mario Puzo.

While Mirabelli, with his novel *The Way In* (1968), enlarges his aesthetic technique with new dimensions of psychological introspection and structural control, he presents the minutiae of the whole range of his daily life. In the wedding scene, for example, he dramatizes the hopeful third-generation Italian American who becomes part of the very fabric of the American environment. This analysis of ethnic assimilation is further pursued by Robert Canzoneri with poems, short stories, and magazine articles best expressed by his autobiography, *I Do So Politely: A Voice From the South* (1965), and the novel *Men With Little Hammers* (1969). Gradually, the themes become of national input, such as Frank Miceli structures in *The Seventh Month* (1969), in which he writes about a Vietnam War veteran's struggle to adjust to civilian life. Thus, Miceli expands the personal theme to universal dimensions. A sound craftsman with glandular language (strong, unashamed, and sometimes poetic), he convinces the reader that the chaos and confusion of one's life is a microscopic view of a national problem.

Assimilation in an Italian American's writing is achieved with the balanced combination of creative artistry, social disposition, and comprehension, a combination in the fiction of Mario Andrew Pei. Connoisseur of linguistics, eminent scholar, academic leader, and governmental genius, Pei is the author of forty-five publications exemplified by *One Language for the World* (1958), *The Story of the English Language* (1967), and *The Many Hues of English* (1967). His genius is unsurpassed in his works of fiction, which include *Swords of Anjou* (1953), *The Sparrows of Paris* (1958), and *The Tales of the Natural and Supernatural* (1971). The works of Pei demonstrate his catholicity of interests, which encompass languages, history, politics, economics, gastronomy, and fiction. He deals a mortal blow to pointless formlessness in fiction by giving it firm organic structure disciplined by the habits of scholarship.

Assimilation, however, demands of the Italian American novelist to be one in two worlds. Some, such as Jerre Mangione, have been able to intensify both worlds by discovering that their identity "belongs" in either place. Others, like Charles Calitri, have sought to explore an elusive ingredient in their Americanism that has made them different from their compatriots. Still others, like Joseph Papaleo, have engaged their entire emotional capacity to experience the concepts of the mother country in order to purge themselves of an undefined dissatisfaction with their "place" in America. On the other hand, some writers, like Robert Cenedella, exorcise the struggle with being "out-of-place" by objectifying it as the problem of a deviant within society. Ultimately, all these motives converge in the type of Italian American writer like Joseph Arleo, who, furious with the whole matter of real and psychic segregation, returns to Italy to finalize an accounting with his father. Arleo's *The Grand Street Collector* (1970) is a compelling document with which the author dramatizes ethnic characteristics and personal distinctions.

Sometimes the conflicts of traditional concepts with those of a new environment intensify so much that they erupt into violence and criminal infraction of established law, as in the case of Frank Canizio's *A Man Against Fate* (1958), or as inflexible restrictiveness evident in Vincent Siciliano's *Unless They Kill Me First* (1970), or as a stronghold of a weakness such as drug addiction in Alexander Trocchi's *Cain's Book* (1961), or as a variety of evils infecting society presented in the books of George Cuomo. A third-generation American whose paternal grandparents came from Italy, Cuomo, after a series of working positions, became professor of English at the State College of Hayward, California, while writing poems, stories, a textbook (*Becoming a Better Reader*), and four books of fiction: *Jack Be Nimble* (1963), *Bright Day, Dark Runner* (1964), *Among Thieves* (1968), and *Sing, Choirs of Angels* (short stories) (1969). Through the actions of his characters, Cuomo points out that nearly everyone is misinformed about crime.

One of the most representative Italian American literary artists is Francis Pollini, who pulls at the very root of rhetoric to expose the American conscience. In addition to a volume of three plays, his novels include *Night* (1961), *Glover* (1965), *Excursion* (1965), *The Crown* (1967), and *Pretty Maids All in a Row* (1968). In his fiction Pollini is realistic with sex and violence, using the aesthetic to intensify the panic that mounts steadily in the development of his themes. His first novel, *Night,* can be compared to Ernest Hemingway's *A Farewell to Arms,* as it is about the brainwashing of American prisoners of war; Pollini exposes the conflict in Korea as Hemingway depicts World War I. In *Glover* he shows, by reference and suggestion, that Italian Americans are now an assimilated part of the national structure. With the novel *Excursion* he adds the dimension of motion to the function of words as he explores the dream and dramatizes the fact that the Italian American must explore his or her roots in order to achieve self-understanding. His increasingly typed protagonist on a platform of crisis is cast in his fourth book, *The Crown,* in which a man of scholarly disposition, who survives military training and combat, has a crippled reflex to engagements in a competitive world of civil accommodation. Then, in *Pretty Maids All in a Row,* he persuades the reader that sex and violence must no longer be the inevitable objectivized areas of inhibited civilized behavior. With this book Pollini brings to culmination his conviction that the Italian American, with his astute perception and ancient-hewn humanity, is helping the nation to amalgamate and, thus, to reduce the extremes of its dichotomy.

For the average reader, the Italian American novel has arrived with Mario Puzo, who demonstrates some violent dynamics of Italian Americanism in *Dark Arena* (1953), *The Fortunate Pilgrim* (1964), and *The Godfather* (1969). In *Dark Arena* he explores the extremes to which military occupation leads both the conquered and the conquerors. Puzo shows that we have made a full circle back to the old ethical theme of the conflict between good and evil that occupied Hawthorne and Melville. The book conveys a formula for the contemporary Italian American novel symbolized in the person and situation of the protagonist. In his second novel, *The Fortunate Pilgrim,* Puzo explores the stresses of Italian American life on New York's Tenth Avenue during the 1930s. He portrays an Italian American who exploits his own people, who are, in turn, rescued by Anglo-Saxon Americans. Basically, Puzo dramatizes the Italian American who is compelled to accept organized pressure in order to survive, but who must hold this relationship in respect, protecting it by silence and unalterable loyalty.

Thus, emerging out of this contemporary disposition, Mario Puzo's *The Godfather* is more than a controversial book. In it the author aims to show that the type of syndicate he portrays is one of the only ways by which the Italian American can survive in the nation. With great sweep, hurtling pace, and electrifying suspense he constructs an inimitable story dealing with the contemporary strategy of gaining and securing power by using the code that controls others in the competition of outlawed enterprises. While kings create and promote warfare, mobilizing armies of mercenaries to seize power from vulnerable monarchies, the American gang leader builds an economic empire in which he attains power by personal warfare, the killing of competitors in the context of loyalty or treachery. One of Puzo's themes is that gangsterism in America thrives through the cooperation of elected government agents, a theme that is dramatized by the competitive forces in the novel. When Michael Corleone commits his first murder, he "makes his bones" and becomes a man to be respected with fear. He gives a new nomenclature to the American dreamer who identifies with the enemy. Aesthetically Puzo carries the reader with hurtling momentum, rendering the most intolerable episode as entirely plausible and natural. Thematically the book challenges America's racial categories, dynastic tendencies, and social prejudices. Structurally, the book abounds with evil incidents, debased sex, primitive terror, and a realistic record of the solecisms and colloquialisms of Italian American characters. By using the brutal themes of contemporary fiction—depravities, crime, lust, sex aberrations, violence, bigotry, racism, and hate— Puzo with *The Godfather* has won acceptance for his other books, which are important works of art and valid documents of American civilization, all of which make evident that the Italian American novel has come of age.

In the context of early American novels, the former distortion of the Italian American was, at least, a recognition of his presence. It was up to the Italian American writers themselves to challenge this distortion. In this way, the art of the writer is evaluated on equal terms with that of other writers. Of current authors oriented to social problems, two examples are Gay Talese and Julia Savarese. The works of Talese include *The Overreachers* (1965), *The Kingdom and the Power* (1969), *Fame and Obscurity* (1970), and *Honor Thy Father* (1971). Julia Savarese writes conventional novels such as *The Weak and the Strong* (1952) and *Final Proof* (1971).

One of the more outstanding writers of instructional form is Gilbert Sorrentino, whose works include *The Sky Changes* (1966), *The Perfect Fiction* (poetry) (1968), *Steelwork* (1969), and *Imaginative Qualities of Actual Things* (1971). In contrast to Gilbert Sorrentino, more rigid narrow themes have been created by Joseph Pilleteri, Don DeLillo, Bill Pronzini, and Paul Gallico. Pilleteri's art has produced *When the Giraffe Runs Down* (1970) and *Two Hours on Sunday* (1971). Don DeLillo renews the American myths of innocence and vitality in *Americana* (1971). A prolific writer of short stories, Bill Pronzini illustrates the well-constructed novel in *The Stalker* (1971). While Paul Gallico exhibits electric writing in his novel *The Zoo Gang* (1970), one of his production of some forty books.

The future Italian American writer of fiction is to be considered an American novelist. The present third- and fourth-generation Italian Americans no longer consider themselves a separate group whose inner-directedness and eventual literary efforts have strictly ethnic themes. As one expands the erstwhile limited subjects to more extensive contemporary themes, it is the quality of the work that admits the writer to the American mainstream.

Rose Basile Green

Bibliography

Barolini, Helen, ed. *The Dream Book: An Anthology of Writings by Italian American Women.* New York: Schocken Books, 1985.

Bona, Mary Jo, ed. *The Voices We Carry: Recent Italian American Women's Fiction.* Montreal/New York: Guernica Editions, 1994.

De Voto, Bernard. *Literary Fallacy.* Boston: Little, Brown, 1944.

Gardaphé, Fred, *Italian Signs, American Streets.* Durham: Duke University Press, 1996.

Green, Rose Basile. *The Italian American Novel: A Document of the Interaction of Two Cultures.* Rutherford, NJ: Fairleigh Dickinson University Press, 1974.

Lesser-Known Novelists

Italian American writers, with certain exceptions (di Donato, Mangione, Talese, and Puzo), tend to be relegated to the becalmed banks of mainstream American literature. Even those well recognized and highly regarded within the Italian American community often remain unknown to the reading audience at large. A general perception that the work (and more specifically, the subject matter) of Italian American authors is of minor relevance or import perpetuates their suppressed literary status. These lesser-known Italian American novelists, then, write on the periphery, twice removed from their literary counterparts who represent other ethnic backgrounds. As Gay Talese asked in a *New York Times Book Review* article, "Where are the Italian American novelists?"

In actuality, there is a formidable bibliography of literature produced by Italian American novelists, who shine varying degrees of interpretive light on the Italian American experience. Often, their novels capture the emotional texture of times and settings that scholarly works on Italian American ethnicity cannot convey. From the beginnings of Italian settlement in the New World up to the present, marginally recognized Italian American writers have presented moving portrayals of the personal and communal experiences of transplanted *Italiani* (Italians).

Pascal D'Angelo's *Son of Italy* (1924), an autobiographical account that depicts life in Little Italy; Edward Bonetti's novella *The Wine Cellar* (1971); Vincent Patrick's *The Pope of Greenwich Village* (1979); Anthony DiFranco's *The Streets of Paradise* (1984); Gilda Ciani Sferra's *Virgilia* (1989); Louisa Ermolino's *Joey Dee Gets Wise: A Novel of Little Italy* (1991), have all offered descriptive accounts of the ever-changing aspects of Italian American life. Yet the preponderance of literature about Italian Americans by Italian Americans continues to achieve minimal levels of mainstream success.

Early writings of Italian American novelists, like Luigi Donato Ventura's *Peppino* (1913), John Antonio Moroso's *The Stumbling Hero* (1923), and Giuseppe Cautela's *Moon Harvest* (1925), focus on the immigrant experience. They recount the dreams that inspired the passage to America and the subsequent feelings of loss—loss of ties to Italy, loss of promised opportunity, loss of hope, and the virtual loss of identity—that assail a stranger in a strange land. Readers empathized with the joys and hardships that defined the newcomers' difficult adjustment to everyday life in America. These early novelists

narrated the interpersonal drama and camaraderie of the *paesani* (fellow countryfolk)
in the tenements, streets, and cafes; and the
wrenching déjà vu of the immigrants' secondary exodus from their Little Italys.

In the next phase of Italian American literature, second-generation peripheral novelists began to focus on assimilation struggles,
marked by first and second intergenerational
conflicts, and at times, the painful rejection of
one's heritage. In such disparate novels as Jo
Pagano's *Golden Wedding* (1943), Michael
De Capite's *Maria* (1943), and George
Panetta's *We Ride a White Donkey* (1944)
and *Viva Madison Avenue* (1957), Italian
Americans faced such identity-searching questions as Who am I? and Who are we?

Many more recent Italian American novels are nostalgic recollections of life in Italian
American neighborhoods. Joseph Vergara's
Love e Pasta (1968), Lucas Longo's *The Family on Vendetta Street* (1968), Joseph Sorrentino's *Up from Never* (1971), and Anthony
Mancini's *The Miracle of Pelham Bay Park*
(1982) all explore the emotional dimensions
as well as the physical settings of Italian
American culture. The novels in this category
all reflect the devotion to family and the ethnic community's sense of order that were unifying developmental factors in the novelists'
early lives. In *Paper Fish* (1980), for example,
author Tina De Rosa honors her immigrant
forebears and grieves over the loss of their
ethnic enclaves. Often, these contemporary
novels come full circle, recapturing the essence
and expressing acceptance of the first generation, including its humor, values, and unique
worldview.

Today's Italian American writers also
deal with more universal themes. Coming-of-
age and passing-into-middle-age works, such
as Jay Parini's *The Patch Boys* (1986), Tony
Ardizzone's *In the Name of the Father* (1978),
Anthony Giardina's *Men With Debts* (1984)
and *A Boy's Pretensions* (1988), and Salvatore
LaPuma's *The Boys of Bensonhurst* (1987), *A
Time for Wedding Cake* (1991), and *Teaching
Angel's to Fly* (1992), look at such perennial
topics as love, hate, and greed from an Italian
American perspective.

Another, and extremely popular, avenue
of expression for Italian American writers is
the detective or mystery story. The heroes of
these books are Italian American detectives
and police officers, whose ethnicity is a vital

component of their character makeup. Ed
McBain's (Salvatore Lombino's) celebrated
87th Precinct Police Procedurals—including
'Til Death (1959), *Bread* (1974), *Vespers*
(1990), *Widows* (1991), and *Mischief* (1993)—
feature squad-room detective Steve Carella,
whose flashbacks to his youth, which included
family and neighborhood situations sprinkled
with foreign phrases, season the pages with
Italian American flavor. Bill Pronzini's long-
running series of mysteries are driven by a
central character known only as "The Name-
less Detective," whose direct references to—
and reflections of—his ethnic past point to his
Italian American identity.

Since the 1980s some of the more productive Italian American mystery writers have
been Eugene Izzi, *Bad Guys* (1988); Anthony
Bruno, *Bad Business* (1991), *Bad Apple*
(1994), *Bad Luck* (1990), and *Bad Moon*
(1992); Jim Cirni, *The Kiss Off* (1987) and
The Big Squeeze (1991); Robert Leuci, *Fence
Jumpers* (1995); and Albert Di Bartolomeo,
The Vespers Tape (1991) and *Fool's Gold*
(1993). These works are all fictionalized accounts of Mafia dealings that intertwine the
lives of Italian American criminals with Italian
American police officers, private investigators,
or private citizens. Standard fare involves the
protagonist's attempt to outwit or imprison
the gangsters, after wrestling with the Italian
American traditions, values, and neighborhood ties that are his legacy, and deciding
where his loyalties lie. These kinds of conflict
resolutions are valid interpretations of Italian
American value orientations.

Most recently, the mystery genre has enjoyed more contributions from female Italian
American writers. Many of these stories place
female protagonists in the spotlight who,
among other major differences, tend to pursue
criminals outside the world of organized
crime. Lia Matera's series, *The Good Fight*
(1990), *A Hard Bargain* (1992), *Face Value*
(1994), and *Designer Crimes* (1995), feature
Laura DiPalma, an intelligent lawyer of Italian American heritage. Camille T. Crespi's
Simona Griffo Mystery Series, including *The
Trouble With a Small Raise* (1991), *The Trouble With Going Home* (1995), and *The Trouble With Thin Ice* (1993), is rich in Italian
American behavioral, cultural, and linguistic
nuances.

Barbara D'Amato's *Cat Marsala Mysteries,* including *Hard Luck* (1992), *Hard Ball*

(1991), and *Hard Women* (1993), further chronicle Italian American women's dual endeavors to maintain their ethnic identity while proving themselves in the traditionally male arena of crime solving. Finally, Sandra Scoppettone's *Lauren Laurano Mysteries,* including *Everything You Have Is Mine* (1991) and *I'll Be Leaving You Always* (1993), raise yet another contemporary women's issue, as the heroine balances her professional crime-solving life with her personal lesbian lifestyle—both of which contradict her traditional ethnic upbringing.

Italian American novelists have gifted their contained reading audience with a multitude of characters, settings, and plots presented against a cultural backdrop. From Charles Calitri's *Father* (1962), which relives a priest's decision to set aside his vows and become a biological father, to Joseph Arleo's *Grand Street Collector* (1970), which tells the story of Carlo Tresca's assassin, to Joseph Caruso's *The Priest* (1978), which tells of an Italian American priest questioning his religious calling, to Anthony Mancini's *Minnie Santangelo's Mortal Sin* (1975) and *Minnie Santangelo and the Evil Eye* (1977), Italian American narratives capture the essence of "Italianicity" and portray the rich depths of cultural heritage in their characters.

It is impossible to list them all here, and their numbers continue to grow, as talented writers add new faces and voices to the ongoing literary panorama of Italian America. Other authors and titles include Valenti Angelo's *Hills of Little Miracles* (1950), *Golden Gate* (1957), and *The Bells of Bleeker Street* (1958); Lawrence Madelena's novel for young readers, *Confetti for Gino* (1959);

Evan Hunter's (Salvatore Lombino's) *Streets of Gold* (1985), the story of a blind Italian American musician from East Harlem; Josephine Gattuso-Hendin's *The Right Thing to Do* (1988), about an Italian American female's bittersweet battle to escape from her father's intellectual and emotional suffocation; and Thomas F. Monteleone's *The Blood of the Lamb* (1992), which tells of an Italian American priest and the miracle cult that surrounds him. All these novelists offer a vast and colorful portrait, as they chronicle the saga and the evolution of Italian Americana.

These so-called peripheral Italian American writers, who have been prolific throughout the period ranging from the immigration era to the present, greatly outnumber those Italian American writers who have been read and have found acceptance outside their ethnic realm. While considered peripheral by many, they have explored complex layers of characters and situations and they have served as crucial narrators and archivists of the Italian American experience.

Salvatore Primeggia

Bibliography

Talese, Gay. "Where Are the Italian American Novelists?" *New York Times Book Review* (March 14, 1993): 1.

Tamburri, Anthony Julian, Paolo A. Giordano, and Fred L. Gardaphé, eds. *From the Margin: Writings in Italian Americana.* West Lafayette, IN: Purdue University Press, 1991.

See also AUTOBIOGRAPHY; LITERATURE; POETRY; WOMEN WRITERS

N

Obici, Amedeo (1877–1947)

A successful entrepreneur, innovative businessman, and noted philanthropist, Amedeo Obici created the Planters Company and built that enterprise into the world's largest manufacturer of nut products. In the process, Obici made peanuts a favorite American snack food.

Born in the village of Oderzo in the province of Treviso, Italy, on July 15, 1877, Obici migrated to the United States in 1888 to work for his uncle, a fruit seller in Scranton, Pennsylvania. He quickly learned English, graduated from grammar school, and mastered the retail fruit trade. Observing the snacking habits of his neighbors and customers, Obici concluded that his uncle's business could profit by adding freshly roasted peanuts to the store's stock. He used his meager savings to buy scrap parts from a local junk dealer and built a crude roaster. Working at night to roast and package the peanuts, Obici soon turned a one-hundred-pound bag of raw peanuts into a profitable addition to the store's inventory.

Obici again visited the local junkyard, bought two used wagon wheels, and fashioned a pushcart upon which he mounted his handmade roaster. He pushed his cart through the streets of Scranton, calling out for people to try his "hot roasted peanuts." While sales exceeded his expectations, the eighteen-hour days took a toll on Obici's voice. Using the steady stream of steam emitted from his roaster, Obici fashioned a tin whistle, the prototype of the peanut vendor's whistle, that produced a distinctive high-pitched sound that announced his presence.

Within a year, profits from Obici's roasted peanut business enabled him to open his own fruit and peanut store in nearby Wilkes-Barre, Pennsylvania. He soon financed the passage of his mother, sister, and brother from Italy to the United States. Obici devoted most of his time to perfecting techniques for blanching raw peanuts, efficiently removing the hulls and skins, and improving roasting techniques. Obici became the major wholesale supplier of roasted peanuts in eastern Pennsylvania.

In 1906, in partnership with fellow Italian immigrant Mario Peruzzi, Obici rented a factory for the commercial production of roasted peanuts and began business as the Planters Peanut Company. While Peruzzi managed the company's production, Obici concentrated on product development and distribution. Using a horse and cart, Obici distributed Planters peanuts to stores throughout the region. By 1908 the flourishing business incorporated as Planters Nut and Chocolate Company with Amedeo Obici as president and general manager.

The inclusion of chocolate into the firm's name reflected Obici's expansion of the business into nut-chocolate confectionery products. He sacrificed quick profits for consumer loyalty. He rejected cheaper European peanuts for the costlier, but larger and tastier, Virginia peanuts. Obici's innovations in the snack food business are best exemplified by the advances in packaging he pioneered. He originated the retail sale of whole salted nuts in penny and nickel bags and introduced glassine, developed in Germany, as grease-proof, see-through packaging for salted peanuts. He introduced cellophane packaging, vacuum jars, and vacuum-sealed cans.

In 1913 Obici established Planters' own processing plant for raw peanuts in Suffolk,

Virginia, soon consolidating all Planters' manufacturing facilities in Virginia, leaving only executive and sales offices in Wilkes-Barre. By 1927 he had expanded his processing facilities and absorbed regional rivals. In the 1920s additional Planters processing facilities were built in San Francisco, California, and Toronto, Canada. Planters became an industrial giant and a dominant factor in the nation's confection and snack food industry.

In the 1930s Obici popularized the use of peanut oil for cooking, implemented commercial peanut oil processing, and automated sorting and processing of peanuts. His automation innovations set the standard for his industry.

In 1916 he sponsored a contest, won by a 14-year-old schoolboy, for an animated symbol for Planters' products. Wilkes-Barre commercial artist Antonio Gentile added a cane, top hat, and monocle to the schoolboy's sketch and "Mr. Peanut" was born, becoming one of the most popular corporate symbols in American business.

Obici was married to Louise Musante. The Obicis endowed a community hospital in Suffolk that provided medical care to all members of the community regardless of ability to pay. The hospital, designated the Louise Obici Memorial Hospital following her death in 1938, included a school of nursing funded by Amedeo Obici.

Frederick J. Simonelli

Bibliography

Bernardo, Stephanie. *The Ethnic Almanac.* Garden City, NY: Doubleday & Co. Inc., 1981, 288.

LoCasio, Ted J. *The Obici Story.* Winston-Salem, NC: Planters and Life Savers Companies, 1982.

Public Relations Department. *The Story of Planters Nuts.* Winston-Salem, NC: The Planters Company of Nabisco, Inc., 1995.

See also BUSINESS AND ENTREPRENEURSHIP

Occupations of Italian Immigrants in Turn-of-the-Century America

It is an indisputable fact that the overwhelming majority of Italian immigrants came to the United States to work, and indeed they became quintessential laborers during the era of mass immigration both in their quantity and in the character of manual labor performed. Entering the workforce prior to labor-saving advances in technology, they frequently supplied the raw brawn and muscle required to build railroads and streets, to mine the deep earth for rich mineral resources, and to construct reservoirs and dams. They were very visible in the construction field not only as laborers, but also as skilled workers.

More than a few Italian immigrants learned their building skills in their homeland and rarely abandoned them or changed their occupations upon entering the American workforce. Accordingly, immigrants from the northern Italian states of Venetia and Tuscany brought with them their mosaic and stucco work skills, those from central Italy their marble and stonecutting techniques, and the rest of Italy supplied carpenters, joiners, woodworkers, painters, and plasters. By 1900 Italian brick and stone masons constituted twice the labor force in this industry as others in the general population. In addition, they were a large part of the laboring class in semiskilled and unskilled work, such as hod carriers and excavators.

From their earliest days Italian workers were employed in huge public works projects including the construction of public utilities, streets, sewer systems, bridges, gas and water pipe-laying, canals, and subways. One example of how important Italian Americans were in construction is late-nineteenth-century Chicago; by 1890 they were estimated to be 90 percent of the public works labor force, and an even greater percentage of street construction. By the turn of the century they were also employed in large numbers in constructing a dam across the Colorado River; in enlarging the Erie Canal in New York; in clearing hurricane-caused debris in Galveston harbor, Texas; and in rebuilding San Francisco after the destructive earthquake of 1906. In a large sense the famed New York City subway system and its counterpart in Boston were built by Italian Americans, as was the Ashokan Dam in New York State.

Their dominance in various aspects of the construction industry· became a backdrop against which more than a few Italian Americans emerged as entrepreneurs as they did, for instance, in New York City. A few examples are in order. Born in Italy, the Paterno brothers followed their father and became builders of handsome New York City edifices such as Casa Italiana at Columbia University and fashionable apartment houses in stylish neighborhoods. Anthony Campagna, brother-in-law of the Paternos, also was an important builder with a famed Times Square theater and high-class apartment houses to his credit. Immigrant teenager Generoso Pope worked his way up the construction ladder from laborer to foreman to owner of the Colonial Sand and Stone Company, at one time the largest construction material company in the world. He owned other construction-related businesses as well.

Italian Americans became prominent in the construction field outside New York. Within three years of his emigration, 14-year-old Dominic Cutrupi of Fort Lee, New Jersey, started his own business as an excavating contractor. Decades later he was acknowledged as a leader in that field, having built many important roads and sewer systems in northern New Jersey towns. Sixteen-year-old immigrant Anthony Farina began a one-man construction business in Newton, Massachusetts, in 1922 that developed into the Farina Brothers Company. Among the important jobs built by the company were tunnels in Boston, facilities at East Boston Airport and Logan Airport, building for the military at various New England bases, and many factories. Ciro Paolella, a penniless immigrant, settled in New Haven, Connecticut, in 1909, where his father taught him to be a mason. As an entrepreneur he had a humble beginning, producing construction blocks. In time he headed one of the ten largest plants producing concrete material in the United States.

The transportation industry is one of the most critical enterprises that an industrial nation can possess. Indeed, railroad transportation was the most vital element among several ingredients that were essential to the phenomenal industrial growth of the United States in the late nineteenth and early twentieth centuries. Historically, various immigrant groups such as the Chinese, Slavic, African, and Irish Americans played important roles in building the railroads of this country to render it the industrial colossus of the world. Although migrating later, Italian immigrants, who frequently replaced the nationalities that preceded them, also became significant factors in the development and expansion of railroads. By the 1890s they had replaced the Irish as the foremost railroad laborers. "It was in fact in the nineties that they first came to be employed extensively. They were scattered over much of the country . . .," wrote Italian immigration scholar Robert Foerster. They were employed by the tens of thousands by railroads in states like Maine, New Jersey, Pennsylvania, Wisconsin, Illinois, Connecticut, and New York. Railroad employment led to settlements of Italian Americans, which eventually influenced the communities at large. For example, so many thousands of Italian Americans provided the labor force for the gigantic Erie Railroad system, that their *padrone* (labor broker) became an important New York State political force.

Italian workers on the Long Island Railroad present another example. Early in the twentieth century they had emerged as the dominant workforce that was responsible for the railroad's extension to the north and south shores as well as penetration of the easternmost part of the island. Encouraging settlement in the eastern areas, the Long Island Railroad developed experimental farms with Italian immigrants as tenants to demonstrate that the seemingly unproductive scrub oak land could be transformed into positive agricultural endeavors.

Italian workers on docks and waterfronts represented another area in which immigrants earned their livelihood. Beginning in New Orleans, where Sicilian longshoremen unloaded fruits, they performed similar duties in ports in Florida. Early in the twentieth century these dock workers were employed in large numbers in ports like Buffalo and to a lesser extent Boston. By the end of the First World War Italian American longshoremen had become the major ethnic workforce in New York, the nation's largest port. They sometimes engaged in violent incidents with competing longshoremen of other nationalities, such as the Irish, for leadership and influence. By becoming the head of New York's Italian American longshoremen, Paul Vaccarella was deemed to be so important to the war effort that he was importuned by the White House to discourage his ethnic dock from striking and thereby impede the war effort.

Although Italian immigrants were not well represented in cotton manufacturing, they were significant in other dimensions of the textile industry. They became the single largest nationality employed in the silk

The Long Island Railroad brought in immigrant Italian labor to extend its tracks in the late nineteenth and early twentieth centuries. Italian work gangs lived in tents on the plains. Courtesy Suffolk County Historical Society, from the Fullerton Collection.

industry by 1919. Italian women worked as weavers, warpers, and silk dyers. Their role in the clothing industry was monumental, as women labored as machine operators and hand sewers of linings, buttonholes, and buttons. Much of this type of work was brought home, where other members of the family, including young children, participated. Furthermore, they were well represented in glove-making, hosiery, and knit-goods manufacturing.

Clearly by the early part of the twentieth century Italian immigrants had become an integral part of the U.S. labor force. While Italian Americans dominated the blue-collar occupations as construction workers, textile manufacturers and longshoremen, they also made great strides in the following selected areas.

The Immigrant Grocer

European immigrants brought with them from their native villages the concept of retailing. Most immigrant retailers served the needs of their fellow countrymen, with some moving aggressively into the wider community to seek out a larger, more diverse clientele with greater purchasing power. By the turn of the century, the number of retail merchants per one thousand employed men in the large cities was greater for the European-born than for natives.

Of the immigrant retailing enterprises, the most common was the grocery. This was especially the case for Italians, who quickly became visible in the grocery, fruit, and meat trades. In Utica, New York, in 1900, twenty-seven Italian grocers and butchers accounted for over 16 percent of the town's businesses. The proportion of Italian grocers in New Orleans was 19 percent in 1900 and 49 percent in 1920. Most of the first Italians to settle in Rochester, New York, in the 1880s and 1890s were fruit vendors.

At first, groceries, fruit, and meat were provided by separate establishments. By the First World War these three businesses were in the process of being combined into one. The Italian food market came into being with the modernization of food retailing in the 1920s and 1930s.

There were many reasons for the popularity of food retailing among immigrant businessmen. Since the Italians knew little English and preferred to deal with merchants from their own background, they needed stores of their own. They were also partial to their own foods. With the creation of immigrant colonies, therefore, came a variety of opportunities for food vendors. The grocery store was an easy-entry business because little capital was required. That capital could be acquired

Italian American grocery store, typical of hundreds of similar establishments that proliferated in Italian neighborhoods in the 1930s. They played a vital social and economic role in the community. Courtesy Salvatore J. LaGumina.

by borrowing from friends and relatives who would charge no interest, since immigrants would often reciprocate lending in kind. Banking among friends was informal; the man who at the moment had the money became the defacto lender. Formal Italian bankers also made loans.

Thus, startup expenditures could be met, and overhead costs, although sometimes burdensome, could be kept low in one-man operations and family-run shops. And, in many cases the owner needed no previous experience. He would purchase goods wholesale, add a markup, display the food, and wait for the customers to come and buy from him.

Customer loyalty was crucial to success in a business that was overcrowded and very competitive. If the grocer failed to please his customers, and his friends did not frequent his shop on a regular basis, the business was in jeopardy. Expanding the range of clientele in an Italian colony was difficult and the small grocery was always at the mercy of customers with little money to spend and a local economy that was often linked to the fortunes of the one industry that supplied the area Italians with steady income. Those few successful Italian grocers would expand to other enterprises, such as a bar, a liquor store, or a cigar shop. As wealth and property were accumulated, some might quit the business entirely, leaving the field open to another immigrant

who was eager to work for himself rather than for others.

The grocer worked on a very close margin. His daily profits were more likely to be measured in pennies rather than dollars. The business had to be a model of economy to survive. A national study of meat markets in 1919 revealed that average net profits were only 2 percent of sales. Half of the markets had gross receipts of under twenty thousand dollars a year, a volume that could sustain only a one-man operation. To produce sufficient volume the grocer had to work longer hours than an immigrant factory laborer. The standard retailer day at the turn of the century ran from early morning to late evening each day except Sunday, when the shop would close at noon. Some grocers worked eighty-eight hours per week. Labor was frequently supplemented by many hours put in by the wives and children of the grocer. Despite this work pace, profit margins could still remain slim and the business could fail.

Yet there were those Italian Americans who made large fortunes as grocers and produce distributors. Substantial profits were earned within the space of a few years. Success in business meant an increase in social prestige. Those who remained in the community often took on leadership roles. Others who saw America as a business opportunity and not as a place of residence returned to Italy with their profits.

Michael LaSorte

Bibliography
LaSorte, Michael. "Immigrant Occupations: A Comparison." In *Italian Americans: The Search for a Usable Past,* edited by Philip V. Cannistraro and Richard N. Juliani, 84–91. Staten Island, NY: American Italian Historical Association.

Sanchirico, Andrew. "Small Business and Social Mobility Among Italian Americans." In *Italian Ethnics Their Languages, Literature and Lives,* edited by Dominic Candeloro, Fred L. Gardaphé, and Paolo A. Giordano, 201–214. New York: American Italian Historical Association, 1990.

———. "Vengo per Fare L'America: The Sojourner Businessman." *New Explorations in Italian American Studies,* edited by Richard N. Juliani and Sandra P. Juliani, 91–99. New York: American Italian Historical Association, 1994.

See also BUSINESS AND ENTREPRENEURSHIP

Mining

The isolated and scattered mining frontiers of the United States, needing a constant supply of skilled and unskilled laborers, attracted thousands of Italian immigrants from the mid-nineteenth to the twentieth century. Companies hired immigrants when they landed. Later through chain migration, young, single Italians sought better wages and working conditions, free from the threat of strikes. The railroads that linked these diverse locations allowed easy access to immigrants.

The California Gold Rush attracted the first large number of Italians beginning in 1849. Within a few years there were over six hundred Italians living in San Francisco alone, where Sardinia opened a consulate. When mining proved to be temporary, immigrants found employment in business and helped to develop California's agricultural potential. Jackson, located in an area known as Mother Lode Country, became the largest Italian mining community in the state.

As other opportunities opened up, Italians began to move to other western mining frontiers. When silver was discovered in Nevada, they moved eastward to Virginia City and elsewhere. As coal and copper mines were opened

in Utah, they followed the call for laborers farther west. Others went north to Alaska in the 1890s, where prospectors like Felice Pedroni (1858–1910), the founder of Fairbanks, and others stayed to work in large gold mines.

In Michigan's upper peninsula, copper and iron were discovered in the 1840s. Although transient Italians settled into communities, it was not until 1860 that the first Piedmontese arrived to stay in "Copper Country." Michigan attracted Italians from Lombardy, Piedmont, Trentino, Tuscany, and Venetia, and this was a trend found in other communities as well.

It was from such mining centers that internal migration sent Italians to the other mining frontiers. Many Michigan copper miners migrated westward to the Minnesota iron ranges, to Butte and Red Lodge, Montana, and farther westward to the silver mines of northern Idaho. Other Italians migrated to the coal mines of Wyoming and Washington, down into Colorado, Arizona, and New Mexico, and eastward to Leadville, South Dakota. As coal mines opened in Illinois, Indiana, Iowa, Kansas, Missouri, Oklahoma, and Texas, Italians pursued job opportunities there. Italians also drifted to the lead and zinc mines of southwestern Missouri.

In the South, Italians were attracted to Appalachian coal mining communities and to the industrial center of Birmingham, Alabama, with its coal and iron mines. Here harsh labor conditions caused many immigrants to move to new mining locations, develop farms, or return to northern urban-industrial areas. During the 1920s, with a decline in mining and the expanding automobile industry, thousands of Italians migrated to Detroit.

The term "miner" is generic, as most Italians were not trained miners who were at the top of the labor hierarchy. The unskilled workers were trammers or loaders of ore, timbermen, and general laborers. With few safety rules, conditions were dangerous, especially in coal mines, where explosions were common. Accident insurance was nonexistent. These conditions caused Italians to leave the area or join in labor strikes and organizations, some radical, to improve working conditions.

Life in these mining communities provided Italians with more freedom than was found in urban centers. The company provided housing, which allowed wives and family members to augment wages by developing small farms and selling the produce. The rural nature of the mining communities allowed men to hunt and fish. In Michigan a number of Italians became involved in local politics as early as 1875. Others developed small businesses and industries and catered to immigrant and larger community needs. In Alabama (coal), Michigan (coal and iron), and Montana (silver) a number of established Italian businessmen had the capital available to invest in their own mines and met with mixed success. Others bought stock in mining companies.

Within these communities various institutions developed to aid the process of assimilation. Fraternal organizations were formed, along with newspapers, and both Catholic and Protestant churches were established. This was especially true of the more permanent frontier of Michigan, where Little Italys were a feature of Calumet and Iron Mountain.

Today many older descendants of Italian miners remain in these communities. With the closing of mines, third and fourth generations had to relocate to find jobs. The legacy of the mining town experience remains with local Catholic churches, Italian restaurants and shops, clubs, summer family visits, and ethnic festivals. Mining sent Italians into the far corners of the United States to develop the nation's industrial potential.

Russell M. Magnaghi

Bibliography

Bailey, Kenneth R. "A Judicious Mixture: Negroes and Immigrants in the West Virginia Mines, 1880–1917." *West Virginia History* 34 (1973): 141–161.

Cofone, Albert J. "Italian Contributions to the Development of Alaska." *Italian Americana* 9 (1991): 167–180.

———. "Themes in the Italian Settlement of Nevada." *Nevada Historical Society Quarterly* 25 (1982): 116–130.

Kathka, David. "The Italian Experience in Wyoming." In *Peopling the High Plains,* edited by Gordon Olaf Henrickson. Cheyenne: Wyoming State Archives and Historical Department, 1977.

Magnaghi, Russell M. "From Michigan to Minnesota: The Internal Migration of Italian Miners." In *Entrepreneurs and Immigrants: Life on the Industrial Frontier of Northeastern Minnesota,* edited by Michael G. Karni. Chisholm: Iron Range Research Center, 1991.

———. *Miners, Merchants, and Midwives: Michigan's Upper Peninsula Italians.* Marquette, MI: Belle Fontaine Press, 1987.

Notarianni, Philip F. "Italians in Utah: The Immigrant Experience." In *The Peoples of Utah,* edited by Helen Z. Papanikolas. Salt Lake City: Utah State Historical Society, 1976.

Rolle, Andrew F. *The Immigrant Upraised: Italian Adventurers and Colonists in an Expanding America.* Norman: University of Oklahoma Press, 1968.

United States Department of Commerce, Bureau of the Census. *Census of Population and Housing.* Washington, DC, 1980, 1990.

Wolfe, Margaret R. "Aliens in Southern Appalachia: Catholics in the Coal Camps, 1900–1940." *Appalachian Heritage* 6 (1978): 43–56.

See also LABOR

Stonecutters

A small fraction of Italian immigration in the United States was made up of a flow of artisans who specialized in cutting and carving stone and marble and who arrived from specific regions in northern and central Italy. The American experience of the stonecutters has been shaped by the character of their skill, by the expansion of the marble industry, and by their expectations connected with emigration.

Italian stonecutters departing from the provinces of Novara, Como, Trento, and the Swiss canton of Ticino first arrived in the main quarries and marble centers after the 1880s, when the marble industry accelerated, helped by the development of railroads. Though quarries were scattered all along the eastern mountains, the main concentrations were in New Hampshire and in Vermont, where the town of Barre soon developed as the granite center of the world. The quarries and the sheds from Maine to Maryland and the new stone buildings and monuments erected in large cities like Boston, Baltimore, and Washington, D.C., formed a mandatory path for the stonecutters and the carvers arriving from Europe.

They worked in teams whose size was determined by the daily work of the blacksmith: the ideal number was twelve men, since it provided a full day's work for the man who sharpened their tools. The assembling of the gangs in order to get the contracts was regulated by

O

an informal network connecting men from the same village or district. Kinship and acquaintanceship provided information and assisted in recruitment for the newly arrived. Since 1877 this chain migration system was helped by the *Granite Cutters Journal* published in Boston by the Granite Cutters Association of America, a monthly magazine that provided information on business in the quarries and the building industry with a full page written in Italian. The character of the work did not allow the men to settle down. Frequent moves were unavoidable since the carvers and stonecutters had to go where the contracts were offered. As a consequence, the high wages earned in this profession were severely reduced by the cost of continuous traveling.

The only chance to escape from this wandering life was offered by the flourishing granite industry in a few towns of New England.

The most prosperous area for granite work was in Barre, Vermont. Here between 1880 and 1890 the marble industry experienced an impressive growth: by 1894 there were seventy sites of excavation employing almost one thousand men, mostly immigrants. Stone manufacturing was concentrated in hundreds of sheds, which were also often set up and run by former laborers. Many immigrants eventually bought and ran the quarries. In 1913 in Milford, New Hampshire, for example, five out of eight quarries were operated by Italians who had arrived from the central and eastern Alps.

In the 1880s the first Italian carvers were engaged by an English entrepreneur; they arrived in Barre from Carrara, the Tuscan town site of the quarries containing a celebrated white marble. In the following years, the largest number of stonecutters and sculptors came from the region of the central Alps surrounding Lake Maggiore and Lake Como. Their skills in the building trade, perpetuated through a long tradition of seasonal migration, had brought these artisans to the main cities of Italy and Europe since the sixteenth century. When the marble industry flourished in the United States, they found a new opportunity to make the best of their hard work. In the last years of 1800 and the first decade of 1900, when the marble industry reached its peak, these artisans migrated consistently to the quarries and the sheds of New England.

In Barre, by 1910, there were more than eighteen hundred stonecutters out of a population of fifteen thousand, with 14 percent Italians, 12 percent Scottish, and 6 percent Canadians. The immigrants clustered in the north end, a neighborhood close to the quarries and the sheds. Such a residential segregation was reinforced by the exclusion of foreigners from social activities of the native born, thereby forcing the Italian community to develop its own organizational network and social life. Both were rooted in a strong class consciousness and socialist political faith as witnessed by the huge building called Socialist Hall, home of the town's Local of the Socialist Labor Party. Most of the labor meetings and dance parties were organized in this building, which hosted also the Union Cooperative Store and the mutual aid society.

The culture shared by these organizations was the heritage of the Italian left: republicanism, anticlericalism, socialism, and anarchism. The most popular Italian anarchist newspaper of the time, *Cronaca Sovversiva,* was published in Barre from 1903 to 1919.

Nevertheless, the actual prospects of these skilled artisans, who thought they had accomplished their dreams of upward social mobility, proved deadly. The stone of New England, with its high silica content, caused severe silicosis in most of the laborers and killed or sickened a whole generation of men. Their intent to work abroad for a few years or for an entire life and to return to their native villages with enough savings to support their years of retirement was jeopardized by silicosis. The funeral monuments they carved in the cemetery of Barre often to celebrate dead companions stand as the sad and significant testimony of their tragic experience.

The flow of immigrants from Italy stopped after World War I and most children of the original immigrants obtained good schooling and better jobs. In the meantime, technological advances in cutting and carving stone reduced demand for skilled labor, and only a few sculptors and carvers remain at work in the town of Barre as a mere memory of the past.

Patrizia Audenino

Bibliography

Audenino, Patrizia. "The Paths of the Trade: Italian Stonemasons in the United States." *International Migration Review* 20, no. 4 (1986): 779–795.

Brayley, Arthur Wellington. *History of the Granite Industry of New England*. 2 vols. Boston: National Association of Granite Industries, 1913.

Fenton, Edwin. *Immigrants and Unions, A Case Study: Italians and American Labor 1870–1920*. New York: Arno, 1975.

———. "Italian Immigrants in the Stoneworkers' Union." *Labor History* 3, no. 2 (1962): 189–207.

———. "Storie di pietra: gli scalpellini di Barre e l' Aldrich Public Library." *Movemento operaio e socialista* 3 (1986): 425–432.

Tomasi, Mari. "The Italian Story in Vermont." *Vermont History* 38 (1960): 73–87.

Vecoli, Rudolph J. "Primo Maggio: May Day Observances Among Italian Immigrant Workers 1890–1920." *Labor's Heritage* 7 (spring 1996): 28–41.

Stonecutters in New England

As mentioned above, Italians excavated granite from the quarries of New England near the end of the nineteenth century and the beginning of the twentieth century. Due to the cheap labor that the *padrone* system was able to provide, immigrants came to the United States from Italy and found jobs in a number of quarries, mostly in the northern parts of New England. In Maine, where a dark granite was excavated, they labored in the quarries of Mount Desert Island and elsewhere. In Massachusetts, Italians found jobs in Milford, which provided a pink granite, and in Quincy, which produced a dark granite. The same was true of Westerly, Rhode Island, where a pink granite was excavated, and Italians were also in New Hampshire, the Granite State.

However, in Barre, Vermont, the center of the world's granite industry, the Italian community was so strong that its stonecutters were able to pull off effective strikes in 1908, and the Italian stonecutters' baseball team won the state championship in 1909. Italian immigrants from Carrara were in evidence in Barre at the beginning of the twentieth century, and the debates they engaged in over issues of common interest are reflected in the newspapers they published, like *Cronaca Sovversiva* (1903), *La Cooperazione* (1910), and *Corriere Libertario* (1914). Fortunately, these stonecutters could rely on at least a dozen Italian printers to help them publish broadsides and pamphlets, as well as newspapers, in that part of New England.

Out of the Italian enclave in Barre came two Italian American women of note, Lena Giudici (1898–1995) and Mari Tomasi (1907–1965). Giudici was a prominent lawyer whose extraordinary involvement in the public service of her time (on local, state, and national levels) flowed out of her family's roots in the granite industry. Tomasi was the author of *Deep Grow the Roots* (1940), a novel that won widespread recognition for its depiction of the Italian American reaction to Benito Mussolini; and of *Like Lesser Gods* (1949), a novel that portrayed life among Italian Americans in Barre.

Vincent A. Lapomarda

Bibliography

Clarke, Rod. *Carved in Stone: A History of the Barre Granite Industry*. Barre, VT: Rock of Ages, 1989.

Mangione, Jerre, and Ben Morreale. *La Storia: Five Centuries of the Italian American Experience*. New York: Harper Collins, 1992.

Occupations, Present Day

Although Italian immigrants were predominately farmers, fishermen, craftsmen, and laborers, Italian Americans today depict drastically different occupations in diverse industries. The 1990 United States Census reports that nearly 80 percent of the Italian American workforce are now in executive, administrative, managerial, professional, technical, and sales occupations.

Of the 15 million Italian Americans in the United States, 8,854,795 are in the workforce. Approximately 6.04 percent of Americans in the workforce are of Italian descent. Fourteen percent of the Italian Americans in the workforce are employed in government operations and 86 percent are working in private industries. Ten percent of the employed Italian American population are working in self-employed occupations, and 6.36 percent of the Italian Americans work in nonprofit organizations. Among government employment, 7.13 percent of Italian Americans are employed in local municipal occupations; 3.34 percent are employed in state governmental service; and 3.51 percent work in federal employment.

Using the Bureau of Census occupational categories (1980), nearly 10 percent of Italian

O

Americans are executives and administrators; 3.85 percent in management-related occupations; 13.22 percent in professional specialties; 3.42 percent in technical and related support occupations; 13.46 percent in sales occupations; 18.19 percent in administrative support occupations; 13.44 percent in service occupations; 1.2 percent in farming and forestry employment; 10.96 percent in precision production, craft, and repair occupations; 11.96 percent as operators, fabricators, and laborers; and 0.02 percent in military occupations.

Of all government workers in the United States, approximately 5.37 percent are Italian Americans, with 6.28 percent of all local municipal workers being of Italian descent; 4.53 percent of state workers are Italian Americans and 4.79 percent of federal workers are of Italian descent, whereas 6.16 percent of private industry employees are of Italian descent. The distribution of Italian Americans within the occupational categories ranging from highest to lowest percentage representation is 7.31 percent executive and administrator occupations; 7.14 percent management-related employees; 7.03 percent sales employees; 6.8 percent administrative and support works; 6.22 percent professional specialty; 6.01 percent technicians and related support worker; 5.99 percent precision, production, craft, and repair workers; 5.51 percent service workers; 4.53 percent operators, fabricators, and laborers; 4.03 percent military occupations; and 2.81 percent farming, forestry, and fishing employees.

Some changes in occupations in New York State, New York City, and Long Island since 1980 are particularly significant. The changes in educational achievement levels of Italian Americans since 1980 have affected their occupational attainment levels. From 1980 to 1990 Italian Americans in managerial and professional positions has increased 6 percentage points in New York State and Long Island and 8 percentage points in New York City. In this period Italian Americans in managerial and professional positions within the three geographic regions changed from one out of five Italian Americans to more than one out of four Italian Americans in these positions in 1990. Since 1980 Italian Americans in managerial and professional positions in New York State increased approximately 48 percent to 443,390 residents in 1990. In this period Italian Americans within these positions changed by 35 percent to 135,964 Italian Americans in New York City and increased in Long Island approximately 62 percent to 107,610 managers and professionals of Italian ancestry in 1990.

From 1980 to 1990, the percentage of Italian Americans working as operators and laborers decreased dramatically from 5 percentage points in New York State and Long Island and 7 percentage points in New York City. In 1980, within all three geographic regions, nearly one out of five Italian Americans were in unskilled positions, while in 1990 only one out of nine were working as operators and laborers. Since 1980 Italian Americans in New York State working in these positions has decreased by 23 percent to 198,324 Italian American laborers and operators in 1990.

Finally, studies show Italian Americans working in federal, state, and local government occupations in New York State, New York City, and Long Island from 1980 to 1990 there is little change, with only a 1 percentage point increase in New York City and a 2 percentage point decrease in Long Island. Nearly one out of six Italian Americans are working in federal, state, and local governmental positions. The decrease in Italian American government workers in Long Island is among local county and municipal positions, although there has been a large increase in Italian American population and educational achievement levels.

In New York State the percentage of Italian American government workers did not change compared to all government workers. From 1980 to 1990 government workers increased 6 percent to 270,561 residents of Italian descent. Since 1980 Italian American government workers in New York City increased 2 percent to 77,552 Italian Americans in 1990. In Long Island the percentage change of Italian American government workers since 1980 was 16 percent, with 65,645 Italian Americans in 1990 working for federal, state, and local government.

Although Italian Americans have done well in most occupations, in some government and academic occupations they are underrepresented. In academia Italian Americans have not been represented according to their labor pool estimates, especially in public universities and colleges. At the City University of New York (CUNY) Italian American faculty and staff have been underrepresented for over two decades since the initial data on Italian Americans was collected in the 1970s. In this period, despite a 1976 protected class affirmative action designation of Italian Americans at CUNY, Italian American representation remained constant at 5 percent of the total faculty and 8 percent of the total administrative positions, compared to labor pool representation of 10 percent and 14 percent, respectively. This resulted in a federal court hearing in 1992 (*Scelsa vs. CUNY*) in which court settlement was entered into in 1994, declaring that CUNY systematically discriminated against Italian Americans and that efforts should be implemented to increase hiring at the university.

Vincenzo Milione

Bibliography

Affirmative Action Availability Data of Post-Secondary Faculty and Administrators in the United States (State Population Counts). New York: The City University of New York, John D. Calandra Italian American Institute, March, 1990.

Milione, Vincenzo. "The Changing Demographics of Italian Americans in New York State, New York City, and Long Island." *Italian American Review* 5, no. 2 (autumn/winter 1996).

———. "Occupational and Educational Attainment of Italian American Professionals in New York City." *Italian Americans in Transition,* edited by Joseph Scelsa, Salvatore J. LaGumina, and Lydio Tomasi, 153–175. New York: American Italian Historical Association, 1990.

National Council of Colombian Associations in Civil Service. *Getting Our Due or Becoming Extinct? New York City and New York State, Report and Recommendations,* edited by Calandra Italian American Institute, The City University of New York, 1994 Philip Cannistraro, 84–91. New York: American Italian Historical Association, 1989.

United States Department of Commerce, Office of Federal Statistical Policy and Standards. *Standard Occupational Classification Manual.* Washington, DC, 1980.

See also BUSINESS AND ENTREPRENEURSHIP; EDUCATION: SOCIOHISTORICAL BACKGROUND; FISHING; WOMEN IN THE WORKFORCE

Onofrio, Carmeno A. (1907–1982)

O

A mechanic and pilot, Carmeno A. Onofrio was the first person ever to land a plane on the summit of Mount Washington, New Hampshire. The son of Italian parents, Michael and Christina Marie (née Civitello) Onofrio, "Carmie," as he became known, was born in Canton, Maine, March 8, 1907, and died in Ludlow, Massachusetts, of complications from diabetes, September 26, 1982. His love for flying developed during his childhood in Andover, Maine, where he had built his first plane in 1923 out of the engine of a Harley Davidson motorcycle. His first flight ended by crashing into a pile of manure. Self-taught, Onofrio became an expert mechanic as well as an exceptional pilot who was called upon to train civilian pilots in Keene, New Hampshire, for the United States Navy during World War II.

Moving to New Hampshire in 1944, Onofrio managed the Berlin Airport at Milan in an area not too far from the Cascades where a number of Italian immigrants had built the railroads, paper mills, dams, and bridges necessary to the economy of the region earlier in the century. It was from Milan, on March 12, 1947, that Onofrio made his historic flight in which he landed a J3 Piper Cub for the first time ever on the summit of Mount Washington. That event alone fixed him in the state's history as a hero of aviation. The flight itself was an experiment to help civilian and military researchers determine the extent to which the readings of altimeters were distorted by mountain winds.

Although he repeated that flight to the top of New Hampshire's highest mountain many times thereafter, Onofrio was also known for his inventions, including an enormous snowblower that he had improvised to keep the airport in Milan free from snow. Though his inventions proved to be very practical, Onofrio failed to take out patents for most of them, following the advice of contemporaries who had discouraged that approach.

Yet, for twelve years, from 1944 to 1956, Onofrio did shape the growth of the regional airport at Milan to such an extent that, after his death, the residents of the area set up a monument in his memory on which were inscribed his own words: I HAVE SEEN THE GREAT AND WONDERFUL HANDIWORK OF OUR CREATOR FROM THE VANTAGE POINT OF A

HIGH-FLYING EAGLE. He was buried in Hill-crest Cemetery in Milan, New Hampshire, and his plane, with which he made the historic flight, was purchased by a resident of Mirabel, Quebec, in 1990.

Vincent A. Lapomarda

Bibliography

Alger, Lois. "Anniversary: The First to Fly to the Top." *Northern New Hampshire Magazine* (March 1997): 4–6.

Batchelder, Jean. *History & Heroes of New Hampshire Aviation*. Spring Hill, FL: Arrow, 1995.

Milan Bicentennial Committee. *Historical Notes and Pictures of Milan, New Hampshire, 1771–1971*. Milan, NH: Courier Print, 1971.

Prichett, Richard. "How to Land a Plane on the Top of Mount Washington." *Yankee Magazine* (March 1978): 101–103, 109.

See also PATENTS AND INVENTORS

Opera

Italian Americans have contributed significantly to the development of opera in the United States. Since opera remained one of Italy's famous exports, Italians and Italian Americans naturally nurtured opera in the New World. Opera developed as a central part of the Italian American cultural experience and provided a link to Italy and its rich humanistic tradition.

One of the first people to transplant opera to the United States was Mozart's librettist, Lorenzo Da Ponte (1749–1838). He wrote the librettos for Mozart's three most famous operas: *Le Nozze di Figaro, Don Giovanni,* and *Cosi Fan Tutte.* Though born in Italy, he moved to Vienna, then London, and eventually New York City. He helped sponsor performances of Italian opera in New York, especially the operas of Mozart. In the fall of 1825 the Garcia troupe, encouraged by Da Ponte, staged Mozart's *Don Giovanni* and other operas at the Park Theater in New York City.

The New World soon attracted renowned Italian singers to its shores. Adelina Patti (1843–1919), though born in Madrid, received most of her vocal training in America and performed often in this country. Luisa Tetrazzini (1871–1940) also performed in the United States at the turn of the century; her amazing coloratura voice filled opera houses, especially in New York. Amelita Galli-Curci (1882–1963) also helped develop audiences for Italian opera in this country through her stellar soprano singing. The tenor Pasquilino Brignoli (1824–1889) sang in New York and in many other American cities.

In 1851 the Pellegrini Opera Company Troupe staged Bellini's *La Sonnambula* at the Adelphi Theater in San Francisco. By 1854 San Francisco, where most of California's Italian Americans lived, supported several Italian opera companies. Clotilda Barili was one of the prima donnas of the period and performed with the Italian Opera Troupe and several other companies. Also in the 1850s, under the impresario P. T. Barnum, Eliza Biscaccianti—known as "The American Thrush"—performed often in San Francisco. In 1854 eleven separate opera seasons were being staged in San Francisco, and California's Italian American miners frequently attended these performances. During this period, Gaetano Donizetti's *The Daughter of the Regiment* became a favorite.

In the 1860s the Bianchi Opera Company staged the premieres in California of Gounod's *Faust* and Verdi's *Un Ballo in Maschera.* Sopranos remained a particular favorite with the California audiences. Among the especially popular sopranos were Signora Brambilla and Euphrosyne Parepa-Rosa. These singers were brought to California by the American impresario Thomas Maguire, then known as "The Napoleon of the San Francisco Stage." San Francisco also attracted during this period the composer Pietro Mascagni and the sopranos Luisa Tetrazzini and Adelina Patti. After stunning successes in eastern cities, Patti succeeded equally as well in San Francisco and Salt Lake City. Her recitals were always sold out. Early in the twentieth century, the Metropolitan Opera began its operatic tours, and often came to California, especially San Francisco.

Later in the nineteenth and early twentieth centuries, Italians and Italian Americans developed many of the major opera companies in America. Giulio Gatti-Casazza (1869–1940) directed the Metropolitan Opera Company in New York from 1908 to 1936, bringing from Italy many singers who popularized America's newest art form. Of these, the Neapolitan Enrico Caruso (1873–1921) became synonymous in America with operatic singing, and his fine tenor voice introduced many roles to Americans. On the evening of April 17, 1906, Caruso sang the role of Don

Verdi Day at Golden Gate Park, San Francisco, March 22, 1914. At the dedication of the Giuseppe Verdi statue, a gift of the Italians of San Francisco to their beloved city; soprano Luisa Tetrazzini, center, sang Verdi's most popular arias to those in attendance. Ettore Patrizi, editor and publisher of L'Italia, *is at left. Andrea Sbarboro, founder of Italian Swiss Colony Wine and pioneer banker, is to Tetrazzini's left. Courtesy Augusto Troiani.*

Jose in *Carmen* in San Francisco's Grand Opera House. That evening, in the middle of the night, the great earthquake occurred, forcing Caruso out of bed and into Union Square. He vowed never to return to San Francisco, and he never did.

Gatti-Casazza also brought to America Arturo Toscanini (1867–1957), who conducted many opera performances at the Metropolitan Opera and later on the NBC radio network. Toscanini became the most famous conductor in America. That reputation, together with his residence in the United States, where he lived until his death in 1957, was the source of special pride among Italian Americans.

Other Italians came to the United States to develop careers. Composer Pietro Mascagni (1863–1945) was heartily welcomed to the United States, especially by Italian Americans, when he came to promote his operas. His most famous opera, *Cavalleria Rusticana* (1890), quickly became popular throughout the United States and has remained in the standard repertoire of most opera companies.

Ezio Pinza (1892–1957) became the Metropolitan Opera's most famous bass and sang there and elsewhere from 1926 to 1948. After his operatic career, he appeared on Broadway in *South Pacific,* where he and Mary Martin made the musical a great success. Pasquale Amato (1878–1942) was a great baritone who was born in Italy but achieved his greatest successes in America, singing with the Metropolitan Opera from 1908 to 1921. The bass Salvatore Baccaloni (1900–1969) also achieved his greatest operatic successes in the United States, singing at the Metropolitan Opera from 1940 to 1962.

Composer Giacomo Puccini (1858–1924) visited New York several times, primarily to oversee the first American productions of his operas, especially *Madama Butterfly.* In addition, his *La Fanciulla del West* had a very successful premiere at the Metropolitan Opera on December 10, 1910. During this period Enrico Caruso sang most of Puccini's tenor roles to great acclaim in America. Fortunato Gallo (1878–1970) began and directed the San Carlo Opera Company, which toured the entire United States. Gaetano Merola (1881–1953) directed the San Francisco Opera Company for many years and helped popularize opera in California. Fiorello H.

LaGuardia, the famous mayor of New York City, helped to found the New York City Opera Company, which began performances on February 21, 1944.

Rosa Ponselle (1897–1981) sang many Italian soprano roles at the Metropolitan Opera and elsewhere in the United States. She was the most popular soprano in New York in the 1920s and 1930s. She was succeeded in the 1940s, 1950s, and 1960s by Licia Albanese (b. 1913), who specialized in soprano roles, especially of Italian operas by Verdi and Puccini. Also in the 1950s the Italian American tenor Mario Lanza (1921–1959) brought opera into mainstream American music, though he did this through film rather than stage performances.

Also in the 1950s and early 1960s, composer Gian Carlo Menotti (b. 1911) had highly successful premieres of his work. His operas *The Telephone* (1947), *The Consul* (1950), *Amahl and the Night Visitors* (1951), and *The Saint of Bleecker Street* (1954) added an Italian American musical voice to the development of composers in this country.

More recently, John Coregliano has written operas in America. His *The Ghosts of Versailles* (1993) had an auspicious premiere at the Metropolitan Opera. The Met was itself directed through most of the 1990s by another Italian American, Joseph Volpe (1908–1994). Italians and Italian Americans helped to make opera a popular and vital performing art in the United States. In addition, Italian Americans achieved a sense of pride in seeing that opera was a significant Italian contribution to American culture and a direct link to Italy and its culture.

John Louis DiGaetani

Bibliography

DiGaetani, John Louis. *An Invitation to the Opera.* New York: Doubleday, 1986.

DiGaetani, John Louis, and Josef Sirefman, eds. *Opera and the Golden West.* Rutherford, NJ: Fairleigh Dickinson University Press, 1994.

Dizikes, John. *Opera in America: A Cultural History.* New Haven: Yale University Press, 1993.

Mayer, Martin. *The Met: One Hundred Years of Grand Opera.* New York: Simon and Schuster, 1983.

Rolle, Andrew. *The Immigrant Upraised.* Norman: University of Oklahoma Press, 1968.

See also ALBANESE, LICIA; BISCACCIANTI, ELIZA (OSTINELLI); CARUSO, ENRICO; DA PONTE, LORENZO; DELLA CHIESA, VIVIAN; GATTI-CASAZZA, GIULIO; LANZA, MARIO; MENOTTI, GIAN CARLO; PATTI, ADELINA; PONSELLE, ROSA; TOSCANINI, ARTURO

Order Sons of Italy in America

The largest and most geographically representative organization of Italian Americans, the Order Sons of Italy in America (OSIA) was founded in New York City on June 5, 1905. While the concept of a nationwide federation for those of Italian ancestry predates the founding of the Order, OSIA has had the longest existence and has been the most successful.

Dr. Vincenzo Sellaro (1868–1932) was born in Sicily and graduated from the medical school at the University of Naples before migrating to the United States in 1897. He called together a group of professionals to effectuate the uniting of Italian mutual-aid societies, some two thousand then extant in the city. Adopting the Enlightenment ideals of "Liberty, Equality, and Fraternity" as its motto, and the nomenclature and ritual of American fraternal organizations, the new group was structured on the pyramid lodge system, with a "Supreme Lodge" at its apex. The professed purposes reflected in the Order's first constitution encompassed group affirmation, "emancipation from every prejudice," cultural attachment to Italy, and civic participation in American political life. Dr. Sellaro served as Supreme Venerable (national president) until 1908.

From the beginning OSIA provided for complete membership parity between men and women; but the Italian version of its corporate name—L'Ordine Figli d'Italia in America—translation unfairly serves as a source of criticism for some. Its institution of English language instruction and citizenship training classes was unique at the time. OSIA also placed an agent at Ellis Island to welcome immigrants.

During the early years, the Order grew rapidly through the issuance of lodge charters to scores of Italian American mutual-aid societies. It soon organized new lodges in surrounding states. By the time restrictive immigration policies were being put into place during the early 1920s (legislation that the Order would battle until repeal of the discriminatory national origins quota system in

1965), OSIA claimed 125,000 members in more than one thousand filial lodges spread throughout the United States and into Canada. Eventually, the Order would charter nearly three thousand local lodges in all but a handful of states, organized under twenty-one American and two Canadian grand lodges; many of the functions of the Order center at this grand (state) lodge level, and a good deal of decentralization allows for activities of a purely local lodge nature. The first grand lodge was founded in New York in 1911. A biennial national convention format commenced in 1917. Far-flung lodges formed in Guam and British island possessions in North America, as well as those in the District of Columbia, are directly under the administration of the Supreme Lodge.

Rudolph J. Vecoli, left, director of the Immigration History Research Center in Minnesota, and Judge Dominic Massaro of the New York State Supreme Court discuss the records of the Sons of Italy that were recently placed in the archives of the IHRC, 1990. Courtesy Frank J. Cavaioli.

Since its founding, assuredly more than a million Italian Americans of various generations have been regular OSIA members. Its far wider, nonvoting social membership category can only be estimated. With growing political significance, OSIA leaders were first received by President Woodrow Wilson at the White House in 1917; every president has followed suit, and a high point was achieved when President Richard Nixon accepted the Order's Marconi Award, its highest, in 1971. President Carter addressed the Order's biennial convention in 1979.

During World War I some twenty-eight thousand members of the Order served in the armed forces of the United States. Subsidies to the families of members at war complemented sick and death benefits that had always been a staple of the Order's early objectives. Mortuary funds would later give way to large-scale, actuarial-based insurance programs still operative in Illinois, Massachusetts, and Pennsylvania. Orphanages that would function into the 1970s were established in New Jersey and Pennsylvania. From its founding until the eve of World War II and the rise of the New Deal beneficent state apparatus, OSIA was perhaps the single most important provider of social welfare programs to Italians in the United States. Likewise, the Order has supported relief efforts for victims of natural disasters in Italy since the earthquake in Sicily in 1914 and established an orphanage at Cassino following World War II.

OSIA was an early and militant supporter of organized labor; it fought the Ku Klux Klan in the South and, in 1927, dispatched an attorney to Massachusetts to assist in the appeal of the "terrible miscarriage of justice" following the conviction of Sacco and Vanzetti. OSIA was responsible for the first Columbus Day measure introduced in Congress in 1932, and annually thereafter until passage of the national holiday in 1984. In 1977 the Order filed a major brief with the Supreme Court of the United States in *Bakke,* opposing the concept of "preferential racial quotas" in admissions to higher education. (A white applicant, Bakke succeeded in convincing the Court that he was denied admission to medical school because the preferential racial quotas unfairly denied him admission in favor of less qualified minorities.) In 1990 it was responsible for preventing the American College Board from canceling Italian language testing as a qualification for advanced college admissions.

As the "golden door" was closed to new immigration in 1924, OSIA turned to the second generation in its recruitment of new members. Junior divisions were established for youngsters to 18 years of age, and one still operates in Massachusetts. More than 350 youth lodges were separately chartered, most of them between the wars, increasingly stressing American-style activities such as sports, bands, and drill teams.

Close political relations with Italy saw the Order officially recognized as the voice of the Italian in America as early as 1922. Student exchanges with and annual pilgrimages to Italy were initiated during this period. In 1935 OSIA mounted intense pressure on Congress and the president to ensure that Ethiopia receive no economic assistance, while simultaneously collecting large sums to aid the Italian incursion there. The Order vigorously opposed League of Nations sanctions against Italy and pressed for a policy of strict neutrality by the United States. These policies of close alignment with the Fascist regime earlier had brought about the most divisive number of schisms in the Order's history. Ten years before, led by Fiorello LaGuardia and Luigi Antonini, a parallel organization was established in New York. The ensuing legal and polemic struggle caused a nationwide division of the Order that would not heal until 1943. In 1928 a split in Pennsylvania led to the formation of the Italian Sons and Daughters in America, which still functions as a separate national fraternal organization comprised of two hundred-odd local lodges, mainly in seven Midwest states. A 1990 effort at reunification was thwarted by objection from Pennsylvania.

Italy's entry into World War II as an Axis partner in 1941 presented a traumatic moment in Italian American history, and focused public attention and hostility on those of Italian ancestry. Dual loyalties were tested, but the Order and its first American-born national president, jurist Felix Forte of Massachusetts, made it abundantly clear that the primary allegiance was to America. Notwithstanding, a brand of infamy, today considered baseless and unjustified, was imposed on Italian language and culture, while indiscriminate curfew, relocation, arrest, and internment of resident Italians, and even naturalized and native-born Italian Americans, was initiated, particularly on the West Coast. The stamp of "enemy alien" was eventually removed in late 1942 largely as the result of the Order's demonstrated unswerving loyalty and its coordinative political initiative. The position of national deputy was established that year to lobby the national government; a Washington office was also opened.

With the fall of Mussolini in 1943, and the rise of a communist threat to the Italian peninsula, the Order was a key element in reordering Italian American priorities. It played a central role in a united Italian American effort committed to support a democratic government for postwar Italy. It exerted pressure on the Roosevelt/Truman administrations in favor of Italian territorial integrity, and played a significant role in interim military government planning for the rebuilding of the war-ravished nation. The *OSIA News,* a monthly newspaper launched in 1946 and published for a half century, articulated these efforts. OSIA successfully lobbied for Italy's inclusion in the Marshall Plan and for its membership in both NATO and the United Nations. Italian American prime minister Alcide De Gasperi (1945–1953) gave the Order high regard. In the "Letters to Italy" campaign of 1947–1948, the Order played an acknowledged role in depriving Communist participation in governing the newly constituted Republic of Italy. Since World War II, OSIA has continued to maintain a lively interest in Italian political affairs, regularly welcoming Italy's ambassadors and engaging in projects like the Douhet Mitchell Award that recognizes joint military cooperation between the two nations. As late as 1996 OSIA was urging the Clinton State Department to accept an Italian plan that would assure Italy a seat on the United Nations Security Council.

From its inception the Order has endeavored to defend the good name of Italians in America. A series of special committees, culminating in 1978 with the creation of a separate, Washington-based legal entity now known as the Commission for Social Justice (CSJ), has vigilantly fought defamatory characterizations by the media. With branches throughout the nation, CSJ serves as an intake and referral agency for such complaints. More recently, as "expressed hostility" toward Italian Americans declines, it has employed a national proactive strategy of promoting positive Italian American imagery based on commissioned research findings. Its cooperative programs with representative organizations of other ethnic and racial backgrounds have become models of intergroup education and understanding.

The Order's membership decline during the 1950s was stemmed by the ethnic revival of the 1970s. The decade witnessed one new grand lodge organized in Arizona and 247 new local lodges, chartered nationwide, confirming prominence in the suburbs as Italian Americans exited from the older, central cities. During this period the Sons of Italy Bank and Trust Company, a Pennsylvania chartered commercial bank, was acquired by Continental Bank and Trust Company of North America; the OSIA Savings and Loan Association continues to function in Philadelphia. Large-scale, federally chartered credit unions, such as that operating in New York, have supplanted earlier forms of loan activity as a member service. The number of new local lodges organized nationally fell to about one hundred during the 1980s. As late as 1995 a new grand lodge was organized in Colorado.

In 1974 OSIA was a founding member of the National Italian American Coordinating Association (NIACA); it continues to play a leadership role in the affairs of this thirty-odd member gathering of national Italian American entities, and the Order has on more than one occasion provided a president for its Conference of Presidents of Major Italian American Organizations. Also in 1974 OSIA was instrumental in the creation of the Italian American Congressional Caucus.

The Sons of Italy Foundation, formed in 1959, has since coordinated support for a multitude of OSIA charitable causes. The principal beneficiary through 1987 was the Birth Defects Program, in the amount of $14 million. When the Order's claim that the sponsoring March of Dimes failed to include an American of Italian descent on its national board was continually ignored, the relationship ended. The Cooley's Anemia Foundation has since received upwards of one million dollars for research and treatment of afflicted youngsters. The Sons of Italy Foundation also funds a vast program of scholastic aid in favor of college-bound youths; this is organized on every level of the Order—national, state, and local—and grants over one-half million dollars annually.

In 1981 OSIA established the full-time position of national executive director; in 1982, a building was purchased in Washington to serve as a national headquarters; permanent staff now coordinate a wide array of programmatic thrusts for OSIA's three main present-day outlets: its Supreme Lodge, the Commission for Social Justice, and the Sons of Italy Foundation. The Garibaldi Meucci Museum, on Staten Island in New York, has been owned and maintained by the Order since 1914. The Sons of Italy Archives, opened in 1989, is housed at the Immigration History Research Center of the University of Minnesota. Surpassing 2,500 linear feet of primary resource material, it is the largest collection of Italian Americana under one roof.

Suffering the general plight of ethnic fraternal organizations—an aged membership and an attendant lessening of interest on the part of the youngest generation—OSIA has sustained an annual net membership loss for at least a decade. It is in a period of retrenchment as the nature of group identity changes and ethnicity becomes an option. In 1995, it established a national membership category as an alternative to the lodge meeting hall; in 1996, it launched a glossy quarterly membership magazine of wider cultural interest than presented in its standard *OSIA News*. Nomenclature, however, was changed only following years of debate, and the use of ritual is still the rule, although more often attenuated or observed in the breach.

Replete with decades of encouragement for the maintenance of *Italianità* in all of its many and varied forms of expression, the Order's efforts "to unite under one banner all those of Italian birth or ancestry," reflect an almost century-old legacy of protest, legislative initiative, and commitment to the collective promotion of the material well-being of American civic life. As intermarriage soars and Italian American needs reflect a new paradigm, OSIA is yet emerging as more of a moral force for an array of pertinent issues.

Notwithstanding the vagaries of time and occasional upstaging by newer Italian American entities, and what now appears to be a separate course for the Order in Canada, OSIA can still boast seventy-five thousand regular per capita dues-paying members organized in 850 local chapters throughout the United States. Its social membership category is presently estimated at fourfold. It can be stated with certainty that the name of practically every major Italian American personality since the turn of the century can be found on an OSIA roster.

Dominic R. Massaro

Bibliography

Andreozzi, John, ed. *Guide to the Records of the Order Sons of Italy in America*. St. Paul: Immigration History Research Center, University of Minnesota, 1989.

Aquilano, Baldo. *L'Ordine Figli d'Italia in America*. New York: Società Tipografica Italiana, 1925.

Biaggi, Ernest. *The Purple Aster*. Philadelphia: Veritas Press, 1961.

Ferrari, Robert. *Days Pleasant and Unpleasant in the Order Sons of Italy in America*. New York: Mandy Press, 1926.

Salvemini, Gaetano. *Italian Fascist Activities in the United States*. New York: Center for Migration Studies, 1977.

See also ORGANIZATIONS

Representatives of Italian organizations in front of the statue of Giuseppe Verdi in Golden Gate Park prior to the start of "Italian Day" concert with the municipal band and artists from the San Francisco Opera Company, June 1986. Courtesy Augusto Troiani.

Organizations

Since the 1820s, when the Unione e Fratellanza Italiana was founded in New York City, Italian immigrants and their descendants have formed thousands of organizations throughout the United States. Over the years a fascinating variety of groups have been established to address the changing needs of Italian Americans, a process that continues to this day.

Many of the original groups founded by Italian immigrants during the nineteenth century focused on providing mutual aid and brotherhood, and this purpose was reflected in their titles. In the 1850s the Nazionale Italiana and Mutuo Beneficenza were founded in New Orleans, and the Associazione Italiana di Mutuo Beneficenza in San Francisco. Like the first group in New York City, a number of the original organizations founded by Italians around the country were named Unione e Fratellanza Italiana. Examples include Chicago and Philadelphia in 1867, Baltimore in 1870, Detroit in 1873, and Buffalo in 1875. Boston's first group, established in 1868, was the Società di Mutuo Soccorso e Beneficenza Italiana. Pittsburgh had the Fraterna Italiana in 1886, and an organization of the same name was formed in Cleveland two years later.

Military organizations were popular in America during the nineteenth century. Among Italian immigrants this was also true, as some had fought in the long series of military struggles that culminated in the unification of Italy, and also in the American Civil War. By 1869 Boston had the Bersaglieri Italiano and New Orleans the Tiro al Bersaglio. Philadelphia Italians founded the Bersaglieri La Marmora, and in Pittsburgh the Legione Giuseppe Garibaldi was formed during the 1880s. When New York City's Italians celebrated Columbus Day in 1892 with a huge parade, the one hundred marching associations included such military groups as Guardia Colombo, Reduci Patrie Battaglie, Guardia Savoia, and the Italian Rifle Company.

Italians, along with Irish Americans who wanted to foster a national Catholic hero, lobbied extensively to get Columbus Day recognized at the local, state, and national level. Italian groups, such as the Columbus Day League of New York City and Baltimore's Columbus Day Association, pursued these goals in the early years of the twentieth century. Eventually, Columbus Day was officially recognized in forty-three states and, in 1934, by the federal government. The single most popular name among Italian American organizations was that of Christopher Columbus. Many Cristoforo Colombo societies were organized at the time of the Columbian Exposition in 1893, when Italians learned that America's civic leaders viewed Columbus as a heroic figure.

The town or provincial origins of Italian immigrants provided the ready focal point for organizing associations. Immigrants met with others who spoke their dialect and socialized in familiar ways. Hundreds of organizations bore hometown names such as Napoli, Agrigento, and Pettorano Sul Gizio. Others were named for Italian provinces and regions in which immigrants had roots. Most of these societies provided economic assistance during times of sickness and a death benefit to the families of deceased members.

Many Italian American associations focused on honoring a hometown saint with a yearly festival that included a Mass, street procession, light displays, fireworks, food booths, games, and entertainment. These groups often functioned independently of the local Italian church. San Rocco, San Giuseppe, San Antonio, and a variety of madonnas, especially Our Lady of Mount Carmel, were some of the more popular patron saints honored in Italian neighborhoods.

Protestant proselytizers attracted a significant number of Italian converts, some of whom organized a national Italian Baptist association. In Wisconsin, Italians in the Evangelical Church founded the Italian Mission Council in 1922 to coordinate activities of churches in three cities. The majority of Italians, however, maintained at least nominal ties with the Roman Catholic Church. The Italian Catholic Federation was established in California as a national organization in 1925 and since then has formed over two hundred chapters throughout the country.

A core group of Italian immigrants were active in leftist political causes. The Italian Socialist Federation was formed in 1905 and established at least eighty sections across the nation. Several dozen Italian anarchist groups were active in the early years of this century. During the 1920s and 1930s Italian Americans who supported the Mussolini government in Italy were active in the Fascist League of North America, while those who opposed the regime joined ranks in the Anti-Fascist League of North America.

The vast Italian American working class took an active part in organizing labor unions. Barbers, terrazzo workers, stonecutters, bootblacks, fruit packers, and construction laborers organized unions or initiated Italian locals of existing labor groups. Italians formed branches of "American" fraternal organizations, such as the Woodmen of America. In New York City alone there were thirteen Italian Masonic lodges, and by 1906 some twenty-one Italian "courts" in the Foresters of America. In California and Michigan the United Ancient Order of Druids had a number of Italian lodges.

As Italian immigrants and their children struggled to survive and advance economically, they formed cooperatives, social welfare groups, orphanages, and hospitals. Learning the lessons of civic life, Italian Americans organized political clubs to lobby politicians for jobs and recognition, and to support their own fledgling candidates. As they moved into government-service jobs they founded organizations to secure their economic niches. Eventually, dozens of Columbian Associations were formed by civil service workers, and by the 1970s New York City was home to the National Council of Columbian Associations in Service to America. Professionals established the Justinian Society of Lawyers, and organizations for teachers and medical personnel. Italian college students founded the Alpha Phi Delta Fraternity in 1914, which later grew to include fifty-four chapters.

By the 1920s many of the small mutual-aid societies were struggling for members. The flow of immigrants had been restricted by new laws and different needs were arising in the Little Italys. An emerging Italian American identity challenged the hometown and provinical identification of earlier organizations. Broader regional affiliations were encouraged by the Federazione Pugliese in America and similar groups. Civic groups and city and county coalitions of Italians focused on civil rights, combated bigotry, and gained recognition for the needs of Italian Americans. Organizations were founded to support Sacco and Vanzetti, challenge discriminatory immigration laws, and proclaim pride in the heritage of Italy. Statues of famous Italians were erected, cultural programs at colleges funded, and visits to Italy arranged. At the national level the Dante Alighieri Society and the Mazzini Society were active in this movement.

In addition to embracing a sense of ethnic identity, other trends emerged that were reflected in Italian organizations during the 1920s and 1930s. As the American-born second generation reached adulthood, it served as a bridge between Italian and American values. With the exception of the Great Depression years of the early 1930s, Italian Americans were struggling less at the level of economic survival and could focus more on recreational and cultural pursuits. Women's organizations and those with mixed gender memberships, which had been rare, were founded in greater numbers. The growing numbers of Italian professionals created societies, such as the Italo American Professional Women's Association in New York City. Many recreational and sports organizations were started by the second generation eager to participate in activities such as Italian theatrical productions and American baseball. These same themes were also reflected in the activities of groups operating at the national level.

Under American and Italian flags, installation of Dell Assunta Society officers, 1980, Westbury, New York. Founded in 1911, the Dell Assunta Society is one of the oldest Italian mutual-aid societies in continuous existence. From left to right, President Poscillico, Durazzano Society; Joseph Piscitelli, Mayor of Westbury; Frank Ciardullo, Vice President, Dell Assunta Society; Carmine Daddio, President, St. Anthony's Society; Charles Fuschillo, North Hempstead Town Councilman; Judge Malloy, Westbury; and Salvatore J. LaGumina, guest. Courtesy Salvatore J. LaGumina.

The idea for a national Italian American federation dates back to 1868, when Italians from seven cities met in Philadelphia to found Unione Italiana negli Stati Uniti. The following year the organization held its first convention in Chicago. The Midwest was the focal point for other early attempts at a national organization. While the Columbian National Exposition was taking place in Chicago in 1893, representatives from twenty-three Italian organizations met in the city to launch the Columbian Federation. The group eventually established its headquarters in Pueblo, Colorado, and created 229 chapters by 1950. In 1895 the Unione Siciliana was organized in Chicago. Changing its name in 1925 to the Italo American National Union, the group grew to 101 chapters, mostly in the Midwest.

Other associations with a national focus were created in the early years of the twentieth century. The Alleanza Italo-Americana degli Stati Uniti, the Sons of Columbus, and the Legione Giuseppe Garibaldi were centered in the northeastern states. The UNICO clubs were organized in Connecticut in 1922, while the National Italian American Civic League began in 1931 and founded chapters in the midwestern and mountain states. These two groups merged in 1947 to become UNICO National. Over the years some 150 local UNICO chapters have been established.

The Order Sons of Italy in America (OSIA) was organized in New York City in 1905. It grew rapidly, taking in existing mutual-aid societies, and became the largest national Italian American organization. Throughout its history the Order has chartered 2,746 adult lodges and 366 youth lodges in the United States and Canada. Several splinter groups broke off from OSIA. In 1907 the Independent Order Sons of Italy was created in New York City. In 1925 another group of dissidents formed the Sons of Italy Grand Lodge, Inc., after a dispute about ties with the Mussolini government. With Italy out of the war in 1943, this faction rejoined OSIA. Twenty lodges in western Pennsylvania left OSIA in 1928 and created the Italian Sons and Daughters of America. The organization, which has its national office in Pittsburgh, has created 270 lodges in ten states during the past seven decades.

The national Italian groups lobbied at the local, state, and federal level for specific causes. Following World War II the focus was on aid to Italy, a just peace settlement, and a more open immigration policy allowing a greater number of refugees into the United States. In the late 1940s members of UNICO, OSIA, and other organizations sent millions of letters to Italy urging relatives to vote against communist candidates. Many Italian American groups supported orphanages in Italy and sponsored relief efforts following floods and earthquakes. Immigration legislation was of particular interest, and Italian groups lobbied for the repeal of the old national origins and quota provisions. The American Committee on Italian Migration (ACIM) was founded in 1952 and within a decade had 125 chapters around the country. ACIM, OSIA, and other Italian groups lobbied successfully to end the discriminatory national origins and quota system in 1965. Ten years later the National Italian American Foundation was set up with the goal of maintaining a continual presence in Washington, D.C., to advocate for an Italian American political agenda.

Since World War II Italians have encountered less of the systematic prejudice endured by immigrants in the early years of this century. However, many local and national groups, such as OSIA's Commission on Social Justice, continue to respond to bigoted and sterotypical depictions of Italian Americans. As a large and well-established ethnic group with a long history in the United States, Italian Americans have focused on preserving their history and accomplishments during the past three decades. Museums, halls of fame for Italian American athletes, historical associations, genealogy societies, and cultural groups have been founded in many regions of the country. One such group, Arba Sicula, Inc., has as its goal the preservation of Sicilian language, literature, and history. The American Italian Historical Association, founded in 1966, promotes research and the preservation of documents and sponsors annual conferences that draw scholars throughout the United States and around the world. It publishes the proceedings of those conferences, which include the latest scientific findings of the Italian American experience.

Societal issues and demographics are also reflected in the Italian organizations founded in recent decades. As part of the general population movement from the northern states to the South and Southwest, Italians have organized civic groups and established new chapters of UNICO and OSIA in Florida and Arizona. Italian American women have formed a number of societies, including the National Organization of Italian American Women, and have risen to the highest national positions in OSIA, which remains the largest Italian American association.

It is estimated that approximately twenty thousand organizations have been established by Italians in the United States during the past 170 years. These associations represent a crucial aspect of Italian American communal life and mirror the changing identity and needs of one of the largest ethnic groups in the United States. The story of Italian organizations reflects the variety and richness in the experiences of Italian immigrants and their descendants throughout America.

John Andreozzi

Bibliography

Andreozzi, John. *Guide to the Records of the Order Sons of Italy in America.* St. Paul: Immigration History Research Center, 1989.

"Le Società italiane all'estero nel 1908." *Bollettino dell'Emigrazione* 24 (1908): 1–147.

"Le Società italiane negli Stati Uniti dell'America del Nord." *Bollettino dell'Emigrazione* 4 (1912): 19–54.

Marchetto, Ezio. *A Directory of Italian American Associations in the Tri-State Area: Connecticut, Eastern New Jersey and New York.* New York: Center for Migration Studies, 1989.

Maselli, Joseph, ed. *Year 2000, Where Will Italian American Organizations Be in the Year 2000?* Washington, DC: National Italian American Foundation, 1990.

Ministero Degli Affari Esteri. *Associazoni Italiane Nel Mondo, 1984.* Roma: Istituto Poligrafico e Zecca Dello Stato, 1984.

National Italian American Foundation. *Directory of Italian American Organizations, 1988–1989.* Washington, DC: National Italian American Foundation, 1988.

O

Tomasi, Silvano M., ed. *National Directory of Research Centers, Repositories and Organizations of Italian Culture in the United States.* Torino: Giovanni Agnelli Foundation, 1980.

See also AMERICAN COMMITTEE ON ITALIAN MIGRATION; AMERICAN ITALIAN HISTORICAL ASSOCIATION; AMERICAN JUSTINIAN SOCIETY OF JURISTS; COLUMBIA ASSOCIATIONS; INDEPENDENT ORDER SONS OF ITALY; ITALIAN AMERICAN CIVIL RIGHTS LEAGUE; ITALIAN AMERICAN LABOR COUNCIL; ITALIAN WELFARE LEAGUE; NATIONAL ITALIAN AMERICAN COORDINATING ASSOCIATION; NATIONAL ITALIAN AMERICAN FOUNDATION; NATIONAL ORGANIZATION OF ITALIAN AMERICAN WOMEN; ORDER SONS OF ITALY IN AMERICA; SOCIETÀ ITALIANA DI MUTUA BENEFICENZA; UNICO NATIONAL

Orlando, Joseph
See CARTOONISTS AND ILLUSTRATORS

Ostinelli, Eliza
See BISCACCIANTI, ELIZA (OSTINELLI)

P

Paca, William (1740–1799)

A signer of the Declaration of Independence, William Paca served as the first Italian American governor from 1782 to 1785. He was born 1740 at Abington, Harford County, Maryland, and died 1799 at his country home, Wye Hall. Paca's ancestors originally came from Italy, moved to England, then migrated to Maryland in the middle of the seventeenth century. The practice of using England as a way station en route to the American colonies was common to many Italians at that time.

Paca received a classical education. He graduated from the College of Philadelphia with a master's degree in 1759. He studied law at Annapolis and completed his legal training at the Inner Temple, London, England, and was admitted to the provincial court in 1764. His successful practice in the law, and prominent role as a civic leader, earned him a place in the Maryland provincial legislature from 1764 to 1774.

Paca joined the revolutionary cause for American independence and became a member of the First and Second Continental Congresses from 1774 to 1778. He served on the Committee of Correspondence in Maryland and made contributions of his own money to outfit troops. In 1778 he was appointed Chief Judge of the state's General Court; two years later Congress appointed him Chief Judge of the Court of Appeals in admiralty and prize cases.

In November 1782 the Maryland legislature elected Paca governor and reelected him unanimously each of the next two years. His last term ended November 16, 1785.

Frank J. Cavaioli

Bibliography

Cavaioli, Frank J. "Charles Poletti and Fourteen Other Italian American Governors." In *Italians in Transition,* edited by Joseph V. Scelsa, Salvatore J. LaGumina, and Lydio F. Tomasi, 137–152. New York: American Italian Historical Association, 1990.

Iorizzo, Luciano J., and Salvatore Mondello. *The Italian Americans.* Boston: Twayne, 1980.

Weaver, Glen. *The Italian Presence in Virginia.* New York: Center for Migration Studies, 1988.

See also GOVERNORS

Pacino, Alfred James (b. 1940)

A widely acclaimed actor in the Method style, Alfred James Pacino was born April 25, 1940, of Sicilian descent to Salvatore and Rose Pacino in New York City. He was two years old when his father left the family, and he was brought up by his mother and grandparents in the South Bronx. He quit school at age 17, taking jobs as a mail delivery boy, a movie theater usher, a porter, and a building superintendent. He attended the High School for the Performing Arts, the Herbert Berghof Studio (where he studied under Charles Laughton), and the Actors Studio in New York City.

Pacino gained experience in Off-Off Broadway productions: *The Peace Creeps* (1966), *America Hurrah* and *Awake and Sing* (1967), and *The Indian Wants the Bronx,* for which he won an Obie as best actor in an Off-Broadway production (1968). In 1969 he made his Broadway debut in *Does the Tiger*

Wear a Necktie? and won a Tony Award as the best dramatic actor in a supporting role. Other plays he appeared in included *Camino Real* and *Richard III* (1973); *The Basic Training of Pavlo Hummel* (1977), for which he won his second Tony; *Jungle of the Cities* (1979); *American Buffalo;* and *Julius Caesar* (1988).

He made his movie debut in *Me, Natalie* (1970). He gained notoriety in *Panic in Needle Park* (1971), but it was his role as Michael Corleone in Francis Ford Coppola's *The Godfather* (1972) that thrust him into stardom and for which he received the best actor award from the National Society of Film Critics and the Academy Award's best supporting actor nomination. The following year he received an Academy Award nomination for best supporting actor for his role in *Serpico*. In 1974 he received an Academy nomination for best actor for his role in *The Godfather II,* and again for his role in *Dog Day Afternoon* in 1975; he did, however, receive the best actor award for these roles from the British Academy. In 1979 Pacino received the best actor Academy nomination for his role in *And Justice for All.*

This prolific Italian American actor has also appeared in *Bobby Deerfield* (1977); *Cruising* (1980); *Author, Author!* (1982); *Scarface* (1983); *Revolution* (1985); *Sea of Love* (1990); *Dick Tracy* (1990), for which he received an Academy Award nomination, best supporting actor; *The Godfather, Part III* (1990); *Scent of a Woman* (1992) for which he received an Academy Award as best actor; *Carlito's Way* (1993); *Two Bits* (1994); *Heat* (1995); *City Hall* (1996); and *Donnie Brasco* (1996).

Pacino has portrayed a wide range of gritty roles emphasizing "spontaneity, improvisation, and a flamboyance of manner." He has often been compared to Italian American actor Robert De Niro, although the latter's "performances seem more completely integrated into the texture of the film, more subordinated to an overall thematic structure." Although Pacino has exhibited nervous energy and childlike vitality in his (often neurotic) roles, as in *Panic in Needle Park* and *Dog Day Afternoon,* he has also portrayed restrained, understated, mature characters, as in several of *The Godfather* films.

In addition to acting, Pacino has worked as writer, director, and producer. He remains active in the development of the Actors Studio.

Frank J. Cavaioli

Bibliography

Cook, David. *A History of Narrative Film.* New York: W. W. Norton, 1996.

Hollows, Joann, and Mark Jancovich, eds. *Approaches to Popular Film.* Manchester: Manchester University Press, 1995.

Maltby, Richard. *Hollywood Cinema.* Cambridge, MA: Blackwell Publishers, 1995.

Yule, Andrew. *Life on the Wire: The Life and Art of Al Pacino.* New York: D. I. Fine, 1991.

See also FILM DIRECTORS, PRODUCERS, AND ITALIAN AMERICAN IMAGE IN CINEMA; MOVIE ACTORS AND ACTRESSES

Padrone
See LABOR

Paglia, Camille (b. 1947)

Born in Endicott, New York, to Pasquale John and Lydia (Colapietro) Paglia, this Italian American writer is also a leading humanities educator. Her father, a professor of Romance languages at Jesuit Le Moyne College in Syracuse, encouraged her to develop her own individuality, assert herself, and "aim for the top." This she did, pursuing a superior education that formed the basis for her literary achievements. She received a bachelor's degree in English from the State University of New York at Binghamton (1968), a master's degree in philosophy (1971), and a Ph.D. in English (1974) at Yale University. While at Yale, scholar/critic Harold Bloom, her mentor, guided her to form her own aesthetic.

Paglia began her teaching career at Bennington College, Vermont, from 1972 to 1980. She has also taught at Connecticut's Wesleyan University and at Yale University. Since 1984, she has been a professor of humanities at the Philadelphia College of Art.

Her major published work, *Sexual Personae: Art and Decadence from Nefertiti to Emily Dickinson* (Yale University Press, 1990), produced widespread critical acclaim and controversy. In it she challenges traditional intellectual and cultural beliefs. She herself considered it the "first female epic" in which she depicts the history of Western art and culture from the time of ancient Egypt to the nineteenth century. She attacks leftist standards and the modern concept that asserts culture has devolved into "meaningless fragments." She believes that the culture of Western society has maintained "its unity and continuity." Paganism, she argues, has continued as a vital force alongside Christianity from the earliest of times to the present, providing a permanent cohesion to the culture of the West.

Paglia has also angered feminists by contending that men exclusively have produced revolutionary achievements. She is critical of feminists who blame men for the plight of women; she rejects sexual victimization and seeks to "bring back the pre-war feminism that stresses self-reliance." As for poet Emily Dickinson, "she's in this patriarchy—she *benefitted* from having this horribly limiting patriarchy around her," a patriarchy that caused the reclusive Dickinson to compose her poetry.

Such provocative concepts have drawn praise and condemnation from critics. Some critics view *Sexual Personae* as original, profound, and revealing. Others see it as simplistic, disregarding the tenets of modern feminist scholarship. Nevertheless, her theories on sexuality and culture have provoked unfettered debate among intellectuals. It is no wonder that she had difficulties in finding a publisher for her book.

Camille Paglia is representative of the modern Italian American woman, devoted to her ethnicity and its traditions, well educated, individualistic, and an original thinker in a changing society.

Frank J. Cavaioli

Bibliography

Bevilacqua, Christina. "Interview: Camille Paglia." *Italian Americana* 11, no. 1 (fall/winter 1992): 69–87.

Paglia, Camille. *Sex, Art, and American Culture: Essays*. New York: Vintage, 1992.

———. *Vamps and Tramps: New Essays*. New York: Vintage, 1994.

Postman, Neil, and Camille Paglia. "Dinner Conversations: She Wants Her TV! He Wants His Book!" *Harpers* (March 1991): 44–51, 54–55.

See also WOMEN IN TRANSITION; WOMEN WRITERS

Pagliuca, Salvatore (1899–1944)

A meteorologist, Salvatore Pagliuca helped to measure the "Great Wind" at the Mount Washington Observatory in 1934. Born in Aversa, outside Naples, Italy, on October 20, 1899, the son of Pasquale and Alfonsina (née Di Maio) Pagliuca, Salvatore died on April 30, 1944, in Asheville, North Carolina. Serving from 1917 to 1919 with the artillery forces of the Italian army during World War I, he fought in the battles at Piave and Vittorio Veneto before he graduated in 1923 from the Regia Scuola Superiore Politecnica in Naples. That same year, he came to the United States and, after six years as an engineer for General Electric, became an American citizen in 1929 and resided in Lynn, Massachusetts.

On April 12, 1934, Pagliuca was the chief observer, as part of the scientific expedition of the Second International Polar Year, when the wind blew at a speed of 231 miles an hour at 1:21 P.M. on Mount Washington. This world record was the result of a southeast storm that struck the mountain and was in excess of the typical measurement of 185 miles per hour. The entry for this strongest wind ever measured can be seen in Pagliuca's log in the Museum of the Mount Washington Observatory along with other memorabilia of him and those of his associates.

Later, after studying at the Massachusetts Institute of Technology from 1934 to 1935, Pagliuca became involved in other scientific work. He was the chief observer at Harvard University's Blue Hill Observatory from 1935 to 1938, founder and director of the Yankee Network Weather Service from 1938 to 1941, forecaster for the weather at what is now Logan Airport in Boston from 1941 to 1942, and a member of the United States Army Air Force from 1942 to 1944. Commissioned with the rank of captain during World War II, Pagliuca was sent to Washington, D.C., and rose to the rank of major before he was tragically killed on Mount Mitchell in the Pisga National Forest of North Carolina. At the time, he was on a weather security mission testing equipment for the Air Force when his jeep struck a boulder. The impact threw him from the vehicle and delivered a fatal fracture to his skull.

In 1937 Pagliuca married Viola Gorizia Amarú, who was of Sicilian parents, and they had two children. He was interred in Westview Cemetery in Lexington, Massachusetts, and a room was named for him at the Mount Washington Observatory.

Vincent A. Lapomarda

Bibliography

Burt, F. Allen. *The Story of Mount Washington.* Hanover: Dartmouth Publications, 1960.

McKenzie, Alexander A. *World Record Wind: Measuring Gusts of 231 Miles an Hour.* Eaton Center: McKenzie, 1984.

Pagliuca, Salvatore, et al. "The Great Wind of April 11–12, 1934, on Mount Washington, N.H., and Its Measurement." *Monthly Weather Review* 62 (1934): 186–195.

See also SCIENCE

Pallotine Sisters

See WOMEN AND THE CHURCH

Palmieri, Aurelio (1870–1926)

Born in Savona, Italy, Aurelio Palmieri joined the religious order of the Augustinians as a friar in 1885, transferred to the Assumptionists in 1890, and returned to the Augustinians in 1902. He was eventually laicized.

Devoting much of his life to Byzantine studies, he was a prolific writer, publishing fifteen scholarly books and writing more than three hundred articles. One of his interests was the relationship between Italian immigrants and religion in the United States. He published six articles on the topic between 1918 and 1923.

In 1918 he published two articles on Italian immigrants and Protestantism in the United States: "Il Protestantesimo e gli emigranti Italiani negli Stati Uniti," in *Rivista Internazionale di Scienze Sociali e Discipline Ausiliarie,* and "Italian Protestantism in the United States," in *The Catholic World.* He described the work done by various Protestant denominations among Italian immigrants in the United States, including the Presbyterians, Methodists, Baptists, and Congregationalists. He concluded that, despite significant Protestant efforts, "the gains of Protestant proselytism after fifty years of hard work, are reduced to hardly more than six thousand souls."

In 1918 he also published "L'Aspetto Economico del Problema Religioso Italiano negli Stati Uniti," in *Rivista Internazionale di Scienze Sociali e Discipline Ausiliarie.* Here he further elaborated on the question of the "Italian problem" in the American Church.

In 1920 and 1923 Palmieri published two articles on the Italian clergy in the United States: "Ii clero italiano negli Stati Uniti," in *La Vita Italiana* (15 February 1920), and "The Contribution of the Italian Catholic Clergy to the United States." In these articles he described the work of Italian priests and nuns among the Italians in the United States. He concluded that the best way to solve the "Italian problem" was "to assist the Italian clergy in their difficult missions, to multiply the Italian churches and the Italian priests, certain that when the process of Americanization has once been achieved, the sons and daughters of the Italian immigrants will add new strength and vigor to the Catholic clergy and laity of the United States."

Palmieri summarized his views on the "Italian problem" in his pamphlet *Il Grave Problema Religioso Italiano Negli Stati Uniti.* He described the Italian religious problem and the American clergy, the necessity for Italian priests in America, and the present condition regarding assistance to Italian immigrants in the United States and hopes for the future.

Palmieri died in Rome on October 18, 1926.

Edward C. Stibili

Bibliography

Tomasi, Silvano M., and Edward C. Stibili, eds. *Italian Americans and Religion, An Annotated Bibliography.* New York: Center for Migration Studies, 1992.

See also APOSTOLATE, ITALIAN; MISSIONARIES OF ST. CHARLES — SCALABRINIANS; RELIGION

Panunzio, Constantine Maria (1884–1964)

The Soul of an Immigrant (1921), Constantine M. Panunzio's classic autobiography, details the author's childhood in Italy and his coming-of-age in the United States as a self-made American. He achieved success as a professor and sociologist.

He was born into a prominent family in Molfetta, Italy, in the province of Bari, October 25, 1884. His grandfather had been a patriotic hero against the Bourbon regime. Panunzio's grandmother plotted the course of her infant grandson's future to honor his famous namesake: he should become first a priest, then a teacher, and then a patriotic statesman. As he candidly details in his autobiography, Panunzio was incapable of complying; the attraction of the sea proved stronger than the pull of books, and he left school at age 13 to join the crew of a coasting schooner. In 1902 his travels led him to Boston, where, through a combination of unfortunate circumstances, Panunzio remained. *Soul of an Immigrant* spares nothing in highlighting the unfair treatment of Italian immigrants. At the mercy of unscrupulous employers, Panunzio quickly lost his youthful naivete. However, even following a brief but unjustified stay in jail, Panunzio preserved a balanced judgment of individual Americans, deciding that he had been exposed to the most corrupt fraction of society.

Encouraged by American friends, Panunzio abandoned his various jobs as laborer and embraced scholarship. After graduating from Kent's Hill Academy in Maine, he worked his way through Wesleyan University, earning a B.A. in 1911 and an M.A. the following year. In 1914 he received a bachelor's of sacred theology from Boston University, and, after studying at Harvard, Columbia, and New York universities, earned a Ph.D. from the Brookings Graduate School of Economics and Government, Washington, D.C., in 1925. Panunzio married in 1911 and became a naturalized U.S. citizen in 1914. The chronology of his autobiography closes in 1920, as Panunzio hoped to improve social conditions for Italian immigrants. From 1915 to 1917 he served as the superintendent of Social Service House in Boston's North End, and from 1917 to 1918 he was the general organizer of the YMCA on the Italian front. Panunzio also investigated the deportation of aliens, as chronicled in his book *The Deportation Cases of 1919–1920,* and testified before several government committees.

He began lecturing professionally on immigrant backgrounds for Hunter College in 1920 and taught social science at Williamette University, Whittier College, the University of California, and San Diego State Teachers College during the 1920s. As a professor of sociology at UCLA from 1931 to 1952, he authored several social science books, including *Major Social Institutions* and *A Student's Dictionary of Sociological Terms,* both of which saw multiple editions. Upon his retirement, Panunzio aimed to reform the professorial pension system, organizing national emeritus groups. At the 1940 New York World's Fair, Panunzio was honored as a foreign-born citizen who had made outstand-

ing contributions to American culture. He died in Los Angeles on August 6, 1964. He had three children.

Camille Cauti

Bibliography

Gardaphé, Fred L. "Writing the Self American: Constantine Panunzio as Model Immigrant and Cultural Critic." *NEMLA Italian Studies* 15 (1991): 163–174.

Holte, James Craig. "Private Lives and Public Faces: Ethnic American Autobiography." *Ethnic Groups* 4 (1982): 61–83.

———. "The Representative Voice: Autobiography and the Ethnic Experience." *MELUS* 9 (summer 1982): 25–46.

Peragallo, Olga. *Italian-American Authors and Their Contributions to American Literature.* New York: S. F. Vanni, 1949.

See also AUTOBIOGRAPHY; LITERATURE

Paolucci, Anne Attura (b. 1926)

An internationally acclaimed scholar in multicomparative studies, Shakespeare, Italian literature, contemporary theater, and dramatic theory, Anne Attura Paolucci is also an award-winning playwright, poet, short story writer, and founder and president of the Council on National Literatures, an educational foundation dedicated to multicomparative literary studies. Born in Rome, Italy, Paolucci learned English at age 8, when she settled in New York City with her widowed mother, a sister, and a brother.

She graduated from Barnard College with a degree in English, and later received a master's degree in Italian literature (under the mentorship of Giuseppe Prezzolini and Dino Bigongiari) and a Ph.D. in comparative literature, both at Columbia University. She returned to her native city and the University of Rome as a Fulbright scholar from Columbia, and later spent two years as a Fulbright lecturer in American drama at the University of Naples. As a Pirandello scholar and president of the Pirandello Society of America for seventeen years, she often visited Agrigento (Sicily) for international conferences dealing with the work of the great Nobel Prize–winning playwright and fiction writer Luigi Pirandello.

Although her dissertation at Columbia University was on *The Women in Dante's Divine Comedy and Spenser's Faerie Queene* (a study that earned her distinction and the first Woodbridge Honorary Fellowship in the Department of Comparative Literature), Dr. Paolucci expanded her scholarly interests over the years to include dramatic theory (especially Hegel), Shakespeare, and the contemporary theater of the absurd, and has won recognition as one of the leading authorities on the plays of Edward Albee. Her major contributions in the field of drama include a translation of Machiavelli's *Mandragola* and what has become a classic in the field, as one of the earliest and most provocative studies on the subject, *From Tension to Tonic: The Plays of Edward Albee* (1972).

Her interest in drama and theater is reflected in her own writings for the stage. Her plays have been produced here and abroad. Her very first full-length play, *The Short Season,* was recently translated into German for Austrian production. A forty-eight-minute video of her play about the ironies of the Columbus story won recognition in 1991 as "Official Project of the Christopher Columbus Quincentennial Jubilee Commission," established by President Ronald Reagan. Her short play *Minions of the Race* (included in *Three Short Plays,* 1994) won an award in 1972. She is an award-winning poet, with four collections to her name. The most recent, *Queensboro Bridge and Other Poems* (1995), was nominated for the Pulitzer Prize in poetry.

In 1981 Paolucci served as an associate director in planning a "Shakespeare Summerfest" and as director of a dozen bilingual dramatic readings and programs. Together with A. Bartlett Giamatti, former president of Yale and former president of the Dante Society, she helped produce two major Dante projects for the American Bicentennial.

Paolucci began her teaching career at Rye Country Day and The Brearley School in New York. She later joined the English department of City College, and in 1969 she moved to St. John's University as professor and university research professor (first of its kind). She was chairperson of the university's Department of English for ten years, and, in 1982, was director of the doctor of arts degree program in English.

The Italian government has recognized her achievements by bestowing on her the titles of *Cavaliere* and *Commendatore* (Legion of Merit, the Republic of Italy), and Canada presented her with its first gold medal commemorating the Columbus Quincentenary cel-

ebrations. Her work has also earned for her an eight-year appointment to the National Council on the Humanities. In 1997, New York Governor George Pataki appointed her to the position of chair of the Board of Trustees of the City University of New York. She was married to the late Henry Paolucci, a historian and foreign policy expert who died in 1998.

Nishan Parlakian

Bibliography

Paolucci, Anne Attura. *From Tension to Tonic: The Plays of Edward Albee.* Carbondale: Southern Illinois University Press, 1972.

———. *Pirandello's Theater: The Recovery of the Modern Stage for Dramatic Art.* Carbondale: Southern Illinois University Press, 1974.

———. *Queensboro Bridge* (and Other Poems). Queens, NY: Potpourri Publication, 1995.

———. *Sepia Tones* (Seven Short Stories). New Zealand: Rimu Press, 1985. Reprint, New York: Griffon House Publications, 1986.

———, trans. with Henry Paolucci. *Machiavelli's Mandragola.* New York: Simon & Schuster, 1995.

See also PLAYS, CONTEMPORARY; POETRY

Paone, Nicola (b. 1915)

Italian American singer, composer, entertainer, and restaurateur, Nicola Paone was born in Spangler, Pennsylvania. His father, a coal miner, was born in Torregrotta (Messina), Sicily. Young Paone came to America in 1931 and resided in the Bronx, New York.

He worked as a shoe shine boy, hat blocker, and dishwasher while attending school and learning English. In his spare time he studied jewelry design, began a successful jewelry business, and studied voice and music. In 1942 he started his own radio program and stage shows, beginning a career as a star entertainer. Paone's great success came as a vocalist and comedian. He wrote his own music and lyrics in English, Italian (dialects also), Spanish, and Portuguese. By 1950 each of his three recordings sold in excess of a million, thus prompting RCA, Columbia, Paramount, and Capitol to seek contracts to produce his work. His business acumen, however, led him to form his own recording company, named Etna, after the Sicilian volcano.

He was known as the Italian Troubadour, performing his own songs and becoming a recording and stage star in America and Argentina. The more than three hundred songs he wrote attest to his talent, versatility, and originality. The songs are a blend of folk and popular styles. His hits included "Uei Paesano," "La Cafetera," and "Yakity Yak Blah, Blah, Blah, Blah"; the latter was the number one song in the country in 1959.

His phenomenal success as a recording star ran parallel to his stage performances and movies. His songs were unique, catchy, and carried a specific message.

Paone performed before 750,000 people on May 1, 1954, in Buenos Aires during the time of an unstable Argentine regime that was being threatened by civil unrest. Paone, who was on a concert tour in that country at the time, was arrested, transported by police to a soccer stadium, and required to perform. His singing distracted the activists, and order was restored to the city. His popularity in Argentina remains strong; as recently as 1992, he was invited by the Argentine television studios for national viewing of his live performances.

Wishing to have a hedge on security in a risky entertainment field, he opened an Italian restaurant in 1958 in New York City. The gourmet type of eatery affords him the opportunity to enjoy daily contact with a wide spectrum of people. His personal acquaintances know him to be knowledgeable, kind, and philosophical. He takes great pride in his wife, son, and grandchildren.

Paone's songs are a valuable documentation of the experiences of the Italian immigrants and their descendants.

Joseph J. Bentivegna

Bibliography

Green, Victor. *A Passion for Polka: Old-Time Music in America.* Berkeley: University of California Press, 1992.

"Nicola Paone: Narrator of the Italian American Experience." In *Italian Americans in a Multicultural Society,* edited by Jerome Krase and Judith N. DeSena, 89–105. Stony Brook, NY.

See also COMEDY

Parini, Jay
See POETRY

Pasquerilla, Frank J. (1926–1999)

Businessman, entrepreneur, and philanthropist Frank J. Pasquerilla was born in Johnstown, Pennsylvania. His parents were from Italy; his father was born in Benevento and his mother in Campobasso. He graduated from the local high school but was unable to attend college because of financial obligations to his family.

He joined the Crown Construction Company within months of its founding in 1950, was named president in 1953, and became sole owner in 1961, changing the direction of the firm. Rather than build projects for others, he decided to concentrate on developing shopping centers and shopping malls. In 1972 Pasquerilla and his associates decided that the word "construction" no longer reflected the company's function and the name was changed to Crown American.

During Pasquerilla's forty-five-year tenure with the company, Crown American developed and owned and/or managed twenty-nine regional shopping malls, thirty community shopping centers, twenty-one motels, and five office buildings.

In 1993 the shopping mall portion of Crown American formed Crown American Realty Trust and became a public company. Trading under the symbol CWN on the New York Stock Exchange, Crown American became the largest equity real estate investment trust on August 10, 1993.

Pasquerilla was a trustee of Notre Dame University, a member of the board of directors of Georgetown University, a member of the board of directors of U.S. BANCORP, and a member of the National Association of Real Estate Investment Trusts (NAREIT).

His numerous awards included the Purple Aster Award as "Man of the Year" from the Pennsylvania Sons of Italy; the Commander of the Order of St. Gregory the Great by Pope Paul II (papal knighthood); the Prime Minister's Silver Anniversary Medal, State of Israel; and the Assisi Award of Saint Francis College (Loretto, Penn.).

The beneficiaries of his philanthropic contributions include Notre Dame University,

University of Pittsburgh at Johnstown, St. Francis College, Georgetown University, and the Altoona-Johnstown Catholic Diocese.

Joseph J. Bentivegna

Bibliography

Apone, Carl. "Notre Dame's $7 Million Man." *Pittsburgh Press Roto,* 23 November 1980, 27.

Clemenson, Brad. "Frank Pasquerilla Turned Adversities Into Opportunities." *Tribune-Democrat Weekender* (Johnstown, PA), 3 September 1993, 2.

Iorizzo, Luciano J. "The R.G. Dun Collection's Assessment of Merchants: A Neglected Source for Italian Americans." In *The Columbus People,* edited by Piero Gestaldo, Lydio Tomasi, and Thomas Rowe. Staten Island, NY: Center for Migration Studies, 1994.

McCreay, Jeff. "Crown Noting 30th Date." *Tribune Democrat* (Johnstown, PA), 21 September 1980, E1.

"Pasquerilla Gift $4 Million." *Tribune Democrat* (Johnstown, PA), 26 February 1987, 2.

Schroeder, M. "Look Who Wants to Buy Bloomies." *Business Week,* 2 October 1989, 30.

See also BUSINESS AND ENTREPRENEURSHIP

Passeggiata

For centuries the *passeggiata* (ritual promenade) has served a singularly important role in Italian culture. At the beginning of the twentieth century the newly arrived Italian immigrants to the United States were well acquainted with the custom of promenading from their home villages. In the Old World the practice involved strolling down to the piazza before supper to chat and talk with the townsfolk. During the promenade men typically milled about the cafes while women performed their ritual laps along the same stretch of pavement. Although everyone took part in the event, the most ardent participants were young women, who put their charms on display in the hope of finding prospective mates. This socially sanctioned opportunity for flirting and courting always took place under the watchful gaze of the community. This ancient and regionally diverse practice of the *passeggiata* has deeply influenced the Italian character. These historical practices

helped form the context for Italian American promenading in the New World.

For early Italian immigrants, East Coast urban centers were full of foreign and hostile elements. Overcrowded tenement housing encouraged people to congregate in the streets and develop the intense community life that has come to be associated with neighborhoods like New York's Lower East Side. The promenade was a crucial element of this street culture. While married women's recreational activities were almost exclusively limited to visiting with family and kinfolk, some Italian immigrant daughters opposed Old World values by taking unchaperoned walks, reinterpreting gender roles in the traditional *passeggiata.* Testimonies of Italian immigrants in New York showed how some women bartered paychecks for greater independence. Even highly supervised Italian girls found ways of eluding parental control by sneaking out to participate in the lively youth culture of the streets.

The street offered a panoply of free amusements, attractions, and sights that helped bring foreigners into American culture. The Bowery styles made famous by Irish Americans in the nineteenth century fit with the working-class sensibility of later Italian immigrants who valued the cosmopolitan practice of putting on finery and promenading. By going out on the town, some Italian women expressed their new wage-earning status and greater sexual freedom. By adapting mainstream American fashion and working-class argot, these women asserted different visions of female respectability. As historian Kathy Piess maintains, the social terrain of the promenade became a site of pleasure, expressiveness, romance, and autonomy. Current data suggest that Italian women participated in these forms of public display, even if they were underrepresented.

While the Italian *passeggiata* underwent substantial changes in the New World, central elements of this practice had a wide-ranging influence on Italian American culture. The *passeggiata* was not merely a walking ritual; it served as an ensemble of culturally specific practices that helped maintain and perpetuate Italian systems of belief in the New World. In the earlier part of the Italian experience, after-church walks, park strolls, and family visits constituted one of the more prominent forms of leisure among newcomers. As in the village, clothing for the Sunday promenade was, according to Piess, a "visible display of social standing and self-respect in the ritual of church going and visiting." The fanciful working-class styles of Bensonhurst residents in the late 1980s described by Donald Tricarico borrow a great deal from the rich repertoire of behavioral styles that have traditionally been used in the promenade.

Many ethnic writers describe persistent Italian parents who tried to maintain their ethnic identity by protecting the family from the influences of the wider culture. The values extolled by the Old World promenade reflect the importance Italian society has historically placed on the presentation of self and the kinds of aesthetic choices individuals make in public situations. For example, the value of *fare la strada diritta* (to walk the straight path) is explicitly enacted in the unique upright posture and forward-thrusting gait, a stance that promenading Italian women are taught to use on their evening walks. The key notion of *fare bella figura* (to cut a fine figure) survives in Italian American life, and the promenade is one of the main areas in which this idea is performed and pursued. Current scholarship emphasizes the idea that culture is less an abstract system of beliefs and more a set of daily practices that establish attitudes and values. A crucial element of daily life, the *passeggiata* has been one of the most important forces for maintaining the continuity of Italian culture in both the Old and New Worlds.

Giovanna P. Del Negro

Bibliography

Del Negro, Giovanna P. *Looking Through My Daughters Eyes: Life Stories of Nine Italian Immigrant Women in Canada.* Toronto: Guernica, 1998.

———. " 'Our Little Paris': Gender, Popular Culture and the Promenade in Central Italy." Ph.D. diss., Indiana University, 1996.

Ewen, Elizabeth. *Immigrant Women in the Land of Dollars: Life and Culture on the Lower East Side, 1890–1925.* New York: Monthly Review Press, 1985.

Piess, Kathy. *Cheap Amusements: Working Women and Leisure in Turn of the Century New York.* Philadelphia: Temple University Press, 1986.

Silverman, Sydel. *Three Bells of Civilization: The Life of an Italian Hill Town.* New York: Columbia University, 1975.

Tricarico, Donald. "Guido: Fashioning an Italian-American Youth Style." *Journal of Ethnic Studies* 19 (1991): 41–66.

See also FOLKLORE, FOLKLIFE

P

Pastore, John Orlando (1907–1994)

A leading statesman of his time, John Orlando Pastore achieved distinction as governor of Rhode Island and was the first Italian American to be elected to the U.S. Senate. He was born in the Federal Hill section of Providence's Little Italy on March 17, 1907. His parents had migrated from the province of Potenza, Italy, eight years earlier.

His father died in 1916, and at age 9 he began working after school to support his mother, brother, and sisters. After completing high school and unable to accept admission to two Ivy League colleges because of financial reasons, he took night classes at a branch of Northeastern University and completed a law degree in 1931, passed the bar examination, and began law practice in Providence. As a member of the Democratic Party, he was elected to the Rhode Island Assembly in 1934. From this point on he became the most popular Italian American politician in Rhode Island.

Appointed state assistant attorney general, Pastore held this position in 1937–1938 and 1940–1944. In 1941 he married Elena Caito, and they had three children. In 1944 he became the first Rhode Island Italian American to win statewide elective office as lieutenant governor. On October 6, 1945, he assumed the governorship at age 38 when Governor Howard J. McGrath resigned to become U.S. Solicitor General. Pastore was elected on his own in 1946 and again in 1948.

His success, much of it due to a large ethnic voting base, helped him win the Democratic Party nomination to the U.S. Senate in 1950, and in a landslide victory he became the first Italian American senator. His first election was for a two-year term to complete an unexpired term. He was reelected in 1952, 1958, 1964, and 1970. The Limited Nuclear Test Ban Treaty of 1963, Nuclear Non-Proliferation Treaty of 1969, Public Broadcasting Act of 1969, and Civil Rights Act of 1964 are some of Pastore's legislative achievements.

He retired in 1976. In 1975, remembering his ethnic heritage, he helped establish the National Italian American Foundation, an

Sign welcoming visitors to Federal Hill, the Italian American community in Providence, Rhode Island, 1982, which provided ethnic support services for immigrants. Courtesy Frank J. Cavaioli.

umbrella group headquartered in Washington, D.C., that provides an agenda for Italian Americans. He also personally appeared at other Italian American forums such as the national conference of the American Italian Historical Association in 1985.

Frank J. Cavaioli

Bibliography

Cornwell Jr., Elmer E. "Party Absorption of Ethnic Groups: The Case of Providence, Rhode Island." *Social Forces* 38 (March 1960): 205–210.

LaGumina, Salvatore J. "John Pastore, Italian-American Political Pioneer." In *The Melting Pot and Beyond, Italian Americans in the Year 2000,* edited by Jerome Krase and William Egelman, 1–14. New York: American Italian Historical Association, 1987.

Lubell, Samuel. *The Future of American Politics.* New York: Harper, 1965.

See also GOVERNORS; POLITICS

Pataki, George E.

See GOVERNORS

Patents and Inventors

Italians have made important contributions to the development of patents and inventions. The sovereign practice of granting patents, which is the right to exclude others from making, using, or selling a particular product or process for a limited time, in return for a public disclosure of an invention, originated in Venice early in the fifteenth century. In 1474 Venice enacted the first patent law, which set forth certain standards that are still recognized: the concept must be novel and original, and the device must be useful and operable.

After the discovery of the Americas by Columbus sailing from Spain in 1492, and the rounding of the Horn of Africa by Vasco da Gama sailing from Portugal in 1498, skilled artisans left Venice for opportunities in the western and northern parts of Europe. When they departed, they took with them their knowledge of the Venetian patent law.

During the sixteenth century, the royal practice of granting patents spread fairly quickly, in much the same form as in Venice, to France, Germany, the Netherlands, and eventually to England. In 1623 the English Parliament enacted the Statute of Monopolies, which granted limited patent rights to inventors who made "new manufactures within this realme."

During the seventeenth and eighteenth centuries, the royal grant of patents continued in England and influenced the breakaway United States of America to formulate a patent clause in its Constitution in 1787. The Congress established a patent system of examination in 1790 but soon replaced it with a mere registration procedure in 1793.

When it became clear that applicants were misusing the procedure by registering about ten thousand "inventions" already established, the Congress reverted to a rigorous examination system in 1836. This Patent Act was the first law anywhere to institute the requirement of filing "claims" for an alleged invention. Acceptance of the new rule was facilitated by a great fire that totally destroyed the United States Patent Office later that year.

The next substantive change in the United States patent law occurred in 1952, when Congress adapted the concept of "nonobviousness" for an invention to be patented. This standard was essentially the brainchild of Examiner-in-Chief Pasquale Joseph Federico (1902–1982) and basically states that a patent may not be obtained "if the differences between the subject matter sought to be patented and the prior art are such that the subject matter as a whole would have been obvious at the time the invention was made to a person having ordinary skill in the art to which said subject matter pertains."

This new hurdle replaced the nebulous rule of "inventiveness" and has been adopted by many industrialized countries.

The following individuals are among the outstanding inventors of Italian origin.

Antonio Meucci (1808–1889) conceived an idea for a type of telephone in Cuba in 1849 after the invention of the telegraph by Samuel F. B. Morse in 1844. Completely lacking in business sense, Meucci did not file a "caveat" for a U.S. patent until December 28, 1871. And, due to a lack of funds, he did not renew it beyond 1874. Alexander Graham Bell applied on February 6, 1876, and obtained United States Patent No. 174,465 on March 7, 1876. As it occurs with every successful invention, infringers abounded and attempted to make a premature profit on the newfangled device before the U.S. patent expired. In 1885 Bell sued a group of infringers. One of them, the Globe Telephone Company of New York, defended on the sole ground that Meucci was the first inventor. After an exhaustive trial with numerous witnesses and mounds of documentary evidence, Judge William James Wallace ruled in favor of Bell on July 19, 1887, because Meucci's alleged invention "was so different that it did not contain any elements of a telephone which would interfere with the Bell patent." Essentially, the trial court agreed with the experts who testified that Meucci had invented a mechanical string telephone for amplifying voices over a short distance, while Bell had invented an electric telephone that converted voices to pulses and transmitted them over long distances before reconverting the pulses back to voices at the receiving end. This decision was not appealed, and the United States Supreme Court ruled unanimously for Bell in all other consolidated appeals on March 19, 1888. Although some people still believe that Meucci was the true inventor of the telephone, an objective review of the available evidence leads one incontrovertibly to the conclusion that Bell invented the telephone as it is known and that Meucci invented something else. However, Meucci can be fairly characterized as an early pioneer in telephone experimentation.

Guglielmo Marconi (1874–1937) transmitted electrical signals through the air from one end of his house to the other and then to his family garden in 1895. These experiments at age 21 began the era of practical wireless

Guglielmo Marconi, the inventor (second row, third from right), visits Marconiville (Copiague), New York, c. 1915. Virtually the entire Italian enclave came to greet him on this occasion. Courtesy Salvatore J. LaGumina.

P

PATENTS AND INVENTORS   449

telegraphy, now known as radio. He applied for and obtained U.S. Patent No. 586,193 in that same year. In 1900 he built a transmitter at Poldhu, England, and in 1901, he installed a receiver at St. John's, Newfoundland. On December 12, 1901, he received signals from across the Atlantic Ocean. News of his achievement electrified the industrialized world, and he was awarded the Nobel Prize for physics in 1909. He later commercialized his patented inventions through the newly established Radio Corporation of America (RCA). After his death, he was inducted into the National Inventors Hall of Fame.

Frank Merlo Bellanca (1882–1962) and his brother, Giuseppe Mario Bellanca (1886–1960), came to the United States in 1911 and together set up the Bellanca Aircraft Corporation on Staten Island, New York. Later, Frank organized his own International Aircraft Company. U.S. Patent No. 2,140,783 was issued to him for a pursuit bomber on December 20, 1938. He later developed military single-engine and multi-engine planes for the war effort against the Axis powers. He devised a twin-engine helicopter in 1943 and also a hydroplane torpedo chaser for the U.S. Navy. Most important, he invented a method of central-beam fuselage construction, which allows high-performance aircraft to withstand the heavy stress loads of fast speeds and sharp turns. Frank and Giuseppe Bellanca rightly deserve to be called the Italian American Wright brothers.

Umberto Nobile (1885–1978) was an aeronautical engineer who built the dirigibles *Roma, Norge,* and *Italia,* for which he was granted U.S. Patent No. 1,513,001 on October 28, 1924. He piloted the second flight ever to reach the North Pole on May 12, 1926. He became a general in the Italian Air Force and was the first man to reach the North Pole twice when he piloted the *Italia* there on May 24, 1928. After an accident the next day, he resigned his commission and left Italy, teaching in the United States from 1939 to 1942. He returned to Italy after World War II, was readmitted to the Air Force, and was elected a deputy to the new Constituent Assembly in 1946.

Rachele Jacuzzi (1886–1937) immigrated to the United States in 1910 and got a job repairing airplanes. In 1915 he invented a metal-tipped, wooden propeller that he dubbed "the toothpick." He opened a machine shop that year in Berkeley, California,

and obtained a government contract when the United States entered World War I. After the war he built a high-winged monoplane, which was the first aircraft to have a fully enclosed cabin. During the last test flight for the United States Air Mail Service on July 14, 1921, the engine exploded and four men were killed, including his 26-year-old brother Giocondo. Rachele and his five surviving brothers then decided to leave the aircraft business. However, his practical knowledge of fluid dynamics led him to develop a crop defroster that was sold under the "Frostifugo" trademark. This machine blew hot air over California fruit orchards via a large propeller driven by a powerful engine. In 1925 he began research on a small steam jet. In the process, he realized that the steam injection principle could be applied to water. In 1926 he built his first water jet injection pump for moving water from below ground in a deep agricultural well. U.S. Patent No. 1,758,400 was issued to him on May 13, 1930. This invention revolutionized the agricultural industry first in California and later throughout the United States, because it allowed farmers to expand and cultivate land that lacked nearby ground-level water sources and had to rely on underground water pumped to the surface. Later that year he exhibited his radical jet pump at the State Fair in Sacramento, where the California Agricultural Society awarded his company a gold medal for "Meritorious Invention."

Candido Jacuzzi (1903–1986) arrived in the United States in 1920 and started working immediately in the family business. After twenty years, he became general manager. His youngest son, Kenneth, born in 1941, developed rheumatoid arthritis as a toddler. When the boy was seven years old, his doctor recommended hydrotherapy. Unfortunately, facilities for such treatment were located only in distant spas and in communal tubs in large hospitals, neither of which was accessible or particularly appropriate for a young boy with severe arthritis. So in 1949 Jacuzzi developed a unique type of pump that created a swirling whirlpool in a bathtub. When his son's suffering was temporarily relieved by the treatment, Jacuzzi patented the invention and assigned it to the family business, which, in turn, assigned 1 percent of the royalties to Jacuzzi's son in order to provide for his well-being. Jacuzzi further modified the invention to make it suitable for mass production and to meet state safety requirements, which had delayed its introduction. The company began commercial marketing of the finished product in the early 1950s as a hydromassage unit for bathtubs of conventional sizes. Jacuzzi later developed the product into a whirlpool pump system for spas and incorporated it into specially designed large baths, now known as hot tubs. Up to 1971, he acquired thirty-one U.S. patents in his own name. Meanwhile, twenty other U.S. patents were issued to eight different Jacuzzi family members. Clearly, he was the creative genius among them. Upon the death of his brother Giuseppe in 1965, Candido became president of the firm and continued the international expansion of the business. During his tenure as president, the Jacuzzi whirlpool baths became so popular that the family name became the generic term for a hot tub. "Jacuzzi" now appears in most English dictionaries.

Enrico Fermi (1901–1954) taught himself about quantum nuclear physics and received his doctorate degree at age 21 from the University of Pisa. He lectured at the University of Florence from 1924 to 1926 before he became a professor of theoretical physics at the University of Rome. While there in 1934, he perfected his theory of beta ray emission in radioactivity and studied the creation of artificial radioactive isotopes through neutron bombardment of elements. His bombardment of uranium with slow neutrons caused reactions that were found later to be atomic fission. For his continued work in this field, he was awarded the Nobel Prize for physics in 1938. He left Stockholm directly for the United States with his Jewish wife and family, much to the embarrassment of the Axis leaders, Hitler and Mussolini. Residing first at Columbia University in New York and then at the University of Chicago, he and his associate, Leo Szilard, began working on the construction of an atomic pile that would make possible the controlled release of nuclear energy. On December 2, 1942, they achieved the first sustained reaction in a neutronic reactor, which he had built on a squash court. He filed a patent application on the reactor, but a government secrecy order withheld issuance of U.S. Patent No. 2,708,656 until after World War II was concluded. After the reactor was perfected, he went to work on the Manhattan Project to help develop atomic bombs in a top-secret laboratory at Los Alamos, New Mexico. He became a United States citizen in 1944 and returned to the University of Chicago after the atomic bombing of Japan to teach as a professor at the Institute for Nuclear Studies. Shortly before his death from cancer, he received a special award from the United States Atomic Energy Commission. Element 100, fermium, is named for him. After his death, he was inducted into the National Inventors Hall of Fame, only the second Italian-born person to be so honored.

Cesare Gianturco (1905–1995) was born in Naples, received his medical degree from the University of Rome in 1929, and migrated to the United States in 1930 to finish a residency at the Mayo Clinic in Rochester, Minnesota. He obtained a master's degree there in 1933 and became a United States citizen in 1934. Later that year he co-founded the Carle Clinic in Urbana, Illinois, and headed its radiology department. During World War II he served as a lieutenant colonel in the Army Medical Corps. While stationed in France, he developed a three-dimensional X-ray visualization technique to assist surgeons in locating shell fragments in the eyes of soldiers, thus minimizing the amount of probing needed to find and remove the metal pieces. After the war concluded, he returned to conduct research at the University of Illinois, where he also served as a clinical professor. While there, he developed three more important inventions: the Gianturco-Roubin coronary stent, a device implanted into the heart to keep the coronary artery open after balloon angioplasty; the Gianturco coil, a tiny winding of wool positioned by a catheter in a blood vessel to block bleeding; and the "bird's nest" filter, which is also positioned by a catheter in a blood vessel to trap loose clots before they reach the heart. He obtained a total of ten U.S. patents. For his pioneering work in interventional radiology to treat illnesses, he received gold medals from the Radiological Society of North America, the American College of Radiology, and the Italian Radiological Society.

Other Inventors

The eight inventors highlighted above are a sample representation of Italians who have obtained U.S. patents and have become well known for their efforts. Others have been more or less successful, and some of them are discussed briefly below. However, the following summaries are not intended to be exhaustive. More detailed information can be obtained from the records at the United States Patent and Trademark Office in Arlington, Virginia. Whereas the foregoing eight inventors were discussed in approximate chronological order of their births, the following six inventors are discussed in alphabetical order.

Bernard Castro (1904–1991) migrated from Italy and opened an upholstery shop in New York in 1931 with his life savings of several hundred dollars. In 1945 he invented the folding sofa bed, which he later patented. He expanded his business under the name of Castro Convertibles until he had forty-eight showrooms in twelve states.

Bernard A. Cousino (1902–1994) was the holder of over sixty U.S. patents and sixteen foreign patents on audiovisual equipment. His most famous invention was the eight-track tape player, which revolutionized the music industry. He developed a special tape lubricant that made it possible for President Dwight Eisenhower to broadcast his famous Christmas message to the world via satellite in 1958. During that same year, he invented the automobile tape deck, which later became a standard dashboard addition. His final invention, for which a patent application was filed just days before his death at age 92, was a continuous loop video cassette that allows videocassette recorders (VCRs) to play tapes repeatedly without rewinding.

Joseph Anthony Mazzitello (1908–1992) was a chemist who worked for the Minnesota Manufacturing & Mining (3M) Company. In 1951 he and two other 3M engineers started searching for a formula to make a magnetic recording videotape. In 1956 they developed a tape on which both image and sound could be recorded for playback. Various U.S. patents were then obtained for the basic tape and improvements developed by him and others. The videotape became an important product marketed by 3M.

George Speri Sperti (1899–1991) was a researcher affiliated with the University of Cincinnati. He invented and patented the hemorrhoid treatment now marketed under the trademark Preparation H. He also developed and patented a process for irradiating starches and milk foods with ultraviolet light. General Foods bought these rights for the lump sum of three hundred thousand dollars. He later discovered a method for enhancing Vitamin D in milk, formulated an arthritis relief compound now sold under the "Aspercreme"

trademark, developed a meat tenderizer, and invented a process for freeze-drying orange juice concentrate.

Ettore Steccone (1897–1984) migrated from Italy to Oakland, California, in 1920. Three years later he started a garage business. While thinking about a quick way to clean the curved surfaces of automobile windows, it occurred to him that a flexible rubber wiper solved the problem. Thus, he developed a handheld tool that he patented and sold under the "Squeegee" trademark. He then opened the Steccone Products Company and began manufacturing the device. He later developed an intermediate wiper for cleaning large glass office windows and a large wiper for pushing along hard floors like a broom. The firm still sells more than one million units annually.

Frank Joseph Zamboni (b. 1921) was born in Suffern, New York, to immigrant Italian parents. After graduating from Yale University in 1943, he served three years as a lieutenant commander in the United States Navy. After he graduated from the Columbia University Law School in 1948, he went to work for the Allied Stores Corp. and was promoted to assistant vice-president in 1967. Subsequently, his enthusiasm for professional hockey led him to develop and patent an ice rink resurfacing apparatus, which became known as the "Zamboni Machine."

Joseph Scafetta Jr.

Bibliography

American Bell Telephone Co. v. Globe Telephone Co. 31 Federal Reporter 729 (C.C.S.D.N.Y. 1887).

Federico, P. J. *Outline of the History of the United States Patent Office,* 18 Journal of the Patent Office Society (hereinafter J.P.O.S.) 251 (1936).

Mandich, G., *Venetian Origins of Inventors' Rights,* 42 J.P.O.S. 378 (1960).

———. *Venetian Patents (1450–1550),* 30 J.P.O.S. 166 (1948).

Rich, G.S., *P.J. (Pat) Federico and His Works,* 64 J.P.O.S. 3 (1982).

Scafetta, Joseph, *Ten Years After Aro II: The Effect of Patent Act Section 271 on the Patent Misuse Doctrine,* 58 J.P.O.S. 69 (1976).

———. "The Jacuzzi Brothers: Pioneering Inventors." *Italian-American Review* 3 (1994): 28.

United States Department of Commerce. *National Inventors Hall of Fame*. Washington, D.C., 1993.

Walterscheid, E.C., *The Early Evolution of the United States Patent Law: Antecedents (Part 1)*, 76 J.P.O.S. 697 (1994).

See also BUSINESS AND ENTREPRENEURSHIP; SCIENCE

Paterno, Joseph Vincent (b. 1926)

While other Italian Americans, such as Carmen Cozza at Yale, have made their mark in coaching football, Joe Paterno holds the record as the most successful football coach in the history of America's colleges and universities.

Joseph Vincent Paterno, the son of Angelo Lafayette and Florence (de LaSalle) Paterno, was born in Brooklyn, New York, on December 21, 1926. His parents, who were also born in this country, sent their son to Brooklyn Preparatory, a Jesuit school, where he became the captain of the football team in his senior year. The school's only loss was to St. Cecilia's, a team coached by Vince Lombardi, and Paterno had distinguished himself as a reputable high school athlete, who was eventually scouted out by Brown University. In his senior year at Brown he played football as a quarterback and, with his brother George as a running back, helped to make the college team famous.

Instead of pursuing a law career like his father, on graduating from Brown in 1950 Paterno took a job as an assistant, coaching football at Pennsylvania State University. He held this position for sixteen years before he became the head coach there in 1966. On May 12, 1962, he had married Suzanne Pohland, and together they had five children.

Paterno's career as a coach at Penn State has covered almost half a century. During his thirty years as head coach, he has won more than 75 percent of the total games he coached. After Penn State won its second national championship (the first was in 1982) in 1986, *Sports Illustrated* honored Paterno as "Sportsman of the Year," a recognition never previously conferred on a college football coach. Other records were broken that same year when the American Football Coaches Association voted Paterno Coach of the Year for the fourth time. In 1991 the National Football Foundation and Hall of Fame gave Paterno its Distinguished American Award.

What has made Paterno particularly attractive to the college football world is his attention to academic achievement as well as to athletic ability in his players. The graduation rate of his players has been over 90 percent and, of his many scholar-athletes, at least fifteen players have won postgraduate scholarships. Paterno has helped to shape the character of his players and to instill in them the importance of intellectual and moral values. For such achievements, Brown University conferred on him an honorary doctor of law degree in 1975. After Paterno and his wife had set up the Paterno Libraries Endowment at Penn State in 1984, Penn State trustees named a new library wing after them.

Vincent A. Lapomarda

Bibliography

Booher, Dennis A. *Joseph Vincent Paterno, Football Coach: His Involvement with the Pennsylvania State University and American Intercollegiate Football*. Ann Arbor: University Microfilms International, 1986.

Denlinger, Ken. *For the Glory: Football Dreams and Realities Inside Paterno's Program*. New York: St. Martin's, 1994.

Newcombe, Jack. *Six Days to Saturday: Joe Paterno and Penn State*. New York: Farrar, Straus & Giroux, 1974.

Paterno, Joseph V. *Paterno: By the Book*. New York: Berkeley, 1991.

See also SPORTS

Patri, Angelo (1877–1965)

Principal of Junior High School 45, in the Bronx, New York, for more than thirty years (1913 to 1944), Dr. Angelo Patri was a pioneering liberal educator. His innovations turned this school from regimentation and rote learning to a loving atmosphere of creative participation. He encouraged children to develop their talents using wood, metal, music, clay, and nature while learning "reading, 'riting, and 'rithmetic."

Patri became directly involved in the relationships between teachers, students, and parents. He was the forerunner of guidance for parents and wrote books about the problems of childhood, school and home, and counseling.

He was born in Italy and came to America in the 1880s. His father, Nicolas, was a laborer but knew many historical figures and was a great storyteller. His mother, Carmela, wanted him to be a priest, but Patri wanted to be a doctor. Later in life, he said he turned out to be a little of both.

His family lived in Little Italy, where Italian was spoken at home. He found school challenging, but he soon made great progress. He graduated from City College of New York at 20 and began teaching in public school. Teaching became a "deadly mechanical grind" for him. At Columbia Graduate School he discovered John Dewey's *Ethical Principles*. Patri said, "No other book had such an influence on my life. It made me feel that I was responsible for children , and not for the facts of the curriculum. . . ." In 1908 Patri became principal of Public School 4, and five years later principal of Junior High School 45.

In 1931 *Parents* magazine presented a medal to Patri for distinguished service in parental education. For a number of years he wrote a syndicated advice column, "Our Children." As teacher, principal, author, and columnist, Patri stressed that the teacher must know the child to help the child become successful.

Many individuals in the arts and professions had their start in Patri's classes: Joy Davidson, poet; John Amore, sculpture; William Hassler, scientist; and John Garfield, actor. Patri encouraged Garfield to participate in debating and dramatics. Although Garfield eventually dropped out of high school, Patri's financial help enabled the budding actor to study at the America Laboratory Theater, which led to a successful career in theater.

Patri received many honors. His own City College of New York awarded him the Townsend Harris medal. He was appointed supervisor of programs for WNYC. The Italian government recognized him for special merit and as director of American War Relief in Italy.

John M. Brindisi

Bibliography

Patri, Angelo. *The Problems of Childhood.* New York: Appleton, 1925.
———. *School and Home.* New York: Appleton, 1925.
———. *A Schoolmaster of the Great City.* New York: Macmillan, 1927.

Patti, Adelina (1843–1919)

Celebrated operatic soprano, born in Madrid on February 19, 1843, Adelina Patti was the daughter of tenor Salvatore Patti and soprano Caterina Chiesa Barilli-Patti, and the younger sister of sopranos Amalia Patti (1831–1915) and Carlotta Patti (1835–1889), all four successful performers. Her mother also had several other children (all notable singers) from a previous marriage.

With both heredity and environment on her side, it seemed almost predestined that Adelina (birth name: Adela Juana Maria) would become a star. Her first lessons in singing came from a family member, baritone Ettore Barilli, a half brother. At age 7 she made her first public appearance at a charity concert in Tipler's Hall, New York. Soon after she toured the United States for three years as a child prodigy, accompanied by Amalia's husband, pianist Maurice Strakosch, who was to be her manager and mentor until Adelina married in 1868.

In 1857 she left the extended family for a period of time, embarking on a tour with the noted American pianist and composer Louis Moreau Gottschalk (1829–1869). When only 16, Patti made her formal operatic debut in New York on November 24, 1859, in the title role of Gaetano Donizetti's famous *Lucia di Lammermoor* (1835). After touring the United States and Cuba, she made her debut in Europe at Covent Garden in London in 1861, followed by debuts in Paris in 1862 and at the famous Milan opera house La Scala in 1877.

With her first London appearance, Patti became the favorite of opera audiences in Europe and America. In 1868 she married the Marquis de Caux; their relationship ended in divorce in 1885. She was wed to tenor Ernest Nicolini from 1886 until his death in 1898. In 1899 she became the wife of the Swedish nobleman Baron Roif Cederstrom. She reached her artistic peak in the 1860s and 1870s, made successful United States tours (after an over twenty-year absence) in 1881, 1882, 1883, 1884, 1886, 1887, 1890, 1892, and 1903, and officially retired in London in 1906. Still responding to public demand, however, she participated in charity concerts until 1914, when she was over seventy. While in her sixties, she made some recordings that preserved her outstanding vocal talents, despite the poor technology of the period. Her voice had a wide range, extensive flexibility, and a pure and even tone, though it lacked strong volume. With roles in many top operas—including Vincenzo Bellini's *La Sonnambula* (1831), Giuseppe

Verdi's *Aida* (1871) and *La Traviata* (1853), and Charles Gounod's *Faust* (1859) and *Romeo et Juliette* (1867)—she was one of the most celebrated singers and operatic actresses of the nineteenth century.

Patti received as much as five thousand dollars for each performance, an enormous sum at the time. Until her death in Wales on September 27, 1919, she was surrounded by adoring fans, fabulous jewels, and various idiosyncracies (including her habit of skipping rehearsals), which made her a most colorful coloratura.

William E. Studwell

Bibliography

Castan Palomar, Fernando. *Adelina Patti: su vida.* Madrid: Generalde Ediciones, 1947.

Klein, Hermann. *The Reign of Patti.* New York: Century, 1920.

See also OPERA

Paulucci, Jeno F. (b. 1918)

The son of Ettore and Michelina Paulucci, who in 1912 migrated from Belisio Solfare in the province of Pesaro to Minnesota, Jeno F. Paulucci is best described as an "incurable entrepreneur," a visionary who applied his talents with the greatest success in business, humanitarian activities, and the promotion of his Italian heritage.

Paulucci first came to national attention when he founded the Chun King Corporation on a loan of $2,500 in 1946. He developed the frozen-food company over the next twenty years. Later, Paulucci sold Chun King to R.J. Reynolds Tobacco Company for $63 million.

Paulucci used his new fortune to move into a wide range of business activities over the next half century, including land development in Orlando, Florida; food and beverage dispensing equipment; advertising; public relations; and research. However, his primary interest has always been the food business.

Paulucci formed Jeno's, Inc., which became one of America's leading hot snacks company and a pacesetter in frozen pizzas. His newest venture, Michelina's, named after his mother, is currently a national leader in frozen Italian food products.

Like countless other Americans of Italian heritage, Paulucci has sought to repay his country for the success he has achieved. Most notably, his home state of Minnesota has been the beneficiary of his efforts. He formed the North East Minnesota Organization for Economic Education (NEMO, Inc.), resulting in the private capital investment of nearly two billion dollars for the area's economy and the distribution of nearly two million dollars to his employees in tax-paid gifts upon the sale of Chun King. Paulucci helped to plan and construct a major recreation center in Duluth and has worked tirelessly to battle the problems of congestion and lack of transportation in Minnesota. Paulucci was the architect of the "New Cities" program aimed at developing a planned environment in some fifty cities and established the Paulucci Family Foundation to fund worthwhile charitable activities.

Paulucci has received numerous awards for his humanitarian and civic activities. He holds the national Horatio Alger Award; has received several honorary doctorate degrees; and in 1973 was named Honorary Swede of the Year by Svenskarnas Dag, Inc., one of the few non-Swedish citizens to receive such an award.

Paulucci has always sought in his business activities to help disadvantaged persons. In recognition of his lifetime efforts in this area, Jeno's, Inc. was selected in 1972 by the President's Commission on Employment of the Handicapped and the National Association of Employers to receive its national award. On behalf of employment practices established by Jeno's, Inc., the company received the Employer of the Year citation by the city of Duluth, state of Minnesota, and the United States of America.

As important as his success in the worlds of business and civic activities has been,

President Ronald Reagan and fast-food magnate Jeno Paulucci at the 1985 NIAF Gala. NIAF has achieved an important presence in the nation's capital. Courtesy of the National Italian American Foundation (NIAF), Washington, D.C.

Paulucci has never forgotten his Italian heritage. He was a founder of the National Italian American Foundation (NIAF) and was its chairman for the first sixteen years of its existence from 1975 to 1991. He served as presidential emissary for Presidents Ford and Carter to evaluate United States disaster relief efforts when earthquakes struck Italy. Paulucci has been honored by three national Italian American organizations as outstanding Italian American of the Year. In recognition of his many services to his ancestral land, he has been accorded the Order of Merit, the highest civilian honor of the Republic of Italy.

Paulucci has been married for fifty years to the former Lois Mae Trepanier. They have three children: Michael, Cynthia, and Gina Jo.

Frank D. Stella

Bibliography

"Jeno's Economic Ego." *Newsday,* 17 March 1986, 52.

Paulucci, Jeno. "NIAF and the Italian American Community." *Ambassador* (Autumn 1989): 21.

Paulucci, Jeno, and Frank Stella. "An Overview of the Italian American in Politics." *Ambassador* no. 2 (summer 1989): 9–13.

See also BUSINESS AND ENTREPRENEURSHIP; NATIONAL ITALIAN AMERICAN FOUNDATION

Pei, Mario Andrew (1901–1978)

Linguist Mario A. Pei was born in Rome, Italy, to Francesco Pei and Luisa Ferri, drugstore proprietors. After his parents' business went bankrupt, the family migrated in 1908 to the United States, where his father became the room-service director at the Buckingham Hotel in New York City.

Critical to his choice of linguistics as a career was his bilingual background in Italian and English. In 1923 he started teaching languages at City College of New York, where two years later he received a bachelor's degree magna cum laude. He enrolled at Columbia University, and in 1928 he published an English translation of Vittoria Ermete de Fiori's *Mussolini: The Man of Destiny.* In 1932 he received his Ph.D. In 1937 he became assistant professor of Romance languages at Columbia University, and four years later he published *The Italian Language.*

During World War II Pei served as a language consultant to the Office of War Information and the Office of Strategic Services. He prepared for military personnel a thirty-seven-language course entitled *War Linguistics.* He followed with a book called *Languages for War and Peace* (1943), which was a detailed guide to seven major languages and a concise description of the other thirty languages. He completed his wartime work with *The American Road to Peace: A Constitution for the World* (1945), which won the First Regional Award in the Ziff-Davis Peace Plan Contest of 1945.

In Pei's *The Story of Language* (1949), he described language as "mankind's most important invention." In this critically acclaimed work, he described the structure of languages in a readily understandable manner for the general public. Using charm and good humor, he made the technical information of linguistics an interesting study. Pei's *The Story of English* (1952) was a sequel to *The Story of Language,* in which he traced the history of English from its Anglo-Saxon roots to its modern form. He was then named professor of Romance philology at Columbia University in 1952. He rewrote *The Story of Language* by summarizing it for youngsters in *All About Language* (1954). Pei quickly followed it with *A Dictionary of Linguistics* (1954), which he edited with Frank Gaynor.

During 1957 he started collaborating with other specialists on the Holiday Magazine Language Series published by Harper for the next two years. This series was a group of guidebooks that started with *Getting Along in French* for travelers. Later works covered German, Italian, Spanish, Portuguese, and Russian.

Pei burst upon the international scene with *One Language for the World and How to Achieve It* (1958), in which he advocated a single language to promote universal understanding and friendship. He proposed that all children be taught a single language in addition to their native tongues. He suggested an artificial language, such as Esperanto.

He then prepared a revised edition of *New Italian Self-Taught* (1959) and wrote *The Book of Place Names* (1959) with Eloise Lambert. He also collaborated with her in writing *Our Names, Where They Come From and What They Mean* (1960).

After publishing *Talking Your Way Around the World* (1961), at age 60, he took a three-year sabbatical from Columbia. He worked as a NATO lecturer for a year at the University of Lisbon and the University of Coimbra in Portugal. Upon his return to the United States in 1962, he wrote *Families of Words, The Meaning and Function of Language,* and *Voices of Man.*

In *Our National Heritage* (1965) he analyzed the characteristics of various immigrant groups in the United States and their contributions to the American culture.

Relentless in his productivity, Pei tackled spelling reform in *The Many Hues of English* (1967). He then released *The Story of the English Language* (1967), which was essentially a new edition that revised 40 percent of his highly successful *The Story of English.*

During his lifetime he became fluent in five languages, competent in twelve more, understandable in thirty others, and had a structural knowledge of about one hundred more.

Joseph Scafetta Jr.

Bibliography

Current Biography. 1968, 1978.
National Cyclopedia of American Biography. Vol. 60, 1981, p. 277.
Obituary, *New York Times,* 5 March 1978.
Science Fiction and Fantasy Literature: A Checklist. Vol. 2, 1979.
Who Was Who in America. Vol. VII, 1981.

Pellegrino, Edmund Daniel (b. 1920)

Physician, educator, and author Edmund Daniel Pellegrino was born in Newark, New Jersey, June 22, 1920, son of Michael J. and Marie Catone Pellegrino. After his graduation from Xavier High School, New York, Pellegrino matriculated at St. John's University, New York, and graduated summa cum laude, with a B.S. in 1941. Three years later he received his M.D. from New York University. He served in the United States Army Air Force from 1946 to 1948.

Dr. Pellegrino's residencies in medicine were served at Bellevue, Goldwater Memorial in New York City, and Homer Folks Tuberculosis Hospital in Oneonta, New York. He was a research fellow in renal medicine and physiology at New York University and held positions as founding chairman and director, founding dean and professor, chancellor and president at medical centers in New Jersey, Kentucky, Tennessee, and Connecticut. Presently, he serves as director of the Georgetown University Center for the Advanced Study of Ethics, director of the Center for Clinical Bioethics, and professor of medicine and medical ethics. He also served as president of Catholic University of America.

He is fellow or member of twenty scientific, professional, and honorary societies, including the Institute of Medicine of the National Academy of Sciences, the Association of American Physicians, and the American Clinical and Climatological Association. He is the editor of *Journal of Medicine and Philosophy.*

His scholarly publications include over four hundred items: articles on medical science, philosophy, and ethics. Married in 1944, Dr. Pellegrino and his wife, the former Clementine Coakley, have seven children.

Margherita Marchione

Bibliography

Cantoni, Serena V., ed. *Who's Who Among Italian Americans.* Washington, DC: The National Italian American Foundation.
Marchione, Margherita, *Americans of Italian Heritage.* New York: University Press of America, Inc., 1995, 165–167.
The Sooner Catholic, 18 May 1997.
Who's Who in America. New Providence: New Jersey, 1992.

See also MEDICAL ETHICS IN MODERN AMERICA; MEDICINE

Perini, Louis R. (1903–1972)

Born in Framingham, Massachussetts, November 29, 1903, Louis Robert Perini, son of Bonfiglio and Clementina (née Marchesi) Perini, was the president of the Perini Corporation, which became a multinational construction business on four continents. His parents, in whose memory the Science Center at St. Anselm College in Manchester, New Hampshire, was erected, were immigrants from northern Italy. Coming to the United States from Milan in 1885, his father founded B. Perini & Sons in 1918. When Bonfiglio died in 1924, Louis, with little more than a grammar school education in Ashland, Massachusetts, but with much experience from working at various jobs for his father's business since age 6, became president of the company. In 1926 Louis married Florence R. Gardetto, daughter of a contractor from

Milford, Massachusetts, and they became the parents of three sons and four daughters.

Working with his brothers, Charles B. as vice-president and Joseph R. as treasurer, Louis expanded the family business into a worldwide construction firm, the Perini Corporation, which is listed on the New York Stock Exchange. This corporation, with its various subsidiaries, has been involved in commercial, educational, highway, industrial, manufacturing, and residential construction. The Perini name has fixed its stamp on a number of sites around the world, not to mention its interest in coal in Pennsylvania and uranium in Canada. Casinos such as the Trump Taj Mahal Casino Resort in Atlantic City, New Jersey; hotels (Luxor Hotel in Las Vegas, Nevada); research centers (MIT Lincoln Laboratory in Lexington, Massachusetts); and the traffic tunnels such as those in Boston, Massachusetts, are products of the Perini Corporation.

The corporation has also made a significant contribution to major league baseball. The Perini brothers have been involved in the ownership of the Braves from 1944 in Boston, when the team was owned by "The Three Little Steam Shovels" (three contractors, Joseph Maney and Guido Rugo, in addition to Louis Perini), until the baseball team moved from Milwaukee to Atlanta in 1962. He served as president of the baseball franchise.

Like other Italian Americans who became successful in business, Perini shared his wealth. Educational institutions such as Boston College; the College of the Holy Cross, from which David B., his son and successor in the corporation, graduated in 1959; and St. Anselm College recognized his contributions with honorary degrees. He was particularly fond of the Jimmy Fund, which he helped launch as president of the Braves. A fellow of Brandeis University (1956) and a Knight of Malta (1959), Perini was also honored by the National Conference of Christians and Jews in 1961. Perini died in West Palm Beach, Florida, April 16, 1972.

Vincent A. Lapomarda

Bibliography

Kaese, Harold. *The Boston Braves.* New York: Putnam, 1948.

Klapisch, Bob. *The Braves: An Illustrated History of America's Team.* Atlanta: Turner Publishing, 1995.

"Lou Perini, Owner Who Took Braves to Milwaukee, Is Dead." Obituary. *New York Times,* 17 April 1972.

MacLaughlin, Curtis D. "He's Building a $350 Million City in Florida." *Worcester Sunday Telegram,* 19 August 1962.

Negri, Gloria. "Jimmy Fund Dedicates Clinic." *The Boston Globe,* 22 May 1994.

Palmer, Thomas C. Jr., "Contractor Pushes Use of Tunnel Technique." *Boston Globe,* 27 August 1995.

Renoff, Richard, and Joseph Varacalli. "Italian Americans and Baseball." *The Nassau Review* 6, no 1. (1990): 92–119.

See also BUSINESS AND ENTREPRENEURSHIP

Pernicone, Joseph Maria (1903–1985)

Bishop Joseph Maria Pernicone provided Italian Americans with service and ethnic pride through his dedicated work in the Catholic Church. He was born in Regalbuto, in the province of Enna, Italy, and was one of six children. Discerning a call to the priesthood at an early age, he began his studies at the diocesan seminary of Nicosia, and later at the archepisocopal seminary of Catania. He migrated to America with his family from Sicily.

He continued his studies at Cathedral College in New York City and at Saint Joseph's Seminary in Dunwoodie, Yonkers. On December 18, 1926, he was ordained a priest of the New York Archdiocese. Two years later, in 1928, he earned a doctorate in canon law from Catholic University in Washington, D.C. His early priesthood was spent as assistant pastor and pastor at churches named in honor of Our Lady of Mount Carmel in Yonkers and in Poughkeepsie, New York.

In 1944 he was appointed pastor to Our Lady of Mount Carmel Church in the heavily populated Italian American Belmont section of the Bronx, New York City, where he dedicated most of his priestly labor, completing his service at that parish in 1966. On May 3, 1945, Pope Pius XII elevated Father Pernicone to the rank of papal chamberlain with the title of very reverend monsignor, and on May 9, 1952, honored him with the title domestic prelate. As pastor of Our Lady of Mount Carmel, Monsignor Pernicone, over a period of a decade, built a block-length school, a youth center, and a convent costing more than $1 million. He paid tribute to a former pastor of Our Lady of Mount Carmel by naming the youth center the Monsignor Cafuzzi Hall. The school was unique, since it served as an auditorium-gymnasium that could accommodate over one thousand persons. At its peak, some 2,000 children were enrolled in the school.

A singular honor was bestowed on Monsignor Pernicone on May 5, 1954, when he was consecrated an auxiliary bishop of the Archdiocese of New York. This appointment made him the third Italian American in the country to become a bishop and the first Italian-born bishop in the New York Archdiocese. In the post–World War II period, 1958, he initiated a successful letter-writing campaign between Italian Americans in the Greater New York area and relatives in Italy urging them to vote for the Christian Democratic Party to defeat the Communist Party in Italy. Earlier, in 1943 during World War II, when the collapse of the Fascist government was imminent, he was also involved in organizing a desperately needed clothing campaign for the people of Italy.

After leaving Our Lady of Mount Carmel Parish in 1966, Bishop Pernicone was appointed the episcopal vicar of Dutchess and Putnam counties and pastor of Holy Trinity Church in Poughkeepsie. In 1978 he retired to the Providence Nursing Home in the Bronx, residing there until his death. Shortly after his death a new blood center at Saint Barnabas Hospital in the Bronx was named in his honor, and a small plaza near Our Lady of Mount Carmel was dedicated to his memory. His parishioners and the people of Belmont attributed their strong sense of community and ethnic pride to Bishop Pernicone.

Nicholas Joseph Falco

Bibliography

Borgatti, Joseph L.J. *Our Lady of Mount Carmel Parish Bronx, NY Golden Jubilee 1906–1956.* New York, 1956.

Brown, Mary Elizabeth. *Churches, Communities, and Children: Italian Immigrants in the Archdiocese of New York, 1880–1945.* New York: Center for Migration Studies, 1995.

———. *From Italian Villages to Greenwich Village: Our Lady of Pompei 1892–1992.* New York: Center for Migration Studies, 1992.

Fogarty, Gerald P. *The Vatican and the American Hierarchy from 1870 to 1965.* Wilmington, DE: Michael Glazier, 1985.

Schiavo, Giovanni. *Italian-American History, The Italian Contribution to the Catholic Church in America.* Vol. 2. New York: Vigo Press, 1949.

See also RELIGION

Pesci, Joe
See MOVIE ACTORS AND ACTRESSES

Petrillo, James Caesar (1892–1984)

Son of an Italian immigrant sewer digger, this labor leader grew up on Chicago's tough West Side. As a young man he played a trumpet given to him at Jane Addams' Hull House, but he soon realized he would never succeed as a musician; instead, he went into the union business. In 1920 he was elected vice-president of the American Musicians Union of Chicago. Three years later, he became president and retained the position until he was elected president of the American Federation of Musicians in 1940. For the next eighteen years, Petrillo was one of the most powerful and controversial labor leaders in America. He often had two bodyguards assigned to protect him when gangsters were waging war against union leaders to gain control of the organizations.

Petrillo ran a closed shop: that is, no one could perform without his consent, regardless of whether it was Liberace or Rubenstein. His inflexibility on this point was adequately demonstrated when he ordered a boycott against the prestigious Boston Symphony, which was attempting to thwart its musicians from unionizing. Union pressure prevented the group from broadcasting for years. In 1942 Petrillo was able to preclude RCA Victor from recording the Boston Symphony, eventually forcing the orchestra to come to terms with the union. His dubious title, "Mussolini of Music," did not weaken Petrillo's power even though some felt he should be restrained by legal action. Again in 1942 Petrillo pulled his musicians out of all recording studios, demanding that they receive a royalty on every record sold. One record company held out for twenty-seven months, and President Franklin Delano Roosevelt's plea failed to get Petrillo to end his strike. Petrillo even refused the War Production Board's request. Petrillo's adamancy paid off and earned the musicians' union one to two and one-half cents' royalty per record. In those years, records cost fifty cents each for a ten-inch platter that transformed seventy-eight revolutions per minute into music and sound. The strike brought in millions of dollars to the musicians' fund.

Petrillo also maintained his opposition to technology that he felt violated the rights of his musicians. He was vehemently against "canned" music, making it clear that he believed that individual radio stations that offered network musical programs and record music should regularly employ live musicians in their studios. Despite a congressional attempt to curb Petrillo and allow broadcasters to hire fewer live musicians, Petrillo persisted. Finally, he authored the contracts that required network stations to hire a quota of live musicians whether or not they were required to play. In 1958 Petrillo resigned in the face of a revolt by some union members who claimed he was preventing them from working in television. At that time more sophisticated labor laws needed to be implemented.

He was faulted by many in his day for using high-handed tactics in courting the support of influential people. In 1937 he was kidnapped, but his four hundred locals were rich enough to rescue him. One of his peccadilloes was a phobia of germs. Legend has it that he would shake hands only with his pinky, and that in his long career he shook hands with only two people, Harry Truman and Celeste Holm. Petrillo died on October 23, 1984, after suffering a stroke.

Charles La Cerra

Bibliography

Leiter, Robert D. *The Musicians and Petrillo.*
    New York: Bookman Associates, 1953.
"Petrillo, Mussolini of Music." *American
    Mercury* 51 (November 1940): 281–287.
Smith, Bernard B. "What's Petrillo Up To?"
    Harper's 186 (December 1942):
    90–97.

See also LABOR

Petrosino, Joseph (1860–1909)

One of the first Italian American detectives, Joseph Petrosino gave his life to rid Italian American communities of crime. Born in Padula on April 30, 1860, he and his family migrated to New York City in 1873. Within a few years, he found work with the Sanitation Department. In 1883 he became a uniformed police officer and two years later was promoted to detective.

Americans stereotyped Italian immigrants as lawbreakers and pieced every incident of Italian criminal activity into a pattern of organized crime. Petrosino was drawn into the investigation of crimes involving Italians, most notably the 1905 New York barrel murder case. In New York City, reformers suspected that all malefactors of whatever ethnicity escaped punishment because the police were corrupt.

In 1908 reform-minded police commissioner Theodore Bingham appointed Petrosino to head a new unit within the New York City Police Department, a supposedly secret service to dismember the Black Hand. Testing the hypothesis of an international criminal syndicate with headquarters in Sicily and a branch in New York, Petrosino immersed himself in Italian community life. He spent hours sitting unobtrusively in restaurants where the criminals were said to congregate. He also studied New York court records, searching for patterns that would indicate organized criminal activity. His work helped to disprove the existence of syndicate crime.

Ironically, Petrosino was shot to death on the evening of March 12, 1909, while visiting Palermo as part of a deportation operation; any immigrants with criminal records in their home countries could be sent back. The assassination resurrected the claim of an international criminal syndicate, whose members on both sides of the Atlantic cooperated to trap Petrosino. Such collaboration was unnecessary; news of Petrosino's upcoming trip had appeared in New York papers, and any criminal who wanted to enhance a local reputation by killing the famous guest had the information that made it easy to do so. The murder remained unsolved. The most likely suspect, Palermo criminal Don Vito Cascio Ferro, died in prison during the Allied invasion of Sicily in 1943.

Petrosino's murder also became a human drama; there were no widow's pensions for police detectives killed in the line of duty, and Petrosino, age 49 at the time of his death, left a young widow, Adele, and an infant daughter. Petrosino's remains were returned to the United States, and he was buried from Saint Patrick's Old Cathedral on Mott Street. A monument over his grave in Calvary Cemetery, Queens, was unveiled March 14, 1910. A plaza north of the former police headquarters at 240 Centre Street is dedicated to his memory.

Mary Elizabeth Brown

Bibliography

Petacco, Arrigo. *Joe Petrosino,* translated by Charles Lam Markmann. New York: Macmillan, 1974.

Pozzetta, George E. "Another Look at the Petrosino Affair." *Italian Americana* 1 (autumn 1974): 81–92.

See also LAW ENFORCEMENT

Philadelphia

Italians have been in Philadelphia since the 1750s, when musicians and composers from Italy first arrived. In the late eighteenth century other Italians joined previous settlers as permanent residents of the city. By 1850 about two hundred Italians, mainly of Ligurian or Tuscan origins, lived in Philadelphia. They were painters and sculptors; casters and vendors of plaster statues; concert hall performers and street musicians; impresarios and beer garden proprietors; importers and merchants; tavern keepers and lodging house operators. In another ten years a number of Italians were beginning to concentrate in the old Southwark and Moyamensing districts, just below the southern boundary of the original city, which had become South Philadelphia after the consolidation of 1854. These neighborhoods eventually became the demographic and cultural center of the Italian population in the entire Philadelphia area.

The growth of the Italian population in Philadelphia increased steadily in the final decades of the nineteenth century. The 1870 United States Census reported only 516 Italian natives in Philadelphia; this figure increased to 1,656 by 1880. Although it was not regularly connected by direct service from Mediterranean ports, large numbers of immigrants from Italy began arriving in Philadelphia in the late 1880s. In 1890 the Census counted the Italian-born population in the city at 6,799, and by 1900 at a total of 17,830. Mainly natives of southern Italy and Sicily, these newcomers were recruited as unskilled laborers for the rapidly expanding railroad systems. By the early twentieth century, Italians were attracted by the major industries of the city, which included the manufacture of clothing, shoes and hats, wood products and furniture, and by the construction trades in the building of city streets, houses, and subways. Even when business cycles moved downward, the diversity of production found in Philadelphia offered steady employment for its workers. By 1910 about one-half of women working in the clothing industry in Philadelphia were Italian. The nearby farms of rural southern New Jersey also provided working opportunities during the harvest season for women and children to supplement household income.

Italian immigrants were also drawn by amenities that distinguished Philadelphia. In contrast to the ubiquitous tenements of other cities, Philadelphia, in its earliest years, had made available by public policy the purchase of relatively modest but inexpensive homes to the families of workers. The residential settlement of Italians rapidly grew into one vast hub of South Philadelphia, with its characteristic row homes. This settlement was augmented by the "satellite communities" of other neighborhoods, such as West Philadelphia, North Philadelphia, Germantown, and Chestnut Hill, as well as those outside the city.

With the peak of immigration from Italy occurring during the first decade of the twentieth century, the Italian-born population reached 45,308 and, when Americans born of Italian parentage were included, the count rose to 77,000 by 1910. The next federal census in 1920 reported 63,223 as Italian-born, with slightly more than 44,000 living in South Philadelphia, and a total population of first- and second-generation Italians of 137,000 for the entire city. The growth of the immigrant population encouraged the exploitation of workers, and the *padrone* (labor broker) system was used extensively in the mining areas of Pennsylvania. The *paesani* (fellow villagers) network was more important in the development of the Italian community in

A section of the Little Italy community in Philadelphia at 9th and Washington Streets, looking north, on a busy Saturday morning, March 17, 1979. Courtesy Frank J. Cavaioli.

Philadelphia, with its own formal institutions and voluntary associations, along with strong leadership, and provided some protection to immigrants and their families.

St. Mary Magdalen de Pazzi, founded in 1853 on Montrose Street, east of Eighth Street, was the first parish for Italian Catholics in the United States, with Father Gaetano Mariani as pastor. Appointed in 1870, Father Antonio Isoleri served as pastor for fifty-six years until his retirement in 1929. The great influx of new immigrants required the formation of another parish, Our Mother of Good Counsel, at Eighth and Christian Streets, in 1898. This church became not only the parish for southern Italians, but extended far larger into the community than the older one, and remained an important part of the Italian settlements until its controversial suppression by the Archdiocese in 1933. Altogether twenty-four nationality parishes were founded for Italians in the city and nearby areas, the last being Our Lady of Loreto in 1932 in Southwest Philadelphia.

Italians in Philadelphia established their first mutual-aid society, the Società di Unione e Fratellanza Italiana, in 1868. Since then, over four hundred organizations, based upon town and regional origins, occupations, political interests, religious devotions, and recreational pursuits, have been founded by residents of Italian ancestry. Of the many Italian language newspapers in Philadelphia, the most important was *L'Opinione,* published by Charles C. A. Baldi, from 1906 until 1935, when it was absorbed by *Il Progresso* of New York City. As individuals and in their group life, through cultural assimilation and social mobility, Italian Americans have achieved success and prominence in the economic, political, and educational institutions of the city. In 1971 voters elected Frank L. Rizzo as the first Italian American mayor of Philadelphia.

In 1980 the number of residents of Italian ancestry in Philadelphia was 192,102, a larger figure than any other American city except New York. By 1990, while their number had declined to 178,315, Italian Americans comprised slightly more than 11 percent of the population, about the same as ten years earlier. South Philadelphia remains the largest residential area of Italian Americans anywhere in the United States. Between 1980 and 1990, although their numbers within the city decreased, the Italian American population and its proportion to all residents in suburban counties increased. Despite many changes, Italian Americans remain, in number, visibility, and influence, an important demographic and cultural factor in the Philadelphia area.

Richard N. Juliani

Bibliography

Juliani, Richard N. *Building Little Italy: Philadelphia's Italians before Mass Immigration,* Pennsylvania State University Press, 1998.

———. "La Comunità Italiana di Filadelfia." *Storia Urbana* (1982): 51–73.

———. "Una comunità in transizione: il caso italiano a Filadelfia." *Le Società in transizione: italiani e italoamericani negli anni ottanta.* Roma: Ministero degli Affari Estero, 1989.

———. "The Italian Community of Philadelphia." In *Little Italies in North America,* edited by Robert F. Harney and J. Vincenza Scarpaci, 85–104. Toronto: The Multicultural History Society of Ontario, 1981.

———. "The Italians in Philadelphia: Problems and Resources." *Newsletter: Philadelphia City Archives* nos. 54–56 (1985).

———. "The Social Organization of Immigration: The Italians in Philadelphia." Ph.D. diss., University of Pennsylvania, 1971. (Reprinted and published under the same title, New York: Arno Press, 1980.)

Phinizy, Ferdinand (1819–1889)

A successful merchant and financier, Ferdinand Phinizy was an Italian American whose family roots go back to the American Revolution.

The son of Jacob and Matilda (Stewart) Phinizy, Ferdinand was born in Bowling Green (Stephens) in Oglethorpe County, Georgia, on January 20, 1819, and died in Athens, Georgia, on October 20, 1889. His grandfather (1761?–1818), Ferdinand Phinizy (Finici or Finizzi was recorded as the original name), who had come to this country with Count Rochambeau to fight in the American Revolution, was a native of Parma, Italy, and, after marrying Margaret Condon, had settled, before the end of the eighteenth century, in Bowling Green.

The eldest of six children (four sons and two daughters), the second Ferdinand grew up in the family homestead and was educated in Bowling Green before his family moved to Athens,

where he graduated with honors from the University of Georgia in 1838. This was a year after John Phinizy, his uncle, was elected mayor of Augusta, a phenomenon that was duplicated in Mobile, St. Augustine, and Texarkana when other Italian Americans were elected mayors in the South before the end of the century.

Managing the family holdings at Bowling Green in his years after college, Phinizy left the area to become successful in business and finance. Before the American Civil War, he had established his own business as a member of the cotton trading firm of F. Phinizy and Company of Augusta, Georgia. As a financial agent of the Confederate government during the war, Phinizy was able to send masses of cotton through the Union blockade of the South and to market bonds to help the Confederate government carry on the war against the North.

The war between the states had taken its toll on his wealth, but Phinizy was able to recoup his losses by reestablishing his business trading cotton and by investing his money in banking, insurance, and railroads so that he had become a millionaire by the time of his death. Though very successful in business and finance, he reflected affability, geniality, and integrity in his relations with others.

Phinizy had married Harriet Hayes Bowdre, on February 22, 1849, and she became the mother of eight of his children, seven sons and a daughter, before she died in 1863. Two years later he married Anne S. Barrett, who bore him three more children.

Although Phinizy's grandfather had worshiped at St. Patrick's Catholic Church in Augusta, the second Ferdinand did not give much attention to religion until later in his life when he followed the beliefs and practices of the Methodist Church and became very much interested in its works. Not only did he support its causes, but he went so far as to entertain Methodist bishops and ministers when their conference met at Athens. A person of simple religious taste, he opposed having instrumental music in the churches and gave only to those churches that refused to install organs.

Of all the descendants of the first Ferdinand Phinizy, it was perhaps the second Ferdinand who was really responsible for anchoring the Phinizy family in the history of Georgia. While a number of its notable members generously served the community in various capacities because of their economic situation in society and had a special esteem for its educational structure, especially the University of Georgia at Athens, the second Ferdinand was the one who had left a rather large fortune. Though his desire to shape his own career had led him to settle in Augusta, he returned to Athens, where, after the Civil War, he made his home and where, in Oconee Cemetery, his remains now rest with those of his first wife.

Vincent A. Lapomarda

Bibliography

Armstrong, Zella, comp. *Notable Southern Families*. 3 vols. Chattanooga: Genealogical Pub. Co., 1918.

Calhoun, Ferdinand Phinizy. *The Phinizy Family in America*. Atlanta: Johnson-Dallis, 1925.

Pierini, Armando (1908–1998)

One of the most accomplished priests and church leaders in the history of Chicago's Italians, the Reverend Armando Pierini was born in Agello, province of Perugia, Italy. He was ordained in 1932 in Piacenza. After a short sojourn as rector for students at the Gregorian University in Rome, Pierini was assigned as assistant to Father Joseph Bernardi at the Santa Maria Addolorata.

Influenced by the presence of Our Lady of Mount Carmel in Melrose Park, Pierini chose the nearby Stone Park as the site for the new Sacred Heart Seminary. The dedication ceremony for the new building in May 1937 drew a crowd of ten thousand people, including the cardinal and apostolic delegates, and received wide coverage in the metropolitan press of Chicago.

Beginning with a class of ten, the fledgling seminary took students from age 14 and stressed liberal arts, philosophy, and the Italian language in its high school- and college-level curricula. A half dozen priest/teachers served the residential student body, which never grew much beyond one hundred. Yet, before the seminary was phased out in the mid-1970s, the institution had trained one hundred Italian American men for the priesthood and for leadership in the Chicago Italian community and beyond. Moreover, the seminary trained a number of men who did not ultimately become priests but who, as laymen, played important leadership roles in Italian American organizations in the city.

During the early post–World War II era the Sacred Heart Seminary was without question the focal center for the Scalabrini movement and the natural place for solving the citywide problems involving Italian Americans. Concerns about the elderly within the Italian American community appeared in the immediate postwar period. One of the first to perceive to instigate a change for the elderly population was Father Pierini. In 1945 he proposed to the lay and clerical representatives of the dozen Scalabrini parishes to build an Italian Old Peoples' Home. The Scalabrini Fathers broke ground for the new retirement home in 1949 and, two years later, opened the doors to Villa Scalabrini.

There followed forty-five years of endless carnivals, banquets, stage shows, bingos, raffles, and every other imaginable method of fundraising. Today the Villa Scalabrini stands as a proud $20 million institution serving 250 residents. The process of striving to achieve this goal has in itself created a community of interest among Italians that has replaced the neighborhood-based geographic communities of the pre–World War II era. In turn, the Villa become a citadel protecting, preserving, and inventing Italian American culture and identity.

In April 1960 Father Pierini won approval from the lay Scalabrini League to support the launching of *Fra Noi*. A modest newsletter during its first few months, the paper's goal was to bring area Italian Americans together once a month and thus rekindle the spirit of cooperation and union created by a common heritage. The hundreds of monthly issues published regularly since 1960 are a rich chronicle of Italian Americana.

At first, *Fra Noi* was a public relations instrument, a house organ that urged financial contributions to the cause. The paper also filled a cultural and political mission for the ethnic group as it became the citywide medium of communication, replacing the informal neighborhood networks of earlier generations. More than anything else, *Fra Noi* held a mirror up to the Italian American community to reveal what it was, to suggest where it should be going, and to encourage Italian Americans to keep identifying with their own. *Fra Noi* became the most important ancillary activity supporting the Villa.

Together, the paper and the home for the elderly formed a focal center for the Chicago Italian American community. In the mid-1980s,

Father Pierini retired, and his work was continued by Father Lawrence Cozzi. Cozzi added an apartment complex, Casa San Carlo, to the Scalabrini holdings in west suburban Northlake and generally continued the course set out by Pierini. In the early 1990s the Chicago Archdiocese and Catholic Charities exercised their right of ownership, and management of the Villa reverted to the Catholic Charities. Although the Scalabrini Fathers, individual Italian Americans, and Italian American organizations continued to play a role in the Villa, *Fra Noi* developed an independent secular identity and the central role of the Villa in the life of the Italian American community of the Chicago area diminished sharply. Nevertheless, Father Armando Pierini has greatly influenced the social, cultural, and religious life of the Chicago Italian American community.

Dominic Candeloro

Bibliography

Candeloro, Dominic. "Chicago's Italians: A Survey of the Ethnic Factor." In *Ethnic Chicago: A Multicultural Portrait,* edited by Melvin G. Hollis and Peter D. James. Grand Rapids, MI: William B. Eerdmans, 1995.

Nelli, Humbert. *Italians in Chicago.* New York: 1970.

See also CHICAGO; CHURCH LEADERS; RELIGION

Pilla, Anthony M. (b. 1932)

Bishop and president of the National Conference of Caholic Bishops, Anthony M. Pilla has genuine roots in the Italian American subculture. Born in Cleveland, Ohio, November 12, 1932, of Italian immigrant parents George and Libera, he was baptized in Holy Rosary Parish, located in the heart of the city's Little Italy. He was raised on Cleveland's East Side, which became a multiethnic neighborhood with strong Italian ties. "The neighbors—we called them 'cousins' because we were so close—and all the families would eat together at all major occasions," he recalled.

Nourished by loving, religious parents with a simple but strong faith, he attended Cleveland's Cathedral High School, where he played various sports and followed a vocation in the priesthood. He was ordained a priest in 1959, served as a teacher for a number of years at St. Charles Borromeo Seminary, and became auxiliary bishop of Cleveland in 1979. In 1980 he was appointed ninth bishop of Cleveland.

From 1992 to 1995 Bishop Pilla served as vice-president of the National Conference of Catholic Bishops (NCCB). In 1996 he became the president of the NCCB. His flock now includes sixty-five million Catholics in the United States and 390 bishops, archbishops, and cardinals. Currently serving as NCCB president and as Cleveland's bishop, he is considered a centrist. For example, while supporting the Vatican's position on a celibate, male clergy, he does speak in favor of a significant role for women in the church. Although his national role frequently requires traveling to other cities or to Rome, he has a strong commitment to his native city and all urban centers. He has instituted an initiative called "The Church of the City," which is essentially a call to remember those of various faiths who live in the inner cities. He personally immerses himself in urban activities and can be seen playing softball in a diocesan charity game or shopping for groceries for his mother.

Salvatore J. LaGumina

Bibliography

Rich, Guerrino Thomas. "Anthony M. Pilla: President of the U.S. Bishops." *St. Anthony Messenger* (June 1997): 36–41.

See also CHURCH LEADERS; RELIGION

Pintauro, Joseph

See PLAYS, CONTEMPORARY

Pisanelli-Alessandro, Antonietta (1869–?)

Singer and stage performer Antonietta Pisanelli-Alessandro was born in Naples. Migrating to New York City, she worked with the early amateur *società filodramatiche* (lovers of the drama). On March 11, 1901, in the Francesco Ricciardi Company benefit for the murdered Mamie Mogavero, Antonietta sang Neapolitan folk songs and duets with Farfariello (Eduardo Migliaccio). She worked outside New York as an actress, singer, and dancer on the Italian American stages of Philadelphia, New Haven, and other cities, including Chicago, where she played Desdemona in 1903 with Il Club Eduardo Scarpetta at Scandia Hall. By November 20, 1904, in

Union, Illinois, she had become the proprietor of Margherita Hall, where she acted in Verga's *Cavalleria Rusticana.*

With the deaths of her mother, her husband, and youngest child, Antonietta and her young son sought a new life in California. By the spring of 1905 she began performing in theater productions at Apollo Hall on Pacific Street in San Francisco. Then she turned Berglieri Hall at Stockton and Union Streets into a *caffe concerto,* which she ran as actress, director, producer, dancer, and singer, and which she called the Circolo Famigliare Pisanelli, San Francisco's first professional Italian American theater. It served as a place for socializing and entertaining and became integral to the Italian community of North Beach.

She brought in companies from the East—Pasquale Rapone, Francesco de Cesare, Antonio Maori, and Eduardo Migliaccio—to perform in other theaters she later ran in San Francisco: the Iris, the Beach, the Bijou, the Washington Square, the Liberty, the Teatro Alessandro Eden. She also toured with her company, billed as "Survivors of the San Francisco Earthquake." With a second husband and a new name, Signora Alessandro continued to produce even as the theater declined due to the Americanization of its audience. She then delved into Mexican and even Chinese theater before retiring from theatrical production by 1925.

Emelise Aleandri

Bibliography

Aleandri, Emelise. *The History of Italian-American Theatre in New York City: 1900–1905.* Ph.D. diss., City University of New York, 1983.
———. "Women in the Italian-American Theatre of the Nineteenth Century." In *The Italian Immigrant Woman in North America,* edited by Betty Boyd Caroli, Robert F. Harney, and Lydio F. Tomasi, 358–368. New York: American Italian Historical Association, 1978.
Estavan, Lawrence, ed. *The Italian Theatre in San Francisco.* First Series, Vol. 10. San Francisco: WPA, 1939.
Seller, Maxine Schwartz, ed. *Ethnic Theatre in the United States.* Westport, CT: Greenwood, 1983.

See also THEATER HISTORY

Piston Jr., Walter (Hamor) (1894–1976)

American composer and Harvard professor Walter Piston Jr. was twice the recipient of the Pulitzer Prize for music. He was born in Rockland, Maine, on January 20, 1894, and died in Belmont, Massachusetts, on November 12, 1976. The son of Walter Hamor and Leona (Stover) Piston, his paternal grandfather was Antonio Pistone (the family name was later Anglicized by dropping the *e*), who had migrated to this country from Genoa. When Walter was 11 years old, his family moved from Rockland to the Boston area, where he continued his education. Graduating from the Massachusetts Normal Art School in 1916, he served with the United States Navy Band in the First World War before his marriage to Kathryn Nason on September 14, 1920. Then, having studied music at Harvard and gaining membership in Phi Beta Kappa, he graduated summa cum laude in 1924. As recipient of the John Knowles Paine Fellowship, Piston went to Paris and continued his musical education with Nadia Boulanger for the next two years.

Returning to the United States in 1926, Piston joined the Harvard music faculty, where he taught for the next thirty-four years and became a very productive composer. In his younger years, he had demonstrated his versatility when he made a living by playing the violin and piano in the cafes and dance halls of metropolitan Boston. When Piston was a professor, Serge Koussevitzky, the famous conductor of the Boston Symphony Orchestra, persuaded him to blend his teaching with his composing. Piston accepted this advice, and a number of his compositions were premiered by the Boston Symphony Orchestra.

Working more in a traditional than in a revisionist style, Piston was very much interested in the manipulation of musical ideas and demonstrated an exceptional flexibility in the variety of his musical compositions. Appointed Walter W. Naumburg Professor of Music in 1948, he won the Pulitzer Prize in music for his composition Symphony No. 3, in 1948, and for his Symphony No. 7, in 1961. He composed eight symphonies during his career; his other works included *The Incredible Flutist* (1938), a ballet; *Psalm and Prayer of David* (1958), a choral work; *Three New England Sketches* (1959), an orchestral suite; the *Lincoln Center Festival* Overture (1962), a hybrid piece; and *Ricercare* (1967), a symphonic composition. Also, his four textbooks on musical theory have become standards for musical study: *Principles of Harmonic Analysis* (1933), *Harmony* (1941), *Counterpoint* (1947), and *Orchestration* (1955). Both his manuscripts and published pieces can be found at Harvard University.

That the Boston Symphony, on its ninetieth birthday, named and endowed a chair in its orchestra for the Walter Piston Principal Flute indicates how highly this Italian American, who had won the praise of Aaron Copland and had influenced Leonard Bernstein, was regarded as a force in the history of American music. Piston's achievements, including his position as a professor emeritus (1960–1976), were a tribute to his heritage as an Italian American. After his death, his ashes were scattered in the historic Mt. Auburn Cemetery in Cambridge, Massachusetts, where the remains of many other icons rest.

Vincent A. Lapomarda

Bibliography

Piston, Walter. *Counterpoint*. New York: Norton, 1947.
———. *Harmony*. Rev. by Mark Devoto. New York: Norton, 1978.
———. *Orchestration*. New York: Norton, 1955.
Pollack, Howard. *Harvard Composers: Walter Piston and His Students from Elliot Carter to Frederic Rzewski*. Metuchen, NJ: Scarecrow, 1992.

See also COMPOSERS, CLASSICAL

Pitino, Richard A. (b. 1952)

Though a successful basketball coach like other Italian Americans (Jim Valvano, Rollie Massimino, Lou Carnesecca, P. J. Carlesimo, and John Calipari), "Rick" Pitino has a unique talent for turning losers into winners.

Richard Andrew Pitino was born of Italian lineage in New York City, September 18, 1952. After growing up in his native city, he went to St. Dominic's High School in Oyster Bay, Long Island, where be became a basketball star under coach Pat McGunnigle. Rising to captain of the basketball team at the University of Massachusetts from which he graduated in 1974, he served as an assistant coach at the University of Hawaii from 1975 to 1976 and at Syracuse University from 1976 to 1978. In the spring of 1976, he married Joanne Minardi, who is the mother of his five children and cofounder with him in 1990 of the Daniel Pitino Foundation in memory of a son who died in infancy in 1987.

Pitino became head coach at Boston University from 1978 to 1983, assistant coach for the New York Knicks from 1983 to 1985, and head coach at Providence College from 1985 to 1987. In these college and professional jobs, Pitino demonstrated his trademark of turning poor teams into winning ones by bringing them into championship competition. Consequently, having achieved greater visibility in coaching college basketball, *Sporting News* named him the "College Coach of the Year" in 1987.

With that background, Pitino was called upon to be head coach of the New York Knicks from 1987 to 1989 and head coach of the Wildcats at the University of Kentucky in Lexington from 1989 to 1997. Again, in these positions, his effectiveness in basketball was evident in bringing the Knicks to the championship of the Atlantic Division in 1989 and the Wildcats to the national championship in 1996.

Having demonstrated repeatedly how he could achieve successful turnarounds under pressure, Pitino stunned the basketball world in May 1997 when he took over the leadership of the Boston Celtics as its coach and president. Coincidentally, at that time, the visibility of Italian Americans was more evident than ever in Boston's history because the mayor (Thomas M. Menino), the lieutenant governor (Paul Cellucci), the state treasurer (Joseph D. Malone), and the state auditor (Joseph DeNucci) were all of Italian heritage.

Vincent A. Lapomarda

Bibliography

Cameron, Chris. *Basketball Pitino Style*. Lexington: Host Communications, 1990.
Pitino, Rick. *Born to Coach: A Season with the New York Knicks*. New York: New American Library, 1988.
Pitino, Rick, with Dick Weiss. *Full-Court Pressure: A Year in Kentucky Basketball*. New York: Hyperion, 1992.

See also SPORTS

Pittsburgh

For more than a century, the Pittsburgh, Pennsylvania, region has been a popular destination for Italian immigrants, who initially came here to find work in the area's expanding industry and later came to join already established family and *paesani* (fellow townspeople). Italians began settling in Pittsburgh in the 1870s, numbering only several hundred. This early community lived in downtown Pittsburgh, along Grant Street and Virgin Alley (today Oliver Avenue), where they found work as laborers in construction, steel mills, and railroads, and also entered into service occupations as grocers, restaurateurs, tailors, barbers, shoe repairmen, and confectioners.

By 1900 Pittsburgh's Italians numbered more than six thousand, with Little Italys thriving in various parts of the city. These included the Lower Hill district, which bordered the downtown and served much of the city's recent immigrant population; East Liberty, a neighborhood in Pittsburgh's east end originally settled by Germans and Pittsburgh's most popular Little Italy by the mid-century, especially around Larimer Avenue, where Italian-owned businesses predominated; Bloomfield, a densely populated neighborhood where many Italians from the region of Abruzzo settled; Oakland, whose Italian community—also

mainly from the Abruzzo region—settled in a small ravine called Panther Hollow; and the Manchester section of Pittsburgh's north side, where many Sicilians located. Other strong Italian communities outside Pittsburgh included McKees Rocks, Mount Washington, Sewickley, Coraopolis, Aliquippa, Braddock, McKeesport, Clairton, Donora, Monesson, and Vandergrift. Many Italians from these communities worked as laborers in the local steel mills.

Of particular note were the Little Italys of Pittsburgh's Lower Hill district and East Liberty. The intellectual, political, and financial life of Pittsburgh's early-twentieth-century Italian community was centered in the crowded Lower Hill district around Webster Avenue. Located here were the offices of Italian attorneys and physicians, the Italian language newspaper *La Trinacria,* and the city's Italian banks and steamship ticket agencies. East Liberty's Italians built the first Italian Catholic church in the city, Our Lady Help of Christians, in 1898. The interior of the Italianate structure was graced with frescos painted by the local Italian artist Pietro Simboli. East Liberty, settled mostly by Italians from the regions of Calabria and Naples, gained a reputation as the mecca of Italian artisans, a place where stonecutters, marble

A picnic of World War I veterans of the Italian Army at Vandergrift Park in western Pennsylvania, August 9, 1931. Courtesy Joseph D'Andrea.

setters, cabinet makers, gardeners, road builders, interior decorators, and skilled workers of all kinds chose to settle.

Italians were the largest immigrant group to Pittsburgh in 1930, numbering over eighteen thousand. By this time, they had become prominent in the building trades, Pittsburgh's produce industry, and in the start-up of small businesses. Italian immigration to Pittsburgh continued into the post–World War II era, but the city's original Little Italys did not thrive. Urban redevelopment destroyed the Italian communities of the Lower Hill district and East Liberty, as did the lure of the suburbs. Many Italian Americans relocated to the Pittsburgh suburbs of South Hills and East Hills.

Today there are about 150,000 Italian Americans living in the greater Pittsburgh metropolitan area, making them the second most populous ethnic group in the region, behind those of German descent. Pittsburgh's Strip district, the site of many of the city's produce warehouses, is lined with Italian food stores, bakeries, and coffee shops, while the old neighborhood of Bloomfield, just east of the Strip and still largely intact, is home to many Italians and Italian-owned food stores and businesses. Visitors to Pittsburgh today will find the contributions and presence of Italian Americans evident practically everywhere.

Catherine Cerrone

Bibliography

Bodnar, John, Roger Simon, and Michael P. Weber. *Lives of Their Own: Blacks, Italians, and Poles in Pittsburgh, 1900–1960.* Urbana: University of Illinois Press, 1983.

Faires, Nora. "Immigrants in Industry." In *City at the Point: Essays on the Social History of Pittsburgh,* edited by Samuel P. Hays, 3–32. Pittsburgh: University of Pittsburgh Press, 1989.

Plays, Contemporary

Some dramatists of Italian descent, in search of patrons and audience and eager for American opportunities, skirted "ethnic" subject matter. Others understood their Italian heritage as a significant contribution to mainstream America. The cultural revolution of the 1960s legitimized the assertion of roots. The Forum, an Italian American playwrights' organization established in 1976, helped resurrect Italian American theater from its eclipse during and after World War II. Noted postwar American dramatists without Italian ancestry also dealt with Italian American and Italian themes or characters. As theater became increasingly international, plays by Italian Americans toured abroad. Italians or binationals who performed on and brought plays to the American stage influenced subject matter and formal innovation.

Leonard Melfi (b. 1935), raised in Binghamton, New York, studied acting before serving in the United States Army. Back from Europe, supporting himself with odd jobs, and pawning his belongings, he wrote plays that were produced Off-Off-Broadway. From the 1950s on, new groups in low-rent buildings offered short innovative new plays, as well as classics, to smaller audiences than Broadway's economy required. Hospitable to Melfi were Ellen Stewart's La Mama Experimental Theatre Club, Theatre Genesis at St. Mark's Church, Playwrights Unit, Actors Studio, and Circle in the Square. His first professionally produced play, *Lazy Baby Susan,* was a smash hit, "all thirty minutes of it," as he wrote, to an audience of about forty. *Coffeecake and Caviar* and *Sunglasses* went over well and became *Birdbath,* which ran for three weeks in 1965 and still enjoys revivals. *The Shirt,* given a staged reading at the Eugene O'Neill Memorial Theatre Foundation in Connecticut in 1966, won Melfi a residency there. In his introduction to *Encounters: Six One-Act Plays,* which included (along with *Birdbath*) *Ferryboat, Lunchtime, Halloween, The Shirt,* and *Times Square,* he wrote that American theater's most important development was taking place in the cellars and lofts of New York City. International recognition followed when *Birdbath* opened simultaneously on June 1, 1967, at La Mama (New York), in Argentina, and in Germany. *Times Square* toured Europe as well as the Frankfurt and Edinburgh festivals; that same summer in 1967, two plays were presented in Spoleto. All six plays are first encounters between two or more characters. Their mode is terror, pity, and laughter. Produced on Broadway in 1968, *Morning, Noon and Night* linked Israel Horovitz's *Morning,* Terrence McNally's *Noon,* and Melfi's *Night,* which is about four individuals who meet to honor the memory of a friend and a fifth mourner who has come to bury his dog. *Porno Stars at Home* ran at the Courtyard Playhouse from November 1978 through January 1979. *Fantasies at the Frick, or The Guard and the Guardess* and *Later Encounters: Seven One-Act Plays* were published in 1980. In another triple bill, Horovitz's *Faith* was linked with McNally's *Hope* and Melfi's *Charity* in a 1988 production in New York.

Joseph Pintauro (b. 1930) published seven volumes of poetry between 1968 and 1973. In his novels *Cold Hands* (1979), singled out by the *New York Times Book Review* as one of the year's best, about intense love between two male cousins, and *State of Grace* (1983), about a Jesuit student in Rome, his protagonists decide to leave the priesthood. Pintauro left the Roman Catholic priesthood after eight years of service. Pintauro's contribution to drama includes the collection of one acts *Plays by Joe Pintauro*. Pithy, apparently starting in the middle of the third act, hence demanding close attention, the short plays were performed seven or eight per evening by New York's Circle Lab in 1987 as *Rapid Fire*. Twelve of them made up four programs for Second Story Theatre's Short Attention Span Workshop in Providence, Rhode Island, in June of 1992. In *Two Eclairs* a happy young wife comes home with briefcase and groceries, after a day of selling real estate, to her self-absorbed husband, a sculptor; bit by bit she uncovers the double betrayal of his affair with her sister. In *Uncle Chick* a gay man declares his love on the night he learns his uncle is also gay. A priest in *Rules of Love* hears the confession of a woman who has been his lover. The curmudgeonly old aunt of *Lenten Pudding* balks at meeting her large family's expectations.

More explicit Italian American content is found in the earlier *Cacciatore* (1981), set on Shelter Island, in which a husband and wife are at odds about their priorities. He has kept her in frantic poverty while hoarding to buy the house where they could "get away from it all," pretending it is his gift to her, while she worries about their son's future and her severed relationships. She cooks chicken cacciatore because "it means home, wherever I smell that smell," but with the stripping away of pretenses maintained through thirty years of marriage, home becomes a new kind of prison. An Italian American chauffeur with a Jewish actress girlfriend generate the action of *Seymour in the Very Heart of Winter.*

Full-length, *Snow Orchid* also deals with Italian American subject matter. Presented at the Eugene O'Neill Playwrights Conference in 1980, it won Pintauro a residency and was staged in New York in 1981 with Olympia Dukakis, Peter Boyle, and Robert Lupone; it has also been staged in London. *Wild Blue* appeared in New York, 1987; in Washington, 1994. In nine sketches presented at the Vineyard Theater as *Moving Targets,* characters come to terms with strained relationships.

In *Beside Herself,* commended by the *New Yorker* as "a real uplifter" in its 1989 Circle Rep staging, a lonely older woman, hungering for sex and self-definition, is given a chance at happiness when a virile young man enters her life. *Raft of the Medusa,* staged as an AIDS group-therapy session, was done Off-Broadway, 1991; in Washington, 1994. An adaptation of Peter Matthiessen's book *Men's Lives,* about the proud history and threatened livelihood of commercial fishermen, premiered at Sag Harbor's Bay Street Theater in 1992. For the same theater, two years later, Pintauro, Lanford Wilson, and Terrence McNally each contributed a one-acter to the trilogy *By the Sea, By the Sea, By the Beautiful Sea.*

Actress-playwright Julie Bovasso (1930–1991), considered the first to introduce the theater of the absurd into America, describes her Italian Albanian American background, Bensonhurst childhood, and subsequent career in a chapter of Linda Brandi Cateura's *Growing Up Italian.* She founded the experimental Tempo Playhouse in New York and also claimed "the distinction of being the first ethnic heroine on a television soap opera." The soap was the series *From These Roots,* which ran in the 1950s. She tried to introduce Italian plays in translation. Ugo Betti's five plays came to the States in the 1950s but were not well received. When she produced his *Island of Goats* and *The Queen and the Rebels,* "out in Middle America," they succeeded. She first took up an Italian American theme in *Angelo's Wedding.* Her other plays include *Gloria and Esperanza* (1969); *The Moon Dreamers* (1969), in which husband, wife, and lover try to decide who should leave the apartment and receive "help" from, among others, the mother-in-law, a French midget, and an Indian chief who is a Japanese Buddhist; *Schubert's Last Serenade* (1972); and *Standard Safety* (1976). Her film acting credits include *Willie and Phil* (1980), *The Verdict* (1982), *Moonstruck* (1987), and *Betsy's Wedding* (1990).

Lewis John Carlino (b. 1932), a native New Yorker, studied drama in California. *The Brick and the Rose* and *Used Car for Sale* were produced by the Los Angeles chapter of ANTA and published in 1959. Carlino wrote and analyzed scripts for West Coast television studios. Through the 1960s he dealt mainly with humble and marginal characters. *Snowangel* and *Epiphany*, combined as *Cages* and produced in 1963, are man/woman encounters, the former about an intellectual prostitute, the latter about a homosexual ornithologist. Other plays include *Doubletalk, The Exercise, Junk Yard, Mr. Flannery's Ocean, Objective Case, High Sign,* and *Sarah and the Sax. Telemachus Clay,* the story of a journey and of a boy's life and tragic death, is dedicated in Italian: *per Aldo, per tutte le cose della nostra [sic] amicicia che non hanno parole"* ("for Aldo, for all the things of our friendship that don't have words"). Its experimental technique, "vocal collage," presents actors seated on stools taking multiple roles. They face the audience only and speak in counterpoint, directed by a narrator. Carlino's plays have been performed internationally.

Frank Gagliano's plays were reviewed and published mainly during the 1960s and 1970s: *The City Scene,* which includes *Paradise Gardens East* and *Conerico Was Here to Stay* (1965), about struggle in a polluted, violent, desperate city; *Night of the Dunce* (1967); *Father Uxbridge Wants to Marry* (1968); and *Big Sur* (1971). *The Hide-and-Seek Odyssey of Madeline Gimple* (1970) is a play for children.

Don DeLillo (b. 1936), Bronx-born son of Italian immigrants, noted as a novelist, opened his first play at American Repertory Theater's New Stages in Cambridge. *The Day Room* (1986) takes place in a hospital ward that also functions as motel room and psychiatric clinic; in the second half, a character in a straitjacket speaks as a television set. Through terror and laughter *The Day Room* explores denial of basic fears.

Rome-born award-winning poet and playwright Anne Paolucci (b. 1926) attended public schools in New York City, Barnard College, and Columbia University. She is longtime president of the Pirandello Society of America, editor of its annual journal, and author of *Pirandello's Theater* (1974). Her one-act *Minions of the Race* was published in 1978. In 1986 she introduced historical programs, cultural events, and publications about the early history of America; three years later, the video recording "Columbus: Countdown 1992" won her Canada's first Gold Medal for the Quincentenary. *Cipango!* is a one-act play in three scenes about Christopher Columbus; she also published a collection of essays, *Columbus: Modern Views of Columbus and His Times* (1990).

Albert Innaurato (b. 1948) was born into a working-class Italian Catholic family in South Philadelphia. A sensitive and precocious child, he composed opera libretti by age 8. His play *Urlicht,* conceived in his late teens, went into print before he turned 21. At Yale School of Drama, he and classmate Christopher Durang collaborated on the 1972 *I Don't Generally Like Poetry, But Have You Read "Trees"?* and the 1974 *The Idiots Karamazov.* He called his early *Wisdom Amok* "frankly crazy"; it offers a generous sample of Innaurato's anticlericalism and gender amorphousness.

Innaurato made his real debut with *The Transfiguration of Benno Blimpie,* based on a nightmare he had that recalled the brutality of parochial school. Written at Yale, it was finished the summer of 1972 in Edward Albee's house for writers, and it extends Albee's own critical perspective on American obsessions, deprivations, and intolerances. The title character loves Renaissance paintings and teaches himself to paint; but he is physically gross, called "pig" and "fat creep" by his own mother. Besides him, his disappointed mother supports a gambler husband and the grandfather she calls a "disgraziato freak." Benno suffers, as the others too suffer, acutely and alone. In America, his ancestral culture, unreinforced, disdained, has dwindled to a few curse words. The grandfather cries, "Aiuto, aiuto." But no one helps. Benno eats himself to death.

Innaurato's first Broadway hit was *Gemini* (1977), begun with support from a Guggenheim grant, a Rockefeller grant, and a series of "mostly humiliating" temporary jobs. It ran for more than four years on Broadway with 1,788 continuous performances. Here an Italian working-class youth facing his twenty-first birthday receives an unannounced visit from two WASP friends from Harvard. Judith speaks "Harvard Italian" that Fran can't understand—for, as he says, "[m]y people over there was the niggers. . . . We're Abbruzzese; so we speak a kinda nigger Italian." In *Gemini,* Innaurato accosts an establishment that was not accepting his plays; and he shows loyalty to his family, the first to support him as an artist. Some critics labeled *Passione* (1981), which followed, a redundant version of *Gemini.*

Coming of Age in Soho (1985) plays with sexual ambiguity, perversity, and permutations of family structure. It jokes about difficulties of maturation in America and about the Mafia. While containing a contrived plot and burlesque tone, it offers serious culture criticism.

Gus and *Al* portray the playwright himself, yanked back to Gustav Mahler's house on the Ringstrasse in Vienna, where he meets and makes a pass at the tutor of Sigmund Freud's children, who, it turns out, will become Al's grandfather. This play, as it splits chronology, investigates both ethnic and sexual aspects of identity. In frolicsome mode it offers reconciliation: Old World culture revitalized by American talent. Produced in Denver, 1987, it ran for twenty-five performances with Playwrights Horizons in 1989 and was ranked by editors of *Burns Mantle Theater Yearbook* among the best plays of 1988–1989.

The Forum staged more than forty Italian American plays, supplemented by dramatic readings, for an ever widening audience. It fostered the talents of Melfi, Louis La Russo, Mario Fratti, and Ted Pezzulo, among others. La Russo has written *Wheelbarrow Closers* (1974); *Lamppost Reunion* (1976); *Mama's Little Angels* (1979), which is about the destruction of a close-knit family, and in a successful run at the Quaig Theater featured Mimi Cecchini, president of the Italian Actors' Union, as Aunt Tillie; *Marlon Brando Sat Right Here* (1980); and *Knockout* (1980). Mel Arrighi (1933–1986) left a number of performed and published plays including *An Ordinary Man* (1969) and *The Castro Complex* (1971). George Panetta is author of *Comic Strip* (1958) and *Kiss Mama* (1965). In *An Evening for Merlin Finch,* produced at Lincoln Center in 1968, Charles Dizenzo showed how insensitive and narrow-minded parents destroy their children; his *A Great Career* of the same year shows a clerical worker trapped in her office life. Henry Salerno (b. 1919) in his *Duck Soup Revisited* showed corruption and hypocrisy reflected in a college bureaucracy.

From Left Field, John Amato's musical collaboration with Joan Harvey, was done by the Fourth Wall Political Theater on East Fourth Street during their 1985–1986 season. Anticolonial and antiracist, it calls attention also to threatened civil rights at home.

Performer and scholar Emelise Aleandri, who has published on popular Italian immigrant theater and its backgrounds, in 1987 directed *The Dream Book Revue,* an adaptation from Helen Barolini's *The Dream Book: An Anthology of Writings by Italian American Women.* Comic and poignant vignettes showed the Italian cultural legacy transformed in surprising ways to meet new expectations and opportunities. Sponsored by the Italian American Institute of the City University of New York and the National Organization of Italian American Women, the show featured Olga Barbato. Aleandri has also directed bilingual productions in connection with her college teaching.

The New York Italian Theater Company still performs bilingually; a 1994 production at the Duality was Gene Ruffini's *Holidays,* whose short vignettes dealt in a range of moods with American holidays. Ruffini's *Angelus,* illustrating the immigrant experience, had a staged reading in New York in 1988. With assimilation, the number of Italian language productions has decreased, as has membership in the sixty-year-old Italian Actors' Union; but the union maintains jurisdiction over Italian language shows and receives referral requests from the entertainment industry for Italian speakers and singers. It is compiling a picture directory of Italian American actors.

Mario Fratti (b. 1927), Italian but a decades-long resident of New York, reviews touring Italian plays; in 1995, he extolled Eduardo DeFilippo's comedy *Napoli Milionara* at the Cocteau and Dario Fò's farce *Non Si paga! Non Si paga!* at the Duality, both of which show that women are braver and more revolutionary than their husbands. He also discussed Italian American Don Nigri's *Lucia Mad,* at the Curracao, which shows James Joyce as a genius who ignores his daughter; she, frail and sensitive, falls in love with Samuel Beckett, is rejected, and ends in a lunatic asylum, where Jung explains her madness to Joyce with lucidity and pathos.

Fratti's own plays are produced internationally. *In the Cage* had its first staging in

Milan as *La Gabbia,* 1963; in New York it debuted in 1966, and in 1970 ran for 126 performances at the Play House. *The Victim* opened in Sacramento, 1968; New York, 1973; also in the Netherlands, Brazil, Germany, Austria, and Spain. Society and family are sharply scrutinized in these and other plays like *The Academy, Refrigerators, The Suicide, The Third Daughter,* and *The Chinese Friend.* In *The Bridge* (1972) his protagonist is a young Puerto Rican. *Mario Fratti's Che Guevara* was first printed in 1970 in the monthly theater magazine *ENACT* in Delhi, India. Six short plays were collected as *Races* in 1972. *Three Plays* (1983) includes *Three Beds, Mothers and Daughters,* and *The Young Wife. Lovers* was staged at Alice's Fourth Floor, New York, 1992. Fratti's language is direct; his characters are often ruthless and immoral, as he tries to enhance audience awareness, criticizing both American and Italian society. Fratti also adapted Fellini's *8½* from the Italian, as *Nine: the Musical,* with book by Arthur Kopit, music and lyrics by Maury Yeston (1983). He wrote both book and lyrics for *Encounter 500: Cristoforo Colombo (or, How the Italians, Jews, Muslims, Portuguese and Spaniards encountered the Indians 500 Years Ago).*

In connection with the Columbus theme, mention should be made of Dario Fo (b. 1926), who was awarded the Nobel Prize for literature in 1997. In his *Johan Padan and the Discovery of the Americas* (1992), a shipwrecked Italian sailor tries to help the Native Americans subvert Christianity into a means of self-defense. In Italy, as a tour de force, Fo performed all the roles himself, portraying a number of Europeans speaking various languages, Native Americans, horses, and a rooster. For years barred from the United States because of his leftist politics, in 1984 he was allowed to attend the New York premiere of *Accidental Death of an Anarchist;* but it took longer before he could himself stand on an American stage. During the past decade, thanks to a successful campaign by the American Civil Liberties Union and others, he has performed here solo and also with his wife and collaborator of over forty years, Franca Rame. During a two-month springtime 1986 tour of the East Coast, he enacted fifteen characters in *Mistero Buffo* (Comic Mystery), including a jaded ticket teller at the raising of Lazarus from the dead. Fo spoke in Gram-

melot, his term for the onomatopoetic language used by fifteenth-century players that mimics other tongues. His kind of popular theater draws on commedia dell'arte and involves direct address to audiences through prologues, intentional narrative interruptions, and quick responses to spontaneous situations onstage or elsewhere in the theater.

English-language translations staged in major American cities make Fo's plays Italian American. Thus *Non Si paga! Non Si paga!* of 1974 (*Can't Pay? Won't Pay!* or *We Won't Pay*), was performed on tour by the San Francisco Mime Troupe and by other "alternative" groups; in February 1993, performed by Alias Stage in Providence, the altered script included well-received references to the Italian American community on Federal Hill. In this popular farce, housewives irked by rising food prices rebel by stealing whatever can be grabbed; they cope with deceiving their husbands too. An anarchist policeman opines that "expropriation is the only defense against robbery." Other plays by Fo include *Accidental Death of an Anarchist, Fo's Fables, Archangels Don't Play Pinball,* the one-acts *Eve's Diary* and *The Story of the Tiger, The Pope and the Witch,* and, with Franca Rame, *Female Parts* and *Orgasmo Adulto Escapes from the Zoo.*

Italian novelist and poet Dacia Maraini (b. 1936) became involved in theater during the 1960s and in 1969 founded the Theater of Centocelle. Activist and populist, it presented theatrical works in Rome's working-class neighborhoods. In 1973 she founded the feminist theatrical association La Maddelena. She brought her play *The Dreams of Clytemnestra* (*I sogni di Clitennestra e altre commedie,* 1981) to New York and California; the 1989 production received mixed reviews.

Italian immigrant laborers on New York City's piers are represented in Arthur Miller's Pulitzer Prize–winning *A View from the Bridge.* Longshoreman Eddie Carbone's incestuous feelings for his niece, Catherine, whom he has raised as a daughter, impel him to betray his illegal immigrant relatives to the authorities in order to get rid of the young man Catherine wishes to marry. His wife intuits the unacknowledged love and stands by helplessly as circumstances gradually force Carbone to a tragic denouement. Often revived in the United States, the play has also been performed abroad. Sidney Lumet made the 1962 film version.

In his autobiography, *Timebends,* Miller (b. 1915) explains the genesis of this play from his interest in how terror reigned in "the sinister waterfront world of gangster-ridden unions, assassinations, beatings, bodies thrown into the lovely bay at night." Peter Panto, who tried to lead a rank-and-file revolt against the corrupt International Longshoremen's Association, was lured from his home and never seen again. Men on the piers, most of Italian descent, were afraid to talk. The hiring system on the Manhattan and Brooklyn waterfront had been imported from the Sicilian countryside, with the arrogant hiring boss replacing the foreman. Vincent James Longhi, a new member of the bar, and his friend Mitch Berenson, who wanted to carry on Pete Panto's work, braved the opposition of the Mafia, which then flourished in the anti-left fever of the late 1940s. They spoke with Miller and provided entry to a world never touched by literature or given stage representation. Longhi mentioned a story of a "longshoreman who had ratted to the immigration bureau on two brothers, his own relatives, who were living illegally in his very home, in order to break an engagement between one of them and his niece." Miller's interest was also reinforced by memories of Carlo Levi's *Christ Stopped at Eboli,* and, after his waterfront wanderings, by a trip to southern Italy and Sicily.

Tennessee Williams (1911–1983) deals with Italian sojourns in his *Memoirs.* In *The Rose Tattoo,* set in a village on the Gulf of Mexico, Sicilian American Serafina della Rosa, a passionate and devout widow, lives with her nubile daughter and an idealized memory of her late husband, a truck driver. For all her defenses and denials, she is forced to recognize facts about his many infidelities. The truth threatens to destroy her, until another truck driver, Alvaro Mangiacavallo, enters her life. Happy again, she affords support for her daughter's delicate romance with a young sailor. The three-act play opened at the Martin Beck in New York in 1951 and ran for 306 performances; Maureen Stapleton played Rosa and Eli Wallach played Alvaro. Williams wrote the play with Anna Magnani in mind; though she declined to play it on stage, she starred in the 1955 film version opposite Burt Lancaster.

In documentary mode, a recent drama connecting Italy and America is the powerful and gripping *Incommunicado,* by Tom Dulack (b. 1935), author of *Breaking Legs, Diminished Capacity,* and *Near the End of the Century.* It centers on Ezra Pound's experiences in a Pisa prison after World War II, where the noted American poet, translator, and literary theorist was incarcerated for his anti-American, anti-Semitic Italian radio broadcasts. It has been produced in Chicago, Washington, and New York.

John Patrick Shanley (b. 1950) directed his comedy about love, loneliness, and the battle of the sexes *Italian American Reconciliation* at the Manhattan Theatre Club in November 1988. John Simon liked it; his review was captioned "Puccini without Music." Other productions followed.

Among musicals with Italian American content, best known is *Most Happy Fella,* based on Sidney Howard's 1924 *They Knew What They Wanted,* both book and songs by Frank Loesser (1910–1969). Sometimes called an operetta, *Most Happy Fella* opened at the Imperial on May 3, 1956, and ran for 676 performances. Set in California's Napa Valley, the comedy has Rosabella arriving to marry a handsome young man who has sent his picture by mail with a proposal. Convinced that she has found love, she learns that she has been deceived: the young man in the picture is only a foreman named Joe, and the real would-be groom is Tony, an aging Italian vintner. He thinks he can win her over and become "The Most Happy Fella," but shock drives her into Joe's arms. Eventually, though, she recognizes Tony's virtues. When he offers to accept her and the baby she now carries, she comes to love him. Despite some reviews demurring that musical comedy had not been successfully merged with opera, the production succeeded. Hit songs were separately performed; revivals in the 1990s were praised.

A recent Broadway musical by Stephen Sondheim drew on unlikely Italian sources. *Passion* is based on director Ettore Scola's 1981 film *Passione d'Amore,* which is derived from an epistolary novel of 1869, Igino U. Turchetti's *Fosca.* Accordingly, it deals with a handsome young army officer involved in a torrid affair with a beautiful married woman. Transferred to a bleak outpost, he is asked to be kind to a sickly woman tormented by her own ugliness. Smitten, she inveigles him until he abandons his mistress. The love letter Fosca entreats the captain to write to her, in Sondheim's song version, is the show's centerpiece.

Theater moved offstage with the long-running 1989 Off-Broadway surprise hit *Tony* 'n Tina's Wedding. It reenacts a working-class Italian ritual in what is part scripted comedy, part improvisation, and part audience participation; the wedding dinner is served to the audience as well, six times a week. First performed at Washington Square Church in New York's Greenwich Village, in late 1992 it starred Lee Mazzilli, a former major league baseball player who turned actor for the role. It was staged that same year at Los Angeles' Park Plaza Hotel, in 1990 at Baltimore's Fells Point Cafe, in 1992 at the First Congregational Church of San Francisco, at Piper's Alley in Chicago in 1993, and at Starcastle Diner Theatre in Gretna, Louisiana, in 1994. Dissolving boundaries between actors and audience, between production and consumption, between life and art, such a play cannot be mass-oriented and hence reinforces a sense of community.

Blossom S. Kirschenbaum

Bibliography

Aleandri, Emelise, and Maxine Schwartz Seller. "Italian American Theater." In *Ethnic Theater in the United States,* edited by Maxine Schwartz Seller, 237–276. Westport, CT: Greenwood, 1983.

Ambrosetti, Ronald. "'Next Door to the Earthly Paradise': Mythic Patterns in Italian-American Drama." *Journal of Popular Culture* 19, no. 3 (winter 1985): 109–118.

DiGaetani, John Louis. "An Interview with Albert Innaurato." In *Studies in American Drama 1945–Present.* State College, PA: Penn State University Press, 1987, 87–95.

DiScipio, Giuseppe Carlo. "Italian-American Playwrights on the Rise." *Journal of Popular Culture* 19, no. 3 (winter 1985): 103–108.

Fratti, Mario. *Four by Fratti.* New York: Samuel French, 1986.

Innaurato, Albert. *Best Plays of Albert Innaurato.* New York: Gay Presses of New York, 1987.

Kirschenbaum, Blossom S. "Albert Innaurato's Plays: Bizarre Behavior in Bizarre America." *Voices in Italian Americana* (spring 1994): 85–98.

———. "Playwright Joe Pintauro: Keeping Faith, Moving On." *Voices in Italian Americana* (fall 1998): 28–50.

Lombardi, John. "Playwrights on the Horizon." *New York Times Magazine* (July 1983): 22–31.

Pintauro, Joseph. *Plays by Joe Pintauro.* New York: Broadway Play, 1989. (Expanded as *Metropolitan Operas: 27 Short Plays.* New York: Dramatists' Play Service, 1997.)

Salerno, Henry, and Ronald Ambrosetti. "Ethnic Theatre: Introduction." *Popular Culture* 19, no. 3 (winter 1985): 91–93.

"'Scrittura femminile': Writing the Female in the Plays of Dacia Maraini." *Theatre Journal* 42 (October 1990): 332–349.

See also FRATTI, MARIO; PAOLUCCI, ANNE ATTURA; THEATER HISTORY

Poetry

Italian American poetry as a category of American literature is only as valid as the dominant culture will allow it to be. Such a seemingly facile statement calls to the fore an array of debatable issues that relate to the discussion of any ethnic category vis-à-vis the larger, mainstream group. Given the sociological changes of the past thirty years, where the notion of the melting pot has been supplanted by a more particularizing notion of smaller distinct groups comprising the whole, one runs the risk of engaging in a type of monolithic or myopic reductionism in claiming that all subgroups eventually transform into something more generic that resembles the mainstream. Second, a question of hermeneutics comes to the fore. Namely, according to whom and which standards do we validate or invalidate a category such as Italian American poetry? Any response is tied to the question of familiarity—who knows what about which poets, and so on. Third, and more significant, in the late-twentieth-century culture of poststructuralism, postdeconstruction, postfeminism, and the like, one now accepts the basic tenet that context is an essential component of one's epistemological or ideological makeup.

Another significant sociological phenomenon to consider is the bipolar notion of the Old and New World. It may be argued that there has been a fundamental change in this couplet of the old vs. the new, a notion of bipolarity that has now transformed itself into the tripolar. Whereas the immigrants and their children contemplated their fate in terms of Italy vs. the United States, today the members of third, fourth, and fifth generations have a third cultural component with which they interact—Italian America. What emerges from such a shift, to paraphrase M. M. J. Fischer, is not simply that parallel processes operate across Italian and American identities; rather, ethnic identities constitute only a family of resemblances for which ethnicity can no longer be reduced to bipolar sociological functions. This said, ethnicity, and specifically Italian American ethnicity, now becomes a process of inter-reference between more than two cultural traditions and, it should be underscored, between two or more generations of the same ethnic/racial group.

One must therefore cast aside the old lens of the monolith and reconsider Italian American poetry through a more prismatic lens that allows one to see the different nooks and crannies of one's ethnicity as it has changed over the decades and across generations from a dualistic discourse to a multifaceted conglomeration of cultural processes transgressing Italian, American, and Italian American cultural borders. One is now compelled to reconsider Italian American poetry as an ongoing written enterprise that establishes an imagistic repertoire of signs, at times, *sui generis,* creating verbal variations that represent different versions—dependent, of course, on one's generation, gender, and socioeconomic condition—of what can be perceived as the Italian American signified, for which one may readily speak of the variegated representations of the Italian American ethos in poetry, for example, in the same fashion in which Daniel Aaron spoke, in more general terms, of the "hyphenate writer."

Self-described as a "pick and shovel poet," Pascal D'Angelo (1894–1934) represents one of the first-generation poets to overcome the trials and tribulations of the immigrant, everyday life. A true autodidact, he taught himself English with the mere aid of a pocket dictionary and went on to write some of the first, poetic renditions of the Italian American immigrant experience. Written mostly in free verse with occasional peculiarities of punctuation, his poetry combines notions of the lofty with that of the mundane in a swirl of images that often contrast the idealized with the harsh reality of his daily life.

Like D'Angelo, Emanuel Carnevali (1897–1944) is one of the early voices that articulated the conflict of hopes and disappointment often confronted by members of the immigrant generation. Unlike Pascal D'Angelo, however, who had little success and died prematurely in his new country, Carnevali met with literary success early on with his newfound language. Carnevali's poetry articulates, in one sense, his headlong collision with his adopted culture. Unable to overcome the daily travails of the immigrant situation, Carnevali returned to Italy after less than a decade living in the United States. "Sorrow's Headquarters," "The Return," and "The Sick Man's Hymn," for instance, exemplify his disillusioned and tired spirit, overwhelmed by the futility of life. Yet, despite such pessimism of content, Carnevali's poetry places him among the notable, especially those nonconventional writers—the American avant-garde—as his style exhibits the free spirit of the modern writer; his disdain for conventions of all sorts is reflected specifically in his lyric style of free verse. His work appeared in numerous journals such as *Poetry,* and he was often courted by the cultural elites of the English-language world.

From working in coal mines in Canada and the United States to the seminary, earning a B.A., to engaging in radical social politics, including the famous textile strike of 1912 in Lawrence, Massachusetts, Arturo Giovannitti (1884–1959) was considered in his time to be the greatest Italian American poet. His only collection of poetry, *Arrows in the Gale* (1914), laments the exploitation of immigrants and, overall, the injustices placed upon the working class. While Giovannitti also wrote poetry of a more formal nature, his compositions in *Arrows in the Gale* are in free verse, often in long rhythmic prose paragraphs, accompanied by an impelling, austere, and realistic style.

The most celebrated of Italian American poets, John Ciardi (1916–1986), the son of immigrants, was the first Italian American writer to rise to national prominence. Not known as a poet of Italian American thematics, Ciardi's early writings nevertheless exhibited general sentiments readily associated with his ethnic group. The very title of his first collection, *Homeward to America* (1940), which won the Hopewell Award in 1939, implicitly sets up the dichotomy of the Old and the New Worlds, where America is now home. Further still, the overall collection questions the possibility of a bright future and fears the darkness that may await. With close to fifty books of poetry, criticism, and translations, Ciardi made an indelible mark on American literature. In addition to his regular creative activity, Ciardi also wrote poetry for children and a good deal of criticism; his volume *How Does a Poem Mean?* (1959) remains fundamental reading for an understanding of the poetic process. Recognition of his Italian heritage may be seen in his translation of Dante's *Divine Comedy* (1954), which has few equals for both its faithful rendition of the original and its overall lyrical quality in English. Full-time lecturer and weekly radio commentator, Ciardi was also editor of the *Saturday Review,* where the poetry of Felix Stefanile and Lewis Turco, to name two other Italian Americans, also appeared.

Felix Stefanile (b. 1920) and Lewis Turco (b. 1934) are, indeed, two other award-winning representatives of the offspring generation of immigrants who have sunk roots in the American literary landscape. To date, Stefanile's career spans close to fifty years of award-winning poetry, prose, essays, and translations. From *River Full of Craft* (1956) to *A Fig Tree in America* (1970), from *East River Nocturne* (1976) to *The Dance at Saint Gabriel's* (1995), Stefanile's poetry has consistently sung the highs and lows of the human condition on a general scale in venues such as the *Saturday Review, Poetry, Sewanee Review,* and *The Formalist.* Yet, be it the fig tree, the aroma of fresh bread, or the bocce ball court on Lewis Avenue, one may easily find references to his Italian heritage and the resultant encounters with the greater United States mainstream culture, as Italian American imagery rises to the surface. More recently, Stefanile finds himself at the forefront of the New Formalist movement in American poetry, as his editorially mercurial magazine, *Sparrow* (1954–), is now dedicated to the sonnet. In addition, like Ciardi and other talented poets of Italian descent (e.g., Jonathan Galassi, Michael Palma, Stephen Sartarelli), Stefanile has translated numerous Italian poets into English, including Cecco Angiolieri and Umberto Saba.

With close to a dozen poetry books to his name, Lewis Turco figures among the most prolific of first-generation, United States–born poets. As is evident with many writers who occupy two cultural worlds—in this case America and Italian America—Turco's verse is informed with a strong dose of opposition that, early in his career, revolves around a discourse on identity that is both personal and literary. Concerned with the structural aspects of poetry and the poets who have preceded him, Turco blends well his strident concern for language with his much impassioned con-

tent. And while concern for his Italian heritage in his poetry may seem to dissipate, metaphor remains an important key in this regard for his readers. Though not explicitly Italianate, "The Ice House," for instance, may be seen as an easy metaphorical rendition of the disappearing Italian America he knew as a child. In addition to his craft, Turco has also written books of literary criticism and "how to" books on poetry (*The New Book of Forms* [1968/1986]) and fiction writing (*Dialogue* [1989]).

Among other poets with a similar creative and intellectual mix, Jerome Mazzaro comes to mind in the category of formalist writing. He, too, is a type of self-reflexive traditionalist who also has a parallel career in critical writing. Other members of this generation worthy of inclusion in an Italian American inventory are John Tagliabue and Gerard Malanga. Whereas Tagliabue periodically invests his poetry with imagery of his Italian Americanness, analogous to Stefanile, Malanga is much more reserved with respect to an explicit ethnic repertoire; similar to Turco, Malanga engages in a poetry of oppositional veneration.

With a migratory experience like his predecessors Carnevali et al., and of the same generation of the likes of Ciardi and Stefanile, Joseph Tusiani (b. 1923) belongs nevertheless to a different category of writer and cultural being than these and other similar co-ethnics; he was already a socialized adult with a university education by the time he moved to the United States. (Others, for example, in this general category of biculturalism and bilingualism would include Peter Carravetta, Rita Dinale, Giose Rimanelli, Paolo Valesio, and Pasquale Verdicchio, to name a few.) With an Italian classical education and, as poet, weaned on the likes of Carducci, Pascoli, and D'Annunzio, as well as an avid reader of others such as Dickens, Hawthorne, Browning, and Dickinson, Tusiani came to the United States with an immense cultural wealth. His polycultural and polylingual experiences contributed to a poetry that has mediated over the years, in both his Italian and English poetry, the rhetoric extravagance of Italy and the linguistic economy of the United States. But Tusiani is a complex figure to say the least. For as he alone among Italian Americans rivals Ciardi in the number of books bearing his name (approximately forty books of poetry, prose, and translation), Tusiani is the only Italian American poet who consistently writes verse in three (four if we count his native dialect) different languages—English, Italian, and Latin. With such a vast linguistic inventory of three distinct languages, Tusiani also exhibits a vast thematic repertoire from the culturally specific immigrant experience of his and his co-ethnics to the more general motifs of solitude and nostalgia that afflict the human condition in general.

In glossing through a category that is Italian American poetry, those associated with the Beat Generation made a significant contribution. Lawrence Ferlinghetti, Gregory Corso, Philip La Mantia, and Diane di Prima are four names that come to mind. Of the first three, Ferlinghetti is the one more readily recognized as having an Italian American mindset. His poem "The Old Italians Dying" (1979) is a kind of swan song to the old Italian neighborhood of North Beach in San Francisco, where flight from the city and gentrification has radically transformed the area. In addition, his City Lights Publishing has been instrumental in getting out not only his Beat Italian Americans but also numerous Italian poets in English translation.

Diane di Prima (b. 1934) is one of the most prolific writers of the nonconformist generation of the 1960s. While her poetry is not steeped in an explicit repertoire of Italian American thematics, her heritage comes through in numerous ways. Poems such as "Backyard" and "April Fool Birthday Poem for Grandpa" stand as excellent examples of reconciling an ideological and formalistic avant-gardist attitude with her Italian heritage. While most Italian American poets flirt with the Italian anarchy of the past, di Prima embraces it whole-heartedly in her poetry, be that anarchy specifically Italian American, as in "April Fool . . . ," or more universal, as is apparent in her poem "Rant," a sort of creative/ideological manifesto. More than queen of the Beat Generation, di Prima exemplifies on a more general scale the counterculture that had its roots in the 1950s and blossomed in the 1960s, with more than one dozen books of poetry, two autobiographies, and numerous chapbooks and pamphlets to her credit.

Similar to some of her predecessors like Ciardi, Ferlinghetti, and Stefanile, Maria Mazziotti Gillan (b. 1940) is also heavily involved in publishing. She is editor of *Footwork: The Paterson Literary Review* and director of the Poetry Center at Passaic County Community College. Together with her daughter, Jennifer, she also edited *Unsettling*

America (1994), the first anthology of contemporary multicultural poetry of the United States that includes a significant number of talented Italian Americans. Mazziotti Gillan's poetry often speaks to the trials and tribulations of the gender issue and a woman's struggle to overcome; often, these themes revolve around issues of the Italian American family. Mazziotti Gillan is very much aware of her style, which in a poem may start out as quite simple and, when necessitated by her narrative, turn into a more complex mode of verse writing. Having won numerous awards for her writing, her self-reflexivity as Italian American female is apparent from her earliest collection, *Flowers from the Tree of Night* (1980), to her latest, *Where I Come From: New and Selected Poems* (1994).

A third Italian American voice that shares the gender dilemma is Daniela Gioseffi (b. 1941). Along with her poetry and prose, her sensitivities to issues of gender and prejudice are also evidenced by her two award-winning, best-selling edited volumes, *Women on War* (1988) and *On Prejudice: A Global Perspective* (1993). Characterized as "one of Whitman's daughters," Gioseffi's poetry is of the more spiritual type, exhibiting an impressive breadth of reading and eloquence. A stylist of sorts, Gioseffi's poetry speaks to the most intense issues of our times while inviting her reader to share in her outrage and wisdom. Be it *Eggs in the Lake* (1979) or *Word Wounds and Water Flowers* (1995), her poetry is accompanied by a compelling amount of frankness for those things she holds dearly.

Considered by *Esquire* as one of the "best of the new generation," as well as the "poet in the gray flannel suit," Dana Gioia (b. 1950) is known as poet, critic, translator, and editor. While his poetry does not exhibit explicitly Italian American thematics, a hue of his ethnic background is present. Work and money seem to occupy a good part of his poetry, where the initial desire to succeed financially—a possible inheritance from the immigrant generation where economic amelioration equaled individual amelioration—transforms itself into the burdensome. But, like the other poets in this limited panorama, regardless of thematic specificity, Gioia is a poet of great sophistication and elegance. A participant in the New Formalist movement, Gioia once stated that while "many American poets reject European influences as distractions from the search for a native voice, most Italian American poets view Europe—sometimes in its Modernistic aspects and sometimes in its older traditions—as a potential source of strength." One would suggest that the same can be said for Gioia himself. As translator of Italian poetry on a broad scale, cognizant or not, he has surely absorbed from the masters of older traditions some of their rhyme and meter.

Along with Ciardi, Jay Parini (b. 1948) is perhaps the most prominent name associated with American poetry that is Italian American. Poet, novelist, critic, professor, radio commentator, and editor, Parini has entered the mainstream of American letters like no other Italian American. While he may not enjoy the glittering fanfare of Mario Puzo or Gay Talese, he has in his own right, as poet especially, surpassed them. Parini's poetry exhibits an immense erudition and familiarity with the master poets. Yet his thematics are very much of the everyday type and transcend ethnic/racial epistemes, allowing members of all groups to appreciate his poetry. Be it the hard work of the mine workers, the praises of family elders, the desire to delve into one's ancestry, any American reader of Parini's can readily identify with and, at the same time, marvel at his craft as poet. Identified with one of the best writing schools in the United States, Bread Loaf, and editor of the *Columbia Anthology of Poetry* (1993), like very few Italian Americans involved in the literary world, Parini is also, in the true sense of the phrase, a cultural broker, as he contributes to the greater history of American literature and to what eventually becomes tradition, the canon, mainstream.

These are just a few of the poets who have made an indelible mark along the trajectory of what one may consider lyric Italian America. Others too numerous to mention here would be added to a more complete inventory. Vincent Ferrini (b. 1913) honed his literary skills at a young age while also working as an instructor of literature for the WPA project from 1935 to 1940. A prolific writer since 1941 whose poetry is steeped in social issues of industrialization, Ferrini figures as the logical successor to Giovannitti. Next to Ciardi, Henry Rago (1915–1969) figures as one of the first to break into mainstream literary America. His poetry appeared in numerous, prestigious journals over the years throughout the United States and in England (e.g., *The New Republic, Commonweal, Horizon*). Having published his first poem in *Poetry* when he was 16, he later went on, with great success, to edit the journal. A third voice of the pre–World War II poets is Elda Tanasso (b. 1917). With poetry published in *Voices, Lyric, Columbia Poetry,* and *New English Weekly* (England), she also had poems in *Poetry* at the early age of 20.

Other poets of the later generation, often labeled as the "baby boomers," those born after the Second World War, would surely include the likes of award-winning David Citino and W. S. Di Piero, the latter also in the category of translators looking back to Italy, as was evident in Gioia, Galassi, and others. In a similar vein is Paul Vangelisti, celebrated poet, novelist, publisher, and translator whose elegant editorial successes include Red Hill Press and Sun and Moon Publishers.

In an attempt to reconcile the ethnic with the general cultural milieu, the more technically conscious and, at times, wistful poets such as Sandra Gilbert and Diane Raptosh deserve their own entry. Likewise, the religious poetry of a Peggy Rizza Ellsberg would also be a necessary inclusion for a more encompassing view of the larger picture. In a different vein, Rose Romano has earned her own place in the history of Italian American poetry both for her own austere creative work and for her unselfish editorial activity dedicated to giving voice to the Italian American lesbian, female, and gay voices that have remained otherwise silent.

Finally, there are those who have sunk roots into the American literary soil and, consequently, consider themselves too American to be ethnic. This, perhaps, appears the most intriguing aspect of all—namely, to uproot their poetry through a poststructuralist, deconstructive lens—in order to demonstrate further how the American literary scene is, among other things, a conglomeration of different voices. All this figures as a pluralistic process of artistic invention and interpretation, which, by its very nature, cannot exclude the individual—artist and reader—who has found an *ars poetica* that does not violate the several components of her or his individual identity, and who has thus (re)created, ideologically speaking, a different repertoire of signs.

Anthony Julian Tamburri

Bibliography

Aaron, Daniel. "The Hyphenate Writer and American Letters." *Smith Alumnae Quarterly* (July 1964): 213–217. Reprinted in *Rivista di Studi Anglo-Americani* 3, nos. 4–5 (1984–85): 11–28.

Alfonsi, Ferdinando P. *Poeti Italo-Americani e Italo-Canadesi/Italo-American and Italo-Canadian Poets.* Catanzaro: Carello Editore, 1994.

———. *Poesia Italo-Americana: Saggi e Testi/Italian American Poetry: Essays and Texts.* Catanzaro: Carello Editore, 1991.

———. *Poeti Italo-Americani/Italian American Poets.* Catanzaro: Carello Editore, 1985.

Barolini, Helen. *The Dream Book. An Anthology of Writings by Italian American Women.* New York: Schocken, 1985.

Clemente, Vince, ed. *John Ciardi: Measure of the Man.* Fayetteville: University of Arkansas Press, 1986.

Gardaphé, Fred L. *The Italian American Writer. Annotated Checklist.* Spencertown, NY: Forkroads, 1995.

Gioia, Dana. "What Is Italian-American Poetry?" *Poetry Pilot* (December 1991): 3–10.

Giordano, Paolo, and Anthony Julian Tamburri, eds. *Beyond the Margin. Readings in Italian Americana.* Madison, NJ: Fairleigh Dickinson University Press, 1997.

———. *Canadian Journal of Italian Studies* 19 (1996). Special issue dedicated to Italian/American literature.

Mangione, Jerre, and Ben Morreale. *La Storia. Five Centuries of the Italian American Experience.* New York: Harper Collins, 1992.

Scapp, Ron, and Anthony Julian Tamburri, eds. *Differentia* 6–7 (1994). Special issue dedicated to Italian American culture.

Tamburri, Anthony Julian, Paolo A. Giordano, and Fred L. Gardaphé, eds. *From the Margin: Writings in Italian Americana.* West Lafayette: Purdue University Press, 1991.

See also AUTOBIOGRAPHY; CIARDI, JOHN; FERLINGHETTI, LAWRENCE; GIOIA, DANA; GIOVANNITTI, ARTURO; LITERATURE; WOMEN WRITERS

Politics

Italian American political participation can be divided into two major chronological periods: the pre–mass immigration era and that commencing with mass immigration.

The first period (pre-1880s) found a number of individuals of Italian descent who made an impact on the body politic. During the era of the American Revolution, for example, Filippo Mazzei played an important role in influencing Thomas Jefferson's writing of the Declaration of Independence while William Paca of Maryland became a signer of that critical document.

Other Americans of Italian extraction to win public office in this era included John Phinizy, mayor of Augusta, Georgia, in 1837; Andrew Houston Longino (1854–1942), member of the Mississippi State Senate and governor of Mississippi, 1900–1904; Charles Antonio Rapallo (1823–1887), Justice of the Court of Appeals in New York State; and Francis B. Spinola, elected to Congress in 1887.

The second Italian American elected to Congress was Anthony Caminetti, an immigrant's son, who first made his mark in California state politics before reaching the national legislature in 1890. Ahead of public opinion in some respects, especially education, Caminetti reflected his times in such other respects as California's anti-Japanese sentiment. Appointed United States Commissioner General of Immigration in 1913, he became known for his anti-alien zeal—a striking paradox for one who was himself descended from immigrant stock. It is significant to note that the acquisition of government influence on the part of these individuals occurred antecedent to the era of mass immigration and the emergence of a substantial number of Italian American voters.

Political participation following the 1880s, when more than four million Italians entered the country, and which included being nominated for and winning public office, has been essentially a story of traversing various stages of ethnic group politics. The first stage, encompassing the generation prior to the First World War, can be called the *periphery* phase because Italian Americans were only occasionally recognizable in the political arena. Like other "new immigrant" people of peasant background who possessed little experience in participatory democracy, Italians Americans

Glen Cove Italian Republican Club. This 1930 certificate of incorporation demonstrates ethnic political activity among Italian Americans. Courtesy Salvatore J. LaGumina.

were ignorant of the English language, understandably preoccupied with earning a living, and, in contradistinction with other immigrant people, frequently intent on returning to Italy to settle permanently. Therefore, their participation in politics was slight. This meant for all practical purposes that they would have to be content to accept elective office primarily within characteristic Italian enclaves and to settle on minor posts. Thus, the election of Michael Rofrano to deputy police commissioner of New York City in 1914 was celebrated as an occasion of great achievement in the city's Italian community. It is interesting to note that in communities outside New York City where they formed small but distinct minorities, deputy sheriffs were the first public positions to which more than a few Italian Americans were appointed.

It was in New York City that Italian Americans were truly looming on the political horizon. New York was at the time the most important political center of the nation as well as the home for the nation's largest Italian American population. Despite their limited conspicuousness in public office during this period, it must nevertheless be recognized that Italian American political leaders were acculturating American political practices, including that of organizing the ethnic group. James March and Paul Vaccarella, for instance, achieved a measure of success and considerable clout by recruiting thousands of immigrants into political clubs within their New York Italian communities, thereby commanding attention of the major political parties. The establishment of this groundwork became an immense benefit to aspiring politicians who reached the peak of their power in the next phase of political maturation.

The 1920s and 1930s may be called the *striving* phase as Italian Americans vigorously contended for more prestigious political posts. Angelo Rossi, a recognized leader within the Italian community of San Francisco, whose political career began with an appointment to a minor public post in 1914, was elected mayor of San Francisco in 1931, by which time the Italian ethnic bloc had become most powerful in the city. Several Italian Americans, including Boston's Henry Selvitelli and Philadelphia's Anne Brancato, became the first of their ethnic background to be elected to their city and state legislatures in 1932. It was during the period between the world wars that Robert Maestri became mayor of New Orleans, while Vincent Palmisano, leader of Baltimore's Little Italy, became the fourth of his nationality elected to Congress in 1926 and was soon joined by Peter Cavicchia of Newark, New Jersey, and Peter Granata of Chicago. Palmisano's successor as Democratic leader of Baltimore's Little Italy, Thomas J. D'Alessandro Jr., gained election to Congress in 1938.

It must be emphasized that Americans of Italian descent constituted significant voting blocs in all these cities and that the candidacies of the aforementioned were direct expressions of ethnic considerations. Simply put, the ethnic neighborhoods were becoming such vital springboards in the direction of political participation that shrewd political bosses, even when otherwise scornful of the Italian element, found it expedient to cultivate them. For instance, when in 1920 Democratic Chicago boss John Powers, who was an alderman in the Chicago City Council, witnessed a significant increase in the Italian American component in his ward, his behavior toward them changed from contempt to outward concern for their plight.

For Italian Americans, Fiorello H. LaGuardia, who was the most important political figure to emerge in the pre–World War II era, became the preeminent political figure in the striving stage. Born in New York City and brought up as a Protestant in western army camps, LaGuardia proffered a half Jewish, but all Italian background and became the hybrid politician par excellence. Firmly embracing an Italian identity, which struck responsive chords within his heavily Italian district in New York City's Lower East Side, LaGuardia won public office as a congressman in 1916. Subsequently, he was elected to Congress repeatedly from East Harlem, in its time the nation's largest Little Italy.

More than all those of his nationality who rose to prominence in the nineteenth century, LaGuardia can be considered an authentic ethnic representative who reflected the emergence of a group that voiced their aspirations. Throughout his long career in public life, he served with distinction in the United States Congress, speaking on behalf of Italy's international aspirations and authoring laws vital to the rights of organized labor such as the Norris–LaGuardia Act. Ascending the mayoralty of New York City in 1933 and winning reelection twice, he established a merited reputation as a progressive, caring government official who worked steadfastly on behalf of constituents confronting the nation's worst depression. He is generally regarded as New York City's greatest twentieth-century mayor.

As political bosses enlarged their cultivation of working relations with the increasingly assertive Italian element in an effort to continue to maintain their own positions, more Italian American political figures surfaced and prepared themselves for loftier political posts. In states where they constituted a significant portion of the electorate such as New York, New Jersey, Connecticut, and Pennsylvania, their numbers in state legislatures showed gains as did their representation in the judiciary. That this was the spawning period for numerous Italian American political aspirants is evident in a number of cases. In 1926 in Maryland and in 1934 in Rhode Island, Thomas D'Alessandro Jr. and John Pastore, spokesmen for their Little Italys in Baltimore and Providence, were elected Democratic state legislators. In 1934 Charles Margiotti was appointed attorney general of Pennsylvania, while New Yorkers Ferdinand Pecora, Edward Corsi, and Vincent Impellitteri were likewise gaining political prominence.

One of the most powerful forces in politics in his time was Generoso Pope. Although he never held a position in public office, he rose in status to become a major power broker. Migrating from Italy as a poor teenager, his meteoric rise in business and political circles was accomplished through his ownership of *Il Progresso Italo-Americano* in 1928. The largest Italian-language paper in the country, its two hundred thousand daily circulation rendered it a major force, especially within the Democratic Party, throughout the 1930s, 1940s, and 1950s. So powerful was the regard for *Il Progresso Italo-Americano* that even President Franklin D. Roosevelt, when running for reelection in 1940, asked Pope to intercede on his behalf before the Italian electorate.

Although both major parties courted the Italian American vote, and big-city Democrats generally were more successful, especially during Roosevelt's New Deal years in the 1930s and 1940s, there were significant exceptions.

La Società Politica James E. March. One of the first Italian American political clubs that was effective in organizing the Italian ethnic bloc vote, it flourished in New York at the turn of the twentieth century. Courtesy Center for Migration Studies.

Elections depended on local situations. For example, despite weighty inroads made by Democrats under the New Deal into Italian American Republican loyalty in Philadelphia's Little Italy, the gains were of short duration. Further, there existed a divergence between the voting behavior of Italian Americans in which they might vote for a Democratic national ticket yet simultaneously vote strongly for Republicans locally.

Simply put, the many shades of the political spectrum were to be found among Italian Americans, with a small but articulate and colorful group promoting a radical/socialist tradition usually outside the mainstream Democratic and Republican parties. Some, like the fiery left-winger Vito Marcantonio, belied his Republican Party label as he began his congressional career in 1934. Indeed, he later became a factor in the leftist American Labor Party. During this era most New York City Italian Americans who achieved public office ran under the Democratic Party emblem, although a smaller but impressive number including LaGuardia and Marcantonio were at least nominally Republicans.

The rise of Fascism in Italy complicated political interaction of Italian Americans. Some like Generoso Pope openly courted Mussolini's favor for a time, while left-wing elements such as the ardent radical Carlo Tresca and labor leader Luigi Antonini emerged as fervent opponents. Whatever division Fascism caused within the Italian community ended with the onset of the Second World War as Mussolini's reckless foreign policy lost him support among Italian Americans. For his part, Generoso Pope now exhibited a staunch loyalty intermingled with Democratic partisanship.

The *assertive* period, which materialized in the years immediately following World War II and lasted through the mid-1960s, found swelling numbers of determined Italian Americans demanding, and in some cases, obtaining their rightful place in the political realm. It has been observed that the war was effectively the watershed for Italian Americans politically. Whereas they were either barely countenanced previously or, with certain exceptions, forced to accept secondary positions, these offices no longer sufficed. Political power brokers realized that as the beneficiaries of improved economic conditions and more extensive education, second and third generations were more likely to adopt American citizenship and exercise voting rights and were, therefore, a major force that could no longer be refused their rightful share of the political spoils.

Furthermore, their outstanding display of loyalty during the difficult war rendered them more acceptable, so that what previously had been denied to them politically, was now within their grasp. In 1945 Rhode Island's John Pastore began his meteoric political career by being elected to the position of governor of his state and in 1950 became the first of his nationality elected to the United States Senate. Notably 1948 saw eight Italian Americans serving in Congress—twice the representation of any previous year. Cleveland, then the eighth-largest city, elected Anthony Celebrezze its first mayor of Italian extraction in 1953, the inauguration of five consecutive terms in that office. Desirous of placating Italian Americans who pressured him for greater prominence, President John F. Kennedy in 1962 appointed Celebrezze a member of the Cabinet as secretary of Health, Education, and Welfare, thereby establishing another milestone for the ethnic group.

It was in this period that Carmine DeSapio, from heavily Italian Greenwich Village in New York City, rose to lead the Democratic Party's Tammany Hall. DeSapio accomplished this after years of representing the local Italian element working in the trenches of the party organization and defeating the long-dominant Irish American leadership. From 1949 on for the next several years he directed the nation's most puissant political machine, thereby having a major role in selecting Democratic nominees for city, state, and national offices, and rendering him the most influential Italian American political leader of his time.

The 1950 election for New York City mayor constituted an extraordinary manifestation of ethnic political presence in that three Italian-born men received nomination for mayor, in large measure because of their nationality. At the insistence of DeSapio, the Democratic Party selected Sicilian-born Ferdinand Pecora; the Republican Party chose Edward Corsi, born in Capistrano; while Vincent Impellitteri, also of Sicilian birth, became the standard bearer for the Experience Party. With his astonishing victory, Impellitteri became the first mayor of Italian birth in the nation's largest city. That background was of pivotal consideration when the United States State Department summoned him to conduct a goodwill tour of Italy in 1951.

The final phase of political participation may be called the *arrival* stage in recognition of both the number and the types of public offices attained. In 1993, Boston, a city dominated politically for years by Irish Americans, elected Thomas Mennino as its first Italian American mayor.

On state levels, Italian Americans held office in proportion or in excess of their percentage of the population. By 1992, 22 percent of the members of the New York state legislature were identified as having an Italian ancestry, although they formed approximately only 16 percent of the state's population. States with large Italian American populations such as New York, New Jersey, and Connecticut elected Mario Cuomo, James Florio, and Ella Grasso governors—the first recognizably ethnic Italians to win those offices locally.

Italian American representation in national government has also undergone significant change. In a momentous development, Geraldine Ferraro became the first woman and the first Italian American to be nominated by a major party for vice-president. For a number of years in the 1980s and 1990s, Mario Cuomo, whose oratorical mastery gained national attention, was considered a potential Democratic presidential nominee. Among other Italian Americans elevated to high national posts were Cabinet members Benjamin Civiletti, Joseph Califano, John Volpe, and Frank C. Carlucci, while Leon Panetta served as the first White House chief of staff of Italian extraction. Although not always indicated by name, by the 1990s the number of Americans of Italian descent in Congress approximated thirty. Individuals such as Senators Patrick Leahy and Rick Santorum and Representatives George Miller and Thomas Downey acknowledged at least a partial Italian background.

Political observers opined that by the 1990s a movement to the right of the political spectrum was becoming the prevailing trend. Whereas prominent Italian American political leaders of yesteryear such as LaGuardia and Marcantonio embodied progressive to radical philosophies, today's leaders tend to be more mainstream or conservative. This is attributed to the transition of the ethnic group from a poor, proletarian, blue-collar working class to one now firmly ensconced in the middle class. The careers of individuals such as Pastore, Celebrezze, and Volpe are cited as exemplifying centrist philosophies, while the careers of people like Philadelphia Mayor Frank Rizzo reflect a conservative propensity. As fascinating as this observation is, it obscures the reality that some of the most persistent progressive voices such as New York governors Mario Cuomo and George E. Pataki and Representative Geraldine Ferraro are also examples of current political expression. In truth, the political leanings of Italian Americans can be found to range across the board of philosophies, mirroring prevailing societal concerns on public issues.

One of the most interesting aspects of Italian Americans in politics revolves around the gender factor. Whereas Italian American women were virtually absent from the political sphere in previous phases, the post mid-1960s finds them playing increasingly prominent roles. Connecticut governor Ella Grasso and vice-presidential candidate Geraldine Ferraro are cases in point. But there are other examples. By 1992 three Italian American women were serving simultaneously in the New York state legislature as opposed to only two in all prior state history. That five members of the United States Congress are Italian American women is another illustration of a major trend. Furthermore, these women manifest solidarity with Italian Americans through family ties and organizational membership. Thus, Rosa De-Lauro of Connecticut has descended from a generations-old Italian area of New Haven; Nancy Pelosi of California is the daughter of Thomas D'Alessandro, the first Italian American mayor of Baltimore; and Susan Molinari of New York, is the daughter of Staten Island borough president and former congressman Guy Molinari.

Another apparent trend is that of a movement from the Democratic Party to the Republican Party. From the mid-1970s on, the number of Italian Americans elected to each congressional term has ranged from twenty-seven to thirty-two. In 1979, twenty-seven of thirty-one congressional members to identify at least in part as Italian Americans were Democrats and four were Republicans. In 1995 figures continued to show a majority of Italian American members of Congress as Democrats, yet only by a very slim majority. If New York State is taken as an example, a similar inclination can be detected. For the better part of this century the overwhelming majority of Italian Americans in the New York state legislature were Democrats, not surprising in view of that party's identification with the prevailing proletarian background of the ethnic group. However, in 1974 there began a persistent trend that demonstrated that Republican Italian Americans outnumbered Dem-ocrats as members of the state legislature.

A final political trend is that of the transition from urban centers to the suburbs. Until the last quarter of the twentieth century, the city was the reference point for assessing political progress, since the metropolis was the main place of residence for the Italian ethnic group. However true that may have been in the past, it is no longer the case. In accord with national demographic changes, Italian Americans currently dwell in suburbia and it is therefore necessary to study their political role in the latter locations. It is significant to note that those Italian Americans who play increasingly important roles in California's legislature reside outside traditional inner cities. Indeed, the careers of United States Senators Dennis DeConcini of Arizona and Pete Domenici of New Mexico in the 1980s and 1990s underscore the ability of Italian Americans to achieve important political offices in areas of the Southwest that do not have enormous Italian American blocs in big cities.

While Italian American suburbanization has frequently led to political realignment and increased presence in the Republican Party, it does not, however, mean complete abandonment of Democratic roots that continue to dominate big cities. Although a dwindling number in major cities, Italian Americans remain an important presence there. It is no longer sufficient to look at their positions in big-city politics to assess their place. For instance, outside the city of Chicago Italian Americans now play meaningful roles in suburbia as county executives, mayors, district attorneys, and legislators. Nassau and Suffolk counties in New York provide another example. Italian Americans constitute approximately 25 percent of the 1.6 million residents of these two counties and are holders of impressive political posts. Indeed, the first Italian American elected United States senator in New York history was Alphonse D'Amato, who rose to power in suburban Nassau County.

The end of the twentieth century found Italian Americans moving from distinctly peripheral to major political positions. The history of their involvement over the course of the past century is one of evolution from the marginal to meaningful, albeit uneven participants in American politics. Conscious of their descent from an immigrant generation, their rising aspirations illustrate something distinctive about their participation. On the other hand, it is remarkable to note that practically within two to three generations, there has been absorption into the prevailing American political culture. Notwithstanding that phenomenon, involvement as candidates and as elected officials still mirrors their areas of concentration. It continues to be a rarity to find Italian names as elected officials or even as candidates in certain parts of the United States, as in much of the South and certain upper midwestern states. However, economic and educational advancement, together with the increase of mobility and exogamy, may alter the pattern.

Salvatore J. LaGumina

Bibliography

Glazer, Nathan, and Daniel P. Moynihan. *Beyond the Melting Pot: The Negroes, Puerto Ricans, Jews, Italians and Irish of New York City.* Cambridge: Harvard University Press, 1963.

LaGumina, Salvatore J. *New York in Mid-Century: The Impellitteri Years.* Westport, CT: Greenwood, 1992.

———. "The Political Profession: Big City Italian American Mayors." In *Italian Americans in the Professions,* edited by Remigio Pane, 77–110. Staten Island, NY: American Italian Historical Association, 1983.

———. *Vito Marcantonio, The People's Politician.* Dubuque, IA: Kendall/Hunt, 1969.

Levy, Mark R., and Michael S. Kramer. *The Ethnic Factor, How America's Minorities Decide Elections.* New York: Simon & Schuster, 1972.

Luconi, Stefano. "The New Deal Realignment and the Italian-American Community of Philadelphia." *Journal of American Studies* 28 (1994): 403–422.

Moscow, Warren. *The Last of the Big-Time Bosses.* New York: Stein and Day, 1971.

Nelli, Humbert, S. *The Italians in Chicago: A Study in Ethnic Mobility.* New York: Oxford University Press, 1970.

Parenti, Michael J. "Ethnic Politics and the Persistence of Ethnic Identification." *American Political Science Review* 61 (September 1967): 717–726.

See also ANFUSO, VICTOR; CUOMO, MARIO M.; FASCISM; FERRARO, GERALDINE ANNE; GIULIANI, RUDOLPH W.; GOVERNORS; LAGUARDIA, FIORELLO H.; MARCANTONIO, VITO; MUSMANNO, MICHAEL A.; POPE, GENEROSO; RODINO JR., PETER WALLACE; ROSSI, ANGELO JOSEPH; SANTANGELO, ALFRED E.

Ponselle, Rosa Melba (1897–1981)

An outstanding operatic soprano, Rosa Melba Ponselle was born in Meriden, Connecticut, May 25, 1897, to parents who had migrated from southern Italy. She became involved with music at an early age. While her father ran the Meriden grocery store he owned, her mother, an amateur singer, taught Rosa about music that enabled her to sing in their local church choir and perform in movie theaters and in vaudeville. With her older sister Carmela (1892–1977), a mezzo-soprano who was to perform as a singer at the Metropolitan Opera in New York from 1925 to 1935, Rosa sang in vaudeville shows in New York and Pittsburgh. The sisters used their real family name, Ponzillo, for these performances.

Rosa took voice lessons with New York teacher and later manager William Thorner. In 1918 Thorner introduced Rosa to the great Italian tenor Enrico Caruso, who arranged for Rosa to audition for the Metropolitan Opera. Impressing the company's impresario, Giulio Gatti-Casazza, Ponselle, who had never before participated in an operatic performance, had her debut on November 15, 1918, to positive critical acclaim. This was quite an achievement for an unknown and inexperienced young woman to be cast as the female lead in a major opera, Giuseppe Verdi's 1862 masterwork *La Forza del Destino,* opposite the world's greatest tenor, Caruso, at the most prestigious opera house in the United States. With a voice described as one of the century's most beautiful, having an even and well-polished technique, a wide vocal range, richness of tone, and the ability to communicate well with audiences, Ponselle was a top star at the Metropolitan until 1937. She sang in a number of famous operas including Carl Maria von Weber's 1826 work *Oberon,* Verdi's *Don Carlos* (1867), *Ernani* (1844), and *La Traviata* (1853), Mozart's 1787 classic *Don Giovanni,* Amilcare Ponchielli's *La Gioconda* (1876), Gioacchino Rossini's *Guillaume Tell (William Tell)* (1829), Giacomo

Meyerbeer's *L'Africaine* (1865), Pietro Mascagni's *Cavalleria Rusticana* (1890), and Vincenzo Bellini's *Norma* (1831).

It was the opera *Norma* that brought the most success, and the one in which she made her foreign debut, at Covent Garden in London, on May 28, 1929. She also sang in Florence, Italy, in 1933. Though she had a very wide repertoire of Italian and non-Italian opera, she never, to her regret, performed in an opera of two of opera's finest masters, Giacomo Puccini and Richard Wagner. Furthermore, despite her brilliant nineteen-year career at the Metropolitan, she had one notable failure, in the title role of Georges Bizet's superlative 1875 work *Carmen,* in 1935. After a reported dispute over the company's repertoire, she retired in 1937. Her final performance, on February 15, 1937, was in *Carmen*.

In 1936 she married Carl Jackson, whose father had been mayor of Baltimore. Jackson built a fine home for her at Green Spring Valley near Baltimore. Ponselle divorced Jackson in 1950. She died at Green Spring Valley, May 15, 1981, after various postretirement activities such as voice instruction, participation in social affairs, and artistic director of the Baltimore Civic Opera. One of the most talented operatic performers of the first half of the twentieth century, Ponselle could be faulted for leaving her profession while still fully possessing her artistic powers. At the same time, she left before age took its inevitable toll. Therefore, the last memories audiences had of Rosa Ponselle were of the soprano at her peak.

William E. Studwell

Bibliography

Hines, Jerome. *Great Singers on Great Singing*. Garden City, NY: Doubleday, 1982.

Thompson, Oscar. *The American Singer*. New York: Dial, 1937.

See also OPERA

Pope, Generoso (1891–1950)

Owner of building supply firms, newspaper publisher, and community leader Generoso Pope was born in Pasquarielli (Benevento), Italy, the son of Fortunato Papa, a small farmer, and Fortuna Covino. In May 1906 he migrated alone to New York City. He worked a number of construction jobs and in 1907 found employment in the Long Island sand pits. In 1911, after having risen to foreman of the Manhattan Sand Company, he joined the Colonial Sand and Stone Company, becoming superintendent in 1914. The following year he became an American citizen. His marriage in 1916 to Catherine Richichi produced three sons: Fortune, Gene Jr., and Anthony. He Anglicized his last name at about this time.

In 1916, when Colonial was at the point of bankruptcy, Pope assumed personal responsibility for the company's debts in return for full management and half ownership of the firm. He fought off the competition, paid the debt, and expanded the company's business. In 1918 Pope and a partner, Lawrence Rukeyser, bought the company, and by 1926 they had taken over most of the leading sand dealerships in New York. In 1927 Pope assumed full control of Colonial.

Pope was part of the network of machine politics, business interests, and labor union affairs that marked the public life of New York in the 1920s. His business success was due in part to his political contacts. In 1925 he helped to establish an Italian American organization for the election of James J. Walker as mayor. Following Walker's election, Pope became a member of Tammany's Democratic County Committee. He also joined the board of directors of the Federation Bank and Trust Company, controlled by the American Federation of Labor. In 1927 Pope expanded into the ready-mix concrete business with William J. McCormack and Samuel R. Rosoff, who built many of the city's subways. In 1929 Walker appointed Pope chair of the city's new subcommittee on Aviation and Airports Program, which planned future airports for New York; Pope's firms supplied the sand and concrete for the new airports as well as for Radio City, Rockefeller Center, and municipal housing projects. Although the Seabury Committee investigated his business dealings with the Walker administration, it brought no charges against him.

In order to organize the Italian vote, Pope sponsored the formation of the Italian American Democratic Clubs of Manhattan in 1929 and the Federation of Italian American Democratic Organizations of the State of New York in 1930. Even though Roosevelt fought Tammany on many issues, Pope supported his reelection in 1930 while simultaneously backing Tammany candidates against Fiorello

P

A check being presented to Generoso Pope at a luncheon in 1935 in New York City by the Committee of Italian Designers for Italian Relief. Courtesy Salvatore J. LaGumina.

LaGuardia in the city's mayoralty campaigns. In 1932 he endorsed Roosevelt for president, and in 1936 was made chair of the Italian Division of the Democratic National Committee.

Pope devoted his wealth and energy to making himself the spokesman for the Italian American community. In September 1928 he purchased for more than two million dollars *Il Progresso Italo-Americano,* the largest and oldest Italian-language daily newspaper in the country with a circulation about ninety thousand. This brought him to the attention of Mussolini, who was concerned about maintaining favorable press for Fascism in the United States. In January 1929 Mussolini awarded him the Commendatore della Corona d'Italia, one of four such awards he eventually received from the Italian government. Within a few years Pope controlled most of the Italian press in New York, purchasing in August 1929 *Il Bollettino della Sera,* whose circulation was about fifty-eight thousand. That summer he went to Italy and Mussolini endorsed his effort to buy the New York daily *Il Corriere d'America* (circulation fifty-six thousand); in 1932 he acquired the Philadelphia daily *L'Opinione* (circulation thirty-five thousand).

Pope's newspapers, which he used to create his own image as the power broker of the ethnic community, were the chief source of political, social, and cultural information for Italian Americans. He encouraged his readers to learn English, become citizens, and vote, and tried to instill pride and ambition to succeed in his fellow Italian Americans. Pope was a lavish spender, sponsoring banquets, civic and religious charities, and scholarships. He was prominent in church affairs; in 1932 Pope Pius XI made him a Knight Commander of the Equestrian Order of the Holy Sepulchre, and Francis Cardinal Spellman appointed him to the Cardinal's Committee on the Laity. Since the mid-1920s Pope had sponsored the celebration of Columbus Day, and in 1944 he founded and served as president of the Columbus Citizens Committee, which ran the Columbus parades in New York City.

Pope's support of Mussolini enhanced his prestige among many Italian Americans but also made him the target of bitter criticism. He tried to put the anti-Fascist newspaper *Il Nuovo Mondo* out of business, and his political enemies accused him of hiring thugs to intimidate anti-Fascist editors. When Mussolini invaded Ethiopia in 1935, Pope organized a campaign that pressured Roosevelt to maintain United States neutrality and raised funds for the Italian Red Cross. As Mussolini drew closer to Hitler, however, Pope came under increasing fire.

Fascist anti-Semitic policies caused Pope's first break with Mussolini. In 1937 the dictator asked Pope in 1937 to reassure Americans that he would not persecute Italy's Jews. When Mussolini announced anti-Semitic measures the next year, Pope, who had political ties to the New York Jewish community, refused, however, to abandon his support for Mussolini until just before Pearl Harbor. A relentless campaign by anti-Fascists to discredit him and force him to give up editorial control of his newspapers failed. Pope rehabilitated himself with Roosevelt by his work on behalf of the American war effort, including the Italian American war bond drive and membership on the New York draft appeals board. He also served on the American Committee for Italian Democracy and the American Committee for Italian Relief.

In the postwar period Pope supported the election of William O'Dwyer for mayor and of Harry S. Truman for president. His business concerns continued to prosper under New York's Democratic administrations, and in 1946 he added the Italian language radio station WHOM to his media holdings. In the early years of the Cold War, he was a staunch anti-Communist, orchestrating a letter writing campaign to prevent the Communists from winning the Italian elections in 1948.

Pope died in New York City shortly after his fifty-ninth birthday, the most important if controversial Italian American leader of his generation. His construction business had played an important part in New York's physical development, his newspapers had encouraged Italian American support for Mussolini, and his leadership had shaped Italian American participation in big-city Democratic machine politics.

Philip V. Cannistraro

Bibliography

Cannistraro, Philip V. "Generoso Pope and the Rise of Italian American Politics, 1925–1936." In *Italian Americans: New Perspectives in Italian Immigration and Ethnicity,* edited by Lydio F. Tomasi, 264–288. New York: Center for Migration Studies, 1985.

Cannistraro, Philip V., and Elena Aga Rossi. "La politica etnica e il dilemma dell'antifascismo italiano negli Stati Uniti." *Storia Contemporanea* 17, no. 2 (April 1986): 217–243.

See also FASCISM; POLITICS; UNITED STATES–ITALIAN DIPLOMATIC RELATIONS, 1776–1945

P

Pop Singers

The first generation of Italian American pop singers was born before the end of World War I and came of age during the swing era: 1935–1945. These singers launched their careers as big band vocalists and, as the swing era ended, made a successful transition as recording artists.

Before his untimely death at age 26 from a gunshot wound, Russ Columbo (Ruggiero Eugenio di Rodolfo Columbo, b. 1908, San Francisco) was the foremost crooner of his time, a major rival of Bing Crosby. Host of a popular weekly radio show, Columbo (known as the "Romeo of the Airwaves") was offered the lead in the first talking picture version of *Show Boat,* but he died before production got started. His softly modulated baritone and smooth reading of popular songs like "Paradise" and "Sweet and Lovely" (1932) set the standard for later singers. Dispensing with handheld megaphones, he relied on the microphone and improved speakers. He made the shouted heroics of an Al Jolson and Rudy Vallee obsolete by softening his delivery, putting more emphasis on key words and phrases, and creating a more intimate style of vocalization.

Frank Sinatra (Francis Albert Sinatra, 1915–1998, Hoboken, New Jersey). *See* separate entry under Sinatra in this volume.

Perry Como (Pierino Ronald Como, b. 1912, Canonsburg, Pennsylvania) and Frankie Laine (Frank Paul Lo Vecchio, b. 1913, Chicago) were born a year apart, but there are interesting parallels in their combined singing careers. Both signed on as big-band vocalists in their early twenties. When Como left the Freddie Carlone Band in 1937, he was replaced by Laine. For both singers recognition did not come early, but when it did, each one turned out a series of gold records. Como was 33 when RCA Victor released his first million-dollar single, "Till the End of Time" (1945), a melody borrowed from Chopin's "Polonaise in A Flat." Laine was 34 when Mercury released "That's My Desire" (1947), his first gold disc. Como gained fame for his big-voiced deliveries of mainstream standards ("Prisoner of Love") and catchy ditties ("Papa Loves Mambo") that consistently made the weekly pop charts. As affable host of his own show on NBC-TV from 1955 to 1963 and as featured star of occasional holiday specials from around the world, he cultivated a secure hold among musically conservative traditionalists who liked their music sweet, sincere, and not too fancy. Laine, on the other hand, built his reputation as the possessor of a powerful, ranging baritone. Like a latter-day Nelson Eddy, he delivered his songs in a pulsating declamatory style. The most famous of these were "Mule Train" (1949), "High Noon" (1952), and "I Believe" (1953). Though his career declined with the coming of rock 'n' roll, he nevertheless sold one hundred million records by 1969, fourteen of which were gold.

Dean Martin (Dino Paul Crocetti, 1917–1995, Steubenville, Ohio) gave up boxing to become a band singer in Cleveland at age 27. His decision to team up with comic Jerry Lewis in 1946 brought them instant fame, but after ten years as a straight man and stooge to his partner's rowdy slapstick humor, Martin elected to go solo. His two most popular early record releases were "That's Amore" (1953) and "Volare" (1958). He improved his acting skills and embarked on a successful screen career, playing diverse and challenging roles in thirty-four motion pictures. In the early 1960s he often made live appearances at the Sands Hotel in Las Vegas in the company of close friends Frank Sinatra and Sammy Davis Jr. (In tabloids they were described as the Rat Pack.) In 1964 he recorded "Everybody Loves Somebody," which became the nation's hit song in mid-August. *The Dean Martin Show* (NBC-TV) made its debut on September 16, 1965, and had an unparalleled nine-year run, averaging fifteen million viewers a week. In 1967 he was the highest paid television performer of his time. Soon after the accidental death of his son, in 1987, he retired to his Beverly Hills home and remained in semi-seclusion until his death on December 25, 1995.

Three other first-generation Italian American pop singers deserve recognition. They are Louis Prima (1910–1978, New Orleans), a jazz trumpet virtuoso and big-band leader, drew a popular following among Italian Americans and others for his novelty songs during the mid-1940s, including "Angelina, the Waitress at the Pizzeria" and "Josephina, Please No Leana on the Bell." He died in New

Orleans on August 24, 1978. Phil Brito (Philip Colombrito, b. 1915, Boomer, West Virginia), sang with a trio of big bands, including the Al Donahue Orchestra (1939–1942) and was once referred to as the "balladeer of the blues." His Musicraft recording of "You Belong to My Heart" ranked in the Top 20 hits soon after its release on September 2, 1944. He will forever be enshrined in the hearts of Italian Americans as the co-writer (in English) and first to introduce the Italian classic "Mama," to an American audience in 1946. Lou Monte (Louis Scaglione, 1917–1989, New York City), was an entertainer and recording artist known as the "Godfather of Italian Humor," who gained recognition with his 1953 release of "Darktown Strutter's Ball." His comic style consisted of blending a mix of English with repetitive Neapolitan idioms. Thus, the opening line, "I'll be down to get you in a pushcart, honey," ends with the punch line, "sott' u' basciment" (under the basement). Over the next three decades of his career, Monte created a gallery of memorable ethnic personalities: Pepino, the Italian Mouse; Lazy Mary ("Won't you get up/We need the bedsheets for the table"); Dominick the Donkey; and Baccigalup, Paul Revere's horse. Lou Monte died in Pompano Beach, Florida, in June 1989.

The next generation of Italian American singers were born between two world wars, survived the Great Depression, and made their impact during the Eisenhower years. With the demise of the big bands, the demand for vocalists declined. When television became a nationwide obsession, trained singers learned to cultivate the small screen to their advantage. Tastes in music changed dramatically during the 1950s. Foot-stomping muscular music with repetitive chords and a thumping beat replaced the more relaxed harmonies of sweet crooners.

Don Cornell (Luigi Francisco Varlaro, b. 1919, New York City) gave up a promising career as a pugilist to play guitar for the Red Nichols Band in 1937. In 1943 band leader Sammy Kaye hired him, discovered his singing talent, and changed his name. After a hitch with the United States Army Air Corps during World War II, he rejoined the Sammy Kaye Orchestra. Major recognition came in 1950 when Cornell's voice helped propel Kaye's recording of "It Isn't Fair" into a hit song, the first of twelve gold records made by Cornell. As a solo recording artist for Coral Records, he was a perennial hit-maker, launching such jukebox favorites as "I'll Walk Alone," "I'm Yours" (both 1952), and "Hold My Hand" (1954). Noted for his vigorous baritone and forceful delivery, Don Cornell has remained popular for more than forty years, drawing large crowds in Las Vegas, Reno, and Atlantic City. In 1996, at 77, he released a double CD album, "Something to Remember Me By," a compilation of forty of his best recordings. Some of these include Italian popular standards, sung in both English and Italian.

Jimmy Roselli (Michael Roselli, b. 1925, West New York, New Jersey) from earliest childhood aspired to sing for an audience. Growing up in Hoboken, he spoke the native tongue of his beloved grandfather who raised him and introduced him to many of the great Neapolitan street songs that "Jimmy" (he took his grandfather's name when he turned professional) later sang and recorded. In his early teens, Roselli performed in local saloons. At 13, he came in first as a contestant on the popular radio show, *The Major Bowes Amateur Hour*. Since he made more money singing in bars than collecting change as a shoe shine boy, he dropped out of school and scrounged around for singing jobs. After his military stint in World War II, he appeared in clubs and began recording with United Artists. Television gave him massive exposure. He was a favorite with TV host and personality Ed Sullivan, making several appearances on Sullivan's variety show. What set Roselli apart from other pop singers was his repertory of time-tested Italian folk songs and ballads. His command of the Neapolitan spoken idiom added authenticity to his parables of love and loss. Unlike most male pop singers of his generation, Roselli is not a true baritone. He possesses a middle tenor range with a powerful reach into the upper register. Like many other trained bel canto singers, he captures the throb in the throat when he wishes to convey heartfelt emotion. His atmospheric songs—like "Vurrie" and "Dicitencello Vuie"—suggest moonstruck landscapes of aching beauty, sometimes linked with a fervid passion for the unattainable. A survivor of quadruple bypass heart surgery in 1992, Roselli continues performing. He set attendance records when he appeared at Carnegie Hall. Now in his early seventies, he tours extensively with his own thirty-five piece orchestra and presides over his own independent recording label.

Tony Bennett (Anthony Dominick Benedetto, b. 1926, Astoria, New York) received the highest accolade from Frank Sinatra: "The greatest saloon singer who ever lived." Bennett's professional singing career began in 1950 when he started recording for Columbia. Recipient of many Grammys and Emmys over a career nearing fifty years, he has recently been discovered by the under-forty MTV generation who flock to his concerts and buy his records. The secret of Bennett's musical longevity is his refusal to alter his style to accommodate changing fashions in pop music. He remains a classicist, giving his own unique interpretation of favorite tunes by great songsmiths such as Cole Porter, Johnny Mercer, and Duke Ellington. Endowed with a husky baritone and with impeccable phrasing and timing, he combines wit and romance in a brilliantly understated style. Bennett's version of "Fly Me to the Moon" and "The Shadow of Your Smile" show why his deceptively casual delivery is more attuned to the sensibilities of younger fans than the super-heated bellowing of onetime favorites Eddy Fisher, Johnny Ray, and Teresa Brewer.

Jerry Vale (Gennaro Luigi Vitaliano, b. 1932, New York) made pin money shining shoes at a Bronx barber shop and entertained

Tony Bennett. One of the most durable and talented of all Italian American singers, Bennett's Italian roots are from Astoria, Queens, New York. His popular and jazz style has appealed to young and old alike, relying on American standards. Courtesy Joseph Fioravanti.

P

customers with snatches of popular songs. The resident barber, impressed with the boy's talent, volunteered to pay for his vocal lessons. In his late teens, while working in a factory, Jerry Vale performed weekends at church dances and weddings. His first professional job at the Club Del Rio convinced him to adopt a more Anglicized name for his growing non-Italian audiences. Columbia Records recruited him to make some albums. Between 1956 and 1958 Vale was responsible for four hit songs. "You Don't Know Me" ranked fourteenth in the nation's Top 20 hits. Blessed with a light baritone that could soar with great resonance into mid-tenor range, Vale continued to build a large constituency in the decades that followed. Between 1962 and 1972 he released twenty successful albums. As a popularizer and revivalist of Italian love songs, he ranks with both Connie Francis and Jimmy Roselli as a master of this genre. Exploiting Jerry Vale's enormous popularity with Italian Americans, Martin Scorsese, the film director, has used this singer's handsome looks (a lean body, silvery mane, boyish features) and instantly recognizable voice in two recent motion pictures, *Goodfellas* (1990) and *Casino* (1995).

Of some half-dozen widely known Italian American female singers, the greatest of these is arguably Connie Francis (Concetta Franconero, b. 1938, Newark, New Jersey). She is the only artist in pop music to have made ten successive gold records in two years. Her first hit, "Who's Sorry Now?" (1957), made her a household name. Her collaboration with songwriters Neil Sedaka and Howie Greenfield resulted in top-grossing hits for three consecutive years, from "Stupid Cupid" (1958) to "Where the Boys Are" (1961). A trained musician (she played accordion at age 4 and sang professionally when she was 11), she has perfect pitch along with the added distinction of vocal clarity, extensive range, and pinpoint timing. In the mid-1960s Connie Francis became an international artist with a series of multilingual recordings of French, German, Spanish, Italian, and Japanese songs. Her diction is flawless. Her definitive recording of "Mama" (1960), in both English and Italian, is one of her most requested songs. Her autobiography, *Who's Sorry Now?* (1984), reveals many tragic episodes in a life plagued with physical abuse, rape, the shocking murder of a beloved brother, and an emo-

tional breakdown that lasted nearly six years. That she survived is a tribute to her courage and resilience. Though her public appearances today are less frequent than before, she always draws enthusiastic crowds wherever she performs.

Bobby Darin (Walden Roberto Cassotto, 1936–1973, New York) was always fascinated by music. Barely out of high school, he wrote and performed radio commercials and then enlarged his considerable talents to include songwriting, arranging, and singing. Darin's rich baritone and deft handling of tricky song lyrics, his accurate timing and perfect pitch all combined to put early listeners in mind of Frank Sinatra—with one crucial difference. While the early Sinatra (from 1940 to 1952) was soulful and intense with a sentimental song, Bobby Darin projected a jaunty indifference to expressive and excessive emotion. He seemed coolly detached from the underlying feeling, focusing instead on the rhythm and tempo. His early rock compositions, "Splish Splash," "Queen of the Hop," and "Dream Lover" (all 1958), clearly defined Darin as a rock Mozart with a penchant for dreaming up hit songs. Still, his recording of "Mack the Knife" (1959) demonstrated that Darin was not merely a rock composer. The playful wit and polished grace of Darin's phrasing make this particular recording a classic of its kind. For all his success as an entertainer, Darin had a lackluster film career except for an Oscar nomination (best supporting actor) in *Captain Newman MD* (1963). As a headliner in Las Vegas and as Capitol recording artist in the 1960s, Darin's reputation grew. He died of congestive heart failure on December 20, 1973, at age 37.

Other Italian American singers of this generation will also be remembered for their unique and individual talents. Mario Lanza (Alfredo Arnold Cocozza, 1921–1959, Philadelphia), a popular MGM musical star of the 1950s was gifted with a powerful tenor voice. His most successful pop song was "Be My Love" (1951), which sold over two million copies and had an extended six-month lease in the pop charts. He died in 1959. Alan Dale (Aldo Sigismondi, b. 1925, New York) once sang with the Carmen Cavallero Orchestra, hosted his own TV show in 1951, and had a major hit recording, "Cherry Pink and Apple Blossom White" (1955), which sold over two million copies.

Al Martino (Alfred Cini, b. 1927, Philadelphia) entered the ranks of romantic baritone singing with "Here in My Heart" (1952). His most popular release, "Spanish Eyes" (1965), was adapted from Bert Kaempfert's melody "Moon Over Naples." He drew much praise when he played a fading singing idol in Francis Ford Coppola's movie *The Godfather* (1974).

Vic Damone (Vito Rocco Farinola, b. 1928, New York) is a superb nightclub singer with a rich and resonant baritone voice. He has had a long, illustrious career doing concerts and club dates. He demonstrated his Italian roots in the recording "You're Breaking My Heart" (1949), from Leoncavallo's popular melody "Mattinata," which Damone sings in English and Italian. His two most popular recordings, "An Affair to Remember" and "On the Street Where You Live" (both late-1950s), still get considerable radio play.

Morgana King (Mary Grace Messina, Pleasantville, New York), a cabaret singer with a rangy soprano, made a career of doing jazz stylings of pop songs in the tradition of Helen Morgan. Her best work may be found in her award-winning album "A Taste of Honey," released in 1963.

Joni James (Joan Carmella Babbo, b. 1930, Chicago) had a brief but memorable career as a rising star for MGM Records from 1952 to 1955. She introduced two gold discs in 1952, "Why Don't You Believe Me?" and "Have You Heard?"

Julius La Rosa (b. 1930, New York City), a regular on the Arthur Godfrey TV show in 1951, had his biggest hit recording in "Eh, Cumpari," a novelty song in which La Rosa, in his best Sicilian dialect, recites an extensive list of musical instruments accompanied by toots, whistles, and thumps. Much more impressive are the Frank Loesser songs La Rosa recorded for the sound track of Danny Kaye's biographical film, *Hans Christian Anderson* (1953).

Around 1955 a generation shift veered away from sweet, sentimental ballads and full orchestra arrangements to a pulsating dance music derived from rhythm-and-blues and gospel shouting. The new teen idols were basically musicians, not trained singers. Among the early pop stars in the forward wave were several Italian Americans.

Sonny Bono (Salvatore Phillip Bono, 1935–1998, Detroit) was a singer, songwriter,

Vic Damone, born in Brooklyn, was a younger contemporary of Frank Sinatra and Perry Como. He became a sensational crooner with a faithful following. He has continued a successful singing career by remaining a current performer. *Courtesy Joseph Fioravanti.*

and popular television host with former wife and co-partner, Cher. Their signature song, "I Got You, Babe," was at the top of the charts during the summer of 1965. For the next decade they reigned among the top performers in pop music. After Bono and Cher divorced, he became deeply involved in politics. He was elected mayor of Palm Springs, California, in 1988. In 1994 he won 56 percent of the popular vote and was sent to the United States House of Representatives from his home district. Sonny Bono died in a skiing accident on January 5, 1998.

Frankie Valli (Francis Castelluccio, b. 1937, Newark, New Jersey), was founder and lead singer of one of the most famous doo-wop vocal groups of the 1960s, The Four Seasons. His two biggest hits were "Can't Take My Eyes Off of You" (1966) and his solo rendition of the title song from *Grease* (1978). Frankie Avalon (Francis Avallone, b. 1939), Bobby Rydell (Bobby Ridarelli, b. 1942), and Fabian (Fabiano Forte, b. 1943), all three from South Philadelphia, were managed by music promoter Bob Marcucci. Their sensational debut on Dick Clark's widely viewed *American Bandstand* television show, airing from Philadelphia during the summer of 1959, briefly made this city the capital of rock music. Blessed with limited vocal range but with a great deal of charm, they heralded what fan magazines called the "Philadelphia Pop Explosion." Avalon recorded his best-seller, "Venus" (1959), then appeared in a series of beach party movies with popular co-star Annette Funicello (b. 1942, Utica, New York). Rydell's hit song was "Wild One" (1960), and he too achieved some celebrity by co-starring with Ann-Margret in the musical film *Bye Bye Birdie* (1963). Fabian, handsome pinup boy for adoring fans, never had a hit record, but he was in great demand in teen-oriented television shows.

Nancy Sinatra (b. 1940, Jersey City, New Jersey), talented daughter and oldest of Frank Sinatra's three children, arrived as a "teen queen" in the mid-1960s. Her hit song, "These Boots Were Made for Walking" (1964), a blend of country and rock music, generated a good amount of airtime and has since been co-opted as a feminist fight song. Three years later she recorded "Somethin' Stupid," a duet with father Frank, which took them both to the top of the charts. She next crossed over to the screen and played Elvis Presley's love interest in *Speedway* (1968). She had a banner year in 1995: *Playboy* did a heavily publicized photo layout of and interview with her in May; and she emerged as an author/editor for her loving chronology and tribute, *Frank Sinatra: An American Legend.*

Jim Croce (1943–1973, Philadelphia) never reigned as a rock star. This folk-oriented musical performer was a serious songwriter and coffeehouse fixture who did not achieve recognition until the release of his first album in 1972. Croce's cerebral music combines a musician's ear and a poet's eye. In a score of earthy ballads he writes about street people ("Bad, bad, Leroy Brown / meaner than a junkyard dog") and unsung heroes (cops, waitresses, truck drivers) who toil and yet retain a core of sweetness and dignity. Two of his best songs were released in 1973: "I Got a Name" (a hymn to ethnic pride) and "Time in a Bottle" (a haunting love song). As the celebrant of ordinary Americans and their indomitable spirit, Jim Croce could be called the Walt Whitman of pop music. On the cusp of a meteoric career after long years of obscurity, Jim Croce, on

tour in Natchitoches, Louisiana, was killed in a plane crash on September 29, 1973.

Felix Cavaliere (b. 1943, Pelham, New York), a musician, composer, and lead singer, organized one of the best-known rock bands in 1965, The Young Rascals. Their three top songs were recorded over the next two years: "Good Lovin'," "Groovin'," and "How Can I Be Sure?" The band's distinguished album "Time Peace and Freedom Suite" (1968) featured two hit songs that reached the Top 10: "A Beautiful Mornin'" and "People Got to Be Free."

The postwar baby boomers matured at a time when ethnic identity mattered least. Suburban lifestyle and the leveling influence of television had a flattening effect on families twice removed from the immigrant experience. In the yawning divide of the turbulent sixties, with bra burning and campus sit-ins, topics once taboo (free sex, drug advocacy, social protest) found general acceptance in a society increasingly tolerant of any deviation from the norm. Popular music, reflecting the alienation of competing and conflicting constituencies, transformed into disco, punk rock, country-western, rap, and "new age" genres, each with its own tribal signature.

Liza Minnelli (Liza May Minnelli, b. 1946, Hollywood, California), as the daughter of legendary entertainer Judy Garland and equally famous film director Vincente Minnelli, and as a product of the movie capital of the world, was destined one day to seek the limelight. Surrounded by prefabricated and technicolored celluloid fantasies, she had what some would consider to be an enviable childhood, but soon enough misfortune dogged at her heels. Judy Garland's losing battle with alcohol and drugs, culminating in her death from a sleeping pill overdose at 47, was nearly more than Liza Minnelli could cope with in her struggle to find her own secure niche. She made her Broadway debut with *Flora, the Red Menace* (1965), a performance that netted the 19-year-old a Tony Award. Glowing reviews followed the release of her first featured role in the Albert Finney film *Charlie Bubbles* (1968). Soon after this she was nominated for an Academy Award for her portrayal of a lonely, love-starved college freshman in *The Sterile Cuckoo* (1969). Three years later she won an Oscar as a much used but feisty saloon singer in the acclaimed movie *Cabaret*

(1972). Like Judy Garland, Liza Minnelli also had to exorcise a few demons along the way: she's been involved in multiple romances and broken marriages; she's had more than one documented encounter with chemical dependency. Yet, for all her misadventures, she has demonstrated fortitude in climbing back from the brink of disaster. Starting with an Emmy Award–winning special, *Liza With a Z* (1972), she made frequent forays into television. Her most memorable appearances occurred when she co-hosted an hour of music with French chanteur Charles Aznavour (1974) and as hostess of a PBS-TV tribute to her father, *Minnelli on Minnelli* (1987). Her greatest career triumph occurred in May 1987 when she was booked for a sold-out engagement of three weeks at prestigious Carnegie Hall. The concert led to a double album, *Liza at Carnegie Hall,* one of the best recordings of a live concert ever issued. Soon after this she toured Europe for five weeks. In 1988 attendance records were broken when Minnelli went on national tour with Frank Sinatra and Sammy Davis, Jr.—immodestly billed as "The Ultimate Event." Equipped with a soaring, theatrical voice and a natural histrionic ability to project strong emotion, Liza Minnelli is closely identified with bravura songs demanding much energy and focused delivery. Her favorite songwriters, Fred Ebb and John Kander, have given her two of her biggest hits, "Maybe This Time" (1972) and the title song from the movie *New York, New York* (1977).

Bernadette Peters (Bernadette Lazzara, b. 1948, New York) is a pop singer and actress whose early career rests chiefly on a string of Off-Broadway and Broadway singing roles in the 1960s. During the next decade she was much in demand on made-for-television musical shows like *George M!* (1970), *Once Upon a Mattress* (1972), and *The Owl and the Pussycat* (1974). She then went to Hollywood and graduated to leading roles in two Steve Martin pictures: the winsome ingenue in *The Jerk* (1979) and the compromised school marm in the black comedy *Pennies From Heaven* (1981).

Singer-songwriter-musician Bruce Springsteen (Ferdinand Joseph Springsteen, b. 1949, Freehold, New Jersey), of Irish Italian ancestry, got his start with several rock bands in local bars. After performing at a Greenwich Village club (1972), he was signed by Columbia Records. Springsteen's early recordings put listeners in mind of Bob Dylan for the cryptic lyrics and long instrumental guitar passages. He formed his own E Street Band and strove for a gritty realism, writing about small-town working types and wanderers. His 1975 album *Born to Run,* within a month of its release, sold a million copies. *Time* and *Newsweek* both ran cover stories about him. One of his own single releases, "Hungry Heart" (1980), was Springsteen's first Top 10 hit. He toured Europe, Asia, and Australia the following year, playing to packed stadiums. He achieved superstar status in 1984 with another album, *Born in the USA,* a searching exploration of a bleak landscape and its celebration of tortured but striving underdogs. Over ten million copies were sold. Five songs featured in this album became hit singles. Always a controversial songwriter, Springsteen has done countless benefit appearances for the indigent and victims of political oppression. Sympathetic to society's outcasts and those afflicted with unpopular pathologies, he won a Grammy in 1994 for "Streets of Philadelphia," his Oscar-winning song for the film depicting lives afflicted by the AIDS epidemic, *Philadelphia* (1993).

Fully twelve years separate Madonna (Madonna Veronica Louise Ciccone, b. 1959, Rochester, Michigan) from Liza Minnelli, but in terms of showmanship, style, and theatrics, a profound cultural gulf separates these premiere artists. Liza Minnelli inherited the MGM tradition of big budget musicals with melodic and finely crafted songs strongly rooted in the romantic tradition of Irving Berlin, George Gershwin, and Harold Arlen, songs projecting a heightened reality and sophistication. Madonna, however, draws her inspiration from rap and techno-pop music combined with street noises and urban settings, a diffused and discursive blend of slang and pulsing disco rhythms.

One of six children, Madonna (given her mother's name) was only 6 when she was desolated by the death of her mother Madonna Horton Ciccone. The oldest of three daughters, Madonna Louise tried to fill the void and become surrogate mother for her younger siblings. Soon after her father remarried, Madonna felt betrayed and nurtured fantasies of escape from her detested stepmother. Though she was raised in a devoutly Catholic home, Madonna often sneaked away with a

P

dance instructor friend to disco clubs in nearby Detroit, discovering her life's mission on the dance floor. Not content with merely dancing, she determined to mold herself into a singer. Enlisting the help of a local disc jockey, she made a demo tape that secured a contract with Sire Records.

Her first album, *Madonna* (1983), spawned three hit single releases. Her second album, *Like a Virgin* (1984), sold three and one-half million copies in just three months. Her dawning notoriety as a provocative performer in downtown dance clubs earned her a chance to go on MTV, the widely viewed music video channel. The video release of "Like A Virgin" caused a minor scandal with its blend of near nudity, erotic imagery, and semi-sacrilegious manipulation of venerated religious props. "Papa Don't Preach" (1986) dramatizes the dilemma of a pregnant single girl who must tell her widowed father about her condition. The release of "Like a Prayer" (1989) provoked a firestorm of protest. Despite good reviews of her first feature-film role, *Desperately Seeking Susan* (1985), Madonna's next four films were poorly received. In *Truth or Dare* (1991), a documentary based on her successful 1990 "Blond Ambition" tour, Madonna freely indulges in profanity and gender-bending conversations with openly homosexual companions and tests the limits of artistic license (she performs fellatio on the head of an empty bottle). In 1992 Time Warner awarded her a sixty million dollar contract to start her own entertainment company, Maverick, making her one of the richest entertainers in the nation.

Possessed of a high-pitched, girlish voice of limited range and flat nasality, Madonna is not a polished singer. Nevertheless, she is a bewitching performer and a fluid dancer with an impressive array of moves. Her music videos, slickly produced and brilliantly choreographed, elevate her to a higher level.

The widely publicized birth of a daughter late in 1996 brought speculation that Madonna was contemplating yet another career move. Her screen performance as Eva Peron in *Evita* (1997), Webber and Rice's spicy blend of passion and politics in Argentina, won many friends and could very well signal a new maturity. The onetime "material girl" seems ready to make the transition from dancing disco queen and sex icon to celebrity artist who uses her exuberant eroticism to explore cultural taboos and redefine gender roles in more challenging and compelling terms for a postwar generation unwedded to the past and uncertain of the future.

Joseph Fioravanti

Bibliography

Balliett, Whitney. *American Singers.* New York: Oxford University Press, 1988.

Bronson, Fred, ed. *The Billboard Book of Number One Hits.* New York: Billboard Books, 1988.

Hardy, Phil, and Dave Laing, eds. *The Faber Companion to 20th Century Popular Music.* London: Faber & Faber, 1990.

Hemming, Roy, and David Hadju. *Discovering Great Singers of Classic Pop.* New York: Newmarket Press, 1991.

Parish, James Robert, and Michael R. Pitts. *Hollywood Songsters.* New York: Garland, 1991.

Paymer, Marvin, ed. *Facts Behind the Songs: A Handbook of American Popular Music from the Nineties to the '90s.* New York: Garland, 1993.

Pleasants, Henry. *The Great Popular American Singers.* New York: Simon & Schuster, 1974.

Tobler, John, ed. *The Rock 'n' Roll Years.* New York: Crescent Books, 1990.

See also COMO, PERRY; FRANCIS, CONNIE; MADONNA; MARTIN, DEAN; SINATRA, FRANCIS ALBERT

Population

With the onset of mass migration from Italy, the immigrants first settled on the East Coast of the United States, primarily in the cities. They worked in the quarries and mills of New England and Italian enclaves cropped up in Boston and Lowell, Massachusetts; in Hartford, New Haven, and Waterbury, Connecticut; as well as in Providence, Rhode Island. Original areas of Italian settlement in New Jersey were established in Newark, Passaic, Paterson, and Trenton.

The major impetus to move westward came from the railroads that needed workers. Along the tracks' route, Italian settlements soon mushroomed in major cities, towns, and villages. Some of these Italian communities sprung up in Omaha, Nebraska; Cheyenne, Wyoming; Santa Fe, New Mexico; Denver, Colorado; and San Francisco.

After World War II Italian Americans joined other Americans in the urban exodus. While many have moved to suburban communities that are predominantly made up of an Italian American population, for the most part, contemporary Italian Americans continue to settle in suburban areas that consist of different ethnic groups.

By the 1980s the trend of older generation Italian Americans was to leave the areas in which they had resided for lengthy periods and flock to the Sun Belt regions as their retirement locale of choice. The Carolinas, Florida, Arizona, New Mexico, and California have drawn these Italian Americans in great numbers. All of this movement, over time, can be seen in the geographic and demographic characteristics of the Italian Americans from the immigrant generation to the present. Categories affecting Italian American population include migration, demography, geography, settlement patterns of the Northeast, and suburban settlement.

Migration

The main flow of Italian migration to the United States was from southern Italy. However, within the three phases of Italian migration to the United States between the seventeenth and twentieth centuries, southern Italians did not always dominate the flow of immigrants. Italians left Italy because of social, political, and economic crises. The attractions of the United States were varied as well, but the main pull was the need for labor.

The first phase began in the 1600s as a trickle of Italian intellectuals, artists, missionaries, craftsmen, and adventurers moved to the Spanish, French, and British settlements in North America. Some who arrived in Maryland came via England, such as Father Blount, who aided in the founding of the colony, and William Paca, a signer of the Declaration of Independence who later became the state's governor, a first for Italian Americans. Italians also came to Jamestown, Virginia, in 1621 as artisans skilled in making glass. In Georgia, Italians planted mulberry trees, launching the production of silk. Others served the Spanish, aiding the conquistadors in Florida and as missionaries. Fra Marco da Nizza and Father Eusebio Kino explored the Southwest. Enrico de Tonti, together with Robert De La Salle, claimed much of the Mississippi Valley for the French.

Italians were also active in supporting the American Revolution. Francesco Vigo landed in Louisiana and made a fortune in fur trading; he was instrumental in financing and guiding the campaign of General George Rogers Clark, who conquered Fort Vincennes and the Northwest Territory for the Americans. Vigo became the first Italian to gain United States citizenship.

Filippo Mazzei was one of the several hundred political activists who came to the Americas. As a friend of Thomas Jefferson, he, along with Italian workers, came to Virginia to cultivate grape and olive production. He wrote revolutionary tracts under the pen name *Il Furioso;* some of his phrases were incorporated into the Declaration of Independence. Mazzei eventually returned to Italy, but others remained in the New World, such as Lorenzo Da Ponte, who helped to change American culture by promoting opera as a viable art form.

This period of the late 1700s coincided with the Industrial Revolution, a movement that transformed Europe. The epicenter was in England, France, and Germany, but tremors were felt in Italy as well. The political and intellectual transformations, coinciding with technological innovations, witnessed the emergence of the modern nation of Italy. The accompanying changes set the stage for the next cycle of emigration occurring from 1850 to 1880.

Between 1851 and 1860 some nine thousand Italians arrived in the United States, a 30 percent increase over the preceding decade with the highest immigration flow (1831–1840). Numbers continued to increase as northern Italians sought their fortunes in the United States. In the south, however, the Bourbon Kingdom of the Two Sicilies prohibited emigration. Those from the Alpine areas and Ligurian coast were free to move. Their destinations included France, North Africa, South American nations, Canada, and the United States. Migration was often temporary, as agricultural workers left during seasons of slack time to later return with money to purchase more land or livestock, earning them the nickname "Birds of Passage."

Their experience foreshadowed that of the southerners. By the 1860s the New York City colony of Italians at Five Points, originally composed of middle-class merchants and political exiles, became increasingly populated by peasant immigrants. This small enclave faced poor working conditions, and Italians became involved in labor disputes with other groups. The myth of lawless Italians emerged during this time, adding to the growing prejudice and discrimination against them. Many did not remain in the East, however, but pushed west to California and other western states.

This phase coincided with the emergence of Italy as a nation in the 1860s. The goals of the intellectuals and liberals who fought for the Risorgimento (resurrection), as the movement was called, were to remove the existing feudal system and introduce modernization and constitutional government.

However, the majority of Italians were peasants, and nationalism had little direct appeal for them; they did not actively support a united Italy. Unification was essentially a civil war between the new, upwardly mobile middle class of the Industrial Revolution and the entrenched aristocracy. The "blessings" of unification came to peasants in the form of increased taxes, military conscription, loss of feudal privileges, and increasing amounts of deforestation and land fragmentation. In 1877 a parliamentary report on rural conditions showed that undernourishment, housing problems, child labor, and illiteracy prevailed; malaria plagued the south and pellagra the north. The government did not respond to these conditions, thus spurring emigration.

The third and largest wave of Italian migration began by the 1880s, a decade in which new arrivals numbered just over three hundred thousand, continuing into the 1920s. The first decade of the new century saw Italian immigration, mainly from the agricultural south, reach its peak at over two million arrivals. The economic and social backwardness of the south, characterized by poverty, compared to the economic development of the north, became known as the "Southern Question."

Furthermore in Italy, the House of Savoy held political power in the north, in Piedmont, and encouraged economic and social modernization there. From 1881 to 1887 modest but steady progress was made in a variety of northern industries, including the cotton, metal, and chemical industries. Unfortunately, the industrial boom coincided with the start of an agricultural crisis, so that as the prices of industrial goods rose, the price of agricultural products declined. Capital was drained from the south; tariffs favored northern industrialists and southern landed gentry. The south retained an obsolete agricultural system.

One effect of modernization that reached the south ironically further encouraged migration. The introduction of modern medicine and sanitation lowered the mortality rates. During the period from 1861 to 1901 the population in the south doubled to twelve million, disrupting the precarious balance between the food supply and population. Finally, migration took away many of the more innovative individuals. The fertility rate was slow to drop in the south, where illiteracy and outmoded institutions flourished.

Other factors triggered emigration: labor recruiters, declining transoceanic fares, and chain migration. Once the pattern of leaving was established, it was difficult to stop. The pull of conditions in an industrializing United States proved a magnet for the migrants, providing a demand of cheap labor following the Civil War. Immigrants from southern and eastern Europe and from Mexico and Asia filled the need for workers.

The first southerners were often men traveling without their families who sought work, planning to return to Italy with their wealth. They moved to areas of rapid economic growth in New York, Rhode Island, Connecticut, Massachusetts, and New Jersey and to the industrial and commercial centers of Detroit, St. Paul, St. Louis, Chicago, and Pittsburgh.

Family-oriented migration transpired by the 1900s. Women began to enter the labor force. Many tried to balance the restrictive southern Italian gender norms with economic needs by doing piecework at home or working in canneries and factories owned by other Italians. Some became active in the growing labor movement of the early 1900s in arenas such as the needle trade unions and the textile unions.

More stable Italian communities began to develop for those who decided to make the move permanent, although conditions were far from ideal. New York City had the largest number of Italians in the United States, and in the early decades some of the worst living conditions. Dense population, poor housing, poverty, and disease were found in the teeming Italian neighborhoods like Mulberry Street; similar conditions could be found in other cities such as Boston, Chicago, and Philadelphia.

Chain migration of *paesani* (town folk) from the same village to a new location in the

United States fostered the development of tightly knit communities. Cleveland's early migrants, for example, first left because of a specific economic crisis, namely the drop in the price of cotton in Sicily, which caused young spinners and weavers to leave. Once established in Cleveland, they sent for relatives and friends in major village chains of twenty or more members. Thus, many Italians in Cleveland, as was the case for other cities, found familiar dialects, family, friends, and organizations that provided indirect parallels to the social structure of the rural communities they left behind in Italy. Chain migration even functioned in western and southern states as well, including Arizona, New Mexico, Washington, California, Louisiana, Texas, Arkansas, and North Carolina.

The third phase of Italian migration to the United States ended in the 1920s amid ethnic slurs and violent tumult created by nativists. Anti-foreign nativist groups formed, beginning with the Native American Group in the 1830s, followed by the Know-Nothing Party in the 1850s, and the American Protective Association in the 1890s. They demanded that the United States end immigration, fearing a negative impact on what they perceived to be the American way. Southern Italian peasants were considered unassimilable because they were Catholic; they were tagged as anarchists, criminals, and "dark skinned," thus racially inferior. These stereotypes contrasted with what the dominant cultural group idealized as "true Americans." Nativists gained force as they allied themselves with labor leaders, who saw foreign workers as a threat to better wages and working conditions.

The peak year of Italian migration was 1914 with 283,738 legal entries, although there were also undocumented entrants. While World War I slowed nativists' agitation because Italy was allied with the United States, the end of the war brought an increase in their wrath. The Immigration Act of 1917 codified all previous exclusions, added the long controversial literacy requirement, and finalized the exclusion of most Asians, a restriction initiated in the latter years of the nineteenth century. When President Harding signed the Quota Act of 1921, a significant turning point was reached in circumscribing Italian immigration, whose quota was limited to 3 percent of their numbers as of the 1910 census. This restriction was not enough for immigration opponents, and in 1924 the Johnson-Reed Act further reduced arrivals from southern and eastern Europe. Each nation's annual quota was established at 2 percent of the group's numbers based on the 1890 census. The quota for Italy was pushed back to about six thousand per year. That act, followed by the 1929 economic depression, which increased deportations and voluntary repatriation to Italy, spelled the end to large-scale migration of Italians. The lowest point in the twentieth century was reached in 1943 during World War II when only forty-nine Italians were admitted.

The Immigration and Nationality Act of 1965 overturned the quota system, setting the stage for new waves of immigrants. A complex preference system emphasizing family reunification and skilled workers emerged. Numerical limits were by hemisphere rather than nation; revisions in 1976 set a cap of twenty thousand per-country annual limit. In addition, close family members did not fall under the limit and were eligible to immigrate. Those groups pushing for this change included European American ethnics, especially Italian Americans, who ironically became the minority in the following decades of immigration as they were overshadowed by Asian and Latin American migrants.

The decade of the 1960s was the height of the new Italian immigration to the United States with some two hundred thousand arrivals; in 1970, the Italian foreign-born population in the United States was second among the top five countries. Subsequently, numbers of Italians arriving dwindled to slightly over sixty-seven thousand in the decade between 1981 and 1990. The reasons behind the decline in Italian migration to the United States are complex. Italy was still an agricultural nation in the post–World War II years, but this changed dramatically by the 1960s with a massive internal migration from the rural south to the northern industrial triangle of Torino, Genova, and Milano. Other Italians left for temporary jobs as "guest workers" in an emerging European Common Market, or to nations such as Australia, where increased migration occurred after the United States restricted Italians in the 1920s.

Ironically, by the mid-1970s Italians were still leaving while Italy became a receiving nation for immigrants primarily from Africa and

Asia. The pattern continues as Italy ranked fifth among European nations receiving foreign-earned remittances in 1989.

As nativism has fanned anti-foreign sentiments in the United States in the late 1990s with fears of dark-skinned, Catholic foreigners from Mexico taking over the western parts of the nation, it should be noted that in the 1901–1910 decade the average annual migration from Italy was 204,588. Mexico's annual average of 70,014 in the period between 1978 and 1988 was slightly one-third of Italian immigration to early-twentieth-century America. The concerns that newcomers will never assimilate echo those claims made earlier against Italians.

Phyllis Cancilla Martinelli

Bibliography

Barton, Josef J. *Peasants and Strangers. Italians, Rumanians, and Slovaks in an American City, 1890–1950.* Cambridge: Harvard University Press, 1971.

Battistelle, Graziano, ed. *Italian Americans in the '80s: A Sociodemographic Profile.* New York: Center for Migration Studies, 1989.

Cinel, Dino. *The National Integration of Italian Return Migration, 1870–1929.* New York: Cambridge University Press, 1991.

Foerster, Robert P. *The Italian Emigration of Our Times.* New York: Russell and Russell, 1919.

Friedman-Kasava, Kathie. *Memories of Migration: Gender, Ethnicity, and Work in the Lives of Jewish and Italian Women in New York, 1870–1924.* Albany: State University of New York Press, 1996.

Higham, John. *Strangers in the Land.* Brunswick, NJ: Rutgers University Press, 1959.

Iorizzo, Luciano, and Salvatore Mondello. *The Italian Americans* (rev. edition). Boston: Twayne, 1980.

Jasso, Guillermina, and Mark Rosenzweig. *The New Chosen People, Immigrants in the United States.* New York: Russell Sage Foundation, 1990.

Mangione, Jerre, and Ben Morrealle. *La Storia: Five Centuries of the Italian American Experience, 1492–1992.* New York: HarperCollins, 1992.

Negri, Vera Zamagni. *The Economic History of Italy: 1860–1990.* New York: Oxford University Press, 1993.

Demography

Italian Americans constitute the sixth largest ethnic group in the United States. Italian migration to North America began as early as the seventeenth century; however, large numbers of Italian immigrants did not arrive until the mid-nineteenth century. The vast majority of immigrants entered through New York and settled in urban areas along the Atlantic seaboard, throughout the Northeast, although some Italians became established in agricultural or mining settlements in rural areas. Migration to North America fell sharply following World War I and did not resume until after World War II.

Settlement patterns of Italians followed those of other European groups. Italians generally settled in central city areas. Sometimes, their settlement areas became well-defined enclaves; when dominated by Italians, such enclaves became known as "Little Italys." Italians eventually moved away from central city areas to other parts of the city, or, more frequently, suburban locations, although somewhat later than other European groups; some of their centrally located neighborhoods continue to exist. Despite the generally humble origins of their forebears and their late arrival in the United States, Italians have attained an educational and occupational status that is similar to or exceeds that of other European ethnic groups.

Migrants came to America from all regions of Italy, but the great waves of Italian immigrants arriving in North America between 1880 and 1920 were mostly southern Italians from regions such as Abruzzi, Campania, Apulia, Basilicata, and Calabria, and from the island of Sicily. Primarily peasant farmers and agricultural workers, these Italian immigrants were largely illiterate and had few technical skills. Many came as families before 1880; however, those who left southern Italy for North America after 1880 were more typically male sojourners between the ages of 16 and 45 who migrated with the express purpose of remaining in the United States for a year or two, earning as much money as they could, then returning to Italy. Of the 3.8 million Italians arriving in the United States between 1899 and 1924, 2.1 million departed in the same time period. The departure rate was somewhat higher for southern Italians than northern Italians. Some of the returnees stayed in Italy until they needed money again, then repeated the process; eventually many settled permanently in the United States, but not before they had made the voyage back and forth several times. After 1900 women and children joined the males migrating to the United States, so that migrations of entire families became more common.

The vast majority of Italians entered the United States through New York, settling in cities principally in the Northeast and Midwest. A large number of Italians stayed in New York; others moved on to cities such as Chicago, Boston, Philadelphia, Baltimore, Pittsburgh, Cleveland, Detroit, Milwaukee, Kansas City, St. Louis, and New Orleans, and farther west to Denver and San Francisco. San Francisco's Italian community was unusual in being predominantly of northern Italian origin. Italians became urban workers in a variety of trades and professions, such as the garment industry. Southern Italians became agricultural workers on sugar, rice, and cotton plantations in states such as Texas, Mississippi, and Louisiana, while northern and southern Italian migrants became tenants or landowners, cultivating vineyards or vegetable farms in California. Italians also became miners in states such as Colorado, West Virginia, and Minnesota.

In 1990, the states with the largest percentage of population of Italian ancestry were (in rank order) New York, New Jersey, California, Pennsylvania, and Massachusetts. For the United States as a whole, 14,664,560 persons claimed to be of Italian ancestry for the 1990 census, a number that represents 5.9 percent of the total population of 248,709,873. Results of the 1990 census show that Italians rank fifth among major groups reporting ancestry (figures rounded to the nearest million):

German	58 million	French	10 million
Irish	39 million	Polish	9 million
English	33 million	Am. Indian	9 million
African	24 million	Dutch	6 million
Italian	15 million	Scotch-Irish	6 million
Mexican	12 million	Scottish	5 million

Italians typically settled in central locations in cities, usually near the city's central business district, because the housing there was cheap and close to work and because, frequently, other Italian immigrants were already residents. Although they tried to settle close to other Italians, the Little Italys were never populated exclusively by Italians. In many cities, such as Baltimore, Italians shared their neighborhoods with other ethnic groups, particularly Germans, Poles, and Jews. In other cities, however, Italians neighborhoods were much more ethnically homogeneous, to the point of being dominated not merely by Italians, but by Italians from the same region. For example, in the period 1900 to 1930, more than 90 percent of the Italian settlement in southwest St. Louis, Missouri, known as "The Hill," hailed from a handful of Lombard and Sicilian villages and towns. Throughout North America, chain migration facilitated the selective migration of Italians to specific urban and rural sites to join relatives and neighbors from the same village.

As Italians improved their economic status, became culturally assimilated, and moved to other neighborhoods, and eventually to the suburbs, newly arrived Italians and other immigrants replaced them. This pattern of dispersal was typical for many immigrants; however, Italians were generally slower to move from their centrally located neighborhoods than other European ethnic groups. Moreover, their dispersal to the suburbs was by no means complete to the extent that Italians are now evenly distributed in suburban settlements. The process of dispersal from centrally located ethnic neighborhoods to the suburbs was activated by the 1920s, then slowed during the 1930s (because of the Depression) and 1940s because of wartime housing shortages. The process accelerated during the 1950s, due to the availability of more housing and for Italian American veterans access to benefits such as favorable rates for mortgage interest and mortgage insurance. Centrally located Italian neighborhoods continue to exist, if not flourish, but are characterized by a much diminished presence of residential Italians; often the only vestiges of Italian American settlement that remain are commercial establishments, such as food stores, and institutions, such as churches.

Few Italians migrating to America during the late nineteenth and early twentieth century had marketable skills, formal education, or an understanding of English. Italian Americans have advanced up the occupational, educational, and social hierarchy so that today their level of schooling and occupational status exceeds that of most Americans. The 1990 Bureau of the Census table presents statistics regarding selected demographic, social, and economic characteristics for persons of Italian ancestry and all persons in the United States. (see Table 1).

Nancy K. Torrieri

P

TABLE 1

Selected Demographic Characteristics for Persons of Italian Ancestry and All Persons, 1990

Characteristic	Persons of Italian ancestry	All persons
Median age	33.8	33.0
Nativity and year of entry	%	%
Native-born	94.3	92.1
Foreign-born	5.7	7.1
Entered 1980 to 1990	8.8	43.8
Entered before 1980	91.2	56.2
Naturalized citizen	72.6	40.5
Not a citizen	7.4	59.5
Occupation, employed persons 16 years and over		
Managerial and professional	29.6	26.4
Technical, sales, and administrative	35.7	31.7
Service	12.0	13.2
Farming, forestry, and fishing	1.0	2.5
Production, craft, and repair	11.1	11.3
Operations, fabrications, and laborers	10.7	14.9
Unemployed	4.9	6.3
Income in 1989 (households)		
Median income (dollars)	$36,060	$30,056
Mean income (dollars)	$44,865	$38,453
Income in 1989 (families)		
Median income (dollars)	$42,242	$35,225
Mean income (dollars)	$51,442	$43,803
Per capita income (dollars)	$17,384	$14,420
Poverty rate	%	%
Families	4.9	10.0
Persons	6.9	13.1
Mortgage status and gross rent		
Specified owner-occupied housing units	100%	100%
Median mortgage (dollars)	$278	$209
Specified renter-occupied housing units		
Median rent (dollars)	$519	$447
School enrollment and type of school	%	%
Persons 3 years and over enrolled	100	100
Preprimary school	8.1	6.9
Elementary or high school	58.3	65.5
College	33.6	27.6
Educational attainment		
Persons 25 years and over	100	100
High School graduate or higher	77.3	75.2
Bachelor's degree or higher	21.0	20.3
Graduate degree or higher	7.4	7.2
Ability to speak English		
Persons 5 years old and over	100	100
Speak a language other than English	12.5	13.8
Do not speak English "very well"	4.2	6.1
Persons 5 years old and over in households	100	100
in linguistically isolated households	1.7	3.5
Marital status		
Never married	27.2	26.5
Now married	57.2	55.5
Separated	1.6	2.3
Widowed	6.9	7.4
Divorced	7.1	8.3

SOURCE: Bureau of the Census.

Bibliography

LaGumina, Salvatore J. "Italian Americans: The Suburban Dimension." In *Italian Americans in Transition,* 27–37. Staten Island, NY: American Italian Historical Association, 1990.

Mormino, Gary. "The Hill Upon a City: The Evolution of an Italian-American Community in St. Louis, 1982–1950." In *Little Italies in North America,* edited by Robert F. Harney and J. Vincenza Scarpaci, 141–164. Toronto: Multicultural History Society of America, 1981.

Nelli, Humbert S. "Italians." In *Harvard Encyclopedia of Ethnic Groups,* edited by Stephan Thernstrom, Ann Orlov, and Oscar Handlin, 545–560. Cambridge, MA: Harvard University Press, 1980.

———. "Italians in Urban America." In *The Italian Experience in the United States,* edited by Silvano M. Tomasi and Madeline H. Engel, 77–107. Staten Island, NY: Center for Migration Studies, 1970.

Smith, Tom W. *A Profile of Italian-Americans: 1972–1991.* Chicago: National Opinion Research Center, 1992.

Torrieri, Nancy K. "The Geography of Ethnicity: The Residential Dispersal of Italians in Baltimore, 1920–1980." In *Italian Americans in Transition,* 49–64. Staten Island, NY: American Italian Historical Association, 1990.

U.S. Bureau of the Census, Ethnic and Hispanic Branch, Population Division, 1990 Census of Population and Housing, CPL-L-149. *Profiles of Our Ancestry: Selected Characteristics by Ancestry Group.* Washington, DC: Government Printing Office, 1990.

U.S. Bureau of the Census, 1990 Census of Population Supplementary Reports, CP-S-1-2. *Detailed Ancestry for States.* Washington, DC: Bureau of the Census, 1992.

Vecoli, Rudolph J. "Introduction." In *Italian Immigrants in Rural and Small Town America,* 1–6. Staten Island, NY: American Italian Historical Association, 1987.

Velikonja, Joseph. "Italian Immigrants in the United States in the Sixties." In *The Italian Experience in the United States,* edited by Silvano M. Tomasi and Madeline H. Engel, 23–39. Staten Island, NY: Center for Migration Studies, 1970.

Ethnic Ancestry and Identity

Assessing ethnic ancestry and identity are complex matters. Richard Alba suggests that in order to assess them correctly they must be measured in different ways. Most national surveys of American ethnic groups such as the General Social Surveys or the National Longitudinal Surveys attempt to do this by asking respondents several questions pertaining to their ancestries and ethnic identification. In these surveys, for example, respondents are usually asked first to enumerate the countries from which their ancestors originated. Then, a second question asks for the name of the one country respondents feel closest to in ethnic origin. The first question measures ancestry; the second assesses ethnic identity.

By this method a large number of Americans report mixed ethnic ancestries. For example, nearly half (46 percent) of the respondents to the 1994 General Social Survey reported two or more different countries of ethnic ancestry. In decennial census studies, by contrast, far higher percentages of respondents report a single country of ethnic ancestry. Why is it that census respondents are more likely to report a single country of ethnic ancestry? The answer revolves around the ethnicity question used in the census.

In the 1990 census only one question was employed to assess ethnic ancestry and identity: "What is [your] ancestry or ethnic origin?" Then, a list of examples follow, enumerating single country name choices. If a respondent was confused by this information they were advised to consult an accompanying instruction guide, "Your Guide to the 1990 Census," which would have shown two countries could be listed in the space provided, or that one could list there the one ancestry group with which the person identifies. Thus, the census combined or confused ethnic ancestry and identification into a single question.

Researchers undoubtedly prefer to use several questions to assess each of the components of ethnic ancestry and identification. Yet none of the available nationally representative surveys come anywhere close to representing adequately each and all of the local regions of the country. The census alone, with its vastly greater coverage of one in six of all households, makes it possible to approximate the distribution of Americans of Italian ancestry in the United States.

P

Map figures 1 and 2 below provide valuable information on the residential patterns of Americans of Italian ancestry. These maps were drawn from 1990 census data, aggregated by counties. Derived from census long forms, respondents provided ethnic origins or ancestry information for themselves (or for that of the householder of their domicile). Respondents were also asked what other languages besides English were spoken in their households.

Of the two maps, Figure 1, which shows the percentages claiming (or attributed to having) Italian ancestry, is the most meaningful one. This map shows Italian Americans concentrated in six states: Connecticut, Rhode Island, Massachusetts, New York, New Jersey, and Pennsylvania. Indeed, over half (56 percent) of those in the United States who identify themselves of Italian descent are located within this six-state region. Table 2 lists the counties with highest concentrations of Italian Americans. Richmond (Staten Island), New York, leads the list with 28 percent of its inhabitants considering themselves as Italian American. Looking over this list of high-ranked Italian American counties and comparing it to a similar list of most populous Italian American counties found in the 1980 census showed great convergence. All of the fifteen counties with the highest percentage of

TABLE 2

Counties With Highest Percentages of Italian Americans, 1990

County	Percent with both parents Italian
Richmond, NY	27.9
Putnam, NY	18.1
Westchester, NY	17.0
Suffolk, NY	16.0
New Haven, CT	15.7
Lawrence, PA	15.6
Nassau, NY	15.5
Bergen, NJ	15.3
Providence, RI	13.3
Ocean, NJ	12.8
Schenectady, NY	12.6
Oneida, NY	12.2
Passaic, NJ	11.9
Morris, NJ	11.8
Las Animas, CO	11.8

SOURCE: 1990 Census of Population and Housing, Summary Tape File 3A.

Italian Americans in 1990 were among the top twenty-five Italian American counties in 1980. Thus, for the last twenty years, if not for longer, Italian Americans have been concentrated in this six-state region.

This data also suggests that Italian Americans are consolidated in the big cities of New

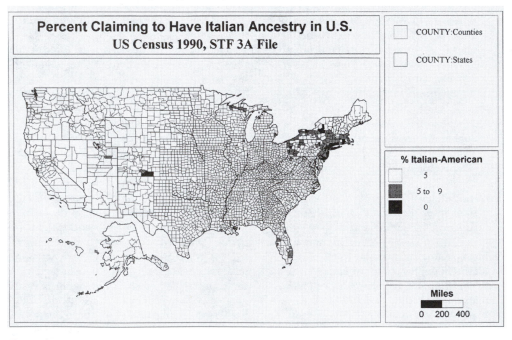

Percent Claiming to Have Italian Ancestry in U.S.
US Census 1990, STF 3A File

COUNTY:Counties
COUNTY:States

% Italian-American
5
5 to 9
0

Miles
0   200   400

Figure 1

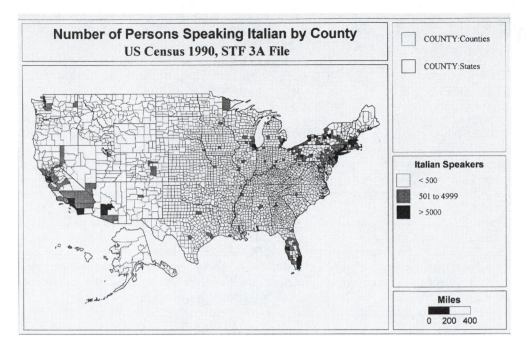

Number of Persons Speaking Italian by County
US Census 1990, STF 3A File

COUNTY:Counties

COUNTY:States

Italian Speakers
< 500
501 to 4999
> 5000

Miles
0   200   400

Figure 2

York, Albany, Rochester, Syracuse, Philadelphia, Pittsburgh, Bridgeport, Hartford, Providence, Boston, and their surrounding suburbs. There is also evidence of high concentrations of people of Italian ancestry in rural New York, New Jersey, and Rhode Island. Yet relying entirely upon the data of those claiming Italian ancestry could lead to a distorted impression of Italian American convergence, which concludes that they are concentrated almost exclusively in the Northeastern states.

According to Figure 2, which displays the counties with five thousand or more who speak Italian in their household's locality, there are large numbers of Italian Americans residing in several other metropolitan regions located in the West: around the San Francisco Bay area; in and around Los Angeles and Southern California; and in Chicago, Detroit, and Buffalo, New York, as well. They are also concentrated in several new Sunbelt locations, such as Tampa–St. Petersburg, Florida, from Miami north to Fort Pierce, Florida, and in the Phoenix and Tucson, Arizona, metropolitan areas. Both figures attest to the trend of Italian Americans to live in metropolitan locations. Table 3, listing the fifteen counties with the highest numbers of Italian speakers, again confirms that the huge convergence of Italian Americans reside from Hartford, Connecticut,

TABLE 3

Counties With Highest Number of People Who Speak Italian, 1990

County	Number who speak Italian
Brooklyn (Kings), NY	78,000
Queens, NY	65,781
Chicago (Cook), IL	46,155
Nassau, NY	41,496
Westchester, NY	36,861
Middlesex, NJ	29,621
Suffolk, NY	29,292
Los Angeles, CA	28,454
Bronx, NY	28,371
Bergen, NJ	27,158
Philadelphia, PA	23,974
New Haven, CT	23,877
Fairfield, CT	19,226
Richmond (Staten Island), NY	18,191
Hartford, CT	18,166

SOURCE: 1990 Census of Population and Housing, Summary Tape File 3A.

to Philadelphia, Pennsylvania. Both maps suggest that among the least preferred areas for Italian American settlement are the Midwest and the South (except for Florida).

William Feigelman

Bibliography

Alba, Richard D. *Ethnic Identity: The Transformation of White America.* New Haven, CT: Yale University Press, 1990.

Davis, James A., and Tom W. Smith. *General Social Surveys, 1972–1994: Cumulative Codebook.* Chicago: National Opinion Research Center, 1994.

Settlement Patterns in the Northeast

Propelled by a host of economic, demographic, and political factors, and attracted by the prospects for a better life, millions of Italians left Italy after its unification in 1870. Nearly fourteen million Italians migrated from Italy between 1876 and 1914, over half of whom crossed the Atlantic. In 1898 the United States replaced South America as the major destination of transoceanic Italian emigrants. From 1902 until the Naturalization Acts of the 1920s, the United States annually attracted more Italians than Argentina and Brazil combined. Although Italians at first settled throughout the United States, by 1910 most Italians lived in the Middle Atlantic states (New York, Pennsylvania, and New Jersey having the most Italians respectively), southern New England (Massachusetts, Connecticut, and Rhode Island), and the Midwest (Illinois and Ohio).

In 1960 New Jersey replaced Pennsylvania as the state with the second largest Italian population, with 10.6 percent of the Italian-born in the country living in the Garden State. By then Italian Americans made up the largest ethnic or racial group in New Jersey.

Between 1899 and 1910 over 80 percent of arriving Italians came from the regions of central and southern Italy; nearly 80 percent were male and over 80 percent were in the prime working ages between 14 and 44. Most of the southern Italian immigrants could not read or write, were of peasant or working class origin, and were poor, often arriving with some seventeen dollars—about two weeks' wages for unskilled workers in the United States.

Nearly all (98.9 percent) of the immigrants from central and southern Italy between 1899 and 1910 knew their destination—to join relatives or friends who had already settled in the country. This chain migration of Italians congregating together form the basis of America's Little Italys, which in turn were

Italian Mutual Aid Society officials prepare for celebration in the Italian enclave of Inwood, New York, in the mid-1930s. Hundreds of such societies flourished among the first and second generations in the Little Italys across the nation. From the collection of Margaret Sciallo Lanza. Courtesy Salvatore J. LaGumina.

characterized by people from particular regions and towns living in close proximity.

The settlement pattern affected organizational, cultural, religious, and political life. In Trenton, New Jersey, for example, many mutual-benefit, cultural, and political clubs reflected the founders' place of origin: The Neapolitan Republican League, Roman Beneficial Society, Società Operaia Mutuo Soccorso Villalbo, Unione e frattelanza Sanfelese, Neapolitan Mutual Benefit Society, Neapolitan Juvenile Dramatic Circle, Monteleonese Society, Favignana Beneficial Society, Società di Mutuo Succorso Caseltermini, Leonessana Abruzzese Society of Mutual Aid, and Società Trento e Trieste, among others. The transplanted Italian American feasts, so important to communal and religious life of the settlers, also reflected place of origin: the feasts of the Madonna S.S. di Cassandrino in Trento, held annually in September, and the Giglio (a huge tower that is danced in the streets) feast of San Paolino of Nola, today celebrated in July in Brooklyn, New York, simultaneously with the feast of Our Lady of Mount Carmel, so important to Neapolitans, are three outstanding examples of surviving feasts.

New York City always has had the largest concentration of Italians. Historically, Italian Americans in New York and Pennsylvania have been more city-oriented that in New Jersey. There Italian Americans have always been dispersed, because the Garden State lacks huge cities and industry, the chief attraction to Italian immigrants.

After World War II Italian Americans became more upwardly mobile in education, economic status, and social position. Many also achieved success as elected officials at all levels of government: local, county, state, and federal. As postwar Americans moved to the suburbs, and as industry and commerce abandoned northeastern cities, many successful Italian Americans joined the exodus to suburbia.

Marconiville, Long Island. Real estate entrepreneur Giovanni Campagnoli advertised Marconiville (Copiague), which he named for his former classmate, the world-renowned wireless inventor Guglielmo Marconi. The community was promoted in Italian newspapers as an "Italian" village near the sea. Courtesy Salvatore J. LaGumina.

The formerly thriving Little Italys shrank in all the big cities, and in some cases have virtually disappeared. The elderly, working class, and small business people dependent on the urban neighborhood clientele now make up the remaining Italian American population in city enclaves.

The urban riots of the 1960s in Newark (1967) and Trenton (1968) accelerated the Italian American exodus from cities and public schools, as race relations became inflamed between the remaining Italian Americans and African Americans. Urban Italian Americans, feeling beleaguered, feared crime and changes in their neighborhood. Meanwhile postwar Italian Americans, now far more educated and prosperous, were more likely to settle in the suburbs than cities.

Today the largest ethnic group on Long Island is composed of Italian Americans. Suburban Philadelphia has seen a dramatic rise in Italian American residents. In New Jersey, not only have the Little Italys in all the six largest cities declined in cities over fifty thousand, but most Italian Americans now live in communities under fifty thousand. This corresponds with the region's general reduction of people living in cities and the shift of industry and commerce to suburban areas.

Dennis J. Starr

Bibliography

Juliani, Richard J. *The Social Organization of Immigration: The Italians of Philadelphia.* Francesco Cordasco, ed. North Stratford, NH: Ayer, 1981.

LaGumina, Salvatore J. *From Steerage to Suburb: Long Island Italians.* New York: Center for Migration Studies of New York, 1989.

Starr, Dennis J. *The Italians of New Jersey: A Historical Introduction and Bibliography.* Newark: New Jersey Historical Society, 1985.

Suburban Settlement

In recording the demographic patterns of immigrants from the late nineteenth to the early twentieth centuries, social scientists identified them as people who settled in urban centers. Eschewing traditional farm life that characterized the earlier immigrants, these latecomers deliberately settled in the large industrial cities of the Northeast (New York, Philadelphia, Boston) and some midwestern cities

(Chicago). The urban affinity was far from unique since these settlement patterns mirrored those of native-born Americans then abandoning farm life for industrial hubs. However, because they were newcomers with widely different cultural patterns from earlier arrivals, the Italian settlement configurations appeared more conspicuous.

Few new immigrant peoples fit the urban model settlement as did Italians, with exception of the minority of Italian immigrants who settled in California and other western and southern states. From the 1880s on, for the following century, commentators on Italian immigration constantly restated the phenomenon to such a degree that Italian immigrants virtually became the epitome of city dwellers. Here in large cities they worked at the lowest rungs of the economic ladders as construction workers, barbers, tailors, and seamstresses. Here, too, they were required to live in the worst neighborhoods in unhealthy, multilevel tenements abandoned by earlier immigrant groups.

However, a couple of generations later, by the late 1940s, Italian Americans joined the exodus from the inner city to the suburbs. Improving their education and economic and social status, an increasing number of Italian Americans followed the path already developed by older stock Americans. Locating in suburbs brought them closer to the land, where they could own their own homes and escape the stressful environment of congested, fast-paced city enclaves. Movement to the suburbs, furthermore, reflected a deliberate choice by second- and third-generation Italian Americans. As one historian put it: "The exodus of Italians to the suburbs was more than the result of favorable material conditions. There was an eagerness to leave the small world of the neighborhood and enter the mainstream of American life."

The trek from inner cities to suburbs found some Italian Americans seeking homes in existing Italian sections of an earlier era; others joined the migration to new suburban communities that were nonexistent in the pre–World War II period. Levittown, New York, is a good example. Developed in the late 1940s from acreage that had been devoted to potato growing, it became one of Long Island's largest communities. By 1980, 25.9 percent of Levittown's population was of Italian ancestry. Even more telling is the case of Shirley, Long Island, that hardly existed before the 1940s, yet by 1980 Italian Americans represented 40.1 percent of its population.

With well over 650,000 Italian Americans living in Nassau and Suffolk counties by the end of the 1970s, they had emerged as the largest single nationality group in the nation's archetypical suburb. This number represented probably the greatest concentration of Italian Americans in any two contiguous counties in the country.

Although Italian Americans remained in large cities for a longer period of time than many other white ethnic groups, and even though a number of distinctive urban Little Italys may still exist, the post–World War II era saw a definite population shift from urban to suburban locations so that currently more Italian Americans live in the latter than in the former sites. Nor should this trend be surprising since so many immigrants had come from small towns and villages where they worked the soil and owned residences, however modest. By opting for the suburbs they were able to satisfy their overwhelming desire to own homes in physical settings similar to the environment they left behind in Italy. They could work the land, although few became permanent, full-time farmers.

To live in the suburban environment represented a number of important achievements. It frequently meant accumulating sufficient capital to finance the undertaking, encountering less discrimination, and experiencing the opportunity for more rapid assimilation. While they did not duplicate the ethnic neighborhoods of the large cities, Italian Americans did exhibit interest in ethnic activities. Many joined organizations such as the Order Sons of Italy in America or other ethnic-oriented civic, cultural, religious, and social societies. They also manifested strong interest and involvement in nonethnic political, social, religious, and labor activities. Along with suburbia's general population, they valued and participated in educational endeavors. Interaction with other ethnic groups was a concomitant of suburban life resulting in increased rates of intermarriages.

Italian Americans in the suburbs exemplify a variegated people, a many-dimensioned populace who offer a range of ethnic behavioral patterns. As such, they reflect the heterogeneity of society as a whole even as they are identified as Italian Americans.

Salvatore J. LaGumina

Bibliography

LaGumina, Salvatore J., ed. *Ethnicity in Suburbia: The Long Island Experience.* Garden City, NY: Nassau Community College, 1980.

———. *From Steerage to Suburb: Long Island Italians.* New York: Center for Migration Studies, 1988.

———. "Italian Americans: The Suburban Dimension." In *Italian Americans in Transition,* edited by Joseph V. Scelsa, Lydio Tomasi, and Salvatore J. LaGumina, 27–37. New York: American Italian Historical Association, 1990.

Scelsa, Joseph V., Salvatore J. LaGumina, and Lydio Tomasi, eds. *Italian Americans in Transition.* New York: American Italian Historical Association, 1990.

Tricarico, Donald. *The Italians of Greenwich Village.* New York: Center for Migration Studies, 1984.

Press, Italian American

In dealing with the Italian American press and its role in American society, there is a vast amount of material in books, newspapers, journals, magazines, and other periodicals printed in the United States. Since the coverage of books on Italian Americans published by such New York houses as Arno Press, Vigo Press, and the Center for Migration Studies would distract from the role of the Italian American press in American society, this entry will restrict itself to the four other types of publications.

Like other ethnic publications in the history of the United States, the Italian American press served a twofold purpose. While it gave its immigrant readers information about the new country, it also provided them with news from their native country. In this way, immigrants were able to settle into a new society in which the press, in addition to neighborhood churches and the schools, played a vital role in helping them to adjust.

"Once almost every city and town with an Italian community from the East to the West had its Italian newspaper," wrote Jerre Mangione and Ben Morreale in their recent history. However, because of changing interests and costs, many of the publications are no longer in existence since they have gone the way of such American publications as *Look, The Saturday Evening Post,* and *Collier's.*

Very little has been written about the Italian American press. To survey the Italian American press properly, it will be helpful to concentrate on those states where, according to the federal census of 1990, most of the fifteen million Italian Americans reside.

New York has the largest concentration of Italian Americans, with 2.9 million, constituting 16 percent of the state's population. In New York City, many Italian American newspapers have been published, such as *L'Eco d'Italia* (1850), the only daily available when the city had twenty-five thousand Italian Americans. Also known as *Rivista Italo-Americano*, it evolved into a weekly and a semiweekly prior to its demise after fifty years. Others were *Il Proscritto* (1851), a weekly dealing with politics, art, and literature; *L'Unione dei Popoli* (1870), a short-lived weekly; *L'Italo Americano* (1871), a weekly; *Cristoforo Columbo* (1887), a daily until 1897; *L'Araldo Italiano* (1889), a daily until 1921; *La Follia* or *Follia di New York* (1893), originally a weekly until 1907, it became a monthly until 1955 and afterward a bimonthly; *L'Italiano in America* (1894), a weekly; *Bollettino della Sera* (1898), a newspaper for the city and the nation until at least 1922, reaching a circulation of sixty thousand in 1920; *La Scintilla Elettrica* (1900), a weekly; *Il Telegrafo* (1902), an evening daily lasting to 1922; *America* or *Bollettino della Domenica* (1903), a weekly; *Il Corriere d'Italia* (1907), a weekly; *La Vita Internazionale* (1908), a weekly; *Corriere della Sera* (1909), a daily until 1933; *Il Corriere Italiano* (1909), a daily until 1921; *Il Cittadino* (1910), a weekly until 1919; *Sicilia* (1911), a weekly, especially for Sicilians in the United States; *Il Pensiero Italiano* (1914), a weekly that ended in 1928; *La Vedetta* (1917), an irregular weekly (also known as *Il Nuovo Vessillo*) for Italians in the Bronx and Long Island, ending in 1938; *Corriere d'America* (1922), a daily; *La Gazzetta del Notaio Italo-Americano* (1922), a monthly; *Il Foro* (1923), a weekly; *Il Popolo* (1923), a weekly turned into a monthly by 1938; *Corriere Siciliano* (1931), a weekly until 1942; *La Voce d'Italia* (1935), a weekly with a short span to 1937; *Il Mondo* (1938), a short-lived monthly closing down in 1941; *La Rassegna Italiana* (1938), a weekly; *La Legione dell'Italia del Popolo* (1942), also known as *L'Italia Libera* (1943), a weekly that became a semimonthly to 1946; and *Italo-American Times* (1964), a bimonthly out of the Bronx, evolving into a monthly by 1977.

While the Italian American press in New York has produced over the years almost sixty publications, perhaps no newspaper dominated readership as did *Il Progresso Italo-Americano* (1880), inaugurated by Carlo Barsotti, an immigrant from Tuscany, who managed it until 1927. Considering itself the "first Italian daily newspaper in the United States," it reached a circulation of more than 125,000 by the 1920s and even more by the early 1940s. Though it declined to half that number by the 1970s, its dominance continued under Barsotti's successor, Generoso Pope, a New York Democrat who used it to defend Fascism during the 1930s. Thereafter, under Pope's sons, especially Fortune Pope, the paper continued until its end in 1989. Its successor, *America Oggi,* functions as the only daily Italian language newspaper into the 1990s.

Other cities in the same state had their own publications. Albany had *La Capitale* (1908), a monthly evolving into a weekly under the Farinacci family, published until 1985, and *L'Internazionale* (1908), a weekly. Amsterdam had *L'Internazionale* (1909), a weekly. Auburn had *Il Sole* (1901), a weekly. Buffalo had *Il Corriere Italiano* (1898), a weekly, and socialist newspapers like *La Fiaccola* (1909) and *Il Pensiero* (1915). Dunkirk had *Il Risveglio* (1928), a weekly. Niagara Falls had *Il Risveglio Italiano* (1920), a weekly, that lasted until about 1945. Rochester had its weeklies, which included *La Tribuna di Rochester* (1906) that evolved into *La Stampa Unita di Rochester* (1920), *The Rochester Press* (1940), *L'Unione* (1917), and *Il Settimanale Italiano* (1928), while the labor voice was raised in such papers as *La Domenica* (1912) and *L'Italiana* (1938). Rome had *La Vita* (1916), a weekly, also known as *Rome Tribune*, until 1931. Schnectady had *L'Internazionale* (1908), a weekly. Syracuse had weeklies such as *La Gazzetta di Syracuse* (1906), *Risveglio Coloniale* (1907), *L'Unione* (1908), and *Il Corriere di Syracuse* (1918). Utica had weeklies like *Utica L'Avvenire* (1900) to 1905, *La Luce* (1901) to 1917 when it joined with *Il Pensiero Italiano* (1914) to 1929, *L'Aurora* (1902), *La Tribuna d'Utica* (1912), *Lotta Operaia* (1913), *La Colonia* (1914), *La Sentinella* (1915), *Il Messaggero* (1921), *Utica Italian News* (1926),

Italian Press (1930), and *La Stella* (1932), all reflecting various interests. And Watertown had *L'Internazionale* (1908), a weekly.

New York's Italian American press also set the tone for other works. There were publications like New York City's *Swiss American Review* (1868), a weekly published in English, French, German, and Romansh, in addition to Italian, with a circulation today of four thousand; *Il Carroccio* (1915), a bilingual magazine until 1937; *Columbus* (1915), a cultural link with Italy; *L'Araldo dei Figli d'Italia* (1916), the voice of the Sons of Italy (for a long time, Albany had its own version, *Il Ruggito*); *Il Corriere Italo-Americano* (1916), an irregular monthly to 1951; *La Parola del Medico* (1916), a monthly for the medical profession; *American and Italian Journal of Commerce* (1919), also irregular; *Italian-American Review* (1921), a bimonthly of the Italian Historical Society; *La Gazzetta del Notaio Italo-Americano* (1922), a monthly to 1925; *Atlantica* (1923), a monthly to 1940; *Il Commerciante Italiano* (1932), a weekly that became a semimonthly; *ENIT News* (1933), a semimonthly for Italian tourists; *Il Prodotto Italiano* (1937), a monthly (also known as *Italamerican Magazine*) to at least 1952; *The Vigo Review* (1938), a journal edited by Giovanni Schiavo and published by Vigo Press, which had launched *The Italian American Who's Who* (1935); *Divagando* (1943), a weekly review in Italian that once had the highest circulation; *American Chamber of Commerce for Italy* (1951), a publication mainly for business; *ACIM Dispatch* (1953), an irregular voice of the American Committee on Italian Immigration; *America Italy Newsletter* (1954), a serial similarly sponsored by the America-Italy Society, Inc.; *Forum Italicum* (1967), a cultural quarterly published at Stony Brook or in Buffalo by the State University of New York; *Italian Quarterly News* (1976) or *Italian Monthly,* a product from Barnard College's Italian Studies Program like *Canale Tre* (1978), a biweekly from the same source; *Attenzione* (1979), a bimonthly of general cultural value to 1987; *National Organization of Italian American Women* (1981), a feminist quarterly; *John D. Calandra Institute* (1986), a newsletter produced at the City University of New York (CUNY); *Italian Journal* (1987), a bimonthly of the Italian Academy Foundation, Inc.; *Arba Sicula* (1990), a journal about the folklore and literature of Sicily

published by St. John's University; *The Italian American Review* (1992), by the Verrazzano Institute at Mercy College and now by CUNY; *Review Italy* (1995); and, not surprisingly, there was a magazine entitled *I AM* (1976).

At least two of the publications out of New York City have subsidiary chapters in other parts of the country. One is *Italica* (1924), a quarterly of the American Association of Teachers of Italian published at Columbia University with Bloomington, Indiana, and Menasha, Wisconsin, listed. The other is the *AIHA Newsletter* (1967), the voice of the American Italian Historical Association founded in 1966 that set up chapters with their own newsletters in California, District of Columbia, Maryland, New Jersey, Metropolitan New York City, Illinois-Wisconsin-Indiana, Long Island (with *L'Isola* as its newsletter), and Minnesota (*Notizie della Stella del Nord* was its newsletter), in addition to its national publication.

In addition to cultural publications, there were religious periodicals based in New York. Catholics had *Corriere della Domenica* (1894), which had a circulation of about twelve thousand in 1930, and *Il Crociato* (1933), a publication of the Roman Catholic Diocese of Brooklyn until about 1976. Among Protestants, Methodists had *Rivista Evangelica, Nord America* (1899), a weekly until 1911 and, then, *La Fiaccola* (1911), a weekly journal until 1933 devoted to religious, moral, and civic reform; and the Evangelicals, through their publication society in Nyack, had *Il Rinnovamento* (1933), a monthly.

Also, given the economic and political concerns of the country during the early half of the twentieth century, it is not surprising to find workers who came up with their own publications. There was *Il Novatore* (1910), a short-lived anarchist semimonthly. The Amalgamated Clothing Workers of America had *Il Lavoro* (1914), a weekly. The International Ladies' Garment Workers' Union had *L'Operaria* (1917) and *Giustizia* (1918) as its publications. The International Workers of the World in New York City published, before 1920, such radical papers as *Il Diretto, Guerra di Classe, Il Martello,* and *Il Proletario.* The latter ran from 1896 to 1942 and was accompanied by *Il Nuovo Proletario* (1918). *L'Adunata dei Refrattari* (1922) was a biweekly with an anarchist voice; *L'Unità del*

San Francisco's North Beach boys preparing to distribute copies of the Italian language daily L'Italia, *which was edited by Ettore Patrizi, 1910. Courtesy Augusto Troiani.*

Popolo (1939), a weekly that soon became a monthly as it continued with a communist slant to 1954; and *Nazioni Unite* (1942), an anti-Fascist semimonthly by the Mazzini Society to 1946. *L'Avvenire* (1943) was a biweekly following the ideas of Carlo Tresca, the originator of *Il Martello,* which circulated from 1916 to 1946.

Next to New York in number of Italian Americans is California, which today has 1.5 million, making up 5 percent of the state's population. In the past, San Francisco has been the leader in Italian American publications with *L'Eco della Patria* (1859), the work of Federico Biesta; *La Voce del Popolo* (1867), once the only daily for Italians in California, which continued until 1943; *L'Unione Nazionale* (1868), a daily; *L'Independente* (1880), a semiweekly; *Almanacco Italo-Svizzero Americano* (1881), an annual; *L'Italia* (1886), a daily originating with Ettore Patrizi and continuing to around 1945; *L'Italia* (1887), a daily that became *The Italian Daily News* (1943) and lasted until 1965; *La Vita Italiana* (1910), a weekly; *L'Unione* (1919), a weekly, also known as *Tribuna; Italian-American News* (1948), a bi-

weekly; *L'Eco d'Italia* (1966), a weekly; and *La Bella Figura* (1988), a quarterly for women published up to 1992. At the same time, *Il Corriere del Popolo* (1911) was an evolving socialist publication that lasted until 1967 after anarchist periodicals like *Secolo Nuovo* (1894), *La Protesta Umana* (1900), and *Nihil* (1909) had vanished.

The religious press was also in California, where Catholics on the West Coast had *Osservatore Cattolico* (1875), the first religious newspaper in Italian. It was followed in San Francisco by others such as *Imparziale* (1891) with a circulation of about a one thousand, *Unione* (1912) with at least seven thousand, and *Bollettino della Federazione Cattolica Italiana* (1924), the voice of the Central Council of the Catholic Federation. For Protestants, *La Pura Verità,* a monthly of the Worldwide Church of God, came out of Pasadena around the early 1960s.

There are a number of cities in California outside San Francisco with Italian American publications. In Los Angeles, there was *L'Italo Americano di Los Angeles* (1908), a weekly (also known as *Gente Italiana in California*) founded by the Fathers of St. Charles in Sun Valley and renamed *L'Italo-Americano Newspaper* (1943), with a recent circulation of thirty-five thousand. In Palos Verdes, an annual is published, *The American Journal of Italian Genealogy* (1989). In Sacramento, *La Capitale* (1907), a weekly, was published until 1945, and *Il Caffè* (1981), a cultural journal, has made a recent appearance. In Sausalito, *Star West* (1969) was published in English, French, German, and Spanish, in addition to Italian. In Stockton, *La Terra* (1906), a socialist weekly, made a brief debut. And, in Riverside, *Italian-American Review* (1957), a cultural quarterly, has been published by the University of California.

Almost equal to California in the number of Italian Americans is New Jersey with 1.5 million, but, unlike California, New Jersey Italian Americans are more prominent, since as a group they constitute 20 percent of the population. Atlantic City had *Popolo Italiano* (1935), which evolved from a daily to a bimonthly, and *Italian-American Herald* (1961), a weekly. Hoboken had *La Sentinella* (1903), a radical weekly that followed the demise of West Hoboken's *L'Aurora* (1899), an anarchist weekly. Morristown recently had the American Italian Heritage Association's newsletter. Newark, where *Monitore Cattolico,* a religious journal of unknown origins once existed, had *Il Corriere della Domenica* (1895), a Catholic weekly also published in Philadelphia; and Bloomfield, New Jersey, had *Italian Tribune* (1931), a weekly, which became *Italian Tribune News* (1969) with a circulation of almost 19,500 in 1970 and 25,000 today. Nutley saw the Stromboli American Heritage Society publish its own *Newsletter* (1987). Paterson had *La Questione Sociale* (1895), a paper that lasted at least to 1908 as an anarchist voice; *L'Era Nuova* (1908), another anarchist paper until 1919; *La Scopa* (1925), an anti-Fascist weekly until 1928; *La Voce Italiana* (1934), which lasted to 1986; and *Star Bulletin* (1959), a weekly. Rutherford had *La Vita Nuova* (1908), an irregular semimonthly. Trenton had *La Nuova Capitale* (1929), a weekly until 1975, and *Il Cittadino* (1942), a weekly that ended in 1951. Recently, Westwood had *America Oggi* (1988), a daily that evolved into *Oggi* (1991) with a circulation of sixty-five thousand, thereby succeeding *Il Progresso* as the leader for Italian Americans.

Ettore Patrizi (1865—1946), editor and publisher of the influential Italian language newspaper L'Italia *in San Francisco from 1897 to 1946. He promoted cultural and community activities benefiting Italians. He also expressed support for Italian Fascism. Courtesy Augusto Troiani.*

In Pennsylvania, where 1.4 million Italian Americans constitute 12 percent of the population, there has also been a strong Italian American press. Altoona had *L'Operaio Italiano* (1910), a voice of labor. Harrisburg had *La Voce Italo-Americana* (1927), a weekly continuing at least until 1941. New Castle had a publication, *La Gazzetta* (1928), a weekly. Philadelphia, of course, dominated with such publications as *La Gazzetta Italiana,* a weekly started in the 1850s; *Il Proletario* (1896), a weekly of the International Workers of the World until 1915; *L'Opinione* (1906), a daily; *Il Momento* (1915), a weekly that went to 1919; *La Libera Parola* (1917), a weekly, published by the Di Silvestro family to 1969; *La Ragione* (1917), an irregularly published work; *La Rassegna* (1917), an irregular weekly; *Il Popolo Italiano* (1934), a monthly that evolved into a bimonthly by the early 1990s; *Il Paese* (1938), an anti-Fascist weekly; and *Italian-American Herald* (1961), a weekly. Pittsburgh had *Il Cittadino Americano* (1894), a weekly; *La Vita* (1926), also known as *L'Era Nuova;* and *Alba* (1929), an anarchist voice. Reading had *Berks-County Italo-American* (1960), a monthly, and *La Voce Italiana* (1978), a weekly. And Wilkes-Barre had *L'Ascesa del Proletariato* (1909), a socialist biweekly.

Religious publications, too, were important for Italian immigrants in Pennsylvania. Out of Philadelphia, Catholics saw *Il Corriere della Domenica* (1895), *L'Osservatore* or *Il Risveglio Italiano* (1905), *Italica Gente* (1908), under the Augustinian Fathers, with a circulation of two thousand in 1930, and *La Verità* (1909), while *La Trinacria* (1900), a weekly, came out in Pittsburgh under Perla Arderio, enjoying a circulation of four thousand in 1930. Protestants, through their Association of Evangelicals for Italian Missions, published, in Upper Darby, *The New Aurora* (1903), which had a circulation of 1,300 in the early 1970s, and *La Verità* (1901), a biweekly evangelical publication out of Philadelphia.

Italian Americans had social organizations with their own publications. From Philadelphia, the Sons of Italy published *Ordine Nuova* (1936), a weekly until 1952, when it evolved into a monthly before becoming *Sons of Italy Times* (1959) with a circulation of almost thirty thousand in the late 1960s, declining eventually to half that number, while the American Sons of Italy published *Italian American Courier News* (1949). And, from Pittsburgh, the Order of Italian Sons and Daughters of America published *Unione* (1890), a weekly, and the Federation of Sons of Columbus of America had *Columbus Press* (1933), a semimonthly.

In Massachusetts, with 845,000 Italian Americans, constituting 15 percent of the population, a number of periodicals were published. Boston had the most, including *Il Corriere di Boston* (1893), a weekly that lasted to 1906; *La Gazzetta del Massachusetts* (1896), a weekly originated by James Donnarumma, became *La Gazzetta del Massachusetts & New England* (1960) before it evolved into *La Gazzetta* (1961) and *The Post-Gazette* (1962) under Caesar Donnarumma; *Il Proletario* (1896), an anarchist weekly for IWW until around 1915; *La Tribuna del Popolo* (1911), a weekly that lasted until World War I; *Il Cronista* (1914), a weekly; *La Notizia* (1916), a daily that evolved into a weekly in 1964, rising to a circulation of nearly twenty-five thousand by the early 1970s; *L'Internazionale* (1917), a

socialist weekly; *The Italian News* (1921), once the state's only Italian weekly in English; *Il Giornale d'America* (1926), a daily for New England; *L'Aurora* (1928), an anarchist semi-monthly that became a monthly in 1929; and *La Controcorrente* (1938), an anti-Fascist paper.

In addition, there were other cities in the Bay State with their own Italian American publications. Lynn published *Cronica Sovversiva* (1912), a revolutionary chronicle started by Luigi Galleani in Vermont, which was read avidly by Nicola Sacco and Bartolomeo Vanzetti and claimed the support of five thousand in 1918 before its demise in 1920. Pittsfield had *Il Corriere del Berkshire* (1930), a weekly for Italians in the western part of the state. Revere provided the Boston area with *Sons of Italy News,* the voice of an organization founded in New York in 1905, which rose in circulation to fourteen thousand in the early 1970s. Springfield had *L'Eco Coloniale della New England* (1913), a weekly until 1920. In Worcester, there was *OSIA News* (1945), a monthly also published for the Order Sons of Italy until 1995.

In Florida, where eight hundred thousand Italian Americans constitute 6 percent of the state's population, the Italian press has been a viable force. From the area of Hillsborough County, for the cigar and tobacco centers at Tampa and Ybor City, Italian workers read *La Voce della Colonia* (1911), the state's only weekly in Italian until 1929; *L'Aurora* (1912), the weekly voice of the Socialist Party; *La Voce dello Schiavo* (1900), an anarchist monthly; *L'Alba Sociale* (1901), a radical biweekly; *L'Organizzatore* (1920), another weekly voice of the workers in the cigar and tobacco industries; and *La Gaceta* (1922), a paper published in English and Spanish as well as in Italian with a recent circulation of eighteen thousand. In Fort Lauderdale there is *The Florida Italian Bulletin,* published by the European Cultural Bureau since the 1950s. In 1991, *Bel Paese,* a monthly newspaper that highlighted Italian and Italian American events, began publication in Boca Raton, and *VIA* (The Voice of the Italian American) publishes in Tamarac. The Sons of Italy publishes monthly *La Famiglia* (1984) and *La Voce Italiana* (1987).

Illinois has 730,000 Italian Americans, who make up 6 percent of the state's population, and it is among the states with an active

Italian American press. Historically, most are Chicago publications like *L'Unione Italiana* (1867), a weekly; *L'Italia* (1886), which evolved into *Il Corriere dell' Italia* (1888); *Il Movimento* (1912), a weekly; *Italian News* (1916) and *Italian News of Chicago* (1942), which became at various times a daily, a tri-weekly, and a weekly; *Il Messaggero* (1888), a semiweekly; *La Tribuna Italiana Trans-Atlantica* (1898), a weekly that existed in the Windy City until 1911; *La Tribuna Italiana* (1909), a biweekly in Herrin; *The Bulletin of Italian Chamber of Commerce of Chicago* (1907), a bimonthly; *La Fiaccola* (1914), a Methodist weekly; *The New Generation* (1923), a monthly; *Italian American Guardian* (1952), a weekly from 1952; *I.A.N.U. Bulletin,* a quarterly of the Italo-American National Union going back to 1958; *Fra Noi,* a successful monthly, started at Northlake in 1961, which was published in Melrose Park in 1965 and continues its circulation into the 1990s; and *Red White & Green Sports* (1982), the publication of the Italian American Sports Hall of Fame published in Arlington Heights.

Furthermore, Chicago had radical newspapers like the IWW's *Il Proletario* (1896), a weekly that eventually became *Il Nuovo Proletario* (1913), evolving into a semimonthly between 1921 and 1928; *La Protesta Umana* (1902), an anarchist paper; *Parola Proletaria* (1906), *La Parola del Popolo* (1908), and *L'Avanti* (1918), three socialist ones; and *Il Lavoratore Italiano* (1919), a communist weekly. In Kensington, *La Gogna,* an anarchist paper, made a brief appearance in 1909.

In Connecticut, Italian Americans number 650,000, or 20 percent of the population. Publications were found in various cities. Bridgeport had *Il Sole* (1901), a weekly; *Corriere di Bridgeport* (1903), a weekly until 1904; *La Tribuna del Connecticut* (1906) a weekly that also served Port Chester and Danbury until 1908; *La Vera Redenzione* (1916), an anarchist biweekly; and *La Vittoria* (1929), also a weekly. Fairfield County had a weekly called *La Voce* (1973). Hartford had *La Capitale Tribuna di Hartford* (1919), a weekly; *The Connecticut Bulletin* (1930), a biweekly; and *The Connecticut Italian Bulletin* (1950), a biweekly with a circulation of five thousand in 1970. Middletown had a bilingual weekly, *Middletown Bulletin* (1947), until 1949. New Britain had *Il Messaggero del New England* (1931), a weekly. New Haven

had two weeklies, *Il Corriere del Connecticut* (1893) and *Italian-American* (1930). Newington came out with *La Voce* (1973), a weekly. And Waterbury, with a strong Italian community, had *La Verità,* a weekly from the early twentieth century; *Il Progresso di Waterbury* (1906), a weekly also entitled *Il Progresso del New England;* and *Il Cittadino del Connecticut* (1924), a weekly until 1942.

Italian Americans number 640,000 in Ohio, making up 6 percent of the state's population. Here there were publications in at least three cities. In Cleveland, there were *L'Italiano* (1908), a weekly until 1910; *La Voce de Popolo Italiano* (1909), a paper that went from a weekly to a daily, then to a triweekly before its demise in 1946; *L'Appello* (1916), a voice of labor; *L'Araldo* (1938), a weekly until 1959; and *L'Eco* (1960), a bilingual weekly. In Columbus, a new serial was started with *Buon Giorno Magazine* (1996). In Steubenville, *L'Avvenire* (1909) spoke in socialist tones. And in Youngstown, *Il Cittadino Italo-Americano* (1902), a weekly to 1938, was important.

Michigan Italian Americans make up 5 percent of the state and have had a prolific press. In Calumet, around 1895, there appeared *La Sentinella,* a socialist paper. In Dearborn, there was *Il Mondo Libero* (1956), a monthly concerned with religion that had a circulation of 1,300 in 1970. In Detroit there were such publications as *La Voce de Popolo,* a national weekly launched by Monsignor Joseph Ciarracchi in 1912 (some put its publication as early as 1910 and designate it a product of the Pious Society of St. Paul), with a circulation of fifteen thousand before its demise around 1970; *La Tribuna Italiana d'America,* a weekly from around 1910 to 1969 (also known as *La Tribuna Italiana del Michigan*); *Il Pilota* (1930), an irregular monthly until 1930; and *La Gazzetta,* a weekly originating in 1972 that also serviced Ontario, Canada.

Texas has 314,000 Italian Americans, who constitute only 2 percent of the state's population. In Austin there appeared a publication entitled *La Dolce Vita* (1987). In Dallas, *La Tribuna Italiana* (1913), a weekly known as "the oldest Italian newspaper in the state of Texas," came out in 1940, and *Texas Tribune* (1941), a weekly to 1944. In Houston, there was *L'Aurora* (1915), a weekly. In Italy, there was *The Italy NewsHerald,* which was a merger of two weeklies that went back to the early 1890s.

In Maryland, where they number 253,000, Italian Americans constitute 5 percent of the population and have published *Il Risorgimento Italiano nel Maryland* (1922) and *The Italian Journal* (1933), both Baltimore weeklies.

Two hundred thousand Italian Americans reside in Rhode Island, yet they constitute 20 percent of the state's population. With Providence so central, it had such publications as *L'Eco d'America* (1894), a weekly (also known as *The Italian American Tribune*) that appears to be the precursor to *L'Eco del Rhode Island* (1897); *La Libertà* (1901), a weekly; *The Echo* (1929); *The Italian Echo* (1930); and *The Rhode Island Echo* (1941), today bearing the name *The Echo* with a recent circulation of 15,300. At the same time, there have been publications such as *La Ragione Nuova* (1909), a socialist monthly; *L'Alba* (1910), a weekly that became a semiweekly (also known as *Il Corriere della Sera*); *The Italian Review* (1924), a weekly started by Alexander Bevilacqua, and *Saluti Amici* (1993), a journal of the Italian American Historical Society of Rhode Island. In 1990 the University of Rhode Island resurrected *Italian Americana* (1974), the cultural and historical review, from its 1986 demise in New York.

In Louisiana, 198,000 Italian Americans constitute 5 percent of the state's population. Its publications in New Orleans have included *Correo Atlantico* (1836), a polyglot newspaper, originally published in Mexico by the Italian Orazio de Attellis; *L'Italo-Americano di Nuova Orleans* (1884), a weekly; *La Gazzetta Italiana* (1889), a weekly; *La Voce Coloniale* (1915), a weekly until it became *Italo-American News* (1955), a monthly that apparently evolved into *Italian-American International Review* (1962), a monthly; *La Voce Italo-Americano* (1941), a weekly; and *Italian American Digest* (1974), a quarterly.

Missouri has 162,000 Italian Americans, who constitute 3 percent of the state's population and have published in its leading cities. St. Louis has *Il Pensiero* (1904), a semimonthly tabloid, the work of Luigi Carnovale, which continues with a recent circulation of seven thousand, and *La Lega Italiana* (1914), a weekly that lasted to 1921. Kansas City had *La Stampa Italiana* (1913), a serial to 1941; *L'Osservatore* (1909), a weekly to 1915; *Il Messaggero* (1921), a monthly; *The American Citizen* (1941), a weekly to 1943; and *Italian American International Review* (1962), a monthly to 1963.

Arizona has 160,000 Italian Americans, who make up 5 percent of the state's population. In Phoenix, there is *La Tribuna Italiana* (1960), a monthly that has become a major publication for the Italian community.

The state of Washington has 158,000 Italian Americans, who account for 3 percent of its population. At least three publications have been relevant, namely, *La Gazzetta Italiana* (1910), a weekly out of Seattle that lasted until 1961; *The Columbus Record* (1918), a monthly out of Spokane; and *Lo Svegliarino dei Figli d'Italia* (1935), later known as *Northwest Italian News,* the monthly published in Seattle by the Sons of Italy for Washington, Idaho, and Oregon.

Colorado has 157,000 Italian Americans, who make up 5 percent of the state. In Denver, they had *La Stella* (1885), a weekly; *La Patria* (1891), a weekly; *Il Roma* (1892), a weekly that existed until 1920; *Il Vindice* (1897), a weekly; *Il Risveglio* (1906), a labor weekly lasting until 1955, when it became *Il Risveglio—L'Unione*, a monthly, after it had combined in 1949 with *L'Unione* of Pueblo; *La Capitale* (1907), a weekly to 1926, lasting much longer than the labor papers *Il Grido del Popolo* (1907) and *L'Italiano* (1912); *La Frusta* (1920), a weekly that became a biweekly; *La Tromba* (1935), a weekly that continued to 1941; and *Tirolian Trentini di Colorado* (1984), a newsletter also found in Arvada and Wheat Ridge. In Pueblo, *L'Unione* (1897), a labor weekly, came out under Hector Chiariglione, lasting until 1947 (it combined with Denver's *Il Risveglio* in 1949); *Il Cooperatore* (1918), a socialist bimonthly; followed by *Marsica Nuova* (1918), a weekly that evolved into a monthly and semimonthly and lasting until 1923; *Abruzzo-Molise* (1924), an anti-Fascist weekly, with links to Rochester, New York, lasting until 1926; and *La Voce del Popolo* (1926), a paper that continued to 1937 until it combined in 1949 with *L'Unione* and Denver's *Il Risveglio*. And, in Trinidad, *Corriere di Trinidad* (1902), a monthly, lasted until 1943, while the labor paper, *Lavoratore Italiano* (1902), ended in 1927.

In Wisconsin, a state with 146,000 Italian Americans, who account for 3 percent of the population, *La Rivolta* (1913), an anarchist paper, appeared irregularly in Madison.

Milwaukee Italian Americans published *La Tribuna Italiana* (1933), a monthly until 1966; *The Italian Leader* (1933), a weekly that evolved into a monthly; and *The Italian Times* (1979), a weekly.

In Indiana, which has 125,000 Italian Americans, who make up 2 percent of the state, there has been a variety of publications. Italians from Gary published *Corriere dell'Indiana* (1910), a product of the steelworkers that lasted to about 1983, and *Americans All* (1925), a polyglot monthly magazine (also known as *Il Corriere del Popolo*). In Indianapolis, a labor weekly, *Il Giornale dell'Unione dei Minatori* (1917), made its debut. And *VIA* (1990) or *Voices in Italian Americana,* a cultural and literary review, is published out of Purdue University in West Lafayette and is, to date, widely circulated.

There are other states with fewer than one hundred thousand Italian Americans where the Italian American press has been active. In Minnesota, where Italian Americans number almost ninety thousand and are slightly more than 2 percent of the state's population, Duluth had *Il Minatore Italiano* (1918) and Minneapolis had *La Campana* (1917), both reflecting the voices of the immigrant labor movement. In Nevada, with 87,500 Italian Americans, who make up nearly 8 percent of the population, Reno produced *Italian-French Colony* (1908), a weekly, and *Bollettino del Nevada* (1915), a weekly that lasted until 1944. In Maine, with about fifty-two thousand Italian Americans, who constitute 4 percent of the state, for the Italian Heritage Center in Portland there is *Rivista Italiana* (1990), a quarterly that continues to circulate. In Utah, with forty-six thousand Italian Americans, who account for almost 3 percent of the state's population, *Il Minatore* (1908), a voice of labor until 1913; *Aurora Socialista* (1910), a socialist weekly; and *Corriere d'America* (1920), the voice of the Italian community, have all been published out of Salt Lake City. In Iowa, with forty-five thousand Italian Americans, who make up less than 2 percent of the state's population, *The American Citizen* (1923) was published in Des Moines. In Kansas, with about forty-five thousand Italian Americans, who make up less than 2 percent of the population, at the University of Kansas in Lawrence, there is *Chimeras* (1967), a journal of its departments of French and Italian, and

at Pittsburg, there has been the *Crawford and Cherokee Italian American* (1901) and *Il Lavoratore Italiano* (1912), a weekly that eventually became a monthly. In Omaha, Nebraska, with thirty-five thousand Italian Americans, who constitute less than 3 percent of the population, *La Stampa* (1914) has been published, a serial until 1931; *The American Citizen* (1923), a semimonthly; and *Omaha Public Ledger* (1932), a weekly.

Moreover, among these smaller states, Vermont, with slightly more than 32,500 Italian Americans, who constitute almost 6 percent of the state's population, has a very prolific history of publications. While *Cronaca Sovversiva* (1902), *Contro-Pelo* (1911), *La Cooperazione* (1911), and *Corriere Libertario* (1914), also known as *Il Libertario,* were newspapers once published in Barre, others like *Il Buffone* (1902), *Il Corriere del Vermont* (1904), *Il Buffoncello* (1908), *Lo Scalpellino* (1915), and *L'Osservatore* (1934) also are part of its history. Although these were short-lived, they indicate how important Italian workers were to an industry based upon the quarries in Vermont just as they were, for example, in the mines of West Virginia, a state where Italian Americans today number seventy-two thousand and are not quite 5 percent of the population. In addition to all the papers from Barre, *L'Informatore del Vermont, New Hampshire e Maine* (1930) was a semimonthly that served Vermont from White River Junction and was still around in 1945.

In this survey of the states, one more can be included, that is, Wyoming, where Italian Americans make up almost 3 percent of the state's population with thirteen thousand. At Rock Springs, the immigrant labor force came up with a weekly *Vita Nuova,* from 1908 to 1911.

Lastly, in the District of Columbia, where Italian Americans number twenty-two thousand and make up 2 percent of the city, there are noteworthy publications due to Washington's symbol as the nation's center. They include the *NIAF Newsletter* (1977), the voice of the National Italian American Foundation; *The Digest* (1991), the law journal of the Italian American Bar Association; and *Italian American* (1996), the voice of the Sons of Italy.

Seventy-five years ago, there were almost one hundred Italian publications in thirty-eight cities. The leading cities were New York with twelve, Philadelphia with seven, San Francisco with six, Chicago with five, Boston with three, Pittsburgh and St. Louis with two each, and Cleveland with one. At least sixty more newspapers and periodicals, according to sociologist Robert E. Park, existed outside those cities.

Even though most of these publications have been vanishing as Italian Americans have adjusted themselves to American society and have climbed higher up the social, political, and economic ladder, their contributions are becoming more evident in the higher forms of the press as the books and the quarterlies of recent years demonstrate. Certainly, the role of the Italian American press in American history demonstrates that it has been incredibly active and diverse.

Vincent A. Lapomarda

Bibliography

Baumgartner, Apollinaris W. *Catholic Journalism: A Study of Its Development in the United States, 1789–1930*. New York: Columbia University Press, 1931.

Cordasco, Francesco. *Italian Americans: A Guide to Information Sources*. Vol. 2. Detroit: Gale Research Company, 1978.

Hoerder, Dirk, *The Immigrant Labor Press in North America, 1840s–1970s: An Annotated Bibliography*. 3 vols. New York: Greenwood, 1987.

Library of Congress. *Newspapers in Microform: United States, 1948–1983*. 2 vols. Washington, DC: Library of Congress, 1984.

Mangione, Jerre, and Ben Morreale. *La Storia: Five Centuries of the Italian American Experience*. New York: Harper Collins, 1992.

Online Computer Library Center. *United States Newspaper Program National Union List: June 1985*. Vol. 7. Dublin, OH: Online Computer Library Center, 1985.

Park, Robert E. *The Immigrant Press and Its Control*. New York: Harper Collins, 1922.

Schiavo, Giovanni. *Four Centuries of Italian-American History*. Reprint. New York: Center for Migration Studies, 1992.

Wynar, Lubomyr R. *Encyclopedic Directory of Ethnic Newspapers and Periodicals in the United States*. Littleton, CO: Libraries Unlimited, 1972.

See also SUCCESSORS TO THE ITALIAN NEWSPAPER

Prezzolini, Giuseppe (1882–1982)

Professor emeritus of Columbia University, a rare example of a self-taught man, a prolific writer, a fearless critic, and a man of untiring energy, Giuseppe Prezzolini was born in Perugia on January 27, 1882, into a family that had cultural and literary interests.

Critics have considered 1903 to 1907 as a period of transition in literature from positivism to idealism when Prezzolini collaborated with Giovanni Papini on the *Leonardo*, one of the more important literary and philosophical periodicals of the century. During this time he began his quest for God by studying the mystical influences of Henri-James Bergson, Henry James, and Saint Augustine, a quest that never ended, as can be seen in his book *Dio è un rischio*, published in 1969.

Prezzolini has a place in the history of Italian literature of this century as the founder and first editor of *La Voce* (1908–1914), a periodical dedicated to the moral, social, and intellectual regeneration of Italy. He became the moving spirit behind a whole generation of writers known as *vociani*. *La Voce* became the rallying point of many of the best minds of Italy—minds of all shades of political thought and religious belief (including agnosticism)—united only by their common desire to promote a spiritual regeneration.

The credo of the *vociani* was action. They had an awareness of social and spiritual issues that enlisted the support of men who differed not only in character but in political and philosophical thought. Among its contributors were Benedetto Croce and Giovanni Gentile, Giovanni Papini and Ardengo Soffici, Benito Mussolini and Giovanni Amendola, Scipio Slataper, Clemente Rebora, and Gaetano Salvemini—leading figures in the Italy of that day and later.

The effect that *La Voce* had on Italian culture was felt in all its fields: literature, music, art, philosophy, and politics. Thus was Italian culture integrated into the entire fabric of the nation. It assumed a true significance in relation to arts and literature, and on a moral plane as well.

When Italy entered World War I, Prezzolini enlisted; he had ample opportunity to witness the ineptitude of old generals and the lack of preparation of the troops. He criticized his country, whose government was responsible for the defeat of Caporetto. In 1925 he went to Paris to direct the League of Nations' Literary and Information Department of the Bureau for Intellectual Cooperation. He left in 1930 to come to Columbia University, where he taught for over twenty years, until his retirement.

An extraordinary exponent of Italy's cultural legacy, Prezzolini made the Casa Italiana at Columbia University a veritable beehive of scholarly and educational activity. Throughout his life he guided and nurtured young men and women. His correspondence with them was an extension of his fascinating diary. In a special way, he loved his students. Indeed, he was the catalyst who skillfully blended literary and philosophical developments with Italian genius that brought forth a new generation of teachers and a twentieth-century Italian renaissance.

Besides dissertations and master's theses, Prezzolini launched several new literary publications: the *Casa Italiana Monthly, Il Giornalino,* the Italian Book of the Month Club, a newspaper and periodical information clipping bureau, and *Repertorio Bibliografico,* in collaboration with some of his graduate students. The latter publication served as the most important critical bibliography of the history and criticism of Italian literature from 1902 to 1942. It is a large, four-volume work, indispensable for those interested in contemporary Italian letters, with 200,000 entries and 150,000 summaries, in addition to cross-references.

Prezzolini awakened in students a great love for culture and literature. By his example of moral integrity, he taught them to appreciate spiritual values. He guided them during research on their books, counseled them in the publication stage, and even assisted them in the correction of proofs.

Giuseppe Prezzolini wrote a remarkable self-portrait in 1922 (*Amici,* Firenze: Vallecchi):

I possess a certain clarity of ideas, the capacity to grasp the character of a man or of a movement, the strength of soul to refuse to be seduced by friendships or to be upset by hatreds in evaluating merits and in measuring defects. At a certain point in my life, having buried the romantic turmoils and aspirations, I de-

cided to become the "useful man" for others; to clarify certain ideas to Italians, to indicate their inferiorities in order to overcome them, to characterize foreign people and foreign movements, to translate from different languages, to reveal promising young men, to point out hidden greatness; that is what one calls work of culture.

Prezzolini was a born educator. He exemplified intellectual stimulation, moral integrity, and spiritual values throughout his life until his death in 1982. His writings, whether scholarly or journalistic, were delightful products of his clear, precise, well-balanced style. He expressed a great variety of interests, and his pen ranged from German mysticism to an erudite history of spaghetti, with biography, criticism, philosophy, scholarship, reportage, allegory, religion, and psychology filling the gap.

Margherita Marchione

Bibliography

Marchione, Margherita. *Giuseppe Prezzolini: The American Years 1929–1962.* New York: Vanni, 1994.

———. *Prezzolini: un secolo di attività.* Italy: Rusconi, 1982.

———. "Prezzolini Recaptures His Past." *The Italian Quarterly* (fall 1970): 75–92.

Prezzolini, Giuseppe. *The Case of the Casa Italiana.* American Institute of Italian Studies, 1976.

See also HIGHER EDUCATION

Protestantism

Although the number of Italian American Protestants has been relatively small from the 1880s to the present, remaining below 2 percent of the population in the New York City area throughout the 1930s and 1940s, the presence of Protestants within the Italian American population cannot be discounted. Moreover, it indicates some important sociocultural characteristics about that population.

Some Italian immigrants and their children, such as the prominent politician and writer Clement Lanni of Rochester, New York, had long ties to Protestantism in Italy. The majority, however, of Italian American Protestants converted to Protestantism in the United States. The basic reason for their conversion was the hostility of the American Irish Catholic hierarchy to the Italian immigrants and their "pre-Christian" religious practices. Some of the migrants moved into the Protestant church to attain stability, feeling that Catholicism had neglected their needs. Among those needs was adjustment to and acceptance by mainstream society. The social life of the Protestant Church was an important aspect in setting oneself apart from other Italian Americans. As in many other cases, the choice of being Protestant came from the mother. Becoming Protestant was often based in an anticlerical sentiment. Protestantism often began as a family affair, with a great deal of socializing among members of Protestant churches, which helped immigrants to learn how to adjust to society and how to get along with people. There were Protestant churches dedicated to an Italian ministry and to Americanizing these new immigrants.

The evangelical missions sought converts among disillusioned Catholics who were upwardly mobile. In particular, they targeted strong women. Protestant missionaries had a rather complex agenda. They sought to combat the growing influence of Catholicism in America, which the incursion of Italians represented. The slums in which most Italians lived personified social evils that the missionaries abhorred. There was a symbolic connection in most missionaries minds, moreover, between physical and moral cleansing. The Presbyterian missionary Mary Remington stated she "would like to put . . . these miserable wretches into a bathtub and clean them up for once." In common with most Americans, and Italians for that matter, the missionaries sought to combat atheism and socialism. They erroneously believed that all Italian men were atheists and socialists and filled with uncontrollable violence. Converting Italians to Protestantism, in effect, Americanized them.

Garibaldi Lapolla's novels, *Fire in the Flesh* (1931) and *The Grand Gennaro* (1935), satirize Protestant missionary activity that sought to buy the immigrants' souls. He points out that the missionaries only wanted those immigrants who fit into their own image. They had to know how to wear and look comfortable in American clothes and speak English with some accuracy. They also had to live up to Protestant moral standards.

However, while this biting satire holds some truth, especially regarding those churches that bordered Italian Harlem, it does a disservice to those breakaway churches that later found homes in the Episcopal Church, such as the Independent National Roman Catholic Church of St. Anthony of Padua in Hackensack, New Jersey. It neglects the work of such evangelical missions as the Brooklyn City Mission or the various Italian evangelical churches found in Rochester, Buffalo, Mt. Vernon, Troy, Albany, and Passaic. It neglects the work of the Italian evangelist Angelo di Domenica and others, who, along with Norman Thomas, were sympathetic to the plight of Italian immigrants and sought to aid their economic progress.

Although the majority of Italian immigrants remained Catholic after their fashion, they shared the anger and frustration of their converted Protestant countrymen with their status as "basement Catholics" in the eyes of the Irish Catholic hierarchy. They knew that their "pre-Christian" practices and "strange" customs were at best tolerated and even openly despised by the Irish Catholic clergy. Even Italian clergy were often ashamed of their fellow Italian laity's "ignorance." Being Catholic, however, was too ingrained in most Italians for them to leave the Church. The movement of even so small a number of Italian immigrants to Protestantism did, however, scare the Catholic hierarchy into making some concessions to the immigrants whose Old World religious practices seemed so foreign. In time, Italian immigrants gained the respect of religious leaders and American society as a whole. They survived and remained Catholics.

Frank A. Salamone

Bibliography

Cordasco, Francesco, ed. *Protestant Evangelism among Italians in America.* New York: Arno, 1975.

———, ed. *Studies in Italian American Social History: Essays in Honor of Leonard Covello.* Totowa, NJ: Rowman and Littlefield, 1975.

Eula, Michael. *Between Peasant and Urban Villages: Italian Americans of New Jersey and New York, 1880–1980.* New York: Peter Lang, 1993.

Juliani, Richard N., ed. *The Family and Community Life of Italian Americans.* New York: Italian American Historical Association, 1983.

Orsi, Robert Anthony. *The Madonna of 115th Street*. New Haven: Yale University Press, 1985.

Tomasi, Lydio F., ed. *Italian Americans: New Perspectives in Italian Immigration and Ethnicity*. New York: Center for Migration Studies, 1985.

Tomasi, Silvano M., and Edward Stabili. *Italian-Americans and Religion: An Annotated Bibliography*. New York: Center for Migration Studies, 1978.

See also Apostolate, Italian; Desmond, Humphrey J.; Palmieri, Aurelio; Religion

Puzo, Mario (1920–1999)

Mario Puzo is probably the best known of Italian American writers, but also the most controversial. The author of several bestselling novels and screenplays that explore the criminal underworld, Puzo was born in New York City, son of a railroad trackman and a housewife. Before becoming a writer, he worked in a variety of civil-servant jobs to support his wife and five children, and also served in the Air Force during World War II in Germany, rising to the rank of corporal.

Before achieving almost instant fame with the enormous success of *The Godfather* (1969), a page-turning thriller about the Mafia in America, Puzo penned two novels that were well received by critics but virtually ignored by the public. *The Dark Arena* (1955) shows how a former American military man views post–World War II German society. *The Fortunate Pilgrim* (1964), considered by many critics to be Puzo's finest work, traces the growth of an immigrant family as it struggles to rise above the poverty of Hell's Kitchen in New York City. Scholars of Italian-American history and literature have compared *The Fortunate Pilgrim* to Pietro di Donato's *Christ in Concrete* (1944) in terms of its depth of characterization and its exploration of a strong woman's attempts to hold her family together in the face of adversity.

Time magazine reported that "[l]ate in 1965 a Putnam editor . . . overheard Puzo telling Mafia yarns and offered a $5,000 advance for a book about the Italian underworld." Disappointed with his lack of commercial success, Puzo admitted in *The Godfather Papers and Other Confessions* (1972) that, like his characters, he too fell prey to an offer that could not be refused: "I was forty-five years old and tired of being an artist." Thus *The Godfather* was born. The novel and its subsequent movie version created an instant sensation. Yet the very elements that contributed to *The Godfather*'s commercial success—the inclusion of sex, drugs, and crime—did not sit well with some members of the Italian American community, who continue to feel that Puzo presented an inaccurate view of the Italian American family and culture by glamorizing domestic violence and the mob.

Yet one could argue that *The Godfather* and its subsequent explorations of the criminal underworld—*Fools Die* (1978), *The Sicilian* (1984), and *The Last Don* (1996)—are important works in the Italian American canon because they explore family ties, the relationship of immigrants to the old country, the insular aspects of the Italian American community, and the crime of breaking silence known as *omerta*. Although criticized for "selling out" to the public's desire for sensational literature, Puzo has also been praised by critics for offering a realistic look at the ethnic underworld.

Puzo, also the author of *The Fourth K* (1991) and *Padrino* (1970), died of heart failure at his home in Bay Shore, New York, on July 2, 1999.

Rita Ciresi

Bibliography

Bell, Pearl K. "Good-Bad and Bad-Bad." *Commentary* 66 (December 1978): 70–73.

Gardaphé, Fred L. *Italian Signs, American Streets*. Durham: Duke University Press, 1996.

Green, Rose Basile. *The Italian-American Novel*. Rutherford, NJ: Fairleigh Dickinson University Press, 1974.

Puzo, Mario. *The Godfather Papers and Other Confessions*. Greenwich, CT: Fawcett Publishers, 1972.

See also Crime and Organized Crime; Literature; Novels and Novelists

R

Radicalism

Emigration and radicalism were contemporaneous responses on the part of workers and peasants to oppressive conditions in late-nineteenth-century Italy. The general causes of both Italian migration and radicalism can be condensed into specific categories: rapid population growth, concentration of land ownership, industrial capitalism, heavy taxes and duties, and chronic agricultural depression. Since the 1870s class consciousness and militancy characterized a growing segment of the working classes. Although immigrants to the United States were drawn predominantly from the ranks of *contadini* (peasants) and artisans, not industrial workers, many had been affected by socialist ideas and movements. The formation of peasants' leagues, socialist groups, and chambers of labor was widespread in the Mezzogiorno (south) as well as the north.

The Kingdom of Italy responded to protests and strikes with harsh repression. Following uprisings in the Po River valley in the 1880s and in Sicily in the 1890s (the *Fasci Siciliani*), large numbers of leaders and rank-and-file activists were imprisoned, while others fled to the United States and other countries. These political refugees carried with them the full spectrum of radical ideologies. Conflicts among the partisans of these various ideologies constitute a substantial chapter in the history of Italian radicalism in the United States.

While Italian immigrants were still few in number, the formation of the Gruppo Socialista-Anarchico-Rivoluzionario ("Carlo Cafiero") in New York City in 1885 manifested the presence of Italian radicalism in the United States. Through its publication, *L'Anarchico,* the group called for social revolution, the emancipation of women, and the liberation of the "ignorant faithful" from the control of priests. With the arrival in 1892 of Francesco Saverio Merlino, a leading anarchist, the movement spread among Italians in the mid-Atlantic and New England states. Through speeches and his publication, *Il Grido degli Oppressi* (The Cry of the Oppressed), Merlino preached anarchist doctrines and attacked the Italian *padroni* (labor brokers) who preyed upon the immigrants.

In a yearlong speaking tour (1895–1896), Pietro Gori, the poet of Italian anarchism, propagated these ideas from coast to coast. Gori also established the Gruppo diritto all'esistenza (The Right to Existence Group) and its publication, *La Questione Sociale* (The Social Question), in Paterson, New Jersey, a silk manufacturing center that attracted many textile workers from northern Italy. During the extreme reaction aimed at radicals in Italy during the 1890s, other refugees came to Paterson, among them prominent anarchists such as Errico Malatesta, Giuseppe Ciancabilla, and Luigi Galleani. Malatesta, the leading exponent of organizational anarchists, advocated the formation of a revolutionary workers' movement, while Ciancabilla and Galleani, as antiorganizational anarchists, opposed labor unions as well as political parties in favor of spontaneous and direct action. When in 1900 Gaetano Bresci, a weaver and anarchist, returned to Italy, where he shot and killed King Umberto I, Paterson gained an international reputation as a hotbed of Italian radicalism.

The most influential of the anarchists, Luigi Galleani was born in Piedmont of a bourgeois family, studied law at the University of Turin, and became a leading practitioner of anarchist communism. Condemned to a penal island, he escaped and arrived in Paterson in 1901. Threatened with arrest for his agitation among the silk workers, he fled to Barre, Vermont, a granite center with a large number of Italian stone workers. Here Galleani published *Cronica Sovversiva* (Subversive Chronicle), in which he expounded his extreme brand of antiorganizational anarchism. A dynamic speaker and writer, he attracted a following of *Galleanisti* that numbered in the thousands.

An Italian socialist movement also appeared on the American scene in the late nineteenth century. Socialist groups led by political exiles sprang up in New York, Pittsburgh, and Chicago, and in out-of-the-way places like Houston and Tampa. In the 1890s the socialists affiliated with Daniel Deleon's Socialist Labor Party, a revolutionary Marxist Party. *Il Proletario* (The Proletariat), the major socialist organ, was established in 1896 and continued to be published until the 1940s. Among the early socialists, Giacinto M. Serrati was the most effective leader, increasing the circulation of *Il Proletario* and initiating the formation of the Federazione Socialista Italiana (Italian Socialist Federation, or FSI) in 1903. Conflicts between anarchists and socialists resulted in ferocious polemics between Galleani and Serrati and bloodshed among their followers, and the FSI itself was torn by the issue of participation in electoral politics. Discouraged, Serrati returned to Europe to pursue a career that was to carry him to leadership in the Italian socialist, then communist, parties.

The split within the FSI widened between those who wished to join the Socialist Party of America (SPA), which pursued a political strategy, and the syndicalists, who believed that the overthrow of capitalism could only be realized by workers organizing in industrial unions. Reinforced by recent arrivals from Italy, such as Edmondo Rossoni and Arturo Giovannitti, the syndicalists gained control of the FSI. While not merging with the Industrial Workers of the World, they subscribed to its program and collaborated with its strikes.

Meanwhile, the social democrats had withdrawn from the FSI and in 1910 established a second Federazione Socialista Italiana (FSI/SPA) as a foreign-language federation within the SPA. Its leaders, Giuseppe Bertelli and Arturo Caroti, believed that the immigrants had to acquire the vote and integrate themselves within the American socialist movement. They also urged the Italians to join the established trade unions, which syndicalists denounced as being controlled by corrupt labor bosses. While sections of the FSI/SPA were scattered about the country, its strength was concentrated in Chicago where the socialist journal *La Parola dei Socialisti* (The Word of the Socialists) was published.

The appeal of the social democrats, however, was limited by the fact that the great majority of Italian immigrants were not naturalized and thus unable to vote. Having been excluded from political life in Italy by the limited franchise, they had a cynical view of politics. Their experience in both Italy and America made them more responsive to anarcho-syndicalist teachings and explains why the FSI/SPA had such a small membership (which was little more than a thousand).

Carlo Tresca exemplified the strengths and weaknesses of Italian radicalism in America. Born of a well-to-do family in Sulmona, Abruzzi, Tresca, while still a student, espoused revolutionary unionism. Coming to the United States to escape a prison sentence, he immediately plunged into the labor struggles of Italian workers. After a brief stint as editor of *Il Proletario,* he published several newspapers, including *Il Martello* (The Hammer). A magnetic personality, Tresca attracted a devoted following, and his fiery orations ignited strikes and resistance. Until his assassination in 1943, Tresca was in the forefront of labor struggles and anti-Fascist resistance, but he did not form a lasting organization.

Through publications and speaking tours, these ideologues disseminated anarchist doctrines among Italian immigrants throughout the United States. Many who were not exposed to these ideas in Italy were converted in America since as workers they were subject to the worst abuses of American industrial capitalism. In addition to such charismatic leaders, some thousands of militant and experienced radicals formed the cadre of the Italian movement. Not only in the large cities, but in towns and mining camps scattered across the country, they formed socialist branches or *circoli di studi sociali* (social studies circles). Loosely connected to each other through the socialist and syndicalist federations and their publications, this militant minority provided grassroots leadership in many labor struggles.

Italian immigrants were a major element in the country's mining labor force by the early twentieth century. In isolated camps, they formed socialist sections, cooperatives, and locals of the United Mine Workers of America, Western Federation of Miners, and Industrial Workers of the World (IWW). On the Mesabi Iron Range in Minnesota, Italian Wobblies (members of the IWW), such as Efrem Bartoletti, were vigorous participants in the strikes of 1907 and 1916.

Italians also became a significant component of the labor force in the textile industry. During the Lawrence woolen mill strike of 1912, Wobbly Angelo Rocco emerged as a local leader, while Giovannitti and Tresca were active in the IWW national leadership. In the Paterson strike of the following year, Eligio Strobino, a weaver and socialist, and Tresca, again, were major figures. In clothing manufacturing, Italians numbered second only to Eastern European Jews among the tailors and seamstresses. Socialists such as Salvatore Ninfo and Luigi Antonini became organizers for and then officers of the International Ladies' Garment Workers' Union (ILGWU), while the Bellanca brothers, Augosto and Frank, rose to important positions in the Amalgamated Clothing Workers of America (ACWA). The origins of the ACWA were in the Chicago clothing strike of 1910. Once again it was socialists Bertelli and Emilio Grandinetti who mobilized the Italian workers during that conflict. Under the leadership of such radicals, Italian workers were conspicuous in the wave of strikes between 1909 and 1916. William D. Haywood, IWW leader during that time, praised them for being in the "front ranks of the revolutionary movement."

Radicalism was more than simply a weapon to be employed in labor struggles; for many it encompassed a worldview and way of life. In places where they were dominant, such as Barre, Vermont, and Tampa, Florida, radical ideas permeated every sphere of daily activity. In Barre the Italians, as stone carvers and sculptors, were the elite of the granite industry workforce. Divided between anarchists and socialists, they engaged in fierce arguments and bloody conflicts. Although members of the Granite Cutters' International Association, they were also members of the IWW and challenged the Anglo leadership as too conservative. There was no Italian church in Barre since it was common knowledge that "almost all are violently anticlerical." Rather, the socialist hall served as the community center with a cooperative store and meeting place, with dances and banquets. Similarly in Tampa, the capital of cigar manufacturing, the Italians (almost all Sicilians) joined with Cubans and Spaniards in forming a pan-Latin radical culture. Under the lector system (as the workers made cigars the lector read radical publications and works of literature and history), the Italians learned Spanish and absorbed ideas on workers' rights. An Italian hall provided a library, theater, and meeting rooms that were devoted to cultivating a radical culture. Italians were prominent in the frequent strikes in Tampa's cigar-making industry. Although the Italians joined the Cigar Makers' International Union, they criticized its leadership as insufficiently radical.

The radicals led the fight not only against American employers but also against the *prominenti* (Italian "big shots") who exploited the workers through their labor agencies and banks. As presidents of the mutual-aid societies and owners of newspapers, they controlled much of the social and political life of the Italian colonies. The radicals exposed the swindles perpetrated by the bosses on the workers and mocked their pretensions. Fervent nationalists, the *prominenti* with the collaboration of Italian priests sought to inculcate patriotism among the immigrants. Antinationalists and antimilitarists, the radicals denounced the imperialist wars of Italy and urged the immigrants not to return for military service. They disrupted the patriotic celebrations of the *prominenti* with counter-demonstrations, flying the red flag. Passionately anticlerical, they ridiculed religious processions, publicized the sexual wrongdoings of the clergy, and urged the workers not to patronize the churches or send children to parochial schools. The colonial elite responded with libel suits, anathemas from the pulpit, and violence. The Little Italys were racked by this internal class struggle during the initial decades of the twentieth century.

Believing that the power of priests and *prominenti* derived from the ignorance of the immigrant masses, the radicals viewed their primary task as educating the workers with modern ideas and imbuing them with a sense of class consciousness. In addition to their newspapers, socialist and anarchist printing houses published hundreds of books and pamphlets, which included writings by Darwin and other scientific thinkers; novels by Emil Zola and other realist writers; and works by radical theorists such as Bakunin, Kropotkin, and Marx. *Università popolare* (people's universities) that sponsored lectures on literary, scientific, and political topics for worker audiences were established in a number of American cities. *Circoli di studi sociali* and socialist halls had well-stocked libraries, including radical publications from Italy. To counter the influence of the *prominenti,* mutual-aid societies were formed on the basis of free thought and working-class solidarity. Such organizations sponsored picnics, dances, and theatrical performances. The singing of labor songs (*l'Inno dei Lavoratori,* "The Hymn of the Workers," was a favorite) was a feature of such events. Plays with a social theme by Ibsen, Gorky, Gori, and others, were performed by amateur drama groups. Rejecting religious ceremonies, the radicals practiced civil marriages and secular baptisms.

The radicals even published their own calendar (*Almanacco sovversivo,* i.e., Subversive Almanac), which commemorated the martyrs and events of revolutionary history rather than the saints of the Church. *Primo Maggio* (May First) was the red letter day on the radical calendar. From 1890 on, this date was celebrated as the harbinger of workers' emancipation with mass processions, demonstrations, and meetings in all parts of Italy. In the United States, social studies circles, anarchist groups, socialist sections, and free-thought societies gathered to listen to speeches on the significance of May Day, to recite radical poetry, to sing labor songs, and to view a performance of Pietro Gori's *Primo Maggio,* but also to enjoy themselves with music, food, drink, and bocce matches. They occasionally paraded through American cities on May Day bearing red or black flags with bands playing revolutionary anthems. The observance of *Primo Maggio* served as a vehicle to express aspirations and dissatisfactions that issued from the immigrants' lives in America. Isolated, despised, and exploited as strangers and workers, May Day, with its message of brotherhood, justice, and equality, offered them a new faith and identity as part of the worldwide proletariat to whom the future belonged.

World War I marked a turning point in the history of Italian radicalism in the United States. The entry of Italy into the war in April 1915 was followed by an upsurge of ethnic nationalism among the immigrants. Although the war was opposed by most radicals as a capitalist and militarist adventure, their ranks were divided over the issue of international working-class solidarity versus loyalty to *la patria* (the homeland). Much ink was spilled as ferocious polemics raged in the radical press, soon blood followed as pro- and antiwar factions clashed. For some, patriotism replaced their ardor for the workers' cause. Edmondo Rossoni, whose career as a radical agitator spanned three continents, embodied the shift from syndicalism to nationalism, and, in his case, to Fascism. Then editor of *Il Proletario,* Rossoni argued for Italy's intervention on the grounds that the war would bring about the revolution. Returning to Italy, he became the head of the prowar Unione Italiana del Lavoro (Italian Labor Union) and subsequently served as director of the Confederazione Nazionale dei Sindicati Fascisti (the National Confederation of Fascist Labor Unions) in Mussolini's regime. Rossoni's trajectory from socialism to fascism was one followed by other Italian radicals and foreshadowed the bitter conflict between Fascists and anti-Fascists, which was to be fought in the Little Italys.

The Red Scare in the United States during and after the war also took its toll among Italian labor activists. From 1917 on, the federal government with the assistance of state and local authorities intensified its surveillance and prosecution of persons, organizations, and publications thought to be subversive. Italian radicals were particularly targeted by these operations. Luigi Galleani, who was identified as "the most dangerous anarchist in the United States," was deported in June 1919, while his followers were arrested en masse. The Galleanisti responded with a series of terrorist acts, culminating with the Wall Street bombing of September 16, 1920. The Federal Bureau of Investigation, under the direction of J. Edgar Hoover, pursued the perpetrators with zeal, although with limited success. Among those caught in the toils of these investigations were Nicola Sacco and Bartolomeo Vanzetti, disciples of Galleani. Their conviction in 1920 and ultimate execution in 1927 for a murder committed during a robbery in South Braintree, Massachusetts, became an international cause célèbre. While the question of their innocence or guilt continues to be debated, as anarchists and Italians, Sacco and Vanzetti were clearly denied justice.

By the 1920s, deportations, disaffections, and deaths had decimated the ranks of Italian radicals. Although Italian anarchists maintained a presence in America, publishing *L'Adunata dei Refrattari* (The Gathering of the Refractories) until 1971, they had lost their base of support among the workers. Similarly, the syndicalist movement was badly bruised by government repression and vigilante action against the IWW. Some Wobblies became organizers for the ACWA, the ILGWU, and the UMWA, while others dropped out of the labor movement. Although *Il Proletario* survived, a much diminished syndicalist FSI was absorbed by a moribund IWW. Meanwhile, the FSI/SPA underwent a schism over the issue of communism. In the struggle within the Socialist Party of America, the majority of the FSI/SPA supported the communist faction which eventually took shape as the Workers' Party of America.

Still the radical belief in the revolutionary potential of the Italian workers appeared to be validated by their vigorous participation in the strikes of 1919. While they walked the picket lines which shut down the steel, coal, textile, and clothing industries, nowhere was their role more central than in the Lawrence woolen mill strike. Accounting for over a third of the labor force, Italian workers constituted the hard core of the strikers during the four-month work stoppage. Italians also constituted a significant element among the strike leaders, none more notably than Nino Capraro. Inspired by the Bolsheviks, Capraro regarded the Lawrence strike as an opening shot in the revolution. Although an organizer for the ACWA, he was a member of the Italian Federation of the Works Progress Administration (WPA) and editor of its organ, *Alba Nuova* (New Dawn). Italians such as Ninfo, Bellanca, and Antonini also continued to play important roles in the ILGWU and the ACWA. In 1919 these unions established the Italian Chamber of Labor in New York City modeled after the *camere di lavoro* in Italy. With Giovannitti as its director, an educational and cultural program was launched to inculcate class consciousness among the Italians. The goal of the chamber was to mobilize and organize all of the Italian workers in New York. However, a postwar depression, government antilabor policies, decline in union membership, and internecine strife soon deflated these aspirations.

Italian American labor leaders Luigi Antonini (left) and E. Howard Molisani. Antonini was responsible for developing Local 89 of the ILGWU into the largest Italian local and became president of the Italian American Labor Council. His successor in the Italian American labor movement was E. Howard Molisani. Photo by Alexander Archer. Courtesy Salvatore J. LaGumina.

Initially Italian radicals hailed the Russian revolution of 1917 as a harbinger of the worldwide emancipation of the working class. Disillusioned by the authoritarian Bolshevik regime, Italian anarchists and socialists were among the earliest and bitterest opponents of the Soviet-controlled Third International. Furthermore, the Communist Trade Union Education League's (TUEL) tactic of "boring from within" to gain control of labor organizations antagonized the established Italian American union leadership. The threat was heightened by the arrival in 1923 of Vittorio Vidali (alias Enea Sormenti and Carlos Contreras). Vidali, who had been a militant leader of the Communists in Trieste and became a dedicated agent of the Comintern, quickly took charge of the Italian Federation of the WPA and its daily newspaper, *Il Lavoratore* (The Worker). The TUEL Needle Trades Workers' Industrial Union (NTWIU) attempt to seize control of the garment unions precipitated a bitter civil war within the ILGWU and the ACWA. In this struggle with the Communists, the Italian union officials supported the conservative Jewish leadership. Although some militants, such as Capraro, sided with the Communists, relatively few Italians, as compared with Jews, seceded to the NTWIU.

In the twenties, an even more serious threat to the Italian Left in the United States came from the triumph of Fascism in Italy. Most Italian Americans, not only the business and professional elite, but those of the working class as well, were predisposed to welcome the rise of Mussolini to power. As a despised minority, Italians could bolster their ethnic pride by identifying with a strong Fascist Italy. The fraternal Order Sons of Italy in America, most of whose members were workers, supported *Il Duce,* as did, by and large, the Italian American press and the Italian clergy.

Italian radicals formed the backbone of the anti-Fascist movement, fighting the Blackshirts (members of the Fascist Party who wore black shirts as part of their uniform) in the press and in the streets of America. Among them were prominent refugees from the Fascist regime, such as Carmelo Zito, Vincenzo Vacirca, and Armando Borghi, but also many common workers fleeing the cudgels of the *squadristi* (Fascist gangs). The core of the anti-Fascist resistance, however, was composed of veterans of the Italian American labor movements, such as Tresca, Giovannitti, and Frank Bellanca. The dressmakers and tailors of the ILGWU and the ACWA constituted the base of the anti-Fascist movement within the Italian American community. However, one can not assume that the rank and file shared the passionate anti-Fascism of their leaders. Ethnic rivalry between Jews and Italians in the labor unions increased the latter's receptivity to nationalistic appeals. Fascist agents were quick to exploit such sentiments among the workers by boring-from-within or establishing dual unions. Although Fascist attempts to gain control of Italian garment unions were repelled, they appear to have made some inroads among longshoremen, barbers, and other trades.

In 1923 a coalition of socialists, syndicalists, anarchists, and communists, formed the Anti-Fascist Alliance of North America (AFANA). The Alliance fought the Fascists with rallies, the printed word, and clubs. It published the daily *Il Nuovo Mondo* (The New World) of which Frank Bellanca was editor. The unity of the anti-Fascist movement, however, was shattered when the Communist Vidali gained control of AFANA in 1926, prompting the secession of the socialist trade unionists who formed the Anti-Fascist League for the Freedom of Italy. The already embattled anti-Fascists were further weakened by fratricidal vendettas.

During the 1920s the Italian American Left fought a rear guard action against antilabor business and pro-Fascist *prominenti.* Much of its energies was absorbed by the struggle to save Sacco and Vanzetti and the campaign to repel the Blackshirts in the Little Italys. Aside from the garment workers' and miners' unions, radicals played a minor role in organized labor during these years. Leadership in the Hodcarriers and Building Laborers' Union and the International Longshoremen's Association was in the hands of corrupt labor racketeers. Also the appeal of socialism was blunted for many Italian Americans by steady wages and a rising standard of living. With the coming of age of the first American-born generation, radicalism was also challenged by the forces of Americanization. Indoctrinated with patriotism in the public schools and seduced by the consumer culture, the children of the immigrants tended to view their parents' ways (including their politics) as Old World and embarrassing.

During the depression of the 1930s, Italian Americans, as did all Americans, suffered long stretches of unemployment; many lost their homes and businesses. Not surprisingly, since they remained predominantly wage earners, Italian Americans were important participants in the revitalized labor movement. They played a major role in the organization of the mass production industries under the aegis of the Committee on Industrial Organization. In the union drives in coal and iron mining, textiles, automobiles, garment manufacturing, and other industries, a notable percentage of the organizers and leaders, as well as rank-and-file, were of Italian origin. Some were veterans of earlier labor struggles, Wobblies, socialists, and communists; others of the second generation had been imbued with family radical traditions. For the most part Italian Americans acted upon a rudimentary sense of class solidarity rather than ideological convictions stemming from the teachings of Marx, Lenin, or Bakunin. In the garment trades, Italian American women and men made up a major portion of the expanded ranks of the ACWA and ILGWU rank and file. Activists, like Angela Bambace, served as organizers among African American and Puerto Rican as well as Italian needle workers. Membership in the ILGWU boomed, and Antonini's Local 89 with forty thousand members became its largest local. By the thirties, however, Italian American workers were acting more as members of an American proletariat rather than as participants in isolated ethnic radical movements.

The relative failure of the Communist Party of the USA (CP) to attract Italian Americans, in comparison to Finns or Jews, is striking. Despite efforts to recruit them, a report of May 1938 on national groups in the CP counted just 600 Italians, while only three of the 212 members of the CP's Central Committee between 1921 and 1961 were born in Italy. Even the Communist International Workers Order (IWO), a confederation of mutual benefit societies organized along nationality lines, attracted only a modest number of Italian Americans. The IWO Garibaldi-American Fraternal Society, organized in 1931, had grown to not quite eight thousand members by 1940. Once the society appeared on the attorney general's list of subversive organizations (the only Italian society to be cited as communist), membership declined rapidly. While its publication, L'Unita Operaia, toed the party line, the Garibaldi Society appealed to national pride both in its namesake and ritual.

Nor did the Communist Party receive significant electoral support from Italian Americans. From 1932 on Italian Americans tended to vote overwhelmingly for Franklin D. Roosevelt, usually the straight Democratic Party ticket. The exceptions were Fiorello LaGuardia and Vito Marcantonio, both of whom first ran as Republicans to break Tammany's grip on city politics. LaGuardia's progressive politics and ethnicity insured him the support of Italian American voters. More controversial, Marcantonio, congressman from East Harlem from 1934 to 1950 (with an interruption of two years), while not a member of the CP, closely allied himself with the party on most issues. Italian Harlem consistently gave him a majority, not because it agreed with his ideology, but because he was a native son who championed its interests. Although Marcantonio became the leader of the American Labor Party (ALP), formed in New York City in 1936 with the support of the garment unions to enable socialists and communists to vote for Roosevelt (and LaGuardia and Marcantonio), the ALP attracted Jewish voters, but few Italians.

One reason for the lack of radical passion among Italian Americans in the thirties may have been their overwhelming enthusiasm for Fascism. In 1939 the historian, Gaetano Salvemini, estimated that 5 percent of Italian Americans were true Fascists, another 35 percent were sympathetic to the Fascists, while only 10 percent were anti-Fascists. The other 50 percent he characterized as apolitical, concerned only with their own affairs. If we accept Salvemini's informed guess, we are still left with the paradox that in the 1930s a very large segment of Italian workers, while participating in strikes, joining unions, and voting Democratic, at the same time, in greater or lesser degree, supported Fascist Italy. A radical minority of anti-Fascists continued to wage an unrelenting battle against Mussolini's followers. The socialist-led garment unions provided the foot soldiers and finances for the campaign against Fascism. While publications such as La Stampa Libera (The Free Press), Il Martello, and La Parola del Popolo (The People's Word) scourged Mussolini and his Italian American sycophants in print, Tresca and his followers wielded baseball bats against the Blackshirts.

Following the attack on Pearl Harbor, the declaration of war by Italy on the United States made pro-Fascist sympathies impossible. The Fascist rhetoric of the prominenti turned out to be bombast, as they pledged their total allegiance to America. As of 1942 only 210 Italians were actually interned as Fascists. Some of the leading apologists for Mussolini, emerged unscathed, deprived neither of liberty nor property. In fact, by and large, the prewar prominenti retained their control over Italian American institutions. During the war, anti-Fascists split into various factions over the status of communists and former Fascists in the movement—and particularly over the character of a liberated Italy. As the U.S. State Department became increasingly anxious about the influence of communism in postwar Italy, Italian American trade unionists, such as Antonini, were enlisted to prevent communists from gaining control of the labor movement in Italy. Given their history of combating communists within their own unions, most Italian American labor leaders easily slipped into a Cold War mentality.

Carlo Tresca, one of the last of the uncompromising radicals, was killed by an "unknown" assassin on January 11, 1943, in New York City. His death may be taken as marking the end of Italian immigrant radicalism. By now many of the old socialists had become labor bureaucrats, while those few who still retained a radical vision were soon to be caught in the toils of the Taft-Hartley Act and McCarthyism.

Ironically, World War II completed the process of incorporation of Italian Americans, particularly of the second generation, into American society. Whether in military service or war jobs, they gained entry on an equal footing with other white Americans. Although the majority were still blue-collar workers, many aspired to middle-class status, middle class signifying a lifestyle keyed to home ownership and consumption. For the most part, union members exhibited their loyalty to the labor movement, derived from a recognition that it was responsible for their relatively high wages. But it was a loyalty largely lacking ideological or cultural content. The anarchism, syndicalism, or socialism that had inspired some in the immigrant generation to heroic resistance persisted only in the memories of an ever-dwindling coterie of aging radicals. An Italian American radicalism that had been forged in desperate strikes during the early decades of the century and renewed in the struggles of the 1930s for all intents and purposes had ceased to exist.

Because anticlericalism was so large a part of radicalism, a bit more amplification is appropriate. Although Italian immigrants were nominally Roman Catholic, with the exception of small minorities of Jews and Waldensians, anticlericalism was widespread among Italian workers. In addition to the traditional mistrust with which many peasants viewed the Church and its clergy (a legacy of its oppressive role as a landlord), many immigrants were influenced by currents of positivism and rationalism. Such ideas were embodied in the ideologies of anarchism and socialism that regarded religion, in the words of Karl Marx, as "the opium of the people." Movements of the Left, in Italy and among the diaspora, actively attacked religious beliefs and practices as hoary superstitions that kept the masses ignorant and servile.

Not all anticlericals, however, were radicals. In the spirit of the Risorigmento, Masonic Lodges, composed of the political and economic elite, embraced principles of liberalism, including separation of church and state. Since the temporal power of the papacy was a major obstacle to the unification of Italy, Italian nationalists were strongly anticlerical. Until the Lateran Pacts of 1929 between the Fascist regime and the Vatican, the papacy denied the legitimacy of the Kingdom of Italy. Immigrants who celebrated the patriotic holiday *XX Settembre* (20th of September), the anniversary of the military conquest of Rome by the Italian army, were denounced by American Catholics. When mutual-aid societies attended Mass for funerals of their members, priests refused to allow the flag of Italy in the churches. The hostility of Irish Catholics toward Italian immigrants can be attributed to their belief that the Italian government kept the pope chained in a cell, forced to sleep on straw and eat gruel.

Radicals and nationalists in the United States carried on a vigorous propaganda against Italian priests who sought to establish churches and schools in the Little Italys. Through speeches, publications, and theater, they challenged clerical influence over the immigrants. In speech and print, Carlo Tresca, Luigi Galleani, Alessandro Mastro-Valerio, Cesare Crispi, and others vividly depicted the misdeeds and crimes of the papacy and its minions. Newspapers such as *La Questione Sociale, La Tribuna Trans-Atlantica,* and *La Parola Socialista* devoted many columns to exposing the wrongdoings (often sexual in nature) of immigrant priests. In addition, the anticlerical *L'Asino,* a satirical and scurrilous journal published in Rome, circulated widely among Italians in the United States. Following a protest by the papal nuncio in 1908, the U.S. Post Office banned the entry of the publication whereupon a New York edition was published for several years. Plays with anticlerical themes, such as *Giordano Bruno* (Bruno, a celebrated martyr, was burned at the stake in Rome in 1600 for his rationalist philosophy), were frequently performed by amateur theatrical groups. At gatherings for *Primo Maggio,* religious beliefs were often mocked by the reproduction of "miracles," for example, the liquification of the blood of St. Janarius, the patron saint of Naples. Rejecting religious ceremonies, radical couples joined in free unions without benefit of clergy and "baptized" their children with names like Ateo and Libera. Anticlericals disrupted religious processions as they wended through the streets of the Little Italys. In certain communities, hostility was so great that Italian priests were physically driven from town.

As in Italy, anticlericalism was also expressed in institutional forms such as *società libero pensiero* (free thought societies) and *Società Giordano Bruno*. Such societies were located in strongholds of radicalism; among stonecutters in Barre, Vermont; cigar makers in Ybor City, Florida; and mining towns scattered from Pennsylvania to Colorado. Popular universities, modeled after the *università popolare* of Milan (to the financial support of which many Italians in America contributed), were established in a number of cities. Through lectures and publications that introduced the immigrants to scientific thinkers, such as Charles Darwin, these institutions also undermined religious faith.

Anticlericalism among the Italians was a source of concern and complaint of American bishops in their reports to Rome as well as of Italian missionaries. The subject, however, took a sensational turn when Giuseppe Alia shot and killed a priest, Father Leo Heinrichs, while he was administering Holy Communion in Denver in 1908. The police and journalists concocted conspiracy theories involving the Giordano Bruno Society of Chicago and even Jane Addams since Hull House was its meeting place. Panic seized many Catholic priests, and in some cities churches were placed under police protection. This incident, and the general reputation of being godless, contributed to the negative stereotype of the Italian immigrants.

The anticlerical tradition did not survive the process of Americanization. In fact, the reconciliation of the Church with the Fascist state led to a nationalist-clerical hegemony over the Italian American community by the 1930s. The second generation, particularly influenced by the religiosity of American culture, either converted to Protestant churches or more likely returned to Catholicism. The children of the immigrants learned that to be accepted as a good American, one had to practice a religion; it did not matter much which religion. By the 1950s only a few *liberi pensitori* (free thinkers) remained, survivors of what had once been a broad anticlerical movement. More diligently than their immigrant ancestors, most Italian Americans now practiced the Roman Catholic faith.

Rudolph J. Vecoli

Bibliography

Avrich, Paul. "Cult and Occult in Italian American Culture." In *Immigrants and religion in Urban America,* edited by T. M. Miller and T. D. Marzik, 25–47. Philadelphia: Temple University Press, 1977.

———. *Sacco and Vanzetti: The Anarchist Background.* Princeton: Princeton University Press, 1991.

Debouzy, Marianne, ed. *In the Shadow of the Statue of Liberty: Immigrants, Workers and Citizens in the American Republic, 1880–1920.* Saint-Denis: Presses Universitaires de Vincennes, 1988.

Fenton, Edwin. *Immigrants and Labor, a Case Study: Italians and American Labor.* New York: Arno, 1975.

Goldstein, Robert J. "The Anarchist Scare of 1908." *American Studies* 15 (1974): 55–78.

———. "Italian Immigrants and Working Class Movements in the United States: A Personal Reflection on Class and Ethnicity." *Journal of the Canadian Historical Association* (1993): 293–305.

Mormino, Gary, and George Pozzetta. *The Immigrant World of Ybor City: Italians and Their Latin Neighbors in Tampa, 1885–1985.* Champaign: University of Illinois Press, 1987.

Pozzetta, George E. *Pane e Lavoro: The Italian American Working Class.* Toronto: Multicultural History Society of Ontario, 1980.

Vecoli, Rudolph J., ed. *Italian American Radicalism: Old World Origins and New World Developments.* New York: American Italian Historical Association, 1972.

———. "Prelates and Peasants, Italian Immigrants and the Catholic Church." *Journal of Social History* 2 (spring 1969): 217–268.

———. "Primo Maggio: May Day Observances among Italian Immigrant Workers, 1890–1920." *Labor's Heritage* 7 (spring 1996): 28–41.

Vezzosi, Elisabetta. *Il Socialismo Indifferente: Immigrati Italiani e Socialist Party negli Stati Uniti nel primo Novecento.* Rome: Edizioni Lavoro, 1991.

See also FASCISM; LABOR; SACCO AND VANZETTI

Radio

The golden age of Italian language radio programming was the period from 1920 to 1950, when it was possible to tune in at almost any hour to some kind of Italian broadcast. In those cities with larger Italian American populations there were a number of stations presenting Italian language programming (for example, New York City had four stations: WHOM, WOV, WEVD, and WBNX). At the same time there were smaller radio stations throughout the United States, meeting the listening demands and entertainment needs of Italian immigrants and their descendants and offering a full range of Italian programming wherever an Italian American population existed.

Italian radio broadcasts brought to the newly arrived Italians their Italy. At the same time, these programs helped immigrants in the transition to understanding their place in America. Accordingly, the eclectic range of programs brought to its listeners information from the fields of labor, religion, politics, citizenship instruction, entertainment, etc. At the outset, these Italian language programs brought news from Italy and the greater American community to those who didn't read (in Italian or English), an echo of the Italian native tongue, and the music that helped listeners take their minds off their work.

While Italian radio shows would be gone by the 1950s, there has been a revival of such programming starting in the 1980s. These programs feature primarily music: contemporary, "golden oldie," and opera. Some of these post-1980 programs have titles such as "The Italian American Serenade," "The Italian American Music Hall," "Ciao Italia," and "Bella Canta." While a full review of the entire field cannot be attempted here, the two following accounts of Italian radio in its heyday in Boston and New York are instructive.

Boston

The most prevalent type of Italian American programming during the late 1920s and early 1990s was broadcasting Italian dramas taken directly from the stage in New York. A number of Italian language theater companies gained extra sponsorship by recording their performances for distribution to radio stations around the country. Professor Gennaro Gardenia (as reported by his son, Vincent) regularly recorded with artists such as Migli-

accio, Sterni, and Baldolatti. The dramas aired for up to twelve hours a day for an entire week on stations such as WOV. In the early years, the transfer of material from stage to radio was relatively direct. Some groups added sound effects in order to replace the lost visual elements of theater performance, but by and large the same text was used for both stage and radio. Plays such as Giacommmetti's *La Morte Civile* were popular on radio as well as stage.

By the mid-1930s Italian American radio used many formats that were popular in mainstream American broadcasting. Full-length dramas did not work as well in a radio programming approach that increasingly required frequent breaks for station identification and messages from sponsors. There was also increasing community interest in a balance of material transferred directly from Italy with performances that reflected a specific Italian American experience. The forces of Italian pride and local corporate support joined to reflect a unique version of the talent show. An example of the Italian American cultural show aired over WAAB in Boston in 1935. Part of the stated aim of the programming was to "bring out the talent in our midst." In a notable response to "Americanization" drives of the period, the Prince company stipulated that eligible contestants were restricted to Bostonians of Italian birth or extraction.

The chance to express an exclusive Italian American culture in broadcasting was short-lived. By 1940 more Italian American programming was focused on news and public service announcements. A concerted effort to encourage Italian Americans to obtain United States citizenship was directed through both newsprint and radio. With the outbreak of the Second World War, radio programs also articulated the special restrictions Italian aliens were obliged to adhere to; they were asked to turn in shortwave radios and cameras. The United States Department of Justice entered into Italian American broadcasting with a bilingual program, "I Hear America Singing." This show promoting American solidarity was written in Washington, D.C., and syndicated by station WOR out of New York in the fall of 1941. The introduction to a half hour of traditional Italian songs (sung by Americans)— "Today's program is dedicated to the loyal Americans of Italian descent, who throughout America are helping to build a stronger and more secure nation"—highlighted a melting pot ideal that was directly aimed at Italian Americans who might have felt schizophrenic loyalties. The songs broadcast ("Cante Pe 'Mme," "Mare Chiaro," "Columbia Gem of the Ocean," and "The Hymn of Garibaldi") attempted to underscore the bond between Italian and American aspirations.

Postwar Italian American programming continued to link Italian and American aspirations. Increasing usage of English language material underscored an inevitable integration with American society. And though Italian American programming maintained the highly popular shows containing traditional songs and dramas, a new genre of advice show became popular as suburban perspectives and growing affluence required Italian Americans to be increasingly familiar with an integrated consumer society. In Boston on WBZ, advice shows dealt with housewives' questions on common repairs, appliance operation, and physical maladies. The type of sponsor of these shows frequently influenced the content, and, unlike "The Prince Macaroni Hour," non-Italians were invited on to assist in various explanations or promotions. Vestiges of the Italian American advice program remain into the 1990s. "Car Talk" broadcast out of Boston on National Public Radio owes its lineage to the original advice shows that presented a combination of practical information and community solidarity through problem solving. Although the hosts of "Car Talk," Bob and Ray Magliozzi, speak to a wider audience than the Italian community, they present a strong image of Italian American values and ethnicity. This emphasis has been a predominant theme throughout Italian American broadcasting.

The Italian American radio program has generally appealed to an older generation. Even in the 1930s the effort to promote young Italian American talent through broadcasting opportunities was met with overwhelming cultural competition from American movies. The postwar period was marked by suburban migration and the rise of television. Many Italian Americans lost touch with the close-knit ties of ethnicity familiar to previous generations who lived in Little Italys. Italian American radio filled a need for those who could not find the necessary cultural link on television. Italian American radio's advantages continue to be its relatively cheap opera-tional costs and its ability to reach members of a community who have moved to a fragmented Little Italy. And even though community leaders continue to fear the disappearance of Italian American broadcasting because younger generations seem disinterested in traditional culture and old-fashioned technology, as generations grow older a surprising number return to tune in to a continually reinvented form of Italian American radio.

Christopher Newton

Bibliography
"The Prince Macaroni Hour." Aired on WAAB, February 15, 1935. *The Italian News,* Boston, February 15, 1935. Immigration History Research Center, University of Minnesota. Loose files.

Station WHOM in New York

Radio has had a pervasive impact on ethnic American life because of its immediacy and flexibility. Radio opened the world to millions when mass listening developed after World War I, and soon grew to be an essential element in family life. Ethnic broadcasting outlets, smaller in scope than mainstream stations, were shaped for specific listener preferences. This technique, called narrowcasting, allowed a particular kind of entertainment and information to reach a particular audience.

One such ethnic station, WHOM, broadcasting in the New York area, was owned and operated from 1946 to 1975 by the Pope family. Generoso Pope, one of the first Italian American millionaires, made his fortune in the construction industry on Long Island. In 1928, he purchased the leading Italian language newspaper, *Il Progresso Italo-Americano,* and made it a vehicle for mobilizing Italian American voters and political clubs in the United States before World War II. In 1946, Pope purchased WHOM; his son, Fortune, managed the station for the first few years. While the newspaper and station were run as separate enterprises with different personnel, the acquisition of WHOM extended the institutional base for his political efforts.

Il Progresso celebrated the acquisition of the radio station with a series of banner headlines. A special inaugural broadcast, on November 22, 1946, from the Biltmore Hotel, featured such performers as Giuseppe de Luca, Licia Albanese, Hilde Reggiani, Vivian Della Chiesa, Era Tognoli, Virgilio Lazzari, and Gino Fratese, and was attended by local notables like Mayor Vincent Impelliteri, Dr. Luigi Nardi, and Judge Ferdinand Pecora. On this occasion, Generoso Pope declared that his first duty as the new owner of WHOM was to serve the interests of the community.

Station WHOM, broadcast in both AM and FM bands, was already multilingual, regularly carrying Yiddish, German, and African American programming. After Pope purchased the station, its ethnic pluralism was retained, but new programming was added, making it the definitive station of Italian Americans in New York City, and linking its news and information services with those of *Il Progresso*. From this point forward, the newspaper carried a diagram of the radio bands with an arrow showing WHOM's location, to assist in finding the station, and a daily listing of the station's offerings.

The content of WHOM's Italian programming, broadcast in both standard and regional Italian and in English, provided some of what might be found on any American radio station: local and national news and information; religious and inspirational programs; popular, classical, and operatic music; and comedy and entertainment. Added to these were regular educational segments about changing immigration regulations, as well as updates from postwar Italy. Foreign language programs were meant for anyone interested in these languages but were generally directed to those who did not speak English so that they could also use radio to be informed. In all these offerings, however, entertainment was always the primary goal.

On a typical day, programming began with a morning devotional, followed by Polish, Italian, Hebrew, and English language features continuing from 6:00 P.M. to 11:00 P.M. with Italian programming, featuring such performers as Nicola Paone and the Teatro Italiano. Some of the most popular programs included an early morning show, hosted by Ralph Constantino, who eventually became the station's program director, and two very successful features: "Pasquale C.O.D.," a down-to-earth comedy about a grocery store owner and the people in his neighborhood, and "The Ciaramellas," another comedy about a quarrelsome married couple, both broadcast in Neapolitan and other dialects. Also popular were a succession of radio dramas and soap operas in Italian. Sunday morning Catholic religious services usually included a sermon from Father Sorrento. News was carried every hour with half-hour news briefs and was tied into prominent stories carried in *Il Progresso*.

WHOM regularly conducted appeals for various charitable causes, including a toy drive at Christmas, and ongoing campaigns to raise funds for war relief efforts and natural disasters in Italy. Extending these efforts, station personnel regularly assisted the numbers of people who called or visited WHOM's offices in New York City with a personal problem, ranging from marital relations to immigration issues, by referring them to the station's legal advisor or to the Italian consulate.

WHOM and other stations like it played an important, multifaceted role in the development of the postwar Italian American community. Radio exerted a strong influence on families and provided a source of cohesiveness that contrasted with other aspects of modern life. In an era of growing industrial and postindustrial capitalism, the immigrant press and later the immigrant radio station served to instruct newcomers in American consumerism. Ethnic radio nurtured Italian American creative resources and provided employment for a variety of performers and artists. It promoted the Italian language, politics, and high culture, especially through classical music and operatic programming. At the same time, it perpetuated a more populist ethic through use of music and other programming in regional dialects.

Radio contributed to the retention of ethnic identity and community by legitimating particular histories, cultures, and traditions. WHOM acted as a kind of social cement for the New York Italian American community, which after World War II was increasingly composed of diverse and even antagonistic elements. By 1950 heavy concentrations of Italians in immigrant neighborhoods began to thin out, as many moved to other urban settlements or to new suburban dwellings. Despite this geographic and social dispersion, radio could still unite Italians by gathering them around special concerns and issues. In a larger sense, the inclusion of other foreign language programming indicates the possible fusing of an ethnic block or working-class interest group.

News and programming about postwar events and disruptions in Italy and the personal troubles of their Italian relatives provided a reference group experience for Italian Americans who could sympathize but also better appreciate their success and good fortune to be living in the United States. At the same time through radio, Italian Americans could experience a continuity with the family and community overseas.

Finally, first through newspaper and then radio, Generoso Pope helped to articulate the immigrant chronicle: rise up from struggle, receive the blessings of this country after hard work, show gratitude for being an American (often expressed as "God Bless America"). Radio has helped to create and maintain the Italian immigrant's saga, which has become the central and defining narrative for this generation of Italian Americans.

Angela D. Danzi

Bibliography

Cannistraro, Philip V. "Generoso Pope and the Rise of Italian American Politics, 1925–1936." In *Italian Americans: New Perspectives in Italian Immigration and Ethnicity,* edited by Lydio F. Tomasi. New York: Center for Migration Studies, 1985.

McDonald, J. Fred. *Don't Touch That Dial: Radio Programming in American Life, 1920–1960.* Chicago: Nelson Hall, 1979.

Park, Robert I. *The Immigrant Press and Its Control.* Chicago: University of Chicago Press, 1922.

Smith, Jeannette, Sayre. "Broadcasting for Marginal Americans." *Public Opinion Quarterly* 6 (December 1942): 588–603.

Sterling, Christopher H., and John M. Kitross. *Stay Tuned: A Concise History of American Broadcasting.* Belmont, CA: Wadsworth, 1978.

Tuchman, Gay. "Mass Media Institutions." In *Handbook of Sociology.* Newbury Park, CA: Sage Publications, 1988.

See also PRESS, ITALIAN AMERICAN; TELEVISION; THEATER HISTORY

Re, Edward D. (b. 1920)

Jurist, lawyer, author, and educator, Edward D. Re was born of Italian immigrant parents in Brooklyn. He received his formal schooling in New York City, including a law degree from St. John's University Law School in 1943 and a doctor of judicial science from New York University's School of Law in 1950.

From 1947 to 1961 Re taught law at St. John's University School of Law and wrote numerous works on the law including eight books and dozens of articles that appeared in prestigious law journals. He also served as interpreter, instructor, and legal officer with the United States Air Force from 1943 to 1947 and continued his legal duties with the armed forces as a judge advocate during the Korean conflict.

Re functioned as a legal specialist on a federal level commencing in 1955 as special hearing officer for the Department of Justice, a post he held until President John F. Kennedy appointed him chairman of the Foreign Claims Settlement Committee in 1961. Simultaneously he served as master in Chancery and Referee before the United States District Court for the Southern District of New York.

After serving in President Lyndon B. Johnson's administration as assistant secretary of state for Educational and Cultural Affairs, he accepted the president's appointment as judge of the United States Customs Court. In 1977 he was named chief justice of the same court by President Jimmy Carter. On November 1, 1980, Re became the first Chief Judge of the United States Court of International Trade.

As indefatigable as he was in public positions, he was equally busy in private organizations as well. He was appointed by the Holy See as consultant in 1961 to its delegation at the United Nations Conference on Narcotic Drugs. He was active in his profession functioning as chairman of numerous committees of the American Bar Association and the New York Bar Association. He lectured extensively in Italy for which he received that nation's honors. He served as president of the American Foreign Law Association (1971–1973), the American Justinian Society of Jurists (1974–1976), and numerous other professional organizations.

Judge Re and his wife, the former Margaret Anne Corcoran, have twelve children.

Joseph J. Saladino

Bibliography

Re, Edward, D. "The Partnership of Bench and Bar." *The Catholic Lawyer* 16, no. 203 (summer 1970): 194–209.

———. "The Roman Contribution to the Common Law." *Fordham Law Review* (February 1961): 447–494.

Reggio, Nicholas (1807–1867)

One of Boston's successful merchants in the nineteenth century, Nicholas (Niccolò) Reggio was once the official consul in that city for five nations.

The descendant of Italians from Genoa, he was born in Smyrna, Turkey. Coming to New York City in 1837, he became an American citizen after residing in Boston for five years. He Anglicized his first name and established the foundation for a lucrative international trading business, Nicholas Reggio and Company, which had a number of fast ships.

In those years before Italy became a united country, Reggio was not only the diplomatic representative for Sardinia, Sicily, Spain, and Turkey, but also for the Papal States. He remained until his death the representative of the latter and became the Italian consul in Boston once Italy was united. In the early 1850s he was influential in having the Catholic publicist Orestes A. Brownson defend the interests of Spain in *Brownson's Quarterly Review* when America was trying to annex Cuba.

In his capacity as a merchant, Reggio helped to make Boston a thriving commercial center. The city welcomed Reggio's imports of goods like dates, figs, nuts, raisins, and wines from the Mediterranean. His trading in imports and exports with the Mediterranean rivaled that of another firm operated by Joseph Iasagi. Their rivalry helped to make Boston a leader in U.S. trade to and from the Near East, establishing the city as a commercial metropolis.

According to Giovanni Schiavo, that rivalry also had an important cultural spinoff evident today in Boston's Louisburg Square. On Beacon Hill, in what was the heart of Boston society, stands a statue of Aristides the Just established by Iasagi while, at the other end, there is one of Christopher Columbus established by Reggio. The Columbus monument was visited annually by Italians on Columbus Day in the first part of the twentieth century and remains today as an enduring legacy from the nineteenth century.

Reggio's success as a diplomat and as a merchant in nineteenth-century Boston was exceptional. Although Italians (cooks, hairdressers, musicians, and others) constituted a fraction of the population in that city, they were confident enough to form their own benevolent society in 1842. In the following year Protestant ministers founded the Massachusetts Philo-Italian Society to counteract the influence of the Roman Catholic Church among Italians throughout the world. Devout Catholics such as Reggio had to live in a hostile atmosphere when adhering to their faith.

Two years after becoming an American citizen, Reggio married into the family of Andrew Carney, another prominent Catholic, by wedding Pamelia Josephine Carney. They parented two daughters and one son. Like Carney, Reggio was a pillar of his faith as one of the city's most exemplary and most wealthy Catholics. His will in the Massachusetts Archives indicates that he left an estate worth over one hundred thousand dollars.

He held the distinguished title of a marquis. Honored by the nations that he represented, he was proud of his Italian heritage and of his two brothers and two sisters who had helped to anchor the family interests, especially in France and in Turkey. Buried from the Jesuit Church of the Immaculate Conception on Harrison Avenue in Boston, Nicholas Reggio's remains rest in Forest Hills Cemetery in New York in the lot of the Carney family (at the corner of Lake and Forest avenues).

Vincent A. Lapomarda

Bibliography

Handlin, Oscar. *Boston's Immigrants: A Study in Acculturation.* Rev. ed. Cambridge: Harvard University Press, 1959.

Schiavo, Giovanni E. *The Italians in America Before the Civil War.* New York: Vigo, 1934.

Stock, Leo Francis. *Consular Relations Between the United States and the Papal States: Instructions and Despatches.* Washington, DC: American Catholic Historical Review, 1945.

Whitehill, Walter Muir, with Katharine Knowles. *Boston Statues.* Barre, VT: Barre Publications, 1970.

Regional Migration and Transplantation

Migration, or the phenomenon of people moving from one part of the globe to another, is accompanied by a transfer of cultural traits, customs, and lifestyles peculiar to incoming immigrants. Thus, in addition to the dynamics of being absorbed by and assimilated into the host society, migrants also bring with them elements of their own culture, commonly and derogatorily referred to as cultural baggage. While the traversed course is common among all immigrant groups, it is of special meaning to Italian immigrants because of a long history of geographical and regional fragmentation in the Italian peninsula that found local communities and regions encompassing the totality of folkways, customs, languages, dress, cuisine and outlooks that definitively distinguished one region from another.

The north–south differentiation in Italy, for example, was so pronounced that it found its way into American immigration laws, which displayed favoritism for northern Italians while demeaning those from the south. Northern Italians were regarded as more industrious, energetic, and self-reliant, while southerners were labeled as indolent, superstitious, and ignorant.

In addition to the geographical distinctions, regional identifications were a fact of life for Italian immigrants. Long before they considered themselves as Italians in America, as Femminella and Quadagno (1976) note, they identified themselves as descendants of particular regions and provinces replete with their own dialects, style of dress, food patterns, and patronage of local saints. Differences between regions were so conspicuous that it was frequently impossible for inhabitants of one region to understand the language used by another.

To comprehend Italian immigration requires an understanding that the peninsula's immigrants were part and parcel of this provincial system and that they transplanted their regional cultures to American locales. Even those ethnic enclaves that were generally referred to as "Little Italys" were more accurately to be identified as "Little Sicilys" and "Little Puglias," for example, since they reflected neighborhoods of descendants from particular regions of Italy. Settlement in these Little Italys was usually along regional and even town lines. Entire streets would mirror a regional background such as Neapolitan, Genoese, or Sicilian, while renters in some apartment houses came from the same town or village in the old country. Immigrants from Naples, Genoa, or Sicily all followed a specific pattern of migration.

Among the Genoese immigrants who were the first Italians to settle in California in the mid-nineteenth century, there emerged a number of individuals who became prominent economically and socially. The great banker Amadeo P. Giannini, for example, descended from Genoese stock as were major figures in the wine industry such as Andrea Sbarboro and the Rossi family. Sicilian immigrants began their trek into California in the 1880s, where many participated in the fishing industry. For at least a generation each of these regional communities repudiated kinship with one another as they used their own dialects, and created their array of institutions such as mutual-aid societies.

Because of an early association of New Orleans with Sicily that supplied fruits and vegetables to that southern port city, Sicilian immigrants formed the bulk of Italian migration to that area. Historian Virginia McLaughlin (1977) has identified immigrants from Bagheria, Termini Immerse, and Cefalu, in Sicily, along with those from Avigliano, Potenza, and San Fele in Basilicata as being numerous among Buffalo's Italian immigrants. Gary Mormino's research (1987) discovered that the Italian immigrants who settled in "The Hill" in St. Louis were largely from clusters of villages around Milan such as Cuggiono as well as southern immigrants from a few towns in eastern and western Sicily. Mormino discovered that approximately 60 percent of Italian migration to Tampa, Florida, in the early 1900s was distinctively Sicilian from the island's southwestern mountainous terrain. Dominic Candeloro found that clusters of Italian immigrants in and around Chicago were made up of regional concentrations. Sicilians from the towns of Catania, Vizzini, and Sambuca-Zabat, surrounding Palermo, dominated Chicago's northwest side, while in Highwood, outside Chicago, the majority of Italians were from Modenese towns of Peligo and Pievepeligo.

The Italians who settled on Long Island, New York, following LaGumina's analysis (1988), tended to establish themselves in enclaves with others from their regional backgrounds. For example, Sardinians settled in the town of Port Washington, where for decades they carried on practices unique to their background, including baking pita bread. Most of the Italians who settled in Westbury emanated from three towns near

Naples: Nola, Saviano, and Durazzano, with each group transplanting its own mutual-aid society and its own feast devotion. For years it was not unusual for Westbury immigrant men to return to their Italian hometown to choose a wife.

Salvatore J. LaGumina

Bibliography

Belfiglio, Valentine. *The Italian Experience in Texas.* Austin: Eakin, 1983.

Femminella, Francis X., and Jill Quadagno. "The Italian American Family." In *Ethnic Families in America,* edited by C. H. Mindel and R. W. Habenstein. New York: E. L. Sevier, 1976.

LaGumina, Salvatore J. *From Steerage to Suburb: Long Island Italians.* Staten Island, NY: Center for Migration Studies, 1988.

McLaughlin, Yans-Virginia. *Family and Community: Italian Immigrants in Buffalo, 1880–1930.* Urbana: University of Illinois Press, 1982.

Mormino, Gary R., and George E. Pozzetta. *The Immigrant World of Ybor City.* Urbana: University of Illinois Press, 1987.

Religion

Religion, particularly Catholicism, has been a consistently important institution in the lives of Italian Americans, although its exact significance has varied depending on historical circumstances. This entry explores the Italian American religious experience, beginning with the Italian background and continuing through the antebellum period, the turn-of-the-century mass migration from Italy, the period of immigration restriction that lasted from the 1920s to the 1960s and the resurgence of interest in immigration and ethnicity that occurred in the 1970s and 1980s.

Three demographic factors shaped religious experience in Italy and carried over into immigrant religious experience in the United States. First, although Italy has a Jewish community dating back to the Middle Ages and is the home of one Protestant denomination, the Waldensians, it is an overwhelmingly Catholic country and most of its emigrants were Catholic. Thus, Italians came to the United States without much religious pluralism. Second, although Italy is largely Catholic, there are tremendous regional variations in its

Catholicism. Four-fifths of the Italian migration to the United States hailed from the peninsula south of Rome and from Sicily. Their religious culture was characterized by an emphasis on lay-led, communal rituals, the annual feast day celebrations of town patron saints, and a folk culture of anticlericalism. Third, not only did one's religious experience depend on one's birthplace in Italy, it depended on one's gender. Women were the links between the family and official Catholicism, the ones who were more regular in attendance at Mass and at devotions such as the rosary. Men were the leaders of the lay-based, communal religious practices, the ones who organized the annual celebration of the patron saints' feast days. Three-fourths of those who migrated from Italy to the United States between 1880 and 1920 were men, and thus the Italian American community had plenty of the traditional practitioners of communal religious rites but few links to the official Church.

Political factors also shaped Italian migration. Two trends in nineteenth-century Italian politics reinforced folk anticlericalism. Fearing the loss of independence necessary for the exercise of its spiritual functions, the papacy opposed Italian unification. Supporters of Italian nationalism thus became opponents of the Church. In the late nineteenth century, the leaders of the new Italian nation imposed heavy taxes and military conscription in an attempt to push Italy into the ranks of the great powers, thus provoking radical, class-based political movements such as anarchism. Again, concerned about the nihilism accompanying anarchism, the Church opposed radical politics. When immigrants came to the United States, American Catholics, who did not have to choose between loyalties to faith, nation, and class, suspected Italians to be unfaithful Catholics.

Finally, socioeconomic factors constrained the practice of the faith. Migration cut across class lines, but the working class, those with the least experience in the lay leadership necessary to the preservation of communal traditions, predominated. During the period of mass migration, migrants were highly transient males who traveled far from churches in search of work. Even if they worked near churches, they labored for long hours at little pay, thus leaving them little time to attend church and little to put in the collection basket.

Prior to 1880, fewer than ten thousand persons migrated from Italy to the United States annually. Historian Howard Marraro has delineated the number of entrepreneurs and professionals among them; such people could assimilate easily and did not need special services from the Church. Marraro has also pointed out the number of political exiles, such as Giuseppe Garibaldi, who were alienated from religion. The development of Italian religious institutions in the United States had to wait for a critical mass of individuals whose education and occupation precluded rapid assimilation, and who either had the skills to exercise leadership or the need for services. Two experiences with Italian parishes demonstrate this trend. In 1852 Bishop John Neumann organized a committee of non-Italians and Italians to purchase a church that would become the nucleus of Saint Mary Magdalene de'Pazzi, a Philadelphia parish to be exclusively used by Italians. The combination of episcopal support, lay leadership, and a body of parishioners to be served led to a stable parish. During the same decade, Father Antonio Sanguinetti attempted to organize a parish for New York's Italians. However, he faced a divided Italian community; a number of anticlerical Italians offered no support, and those that were interested in the parish divided into different groups with different plans for the church's organization. Nor did Archbishop John Hughes support Father Sanguinetti; the New York ordinary feared the divisive effect of St. Anthony's would spread to parishes for every ethnic group in that heterogeneous city. Although St. Anthony's was incorporated in 1859, there was no actual parish; Father Sanguinetti had already returned to Italy. Not until 1866 did New York get an Italian parish. St. Anthony's was reincorporated, this time with some changes intended to stabilize it. The parish was given to the Franciscans, who could provide a steady stream of Italian-speaking clergy. While St. Anthony's ministered to any Italian who came to the parish, it also had a base of Irish American Catholics to minister to and draw support from.

By the 1880s the demographic situation had changed. During that decade, the number of Italians migrating to the United States rose above ten thousand per annum. At the beginning of the twentieth century, Italian migration increased to one hundred thousand per annum, and during half of the years between 1900 and World War I, it rose to two hundred thousand. So many people arriving in such a short space of time guaranteed that Italian migration would become an issue; a slower pace of migration might have given the early migrants time to assimilate themselves and thus allow the country to absorb later migrants. In addition to the sheer numbers, other factors made this a group in need of special attention. Usually men migrated alone and either returned for their families or sent for them. Besides placing stress on individuals and families, this type of migration disrupted the gender division of religious labor and left the most regular churchgoers in Italy. Poverty kept the migrants away from church and reduced their welcome when they did come. Finally, the Italians practiced chain migration, meaning that a pioneer would set out from a specific place in Italy, settle in a specific place abroad, and would attract compatriots to the new area, so that numerous people from the same region settled in enclaves.

Mass migration from Italy presented a possibility of a religiously heterogeneous Italian community. Several American Protestant denominations conducted missionary work among the immigrants. In some cases, for example, that of Antonio Arrighi, their efforts were rewarded by converts who went on to careers in the Protestant ministry. In other cases, they at least provided some much needed practical aid; Judson Memorial in Greenwich Village converted few Italians to the Baptist faith of its major sponsor, John D. Rockefeller, but it did provide a range of services for the neighborhood. However, denomination efforts did not lead to mass evangelization. Some Italians were alienated from all religion, not just Catholicism. Even though many American Catholics feared the Italians to be so badly educated in their faith that they might fall prey to proselytism, what actually happened was the folkways of Italian religion tended to keep the Italians close to Catholicism.

The migrants re-created the lay-led, communal religion they had known in Italy. The men formed mutual-benefit societies. These societies collected dues and distributed cash benefits in case of illness, injury, or death, functioning as insurance companies. The societies also perpetuated religious traditions, for they were the principal organizers of feast day celebrations of hometown patron saints. In

R

Holy Rosary Catholic Church May Procession, Washington, D.C., May 16, 1915. Courtesy Center for Migration Studies.

some cases, the number of Italians and their organization were enough to perpetuate this Old World tradition. For example, the San Gennaro Society began celebrating its patron's feast day on Manhattan's Mulberry Street late in the nineteenth century. In other cases, the mutual-benefit societies became incorporated into the parish structure. Saint Joachim's, an Italian parish on the Lower East Side of New York that functioned between 1888 and 1958, had agreements with a number of neighborhood mutual-benefit societies: the societies received the services of the clergy for feast days and for the funerals of society members, and the parish got a nucleus of parishioners and a basis for financial support. In still other cases, the relationship was even closer. Laity had been celebrating an annual *festa* to honor Our Lady of Mount Carmel in East Harlem since 1881; in 1884, the archdiocese erected an eponymous parish, which became thoroughly identified with the feast.

The parishes that served Italians were erected and staffed in different ways. Some were Italian national parishes, that is, erected to serve those who needed special linguistic services. Some were regular territorial parishes, which meant they ministered to Catholics in a particular neighborhood, and often that neighborhood happened to be predominantly Italian. Very few were staffed by Italian secular or diocesan clergy, because few

clergy migrated in proportion to the need for their services, and because the American clergy's image of their Italian confreres was as unflattering as their stereotype of the Italian laity, although some secular Italian immigrant clergy, such as Nicholas Odone in the Archdiocese of Minneapolis and Saint Paul, were well respected and effective. More were staffed by clergy from male religious orders. Some of these orders, such as the Servites, who staffed many Chicago Italian parishes, had sent clergy out of Italy to escape difficulties with the new anticlerical national government. Others, such as the Salesians of Don Bosco, who staffed San Francisco Italian parishes, came because they were new orders and this was an opportunity for expansion. Unique was the Society of Saint Charles, formed especially to minister to migrants. In addition, female religious orders found work in Italian communities, providing orphanages, hospitals, day-care centers, and schools, and assisting in parochial work.

The development of Italian national parishes has been subject to several historical interpretations over the years. American Catholics witnessing the Italian mass migration referred to an "Italian problem" that they "solved" by recruiting religious orders that supplied Italian-speaking clergy and sisters. Some historians have charged that the real "problem" was the anti-Italian attitudes that alienated migrants already disaffected by anti-radical and antinational politics in Italy. Other historians have dismissed the question of whether the Italians or the American hierarchy was the problem by pointing out that both groups had reasons for wanting national parishes: the Americans used them to provide specialized language services, and the Italians used them as a setting for preserving a rich cultural heritage.

World War I, the adoption of national quotas to control immigration to the United States, Fascist Italy's reluctance to let men of military age migrate, the Great Depression, and World War II all reduced Italian migration to the United States in drastic measures; migration averaged under five thousand per annum between 1921 and 1945. Nevertheless, this was an important period in the development of an Italian American Catholic identity. The Lateran Treaty reconciled the conflict between religion and nationalism in Italian life; after 1929 it was possible to be a patriotic, active citizen and a faithful Catholic. The Cold War that developed between the United States and the USSR served to reconcile all three identities, as American patriotism, Italian patriotism, and Catholic loyalty all led individuals to oppose communism. Periods of prosperity in the 1920s and the postwar period, fleeting though they were, allowed Italian parishes to build commodious churches and decorate them in a style that reflected their heritage and to erect parochial schools and other community institutions. It is also during this period that one sees examples of ethnic action that became even more prevalent in the 1960s. The American Committee on Italian Migration, or ACIM, was formed in 1953, and affiliated with the National Catholic Welfare Conference (now the United States Catholic Conference). ACIM extended charitable assistance to those Italians who were able to migrate to the United States, and also lobbied to increase opportunities for Italian migration.

Three developments of the 1960s marked a new era in Italian American religion. In 1965 the United States adopted two new systems: one that gave every nation a quota of twenty thousand migrants per year and another for prioritizing potential migrants by their degree of relation to American citizens and by their prospective contribution to the American economy. Some relatives of American citizens, such as wives, could be admitted even if a particular nation went above the twenty thousand per annum quota. For a few years after the adoption of these rules, Italy was one of the ten leading countries in terms of sending migrants to the United States. Migration from Italy has slowed but has not ceased, and new migrants have continued to need religious services in Italian.

The Second Vatican Council held annual sessions in 1962 and in 1964, and the Vatican continued to issue directives based on Council discussion throughout the 1970s. Vatican II affected Italian American Catholics in much the same way that it affected American Catholics of other ethnic backgrounds. The Council called for profound changes in long-standing religious practices. In some instances, the changes could be read as increasing the distance between the descendants of Italian immigrants and their traditional religious practices, thus completing their assimilation. In other ways, such as its emphasis on the diversity of faith experience and on the importance of community in worship, the Vatican Council reinforced historical developments in the United States, in which Italian Americans maintained national parishes not because they needed the special language services but because their need for a worship community was being met.

By the late 1960s the Black Power movement had inspired similar movements in other groups. Among Italians, two factors led to the development of an ethnoreligious group. To a certain extent, forces outside the Italian community, especially the persistent stereotyping of Italians in the mass media, made people of Italian descent realize that they all had much in common. Also, nearly three generations after the mass migration, the Italians were entering into the phase of ethnic history first described by historian Marcus Hansen, who observed that what the grandparents try to forget the grandchildren try to remember. The upsurge in interest in ethnicity coincided with developments in Italian Catholic national parishes. Many of these parishes were in neighborhoods that were losing parishioners to the suburbs. At the same time that their base of support was shrinking, the need for funds, to maintain aging buildings or to operate in an age of inflation, was increasing. At this point, the traditional Italian practice of an annual feast day in honor of a patron saint

R

became a tremendous advantage. Feast days became prominent parts of church calendars, with the week leading up to the feast day being taken up with a fund-raising street fair.

The American environment shaped the development of the Italians' religious practice. As sociologist Nicholas John Russo has observed, successive generations of Italian Americans increasingly emulated other American Catholics in matters such as Mass attendance. The positions of politicians such as Geraldine Ferraro on issues such as abortion suggest Italian American Catholics emulate some of their coreligionists in their selective adherence to Church teaching. What has been the nature of the Italian contribution to American Catholicism? Some have argued that there has been no concerted contribution; when sociologist Francis X. Femminella hypothesized that traditional Italian anticlericalism may have mellowed into a certain healthy independence of mind among the laity, sociologist Andrew M. Greeley responded that any independence of mind among the American laity was first cultivated by the descendants of Irish and German immigrants who reached the middle class and the higher levels of education. Others have argued that any Italian influence may have been somewhat negative; sociologist Joseph A. Varacalli has used the "Italian problem" as a metaphor for the larger questioning of hierarchical authority in American Catholicism. It may be that the Italian contribution is too diverse to characterize: Italian Catholics are as diverse as Joseph Cardinal Bernardin and Anthony Cardinal Bevilaqua. Italians have maintained unique devotions in the United States, such as the dancing of the giglio in honor of San Paolino (Paulinus) di Nola in Brooklyn. Italian Catholics have also organized many parishes that have become important institutions serving many populations in their neighborhoods.

Mary Elizabeth Brown

Bibliography

Browne, Henry J. "The 'Italian Problem' in the Catholic Church of the United States, 1880–1900." United States Catholic Historical Society. *Historical Society Records and Studies* 35 (1946): 46–72.

Di Giovanni, Stephen Michael. *Archbishop Corrigan and the Italian Immigrants.* Huntington, IN: Our Sunday Visitor, 1994.

Primeggia, Salvatore, and Joseph A. Varacalli. "The Sacred and Profane Among Italian American Catholics: The Giglio Feast." *International Journal of Politics, Culture and Society* 9 (1996): 423–449.

Russo, Nicholas John. "The Religious Acculturation of the Italians in New York City." Ph.D. diss., Saint John's University, 1968.

Tomasi, Silvano M. *Piety and Power: The Role of the Italian Parishes in the New York Metropolitan Area, 1880–1930.* New York: Center for Migration Studies, 1975.

Tomasi, Silvano M., and Edward C. Stibili. *Italian Americans and Religion: An Annotated Bibliography.* 2nd ed. New York: Center for Migration Studies, 1992.

Varacalli, Joseph A. "The Changing Nature of the 'Italian Problem' in the Catholic Church of the United States." *Faith and Reason* 12 (1986): 28–73.

Vecoli, Rudolph J. "Prelates and Peasants: Italian Immigrants and the Catholic Church." *Journal of Social History* 2 (1969): 217–268.

See also AMERICAN COMMITTEE ON ITALIAN MIGRATION; APOSTOLATE, ITALIAN; BANDINI, PIETRO; BERNARDIN, JOSEPH CARDINAL; BEVILACQUA, ANTHONY CARDINAL; CABRINI, MOTHER FRANCES XAVIER; CALIANDRO, BRUNO L.; CHURCH LEADERS; DEMO, ANTONIO; DESMOND, HUMPHREY J.; FESTA; FOLKLORE, FOLKLIFE; GAMBERA, GIACOMO; LIGUTTI, LUIGI GINO; MAZZUCHELLI, SAMUEL; MISSIONARIES OF ST. CHARLES–SCALABRINIANS; MUGAVERO, FRANCIS J.; PALMIERI, AURELIO; PERNICONE, JOSEPH MARIA; PIERINI, ARMANDO; PILLA, ANTHONY M.; PROTESTANTISM; RIZZO, RITA ANTOINETTE; STURZO, DON LUIGI; WOMEN AND THE CHURCH

Religious Venerini

See WOMEN AND THE CHURCH

Restrictionist Immigration Laws in the United States: The Literacy and National Origins Quota Acts

The immigration restriction problem was summarily stated in the 1953 *Report of the*

President's Commission on Immigration and Naturalization: "What started out as a debate on a literacy requirement developed into a move to end all immigration, became a temporary emergency measure, and ended up without much discussion as the national origins systems."

Primary Dates of Immigration Restriction Efforts

In the late 1890s, a bill that would require immigrants to pass a literacy test before being admitted to the United States was introduced in both houses of Congress. In 1897 the bill, which was introduced by Senator Henry Cabot Lodge, was vetoed. In 1901, after the assassination of President William McKinley, President Theodore Roosevelt instigated a call to rewrite immigration laws. In 1903 the Lodge literacy test clause was sacrificed in order to push through immigration restrictions on anarchists and persons of "low moral character." Between 1905 and 1914 an influx in immigration occurred, creating greater pressure in a 1914 vote to pass a bill that would require new immigrants to pass a literacy test. In 1907 a commission on immigration was formed, chaired by Senator William P. Dillingham. Literacy bills were then vetoed in 1913 by President William Howard Taft, and President Woodrow Wilson vetoed two more, one in 1915 and one in 1917, with the latter veto overturned. In 1917 Congress passed a bill containing a literacy test, giving the restrictionists their first major victory. The application of the bill was subsequently considered insufficient. After World War I restrictionists pushed for more restrictive measures. In 1921 Congress passed an emergency immigration exclusion of Europeans using a national origin quota system (NOQA), an act based on 3 percent of foreign-born U.S. residents contained in the 1910 census. In 1924, the NOQA was revised for European immigrants based on 2 percent of the 1890 census. NOQA was put into effect in 1929 and caused immediate reaction, with attempts to extend the system to the Western Hemisphere, particularly in restricting Mexicans.

History of Immigration Laws

A survey of related writings reveals the intricate complexity of views on the immigrant restriction question. As literature contemporary to nineteenth- and early-twentieth-century restriction movements often served specific partisan allegiance, it represents arguments rich in supporting details related to its function. Nonetheless, a well-defined, impartial study remains an arduous undertaking given the range of contributing factors: practical (economic, population concerns, and capacity to absorb the influx); political (national sovereignty and international relations); sociological (eugenic or racial concerns, similarities or dissimilarities of physical types, assimilation); and cultural concerns (educational suitability, humanitarian and idealistic principles). In addition, an overall view is further complicated by specific interests expressed both in individual and group opinion, which formed the basis for powerful lobbying tactics by influential persons or groups before boards and commissions and served as the mainstay of theories moving from laissez-faire principles to explicit policies of the state to restrict immigration for specific political purposes.

While not all these elements may have coexisted in a specific historical period, all have contributed to the formulation of justifications necessary to instituting laws that govern movement into the United States. Restrictive laws are a direct consequence of all theories professing the need to maintain the identity of the nation and maintain that alien persons do not have a "right" to immigrate. This dilemma has played a role from the earliest days of immigration, and recent writers suggest the probability that, even under more communitarian laws (theories based not on consent by sovereign government but grounded in social relations and substantive justice), restrictionist measures of exclusion from the community will continue to exist.

The difficulties of adequately comprehending the problem are evident, for over the years a myriad of contributors have debated this complex question in literature of all types: from opinionated papers to popular magazines, in reviews published by elite institutions, in official publications of the government offices, and, of course, in numerous books. These works range from those commentators who limit their vision to the difficulties met by individual groups, such as the Italians, to broader views that reevaluate the restrictionist policies of the United States as only part of a much larger, more complex interrelated phenomenon of mobility.

In fact, the desire to intensify selective restrictionist laws, such as the literacy act in the late nineteenth century, did coincide with a particularly high influx of southern Italian immigration. This means that while it is necessary to examine the individual case of the large Italian influx of the 1890s–1920s, in the end, this trend of Italian migration must also be related to the complex interchanges that contributed to the making of that specific law, as well as to successive ones, such as the National Origins Quota Act, which further and more severely limited southern Italian immigration. In addition, such studies cannot be limited to immigrants arriving in a U.S. port; they must also consider conditions and debates related to general migration or emigration patterns and selective or restrictive immigration trends occurring on the other side of the Atlantic, in the Western Hemisphere and beyond.

From an early period, the 1830s until the 1860s, exclusion tendencies and nativist sentiments surfaced as the immigrant volume rose. For the immigrants of that period, the stigma of "unwanted alien" might refer to their race, religion (Catholic), willingness to accept low wages that undercut the local labor standard, or their compliance in voting. This latter case was considered dangerous by a nativist group, the Know-Nothings, to their own political goals. To mask their agenda, the group suggested an exclusionary tactic: the institution of a literacy test, thus setting in motion the forces that later developed into a series of complex immigration laws.

In a general way, the earliest notions viewed choice of migrant entrance as a selective process, a matter of establishing individual prerequisites compatible to the needs of the nation. Later, more restrictive trends prohibited migration based on characteristics that coincided with qualities typical of specific groups of people that, therefore, made them undesirable to the development of the United States. In the former sense, anti-immigration sentiment became official under the August 3, 1882, congressional law barring lunatics, idiots, and possible public charge cases, while later acts strengthened the previous ones and met more selective measures by barring Chinese and contract labor. And as the nativist attitude intensified along with the 1890s massive rise of immigration, other defensive mechanisms began to appear in an effort to suppress the flow of immigration from southern and eastern Europe.

By the beginning of the twentieth century, discussions centered on how these immigrants would harm the country. Motives ranged from their damage to the native workforce as ignorant, unskilled labor who would undercut living standards and base wages, to eugenics, and, consequently, racially based discussions. At the same time, however, for industry and business, immigration was felt to be necessary for expansion. In the ensuing battles over the contributions of the unskilled immigrant to the building of the country, interest also gravitated to the effect of their presence on the racial, intellectual, and moral development. While the doors remained open to those from "old" familiar areas of immigration (north and northwest Europe), the increasing tide of "new" southern and eastern European immigrants produced hostile reactions. In this atmosphere of fear for the "progress of the nation," a future, unrecognizable national complexion in terms of "instincts" and "institutions," mounting anti-immigration campaigns garnered a consensus favoring restriction stronger than any before.

In light of the 1895 *Report of the Immigration Investigating Commission,* the 1893 laws seemed inadequate, useful for only a summary application by port immigration officers faced with an increasing number of arrivals. Therefore, those who considered the immigration issue central to the economic, social, and genetic health of the country sought new methods for culling desirable from undesirable immigrants. In this tense atmosphere, the literacy test proposal appeared to many as the most objective and least objectionable method; while some restrictionists found it selective without being exclusive, others viewed the literacy test as a practical restriction tool, a way to deter or, at least dissuade, the arrival of ever-growing numbers of "new," ignorant, and, therefore, undesirable immigrants. In some thinking, the application of restriction paralleled the tariff principle: the immigrant was analogous to an imported product, subject to demand and quality of work required.

Early references proposing an intelligence or literacy test are present in the ideas of the Know-Nothing Party, in the 1888 writings of Edward Bemis, and in a Senate bill of 1893. The idea, however, was core to the concep-

Members of the American Committee on Italian Migration surround President John F. Kennedy at the White House during the two-day ACIM Symposium, June 1963. This event represents lobbying efforts Italian Americans used to end the discriminatory national origins quota system. Courtesy Immigration History Research Center, Minnesota.

tion of the Immigration Restriction League. Founded in 1894 by a group of Bostonians, this group publicized the dangers of "new" immigrants to America and formulated the ideas central to application of the literacy test. The bill is generally associated with its primary proponent, Henry Cabot Lodge, but from 1895 to the passage of the bill in 1917 the bill was reformulated and re-presented under various names and in different forms in both houses of Congress.

As this bill developed through successive variations, it gained notoriety from the contentious debates involving a variety of sources: commissions, the political stances of Presidents Cleveland and Theodore Roosevelt, the American Federation of Labor and its leader, Samuel Gompers, opinions within the ranks of the social reformers, the National Manufacturers Association, the steamship companies, and also immigrant lobbies; the literacy test project, therefore, reflects a multi-faceted view of America in serious confrontation with a significant transformation in immigration policy.

Already in 1893 the proportion of illiterates entering the United States seemed, to the restrictionists, to be incompatible with the educational expectations of future residents or citizens. Thus the bill in the Senate Reports of the 52nd Congress declared that all persons of suitable age be required to read and write. Later, in 1895, the bill of the Immigration League established the literacy age level as being between 14 and 60 with an ability to read forty words. The literacy bills generally aimed to contain immigration of males; thus, illiterate parents or grandparents could enter without being tested. In February 1897 a version of the Lodge bill passed in both houses of Congress; it set the minimum age at 16, the maximum at 50, and required immigrants to read and write twenty-five words of the United States Constitution in the immigrant's own language. Before leaving office, President Cleveland on March 2, 1897, affixed his veto explicitly disapproving this restriction bill as an unworthy reversal of America's asylum principles. Furthermore, Cleveland believed the bill contradicted the established national policy requiring of immigrants only physical and moral soundness and a willingness and ability to work.

Apart from the drive of the Immigration League, the strong surge of approval for restriction in the 1890s is also viewed as a product of the 1880s: social disturbances outside the urban areas, concern that the "new" immigrants would not assimilate, "aggressive nationalism," and "jingoist outbursts" that sparked movements culminating in the 1886 Haymarket affair and the 1891 New Orleans lynchings. These events, in consequence, focused more attention on southern and eastern Europeans, immigrants of a peasant class associated by restrictionists with "serfdom" conditions, considered to be "socially backward," and "bizarre in appearance." In this context, Italians were marked as an ethnic target. Furthermore, it is also important to consider the significant role of trade and labor unions in passing the Lodge bill of 1897; these same organizations applied forceful pressure for severe restrictionist measures in the following decade. The literacy test underwent some skepticism as a means of selection in 1896 by Dr. J. H. Senner, commissioner of the port of New York. Previously believing that illiteracy reflected a low standard of living, he attempted to use the educational test to restrict entry. However, after leaving the government, Senner, in his work for the Immigration Protective League, held the opposite view: an educational test would exclude "sturdy" but "ignorant" immigrants.

While the battle in the nineteenth century was inconclusive, restrictionists' efforts to pass a bill that included a literacy test in the twentieth century, though not diminished, met stronger, organized opposition from business groups, such as the National Association of Manufacturers, and immigrant groups, in particular, the Russian Jews. The National Board of Trade also registered their disapproval of the literacy test in 1903–1904. In addition, the period between the two centuries, from the Spanish-American War to the onset of World War I, was a period of growth, leading observers to conclude that a decline in nativist anxieties was accompanied by a confident belief in the possibility of assimilation. This theory culminated after the 1920s into the fusion theory of the melting pot. But running parallel with this trend, in the opening years of the century, were new intellectual ideas and philosophies about race, eugenics, and heredity. Later, these ideas took on a disquieting aspect with dire predictions that undesirable hereditary factors would lead to the decline of the race.

During this period, the National Civic Federation in 1905 held a conference on immigration in New York where the participants approved President Roosevelt's program to amend and enforce immigration laws and called on Congress to pass new laws. In 1906 Senators Lodge and William P. Dillingham presented a bill in Congress. It was backed by Gompers and the American Federation of Labor, but was bitterly opposed by the Liberal Immigration League that favored an absolute laissez-faire attitude toward immigration in response to the needs of the labor market. In response to the increasing social ills in the cities, the only compromise the league would consider was an alternative program aimed at distributing new immigrants throughout the country. Although the Lodge-Dillingham bill passed in 1907, the literacy test was sacrificed in the interest of political solidarity within the Republican ranks. But, as immigration had become a question to be resolved at the national level, Congress formed a commission of experts, chaired by Senator Dillingham, to gather material useful for formulating a credible immigration policy.

The commission reports provided the grounds for defining undesirable immigrants, which evoked a collection of diverse responses. Some found the experts capable of viewing the problem only in racial terms, but others, with more equanimity, found the results coherent with the commission hypotheses: immigrants *could* be divided into "old" or "new"; as the latter represented the problem, the study focused on them. Thus, the forty-one volumes of material, published in 1911, reflect this concern. They include a dictionary classifying races in Europe (southern Italians: Mediterranean group of "Iberian" stock, inhabiting Genoa, the peninsula, and islands south of the Apennines; northern Italians: "Keltics"), which also states that Italy is one of most illiterate countries in Europe, especially in the southern area: in Calabria, for example, 78.7 percent over the age of 6 are illiterate. A number of volumes focus on immigrants in relation to industry and trade, to agriculture, to life in the cities; others discuss their fecundity, their children in relation to the school system, their tendencies to seek charity, and their relation to crime.

President Lyndon B. Johnson with congressional delegation at the White House for a meeting on immigration legislation, January 13, 1964. New Jersey Congressman Peter Rodino, fourth from left in front, helped secure passage of the 1965 Immigration Reform Act, which ended the national origin quota system. Courtesy Lyndon B. Johnson Library.

In practice, this complex study supplied adequate material for justifying and confirming restrictive immigration legislation: the experts had concluded that "new" immigrants came to the United States primarily for economic reasons, were prime contributors to crime, and were prone to ill-health and poverty. One solution was ready-made: the institution of the literacy test; another emerged: restriction based on country-of-origin quotas. While the commission report gave credibility to these initiatives, the pre–World War I atmosphere reinforced and lent a sense of propriety to that aim: "Old World ties" were suspect, heterogeneous cultural attitudes represented disaffection, 100 percent Americanism was expected, the United States educational system had cost millions and stood threatened by outside sources, illiterates would only further burden the system and would have no interest in acquiring knowledge of, or aspiring to, the American system of government. In this latter sense, the literacy test seemed a reasonable means by which to select individuals, but these "undesirables," numbering in the millions, also formed well-defined groups (alternatively viewed as "races" or "nationalities") whose origins were, primarily, southern and eastern Europe. The literacy test

passed, after a veto by Wilson, in February 1917; in April the United States entered the war.

The restrictionist movement triumphed, but the approval of the literacy test served little purpose. Italy, in 1914, had already suspended emigration for men of military age and also refused emigration for women and children attempting to join these men abroad. In addition, travel had become dangerous, and steamships were no longer available for emigrant passage; these factors, not the literacy test, temporarily halted the great tide of immigration. And later, postwar restrictions, in response to fears of new immigration invasions, accelerated the formulation of stringent restrictive laws: group selection explicitly defined by national and racial affiliations rather than individual qualifications. On May 29, 1921, President Warren Harding signed the first bill restricting European immigration; this bill and later forms finally crystallized into the National Origins Quota Act of 1924 establishing visas for nonquota and quota categories, and, finally, the 1927 plan that became effective in 1929. The 1952 McCarran-Walters Act continued the basic policy of earlier acts but set a cap of 150,000 immigrants for Europe. A reform of the NOQA and removal of quotas occurred only in 1965.

Following the 1921 quota act, the Italian emigration commission spent much time and effort seeking ways to supply an emigrant product that would satisfy the request of the host country. The commission's official publication, the *Bollettino dell'Emigrazione,* reports that in 1921–1923, Italy preferred to maintain a liberal emigration policy, but uncontrollable speculative ventures by intermediaries, interested in profits rather than rational emigration criteria, forced the government to assume responsibility. As the work markets continued to close their doors, Italy's concern for emigration increased; the January 1924 bulletin writes of its new policy: economic considerations should take precedence over sentimental ones involving family reunion; requests made to the government will enter a classification list in reference to available posts evenly distributed over the territory; preference to be given to able-bodied young males, 80 percent, capable of maximum return—savings sent back to Italy—over family members and single females 20 percent. Although this initiative met favorable responses in the United States, stricter laws followed. By 1927 Italy's quota had dropped to under four thousand. Furthermore, in 1927, both Italy and the United States entered a new political era: the Italian emigration commission ceased to exist as Mussolini's political policies began to transform the development of the country, and the doors closed even more to immigrants in the United States.

Carol J. Bradley

Bibliography

Caroli, Betty Boyd. "The United States, Italy and the Literacy Act." In *American Immigration & Ethnicity. Law, Crime, Justice: Naturalization and Citizenship,* edited by George E. Pozzetta. Vol. 17. New York: Garland, 1991. (First published in *Studi Emigrazione* 41 (Marzo 1976): 3–22.)

Cavaioli, Frank J. "Italian Americans Slay the Immigration Dragon: The National Origins Quota System." *Italian Americana* 5 (fall/winter 1979): 71–100.

Higham, John. *Send These to Me, Immigrants in Urban America.* Baltimore: Johns Hopkins University Press, 1985.

Jones, Maldwyn Allen. *American Immigration.* Chicago: University of Chicago Press, 1960.

United States Congress, Senate. Reports of the Immigration Commission. *Emigration Conditions in Europe.* Washington, DC: Government Printing Office, 1911. Reprint: New York: Arno, 1970.

———. *Whom We Shall Welcome.* Report of the President's Commission on Immigration and Naturalization. New York: Da Capo Press, 1971.

See also AMERICAN COMMITTEE ON ITALIAN MIGRATION; ANTI-ITALIAN DISCRIMINATION; REGIONAL MIGRATION AND TRANSPLANTATION; RETURN MIGRATION

Return Migration

Although many European immigrants chose to return home after living and working in the United States, Italians did so in particularly high numbers. Part of the reason was timing. The Italian flow to the Western Hemisphere began to climb in the late nineteenth century when steamships were replacing sailing vessels on the Atlantic, which shortened the time and expense of the trip. Economic problems in the newly united Italy remained unsolved, and by the 1890s many workers looked for jobs abroad. The Italian government encouraged temporary emigration in a number of ways: they regulated the ships that carried immigrants, established channels for transmission of remittances back to Italy, and protected Italian citizenship for those who left. On the part of the United States, a huge market for unskilled labor served as a magnet.

The exact number of Italians who journeyed to the United States and then returned to live in Italy is impossible to determine because neither country kept accurate records. Italy based its estimates on the numbers of nationals disembarking in Italian ports after traveling in third class across the Atlantic (the assumption being that only immigrants would choose third class) and on the number of emigrants who applied to local registries for reinstatement after residence abroad. The United States began collecting data in 1908 on "departing aliens," but these reports are suspect for many reasons, and they do not include information on how many times the same alien sailed from an American port. The heavily male Italian immigration to the United States after 1890 is of-

The Hicks Nursery in Westbury, New York, was one of the largest nursery companies on the eastern seaboard of the United States. Hicks employed hundreds of manual workers, the bulk of whom were Italian immigrants who frequently worked during the growing seasons and returned to Italy in the winter. Courtesy Salvatore J. LaGumina.

ten cited as evidence that many intended to return home. If they had planned to stay, they would have brought their families. Estimates vary greatly, and return migration was higher to some southern regions of Italy than to the north, but it is generally agreed that more than half of all Italians who came to the United States between 1900 and 1914 returned to live in Italy.

The effect on both countries was enormous. The United States gained from an elastic labor supply. Adult men arrived ready to go to work, but they would quickly leave for home when jobs became scarce. Italy benefited from having a place where its young men could find jobs and then send their remittances back to their families who remained in Italy. But return migration had a darker side. In Italy local governments complained that the men often returned sick and more inclined to commit crimes than when they left. The money they brought back drove up local land prices. In the United States, observers noted that temporary immigrants had little reason to join unions, change their citizenship, or "commit" to their new country.

Although small numbers of Italians continued to opt for temporary migration, the large volume of returnees dropped after 1914. First the war slowed emigration in general, and then, in the 1920s, conditions on both sides of the Atlantic applied a brake. Restrictive quota laws in the United States made entry more difficult, especially for Italians, whose own government raised obstacles to their exit. The Great Depression and World War II deterred immigration. Temporary residence in the United States had a brief popularity in the 1960s when some Italians worked long enough to qualify for social security benefits that they then opted to receive in Italy. By the 1980s, when jobs and benefits were more plentiful in Italy, interest in immigration diminished, and return migration has practically disappeared.

Betty Boyd Caroli

Bibliography

Caroli, Betty Boyd. *Italian Repatriation from the United States, 1900–1914.* New York: Center for Migration Studies, 1973.

Cinel, Dino. *The National Integration of Italian Return Migration, 1870–1929.* Cambridge: Cambridge University Press, 1991.

See also POPULATION; RESTRICTIONIST IMMIGRATION LAWS IN THE UNITED STATES: THE LITERACY AND NATIONAL ORIGINS QUOTA ACTS

Rhode Island

In April 1524, Giovanni da Verrazzano, a Florentine mariner commissioned by the king of Francis, provided the first recorded visit to what is now Rhode Island. For fifteen days he explored the region of Narragansett Bay including Block Island, which he thought looked like the island of Rhodes, an observation that later gave Rhode Island its name.

Large-scale Italian immigration to Rhode Island began in the late nineteenth century. In 1850 records show that there were only twenty-five Italian residents in the state, most from the north of Italy. By 1900 this number reached nine thousand. Because of the large turnout during the 1910 Columbus Day celebration, historian Charles Carroll observed: "Rhode Island had become conscious of its Italian population in a day."

Attempting to replicate Old World communities, Italian immigrants collected in the communities where their relatives and friends had settled. Immigrants from Fornelli chose West Warwick's village of Natick; those from the mountain towns of Aliano, Raviscania, and Sant'Alife settled in West Barrington. From Calabria, Cosenza, and Acri the new arrivals went to Westerly; from Itri they made Cranston's village of Knightsville their new home. By 1920 Italians were recorded as the largest number of foreign-born in the state with 19 percent of the population. As they poured into the port of Providence, they displaced the Irish on Federal Hill, spread to Eagle Parke and Charles Street in the North End, and eventually populated Silver Lake.

They settled in every city and town in the state. The 1980 census showed how "Italian" Rhode Island had become. Eighty percent of those claiming Italian ancestry resided in ten states; of these, Rhode Island's proportion of Italians—nearly 20 percent—was the largest. Of the twenty-three United States cities with the highest concentration per capita of Ital-

ians, Cranston, where Italians numbered 38 percent, led all the rest. According to the 1980 census, which first posed the question of ancestry, 185,000 Rhode Islanders claimed Italian heritage, placing them third in size behind the Irish and English. The 1990 census counted 199,028 Italian Americans in Rhode Island.

Although most Italian immigrants were unskilled, comparatively few worked in unskilled labor or construction by 1915. The larger number found employment in skilled or semiskilled jobs in foundries, textile plants, building trades, and jewelry manufacturing firms. By 1930 more than 35 percent of Italian shopkeepers owned their own businesses—general stores, clothing stores, macaroni factories, and bakeries—while others served the community as independent craftsmen, such as barbers, tailors, cobblers, carpenters, and tinsmiths. Their entrepreneurship gave the Italian Americans in Rhode Island a high rate of upward mobility.

Federal Hill, a neighborhood of 350 acres west of downtown Providence, is the most famous Little Italy in Rhode Island. Residents shopped for their daily needs in open air markets and neighborhood stores. It was not unusual to see rabbits or lambs hanging from shop windows and buckets of codfish on sidewalks. There was a constant activity of women shopping, children playing, and men socializing. Religious events played an important role, and on special holidays church attendance spilled into the streets as processions halted traffic.

Federal Hill experienced its heyday before World War II. Then from 1950 to 1965 there was an exodus from the community, with a loss of 46 percent of the population. Factors accounting for exodus were: deterioration of housing conditions, the assimilation process, and the accumulation of wealth. In Mount Pleasant, North Providence, Cranston, and Warwick, Italian Americans could enjoy homes with yards, garages, swimming pools, and play areas for their children. From 1950 to 1970, Providence as a whole experienced a greater out-migration relative to its population than any other major city in the nation.

Those who remained in Federal Hill worked to restore the ethnic flavor of the past. In 1975 a beautiful new park named for Giuseppe Garibaldi graced the entrance to the neighborhood, replacing the public bathhouses that had been used by the older residents. Today Federal Hill has become a popular tourist attraction known for its fine Italian restaurants, food stores, and ethnic ambience. Federal Hill has provided Rhode Island with most of its successful and famous Italian American citizens.

The granite industry attracted Italian immigrants to the city of Westerly. When the quarries opened and prospered, the demand for skilled workers increased. Craftsmen were recruited from other American regions, Scotland, and Ireland; but it was Italy that provided the talented carvers who chiseled life into stone. In the 1870s and 1880s stonecutters migrated from places such as Carrara in northern Italy. Although the granite industry declined in the early twentieth century, Italians continued to migrate to Westerly. They came from Naples and the Abruzzi, followed by immigrants from Sicily and Calabria. Today, pride in Italian heritage is reflected in one of the most active cultural societies, the Società Dantesca di Westerly.

Central to each settlement was the Catholic Church. The first Italian immigrants founded a Catholic Church controlled by Irish priests and bishops, hostile to their distinct practice of religion, particularly the *festa* and other rituals. The language barrier was another source of friction. In 1889 the first Italian parish in the Providence Diocese was established, and Bishop Matthew Harkins invited the Reverend Luigi Paroli, a Scalabrini priest from northern Italy, to minister to his countrymen. The first Mass was celebrated in a small chapel on Brayton Street, September 22, 1889, and the Holy Ghost Church was dedicated the following year, August 17, 1890. Subsequently, other Italian churches were established throughout Rhode Island. From these parishes came parochial schools, and, later, day-care centers and youth centers.

The American Baptist Church attempted to convert Italian immigrants and established the First Italian Baptist Church in the North End of Providence in 1897. Five years later the Methodist Church established an Italian mission on Federal Hill. Another Italian Baptist church opened there in 1904. Despite these efforts, Protestantism did not attract many Italian American followers in Rhode Island.

One of the Italian American Catholic churches that had a considerable effect on the residents from Itri is St. Mary's in the Knightsville section of Cranston where the Festa Della Madonna Della Città is celebrated on July 21. The strong ties between Cranstonians and Itrani prompted Rhode Island filmmaker Salvatore Mancini to make the film *The Americanization of Itri* (1985).

Among the earliest organizations formed by Italian immigrants were mutual assistance societies, the first of which was the Unione e Benevolenza Society of Providence, founded in 1882 to dispense emergency aid and to provide death benefits. Six years later the Roma Society was established, followed by the Società Fratellanza Militare Italiane Bersagliere in 1890. Other kinds of organizations emerged: the Order Sons of Italy (1919), Young Italian Imperial Club (1901), Italo-American Club (1896), Aurora Civic Association (1932), Clavis and Colita Club (1935), Convivio (1935–1978), Alpine Club (1962), Verrazzano Day Observance Committee (1962), Unitam (1978), and the Rhode Island Italian American Historical Society (1978).

The Italian American voice was heard through *The Echo,* begun in 1895 as a biweekly newspaper *L'Aurora,* later a weekly newspaper, written in Italian and English. This publication has been an important source of information about Italianità in Rhode Island.

Great strides in government were made in the second half of the twentieth century. John O. Pastore became the first Rhode Island Italian American governor (1945) and the first Italian American United States senator (1950). Cranston got its first Italian American mayor with the election of James Di Prete (1963) and subsequently Vincent A. Cianci Jr. in Providence (1975). Joseph R. Paolino became mayor of Providence in 1984. In 1989 five communities elected Italian American mayors. Other elected Italian American governors in Rhode were Christopher Del Sesto (1959), John A. Notte (1961), Philip Noel (1973), and Edward D. Di Prete (1985).

Italian Americans in Rhode Island, particularly Providence, have been leaders in jewelry manufacturing as founders, designers, and craftsmen. They are the backbone of the industry for which the state—"The Jewelry Capital of the World"—is renowned. Among the best-known jewelry firms is the Uncas Manufacturing Company, one of the largest ring factories in the world, founded by Vincent Sorrentino.

R

In the arts, Antonio Cirino, born in Serino, Italy, in 1888, was a leading educator at the Rhode Island School of Design. Aristide Cianfarani was born in 1895, arrived in Rhode Island in 1913, was educated for three years at the School of Design, and was employed as a modelmaker and designer of silverware and bronze statuary. Among his works is a bust of Edgar Allan Poe, created for the John Hay Library at Brown University. Leading artist Gino Conti, born in Barga, Italy, in 1900, exhibited his paintings in Europe and America, and during the Great Depression undertook numerous WPA projects. Two of the earliest teachers of music in the Rhode Island Italian American community were Oscar Lozzi and Danilo Sciotti. In the field of popular music and entertainment, Rhode Island has produced band leader Frankie Carle, who was born in Providence's Eagle Park as Francesco Carlone. Denise Mainelli, a native of Federal Hill, and performer Ruth Buzzi of Westerly have achieved national fame. Locally, Frank J. Russo has emerged as Rhode Island's premier promoter of popular music concerts and entertainment events.

There has been a reawakening among Italian Americans in Rhode Island as the grandchildren and great-grandchildren become interested in their heritage. In 1994 the Italian American Genealogical Society was founded. In 1990 Rhode Island had the fourth highest enrollment of high school students studying Italian. In November 1983 the American Italian Historical Association held its eighteenth annual conference in Providence.

Carmela E. Santoro

Bibliography

Bardaglio, Peter W. "Italian Immigrants and the Catholic Church in Providence, 1890–1930." *Rhode Island History* 34 (May 1975): 47–57.

Carroll, Leo F. "Irish and Italians in Providence, Rhode Island, 1880–1960." *Rhode Island History* 28 (August 1969): 66–74.

LaGumina, Salvatore John. "John Pastore, Italian American Political Pioneer." In *The Melting Pot and Beyond: Italian Americans in the Year 2000,* edited by Jerome Krase and William Egelman, 1–14. New York: American Italian Historical Association, 1987.

Santoro, Carmela E. *The Italians in Rhode Island.* Providence: Rhode Island Publications Society, 1990.

See also GOVERNORS; PASTORE, JOHN ORLANDO; VERRAZZANO, GIOVANNI DA

Rimanelli, Giose (b. 1926)

A leading poet, novelist, and literary critic, Giose Rimanelli is professor emeritus of Italian and comparative literature at the State University of New York at Albany and lives in Pompano Beach, Florida. He was born in Casacalenda, Italy, on November 28, 1926, of a Molisan father and a Canadian mother, and has written novels, poetry, plays, and literary criticism in both Italian and English. His books have been translated into many languages, and some of his stories have been made into films, among them *The Day of the Lion* (1954) and *Original Sin* (1957). He has traveled extensively in Europe and North and South America, giving lectures and writing for newspapers and magazines. In 1960, invited to Washington by the Library of Congress to deliver a prestigious lecture on contemporary Italian literature, he chose the United States as his primary residence, teaching in colleges and universities such as Sarah Lawrence College, Yale University, University of British Columbia, and University of California at Los Angeles. He has also translated into Italian Lincoln's Gettysburg Address for the Library of Congress. One of his novels in English, *Benedetta in Guysterland* (1993), was selected by The Before Columbus Foundation to receive the American Book Award 1994.

Rimanelli's first novel, *Tiro al piccione* (1953, 1992), was written when he was barely 20 years old. His literary output has continued with *Peccato originale* (1954), *Biglietto di terza* (1958), *Una posizione sociale* (1959), *Graffiti* (1977), *Il tempo nascosto tra le righe* (1986), *La stanza grande* (1996), and *Detroit Blues* (1996). Essays include *Il mestiere del furbo* (1959), *Modern Canadian Stories* (1966), *Tragica America* (1968), *Italian Literature: Roots and Branches* (1978), and *Dirige me Domine, Deus meus* (1996). Dramatic writings include *Tea at Picasso's* (1961), *The French Horn* (1962), and *Lares* (1962). Poetry includes *Carmina blabla* (1967); *Monaci d'amore medieval* (1967), *Poems Make Pictures, Pictures*

Make Poems (1971), *Arcano* (1990), *Moliseide* (Campobasso, 1960; New York, 1991, in the Molisan dialect), *Alien Cantica* (1995), *I rascenije* (1996, in the Molisan dialect), and *From G. to G.: 101 Sonnets* (1996, with Luigi Fontanella).

Franco Mulas

Bibliography

Gardaphé, Fred. *Italian Signs, American Streets*. Durham: Duke University Press, 1996.

Rimanelli, Giose. *Benedetta in Guysterland* Montreal: Guernica, 1993.

See also LITERATURE

Rizzo, Rita Antoinette (Mother Angelica) (b. 1923)

This Catholic nun developed a broadcasting operation into a global network so that it became during the 1990s the most extensive religious telecommunications system in the United States.

The daughter of John and Mae Helen (Gianfrancisco) Rizzo, Rita Antoinette Rizzo was born in Canton, Ohio, on April 20, 1923. Faced with adversity from age 6, when her parents were divorced, Rizzo learned how to cope with hardships. After she encountered discrimination at a Christmas party in St. Anthony's School because of that divorce, her mother withdrew her child from the parish school. However, Rizzo's near miraculous escape from injury when, in grade school, she had been hit by a speeding car, convinced the young girl that, despite her many disappointments, her life was not abandoned by God.

Upon enrolling in McKinley High School in Canton, she was still confronted by poverty and the need to help her mother, and, consequently, her grades suffered during those years. Though Rizzo did not measure up to her potential in her studies, she did reflect, at age 16, the courage, determination, and stamina that have characterized her later years. Before graduating from high school in 1941, she had successfully obtained a job for her mother at city hall, thereby alleviating their plight.

Later, in the fall of that same year, when Rizzo's health was threatened by a calcium deficiency that caused severe pain in her stomach, her mother brought her to Rhoda Wise, a local mystic. The latter encouraged Rizzo to pray a novena, and she was cured on January 17, 1943, through the intercession of St. Therese of Lisieux. Consequently, having undergone a complete religious conversion, Rizzo joined the Franciscan Sisters or the Poor Clares of Perpetual Adoration at St. Paul's Shrine in Cleveland, on August 15, 1944, and took the religious name of Sister Mary Angelica of the Annunciation.

Having helped to establish the Santa Clara Monastery in her native Canton during 1946, Sister Mary Angelica lived a quiet life in the cloister before she formally opened Our Lady of the Angels Monastery in Birmingham, Alabama, on May 20, 1962. In subsequent years she was inspired by the teachings of the Second Vatican Council to employ modern means of communications to spread the Word of God. As a result, Mother Angelica turned the monastery, as its abbess, into the center of her apostolate by printing booklets and recording tapes. Through the Catholic Family Missionary Alliance, her work became widespread, yet her life was not free from adversity and pain.

With the formal dedication of Eternal Word Television Network, on August 15, 1981, Mother Angelica's work of evangelization spread across the nation and eventually around the world, through both EWTN and the shortwave radio ministry, WEWN, in English and Spanish. Her ministry eventually became available on the World Wide Web. The community of priests and brothers, the Franciscan Missionaries of the Eternal Word, which she founded in 1987, has helped her to carry on a worldwide ministry of religious programs for the whole family, including her own talk show, "Mother Angelica Live," and the "Rosary."

At the same time, Mother Angelica has won a number of awards, including the prestigious Gabriel Personal Achievement Award in 1984. Next to the late Mother Teresa of Calcutta, she has become the most recognizable nun in the world. Primarily because of her conservative views, Mother Angelica is more controversial among Roman Catholics than the former despite the widespread support of her ministry through generous donations and encouragement.

Vincent A. Lapomarda

Bibliography

Angelica, Mother, with Christine Allison. *Mother Angelica's Answers, Not Promises.* New York: Harper & Row, 1987.

"Mother Angelica: Nun Better." *Christianity Today* 39 (2 October 1995): 99 ff.

Noonan, Daniel P. *The Catholic Communicators.* New York: Xavier Society for the Blind, 1990.

O'Neill, Dan. *Mother Angelica: Her Life Story.* New York: Crossroad, 1986.

See also RELIGION; WOMEN AND THE CHURCH

Rochester

The first center of Italian settlement in Rochester, New York, occurred in the 1880s in an area termed "Sleepy Hollow." It was in a rundown district between St. Paul Street and the Genesee River. Domenico Sturla was the first Italian in Rochester. The next major settlement area was also near the river on Front and Mill streets. Because of a language problem, *padroni* (labor brokers who hired workers and offered protection and other services) served as labor recruiters and go-betweens. When Italian immigrants sought to learn English in night school, they were frequently turned away because they did not know the language. The irony of the situation led a group of prominent Rochester women to found a mission to aid Italian men.

Landlords and employers joined forces to oppose housing reforms since they benefited from high rents charged to workers desperate for employment. Nevertheless, immigrants kept coming and Italians formed a large percentage of the population in a city made up of various immigrant groups. The first Italian to become an American citizen in Rochester was Paul Rigali in 1876. Between 1920 and 1960 approximately half of all people naturalized as citizens in Rochester came from Italy. As early as 1910 Italians formed over 10 percent of Rochester's white population of foreign birth or of those who had at least one parent born outside the United States. There were 142,680 foreign-born people by that definition in Rochester's total population of 218,000; 14,816 of those people were from Italy, most of whom came from the south, the vast majority of southerners coming from Sicily.

The Lewis Street Center founded in 1907 was part of the settlement house movement that worked to integrate immigrants into the mainstream of American life. It focused on domestic skills, the teaching of housekeeping, American cooking, and child rearing. The theory was that the quickest way to Americanize Sicilian families was to Americanize the mother. Elite Rochester women became a major force, if not *the* major force, in modifying Italian family values and in determining Italian immigrants' perceptions of an American household.

In all of Rochester in 1914 there were nineteen people per acre, while in the Italian seventh ward there were fifty-five people per acre. In the Lewis Street section of the basically Sicilian sixteenth ward, containing a population of 2,357, there were seventy-four people per acre. The effects of overcrowding took their toll. Garbage collections were irregular, and trash was often piled under the outside staircases of homes, presenting health and fire hazards. Spontaneous combustion occurred frequently. Even schools in the area suffered under the erratic regime of refuse collection. Food spoiled quickly in homes without refrigeration, and contaminated milk often caused tuberculosis. In schools, common cups were used regularly for drinks. Canned milk replaced breast milk for babies in many families.

A 1911 survey showed fifty-four of two hundred families had both parents working all day, and more than 25 percent of mothers of young children found it necessary to work to balance the family budget.

Rochester attracted laborers and masons for the construction projects that were taking place in a growing economy. Later, tailors were needed for the clothing factories. But not everyone who came to Rochester had been a laborer or a tailor in Italy. Many picked up skills in America in order to provide for their families. Many men who had worked in the sulphur mines of Sicily initially came to the Pennsylvania coal mines. They soon left the area so that their families could live in a better environment and breathe healthier air. Women, whose place presumably was "in the homes," worked in clothing factories so that their children could have food, clothes, and, eventually, college educations.

Italians participated in cultural activities in Rochester. They formed various associations, including the Good Time Club (Buontempone), the Cristoforo Colombo Society, and a host of mutual-aid societies. As early as 1909, they organized a Columbus Day Parade in which twenty thousand people participated. Along with cultural societies, Italian political associations also soon sprang up.

The first recorded incident of discrimination in Rochester occurred in 1897. A workman, John Ronzone, "declared that contractors at the canal work refuse to employ Italian labor." Angelo Maggio and eleven other Rochester men met together one October night to form the Italian American Business Men's Association. When the chamber of commerce did not recognize them, they formed their own organization, which consisted of insurance agents, doctors, lawyers, judges, and other professionals who were refused admittance into mainline professional associations. They sought to achieve group aims that also advanced individual benefits. Seeing a need for greater protection of its ethnic interests, the Italian Civic League was organized. At its fiftieth anniversary in 1985, the Italian Civic League attracted four hundred people to its dinner, a testament to its success.

Frank A. Salamone

Bibliography

Briggs, John. *An Italian Passage: Immigrants to Three American Cities, 1890–1930.* New Haven: Yale University Press, 1978.

Lanni, Clement G. "The History of the Italians of Rochester from 1876–1926." *Rochester Historical Society Papers.* First Series 6 (1927): 183–199.

Mangione, Jerre. *An Ethnic at Large.* New York: Putnam, 1978.

———. *Mount Allegro.* New York: Crown, 1942.

Salamone, Frank A. "Moral Familism: Italian Americans and Their Società." In *New Explorations in Italian American Studies,* edited by Richard N. Juliani and Sandra P. Juliani, 209–226. New York: American Italian Historical Association, 1994.

———. "Power and Dominance in Sicilian Households in Rochester, NY (Lewis Street Center)." *Studi Emigrazione* 31 (1994): 64–90.

———. "Reflections on Ethnicity." *Multiculturalism and Diversity in America.* Westport, CT: Greenwood Press, 1996.

See also FAMILY LIFE; ORGANIZATIONS

Rodia, Sabatino (1879–1965)

Bricklayer, tile setter, and primitive artist, Sabatino Rodia (also called Simon or Sam) is famous for building the Watts Towers in Los Angeles.

Rodia's days were filled with hard work and innovative use of his materials. At the end of each day he saved all the broken tiles, scraps of mosaics, and broken pieces of glass. Out of the broken pieces he built towers for thirty-three years; they stand 99-, 97-, and 55-feet tall. The Watts Towers have received wide acclaim and have been protected from destruction by the nonprofit Committee for Simon Rodia Towers, and an annual Simon Rodia Watts Towers Music and Arts Festival has been held for many years.

Rodia was born in Serino (Avellino) and died in Martinez, California.

Frank J. Cavaioli

Bibliography

Rolle, Andrew. *The Immigrant Upraised.* Norman: University of Oklahoma Press, 1967.

Soria, Regina. *American Artists of Italian Heritage, 1776–1945.* Rutherford, NJ: Fairleigh Dickinson University Press, 1994.

See also ART

Rodino Jr., Peter Wallace (b. 1909)

After having been almost ignored by the mass media during his first twenty-five years in Congress, Peter Rodino won his place in history as the chairperson of the Judiciary Committee that voted to impeach President Richard M. Nixon in 1974. Yet aside from his outstanding role in the impeachment inquiry, his four decades in the House of Representatives made Rodino one of the most influential legislators in the postwar years.

Rodino was born in Newark, New Jersey, on June 7, 1909, received an LL.B. from New Jersey Law School in 1937, and served in World War II, rising to the rank of colonel. After discharge, his legal practice provided him with a springboard to wage a successful campaign for Congress in 1948 as a Democratic candidate. Rodino's political stronghold during his twenty consecutive terms in the House of Representatives was Newark's North Ward with its large Italian American community. The support of his fellow ethnics remained pivotal to Rodino's reelection in the 1970s and 1980s, even after African Americans had become the largest cohort of voters in his district in 1972.

In return for the endorsement of the law-and-order Italian Americans of his native city and in response to the spread of violence in Newark, which climaxed in a major urban riot in 1967, Rodino supported the passing of strong anticrime measures in Congress. Yet he sided with liberals on civil rights legislation (voting, for instance, for school busing) and refused to pander to the racist feelings of that impoverished blue-collar wing of the Italian American community that resisted black migration into its neighborhoods and found its own champion in Anthony Imperiale.

Although Rodino had already distinguished himself by making the case against the confirmation of Gerald Ford as vice-president, his involvement in the hearings on the impeachment of President Nixon constituted his own political trial. He mastered his arguments with unexpected skills and remarkable fairness. He was persuaded that the president had to be removed from the White House. Yet he granted the Republican minority on the House Judiciary Committee any opportunity to present its views. He also endeavored to forge a bipartisan majority for the impeachment resolution in order to demonstrate that the misconduct of the president in the Watergate case was an objective fact and that the impeachment was not the product of arguable party politics.

After Nixon's resignation Rodino used his prestige and influence to shape the legislation of the following years. For instance, he was instrumental in killing proposed constitutional amendments to outlaw abortion and allow school prayer. He also cosponsored the 1986 Immigration Act, became the congressional authority in the field of bankruptcy, and served on the special committee investigating the Iran-Contra scandal.

Rodino retired from the House in 1988. His career refuted Nixon's notorious allegation that "you can't find one [Italian American] that's honest."

Stefano Luconi

Bibliography

Barone, Michael, and Grant Ujifusa. *The Almanac of American Politics.* Washington, DC: National Journal, 1987.

Drew, Elizabeth. *Washington Journal: The Events of 1973–1974.* New York: Random House, 1975.

MacNeil, Neil. "The Man for the Times." In *Dream Streets: The Big Book of Italian-American Culture,* edited by Lawrence Di Stasi, 210–212. New York: Harper & Row, 1989.

Sussman, Barry. *The Great Coverup: Nixon and the Scandal of Watergate.* Arlington, VA: Seven Locks Press, 1972.

See also POLITICS

Rodney, Caesar (1728–1784)

One of two Italian Americans who signed the Declaration of Independence, Caesar Rodney held more public offices than any other citizen in the history of Delaware and showed himself to be a true hero and patriot.

The son of Caesar and Elizabeth (Crawford) Rodney, he was born on October 7, 1728, in Dover, Delaware, and died of cancer there on June 26, 1784. While he was clearly of English ancestry on his mother's side, his Italian lineage is obscured in his father's ancestry, which goes back several generations to the Adelmare family of Treviso, Italy, but emerges in the Rodney genealogy with the perdurance of the name Caesar passed from one of his early ancestors down through subsequent generations, including that of his father, himself, and his nephew. Rodney's family roots in Delaware go back to his grandfather who came in 1682, after converting to Quakerism, and settled in Kent County on land granted to William Penn by the Duke of York.

After becoming a sheriff in Kent County in 1755, Rodney's life was distinguished for public service during the next three decades. A captain in the French and Indian Wars in 1756, he became a legislator for the colony of Delaware in 1762, a justice in its supreme court in 1766, and a delegate to the Continental Congress in 1774. In this capacity, along with Italian American William Paca (1740–1799) of Maryland, Rodney signed the Declaration of Independence. To achieve this, he rode the eighty miles to Philadelphia to be present for the crucial vote that broke the tie in his delegation on the issue of independence. Then, as the speaker of the assembly in Delaware, he became its chief executive, based on his position as top public official when it decided for independence from England.

Moreover, during the American Revolution, Rodney rose to major general in the Continental Army as well as to chief executive of Delaware. For his unique contribution in serving it with courage before and after the Revolutionary War, Delaware chose him as one of the state's two historic figures to represent it in the National Statuary Hall in Washington, D.C. An Episcopalian, his remains, originally interred on the family farm, were transferred in 1889 to the cemetery of Christ Church in Dover.

Vincent A. Lapomarda

Bibliography

Frank, William P. *Caesar Rodney Patriot: Delaware's Hero for All Times and All Seasons.* Wilmington: Delaware American Revolution Bicentennial Commission, 1975.

Haas, John H. "Caesar Rodney: Delaware's Prudent Engineer of Revolution." Ph.D. diss., Claremont Graduate School, 1994.

Johnson, Roger D. "The Public Career of Caesar Rodney." Master's thesis, University of Northern Colorado, 1979.

See also PACA, WILLIAM

Rosati, Joseph (1789–1843)

Pioneer Catholic missionary in the American Midwest, first American bishop of Italian origin, administrator of the Diocese of New Orleans (1826–1830), and first bishop of St. Louis (1827–1843), Rosati was born January 12, 1789, at Sora, province of Frosinone (then in the Kingdom of Naples), the son of Giovanni and Vienna Senese Rosati. He took vows in the Congregation of the Mission (Vincentians) in Rome (1808) and was ordained priest by the papal sacristan, Bishop Giovanni Bartolomeo Menochio, on February 10, 1811. He was assigned to parish work and conducted spiritual revivals for laity and retreats for clergy around Rome and Naples.

Bishop Louis William DuBourg of Louisiana obtained Pope Pius VII's permission to recruit Italian Vincentians for his diocese. Among them was Rosati, who arrived in America in 1816 and immediately took up missionary work around Bardstown, Kentucky, and at Vincennes, Indiana. He reached St. Louis for the first time in October 1817. The Vincentians organized a seminary and college at the Barrens, near Perryville, Missouri (1818), and Rosati became its first president.

DuBourg consecrated Rosati coadjutor bishop at Donaldsonville, Louisiana, on March 25, 1824. Upon the division of the Diocese of Louisiana into two dioceses (New Orleans and St. Louis), Rosati was appointed to St. Louis. He exercised spiritual jurisdiction from the Mississippi River valley to the Rocky Mountains and from Arkansas to the Canadian border. He welcomed several communities that operated schools, orphanages, and hospitals in his diocese: Sisters of Loretto, Jesuits, Religious of the Sacred Heart, Sisters (Daughters) of Charity, Sisters of the Visitation, and Sisters of St. Joseph. He encouraged Jesuits to staff Native American missions in Kansas and the West, and dispatched the Milanese Dominican Samuel Mazzuchelli to Iowa Catholics. From 1831 to 1834 Rosati oversaw construction of a stone and marble cathedral with a 90-foot steeple at a cost of over sixty thousand dollars (the present Basilica of St. Louis, the King, "the Old Cathedral" near the Gateway Arch).

Rosati was an active participant in the Baltimore provincial councils of 1829, 1833, and 1837, preparing translations and documents for the approval by other bishops and the Holy See. The Fourth Provincial Council of Baltimore (1840) entrusted Rosati with its documents and memorials for Pope Gregory XVI. The trip to Europe provided him an opportunity to raise funds for his growing diocese (estimated at the time to number thirty thousand Catholics). Pope Gregory, however, delayed his return to St. Louis by appointing him apostolic delegate to Haiti. Since Rosati spoke Italian, French, and English, the pope charged him with negotiating the reestablishment of an ecclesiastical hierarchy in the island nation.

After returning to Rome (1842) to report the successful conclusion of negotiations with the president of Haiti and the preparation of a draft concordat, Rosati suffered several sharp attacks of coughing with accompanying fever. He died on September 25, 1843, at the Vincentian House on Montecitorio. His remains were subsequently transferred from Rome to St. Louis and, in 1970, they were reburied in the crypt of the cathedral he had built.

James J. Divita

Bibliography

Easterly, Frederick John. *The Life of Rt. Rev. Joseph Rosati, C.M., First Bishop of St. Louis, 1789–1843.* Washington, DC: Catholic University of America Press, 1942.

See also HIGHER EDUCATION

Rossi, Agnes (b. 1959)

A fiction writer, Agnes Rossi was born in 1959 in Paterson, New Jersey, of Italian and Irish parents. She was raised in Upper Saddle River, New Jersey, and currently lives in Brooklyn, New York. Her paternal grandfather left the family farm in Gubbio, Italy, to come to the United States in 1911, where he worked as a coal miner in Scranton, Pennsylvania. Like other miners, many of them Italian, Rossi's grandfather died thirty-five years later of black lung disease. Rossi's parents, members of the transitional generation that maintains strong economic and cultural ties with its working-class origins, struggled to move into the middle class to fulfill the American dream of success.

Rossi received a bachelor's degree from Rutgers University and a master's degree in English from New York University. Her authorial debut, a collection of short stories entitled *Athletes and Artists* (1987), won the New York University Prize for Fiction. These stories, pervaded by a dark humor, begin to explore an issue that is central to *The Quick: A Novella and Stories* (1992): the search for human connection in order to fight the anonymity and solitude to which her characters are often doomed. The novella from which the collection takes its name, "The Quick," offers Rossi's most explicit exploration of Italian American themes. Set in New Jersey, "The Quick" traces Marie Russo's ascent to the materialistic comfort of middle-class life, which she achieves through marriage, only to eventually fall back into the financial precariousness of her working-class origins. Opting for the anonymity and solitude of life in an empty apartment in a dilapidated neighborhood, she initiates a more honest search for selfhood. Scattered traces of ethnicity in Rossi's novella reveal a disconcerting sense of loss and displacement, one that articulates its protagonist's ambivalent relationship to a cultural heritage that she experiences only indirectly, through old souvenirs and thin airmail envelopes from her parents' relatives.

Rossi's first novel, *Split Skirt* (1994), translated into Italian (Mondadori, 1995), advances Rossi's exploration of identity through the filters of gender, class, ethnicity, and age. The novel tells of two women, the 27-year-old, lower-middle-class Rita and the wealthy and middle-aged Mrs. Tyler, whose friendship develops during their three-day stay in the Hackensack county jail. Narrated from a dual narrative perspective that eventually enlarges to include a third character's point of view and a detached third-person perspective, the novel depicts the two characters' attempts to transcend their self-contained, isolated, and isolating worlds, to establish a relationship with each other that in turn promotes a more fulfilling process of self-exploration for each. The last draft of the novel omits the explicit references to Rita's Italian American identity evident in an early draft, allowing only for the Irishness of Mrs. Tyler to emerge unambiguously. Yet the presence of an apparently minor Italian American character, Rita Gennaro, demonstrates Rossi's continuous preoccupation with examining the ways in which to define ethnic identity, especially as a third-generation and culturally displaced Italian American. Rossi's most recent novel, to be titled "Fancy," focuses on the author's Irish ancestry, though again earlier drafts contained references to Italian American themes.

Rossi's concern with investigating ethnic intersections, her rejection of simplistic notions of ethnic identity, and her exploration of narrative strategies make her one of today's significant contemporary Italian American authors. Her works, especially *The Quick,* have received much critical praise. Both *The Quick* and *Split Skirt* were published in England as well as translated into other languages. Norton reprinted *The Quick* in paperback in 1996.

Edvige Giunta

Bibliography

Dybek, Stuart. "Loving the Ruthless Truth." *The New York Times Book Review,* 14 June 1992, 14–15.

Giunta, Edvige. "Narratives of Loss: Voices of Ethnicity in Agnes Rossi and Nancy Savoca." *Canadian Journal of Italian Studies* 19 (1996): 55–73.

———. "Reinventing the Authorial/Ethnic Space: Communal Narratives in Agnes Rossi's 'Split Skirt'." *Literary Studies East and West* 12 (1996): 90–102.

See also LITERATURE; NOVELS AND NOVELISTS

Rossi, Angelo Joseph (1878–1948)

The first Italian American mayor of San Francisco, Angelo J. Rossi held that office from 1931 until 1944. His parents migrated in the 1860s from Genoa, Italy, to Volcano, California, a small mining town in Amador County, where Angelo was born on January 22, 1878, one of seven children. The elder Rossi worked in the mines and later bought a farm and a general merchandise store. When his father died in 1884, his mother and the children continued to operate the store and farm. In 1890 the store burned, and, subsequently, the family moved to San Francisco. There he attended school and worked in a florist firm after school, became a full-time employee, then the sole owner, renaming the firm Angelo J. Rossi Florists. He married Grace Allen in 1902; they had three children and eight grandchildren.

A leader in San Francisco business circles, active in the advertising and rotary clubs, he was a founder and later president of the Downtown Association, a business and professional group. In 1914 he began his public service career as an appointee on the Playground Commission, where he served until his election to the City and County Board of Supervisors seven years later. After a hiatus of one term, Rossi won reelection in 1929, and when Mayor James Rolph was elected as governor of California in 1931, the board appointed Rossi as mayor. He won reelection to that office in the following three elections.

Rossi was mayor of San Francisco longer than any other politician except his immediate predecessor, notable in that this was a troubled period: economic depression, labor unrest, and World War II, when Italians in the United States were briefly classified as "enemy aliens." During an era of many federally financed public projects, Rossi's reign is known for the municipal purchase of the street railway system, the completion of a major water project, the Golden Gate and Bay Bridges, the Municipal Opera House, and the Golden Gate Exposition of 1939–1940.

Labor unrest provided the most difficult challenge of Rossi's career. Many strikes were called; the most widespread was that of the twelve thousand member International Longshoremen's Association and the general strike of 1934. Local newspapers accused Rossi of ineffectiveness; the general strike was settled by a federal mediator. A long-lasting enmity developed between Rossi and Harry Bridges, longshoreman president, which was reflected in critical remarks about each other in the newspapers: Bridges was accused of being a communist, and Bridges called Rossi anti-labor.

During the first years of World War II, when Italy was one of the enemy nations, a union official gave hearsay testimony before the State Un-American Activities Committee that Rossi had used the Fascist salute at public meetings. Although this was not substantiated, Rossi considered this charge a personal affront and gave an emotional response before the committee. Although the Board of Supervisors passed a resolution expressing confidence in the mayor, Rossi was humiliated. It is notable that, at the time, both San Francisco and New York City (Fiorello LaGuardia) had Italian American mayors. Except for this wartime incident, the media gave little attention to Rossi's ethnic heritage. Even though he was the first Italian American mayor in the city, many others of his ethnic group had served on the Board of Supervisors, and Italian Americans had been integral in the development of the city. In later years, two other Italian Americans became mayor: Joseph L. Alioto in 1967 and George Moscone in 1976.

Although Rossi enjoyed general support in the city throughout his thirteen years as mayor of San Francisco, there were two failed recall attempts in 1934 and in 1942, and Rossi lost his reelection bid for a fourth term in 1944. At his funeral in 1948 he was eulogized as a hardworking, farsighted man of integrity who had devoted much of his life to public service. Rossi's official papers are on file in the City Hall Archives; a Rossi collection is on deposit in the San Francisco History Room of the Public Library, Main Branch.

Rose D. Scherini

Bibliography

California State Legislature. Senate. *Report of the Joint Fact-Finding Committee on Un-American Activities in California*. Sacramento, 1943.

Gumina, Deanna Paoli. *The Italians of San Francisco, 1850–1930*. New York: Center for Migration Studies, 1985.

Martinelli, Phylis. "Mayor Rossi—An Ethnic Politician." *Gazzetino* 2, no. 3 (1975): 10–11.

See also POLITICS; SAN FRANCISCO

Ruotolo, Onorio ("Bayard") (1883–1966)

Born in Cervinara (Avellino), Onorio Ruotolo achieved distinction as a sculptor, author, poet, and teacher. At age 12, he studied for six years at the Academia di Belle Arti. As he became disenchanted with academic studies, he was inspired by the great Neapolitan sculptor Vincenzo Gemito to pursue art as a vocation.

While living in the United States, Ruotolo captured the pathos that embodied the sadness and suffering of Italian immigrants in his poems, articles, and sculpture. He co-directed *Il Fuoco,* a magazine on art and politics, with radical poet Arturo Giovannitti. In 1921 he began *Minosse,* a social and literary publication. He founded and became president of La Scuola d'Arte Leonardo Da Vinci, which met in the chapel of St. Mark's Church in the Bowery. The purpose of the school, which operated until the 1940s, was to advance the arts and applied arts to children of Italian parentage, and others, and to men and women of all races and creeds.

In his early years in the United States, Ruotolo, under the pseudonym of Bayard, drew cartoons to criticize society. From the 1940s until his death in 1966 in New York City, his writings appeared in newspapers and periodicals. A collection of poems, *Accordi e Dissonanze,* was published in 1958. He served as education director of the Amalgamated Shirt and Leisure Wear Joint Board from 1950 to 1957.

In his sculptures during World War I, he combined realism with sociological interests. They include *And Jesus Wept* (1914), *The Other Heroism* (1916), *Red Cross* (1917), and *Les Emurees* (The horrors of the war) (1918). In the 1920s Ruotolo produced busts of Don Ciccio Sisca, Helen Keller, Enrico Caruso, Arturo Toscanini, Theodore Dreiser, Dante, Albert Einstein, and Abraham Lincoln. The works of this multitalented Italian American artist have been widely acclaimed in the United States and Europe.

Frank J. Cavaioli

Bibliography

Craven, Wayne. *Sculpture in America*. New York: Thomas Y. Crowell, 1968.

Soria, Regina. *American Artists of Italian Heritage, 1776–1945*. Rutherford, NJ: Fairleigh Dickinson University Press, 1994.

See also ART

S

Sabelli, Cesare (1897–1984)

A participant in the saga of long-distance flying that captivated the world during the early decades of the twentieth century, Cesare Sabelli was born in Montepulciano of a venerable Abruzzese family. The beneficiary of a formal education, including two technical degrees, the young Cesare embraced the romance of aviation by reading stirring accounts of aviation feats. He translated his dreams of aviation into reality by enlisting in the air wing of the Italian army in 1915 when Italy entered the First World War.

Assigned to combat duty, his activity, primarily that of reconnaissance and observation, was sufficient for him to win several air medals and to be recognized as an *Asso* (Ace) of the Italian Air Force. During his wartime service he came into contact with an American Army Air unit assigned to duty in Italy then under the leadership of Fiorello H. LaGuardia, destined to become the most famous Italian American politician. At the conclusion of the war, Sabelli spurned an opportunity to join the emerging Fascist Party and decided to immigrate to the United States. Cognizant of his ethnic roots, he stated, "I decided to come across the ocean to that land that was discovered by an Italian, which bore the name of another Italian and in which lived millions of Italians."

In the United States he advanced his notion of flying nonstop from New York to Rome—a concept considered too risky in 1920. Determined to prove that this was a feasible operation, he realized that it would take years of preparation before it could be accomplished. In the meantime, he continued to fly and remained in contention as a bona fide aviator via the "barnstorming" route. Teamed up with another intrepid Italian American named Cavicchia, for several years he launched an uncertain, erratic career in exhibition flying.

The mid-1920s witnessed an escalating interest in transatlantic crossings as nations vied with each other to make aviation history. Until then the only nonstop transatlantic flight had been that of a British team in 1919. That feat, however, had not removed the hazards involved, and several subsequent failures had followed before the success of Charles Lindbergh's New York to Paris flight in 1927. Sabelli dreamed of surpassing Lindbergh's feat by being the first to fly nonstop from New York to Rome, a much greater distance.

By 1929 Sabelli brought together a group of Italian Americans, including opera luminaries Tito Schipa and Beniamino Gigli, to finance the flight of the *Roma*. Designed as a radically new sesqui-plane by the Sicilian immigrant inventor Giuseppe Bellanca, the *Roma* was to have Sabelli as the pilot and a crew of three other Italian Americans. The project was designed to be "Italian" since all connected with the flight—builder, owner, backers, and crew—were of Italian heritage. By September 20, 1928, the date of the proposed flight of the *Roma,* attention had developed to guarantee extensive press coverage. A successful flight would also provide financial gains as various industrial companies provided monetary incentives. Unfortunately, due to a mechanical engine problem, the *Roma* was forced to abort its mission.

Refusing to concede defeat, Sabelli made plans for a new plane. By 1932 Giuseppe Bellanca had designed another plane, the *Leonardo DaVinci,* that was capable of reaching over forty hours of nonstop cruising.

The Roma sesqui-plane built by leading aircraft designer Giuseppe Mario Bellanca for Cesare Sabelli, 1928. Courtesy Salvatore J. LaGumina.

Untimely problems and postponements consumed another two years. Finally, on May 14, 1934, with Sabelli at the helm and with George Pond of the famous cosmetic manufacturing family as copilot, the *Leonardo DaVinci* took off from Brooklyn's Floyd Bennett Field. Sabelli and Pond were aware that thirteen others had perished in prior unsuccessful efforts to fly nonstop from New York to Rome. Nor were they destined to complete the feat themselves as their plane crash landed in Ireland after crossing the Atlantic Ocean. Nevertheless, the flight was considered an authentic transatlantic air flight, and Sabelli became the first Italian-born pilot to fly nonstop across the Atlantic Ocean.

Salvatore J. LaGumina

Bibliography

Hamlen, Joseph. *Flight Fever.* New York, 1971.
LaGumina, Salvatore J. "Cesare Sabelli: Italian American Aviation Pioneer." *La Parola del Popolo* (Maggio/Giugno 1979): 49–63.

See also BELLANCA, GIUSEPPE MARIO

Sacco and Vanzetti

On April 15, 1920, two bandits ambushed and killed the paymaster and guard who were transporting the weekly payroll (almost $16,000) of a small shoe factory in South Braintree, Massachusetts. Three weeks later, the shoe worker Nicola Sacco and the fish peddler Bartolomeo Vanzetti were arrested and charged with the crime. At the outset questions were raised about the handling of the case. In the aftermath of the First World War and the Bolshevik Revolution, America was experiencing its first "Red Scare." Radicals—especially those foreign or foreign-born—were being hunted, arrested, imprisoned, or deported by the U.S. attorney general, A. Mitchell Palmer. A year earlier, a bomb had exploded in front of Palmer's Washington home that was tied to anarchist organizations.

It was in this political context that the Sacco and Vanzetti case unfolded between 1920 and 1927. Sacco and Vanzetti were both anarchists who were followers of Luigi Galleani and subscribed to his newspaper, *Cronica Sovversiva.* Both had fled to Mexico to avoid the draft in 1917 and later returned to Massachusetts. While being held for the South Braintree crime, Vanzetti was tried and convicted for an attempted robbery committed on December 24, 1919, even though many witnesses testified that he was selling eels that day—the traditional dish for Italians on Christmas Eve. Judge Webster Thayer imposed a sentence of fifty years, rather than the usual eight to ten that were customary for attempted armed robbery. Then the same

Judge Thayer presided over the murder trial of Sacco and Vanzetti, which began on May 31, 1921. A jury found both men guilty.

Over the next several years, motions were filed for a new trial based on evidence that was not presented at the first trial; Judge Thayer denied the material. In late 1925 Celestino Madeiros confessed to having participated in the South Braintree crime; he insisted that Sacco and Vanzetti were not involved, but Thayer again denied a motion for a new trial. Two years later, a final attempt was made after Felix Frankfurter, a professor of law at Harvard University and future Supreme Court Justice, published an essay in the *Atlantic Monthly,* which pointed to the judicial discrepancies in the trial and the probability that both men were innocent. This last motion for a new trial was also denied and in April 1927 Judge Thayer imposed the death sentence on Sacco and Vanzetti.

Frankfurter's involvement in the affair was typical: the Sacco and Vanzetti case galvanized American liberals and the European Left. Workers and intellectuals shared a common passion. The literary world began to intercede; besides support from the *New Republic* and the *Nation,* Sacco and Vanzetti were the subjects of works by Katherine Anne Porter, Upton Sinclair, John Dos Passos, Maxwell Anderson, Edna St. Vincent Millay, and a cycle of paintings by Ben Shahn, entitled *The Passion of Sacco and Vanzetti.* Under pressure, Governor Alvan T. Fuller appointed a special three-man commission of Harvard President A. Lawrence Lowell, M.I.T. President Samuel W. Stratton, and Judge Robert Grant to review the proceedings; the commission found no reason for a retrial and Governor Fuller denied a petition for amnesty on August 3, 1927. Shortly after midnight on August 23, Sacco and Vanzetti were executed in the electric chair. Worldwide protests could not stop the sentence; the executions were followed by a massive funeral conducted through the streets of Boston.

The case became the subject of innumerable studies over the decades; many reached the conclusion that Sacco may well have been guilty but that Vanzetti was most probably innocent. In 1977, on the fiftieth anniversary of their executions, Massachusetts Governor Michael Dukakis issued a proclamation "that any stigma and disgrace should be forever removed from the names Nicola Sacco and Bartolomeo Vanzetti. . . ." The proclamation actually ignited more flames of debate. In the last decade of the twentieth century several new works have appeared, ranging from those that condemn both men to those that exonerate both.

Stanislao G. Pugliese

Bibliography

Avrich, Paul. *Sacco and Vanzetti: The Anarchist Background.* Princeton: Princeton University Press, 1991.

Russell, Francis. *Sacco and Vanzetti: The Case Resolved.* New York: Harper & Row, 1986.

———. *Tragedy in Dedham: The Story of the Sacco-Vanzetti Case.* New York: McGraw-Hill, 1971.

Sinclair, Upton. *Boston: A Documentary Novel of the Sacco-Vanzetti Case.* Reprint, Cambridge: Robert Bentley, 1978.

Young, William, and David E. Kaiser. *Postmortem: New Evidence in the Case of Sacco and Vanzetti.* Amherst: University of Massachusetts Press, 1985.

See also ANTI-ITALIAN DISCRIMINATION; RADICALISM

Saints

The belief in, and worship of, the saints historically has occupied a significant place in the lives of Italian Americans. With assimilation into a secular, non–southern Italian and non-Catholic worldview, however, this tradition has been attenuated, especially on the part of the third and fourth generations.

John J. Delaney has spoken of saints, from the Catholic perspective, as "real men and women who struggled desperately, sometimes against incredible odds, sometimes against a most mundane background, to live lives of perfection to the best of their . . . [various] . . . abilities in the service of the Master, . . . Jesus Christ." In the same vein, the *Dogmatic Constitution on the Church* (No. 50) in *The Documents of Vatican II* (1967) discusses not only the Catholic conception of the communion of saints as linking this world to the other side but also the need to venerate and seek out the intercession of the saints.

A scholarly investigation of the saints in the lives of Italian Americans points to at least six major issues. First, to study the saints as a central entity addresses the issue of what provides meaning to individuals and communities. A second issue is that the study of the saints sheds important light on the issue of social change over time among Italian American Catholics. Third, such an analysis is informative regarding the changing definitions of social reality operant in the broader American culture. Fourth, such an endeavor provides evidence about the transformation—whether officially sanctioned or not—of the Catholic Church in the post-Vatican era. Fifth, such a study demonstrates how a belief in saints serves to maintain symbolic boundaries between certain categories of people: believers from nonbelievers, Catholics from most non-Catholics, traditional Catholics from progressive Catholics, and southern Italians who have maintained *la via vecchia* (the ancient way of life) from those highly assimilated into American culture. Finally, to study the saints is one way to correct what Pitirim Sorokin termed the "one-sidedness of sensate social science," the latter discipline emphasizing the negative and pathological qualities of human life. In other words, the study of the saints, with their assorted virtues and positive role models, is one useful way to highlight the positive in a culture permeated increasingly with cynicism and despair.

That the saints have historically played a prominent role in the religion both of premodern southern Italians and the first and second generations of Italian Americans is attributable at least as much to cultural background as to any immersion into an official, institutional Roman Catholicism. As Primeggia and Varacalli noted, two key traditional southern Italian values have been those of "personalism" and "familism." The first encourages a religious orientation stressing the concrete and the experiential; the saints, for southern Italians, have represented palpable, immediate, warm, and accessible intercessors to a cosmos otherwise seen as too alien, distant, cold, and abstract. The southern Italian reliance on familism is similarly conducive to embracing the saints; the saints were seen by many in the southern Italian tradition as supernatural extensions of the family. In this sense, then, the "low tradition" of southern Italian thought with its emphasis on community mirrored the "high tradition" of a Catholic social thought that included in its corpus the concept of the "communion of saints." For many southern Italian peasants and immigrant Italian Americans these "extensions," like family members, could be coerced and "bargained" with as well as loved and venerated. It should come as little surprise, then, that at the center of the panopoly of saints that southern Italians and Italian Americans have been attracted to is the Holy Family: surrounding baby Jesus is Mary (mother), Joseph (father), and Ann (grandmother). The special attraction of the Italian American to the Blessed Mother, relatedly, is in part a function of the matriarchal nature of southern Italian society.

Given the basic demographics of the transatlantic voyage, the baseline for the Italian American experience vis-à-vis the saints was both the traditional, isolated village existence and, relatively speaking, the more modern, open urban centers of south Italy that shaped social life prior to migration to the United States. Each village had its local Marian devotion, saint, or saints. Given the imperfect institutionalization of an official Catholic presence in such premodern settings, the worship of saints were oftentimes viewed as far more central to the religious and cultural celebrations and *la via vecchia* than were specifically Catholic practices (for example, full participation in the sacramental system) and Catholic doctrine. Furthermore, following a host of scholars including Rudolph J. Vecoli, Paul McBride, Richard Gambino, and Nicholas J. Russo, the worship and reliance on the saints was part of a matrix of folk religiosity that fused with Catholic components of magic, superstition, the occult, and paganism. Regarding the latter, Richard Gambino argues that saint worship served, for many premodern southern Italians, as the functional replacement for formerly important Roman pagan gods or other indigenous religious beliefs. For Gambino, "as was true of ancient gods, each saint was seen as having domain over a specific area of life and often to be in competition or rivalry not only with other saints but with Satan and other demons, with witches and even on occasion with God." In any event, it is clear that the southern Italian appropriation of the saints was used, in the peasant mindset qua folk religion, in a practical, world-affirming way as a vehicle to defend oneself from an otherwise hostile, poverty-ridden, and politically oppressive social order (*la miseria*). Conversely put, such a utilization underplayed the characteristic Catholic emphasis on selfless service and surrender to God as well as conformity to doctrine. The specific approach of southern Italians to the idea and practice of the saints was part of the generally recognized "Italian problem" in the Catholic Church of the turn-of-the-century United States as immortalized especially in the scholarship of Henry J. Browne.

Of the multitude of local southern Italian saints, some were successfully transplanted to American shores. According to Primeggia and Varacalli, for instance, the famous *giglio* (lily) feast of Nola, Italy, with its central focus on the veneration of St. Paulinus, has now been celebrated for over one hundred years in Williamsburg, Brooklyn. But this is certainly more the exception than the rule. As Rudolph Vecoli had astutely observed in 1977, "as the multiple identities of the hundreds of groups of *paesani* (fellow townfolk) have merged into a general Italian-American identity, so too the devotions to the multitude of local patrons have merged into the cult of a few favored saints and madonnas."

It is important to point out, however, that northern Italians also had their saints, some of them successfully being transplanted to America. Carol Field, for instance, reports that, in one way or another, St. Orso is honored in Osta, St. Ippolitio and St. John the Baptist in Tuscany, St. Mark in Venice, St. Margherita Ligure in Liguria, and St. Ambrose in Milan. In her work on the Italians of San Francisco, Deanna Paoli Gumina notes that the immigrants and their descendants from the vicinity of Lucca in Tuscany held an annual fair in September in honor of St. Croce; formed a society dedicated to a Tuscan woman who had attained sainthood, Gemma Galgani; and celebrated numerous devotions to the Blessed Mother, such as the Madonna della Guardia and the Madonna della Grazia.

However, it is fair to conclude that the veneration of the saints both in northern Italy and among Italian Americans from the north was not as strong as the southern Italian devotion given both the impact of modern ideologies and other social-structural realities. As Sensi-Isolani and Martinelli state, for instance, "[M]any northern Italian immigrants . . . [to California] . . . were from families of small town craftsmen and tradesmen who thus came with some money and entrepreneurial skills. They were more likely to be literate and had a tradition of political and labor activism that generally did not exist in the feudal South." As Sensi-Isolani reports in her case study of the Sonoma County village of Occi-

dental (about 60 miles north of San Francisco), the majority of Lombards were religiously unmusical and embraced a secularized socialistic worldview. Moreover, many northern Italians felt ashamed of their impoverished conationals from *Il Sud* (the south) and, especially, of their specific brand of folk religiosity. As Joseph Giovinco recounts, in 1911 some elite elements of the northern Italian community in San Francisco leveled a vigorous protest against an anticipated religious celebration and public procession by Sicilians in honor of St. Anthony on the grounds that it represented "superstition and ignorance . . . which would cast a disagreeable light on our colony and threaten to transform it into a resemblance of the sister colonies of the East" in which southern Italians predominated. It should be pointed out, however, that not all southern Italian immigrants were believers and practitioners in the concept of sainthood. Rudolph J. Vecoli claims that, in addition to widespread anticlerical attitudes, some immigrants from throughout the Italian nation were influenced by currents of rationalism and positivism and celebrated May Day observances—a form of secular *festa*—in Italian American communities.

Some of the saints that survived the transatlantic voyage and flourished in the land of Columbus have, more or less, a distinctive appeal to Italian American Catholics, while the attraction of other saints extends through this specific ethnic community to the total Catholic world. Among the latter saints with more universal appeal are St. Anthony of Padua, St. Francis of Assisi, St. Therese of Lisieux, St. Michael the Archangel, St. Lucy, St. Rita, and St. Blaise. Among those with, relatively speaking, a more specific appeal to Italian Americans are St. Janarius, St. Filomena, St. Rosalia, St. Paulinus, and St. Rocco. Probably the most popular expression of Mary for Italian-Americans is Our Lady of Mount Carmel; some others include Our Lady Assumed into Heaven, the Immaculate Conception, Our Lady of Loretto, Our Lady of Pompeii, and Holy Rosary. Mention also should be made here of the Italian-born St. Frances Xavier Cabrini, or Mother Cabrini, who in 1946 became the first American to be canonized.

Not all of these saints were born in Italy. St. Anthony, for instance, was a native of Portugal, St. Donato came from Ireland, while St. Rocco originated in France. St. Blaise is believed to have come from Armenia. Some are popularly but not officially recognized as saints; St. Filomena is one such example, losing her official status in 1961. While having a general appeal to all Italian American Catholics, some of these saints still maintain a special attraction to a particular region of Italy (for example, St. Janarius for Neapolitans; St. Rosalia for Sicilians; St. Filomena for Sardinians). All of these saints, in addition to having a strong attraction to Italian Americans, are believed to possess special intercessory powers (for example, St. Lucy for eyesight, St. Blaise for throat ailments, St. Rocco for plague, St. Rita for hopeless causes, St. Francis for animals, St. Michael for protection from Satan, St. Onofrio for the healing of burns, St. Apollonia for toothaches). Many saints also served as patrons for specific occupations (for example, St. Joseph for carpentry, St. Damiano for barbers, St. Crispino for shoemakers, St. Paolino for gardeners). Certain Italian American enclaves venerate St. Benedict the Moor, a saint of African origin. (See following entry.)

The worship and veneration of the saints has taken place through many different social contexts and venues in the Italian American community. Scapulars of Our Lady of Mount Carmel with St. Simon Stock adorn the neck and chest of many Italian Americans—sometimes along with such superstitious symbols as *il corno* (the twisted horn), worn to ward off *il malocchio* (the evil eye). The saints are found in and outside homes. They are central in the celebrations of *feste* (feasts). They are found in the neighborhood storefronts of some Italian American organizations such as religious and mutual benefit societies. They are, of course, found within all Catholic parishes. The saints have threaded and, in some cases, mutually supported aspects of both official Catholic and folk religiosity. Indeed, the establishment of national and de facto Italian ethnic parishes in the United States started a process that encouraged not only the maintenance of Old World religious beliefs but their development within an authentic Catholic framework.

Systematic social scientific as well as an abundance of anecdotal evidence suggests that the saints are steadily marching out of the minds, hearts, and lives of many contemporary Italian American Catholics. In his study of three generations of Italian-Americans in New York City, sociologist Nicholas J. Russo confirms a severe attenuation in the attachment to the saints. In his study comparing middle-class and working-class sensibilities toward the saints, David Halle finds that the display of religious iconography in homes is both quantitatively less and highly privatized in the former as compared to the latter category.

There are, undoubtedly, many causes for this attenuation. One is the general rationalization and secularization of the larger American culture, which makes belief in any supernatural conception seem less plausible. Related to this is the assimilation of many highly formally educated Italian Americans into this culture of unbelief. This assimilation brings with it the pressure to conform to external indices of "success," thus pressuring many upwardly mobile Italian Americans to reject allegiances to any "Old World" practice, the saints included. Related to this, as noted by David Halle, is the increasing reluctance of many middle-class Italian Americans to place a statue of Mary or some other saint in front of their homes lest they offer "offense" to their non-Catholic neighbors and friends. Halle also reports that many Italian Americans, just entering the category of the nouveau riche, refuse to prominently or publically acknowledge any symbol associated with their previous state of material poverty.

Additionally, the hibernization of Italian American Catholics, strong between the 1930s and 1960s in American society, as discussed by Nicholas J. Russo, may have slightly deemphasized the southern Italian attraction to the saints in favor of other (for example, sacramental and doctrinal) components of the official Catholic worldview. Finally, and very importantly, many contemporary Catholic leaders—clergy, religious, and laity alike—have downplayed the significance and, indeed, the "reality" of the conception of sainthood itself. In some cases, the motivation for this downplaying has included legitimate theological and liturgical reform, that is, a stronger emphasis and focus on the worship of Christ. In other cases, this rejection/attenuation is the result of an internal secularization within significant progressive sectors of the Catholic Church itself, of accepting the claim that the veneration of the saints is indicative of the acceptance of retrograde and irrational beliefs and practices. In this latter case, then, the saints have been pushed to the periphery of the Catholic Church and local parish by those individuals rejecting the devotions of the mid-twentieth century and identifying the main purpose of Catholicism to be that of pursuing more worldly social justice causes and personal therapeutic pastoral concerns.

Any resurrection of the centrality of the saints in the lives of Italian Americans and within the Catholic Church in general would necessarily entail a reversal of these secularizing movements. The present-day emphasis on the concept of "multiculturalism," especially on the part of the very formally educated middle classes who have for the most part abandoned the saints, might very well afford a window of opportunity for them to come marching back into the hearts and minds of Italian Americans and other Catholics alike.

Joseph A. Varacalli

Bibliography

Abbott, Walter M., S.J., and Monsignor Joseph Gallagher, eds. *The Documents of Vatican II.* Washington, DC: America Press, 1967.

Browne, Henry J. "The 'Italian Problem' and the Catholic Church in the United States, 1880–1900," *Records and Studies,* Vol. 35, United States Historical Society, 1946.

Delaney, John J. *Dictionary of the Saints.* Garden City, NY: Doubleday, 1980.

Field, Carol. *Celebrating Italy.* New York: William Morrow, 1990.

Gambino, Richard. *Blood of My Blood.* Garden City, NY: Doubleday, 1974.

Giovinco, Joseph. "'Success in the Sun?': California's Italians During the Progressive Era." In *Struggle and Success: An Anthology of the Italian Immigrant Experience in California,* edited by Paola A. Sensi-Isolani and Phylis Cancilla Martinelli. Staten Island, NY: Center for Migration Studies, 1993.

Gumina, Deanna Paoli. *The Italians of San Francisco, 1850–1930.* Staten Island, NY: Center for Migration Studies, 1978.

Halle, David. *Inside Culture.* Chicago: University of Chicago Press, 1993.

McBride, Paul. "The Solitary Christians: Italian Americans and Their Church." *Ethnic Groups* 3, no. 4 (December 1981): 333–353.

Primeggia, Salvatore, and Joseph A. Varacalli. "Community and Identity in Italian American Life." In *The Ethnic Quest for Community: Searching for Roots in the Lonely Crowd,* edited by Michael Hughey and Arthur Vidich. Greenwich, CT: JAI Press, 1993.

———. "The Sacred and Profane Among Italian American Catholics: The Giglio Feast." In *International Journal of Politics, Culture, and Society* 9, no. 3 (spring 1996): 423–449.

Russo, Nicholas John. "Three Generations of Italians in New York City: Their Religious Acculturation." In *The Italian Experience in the United States,* edited by Silvano M. Tomasi and Madeline Engel. Staten Island, NY: Center for Migration Studies, 1970.

Sensi-Isolani, Paola A. "Tradition and Transition in a California Paese." In *Struggle and Success: An Anthology of the Italian Immigrant Experience in California,* edited by Paola A. Sensi-Isolani and Phylis Cancilla Martinelli. Staten Island, NY: Center for Migration Studies, 1993.

Sensi-Isolani, Paola, and Phylis Cancilla Martinelli, eds. *Struggle and Success: An Anthology of the Italian Immigrant Experience in California.* Staten Island, NY: Center for Migration Studies, 1993.

Sorokin, Pitirim A. *Altruistic Love: A Study of American 'Good Neighbors' and Christian Saints.* Boston: Beacon Press, 1950.

Varacalli, Joseph A. "The Changing Nature of the 'Italian Problem' in the Catholic Church of the United States." *Faith and Reason* 12, no. 1 (spring 1986): 38–72.

———. "Italian American Catholic: How Compatible?" *Social Justice Review* 83, nos. 5–6 (May–June 1992): 82–85.

Varacalli, Joseph A., Salvatore Primeggia, Salvatore J. LaGumina, and Donald E. D'Elia, eds. *The Saints in the Lives of Italian-Americans: An Interdisciplinary Investigation.* SUNY-Stonybrook, NY: Forum Italicum, 1999.

Vecoli, Rudolph J. "Cult and Occult in Italian American Culture." In *Immigrants and Religion in Urban America,* edited by Randall M. Miller and Thomas D. Marzik. Philadelphia: Temple University Press, 1977.

———. "Prelates and Peasants: Italian Immigrants and the Catholic Church." In *Journal of Social History* 2, no. 3 (spring 1969): 217–268.

S

———. "Primo Maggio: May Day Observances Among Italian Immigrant Workers, 1890–1920," *Labor's Heritage* 7 (spring 1996): 28–41.

Feast of St. Benedict the Moor

One striking example of the variety of street festivals found in the numerous Italian American enclaves in the United States is that of St. Benedict the Moor. San Fratello, the birthplace of St. Benedict the Moor, is a village within the province of Messina, Sicily. His parents, Christopher and Diana Manasseri (given name of San Fratellan owners), were black slaves, understood, by tradition, to have been brought from Ethiopia to Sicily. Born in 1526, Benedict was eventually granted freedom at the age of 18. He then became a day laborer, sharing his earnings with the poor and spending free time with the sick. He became known as "the Holy Negro." Later, becoming a hermit in the hills near San Fratello, Benedict lived under the direction of Jerome Lanza, and, following Lanza's death, he became the superior of a growing number of hermits.

In 1562 Pope Pius IV ordered Benedict's independent eremetical group, as well as others, to join established religious orders. Benedict joined the Order of Friars Minor of the Observance (the Franciscans) shortly thereafter. At the friary of St. Mary of Jesus in Palermo, Benedict lived his days, primarily as a cook, though for a period as guardian and novice master. In brief, he was an austere man, with exceptional gifts of prayer.

At age 63, he died in Palermo. April 4, 1589, his date of death, is marked as his feast day by the Catholic Church. The villagers in his birthplace of San Fratello, however, have marked September 17 as his feast day, in recognition of his date of birth.

Many villagers from San Fratello migrated to the United States, primarily New York City, in the first half of the twentieth century, bringing with them their devotion to St. Benedict the Moor. The devotion was thus made manifest in East Harlem, on Manhattan Island in New York City. East Harlem, or "Italian Harlem," was a term used to describe the area in the first half of the twentieth century extending from Third Avenue to the river, west to east, and 104th Street to 120th Street, south to north.

As the streets of Italian Harlem were understood to be Italian village–oriented, the immigrant villagers of San Fratello principally settled in the tenement buildings on 107th Street between First and Second Avenues. As each of the village-oriented streets commonly honored the patron saint or Madonna of one's particular village, or *paese,* in the form of a street festival, the immigrants from San Fratello celebrated the Feast of Saint Benedict the Moor on 107th Street.

The Società di San Benedetto, a local Sicilian society, conducted the feast, holding it for three days in mid-September around September 17, the birthday of the saint. During the procession with the statue of the saint, it was not uncommon to see San Fratellan women, barefoot and in prayer, honoring the black saint. The feast was celebrated on 107th Street from approximately the mid-1920s to the late 1940s. As the ethnic make-up of East Harlem began to change with many San Fratellan immigrants and their children moving out of East Harlem, the feast became a one-day block party in the 1950s and, later, ceased to exist as a street feast.

There was formal and informal participation of African Americans, though few in number, at the feast. It was a unique endeavor by Italian Americans to worship a saint of African descent.

Anthony D'Angelo

Bibliography

D'Angelo, Anthony. "Italian Harlem's Saint Benedict the Moor." In *Through the Looking Glass: Italian & Italian/American Images in the Media,* edited by Mary Jo Bona and Anthony Julian Tamburri, 235–240. Staten Island, NY: American Italian Historical Association, 1996.

Davis, Cyprian. *The History of Black Catholics in the United States.* New York: Crossroad, 1990.

Hardison, Inge. "Italians Honor Negro Saint." *Color* (March 1953): 34–37.

Lynch, C. "Benedict the Moor, St." In *New Catholic Encyclopedia,* Vol. 3, 282–283. New York: McGraw-Hill Book Company, 1967.

Orsi, Robert Anthony. *The Madonna of 115th Street.* New Haven: Yale University Press, 1985.

———. "Religious Boundaries of an In Between People." In *American Quarterly* 44, no. 3 (September 1992): 313–347.

See also FESTA; FOLKLORE, FOLKLIFE; RELIGION

Salvemini, Gaetano (1873–1957)

Born in Molfetta, a small southern Italian town, on September 8, 1873, Gaetano Salvemini adopted the traditional Roman Catholicism of his parents and received a clerical education before moving on to the University of Florence, beginning a brilliant career as historian, professor, and political activist. While in Florence, he embraced the political Left.

A man of indomitable courage, he withstood cruel blows of personal fate and rose time and time again to champion victims of tyranny and exploitation. In 1908, while teaching at the University of Messina, he lost his wife, five children, and a sister to a terrible earthquake occurring that year. His early historical works are characterized by a crusade for the voiceless peasants of the south and an endless battle for social reform and relief to the beleaguered Mezzogiorno of Italy. In fact, he forever remained a crusader for justice and champion of freedom, best known for his outspoken and courageous attacks against Mussolini and Fascism. He was arrested as an antifascist and left Italy in 1925.

After spending the years 1925–1934 in London and Paris, Salvemini came to America, where he lectured at Harvard from 1934 to 1948, becoming a United States citizen in 1940. He ultimately retired to Sorrento in Italy, where he died in 1957 to accolades for his scholarship and heroism from both sides of the Atlantic.

Salvemini is remembered for his historical works on medieval Italy, Giuseppe Mazzini, the French Revolution, and his studies on history and science. But for many, he is best remembered for his unrelenting attacks against Fascism in *The Fascist Dictatorship in Italy* (1928), *Under the Axe of Fascism* (1936), *Prelude to World War II* (1954), and *Italian Fascist Activities in the United States* (1977). Reacting to criticism that historians should be objective observers and not knightly crusaders, Salvemini mused that in the next world individuals go to hell, or purgatory, or to paradise. But since there is no paradise on earth, they will surely end in hell if they scorn purgatory. If he sinned as a scholar and historian in revealing his animosity toward his subject, he willingly suffered the criticism. But few have combined the balance between thought and action, scholarship and political activism as Gaetano Salvemini.

Paul J. Devendittis

Bibliography

DeCaro, Gaspare. *Gaetano Salvemini*. Turin: Unione tipografico, 1970.

Puzzo, Dante. "Gaetano Salvemini: An Historiographical Essay." *Journal of the History of Ideas* 20 (April 1959): 217–235.

Salomone, A. William. *Italy in the Giolittian Era*. 2d ed. Introduction by Gaetano Salvemini. Philadelphia: University of Pennsylvania Press, 1960.

Salvemini, Gaetano. *The Fascist Dictatorship in Italy*. London: Jonathan Cape, 1928.

———. *Historian and Scientist*. Cambridge, MA: Harvard University Press, 1939.

———. *Italian Fascist Activities in the United States*. New York: Center for Migration Studies, 1977.

See also FASCISM

Sammartino, Peter (1904–1992)

Founder, president, and chancellor emeritus of Fairleigh Dickinson University, Dr. Peter Sammartino epitomizes a success story that has few equals in the history of higher education.

Around the beginning of the twentieth century, Gaetano and Eva Amendola Sammartino migrated from Salerno, Italy, to the United States. Their first child, Peter, was born in New York on August 15, 1904. He graduated from the College of the City of New York in 1924, received a Ph.D. from New York University in 1931, then studied at the Sorbonne in Paris. He married Sally, the daughter of Anna Bianchi and Louis Joseph Scaramelli, a prominent and successful businessman in Rutherford, New Jersey. Among Peter Sammartino's many books dedicated to Sally, the most significant dedication is found in *Of Castles and Colleges* (1972): "To my wife, Sally, who has always done half of the work but who has rarely gotten any of the credit."

His experiences during the 1930s as a participant in the experimental New College

Peter Sammartino founded Fairleigh Dickinson University, New Jersey, and with his wife, Sally, made it a leading institution of higher learning. The Sammartinos were prominent promoters of Italian contributions to American cultural life. Photo by Peter Fink, New York. Courtesy Frank J. Cavaioli.

movement at Teachers College, Columbia University, influenced his life work. He applied these ideas to the multiple-campus expansion of Fairleigh Dickinson University he founded in 1941, which developed into five campuses and America's eighth largest privately supported university. Peter and Sally Sammartino visited and assisted colleges and universities in twenty-one countries throughout Africa, Asia, and Europe. He received honorary degrees from colleges and universities in five countries and has been honored by seven others.

As an international educator, he disseminated culture, promoted research and scholarship, and spearheaded several literary and historical institutions in the New York City metropolitan area. He was founder-president of the International Association of University Presidents and national chairman of the International Columbus Quincentennial Commission. Among his thirty books, Sammartino wrote *Columbus* (1988) to promote interest in the 1992 Columbus Celebrations.

In 1974 Peter and Sally Sammartino began a nationwide campaign and ultimately convinced Congress to authorize funds for the restoration of Ellis Island. He planted the seed for the restoration and obtained the first grant of $1.5 million, which was followed by an additional $5 million, toward restoring America's most famous shrine for immigrants.

Peter and Sally Sammartino coped with the many problems involved with building, equipping, staffing, and integrating Fairleigh Dickinson University. When they retired in 1967, Fairleigh Dickinson University boasted twenty thousand students, fifty-two buildings, and seven campuses valued at $250 million with an endowment of $62 million consisting of stocks, bonds, and real estate.

A staunch promoter of the Italian contribution to the creation of the United States of America, Dr. Sammartino advocated studies in Italian culture. He was one of the group of students responsible for the establishment of the Casa Italiana of Columbia University, and he organized the first Italian Honors Society. In his later years, he donated his voluminous library of rare books on Italian Americans and Italian culture to the Casa Italiana Zerilli-Marimò of New York University, his alma mater.

He spearheaded the Philip Mazzei Project at Fairleigh Dickinson University; he also encouraged studies on Giuseppe Garibaldi, William Paca, and other Italian patriots and explorers. As vice-president of the Northeastern Region of the National Italian American Foundation, which he had helped establish, Dr. Sammartino sponsored seminars and conferences to disseminate Italian culture in the United States. His sound guidance as a member of the American Italian Historical Association rendered important scholarship in the field of ethnic studies.

Peter Sammartino was an internationalist and yearned for a world organization that could enhance communication among educators worldwide. His dream became a reality in 1964: he founded the International Association of University Presidents. Today the group consists of over six hundred university presidents from over fifty countries, organized into regional councils and allied with the United Nations.

On the occasion of their tragic deaths, March 29, 1992, in Rutherford, New Jersey, Governor James Florio expressed the condolence of the entire State of New Jersey: "The Sammartinos lived their lives with purpose, committed to the values which define our species as compassionate, civilized, and humane. Their devotion to education, the arts, and the humanities will have lasting effects on our State and beyond."

The Sammartinos established the Peter and Sally Sammartino Charitable Remainder Unitrust, and they bequeathed their estate to Fairleigh Dickinson University in order to provide scholarships for students interested in the teaching profession.

Margherita Marchione

Bibliography

Cavaioli, Frank J. "Peter Sammartino." In *Italian Americans and Their Public and Private Life,* edited by Frank J. Cavaioli, Angela Danzi, and Salvatore J. LaGumina, 2–8. New York: American Italian Historical Association, 1993.

Marchione, Margherita. *Peter and Sally Sammartino, Biographical Notes.* New York: Cornwall, 1994.

Sammartino, Peter. *I Dreamed a College.* New York: A. S. Barnes, 1977.

———. *Of Castles and Colleges, Notes toward an Autobiography.* New York: A. S. Barnes & Co., 1977.

See also HIGHER EDUCATION

San Francisco

The 1848 discovery of gold in the Sierra Nevada foothills was the impetus that brought thousands of adventurers to San Francisco. Among them were Italian speculators eager to pan for the precious mineral that promised them wealth. But few speculators made the expected quick fortunes, and by the mid-1860s many packed their belongings and settled in lumber camps, silk farms, fruit ranches, farms, and fishing communities of northern California. Others returned to San Francisco with hopes of earning the price of a ticket home.

The Italian speculators who returned to San Francisco were welcomed by a small number of fellow countrymen, mostly from the northern regions of Italy, who migrated during the same period but had chosen to remain in San Francisco. An Italian settlement developed along the base of Telegraph Hill in the North Beach district, a mercantile and semiresidential neighborhood situated close to the waterfront and the city's financial center. It was within this area that the essential outline of the Italian community was formed. Similarly, a concurrent settlement was in the Outer Mission district, an urban agricultural district at the southern end of the city wherein Italian urban gardeners and truck farmers spread out, growing flowers and produce in the sandy soil.

The Italian community's physical expansion in these two geographic directions eased its integration into the city's, and later the state's, commercial markets that contributed in enormous measure to the economic growth of San Francisco as well as California. A measure of modest prosperity followed the geographic settlement that enabled the Italians to establish a socioeconomic system based on a fortuitous match between the Italians' agricultural and fishing expertise and the manpower needs and opportunities available in the young American city of San Francisco. It was the convergence of these factors that resulted in the prominence of Italians in the Bay fishing industry and the commercial produce markets that gave them a springboard into larger enterprises: notably, banking, a municipal contract for the collection of refuse, commercial canneries, and import-export companies that directly exported California produce to Italy and imported Italian foods and dry goods. Italians became active in San Francisco's politics electing Angelo Rossi mayor. They built churches and sent their sons to Jesuit universities.

Accompanying this economic expansion based on geographic opportunities, these Italian pioneers created for themselves a rudimentary social services network, including medical and welfare assistance, for needy Italians in order to keep them off the streets, while finding them work in rural locales where they were needed and wanted. It was these early successes that gave Italians the sense that they were pioneer builders, and they proudly referred to their community as the Italian Colony of San Francisco.

The Italian immigrant experience in San Francisco can be divided into two major periods that coincide with this geographic expansion: 1850 through 1870, in which there were 1,621 Italians, and 1880 to 1930, in which the Italian community grew to 30,710. The first period began with the gold rush and

Members of the "Cantori di Assisi" chorus from Italy after their recital at the Italian Mausoleum. The chorus visited San Francisco in 1982 as part of a year-long series of cultural events to celebrate the eight-hundredth anniversary of the birth of St. Francis of Assisi, the city's namesake. Courtesy Augusto Troiani.

terminated during a transitional social and economic period for both California and San Francisco. During these first decades, the Italian immigrants came in steady, though small, numbers as they settled predominantly in the northern interior regions of California. The second period, beginning in 1880, saw the doubling of the number of Italians and ended with the passage of national restrictive immigration laws in the 1920s that curtailed the influx of southeastern Europeans. By 1930 Italians ceased to be California's largest European immigrant group.

The next period in the history of the Italian Colony was overshadowed by the events of World War II as many Italian aliens were interned and sons were drafted. World War II, however, brought economic growth along with increased personal incomes. This, combined with government subsidies to returning servicemen, enabled many to obtain college educations and buy homes. Afterwards, there was a movement out of the North Beach and Outer Mission districts as Italian Americans moved to more affluent neighborhoods in San Francisco or to communities throughout the Bay Area where they found affordable housing and quality education for their children. They were less campanilistic (parochial),

spoke English, intermarried, and enrolled in colleges. Again, these trends continued in the aftermath of the Korean and Vietnam wars.

By the 1970s the third and subsequent generations of the ancestral Italian immigrants came to ethnically identify themselves in symbolic ways. Through a number of organizations devoted to the preservation of Italian culture and the learning of the Italian language, those who have chosen to perpetuate their heritage now represent the spirit of those pioneer Italian immigrants who helped to build San Francisco.

Deanna Paoli Gumina

Bibliography

Di Leonardo, Michaela. "Five Families from the 1920s to the Present." In *Struggle and Success,* edited by Paola A. Sensi-Isolani and Phylis C. Martinelli, 175–198. New York: Center for Migration Studies, 1993.

Gumina, Deanna Paoli. *The Italians of San Francisco, 1850–1930.* New York: Center for Migration Studies, 1985.

See also AGRICULTURE; FISHING, WEST COAST FISHING; FUGAZI, GIOVANNI F.; GIANNINI; AMADEO P.; SBARBORO, ANDREA; SOCIETÀ ITALIANA DI MUTUA BENEFICENZA

Sanguinetti, E. F.
See Business and Entrepreneurship

Santangelo, Alfred E. (1912–1978)

This distinguished Italian American served four terms as a New York state senator (1947–1950, 1953–1956) and three terms as a U.S. congressman representing the 18th congressional district in Manhattan (1957–1962). Santangelo's parents were Italian immigrants whose belief in the value of education for their ten children produced a successful family; virtually all of their children became professionals. Santangelo attended City College and Columbia University Law School and became an assistant district attorney in New York City's homicide division. At age 35 he was recruited by the Democratic Party to run for the state senate. In his six years in Congress, he campaigned to reform abuses of military spending, and championed the cause of labor and programs for youth.

Congressman Santangelo and other Italian Americans fought to have Italian Americans appointed to federal posts. In 1962 Anthony Celebrezze became a cabinet member when he was appointed Secretary of the Department of Health, Education, and Welfare. Due to Santangelo's position on the Appropriations Committee, he, John LaCorte, and the Italian American community helped in efforts to name the Verrazano-Narrows Bridge.

Santangelo fought against anti-Italian prejudice. As president of the Federation of Italian American Democratic Organizations (FIADO), Santangelo enlisted the support of the Order Sons of Italy and UNICO to stop Italian American character defamation in the ABC television program *The Untouchables* (1959–1963). He successfully organized a boycott against Liggett & Myers, the sponsors of the program. FIADO called off the boycott only after Desilu Productions agreed to reduce the number of individuals with Italian surnames who were stereotyped as criminals. Santangelo also fought discrimination against the Jewish community, for which he later received the B'nai B'rith award.

In 1970 Santangelo became president of AID (Americans of Italian Descent), a group that published a national newspaper called *The Challenge* to expose defamation and bigotry. That year, the officers of AID went to Washington to discuss the failure of the Nixon administration to appoint qualified Americans of Italian descent to federal posts, after which President Nixon appointed John Volpe the ambassador to Italy. President Nixon also directed Attorney General John Mitchell to ban the odious terms *Mafia* and *La Cosa Nostra* from government documents. Santangelo was also active in efforts to establish the Enrico Fermi Library and Cultural Center, which was later built in the Belmont section of the Bronx.

Santangelo supported the National Italian American Foundation, a national group of leading Italian Americans dedicated to stopping discrimination, enabling young Americans with a scholarship outreach program, conducting research initiatives, and setting an Italian American agenda in the nation's capital.

Patricia Santangelo
Betty Santangelo

Bibliography

Colello, Joseph V. *Outlines of Greatness.* Kearney, NE: Morris, 1993.

Lepis, Louis. *Italian Heroes of American History.* New York: AID, 1976. Reprint, 1992.

See also Politics

Sarazen, Gene (1902–1999)

A golfing champion who broke records in his youth, Sarazen was born on February 27, 1902, in Harrison, New York, the son of Federico and Adela Saráceni. Eugenio began caddying at the early age of 8 in nearby Rye and quickly learned the intricacies of golf, especially after he dropped out of school in 1913. Then, after he saw his name in print following his first hole in one in 1918, he Anglicized his name to fit in better with the game that became his career.

At age 20 Sarazen was able to enter the U.S. Open and immortalized himself in the history of the game by winning that title, thereby making him the youngest champion ever. That same year, he defeated Walter Hagen to become the world champion. Sarazen's list of championship victories became very impressive.

Sarazen's success as a golfer was both as an individual player and as part of a team. Individually, he won the U.S. National Open

(1922 and 1923), the Professional Golf Championship (1922, 1923, and 1933), the British Open (1932), and the Masters (1935). Though Lawson Little beat him in 1940 during a playoff that would have earned him a third U.S. Open title, Sarazen was able twice to win the Professional Golf Seniors Championship (1954 and 1958). He participated in the Ryder Cup as part of the American foursome six times, winning four times (1927, 1931, 1935, and 1937) and losing twice (1929 and 1933).

Sarazen was one of the giants of the golf world at a time when both Bobby Jones and Walter Hagen were in their prime. Not only did he become the youngest champion of all time by winning the U.S. Open and the PGA championships in 1922, but he became the first player to do so. His fame led Benito Mussolini to invite Sarazen to Rome, where he played golf in 1927. By 1935 Sarazen was the first player ever to win the sport's four major tournaments (U.S. Open, PGA, British Open, and the Masters).

Perhaps Sarazen's moment of true glory came the day he fired a two for a double eagle on the fifteenth hole in the final round of the Masters in Atlanta in 1935. That opened the way for his playoff against Craig Wood and his victory in the Masters that year. Out of this was born his plan to bring together annually the world's champions in golf. This vision became a reality in the fall of 1994 with the inauguration of the Sarazen World Open Championship. His wife of sixty years, Mary Catherine (Henry) Sarazen, died in 1986. In 1978 a scholarship fund in their name was established at Siena College in Loudonville, New York. Sarazen died on May 13, 1999, at Naples, Florida.

Vincent A. Lapomarda

Bibliography

Alliss, Peter. *Peter Alliss' Supreme Champions of Golf.* New York: Scribner's, 1986.

Galvin, Terry, and others. "The Squire: The Golfing Life of Gene Sarazen." *Golf World* (Special Vintage Issue, 24 November 1995), *New York Times* Sports, Leisure Magazines, 1995.

Olman, John M. *The Squire: The Legendary Golfing Life of Gene Sarazen.* Cincinnati: Olman Industries, 1987.

Sarazen, Gene. *Golf: The New Horizons.* Rev. ed. New York: Crowell, 1968.

See also SPORTS

Savio, Mario (1942–1996)

Mario Savio, who launched the free speech movement, helped to set off student-run political protests against abuses in American society. The son of Joseph, a Sicilian immigrant, and his wife, he was born in Queens County, New York City, on December 8, 1942, and died in Sebastopol, California, on November 6, 1996.

Coming from a working-class family in that same section of New York that has produced such prominent Italian Americans as Mario Cuomo and Geraldine Ferraro, Savio graduated from Martin Van Buren High School. After studying at Manhattan College and Queens College, he entered the University of California at Berkeley, where, on October 1, 1964, standing on the top of a police car, he sparked the free speech movement by encouraging his fellow students to disrupt the university for denying their right to discuss political issues.

On December 2, 1964, inspired by the words of its leader, the free speech movement erupted into a full-scale confrontation at Berkeley between Savio, symbol of the anti-establishment protest, and Chancellor Clark Kerr of the University of California, symbol of the establishment, in the greatest student strike in the nation's history. Though it resulted, on the next day, in the arrest and subsequent prosecution of Savio with a sentence of four months in the Santa Rita Jail, the university conceded to the movement when, on December 8 of that year, Kerr recognized the right of its twenty-six thousand students to engage in political protest on campus.

Setting the model for organized political protests by students in the United States, the free speech movement spread nationwide with protests against the Vietnam War. Tom Hayden, a California state senator at the time of Savio's death and once an activist with Savio, said: "In the sixties, he was a powerful symbol of how an ordinary person could stand up and make history."

Before the protests at Berkeley, Savio had been involved in the civil rights movement in both the West and South. In the spring of

1964, in San Francisco, he was demonstrating to have hotels give decent jobs to blacks, and in the summer of 1964, in Mississippi, he took up the cause of voter registration for blacks in the South. "I saw," he said with respect to the latter, "groups of men in the minority working their wills over the majority."

After a number of years in oblivion, Savio emerged again. He protested United States involvement in Nicaragua in 1984 and agitated against apartheid in South Africa in 1985. During political campaigns in California in 1994, he condemned Proposition 187 because it limited public benefits for illegal immigrants, and, in 1996 he attacked Proposition 209, which was designed to undercut affirmative action programs in California. Having earned a bachelor's degree from San Francisco State University, graduating summa cum laude in 1984 and, in 1985, a master's degree there, both in physics, he taught at Modesto Junior College and, for his last three years, at Sonoma State University, where he was still leading protests, this time against higher tuition fees for students.

Savio married and divorced Suzanne Goldberg, the mother of two of his children, before he married Lynne Hollander, by whom he had a third son. Both women were veterans of the movement that he had launched and for which Mario Savio is best remembered.

Vincent A. Lapomarda

Bibliography

DeLeon, David, ed. *Leaders from the 1960s.* Westport, CT: Greenwood Press, 1994, 222–225.

Jerome, R. "Radical Creak." *People Weekly* 42 (19 December 1994): 44–45.

Phillips, Donald. *Student Protest, 1960–1969.* Washington, DC: University of America Press, 1980.

Savio, Mario. *The Free Speech Movement and the Negro Revolution.* Detroit: News and Letters, 1965.

———. "Organizing 'The Movement'." *North Coast Xpress* 3, no. 3 (April/May 1995): 15–17.

Savoca, Nancy (b. 1959)

Director of three films, Nancy Savoca was born in the Bronx, New York, of a Sicilian father and an Argentinean mother. She lived in her old neighborhood (which she depicted in her first film, *True Love* (1990) until the early 1990s and currently lives in Westchester County, New York, with her husband and three children.

In 1980, soon after marrying Richard Guay (her co-writer and co-producer), Savoca entered the film school of New York University, from which she graduated in 1982. Before working as a director, Savoca took various jobs as a production coordinator, storyboard artist, assistant editor, and assistant auditor. After filming a nine-minute trailer of *True Love,* Savoca and Guay found producers willing to finance her project, which was produced on the low budget of $750,000.

Savoca's first film, which won the Grand Prize at the 1989 United States Film Festival in Park City, Utah, defies the romanticized views of Italian Americans maintained by films such as *Moonstruck* (1987) and *Married to the Mob* (1989). Savoca delves into the dynamics of an Italian American working-class family getting ready for the upcoming wedding of Donna and Michael.

In *Dogfight* (1992) Savoca departs from the ethnic subject. Based on an autobiographical script by ex-Marine Bob Comfort, the film recounts the encounter between a Marine about to leave for Vietnam and a young waitress in San Francisco in 1963. *Dogfight* examines questions of identity and self-definition, which in *True Love* Savoca had linked to the ethnicity of her characters.

Household Saints (1993) is based on Savoca's adaptation of Francine Prose's novel of the same title. Set in New York's Little Italy, the film covers the lives of the members of an Italian American family between 1949 and 1972. While Savoca returns to Italian American themes, she also begins to explore her Argentinean heritage. Savoca's third film re-creates the story of Saint Therese of Lisieux, the "Little Flower," in a modern-day context.

Savoca's depiction of three generations of Italian American women in *Household Saints* expresses a concern with understanding intergenerational relationships, one she shares with authors such as Helen Barolini, Tina De Rosa, and Agnes Rossi. In addition, Savoca's portrayal of the neighborhood from the past typifies the reconstructive work evident in the autobiographical writings of authors such as Tina De Rosa and Louise DeSalvo (*Vertigo,* 1996). Her experimentation with various forms of narration illustrates the commitment of Italian American women artists to document histories and stories that would otherwise be lost. In addition, her focus on gender and domesticity provides an alternative to the Mafia, male-centered nar-ratives popularized by directors such as Francis Ford Coppola and Martin Scorsese as well as by non–Italian American Hollywood directors.

Edvige Giunta

Bibliography

Giunta, Edvige. "Narratives of Loss: Voices of Ethnicity in Nancy Savoca and Agnes Rossi." *The Canadian Journal of Italian Studies* 19 (1997): 55–73.

———. "The Quest for True Love: Ethnicity in Nancy Savoca's Domestic Film Comedy." *MELUS* 22, no. 2 (spring 1997): 75–89.

Nardini, Gloria. "Is It *True Love?* or Not? Patterns of Ethnicity and Gender in Nancy Savoca." *VIA: Voices in Italian Americana* 2 (spring 1991): 9–17.

Reich, Jacqueline. "Nancy Savoca: An Appreciation." *Italian Americana* 13 (winter 1995): 11–15.

See also FILM DIRECTORS, PRODUCERS, AND ITALIAN AMERICAN IMAGE IN CINEMA

Sbarboro, Andrea (1839–1923)

Andrea Sbarboro, grocer, banker, and viticulturalist, came to San Francisco ten years after his 1842 arrival in New York. Born in Acero, Genoa, Italy, on November 26, 1839, he worked for years as a San Francisco grocer before entering the loan association business and the corporate world.

In April 1861, while he and his brother Bartolomeo were operating a grocery at 531 Washington Street, Andrea married New Yorker Maria Dondero. The marriage lasted until her death, seven years later. In the early 1870s he visited Italy; there he met and married Romilda Botto on September 12, 1872. The couple had five children.

While Sbarboro's grocery business and family were growing, he ventured into cooperative loan associations and established other businesses. The loan associations pooled money and helped families to build homes in Alameda, San Francisco, and Sonoma counties. Elected secretary of West Oakland Mutual Loan Association, San Francisco Mutual Loan Association, San Francisco and Oakland Mutual Loan Association, and San Francisco Home Mutual Loan Association, Sbarboro oversaw their fiscal success. He also helped establish a garbage disposal firm, the Sanitary Reduction Works of San Francisco, and two corporations, Italian Swiss Agricultural Colony and Italian American Bank.

Headquartered in San Francisco and incorporated in 1881, Italian Swiss Agricultural Colony bought agricultural land and sold wine, spirits, and stock. The Colony purchased the Truett sheep ranch in Sonoma County to grow grapes. Renamed Asti, the ranch employed Italian workers to tend the grapevines and to make wine. Sbarboro invited Pietro C. Rossi to Asti from Italy to assume the duty of Colony winemaker and chemist. Steady growth over twenty-five years permitted Colony to increase its capital stock in 1909. Two years later Colony president Rossi died in an accident; Sbarboro and Rossi's sons restructured its stock in 1913 and 1915. Although the Colony encountered competition from other producers, society's move toward the prohibition of alcohol at the turn of the century challenged the winery's survival. To combat prohibition, Sbarboro wrote a booklet entitled *The Fight for True Temperance* (1908). In it he boldly stated that wine-drinking countries had lower rates of alcoholism, and America should follow the example. The Eighteenth Amendment (1919) became law, and, by 1923, Prohibition forced the Colony to dissolve. Enrico Prati and Rossi's sons, Robert and Edmund, purchased what remained.

Sbarboro's winery interests did not deter him from his next corporate enterprise, a bank. Sbarboro incorporated the Italian American Bank (IAB) in 1899 with capital of five hundred thousand dollars. It grew steadily and survived the catastrophic 1906 earthquake and fire that left the bank building in ashes. Sbarboro quickly reassured customers that the bank could meet "any possible call for money. . . ." In that devastating year, he joined San Francisco's Committee of Fifty to oversee the rebuilding of the city. By 1909 San Francisco's banking industry was recovering, and IAB increased its capital to $750,000. Ten years later its assets totaled $11,244,709.05. IAB also joined the Federal Reserve System, opened three branches, and purchased Columbus Savings and Loan bank. When Sbarboro died on February 28, 1923, his bank's assets topped $15 million; four years later, Amadeo Giannini's Bank of Italy absorbed IAB.

Philip M. Montesano

Bibliography

Gumina, Deanna Paoli. "Andrea Sbarboro, Founder of the Italian Swiss Colony Wine Company." *Italian Americana* 2, no. 1 (autumn 1975): 1–17.

Sbarboro, Andrea. "Life of Italian American Pioneer." Master's thesis, Bancroft Library, Berkeley, CA, 1911.

See also BUSINESS AND ENTREPRENEURSHIP

Scalabrini, Giovanni Battista (1839–1905)

Born in Fino Mornasco, Como (Italy), Giovanni Battista Scalabrini was ordained a priest in 1863, became professor and rector of the minor seminary in Como, where he served until 1870, and was appointed pastor of St. Bartholomew in Como, where he served until 1875. In 1870 Scalabrini was consecrated bishop of Piacenza, where he remained until his death. Scalabrini was above all a pastor. He implemented the Tridentine Reformation in restructuring catechism and seminaries, clergy and liturgy, synods, and pastoral visitations. Yet Scalabrini was also the precursor of new times. He dealt courageously and farsightedly with major issues of his epoch: promoting freedom of opinion in philosophical matters, participation of Italian Catholics in politics after the unification of Italy, rights for the working class, and social justice. However, Scalabrini is remembered especially for his activity in the field of migration.

When mass immigration was met by indifference on the part of the state and by embarrassment on the part of the church, Bishop Scalabrini emerged as the principal actor in developing a global approach for the religious and social assistance to migrants, particularly in North and South America. He visited towns and countrysides left by emigrants; called a diocesan synod to conscien-tize the clergy; wrote extensively on emigration, the conditions of emigrants, and proposals for new immigration laws; lectured throughout Italy to arouse public opinion; organized the St. Raphael Society of lay people for the assistance to migrants; founded the Congregation of the Missionaries of St. Charles–Scalabrinians for the religious and social assistance to migrants; undertook two "pastoral visits" to the emigrants—in 1901 to the United States and in 1904 to Brazil; and sent a memorandum to the Vatican secretariat of state outlining the plan for the pastoral care of migrants of all nationalities.

In his writings, Scalabrini worked out a clear and complete theory on the immigration problem, its causes, effects, and the development of its various elements. He outlined directives for its solution, with respect not only to its religious aspects, but also to its social, economic, legal, and political aspects. Contemporary sociologist Giuseppe Toniolo called Scalabrini the "Apostle of the Emigrants" with "an intuitive sense of the future." In 1997 Bishop Scalabrini was declared venerable, which is the last step before being declared a saint by the Catholic Church.

Lydio F. Tomasi

Bibliography

Caliaro, Marco, and Mario Francesconi. *John Baptist Scalabrini, Apostle to the Emigrants.* New York: Center for Migration Studies, 1987.

Francesconi, Mario. *Bishop Scalabrini's Plan for the Pastoral Care of Migrants of All Nationalities.* New York: Center for Migration Studies, 1973.

———. *Giovanni Baptista Scalabrini, Vescovo di Piacenza e degli emigrati.* Roma: Citta' Nuova Editrice, 1985.

Scalabrini, Giovanni Battista. Scritti: Vol. 1–2; Missionari, Emigrazione; Vol. 3: Carteggio Scalarni-Bonomelli, Intransigenti; Vols. 4–5: Lettere; Vol. 6: Concillio Vaticano, Catechismo; Vol. 7–9: Pastoralli; Vol. 10–13: Discorsi; Vol. 14: Processo Beatificazione, Scritti Vari. Roma: Congregazione Scalabriniana, 1980.

Signor, Lice Maria. *John Baptist Scalabrini and Italian Migration.* New York: Center for Migration Studies, 1994.

See also APOSTOLATE, ITALIAN; CHURCH LEADERS; MISSIONARIES OF ST. CHARLES–SCALABRINIANS; RELIGION

Scalia, Antonin (b. 1936)

The first Italian American to serve as associate justice of the United States Supreme Court,

President Ronald Reagan with Antonin Scalia, the first Italian American to serve on the United States Supreme Court. Courtesy of the National Italian American Foundation (NIAF), Washington, D.C.

Antonin Scalia was born in Trenton, New Jersey, March 11, 1936, and was raised in Queens, New York. His mother, Catherine Louise Panaro, was a first-generation Italian American. Scalia's father had migrated from Sicily when he was 15 years old. Both his parents became educators: his mother taught elementary school, and his father became professor of Romance languages at Brooklyn College.

Young Scalia graduated first in his class from Xavier High School, New York City; and again at Georgetown University in 1957. His education included six years of Latin and five of Greek, which gave him a strong historical and philosophical perspective. At Harvard Law School, Scalia became note editor of the *Law Review.* While at Harvard, he met Radcliffe student Maureen McCarthy, whom he married in 1960, the same year as his graduation. Nine children would be born to the Scalias.

Antonin Scalia accepted a position as law professor at the University of Virginia, where he taught from 1967 to 1971. Scalia then went to Washington, D.C., first as general counsel of the White House Office of Telecommunications Policy, then as chairman of the Administrative Conference of the United States, and finally as assistant attorney general in charge of the Justice Department's Office of Legal Counsel. He returned

again to academia from 1977 to 1982, when he taught at the University of Chicago Law School and, as visiting professor, at the Stanford Law School and at the Georgetown Law Center. During that same period Scalia, a valued specialist in administrative law, was named editor of *Regulation,* the magazine published by the American Enterprise Institute for Public Policy Research.

The Reagan administration tapped Scalia for a judgeship on the Federal Appeals Court in Washington, D.C., and he served in that capacity from 1982 to 1986. When the president nominated him as associate justice of the United States Supreme Court, he sailed smoothly through the Senate hearings and was confirmed 98–0.

Justice Scalia has distinguished himself as an eminent authority on constitutional law, an aggressive interrogator, and an intellectual dynamo. Scalia's crusades are notably vehement against judicial overreaching, especially when the Supreme Court trespasses on legislative terrain. He adamantly believes legislatures, not courts, should rule on a terminally ill patient's right to die, on whether the public schools have the right to teach "creation science," and whether criminals who are clearly guilty should be allowed to go free on technicalities. He is convinced the Supreme Court should play a less dramatic role in the daily life of the average American. Although he terms himself "a thoughtful moderate," Justice Scalia's conservative positions are often diametrically at odds with the viewpoint of liberals on such issues as the constitutional power of legislatures to adopt abortion restrictions and the legality of race-based preferential hiring.

Margherita Marchione

Bibliography

Barnes, Fred. "Top Gun of the High Court." *Reader's Digest* (July 1991): 91–95.

Scalia, Antonin, et al. "Excerpts from U.S. Supreme Court Decision in Veronia v. Acton." *Education Week* 14 (12 July 1995): 24–25.

———. "Text of U.S. Supreme Court Decision: Ronald W. Rosenberger, et al. v. Rector and Visitors of the University of Virginia, et al." *Journal of Church and State* 37 (summer 1995): 690–727.

Scaravaglione, Concetta Maria (1900–1975)

One of nine children raised by southern Italian parents, Concetta Maria Scaravaglione was one of the first American sculptors to explore the technique of welding metal. Her education included the National Academy of Design, at age 16, and American sign language, at age 21, with Boardman Robinson.

Scaravaglione taught at the Educational Alliance and Masters Institute, both in New York City; New York University; Sarah Lawrence College; Black Mountain College; and Vassar College. She was the first woman to receive the Prix de Rome at the American Academy in Rome. Other awards included the Widener Gold Medal and Pennsylvania Academy of Fine Arts (PAFA). She was also a frequent judge in art contests in New York and New Jersey during the 1950s and 1960s.

Her major works are *R.R. Express 1862* in the Main Post Office (1936) and an agricultural relief in the Federal Trade Commission Building (1940), both in Washington, D.C.; *Girl with Mountain Sheep,* U.S. Government Building (1939), New York World's Fair; *Woman Walking,* Vassar College (1961); and *Girl with Gazelle* (1938), in several high schools, New York.

As her reputation grew as a sculptor, Scaravaglione had exhibits shown at the Art Institute of Chicago, Vassar College, Museum of Modern Art, Whitney Museum, Brooklyn Museum, Corcoran Gallery of Art, and PAFA. Her collections are included at the Glasgow Museum, MOMA, PAFA, Roerich Musem, Whitney Museum, Arizona State College, Dartmouth College, and Art Gallery of Hamilton, Ontario.

She was born in New York City, July 9, 1900, and died there on September 24, 1975.

Frank J. Cavaioli

Bibliography

Scaravaglione, Concetta M. "My Enjoyment in Sculpture." *Magazine of Art* 32 (August 1939): 451–455.

Soria, Regina. *American Artists of Italian Heritage,* 1776–1945. Rutherford, NJ: Fairleigh Dickinson University Press, 1994.

See also ART

Scarne, John (b. 1903)

Magician and master card manipulator, John Scarne (John Orlando Carmelo Scarnecchia) was born in Steubenville, Ohio, of immigrant parents Maria and Fiorangelo Scarnecchia from Abruzzi, Italy. He became one of the most accomplished gambling experts in the United States. Growing up in Fairview, New Jersey, at an early age John was fascinated with the techniques involved in manipulating a deck of cards. Through the nurturing care of deeply religious Catholic parents, he abandoned his boyhood dream of becoming a gambler, and settled instead on a career analyzing a variety of games of chance. In the process he mastered many tricks and created many of his own. He was able to detect charlatans and frauds, and he benefited the public by sharing his knowledge through his demonstrations, lessons, and books.

His deftness with cards brought unusual attention to him while still a young man. During the 1920s, for example, he was called to demonstrate to expert card players and gamblers, such as Al Capone and Arnold Rothstein, who were unable to detect how he performed some tricks such as producing four aces whenever he desired. Despite importuning, Scarne did not succumb to a gambling career.

In addition to cards, Scarne sought to perform magic tricks by watching and learning from the best magicians, whose friendship he cultivated. One case in point was his relationship with the famous Harry Houdini, who treated him as a fellow professional. At one point Scarne had himself tied up in ropes, placed in a bag, and thrown off a bridge into the water, where he quickly freed himself. Accordingly, Scarne became a performer on the vaudeville circuit, movies, and later television. He gave personal performances for many notable public figures including New Jersey governor A. Harry Moore and President Franklin D. Roosevelt. As gambling consultant to the United States Armed Forces during the Second World War, he went on tours giving demonstrations and lessons to soldiers in order to protect themselves against card sharks and dice cheats that abounded in army camps.

Scarne's uncanny success with cards, even when he did not personally handle them as in the case of casino black jack, prompted virtually all of Las Vegas's casinos to prohibit him from playing there. He used his talent, however, by becoming gambling consultant to Conrad Hilton's casinos. He also served in similar capacities in Panama, Cuba, and Puerto Rico.

Scarne took great pride in creating three parlor board games: Teeko, Scarney, and Follow the Arrow. He claims that with Teeko he became the first American to have invented a sound mathematical skill game that surpasses checkers. Thousands of these games have been sold over the years. In addition to creating games, Scarne wrote a number of books on gambling including *Scarne on Dice* (1969), *Scarne on Cards* (1949), *Scarne on Card Tricks* (1950), *Scarne on Magic Tricks* (1951), and *Scarne's Complete Guide to Gambling* (1974). The U.S. Senate Committee that held hearings on gambling and organized crime called him to testify as "the nation's outstanding gambling authority." Thus, Scarne's fascination with gambling was put to good use: he exposed the many ways innocent people can be cheated by gambling.

Salvatore J. LaGumina

Bibliography

Scarne, John. *The Odds Against Me.* New York: Simon & Schuster, 1966.

Schiavo, Giovanni Ermengildo (1898–1983)

Journalist and writer who documented the saga of the Italian immigrant experience, Giovanni E. Schiavo was born in Castellamare del Golfo, province of Trapani, Sicily. He was a precocious child who learned to read and write before he went to school. His father, like his grandfather before him, was a tailor; his mother (Giuseppina Fazioli) was from Palermo.

In 1916 Schiavo migrated to the United States and lived with his family in Baltimore, Maryland. He received a bachelor's degree from Johns Hopkins University in 1919 and later became a Ph.D. candidate at Columbia University. He became a United States citizen and worked in various financial and journalistic positions, becoming involved in the production of such Italian American media as *La Domenica Illustrata* and *Il Corriere del Wisconsin.*

His early journalistic experience confirmed in his mind that, from 1926 on, writing and publishing would be his profession. The result was the production of over thirty volumes of documentation of the Italian experi-

ence in America. His first book, *The Italians in Chicago,* with a preface by the famous Jane Addams, underscored his determination to record the history of the Italian immigrant population. In the 1930s Schiavo converted *La Rivista d'Italiano* into the Italian American monthly *Atlantica Magazine,* while simultaneously serving on the editorial staff of the *New York Herald Tribune* and *Il Progresso Italo-Americano.* In 1933 he married Anne Maher of New Jersey, and they had two daughters, Giovanna and Eleanor, who subsequently relocated to Texas.

The year 1934 was a milestone in Schiavo's life as a chronicler of the Italian American saga. It was the year in which Schiavo decided to dedicate himself completely to the study and publication of the Italian American experience, and for this purpose he organized his own Vigo Press. The first publication with the Vigo imprint was *The Italians in American Before the Civil War* (1934) in which Schiavo presented a vast procession of heroic Italians who were prominent contributors to American history: Fra Marco da Nizza, Father Eusebio Kino, Giacomo Beltrami, the Tonti brothers, Paolo Busti, Francesco Vigo, and Filippo Mazzei. It was Schiavo who first associated Mazzei with Thomas Jefferson's Declaration of Independence. Subsequent books dealt with the contribution of Italians to music in America, to the Catholic Church in America, and to public life. Most of this is summed up in his monumental *Four Centuries of Italian American History* (1952), which subsequently went through five editions. Other important works published by Schiavo are *Philip Mazzei: One of America's Founding Fathers* (1952), *Antonio Meucci: Inventor of the Telephone* (1958), *The Italians in America Before the Revolution* (1976), and *The Truth About the Mafia and Organized Crime in America* (1952).

The American Italian Historical Association at its fifteenth annual conference held at St. John's University in October 1982, unanimously voted Schiavo an Award of Merit.

Schiavo died on March 4, 1983.

Remigio U. Pane

Bibliography

Pane, Remigio U. "In Memoriam Giovanni Schiavo (1898–1983)." In *Italians and Irish in America,* edited by Frank Femminella. Staten Island, NY: American Italian Historical Association, 1985, 5–11.

Peter Sammartino, left, founder of Fairleigh Dickinson University, and Giovanni Schiavo, pioneer in chronicling Italian American history, at Rutgers University, October 26, 1979. They are discussing the Italian contribution to early America. Courtesy Frank J. Cavaioli.

Schiavo, Giovanni. *Four Centuries of Italian American History.* New York: Vigo Press, 1952.

———. *Italian American History,* Vol. 1 and 2. New York: Vigo Press, 1947 and 1949.

———. *The Italians in Chicago: A Study in Americanization.* Chicago: Italian American Publishing, 1928.

———. *The Italians in Missouri.* Chicago: Italian American Publishing, 1929.

Science

In the development of the sciences (which includes astronomy, biology, engineering and technology, geology, and mathematics), Italian Americans have been somewhat underrepresented. While there is a plethora of talented contributors to art and music, and aside from one instance where an Italian is listed first in a chronology of scientific breakthroughs, there are few Italian American names recorded in the annals of well-known scientists.

The paucity of research into Italian American contributions to science, and the biases of such investigations, adds to this dilemma. The sequence of scientific entries is uneven, and interconnections are complex and profound, such as when scientists migrate to countries that award research grants and laboratories for experimentation. Many Italian American scientists work for government and individual laboratories where the work is done almost anonymously. Consequently, research on the subject of Italian Americans in science is near impossible. These common situations preclude isolating contributors by national origin. More importantly, sociopolitical events have had decisive influences on their careers and, consequently, on the nature, production, and dissemination of their discoveries.

As far as major breakthroughs are concerned within the history of science, 150 Italian names are listed in a directory spanning from 1200 to 1930 (Parkinson, 1985). Major contributions by Italians were made during the sixteenth and seventeenth centuries. Italy's economic and sociopolitical history, undoubtedly, accounts for this trend. From ancient Rome to the modern era, there have been periods in its history when scientific pursuits proliferated as a result of a sustaining economic and ideological order. On the other hand, similar structures did much to inhibit, and at times curtail, scientific investigations. In each of the subfields of science, a somewhat different and complex history evolved that can lend insight to the lack of Americans of Italian descent in the sciences.

Despite their astonishing ability in geometry, physics, and mathematics, the Greeks were unable to make advances that supported architecture and civil engineering. The Romans put the arch to full use in the design and construction of aqueducts. They were thus able to set up an infrastructure and communications network that gave them an unprecedented standard of living. This bent in mechanical engineering continued to include the development of weaponry in the fifteenth century demanded by the feuding states of Italy. Engineering, however, eluded Italy as discoveries of the press in Germany, steam and industrial power in England, and the technological revolution in America overrode Italian ingenuity.

Yet one of the most renowned names from the early days of science was Italian. Leonardo da Vinci (1452–1519) was a painter, sculptor, architect, musician, engineer, and scientist. His versatility marks him as perhaps the supreme genius of all time. Hundreds of his drawings indicate his advanced scientific investigations. The problems he approached in geology, botany, hydraulics, and mechanics continue to intrigue scientists today.

Although a comprehensive philosophy of the earth began to develop from antiquity, Italy, as followers of the Christian doctrine of creation as set out in Genesis, curtailed new ideas about the earth. Consequently, unlike the modern states of Germany, England, and later the United States, the funding of scientific education and research organizations was minimal. During the sixteenth and seventeenth centuries, scientific studies of the Earth caused significant change in a theocentric society. Copernican astronomy sabotaged the old notion that the Earth was the center of the system. For enlightened naturalists, the Earth came to be viewed as a machine, operating according to fundamental laws.

Roman Catholics decided that the geocentric explanation was the only theory compatible with their beliefs, and that those who attempted to put the Sun at the center of the universe were guilty of heresy, which was punishable by death. In spite of such devastating odds, Galileo Galilei (1564–1642) utilized the telescope invented by Kepler and located Venus, Jupiter, and established the stellar nature of the Milky Way. Disputing the platonic dogma that dominated and inhibited astronomy for so long in Italy, he insisted that the planets revolve around the Sun and was threatened with torture by the Vatican in 1633. It is this history that discouraged scientific investigations, allowing other nations to take the lead.

Readings in the history of science confirm that the greatest contributions in science by Italians were in the field of biology (including practical botany, dissection, and surgery). For example, Morgagni (1682–1771) was known as the "father" of pathology because of his work in postmortem autopsies. Ancient writings of the Greek physician Galen were discovered in southern Italy. Hundreds of significant breakthroughs were made in anatomy, physiology, and early chemistry, metallurgy, mechanics, and physics. The Italian Porta (1540–1615) experimented in and wrote about physics and developed a "magic lantern." Galileo Gallei (1564–1642), called the greatest physicist of his age, invented the air thermometer and the hydrostatic balance as well as the astronomical clock. Frascaturo advanced blood circulation theory. In the early seventeenth century, Santorio adopted Galileo's thermometer to the measurement of body temperature. He also devised an apparatus for comparing pulse rates. Malphigi (1628–1694) extended William Harvey's (1578–1657) work on the heart and blood and advanced understanding of the circulation of blood from the heart to the arteries and veins. He was also the first to realize that capillary channels enable blood to pass from arteries to veins. Toricelli (1608–47) discovered the principle of the barometer.

Developments in organic chemistry and modern atomic theory were primarily the work of Germans and Englishmen. However, in 1934, Enrico Fermi (1901–1954) bombarded uranium to see whether he could produce any elements of higher atomic numbers. He postulated the existence of an atomic particle, which he called the neutrino, and discovered element 93, now called neptunium.

Fermi came to the United States in 1939 as a professor of physics from 1939 to 1945 at Columbia University, and later at the University of Chicago. For his work on radioactive substances he received the 1938 Nobel Prize in physics. The atomic bomb project was materially aided by his early research and after 1939 by his active participation. Other Italian Americans associated with the Atomic Energy Commission include Alfonso Tammaro, Joseph T. Gemmi, Armando Spadetti, and Albert Ghiorso.

Another renowned physicist, Guglielmo Marchese Marconi (1874–1937) developed wireless telegraphy and invented a practical antenna. In 1895, he sent long-wave signals over a distance of more than a mile. He patented his system (1896) and organized a wireless telegraph company (1897). After World War I, he concentrated on short waves, and around 1930 focused his attention on microwaves. He received, jointly with K. R. Braun, the 1909 Nobel Prize in physics for his work in wireless telegraphy. Italian American admiration for Marconi is reflected in a real estate venture on Long Island, New York, that was popularly known as Marconiville.

Alessandro Volta (1745–1827) devised instruments used by another Italian (Luigi Galvani, b. 1737) in experiments to measure the electrical stimulation of muscle contraction. Using different metals, he measured the flow of electricity (Volta Pile). Terms derived from the names Galvani and Volta have become essential parts of scientific vocabulary.

Engineers were, undoubtedly, among the early immigrants to America. Although few in number, they contributed to building bridges and worked in city and state governments improving the environment. Records indicate that Luigi D'Auria, who came to the United States in 1876, invented a pumping engine still in use today. Gaetano Lanza was a graduate of the University of Virginia and on the faculty of Massachusetts Institute of Technology, where he was noted for his work in mechanical engineering, for over forty years. Other noted engineers are numerous and listed in professional directories; many have served as top executives for companies such as AT&T, Westinghouse, IBM, and General Electric.

In colonial America there were few Italian immigrants, relatively few colleges where scientists could be trained, and virtually no centers of scientific inquiry. Consequently, many Americans interested in science studied abroad and the few individuals making contributions in science or medicine were early immigrants who studied in the medical schools throughout Italy. Most of the scientists came from Turino and the Piedmont region, which had established major research centers in physics and engineering by the end of the nineteenth and early twentieth centuries. It is these centers in Italy that provided the pool of scientists that have served the major research institutes (including Harvard, MIT, Princeton, and Stanford) throughout the twentieth century.

As a result of two world wars and the Fascist regime in Italy, many scientists left Italy for academic and research positions in the United States. Renato Bulbecco (b. 1914) worked in the Resistance movement during World War II. In 1947 he migrated to the United States, securing appointments at Indiana University and then at California Tech. From 1972 to 1977, he served as assistant director of Research at the Imperial Cancer Research Fund in London. He then returned to the United States as professor of pathology and medicine at the University of California (1977–1981) and is presently professor at the Salk Institute. Dulbecco demonstrated how certain viruses can transform some cells into a cancerous state. For this discovery, he was awarded the Nobel Prize for physiology in 1975.

Cesare Emiliani (b. 1922) migrated to the United States in 1950 to become a research associate in geochemistry and associate professor at the University of Chicago. Carlo Floriani (b. 1940) is a chemist whose work is important in opening up the chemistry of the widely known but unreactive molecule (formaldehyde, dioxygen, and carbon monoxide). William V. Consolazio, a former Harvard biochemist and chief chemist of the National Naval Medical Research Institute, perfected the process for making sea water drinkable.

Other Italian Americans who have won Nobel Prizes in physics include Ricardo Giaconni (b. 1931), an astrophysicist who migrated to the United States in 1956 with academic research positions in Indiana and Princeton. In 1960 he and an Italian colleague, Bruno Rossi, proposed the use of a paraboid of revolution as a space X-ray telescope mirror. He discovered the first extrasolar source of X-rays and extragalactic background radiation. Giacconi's group built the first orbiting X-ray detector, a small astronomy satellite called *Uhuru*. Guilio Natta won the Nobel Prize in 1963 for chemistry with his invention of a process for making isostatic hydrocarbon polymers.

Edward Salvador Luria (1912–1991) was awarded the Nobel Prize in 1952 for his work on the role of DNA in bacterial viruses. Carlo Rubia (b. 1934) accepted a chair in physics at Harvard University, and for his work on W and Z bosons, he shared the 1984 Nobel Prize in physics. He was the driving force behind the LEP (an electron-positron collider) and LHC (Large Hadron Collider) projects. Emilio Segrè (1905–1989) was another American physicist born in Rome who worked with Fermi in Rome until 1936. Dismissed from his post at the University of Palermo under Mussolini's regime, he moved to the University of California at Berkeley and worked on the Manhattan Project (atom bomb) during World War II. In 1937 he discovered the first entirely man-made element, technetium. Three years later he was involved in the discoveries of astatine and plutonium. For his work, he shared the 1959 Nobel Prize for physics with Owen Chamberlain.

Rita Levi-Montalcini (b.1909), a neurobiologist, gained acclaim for her research on the nerve growth factor. She became the first woman to acquire membership in the Pontifical Academy and received the Nobel Prize in physiology in 1986.

Antonio Meucci (1808–1889) was an inventor who succeeded in building a rudimentary telephone in Staten Island, New York. Due to lack of funds, Meucci was unable to pay the considerable sum necessary for obtaining a patent. In 1888 the Supreme Court awarded possession of the patent to the Bell Company. Meucci died a poor man. His house is a landmark in Staten Island, New York.

There are many other Italian American scientists who have won awards or published major articles. More than half migrated to the United States, assuming research positions at major institutions. A small percent of Italian American scientists had graduated from American universities prior to 1970. Although the numbers of Italian Americans receiving their Ph.D.'s in mathematics and other sciences have increased somewhat since then, their numbers are still relatively small. Other science-related fields outside of research, such as medicine, psychology, and education, have incorporated Italian Americans in greater numbers.

Rosanne Martorella

Bibliography

Bynum, W. F., E. J. Browne, and Roy Porter, eds. *Directory of History of Science.* Princeton: Princeton University Press, 1981.

Kuhn. T. S. *The Structure of Scientific Revolutions.* Chicago: University of Chicago Press, 1970.

Martorella, Rosanne, and Patricia Perri Rieker. "A Sociological Profile of Italian-Americans in Medical Education." In *The Melting Pot and Beyond,* edited by Jerome Krase and William Egelman, 151–164. New York: American Italian Historical Association, 1987.

Parkinson, Claire L. *Breakthroughs: A Chronology of Great Achievements in Science and Mathematics 1200–1930.* Boston: G. K. Hall, 1985.

Plescia, Otto. *Contributions of Italians to Science in the United States Prior to the Civil War.* Washington, DC: National Italian American Foundation, 1980.

See also FERMI, ENRICO; MEDICINE; PATENTS AND INVENTORS; SEGRÈ, EMILIO

Scorsese, Martin (b. 1942)

Born in Flushing, New York, on November 17, 1942, to Charles and Catherine (Cappa) Scorsese, Martin Scorsese has achieved success as a screenwriter and director of American film. In 1960 he graduated from Cardinal Hayes High School and from New York University, where he earned a B.S. (1964) and an M.A. (1966) in film communications. He taught film at NYU from 1969 to 1971 and worked on short films, feature films, commercials, and documentaries. In a short span of time he won acclaim as one of the most innovative filmmakers.

As he developed his knowledge and skill in the demanding field of cinema, Scorsese received numerous honors for his work: Edward L. Kingsley Foundation Award (1964), First Prize from the Rosenthal Foundation (1964), First Prize from the Screen Producer's Guild (1965), First Prize in the Brown University Film Festival (1965), Best Director from the National Society of Film Critics for *Taxi Driver* (1976), Best Director from the National Society of Film Critics for *Raging Bull* (1980), and was named Best Director at the Cannes Film Festival (1986). By the 1990s critics regarded Scorsese as the greatest director of his generation.

His Italian American heritage has inspired some of his most important films: *Mean Streets* (1973), *Raging Bull* (1980), *Goodfellas* (1990), and *Casino* (1995). He also made a film documentary, *Italianamerican* (1974). Many of his films are innovative in that they attempt to capture the underlying implications of contemporary cultural change. He has defied the typical Hollywood genre film. *Taxi Driver* (1976), *Alice Doesn't Live Here Anymore* (1975), *The Last Temptation of Christ* (1986), *The King of Comedy* (1982), *The Color of Money* (1986), *The Grifters* (1990), *Cape Fear* (1991), *The Age of Innocence* (1993), *Mad Dog and Glory* (1993), *Naked in New York* (1994), and *Clockers* (1995) are among Scorsese's films that challenge the tradition of filmmaking.

Scorsese's mother, a daughter of Sicilian immigrants who was born in New York City's Little Italy, where she met her husband who worked in the garment industry, appeared in cameo roles in some of her son's films: *Mean Streets, New York, New York, Goodfellas, Cape Fear.* She also appeared in Francis Ford Coppola's *Godfather III.* She was the central figure in Scorsese's documentary, *Italianamerican.*

His first marriage (1965) to Laraine Brennan ended in divorce; they had two daughters. His next marriage, to Julia Cameron (1975), also produced two daughters and ended in divorce. His marriage to Isabella Rosellini in 1979 ended in divorce in 1983. Two years later he married Barbara DeFina.

Frank J. Cavaioli

Bibliography

Casillo, Robert, et al. "Italian Filmmakers." *Italian Americana* 13, no. 1 (winter 1995): 5–23.
Cook, Daniel. *A History of Narrative Film.* New York: W. W. Norton, 1996.
Kelly, Mary Pat. *Martin Scorsese: A Journey.* New York: Thunder Mouth, 1992.
Maltby, Richard. *Hollywood Cinema.* Cambridge, MA: Blackwell, 1995.

See also COPPOLA, FRANCIS FORD; DE NIRO, ROBERT; FILM DIRECTORS, PRODUCERS, AND ITALIAN AMERICAN IMAGE IN CINEMA; MOVIE ACTORS AND ACTRESSES

Scotto, Anthony
See LABOR

Scottsdale, Arizona

The movement of Italian Americans to the suburban city of Scottsdale, Arizona, began after World War II. This shift in population runs parallel with recent migrations to other Sunbelt states. The 1960 census indicated that 84 percent of Italian Americans still lived in the established areas of the Northeast and North Central United States. By 1990, however, this number had dropped to about 56 percent, with dramatic population growth in the West (Arizona, southern California), the Northwest, and Florida in the Southeast.

Italian Americans relocating to new areas left behind their ethnicity and merged into the mainstream, or they established a presence in a new setting, which is the case with Scottsdale. Scottsdale was a small agricultural town with a population of slightly over two thousand when it was incorporated in 1951. It grew as a result of the population boom in Phoenix and the Southwest. Phoenix's initial growth was launched by wartime industry in the 1940s, followed by the electronics industry in the postwar years. Phoenix had a small but active Italian community, with many immigrants from Liguria and Piedmont. However, they never established community structures such as a neighborhood or church. One of the first few Italian settlers in Scottsdale was George Cavalliere, who arrived in 1909. His brother John settled in Phoenix. Both had blacksmith shops; George's adobe shop still stands in old Scottsdale. Although the family was accepted by most in the 1920s, the Klu Klux Klan targeted the Cavalliere home in the only local cross burning incident in Scottsdale.

The recent Italian American community in Scottsdale does not represent an overflow from the Phoenix community; it is a new growth primarily from eastern and midwestern states, especially New York, Illinois, and New Jersey. In 1960 the U.S. census counted only fifty-five Italians in Scottsdale. This number grew to 5,252 by 1980 (including those of Italian and Italian-mixed ancestry). Italian Americans eventually made up almost 6 percent of Scottsdale's total population of 88,364, higher than the 3.5 percent of Italians in Arizona. These numbers allowed the community to establish a local presence, although the new arrivals did not cluster into any one area. The suburban sprawl of the city and arrival of Italian Americans from other states worked against the formation of a highly localized ethnic neighborhood.

Nevertheless, contact with fellow Italian Americans led to the emergence of several clubs. The Order Sons of Italy in America

(OSIA) was the most active of these. John Suardini was instrumental in establishing both the Scottsdale lodge and the Grand Lodge of Arizona during the 1970s. The OSIA lodge aided the city of Scottsdale in building bocce courts in a local park. Members were also active in local ethnic festivals and in working with other groups in the Phoenix area on projects promoting Italian language schools and the 1992 Columbus Day events.

Italian Americans have made themselves visible in Scottsdale by establishing numerous Italian restaurants, delicatessens, and pizza places in a city where steak and potatoes has been the norm. Perhaps the most Italian of all is a shopping complex modeled after San Gimignano, Italy, called Mancuso's, located in the Borgata section of Scottsdale. The idea of such a complex was originated by Salvadore Cudia.

Italian Americans also gained notable visibility as prominent public servants in the community. Dick Campana became known as "the councilman's councilman" in the eight years (1972–1980) he helped guide Scottsdale's growth. Joe Garagiola, famous for his baseball and television career, established a popular golf tournament when he relocated to Arizona. The Del Duca sisters, Pam and Sharon, gained recognition for their business expertise. In 1986 the sisters simultaneously became the first women to be elected as heads of their respective chambers of commerce. Pam led the Scottsdale chamber, while Sharon presided over the nearby chamber in Paradise Valley. Pam Del Duca was also honored as one of the country's top three small business owners in a national competition.

A maintained ethnic identity, the continued importance of family, support for traditions, and ties with fellow ethnics indicate that for many Italian Americans in Scottsdale their heritage is still relevant. At times it has formed the basis for action, as when Italian Americans throughout the state rallied to keep Columbus Day an official holiday in 1989. However, it is now usually maintained as a more individualistic, private form of ethnicity than that of the earlier immigrants.

Phylis Cancilla Martinelli

Bibliography

Johnson, G. Wesley, ed. *Phoenix in the 20th Century.* Norman: University of Oklahoma Press, 1993.

Martinelli, Phylis Cancilla. *Ethnicity in the Sunbelt: Italian American Migrants to Scottsdale, Arizona.* New York: AMS Press, 1989.

———. "Exploring Ethnicity in the Sunbelt: Italian Americans in Scottsdale, Arizona." *Humbolt Journal of Social Relations* (spring/summer 1985): 143–162.

Segrè, Emilio (1905–1989)

Awarded the Nobel Prize for physics for his discovery of the antiproton, a fundamental element of antimatter, Emilio Segrè is also credited with the codiscovery of three chemical elements, technetium, astatine, and plutonium.

He was born on February 1, 1905, in Italy, the son of Giuseppe Segrè, a manufacturer, and Amelia Treves. He graduated in 1922 from the Liceo Mamaiani in Rome. He entered the University of Rome to study engineering, but his association with mentor Enrico Fermi influenced him to change his major to physics. Segrè later became Enrico Fermi's first doctoral student.

He served a term in the Italian army upon graduation and then returned to the University as a faculty member. He left Rome for two years to study in Hamburg and Amsterdam, but returned to his faculty position in 1932 and worked with Fermi on neutron physics. During this research, he discovered that slow moving neutrons were more effective in causing fission than fast neutrons. Segrè became chairman of the Department of Physics at the University of Palermo in 1936.

Segrè visited Ernest Lawrence at the University of California. He shared with Lawrence his theory that element 43 could be obtained by bombarding element 42 with neutrons. Lawrence gave him a sample of element number 42, molybdenum, which had been bombarded, and when he returned to Italy he discovered a new element within the sample. Since this was the first artificially created element, it was called "technetium." His colleague C. Perrier assisted him in this discovery.

In 1938 he returned to California to work with Lawrence. He devised an experiment to create element 85. He bombarded polonium with neutrons and produced element 85, astatine since the element appeared to be unstable. Since he was a Jew, he was prevented from returning to Italy because of Fascist restrictions.

In 1944 he became a citizen of the United States. He remained at Berkeley, working on yet another new element, 94, plutonium.

In 1943 he was reunited with Fermi in the Manhattan Project at the Los Alamos Scientific Laboratory. His work on neutron physics made him an essential part of the development of the atomic bomb.

Antimatter had been theorized in 1928 and proven to exist as early as 1932 with the discovery of the positron, the antimatter subatomic particle equal in mass but opposite in charge to the electron. Working with a powerful particle accelerator, Segrè and Owen Chamberlain discovered the antiproton in 1955 and four years later shared the Nobel Prize for physics.

Segrè and his first wife, Elfriede Spiro, had three children. Elfriede died in 1970. He later married Rosa Mines.

Segrè received numerous awards for his nuclear physics research including the Hofmann Medal of the German Chemical Society in 1954 and the Cannizzaro Medal of the Accademia Nazionale de Lincei in 1956. He suffered a heart attack and died on April 22, 1989, ending an extremely productive research career. In his lifetime he codiscovered three new elements and codiscovered the positron.

Sean A. Fanelli

Bibliography

Segrè, Emilio. *Enrico Fermi, Physicist.* Chicago: University of Chicago Press, 1970.
————. *From X-Rays to Quarks: Modern Physicists and Their Discoveries.* New York: W. H. Freeman, 1970.
Weber, Robert L. *Pioneers of Science: Nobel Prize Winners in Physics.* College Park: American Institute of Physics, 1980, 177–178.

See also SCIENCE

Sellaro, Vincenzo (1868–1932)

A medical doctor and founder of the Order Sons of Italy in America, Vincenzo Sellaro was born in Polizzi Generosa in the province of Palermo, Sicily, to Giuseppe Sellaro, a shoemaker, and his wife, Serafina Polizzotto.

He received his medical degree in 1895 from the University of Naples and migrated in 1897 to the United States, settling in New York City. After postgraduate courses at the Cornell Medical School, he obtained his medical license in 1898. When establishing his private practice at 203 Grand Street in the Little Italy section of Manhattan, he noticed that many Italian immigrants were often placed in life-threatening situations because of difficulties in communicating with medical personnel at local hospitals. For this reason he organized a group of bilingual doctors who raised private financing from mutual-aid societies in the large Italian American community. They founded the Columbus Italian Hospital. By 1902 the building was completed, and he became the chief gynecologist.

Subsequently, Sellaro organized a school for midwives under the auspices of the New York City Health Board. This school was one of the first of its kind and was merged with other training programs into the famous School at Bellevue Hospital a decade later.

Sellaro realized that for most immigrants in the United States and Canada, mutual-aid societies had provided opportunities for them to speak their native tongues and to keep their "old country" customs alive. The mutual-aid societies were tightly knit by ties to the same town or province. Italian American mutual-aid societies were important outlets for assistance to the immigrants. Such assistance took the form of providing information about job opportunities, giving English-language classes, conducting social events on weekends, and rendering financial aid to members during illnesses or to families when members died. There were about two thousand mutual-aid societies in New York City alone by the turn of the century.

During 1904 Dr. Sellaro conceived the idea of uniting all Italian Americans into one large fraternal organization. On June 7, 1905, an organizational meeting was held at Dr. Sellaro's home. The attendees were a lawyer, Antonio Marzullo; a pharmacist, Ludovico Ferrari; a sculptor, Giuseppe Carlino; and two barbers, Pietro Viscardi and Roberto Merlo. The first formal meeting was held three weeks later. At that meeting, Dr. Sellaro was elected Supreme Venerable (i.e., national president) of the Supreme Lodge of the Sons of Italy. The name of the group was soon changed to the Order Sons of Italy in America (OSIA). A golden lion was adopted as its emblem, and "Liberty, Equality & Fraternity" was chosen as its motto. He served until 1908.

S

Sellaro later became interested in the Masons, even though they were reputedly anti-Catholic, and was elected by the Garibaldi Masonic Lodge as a Grand Master. When questioned about this affiliation, he would later write that he joined "in order to emancipate [them] from every prejudice." In 1928 Governor Alfred E. Smith gave Sellaro the key to New York State in recognition of the medical and social contributions.

On September 18, 1932, Sellaro was admitted as a patient to the hospital that he had founded and died there at the age of 64. His greatest contribution remains the founding of the OSIA, which continues to be the largest and longest surviving Italian American organization.

Joseph Scafetta Jr.

Bibliography

Andreozzi, John. *Guide to the Records of the OSIA.* St. Paul: University of Minnesota Press, 1989.

Aquilano, Baldo. *L'Ordine Figli d'Italia in America.* New York: Società Tipografica Italiana, 1925.

See also ORDER SONS OF ITALY IN AMERICA; ORGANIZATIONS

Serpico, Frank
See LAW ENFORCEMENT

S. F. Vanni (Publishers)

Also known as Italian Publishers, S. F. Vanni, Inc., S. F. Vanni (Ragusa), and S. F. Vanni Publishers and Booksellers, this company is the longest existing Italian bookstore in the United States. Founded by S(ante) F(ortunato) Vanni in 1884, its roots lie in the heyday of Italian immigration when it was not unusual for printed matter (newspapers, periodicals, calendars, postcards, popular fiction, religious books, technical manuals, and compendia of useful information) to be in demand, sometimes alongside other products from Italy in general stores, occasionally in specialized stores that catered to the writing and reading needs of an often barely literate population unable to communicate in English. Originally located at 548 West Broadway, New York City, at the southern edge of Greenwich Village, the bookstore had moved to 135 Bleecker Street when in 1931–1932 the heir of the original owner, Charles J. Vanni, sold it to Andrea Ragusa (1896–1974), who thoroughly transformed it.

Ragusa had come to the United States not as an immigrant but on a commercial visa, and had behind him a successful career in Italian publishing. In Italy he had been employed as general director of the Milanese publisher Fratelli Treves, also later known as Treves-Treccani-Tumminelli, who, together with Italy's Minister of Public Education, Giovanni Gentile, and the industrialist Senator Giovanni Treccani, had been instrumental in founding in 1925 the *Istituto per la pubblicazione dell'Enciclopedia Italiana,* a major reference work that would rival comparable ones already in existence in other European countries. Ragusa's connection with the *Enciclopedia Italiana* gained him an entrance to the American academic world concerned with Italian studies, reminiscent of Lorenzo Da Ponte, librettist for Mozart, who one hundred years earlier became the first importer of Italian books in America and first professor of Italian at Columbia University.

While continuing to import and sell a wide selection of books, Ragusa, as the new owner of S. F. Vanni, also installed a printing establishment that enabled him to expand into publishing. Thus, in 1932, the renamed Italian Publishers entered into an agreement with the Casa Italiana of Columbia University to publish its monthly *Bulletin,* the initial step in a long association that led to a whole cluster of publications, including the three collections *Casa Italiana Library of Italian Classics, Paterno Library Collection of Italian Studies,* and *Old and New Sheaves.* Many other scholarly works in the field of Italian followed, as well as important contributions to the study of literature and linguistics in general. The Vanni list was enriched over the years with textbooks for the study of Italian at the high school and college levels, and also for the study of other languages: Spanish, French, German, and English as a second language. In 1945 S. F. Vanni moved to its present location at 30 West 12th Street, New York City, finding its place among the rich flowering of literary activity and publishing in Greenwich Village during the subsequent decades. As a bookstore it continued to serve the expanding needs of students and libraries both in the New York area and in the United States and Canada at large. The business has been maintained since 1974 by Olga and Isa Ragusa.

Olga Ragusa

Bibliography

Gisolfi, Anthony. "In Memoriam: Andrea Ragusa (1896–1974)." *Italica* 51 (1974): 504.

Morris, Ronald L. "The Last Ethnic Bookstores in New York." *Book Source Monthly* 10 (March 1995): 16–18.

Phelps, Robert. "Worth Every Inch of Sootfall." *Sunday Herald Tribune*. Book Week Section, 20 October 1963.

Prezzolini, Giuseppe. "Trovo un editore che mi rassomiglia." In *L'italiano inutile,* 315–322. Milan: Longanesi, 1953.

See also BUSINESS AND ENTREPRENEURSHIP

Shire, Talia
See MOVIE ACTORS AND ACTRESSES

Sinatra, Francis Albert (1915–1998)

Born December 12, 1915, in Hoboken, New Jersey, Frank Sinatra's father (Anthony Martin Sinatra) had migrated from Catania and his mother (Dolly Natalie Della Gravante) from Genoa. His father had fought professionally under the name "Marty O'Brien" before finding steady work as a boiler maker, stevedore, saloon keeper, and fireman; his mother supplemented the family income working as both midwife to immigrant mothers and ward chief for the Democratic machine of Mayor Frank Hague.

Young Francis, in frail health, spent mornings and afternoons shuttling between the homes of his married aunt and his maternal grandmother. A life-threatening mastoid infection required surgery that left him partially deaf while inflicting a massive scar behind his left ear.

At David E. Rue Junior High School, Frank regaled his classmates and annoyed his teachers by doing imitations of popular movie stars and radio comics. He was 15 when he dropped out of A. J. Demarest High School after attending the first forty-seven days. He enjoyed singing in the glee club.

At 17, he vowed to emulate the success of idol Bing Crosby. He and three friends formed a singing quartet, The Hoboken Four. They competed in local contests. In 1935, while performing at a talent audition at New York City's Capitol Theatre, they came in first, and soon after were invited to perform on radio's Major Bowe's Original Amateur Hour, winning again and earning a spot on the show's national touring company. Throughout his late teens, Sinatra sang at weddings and house parties.

At 21 he was hired to wait on tables at the Rustic Cabin in Alpine, New Jersey, but during the evening show he doubled as emcee and vocalist with the house band. In 1939 trumpet player Harry James, then organizing his first band, was looking for a male singer. He was advised to see the evening show at the Rustic Cabin. Sufficiently impressed, James hired the singing waiter for seventy-five dollars a week.

In 1940 bandleader Tommy Dorsey lured the young singer away from the James band. He played one-night stands, did radio remotes, appeared with the band in two motion pictures, and recorded more than a hundred songs as featured vocalist and lead singer with Dorsey's choral group, the Pied Pipers. It was Dorsey's celebrated trombone technique, with its stretched notes and seemingly effortless breathing, that profoundly influenced the young vocalist's singing style. Sinatra's purring notes and soft delivery personalized the message of romantic yearning, a heady brew for giddy bobby soxers and lonely war brides.

Sinatra quit the Dorsey band in September 1942 determined to go solo. There was no guarantee that younger audiences, who loved dancing to big band swing arrangements, would sit still long enough to listen to a crooner. Yet, by 1945, Sinatra had already set attendance records for stage appearances at the New York Paramount; he had signed a lucrative recording contract with Columbia Records; he was heard weekly on his own radio show and as cohost for the popular "Your Hit Parade"; and he was a recognized movie star in MGM big budget musicals.

For the fifth consecutive year, the 1948 *Down Beat* Annual Poll rated Sinatra "best male vocalist." During Sinatra's peak success, he was hailed by several catchy titles: "Swoonatra," "King of the Baritones," "The Voice." It would not be long, however, before his popularity skidded and scandal would forever shatter the squeaky clean homegrown boy image sedulously engineered by studio flacks and Hollywood fan magazines.

In 1949 Sinatra had plummeted to fifth position in the *Down Beat* poll. Not a single Sinatra recording that year made it to the top of the weekly pop charts. Teenagers, long a staple of the Sinatra cult, by 1950 had switched allegiance to a new breed of singers influenced by the growing popularity of rhythm and blues, a derivative of black gospel music that demanded a more muscular delivery against a heavy bass beat. The muted crooning style of Sinatra fell victim to changing times.

Even before his popularity slumped, Sinatra was pursued by tabloid journalists and often became embroiled in sensational disclosures. In April 1947 the Hearst newspapers ran banner headlines for five successive days following a nightclub brawl in which Sinatra punched a Hearst writer over an alleged slur of his character. Gossip columnists uncovered lurid details and speculations regarding his "womanizing" and questionable contact with gangland figures. His publicly anointed "perfect marriage" to childhood sweetheart Nancy Barbato became unglued after his publicized affair with movie queen Ava Gardner. After a long separation, Nancy consented to a Reno divorce, granted October 30, 1951. Several days later Sinatra married Gardner in Philadelphia. Theirs was a tempestuous relationship. When she traveled to Spain to shoot a film, there were rumors of an alliance with her costar, a matador. Sinatra seemed inconsolable. Reported bouts with depression and the possibility of a suicide attempt seemed like the final stages of a once brilliant career on the verge of total meltdown.

Columbia Records refused to renew his contract in 1952. Although Sinatra had played leading roles in four major musical pictures from 1945 to 1949, his movie career faltered after his popularity dipped. After appearing in two successive flops in 1951, Sinatra was ignored by every major studio. MCA, his talent agency, dropped him as a risky client.

Never one to admit defeat, Sinatra fought back. He was convinced that his best years were still ahead of him and took a major step when he badgered studio chiefs at Columbia Pictures into giving him a screen test for the eagerly anticipated war drama *From Here to Eternity* (1953). Sinatra not only won the coveted role of Private Angelo Maggio but also received accolades for a performance that earned him an Academy Award for best supporting actor. More important, he no longer relied solely on his singing for his livelihood. As a recognized serious actor, he could hold out for more challenging roles. For the next three decades, Sinatra would appear in forty-one motion pictures, teaming up with big screen personalities and creating a gallery of memorable misfits, social outsiders, and tough guys whose veneer of cynicism masked an ambivalent romanticism.

Music critics largely agree that Sinatra's vintage singing years came to fruition over the next fifteen years. When he switched to Capitol Records in 1953, he had available to him the best music arrangers in the business. Over the next decade, in close collaboration with Gordon Jenkins, Billy May, and Nelson Riddle, Sinatra crafted more than a few score of timeless gems, including "Young at Heart" (*Billboard*'s best song for 1954), *Swing Easy* (best album for 1954), "All the Way" (Oscar-winning song from the Sinatra movie, *The Joker Is Wild*, 1957), "The Lady Is a Tramp," "Witchcraft," "Learnin' the Blues," and "High Hopes" (another Oscar-winning song, 1959). He was given a Grammy Award for best vocal performance for that year's top-selling album, *Come Dance With Me*.

As Capitol's premier recording artist, Sinatra reinvented himself. He became a cocksure hedonist and cool hipster, a mid-century minstrel with a jaunty charm, a reformed sentimentalist with a practiced disdain, laughing at all pretension and poking holes in the vagaries of modern courtship. Yet, in several recording sessions with Gordon Jenkins, he is a mournful herald of love and loss. In "Lonely Town" (1957), "I'm a Fool to Want You" (1957), and "Here's That Rainy Day" (1959), a tristful Sinatra distills the trauma of damaged love with a knifelike raspiness, giving an added edge to his blue notes. Not surprisingly, Sinatra appears on the album cover of "Only the Lonely" (1958) as the painted jester of the woeful countenance, a sad-eyed harlequin musing on his own misfortune.

After Sinatra's second marriage ended in a Mexican divorce in 1957, celebrity watchers took note of his fraternization with a select circle of friends. With Sinatra in the designated role of master of the revels, he was nearly always accompanied by some or all of the following: Dean Martin, Sammy Davis Jr., Peter Lawford, and Joey Bishop. In public they adopted a free-wheeling and studied indifference to social protocol, committing pranks on each other and toward unsuspecting dupes. They even carried their puckish humor onto the screen in films like *Ocean's Eleven* (1960) and *Robin and the Seven Hoods* (1964). They were known as the "Rat Pack" or merely the "Clan." During the early sixties they performed regularly at the Sands Hotel, drawing many honeymooners and starstruck tourists to Las Vegas, making it a favorite watering hole for years to come.

Sinatra launched Reprise, his own record company, in 1961. Three years later Reprise merged with Warner Brothers, with Sinatra retaining one-third financial interest and freedom to produce independent films of his own choosing. By the fall of 1961 gross returns on his multiple holdings approached $20 million. In addition to Reprise Records, he also controlled Essex Productions, four music publishing houses, a string of radio stations (with copartner Danny Kaye), two casino/hotels in Nevada, and investments in real estate, banks, and loan companies. In his mid-forties, Sinatra had total artistic control as well as financial stability. While operating as a successful entrepreneur, he still maintained a productive singing career. His stature as a jazz stylist was greatly enhanced in the late sixties by a series of live sessions and subsequent releases of songs recorded with the Count Basie Band, Antonio Carlos Jobim, and the Duke Ellington Orchestra.

With the issuance of *September of My Years* (*Billboard's* best album of 1965), Sinatra proved that time had not diminished his artistry. He won a Grammy for best vocal performance/male (for "It Was a Very Good Year," one of the album's most requested songs). With his middle-age years creeping up on him, Sinatra emerged as an august presence, wistfully reminiscing over the follies and excesses of prodigal youth, savoring the sweetness of life's transcendent joys like "vintage wine from fine old kegs."

"Strangers in the Night" (1966) was his first hit single in eleven years. The following year he cut another hit single, "Somethin' Stupid," a father-and-daughter duet with Nancy Sinatra.

Nine years after his divorce from Ava Gardner, Sinatra married 20-year-old actress Mia Farrow. Their May-December union was dissolved by mutual consent two years later, in 1968.

In a salute to the dean of songdom's survival skills, Paul Anka added new lyrics to a popular French ballad and dedicated it to Sinatra. "My Way" (1968), a nonapologetic defense of fierce self-determinism, gave every indication toward becoming the legendary showman's valedictory. Within a short time it became his signature song, the most requested title in his songbook.

Despite a heavy schedule, Sinatra found time to appear on network television. He hosted his own weekly show, starting with the *Frank Sinatra Show* (1950) and continuing on to *Sinatra and Friends* (1977). He also appeared on variety shows as featured guest and headlined seasonal specials. He was a memorable narrator for the musical remake of Thornton Wilder's *Our Town* (1955). He received an Emmy and Peabody Award as producer and host of *A Man and His Music* (1965).

Though he declared his intention of quitting show business in June 1971, Sinatra was forced out of seclusion time and again by fans and colleagues. In April 1973 President Nixon coaxed him to perform at a White House reception honoring the prime minister of Italy. Sinatra's first album in three years, *Ol' Blue Eyes Is Back,* appeared in autumn, timed to draw attention to an NBC-TV Sinatra special airing November 18. The following January, he opened at the newly refurbished Caesar's Palace, Las Vegas. An enthusiastic opening night audience gave him five standing ovations. Over the next two years he resurfaced in New York's Madison Square Garden ("Sinatra, The Main Event") and then embarked on an extensive tour of major European cities, which took him as far as the Middle East.

Sinatra, on the verge of sixty, married for the fourth time on July 11, 1976, to Barbara Blakely Marx, widow of comic actor Zeppo Marx.

The death of matriarch Dolly Sinatra (killed in a plane crash on January 6, 1977) momentarily derailed her son's resurgent career. In late February he did a benefit in London, a concert in Amsterdam, and road shows across the United States. His appearance at a soccer stadium on January 26, 1980, in Rio de Janeiro, proved to be a historic event. He performed before a vociferous crowd of 170,000 fans—at the time the largest live audience ever to hear a solo performer.

Sinatra raised close to two billion dollars in benefits for battered children, scholarships, and medical centers. His global fund-raisers have had worldwide impact: orphanages in Japan, a nursery in Athens, pediatric hospitals in Hong Kong and Paris, a Boys' Town in Rome.

His last feature film, *The First Deadly Sin* (1980), and a walk-on role in *Cannonball II* (1984) may have ended his screen-career, giving him more time for leisurely pursuits like golf and marketing his own spaghetti sauce. He also cultivated a deep, abiding interest in painting. Over the past few decades, he achieved a high degree of sophistication in abstract art. His canvases are eagerly sought by serious art collectors. The proceeds, in most cases, go to his favorite charities.

A week's engagement at Carnegie Hall (September 1987) sold out immediately. On March 13, 1988, Sinatra, Dean Martin, and Sammy Davis Jr. launched a nationwide tour. When Dean Martin was forced to cancel, Liza Minnelli replaced him. The tour was billed as "The Ultimate Event" when footage was compiled and showcased on cable TV. In 1991 Sinatra performed to capacity crowds for his "Diamond Jubilee" tour, commemorating his 75th birthday. Though his weathered vocal cords had lost some of their resilience, he still captivated the crowds with his boundless enthusiasm and masterful phrasing.

In October 1993 Capitol Records released *Duets I*, Sinatra's first studio album in ten years. Within four months it went multi-platinum (sales in excess of two million copies). Through the magic of hi-tech dubbing, thirteen contemporary pop singers had their voices grafted onto the sound track laid down by Sinatra and a studio orchestra. The success of *Duets I* invariably led to the release of *Duets II* (1994). Though *Duets II* did not do as well as its prequel, it did garner a Grammy for best performance in traditional pop.

The music industry bestowed its Lifetime Achievement Award on Sinatra on March 1, 1994, acknowledging his track record in an industry where competition is fierce and success short-lived.

Frank Sinatra died on May 14, 1998. The probability is that his legend will long outlive any future trends in music. Music critic John Rockwell stated that Sinatra was "by any reasonable criterion the greatest singer in the history of American music."

America's reaction to Sinatra's death at 82 in 1998 was marked by extensive coverage in the media, expressions of sorrow from national leaders, and the reissuing of many of his musical pieces. He was perhaps the foremost popular star the Italian American community produced in the twentieth century.

Joseph Fioravanti

Bibliography

Balliett, Whitney. *American Singers*. New York: Oxford University Press, 1988.

Friedwald, Will. *Sinatra! The Song Is You: A Singer's Art*. New York: Scribner, 1995.

Hemming, Roy, and David Hadju. *Discovering Great Singers of Classic Pop*. New York: Newmarket Press, 1991.

Irwin, Lew. *Sinatra: The Pictorial Biography*. Philadelphia: Courage Books/Running Press, 1995.

Parish, James Robert, and Michael R. Pitts. *Hollywood Songsters*. New York: Garland, 1991.

Paymer, Marvin, ed. *Facts Behind the Songs: A Handbook of American Popular Music from the Nineties to the '90s*. New York: Garland, 1993.

Petkov, Steven, and Leonard Mustazza, eds. *The Frank Sinatra Reader*. New York: Oxford University Press, 1995.

Rockwell, John. *Sinatra: An American Classic*. New York: Random House/Rolling Stone, 1985.

Sayers, Scott Jr., and Ed O'Brien. *Sinatra: The Man and His Music*. Austin: TSD Press, 1992.

See also MOVIE ACTORS AND ACTRESSES

Sirica, John Joseph (1904–1992)

Named "Man of the Year" by *Time* magazine (January 7, 1974), Judge John Joseph Sirica was born in Waterbury, Connecticut, on March 19, 1904. His father, Federico Sirica, was 7 years old when, in 1887, he migrated from a small village near Naples. He married Rosa Zinno from New Haven, Connecticut. Federico was a barber, and his wife ran a small grocery store.

Life was not easy for the Sirica family as they moved from Ohio to Georgia to New Orleans to Los Angeles to Richmond to Washington, D.C. John earned his law degree in 1926 from Georgetown University. He joined a Washington law firm, served as a counsel for a congressional committee, and became interested in Republican Party affairs. In 1957 President Eisenhower appointed Sirica to the federal bench.

In the early 1930s Sirica helped start a boxing club and began a lifelong friendship with Jack Dempsey. In fact, the former heavyweight champion was his best man when Sirica married Lucille Camalier in 1952. They had three children.

He showed stamina and character as a tough but fair judge. In his book, *To Set the Record Straight* (Norton, 1979), Sirica revealed details of the Watergate case involving the Nixon Administration. In his five-year association with Watergate, Sirica dealt with the break-in, coverup trials, indictments, guilty pleas, battle over the tapes, the unraveling of the Nixon presidency, and jailing of men who were among the most powerful in the nation. At the time of the Watergate burglary on June 17, 1972, Sirica was chief of the fifteen-judge federal court in the District of Columbia.

Sirica died August 14, 1992, at the age of 88.

Margherita Marchione

Bibliography

Marchione, Margherita. *Americans of Italian Heritage.* New York: University Press of America, 1995.

Sirica, John. *To Set the Record Straight.* New York: Norton, 1979.

Siringo, Charles Angelo (1855–1928)

A cowboy, detective, memoirist, and biographer who became popular in Wild West lore, Charles Angelo Siringo was born February 7, 1855, in Matagorda County, Texas. Baptized Charlie, his mother was Irish and his father was born in Italy. As a child Siringo worked at odd jobs and drifted from Texas to Louisiana to Missouri to Illinois and back to Texas. By age 14 he had developed into a full-fledged cowboy.

The open range became Siringo's classroom during the growth of the cattle industry. He earned his spurs riding for the colorful "Shanghai" Pierce and learned the cowboy trade from older hands. Pierce was a cattle baron who rounded up and shipped tens of thousands of longhorn cattle northward to Kansas. Siringo drove cattle along the Chisholm Trail from San Antonio to Abilene and helped to establish the LS Ranch in the Texas Panhandle. He married Mamie Lloyd at Wellington, Kansas; she died six years later, leaving one daughter.

In the 1880s he retired from the cowboy business, became a restaurateur in Caldwell, Kansas, and wrote his autobiography, *A Texas Cowboy: or Fifteen Years on the Hurricane Deck of a Spanish Pony.* The book appeared in 1885 and became the first authentic autobiography in cowboy history. A paperback, it became a best-seller throughout the West and East, eventually selling over one million copies. The book was reissued and rewritten five different times during his lifetime.

Siringo left Kansas in 1886 to join the Pinkerton National Detective Agency in Chicago. He retired from this business in 1912 and wrote a second book, *A Cowboy Detective: A True Story of Twenty-Two Years with a World-Famous Detective Agency.* Since the book divulged Pinkerton methods of operation, he was enjoined from releasing it. In 1915 he wrote *Two Evils: Pinkertonism and Anarchism,* which again brought to light the unsavory tactics used by the Pinkertons. The Pinkerton Agency again went to court to stop circulation of the book and forced Siringo to surrender the plates and remaining copies of the book.

In 1909 he wrote *A Song Companion of a Lone Star Cowboy,* which contained old ballads of the cow camps, and eleven years later *History of "Billy the Kid,"* a book he said presented the true life of the most daring cowboy in the West. His first book, *A Texas Cowboy,* was revised with a new title, *Riata and Spurs, The Story of a Lifetime in the Saddle as a Cowboy and Detective,* and was published by Houghton Mifflin in 1927. It achieved the recognition the author had long sought. Siringo died in Hollywood, California, in 1928.

Despite his personal heroics and experiences in the Wild West, Siringo's enduring contribution lies in his genuine literary narrative depicting life in that part of the country. Simple and direct, his recollections graphically set down one of the most colorful periods in American history. The original *A Texas Cowboy* is considered a classic.

Frank J. Cavaioli

Bibliography

Cavaioli, Frank J. "Charles Angelo Siringo, Italian American Cowboy." *Italian Americana* 7 (spring/summer 1983): 35–45.

Peavy, Charles D. *Charles Angelo Siringo, A Texas Picaro.* Southwest Writers Series 3. Austin: Steck-Vaughn, 1967.

Pingenot, Ben E. *Siringo.* College Station: Texas A&M University Press, 1989.

Siringo, Charles Angelo. *A Texas Cowboy: or Fifteen Years on the Hurricane Deck of a Spanish Pony.* 1885. Reprint, New York: William Sloan, 1950.

Smeal, Eleanor Cutri (b. 1939)

President of the National Organization for Women (NOW) from 1977 to 1982 and from 1985 to 1987, this social activist was born in Astabula, Ohio, to Peter Anthony Cutri, who had migrated from Calabria, Italy, and Josephine E. Agresti, also from an Italian immigrant family. Eleanor Cutri Smeal commented that she excelled in debating and public speaking because she started at "age four or five, like in any good Italian family." Although raised as Roman Catholics, she and her sibling attended public schools. A diligent student, Smeal achieved excellence in high school and subsequently at Duke University, where in 1961 she graduated with a Phi Beta Kappa key and a bachelor's degree.

She considered pursuing a career in law; however, after becoming aware of the discrimination that women endured, she changed the direction of her career. When she learned that women attorneys seldom practiced in courtrooms, she took classes in political science and public administration at the University of Florida, where she received a master's degree in 1963. It was there that she met and married her husband, Charles R. Smeal, a student in metallurgical engineering. They have a son and a daughter.

Illness forced her to stop work on her doctoral thesis, an investigation into the attitudes of women toward female political candidates. It was at this point she faced the difficulties encountered by working mothers. After moving to the Pittsburgh area in 1969, a back ailment forced a year of complete bed rest. She became aware of the need for disability insurance for wives and mothers. Both she and her husband delved into the history and significance of the women's movement. Their conversion to confirmed radical feminists was now complete.

Among her civic activities, Eleanor Cutri Smeal served as secretary-treasurer to the Allegheny County Council from 1971 to 1972 and was a member of the board of the Upper St. Clair, Pennsylvania, chapter of the League of Women Voters from 1968 to 1972. In 1970 she and her husband joined the National Organization for Women. She became a convenor and first president from 1971 to 1973 of a NOW chapter in South Hills, a Pittsburgh suburb. At this time she established her feminist priorities, especially as they affected her personally. The Smeals organized a nursery school in that community. Elected president of Pennsylvania NOW in 1972, she made educational injustice a target, leading the fight for equal opportunity for girls in physical education and sports in the Pennsylvania schools.

In 1973 Smeal was elected to the national board of directors of NOW, and two years later became its chairperson. She saw her election as a symbol of housewives' support for women's rights, asserting that the economic security of home is vital and that passing the Equal Rights Admendment was an important step toward achieving that goal. Ratification of the ERA was a high NOW priority. She was designated chief of a national strike force in 1977, charged with developing strategy to fight for ratification of the amendment. Other NOW goals addressed by Smeal were establishing congressional committees on discriminatory health care, the Susan B. Anthony dollar, job preference for veterans, and eliminating employment discrimination for women. In 1978 President Carter appointed Eleanor Smeal to the National Advisory Committee for Women and in 1979 to the national advisory committee to the White House Conference on Families. The 1978 *World Almanac* listed her as one of the twenty-five most influential women in the United States, and she was listed as one of the thirteen women among the persons chosen for "50 Faces for America's Future" by *Time* magazine in its cover story of August 6, 1979.

Anne T. Romano

Bibliography

Smeal, Eleanor Cutri. *Why And How Women Will Elect the Next President.* New York: Harper and Row, 1984.

See also NATIONAL ORGANIZATION OF
ITALIAN AMERICAN WOMEN; WOMEN IN THE
WORKFORCE

Soccer

The most popular sports game in virtually every country in the world, except the United States where it has begun to emerge in the last third of the twentieth century, soccer's claim on the sports-minded public is most extensive in Italy as Italian soccer stars reign in popularity in a manner similar to the most famous baseball, football, and basketball luminaries from the United States.

Although soccer was not a vital part of the immigrant cultural baggage at the turn of the twentieth century, it nevertheless was present in Italian immigrant neighborhoods in the pre–World War I era as reflected in the establishment of many soccer clubs in eastern seaboard cities such as New York. Little Italy soccer clubs increased throughout the country during the 1920s and 1930s—the 1929 Italian soccer organizations of Chicago and St. Louis being the most prominent. It was, however, in the post–World War II period that soccer became more central to Italian Americans as increased numbers of postwar Italian immigrants possessed substantial experience and familiarity with the game. From the 1960s on, it was not unusual for soccer clubs, founded and supported by Italian American organizations, to be fixtures in Italian neighborhoods. Italian American players, moreover, became more involved in the game as youngsters increasingly enrolled in soccer youth leagues.

This background encouraged the notion that it was time for big league professional soccer to compete with other major sports. U.S. promoters sought to attract immigrant Italians and other immigrant groups to the games by introducing famous professionals from European soccer. For example, in 1976 Giorgio Chinaglia was brought in to play for the New York Cosmos team in an attempt to attract Italian Americans in the New York metropolitan area to attend games. Unfortunately this effort was discouraged by limited response as the league proved to be short-lived, thereby compelling professional soccer enthusiasts to await a more propitious time to introduce the sport on that level.

The accomplishments of Italy's national soccer team in the World Cup finals of 1982 struck a responsive chord among Italian Americans. By defeating arch rival West Germany, and winning the world championship, the Italian team ended a forty-four-year gap since its last championship and elated those of Italian ancestry throughout the world. Italian American neighborhoods across the nation enthusiastically hailed news of the victory with unusual proprietary pride. On July 12, 1982, Italian flags were ubiquitous in New York's Mulberry Street, Little Italy, and Brooklyn's Bensonhurst, while numerous motorcades and parades marked celebrations in Boston's North End and the Little Italys of Baltimore and Newark. In these and other Little Italys, thousands jammed the streets shouting, "Italia, Italia," while waving the red, white, and green tricolors.

The 1994 World Cup Soccer Tournament finals, hosted by the United States, represented another example of how the Italian national team elicited pride in Italian Americans. Ardent Americans of Italian descent flocked to major stadiums from California to Boston, where they displayed their Italian colors along with vibrant banners proclaiming their home communities and organizations as they cheered on the Italian team.

Soccer, the world's most popular sport, while not exclusive to Italy, is played by numerous Italian Americans within various clubs and leagues. Because of Italy's prowess in the sport, it has been the basis for continuous identification between Italian Americans and the land of their ancestry.

Salvatore J. LaGumina

Bibliography

Eisen, George, and David K. Wiggins, eds. *Ethnicity and Sport in North American History and Culture*. Westport, CT: Greenwood, 1994.

See also BOCCE; SPORTS

Social Class Characteristics

With reference to the Italian Americans as a socially identifiable group, the relevant questions that have been addressed in research are: What changes in class composition of this group have occurred over the past century? Since large-scale immigration began, how do Italian Americans rank in the present scenario

Grace Mirabella, who served as editor of Vogue *and* Mirabella, *has influenced the publishing and fashion worlds. Courtesy of the National Italian American Foundation (NIAF), Washington, D.C.*

of class distribution in America? What has been the Italian American pattern in terms of intergenerational social mobility, as well as occupational and educational achievements of the group? What differences have been brought about by increasing rates of intermarriage and assimilation? How much congruity exists between the wealth, prestige, and power of Italian Americans as a group? Finally, but of crucial importance, who is an Italian American and what image does he/she project in American society? Frequently left out of the research interest is the notion of lifestyle ("that touch of class"); its fluidity has befuddled and often eluded most scholars.

Earlier studies on these topics could not be based on hard data, so results were tentative and impressionistic. Major breakthroughs have occurred from the confluence of several factors: (1) the inclusion of variables such as ethnicity, country of origin, ancestry, etc., in the U.S. decennial census; (2) the ongoing research findings of the General Social Survey (NORC of Chicago); and (3) the research efforts on this subject by several competent scholars and qualified institutions, e.g., the National Italian American Foundation, Agnelli Foundation, Center for Migration Studies, and American Italian Historical Association.

From the abundance of studies, the overall picture that emerges is that the Italian American community is characterized by a steady trend of upward mobility whose momentum increases as the community moves away from the large-scale immigration period. Like most other ethnic communities of European descent, the Italian Americans progressed at a steady pace in the direction of achieving equal status with groups that had preceded them chronologically. Although the pace of development may have been slow at the beginning (for various reasons), by the closing of the twentieth century Italian Americans have managed to achieve, and even surpass, the goal of parity with other ethnic groups in several sectors of life. All evidence points out to the fact that the collective development of Italian Americans has converged steadily with the wider Anglo-American society.

This convergence includes also the skewing of the distribution of Italian Americans toward the middle and upper class, while the nation as a whole is moving somewhat toward a U-shaped polarization that tends to squeeze out the middle class. The percentage of Italian Americans below the poverty level has diminished consistently over the past one hundred years to the current level in the single digits.

While such gains were not achieved without heavy cost and sacrifice, they are clouded by discontinuities and incongruities that underpin some of the questions posed at the beginning. A consideration that lies at the root of the whole issue of social class is the systematic undercounting of Italian Americans; the answers to the questions posed earlier hinge decidedly on the outcome of who should be counted as Italian American at a given stage in the process of assimilation. Richard Alba and Gwen Moore note that "the discrepancy between the size of the population with at least some Italian ancestry and the number of persons who identify in some sense with the Italian American group is bound to increase." This is attributable not only to the effect of intermarriage, but more specifically to the fact that persons who are of mixed ancestry that include Italian ancestry appear to be less likely to acknowledge this fact to census and General Social Survey interviewers.

This is one plausible explanation for the striking difference in the number of those claiming Italian, German, and Irish national origin (to consider but three comparable ethnic groups). According to the 1990 United States Census Summary Data on reported ancestry, 80,659,530 Americans indicated that they are of single, first, or second German ancestry; 51,069,901 of single, first, or second Irish ancestry; but only 22,013,987 Americans indicate that they are of single, first, or second Italian ancestry. These data leave the researcher perplexed, especially if one keeps in mind that from 1820 to 1967 there came to the United States 6,879,495 Germans, 4,289,215 Austro-Hungarians, 4,708,845 Irish, and 5,096,204 Italians. If one takes into consideration the birth and death rate alone of these groups over the past one hundred years, it would be difficult to accept the census figures at their face value.

Literature on the subject shares the opinion that cross-ethnic comparisons that highlight most tables and statistics do not make much sense; the data rarely refer to comparable cohorts, or generations equally removed from the beginning years of large-scale immigration. Nonetheless, this particular situation raises considerable concern and calls for suitable explanations. A partial explanation of the discrepancy between the number of Americans who in 1990 claimed German and Irish ancestry and those who claimed Italian ancestry can be found in the light of four hypotheses, for which more precise data could be gathered. One explanation would imply a hypothetical higher fertility rate among Americans of German and Irish descent, for which there exists no cogent evidence; another hypothesis is a possible higher rate of German/German, Irish/Irish marriages occurring over a longer period of time than is the case among Italians (there is some evidence to this effect but not such that would create the disproportion seen above); yet another hypothesis would attribute the difference to the significantly high rate of returns to Italy among immigrant Italians; but a final, and rather unpleasant, hypothesis would attribute at least part of the discrepancy to the low self-esteem among Italian Americans of multiple ancestry that prompts them to ignore or negate their partial Italian descent.

Alba has conceptualized this phenomenon, in part, as the increasing "twilight of ethnicity" in which "the force of ethnicity is dissipating." Undoubtedly among Italian Americans the current high rate of intermarriage, the mobility out of the ghetto, and the waning of the family-centered ethos, all work to dissolve the sense of ethnic belonging at a higher rate than that experienced by other ethnic groups.

This argument, however, does not take away from the fact that the Italian American community as a group succeeded in catching up with "native" Americans as well as older immigrant groups in a relatively short span of time. It is clearly valid when one looks at family income and class appurtenance on the basis of subjective self-classification. The most recent studies, conducted by scholars using the census data and data from the General Social Survey, indicate that Italian Americans as a group enjoy one of the highest per capita and per family income in the country, although they may not occupy positions of prestige and power in all professional and occupational areas in proportion to their numbers. In 1990, while the average family income for the entire country was $43,803 and the per capita income was $17,722, the corresponding number for Italian Americans was respectively $51,442 and $17,381, comparable, that is, to that of the leading ethnic groups of the nation.

However, when indicators other than income are taken into consideration, there emerge discontinuities and major dissonances. Indicators usually associated with the variable of power have been of two kinds: political office and positions of authority and power in institutions. The expected lag between social mobility of a group and political advancement has been hypothesized, but hardly measured. In the case of Italian Americans, the lag has been rather noticeable. Until 1960 Fiorello LaGuardia (mayor of New York) and John Pastore (first Italian American senator and governor) were the only two names worth mentioning. Starting from 1960 the situation moved at an accelerated pace.

The characteristic underrepresentation of Italian Americans in the political and business institutions, including the Roman Catholic Church, can be explained by the fact that a much more profound change had to take place at the economic and educational level. The masses of immigrants were the heirs of the Italian social underclass that for centuries had been exploited by a cruel governing class toward which they felt alienation and enmity.

Giovanni Schiavo was the first to point out the significant class distinction between the Italian immigrants who arrived before 1870 and those who came during the rush decades of 1880–1920. While the relatively few immigrants from Italy to the United States prior to 1880 originated from a variety of regions and belonged, in general, to the professional and upper middle class, the flow of immigrants that began after 1880 was characterized by an overrepresentation of peasants, *contadini*, and unskilled manual laborers from the southern regions, mixed with a generous sprinkle of artisans and a handful of professionals. During the first three decades of Italian immigration the average immigrant entered the United States with an average of seventeen dollars. Their most widely held occupations were manual and menial jobs, poorly paid. Discrimination was widespread.

Unlike some other immigrant groups, Italian immigrants labored under a triple handicap: they came from a country with one of the lowest upward mobility of all developed societies; they had to maintain themselves; and they had to provide sustenance to the families they had left behind in Italy. After sending whatever they could spare to their families, not much was left for the immigrants to plough into autonomous enterprise, or life improvement. Moreover, the initial resistance to avail themselves of American educational opportunities slowed down the economic activity of the first and, in part, second generation of Italian immigrants, who, with few notable exceptions, remained solidly in the low or lower middle class for decades.

Little more than a century later, these "low class" masses had so progressed that by 1994, 45.7 percent identified themselves as middle class, 46.1 percent identified themselves as working class, and only 5.2 percent identified themselves as belonging to the lower class. In the official records of American occupational distribution, Italian Americans of the first and part of the second generation are identified mostly as laborers, manual workers, and, only occasionally, as lower-rung professionals. Over the decades, however, through increased earnings and/or access to higher education, Italian Americans have achieved an occupational distribution that does not deviate significantly from other ethnic groups of European ancestry, with the exception of members of the Jewish community.

The internal mobility of Italians indeed reflects the pattern of the American population as a whole. They participated in the post–World War II exodus to the suburbs, or were evicted from those neighborhoods that became prime targets for the urban-renewal movement of the 1950s and early 1960s. In the 1970s, as Graziano Battistella points out, they participated to a limited extent in the movement from the Northeast and Midwest toward the South and the West, though recent data show that two Italian Americans out of three still live in the northeastern region. While some specific ethnic characteristics, such as their familial ties, originally slowed the achievement of Italian Americans, other factors contributed greatly to accelerate the process: the increasing rate of intermarriage with other ethnic groups, the lowering of fertility rate, and the growing appreciation of education.

A deciding factor in the social class condition of Italian Americans has been their attitude toward education. While Italian missionaries who had come to this country before the unification of Italy distinguished themselves by their contribution to American education (Father Giovanni Grassi was the first president of Georgetown College, Father Anthony Maraschi founded the University of San Francisco, and Father Joseph Cataldo started Gonzaga University in Spokane, Washington), the educational background of most pre–World War II immigrants was poor or totally lacking, and the number of immigrants that went to school was small. As Francis X. Femminella notes, education was not the main avenue of success for Italians of the first and second generation, nor was it the major means of upward mobility. As recently as 1980, Italian participation in education was lower, overall, than that of most other European ancestry groups. Since then the involvement of Italian Americans in the educational enterprise has increased considerably. Nonetheless, their increased participation in education notwithstanding, higher education has been seen by Italian Americans more as a means of making a living and a way of personal enrichment rather than as a contribution to society or to the pursuit of knowledge; education is a means to obtaining a job rather than as the basis of a career.

In the 1990s renewed attention has been paid to a disturbing paradox: while the average income of Italian American households is

Proud members of the CENACOLO, the Italian Cultural Club, organized in San Francisco, 1920. The CENACOLO continued the creative cultural tradition of Italy that was so important to Americans of Italian descent. Courtesy Augusto Troiani.

among the highest in the nation, and while Italian Americans are enrolling in colleges at a higher percentage than all other ethnic groups, except the Polish, Italian Americans still have very high dropout rates among high school students. This is so especially in the Northeast, a condition that had already been evident at the beginning of the twentieth century, suggesting that the familistic culture of Italian Americans in nearly a hundred years of acculturation has not completely lost its traditional antieducation bias.

Yet another factor that had a profound impact on the social mobility of Italian Americans during the first two generations is their family-centered ethos, which has prompted them to mobilize the resources of every member of the family. Census data show that, in Italian American families, a higher number of members are employed and contribute to the family income than is the case with most other American ethnic groups. Among Italian Americans there has never occurred anything like the feminization of poverty noticeable in some other ethnic groups. Data from the 1980 census, as dis-

cussed by Battistella, confirmed Andrew Greeley's findings that Italian Americans have a very low rate of divorce, the lowest among Americans of European ancestry. Considering the negative contribution of divorce to family economics, this factual consideration explains in part the high economic success rate of Italian Americans.

As indicated before, single or multiple ancestry is a crucial variable in the discussion of social class in America and certain characteristics of Italian American behavior can be explained by reference to it. As generations pass and the rate of intermarriages increases, the level of educational achievement rises and the lifestyle of ethnic groups changes dramatically. Although the relationship is unclear, some significant association appears to be involved that deserves further research and analysis, especially considering the limitation of the data.

In 1972, 8.8 million Americans claimed to be "of Italian origin." By 1980, twelve million persons (5.4 percent of the nation's population) claimed some Italian ancestry. Of these, 51.1

percent were of multiple ancestry and 48.9 percent of single ancestry. By 1990, 14,665,000 Americans claimed some Italian ancestry. Of these, 2,085,000 indicated Italian as their leading ancestry group, 199,000 indicated it as second leading ancestry group, and 7,885,000, most of them from the Northeast, indicated it as third leading ancestry group. Evidently, not all Americans whose ancestry is partly Italian are aware of it or willing to recognize it.

The resulting question is: To what extent have the numerical consistency of Italian Americans and their ethnic consciousness contributed to facilitate their entry into the power elite of the nation? Alba notes that a few Italian Americans have managed to break through into the higher echelons, but that the group remains quite underrepresented at this level. With the notable exception of Cardinals Bernardin and Bevilacqua, and several bishops, Italian Americans have been slow to gain even a proportionate share of the American Catholic Church hierarchy, where they are notably underrepresented in proportion to their number as parishioners in the Roman Catholic Church. Their presence in the "Social Register" is insignificant.

Therefore, even though some individuals have managed to reach high positions in the political and social arena, the collective prestige of the group remains disproportionately low in relation to its accomplishments. This could be attributed mainly to two factors: the enduring association of the Italian American community with organized crime and the tardiness with which the group has succeeded in creating powerful national organizations and institutions that could represent the group as a whole in proportion to its numerical and economic strength, thus exerting effective political pressure.

A recent study by DiLorenzo indicates that, while Italian Americans represent over 6 percent of the total American population, their presence in the faculty of twelve leading law schools in America amounts to only 1.4 percent, and they are totally absent in seven of the top-ranking schools. However, research in progress on the presence of Italian Americans in the editorial staff of one hundred leading American periodicals put their number at nearly 6 percent, which appears to come close to the total proportion of Italian Americans in the United States population.

A valid indicator of the overall prestige profile of the Italian American can be gleaned by viewing the content of the *Who's Who among Italian Americans* compiled by Serena Cantoni of the National Italian American Foundation in 1995. The volume lists a short biography of thirteen hundred "prominent Italian Americans." Nearly half of them are found in the northeastern corridor, while the other half is spread in very small numbers in the remaining states, with the exception of Louisiana and California, which contain a significant number.

The professional distribution, however, is of greater significance. Nearly one-third of these "prominent" Italian Americans (483) are in education and/or administration; 139 are in business leadership; 123 are in public service (elected or appointed offices); 87 in business owner/entrepreneurship; 172 in law and law enforcement; 55 in entertainment; 46 in financial services; 94 in health care; 64 in writing and publishing; 29 in the media; 20 in the arts; and 22 in science.

The volume is indicative in three ways: whatever the reason, many prominent Italian Americans, especially those in business and the media, are not listed; people in education and educational administration are disproportionately represented; and territorially, the Italian American leadership is unevenly distributed. For all its shortcomings, however, the *Who's Who* negates the image of the Italian American as being associated with the low-class mode of marketing Italian food, stereotyped use of broken English, and boisterous gesticulating demeanor in social interaction.

One last consideration needs to be made concerning the notion of lifestyle. Economic and professional success has given Italian Americans the opportunity to provide themselves with material goods, positive living conditions, and favorable life experiences. Expenditure on food, education, and housing have consumed a relatively larger portion of their budget than books, travel, or artistic endeavors. Where they live and what kind of status symbol they prefer is also very crucial in determining social class. Available statistics are relatively scanty and present research does not permit us to draw any valid generalization that would have more solid grounding than the stereotyped image frequently portrayed by the mass media.

Rocco Caporale

Bibliography

Agnelli, G. Fondazione. *The Italian Americans: Who They Are, Where They Live, How Many They Are.* Torino: Fondazione G. Agnelli, 1980.

Alba, Richard. *Italian Americans Into the Twilight of Ethnicity.* Englewood Cliffs, NJ: Prentice-Hall, 1985.

Alba, Richard, and Gwen Moore. "Ethnicity in the American Elite." *American Sociological Review* 47, no. 3 (June 1982).

Battistella, Graziano, ed. *Italian Americans in the '80s. A Sociodemographic Profile.* New York: Center for Migration Studies, 1989.

Cantoni, Serena V., ed. *Who's Who Among Italian Americans.* Washington, DC: National Italian American Foundation, 1995.

Cordasco, Francesco, and Eugene Bucchioni. *The Italians: Social Background of an American Group.* Clifton, NJ: Augustus M. Kelley, 1974.

Crispino, James A. *The Assimilation of Ethnic Groups: The Italian Case.* New York: Center for Migration Studies, 1980.

DiLorenzo, Vincent. "The Impassable Road From Boston's North End to Harvard Square: Italian American Faculty in the Nation's Top Law Schools." *The Italian American Review* 5, no. 1 (spring 1996): 60–66.

Femminella, Francis X., ed. *Power and Class: The Italian American Experience.* New York: American Italian Historical Association, 1973.

Gans, Herbert J. *The Urban Villagers: Group and Class in the Life of Italian-Americans.* New York: The Free Press, 1982. Updated and expanded edition.

Kessner, Thomas. *The Golden Door: Italian and Jewish Immigrant Mobility in New York City, 1880–1915,* New York: Oxford University Press, 1977.

Pane, Remigio U., ed. *Italian Americans in the Professions.* New York: American Italian Historical Association, 1983.

Pozzetta, George E., ed. *Pane e Lavoro: The Italian American Working Class.* Toronto: The Multicultural History Society of Ontario, 1980.

Schiavo, Giovanni. *Four Centuries of Italian-American History.* New York: Center for Migration Studies, 1992.

Tomasi, Lydio F., ed. *Italian Americans: New Perspectives in Italian Immigration and Ethnicity.* New York: Center for Migration Studies, 1985.

Tomasi, Lydio, Pietro Gastaldo, and Thomas Row, eds. *The Columbus People: Perspectives in Italian Immigration to the Americas and Australia.* New York: Center for Migration Studies, 1994.

See also ASSIMILATION; BUSINESS AND ENTREPRENEURSHIP; CRIME AND ORGANIZED CRIME; POLITICS

S

Società Italiana di Mutua Beneficenza

On October 17, 1858, 164 Italians gathered at 246 Dupont Street, San Francisco, to organize the Italian Mutual Benevolent Society, an organization committed to providing mutual help, relief, and comfort to its sick members and the families of the departed. To carry out the organization's objectives, first society president Nicola Larco and chocolatier Domenico Ghirardelli began a money-raising campaign that obtained the sum of $1,404.00. This money allowed the society to hire a physician, Dr. Emanuel D'Oliveira, and to contract with La Société Française de Biefanisance Mutuelle's French Hospital (est. 1851) to provide care.

In the 1860s society members expressed a desire to hire an Italian-speaking doctor and to build their own hospital. The society selected Dr. Antonio Rottanzi but needed more time to accomplish its second goal. The society incorporated on December 31, 1867, and then secured San Francisco land at Vale, Dale, Noe, and Castro streets, suitable for building a hospital. There the Italian Hospital opened to great fanfare on May 10, 1869. The Italian Hospital cared for patients until the mid-1870s, when the society's financial condition deteriorated, and it had to close the facility and sell the property. No buyer emerged; instead, St. Paul's Catholic Church used the building for parish facilities until its own buildings opened in the 1880s. The hospital stood abandoned and unsold into the twentieth century.

During the years the hospital operated, the society continued to help families. When the city of San Francisco opened a section of its cemetery located at Lands End (Lincoln Park today) to benevolent associations in 1879, the society applied for and received a plot to bury deceased members. The society

In the foreground is the Italian Hospital built in 1869 in San Francisco by the Società Italiana di Mutua Beneficenza. It is the first hospital built by Italians in the United States. Photo taken in 1875. Courtesy Augusto Troiani.

maintained the plot until 1897, when the city of San Francisco decided to close the city cemetery to future burials. Society president Vincenzo Ravenna prompted the organization to purchase land in Colma, California, and open its own cemetery.

While continuing to provide physician and other medical services, the society opened a cemetery on F Street in Colma in 1899. Society and cemetery business ran smoothly until the earthquake and fire of 1906. That calamity destroyed records housed in San Francisco and the receiving vault in Colma. The society could not reconstruct its records, but it did rebuild the receiving vault at a cost of fifteen thousand dollars.

In June 1940 the society amended its articles of incorporation to exist in perpetuity. Eight years later in 1949 it purchased land on F Street adjacent to the cemetery. In the 1950s, 1960s, and 1970s, the association started building outdoor crypts and mausoleums, exemplified by the cross-shaped Chapel/Mausoleum and the El Camino mausoleum adjacent to a blue-colored map of Italy. In 1962 the society moved its headquarters from San Francisco to 540 F Street in Colma.

An important change occurred in 1978, when the society split into two corporations: the society, with medical/pharmaceutical ben-

efits, and the Italian Cemetery. The society transferred its properties, Endowment Care Fund, and Special Care Fund to the Italian Cemetery. In August 1978 the State Cemetery Board granted it authority to operate as a cemetery. The new corporation began building the Skylight Mausoleum in the 1980s and, in the 1990s, planned new mausoleums and additions to the El Camino and Skylight buildings, projects scheduled for completion from 1997 to after 2000.

Philip M. Montesano

Bibliography

Gumina, Deanna. *The Italians of San Francisco, 1850–1930.* New York: Center for Immigration Studies, 1978.

Montesano, Philip M. "Italian Mutual Benevolent Society of San Francisco." *Columbus Historical Issue: Italians in California.* San Francisco: Columbus Publications, 1977, 189–191.

———. *Società Italiana di Mutua Beneficenza: The First Fifty Years.* Colma, CA: Società Italiana di Mutua Beneficenza, 1983.

Montesano, Philip M., and Sandra R. Montesano. *La Società Italiana di Mutua Beneficenza: The Italian Hospital, 1858–1874.* Colma, CA: Società Italiana di Mutua Beneficenza, 1978.

Bronze plaque commemorating the 120th anniversary of the Società Italiana di Mutua Beneficenza (1858–1978) in San Francisco. The society was formed to aid its Italian members. It later started the Italian Cemetery, where over forty thousand are buried. The society continues to conduct cultural and community events. Courtesy Augusto Troiani.

See also SAN FRANCISCO; SBARBORO, ANDREA

Soleri, Paolo (b. 1919)

Architect, environmentalist, and visionary of future cities, Paolo Soleri was born in Turin, Italy, on June 21, 1919, and received his training at Turin Polytechnic, graduating with a doctoral degree in architecture in 1946. Awarded a scholarship, he migrated to the United States, where he apprenticed in Arizona with the famous architect Frank Lloyd Wright. In 1949, having just married Carolyn Woods, he constructed his first building, a remarkable masonry and dome house for his mother-in-law at Cave Creek, Arizona (The Dome House). The following year Soleri returned to Turin with his wife, where they designed craft objects and built a Leoncino, which incorporated a solar device. In it they moved to southern Italy in 1951 and built a ceramics studio and workshop, the Artistica Ceramica Solimene Ceramics Factory.

Soleri and his wife returned to the American desert in 1955 and settled in Scottsdale, Arizona. On a flat, arid, five-acre site, Soleri began to build his Cosanti Foundation and sketch out his blueprints for alternative urban environments. Soleri views all cities as absurd, unworkable, obsolete megalopolises eating up the surface of the earth and polluting the environment. He believes suburbs enslave people by depriving them of the dynamism of urban life and the complexity of nature. He feels that by compressing the environment into a single, highly efficient structure surrounded by open country, the cultural excitement of the urban areas can be merged with the beauty of nature. For this Soleri has coined the term *arcology.*

In his definitive book about arcology, *The City in the Image of Man,* published by the Massachusetts Institute of Technology (1970), are printed detailed diagrams of thirty Soleri archaeologies. His marvelous, controversial images are detailed page after page including archaeologies with names such as Arcoforte, Arc-Village, Logology, Babel, Babel Canyon, Arckibuz, Arcodiga, and Babeldiga. His Novanoah is a mile-high, 6,900-acre floating ocean arcology designed for 2.4 million people. His ultimate arcology, Babelnoah, holds a population of six million living in a complex of mile-high skyscrapers spreading over eighteen thousand acres. His arcology/asteroid, Asteromo, would spin through space, housing seventy thousand scientists and their families, doing research in astronomy, physics, and space biochemistry.

A recurring design theme in Soleri's work has been on bridges and cities. He first achieved recognition in this engineering field through the publication of some of his designs in the book *The Architecture of Bridges,* issued by the Museum of Modern Art in New York (1948). His work came to the wider attention of the American public through a large-scale exhibition of his arcology and bridge projects held at the Corcoran Gallery, Washington (1970). That same year, Soleri began building his arcology Arcosanti on 860 acres in Arizona. Arcosanti was designed to accommodate about five thousand people and to rise twenty-five stories. It will be pedestrian oriented and cover only thirteen acres.

His writings and philosophies on the untenable situation of modern people and modern cities are documented in his books, *The City in the Image of Man* (1970), *The Sketchbooks of Paolo Soleri* (1971), *The Bridge Between Matter and Spirit Is Matter Becoming Spirit* (1973).

Anne T. Romano

Bibliography

Hillinger, Charles. "Paolo Soleri's Cities of Tomorrow, Environments for the Future." *Mainliner Magazine* 11 (1976).

Sharp, Dennis. *Contemporary Architects.* New York: Macmillan, 1980.

South, The

From the daring sixteenth-century explorations of Giovanni da Verrazzano to scattered late-nineteenth-century agricultural colonies to Charleston's celebrated Spoleto festival, Italians have contributed to the diversity and vitality of the American South.

Three distinct stages have marked the migration of Italians to the American South, the result of a complex interplay of variables involving the social and economic health of Italy, the southern demand for industrial and agricultural laborers, fluctuating levels of nativism, and, most recently, retirement patterns and new economies.

Italians appeared prominently in the American South on an individual basis, rather than as a group experience, in the three centuries between the Hernando de Soto expedition (1539–1542, that effectively explored the South) and the Civil War. Individual Italian adventurers appeared as *condottieri* (leaders) and navigators under the Spanish, English, and French flags. Most prominently, Giovanni da Verrazzano charted the Atlantic coast and Henri de Tonti explored the southern interior.

A remarkable chapter of Italian immigration occurred in the 1760s in the then isolated fourteenth colony of Florida. In 1763 an English physician, Andrew Turnbull, encouraged fifteen hundred Italians—largely from the Ligurian coast—to come to British East Florida and labor on his New Smyrna plantation. The Italians, joined by Minorcans, rebelled at the harsh conditions, and a handful of survivors managed to escape to Saint Augustine, where they remained and thrived.

The influence of Italian artists and intellectuals, such as Andrea Palladio and Philip Mazzei, deeply influenced southern architectural styles and thought. William Paca of Maryland signed the Declaration of Independence, while Mazzei enjoyed a long friendship with Thomas Jefferson and inspired his famous "all men are equal" declaration.

On the eve of the Civil War, relatively few Italians resided in the American South. Louisiana was home to 915 Italians, but most other southern states counted only handfuls of Italians.

The second stage of immigration to the South, from 1880 to 1920, paralleled the massive surge of millions of Italian migrants to the Americas. In comparison to the extraordinary presence of Italians in Buenos Aires, New York, or Philadelphia, the number of Italians in the American South was limited. Yet the influence of Italians in the South was disproportionate to their numbers.

Louisiana served as home to the largest concentration of Italians in the south. By 1914 at least sixteen thousand Italians, largely Sicilians, migrated to the Bayou State to cut sugarcane, establish truck farms, and peddle produce. Many more Italians migrated in and out of Louisiana, working on and traveling on the Illinois Central, with New Orleans serving as the center of a vast labor market. Italians helped pioneer a successful strawberry industry in Hammond, Louisiana. New Orleans boasted a thriving Italian community—5,866 Italians by 1900—and quickly dominated the fruit and vegetable markets and helped shape the Cresent City's character.

Louisiana's treatment of Italians also added a dark chapter to the history of American intolerance. In 1890 the assassination of the police chief of New Orleans sparked nativist fears of immigrants and led to the lynching of eleven Italians, still the greatest mass lynching in American history. Nativist violence was not limited to New Orleans. In 1899 a mob lynched five Italians in Tallulah, Louisiana. Louisiana's rich agricultural lands of "Bloody" Tangipahoa Parish attracted several thousand Italians, who maintained an uneasy relationship with native southern planters. In this era Italians were victims of lynching in Hahnville, Louisiana, and Walsenburg, Colorado.

Throughout the agricultural South, Italian immigrants faced perilous conditions. On the large plantations and railways in Louisiana, Mississippi, Alabama, and Florida, Italians confronted peonage, fraud, and violence. Courts offered little solace, and because of the sparsely populated and isolated settlements, Italians had few opportunities to create institutions similar to the ones that had ameliorated their lives in northern cities. In the 1920s Alabama Congressman John Burnett called Italians an "undesirable, dirty class of people."

The most celebrated agricultural settlement experiments occurred in Arkansas. Between 1895 and 1897 several hundred northern Italian laborers migrated to Sunnyside, Arkansas. Organizers hoped to recruit Italian families and sell them lots where they would cultivate cotton. The experiment was doomed. Fevers wracked the colony, critics charged the owners with peonage, and finally, Father Pietro Bandini encouraged the survivors to relocate to Tontitown, Arkansas, which became a successful agricultural colony. In Valdese, North Carolina, a group of Waldensians (Italian Protestants) established a cooperative to plant and market tobacco. Italians also established large and successful farming colonies in Dickinson and Bryan, Texas.

Italian immigrants found more success and stability in the emerging southern industries of coal, steel, and cigars. Birmingham, Alabama, became a magnet for Italians fleeing plantation life and offered employment in the coal mines and steel mills. By 1900, two hundred Italian immigrants were laboring in the Tennessee coal and iron mines of northern Alabama. Italians from the north lived in Little Italys in company towns such as Blocton, Alabama. Many miners left the small boom towns, migrating to Birmingham. Sicilians from Bisacquino, Campofranco, and Sutera also migrated to the Birmingham mills and Little Italy. By 1920 more than two thousand Italians resided in Jefferson County, Alabama.

Tampa, Florida, also offered an unusual refuge for Italian immigrants. In 1886 a Spanish entrepreneur, Vicente Martinez Ybor, founded an industrial town, Ybor City (which merged into Tampa). By the 1890s Ybor City had become one of the great centers for the manufacture of hand-rolled cigars. Large numbers of Cubans and Spaniards helped pioneer the enterprise, joined by small numbers of Sicilians in the early 1890s. By 1910, twenty-five hundred Italians helped make Ybor City a Latin community. In Tampa, Italians learned Spanish, embraced a radical industrial culture, and contributed to a remarkable flowering of Italian-language arts.

The third and still evolving phase of Italian migration began in the 1950s and continues to grow. Many Italian Americans encountered the South for the first time during World War II. Many would return. Buoyed by postwar prosperity, newfound leisure and recreation, and pension and retirement benefits, Italian Americans came southward in increasing numbers, as tourists, new residents and workers, and retirees.

The South's Sunbelt dynamic economy has attracted large numbers of young Italian Americans, most lured from "Rustbelt" cities. This more recent migration has had a tremendous impact on cities without historic Italian populations, such as Miami, Atlanta, and Fort Lauderdale. Italian Americans have brought some of their institutions with them; note the proliferation of ethnic restaurants and the Sons of Italy chapters.

The 1990 census revealed the extraordinary changes wrought by decades of demographic shift. Most dramatic is the emergence of Florida as an irresistible magnet for Italian Americans. Nearly eight hundred thousand Italian Americans called Florida home in 1990, a figure surpassing the Italian American populations of Connecticut and Illinois, and only slightly less than Massachusetts. Indeed, Florida's Italian American residents increased by 370,000 during the 1980s. Today, the Miami–Fort Lauderdale metropolitan area

Historical marker in Tampa, Florida, indicating how the mutual-aid society has provided important social services to Italians in a new land. Courtesy Frank J. Cavaioli.

accounts for two hundred thousand Italian Americans, this in a region that witnessed little Italian presence from 1890 to 1920.

Other southern states have drawn large numbers of Italian American retirees and families. Texas boasts 313,000 Italian Americans, followed by Virginia and Louisiana, with two hundred thousand each. North Carolina and Georgia, which had drawn little interest from new immigrants during the great migrations, now each claim 112,000 Italian American residents.

Gary R. Mormino

Bibliography

Baiamonte, John V. Jr. *Spirit of Vengeance: Nativism and Louisiana Justice, 1921–1924.* Baton Rouge: Louisiana State University Press, 1986.

Belfiglio, Valentine. *The Italian Experience in Texas.* Austin: Eakin Press, 1983.

Ellison, Rhoda Coleman. "Little Italy in Rural Alabama." *Alabama Heritage* 2 (fall 1986): 34–35.

Fede, Frank Joseph. *Italians in the Deep South.* Montgomery, AL: Black Belt Press, 1993.

Gambino, Richard. *Vendetta: A True Story of the Worst Lynching in America.* New York: Doubleday, 1977.

Haas, Edward F. "Guns, Goats, and Italians: The Tallulah Lynching of 1899." *Northern Louisiana Historical Association Journal* 13 (1982): 45–58.

Milani, Ernesto. "Peonage at Sunnyside and the Reaction of the Italian Government." *Arkansas Historical Quarterly* 50 (spring 1991): 30–40.

Mormino, Gary R., and George E. Pozzetta. *The Immigrant World of Ybor City: Italians and Their Latin Neighbors in Tampa, 1885–1985.* Urbana: University of Illinois Press, 1987.

Scarpaci, Jean. "Immigrants in the New South: Italians in Louisiana's Sugar Parishes, 1880–1910." *Labor History* 16 (spring 1975): 165–183.

Wyatt-Brown, Bertram. "Lord Percy and Sunnyside: Planter Mentality and Italian Peonage in the Mississippi Delta." *Arkansas Historical Quarterly* 50 (spring 1991): 60–84.

See also AGRICULTURE; NEW ORLEANS; TEXAS

Speranza, Gino Carlo (1872–1927)

As a civil rights advocate and lawyer, Gino Speranza's ethnic name belied his assimilationist convictions. He was born in Connecticut on April 23, 1872, to Professor Carlo L. Speranza and his wife, Adele Capelli. He received a B.S. from City College of New York (now City University of New York) in 1892, an LL.B. from New York Law School in 1894, and an M.S. from his undergraduate alma mater in 1895. That same year he was admitted to the bar in New York State. He maintained a practice and spent fifteen years as legal advisor to the Royal Consulate General of Italy in New York.

Speranza's career reflected both the bright and the dark sides of his loyalty to the United States. He thought the United States should inspire in the immigrants a love and a desire for citizenship. If Americans exploited immigrants in transit through New York Harbor or in labor camps, Speranza believed such practices should be investigated and halted. On the other hand, he thought the immigrants should make every effort to become good citizens. He accepted the stereotypical connection between Italians and crime and feared it would hinder Italian progress toward U.S. citizenship. Witnessing Italian American support for Italy during World War I developed in him a concern that immigrants might never really obtain what he called "heart's allegiance," which was overcoming the accident of being born into a "foreign" race and voluntarily adopting a national ideal.

During the 1900s Speranza began working with organizations to prevent the exploitation of Italians and encourage their assimilation. His positions with private-sector agencies included director of the Prison Association of the New York Society for Italian Immigrants and chairman of the Committee on Crime and Immigration of the American Institute of Criminal Law. His collaboration with Italian government agencies began in 1906, when the Royal Italian embassy commissioned him to investigate labor conditions in West Virginia camps. He volunteered his services to the U.S. government in World War I and served as assistant to the military attaché of the American Embassy of Rome and attaché of the Embassy's Political Intelligence Division.

Speranza also wrote extensively on issues concerning Italians and immigrants in general. During World War I he was the special correspondent in Italy for *Outlook* and for the *New York Evening Post*. He contributed on a freelance basis to journals such as the *Atlantic Monthly*. He published one book, *Race or Nation?* (1925).

In 1909 Speranza married Florence Colgate, heiress to the toiletries fortune. They made their home in Irvington, New York. He died July 12, 1927. His widow donated his books to Stanford's Hoover Institute. His papers went to the New York Public Library.

Mary Elizabeth Brown

Bibliography

Salerno, Aldo E. "America for Americans Only: Gino C. Speranza and the Immigrant Experience." *Italian Americana* 14 (summer 1996): 133–147.

Spinola, Francis Barretto (1821–1891)

The distinguished Italian American politician Francis Spinola holds the record for many firsts, such as the first of his heritage to be elected to the United States Congress, New York State Assembly, and New York State Senate. In addition, he was one of the few generals of Italian descent to serve in the Civil War.

He descended from a venerable Genoese family on his father's side, while his mother was American-born of Irish descent. Born in Stony Brook, Long Island, in 1821, a time when very few Italians resided in that area and throughout the country, he was raised and educated in a predominantly rural and agricultural environment. As a teenager, he moved to the then separate city of Brooklyn and tried his hand at various occupations before being appointed a clerk to the Brooklyn City Council. Admitted to the bar in 1844 at the age of 22, he was elected a Brooklyn alderman and served in that position for five years.

Immersed in the political whirligig of his day, he was originally a member of the Whig Party in contradistinction to the majority Democratic Party. Within a short time he joined the latter party and remained an obdurate, inveterate and loyal Democrat for the rest of his life—a position for which he was censured by the media. His attachment to the local Democratic Party was reflected in his association with local firehouses that were synonymous with politics. He even adopted the shirt worn by firemen as his own trademark and was known as "Shirt Collar Spinola."

In 1855 he moved from local to state politics, winning office as a New York state assemblyman and, after a few years, a state senator representing poor German and Irish immigrants in Brooklyn. As a state senator, he was instrumental in urging the New York State legislature to approve enactment of measures that would enable the state to fill its quota following the call for troops requested by President Lincoln. Though he was a strong Democratic Party leader who opposed the Republican administration, his loyalty to the Union overcame political partisanship. Spinola forthwith left his legislative post and proceeded to raise levies of men for the Union army, including four regiments of troops that became known as the "Spinola Empire Brigade." He was assigned to the unit and became a brigadier general. His wartime service was remarkable in that, without military education or experience in the field, he proved himself to be courageous in combat, playing a critical role in the Battle of Wapping Heights, Virginia, July 23, 1863. He was twice wounded.

Following the war he moved to New York City, where he engaged in a number of business enterprises that brought him prosperity; his estate was valued at over a million dollars at the time of his death. Spinola also developed formidable and lasting ties with the Tammany political organization and in 1876 won a seat in the New York State Assembly. Continually reelected to the post, he became conspicuous in a number of public issues. The heavily partisan nature of city politics earned him, however, an opprobrium usually reserved for rascals. In 1886 he was elected to Congress, representing the 10th Congressional District in New York, also known as the "Gas House" district. He was reelected to the position in 1888 and grudgingly earned praise even from his critics. During his time in Congress he sought to secure a fitting monument for American servicemen of the Revolution who perished on British prison ships docked in Brooklyn. In doing so he linked the cause with that of his Italian heritage, eliciting a comment by one of his colleagues that "Spinola loved America with an Italian devotion."

Salvatore J. LaGumina

Bibliography

Fox, Dixon Ryan. *The Decline of Aristocracy in the Politics of New York, 1801–1840.* New York: Harper and Row. 1965.

Handlin, Oscar. *Al Smith and His America.* Boston: Little, Brown, 1958.

LaGumina, Salvatore J. "Francis Barretto Spinola, Nineteenth Century Patriot and Politician." In *The Italian Americans Through the Generations,* edited by Rocco Caporale, 22–34. New York: American Italian Historical Association, 1986.

Marraro, Howard R. "Lincoln's Italian Volunteers from New York." *New York History* 24 (January 1963): 56–57.

See also POLITICS

Sports

The most prominent Italian American athletes picked up American sports either as immigrant children or as part of the American-born second, third, or fourth generations. Numerous world-renowned sports figures claim a full or partial Italian American heritage: Ray Barbuti (1905–1988), Joe DiMaggio (1914–1999), Rocky Marciano (1923–1969), Willie (Papaleo) Pep (b. 1922), Mary Lou (Rotundo) Retton (b. 1968), and Gene (Saraceni) Sarazen (1902–1999), as well as local heroes such as baseball's Phil Cavaretta (b. 1916) and Carl Furillo (1922–1989). Professional boxing champion Johnny (Giuseppe Carrora) Dundee (1893–1965) was born in Europe but learned to box as a boy in New York City. Southern Italian norms and values have played an important part in establishing the necessary preconditions for participation and achievement in American sports.

Contrary to disparaging stereotypes that described Italian immigrants as amoral, Calabrese, Neapolitan, Sicilian, and other regional groups had numerous strict mores both within and external to the family. They also had rules governing games like bocce and *il formaggio.* Immigrants practiced the ethics of hard work and discipline, which transferred well into the rigors of athletic training. Nationwide publicity given to baseball's Tony Lazzeri (1903–1946) and boxing's Tony Canzoneri (1908–1959) and Fidel LaBarba (1905–1981) provided inspiration for upcoming generations of athletes.

By the 1930s second-generation Italian Americans were sociologically ready to compete in American sports despite the tepid feelings of their elders. As Lawrence Pisani has noted, games in Italy were social occasions and Italian Americans took readily to club and industrial team sports. Donna Lopiano (b. 1947) pitched for the legendary Raybestos Brakettes softball team during the 1960s, coached three sports at Brooklyn College during the early 1970s, and was women's athletic director at the University of Texas from 1972 to 1992, illustrating Italian American mobility into leadership positions in sports. Men, women, girls, and boys, inspired by the accomplishments of the DiMaggio brothers, Marciano, Retton, Sarazen, and other Italian American athletes, have filled arenas and stadiums, gathered around radios and televisions, and perused sports pages.

Baseball is the classic American sport; therefore, success in baseball signified success in American society. The Americanized second generation tended to reject their elders' disdain for baseball and competed in this cooperative yet individualistic game, or became enthusiastic spectators. Joe DiMaggio, a second-generation Sicilian who played from 1936 to 1951, served as a role model for teenage urban ballplayers. Although his own identification with the Italian American community may have been tenuous, his grace and consummate skill helped weaken stereotypes of Italians as buffoons, criminals, and semiliterates. He was an American folk hero.

A professional baseball career has in principle been open to the most skilled players regardless of race, religion, ethnic background, place of birth, or social class. City slicker or farm boy, patrician or pauper, old-stock American or son of immigrant, Christian, Muslim, or Jew, white or nonwhite could become a major leaguer if he possessed major league ability. Before 1946 African Americans were an exception. But professional baseball has functioned as a means of upward social and economic mobility for young men of minority background, including Italian Americans. Pioneer Italian American major league players included Ed Abbaticchio (1877–1959), Ping (Pezzolo) Bodie (1887–1961), and umpire "Babe" Pinelli (1895–1984). Following Pinelli, the most famous Italian American of the 1920s in baseball was Tony Lazzeri, who played second base on the great Yankee teams from 1926 to 1937. Of the handful of Italian American players who broke into baseball prior to 1933, only infielder Tony Cuccinello (1907–1995) and Hall of Fame catcher Ernie Lombardi (1908–1986) played more than ten years in the majors. Others prominent in the 1930s were Dolph Camilli (b. 1907), Frank Crosetti (b. 1910), Gus Mancuso (1905–1984), Oscar Melillo (1899–1963), and Ernie Orsatti (1902–1968). However, by 1942 (the last year before most skilled players entered World War II service), over 8 percent of players listed in that year's *Baseball Register* were Italian American, notably Joe DiMaggio, Dominic DiMaggio (b. 1917), Vince DiMaggio (1912–1986), and Phil Rizzuto (b. 1917).

A long-term decline in the percentage of Italian American major leaguers began around 1946. This decline was probably due to increased opportunities outside baseball. The fifteen years following World War II witnessed fewer Italian American players. Typically, they were born in the urban, industrial East or the San Francisco Bay area and raised in an ethnic enclave. These men had little opportunity for social and economic success outside of baseball. Contemporaneous with the decline of the second-generation Italian American player was the decline of the folk hero. The dissolution of urban neighborhoods, urban blight, and suburbanization led to the closing of old inner-city ballparks and the expansion of major league baseball to the Pacific Coast. Fewer players would spend their entire career with one team in the same city as did Cavaretta, Crosetti, and Dom and Joe DiMaggio. The necessary conditions for the persistence of folk heroes had dissolved. Yogi Berra (b. 1925), Roy Campanella (1921–1993), Carl Furillo, Sal Maglie (1917–1992), and Vic Raschi (1919–1988) were among the last to be regarded as *Italian American* players both by Italian American and non–Italian American fans. Several men with Italian surnames were popular during the 1970s: Rick Cerone (b. 1954), Lee Mazzilli (b. 1955), Joe Pepitone (b. 1940), Rico Petrocelli (b. 1943), Frank Torre (b. 1931), Joe Torre (b. 1940), and Ron Santo (b. 1940). Yet the percentage of Italian American players continued to fall. Due to increased educational attainment and economic prosperity of the 1960s, many potential players concentrated on other skills and entered white-collar occupations. The post–World War II Italian American generation achieved dramatic societal success.

By the 1980s evidence suggested that the percentage of players with Italian surnames was increasing due to favorable changes in the salary structure. During the 1990s there appeared a sprinkling of Italian names: Craig Biggio (b. 1965), Rico Brogna (b. 1970), Ken Caminitti (b. 1963), Tom Candiotti (b. 1957), John Cangelosi (b. 1958), Gary Gaetti (b. 1958), Dave Righetti (b. 1958), John Franco (b. 1960), Frank Viola (b. 1960), Joe Girardi (b. 1964), and Mike Piazza (b. 1968).

More prominent, however, were the Italian American managers. Chicago native and Cubs' star Phil Cavaretta became the first when he took over that team in 1951. Up to 1964 there were only three others: Yogi Berra, Harry Lavagetto (1912–1990), and Sam Mele (b. 1923), but by the 1980s and 1990s there was a sizable number of managers and coaches. Among them were Berra, Tony La Russa (b. 1944), Joe Torre, and Bobby Valentine (b. 1950). Noteworthy umpires have been Lou Di Muro, Augie Donatelli, Ron Luciano, Dave Pallone, and Art Passarella.

Less numerous have been executives. The pioneer club owner was Lou Perini (1905–1972) of the 1942 Boston Braves, and later the Bavasi family was prominent. During the 1980s, there were accusations of ethnic discrimination when Cleveland entrepreneur Edward DeBartolo Sr. (1919–1994) was rejected as purchaser of the Chicago White Sox. A. Bartlett Giamatti (1938–1989) served as National League president shortly thereafter.

Occasionally, a baseball celebrity publicly expresses interest in his Italian heritage, illustrated by Tom Lasorda's serving as grand marshal of a Columbus Day parade and Phil Rizzuto's uninhibited references to Italian cuisine and culture. Nevertheless, at the end of the twentieth century, baseball personnel of Italian heritage were not normally thought of as manifesting ethnic culture and identity.

Turning to the sport of basketball, compared with the numbers of successful German Americans, Irish Americans, and Jewish Americans of an earlier era, and more recently African Americans, standout Italian American college and professional players have been sparse. Unlike baseball, where minor leaguers could be professionals as teenagers, basketball

players played for college teams. Lack of emphasis upon the practical worth of a college education and insufficient funds deterred entrance into this venue. During the early twentieth century, basketball was popular at the local community level, and clubs such as De Neri of South Philadelphia and St. Anthony's Knights of Williamsburg, Brooklyn, provided excellent opportunities for Italian American players. Agnes Iori made the first women's college All-American team in 1920.

Only a handful of Italian Americans were collegiate players before World War II. Angelo "Hank" Luisetti (b. 1916) gained national attention at Stanford during the 1930s when he used his innovative running, one-handed shot that changed the game's style. He was twice voted All-American. He played for the legendary Phillips 66 Oilers before World War II. He contracted spinal meningitis while serving in the navy, thus ending his career. Al Cervi (b. 1917) did not attend college but began professional ball with the Buffalo Bisons in 1938. Best known as player-coach and coach of the Syracuse Nationals from 1948 to 1953, he was elected Coach of the Year four times, a great scorer, defender, and clutch player. He stood 5 feet 11½ inches and played guard.

Sports' pundits often argue that the greatest players are rarely successful coaches. While Cervi is a clear exception, the typical Italian American basketball coach was not a famed player. Dick Motta (b. 1931), cut from his high school team, worked up from being a junior high, high school, and college coach to pilot the successful Chicago Bulls' teams during the late 1970s. Another famous coach is Lou Carnesecca (b. 1925), who led the New Jersey Nets from 1970 to 1973 and became one of the game's most successful college coaches with St. John's University (1966–1970; 1974–1992). Carnesecca ranked twenty-fourth in winning percentage among the all-time Division I winningest basketball coaches through 1996. Ben Carnevale (b. 1915), longtime U.S. Naval Academy skipper, subsequently became athletic director at New York University and William and Mary. Other coaches include John Calipari (b. 1958), P. J. Carlesimo (b. 1949), Mike Fratello (b. 1947), Rollie Massimino (b. 1934), Rick Pitino (b. 1952), and Jim Valvano (1946–1993), whose father, Rocky, and uncle, Bruno, were successful New York high school basketball coaches. Massimino and Valvano won National Collegiate Athletic Association championships. Additional contributors to basketball are Dan Biasone (1909–1992), inventor of the twenty-four-second clock; Al Bianchi (b. 1932), National Basketball Association coach and executive; and Johnny Nucatola (b. 1907), college and professional referee who has been called basketball's greatest official. During the 1970s, 1980s, and 1990s, the NBA's Vinnie Del Negro (b. 1966), Ernie DiGregorio (b. 1951), and Tom Gugliotta (b. 1969) have been outstanding players. Jennifer Rizzotti (b. 1974) starred for the University of Connecticut before turning professional in 1996 with the New England (Hartford) Blizzard of the American Basketball League, helping to make women's basketball a respected professional sport.

Italian Americans have been more successful in boxing than in any other sport except baseball. Pugilists of this background have been undisputed world champions in all eight traditional weight divisions with an overrepresentation in the lighter classes. Among the best remembered champions and their reigns are Rocky (Marchegiano) Marciano, heavyweight 1952–1956; Jake LaMotta, middleweight 1949–1951; and Willie (Guglielmo Papaleo) Pep, featherweight 1942–1948, 1949–1950. Tony Canzoneri, lightweight, 1930–1933, 1935–1936, and Pete (Gulotta) Herman, bantamweight, 1917–1921, made outstanding names for themselves earlier in the century. Rocky (Barbella) Graziano, middleweight 1947–1948, used boxing fame as an entree into show business.

Pugilism in Italy at the time of the mass migration of southern Italians to America existed on a small scale and only in the northern region. Most Italian-born boxers, successful or unsuccessful, learned the art in the urban New World. An early Italian American champion, Johnny (Giuseppe Carrora) Dundee, featherweight, 1923–1924, was born in Sicily but began his career in New York in 1910. Boxing is an individual sport, the popularity of which was enhanced by the first generation's interest in individual rather than team sports.

Boxing illustrates ethnic succession with Italian Americans generally displacing Jewish Americans just before World War II and African Americans displacing Italian Americans and others by the early 1960s. However, Jewish American success (with some notable

Lou Carnesecca. One of the winningest college basketball coaches of all time and a popular sports personality, Carnesecca coached at St. John's University. He is from an Italian American background in New York City. Courtesy Richard Renoff.

exceptions) was more concentrated in the two decades from 1920 to 1939, whereas a modicum of Italian American success persisted into the 1980s and 1990s, as illustrated by Arturo Gatti (b. 1972), Ray Mancini (b. 1961), Vinny Pazienza (b. 1963), and Lou Savarese (b. 1965). By the 1950s many Italian Americans had become successful as promoters, managers, trainers, and referees. This upward mobility within boxing is exemplified by early promoter and travel agency founder Jack Fugazy (1889–1966); promoter Chris (Mireno) Dundee (b. 1911); managers Cus D'Amato (1908–1985), Don Duva (1951–1996), and Lou Duva (b. 1922); trainers Angelo (Mireno) Dundee (b. 1921) and Richie Giachetti (b. 1940); and referee Arthur Mercante (b. 1920).

Persons striving for occupational mobility sometimes change their names to identify with an ethnic group that had previously been prominent in their chosen field. Some Italian, Jewish, and other boxers assumed Irish names. Italian American examples are Packey (Pasquale Agati) O'Gatty (1900–1966) and

Tippy (Tony Pilleteri) Larkin (1917–1991). Lightweight champion Sammy (Mandello) Mandell (1904–1967), who was actually Italian Albanian, was sometimes thought to be Jewish and half-Italian and half-Jewish. Mike (DiPiano) Rossman (b. 1956) used his mother's given surname as a marketing tool. Several Italian American boxers have taken the Scottish name Dundee. It is unknown whether these name changes actually aided popularity and gate appeal, but this phenomenon does signify Italian American identification with the greater American society. As with actors and entertainers using stage names, the practice waned after World War II.

Boxing has both fostered and broken down ethnic stereotypes. The long-standing link between the boxing business and shady practices, the control of many boxers by organized criminals, and the Senate Kefauver subcommittee hearings in 1960 reinforced the pervasive image of the Italian American racketeer notwithstanding the fact that two notorious principals convicted of illegal schemes were non-Italian. At the same time, the manager of heavyweight champion Floyd Patterson, Cus D'Amato, was kind and scrupulously honest. Italian boxers share with non-Italians the stereotype as being the semiliterate, grammatically maladroit fighter. Yet Jake LaMotta (b. 1921) was well read, Fidel LaBarba was a Stanford graduate, and Chico Vejar (half-Italian) (b. 1931) attended New York University.

National and international ethnic rivalries are often symbolized in boxing matches. Primo Carnera (1906–1967) fought most of his major bouts in America including his 1933 heavyweight title knockout loss to Max Baer. Despite his modest skills, Carnera was quite popular among Italian American and other fans. Amid rumors of the impending Italian-Ethiopian war in East Africa, he was severely beaten in June 1935 by Joe Louis, whose African American heritage was cited numerous times by sports writers. Perhaps for stylistic and political reasons, Carnera was dubbed "Mussolini's Muscleman" by a New York reporter. African American papers such as the Chicago *Defender* emphasized ethnic and political symbolism, and law enforcement officials feared African American versus Italian disturbances in the Yankee Stadium crowd attending the fight, but none occurred. Carnera had been financially exploited by managers and promoters but became financially successful when he switched to professional wrestling after World War II.

Rocky Marciano was the only Italian American heavyweight champion. Son of an immigrant shoe factory worker and a homemaker who settled in Brockton, Massachusetts, he won universal recognition via a thirteen-round knockout of Joe Walcott in 1952. An "up-and-coming" Rocky had knocked out former champ Joe Louis in 1951 after winning a disputed verdict over Italian American Roland La Starza (b. 1927), and later outclassed La Starza with a 1953 title bout knockout. He became renowned by winning a close, brutal defense against ex-champion Ezzard Charles in 1954 and retired undefeated after stopping light-heavyweight champ Archie Moore in 1955. Marciano was a dedicated, well-conditioned athlete whose spartan work habits and loyalty to family and friends were congruent with Italian American values. Like baseball's Joe DiMaggio, he represented the Americanized second generation and was nationally admired and respected. By 1997 sixteen Italian Americans had been inducted into the International Boxing Hall of Fame in Canastota, New York.

Turning to football, Italian Americans initially were not well represented because of the sport's limited popularity in inner cities and the paucity of Italian American college students. Nonetheless, Vincent "Pat" Pazzetti (1890–1972) quarterbacked at Lehigh in 1912 and 1913, made All-American on Walter Camp's second team, and was the first Italian American star. During sports' "Golden Age," Ray Barbuti captained and played halfback at Syracuse University in 1927 and 1928 and became a popular official. George Musso (b. 1910) was all-pro with the Chicago Bears around 1940. Pre–World War II collegiate standouts were Angelo Bertelli (b. 1921), Heisman Trophy–winning Notre Dame quarterback (1943); Paul Governali (1921–1978), Columbia University quarterback (1941–1943); and Charley Trippi (b. 1922), Georgia halfback (1942; 1945–1947). Trippi reached his peak after the war and set several records with the NFL Chicago Cardinals. Dante Lavelli (b. 1923) played end for Ohio State under Coach Paul Brown, but did not return to college. He then became a sure-handed end for the postwar Cleveland Browns.

Nicholas Buoniconti (b. 1940) was one of the most heralded football players of Italian descent. Born in Springfield, Massachusetts, the 5' 11", 220-pound athlete went to famed University of Notre Dame, where he became All American in 1961. A strong pass rusher, he excelled in professional football, first with the Boston Patriots (1962–1968) and then with the Miami Dolphins (1969–1973), where he became Miami's first All League player. He caught thirty interceptions during his thirteen-year career and was selected to play in All-Star games six times. Buoniconti now holds a law degree and is a practicing attorney.

Many did attend college through the G.I. Bill. Notable during the late 1940s and early 1950s were Andy Robustelli (b. 1926), University of Bridgeport defensive end, and Gino Marchetti (b. 1927) of the University of San Francisco; each attained greater fame as professionals. Italian-born Leo Nomellini (b. 1924) did not play in high school but perfected his skills on a Marine Corps team before entering college. He played both offensive and defensive tackle without protective padding. During the 1960s, Brian Piccolo (1943–1970) set rushing records at Wake Forest but died of cancer at age twenty-six. Ed Marinaro (b. 1950), a 1970s professional, became a television actor in the 1980s.

Italian Americans attained numerous leadership positions within the sport by the 1960s. Professional quarterbacks Dan Marino (b. 1961) and Joe Montana (b. 1956) are part Italian but generally considered Italian American. Gino Torretta (b. 1970) and Vinnie Testaverde (b. 1963) each won the Heisman and Maxwell awards as Miami (Florida) quarterbacks. Highly respected coaches include Columbia's Lou (Piccola) Little (1893–1979), Penn State's Joe Paterno (b. 1926), Yale's Carmen Cozza (b. 1930) and the NFL's Vince Lombardi (1913–1970). Edward DeBartolo, Jr. (b. 1946) owned the San Francisco 49ers, and Paul Tagliabue (b. 1940) served as NFL commissioner. By the end of the twentieth century, Italian Americans were neither dominant nor infrequent participants in the sport.

Few golf courses existed in Italy during the 1920s prior to the restriction of the mass immigration from the Mezzogiorno. All except one were in the extreme north—in the mountainous territory near Switzerland where cold winters prevent the courses from

Nick Buoniconti was one of the most valuable football players on the highly successful Miami Dolphins. A graduate of the University of Notre Dame, he was considered one of the most talented players of his time. Courtesy Miami Dolphins.

being open all year. Hence, the first successful Italian American golfers learned their skills in America while they were caddies or they (or their fathers) were greenskeepers and groundskeepers at country clubs. In these positions they had the opportunity to learn techniques and etiquette from club members and to practice on the links. The most outstanding examples of this type of socialization are Gene Sarazen, designer of the sand wedge and the most successful Italian American golfer, and the seven Turnesa brothers. Some of whom became successful after World War II followed a different path, such as Donna Caponi (b. 1945), whose father was a teaching pro, and Ken Venturi (b. 1931), son of an equipment shop manager.

Golf is an expensive pastime because of club membership expenses, greens fees, and equipment costs. Nonetheless, many successful entrepreneurs and professionals took up golf. An outstanding professional in the 1990s with this family background is Danielle Ammaccapane (b. 1965). Few post–World War II immigrants or their children have been prominent in American tournaments.

Italian American golfers have succeeded in ancillary areas. George Fazio (1911–1986), a well-known 1950s touring professional, earned a reputation as an architect and builder of courses; and Jim Dante (1898–1951), New Jersey PGA president during the 1940s, co-authored the popular instructional book *The Nine Bad Shots of Golf.*

There is less opportunity for employees at clubs and public courts to observe tennis matches than there is at golf courses. Also, tennis has been less popular in America than golf. Still, 1980 French Open winner Kathy Rinaldi (b. 1967) and Jennifer Capriati (b. 1976) have been illustrative of the sport's successful female teenagers in the late twentieth century.

A number of Italian Americans have been journalists and sports broadcasters on radio and television. During the 1920s and 1930s, Paul Gallico (1897–1976), American-born son of an Italian composer and musician, was sports editor for the *New York Daily News.* His 1938 memoir, *Farewell to Sport,* raised issues pertinent to a half century later, including gender identity of female athletes, discrimination against African American athletes, and payment for college athletes. Gallico also wrote short stories, novels, and the screenplay for *Pride of the Yankees,* the story of Lou Gehrig.

Broadcasters Joe Garagiola and Phil Rizzuto began their careers as baseball players and later became recognized media personalities. Talented writers include Joseph Durso, Mike Lupica, and Phil Pepe, among others.

Motor sports competition in Italy predates World War I. Enzo Ferrari (1898–1988) was a driver during the 1920s and founded a successful company in Modena in 1929. His cars have won a number of world championships. Northern Italian racing tradition is illustrated by Istria-born Mario Andretti (b. 1940), who began racing in Italy but, after moving to Pennsylvania at age 15, won the 1969 Indianapolis 500; he is among the all-time top money winners. An earlier native Italian who fared well in America was Ralph De Palma (1883–1956), 1915 Indianapolis winner. Many of the third and fourth generation compete in less renowned meets since they cherish their cars as other Americans do.

Phil Rizzuto, member of the Baseball Hall of Fame. He played shortstop during the New York Yankees' glory years in the 1940s and 1950s and later continued his association with the team as a popular announcer. Courtesy New York Yankees.

Italian Americans also have distinguished themselves in individual sports that generally do not have mass spectator appeal. Among them are Charles (Angelo Siciliano) Atlas (1893–1972), body building; Joe Falcaro (1896–1951), Millie Martorella, Robin Romeo, Carmen Salvino (b. 1933), Andy Varipapa (1891–1984), and John Venturelli (1889–1994), bowling; Brian Boitano (b. 1963) and Linda Fratianne (b. 1960), figure skating; Mary Lou (Rotundo) Retton, gymnastics; Ray Barbuti, Marty Liquori (b. 1949), and Lindy Remigino (b. 1931), track and field; and Primo Carnera (1906–1967), Antonino Rocca (b. 1923), and Bruno Sammartino (b. 1935), wrestling. Barbuti, Boitano, and Retton are Olympic gold medalists.

Few Italian Americans have been leading professional hockey players. John Mariucci (1916–1987) was one of the first Americans to play in the National Hockey League, and Al Iafrate (b. 1966) is the Michigan-born son of an immigrant father. Canadian-born Alex Del Vecchio (b. 1931) and Phil

Esposito (b. 1942) settled in the United States. Thoroughbred racing's Eddie Arcaro (b. 1916) and billiard's Willie Mosconi (b. 1913) are considered peerless.

Italian American participation in sports was initially in competitive arenas that stressed individual achievement. Bicycle racing, for example, was very popular in America during the late nineteenth century, and many racers and spectators were Italian immigrants. Auto racing, Greco-Roman wrestling, and the northern Italian sport of bocce were other popular individual sports. Boxing had greater appeal to the general American sporting public, and numerous Italian American young men were outstanding as amateurs and professionals.

Baseball, which is an individual as well as a team sport, witnessed many Italian American major leaguers whose achievements were admired by Italian American fans and others. Basketball and football have produced fewer Italian Americans. However, after World War II a fair number of Italian Americans were successful coaches, executives, and officials in these sports.

By the end of the twentieth century, Italian Americans have become nationally known in professional golf and tennis, and for decades there have been auto racers, bowlers, harness racing drivers, thoroughbred jockeys, and track and field athletes. In future years, upward mobility could lessen Italian American participation in professional sports but increase involvement in recreational sports, while more Italian Americans field the professional arena as executives and mass media specialists.

Richard Renoff

Bibliography

Bazzano, Carmelo. "The Italian-American Sporting Experience." In *Ethnicity and Sport in North American History and Culture,* edited by George Eisen and David K. Wiggins, 103–116. Westport, CT: Greenwood, 1994.

Cavaioli, Frank J. "The Italian American Chariot of Fire." *Italians and Irish in America,* edited by Francis X. Femminella, 35–42. New York: American Italian Historical Association, 1985.

Johnson, Anne Janette, comp. *Great Women in Sports.* Detroit: Visible Ink Press, 1996.

Mangione, Jerre, and Ben Morreale. *La Storia, Five Centuries of the Italian American Experience.* New York: Harper, 1992.

Pisani, Lawrence. *The Italian in America.* New York City: Exposition Press, 1957.

Renoff, Richard. "Italian Americans and Professional Boxing in Connecticut." In *Italian Americans and Their Public and Private Life,* edited by Frank J. Cavaioli, Angela Danzi, and Salvatore J. LaGumina, 212–227. New York: American Italian Historical Association, 1993.

Renoff, Richard, and Joseph A. Varacalli. "Italian Americans and Baseball." *Nassau Review* 6 (1990): 92–119.

Roberts, James B., and Alexander G. Skutt, comp. *The Boxing Register: International Boxing Hall of Fame Official Record Book.* Ithaca, NY: McBooks Press, 1996.

See also ANDRETTI, MARIO; ATLAS, CHARLES; BERRA, LAWRENCE PETER "YOGI"; BOCCE; COZZA, CARMEN; DiMAGGIO, JOSEPH PAUL; LOMBARDI, VINCENT THOMAS; LUISETTI, ANGELO JOSEPH; MARCIANO, ROCKY; MERCANTE, ARTHUR L.; MOSCONI, WILLIAM; PATERNO, JOSEPH VINCENT; PITINO, RICHARD A.; SARAZEN, GENE; SOCCER; VALVANO, JAMES THOMAS

Stallone, Sylvester

See MOVIE ACTORS AND ACTRESSES

Stefanile, Felix (b. 1930)

Since his first book of poetry, *River Full of Craft* (1956), Felix Stefanile has labored steadily, quietly, and independently in the field of American letters. In 1954, with his wife Selma, he founded *Sparrow,* a journal of poetry. One of a handful of the more well-known "little magazines," *Sparrow* still thrives without a cent of government funding and has taken on new significance through the Stefaniles' decision to focus on such ideas as "The Revenge of the Sonnet." In 1966 Felix published an important chapbook, "The Imagination of the Amateur," in which he stated that the "little magazine" expresses "what otherwise would not be expressed" and that the dedicated work of its producers "make for dialogue with a vengeance." Stefanile viewed the little magazine as "one of the last refuges of American pluralism in an age which has elevated the twin religions of Conformity and Comfort to the heights of unassailable dogma."

His strong connection to his ancestral culture has prompted him to bring the voices of the leading poets from Italy to America. He has translated Italian poetry into English: *Umberto Saba: Thirty-one Poems* (1978), *If I Were Fire: Sonnets of Cecco Angiolieri* (1985), and *The Blue Moustache: Some Futurist Poets* (1980). He has regularly contributed essays and criticism to national publications.

Stefanile's literary honors include professor emeritus of Purdue University, the Balch Prize awarded by the *Virginia Quarterly Review* (1972) for a group of poems published that year, and the republication of his essay "The New Consciousness: The NEA and Poetry Today" in the *Pushcart Press Prize Anthology* (1974). His poetry has appeared in many of this country's most prominent journals, but he has always maintained a low profile, focusing his time and effort on his art. His major poetry collections include *A Fig Tree in America* (1970) and *East River Nocturne* (1976).

His latest collection, *The Dance at St. Gabriel's* (1995), combines the best of his past works with the beauty of his present talent. The book's first section opens with the poem "On Theory and Practice," which is both a manifesto on formalism and his assessment of the poet's responsibility: "To make the familiar strange, that is a touch / that can annoint, that can transform the self. / Make the strange familiar, agitate / the consciousness / . . . What is tame is shame, the absence of a probing mind." Stefanile uses personal experiences and familial stories, and through the magic of his poetics he transforms the common into the mythic.

In the second section, the heart of the collection, is a seven-part poem, "The Bocce Court on Lewis Avenue," which recounts the history of his boyhood New York City neighborhood of Corona. In this poem Stefanile transcends the narrow confines of the Italian American ghetto and the usual nostalgic references to "Little Italys" by creating beautiful art out of common words, reminding us that heroic deeds can come from everyday actions. This poem, which follows life from the Great Depression era through World War II, is a mini-epic of working-class culture done up in the formal attire of high culture. This is Stefanile's genius. He can take experiences from his birth culture and translate them into the high art of American literati.

Fred L. Gardaphé

Bibliography

Stefanile, Felix. "The Culture of Descendants: Archeology and Ontology." In *Romance Languages Annual,* edited by Jeanette Beer, Charles Ganelin, and Anthony Julian Tamburri, 353–356. West Lafayette, IN: Purdue Research Foundation, 1993.

———. *The Dance at St. Gabriel's.* Brownsville, OR: Storyline Press, 1995.

———. *East River Nocturne.* New Rochelle, NY: Elizabeth Press, 1976.

———. *A Fig Tree in America.* New Rochelle, NY: Elizabeth Press, 1970.

———. *The Imagination of the Amateur.* New Rochelle, NY: Elizabeth Press, 1982.

———. *In That Far Country.* West Lafayette, IN: Sparrow Press, 1982.

———. *River Full of Craft.* New Orleans: The New Orleans Poetry Journal, 1956.

See also LITERATURE; POETRY

Stella, Antonio

See HEALTH MENACE AND THE ITALIAN IMMIGRANT

Stella, Frank (b. 1936)

Rated as a preeminent American artist since the 1970s, Frank Stella was born in Malden, Massachusetts, son of a medical doctor of Sicilian heritage. He studied at Phillips Academy with Patrick Morgan and at Princeton University with William Seitz and Stephen Greene. He was artist-in-residence at Dartmouth College (1993), lectured at Yale University and Cornell University (1965), and was an instructor at the University of Saskatchewan (1967) and Brandeis University (1968). In 1970, at age 33, he was the youngest painter ever to be given a retrospective by the Museum of Modern Art in New York.

Stella was a representative of the minimalist art movement, which made abstract art out of simple and geometric forms that continued the tradition of austere abstraction. Later in the 1970s he broke away from the hard-edged style of his earlier work and created sensuously colored mixed media reliefs. As a minimalist his simple paintings consisted of black chevrons from which nearly all content was eliminated. These "black paintings" were austere and monumental in design.

One of his earlier works, *Empress of India* (1965), which helped to establish him as a leading painter, contains four countervailing chevrons that are identical in size but different in coloration and relation to the whole. The powdered metallic paint produces an iridescent sheen. The dimensions of this unique painting are 6 feet 5 inches by 18 feet by 8 inches. It is part of the Museum of Modern Art collection.

His canvases are massive, full of geometric shapes, such as stripes of color outlined in white. He has also designed his paintings with arcs, zigzags, and various other shapes with structures revealing complex nuances to the eye. The colors on his canvases change subtly to the viewer's eyes, and the colors and shapes seem altered as they relate to each other. Such artistic creativity has won wide acclaim for this Italian American painter.

Stella's works are in the permanent collections of the Museum of Modern Art; Whitney Museum of American Art; Pasadena Art Museum; Walker Art Center in Minneapolis; Albright-Knox Gallery, Buffalo; Stedelijk Art Museum, Amsterdam; Art Institute of Chicago; Detroit Institute of Art; San Francisco Museum; and Los Angeles County Museum. He has had exhibitions at the Leo Castelli Gallery, New York; Galerie Lawrence, Paris; Fergus Gallery, Los Angeles; Kasmin, Ltd., London; David Mirvish Gallery, London; Pasadena Art Museum; Seattle Art Museum; Gallery of Modern Art, Washington; Museum of Modern Art; Corcoran; Philadelphia Museum of Art; Houston's Museum of Art; Virginia Museum of Fine Arts; and Walker Art Center.

This prolific artist is the recipient of numerous awards, among which are First Prize at the International Biennial Exhibition of Painting, Tokyo; Museum of Modern Art; Whitney Museum; Phillips Academy; and Princeton University. In 1983 Harvard University chose Stella to deliver six celebrated Charles Eliot Norton Lectures.

Frank J. Cavaioli

Bibliography

Axon, Richard H. *The Prints of Frank Stella: A Catalogue Raisonné, 1967–1982*. New York: Hudson Hills, 1983.

Rubin, Lawrence. *Frank Stella: Paintings, 1959–1965*. New York: Stewart, Tabori & Chang, 1986.

Rubin, William Stanley. *Frank Stella, 1970–1987*. New York: Museum of Modern Art, 1987.

See also ART

S

Stella, Joseph (1877–1946)

A leading painter of pastel and crayon drawings of miners and steel workers, Joseph Stella is best known for works that are inspired by cubist and futuristic motifs. Born on June 13, 1877, in Muro Lucano, a mountain village near Naples, he migrated to the United States in 1896 to join his brother Antonio, a physician, and other family members. Following a year each of medical and pharmacology education, he studied at the New York School of Art under William Merritt Chase (1898–1900). Much of his life was spent in lower Manhattan, although he did live in the Bronx and Brooklyn, where he taught Italian at Baptist Seminary in the Williamsburg section. He traveled extensively to Rome, Florence, and Paris, where he met major contemporary artists: Mancini, Matisse, Carra, Modigliani, Severini, Cucovini, and other avant artists.

Sensitive to his Italian roots, Stella's first drawing was published in the *Outlook* (1905) and it depicted immigrants at Ellis Island. In West Virginia he drew scenes of the Monongah mine disaster for *Survey* (1907). Two years later, his drawings of the mining environment in Pittsburgh appeared in *Survey*.

Stella earned a prominent reputation with his many exhibitions. He participated in the 1913 Armory Show and had a one-man exhibition at the Italian National Club in New York City. His exhibition of modern art included *Battle of Lights, Coney Island, Mardi Gras* (1913), a dazzling cubist painting that the public derided but won critical respect. The Bourgeois Galleries exhibited his first *Brooklyn Bridge* in a one-man show (1920). This work exemplifies his many depictions of New York City skylines and structures that were organized along the lines of precisionism. His monumental masterpiece,

The Voice of the City of New York Interpreted (1920–1922), consists of five paintings on oil and tempera: "the Port," "the White Way I," "the Skyscrapers," "the White Way II," and "the [Brooklyn] Bridge." In this breathtaking collection, Stella captures concepts of iconography, light, and motifs of the New York environment. Later, he exhibited twelve religious paintings in the International Exhibition of Religious Art in Rome (1934).

He began his career as a realist, turned to abstractionism, and finally to "lyric fantasy." Similar to the futurists, Stella sought to capture the dynamism of modern urban life. His later works were increasingly romantic, mystical, and symbolic.

Because of an illness, he moved to Astoria, New York, to live in an apartment near his nephew, where he died November 5, 1946. Joseph Stella's reputation and influence as an artist continued to grow after his death. In 1963 the Whitney Museum of American Art honored him with a retrospective. Cynthia Jaffe McCabe recognized the core focus of his life in *The Golden Door. Artists–Immigrants of America, 1876–1976* (1976).

Frank J. Cavaioli

Bibliography

Bauer, John I. H. *Joseph Stella*. New York: Praeger, 1971.

Jaffe, Irma B. *Joseph Stella*. Cambridge: Harvard University Press, 1988.

———. *Joseph Stella's Symbolism*. San Francisco: Pomegranate Artworks, 1994.

See also ART

Stereotypes

See LABELS AND STEREOTYPES

Stonecutters

See OCCUPATIONS, STONECUTTERS

Sturzo, Don Luigi (1871–1959)

Born in Caltagirone, Sicily, on November 26, 1871, and ordained in 1894, Catholic priest Don Luigi Sturzo was a noted Italian populist political leader who founded *Il Partito Populare* in 1919. He is considered not only the father of Christian Democracy in his home country but an important inspiration for the formation of other Christian Democratic parties in post–World War II Europe and Latin America. Sturzo's political activity should be seen as inextricably intertwined with his equally impressive accomplishments as a Catholic social theorist, sociologist, and social activist. Praising Giambattista Vico, Don Sturzo consciously affirmed the necessary connection between knowledge and action. He spent over twenty years in exile from Mussolini's fascist government, first in France, mostly in England and, from 1940 and 1946, in the United States. Characteristically, he used his years in exile well: organizing antifascist activities, constructing the blueprint for the reemergence of his political movement after the defeat of the Axis powers, and authoring numerous volumes on diverse subjects, including his evolutionary theory delineating the dynamic relationship between history, society, and personality. After the war he returned in triumph to Italy to see his former lieutenant, Alcide De Gasperi, lead the Christian Democratic Party to dominance in Italian politics. Sturzo settled in Rome, where he died on August 8, 1959.

After ordination, Sturzo quickly abandoned his mostly academic career as a seminary professor to champion the cause of the urban poor (first in Rome) and a neglected rural peasantry (initially in Sicily). This transformation was the result of several forces acting in concert. Most generally, the young priest was influenced by Pope Leo XIII's *Rerum Novarum* (1891). More specifically, he was exposed to the Christian vision of society as articulated by economist Giuseppe Toniolo. It was the pervasive social injustice around him, however, that energized Sturzo to convert Christian principles into concrete actions. Among other initiatives, the young priest created all types of cooperatives, associations, credit banks, unions, and newspapers intended to empower the otherwise disenfranchised. From 1905 to 1920, he served as mayor of his hometown.

The first singularly great achievement of Sturzo was the founding of his nonconfessional Catholic Populist Party that made both an immediate and significant impact. This achievement, however, presupposed the withdrawal by the papacy of its injunction against active Catholic participation in Italian political life, an injunction that represented the Catholic Church's inward response to the victorious forces of the Risorgimento. The attraction of *Il Partito Populare* to many Catholics, especially to the working classes, was that it provided an alternative to the then currently reigning options of an anticlerical liberalism, a violent and totalitarian Marxism and Fascism, or a clerical traditionalism. While some secular scholars see Sturzo as attempting to reconcile a medieval Catholicism with such modern ideas as democracy, citizenship, and individualism, Sturzo himself saw the latter ideals as products of the Catholic faith working itself out in history. The advent of Mussolini to power sealed Sturzo's fate by exile abroad in 1924 and led to the subsequent dissolution of *Il Partito Populare* by fascist decree.

Suffering from heart problems and seeing his home in London bombed by German aircraft, Sturzo left England for the United States in 1940. After a year-long period of hospitalization in Florida, he moved to a small house in Brooklyn's Bensonhurst community. His home became the base through which he launched a whirlwind of antifascist, pro-Christian democratic activities. These activities ranged from the constant receiving of visitors, to radio broadcasting and journalistic endeavors in the Italian language, to writing scholarly articles in such important Catholic vehicles as *Commonweal, Thought,* and the *Review of Politics,* to the authoring of major monographs. These activities were addressed not only to the Italian American and American Catholic communities but also to American government leaders who realized that the implementation of Sturzo's vision represented the best guarantee in preventing a Communist takeover in post–World War II Italy. Don Sturzo chronicled these multifaceted activities during the years 1943–1946 in his celebrated *La Mia Battaglia da New York* (1949). Even more importantly, during his American stay, he articulated his blueprint for a future Christian Democratic Italy in what many scholars consider his most important treatise, *Italy and the Coming World* (1945). As Sturzo stated, "[L]iberty and democracy must today be reviewed in the light of Christianity even by those who are without religious faith; they cannot but recognize the incoherence of modern society as founded on scientific materialism, or pragmatic positivism, or state, national, or racial pantheism. . . ."

The major thrust of a Sturzian sociology is both historistic and personalistic, stressing the dignity and creativity of the individual person. Sturzo's major sociological treatises include *Essai de Sociologie* (1935), *The Inner Laws of Society* (1944), *The True Life* (1947), and *Del Metodo Sociologico* (1949). Other important volumes in the large Sturzian corpus are his *Dall' Idea al Fatto* (1910), *Riforma Statale e Indirizzi Politici* (1923), *Italy and Fascismo* (1926), *The International Community and the Right of War* (1930), *Church and State* (1939), and *Les Guerres Modernes et La Pensée Catholique* (1942).

Joseph A. Varacalli

Bibliography

Amfitheatrof, Erik. *The Children of Columbus: An Informal History of the Italians in the New World.* Boston: Little, Brown, 1973.

Caponigri, A. Robert. "Don Luigi Sturzo." *The Review of Politics* 14 (1952): 147–165.

Murphy, Francis J. "Don Sturzo and the Triumph of Christian Democracy." *Italian Americana* 7 (1981): 89–98.

Pollock, Robert C. "Luigi Sturzo." *New Catholic Encyclopedia.* New York: McGraw-Hill 13 (1967): 749–750.

Sturzo, Don Luigi. *Italy and the Coming World.* New York: Roy Publishers, 1945.

Timasheff, Nicholas. "Don Luigi Sturzo's Contribution to Sociological Theory." *The American Catholic Sociological Review* 22 (1961): 11–34.

Successors to the Italian Newspaper

Italian immigrants eventually became involved in or helped influence the publication of various journals, magazines, and newsletters. Unlike mainstream newspapers, which appealed to a broader readership and thus maintained a larger base of support, issuing Italian American publications entailed risks and uncertainty, and, indeed, most of the efforts in this direction were short-lived. Nevertheless, one of the earliest mediums Italians embraced was the journal, though sometimes distinctions between newspapers, journals, and magazines were somewhat blurred in nineteenth-century publishing. The earliest of these newspaper-journal type publications was *El Correro Atlantico,* which appeared in New Orleans in 1836. Though several others also made their appearances soon after, most never survived for any length of time.

An exception for longevity has been the New York City–based *La Follia di New York*. Founded by two brothers, Alessandro (also known by the pseudonym Riccardo Cordiferro) and Marziale Sisca in 1892, the journal sought to be both literary and popular, appealing to the readers' nostalgia for the homeland, while encouraging readers to assimilate into the mainstream of American life. Its masthead exclaimed: "Satirico, Politica e Literario"; thus, it also drew in the immigrant's passion for the politics of the period.

In 1908 in Chicago, a newspaper was published that would eventually turn into a bimonthly magazine, *La Parola del Popolo*. Its intention was not literary, but rather emphasized labor and *dei Socialisti*, as the original name stated on its first masthead. Indeed, the magazine's founder and first editor was the Trieste-born Giuseppe Bertelli, who a few years earlier had edited *Il Proletario*, the official organ of the Autonomous Italian Socialist Federation in Philadelphia. *La Parola del Popolo*, under the leadership of E. Clemente, published continuously into the last quarter of the twentieth century. *Il Carroccio*, appearing in 1915, was a literary journal with a fascist political stance. It lasted until 1935. The *Vigo Review* was an example of a journal of the 1930s that proclaimed to be an American journal of Italian life and achievements.

In the 1970s to the early 1990s, other literary and cultural journals appeared, for example, *Italian Americana* and *VIA*. They stressed history, literature, and art, and though the language was now English, on occasion an article in Italian appeared. *Italian Americana* was temporarily discontinued, but through the support of Joseph DeAngelis, speaker of the Rhode Island House, it has resumed publication. Journals that do not deal exclusively with Italian Americans, such as the *International Migration Review*, founded in 1964, and *Migration Today*, founded in 1973, have carried articles on Italian Americans. These two publications are published under the auspices of the Center for Migration Studies, a research institution established by the Scalabrini Order, a religious order founded in the late nineteenth century to help Italian immigrants adjust to their new environment.

In the late 1960s and early 1970s, a number of Italian American magazines appeared that aimed at appealing to a wider readership. *Divigando, I AM, Identity, Red White Green*

Sample of Italian American newspapers. Early in the twentieth century hundreds of Italian language newspapers of various ideological and political viewpoints could be found in every Italian American community. Courtesy Salvatore J. LaGumina.

Magazine, *L' Italiano,* and *Attenzione* were among these, but all were relatively short-lived, though *Attenzione* achieved a circulation of one hundred thousand or more. These magazines carried articles on famous Italian Americans, business enterprises, travel, food, and other items of general interest. At the same time throughout the twentieth century, several religious magazines appeared that were founded by Catholic religious orders. In 1983 the Italian-published magazine *Italy, Italy* appeared in an English edition and soon became popular in the United States. In 1995 *Mondo Italiano,* a bilingual magazine published in England and dealing with contemporary Italian life, began distribution in the United States.

With the beginnings of professional organizations, especially in the mid-twentieth century, specialty journals appeared. Among these were *Italica,* "The Journal of the American Association of Teachers of Italian," which began publication in 1924; the *Justinian Law Journal* (1965), issued by the Italian American Association of Lawyers and Jurists; and the *American Italian Historical Association Proceedings,* which appeared in 1968 soon after the organization had been founded. Other specialty journals include *Arba Sicula,* established in New York City in 1979 to advance the cause of Sicilian language and culture; *Italian Quarterly,* issued by the Department of Italian at Rutgers University in 1979; *Forum Italicum,* a bilingual quarterly founded in 1967; and *The Italian American Review,* a semiannual commentary on Italian American achievement, founded in 1992.

Newsletters issued by cultural or professional groups with a limited membership base also came into existence, for example, *Tradizioni,* published by the Italian Folk Art Federation of America, the *Italian Heritage Newsletter,* and the newsletter of the American Italian Cultural Roundtable, founded in 1984 in New York City. Of wider appeal was the newsletter of the America-Italy Society founded in 1949, also in New York City. Other cultural organizations in different parts of the country issued newsletters with varying degrees of success, such as the Connecticut Italian American Cultural Association, founded in 1978, the Dante Alighieri Society of the State of Washington, founded before World War I, and the Italian Heritage Society of Loretto, Pennsylvania, founded in 1974. Social and fraternal organizations such as the Sons of Italy, founded in 1905, and UNICO, established in 1922, also joined in publishing local chapter newsletters.

A random sampling of other publications include the Stone Park, Illinois, Italian Cultural newsletter, begun in 1974; the National Italian American Foundation newsletter, begun in 1978 and later published in magazine format with the title *Ambassador;* the NOIAW newsletter, begun in 1983 by the National Organization of Italian American Women; and the "Forum," begun in 1987 by the Association of Ligurians in the World, New York, chapter. Though not as numerous, Italian Americans in a number of business enterprises also joined together to issue newsletters. As early as 1907 the *Bulletin of Italian Chamber of Commerce of Chicago* made its debut, and in 1936 the *Italian Bakers Review.* In some cases, professional groups such as the American Italian Historical Association also issued newsletters nationally and at the chapter level. Moreover, virtually every Italian parish issued a weekly or monthly newsletter, often from their earliest foundations. In many instances these were written in Italian as well as in English.

Data gathered in 1980 indicated that at the turn of the century, when Italian immigrants were coming to America in increasing numbers, Italians were issuing about thirty-five periodicals. The same research indicated that at the close of the 1970s at least eighteen journals and magazines and approximately fifty newsletters were being issued. Though many Italian American publications did not always last, their input was of inestimable value in several ways. They encouraged a cohesiveness among a people in a new land, and they informed readers of contributions made by their countrymen in America. These publications provided a vehicle for literary, artistic, and notable achievement, inspiring and sustaining Italians to adapt to their American environment.

Nicholas Joseph Falco

Bibliography

Briani, Vittorio. *La Stampa Italiana All'Estero Dalla Origini Ai Nostri Giorni.* Rome: Instituto Poligrafico Dello Stato, 1977.

Russo, Pietro. *Catalogo Collettivo Della Stampa Periodica Italo-Americana, (1836–1980).* Rome: Centro Studi Emigrazione, 1983.

Tomasi, Silvano M. *National Directory of Research Centers, Repositories and Organizations of Italian Culture in the United States.* Torino, Italy: Fondazione Giovanni Agnelli, 1980.

Wynar, Lubomyr, and Anna T. Wynar. *Encyclopedic Directory of Ethnic Newspapers and Periodicals in the United States.* 2nd ed. Littleton, CO: Libraries Unlimited, 1976.

See also PRESS, ITALIAN AMERICAN

T

Talese, Gay (b. 1932)

Author and founder of the "New Journalism," Gay Talese is one of the most widely read Italian American writers of the twentieth century.

His latest book, *Unto the Sons* (1992), is the most autobiographical of his eight books, and most concerned with Italian American culture. It chronicles his father's migration from the Calabrian village of Maida in 1920 and his quest for success in America, placing the immigrant saga in context of the Talese family history and the history of southern Italy. *Unto the Sons* also relates Talese's own experiences to 1944, shortly before he began contributing articles to his hometown newspaper, the *Ocean City Sentinel,* in New Jersey. After high school, Talese attended the University of Alabama, where he majored in journalism and wrote a sports column for the campus newspaper. Upon graduation in 1953, Talese entered the United States Army. While on furlough, he visited his father's native village and was inspired to begin a novel about the elder Talese's journey to America, a novel he ultimately put aside. In 1955 he went to work, first as a copy boy, then a reporter, at the *New York Times.*

When he began freelancing his work, an editor wary of anti-Italian prejudice advised him to publish under the pseudonym Hyman Goldberg. Before long, though, Talese had established his own name as a journalistic pioneer. Early articles reflect his signal approach; in them, he applies techniques of fiction—invention of dialogue, elaboration of scene, and unexpected, shifting points of view—that he admired in the work of writers such as John O'Hara and Irwin Shaw. Talese's application of these techniques established the New Journalism. His pieces "The Loser" (1962) and "Frank Sinatra Has a Cold" (1965), both published in *Esquire,* are classics of the genre.

Talese's first book, *New York: A Serendipiter's Journey* (1961), collected a number of his articles from the *Times* and was well received by critics. His second book, *The Bridge* (1964), an account of workers who built the Verrazano-Narrows Bridge, appeared in 1965. That same year, Talese left the *Times* to concentrate on books and freelance articles. By 1971 he had published two critically acclaimed best-sellers, both bearing the author's trademark biblical titles: *The Kingdom and the Power* (1969), a critical history of the *New York Times,* and *Honor Thy Father* (1971). For six years, he conducted characteristically exhaustive research for *Honor Thy Father,* the story of crime boss Joseph Bonanno and his son Bill; during this period, he recorded intimate details of mobsters' business and private lives. The fruit of his efforts is a complex, humane portrait of mafiosi men and women. Talese's next book, *Thy Neighbor's Wife* (1980), examines America's changing sexual mores. In the wake of media speculation about the book and his involvement with its subject, Talese returned to a less sensational project: his father's story and the familiar theme of father-son conflict in *Unto the Sons.*

Recently, Talese has published several articles on Italian American culture, including the 1993 essay in the *New York Times Book Review* "Where Are the Italian-American Novelists?" He continues writing and speaking on Italian American issues.

George Guida

Bibliography

Eason, David L. "New Journalism, Metaphor and Culture." *Journal of Popular Culture* 15, no. 4 (1982): 142–149.

Lounsberry, Barbara. "Gay Talese's Fathers and Sons." In *The Art of Fact: Contemporary Artists of Nonfiction*. New York: Greenwood, 1990.

Murray, William. "Honor His Father." *New York Times Book Review,* 9 February 1992, 3, 25.

Talese, Gay. *Unto the Sons*. New York: Alfred A. Knopf, 1992.

See also LITERATURE

Taliaferro Family

This prominent Italian family migrated to the American South by way of England. Richard Taliaferro, who died March 15, 1781, was a freeholder in James City County, Virginia, and was elected a member of the Committee to enforce the Continental Association (devoted to prohibiting British imports). Serving as a colonel with Patriot forces during the War for American Revolutionary War, he fell mortally wounded on March 15, 1781 at the Battle of Guilford Hall. His name is inscribed, with others killed that day, at Guilford Courthouse, Greensboro, North Carolina.

Benjamin Taliaferro (1754–1821) served as a Revolutionary War officer under General Daniel Morgan and was with General George Washington in the November 1776 New Jersey campaign. He served in the Georgia state legislature, as a delegate to the Georgia State Constitutional Convention, as a judge of the superior court, and from 1799 to 1802 as a member of the United States House of Representatives. He was a trustee of Franklin College, now the University of Georgia.

While serving as a captain in the second Virginia Detachment Continental Line, he authored a valuable orderly book that he kept during the siege of Charleston, South Carolina, in 1780, which has served as a valuable for military historians. Taliaferro was born to Zachariah Taliaferro and Mary Boutwell in Albermarle County, Virginia. His father was a ship's captain, justice, and sheriff, and was a member of the local Committee of Safety during the Revolutionary War.

Commissioned a second lieutenant in 1776 in Captain Samuel Jordan Cabell's Seventh Company of the Sixth Virginia Regiment of Foot, Benjamin rose quickly to the rank of captain when his unit was bloodied in fierce combat in New York and New Jersey.

Returning home to Amherst County, Virginia, Taliaferro married Martha Meriwether, his brother Zachariah's fiancée, causing bad feelings that the two brothers never overcame. Zachariah, an attorney, left Virginia for Pendleton, South Carolina, where he married and had four children. Benjamin also left Virginia and settled in Wilkes County, Georgia. As a superior court judge, he bravely opposed land speculators at every turn, even to the point of wounding one of them, a Colonel Willis, in a duel. Four years after he died in 1821, a county was named in his honor. Benjamin Taliaferro had ten children by his first wife, and one by his second.

Nicholas Taliaferro (1757–1812), Revolutionary War officer, served as a second lieutenant with the Sixth Virginia, Second Virginia detachment. Taken prisoner by the British at the siege of Charleston, Taliaferro was later exchanged and promoted to first lieutenant. He fought again at Yorktown. Retiring from the service in 1783, Taliaferro went west to Kentucky, where he died in 1812.

Lawrence Taliaferro (1794–1871) was a respected Indian agent known affectionately by Native Americans as the "Iron Cutter." He was so named because of his integrity and protection of the tribes against corruptionists, especially those representing the American Fur Company near Fort Snelling at what is today the mouth of the Minnesota River. Taliaferro was born of James Garnett and Wilhelmina Taliaferro at Whitehall in King George County, Virginia. He joined a volunteer company of light infantry during the War of 1812 and attained the rank of first lieutenant by the war's end. His military service at frontier posts enabled him to win appointment as an Indian agent by President James Monroe in 1819. In that office he was so successful at keeping the peace and safeguarding the interests of the Native Americans that he was reappointed six times, despite intense opposition from the American Fur Company. Leaving Indian country in 1839, Taliaferro retired to Bedford, Pennsylvania, the hometown of his wife, Eliza Dillon. He served again with the quartermaster department of the army in 1857 at San Antonio; Fort Leavenworth; and Bedford, Pennsylvania. A slaveholder before the Civil War, Taliaferro converted to a stalwart Unionist when war broke out. In Bedford, Taliaferro was a Mason and deacon in the local Presbyterian church.

William Booth Taliaferro (1822–1898) served as a colonel and brigadier general in the Confederate States Army. A graduate of William and Mary College and a Harvard law student, Taliaferro won distinction early in his military career while serving as a captain of infantry in Mexico. After several years of activity in Virginia politics, in 1856 he became a Buchanan presidential elector. Taliaferro was at Harpers Ferry in November 1859 as a militia officer, after the failure of John Brown's Raid. Later, serving under General Stonewall Jackson during the Valley Campaign, he impressed Jackson and was rewarded with great military responsibilities, despite the general's strong disagreements with Taliaferro over certain military matters. Taliaferro received serious wounds at the Battle of Groveton but continued his distinguished career as a commander at Fredericksburg. He finally suffered the humiliation of having to surrender to the Union Army during combat in eastern Florida and Savannah with General Joseph E. Johnson in April 1865. Taliaferro married Sally N. Lyons of Richmond, Virginia, in 1853, and they had eight children. A tall Virginia gentleman in the "Old Dominion" tradition of Washington and Lee, Taliaferro spent his final years as Grand Master of the Virginia Masonic Order and as a Gloucester County judge and farmer-lawyer. He was for many years a member of the board of visitors of the College of William and Mary and the Virginia Military Institute.

Donald J. D'Elia

Bibliography

Schiavo, Giovanni. *Four Centuries of Italian-American History.* New York: Center for Migration Studies, 1993.

Wallace, Lee A. Jr., ed. *The Orderly Book of Captain Benjamin Taliaferro.* Richmond: Virginia State Library, 1980.

Television

Italian Americans have had a profound impact on the development of television. Many shows have been named after and built around memorable and equally forgettable Italian American characters, while others have portrayed Italian Americans in secondary and sometimes demeaning roles. Additionally, television program schedules have featured the names of famous Italian American actors, singers, and comedians, some with their own shows, others as regular guest performers. Some of these talents seemed out of their element appearing on television, notably boxing champion Rocky Graziano, who cohosted the *Henny and Rocky Show* and had a stint as a regular on *The Martha Raye Show,* or opera singer Ezio Pinza, who played the title role in NBC's *Bonino* in 1953.

The depiction of Italian Americans on television has been the subject of many controversies. In the earliest days of the medium, television followed film and stage in identifying Italians as the criminal element. A study of daytime serials done by Dallas Smythe in 1951–1953 found that only 44 percent of all Italians portrayed were shown as law abiding. Smythe noted that no other minority/foreign group had been singled out like that. Perhaps one of the shows that brought the loudest outcries from the Italian American community was *The Untouchables,* which aired from 1959 to 1963 on ABC. Originally a two-part series on the *Westinghouse Desilu Playhouse,* the popular program about Chicago's underworld during the Prohibition era featured many gangsters with Italian names.

By the 1970s the situation supposedly had changed as television executives increasingly employed an inoffensive criterion in structuring programs, leading to what some critics cited were unrealistic portrayals. Frank Mankiewicz and Joel Swerdlow, in their book *Remote Control* (1978), wrote, "It is well known that many members and particularly leaders of organized crime have Italian names. . . . But on those television shows that portray organized crime, nobody has an Italian name except the occasional policeman." A 1980–1981 survey of 263 prime time episodes, conducted by Robert and Linda Lichter, revealed that Italian Americans did not fare well on television despite the network's newly instituted politically correct policy. The Lichters reported that Italian Americans were either gangsters or gagsters on the small screen, either villains or "lovable or laughable dimwits who worked in jobs that offered little pay and less prestige." Among their major findings were negative portrayals of Italian Americans outnumbered positive ones by two to one;

most Italian Americans could not speak proper English; one in six engaged in criminal activities; and only one in seven worked as an executive, manager, or professional.

Throughout the 1970s there was a spate of detective shows that carried Latin-sounding, most likely Italian, names. One of the most popular was *Columbo,* carried by NBC from 1971 to 1977; it was probably the object of Mankiewicz and Swerdlow's reference to "slow-witted, but keen-eyed and remorseless Italian American detectives." Other shows, mostly of the police/detective genre, that carried seemingly Italian names were *Johnny Staccato* (1959–1960, NBC), starring John Cassavetes as a modern jazz pianist who also fought crime; *Toma* (1973–1974, ABC), with Tony Musante as David Toma; *Calucci's Department* (1973, CBS); *Baretta* (1975–1978, ABC); *Petrocelli* (1974–1976, NBC); *The Montefuscos* (1975, NBC); *Bert D'Angelo/Superstar* (1976, ABC); *Sirota's Court* (1976–1977, NBC); *Serpico* (1976–1977, NBC); *Rosetti and Ryan* (1977, NBC); and *Mrs. Columbo* (1979, NBC).

Italian American characters have popped up in countless situation comedies and dramas. One of the earliest programs was *Life with Luigi* (1952–1953, CBS), which dealt with a big city Italian immigrant and his Old World ties. J. Carrol Naish played Luigi Basco. In the 1970s the main character on the glorified tribute to the 1950s *Happy Days* was the "cool" Arthur "Fonzie" Fonzarelli, who hung out occasionally with his cousin, Chachi Arcola, at Alfred "Big Al" Delvecchio's soda fountain. Delvecchio was played by Al Molinaro, who added to his fame with the role of Murray the Cop in the 1970s series *The Odd Couple*. A *Happy Days* spinoff, *Laverne and Shirley* (1976–1983, ABC), starred Penny Marshall as Milwaukee brewery worker Laverne Di Fazio; a number of episodes featured her father, Frank. About the same time, John Travolta portrayed Vinnie Barbarino, one of the academic misfit "Sweathogs" in *Welcome Back, Kotter* (1975–1979, ABC); Richard Castellano played Joe Vitale, an Italian American widower, in *Joe and Sons* (1975–1976, CBS); and Bonnie Franklin was Ann Romano in *One Day at a Time* (1975–1984), a Norman Lear story of a divorced career woman trying to raise two teenage daughters. Valerie Bertinelli played the younger daughter, Barbara.

At the beginning of the 1980s, other Italian American characters appeared, such as the dedicated police captain Frank Furillo on *Hill Street Blues,* played by Daniel Travanti; the aggressive reporter Joe Rossi on *Lou Grant;* and numerous individuals on *The Gangster Chronicles. Taxi* (1978–1983, ABC, NBC) also featured Italian American characters, the most ubiquitous being the cynical dispatcher at the Sunshine Cab Company, Louie Di Palma, played by Danny DeVito. Tony Danza's long career in television sitcoms also got its boost on *Taxi,* where he played the part-time boxer Tony Banta. Besides DeVito and Danza, other Italian Americans whose big break can be credited to television shows are Joe Piscopo, *Saturday Night Live;* Brenda Vaccaro, a guest appearance on *The Greatest Show on Earth* in the early 1960s, and later, *Sara;* Danny Bonaduce, *The Partridge Family;* and Susan Sarandon, *Search for Tomorrow* and other drama specials. Perry Como, Liberace, Jimmy Durante, and Ernest Borgnine, all of whom had careers in other fields of entertainment with varying degrees of success, owed great debts to television.

One of thirteen children, Pierino Roland Como was born in western Pennsylvania in 1912. An enterprising lad, he opened his own barber shop when he was 14. His singing career began with the Freddy Carlone Band; later, he joined the Ted Weems Band, and by the late 1940s, was featured on NBC radio's "Chesterfield Supper Club." On December 24, 1948, he was given an unprecedented twelve-year contract with NBC TV and Kraft Foods; his show lasted until June 12, 1963. Como's recent election to the Television Hall of Fame is testimony that the small screen was his chief medium.

Certainly responsible in no small measure for advancing television's golden era was pianist Wladziu Valentino Liberace, whose candelabrum, bejeweled clothing, toothy smile, and blond locks made him one of the most watched performers of the 1950s and 1960s. His weekly television audience exceeded 35 million. *The Liberace Show,* which began in 1951 on KLAC TV in Los Angeles, was nationally syndicated on February 13, 1953. With some lapse time, it ran until September 16, 1969. By the time of his death in 1987, Liberace's records sold more than 60 million copies, and credit was given to him for influencing rock stars of the 1970s and 1980s through his use of innovative lighting and sound techniques, props, and costumes.

Jimmy Durante had also been around for a considerable time, performing in vaudeville, nightclubs, Broadway, movies, and radio, before debuting on NBC's *Four Star Review* in 1950. Even then, he did not have his own show per se, as he alternated with three other performers as host. On October 2, 1954, *The Jimmy Durante Show* was telecast as a separate entity on NBC; it shifted to CBS, where the show ended in 1957. Durante was born in New York's Lower East Side in 1893. His father, Bartolomeo Durante, was a native of Salerno, Italy. Durante spent much of his career, including some television, as part of a vaudeville act with Lou Clayton and Eddie Jackson. His television skits often called attention to his outsized nose ("Schnozzola"), his gravel voice, fractured English, and theme song, "Inka Dinka Doo." His sign-off was one of the best remembered and most curious in television: "Goodnight, Mrs. Calabash, wherever you are."

Ernest Borgnine, born Ermes Effron Borgnino in Hamden, Connecticut, in 1917, spent the first ten years of his adulthood in the United States Navy. After leaving the military, he performed on stage before becoming one of the stalwarts of early television drama. In 1955 he won a best actor Oscar for his role in *Marty*, the story of a gentle, lovelorn butcher. A versatile actor, Borgnine befuddled Hollywood directors who could not decide what type of role best suited him. He made up their minds for them by returning to television and a role he was at home in, the commander in *McHale's Navy* (1962–1965).

Besides those already mentioned, other musical variety shows starred Italian Americans such as Frank Sinatra, Tony Bennett, Julius La Rosa, Dean Martin, and Sonny Bono. Sinatra's first television series came after his phenomenal radio, recording, concert, and film stardom of the 1940s, and during the lowest part of his career in the early 1950s. ABC's strategy for *The Frank Sinatra Show* was to put it opposite the Saturday night hit, NBC's *Your Show of Shows*, during the 1950–1951 season and *Texaco Star Theater* the following year. The tactic backfired and when the show ended April 1, 1952, Sinatra vowed that he would never do another weekly television series. However, he changed his mind and *The Frank Sinatra Show* re-commenced on October 18, 1957, lasting eight months.

Son of a Queens tailor, Tony Bennett (Anthony D. Benedetto) was born in 1926 into a loving family. Besides his concert and recording work, he performed consistently on all the television variety and talk shows, including the very first Johnny Carson *Tonight Show*.

Singer Julius La Rosa carved out a niche in television on the *Arthur Godfrey Show* in 1953–1954; his firing by Godfrey was tabloid fodder for weeks. La Rosa appeared as a guest on other television shows before doing, in 1954, the first of three musical variety programs he would host over the years.

Another headline-grabbing split up of the period led to *The Dean Martin Show* (1965–1974, NBC). Martin, who had teamed with Jerry Lewis in a number of popular slapstick movies, created a new persona built around a casual approach with booze, cigarettes, and the curvaceous "Golddiggers" always at hand. One of his regular guests was Dom DeLuise, who had his own show, *Lotsa Luck,* on NBC in 1973–1974. *The Sonny and Cher Comedy Hour* was a top draw from August 1971 to May 1974, when Cher began to advance her career primarily in movies, and Sonny eventually went into politics.

Italian Americans played other key roles in the history of television. Guy Lombardo and his "Royal Canadians" helped an entire generation usher in each New Year. He also hosted his own show on CBS for three months, *Guy Lombardo's Diamond Jubilee*. Peter Gennaro topped the list of television choreographers, working with big names such as Perry Como, Andy Williams, Judy Garland, and Bing Crosby; Joe Barbera and his partner, Bill Hanna, created television's first prime-time animation series, *The Flintstones,* which had an astonishing six-year run in the 1960s, and Canadian-born Paul Anka, a popular singer from age 14, wrote one of the best-known themes ever done for television: Johnny Carson's *Tonight Show*.

The person who dominated music composition for the movies and television, however, was Enrico Nicola (Henry) Mancini. Born in Cleveland, Ohio, in 1924, Mancini was given a shove into music early on by his steelworker father, who loved music. After serving in the infantry in World War II, and playing in the Glenn Miller Band, Mancini began to score and write songs for movies in the 1950s. His credits were on dozens of movies, including *Breakfast at Tiffany's, The Pink Panther,* and *Days of Wine and Roses;* overall, he received seventeen Oscar nominations. His first big break, however, was in television, when Blake Edwards asked him to write the score for the detective series *Peter Gunn,* and Mancini obliged with a provocative jazz theme.

Liza Minnelli, daughter of film director Vincente Minnelli and actress/singer Judy Garland, added to her stage, concert, and film success with numerous television appearances, including her Grammy-winning special of 1972, *Liza with a Z.* Multimedia performer Don Ameche (Dominic Felix Amici) also was seen regularly on television. Joseph Campanella had a number of television roles, commencing when he was added to the cast of CBS's *The Nurses* (which later became *The Doctors and the Nurses*). He was Mannix's boss in the 1967 show by that name, and starred in *The Lawyers* (1969–1973, NBC), along with James Farentino.

Obviously, it is impossible to list every Italian American who contributed to the advancement of television. There are numerous others who are mainstays of the medium. Today, they work in a different climate as many shows feature homogenized characters almost devoid of nationality; and singers and comedians are not apt to call attention to their ethnicity as they did at an earlier time. It is clear, however, that a greater sensitivity has evolved in the depiction of Italian Americans in television.

John A. Lent (Zinghini)

Bibliography

Corte, Robert. *They Made It in America.* New York: William Morrow, 1993.

Fans, Jocelyn. *Liberace: A Bio-Bibliography.* Westport, CT: Greenwood, 1995.

Greenfield, Jeff. *Television: The First Fifty Years.* New York: Crescent, 1981.

Lichter, S. Robert, and Linda Lichter. *Italian American Characters in Television Entertainment.* West Hempstead, NY: OSIA Commission for Social Justice, 1982.

Mankiewicz, Frank, and Joel Swerdlow. *Remote Control: Television and the Manipulation of American Life.* New York: Times Books, 1978.

See also COMEDY; COMO, PERRY; DURANTE, JIMMY; LIBERACE; MARTIN, DEAN; POP SINGERS; SINATRA, FRANCIS ALBERT

Terra, Daniel J. (1912–1996)

Born in Philadelphia in 1912, Daniel J. Terra was the son and grandson of lithographers who immigrated from Italy to the United States. His mother, Mary DeLuca, was a dancer. Daniel grew up and received his education in Philadelphia. In 1931 he received a bachelor's degree from Pennsylvania State University. Continuing in the craft of his forebears, Terra moved to the Midwest at a time when that geographic area was the printing center of the nation. After gaining several years of experience, he borrowed $2,500 and founded the Lawter Chemicals International Company, a printing/chemical enterprise. There he developed a revolutionary process to reduce the time required to print magazines from the previous process of twenty-five days to twenty-four hours. This made possible the publication of *Life* magazine in 1936, the first photojournalistic periodical in history.

Terra's success helped propel Lawter Chemicals International into one of the foremost firms in the field. His fortune (estimated at 790 million dollars in 1995) grew impressively and enabled him to achieve the rank of 138th among the four hundred richest Americans. Because of his success in raising funds for the Republican Party in the 1980 presidential election of Ronald Reagan, he was appointed ambassador-at-large for cultural affairs—the first and only such post in U.S. history.

Terra's marriage to Adeline Evans Richards, a woman with an art history degree, opened a new avenue of interest that was to remain with him throughout his life. He and his wife became avid art collectors, interested especially in American paintings largely by late-nineteenth- and early-twentieth-century artists. Among the important paintings in their collection are works by Samuel F. B. Morse, Mary Cassatt, and John Lafarge. In 1987 Terra opened the Terra Museum of American Art in Chicago. In 1992 he also opened an art museum in Giverny, France, which features American impressionist artists.

After the death of his first wife in 1982, he remarried. He died in June 1996 due to complications following a heart attack and was survived by his second wife, a son, stepson, and stepdaughter.

Salvatore J. LaGumina

Bibliography

"Canada's Threat to Donations." Art News 92 (January 1993): 30.

"Chicago: Problems at the Terra." Art News 89 (January 1990): 59–62.

See also BUSINESS AND ENTREPRENEURSHIP

Tesoro, Guiliana C. (b. 1921)

Internationally recognized as an expert on the science and technology of polymers, Guiliana C. Tesoro holds more than one hundred patents in fields that affect the strength, durability, and color qualities of textiles. Her research has involved synthesis of pharmaceuticals, textiles, chemicals, chemical modifications of fibers, and polymer flammability and flame retardants.

Tesoro received her Ph.D. degree in organic chemistry from Yale University in 1943. Following graduation she worked for several textile firms. In 1969 she became a senior chemist for Burlington Industries and was appointed director of chemical research in 1971. Since 1982 Tesoro has been a research professor at Polytechnic Institute.

Joanna Bevacqua

Bibliography

Bailey, Marthe J. *American Women in Science.* Denver: ABC-Clio, 1994.

Herzenberg, Caroline L., ed. *Women Scientists from Antiquity to the Present.* West Cornwall, CT: Locust Hill Press, 1986.

See also SCIENCE; WOMEN IN THE WORKFORCE

Texas

Italians who came to Texas during the seventeenth, eighteenth, and early nineteenth centuries were mainly explorers, missionaries, and adventurers. Those who chose Texas as their home before the American Civil War came from the north of Italy, and they settled in the southern or southeastern part of the state. There were forty-one Italian-born immigrants living in Texas in 1850 and sixty-seven ten years later, including Charles Angelo Siringo (1855–1928), the Italian cowboy, and John B. (Giovanni Battista) Costa, an attorney born in Italy in 1807 who settled in Austin.

Italians began arriving in the Lower Brazos Valley in the 1870s and Thurber in the 1880s. By the time of World War I, their numbers had increased to nearly fifteen thousand, most of whom were born in western Sicily and southern Calabria, and they settled primarily in the eastern part of the Lone Star state. The immigrants' goal was to provide a higher standard of living for themselves and their families.

A few Italian men provided the initial direction of the migration, and other pioneers acted upon their advice. Railroad and steamship advertisements and notices published in the Italian press supplemented letters and word of mouth information. Most Italians worked as farmers, railroad hands, and miners. The immigration to Texas was part of a movement of Italians to the vast expanses of the West and South region; and many others also settled in and around New Orleans and the Gulf Coast, forming one of the principal centers for Italian immigrants. Seventy-eight percent of the Italians who moved to the United States before 1910 were young males between the ages of twenty and thirty-four. The elderly, destitute, fainthearted, lazy, or feeble usually remained behind.

They moved to cities such as Dallas, Houston, San Antonio, and El Paso, where they opened retail grocery, confectionery, and fruit stores, shoe shops and restaurants. Salvatore (Sam) Lucchese, for example, who was born in Sicily in 1866, migrated to San Antonio, and in 1883 established the famous Lucchese Boot Company in San Antonio. Fossatti's Restaurant and Delicatessen, founded in 1882 by Frank Fossatti, an immigrant from Brescia, is the oldest business in Victoria. Joe Grasso, who was born in Sicily in 1883, settled in Galveston, where he developed a successful shrimp business that was eventually sold after his son died in 1975. Louis Cobolini (1845–1928), who was born in Trieste, is credited with developing the ports of Corpus Christi, Rockport, and Brownsville. The children of Italian immigrants also became physicians, attorneys, engineers, and teachers.

They fought in all the major Texan and American wars. Prospero Bernardi fought with the Texans at the Battle of San Jacinto in 1836 during the Texan War for Independence.

He is listed in Sam Houston Dixon's *The Heroes of San Jacinto* (1932). A large bust of Bernardi stands in front of the Texas Hall of State, Fair Park, in Dallas.

There are three reasons why Italians succeeded in commerce in Texas. First, many northern Italians were businessmen who came to Texas for the purpose of establishing capitalistic enterprises. Second, most of the immigrants had spent a few years in other parts of Texas or other states before moving to Texas, and they possessed language and business skills superior to those of newly arrived immigrants. Third, Italians shared a culture and social organization that provided for the welfare of the Italian community. These groups and customs helped to contribute to the emotional, financial, and social support necessary to make the transition from indigent immigrants to successful Americans. They continued the folk traditions of the old country.

Five basic factors formed the backbone of Italian Texan culture: membership in the Catholic Church; a belief in the importance of the family; the social context in which Italian food was prepared, served, and eaten; the Italian language press; and benevolent-fraternal organizations.

Italians who moved to Texas were very religious people. Most of them believed in Catholicism with its emphasis on the hierarchy, the sacraments, and elaborate rituals. In 1845 the Reverend Bartholomew Rollando was the first Italian-born missionary to come to Texas. Father Augustine D'Asti, who was born in Piedmont, was pastor of St. Vincent's Catholic Church in Houston during the Civil War. Jesuit priest Carlos M. Pinto (1841–1919), born in Salerno, helped build six parish churches and three parochial schools in El Paso. And Jesuit priest Carmelo Tranchese, Italian-born, served the spiritual and economic needs of his parishioners, mostly Mexican, during the Great Depression. Also, in 1929, Italian Protestants in Galveston formed the Valdese Presbyterian Church. The Reverend Arturo D'Albergo tended to their spiritual needs until 1943, when its membership was absorbed into the First Presbyterian Church in Galveston.

The family unit was the most important institution. Southern Italians recognized a restricted network of relevant kin. Family units were strong, and divorce was virtually unknown. Italians formed organizations, an adaptation of *comparaggio* (godparentage), and members became part of a quasi-extended family. Participants felt a "consciousness of kind" that allowed them to easily confront the stress associated with moving to a new environment. They formed such organizations as UNICO, American Committee on Italian Migration, Christopher Columbus Italian Society, cultural associations, and mutual benefit societies. Adam E. Janelli, born in Parma, brought the Salvation Army to Texas in 1889.

To Italians, food is the symbol of life, of all that is good and nourishing. The social context in which meals are prepared, served, and eaten has been central to their lives. In the Italian immigrant communities of Texas, food, family, and religion merged during the feast of St. Joseph on March 19 of every year. Wine usually accompanied their meals, and a Texas wine industry developed: the Val Verde Winery at Del Rio has been in continuous operation since Francesco and Mary Qualia (from Milan) established it in 1883.

Italian artists have influenced important aspects of high culture in Texas. Some, such as Louis Amateis (1855–1913), Enrico Cerracchio (1880–1956), and Pompeo Coppini (1870–1957), have sculpted state monuments. Architect-brothers Oscar Ruffini (1858–1957) and Frederick Ruffini (1851–1885) produced works of innovative style and design. They were also painters. Italian-born (Florence) Rodolfo Guzzardi (1903–1962) painted landscapes and scenes depicting frontier life.

The 1990 census reported 312,294 persons of Italian ancestry living in Texas.

Valentine Belfiglio
Frank J. Cavaioli

Bibliography

Belfiglio, Valentine. *The Italian Experience in Texas: A Closer Look.* Austin: Eakin, 1995.

Forrester-O'Brien, Esse. *Art and Artists of Texas.* Dallas: Tardy, 1935.

Pingenot, Ben E. *Siringo.* College Station: Texas A&M University Press, 1989.

Rolle, Andrew. *The Immigrant Upraised.* Norman: University of Oklahoma Press, 1968.

See also AGRICULTURE; COPPINI, POMPEO; SOUTH, THE

Theater History

The connection of Italian Americans to theater in America is a long one and is based in the commedia dell'arte performances as well as the reenactment of Italian plays and melodramas in their immigrant community theaters. In addition, Italians in America created amateur and professional Italian theater groups. In each case, they hoped to keep the tradition of the Italian theater alive in the New World, even as a new Italian American theater tradition was emerging in the cities and enclaves where Italians resided.

Italian American theater began in New York City. In 1808 the first Italian American playwright, Lorenzo Da Ponte (famous as Mozart's librettist), staged Vittorio Alfieri's play *Mirra* and wrote short plays in Italian performed by his American students at Columbia University in a small theater he had constructed in his home. But the first real phase of this vital ethnic theater emerged when the waves of Italian immigrants began pouring into this country in the 1870s, bringing both the performers and audiences necessary for theatrical entertainment.

Arriving in the United States, immigrants chose for the most part to settle in the larger cities on the eastern seaboard with the greatest concentration of Italians in New York City. Many of them had no desire to assimilate into their new surroundings, even if they had been welcome to do so. They retained their regional speech, their social and religious customs, their eating habits, and congregated in communities that allowed them some free expression: hence, the Little Italys of America.

All these factors contributed to creating an original theatrical expression: the Italian American immigrant theater of New York City. Its audiences were the displaced men and women of Italy, and they were hungry for entertainment, a support system, and social intercourse, all emotional needs that the Italian theaters and the nightclubs helped to satisfy.

The Italian immigrant community, located in tenement Little Italys throughout the city, supported itself through a network of fraternal and benevolent associations that often sponsored dances, concerts, and lectures to celebrate holidays and benefit social causes in New York City and in Italy. Soon amateur theatrical clubs evolved. The earliest and most prolific prototype was the Circolo Filodrammatico Italo-Americano (The Italian American Amateur Theatre Club), which mounted the first Italian American production, the Italian play *Maria Giovanna* by Giovanna Marni, on October 17, 1880, at Dramatic Hall on East Houston Street.

During the nineteenth century, a great variety of dramatic forms and entertainments were essayed on the stages of the Italian American theater. Italian and European writers were introduced to immigrant audiences, many of whom had never before experienced the theater or the classics of literature. They heard the plays of their homeland and other European theaters spoken, if not in Italian, then translated into their own Neapolitan, Sicilian, or other regional dialects. They heard the familiar operatic arias and duets, known by most Italians, in their local bistros.

The Italian American experience furnished the subject matter for original plays written by Italian immigrant playwrights. Among them, Eduardo Migliaccio, made the Italian American immigrant the hero of his dramatic creations; and Riccardo Cordiferro, the pen name for the journalist and political activist Alessandro Sisca, who concerned himself in his plays and philosophical writings with the social conditions of the Italian immigrant.

Not all immigrants were uneducated. Many intellectuals also migrated from Italy, where they had been professors, writers, or theatrical artists. For them the theater was a natural attraction, outnumbered though they were by their working-class countrymen and women. The theater provided them with a forum for literary and artistic expression. The women in the theater also enjoyed a freedom and an outlet for creativity that was not shared or available to their sisters who played out their lives in the more traditional domestic roles. Many women became writers, directors, and entrepreneurs in their own right, as well as popular actresses and singers.

In general, the nineteenth-century phase of the Italian American theater represents a breaking of ground for the more ambitious, professional twentieth-century endeavors. In 1900 the theater had just begun to emerge from its predominantly amateur phase. By 1905 the Italian American theater had become firmly rooted in its professional phase, which would continue for at least five more decades until its decline.

By far the professionals outnumbered the amateurs during the twentieth century, with respect to both performers and performances. Amateur or professional, the theater continued to serve the same functions: entertaining its audiences, educating them to the best literatures of Europe, raising money for worthy causes, perpetuating Italian language and culture, and providing a forum for socializing with other members of the immigrant community.

By 1900 the community had produced the major forces that created the theater of the ensuing decades: Antonio Maiori, who introduced Shakespeare to his immigrant audiences in his southern Italian dialect productions; Francesco Ricciardi, who held sway as the "Prince of Pulcinellas" in the nightclub arena; Eduardo Migliaccio, whose stage name, "Farfariello," translates as "Little Butterfly," who created the unique art form—the Italian immigrant character sketch; Guglielmo Ricciardi, who created Italian American theater in Brooklyn and went on to a successful career in the American theater and cinema; Antonietta Pisanelli Alessandro, who started in New York, performed in Chicago, and then in San Francisco, where she single-handedly created Italian American theater there, to name a selection. Many professional liaisons, marriages, and business partnerships took place between these major families, creating a strong theatrical network in later years. More often than not, children in these families started their careers early and continued the family theatrical tradition for as long as there were audiences who needed entertainment.

The artists of the early Italian American theater had to resort to their wits to keep themselves and the theater alive. Financial problems were an ever-present worry for these young companies. Groups appeared and, with equal facility, disappeared. The more stable theater companies tried everything to "make a go" of business: they would flourish one year, only to have a lean year the next, which would prompt them to go on the road to try new audiences, sometimes returning poorer than when they left; they would move to smaller or bigger theaters in the hopes of juggling finances to better advantage; they would change their theatrical offerings, from the classics to comedy and vaudeville, or vice versa; nightclubs would easily change ownership, renovate, bring in stars from Italy. Suc-

cessful or unsuccessful as these attempts might have been, efforts to create theater were constantly in force and constituted an enormous output of energy during the seventy odd years of its existence in New York City.

Actors ventured outside the city limits, up and down the eastern seaboard to the Midwest, and inevitably to California. The abundance of theatrical energy spilled out over the city's boundaries with the effect that professional New York City companies were bringing professional theater experiences to Italian immigrants who lived in rural and suburban areas. Most of the major figures, such as Antonio Maiori and his comic sidekick, Pasquale Rapone; Guglielmo Ricciardi; Giovanni De Rosalia, who created the comic halfwit "Nofrio"; the itinerant actor and singer Rocco De Russo; Eduardo Migliaccio; and Clemente and Sandrino Giglio, to name a few, made excursions out of town to reach new audiences and get the most mileage out of their productions.

One effect of this theatrical migration was to inspire the formation of amateur theatrical groups in other cities. During the nineteenth century several amateur groups existed in New Jersey, Boston, and Philadelphia. By the early twentieth century there were over eighty amateur groups scattered throughout small and large cities throughout the United States. Some became professional. But many followed the pattern already established by amateur clubs in New York: they formed either for the sole joy of performing theater, to raise money for worthwhile social causes, for socializing, for entertainment, and for a support system in the difficult process of assimilation. These clubs have often been associated with some religious, fraternal, or educational organization.

Of course, not all amateur groups outside New York City owed their existence to the example set by traveling professionals. The great numbers of new immigrants alone would have inevitably resulted in the emergence of new theater clubs. But what is certain is that major performers from the city came in contact with actors outside and often used them in their productions, thereby creating temporary marriages between companies. New York's Francesco Vela, for example, taught at a drama school in Providence, Rhode Island. It is conceivable that New York's ready access to the latest printed scripts, songs, and sheet music found their way to other cities via the traveling companies, thereby increasing the repertoire of local amateur clubs. Journalist and playwright Riccardo Cordiferro brought scripts of his play *L'onore perduto* (Lost Honor) to many out-of-town theaters.

Being "on the road" made reporters out of some New York actors and directors. The actor-playwright Salvatore Abbamonte sent in information about his activity in Asbury Park to *L'araldo Italiano,* as did the actor Salvatore Melchiorri when he performed in Chicago. Riccardo Cordiferro included frequent out-of-town notices in his radical newspaper *La Follia.* Many of the anonymous notices of productions done out of town came from the pens of well-known New York personalities. Furthermore, many regional reporters, who may also have been actors and directors, reported to the New York dailies about shows in their towns and about their own local stars. New York City's Italian American theatrical consciousness was not a parochial one. It included an awareness and a sharing of the theatrical tradition with other immigrants who no doubt went to the theaters in their respective cities for the same reasons Italian American New Yorkers did.

We know that Riccardo Cordiferro was a castigating critic of the amateur theater clubs that flourished at the turn of the century. Serious criticism, of which Cordiferro was capable, was the exception and not the rule among Italian American theater reviewers. The reviews of performances continued for the most part in the patterns established in the nineteenth century. Glowing reviews appeared with annoying frequency, possibly because the reporter hoped to encourage groups who often performed benefits for worthwhile social causes. The attitude is best summed up in a remark made by *L'araldo*'s Philadelphia correspondent about the efforts of La Compagnia Filodrammatica Silvio Pellico of that city. His comments about their production of *Tosca* were gentle: "Criticism, if there should be any criticism, I leave to the critics, that is to say, to those who are difficult to please."

No writer formally and systematically encoded a poetics or theory of theater, but many other factors contribute to recreating the idea of what critics, audiences, and directors expected theater to be. In the nineteenth century the stated aim of the Italian American theater was to delight and instruct. These two concepts continued to be important after 1900, but to them may be added a third factor: the concern for social justice.

First and foremost, audiences came to the theatre expecting to be entertained. The hardworking laborers came to the theater either alone or with families in tow to escape the harsh reality of their lives; to be dazzled by the glamour of the costumes and the beauty of the performers; to be reminded of home by hearing familiar folk songs, ballads, and operatic arias; to hear Italian spoken, as well as their own regional dialects; to laugh at the antics of their own regional stock character of the commedia dell'arte tradition; to be stirred by the patriotic sentiments and grandeur of the historical dramas; to be moved by the emotions played out in the melodramas; and to be reassured by the well-ordered universe depicted therein. The average audience was quite dispassionate, or at best ambivalent, about whether a production was educational or socially relevant.

These concerns instead were voiced by the writers and directors. When Paolo Cremonesi and Giovanni Flecchia formed a company to perform for Hoboken's Italian immigrants, they called the group The Club for Instruction and Entertainment and also The Study and Work Club. Salvatore Abbamonte called his group The Club of Young Studious Italians, whose stated purpose was the propagation of Italian culture overseas, as well as entertainment.

Intentionally or unintentionally, Italian American theater did play an educational role in the life of the immigrant. The history, literature, and culture of Italy were paraded across the stages of Little Italy. Furthermore, dramatic literature of other European countries was equally accessible. The actor and director Antonio Maiori introduced Shakespeare in dialect to Italian immigrant audiences.

The gentle, humorous satire of Eduardo Migliaccio provided another type of education. Farfariello, the character he created, was a comic stock character: a *carraterista* in the tradition of the commedia dell'arte, only this character, instead of originating in Naples or Bologna or Calabria or any other Italian region, was a product of New York City's immigrant community and spoke a curious new, but familiar, regional dialect, which has been called "Italo-Americanese." Farfariello was the typical newly arrived immigrant, the bewildered greenhorn, trying to make his way in a strange and inhospitable country.

Education was an incidental byproduct of Migliaccio's characterizations, or *macchiette*. Migliacco's skit "Pasquale Passaguai" showed the immigrant how to avoid being duped by thieves, while his parody of "Il Presidente della Società" cured many community leaders of their habit of wearing pretentious military uniforms at public functions. Migliaccio's creations in particular, and the immigrant theater in general, helped ease the tensions and anxieties of living in a foreign country and indirectly helped the immigrant in the process of assimilation.

The task of education was imposed on the theater by its more educated and literate observers and participants. It was not long before the literati of the day obligated the immigrant theater to spread propaganda. The actor Salvatore Abbamonte told of "red" evenings of theater that included radical speakers, revolutionary songs, plays on social topics. He claimed that, for love of the theater, he too had become a revolutionary. His play, *Senza Lavoro* (Unemployed), dealt with a contemporary social problem. Theater groups identified themselves by names reflecting their political leanings. New York City had La Filodrammatica dell'Unione Socialista (The Drama Club of the Socialist Union), while Paterson, New Jersey, the home of King Umberto I's assassin, Gaetano Bresci, was also the home of Il Teatro Sociale (The Social Theater). Il Nuovo Club Democratico Italiano (The New Italian Democratic Club) was located in Washington, D.C. New Haven, Connecticut, had La Sezione Socialista Italiana (The Italian Socialist Department), and New Castle, Pennsylvania, had Il Circolo Socialista Enrico Fermi (The Enrico Fermi Socialist Club).

On Italian American stages, immigrant audiences were confronted with contemporary social concerns, among them the exploitation of laborers by American bosses and Italian *padroni* (labor brokers) and the miserable living conditions of crowded tenement slums, corruption, and social injustice. At the turn of the century the left-wing journalist Riccardo Cordiferro began writing what would become a formidable list of social protest plays. His dramatic monologue *Il Pezzente* (The Beggar) described the plight of the beggar. His drama *L'onre Perduto* (Lost Honor), using the structure of domestic melodrama, examined the dishonesty of some Italian American bankers and its tragic effects on the newly arrived immigrant. The play also touched, however lightly, on the emancipation of women, and was produced in many eastern cities for Italian immigrant audiences. Even the regular professional theaters would sometimes put on productions of plays they described as "social dramas."

However significant these plays might have been, however satisfying their enactment may have been to the more educated members of the audience, they never achieved the popularity of the comedies, the variety shows, and the classics of the European theater. In the theater at least, Cordiferro was no match for Farfariello, in terms of popularity and exposure. But in the years that follow, the class struggle became more desperate and the voice of reform more insistent, all of which was reflected in the theater.

The Italian American theater of the early twentieth century made outstanding progress. First, the theater transitioned from an essentially amateur status to its predominantly professional phase; second, audiences saw an enormous output of activity and the participation of thousands of theater artists; third, theater proliferated within Italian American communities outside New York City, as far as California, partially as a result of traveling professional and amateur companies from New York City; fourth, a distinctly Italian American language and literature developed; fifth, the theater was responsible in part for the evolution and celebration of a uniquely Italian American identity; finally, this new identity contributed, in the characterization of Farfariello, a new comic stock character in the tradition of the commedia dell'arte. By 1905, despite the vagaries of artistic life, the Italian American theater had, with persistence and devotion, "arrived."

Throughout the first quarter of the twentieth century, immigration statistics for these years reveal a steady flow of new immigrant arrivals from which emerged eager new audiences. The major impresarios were still actively engaged in production for the better part of these years: Maiori, Francesco Ricciardi, De Rosalia, Cremonesi, Costantini, Migliaccio, Ragazzino, De Russo, the Marrone brothers, Imperato, Minciotti, Cunico, Giglio. Their ranks were enlarged and infused with the energies of new recruits and entrepreneurs, among them: Ilario Papandrea, Alberto Campobasso, Gennaro Gardenia (father of Vincent Gardenia), Francesco De Cesare, Gino Caimi, Giuseppe Sterni, Ettore Mainardi, and a host of amateur clubs as well. The immigrant community needed a theater, and the Italian American theater needed an immigrant population to exist.

The new immigration quota laws of 1924 restricted the annual importation of new Italian immigrants into the United States to a figure not in excess of 2 percent of the total number of new arrivals in 1890. The Italian American theater gradually began to see the effects of the restrictive quotas in their dwindling audiences. Furthermore, as the second and third generations of Italian Americans became acculturated, they turned to the new and readily available popular forms of entertainment: radio, movies, and eventually television. Giglio, who worked into the 1940s, and Gardenia, into the 1950s, were two of the last holdouts. Some, like Guglielmo Ricciardi long ago, managed to cross over into American spheres. Esther Minciotti, for instance, played Ernest Borgnine's mother in the film *Marty*. The late Vincent Gardenia, who played in the Italian American Theatre until the 1950s, and Olga Barbato of the Dona Vicenza Company are still highly visible in television and films.

But the Italian American theater is virtually nonexistent today. The Italian Actors' Union still exists, conducts meetings, and functions minimally as a liaison for visiting Italian professional entertainers. Our modern technological age has manufactured other diversions which assure that a popular immigrant theater is now impossible. The playwright Mario Fratti, who writes in Italian and English and whose plays are performed all over the world, still stages Italian plays at Hunter College, using as actors his students of Italian, in the tradition started by Lorenzo Da Ponte at Columbia University in 1808.

Emelise Aleandri

Bibliography

Aleandri, Emilese. "The History of Italian-American Theatre in New York City: 1900–1905." Ph.D. diss., City University of New York, 1983.

———. "Little Italy at the Turn of the Century." In *Little Italy Souvenir Book,* New York, 1981.

Aleandri, Emelise, and Maxine Schwartz Seller. "Italian American Theatre." In *Ethnic Theatre in the United States,* edited by Maxine Schwartz Seller, 237–276. Westport, CT: Greenwood, 1983.

Sogliuzzo, Richard A. "Notes from the History of Italian American Theatre." *Theatre Survey* 14, no. 2 (1973): 59–75.

See also CORDIFERRO, RICCARDO; MIGLIACCIO, EDUARDO (FARFARIELLO); PISANELLI-ALESSANDRO, ANTONIETTA; PLAYS, CONTEMPORARY

Tommasini, Maria Luigia Angelica Cipriana Stanislas

See WOMEN AND THE CHURCH

Tonti, Enrico di (ca. 1649–1704)

Born of Neapolitan stock, Tonti (or Tonty) served the king of France and was brought to the New World by the much better known explorer Robert Cavelier de LaSalle, who dreamed of creating a great entrepôt at the mouth of the Mississippi. Tonti's father, Lorenzo, a banker by trade, was a leader in the popular revolt of the Lazzaroni against the Spanish viceroy in 1647 and fled with his family to France when the uprising was crushed.

After a short time as cadet in the French army, Tonti joined the navy and rose to the rank of captain-lieutenant, distinguishing himself by his courage: he lost his right hand to a grenade in action against the Spaniards. He became known afterwards as the "Man with the Iron Hand."

In 1678 LaSalle was in Paris using his influence at the French Court to promote the idea of a chain of forts in the Mississippi Valley to protect French interests against Spain and England. Tonti was recommended to LaSalle and became his trusted lieutenant. The Italian explorer was with LaSalle when on April 9, 1682, he claimed Louisiana for France.

From Fort Saint Louis, constructed by him and LaSalle a year later on a bluff of the Illinois River, Tonti conducted a fur trade that was so successful, Clarence W. Alvord, a leading historian of the region, called him "the first promoter of big business in the west." In 1686 as part of his growing commercial empire, he

Enrico di Tonti was an early explorer in America. He is shown here with an Indian guide in East Texas in a painting by Bruce Marshall, 1973. Courtesy U.T. Institute of Texan Cultures, San Antonio, Texas.

established a trading post on the Arkansas River, the first on the lower Mississippi. Tonti promised the Jesuits two tracts of land if they would send missionaries, an offer on which he made good three years later.

Among his efforts, Tonti sought to create a commercial empire linking the West with the Gulf of Mexico. The Iroquois, acting as middlemen for the English and the Dutch fur trade, were seen by him as his rivals, and he was constantly at war with them. With his metal hand, which he became famous for using as a weapon, Tonti was feared as "powerful medicine" by his Indian enemies. Otherwise, his Indian policy was one of peace, especially with the Illinois, whose trade he sought. He was reported to be a master of Indian languages, and he negotiated with tribes as distant as the Assiniboins near Hudson's Bay, the Chickasaws and Choctaws along the southern Mississippi, and the Cenis of the Southwest.

Tonti's unrivaled knowledge of the Mississippi Valley, so important in the history of North America, is attested in a letter of a missionary priest to his bishop in Quebec.

Father St. Cosme had been taken by the Italian explorer to Arkansas country. He wrote that Tonti was the man "who best knows the country . . . he is loved and feared everywhere. . . . Your grace, Monseigneur, will, I doubt not, take pleasure in acknowledging the obligations we owe him."

But Enrico di Tonti was not only an explorer, pioneering businessman, mediator, and empire-builder. His memoirs, published in Paris in 1697 as a tribute to LaSalle, have been hailed as the "first accurate extensive descriptions of the geography, Indians, and resources of the Mississippi basin."

Later, in 1898, Father Pietro Bandini founded Tontitown, Arkansas, a community of Italian immigrants, in honor of the great Italian explorer who in 1686 founded the first white settlement in the Arkansas wilderness.

Donald J. D'Elia

Bibliography

Murphy, Edmund R. *Henry DeTonty. Fur Trader of the Mississippi.* Baltimore: Johns Hopkins Press, 1941.

Sammartino, Peter. *Seven Italians Involved in the Creation of America*. Washington, DC: National Italian American Foundation, 1984.

See also BANDINI, PIETRO; EXPLORERS

Toscanini, Arturo (1867–1957)

Born in Parma, Italy, on March 25, 1867, Arturo Toscanini studied cello, piano, and composition starting at age 9 at the Parma Conservatory. After graduating in 1885 with high distinction, he became a cellist with the Italian opera in Rio de Janeiro, Brazil, in 1886. In June of that year he was called upon to substitute for the conductor of the orchestra after the start of the performance of Giuseppe Verdi's *Aida*. At age 19, Toscanini was given an ovation after his masterful conducting (without a score in front of him) and became the conductor for the remainder of that season.

His meteoric rise to fame continued upon his return to Italy. He successfully conducted at various Italian opera companies from 1887 to 1896, when he made his first appearance as a symphonic conductor in Turin. In 1898, Giulio Gatti-Casazza, the new impresario of the prestigious La Scala opera company in Milan, invited Toscanini to become the chief conductor. Toscanini was at La Scala from 1898 to 1908, with a three-season absence between 1903 to 1906. During his leave from La Scala he was an operatic conductor in Buenos Aires, Argentina, and also conducted in Turin and Bologna.

Toscanini's biggest career move was in 1908, when he followed Gatti-Casazza to New York. The impresario had become manager and director of the Metropolitan Opera and took Toscanini with him as principal conductor. After an outstanding seven years at the New York company, Toscanini returned to Italy in 1915. He toured the United States and Canada with the orchestra of La Scala in 1920 and 1921, and from 1921 to 1929 was La Scala's artistic director. For the 1926–1927 and 1928–1929 seasons he was a guest conductor for the New York Philharmonic. (He had had his first American experience as a symphonic conductor in New York in 1913.)

Arturo Toscanini, considered the greatest symphonic conductor of his time, led the National Broadcasting Company's orchestra during the later years of his life. His recordings, heralded as master works, continue to be studied by other conductors and appreciated by music lovers. Courtesy NBC.

In 1930 he became the conductor of the Philharmonic and stayed there, with guest appearances in Palestine, Salzburg, and London until 1936. Toscanini refused to conduct concerts in Germany and Italy during the 1930s in protest against Nazism and Italian fascism. The 1936 concert he gave in Tel Aviv, Palestine, grew out of Toscanini's sympathy for the plight of Jewish musicians fleeing from Nazism. His next engagement was as music director of the National Broadcasting Company Symphony Orchestra from 1937 until 1954, when he retired at age 87. The NBC orchestra had been specifically organized for his considerable talents and spread his fame further via radio. He died in New York less than three years after retiring, always retaining his Italian citizenship.

Toscanini was one of the greatest conductors of all time, having an amazing ear and memory for music, a considerable ability to concentrate, a passion for perfection, a strong character, and perhaps most of all, great energy. One of his few foibles was his tendency to hum during concerts, which some of his many fine recordings picked up in the background. Yet this curious habit just adds to his sizable legend as the incomparable "Maestro" of two continents, the versatile genius who so capably handled a wide variety of serious music. He died on January 16, 1957.

William E. Studwell

Bibliography

Chotzinoff, Samuel. *Toscanini: An Intimate Portrait*. New York: Da Capo, 1976.

Freeman, John W., and Walfredo Toscanini. *Toscanini*. New York: Treves, 1987.

Hoeller, Suzanne. *Arturo Toscanini: A Photobiography*. New York: Island, 1943.

Horowitz, Joseph. *Understanding Toscanini: How He Became an American Culture-God and Helped Create a New Audience for Old Music*. New York: Knopf, 1987.

Marek, George Richard. *Toscanini*. New York: Athenaeum, 1975.

Sachs, Harvey. *Toscanini*. Philadelphia: J. B. Lippincott, 1978.

See also OPERA

Trade Policy

See BUSINESS INTERRELATIONS WITH ITALY

Traditional Songs in Italian American Communities

Even after the end of World War II, a visitor to Italian American communities in large and small cities throughout the United States could hear the melodic strains of a song from some region of Italy. Some of the songs would be familiar to anyone who was knowledgeable about music, for the compositions were world famous, while some of the songs originating from a specific region and dialect would be unfamiliar to even a selection of individuals born in Italy. Despite the many songs that were well known in only one region, particularly folk songs, there were pieces that were familiar to most Italian immigrants in America.

Without a doubt, there is one field of music in which Italy surpassed all other nations—opera. With an operatic tradition reaching back to the sixteenth century, with opera houses a fixture of every sizable Italian city, with many world-famous opera composers including Antonio Vivaldi, Giovanni Pergolesi, Allesandro Scarlatti, Gioacchino Rossini, Giuseppi Verdi, and Giacomo Puccini, opera was not just a national institution, it was a national passion.

Although the arias and songs of older operatic composers were not forgotten, the operatic pieces that were most popular among Italian American immigrants appear to be those of the more recent masters, Gioacchino Rossini (1792–1868), Giuseppe Verdi (1813–1901), and Giacomo Puccini (1858–1924). This was not just because these three were arguably the best and best-known Italian operatic composers, but because they wrote their fine works somewhat before and during the period most Italians migrated to America, that is, the late nineteenth and early twentieth centuries. Pieces from operas such as Rossini's *Il Barbiere di Siviglia* (*The Barber of Seville*) (1816) and *Guillaume Tell* (*William Tell*) (1829), Verdi's *Rigoletto* (1851), *La Traviata* (1853), and *Aida* (1871), and Puccini's *La Bohème* (1896) and *Madame Butterfly* (1904) were not just excerpts of excellent artistry but succulent reminders of the land from which the immigrants had come. Even if life in the New World was difficult, which it frequently was, or even if the golden shores of the United States did not in reality share sufficient amounts of its wealth in the early years, Italian Americans had a fantastically rich musical resource to fall back on.

Although operatic songs were a mainstay of everyday cultural life of Italian Americans, other songs, folk and mainstream, also brightened the lives of the immigrants and their descendants. Three of the most notable songs came from the Naples region, an area from which many persons emigrated to the United States. Like the operatic pieces by Rossini, Verdi, and Puccini, they were created somewhat before and during the peak period of Italian immigration and therefore were very familiar to Italian Americans. The gentlest composition of the three was "Santa Lucia," written to honor the Sicilian virgin martyr who died around the year 304. Its creator was Teodoro Cottrau (1827–1879), a musician, journalist, and politician in Naples who published his eventually world-famous love ballad in 1850 or 1851.

Much more vigorous and somewhat more famous was "Funiculì, Funiculà," which was created in 1880 to honor the completion of a funicular railway (cable cars) for tourists on Mount Vesuvius near Naples. While there is considerable reason to question why anyone would want to build a railway on an active volcano that had buried Pompeii and other towns in A.D. 79, there can be no question about the quality of the song written for the occasion. The jubilant and hard-driving melody by the noted composer Luigi Denza (1846–1922), coupled with lyrics by the obscure G. Turco, resulted in one of the world's most energetic and artistic songs.

The third in this esteemed trio is the passionate love ballad "O Sole Mio" (My Sun). Published in 1899 though possibly performed as early as 1894, "O Sole Mio" was the work of Neapolitan composer Edoardo di Capua (1864–1917) and lyricist Giovanni Capurro (1859–1920), also a Neapolitan. A favorite in Italy and in America, the piece had an operatic feel to it. In 1949 it became a popular hit in the United States after the lyrics were revised and the title changed ("There's No Tomorrow") by Al Hoffman, Leo Corday, and Leon Carr.

With so much excellent music from operas, other classical works, the folk domain, and popular culture in Italy, Italian immigrants had a rich repository of songs to help manage the challenges of life in a new land. The compositions highlighted above not only served the needs of new immigrants but are still popular among subsequent generations of Italian Americans and others as the twentieth century comes to a close.

William E. Studwell

Bibliography

Fuld, James J. *The Book of World-Famous Music: Classical, Popular, and Folk.* 4th ed., rev. and enlarged. New York: Dover, 1995.

Leydi, Roberto. "Italy, Folk Music." *The New Grove Dictionary of Music and Musicians.* Vol. 9. London: Macmillan, 1980, 382–392.

Nakamura, Julia Volpelletto. "Canzone Napoletane: The Stories Behind the Songs." *Italian Americana* 15 (summer 1997): 143–156.

Studwell, William E. *The National and Religious Song Reader.* New York: Haworth, 1997.

Studwell, William E., and David A. Hamilton. *Opera Plot Index: A Guide to Locating Plots and Descriptions of Operas, Operettas, and Other Works of the Musical Theater, and Associated Material.* New York: Garland, 1990.

See also COMPOSERS, CLASSICAL; FOLKLORE, FOLKLIFE; OPERA

Travanti, Daniel J.
See TELEVISION

Travolta, John
See MOVIE ACTORS AND ACTRESSES

Trenton's Chambersburg

The city of Trenton annexed the borough of Chambersburg in 1888, and, beginning in the 1880s, growing numbers of Italians from small towns in southern Italy settled in the southern portion of Chambersburg. It became and remains the largest Italian American community in central Jersey.

The many industries in and adjacent to Chambersburg attracted and employed most of the Italian settlers. Since 1910 initially, unskilled Italian industrial workers have played an important part in Trenton's labor history. In 1910 unskilled Italian and Hungarian immigrants launched the first major strike against the John A. Roebling's Sons Company in Chambersburg, Trenton's largest employer. This strike ended disastrously, with many Italians being dismissed.

The Italian community contained a small elite of professionals, prominent businessmen, small businessmen, self-employed artisans, and a larger working class employed in the mills, on the railroads as section hands, and as workers on public construction projects.

Chambersburg's Italians formed many mutual-aid, cultural, and political societies (the oldest dating from 1886), established three churches (two Protestant and one Roman Catholic), and one parochial school. The Maestre Pie Filippini teaching order arrived in 1910 from Rome to teach at St. Joachim's School, the first assignment for these nuns in the United States. The communal highlight of the year is the celebration of the feast of the Madonna S.S. di Casandrino, held annually in early September since 1906.

After World War II, Trenton's many industries closed or moved, and Trenton lost its mostly upper and middle classes to suburbia. By the 1960s Italian Americans constituted Trenton's largest European-ancestry group and dominated city government. In 1966 Carmen J. Armenti was elected Trenton's only Italian American mayor. He lost his reelection bid in 1970. Since then, economically and socially upwardly mobile Italian Americans have moved to suburbia, attracted by the status of a single-family home, better public schools, lower taxes, and proximity to jobs. Chambersburg's Italian Americans are now fewer in number. Many are elderly, living in the same row house that has been owned by the family for generations, and with children living in suburbia. Most Italian American school-age children attend parochial schools.

The years immediately before and after the 1968 riot witnessed growing tensions in the community between Italian Americans and African Americans. The result has been the abandonment of the city by Italian Americans and others of European ancestry. The public schools, attended by predominantly African Americans and Hispanics, are plagued by numerous problems.

A shrinking Italian American population remains in the heart of the Trenton Chambersburg Little Italy. The Italian Americans remain attached to their community and well-maintained homes, while St. Joachim's Church and School are anchors of the community. The annual feast of the Madonna S.S. di Casandrino still attracts large crowds, and its procession draws many participants and observers. The renovation of the Roebling works into a multi-use site could possibly rejuvenate this old but proud community.

Dennis J. Starr

Bibliography

Ciccolella, Erasmo S. *Vibrant Life: 1886–1942 Trenton's Italian Americans.* New York: Center for Migration Studies, 1986.

Ferri, May Nicola, and Erasmo S. Ciccolella, eds. *Italian American Vignettes.* Princeton: Central Jersey Chapter, American Italian Historical Association, 1983.

Peroni, Peter Aloysius, II. *The Burg: An Italian-American Community at Bay in Trenton.* Washington, DC: University Press of America, 1979.

Tresca, Carlo (1879–1943)

A radical leader in the labor struggles of the early twentieth century, Carlo Tresca is remembered by the political left as a fearless fighter against injustice and a tireless friend to those arrested in labor demonstrations and strikes.

Tresca arrived in New York City in 1904, having left his home in Sulmona/Abruzzi, Italy, to evade a prison sentence for libel based on his report in a regional socialist newspaper on the torture of prisoners in the local jail. While a teenager, his affluent family had lost their fortune and their home, and Tresca—already a free thinker—had joined the socialists. By age 20, he was organizing peasants and leading protests against the government, becoming secretary of the railroad workers union the following year.

Within a few months of migrating to America, Tresca became editor of *Il Proletario,* another socialist newspaper. Later, he started his own newspaper, *L'Avvenire,* succeeded by *Il Martello,* which he published until his death. He attacked the Catholic clergy, police corruption, and labor conditions, and he published information on the availability of birth control—the latter being considered so scandalous that it led to his arrest.

Throughout his life, Tresca was active in political protests and labor strikes, being arrested and jailed numerous times, including the strikes of the Lawrence textile workers in 1912, Paterson, New Jersey, silk workers the following year, and mine workers in Colorado and Minnesota in 1914 and 1916. He was also a frequent speaker at antiwar rallies during the First World War.

Tresca was a radical hero among many Italian exiles in the United States. Often described as an anarcho-syndicalist, he did not fit any narrow category. He associated with the intellectual free thinkers of his day whether socialist, anarchist, or communist, including Norman Thomas, Elizabeth Gurley Flynn, Roger Baldwin, Luigi Antonini, and John Dos Passos. He opposed communism as well as fascism, but he supported many persons and causes even when their views differed from his. However, others were not so tolerant of his criticisms, and he acquired many enemies. Tresca is best known for his support of the Sacco-Vanzetti case of the 1920s, opposition to Mussolini's policies, and advocacy of the republicans in the 1936 Spanish Civil War.

Frequently invited to speak at public gatherings, his outspoken nature provoked the wrath of many, and several attempts were made on his life beginning in 1909. Personal danger did not deter him from speaking out against individuals and groups he believed antagonistic to working-class interests. He cooperated with groups such as the Industrial Workers of the World, other labor organizations, and the American Civil Liberties Union.

His wife—whom he married in Italy—and young daughter joined him in New York shortly after his arrival. Later they separated and he had several liaisons; he fathered a son in 1923.

In 1943 Tresca was assassinated—shot down in the street near his newspaper office in New York City. Although a known criminal was arrested, the murder has not been solved, and the suspect was released after being held several months for parole violation. Many theories exist about his murder: both fascists and communists have been accused.

Carlo Tresca was 63 at the time of his death. He was eulogized as a friend to everyone and a man of action who gave unstintingly of himself for many causes. He allowed radical groups to use space in his newspaper offices, raised money for many individuals and group efforts, and arranged political and legal help, being known as a "fixer" among the Italian radicals. A man of fiery temperament, he could be a fierce opponent as well as a true comrade.

Rose D. Scherini

Bibliography

Avrich, Paul. *Anarchist Voices: An Oral History of Anarchism in America.* Princeton: Princeton University Press, 1995.

Diggins, John P. *Mussolini and Fascism: The View from America.* Princeton: Princeton University Press, 1972.

Gallagher, Dorothy. *All the Right Enemies: The Life and Murder of Carlo Tresca.* New Brunswick, NJ: Rutgers University Press, 1988.

Mangione, Jerre, and Ben Morreale. *La Storia: Five Centuries of Experience.* New York: Harper Collins, 1992.

Pernicone, Nunzio. "Carlo Tresca and the Sacco-Vanzetti Case." *The Journal of American History* 66 (1979): 535–547.

See also LABOR; RADICALISM

Trombetta, Domenico

See FASCISM

Trosino, Earl (b. 1906)

Rear Admiral Earl Trosino, a decorated hero in World War II, the second of nine children of Angelo Michael Trosino and Domenica Rosa Bozzi, was born in Port Deposit, Maryland. His father migrated from the province of Benevento, and his mother migrated from the province of Teramo.

The family moved to Chester, Pennsylvania, in 1910. Trosino left high school, enrolled in the Pennsylvania Nautical School to study marine engineering, and graduated in 1928. He married Lucia Bianca DiRenzo.

Trosino obtained his license from the United States Coast Guard, rose to chief engineer in the U.S. Maritime Service, was accepted by the Naval Reserve, and was granted a senior lieutenant's commission. In June 1941 he received orders for active duty from the U.S. Navy.

His first assignment was as assistant engineering officer aboard the U.S.S. *Alcyone*. He engaged in combat with a German U-boat wolf pack before the United States formally entered World War II. Trosino was promoted to lieutenant commander after being assigned to the U.S.S. *Long Island*. He was assigned to the U.S.S. *Guadalcanal* and was promoted to full commander.

Commander Trosino distinguished himself by directing an inexperienced crew to take over a slowly sinking German submarine. His knowledge of German enabled him to identify various bulkhead devices and thereby prevent the craft from sinking. As the submarine was being towed toward Bermuda, ten mail bags and a sea chest were dispatched by a destroyer escort to Washington, D.C. They were filled with captured documents, including secret German radio codes for directing U-boat operations. Electric torpedoes, which left no telltale wakes, were also recovered from the sub. Information about them provided some of the most valuable intelligence captured during World War II. For his heroism, Commander Trosino received the Legion of Merit with a "V" (Earned under Combat).

Trosino was next attached to the U.S.S. *Wasp* in the Pacific Fleet, a front-line aircraft carrier with approximately one hundred planes and three thousand men on board. After the war ended, the ship was used to return Italian prisoners of war to Naples, Italy, and transported American soldiers home to the United States.

In 1949 Trosino was promoted to captain. Prior to retirement in April 1959, he was promoted to rear admiral, one of the first Italian Americans ever to achieve this rank.

Joseph Scafetta Jr.

Bibliography

Gallery, Daniel V. *Clear the Decks*. New York: William Morrow, 1951.

———. *Twenty Million Tons under the Sea*. New York: Henry Regnery, 1956.

See also WARTIME MILITARY AND HOME FRONT ACTIVITIES

Tusiani, Joseph (b. 1924)

Professor emeritus of Italian and internationally known poet, translator, and scholar, Joseph Tusiani was born in San Marco, Lamis (Foggia), in 1924. After receiving his doctorate in English literature from the University of Naples, Tusiani migrated to the United States in 1947 at age 23. In the United States he

began a long distinguished career in academics. From 1948 until 1971 he taught Italian and served as chairman of the Italian Department at the College of Mount Saint Vincent. In 1971 he accepted a position at the Herbert H. Lehman College of the City University of New York, where he remained until his retirement in 1983. Professor Tusiani also taught at Hunter College, Fordham University, and New York University.

Among Tusiani's most ambitious translations are *The Complete Poems of Michelangelo* (1960), Torquato Tasso's *Gerusalemme Liberata* (*Jerusalem Delivered*, 1970) and *Il mondo creato* (*Creation of the World*, 1982), Giovanni Boccaccio's *Ninfale Fiesolano* (*The Nymphs of Fiesole*, 1971), *Italian Poets of the Renaissance* (1971), *From Marino to Marinetti* (1974), *The Age of Dante* (1974), and *Dante's Lyric Poems* (1992), and the recently completed translation of Luigi Pulci's *Morgante* (1996). Into Italian he has translated *Poesie Inglesi*, by Giuseppe Antonio Borgese. Writing in English, Latin, Italian, and in his native dialect of the Gargano region of Puglia, he has completed several collections of poems. His selections in English include *Rind and All* (1962), *The Fifth Season* (1963), and *Gente Mia and Other Poems* (1981); in Latin, *Melos Cordis* (1955), *Rosa Rosarum* (1984), *In Exilio Rerum* (1985), *Confinia Lucis et Umbrae* (1992), *Carmina latina* (edited by Emilio Bandiera, 1994); in Italian, *Lo speco celeste* (1956), *Odi Sacre* (1958), and *Il ritorno* (1992); in dialect, *Làcreme e sciure* (1955), *Tìreca tàreca* (1978), *Bronx, America* (1991), and *Annemale Parlante* (1993).

Tusiani also published a novel, *Envoy From Heaven* (1965), and a three-volume autobiography: *La Parola Difficile* (1989), *La Parola Nuova* (1991), and *La Parola Antica* (1992), with the unifying secondary title *autobiografia di un emigrante*.

He has received many honors for his writings and for his dedication to education. In 1956 he was the first American to win the Greenwood Prize of the Poetry Society of England. In 1968 he received the Alice Fay di Castagnola Award from the Poetry Society of America and was awarded the Spirit Gold Medal from the Catholic Poetry Society of America. The honor of Cavalliere Ufficiale della Repubblica was bestowed upon him in 1973, the Leonardo Covello Educator Award in 1980, and the Leone di San Marco Award in 1982. In 1986 the American Association of Teachers of Italian chose Professor Tusiani as the recipient of the first American Association of Teachers of Italian Distinguished Service Award "in recognition of outstanding teaching and/or published research in the fields of Italian language, literature, and civilization." In 1996 he was honored with the Lyons Club Melville Jones Medal for outstanding service and the Enrico Fermi Award presented by the Enrico Fermi Cultural Center of the Bronx.

Like all writers who are born in one country and received their education in the country of birth, but are culturally and intellectually active in another, Tusiani operates in a reality that is bilingual and bicultural. He has created literature that explores, is influenced by, and is sensitive to the different cultural and linguistic referents that help mold it. He is a writer writing on and across cultural borders.

With the well-known verses from "Song of the Bicentennial," from *Gente Mia,* "Two languages, two lands, perhaps two souls . . . / Am I a man or two strange halves of one?" Tusiani perfectly verbalizes the plight of the emigrant/immigrant. In *Gente Mia and Other Poems,* and in the autobiographical trilogy, *La Parola Difficile, La Parola Nuova,* and *La Parola Antica,* Tusiani addresses, with eloquence and dignity, the experience of immigration to the United States. In these works, his muse inspires him to examine the major themes that are associated with immigration: the spiritually and psychologically violent act of division from one's family and native land (which is the first experience of the new emigrant), the dreams of the emigrant/immigrant, the prejudice he or she encounters, the process of Americanization, the question of language, the alienation, and the realization that the New World is not the "land of hospitality" he or she believed it would be.

As a translator of Italian poetry, Tusiani is clearly the most prolific and one of the most accomplished in the world. His translations encompass all eight centuries of Italian poetry, from short lyrical compositions to some of the most demanding and challenging of the major works, such as the twenty cantos of Torquato Tasso's epic *Jerusalem Delivered,* to the forty-eight cantos of Luigi Pulci's mock-epic *Il Morgante.*

Paolo A. Giordano

Bibliography

Fontanella, Luigi. "Poeti italiani espatriati negli Stati Uniti: il caso di Joseph Tusiani." In *La Letteratura dell'emigrazione,* edited by Jean-Jacques Marchand. Torino: Fondaz. G. Agnelli, 1991.

Giordano, Paolo A. "From Southern Italian Emigrant to Reluctant American: Joseph Tusiani's *Gente Mia and Other Poems.*" In *From the Margin, Writings in Italian Americana,* edited by Anthony Julian Tamburri, Paolo A. Giordano, and Fred L. Gardaphé. West Lafayette: Purdue University Press, 1991.

——— . "Images of America and Columbus in Italian American Literature." *Annali d'Italianistica* 1 (1992): 280–296.

——— . *Joseph Tusiani Poet Translator Humanist an International Homage.* West Lafayette, IN: Bordighera, 1994.

Petracco Sovran, Lucia. *Joseph Tusiani: Poeta e Traduttore.* Perugia: Editrice Sigla Tre, 1984.

Rimanelli, Giose. "Tusiani a Mesmeric Sculpture." In *Italian Ethnics: Their Languages, Literature and Lives,* edited by Dominic Candelord, Fred L. Gardaphé, and Paolo A. Giordano, 9–11. New York: American Italian Historical Association, 1989.

See also LITERATURE; POETRY

T

U

UNICO National

Founded in 1922 in Waterbury, Connecticut, as an Italian American service organization similar to the Rotary and the Lions, UNICO National's headquarters are in Bloomfield, New Jersey; its membership is open to business or professional males of Italian descent, a condition that has been modified recently to include those men married to females of Italian descent as well. Some local affiliates have female members, but those members are not national members. There are about eight thousand members in UNICO National.

The word *unico* in Italian means "unique," perhaps distinguishing it from other Italian societies founded in the early years of the twentieth century that were more concerned with mutual-aid activities. UNICO and its service orientation spread throughout the eastern cities of the United States. Its first convention was held in 1930 in New York City. Meanwhile, in 1931 the National Italian Civic League was founded in Omaha, Nebraska, with a program similar to that of UNICO. After World War II the two groups began to explore the possibility of a merger. On July 4, 1947, the eastern and western service organizations fused into UNICO National.

UNICO National sponsors a National Project in Mental Health and scholarships for deserving Italian American students. It is also quite active in raising money for research into Cooley's anemia, a disease that is mainly found in people of Mediterranean ancestry. UNICO has been active in sponsoring Hope University UNICO National College for the gifted and mentally challenged. It sponsors a number of scholarships, including the Alphonse A. Miele Memorial Scholarship,

Theodore Mazza Memorial Scholarship, John Basilone Memorial Post Graduate Scholarship, Dr. D. M. Nigro Amateur Athletics Memorial Award, Vincent Lombardi Memorial Award, Brian Piccolo Memorial Award, Philip Mazzei Americanism Awards, Ella T. Grasso Literary Award, Joseph P. Cianci Humanitarian Award, Antonio R. Rizzuto Gold Medal Award, and Dr. Anthony P. Vastola Gold Medal Award. UNICO National also publishes a journal, *ComUnico,* eight times a year.

In addition to its national projects, UNICO National also endorses local community projects that advance the image of Italian Americans. These efforts are encouraged through the Italian Heritage and Cultural Matching Grant Program. Local chapters also promote service efforts in their communities and seek to combat the portrayal of Italian stereotypes that often occur in the various media.

Along with other Italian American organizations, UNICO has had its successes in ending blatant insults to Italian honor. In 1990, for example, a Camarillo, California, woman contacted UNICO to have the sheriff's department stop displaying its dog's name, "Dago," on its patrol cars. More positively, UNICO has sought to associate its efforts with projects that promote goodwill toward the Italian American community. Its Hope University UNICO National College has been an outstanding success in this regard. Hope University is a successful arts college for individuals who are mentally challenged but gifted. Within one year, the community of Anaheim, California, changed from protesting the project to embracing it and its Hi-Hopes troupe of entertainers. The $2.2 million invested in the Hope University project has been more than worth the goodwill that has returned to UNICO National and the Italian American community.

Frank A. Salamone

Bibliography

Maselli, Joseph. *Year Two Thousand, Where Will Italian American Organizations Be in the Year 2000?* Washington, DC: National Italian American Foundation, 1990.

UNICO National. *UNICO National: The Largest Italian-American Service Club in the United States.* Bloomfield, NJ: UNICO National, n.d.

See also NATIONAL ASSOCIATION OF THE WOLVES; ORGANIZATIONS

United States–Italian Diplomatic Relations, 1776–1945

America's independence and ideals of liberty, popular democratic representation, and constitutional rights influenced Europe and stimulated the 1789 French Revolution. A few Italians helped in the fight to build the new America, such as Filippo Mazzei, confidant of Thomas Jefferson and James Madison, both influential revolutionary leaders and later presidents of the United States. But the six sub-Italian regional states (Savoyard Piedmont, Tuscany, Venice, Genova, Papal Rome, and Bourbon Naples) condemned any American and French revolutionary ideals. When Italy was conquered by Napoleon during the 1789–1815 French Revolution and Napoleonic Wars, Britain's naval blockade of Europe kept Italy's economy depressed, while young America became isolationist. American neutrality was breached only by the 1812–1815 Anglo-American War. Until 1914 American presence in Italy and Europe remained commercial, artistic, and touristic.

The fall of Napoleonic France in 1815 left America the only surviving liberal democracy, while the liberal-nationalist flame was kept alive in Italy during the 1820–1870 Risorgimento (national unification) against the Congress of Vienna's reactionary restoration of absolutist rule (1815–1848). But as the American and French examples spurred Latin America

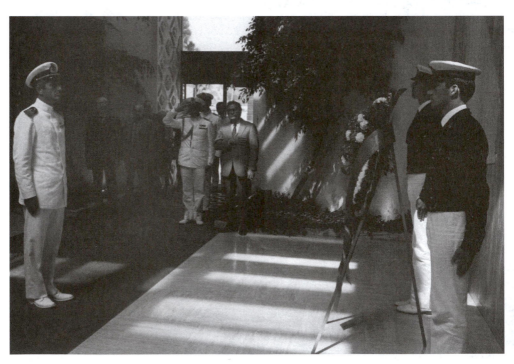

Officers and cadets from the Italian Navy destroyer Caio Duilio *at a ceremony at the Italian Mausoleum in San Francisco honoring the Italian pioneers of California. Captain Achille Zanoni, commander of the* Caio Duilio, *stands at attention after having presented the wreath. Courtesy Augusto Troiani.*

to gain independence from Spain and Portugal (1820-1830), Italy was consumed by failed revolutions (1820s, 1830s, 1848–1849). Although America opposed European designs to reconquer the new Latin American republics (1823 Monroe Doctrine), foreign policies remained isolationist, while settling the West at home against nomadic Native American tribes (Manifest Destiny). Even the presence of a United States naval squadron in the Mediterranean (1800–1805, 1815–1860s) was designed only to protect United States trade against North African Barbary pirates, not to support any liberal revolution in Europe. Yet the reactionary sub-Italian states distrusted American liberal ideals and trade, which they countered with censorship and import tariffs. Only when Piedmont embraced liberalism in 1847 and cut tariffs did America gain a foothold in Italy. During the First Italian Independence War (1848–1849) both the U.S. government and public opinion backed Piedmont's claims for national unification against Austrian domination. Scores of American residents, tourists, writers, artists, and a few U.S. consuls fought and died alongside the Italian insurgents: Consul J. Sparks in Venice died during the Austrian siege, while Consul T. Brown was expelled from Papal Rome after a joint Franco-Austro-Neapolitan army crushed Giuseppe Mazzini's and Giuseppe Garibaldi's liberal Roman Republic, reinstating Pope Pius IX. Some United States warships were even dispatched to deter Austrian and French forces, while spiriting away Italian revolutionaries. The repression of the 1848–1849 revolutions left American trade in shambles, while many Italian political refugees were forced to emigrate to America as condition for their release from Austrian jails. (Piedmont likewise shipped out most revolutionaries, whose proselytism threatened to destabilize its isolated conservative monarchy.)

Although neutral, unofficial U.S. governmental and popular support for Italy never abated in 1848–1870. First, Americans backed Italy's unification, believing that all oppressed nationalities should gain freedom and independence, and Italy's revolutionary values were ideologically akin to America's views of liberty, liberalism, and federalism. But such symbolic support of "right" (the "underdog's" fight for independence, unification, and democracy) against "wrong" (local and foreign monarchical oppression) did not fully grasp either the complexities of international politics (the Great Powers, including Great Britain, Germany, France, Russia, and Austria-Hungary, feared that Italy's unification would destroy Europe's balance of power through a total war), or the ideological rivalries among Italian patriots: Premier Camillo Cavour wanted Piedmont's Savoyard Kingdom to unify a liberal-conservative Italy, while radicals under Mazzini (who influenced Italian and European revolutionaries, including America's John Brown) and General Garibaldi (the "Hero of the Two Worlds" who fought for South American liberty and then joined Mazzini) sought a republican liberal Italy as a beacon of democratic revolution abroad. America's republican democracy appealed only to the revolutionaries, not to Cavour's moderate-conservative patriots who favoured a British-style constitutional monarchy. Second, both the United States government and mercantilist circles saw a strong, unified liberal Italy as a key ally in Europe to expand trade and diplomatic cooperation against the conservative powers (such as Germany and Austria-Hungary). Finally, America's Protestant churches backed Italy's unification, hoping that Papal Rome's collapse would unleash mass conversions to Protestantism. Under these powerful domestic influences the U.S. Senate denounced in 1867 Papal Rome's domestic repression and broke diplomatic relations.

Nearly all American groups backed Italy's unification: northern Abolitionists, Yankee Protestants, mercantilist cities, and even the slave-owning South (whose highly educated land gentry revived their historical passion for liberty and independence in far-away causes, rather than acknowledge the widening national chasm over slavery). Only the Irish and American Catholics opposed Italy's unification, fearing it would destroy Papal Rome. But whenever Italian revolutions erupted (1848–1849, 1859–1861, 1866, 1870) American support poured out: mass demonstrations in New York (1847, 1849, 1860, 1871), diplomatic forays, volunteers in the war effort, donation of funds, and sporadic shipments of weapons. Once Cavour's Franco-Piedmontese alliance defeated Austria (Second Italian Independence War, 1859), European hostility kept Piedmont from openly backing Garibaldi's 1860–1861 daring, lightning revolutionary conquest of Bourbon Naples (Mille Expedition). Instead, ships carrying Italian volunteers to Garibaldi's army in Sicily were masked with American captains, flags, and names, with the undercover backing of Cavour and the U.S. government. During the 1860 Battle of Palermo, American ships secretly passed vital ammunition to Garibaldi, who had run out of supplies, thus securing his victory. Although the British Mediterranean Fleet later protected Garibaldi, he never forgot that first critical American help, and he claimed honorary U.S. citizenship while sojourning in New York.

After Piedmont annexed Garibaldi's revolutionary south in 1861, Britain and the United States were the first to recognize the new Italian state in contrast to Europe's diplomatic hostility. Italy always remained grateful for America's diplomatic support during the Risorgimento (even if its material impact was limited to selected groups), repaying it with increased bilateral trade; lower tariffs on United States goods; expanded rail and sea routes as trade links between America, Italy, and Europe; and by home porting the U.S. Mediterranean squadron at La Spezia in 1848–1864 (which provided a military deterrent against hostile Austrian and French fleets). In 1864, when Italy based at La Spezia its new unitarian navy (the world's fourth largest), the U.S. Mediterranean squadron was recalled home and disbanded during the Civil War (only in 1946 did the U.S. Sixth Fleet reestablish a permanent presence in the basin from its Italian base in Naples). During the Civil War only Russia and Italy diplomatically supported the Union and curbed Confederate trade, while all European powers (France, Britain, Austria, Prussia, Spain, Portugal, Papal Rome) backed the Confederate secession and slavery. Garibaldinian volunteers enrolled with the Union Army, as did the small Italian community of New York, while Italians of New Orleans sided with the Confederacy to "fit in." President Abraham Lincoln even offered twice a top military command to Garibaldi (most of the United States officer corps had defected to the South). But Garibaldi's request for supreme command of the U.S. Army and immediate abolition of slavery were conditions that Lincoln could not meet politically at the time, so Garibaldi returned home to complete Italy's unification in 1864–1870.

Up to 1870, United States/Italian relations were characterized by local warfare and individual efforts, rather than by any form of trans-Atlantic intervention. For both nations, diplomatic support had to suffice. After 1870, an era of expanding industrialization, liberalism, and democracy began, and each country, no longer isolated diplomatically or ideologically, focused upon more pressing problems of domestic economic development and divergent foreign policies: America colonized the West and economically penetrated Latin America and China; Italy sought "Irredentist" borders, economic and administrative unification, and Mediterranean colonies.

Yet both countries were labeled as brash, second-class young powers. America's moral self-righteousness, demobilization of the vast Civil War army and navy, and isolationism (geographically secluded behind the Atlantic and Pacific Oceans, and weak Mexican and Canadian neighbors) confirmed the Great Powers' disdain for an immature new power unable to channel abroad its immense economic strength. Italy's 1859–1861 emergence as a European power altered the regional balance and awakened the dreams of ancient Rome's glories (until Fascism's reenactment in 1923–1943). But as the "least of the powers," Italy's politico-economic backwardness and diplomatic-military hesitations kept it from acting as a Great Power in Europe and the Mediterranean. Italy's national security always required alliances both with Europe's hegemonic land powers (Germany in 1882–1914, 1936–1945; France in 1848–1866, 1914–1918, 1935; the Allies in 1915–1922, 1943–1947; United States/NATO in 1949), and with the Mediterranean's maritime hegemony (Britain in 1848–1935). Thus, Italy joined German Chancellor Otto von Bismarck's Triple Alliance in 1882–1914 (Germany, Austria-Hungary, Italy) to protect its porous Alpine borders, while its friendship with Britain secured its colonies and vital sea trade (85 percent of imports and 70 percent of exports). Until 1943 Italy's economic and diplomatic weakness contrasted dramatically the cyclical attempts to revamp its regional importance through massive, yet halting, industrial, naval, and technological races, while pursuing hasty colonial campaigns. But if Italy's new "high-tech" navy was briefly the world's third strongest (1865–1866, 1878–1890s), its prohibitive cost and unexpected colonial reversals in Ethiopia (1896) spurred heated criticism at home, in Europe, and in America over such futile attempts in securing global power.

United States–Italian relations became strained in the period 1870s through 1945 under the impact of massive Italian and European immigration, nativist American racism, ideological differences, and contrasting diplomatic goals, which destroyed the old veneer of cooperation and sympathy and left behind misunderstandings, distrust, and rivalries culminating in two world wars. America's industrial expansion and protectionism undercut traditional mercantilist interests in bilateral trade, while the flood of unskilled Italian emigrants to the New World (1870–1914, 1919–1921) sparked domestic resentment and diplomatic embarrassment. Earlier Italian settlers had been mostly northerners, few, often well-educated, or revolutionary patriots, all easily accepted socially within the American fabric, while the original Italian ethnic communities existed only in New York, New Orleans, and San Francisco. But overpopulation and economic impoverishment in Italy stimulated a steady outpouring of emigrants to the Mediterranean, France, and South America in the 1860s–1890s, and to the United States in the 1870s–1920s after the economic decline of Argentina and Brazil. Southern Italian peasants concentrated in North American cities because they were too poor to buy farmland in the West, and Italian American communities rose in the 1870s from fifteen thousand to forty thousand and exploded in 1880–1914 to over three million (with annual inflows of one hundred thousand immigrants after 1900 and an all-time high of three hundred thousand in 1913).

As one of the largest "instant" ethnic communities flooding America, the Italians spearheaded the turn-of-the-century massive influx of poor immigrants from southern and eastern Europe. Thus, local xenophobic racism and nativist militancy against the poor, ignorant, dirty, "dark-skinned" Catholic Italians fed upon American cyclical fears of being swamped by "unassimilable" foreign cultures. Soon this distorted view poisoned even traditionally pro-Italian circles in Boston and New York, where many Italian immigrants (including earlier Italian residents) were now discriminated as being either "acceptable" northern Italians or "dangerous" southern Italian "dagos." Such chasm in attitudes ran all the way to the White House, irrespective of party affiliations: international statesmen like presidents Theodore Roosevelt (Republican, 1901–1909) and Woodrow Wilson (Democrat, 1913–1921) often voiced their anti-Italianism, while Benjamin Harrison (Republican, 1889–1993), William H. Taft (Republican, 1909–1913), and Grover Cleveland (Democrat, 1885–1889, 1893–1897) courageously vetoed popular anti-immigration laws.

Most new Italian immigrants worked hard, were frugal, and saved painstakingly, hoping to gain wealth and return home to Italy. Yet in the pre–World War I period they rarely made it in America, remaining beset instead by crime, poverty, and segregation in ethnic ghettos, due to sociocultural and linguistic barriers (often only third-generation Italians became truly fluent in English and educated, given the traditional Italian indifference to education in favor of immediate jobs and earnings). The annoying "visibility" of these impoverished Italian peasants (like Russia's Jews and other eastern European immigrants) condemned them to marginal jobs and hard lives in ethnic ghettos in Boston, New York, Philadelphia, Baltimore, New Orleans, and San Francisco, all international harbors, where they settled as unskilled workers, bricklayers, artisans, and small shopkeepers. Later on, Italians spread across the East Coast and Midwest following the construction of railways and urban sewage systems that employed them, while others became blue-collar workers in industrial centers. But hostility and intercultural incomprehensions cut across classes: nativist snobbery by the American bourgeoisie bemoaning a lost "classical" vision of Italy, was backed by hostile nativists who feared the Italians' stubborn attachment to their old ways, while the working class resented Italians as cheap labor, strike-breakers, and tools of capitalist oppression undercutting strikes over wages and hiring policies. The many Little Italys flourishing throughout North America were also fragmented at their core by internecine rival provincial heritages: barely united at home under Piedmontese rule, Italians abroad remained split between several predominant southern subgroups (Neapolitans, Sicilians, Calabresi, Abruzzesi), each with its own subcultures, rivalries, and dialects distinct from literary Italian, yet all equally incapable to forge a common cultural linguistic identity, or a united front against outside prejudice.

Italians were particularly abused in the American South, where they were labeled "as bad as Negroes," attacked and often lynched (Louisiana, Mississippi, West Virginia) whenever they fraternized with local blacks, or were accused of crimes. The worst such incident was the infamous March 14, 1891, New Orleans lynching of eleven imprisoned Italians, members of a Mafia-type gang acquitted of killing Police Superintendent David Hennessy, by an organized mob of eight thousand with political support at the highest levels in Louisiana. Italy strongly condemned the New Orleans lynching as a violation of international law's safeguards toward foreign residents in host countries but was rebuffed by President Benjamin Harrison, who faced a deeply split country where North and West mostly decried the lynching, while the South praised it and turned it into a political tool to derail Harrison's reelection. Thus, United States–Italian diplomatic relations were nearly broken for a year; a war scare raged over "impending" Italian naval raids against an undefended America; and local Italian communities found themselves isolated, defiant, and embittered against the host country. Only in 1892 did Italy receive scant satisfaction through limited United States reparations. The New Orleans crisis and continuing tensions over immigration were all the more painful given Italy's close cooperation with the United States in regulating visas and blocking or repatriating the sick and criminals, while only demanding equal legal treatment for emigrants. Italy kept a routine low-key diplomatic profile on lynchings by routinely requesting reparations for the victims and prosecution of the guilty, but met constant American refusals to admit responsibility under international law. The risk of alienating such a vital emigration outlet muted Italy's diplomatic response. Thus, Italy never sought to mobilize politically its communities abroad, except to preserve its national language and culture in organizations like the Dante Alighieri Society and Sons of Italy Grand Lodge. Because the organization leaders and ethnic newspapers remained split by rancorous rivalries, they exercised scant political influence.

Accordingly, Italy could do little to keep diplomatic relations from unraveling with its old American friend, nor was any "gunboat diplomacy" advisable to protect Italy's interests in the New World. Although in the period between 1880 and 1990 the Italian navy was the third largest worldwide and kept a permanent naval squadron in South America (1860–1911) to protect the millions of emigrants from local xenophobic massacres (the 1893–1996 Italo-Brazilian crisis is an example), Italy remained a semi-industrialized medium power, geographically remote and unable to mount any major military reprisal beyond naval raids against enemy coastlines and sea trade. The United States instead, even with a skeletal army and obsolete navy, was already by 1895 a leading world industrial power, overtaking Britain and Germany, while economically dominating Latin America. The 1891 United States–Italian war scare spurred Washington to quickly build a modern, strong navy, which proved instrumental in winning the 1898 Spanish–American War and in seizing Cuba, Puerto Rico, the Philippines, and the Pacific, turning America into a world power. But at home hostility to Italian, Chinese, Japanese, Hispanic, Slavic, and Jewish immigrants reflected hysterical fears that the "melting pot" could not absorb such a massive influx of poor, uneducated "unassimilable aliens." Since 1891 nativist xenophobia waged for thirty years a domestic political battle to stop immigration, regardless of the needs of labor-hungry industries. During World War I all trans-Atlantic travel and emigration collapsed; then in 1921–1924 sweeping postwar U.S. anti-immigration laws kept the door shut. (Italy's annual immigration fell from 300,000 in 1913 to 5,800 in 1929.)

United States–Italian diplomatic relations reached an all-time low since the 1911–1912 Italo-Turkish War, when Europe and America condemned Italy's conquest of Libya, which was to prevent France's rival colonial expansion in North Africa from cutting Italy off the Mediterranean Sea. Sympathy from the United States for the Turks, despite the latter's well-known atrocities and corruption, reflected America's traditional anti-colonialism, which created opposition to Italy's nationalist expansion in the period between 1911–1914. This incident was more significant than earlier tensions (1885–1896 Italo-Ethiopian Wars), given America's global economic leadership and role in easing Italy's overpopulation. But Italy was still too distant and marginal in U.S. foreign policy, while America's isolationism from Europe's "immoral" power politics prevented any real bilateral showdown, at least as long as American global assertiveness and

Italian regional ambitions did not clash in the Mediterranean, as happened during both world wars.

At the onset of World War I, the United States and Italy became neutral, while the Entente/Allies (France, Britain, Russia, Serbia, and Japan) fought for European supremacy against the Central Powers (Germany, Austria-Hungary, Turkey, and Bulgaria). Notwithstanding its thirty-three-year membership in Germany's Triple Alliance, Italy's neutrality in 1914–1915 reflected an irredentist opposition to any Balkan war against Serbia unless Austria traded its disputed Italian provinces for support. Moreover, as Germany and Austria-Hungary were fighting for hegemony over Europe, Italy's security remained conditioned by British friendship for naval security and uninterrupted sea trade. Thus, Italy switched to the Allies when they promised Italy the Irredenta (Trentino, Istria, Dalmatia, and Fiume) and Adriatic Sea (1915 Treaty of London): Italy blocked a third of Austria-Hungary's army from the Balkans and Russia, delaying the Austro-German defeat of Russia. But Italy's unwillingness to back France against Germany alienated the Allies.

Also, the United States soon compromised its neutrality. At first, isolationism seemed best for a country heavily inhabited by European immigrants still passionately split along ethno-political lines by World War I (Anglo-Saxons, most Slavs, and Italians supported the entente; Germans, Hungarians, Poles, Irish, and Jews backed the central powers or noninterventionism). Woodrow Wilson, who was sympathetic to the entente, was reelected in 1916 on the pledge to "keep America out of the war," while fruitlessly mediating for peace between 1914 and 1916. Yet since 1914, the pull of United States war loans and exponential trade growth with the Allies doubled America's gross national product and set it in all but name on the entente's side (never challenging the Allied naval blockade of American and all-neutral trade with the central powers). Wilson then became convinced that peace was possible only by defeating Germany through direct American military intervention in 1917–1918 to rescue the demoralized Allies from collapse after the Russian Revolution and Italy's rout at Caporetto. Finally, fresh American troops and massive aid allowed the Allies to win the Great War by late 1918.

Wilson's Fourteen Points (1918) and Allied vindictiveness at Versailles (1919–1920) imposed a harsh peace treaty: Turkey and Austria-Hungary were dismembered and their oppressed Slavic nationalities became new independent states; Germany was demilitarized, occupied, and weakened under heavy reparations; Bolshevik Russia was isolated; international peace and disarmament were guaranteed by a "League of Nations." Wilson hoped to correct the Versailles Peace Treaty's harshness through the United States–led League of Nations as guarantor of the world's "collective security," but in order to achieve his moral internationalist vision he had to accommodate Allied vindictiveness and promise bilateral alliances with Britain and France to gain their support. This, however, exposed him to American criticism, while his intransigence toward Italy's nationalist claims on mixed Italo-Slavic lands (the Irredenta) precipitated the latent United States–Italian clash beginning in 1917: America and the Allies now supported Yugoslavia's rival border claims (which Italy saw as a reincarnation of its old Austrian enemy's regional influence), while Italo-Yugoslav nationalist rivalry and Rome's condemnation of Wilson's interference on behalf of Yugoslavia worsened Italy's isolation among the Allies. World War I had strengthened the bonds between America and the British and French, who jointly saw the Italians as poor soldiers (yet very few Allied troops were deployed in Italy). Wilson exploited the delirious enthusiasm his presence aroused among Europe's crowds in Europe by appealing directly to the Italian public opinion, seeking to turn it against its own government. Yet Rome resisted all Allied pressures until Wilson put the financial-commercial squeeze on American aid to Italy, exposing its extreme economic fragility. This breach between Italy and America was never fully healed, and although Versailles still gave Adriatic supremacy to Italy, the loss of Dalmatia and Fiume accelerated the postwar domestic collapse into political instability, massive socioeconomic turmoil, and a nationalist sense of betrayal (Mutilated Victory), which few in America and Europe understood or cared about.

Wilson's League of Nations was also seriously weakened when he was politically demoted in 1921 by Republican opponents who advocated neo-isolationism and rejected any

American involvement to protect "collective security," or the Anglo-French. United States–European relations deteriorated as budget-minded Republicans restricted trade and emigration and sought repayment of Allied war loans; although the United States had benefited most from Allied war trade, becoming the richest world power with negligible losses compared to millions of Allied lives, America always opposed writing off war loans as dutiful financial contribution to the Great War. United States–European relations broke down in 1931 when the Europeans, savaged by the 1929–1933 Great Depression, stopped payments and America prohibited future loans and supplies until all debts were repaid.

In Italy, as democracy and governmental authority collapsed in 1919–1922, attacked from both left-wing and right-wing groups, Benito Mussolini's paramilitary Fascist Blackshirts seized power in a bloodless 1922 coup (March on Rome) by skillfully wielding nationalist resentment against the Allies and Yugoslavia, while attacking the Left at home. Mussolini's Fascist regime eliminated domestic oppositions and renewed Italy's quest for prestige and territorial gains against France and Britain in the Mediterranean, while supporting Germany's demands to revise the Versailles Treaty. Mussolini's policy of balancing one threat with another to magnify Fascist Italy's international importance and exalt a diplomacy of violence as a means for prestige and power slowly destabilized the fragile peace between the two world wars through cyclical crises: the 1923 Corfù crisis; the 1920s contrasts with Yugoslavia and France; the 1935–1936 Italo-Ethiopian War; the 1936–1939 Spanish Civil War; the 1936–1945 Italo-German Axis. Bereft of American leadership, the West and League of Nations were unable to prevent the 1930s collapse of the Versailles system under the parallel destabilizing expansion of Fascist Italy, Nazi Germany, and Japan.

Throughout the 1920s and 1930s, most Americans lost interest in European politics. Instead, Mussolini, between 1923 and 1935, was often praised in the United States, Britain, and most countries as a champion of anticommunism, law and order, and opposing "subversive" radical strikers and unions. In America the business and banking sectors cheered Mussolini; the press was generally obtusely acritical when not swayed by Fascist propaganda and bribes; while Catholic, Protestant, and Jewish communities remained split. Only the unions and academic circles remained generally critical of Nazi-Fascist totalitarianism, except for Columbia University's overt pro-Fascism. American tourists flocked to Italy in the 1920s–1930s, but being less cultured in the Italian language than their predecessors in the 1700s–1900s, their contacts were superficial and easily manipulated by Fascist propaganda into praising Italy's "achievements." While some writers like Ezra Pound keenly backed Mussolini, the majority remained acritical, except for Ernest Hemingway's strong anti-Fascism and involvement in the 1936–1939 Spanish Civil War, which spearheaded the delayed ideological shift of America's *intelligentizia* against Fascism. Among most emigrant communities (United States, Latin America, North Africa) Italy's consulates now controlled Italian schools abroad, and the Fascists eagerly established local party sections (*Fasci*), promoted pro-Italian nationalist demonstrations, and used radio broadcasts and educational materials to indoctrinate the emigrants, while harassing and organizing covert terrorist assassinations to muzzle exiled anti-Fascists (*Fuoriusciti*).

In the nostalgic void of emigration, hard times, and cultural shock of assimilation into foreign realities, Mussolini's grandeur capitalized on the misguided naive sense of national pride that an apparently strong and braggart Fascist Italy enticed among her distant, lost sons, soothing the wounded nationalist pride of Italian Americans (4.5 million by 1940) who grieved the discriminating 1924 United States anti-immigration laws. Mussolini first formed the Fascist League of North America (1923–1929), which was eventually disbanded under charges of subversion by the American media and Congress; it was replaced in 1930 by the Lictor Federation, soon under scrutiny by the Federal Bureau of Investigation. Although both were limited in membership, their propaganda influence was strengthened since 1922–1925 by the Fascist's virtual takeover of the largest and oldest Italian-American organization, the Sons of Italy Grand Lodge (three hundred thousand members), and the Dante Alighieri Society after expelling their anti-Fascist members (politician and first New York City Italian American mayor Fiorello LaGuardia was among the few condemning Fascism's penetration in America). By 1936–1937

Italo-American Fascists cooperated with the smaller pro-Nazi German American Bund, and by 1940 controlled two hundred groups with some ten thousand local Blackshirts and one hundred thousand active supporters (or 5 percent of the Italian American community), while opponents feared that Fascist sympathizers numbered between 10 percent (450,000) to even 35 percent. But with 50 percent more indifferent to politics and just 10 percent opposed to Fascism, anti-Fascist rallies never attracted more than two thousand participants. While quite influential in France under the exiled Rosselli brothers and Catholic leader Luigi Sturzo, the anti-Fascist *Fuoriusciti* in America under ex–foreign minister Count Carlo Sforza found it difficult to overcome local hostile indifference by the U.S. government, Italian communities, and American public opinion. The moderate Sforza was still stigmatized by American and British intelligence as an anti-Fascist as late as the beginning of World War II when he reemerged as a key exiled leader. In the United States, Fascist propaganda wisely never portrayed anti-American sentiments, but cultivated the similarities between Italy's nationalist imperialism in the Mediterranean and United States control of Latin America. Yet Italian American Fascists remained fractured by internecine rivalries and although they answered Mussolini's patriotic calls, sending two small volunteer brigades during the 1935–1936 Italo-Ethiopian War, their influence collapsed by 1940–1941 and no Fascists joined Italy in World War II, deserting the cause altogether once the Axis attacked America (December 7–11, 1941).

Notwithstanding brief intermittent American criticism of Fascist imperialism, United States–Italian relations remained nearly friendly, while Britain also backed Mussolini in 1923–1935 as a useful Mediterranean bulwark against France. The peak of America's friendship with Fascist Italy was reached during the two highly propagandized trans-Atlantic flights in 1930 and 1933 of Italo Balbo's Atlantic Air Squadron fleet of thirty-five seaplanes, enthusiastically received by all Italian American communities in the United States and Latin America. A Fascist leader (1920–1940), air force minister (1929–1933), and Mussolini's keenest rival, Balbo revamped the Italian air force as a tool of nationalist prestige and his trans-Atlantic flights to the Americas were carefully orchestrated to boost Fascist Italy's image abroad as a right-wing, brazen world power, while consolidating Fascist politico-ideological control over the emigrated Italian communities in the United States and South America (with 40 percent of the population of Italian stock, Argentina became Fascist in the 1930s under the dictatorship of Juan Perón, a friend of Mussolini and Hitler until 1945). Balbo's zigzagging trans-Atlantic feat was also the first of that kind since German American flyer Charles Lindbergh had completed the first trans-Atlantic solo flight from America to France less than a decade earlier on a shorter route. However, after the 1933 Chicago triumph, Mussolini demoted his powerful rival, sending Balbo to a "golden exile" as governor of Libya in 1934–1940. Balbo opposed World War II and died when his plane was accidentally shot down by Italian defenses fearing a British air raid.

During the 1935–1936 Italo-Ethiopian War, Democratic President Franklin D. Roosevelt and America's public opinion slowly woke up to the threat of Fascist power politics, fearing thereafter any Italian American nationalist revival to be hostile fifth columns. But American diplomacy still remained essentially isolationist and neutralist; against Roosevelt's wish, an isolationist Congress responded to the Ethiopian War and Spanish Civil War with five Neutrality Acts prohibiting arms shipments to any side in war, while U.S. businesses ignored Roosevelt's pleas to voluntarily back the League of Nation's economic sanctions against Fascist Italy. Although the United States was not a member, the unimpeded flow of American oil and the League's abysmal failure to enforce either sanctions or international military reprisals allowed an isolated but defiant Italy to defeat Ethiopia. United States–Italian relations cooled further when Mussolini's Axis alignment with Nazi Germany led a joint propaganda rhetoric. The ideological-imperialist clash between Nazi-Fascism and democracy would soon present an additional threat to an enfeebled West. International tensions skyrocketed in 1938–1939 following Germany's annexation of Austria, the Munich Pact, and Italy's seizure of Albania. With the 1939 Italo-German Pact of Steel, the alliance also planned World War II after completing their rearmament: Nazi Germany would conquer Europe, and Fascist Italy the Mediterranean with an expanded colonial empire (Dalmatia from Yugoslavia; Tunisia, Djibouti, Corsica,

Nice, and Savoy from France; Malta, Somaliland, Sudan, and North Kenya from Britain).

As World War II broke out in 1939, both Italy and the United States reconfirmed their neutrality. But Roosevelt slowly eroded domestic isolationism: America gave supplies to China during the 1937–1945 Sino-Japanese War and in 1940 imposed a trade embargo on Japan; national rearmament was initiated; and the Neutrality Acts abrogated. The fall of France in June 1940 and Fascist Italy's entry into war shocked America's public opinion into finally allowing Roosevelt to support Britain with United States war matériel shipments (1940 Cash and Carry Act and Destroyers Deal; 1941 Lend-Lease Act to Britain and the USSR). Roosevelt's political interventionism against Germany (Four Freedoms and Arsenal of Democracy) and his secret 1940–1941 negotiations to join Britain in war to defend democracy included the freezing of Axis assets in America, the closing of their consulates, the seizure and internment of Axis ships in U.S. ports, and the 1941 secret naval harassment in the Atlantic's international waters of German submarines.

Fascist Italy's military inferiority (the 1935–1939 wars had exhausted it) led to its brief neutrality until 1940, when Mussolini joined Hitler, believing the West was doomed and an easy, quick war would allow the Axis to partition Europe. Instead, Britain continued to fight alone after France's collapse, locking Fascist Italy in a desperate naval struggle for Mediterranean supremacy (1940–1943), while Mussolini's ill-planned offensives in France, Libya, Ethiopia, and Greece turned into humiliating defeats, notwithstanding the 1940 Tripartite Pact (Germany, Italy, and Japan) and Axis successes in North Africa, Yugoslavia, and the USSR. Finally, when in December 1941 the Japanese sunk the U.S. Fleet at Pearl Harbor, Hawaii, and demoted America's rival presence in the Pacific, Hitler and Mussolini gratuitously declared war on the United States, thus "freeing" Roosevelt from domestic pressures to wage an American war exclusively against Japan (leaving Britain and Russia alone against the Axis). Roosevelt and Churchill focused on rescuing Stalin and first win the vital European war against the Nazi-Fascists, while halting Japan in the Pacific. Tens of thousands of Italians were briefly detained in United States relocation camps in the West, while Japanese Americans were detained for the entire war. By 1943 the Allies conquered North Africa and Sicily, securing Mediterranean sea routes to India via the Suez Canal. Then Allied landings in southern Italy provoked a military monarchist coup d'état, replacing Mussolini with General Pietro Badoglio (July 1943), who secretly negotiated with the Allies to switch sides. But British hostility and the Allied 1943 Casablanca Declaration of "unconditional surrender" forced Italy into the humiliating September 1943 armistices, tempered by Anglo-American promises to land near Rome and protect the city from Hitler's wrath. Instead, Germany's rapid seizure of north central Italy and Rome forced the Allies to land south at Anzio, while Italy's royal government fled to Allied-controlled areas. Left by Badoglio without orders or leadership, Italy's army was totally wiped out in a few days by German attacks and widespread dissertions, while only the navy remained to face the Allies at Malta. Italy's collapse forced the Allies to fight a long campaign in 1943–1945 on hard mountainous terrain, while a spontaneous Italian partisan war engaged German forces and Mussolini's north Italian republic of Salò.

To conquer impoverished southern Italy, the United States relied heavily on both pardoned Italian American gangsters (using the Cosa Nostra's criminal ties to the Sicilian Mafia to gather intelligence and sabotage the enemy) and Italian American soldiers (to fraternize with the ex-enemies). Paradoxically, notwithstanding the large Italian American immigrant population, America was lacking Italian experts compared to Britain: most ethnic Italian Americans spoke only broken dialect and had scant contacts with the "old country," toward which they displayed offputting superiority and contempt (due in part to their legacy as descendants of poor emigrants kicked out of Italy and now returning as well-off "cousins" to a despised, defeated country). But while many found their roots, all saw southern Italy as a strikingly alien, backward land (socially and culturally). Only in time did American contempt melt away under the impact of close interaction with long-lost semi-relatives and new friends, as well as a high rate of intermarriages and generous American aid. By contrast, British hostility remained unrelenting: from 1935 to World War II Britain had been besieged by Mussolini's expansionism and the Axis, so London now sought to lead postwar Europe against Germany and Soviet influence, while dominating the Mediterranean, Spain, Greece, Turkey, and Italy. Britain opposed any pro-Allied Italian military role, systematically undercut the anti-Fascist partisan-democratic front (CLN/National Liberation Committee), and kept Italy weak and monarchical, rather than allow Sforza and the CLN to forge a republican, democratic Italy. America deferred to British local interests but later supported Italy's cause.

World War II ended once the Anglo-American invasion of France and Western Europe in 1944–1945 met the Soviet advance, crushing Nazi Germany from the East in 1943–1945, while Japan collapsed by late 1945. An independent democratic Italian republic emerged in 1946 after local partisans and anti-Fascists prevailed in 1943–1946 over the conservative Badoglio and Savoyard regime (representative of the ex-Fascist "old order") and oppressive Allied controls. But British efforts to isolate Italy were backed by the USSR, France, Yugoslavia, Greece, Albania, and Ethiopia: the 1947 Paris Peace Treaty left Italy demilitarized and without a navy, colonies, and borders. Yet soon the 1946–1991 East–West Cold War against the USSR allowed Italy's national security to benefit from America's economic aid and military protection, becoming an equal Western member of the United States–led NATO alliance (1949–2000).

Marco Rimanelli

Bibliography

Diggins, John P. *Mussolini and Fascism: The View from America*. Princeton: Princeton University Press, 1980.

Kogan, Norman. *A Political History of Italy, 1945–1980s*. New York: Praeger, 1983.

Rimanelli, Marco. *Italy between Europe and the Mediterranean: Diplomacy and Naval Strategy from Unification to NATO, 1800s–2000*. New York: Peter Lang, 1997.

Rimanelli, Marco, and Sheryl L. Postman, eds. *The 1891 New Orleans Lynching and U.S.–Italian Relations: Diplomacy, Mafia, Immigration*. New York: Peter Lang, 1992.

Sassoon, Donald. *Contemporary Italy: Politics, Economy and Society Since 1945*. New York: Longman, 1986.

Smith, Mack Denis. *The Making of Italy, 1796–1870*. New York: Harper & Row, 1968.

Spots, Frederic, and Theodor Wieser. *Italy: A Difficult Democracy*. London: Cambridge University Press, 1986.

Tannenbaum, Edward R. *The Fascist Experience: Italian Society and Culture, 1922–1945*. New York: Basic Books, 1972.

See also COLD WAR: ITALIAN AMERICANS AND ITALY; COLD WAR: UNITED STATES FOREIGN POLICY TOWARD ITALY

Utah

Italian immigrants formed one of the largest settlements of southern and eastern Europeans in Utah. Some Protestant Waldensians from northern Italy had immigrated in the 1870s as Mormon converts. However, the bulk of these immigrants, primarily Catholic, journeyed to Utah during the years spanning from the 1890s through the 1920s in response to demands for labor in the mining and railroading industries. Italians continued to trickle into the state after World War II, and in the 1980s and 1990s some continued to arrive due to religious beliefs.

Italians came to Utah primarily from the regions of Piemonte, Veneto, Lombardia, Abruzzi, Lazio, Calabria, and Sicilia. They settled in the four main counties of Carbon, Salt Lake, Tooele, and Weber. These immigrants found employment in metal mining, coal mining, mills, smelters, refineries, railroads, farming, goat ranching, service-related industries, and businesses. The highest point of Italian foreign-born population in Utah occurred in 1920 with 3,225 immigrants. By 1990 those of Italian heritage in Utah numbered over ten thousand individuals.

In Carbon County, Italians settled in coal towns such as Castle Gate and Sunnyside and in the farming/railroading locales of Spring Glen, Price, and Helper. Italians migrated to the railroad hub of Helper after a labor strike in 1903, many leaving the labor ranks and entering into the professions and businesses.

Salt Lake County Italians resided in Salt Lake City and the mining towns of Bingham Canyon, Garfield, Magna, Midvale, and Murray. The west side of Salt Lake City harbored a Little Italy. In the southern portion of the city Italians owned truck farms that supplied fruit and produce. Others operated goat ranches. Those who lived in Tooele County worked in the mining town of Mercur or located in the city of Tooele, where many labored in the local smelter.

Tyroleans settled in the Ogden area, a railroad hub known as "Junction City." Many worked first in Rock Springs, Reliance, and Superior, Wyoming, before migrating to Utah. In Ogden some established dairies, farms, or other businesses. Other Italians labored as railroad section hands, later entering other occupations.

Italians arrived in Utah primarily as single men with the intent to remain sojourners. However, with opportunities abounding, many of these men in the 1910s decided to remain in Utah and establish families. Italian social and fraternal organizations developed in Utah to provide these immigrants with insurance and death benefits, as well as companionship. In time, such groups provided Italians with the tools to move into the larger society. These associations included the following: Stella D'America, Castle Gate (1891); Principe Di Napoli, Castle Gate (1902); Fratellanza Minatori, Sunnyside (1902); Società Cristoforo Colombo, Castle Gate (ca. 1919); Italian Americanization Club, Price (1919); Società di Beneficenza, Bingham Canyon and Mercur (1896); Società Cristoforo Colombo, Salt Lake City (1897); Club Dante Alighieri, Salt Lake City (1908); Figli D'Italia, Salt Lake City (1915); the Italian-American Civic League, Salt Lake City (1934); the Friendly Club (Tyrolean-Italians), Ogden (1937); Società Cristoforo Colombo, Ogden (ca. 1930s); and Club Italia, Salt Lake City (1992).

Italians played an active role in the state's labor history. In the 1903–1904 coal miners' strike in Carbon County, organizer Carlo Demolli, from Como, assumed a leadership role for the United Mine Workers of America. Frank Bonacci, born in Decollatura, led a tireless effort for union recognition from the late 1910s through the 1930s. Italians also became active in the Western Federation of Miners, later to become the International Association of Mine, Mill, and Smelter Workers.

An Italian press enjoyed an ephemeral life in Utah. The newspapers, with their editors, included the following: *Il Minatore* (Mose Paggi), *La Gazzetta Italiana* (G. Milano), *La Scintilla* (Alfonso Russo and Milano), and *Il Corriere D'America* (Frank Niccoli and Russo). Italian papers from other regions circulated, and continue to circulate, into Italian homes: *Il Vindice* (Pueblo, Colorado), *Il Lavoratore Italiano* (Trinidad, Colorado), *L'Italia* and *Protesta Umana* (San Francisco, California), *La Follia di New York* and *Il Progresso Italo-Americano* (New York), and *Italo Americano* (Los Angeles).

Italians in Utah reached an accommodation with the dominant society but have maintained vestiges of their ethnic culture. Religious and secular holidays, feast days, and celebrations, with accompanying folk foods and music, provide Italians some continuity with the past. Connections between places of origin and destination continue for many Utah Italian Americans.

While restrictive immigration legislation of the 1920s effectively cut the flow of immigrants into Utah, Italian immigration has continued from the 1950s through the 1990s. Some immigration persists in Utah due to missionary efforts of the Mormon Church in Italy.

Philip F. Notarianni

Bibliography

Notarianni, Philip F. "Italian Fraternal Organizations in Utah, 1897–1934." *Utah Historical Quarterly* 43 (spring 1975): 172–187.

———. "Italian Involvement in the 1903–04 Coal Miners' Strike in Southern Colorado and Utah." In *Pane e Lavoro: The Italian American Working Class,* edited by George E. Pozzetta. Toronto: Multicultural Center of Ontario, 1980.

———. "Italianità in Utah: The Immigrant Experience." In *The Peoples of Utah,* edited by Helen Z. Papanikolas. Salt Lake City: Utah State Historical Society, 1976.

———. "Italians in Utah." In *Utah History Encyclopedia,* edited by Allan Kent Powell. Salt Lake City: University of Utah Press, 1994.

Raspa, Richard. "Exotic Foods Among Italian-Americans in Mormon Utah." In *Ethnic and Regional Foodways in the United States,* edited by Linda Keller Brown and Kay Mussel. Nashville: University of Tennessee Press, 1984.

Taylor, David A., and John Alexander Williams, eds. *Old Ties, New Attachments: Italian-American Folklife in the West.* Washington, DC: American Folk Life Center, 1992.

V

Vacchiano, William (Anthony) (b. 1912)
A member of the New York Philharmonic for many years, William Vacchiano became one of America's most accomplished trumpeters and teachers of music. He was born in Portland, Maine, on May 23, 1912, the son of Ralph and Anna (née Crispi) Vacchiano, Italian immigrants from Cicciano, near Naples. At an early age, William came under the influence of a professor who conducted a band of local Italian musicians. Later, at age 14, his talent as trumpeter was recognized when Frank Knapp, the trumpeter of this local band, had him play for the developing Portland Symphony Orchestra. Having distinguished himself in the band at Portland High School from which he graduated in 1930, Vacchiano had sought but failed to receive a scholarship from St. John's University because of a difference in the academic point systems between Maine and New York.

Fortunately, music professor Max Schlossberg recognized his talent and obtained a scholarship for William at the Institute of Musical Art, now known as the Juilliard School of Music. Here the Maine native studied until 1935 under Schlossberg who was not only a fine teacher but an excellent trumpeter. During these years Vacchiano met Josephine LaPrade, whom he married before he finished his studies and received a bachelor's and a master's from the Manhattan School of Music. Thereafter, Vacchiano launched into a lengthy musical career that centered on the concert hall and the classroom. Not only did he rise to trumpeter extraordinaire with the New York Philharmonic Orchestra from 1935 to 1973, but he served on the faculty of both the Juilliard School of Music and the Manhattan School of Music from 1936 to the present, while also teaching at the Mannes School of Music from 1940 to 1975.

Sensitive to the potential of ranges that could be reached by each performer, Vacchiano saw the need to develop various mouthpieces to suit the individual trumpeter. "These mouthpieces were designed especially for the high trumpets," he once explained. "All models have special features in rim, cup, bore, and backbore that give excellent support for sustained playing in the upper register while maintaining a big symphonic sound." Along with his expertise in improving the quality of performance by trumpeters, Vacchiano also made a major impact as a teacher of more than fifteen hundred students. Among them are such talented individuals as Mel Broiles, Armando Ghitalla, Manny Laureano, Wynton Marsalis, Philip Smith, and Gerard Schwarz.

Vacchiano has been prominently featured in a number of recordings with the New York Philharmonic. One of the better-known recordings was his long-playing rendition of Johann Sebastian Bach's Brandenburg Concerto no. 2. He has also specialized in the music of Anton Bruckner, Aaron Copland, George Gershwin, Gustav Mahler, Richard Strauss, and Igor Stravinsky. In forty years Vacchiano has performed under eighty conductors, including such great twentieth-century conductors as Arturo Toscanini, Fritz Reiner, and Leonard Bernstein. His musical career has reflected his talent as an extraordinary performer and his genius as an exceptional teacher.

Vincent A. Lapomarda

Bibliography

Meckna, Michael. *Twentieth-Century Brass Soloists.* Westport, CT: Greenwood Press, 1994.

Silberschlag, Jeff, and John Irvine. "William Vacchiano, Trumpeter." *International Trumpet Guild Journal* 16 (December 1991): 4–11.

Smith, André M. "William Vacchiano, An Appreciative Recollection of His 83rd Birthday: 23 May 1995." *International Trumpet Guild Journal* 19 (May 1995): 4–33.

See also HIGHER EDUCATION

Valachi, Joseph

See CRIME AND ORGANIZED CRIME

Valenti, Jack (b. 1921)

Born in Houston, Texas, in 1921, Jack Valenti has worn many hats: wartime bomber, advertising agency founder, political consultant, White House assistant, and film industry leader.

During World War II as a pilot in the Army Air Corps, Lieutenant Valenti flew fifty-one combat missions as the pilot-commander of a B-25 attack bomber with the 12th Air Force in Italy. He was decorated with the Distinguished Flying Cross, the Air Medal, the Distinguished Unit Citation, and the European Theater Ribbon with four battle stars. France awarded him its highly prized the French Legion of Honor.

Valenti received a B.A. from the University of Houston and an M.B.A. from Harvard University. As an undergraduate, he worked during the day and attended classes in the evening. In 1952 he co-founded the advertising and political agency of Weekly and Valenti. Three years later Valenti met Lyndon B. Johnson, the majority leader of the U.S. Senate. The meeting between these two men led to Valenti's close association with Johnson throughout the latter's presidency. Valenti was in the motorcade in Dallas on November 22, 1963, when President John F. Kennedy was shot. Within hours of the president's assassination, Valenti flew back on Air Force One to Washington as the newly hired special assistant to the new president.

In 1966 Valenti resigned from his White House post to become the third president and chief executive officer of the Motion Picture Association of America. He has presided over enormous change in the industry as new technology and the rise of world markets have drastically changed the American film and television industries.

Valenti was one of the founding board members of the National Italian American Foundation (NIAF) in 1976. He is the author of three books: *The Bitter Taste of Glory* (1971), *A Very Human President* (1975), and *Protect and Defend* (1992). He and his wife, Mary Margaret, live in Washington, D.C., though he spends half his time in Los Angeles. The Valentis have three children.

Elissa Ruffino

Bibliography

Valenti, Jack. *The Bitter Taste of Glory.* New York: World, 1971.

———. *Protect and Defend.* New York: Doubleday, 1992.

———. *A Very Human President.* New York: Horton, 1975.

Valentino, Rudolph (1895–1926)

Rodolfo Alfonzo Raffaelo Pierre Filibert Guliemi di Valentina d'Antonguola, destined to become the most popular male star of the silent film period, was born on May 6, 1895, in Castellaneta, a small village in the Apulia region of southern Italy. After failing to gain admission to a naval academy, he attempted agricultural studies. In 1912 he settled in Paris but again met failure. He arrived in New York in late 1913 and settled briefly among Italian immigrants in Brooklyn, where he worked as a landscape gardener, dishwasher, and waiter. He was also arrested several times on suspicion of petty theft and blackmail. Eventually he obtained work as a taxi dancer in the dance halls and nightclubs of Manhattan by virtue of his skill as a ballroom dancer. He had a big break when he replaced Clifton Webb as the partner of a popular dancer of that time. He left New York to join the cast of a musical that eventually folded in Ogden, Utah. He traveled to San Francisco, where he continued his career as a dancer, finally arriving in Hollywood in 1917.

At first he found employment in the movies by playing extra roles and bit parts. By 1920 his roles had improved. The following year, Metro-Goldwyn-Mayer gave Valentino the lead in *The Four Horsemen of the Apocalypse*. The film was a huge box office hit, and he became an overnight Hollywood star. Within a few years his fame had reached such a level that his strikingly handsome face was recognized all over the world wherever American movies were shown. The year 1921 also saw the release of *The Sheik* (Paramount), which is considered his biggest success. This was followed in 1922 by *Blood and Sand* and *Monsieur Beaucaire* in 1924, also popular hits.

Valentino is considered the first of a long line of male film stars who exuded a sex appeal to female movie audiences. His handsome features, grace of movement, and provocative gaze established him as a new-style foreign leading man (often in exotic costume) who created fantasies of illicit love and erotic adventures in the minds of his women admirers. *The Sheik* created such a sensation that women fainted in the aisles of theaters where it was shown and Arabic designs influenced fashions and home decorating. Valentino's film persona helped establish the image of the Italian as the archetypical "Latin lover." In contrast, male audiences and critics generally judged his acting as exaggerated and his style foppish and often effeminate.

Regardless of his reputation as a silent screen actor, Valentino's popularity was crucial to the early development of the movie industry and to the survival of three major studios, including MGM, which was saved from bankruptcy by Valentino's first major film. He is also credited with helping to establish the star system (wherein top actors receive special consideration) as a result of his pay disputes and two comebacks. In sum, he portrayed minor and major roles in thirty-two films in approximately nine years—a record that is notable even by modern standards.

In his personal life Valentino was not so successful. In 1919, before he became famous, he married Jean Acker, an actress. He was locked out on their wedding night, and the marriage was never consummated. His second marriage to Natasha Rambova was declared bigamous since his first marriage had not been dissolved, and he was arrested. He avoided prosecution on the grounds of nonconsummation of his first marriage. He married Rambova again, legally, in 1923; however, the couple soon separated. Valentino's second wife proved to be ambitious and strong-willed with regard to his career. She took charge and interfered in career decisions that proved disastrous by rendering Valentino's film image increasingly effeminate. Eventually studio executives barred her from the set in order to curtail her influence and to salvage his popularity, which had begun to wane. This situation was reversed with two box office hits: *The Eagle* (1925) and *The Son of the Sheik* (1926). At the peak of his comeback, before the release of *The Son of the Sheik,* he died suddenly on August 23, 1926, of a perforated ulcer. His death at age 31 caused a wave of mass hysteria among his female fans. Thousands lined up to view his casket and funeral. To date people still visit his crypt, especially on the anniversary of his death. His enduring fame as an icon of the silent screen is attested by several biographies, two film biographies (1951 and 1977), and an opera (*The Dream of Valentino,* 1994). Valentino's name lives on as silent film's leading male star.

Angelo Tripicchio

Bibliography
Shulman, Irving. *Valentino.* New York: Trident, 1967.
Walker, Alexander. *Valentino.* New York: Stein and Day, 1976.

See also FILM DIRECTORS, PRODUCERS, AND ITALIAN AMERICAN IMAGE IN FILM; MOVIE ACTORS AND ACTRESSES

Valvano, James Thomas (1946–1993)

One of the exceptional coaches of college basketball, Jim Valvano set an example for his generation with his spirited fight against cancer.

The son of Rocco and Marie Angela (née Vitale) Valvano, he was born March 10, 1946, in Queens, New York City, and died at Duke University Medical Center in Durham, North Carolina, on April 28, 1993. Growing up on Long Island, he received his secondary education at Seaford High School, where he played basketball under his father who was the school's coach.

Entering Rutgers in New Brunswick, New Jersey, where he majored in English and played basketball, Valvano helped to lead the Scarlet Knights to the National Invitational Tournament, where they finished third. Named senior athlete of the year, he graduated in

1967 with a bachelor's degree and married Pamela Susan Levine, who became the mother of his three daughters.

Valvano chose for his model football's Vince Lombardi, who emphasized commitment to one's family, faith, and team. From coaching freshmen at Rutgers in the next two years, Valvano moved to Johns Hopkins, where he became the youngest head coach ever and, during the 1969–1970 season, led the basketball team to its first winning season in a generation. He spent the next two years as an assistant coach at the University of Connecticut before be became head coach, from 1972 to 1975, at Bucknell University. Subsequently, he became head coach at Iona College in New Rochelle, New York, from 1975 to 1980. His teams won almost one hundred games while losing fewer than fifty and appeared in two National Collegiate Athletic Association tournaments. However, the NCAA achievement in 1980 was marred after it was learned that one of his players had violated NCAA rules.

Nevertheless, Valvano's coaching career rose swiftly to the top at North Carolina State University, where he took its basketball team into the finals of regional and national tournaments. In 1983 his team won the NCAA tournament by defeating Houston 54–52, and in 1989 he was voted basketball's college coach of the year. Unfortunately, the troubles that had emerged at Iona only increased at North Carolina State because he tended to regard his players more as recruits for an athletic team than as students preparing for an academic degree. By 1990 his coaching career ended, and he took a position as a basketball expert for television networks ABC and ESPN.

Because of his courageous fight against bone cancer during the last year of life, he received the Arthur Ashe Award for Courage. Before his death, Valvano established, with ESPN's help, The Jimmy V Foundation to help cancer patients. The foundation is located in Cary, North Carolina, where he was buried.

Vincent A. Lapomarda

Bibliography

Golenbock, Peter. *Personal Fouls: The Broken Promises and Shattered Dreams of Big Money Basketball at Jim Valvano's North Carolina State*. New York: Carroll & Graf, 1989.

Kirkpatrick, Curry. "How King Rat Became the Big Cheese." *Sports Illustrated* 59 (5 December 1983): 76–90.

Smith, Gary. "As Time Runs Out." *Sports Illustrated* 78 (11 January 1993): 10–20.

Valvano, James T. *Too Soon to Quit: The Story of N.C. State's 1983 National Championship Season*. Raleigh: Coman, 1983.

———. *Valvano: They Gave Me a Lifetime Contract, and Then Declared Me Dead*. New York: Pocket, 1992.

See also SPORTS

Venturi, Robert Charles (b. 1925)

Credited with founding the postmodern movement in architecture, Robert Charles Venturi was born in Philadelphia on June 25, 1925. His father, Robert Venturi Sr., was a successful Philadelphia food merchant who had migrated in 1890 at age 9 to the United States from the town of Atessa, Abruzzi; his mother, Vanna Lanzetta, was born in Washington, D.C., and her parents came from Apuglia. Both parents were nominally Catholic but became Quakers when their only son was 5 years old. At an early age, Robert aspired to become an architect, and his parents encouraged this aspiration.

Young Venturi attended the Lansdowne Friends School and graduated from the more traditional Episcopal Academy in Philadelphia in 1943. Four years later, he graduated summa cum laude from Princeton University with a B.A. in architecture. In 1950 he received a master's degree at Princeton's Graduate School of Architecture. While at Princeton, Venturi was influenced by social and architectural historian Donald Drew Egbert and architectural design critic Jean Labatut. He broadened his education with a visit to England, France, and Italy in the summer of 1948. Venturi won the prestigious Rome Prize Fellowship in architecture and spent 1954–1956 in Italy. This personal and professional experience greatly influenced his development as an architect. From 1950 to 1958 he worked as a designer in the architectural firms of Oscar Stonorov of Philadelphia, Eero Saarinen of Bloomfield Hills, Michigan, and Louis I. Kahn of Philadelphia. He was a partner in the firm of Venturi, Cope, and Lippincott in Philadelphia, 1958–1963; Venturi and Short in Philadelphia, 1961–1964; and Venturi and Rauche in Philadelphia, 1964 to the present.

From 1957 to 1965, he taught architectural theory and design at the University of Pennsylvania, where he developed his ideas on architectural postmodernism. He met Denise Scott Brown, a British-educated professor from South Africa, whom he married in 1967; they have one child, James Charles. She collaborated with Venturi and became a member of the firm of Venturi and Rauche in 1967. Venturi joined with Scott Brown and Steven Izenour to write *Learning from Las Vegas* (Cambridge, MA: MIT Press, 1972, 1977). Its purpose was to humanize architecture by examining the rising city of Las Vegas with its sprawl, automobile-dominant culture, billboards, neon-lit signs, and commercial architecture. Venturi stated in this work that "learning from popular culture does not remove the architect from his or her status in high culture. But it may alter high culture to make it more sympathetic to current needs and issues." He demanded a "people's architecture," an appreciation of mass culture, and an eclectic approach to architectural design over the functional boxlike structures that were destroying the urban unity of American cities.

Venturi's basic philosophy had emerged in his influential book *Complexity and Contradiction in Architecture* (New York: Museum of Modern Art, 1966, 1977), when he criticized modern architecture as vapid, without meaning, puritanical, simplistic, and lacking historical tradition. Younger architects took note of Venturi's call for change, and even modernists were transformed to postmodernism. In 1972, when several modern-designed fourteen-story "apartment blocks" in St. Louis were destroyed, the postmodern age began. Other similar buildings were destroyed because of the dissatisfaction of modernism. Venturi's influence was profound.

Among the buildings he has designed are Guild Hall (Philadelphia, 1961); Vanna Venturi House, designed and built for his mother, (1964, Philadelphia); Humanities Building (SUNY Purchase, 1972); Franklin Court (Independence National Historical Park, Philadelphia, 1976); Gordon Wu Hall (Princeton University (1981); Seattle Art Museum (1984); National Gallery Sainsbury Wing (London, 1986); Charles P. Stevenson Jr. Library at Bard College (1989); Regional Government Building (Toulouse, France, (1992); and Kirifuri Resort Facilities (Nikko, Japan, 1992).

Venturi has also written *Iconography and Electronics upon a Generic Architecture* (Cambridge, MA: MIT Press, 1996). He is the recipient of numerous awards and honorary degrees.

Frank J. Cavaioli

Bibliography

Cook, John Wesley. *Conversations with Architects*. New York: Praeger, 1973.

Eldefield, John. *American Art of the 1960s*. New York: Museum of Modern Art, 1991.

Lawson, Bryan. *Design in Mind*. Boston: Butterworth Architecture, 1994.

Mead, Christopher, ed. *The Architecture of Robert Venturi*. Albuquerque: University of New Mexico Press, 1989.

Schwartz, Frederic, ed. *Mother's House: The Evolution of Vanna Venturi's House in Chestnut Hill*. New York: Rizzoli Publishers, 1992.

Steele, James, ed. *Museum Builders*. New York: St. Martin's, 1994.

Verrazzano, Giovanni da (1485?–1528)

This Florentine navigator-explorer was the first European to chart the Atlantic coast from South Carolina to New England. Sailing under the French flag, he laid the foundation for a French claim to the entire North American continent. He received a fine Italian Renaissance education in literature and mathematics.

King Francis I became interested in finding a direct route to Cataia (Cathay or China) and establishing trade in spices and silk. Since the Spanish and English kings had employed successful Italian navigators, Francis also wanted to employ one. Verrazzano (or Verrazano), who apparently had experience sailing the eastern Mediterranean and may have known Ferdinand Magellan at Seville, came to the king's attention. Financed by Florentine bankers in Lyon and Rouen (including presumed relatives Rucellai and Guadagni), Verrazzano left Dieppe in the caravel *La Dauphine* for Madeira. He departed from this Portuguese island on January 17, 1524, and sailed almost directly west until he sighted North America at present Cape Fear, North Carolina, about March 1. He turned south, but wishing to avoid contact with the Spanish, turned back before reaching present Charleston, South Carolina.

Charting the Outer Banks, the explorer concluded that they were a very long isthmus and that Pamlico Sound west of the Outer Banks was the Pacific Ocean. For many decades, because of his observations, European cartographers showed this portion of North America as a narrow strip of land separating the two oceans. The Kitty Hawk area reminded Verrazzano of the hilly, treed setting in Jacopo Sannazzaro's pastoral romance *Arcadia* (1504); cartographers transferred his designation L'Acadie continually northeastward until it applied to the present Nova Scotia region. Missing Chesapeake and Delaware Bays, he entered New York Bay and anchored in the Narrows, which separate Staten and Long Islands. Today an interstate highway bridge linking the two islands is called the Verrazano-Narrows Bridge.

In Narragansett Bay, Verrazzano explored an island that he concluded had contours similar to the Mediterranean island of Rhodes. In the seventeenth century, Roger Williams named his colony after the explorer's designation. After passing Cape Cod and admiring the Maine coast, he sailed wide of Nova Scotia and reached Newfoundland. Running out of victuals, he then decided to return home and arrived at Dieppe on July 8.

Verrazzano returned to America two more times. Merchants financed a voyage (1526–1527) to obtain spices and other valuable merchandise. He sailed the coast of South America, noted Guanabara Bay (Rio de Janeiro), and obtained brazilwood, which the clothiers of Rouen used for dyeing cloth. In 1528 he sailed into the Caribbean in search of a passage to the Orient. Landing on the island of Guadeloupe, he was killed and eaten by natives.

James J. Divita

Bibliography

Morison, Samuel Eliot. *The European Discovery of America: The Northern Voyages,* A.D. *500–1600.* New York: Oxford University Press, 1971.

Wroth, Lawrence C. *The Voyages of Giovanni da Verrazzano, 1524–1528.* New Haven: Yale University Press, 1970.

See also EXPLORERS

Vigo, Francis (1747–1836)

Italian-born merchant who facilitated George Rogers Clark's capture of Vincennes, Indiana, during the American Revolution, Giuseppe Maria Francesco Vigo was born in Mondovi, province of Cuneo, Piedmont, the son of Matteo and Maria Maddelena Vigo, on December 3, 1747, the feast day of St. Francis Xavier.

He enlisted in the Spanish army and was stationed in Havana and then New Orleans (1769). He left the military to engage in profitable fur trading with Native Americans and to supply settlers in the Arkansas country. By 1772 he became a business partner of the Novarese Emiliano Yosti in St. Louis. Then he became a partner of the Spanish lieutenant governor and was guaranteed that local authorities would not curtail his lucrative trade with the British-held east bank of the Mississippi.

In July 1778 Clark captured Kaskaskia in present Illinois and obtained for Virginia the allegiance of Canadiens at Vincennes on the Wabash River. Spanish officials apparently encouraged Vigo to extend Clark twelve thousand dollars' credit for supplies, because other Mississippi River merchants remained reluctant to provision Clark's army in return for Virginia notes of questionable worth. Then Vigo set out for Vincennes on business unaware that the British had returned there. On December 24, 1778, he was arrested and confined for three weeks, during which time he observed the weaknesses of the British military, gauged the attitudes of the Canadien inhabitants, and ascertained future British plans. Upon release, Vigo informed Clark that the British did not expect a winter attack; thereupon, Clark surprised them and recaptured Vincennes on February 25, 1779. Vigo's provisions and information facilitated Clark's military action, which helped establish an American claim to the region.

Moving to Vincennes, Vigo or his agents traveled annually to eastern cities to sell furs and acquire merchandise for resale (1788–1798). He conferred with George Washington in Philadelphia (1790) about federal Native American policy. Active in local politics, he became a trustee of Vincennes University and a shareholder of the town's circulating library (1806).

Vincennes' largest landowner, Vigo married Elizabeth Shannon (1770–1818) but had no children. After 1804 he suffered major financial reverses. He lost a court suit over several business debts and was forced to dispose of twelve thousand acres of land and his prized home to pay the judgment. He died destitute March 22, 1836, in Vincennes at age 89. Once active in Catholic parish life, he became disaffected from the Church and was buried in the public cemetery. His only asset was a nine thousand dollar note from the Clark expedition. Finally, in 1876, the federal government redeemed this note and paid Vigo's heirs almost fifty thousand dollars (original value plus interest).

The Indiana state legislature named a county after Vigo (1818). His heirs donated the bell for the Vigo County courthouse in Terre Haute. Near the George Rogers Clark memorial in Vincennes is a sculpture of a seated Vigo resting against a pile of money bags (1932). The Italian and United States postal administrations jointly saluted Vigo by issuing commemorative postcards in his honor on the bicentennial of Clark's capture of Vincennes (1979).

James J. Divita

Bibliography
Riker, Dorothy. "Francis Vigo." *Indiana Magazine of History* 26 (1930): 12–24.
Roselli, Bruno. *Vigo: A Forgotten Builder of the American Republic*. Boston: Stratford, 1933.

See also EXPLORERS

Villella, Edward (b. 1936)

One of America's most popular and critically acclaimed ballet dancers, Edward Villella was born in Elmhurst, New York, the son of first-generation Italian Americans Joseph Villella and Mildred Di Giovanni. At age 10, he was granted a scholarship to the School of American Ballet. The young Villella was intrigued with the ballet world, but he felt himself to be a rough street kid from Queens County who did not belong with the sophisticated, bohemian, high-brow men and women who peopled the halls of the prestigious dance academy. However, he had a natural dance talent and, in 1957, was invited to join the New York City Ballet. After only one year with the company he was promoted to the rank of soloist and, in 1960, to the rank of principal dancer. In 1962 Villella married Janet Greschsler, with whom he had a son. The couple divorced in 1970.

Villella graduated from the State University of New York's Maritime College, where he earned a varsity letter in baseball and was the school's welterweight boxing champion. Villella's athleticism was a distinguishing feature of an extraordinarily virile dance style that did much to popularize the role of the male ballet dancer. He brought the sense of a tough, self-reliant, streetwise New Yorker to the ballet stage and challenged the stereotype of the effeminate male ballet dancer.

The legendary choreographer George Balanchine was inspired by Villella's passionate style and exceptional technical abilities and created many roles to showcase Villella's talents, including the furiously paced, technically demanding *Tarantella* (1964), the commedia dell'arte–style ballet *Harlequinade* (1965), the "Rubies" section of *Jewels* (1967), the "Divertimento Brillante" section of *Glinkiana* (1967), and *Symphony in Three Movements* (1972). Villella is probably best known, however, for the international acclaim he received for his performance of the title role in the 1960 revival of Balanchine's *Prodigal Son*. In addition, choreographer Jerome Robbins created roles for Villella in *Dances at a Gathering* (1969) and *Watermill* (1972).

Throughout his career Villella worked to increase Americans' awareness of ballet by dancing on television programs, in Broadway musicals, and in guest appearances across the country. He also danced at President Kennedy's inauguration and for Presidents Johnson, Nixon, and Ford. Injuries forced Villella to stop dancing in the late 1970s. In 1980 he married Linda Carbonetto, with whom he had a daughter. During the early 1980s, Villella taught at colleges and universities, including the United States Military Academy at West Point and the University of California, Irvine. He has also been a member of the National Endowment for the Arts' Dance Advisory Panel and the Board of Trustees' Executive Committee of the Wolf Trap Foundation for the Performing Arts. In 1986 Villella became the founding artistic director of the Miami City Ballet, which has achieved critical acclaim under his leadership.

Lisa Jo Sagolla

Bibliography
Villella, Edward, and Larry Kaplan. *Prodigal Son: Dancing for Balanchine in a World of Pain and Magic*. New York: Simon & Schuster, 1992.

See also DANCE

V

Viscardi Jr., Henry (b. 1912)

Born with only stumps for legs and hospitalized for the first six years of his life, Henry Viscardi Jr., founder of the Human Resources Center in Albertson, New York, grew from a severely handicapped child of Italian immigrant parents to become a world-renowned educator, advocate, and friend of the disabled.

He was born on May 10, 1912, in New York City, to Henry and Ann (née Esposito) Viscardi. His parents were, in his own words, "simple immigrants," and his father, a barber, died when he was very young. Henry lived the first six years of his life in the Hospital for Deformities and Joint Diseases. Throughout his life he has borne the scars and pain from early surgical procedures to straighten and strengthen his severely twisted legs. He also struggled to overcome the ridicule and bigoted attitudes that were regularly directed at the handicapped—a struggle that prepared him well for his lifelong work of helping others to rise above their disabilities and achieve their potential.

Having excelled in elementary and high school, Viscardi attended Fordham University in the Bronx for three years but ran out of money before he could complete his degree. He obtained a well-paying job doing tax work for the Home Owners Loan Corp. At age 25, his deformed legs all but worn out, he was fitted with artificial aluminum legs and feet. It was a revolutionary concept at the time (1934), and it had a revolutionary impact on his life. For the first time, he could stand up straight and really walk. "I knew nothing but disability for twenty-seven years," he recalled. "I was determined I was going to be free." His doctor did not charge him for the artificial limbs, but instead urged him to "make a difference" for someone else.

World War II started Viscardi on his lifelong mission of aiding and advocating for the disabled. Unable to enter military service, he instead joined the Red Cross, where he was able to use his personal experience to assist amputees returning from the war: he helped them to learn how to use artificial limbs, and also offered emotional support and counsel to them and their families. He was also outspoken in demanding that more be done for these wounded veterans, and his complaints got the attention of First Lady Eleanor Roosevelt as well as several high-ranking officials in the United States Air Force. The result was improved and expanded rehabilitation programs for amputees and the beginning of Viscardi's services as an advisor on disability issues to every president from Franklin D. Roosevelt on.

Following the war, on November 16, 1946, Viscardi married Lucile Darracq, whom he had met while sailing—a lifelong avocation that he and his wife have both shared. The marriage produced four daughters—Lucile, Lydia, Donna, and Nina—and eventually nine grandchildren. Emotionally drained by his work with the disabled during the war years, Viscardi moved on to different vocations after the war. After working for the Mutual Broadcasting System reporting sports and special events, he became personnel manager for Burlington Industries. But he was disturbed by the ongoing job discrimination against the disabled, including many of the war veterans whom he had helped to rehabilitate. He began speaking throughout the country as an advocate for the disabled. He was then approached by Dr. Howard Rusk, a pioneer of rehabilitation programs in the Air Force during World War II, who encouraged Viscardi to start Just One Break (JOB), an employment search program for the disabled.

The program encountered great resistance from industry, however, and Viscardi realized the need to demonstrate the working capabilities of the handicapped. So in 1952, in a garage in Hempstead, he and a small group of businessmen started Abilities, Inc., which employed handicapped workers in electronic assembly. From that small beginning has evolved the National Center on Employment and Disability, Human Resources Center, "the most comprehensive program in the country" for disabled children, in the words of Dr. Edward Martin, Viscardi's successor as CEO and president of the center.

Today, the center includes Abilities Health and Rehabilitation Services, a licensed diagnostic and treatment center with outpatient services in physical therapy, occupational therapy, speech therapy, and psychological services; Career and Employment Institute, which evaluates, trains, and counsels over six hundred adults each year to help them gain productive employment; and the Henry Viscardi School, a New York State chartered school, which educates more than two hundred handicapped children each year, in early childhood, elementary, and secondary levels. The school also serves more than two thousand adults each year through an evening and weekend continuing education program, and has a Research and Training Institute to study education and career employment opportunities for the handicapped.

The Human Resources Center has become a worldwide model for service programs for the disabled, while Viscardi's role as an advocate and an educator for the disabled has taken him throughout the world as a much sought after speaker. He is also a prolific author, having written numerous articles and eight books, detailing the struggles he and other disabled people have endured and some of the challenges he has faced in establishing support services for the disabled. He is also credited with paving the way for the passage of the national Americans with Disabilities Act in 1990.

Richard Hinshaw

Bibliography

Hinshaw, Rick. "Video Documents Extraordinary Life." *The Long Island Catholic,* 21 April 1993, 1, 3.

Murray, Barbara. "Dr. Henry Viscardi, World Citizen." *LIBNews,* 18 May 1992, 12–13.

Program Guide & 1992 Annual Report. Albertson. NY: National Center for Disability Services, 1992.

Volpe, John A. (1908–1994)

A successful businessman and public figure, John A. Volpe distinguished himself in high political positions such as governor of Massachusetts, first federal highway administrator, U.S. secretary of transportation, and ambassador to Italy.

He was born in Wakefield, Massachusetts, December 8, 1908, son of Vito and Filemena Volpe, both of whom had migrated from the Abruzzi region of Italy. His father, working as a hod carrier and plasterer, began a construction company that he converted into a successful enterprise. The Volpe Company became a multinational company under his son's leadership.

In 1934 Volpe married Jennie Benedetto, and they eventually had three children. He graduated from Wentworth Institute and hoped to attend college, but his father, who needed him in his company, said, "I think MIT can do without you, but I can't." During World War II he served in the United States Navy Civil Engineering Corps.

Volpe entered public life as a Republican and became chairman of the Massachusetts Republican State Committee and public

Former industrialist, governor, cabinet member, and ambassador to Italy, John Volpe, seated third from left, is honored by his fellow Italian Americans in Washington, D.C. Poet-scholar Rose Basile Green is seated fifth from left. Courtesy of the National Italian American Foundation (NIAF), Washington, D.C.

works commissioner. He became the first federal highway administrator for the interstate highway system instituted by the Eisenhower administration. He was a delegate to the Republican national conventions of 1960, 1964, 1968, and 1972.

Volpe won the Massachusetts gubernatorial election in 1960. He lost a disputed election to Endicott Peabody two years later. In 1964 he defeated Francis X. Bellotti in another close election. In 1966 he won a landslide victory, this time to a four-year term. As a result, he received serious consideration as a Republican vice-presidential candidate in 1968. In January 1969 he resigned from the governorship to become President Nixon's secretary of transportation. Four years later President Nixon appointed him ambassador to Italy.

Volpe's attachment to his ethnic roots was evident in his efforts to establish the National Italian American Foundation in the nation's capital and then serving as an active executive in this advocacy organization for Italian Americans.

Frank J. Cavaioli

Bibliography

Cavaioli, Frank J. "Charles Poletti and Fourteen Other Italian American Governors." In *Italian Americans in Transition,* edited by Joseph V. Scelsa, Salvatore J. LaGumina, and Lydio F. Tomasi, 137–152. New York: American Italian Historical Association, 1990.

Kilgore, Kathleen. *John Volpe: The Life of an Immigrant's Son.* Dublin, NH: Yankee, 1987.

Musmanno, Michael A. *The Story of the Italians in America.* New York: Doubleday, 1965.

See also GOVERNORS; POLITICS

Vuono, Carl Edward (b. 1934)

A U.S. military career officer, Carl Edward Vuono was born in Monongahela, Pennsylvania, on October 18, 1934. His father's parents migrated from Calabria, Italy, while his mother's parents came from Naples. Vuono credited his close-knit Italian American family with instilling in him the values that motivated him throughout his life.

As a young boy, he was impressed by soldiers and military parades. While a student at Monongahela High School, he received an appointment to the United States Military Academy at West Point, New York, from which he graduated in 1957. He received his B.S. in engineering and was commissioned a second lieutenant on June 4, 1957.

After finishing the field artillery officer's course at Fort Sill, Oklahoma, he was assigned to a howitzer company at Fort Meade, Maryland. While serving as first lieutenant he met and married Patricia H. Hall in 1960. They have three children.

In August 1960 he was transferred to Korea, where he served as a battalion operations officer. He was promoted to captain in 1961 and was transferred the following year to Fort Bragg, North Carolina, to serve with the Airborne Artillery. In 1963 he became commander of the headquarters battery. Several months later he was sent to England as an exchange officer with the British Royal Horse Artillery (Parachute) as a troop commander and subsequently was promoted to major.

He was next assigned to Vietnam as an executive officer to the First Battalion, 77th

General Carl Vuono. The first Italian American to become Army Chief of Staff was the son of Italian immigrants. Courtesy Carl Vuono and Joseph Scafetta Jr.

Artillery, First Infantry Division. While there, he won the Bronze Star Medal for Valor. In 1968 he was assigned to the Pentagon. His next destination took him back to Vietnam in July 1970, where he was awarded the Legion of Merit. After he completed this second tour of duty in the war zone in July 1971, he was assigned to the office of the vice chief of staff in the Pentagon, where he served as a staff officer.

In 1972 he attended the Army War College at Carlisle Barracks, Pennsylvania. He also earned an M.S. in public administration at Shippensburg State College. In 1981 he became the commanding general of the Eighth Infantry Division (Mechanized) in Germany and served there until 1983.

On July 1, 1986, he was promoted to four-star general and was appointed commanding general of the Army Training and Doctrine Command at Fort Monroe, Virginia. President Ronald Reagan appointed him to be the thirty-first chief of staff of the United States Army, a post he assumed at the Pentagon on June 23, 1987. He became the first Italian American to achieve this position.

General Vuono directed the preparation and deployment of American forces during Operation Just Cause in Panama during December 1989. Later, President George Bush authorized Operation Desert Shield on the Arabian peninsula from August 1990 to February 1991 and Operation Desert Storm in Kuwait and Iraq during February 1991. Again, General Vuono prepared units for the field commanders. He led the United States Army in the National Victory Parade in Washington, D.C., June 1991.

He retired from active military duty autumn of that year. In 1992 he became vice-president and general manager of an international group for a training and education company, Military Professional Resources, Inc. (MPRI), in Alexandria, Virginia.

Joseph Scafetta Jr.

Bibliography

"Generals for Hire." *Time*, January 15, 1996, 34–36.

See also WARTIME MILITARY AND HOME FRONT ACTIVITIES

V

Wartime Military and Home Front Activities

To shed blood for one's country exemplifies the epitome of patriotism—a deed that earns the gratitude of the nation at large, and an act that Italian Americans have performed repeatedly since the earliest days of the republic.

In his classic book *Four Centuries of Italian American History* (1955), the eminent scholar Giovanni Schiavo shows that of the thousands of people of Italian origin living in the American colonies in 1776, many fought in the American Revolution. Examples include Lieutenant James Bracco of New York and Colonel Richard Taliaferro of Virginia, both of whom were killed in action. The Taliaferro name is inscribed in stone in the Guilford Courthouse National Military Park at Greensboro, North Carolina. Another Taliaferro, Benjamin, served in General Daniel Morgan's rifle corps. Schiavo also cites Joseph DeAngeles, who entered the colonial army at the age of 13 and served from 1776 to 1783.

Another scholar, Angelo Flavio Guidi, examined the historical files of the United States Army, the lists of American Revolutionary War sailors, and state historical records. He found many colonial soldiers with Italian surnames, including Stefano Almero, Vincenzo Curria, Dallino Guglielmo, and Giovanni Norile.

In an attempt to compile a complete list (1959) of known military dead during the American Revolution, Clarence Peterson utilized hundreds of sources including national and state archives, military records, and state and local historical societies. Among the list of thousands are a number of Italian names such as Private William Mellone of Maryland and Colonel William Taliaferro.

Among the outstanding patriots of the Revolution is Philip Mazzei, who was born in Poggio a Caiano, Tuscany, in 1730. An expert agronomist, he came to Virginia in 1773 and conducted farm experiments in a homestead next to Thomas Jefferson in Monticello. Mazzei became a naturalized citizen of Virginia in 1774. Together with Jefferson he published a series of articles in support of the colonial cause, which contained many words and ideas later found in the Declaration of Independence. Mazzei also enlisted in Virginia's Albemarle County volunteer company. At the behest of Virginia governor Patrick Henry, Mazzei visited high officials in Genoa and Florence and wrote numerous discourses in support of the American cause.

Francis Vigo, born in Mondavi (Cuneo), Piedmont, in 1747, was another Italian American patriot of the American Revolution. In 1778 he joined Colonel George Rogers Clark in an effort to drive the British out of the Northwest Territory. At Vigo's urging Clark's forces defeated the British garrison at Vincennes the following year, thus assuring American claim to the region. Vigo gave his entire personal fortune of $8,616.00 to help supply Clark's soldiers. In 1783 Vigo became a naturalized citizen of the United States and spent his declining years in poverty until he died in 1836.

Italian Americans also fought in the War of 1812. Lieutenant Lawrence Taliaferro (Tagliaferro), born in 1794 in King County, Virginia, enlisted in a volunteer company of light infantry in 1812 and saw action on several fronts. Also, Virginia-born (1792) Private Henry Modena fought with the Virginia militia. Private Francis Como of New Hampshire served in the military during the war, as did a number of Italian American citizens from Louisiana, such as Privates Joseph Antonio, Joseph Carpentero, Joseph Colombi, Louis Ferrara, Amed(e) Reggio, and musicians Antonio and Francesco Caponi.

It is impossible to determine how many Italian Americans fought for the United States during the Mexican War, especially since many Italian surnames were Anglicized. Lewis C. Sartori, an Italian immigrant's son born in New Jersey in 1812, was one of them. Sartori entered the navy in 1829 and subsequently was promoted to lieutenant. During the war he served aboard the bomb-brig *Stromboli* and participated in the capture of Goatzacoalcas and Tobasco in 1847 and 1848. Among other Italian Americans who served were First Lieutenant John Phinizy (Giovanni Finnizzi) of Georgia, Lieutenant Colonel Christian C. Nave of Indiana, Major Charles Fiesca, Colonels Henry Forno and Louis Gally (Luigi Galli) of Louisiana, and N. C. Barbarino, a surgeon in the U.S. Navy.

Although most of the Italian men-at-arms who fought for the Union during the Civil War are forever lost to historians, a few remain as representatives of those unknown soldiers. From New York, Antonio Ferrari, Domenico Cavagnaro, Joachim Gafferalli, Carabino Polidrotti, and seaman Antonio Cutormini served the Union cause, as did P. E. Benzi of Connecticut.

The highest ranking Union officer of Italian birth was Brigadier Luigi Palma DeCesnola, born in 1832 in Rivarolo Canavase (Turin). After service as an officer in the Sardinian army, he migrated to New York and became a lieutenant colonel and then a colonel of a New York cavalry regiment. Praised for his valor in action, he was also seriously wounded and incarcerated in the infamous Libby prison in Richmond. After his release from prison he fought alongside General Philip Sheridan. In April 1865 President Abraham Lincoln promoted Cesnola to brigadier general and offered him the American consulship at Cyprus, upon his agreement to become an American citizen.

The highest ranking Union naval officer of Italian descent was Rear Admiral Bancroft Gherardi, born 1832 in Jackson, Louisiana. After graduation from the Naval Academy in 1853, he rose in 1862 to lieutenant commander, serving on the warship *Mohican* with orders to search and destroy Confederate ships. Highly commended by superiors for his wartime service, he remained a career officer after the war and became commander-in-chief of the North Atlantic Squadron in 1884.

Major General Edward Ferrero, born in Spain of Italian parents in 1831, became the highest ranking officer of Italian descent to serve with the Union forces. Brought to New York as an infant, Ferrero was later mustered into the volunteer service as colonel of the 51st New York Infantry in 1861. He saw action in North Carolina, the second battle of Bull Run, Chantilly, South Mountain, Antietam, and Fredericksburg. Promoted to a brigadier general in 1863, he played an important part in General Ulysses S. Grant's Vicksburg campaign, when Ferrero's troops made a gallant stand against Confederate assaults at Knoxville. He was then promoted to major general.

The son of an Italian immigrant from Liguria, Francis B. Spinola was born in Stony Brook, New York, in 1821. After a career in politics as a state assemblyman and state senator, Spinola received a commission in 1862 as a brigadier general of volunteers. He was twice wounded in combat and after the war was elected the first of his nationality to the U.S. Congress. Other Italian Americans who were cited for valor in the Union cause were Brigadier General Enrico Fardella, Naval Commander Louis G. Sartori, and Colonel Alberto Maggi.

Although much smaller in number when compared to their counterparts who fought for the Union, hundreds of Italian Americans also fought for the Confederacy. Decimus et Ultimus Barziza was born in Williamsburg, Virginia, in 1838, the son of an Italian viscount who came to America in 1814 and who provided his tenth and last child with the unusual appellation. After studying law at Baylor University, Decimus's legal career was interrupted by the Civil War. He became a first lieutenant, saw action, and was captured at Gettysburg. Imprisoned on Johnson's Island, he engineered a daring and successful escape by diving through the window of a moving train. He recorded his wartime experiences in *The Adventures of a Prisoner of War*.

Italian Americans continued to serve in the armed forces following the Civil War. Trumpeter John Martini and Lieutenant Charles C. DeRudio took part in Native

American campaigns, including service with General George A. Custer during the campaign against the Sioux in 1876. Custer had sent Martini to appeal for reinforcements on the fateful day when the general and two hundred of his men were killed. Lieutenant DeRudio also fought at the battle of Little Big Horn and even though his horse was killed, DeRudio managed to escape to join the few survivors of the battle.

The highest ranking Italian American to serve during the Spanish-American War was Luigi Lomia, who was born in Canicatti (Agrigento), Sicily, in 1843. His family migrated to America in 1857. Luigi graduated from West Point, served in Cuba, and rose to the rank of colonel. He taught military science and languages at several universities and became military attaché in Rome in 1898.

Among the lesser known Italian Americans to serve in this war was George Minetty, who was born in San Giorgio, Cannavese, in 1868. Minetty attended the military academy at Pisa and upon graduation became a lieutenant in the Italian army. He emigrated to the United States. With the outbreak of the Spanish-American War he enlisted in the army, saw action in Cuba, was wounded, and received the Purple Heart as a result of his heroics during Theodore Roosevelt's charge up San Juan Hill. He also served in the Philippines during the Filipino insurrection and finally in China during the Boxer Rebellion.

More than 4.5 million men served in the American armed forces during World War I, about three hundred thousand of whom were Italians or Italian Americans. Although they constituted only 4 percent of the U.S. population, 10 percent of those killed in action were of Italian descent. While thousands of Italian immigrants returned to their homeland to fight for Italy when it entered the war in 1915, many entered the American armed forces. Automatic citizenship was conferred on those enlistees who were not yet citizens. The role played by Italians and Italian Americans during this war may be gleaned by figures that indicate that eighty-three Distinguished Service Crosses were awarded to natives of Italy while another score were presented to American soldiers of Italian heritage exclusive of those whose names had been Anglicized. Among those worthy of note are John Isadore Eopolucci, the first American seaman to die for his country, and Private Michael Valente

of New York, who was awarded the Congressional Medal of Honor for his heroism.

Among the more famous Italian Americans who fought with distinction in the war were two future mayors of New York City, Fiorello H. LaGuardia and Vincent R. Impellitteri. Congressman LaGuardia was only one of a handful of members of Congress to volunteer, serving as major in the Army Air Force, stationed in Italy. Impellitteri joined the navy and served on a destroyer that successfully repelled enemy attacks.

For thousands of other Italian Americans who served in the armed forces, their wartime effort served to strengthen bonds of loyalty. Thus they became active supporters of veterans organizations and promoters of patriotic acts. One example was that of the Thomas Jefferson American Legion Post based in heavily Italian East Harlem, which for years was headed by Mr. Casamento whose son was to become a World War II Medal of Honor winner.

This monument, in a park at the entrance to the Long Island Railroad station in Copiague (also known as Marconiville), New York, is testimony to the pride Italian Americans took in defense of the United States during World War I—and to the sacrifices they made in the service of their adopted country. Courtesy Salvatore J. LaGumina.

World War II proved to be a testing time for Americans of Italian descent. Because Italy was formally an enemy nation, actions that seemed to celebrate Italianità were barely tolerated when they were not condemned outright. Prudence and inconspicuousness became the norm, especially since hundreds of thousands of Italian immigrants, lacking American citizenship, were initially registered as enemy aliens, a practice that continued until October 1942. Demonstrations of unquestioned loyalty were the best bulwarks against the prevailing atmosphere of distrust and suspicion. While working in war plants to produce war equipment and purchasing war bonds to support the war effort were welcome, participation in the armed forces remained the principal test of devotion, one which Italian Americans responded to convincingly.

Whether via the draft or enlistment, Italian Americans were conspicuous in all branches of the armed forces. They fought in every theater of the war including Italy, even risking the chance that they might be fighting against friends and relatives. The countless instances of American soldiers on duty in Italy meeting with Italian family members who had served with the Italian forces underscore the dilemma confronting Italian American soldiers who, nevertheless, proved their loyalty to the United States. While accurate figures are elusive, some estimates place the number of Italian Americans in the armed forces at a million or more, while others indicate five hundred thousand; in either case these are figures far in excess of their percentage of the U.S. population. The number of Italian American families with multiple representatives in the armed forces is instructive. While many families had five or more children in the armed forces, few could match the record of Sorrento-born Frank Maresca's family. Of his fifteen children, three sons fought for the United States in World War I, one of whom was killed in action in France, and six more were in the armed services during World War II. Another example would be that of widow Assunta Ioli of Corona, New York, whose four sons served in the army, two of whom died defending the nation adopted by their parents. Equally instructive is the realization that "Gold Star" Italian American mothers who had lost sons in action were enlisted to appear at war bond rallies and hailed in the Italian language press.

Four Italian Americans held the rank of brigadier general during the war. They were Daniel Noce of Denver, Colorado; Robert V. Ignacio of Boston, Massachusetts; Ralph Palladino of Winchester, Massachusetts; and Joseph T. Michela of Duluth, Minnesota. For the prominent role he played as chief of amphibious operations in the European theater, General Noce was awarded the Distinguished Service Medal.

There were many instances of extraordinary military achievements on the part of Italian Americans during the Second World War. One example was that of Max Corvo of Middletown, Connecticut. Born in Sicily, he immigrated to Connecticut with his family as a youngster and helped his father publish an antifascist Italian American newspaper. With the outbreak of the war, he volunteered for the army and as a buck private proceeded to convince army superiors to follow his plan to infiltrate Sicily, Sardinia, and the Italian mainland, in order to gather necessary intelligence preparatory to a successful invasion. He was promoted to an officer rank and put in charge of the Special Intelligence (SI) unit of the newly created Office of Strategic Services (OSS), the nation's first professional intelligence system. In due course, he gathered and

Letter from a diary of a newly naturalized citizen-immigrant-barber affirming loyalty to the United States on the day that Pearl Harbor was attacked, December 7, 1941. It is a representation of the unhesitating allegiance of Americans of Italian descent even while their native country was at war with their adopted country. Courtesy Salvatore J. LaGumina.

trained a unit consisting mainly of Sicilian Americans who obtained valuable information that helped facilitate the Allied operation in Italy. The uniqueness of Corvo's operation can be seen in that it was designed by Italian Americans to focus on Italy; its main operatives were Italian Americans and it interacted with Italians as it helped liberate Italy and expedite its alignment with the United States.

Among the countless instances of magnificent military achievements, several attracted widespread renown. Major Allen V. Martini of San Francisco received the Silver Star, the Air Medal, and the Distinguished Flying Cross for destroying twenty-two enemy planes in dozens of missions. Few Americans received the publicity accorded Captain Don Gentile of Ohio. He was credited with destroying a total of thirty enemy planes, thereby becoming the first World War II pilot to break Eddie Rickenbacker's World War I record.

At the peak of medals for bravery stands the Congressional Medal of Honor, which was awarded to thirteen Italian Americans who served in the war, seven posthumously. Lieutenant Willibald C. Bianchi of Minnesota was the first Italian American to receive one for his courage and leadership in Bataan's jungles in February 1942. Sergeant John Basilone of New Jersey emerged as the most famous Italian American Medal of Honor winner and hero. The son of Italian immigrants and one of ten children, he received his award for extraordinary bravery against the Japanese in the September 1942 battle of Guadalcanal. Assigned for a time to the Treasury Department to encourage Americans to purchase war bonds, he requested reassignment to the Pacific front, where he was killed in subsequent military action. Basilone's name was given to a destroyer, several monuments in New Jersey, and to a Sons of Italy Lodge. For Anthony Casamento the road to winning the coveted award was long and tortuous, encompassing nearly four decades, until finally he was presented with the Congressional Medal of Honor by President Jimmy Carter in 1980. He also has a Sons of Italy lodge named after him. Other Congressional Medal of Honor winners during this war were Frank J. Petrarca of Cleveland; Ralph Cheli of San Francisco and Brooklyn; Arthur DeFranzo of Saugus, Massachusetts; Anthony Damato of Shenandoah, Pennsylvania; Peter J. Dalessandro of Watervliet, New York; Vito Bertoldo of Decatur, Illinois; Robert F. Viale of Bayside, California; Joseph J. Cicchetti of Waynesburg, Ohio; and Mike Colalillo of Duluth, Minnesota.

Although the number of Italian Americans who served during the Korean War and the Vietnam War is unknown, their contributions are made apparent by the number of major citations awarded. During the Korean War it is known that six Italian Americans received the Congressional Medal of Honor and four received the Navy Cross. It is estimated that during the Vietnam War eight received the Medal of Honor and eighteen received the Navy Cross. Italian names also served with distinction in Desert Storm. Female officer Major Marie Rossi, who died in the operation, is recalled in the epitaph on her tomb: "First female combat commander to fly into combat: Operation Desert Storm." Finally, in the Somali peace-keeping mission of 1995, Lieutenant General Anthony Zinni headed the Marine forces that evacuated United Nations troops.

Valentine Belfiglio
Salvatore J. LaGumina

Bibliography

Keefer, Louis. "Italian POW's and the Italian American Community, 1943–1945: An Overview." In *Italian Americans and Their Public and Private Life,* edited by Frank J. Cavaioli, Angela Danzi, and Salvatore J. LaGumina, 48–53. New York: American Italian Historical Association, 1993.

LaGumina, Salvatore J. "Camp Wikoff, That Accursed Place." *Long Island Forum* 44 (July 1981): 144–150.

———. "Enemy Alien: Italian Americans During World War II." *The Italian American Review* 3 (12 October 1994): 38–44.

Mormino, Gary. "The House We Live In, Italian Americans and World War II." *Ambassador* 26 (summer 1995): 12–18.

Nelli, Humbert S. *The United States and Italy: The First Two Hundred Years.* New York: American Italian Historical Association, 1976.

Peterson, Clarence S. *Known Military Dead During the Revolutionary War, 1775–1783.* Baltimore: Peterson, 1959.

Pierson, Marion John Nennet. *Louisiana Soldiers in the War of 1812.* Baton Rouge: Louisiana Genealogical and Historical Society, 1963.

Proft, R. J. *United States of America's Medal of Honor Recipients.* Columbia Heights, MN: Highland House II, 1994.

Schiavo, Giovanni. *Four Centuries of Italian American History.* New York: Vigo Press, 1955.

———. *The Italians in America Before the Civil War.* New York: Vigo Press, 1934.

Wagner, Anthony, and F. S. Andrus. "The Origin of the Family of Taliaferro." *Virginia Magazine of History and Biography* 77 (1969):

See also MEDAL OF HONOR WINNERS; WORLD WAR II, INTERNMENT, AND PRISONERS OF WAR

Waterbury

The fourth largest city in Connecticut (1990 census: nearly 109,000), Waterbury is a diverse community represented by eighteen ethnic groups living in middle-class neighborhoods on its seven hills.

Italian Americans constitute the largest ethnic group in Waterbury. Nearly one-fourth of the population, or twenty-seven thousand, identified themselves as Italian American in the 1990 census. Hispanics ranked second with 20.2 percent, followed by Irish with 12.2 percent. During the 1980s, the Hispanic population increased 111 percent. The African American population grew 17 percent. Waterbury was the only large city in Connecticut to increase in population during the decade. Also, fewer families left Waterbury in this period than any other large Connecticut city.

The Waterbury downtown historic district is enhanced by elements of Italian architecture: Medieval Revival, Renaissance Revival, and Palladian style. The most impressive buildings include the Waterbury Republican American Building, a fine copy of the Mangia campanile at Siena's Palazzo Pubblico, and the Church of the Immaculate Conception and the Church of Our Lady of Lourdes (Italian), both excellent copies of churches in Rome, Italy.

In 1776 Waterbury's population was thirty-five hundred. The character of the city changed in the mid-1800s with the arrival of Irish immigrants. Small brass industries developed, and immigrants from France, Germany, Quebec, Italy, and eastern Europe flocked to the local workplaces. Thousands worked in the city's clock shops, producing "the watch that made the dollar famous." Waterbury became known as the "Brass Center of the World."

In 1876, during the Centennial celebration, a house-to-house census showed that only two Italian families lived among the city's 16,039 inhabitants: Peter and Joseph Bauby and their respective wives. Their names (DiBarbieri) had been changed by immigration officials. The brothers set up a fruit business upon arriving in 1872. Their sixteen children worked in their two stores: Waterbury's first mom-and-pop stores. Two of Peter's sons graduated from Holy Cross College and Yale Law School.

By 1910 Waterbury's Italian population reached twelve thousand, with sixteen fraternal, social, and mutual-aid societies participating in the first Columbus Day celebration as a state legal holiday.

For decades, the companies Scovill Manufacturing, American Brass, and Chase Brass & Copper dominated the economy. By the 1970s aluminum, plastics, and light industries replaced the brass mills. Waterbury's industrial base, however, remained in eyelet and screw machine companies, many of which were staffed and owned by Italian Americans.

UNICO National, the largest service organization for Italian American men, was founded in Waterbury by Anthony P. Vastola. The Connecticut Grand Lodge, Order Sons of Italy in America, was founded there in 1914. The first convention of Connecticut posts of the Italian American War Veterans was held in Waterbury in 1935. A Pro Patria Committee, spearheaded by Waterburians in the Italian Army during World War I, raised funds in the 1930s for the Italian Red Cross. In February 1942 nearly 4,300 unnaturalized Italians had to register as enemy aliens during World War II.

An Italian American presence has been kept alive by the annual celebrations of four summer Italian festivals: Festa di San Donato of Pontelandolfo (first weekend of August); Festa of Madonna della Libera of Cercemaggiore (last weekend of June); Our Lady of Mount Carmel Festival (closest weekend July 16); Italian Heritage Club Festival (third weekend of August).

Italian is spoken at meetings of the Pontelandolfo Community and Cercemaggiore clubs. Their clubhouses and property are among the largest in New England. An estimated six thousand residents of Pontelandolfo, province of Benevento, and Cercemaggiore, province of Compobasso, migrated to the Waterbury area when immigration restrictions were liberalized in the 1950s and 1960s. The construction industry is dominated by Pondelandolfesi and Cercesi.

Italian is taught in Waterbury's three public middle and three public high schools, Holy Cross High School, Naugatuck Valley Community and Technical College, Teikyo Post University, and Waterbury Adult Education Program. Special classes are held for immigrant children.

Patrick Perriello, a native of Frigento, province of Avellino, was mayor for four months in 1939. Other Italian American mayors of Waterbury were Frederick W. Palomba Jr. (1965–1968), Victor Mambruno (1971–1975), and Joseph Santopietro Jr. (1985–1991). Philip Antonio Giordano, originally a native of Caracas, Venezuela, was elected mayor in 1995.

Sando Bologna

Bibliography

Bologna, Sando. *The Italians of Waterbury.* Portland, CT: The Waverly Press, 1993.

Wine Industry

In 1773 Thomas Jefferson, then a 30-year-old lawyer and gentleman farmer, met Filippo Mazzei, a visiting Tuscan wine merchant seeking a site to grow wine grapes and olive trees. Jefferson offered him a 2,000-acre parcel adjacent to Monticello. The following year Mazzei and ten viticulturists planted cuttings of grapevines and lemon and olive trees they had brought from Italy. The first year a severe frost killed the new shoots, and Mazzei planted again, but the venture never succeeded. While Mazzei was abroad raising money for the American revolution, his vineyards were trampled and destroyed by a "troop of Hessian cavalry." Mazzei was able, finally, to produce some wine in Virginia from the native American *labrusca* or Concord grape.

Mazzei was probably the first Italian to grow grapes on this continent, and his story is representative of East Coast wine history, where conditions were not conducive to growing the European *vinifera* grape. In California, almost a century later, Italian immigrants found a Mediterranean climate and affordable land that eventually led to a flourishing wine industry. Italians in several other regions have also succeeded in wine production, especially in recent decades. Today, New York and the northwestern states of Washington, Oregon, and Idaho are two rapidly developing wine regions.

In New York, Italian settlers were originally drawn to the economic opportunities in the cities; the wine industry there has developed primarily in the last half of the twentieth century. In Brooklyn one of the early wineries, Delmonico's, has been operated by the same family since 1912 with Gerald Della Monica as current president; and the Transamerica Winery has been headed by the Boccafoglio family since 1940. Then in the 1970s, Italian names began to appear in the Finger Lakes region in the west-central section of the state. Andrew Colaruotolo, a home builder, founded the Cass Larga Vineyards near Rochester in 1978 and runs it as a family enterprise. At least twenty of New York's wineries have principals who are Italian Americans; these include John Mariani, president of Anthony Road Winery, founded in 1990 near Watkins Glen; Bob Mazza, vice-president of Olde Germania Wine Cellars, Hammondsport, founded in 1994; and Steve deFrancesco, wine maker and microbiologist at Glendora Wine Cellars, Seneca Lake, established in 1977.

In the Pacific Northwest, a fast-growing wine region with 220 wineries, there have been few Italian settlers; still, a small number of Italian Americans are principals in several wineries including Ponzi Vineyards of Oregon and Leonetti Cellars of Washington, both in operation for twenty years or more.

Wherever Italian immigrants settled in the United States, they grew grapes on arbors or small plots and made wine for home use. Wineries in states around the country bear Italian names from the past or present. In Texas, immigrant Frank Qualia founded Val Verde Winery in 1889, and a family member still runs it. Val Verde is one of several working wineries in the nation today dating from the nineteenth century.

It is in California where Italian family businesses have been in the forefront of the wine industry since the 1860s. Although Spanish missionaries were the first to plant grapes in the state a hundred years earlier, and the major commercial wine producers in the 1800s were primarily German, French, and Hungarian immigrants, Italians played an important role in establishing the state's wine industry. While Italian American wine producers have been a minority in the wine business, they have owned some of the largest wineries and were often responsible for the continuation and expansion of the industry through hard times. The history of Italian Americans in the wine business typifies the usual immigrant story of individual ingenuity, hard work, and family and community interdependence.

The 1850 discovery of gold provided the first major impetus for expansion of the California's wine industry. Unsuccessful gold prospectors turned to providing food and drink for the miners. Some Italians, such as Andrea Arata in Amador County, planted grapes near the mines. Others—Domenico Ghirardelli was one—distributed supplies to the miners in the port city of San Francisco.

Other Italian wine makers appeared in the 1860s: Battista Frapotli was a wine dealer in San Francisco; Giovanni Migliavacca, first selling his wine from his Napa grocery store, built a stone winery in 1874 and won a gold medal for his wine in Paris; Battista Salmina began making wine in 1867 and built a winery in 1895. An 1880 list of fifty-two Napa wineries included more than 10 percent Italian names. Wine making was concentrated in the north-central coastal valleys and in the south. The vineyard laborers then were primarily Chinese, but after a series of Chinese exclusion acts, plus an increase of Italian immigrants, the workers were almost exclusively Italian by the turn of the century.

In 1881 Andrea Sbarboro founded the Italian Swiss Colony, one of the first "integrated" units made up of vineyards, winery, and marketing operations. With the assistance of a talented enologist, Pietro C. Rossi, Italian Swiss wines won many awards and eventually became the second largest wine producer in California. By 1890 more Italians opened wineries around the state, and one hundred years later the Nichelini and the Segheslo families still operate their wineries.

The early twentieth century brought many problems to this industry. Phylloxera, a pest that attacks and destroys grape stock, be-

came a periodic epidemic in the vineyards, allowing Italian immigrants to buy land at lower prices as many vineyard owners gave up. Then, in 1906, the San Francisco earthquake destroyed many wine warehouses in that city, creating new economic hardships for the wine makers. In that same year, Antonio Forni completed a stone winery in Napa and shipped most of the wine to Vermont to sell to Italians working in marble quarries.

Disaster occurred in 1919 with the advent of Prohibition, the constitutional amendment banning the production of alcoholic beverages. This would have effectively destroyed the wine industry had it not been for Italian and other European immigrants who continued to buy wine grapes. Because home use of wine was permitted—a household was allowed to make two hundred gallons of wine per year—grape growers flourished as the price of grapes escalated. Some wineries survived by producing grape concentrate and sacramental wine during those fourteen years of Prohibition. Then the 1929 crash and subsequent Great Depression drove down the price of grapes by two-thirds. When the amendment was repealed in 1933, few wineries remained.

In the post-Prohibition era, many new wineries opened. One of the newcomers was Louis M. Martini, who migrated to America as a boy in 1900. He and his father began selling wine in San Francisco in 1910; he returned to Italy to study enology, and after owning a winery in Kingsburg, built his Napa Valley winery in 1933. He was a wine industry leader and a founder of the Wine Institute, a trade association, in 1944. Today, later generations of his family own and operate the Martini Winery in St. Helena.

Also in the 1930s, the brothers Ernest and Julio Gallo began a winery of their own in Modesto after having worked in their father's vineyard. Gallo wines won numerous awards and by the early 1990s was the largest wine producer in California, still managed by members of the Gallo family.

Antonio Perelli-Minetti's story is representative of the contribution Italians have made to this industry. An oenology graduate in Italy, he migrated to San Francisco in 1901. He was first employed in the Italian Swiss Colony warehouse washing and mending wine barrels; soon, he was appointed assistant wine maker at the Asti winery in Sonoma County. Later, having worked in several Italian-owned wineries, he purchased his own facility with two of his brothers and another Italian, Mario Tribuno, as partners, having obtained loans from the Bank of Italy (later Bank of America) and from Tribuno's father-in-law. Even though some of his ventures failed over the years, Perelli-Minetti was extremely successful as the owner of several wineries. From 1924 he headed A. Perelli-Minetti & Sons in Delano and was active in the wine industry until his death in 1976 at age 95. Family members continue to run the Perelli-Minetti Winery in the Napa Valley.

In the mid-1960s, over half of the wine cooperage in California was controlled by the four largest producers, all of Italian immigrant origins: DiGiorgio, Franzia, Gallo, and Petri. Some writers assert that Italian Americans are primarily responsible for the continuity and success of the California wine industry. In fact, through all the problems of the early twentieth century—earthquake, phylloxera, Prohibition, Great Depression—many Italian family wineries hung on. These immigrants managed to weather economic uncertainty and other hardships even when others gave up.

In the second half of the twentieth century, another major issue came to the forefront: Could family wineries survive corporate takeovers? Corporations absorbed some large wineries: Schenley Distillers bought Italian Swiss Colony and Roma Wine; Heublein bought Gallo Wines; and United Vintners absorbed Cella Wines. Nonetheless, many family wineries continue to prosper: Cadenasso, Guglielmo, Pedrizetti, Pedroncelli, Sebastiani, Seghesio, and Trinchero (Sutter Home). Today, Italian names are still common among winery managers, consultants, grape growers, and industry associations.

In the mid-1990s, there are 684 bonded wineries throughout California that produce 92 percent of this country's wine. Forty percent of the wineries are in the Napa and Sonoma Valleys. Twenty-five wineries still in operation began in the latter half of the 1800s. Two-thirds of today's California wineries were established since 1975 when an increased demand for wine resulted from a shift in American drinking habits away from spirits to wine and beer. Italian Americans own or manage 15 percent of California's wineries, including three of the largest and ten of the oldest. Thus, Italian Americans continue to play a significant role in the nation's wine industry.

Rose D. Scherini

Bibliography

California Wine Pioneers. Profiles of forty-one wine makers based on oral histories in the wine industry series of the Regional Oral History Office Bancroft Library, University of California, Berkeley. San Francisco: Shanken Communications, 1990.

Carosso, Vincent P. *The California Wine Industry: A Study of the Formative Years, 1830–1895.* Berkeley: University of California Press, 1951.

Ensrud, Barbara. *American Vineyards.* New York: Stewart, Tabori and Chang, 1988.

Heintze, William F. *Wine Country. A History of Napa Valley. The Early Years: 1838–1920.* Santa Barbara: Capra Press, 1990.

Hiaring, Philip E. "New York! Finger Lakes District." *Vines and Wines* 78, no. 2 (February 1997): 16–32.

Jacobs, Julius L. "California's Pioneer Wine Families." *California Historical Society Quarterly* 59 (1975): 139–174.

Martini, Louis M. "Wine Making in the Napa Valley." Regional Oral History Office, Bancroft Library, University of California, Berkeley, 1973.

Morton, Lucie T. *Winegrowing in Eastern America.* Ithaca, NY: Cornell University Press, 1985.

Palmer, Hans C. *Italian Immigration and the Development of California Agriculture.* Ph.D. diss., University of California, Berkeley, 1969.

Perelli-Minetti, Antonio. "A Life in Wine Making." Regional Oral History Office, Bancroft Library, University of California, Berkeley, 1976.

Rolle, Andrew F. *The Immigrant Upraised.* Norman: University of Oklahoma Press, 1968.

Walker, Larry. "Pacific Northwest Shows Astonishing Growth." *Vines and Wines* 78, no. 7 (July 1997): 47–50.

"Wines and Vines." *1995 Buyer's Guide.* Directory of wineries by state. San Rafael, 1995.

Author's Note: Major reference collections are (1) the California Wine Industry Series of the Regional Oral History Office, Bancroft Library, University of California, Berkeley, and (2) the wine sections of the public libraries of St. Helena and Santa Rosa, California.

See also WINE MAKING TRADITION

Wine Making Tradition

Wine making has been a tradition for Italian Americans since the middle of the nineteenth century when the first Italian immigrants arrived in this country. Although commercial vineyards and wine making play a significant role in the wine making enterprise, most of the world's wine is made at home. It is a tradition that has evolved over the centuries. From the biblical lands of the Near East to the far reaches of the Orient, the householder has made wine from grapes, fruits, herbs, and grains. Throughout Europe, including Italy, and the United States, a significant amount of wine is made and consumed at home.

Wine making in the United States originated in the early seventeenth century, but wine produced from native American grapes indigenous to the eastern United States (*vitis labrusca*) was considered low quality. In an effort to solve this problem, colonists imported cuttings of classic grapes from native European vines (*vitis vinifera*). In 1773 Thomas Jefferson sent for his friend, Philip Mazzei, of Florence, Italy, to plant an extensive grape vineyard at Monticello, Jefferson's Virginia home. Mazzei brought sixteen experienced Italian vineyard chiefs (vignerons) with him to plant the new vineyard. After a few years, the venture proved to be unsuccessful. It was determined that European grape varieties lacked the qualities and hardiness that enabled native American grapes to survive in the colonies. This experiment was, however, the initiation of Italian involvement in growing grapes in the United States for the sole purpose of making wine.

In 1769 Father Junipero Serra founded a mission near San Diego, California, and it was here that he planted the first known wine grapes for the purpose of producing wine used in the celebration of a Catholic Mass. Weather conditions, soil, and climate were conducive to growing *vitis vinifera* grapes. For more than one hundred years the wine industry grew steadily, and by 1880 California was a powerful grape and wine producing region. From the 1880s through the middle of the twentieth century, most immigrants preferred to make wine from California grapes. They included red varietals such as Zinfandel, Alicante, Carignane, and Muscat, a white grape, all of which were available at farmer's markets in major cities.

The influx of Italian immigrants between 1885 and 1925 brought to America the skill of producing wine at home, which was commonplace in the old country. The largest number of Italians migrated from Italy in 1907, when 285,731 persons, mostly from southern Italy, entered the United States. Of this number, it is estimated that more than 78 percent were young men in their teens or early twenties. By the time they arrived, they were well versed in the art of making wine. The timing of the mass exodus of Italians from southern Europe coupled with the rapid growth of California's grape industry was a phenomenon that enabled Italian immigrants to make wine at home.

The commercial wine industry throughout the United States, which consists of hundreds of wineries and thousands of acres of vineyards, has been influenced by Italian immigrants as well as Italian Americans. The greatest concentration of commercial wineries is in California, where the Ernest and Julis Gallo Winery is located. This winery, the world's largest, produces in excess of sixty million cases of wine annually. The Louis M. Martini vineyard and winery has been in existence since 1922, and the Robert Mondavi family has been producing wines since 1966. A representative example of California wineries that were originally or are currently owned or operated by Italian Americans include the Robert Pepi, Foppiano, Robert Pecota, Carlo Rossi, Signorello, Cambria, Sebastiani, and Ferrari-Carano wineries. New York, the second largest wine producing state, boasts more than one hundred wineries. The Casa Larga Winery was formed by an Italian immigrant and is now managed by Italian Americans.

Wine is central to life in the Italian family as well as in the Italian community at large, and is considered a staple as a food and a beverage. For most Italian Americans, wine with food makes a meal complete. It provides a forum for conversation, a venue for meeting people, and a reason for making new friends. It can be a social event that may last a few minutes to several hours in length. For home wine makers, this art was an inexpensive method of producing a food beverage that could be enjoyed and shared with others.

Until the middle of the twentieth century, a small number of immigrant Italian wine makers were fortunate enough to possess their own vineyard. Others had a few rows of vines or a grape arbor in their yard that would produce a few gallons of wine, at most. For this group it meant careful pruning of the vines in the late autumn or early spring of the year as well as making certain that during the growing season birds and animals and diseases of the vine were controlled.

Wine making was and still is prevalent in Italian American neighborhoods in the fall of the year, a time when the wine making process begins. For the majority of wine makers, late September or early October is when fathers and sons trod down to the local wine grape merchant or to the farmer's market to examine the grape quality and to compare costs of grapes shipped in from California. Currently, one would also find wine makers purchasing fresh fruit, grape juice, or a grape concentrate from local vineyards, wineries, and wine shops, as well. It is not unusual for several families to jointly purchase grapes as well as to assist each other in the crushing and the pressing operation in the wine making process.

Italian immigrant wine makers purchased used white oak wine barrels from local coopers. The wine making process required the use of two barrels, one which was open at one end, for the primary fermentation of the crushed grapes, and a second barrel for wine aging purposes. After several months to a year or more in the barrel the wine was ready to drink. It was not uncommon to tap wine directly from the barrel for the family's daily consumption. Early on, the yeast used to provide fermentation was the type used for baking purposes. Hot water and baking soda were used for cleaning equipment, while lighted sulfur sticks placed in the empty barrel provided sterilization.

The success of the wine maker's art depends upon the source and quality of the fruit and the conditions under which they are made into wine. Wine making at home has changed over the years. Early on, methods were crude and the wine was of a high alcohol content, or *vino forte*. As a result of vigorous research programs in oenology conducted at the University of California at Davis and Cornell University in New York, thousands of grape varieties, including *vinifera* from Italy, are under evaluation for wine producing characteristics and for grafting possibilities. As a result of the theory, practice, and science of grape growing (viticulture) and wine making (viniculture) at these schools, there have been a variety of wine yeasts available for fermentation as well as chemicals for equipment sterilization, wine preservation, and stabilization.

The Qualia Wine Press in Del Rio, Texas, was brought from Italy and is still in use. Started in 1883 by Frank and Mary Qualia, who had migrated from Milan, the winery is still a successful business enterprise. Courtesy U.T. Institute of Texan Cultures, San Antonio, Texas.

In addition to fresh fruit, grape concentrate, and grape juice, frozen crushed grapes are available for wine making. At one time wine was aged only in barrels. Currently, wine may also be found fermenting in food-grade plastic containers and aging in large glass carboys and demijohns in the cellars of wine makers. In addition, short courses and seminars are available to prospective wine makers at universities and cultural institutions as well as through the American Wine Society, which boasts nearly twenty-seven hundred members, 60 percent of whom are home wine makers.

Edward Albert Maruggi

Bibliography
Adams, Leon D. *The Wines of America*. New York: McGraw-Hill, 1990.

Hardwick, Homer. *Winemaking at Home*. New York: Funk & Wagnalls, 1972.

Kraut, Alan M. *Silent Travelers*. New York: Basic Books, 1994.

Wagner, Philip M. *Grapes Into Wine*. New York: Knopf, 1982.

See also WINE INDUSTRY

Winwar, Frances (1900–1985)

Encouraged by her editor to Anglicize her name, Francesca Vinciguerra reluctantly changed her name to Frances Winwar, a pseudonym that appeared on her first novel, *The Ardent Flame* (1927), and publications thereafter. A prolific novelist and biographer, Winwar was born in 1900 in Taormina, Sicily, where she spent the first seven years of her life playing near the Greek theater of her native town, a site considered one of the most beautiful and renowned in Italy. Winwar was fascinated by the beauty of her town and by the many foreign visitors, who inspired her love for other cultures and languages. Her family migrated to America in 1907, where she quickly learned to speak English and impressed her teachers with her writing skills. She continued to write during high school years and later at Hunter College and Columbia University, which she left before getting a degree.

Before she became a naturalized citizen in 1929, Winwar had written three novels, including *Pagan Interval* (1929); she served regularly as a book reviewer for the *New York World* (1923–1925); she cofounded the Leonardo da Vinci Art School in New York City (1923); and she married and had a son. Though she continued to write fiction throughout the next thirty years—*Gallows Hill* (1937), *The Sentimentalist* (1943), *The Eagle and the Rock* (1953)—Winwar is known primarily for her historical biographies, the most famous being *Poor Splendid Wings* (1933), for which she won the prestigious Atlantic Monthly Award for the best nonfiction book of the year. *Poor Splendid Wings,* a biography of the Rossetti family and their pre-Raphaelite circle, follows the lives of young artists during Queen Victoria's reign and centers around such figures as Dante Gabriel Rossetti and Algernon Swinburne.

Three other biographies followed: *The Romantic Rebels* (1935) is a composite biography of Shelley, Byron, and Keats; *Farewell the Banner* (1938), another composite biography, closely examines the personal and intellectual relationships of William Wordsworth, his sister Dorothy Wordsworth, and Samuel Taylor Coleridge; completing the trio is the biography *Oscar Wilde and the Yellow Nineties* (1940), in which Winwar contextualizes Wilde's work within the aesthetic movements of his time and against the background of Victorian propriety.

Subsequent biographies followed in remarkably rapid succession: Walt Whitman, George Sand, Joan of Arc, Elizabeth Barrett and Robert Browning, Gabriele D'Annunzio, Edgar Allan Poe, Jean Jacques Rousseau, and Napoleon Bonaparte. Reviewers praised Winwar's ability to maintain historical veracity amid narratives that read like fiction. That Winwar was interested in the historical and literary achievements of America is attested by her biographies of Whitman and Poe, and also by her works on seventeenth-century Massachusetts, *Gallows Hill* (1937) and *Puritan City* (1938).

Winwar published numerous other works, including a history of Italy for juvenile readers, translations of libretti for the Metropolitan Opera Association, and a translation of Boccaccio's *The Decameron* (Modern Library, 1955). She was a highly dedicated writer, who never forgot her deep reverence and love for her homeland of Italy. By incorporating references to the Italian language and describing the beauty of the Mediterranean, for example, Winwar maintained her connection to Italian culture. Winwar died on July 24, 1985, leaving a legacy of work that honors the importance of the historical past.

Mary Jo Bona

Bibliography

Belli, Angela. "Frances Winwar." In *American Women Writers: From Colonial Times to the Present,* edited by Lina Mainiero, 449–451. New York: Frederick Ungar, 1982.

Green, Rose Basile. *The Italian-American Novel: A Document of the Interaction of Two Cultures.* Rutherford, NJ: Fairleigh Dickinson University Press, 1974.

Peragallo, Olga. *Italian-American Authors and Their Contribution to American Literature.* New York: S. F. Vanni, 1949.

See also LITERATURE; WOMEN WRITERS

Women and the Church

Although Italy's religious heritage has been shaped by many religious forces, to say

"Women and the Church" is to presume women and Roman Catholicism. The Catholic Church shaped traditional conceptions of womanhood everywhere on the Italian peninsula. The institutional Church also provided some women with an alternative to this traditional role and an opportunity for advanced education and professional training. Catholicism has shaped Italian and Italian American understanding of womanhood, the role Italian family women played in Italian American parish life, and Italian women in religious vocations.

The specific role of women in Italian American Catholicism has long been a neglected topic. Following the lead of historian Henry J. Browne, Italians were considered a "problem" for American Catholicism. Rudolph J. Vecoli has described some of the historical circumstances that fostered the image of the irreligious Italian: many Italians were indeed anticlerical, an attitude influenced by southern Italian folk culture and nineteenth-century political experience. Statistics suggest another reason for the perception of Italians as irreligious: early migrants were overwhelmingly male, four out of five in the 1880s, 1890s, 1900s, and 1910s. Not until after World War I did women and children come in large numbers.

The arrival of women and children did not resolve the "Italian problem," for Catholic teaching upheld the same standards of religious observance for both sexes. It did, however, allow a fuller picture of Italian Catholicism. Modern gender research, which emphasizes the sex-specific roles of men and women, have inspired more scholarly analysis of the gendered nature of Italian Catholicism, and of women's roles within it.

Italian Catholic concepts of womanhood actually incorporate elements of pagan and folk culture on the Italian peninsula. Lucia Chiavola Birnbaum has documented the pervasive influence of the Black Madonna. The earliest pre-Christian sources of this image of womanhood date from 20,000–10,000 B.C. The image was of a woman who was doubly powerful: she was in command of her own sexuality and she was fertile; men admired her for both the passion she aroused and the children she produced. With the introduction of Roman Catholicism into southern Italy, a partial syncretization took place. The Catholic Church recognized the importance of one woman, Mary, and celebrated her as the

Mother of God. The Italian laity emphasized how Mary's maternity made her a powerful intercessor.

Mary provided an ambiguous model for Italian and Italian American women. According to Robert Anthony Orsi, the veneration of Mary placed all women in a double bind. Women were honored for their role in maintaining family life. Yet they were also held responsible when things went wrong, and there were many things that could be interpreted as going wrong in impoverished migrant families. This dilemma was acted out in the rituals surrounding the celebration of such feast days as Our Lady of Mount Carmel in East Harlem. Veneeta-marie D'Andrea has described how the Italian Catholic image of womanhood could also have the opposite effect. Simply being thought of as capable of handling such responsibilities developed in women a sense of themselves as serious-minded, assertive in protecting others, and practical. Such a self-image enhanced self-esteem and promoted the individual woman's mental health and sharpened the skills needed for individual social and economic advancement.

An increasing body of research has elaborated how Italian immigrant women and their American-born and -raised daughters acted upon the inherited notion of the role of the Italian American woman as mainstay of the family circle, especially the woman's role in the family's religious life. Italian immigrant women were the links between the institution of the home and the institutional Church. As Italian men would readily admit, it was the women in the family who fulfilled the Catholic responsibility to hear Mass on Sundays and holy days of obligation, to go to confession and receive communion, to see that children received the sacraments, and to tend to children's religious education. As Maxine Schwartz Seller has shown, Protestant denominations emphasized the importance of converting Italian Catholic women in order to secure the conversion of other family members.

Men and women had sex-specific roles in Italian paraliturgical devotional life. Men were the community's public face, organizing mutual-benefit societies that took responsibility for the annual feast day observances of the hometown patron saint in Italy and for transplanting such *feste* to the United States. Within the context of the *festa* or the parish church, women performed the devotional activities that linked their families to the institutional Church. The feast day was a time for rituals signifying petitions for favors or humble gratitude for favors received. To thank the patron saint or Madonna for past favors received, women sometimes walked barefoot in the procession. To petition for favors, women carried lighted candles, sometimes as heavy as the person for whom they were praying, or they purchased and laid before the altar the wax image of the body part they wished healed. During the rest of the year, women visited either their own parish church or the shrine of their patron saint, lighting candles and participating in devotions such as novenas, First Friday devotions to the Sacred Heart, or the thirteen Tuesdays of Saint Anthony. Women could also carry out religious rituals at home, setting up a statue of the Madonna or patron saint and keeping a lighted candle before it, or reciting the rosary. By praying for family members in need, women discharged a culturally mandated obligation that made them responsible for family health and welfare.

Earthly help was also available at the local church. Parishes provided numerous services for families. Saint Vincent de Paul societies gave grants of cash, food, fuel, and clothing. Nurseries took in working mothers' preschoolers. Parochial schools provided both education and child care for youngsters in grades one through eight. Sports, drama clubs, choirs, and altar boys' rehearsals kept the youngsters busy outside of school hours. Services not available at the parish could be found at other Catholic institutions. Men and women in religious orders ran infant asylums, orphanages, boarding schools, homes for delinquent or handicapped youth, rest homes for senior citizens, and hospitals for both emergency and long-term care. If help was not available from the Catholic Church, it might be available in a non-Catholic private philanthropy or a city or state welfare agency. By consulting the pastor, family women could provide practical assistance for their husbands and children.

There are few cases of individual women assuming leadership roles in public religious life. Rudolph J. Vecoli has documented that of Emmanuella Di Stefano. Her husband, Emilio, migrated from Laurenzana Potenza to Chicago in 1873. He was a pioneer of the migration of Laurenzanesi to Melrose Park, a Chicago suburb. In gratitude for his recovery from an illness, Emmanuella vowed to establish an annual feast day celebration of Our Lady of Mount Carmel (that is, of Mary and Jesus bestowing the scapular of Mount Carmel upon Saint Simon Stock and thus on the world) and erected a chapel to house it. In 1903 the devotees became the basis for the parish of Our Lady of Mount Carmel in Melrose Park.

More often, women exercised community leadership via the method of collective action. One example is Saint Ann's Church in the North End of Providence, Rhode Island, in 1901. The local bishop had decided to transfer Saint Ann's pastor and appoint a new one. Dissatisfied parish women took action. When a van and furniture movers arrived to take away the old pastor's furniture, parish women returned the furniture to the house as soon as it was carried out. The old pastor himself intervened to end the parish women's action, but he could not end their passive resistance; his departure resulted in a drop in church attendance. Such female crowd protests have been noted in other large cities with sizable Italian neighborhoods in the 1900s.

Pastors preferred that women act in organized fashion under pastoral direction. Pastors usually organized sodalities, or religious societies, which parishioners joined according to their age and marital status. The principal sodality for unmarried women was the Children of Mary. The names for sodalities for married women in Italian American parishes varied. In the late nineteenth and early twentieth centuries, many parishes had Rosary Societies for the married women. By the 1930s Christian Mothers' Society was a common name. Women also formed organizations that reflected the devotions they or their mothers had practiced in Italy. For example, women from near Genoa had a devotion to Our Lady of Guadalupe. When these women migrated to New York City and became members of Our Lady of Pompeii in Greenwich Village, they organized an annual *festa* to Our Lady of Guadalupe there. Whatever the sodality's name, the functions were similar. Women came together for prayers. The sodality usually had one Sunday a month during which its members received communion as a group, which meant it had an unofficial Saturday for monthly confessions. The sodality helped add to the dignity and solemnity of Sunday or special-occasion Masses by entering the church in a procession, with the sodality banner in the lead and each woman wearing a distinctive piece of clothing. Sodalities helped to raise money for their parishes. Sometimes, the Children of Mary were part of the pool from which Sunday school teachers were selected.

One consequence of neglecting women's history is the scarce data on Italian women's impact on Italian religious vocations. Both Italian and non-Italians have thought that Italian and Italian American men did not enter the priesthood and religious life in the same numbers as men of other ethnic groups. A search of the literature has yet to yield similar charges against Italian women. Although individual families might have preferred their daughters not enter the convent in order to be free to care for elderly parents, Italian culture had no "anti-nunism" comparable to its anticlerical component. Histories of communities, though, have documented the impact of the religious Italian woman tradition on American Catholicism. Biographies demonstrate how individual Italian and Italian American women shaped the Italian religious tradition for that ethnic community.

The first Italian Catholic women to enter religious vocations in America were members of institutes that did not have strong Italian ethnic identity. Giovanni Schiavo has provided the example of Maria Luigia Angelica Cipriana Stanislas Tommasini (1827–1913). Born into an educated Parma family, she joined the Society of the Sacred Heart. In 1848 the Italian liberal revolutions forced Mother Tommasini out of Italy and to France and then to the United States, where she began teaching at Manhattanville. She went on to serve in several administrative positions in her institute.

Italian American girls born or raised in the United States also gravitated to religious institutes. Perhaps the most famous of these is Blandina Segale (1850–1941), who ministered to Indians in New Mexico.

Italian women were also pioneers in the establishment of contemplative institutes. In 1875 Mother Mary Magdalen Bentivoglio and Mother Mary Constance Bentivoglio, blood sisters, natives of Bologna, and members of the Order of Saint Clare, came to erect a monastery in the United States. They settled in Omaha, Nebraska. Mother Mary Con-stance died at Omaha on January 29, 1902, Mother Mary Magdalen at Evansville, Indiana, on August 18, 1905.

The nineteenth century saw an interesting development in the history of religious institutes in Italy. As the unification of Italy came about, political leaders denounced Catholicism as an obstacle to national unity, and there were incidents of appropriation of Church property and of the ousting of religious communities. These antireligious actions were accompanied by the development of free-market capitalism and a minimum of state responsibility for citizens' welfare. These secular developments shaped new religious institutes. The new institutes needed to be self-supporting rather than relying on inherited property or charity. They were also more likely to be concerned with the social issues of the day, not in the sense of advocating social change but in the sense of tending to those who could find no other source of social services. Many Italian communities established foundations in the United States, where members could labor both for the good of the institute and for the good of the Italian immigrants whose lives had been disrupted.

A number of institutes erected in nineteenth-century Italy established foundations in the United States during the period of Italian mass migration and worked in areas pertinent to the migrant apostolate. However, they did not all work with Italian immigrants. The first such organization, the Franciscan Missionary Sisters of the Sacred Heart, was founded in 1861 and came to the United States in 1865. Actually, it was founded near the Italo-Austrian border by a French countess and a Roman priest, and its first U.S. mission was to the German parish of Saint Francis of Assisi in New York City. The Adorers of the Blood of Christ (Sister Adorers of the Most Precious Blood) was founded in Acuto in the Diocese of Anagni in 1834 and came to Piopolis, Illinois, in 1870. The Sisters of the Holy Family of Nazareth was founded in Italy by a Polish noblewoman in 1875 and came to Chicago in 1885. The Sisters of the Sorrowful Mother (Third Order of Saint Francis) began in 1883 and came to the United States in 1889. The Daughters of Charity of the Most Precious Blood was founded in Pagani in 1872, and the Daughters of the Most Holy Cross in Mornese the same year; both came to the United States in 1908. The Sisters of the

Resurrection, founded in Rome in 1891, came to the United States in 1910. The Institute of the Sisters of Saint Dorothy was founded in Quinto in 1834 and came to New York and Providence in 1911. The Mantellate Sisters, Servants of Mary of Blue Island, founded in 1861, came to the United States in 1916. The Daughters of Our Lady of Mercy, founded in 1872, came to the United States in 1919, the same year that the Franciscan Sisters of Saint Elizabeth came to Newark. The Nuns of the Perpetual Adoration of the Blessed Sacrament, founded in Rome in 1907, came to the United States in 1925. The Pious Daughters of Saint Paul, founded in Alba, Piedmont, on June 15, 1915, arrived on Staten Island in June 28, 1932.

The most famous of the institutes that worked directly with Italian immigrants was that of Saint Frances Xavier Cabrini (1850–1917), whose Missionaries of the Sacred Heart, founded in Italy in 1880, came to New York in 1889. Other institutes also worked with Italian immigrants. The Pallottine Sisters of Charity also arrived in New York in 1889. The Apostles of the Sacred Heart, founded by Clelia Merloni in 1894, came to the United States in 1902. The Religious Venerini Sisters, founded in the seventeenth century and dedicated both to religious life and to education, sent sisters to staff a parochial school in Lawrence, Massachusetts, in 1909. The Religious Teachers Filippini, whose origins are connected with those of the Venerinis, came to Trenton in 1910. The Daughters of Saint Mary of Providence, which grew out of a group of women who began work in 1872, came to Chicago in 1913.

Since the end of Italian mass migration, a number of other Italian communities have come to the United States. The Oblates of the Mother of Orphans, founded in 1945, came to the United States thereafter. The Institute of the Sisters of Our Lady of Mount Carmel, founded in 1854, and the Sisters of Our Lady of Sorrows, founded in 1839, came in 1947. The Little Workers of the Sacred Heart, founded in 1892, came in 1948. The Little Missionary Sisters of Charity, founded in 1915, came in 1949. The Camboni Sisters, founded in 1872, came in 1952. The Consolata Missionary Sisters, founded in 1910, and the Xaverian Missionary Society of Mary, founded in 1945, both came in 1954. The Handmaids of Reparation of the Sacred Heart of Jesus, founded in 1918, came to Steuben-

ville in 1958. Three institutes came in 1961: the Canossian Daughters of Charity, founded in Verona in 1808; the Sisters of Charity of the Immaculate Conception of Ivrea, founded in the eighteenth century; and Franciscan Missionary Sisters of the Infant Jesus, founded in Aguila in 1870. The Daughters of Divine Providence, founded in Rome in 1832, came to the United States in 1964. The Vocationist Sisters, founded in 1921, came in 1967. The Sister Oblates of the Blessed Trinity, founded in 1923, came in 1987.

Perhaps ethnic people assimilate when their ethnicity no longer predicts their position in American life. This seems to have happened to Italian American Catholic women, but not without cost. In 1984 vice-presidential candidate Geraldine Ferraro was considered a groundbreaker for women and Italian Americans. Among the critics of Ferraro's positions was the principal broadcaster on the Eternal Word Television Network, Mother Angelica, born Rita Rizzo.

Mary Elizabeth Brown

Bibliography

Birnbaum, Lucia Chiavola. *Black Madonna: Feminism, Religion, and Politics in Italy.* Boston: Northeastern University Press, 1993.

Browne, Henry J. "The 'Italian Problem' and the Catholic Church in the United States, 1880–1900." In *Records and Studies* 25. New York: United States Catholic Historical Society, 1946.

D'Andrea, Veneeta-marie. "The Social Role Identity of Italian-American Women: An Analysis and Comparison of Families and Religious Expectations." In *The Family and Community Life of Italian Americans,* edited by Richard N. Juliani, 61–68. New York: American Italian Historical Association, 1983.

Orsi, Robert Anthony. *The Madonna of 115th Street: Faith and Community in Italian Harlem, 1880–1950.* New Haven: Yale University Press, 1985.

Raptosh, Diane. "Italian/American Women on the Frontier: Sister Blandina Segale on the Santa Fe Trail." In *Italian Ethnics: Their Languages, Literature and Lives,* edited by Dominic Candeloro, Fred L. Gardaphé, and Paolo A. Giordano, 91–107. New York: American Italian Historical Association, 1990.

Schiavo, Giovanni [Ermenigildo]. *The Italian Contribution to the Catholic Church in America.* New York: Vigo Press, 1949.

Seller, Maxine Schwartz. "Protestant Evangelism and the Italian Immigrant Woman." In *The Italian Immigrant Woman in North America,* edited by Betty Boyd Caroli, Robert F. Harney, and Lydio F. Tomasi, 124–136. Toronto: The Multicultural History Society of Ontario, 1978.

Sullivan, Mary Louise, M.S.C. *Mother Cabrini: Italian Immigrant of the Century.* New York: Center for Migration Studies, 1992.

Vecoli, Rudolph J. "The Formation of Chicago's Little Italies." *Journal of American Ethnic History* 2 (spring 1983): 5–20.

See also CABRINI, MOTHER FRANCES XAVIER; FAMILY LIFE; RIZZO, RITA ANTOINETTE; WOMEN IN TRANSITION

Women in the Workforce

Italian American women have made a constant and stable progression in the American workforce. Immigrant women of the early 1900s built a cornerstone for future generations by overcoming oppressive work conditions. Second-generation women merged into the American workforce by balancing Old World cultural traits and skills with New World values of personal fulfillment and independence. Third-generation women overcame traditional barriers and succeeded in a changing workplace. Fourth- and fifth-generation women continue to meet new challenges of the "high-tech" work force into the twenty-first century.

From the late 1700s to mid-1800s some twelve thousand Italians, mainly well-educated males from northern Italy, migrated to America. With the exception of a few prominent artists, teachers, tradesmen, and entrepreneurs, little is known about them. From 1870 to 1880 over fifty-five thousand Italians left the poverty-stricken agricultural regions south of Rome, the Mezzogiorno, for the United States, starting a mass migration. The number escalated to over two million from 1900 to 1910. Once in America the majority of men could find work only as unskilled laborers. Women who had been schooled exclusively in domestic necessities for the survival of the family in the Mezzogiorno now became wage earners and equal partners in the economic success of their families.

Unlike married Jewish women who were seldom allowed to do outside work at home, common sources of income for Italian immigrant women were the home piecework industry and the taking-in of boarders. Irish immigrant women, who were not as restricted by traditional cultural barriers as Jewish and Italian women, had the advantage of English-speaking skills. They were more likely to be employed in personal service occupations, which included domestics. Compared to young Jewish women who were encouraged to develop careers, young Italian women were expected to sacrifice career opportunities for the welfare of the family. Once married, both Italian and Jewish women were expected to devote themselves to husbands and families. However, where only 2 percent of Jewish women worked outside the home, a larger number of Italian women did.

By the early 1900s Italian women joined other immigrant women working outside the home in the manufacturing trades. While Polish, German, Hungarian, and Slavic women gravitated toward laundries, cigar making, and the metal industries, Italian women were more frequently found in operative positions in the garment, artificial flowers, lace, tobacco, paper products, and candy industries. Because of their strong work ethic and frugality, Italian American women were more easily exploited, often receiving the lowest wages. Discrimination was rampant and working conditions were deplorable. Unsafe work conditions caused the deaths of 145 workers, of which seventy-five were young Italian women, in the Triangle Shirt Waist Company fire on March 25, 1911, in New York City. This tragedy was instrumental in convincing workers that women must be part of unions and that unions were necessary for the protection of all workers' rights and safety.

Prior to the 1913 and 1919 garment strikes, Italian American women, generally, were not involved in the labor movement as actively as other women. These strikes gave rise to their militancy and the establishment of the International Ladies' Garment Workers' Union's Local 89, a separate Italian-speaking local. Angela and Maria Bambace were key organizers in the 1919 strike and in the formation of Local 89. Angela later became vice-president of the International Ladies' Garment Workers' Union and an effective leader in the American labor movement.

In addition to improving economic conditions, unions had a positive impact on the assimilation of Italian American women by providing contact with other ethnic groups, exposing them to new ideas, and broadening their social focus. The unions sponsored educational programs and afforded career opportunities for Italian American women who rose to positions of leadership. Along with the Bambace sisters, Grace de Lusise-Natarelli, Margaret DiMaggio, and Tina Catania were but a few of the Italian American women organizers and leaders whose efforts contributed to the success of the American labor movement.

During the 1930s and the 1940s, many second-generation Italian American women, who were better educated, moved from the factories to clerical, sales, and professional positions. The move into the larger American work force caused conflict for these women who had to balance the cultures of two worlds: American education, work experience, and social contact with that of Italian family solidarity and traditional female roles. Reflecting this change, the 1950 United States census shows 5 percent of Italian American second-generation women were in professional positions as compared to 2 percent of immigrant women. Perhaps more indicative of change, the census reflected 40 percent of the second generation, but only 8 percent of the immigrant women, in clerical/sales positions. Though second-generation women had a representation of 44 percent in operative positions, 77 percent of immigrant women were in the same category.

After World War II and well into the 1960s, Italian Americans continued to gain middle-class status. An increasing number entered college and attained professional positions as they moved from the ethnic enclaves of the cities to the suburbs. The 1970 census counted 10 percent of Italian American women in professional and technical categories with many entering nursing, social work, and teaching; the number in operative positions dropped to 25 percent.

During the years following the 1970s women's movement, which had a positive impact upon career choices and attitudes, third-generation Italian American women made major career and educational advancements. According to the 1980 census, 29 percent of Italian American women were employed in full-time positions. They were most frequently employed in professional services, 29 percent; retail trade, 22 percent; and manufacturing industries, 16 percent. Nineteen percent were in professional positions, and 52 percent were in clerical/sales positions. As with all other women, Italian Americans' incomes were, generally, less than half of men's, creating a financial gender gap where white women received $415 for every $1,000 received by white men. Forty-one percent of Italian American women completed four years of high school, 10 percent completed one to three years of college, and 5 percent completed four years of college.

Unlike previous generations, modern Italian American women were encouraged to pursue higher education and greater economic roles. They also were taught, as those had been before them, that womanhood revolved around their roles as wives and mothers. Despite this dichotomy, they overcame restrictive

Rose Marie Bravo, outstanding Italian American businesswoman who achieved the position of president of Saks Fifth Avenue. Courtesy of the National Italian American Foundation (NIAF), Washington, D.C.

gender barriers and balanced demanding workplace and familial responsibilities. For some, these advancements were in conflict with their sense of ethnicity, but for others, especially those born after World War II, ethnicity became more personal in nature rather than a living culture. Ethnicity was viewed with pride and a bittersweet nostalgic memory of their immigrant grandparents' experiences and traditions.

Italian American women moved up the career ladder in greater numbers to white-collar, executive, and professional positions. The 1990 census shows the percentage of Italian American women in professional positions increased significantly to 30 percent. Representation in the operative category reached a low of 5 percent, while 49 percent were in clerical/sales positions.

As today's fourth- and fifth-generation Italian American women enter a changing workforce symptomatic of the 1990s, they are better prepared than the generations before. They are more educated and technically trained. According to the 1990 census, 16 percent of Italian American women have some college experience and 7 percent hold associate degrees. Twelve percent hold bachelor degrees and over 5 percent hold graduate and professional degrees. They have greater mentoring and support networks through professional and occupational organizations, many whose memberships are exclusively female. Within the Italian American community there are professional and educational organizations, programs, and services offering occupational networking and mentoring opportunities, as well as scholarships.

Growing up in a multicutural society that recognizes ethnic diversity, Italian American women are more comfortable about expressing ethnic sentiments. The nature of ethnicity has become less restrictive and more consistent with occupational, educational, and social mobility. Equally important, fourth- and fifth-generation women now have the example of successful Italian American female role models to guide them into the twenty-first century.

Bridget Oteri Robinson

Bibliography

Battistella, Graziano, ed. *Italian Americans in the 1980s: A Sociodemographic Profile*. New York: Center for Migration Studies, 1980.

Gambino, Richard. *Blood of My Blood, The Dilemma of the Italian Americans*. New York: Doubleday, 1974.

Kessner, Thomas. *The Golden Door: Italian and Jewish Immigrant Mobility in New York City, 1889–1915*. New York: Oxford University Press, 1977.

Mangione, Jerre, and Ben Morreale. *La Storia, Five Centuries of the Italian American Experience*. New York: Harper Collins, 1992.

Nelli, Humbert. *From Immigrants to Ethnics, The Italian Americans*. New York: Oxford University Press, 1983.

Tomasi, Lydio F. ed. *Italian Americans: New Perspectives in Italian American Immigration and Ethnicity*. New York: Center for Migration Studies, 1985.

United States Department of Commerce. Economics and Statistics Administration. *1990 Census of Population—Ancestry of the Population in the United States*. CP-3-2. Washington, DC: Bureau of the Census, 1990.

Weatherford, Doris. *Foreign and Female: Immigrant Women in America 1840–1930*. New York: Schocken, 1986.

See also BONAVITA, ROSE; LABOR; OCCUPATIONS OF ITALIAN IMMIGRANTS IN TURN-OF-THE-CENTURY AMERICA, OCCUPATIONS, PRESENT-DAY

Women in Transition

Cross-cultural psychologists and ethnographers believe that history and individual development are linked and that historical events affect personality development, emotional functioning, and psychopathology of the immigrant group and subsequent generations. In their country of origin and in the United States Italian immigrant women exemplify this dynamic by the difficulties they have endured.

Geographically and culturally, Italy has been divided into two countries, north and south. Pervasive racial prejudice by northerners toward southerners has prevailed throughout the centuries. The major migration to the United States originated from towns and villages of southern Italy. The southern Italian who migrated to the United States at the turn of the century emerged from a feudal system in which political power and social influence were based on hereditary possession of land and opportunities for upward mobility and

United States Congresswoman Nancy Pelosi, Democrat, from California. Born into the politically active D'Alessandro family from Baltimore's Little Italy, Pelosi is an example of the rising status of Italian American women in public life. Courtesy of the National Italian American Foundation (NIAF), Washington, D.C.

individual achievement were nonexistent. They were exploited by landowners, the middle class, and nobility; the clergy tended to support the nobility, so they, too, were perceived by the southern Italian as part of a hostile, exploitative world.

Southern Italians who migrated to the United States to make a better life most likely carried with them deep-seated feelings of inferiority and low self-esteem rooted in their powerlessness to influence or control the political, educational, or social systems that had subordinated them for many generations. Centuries of exploitation led to a realistic mistrust of social institutions outside the family. In the setting of these historical experiences, the family was the only social structure on which the southern Italian could depend for survival. Loyalty to anyone or any institution outside the family was considered unwise.

The distress that was associated with acculturation in the United States where Italian immigrants experienced educational and occupational discrimination based on ethnicity,

class, and gender, was compounded by their occupational disadvantage in the labor force as semiskilled and unskilled laborers and by poor communication skills in English.

The Italian immigrant's desire for the economic stability of the family shaped their occupational preferences in the United States for several generations. These preferences, in turn, created a multigenerational pattern of educational and occupational cultural marginalization. For immigrants and second-generation Italian Americans, upward occupational and social mobility and its corollary, residential mobility, meant separation from the family and peer group. Between the first and second generations, most Italians filled blue-collar occupations in the skilled, semiskilled, and unskilled labor categories. There was little occupational mobility among Italian women into professional and managerial categories in the second generation: 42 percent of second-generation Italian men advanced into white-collar jobs, while second-generation females remained underrepresented in professional categories (9 percent) and overrepresented in the ranks of clerical (39 percent) and operative (25 percent) categories.

Work was viewed less as an opportunity to excel individually and more as a means to economically provide for one's family. Antithetical to the values of the mainstream American family cultural values, where independence, individual achievement, and privacy of the nuclear family are valued, the dynamics of the Italian American family have been characterized by a pattern of family relations in which family loyalty, affiliation, and cooperation are valued over pursuit of individual rights and feelings, confrontation, and competition. As a result, many Italians in America invoked the Old World tradition that children should share in the economic upkeep of the family. To some extent, the American compulsory school attendance law conflicted with the children's ability to contribute earnings to the family income. Hard work, earning wages, and saving income were viewed by many Italian Americans as the formula for economic security in America.

The pursuit of higher education was not traditionally a birthright nor was it considered a very practical means to obtain financial security. Consequently, educational attainment was not a priority for many Italians. A 1969 census survey of educational attainment showed that Italian Americans ranked behind all other groups except Mexicans and Puerto Ricans. A 1979 survey conducted by the United States Department of Commerce on Ancestry and Language in the United States reported that the proportion of Italian Americans completing high school continued to be lower than the national average (62 percent). Nevertheless, educational and occupational disadvantage did not translate into income disadvantage: Italian American income has and continues to be above the national average.

Thousands of women augmented family income by entering sweatshops in the garment trade, working in factories, cellars, and attics. In 1910 Italian women represented 36 percent of female labor in New York City and 72 percent of the labor force in the artificial flower cottage industry. They displaced other workers by accepting lower wages. Additionally, in 35 percent of Italian homes, the wives took in boarders.

Italian immigrant women successfully assumed multiple roles as wage earners, strong maternal figures, and managers of the home and family. In addition to contending with cultural barriers that have interfered with and affected Italian American's educational aspirations and occupational preferences for several generations, the Italian American woman's socialization, in particular, attenuated her education and career aspirations. Historically, the Italian American woman was socialized to cultivate her maternal role over career and to favor her family's needs over her own desires, needs, and aspirations. Social pressures reinforcing the behaviors associated with adopting traditional feminine roles may have also limited the Italian American woman's development of her potential in the traditionally male-oriented domains of educational and occupational achievement. These cultural parameters are critical to an understanding of labor force participation of the female Italian American immigrant.

As a group, Italians have achieved considerable economic, occupational, and educational progress since their immigrant days. More recent studies demonstrate that third- and fourth-generation Italians have achieved greater educational, social, and occupational mobility than previous generations but continue to adhere to many of the traditional family norms and values that are in conflict with their roles in mainstream culture.

The traditions of an agrarian feudal society and Catholicism have influenced southern Italians who migrated to the United States. These traditions are linked in that they share a similar conception of the family and the status of women. Both view the family as the basic social unit that provides for the survival of the individual. The woman is the binding force of this social structure. Individual needs, particularly those of the mother, are subordinated to the needs of the family. The traditional immigrant view of the outside world as hostile and threatening promoted bonding patterns with children that emphasized primary loyalty to the family, in general, and to the mother, in particular.

Because political power and social influence were not a birthright of the southern Italian, masculine identity could not be defined on the basis of occupational achievement. Instead, male status was derived principally from his authoritarian role in the home, which was maintained through fear. However, the widespread economic marginality of males in southern Italian culture concentrated de facto authority of the home in the mother; therefore, the Italian American family has been described as "father dominated but mother centered." A woman learned to exercise her emotional power and authority indirectly in order to preserve the appearance of her husband's social authority. This required that she create the impression to neighbors and family that she deferred to her husband when in fact, emotionally, she ruled the home.

Historically, for women, the more immediate practical considerations of taking on the roles of wife and mother through marriage had ascendancy over expectations of emotional or sexual intimacy in the marital relationship. Romantic expectations of emotional fulfillment in the marital relationship were not aspired to and not cultivated. The ideal wife was expected to be obedient, chaste, fertile, and the bearer of healthy children. Anecdotal clinical evidence suggests that among Italian Americans, husband and wife appear to give more priority to their relationship as parents than as a couple.

Historically, Italian Americans have had one of the lowest divorce rates in the United States. Over the centuries, the Italian legal system and the Catholic Church created a marriage-unto-death norm that, some might say, has placed women in a powerless bind.

Civil and religious laws prohibiting divorce, contraception, and abortion, ensured a woman's obedience to her husband. Divorce and abortion were not legally permitted in Italy until 1970. Until recently in the Mediterranean, a woman's chief bargaining power for marriage was her virginity. Excessive sexual repression of a woman's impulses prior to marriage was the norm. Only marriage legalized and sanctified her sexuality.

For southern Italians, and most of the Mediterranean, masculine honor and feminine shame were inextricably linked to a woman's sexuality. A man's social power was derived from the public appearance of control and sexual domination over a woman. A wife's infidelity and a daughter's loss of virginity outside marriage dishonored the man in his role as husband and father. Obedience to the male was often maintained through fear. Punishment, often violent, was exacted, if the sexual code of the obedient, chaste, sexually faithful daughter or wife was violated.

Italian laws have promoted a morality sanctioning a double standard that was discriminatory against women until the women's movement in Italy achieved legislative victories in the early 1970s. Up until 1971, under Italian law, a husband's honor was considered to be more important than that of his wife. Adultery was assessed according to whether it was committed by the husband or wife; the law favored the husband. "Crimes of passion" (the murder of a spouse, or the murder of a daughter by her father, or the murder of a sister by her brother) were considered second-class homicides if the murderer could prove a serious offense to his "honor."

The social structure of southern Italy over hundreds of years undermined the autonomy and self-esteem of men and women not born into nobility. Some theorists believe men who have been emasculated by their culture will frequently assert their power over women to compensate for their powerlessness in the social order. Women, economically dependent on their husbands for survival, became economically and psychologically subordinated to their husbands. The machismo complex is rooted in this pattern of socialization. This compensatory complex is conceptualized as a male-centered defensive ideology that encourages men to be sexually aggressive, to sexually dominate women, and to brag about their sexual prowess. There are many definitions of machismo. They range from the more benign definition of the male as the protector and family breadwinner, where male and female activities in the home are clearly demarcated, to the extremely rigid form of machismo that is manifested in a defensive, pathological subordination of the woman. Italians and Italian Americans vary a great deal in the degree to which machismo characteristics and their sequelae have been integrated into family functioning and individual psychological development.

A double sexual standard in Italian culture is sustained psychologically by cultural norms that are defined by the concepts of machismo and its corollary, the madonna complex. The madonna complex stipulates that a woman should be chaste and virginal prior to marriage, sexually faithful when married, and both tolerant and forgiving of her husband's macho behavior, including his sexual infidelities, in order to preserve family solidarity.

Southern Italian culture encouraged women to emulate the Virgin Mary, *La Madonna,* in her roles as wife and mother. The Madonna's power derives from her asexuality (she conceived a child without sexual intercourse) and by her self-sacrificing motherhood. The madonna complex in Italian culture infers female spiritual superiority to males and is based on an ideal and ethic of suffering and self-sacrifice of a woman's needs as an individual, in favor of her children and family. The cultural respect for maternal authority entails several behavioral norms: in return for her children's and husband's respect, the mother is expected to develop and endure hardship and suffering without complaint. She is expected to accept the obligation to provide for their care, whenever it is needed throughout the life cycle, and she is expected to demonstrate unconditional love and forgiveness of family members regardless of their behavior toward her and the suffering their behavior may inflict.

Family solidarity appears to be maintained at considerable psychological cost to the Italian American woman. Although there is no empirical data available that demonstrates the impact of the madonna complex on Italian American women's psychological functioning, or the interaction effects of the machismo complex on their sexual functioning, clinical and anecdotal evidence suggests that they have internalized the madonna complex and have psychologically subordinated their needs. This, in turn, discourages direct expression of their feelings or assertion of their needs. Conceptually there is good reason to suspect that the cultural factors mentioned play a crucial role in the Italian American woman's psychological makeup, but to date there has been no attempt to examine this hypothesis empirically.

One stereotypical image of the Italian woman is that of a sensuous, passionate, generous, born-for-love partner who gives herself to man with simplicity and naturalness. In 1960 A. Parca surveyed eight thousand women in Italy and reported her findings in her book *Italian Women Confess* (1963). Parca's findings revealed that most women in Italy did not believe that they had a right to sexuality apart from procreation and were ignorant of the most elementary physiology of the sex act. The reality of the women she surveyed was that they were obsessed by sexual problems and overcome with doubts and fears. Ann Cornelisen studied the patterns of peasant women's behavior in Lucania, Italy, and concluded that most women perceived sexual relations with their husbands as a non-passionate, necessary duty.

An ethnographic study of a small group of elderly Italian immigrant women in New York City revealed the persistence of similar attitudes toward sex and sexuality. The marriages of the immigrant women ranging in age from 72 to 95 interviewed in Little Italy, New York, like those of their parents, appeared to have been based on a mutual system of obligations to family members with little or no expectation of emotional intimacy and sexual fulfillment. Sex was primarily a matter of procreative duty rather than pleasurable activity.

As a result of both the excessive sexual repression required of these women prior to marriage, and the imperative that they bear children in marriage, many of them became mothers without ever experiencing orgasmic and sexual pleasure. The narratives revealed that these women were well acquainted with the duties, and very few of the pleasures, of conjugal relations. There were few if any opportunities to develop knowledge of sexual and emotional intimacy. Mothers did not discuss their daughters' sexuality with them and, not surprisingly, many women carried the norms learned in the parental home into their marriage relationships. Italian culture traditionally encouraged women to emulate the asexual Madonna. It appears that the women internalized their mother's cultural ideal of the asexual Virgin in their roles as wives and mothers.

Today in contrast, the modern "goddess" third-generation Italian American rock singer Madonna embodies the contradictory elements of lusty sexuality, passion, and bodily earthiness of the whore, while satirizing the virginal innocence and feminine fragility of the Roman Catholic Madonna. However, Madonna's cultivation of her erotic persona seems more related to a desire for power and need for control than a desire for an emotional connection that honors the mystery of the feminine. According to Mary Simeti-Taylor, in Greek and Roman mythology goddesses who assumed power in the patriarchal hierarchy learned to hide their maiden vulnerability behind their worldly, armored self. Like the goddesses of mythology, Madonna's vulnerability is hidden behind an armored erotic shield.

Currently there is no research that assesses the psychological affect in Italian American women of the recent American cultural shifts in attitudes toward various aspects of a woman's sexuality and functioning both within and outside the context of a marriage relationship. A national opinion survey in 1984 indicated that Italian American respondents, compared to all other ethnic groups surveyed, had the most liberal attitudes toward premarital sex: only 24 percent of Italian Americans surveyed indicated that premarital sex is always or almost always wrong. However, it is difficult to interpret the significance of this finding without also assessing the impact of these attitudes on sexual behavior. This is certainly an area worthy of more systematic future research.

The challenge for the Italian American woman today is to integrate aspects of her sexuality that have been split and dissociated for centuries: in her psychological life the static protective elements of the Virgin Mary conventionally associated solely with the maternal aspect of the feminine could be transformed into a more vibrant fullness. It is possible to integrate the dynamic elements of her sexuality with the spirituality and creative power of the Virgin such that instinctive sexual expression is transformed into lovemaking and the birth of new forms of femininity.

In the United States it is expected that adult children will be independent and relatively free from parental control in adult-hood. Not surprisingly, the focal point of conflict revealed across psychological studies of adult Italian Americans centers on problems related to continuing dependence on the mother and the family. These studies suggest that adult Italian Americans experience greater conflicts related to emotional dependency on their parents than non-Italians. Research evidence indicates that Italian American family dynamics create bonding and attachment patterns with children that are less tolerant than those in the dominant American culture regarding the child's striving for emotional separation and independence from the family, in general, and from the mother, in particular. Moreover, the research suggests that these separation difficulties are shared by both the parent and the child and may lead to lifelong conflicts as the adult child aspires to full independence. For the traditional Italian family, the moving away of young adult and adult children is frequently psychologically translated as an emotional abandonment of the family and mother.

The traditional cultural expectation is that the mother will devote herself exclusively to the child and that her satisfactions derive primarily from her nurturing and caretaking roles. The overwhelming cultural emphasis on an exclusive maternal relationship could undermine the mother's ability to accept the child's separation from her. Several studies support this hypothesis and suggest that Italian mothers are high in nurturing but less tolerant and encouraging of their children's emotional independence than non-Italian mothers throughout the life cycle.

Research also suggests that the developmental task of separation is extremely difficult for the Italian American adolescent. Italian American mothers, compared to non-Italian mothers, tend to give priority to the maternal role to the exclusion of most outside interests and are more protective, attentive, and stricter disciplinarians than non-Italian mothers. According to Colleen Johnson, Italian American parents did not expect that their adolescent children would want to leave the warmth and protection of family and mother to attend college away from home. A popular solution to the family's difficulty with separation is for young adults to live at home while commuting to college. In a comparative study of college students by McGoldrick, Pearce, and Gior-

dano, Italian Catholics demonstrated the most difficulty in the experience of separation from the family. They experienced more instances of separation anxiety, tended to live in their parents' home while attending college, and if they did leave home, started college feeling mostly sad and expecting to be homesick.

American culture encourages a discontinuity in parent-child ties subsequent to marriage. If the adult female or male has not adequately separated from his or her family, this invisible bond of loyalty will continue to interfere with succeeding phases of the individual's and the family's life cycle. Psychologically, difficulties in separation for the Italian American of both genders may result in an invisible conflict of unresolved loyalties between the marriage partner and the natal family. Developmentally, marriage should signify that significant progress has been made in the task of becoming emotionally independent of the natal family. In the traditional Italian American family, marriage may not interrupt the close tie to the natal family and parent. Mother, in particular, may expect close involvement with a daughter or son even after he or she has married.

Emerging research suggests that Italian American women of achievement, compared to non-Italian achieving women, experience considerable conflict related to the reconciliation of career roles with traditional nurturing roles within the family. In a survey by Geraldine Battista-Lanzalli, responses revealed that 70 percent of Italian American women compared to 25 percent of non–Italian American women experienced considerable conflict between these roles. There is no data on the psychological effect of these dual roles on the Italian American woman's psychological quality of life, her marital satisfaction, or relationships with children and parents. It is likely, however, that Italian American women who have become economically and socially emancipated struggle with trying to function in a face-paced, competitive culture with expectations that differ from the traditional sex-role expectations of her family.

In psychology literature, the traditional focus of inquiry has been on Italian and Italian American women in their nurturing, maternal roles. Psychopathology in the family was thought to be rooted in the mother's dominant role in the psychological lives of family members. For example, in 1963 Jungian analyst Ernst Bernhard observed that most neurotic disorders in Italy were primarily conditioned by excessive maternal attachment. According to Bernhard, this resulted in male disorders of potency, Don Juanism, homosexuality, and disturbed relationships between the sexes. In women, the complex was manifested in psychosomatic disorders, and a lack of confidence in their biological and sexual fulfillment.

In 1969 social anthropologist Anne Parsons investigated the psychodynamic characteristics of working-class Neapolitan families and in first- and second-generation Italian American working-class families. She found that conflicts related to the young adults' difficulties in modulating expression of intense feelings and impulses and identity formation associated with acculturation to the American culture were major sources of psychopathology. Additionally, she observed that prolonged dependency on parents was one source of low occupational mobility among second- and third-generation Italian Americans. Further, she observed that pathology usually developed in those families that produced exclusive and restrictive environments that interfered with the efforts of adolescents and young adults to achieve independence in the wider community.

Though familial barriers to occupational mobility are changing as third- and fourth-generation Italian Americans achieve greater educational and occupational mobility, the psychologically dynamic remnants of these patterns described by Parsons remain a source of intergenerational psychological conflict between upwardly mobile Italian Americans and their families as described in the psychological studies cited earlier.

Italian American women today are in the midst of a powerful psychological transition: they are being challenged to achieve a level of development and integration in their feminine identities that may ultimately require them to transform many aspects of their psychological functioning. As the Italian American woman avails herself of opportunities to achieve levels of educational and professional success historically denied to her mother and grandmother, she is confronted with the developmental challenge of facing her many hidden emotional needs, feelings, and sexual desires that may conflict with her culture's traditional ideals of femininity. Most Italian American grandmothers and great-grandmothers were trapped in social systems that denied them political power and access to higher education and that prevented them from freely selecting marital partners, owning property after marriage, and expressing their sexuality or limiting their control over reproduction. Yet despite these constrictive historical circumstances, many of them developed a measure of psychological self-sovereignty even though the psychological accommodation that was necessary for survival over many centuries required that many parts of their inner selves remain hidden and repressed. Their opportunities for self-development and achievement were compromised by their struggles to provide for the family's well-being. The changing economy and the changing role of women in the 1990s is altering the family life-cycle patterns that have been historically adaptive up until the current generation. The Italian American women's ability to grow and change and redefine their connections to their families will profoundly influence the growth, development, and adaptation of future generations of Italian Americans.

Elizabeth G. Messina

Bibliography

Battista-Lanzalli, Geraldine. "Family vs. Career: A Dilemma for the Italian-American Woman of the 80s." In *Italian Americans in Transition*. Edited by Joseph Scelsa, S. La Gumina, and Lydio Tomasi, 115–126. Staten Island, NY: The American Italian Historical Association, 1990.

Bernhard, Ernst. "The Tasks Confronting Analytic Psychology in Italy." In *Contact with Jung,* edited by Michael Fordham, 97–110. London: Tavistock Press, 1963.

Comas-Diaz, Lillian, and Ezra E. H. Griffith, eds. *Clinical Guidelines in Cross-Cultural Mental Health*. New York: John Wiley & Sons, 1988.

Cornelisen, Ann. *Women of the Shadows*. New York: Vantage Books, 1977.

Gambino, Richard. *Blood of My Blood, The Dilemma of the Italian Americans*. Garden City, NY: Doubleday, 1975.

Johnson, Coleen Leahy. *Growing Up and Growing Old in Italian American Families*. New Brunswick, NJ: Rutgers University Press, 1985.

———. "The Maternal Role in the Contemporary Italian American Family." In *Italian*

Immigrant Women in North America,
234–244. Toronto, Canada: The Multicultural History Society of Ontario, 1982.

McGoldrick, M., M. Pearce, and J. Giordano.
Ethnicity and Family Therapy. New
York: Guilford, 1982.

Messina, Elizabeth G. "Life Span Develop-
ment and Italian American Women." In
*Italian Americans in a Multicultural So-
ciety,* edited by Jerome Krase and Judith
N. DeSena. Stony Brook, NY: Forum
Italicum, 1994.

Parca, A. *Italian Women Confess.* Translated
by Carolyn Gaiser. New York: Farrar,
Straus, 1963.

Parsons, Anne. *Belief, Magic and Anomies:
Essays in Psychological Anthropology.*
New York: The Free Press, 1969.

Rolle, Andrew. *The Italian Americans: Troubled Roots.* New York: Macmillan,
1980.

Simeti-Taylor, Mary. *On Persephone's Island.*
New York: Alfred A. Knopf, Inc., 1986.

See also ASSIMILATION; FAMILY LIFE;
MADONNA; MENTAL HEALTH; WOMEN IN THE
WORKFORCE

Women Writers

Olga Peragallo's 1949 compilation *Italian-
American Authors and Their Contribution to
American Literature* includes fifty-nine authors, of which only eleven are women. Peragallo's book (completed by her mother and
brother after she died) remains important for
its bibliographic accuracy and detail. It is a
study authored by a woman who believed in
the importance of the literary activities of Italian Americans. It has acted as a beacon for
other scholars equally devoted to shedding
light on the literary productions of Italian-
descended writers in America.

In the past twenty years, women scholars, themselves creative writers, have been at
the literary helm, introducing and disseminating information about Italian American writers, including women writers. Rose Basile
Green's survey of the relationships between
two established cultures—Italian and American—is thoroughly detailed in her book *The
Italian-American Novel: A Document of the
Interaction of Two Cultures* (1974). Green
analyzes autobiographical accounts of the
early Italian immigrants (Constantine Panunzio and Pascal D'Angelo, for example) and the
emergence of the Italian American novel, in
which the experiences of immigration and assimilation occur in a context of the individual's "moral power to triumph in the struggle
against a hostile environment." Although she
only includes commentary on four Italian
American women writers (Frances Winwar,
Mari Tomasi, Marion Benasutti, and Julia
Savarese), Green was instrumental in extending Peragallo's bibliographical compendium
to include an analysis of recurring motifs that
occur in the narratives, such as the isolated
immigrant/alien marginalized by the established society.

Yet it was not until 1985 that the first
thoroughgoing anthology solely dedicated to
women writers was published. A novelist and
essayist herself, Helen Barolini's *The Dream
Book: An Anthology of Writings by Italian
American Women* presents the literary contributions of a cultural group that had gone un-
recognized. *The Dream Book* won the American Book Award in 1986. This collection is
much more than a guide book: featuring the
writings of fifty-six Italian American women,
including five separate genres (memoirs, nonfiction, fiction, drama, and poetry), Barolini
further broadens the analysis of Italian American writers by placing them in a historical, social, and cultural context, bringing to light the
impingements of class and gender on the
women's lives. Barolini's stupendously conceived introduction merits the back-cover
commendation she receives from Alice Walker,
who describes the anthology as "a book of
heroic recovery and affirmation." The publication of *The Dream Book* has spawned
an increased awareness of and discussion
about the literary talent of Italian American
women writers.

As a result of Barolini's auspicious publication, scholarly publications on women writers have increased, appearing in such journals
as *Melus* (The Journal of the Society for the
Study of Multi-Ethnic Literature of the United
States), *Italian Americana,* and *VIA* (Voices in
Italian Americana). Two subsequent anthologies, the 1991 *From the Margin: Writings in
Italian Americana* (edited by Anthony J. Tamburri, Paolo Giordano, and Fred L. Gardaphé) and the 1994 *The Voices We Carry:
Recent Italian/American Women's Fiction*
(edited by Mary Jo Bona) continue to showcase the contributions of Italian American

writers, aware of the absolute necessity of advocacy in keeping these voices audible and viable. Without the groundbreaking work of Barolini and the editorial work of Rose Romano (whose journal *la bella figura* was instrumental in promoting the works of women poets) the analysis of Italian American women writers might still, unhappily, be consigned to a backwater of one's academic or literary career. Instead, it is the work of such scholars and writers mentioned above that makes continued discussion of Italian American women writers possible.

Rosa Maria Segale, Frances Winwar, and Rosa Cassettari represent the options opened to women in the mid to late nineteenth and early twentieth centuries. That each woman was devoted to telling stories attests to the importance of oral traditions in Italian culture. For Segale, born in 1850 in the northern Italian village of Cicagna (fifteen miles above Genoa), the example she observed from the Sisters of Charity in Cincinnati after she and her family migrated to America unequivocally determined her decision to become a nun. At the age of 16, Rosa Maria, now renamed as Sister Blandina, entered the Sisters of Charity novitiate, followed by her older sister, Sister Justina. For twenty-one years, Sister Blandina Segale lived in the Southwest (Trinidad, Colorado; Santa Fe and Albuquerque) doing missionary work: establishing schools and hospitals, working among the Indians, and suppressing the lynch law in Trinidad. Out of that experience, Sister Blandina was encouraged to publish the journal she kept about events and mores in the Southwest. The journal, whose entries are addressed to her sister, Justina, reveals the strength of a woman emboldened by her desire to help others.

Because she chose the vocation of a nun, Sister Blandina was liberated from the constraints placed on Italian women of her generation: marriage and motherhood. Aware of the importance of educating her daughters, Sister Blandina's mother, Giovanna, hired an English teacher (despite the family's dire poverty in the early Cincinnati days), preparing them for further educational training at the Catholic grammar school. Though she considered herself foremost a Sister of Charity, Sister Blandina's journal more than records the educational and charitable work in which she was involved for over twenty years in the Southwest. Her penchant for set-

ting the scene, employing dialogue, and describing the kinds of people she meets out West, especially the typical cowboy, makes *At The End of the Santa Fe Trail* an important contribution to literature of the West, including the travel narrative, accounts of female pioneering in the West, and the influence of Catholicism in the American West. Even if she did not consider herself a writer per se, Sister Blandina's contribution to American letters is imbued with both an Italian and a Catholic ethos, elements that are prevalent in the Italian American novel.

Perhaps it is an example of the Italian American woman's subordination of the self to others that made Frances Winwar consign her autobiography to the flames of her studio fireplace. Yet it did not prevent her from writing and producing a prolific resume of biographical works and historical novels throughout her long life (1900–1985). Born Francesca Vinciguerra in Taormina, Sicily, Winwar migrated to America with her parents in 1907. She never forgot her beloved Sicily, which is memorialized in *Pagan Interval* (1929), a novel set on the Mediterranean island of Ennios. Frances Winwar's primary vocation was that of a writer. Her quick acquisition of the English language and recognized talent for writing in school made the choice to write throughout her career a seemingly effortless one. Early on Winwar worked as a book reviewer, but she eventually claimed a reputation as a biographer and novelist. Reluctantly, she agreed to Anglicize her name to Winwar (a literal translation of her surname, Vinciguerra) for her first novel, *The Ardent Flame* (1927).

Winwar obviously did not see a contradiction between being a full-time writer and becoming a mother to her only son. But perhaps her four marriages indicate a conflict between literary aspiration and devotion to a spouse. Her book *Poor Splendid Wings* (1933) is a biography of the Rossetti family and achieved international recognition and received the prestigious Atlantic Monthly Award for best nonfiction book. Along with several other works, Winwar displays keen interest in things Italian, evidenced by her Italian settings and her subjects. *Poor Splendid Wings* details the lives of the pre-Raphaelite circle and the artistic movement in England in the late nineteenth century, which centered around such figures as Dante Gabriel Rossetti

W

and Algernon Swinburne. Winwar's ability to breathe life into these personages was the product of thorough research and an imagination fired by probing the psychology of her characters. She later wrote a biography on Edgar Allan Poe called *The Haunted Palace* (1959), which further demonstrates her interest in a writer's psychological journey. Frances Winwar's early achievements represent an important contribution to Italian American writing: her prolific imagination, her belief in her creative ability, her fascination with the internal workings of the writer's mind all anticipate later treatments of Italian American characters by such writers as Mari Tomasi and Octavia Waldo.

Both educated and well-read, Segale and Winwar reaped the benefits of their parents' belief in the intellectual development of their girl children. Yet the accounts of successful transplantation and assimilation into American culture would be incomplete without the story of Rosa Cassettari, an unlettered immigrant woman, who arrived in America in 1884. Born in a small village in the region of Lombardy, Rosa tells her story of unabated manual labor: from the silk-making factory in Bugiarno where the 7-year-old Rosa worked from dawn till dusk to the settlement house called the Chicago Commons, where she washed, scrubbed floors, and occasionally served as a cook. Though she never learned to read or write in Italian or English, Rosa gained fame as a storyteller and entertained guests at the Commons and at Hull House and Northwestern University. Narrating her story to friend and social worker Marie Hall Ets, Rosa recalls minute details of her life in *Rosa: The Life of an Italian Immigrant* (1970). Rosa's story depicts the epic saga of immigration and shares similar themes with many Italian American novels: the journey to America and the attendant difficulties of leaving the homeland and adapting to American ways; a strong and abiding belief in the efficacy of the Madonna, a figure of enormous strength for all believers, not only the peasant class; a determination to survive insurmountable odds—poverty, prejudice, lack of education—with resiliency and force of character; and, finally, a belief in America as a promised land, despite ceaseless struggle and privation.

A nineteenth-century nun, a twentieth-century woman of letters, and an unlettered storyteller—each emigrated from Italy to America in girlhood and documented her relationship to both her homeland and adopted countries. Their differences are instructive, clarifying the point that there is no monolithic identity for the Italian American woman or the writer. In various and complicated ways, each of these writers anticipated the stories told about Italian American lives by future generations of writers.

Moving to the fiction writers, Italian American women have overwhelmingly written novels about the family. Reared in families who struggled against poverty and worked hard to make life better for their children in America, it is no wonder that so many women have written about the domain to which they were tied. Of the over two million immigrants who arrived from Italy between the years 1899 and 1910, nearly 85 percent migrated from the Mezzogiorno, areas south and east of Rome. According to historians of southern Italian culture, the family was the only institution that provided comfort and trust. As a result, the emphasis on *la famiglia* and the rules attendant therein survived the transatlantic crossing, but not uniformly. Raised in an American milieu with its alluring emphasis on individualism and independence, the children of immigrants often felt confused by two contradictory value systems. Although the code of silence (*omertà*) was imposed within families to maintain honor and to keep families protected, Italian American women novelists chose the family as their subject, concomitantly breaking the silence and commemorating their cultural heritage.

Mari Tomasi's *Like Lesser Gods* (1949), Antonia Pola's *Who Can Buy the Stars?* (1957), and Marion Benasutti's *No Steady Job for Papa* (1966) share features of what may be called the immigrant saga. In each of these novels, the story of immigration and assimilation is viewed optimistically, the negative occurrences of prejudice and restriction deemphasized. In their attempts to portray successful examples of Italian immigrants' adjustment to American ways, Tomasi, Pola, and Benasutti deliberately underscore the *promise* of living in America, not the privation. The authors share several thematic and structural characteristics that are repeated and expanded on by the next generation of writers. Writing about emigration from northern Italy, the authors unfortunately succumb to spurious distinctions between the north and the south, reinforced by the northern Italian government and immigration authorities in America. Though they claim a northern Italian origination, the characters in these novels are subject to derogatory ethnic nomenclatures, forcing them to reconsider their positions as Italians in America and as ethnic Americans.

These novels focus on the development of the Italian family in America, not just the personal growth of the protagonists. By incorporating the family into their novelistic structure and theme, these writers enlarge the novel of formation or bildungsroman so that it includes a depiction of communal development, not just individual growth. Tomasi's second novel, *Like Lesser Gods,* insistently concerns itself with the development of a first- and second-generation Italian American family, whose assimilation into American society is aided and enriched by the development of a godparent figure. The use of such a figure is no anomaly in the Italian American literary tradition. Originally chosen to function as godparents at baptism or sponsors at confirmation, these figures take on a new role in America. Benasutti and Tomasi create such characters to function as mediators between homeland and inherited cultures. Second-generation children, often confused by their roles as Italian Americans, seek the help from an older, wiser figure, whose mediation is based on a love of the Italian culture and an awareness of the necessity of acquiring American traditions.

The conflict between generations, a prevailing theme in Italian American women's novels, is often resolved by the helpful ministrations of a godparent figure. When no such figure is available or when a godparent is ineffective, later writers such as Octavia Waldo and Josephine Gattuso Hendin explore the more severe ramifications of being Italian in America. Early in the tradition, however, Pola, Tomasi, and Benasutti hint at two themes that are more fully developed in later texts. The first is an emphasis on a double marginality for Italian immigrant women in America. The mothers in particular in these texts suffer because their roles as caretakers and teachers have been attenuated, though not destroyed, by what might be seen as rival institutions: the public school and the workplace. As their children learn another language and live more directly in another cul-ture outside the family, the mothers often lose the absolute control they had as sustainers of the household. Nonetheless, each novel—*Like Lesser Gods, Who Can Buy the Stars?,* and *No Steady Job for Papa*—celebrates the immigrant mother's resourcefulness and determination as she helps her family achieve emotional and financial stability in a new country. Benasutti deliberately emphasizes that the strength of the family belonged to its most determined achiever: the mother. While these mothers are able—with difficulty—to maintain their inviolate status as caretakers inside the family, they are nonetheless not highly valued outside the home as women or as Italians.

A second theme of concern to these writers has to do with the realistic occurrence of illness and its impact on the Italian American family. In each novel, actual instances of illness occur: the loss of an infant, a child, a husband. But what remains distinctive to these novels and to the Italian American women's tradition is the use of illness as a metaphor for living in America. Pola, Benasutti, and Tomasi embody this idea in characters whose relationships to the "old country" remain central to their understanding of themselves. For the mother in Pola's *Who Can Buy the Stars?* and the grandmother in Benasutti's *No Steady Job for Papa,* for example, Italy remains the country of health and beauty. America, for each of them, becomes equated with illness and death; Italy remains untarnished, the land of redemption. In ironic contrast to nineteenth-century American writers such as Hawthorne and James, who place their characters in Italy for lessons in decadence, the writers of Italian descent in twentieth-century America reverse this trend. As much as America has been promoted as a Garden of Eden, actual life for Italian immigrants has been more akin to a Dantean hell. Later writers in the Italian American tradition return to Sicily and Italy and are able to test their grandparents' unmediated vision of Italy against actuality. Such writers as Susan Caperna Lloyd (*No Pictures in My Grave,* 1992), Barbara Grizzuti Harrison (*Italian Days,* 1989), and Anna Monardo (*The Courtyard of Dreams,* 1992) return themselves or create characters whose return to Italy forces a reconsideration of the earlier novels in the tradition. Nonetheless, for Pola and Benasutti, especially, Italy remains the land of milk and honey; America becomes the country of suffering and death.

W

For the writers such as Helen Barolini, Dorothy Bryant, Diana Cavallo, Julia Savarese, Octavia Capuzzi Waldo (Locke), Tina De Rosa, Carole Maso, and Josephine Gattuso Hendin, the family remains central to the characters' sense of identity, but with important distinctions. Barolini's multigenerational novel, *Umbertina* (1979), covers four generations of women's development, spanning the years 1860 through approximately 1975. What makes this novel pivotal in the Italian American women's tradition is its ability to embrace the traditional subject (family) and the traditional form (immigrant saga, bildungsroman) and endow them with a distinctively feminist perspective, without being anachronistic or polemical. The Italian American women's tradition needed a big novel with a focus on women's development throughout the generations, and Barolini's *Umbertina* provides the material. Because the family remains central to these novels, one of the figures that takes preeminence is the grandmother. Barolini's *Umbertina,* De Rosa's *Paper Fish* (1980), and Maso's *Ghost Dance* (1985) reconstruct the essential relationship between grandmother and granddaughter. Writing from the perspective of the third generation, Barolini, De Rosa, and Maso suggest that granddaughters receive life-sustaining legacies from these ancestors. From grandmothers, girl characters are given the cultural heritage through stories, rituals, and symbols. Able to retrieve the past through their grandmothers and invent a viable ethnic identity for themselves, the granddaughters (the great-granddaughter in *Umbertina*) enter adulthood with a fuller understanding of cultural identity and the language to maintain and nurture that identity.

Without the benefit of godparents and/or grandparents, the characters' development is subject to conflict and anguish. Julia Savarese's *The Weak and the Strong* (1952), Octavia Waldo Locke's *A Cup of the Sun* (1961), and Josephine Gattuso Hendin's *The Right Thing To Do* (1988) portray Italian American families suffering in various ways: unabated poverty and squalor in New York City's tenements during the Great Depression of the 1930s in Savarese's novel; psychological torment and madness in an Italian American community on the outskirts of Philadelphia during World War II in Locke's novel; and father-daughter conflict, which becomes sym-

bolic of the fate of the Italian American family in Astoria and Manhattan's Little Italy in Hendon's novel. Each of these novels offers another reading of Italian American culture. Savarese refuses to structure her novel around the dictates of the bildungsroman; she instead depicts families who are unable to develop, despite hard work and good intentions. Locke explores the Italians' belief in *destino* (destiny, fate), *mal'occhio* (evil eye), and *onore* (honor) in order to dramatize the conflict between Italian and American cultures and between immigrant parents and their increasingly Americanized children. In a similar way, Hendon explores the implications of the father's belief in *onore* and how his behavior both harnesses and liberates his only daughter. Locke and Hendon in particular are unafraid of probing the sometimes negative and always complicated results of being raised a female in a male-dominated Italian American family. They offer the flip side of Tomasi, Benasutti, Barolini, and DeRosa in their emphasis on demanding and interrogating fathers.

While upon first reading, it may seem as though Diana Cavallo (*A Bridge of Leaves,* 1961) and Dorothy Bryant (*Miss Giardino,* 1978) have jettisoned the Italian American family in favor of exploring individual development, both novels are fundamentally concerned with the family's impact on a young person's formation. Both writers in fact anticipate the narratives written in the nineties in their emphasis on a kind of submerged or covert ethnicity. For the 30-year-old male narrator of *A Bridge of Leaves* and the 68-year-old retired high school teacher of *Miss Giardino,* healthy development means returning in memory to a past that hurt, confused, angered, and nurtured them. What they discover is vital to their development: features of *Italianità* that they had buried, suppressed, and willfully forgotten. Cavallo and Bryant extend the theme of illness by focusing on how their protagonists recover from illnesses related specifically to their personalities. Each novel traces the characters' struggle to recuperate mentally as they wrestle with painful memories of loss (of grandparents, parents, siblings) and repudiation (for their "Americanness," for their education, for their rebellion against the Italian family). In this way, Cavallo and Bryant foreshadow two novels written in the 1980s: Dodici Azpadu's *Saturday Night in the Prime of Life* (1983) and Rachel Guido deVries's *Tender Warriors* (1986). As in so many novels of the Italian American women's tradition, these also focus on the family's effect on the development of the female protagonist. Azpadu and deVries further complicate the family narrative by introducing a lesbian character who refuses to abide by the imposition of *omertà* and openly reveals her sexual orientation. Other writers have also incorporated the issue of lesbianism into their narratives about the family: Susan Leonardi's collection, *Nun Stories,* Giovanna (Janet) Capone's "Holy Ghosts," and Rita Ciresi's "La Stella d'Oro" are recent examples of such works.

Describing only those novels that overtly emphasize Italian American ethnicity overlooks several other works that only tangentially, if at all, touch on the topic. In particular, Helen Barolini, Dorothy Bryant, and Carole Maso continue to write novels about other subjects, demonstrating their talent in equally interesting arenas. *Love in the Middle Ages,* Barolini's second novel (1986), focuses on the relationship between a middle-aged widow and a divorced businessman. Throughout her career, Barolini's creative interests have taken her into other genres, including the essay. She has written about topics as wide-ranging as the Italian literary-prize business, humorously portrayed in "Neruda vs. Sartre at the Sea," and her mother's inclination for collecting Americana in "The Finer Things in Life," both of which are published in a collection of her essays, *Chiaroscuro: Essays on Italian-American Culture,* which is being republished by Guernica Editions. Barolini's volume of recipes called *Festa: Recipes and Recollections of Italian Holidays* (1988) is more than merely a listing of favorite Italian foods. It represents Barolini's passion for Italian culture as she offers readers delectable recipes, taking us on a sacred and secular excursion, by recalling the holidays and saints' days celebrated by Italians throughout each month of the year. Like her book *Festa,* Barolini's *Aldus and His Dream Book* (1992) is learned and thorough, a beautifully written tribute to the late-fifteenth- and early-sixteenth-century Venetian scholar-publisher Aldus Manutius. Speaking about her novel *Umbertina,* Barolini once explained that she was not a linguistic stylist first and foremost. However, Barolini's essayistic prose style in *Festa* and her sundry writings belie that statement by proving their stylistic virtuosity.

Likewise, Dorothy Bryant remains a prolific writer, having written ten novels, three plays, and one nonfiction book about writing, *Writing a Novel* (1978). Though *Miss Giardino* remains centrally located in the Italian American literary tradition, other novels of hers such as *A Day in San Francisco* (1982), *The Test* (1991), and *Anita, Anita* (1993) use elements of Italian and Italian American culture. Skilled at focusing on one character's troubled situation, Bryant incorporates modernist narrative strategies such as overlapping stories and internal monologue to flesh out the complications between characters. Highly interested in the marginal figure—a staple of American literature—Bryant regularly makes central to her fiction disenfranchised women, gay men, aged, ill, and disabled people, including a blind woman, who births her own baby in *The Garden of Eros* (1979). For Bryant, making marginal characters central to her narratives repositions them in American culture as valid and necessary, without which the world of the text is incomplete.

Carole Maso explores the multidimensional text skillfully in her novels *Ghost Dance* (1986), *The Art Lover* (1990), *Ava* (1993), and *The American Woman in the Chinese Hat* (1994). Awarded the prestigious Lannan fellowship of $50,000 for writers who demonstrate potential for outstanding future work, Maso has already proven to be a remarkably versatile writer. Only *Ghost Dance,* the most modernist of her novels, overtly incorporates Italian American characters and themes, though this is only one of the threads interlaced throughout the novel. Like Bryant, Maso is fascinated by the marginal character—the lesbian, the AIDS victim, the poet who struggles with mental illness, the woman dying of a rare blood disease. Equally fascinated by contemporary French feminist theory, Maso's innovation with language, especially in *Ava,* takes her well beyond the modernist text. Believing, like Helene Cixous, that she must arrive at a language that heals as much as it separates, Maso experiments with multiple and interacting layers of plot and character and repeated phrases and imagery to produce a poetic and musical language that resists closure.

Writers in the 1990s continue to produce both traditionally realistic novels about Italian American themes and modernist and postmodern texts that inscribe ethnicity in subtle and innovative ways. Writers such as Anne Paolucci (*Sepia Tones,* 1985) and Anna Monardo (*The Courtyard of Dreams,* 1993) continue in the tradition of characterizing Italian American lives with poignancy and lyricism. Other writers such as Denise Giardina (*Storming Heaven,* 1987), Lynn Vannucci (*Coyote,* 1987), and Mary Caponegro (*The Star Cafe & Other Stories,* 1990) do not choose overtly to focus on Italian American themes. However, a story like Caponegro's "Materia Prima" is about the family and the child's imaginative ability to re-create the family in prose. Other collections of short stories continue to impress and receive literary awards: Rita Ciresi's *Mother Rocket* (1993) won the Flannery O'Connor award for short fiction; Anne Calcagno's *Pray For Yourself and Other Stories* (1993) received the James D. Phelan Award; Renee Manfredi's *Where Loves Leaves Us* (1994) won the Iowa Short Fiction Award. Once again, these stories deserve serious consideration for their emphasis on the instability of relationships and families in the late twentieth century. A story like Ciresi's *Mother Rocket* is a tour de force about being different—being ethnic. Agnes Rossi's *The Quick: A Novella and Stories* (1992) and *Split Skirt* (1994) similarly focus on troubled relationships, the category of class position often influencing the characters in crisis. Although submerged, the Italian American ethnicity of Marie Russo's complicated familial life in Rossi's *The Quick* encourages an analysis of family and identity through the lens of class.

Italian American women writers of prose continue producing a plethora of literary works, incorporating issues of identity and ethnicity in daring and innovative ways. For example, Gloria Vitanza Basile's *The House of Lions* (1976), Nancy Maniscalco's *Lesser Sins* (1979), and Louise Ermelino's *Joey Dee Gets Wise* (1991) tackle a topic formerly limited to male writers and directors: the Mafia and its dire implications on family and community.

Several women writers of Italian American descent have produced works in more than one genre, including poetry. Some of them include Rose Basile Green (*To Reason Why,* n.d.); Anne Paolucci (*Riding the Mast Where It Swings,* 1980; *Queensboro Bridge and Other Poems,* 1995); Diane di Prima, who selected poems from her many publications for *Pieces of a Song* (1990); Sandra

Gilbert (*Emily's Bread,* 1984; *Blood Pressure,* 1988); Daniela Gioseffi (*Eggs in the Lake,* 1979; *Word Wounds and Water Flowers,* 1995); and Rachel Guido deVries (*How To Sing to a Dago,* 1996). Along with the generous representation of Italian American women poets in *The Dream Book* and *From the Margin,* individual female poets have been instrumental in bringing to recognition the contributions of Italian Americans.

Rose Romano, former editor of the journal *la bella figura,* published a series of chapbooks out of *malafemmina* press to insure that the voices who spoke so eloquently in the journal continued to be heard: Maria Mazziotti Gillan's *Taking Back My Name* (1991); Maria Fama's *Identification* (1991); Carmela Delia Lanza *Long Island Girl* (1992); Rina Ferrarelli's *Dreamsearch* (1992); and Lenore Baeli Wang's *Born in the Year of the Pink Sink* (n.d.). Romano, a poet herself, has written extensively and passionately on the intersection between Italian American and sexuality identities in *Vendetta* (1990) and *The Wop Factor* (1994). Her anthology, *la bella figura: a choice,* represents yet another attempt to collect the prose and poetry that appeared between the years 1988 and 1992 in the journal of that name. Introduced by scholar and critic Lucia Chiavola Birnbaum, Romano's collection functions as a recovery, a "rescuing [of] the memory in this country [America]," as Birnbaum puts it. Mary Russo Demetrick (*First Pressing,* 1994) and Maria Fama collaborated on a book of poems that share topics such as the Catholic Mass and visits to Italy and Sicily. Their book is entitled *Italian Notebook* (1995).

Maria Mazziotti Gillan has been highly instrumental in promoting the contributions of Italian American women poets. Gillan's editorship of *Footwork: The Paterson Literary Review* continues to be a place where ethnic voices are heard, including Italian American. Writers such as Phyllis Capello, Mary Cappello, Rita Ciresi (fiction), Lisa Ruffolo (fiction), Vittoria Repetto, Roseanne Lucia Quinn, Jennifer Lagier, Maria Fama, Daniela Gioseffi, and Diane di Prima continue to sprinkle the pages of this impressive journal. Gillan demonstrates her awareness of the necessity of presenting the contributions of Italian American poets in the larger arena of American literature. Her collection, co-edited with her daughter, Jennifer Gillan, is called *Unsettling America: An Anthology of Con-*

temporary *Multicultural Poetry* (1994). What makes this anthology so important is its emphasis on multiculturalism; that is, bringing the diverse voices of America together in an effort to examine shared themes about the relationship between identity and ethnicity. Gillan uses Italian American themes in many of her own poems, which have been collected in *Where I Come From: Selected and New Poems* (1995). One of Gillan's chapbooks, *The Weather of Old Seasons* (1989), focuses on the ongoing importance of cultural heritage to this poet's life. *Flowers from the Tree of Night* (1981) and *Winter Light* (1985), earlier books of poetry, anticipate Gillan's devotion to Italian American ethnicity in such poems as "Betrayals" and "Public School No. 18, Paterson, New Jersey." Cognizant of the importance of establishing a continuing relationship between Italian America and Italy, Gillan was the 1987 recipient of the ALTA (American Translators Association Award) for the translation of her second book of poetry, *Winter Light,* which is called *Luce d'Inverno* (1988) in its bilingual publication.

Poets such as Daniela Gioseffi, Maria Gillan, and Rose Romano often use the topic of their ethnicity as an entry way into the language of poetry. But they are not limited by such a topic, nor do they limit themselves to writing narrowly about Italian American identity. In a similar way, the topic of family and the country of Italy remain vital places where the poetic imagination is fueled for poets Diane Raptosh and Jean Feraca. Raptosh's *Just West of Now* (1992) and Feraca's *South From Rome: Il Mezzogiorno* (1976) and *Crossing the Great Divide* (1988) incorporate scenes of Italian American life and the moral and literal topography of America and Italy. Like Raptosh and Feraca, Kathryn Nocerino (*Death of the Plankton Bar & Grill,* 1987) and Claudia Menza (*The Lunatic's Ball,* 1994) are equally interested in the effect of place on the poetic imagination. Urban scenes dominate their poetry, offering surrealistic images of the harshness and absurdity of city living.

A poet like Leslie Scalapino (*Considering How Exaggerated Music Is,* 1982) does not ostensibly use Italian American themes, but her innovative use of the prose-like poem and utter lack of predictability in her poetic line make her an important contributor to modern poetry. Likewise, Diane di Prima is considered one of the foremost voices of the sixties Beat generation. She captures that era quite well in her prose work, *Memoirs of a Beatnik* (1969), and she has recently written an autobiography that details her life in an Italian American family before she left home (*Recollections of My Life as Woman,* 1996). Di Prima remains preeminently an extraordinarily gifted poet, some of whose elegiac poems at times recall her familial past: "To My Father," "Prayer to the Ancestors," "Minnesota Morning Ode," and "To My Father–2." Like many poets in the Italian American tradition, di Prima uses the topic of ethnicity as one of many strands in the multitextured layers of her poetry. Italian American identity does not limit writers like Gillan, Paolucci, and di Prima; rather, it enriches their language.

It is clear that Italian American women writers have significantly contributed to the mosaic that constitutes American literature. Recognizing that they share a tradition further inspires literary activity and collegiality among scholars, creative writers, and reviewers. Serious attention and advocacy need to be given to these writers, ensuring that they stay in print and therefore remain accessible to future writers and critics. The above listing of authors does not pretend to be exhaustive; rather, it contributes to the ongoing conversation about Italian American culture in an attempt to give women's writings a prominent position in that tradition.

Mary Jo Bona

Bibliography

Ahearn, Carol Bonomo. "Interview: Helen Barolini." *Fra Noi* (September 1986): 47.

Barolini, Helen, ed. *The Dream Book: An Anthology of Writings by Italian American Women.* New York: Schocken, 1985.

Bona, Mary Jo, ed. *The Voices We Carry: Recent Italian/American Women's Fiction.* New York: Guernica, 1994.

Gabaccia, Donna. "Italian American Women: A Review Essay." *Italian Americana* 12 (fall/winter 1993): 38–61.

Gardaphé, Fred L. *The Italian-American Writer: An Essay and an Annotated Checklist.* Spencertown, NY: Forkroads, 1995.

Green, Rose Basile. *The Italian-American Novel: A Document of the Interaction of Two Cultures.* Rutherford, NJ: Fairleigh Dickinson University Press, 1974.

Peragallo, Olga. *Italian-American Authors and Their Contribution to American Literature*. New York: S. F. Vanni, 1949.

Tamburri, Anthony Julian, Paolo A. Giordano, and Fred L. Gardaphé, eds. *From the Margin: Writings in Italian Americana*. West Lafayette: Purdue University Press, 1991.

See also AUTOBIOGRAPHY; LITERATURE; NOVELS AND NOVELISTS; POETRY

World War II, Internment, and Prisoners of War

The approaching Second World War brought a resurgence of anti-Italian sentiment that had largely declined in the 1930s with the virtual end of immigration from southern Europe. Americans perceived that first- and second-generation Italian Americans still clung to their ethnic identity and remained in contact with relatives in the homeland. Some Italians took pride in Mussolini's success overseas and supported Italian American newspapers that urged immigrants to help the *patria* (country, fatherland) financially and morally. Americans questioned why Italians had the largest number of noncitizens of any immigrant group—six hundred thousand in 1942—and saw this as an indication of disloyalty. Americans looked with increasing suspicion on the ethnic cohesiveness of Italian communities throughout the country.

The first indication that Italian Americans might suffer discriminatory treatment as a result of the war came with the fall of France in June 1940. Congress passed the Alien Registration Act (Smith Act), requiring all noncitizens 14 years and older to be fingerprinted and to register at the nearest post office. This was relatively mild when compared to what would follow after the bombing of Pearl Harbor on December 7, 1941. When the United States entered the war, President Franklin Roosevelt ordered the arrest of Italian and German aliens who had been identified by the Federal Bureau of Investigation as potentially dangerous. During the next few weeks, enemy aliens had to surrender firearms, cameras, radios, ammunition, explosives, maps, signaling devices, and other "dangerous" items. Government officials promised to return these possessions after the war, a promise that was not kept in many cases. A ban prohibited aliens from traveling five miles beyond home or work without special permission. On January 15, 1942, Attorney General Francis Biddle ordered nationwide registration of aliens 14 years and older, which went beyond that of the Smith Act by requiring aliens to carry an identification card with their fingerprint and photograph. Italians countered this show of racism by expressions of loyalty. Shop owners displayed President Roosevelt's photo, Italian American newspapers professed support for the Allied war effort, Italian American organizations passed resolutions of loyalty to the United States, and thousands of Italian American men enlisted.

Fear of internment overshadowed Italian communities in the first several months of war. Local governmental groups and officials, citizen groups, and newspapers became involved in the debate over whether entire alien groups or just individual aliens should be interned as well as which of the alien groups was the most dangerous. A bitter struggle developed between General John L. DeWitt, who argued for internment of Italians, Germans, and Japanese, and Attorney General Biddle, who questioned the internment of all aliens as opposed to just selected individuals. The severest blow came in late January 1942, when the government announced that eighty-six prohibited and restricted zones on the west coast had to be cleared of aliens.

Restrictions placed on California's fifty-two thousand Italian aliens were more severe than on the East and Gulf coasts because of a greater fear of invasion plus the suspicious nature of General John DeWitt, commander of the Army's Western Defense, who wanted all enemy aliens relocated. In fact, an estimated ten thousand Italians in "prohibited" coastal and military areas did have to relocate. Included were families whose Navy sons had been killed when the Japanese attacked Pearl Harbor. Even though the spouse or other family members might be United States citizens, the enemy alien—often elderly—had to leave the family and find housing out of the designated zones between February and July 1, 1942, when, without explanation, they were allowed to return home.

All enemy aliens were required to register at local post offices, carry photo-identification cards, and surrender to local police certain contraband items (guns, shortwave radios, cameras, and signaling devices). In most areas in California, they were also subject to curfew from 8:00 P.M. to 6:00 A.M. and forbidden to travel more than five miles from home. The FBI searched their homes and arrested aliens for possession of contraband items not already turned in. Those who violated curfew hours were liable to arrest; no exceptions were granted, not even to those whose work was located in prohibited areas or where work hours exceeded the curfew. Many coastal fishermen were Italian aliens now forbidden to fish in coastal waters, and many of their boats were commandeered by the U.S. Coast Guard for the war's duration. These restrictions were lifted in October 1942, when the attorney general announced that Italians had proven themselves to be "responsible" citizens. Some analysts suggest that this decision was made just prior to the November elections in order to win support of the large Italian American vote.

The most egregious action was the arrest and internment of several hundred Italian aliens who were deemed dangerous. While other actions regarding enemy aliens derived from executive orders or army proclamations issued after the declaration of war, the internment was based on Title 50 of the United States Code, a statutory provision with origins in the 1798 Alien and Sedition Acts. The dangerous list consisted primarily of members of the Federation of Italian War Veterans and staffs of formerly pro-Mussolini newspapers or Italian language schools. Even some naturalized citizens were listed as "dangerous," and twenty-four naturalized Italians were ordered in the fall of 1942 to move out of California's prohibited zones—by then extended to most cities in the western half of the state. This happened nine or ten months after the war's start and lasted before Italians were dropped from the enemy alien category. Those interned or excluded, however, did not regain their freedom until late 1943, after Italy had joined the Allies.

Researchers have found no evidence in FBI and other archival records indicating that any of these dangerous persons had acted or would have acted in any way inimical to this country. In fact, the evidence was to the contrary: most had American-born children or spouses, were law-abiding, and would have done nothing to endanger the United States. Some were even anti-fascist; others were apolitical. The Italian War Veterans fought with the Allies against Germany in World War I and, although they collected funds for Italy prior to U.S. entry into the Second World War, there was no evidence they planned to help Germany. Most were longtime residents of this land; their failure to obtain final citizenship papers was not due to lack of patriotism.

This World War II story has not been completely resolved more than fifty years later. Many have wanted to forget their experiences, and some families still will not talk about this aspect of the war. Only recently have scholars begun to investigate the topic, unknown even to many Italian Americans. Government archives have not revealed the entire experience and some documents are still classified or censored. What is known is that three thousand Italian Americans were arrested in California: several hundred from the dangerous list, half being released after short detentions, and the others interned for up to two years; still others were arrested and detained for up to two months for curfew violations or possession of contraband.

While some Americans believe these governmental actions were justified during wartime, scholars generally conclude there were severe violations of civil rights, unnecessary even in war. Aliens were, in fact, subjected to unreasonable search and seizure, not permitted legal counsel at internment or exclusion hearings nor informed of evidence against them, thus being denied due process. Even Attorney General Francis Biddle wrote in a 1943 memo that the "dangerous" classification was invalid as it had no statutory authorization, was unreliable in the absence of evidence, and should never again be used. Moreover, the application of the emeny alien regulations was uneven and unfair, affecting Italians randomly. Although West Coast Italians were subject to more restrictions, the much larger eastern population—although geographically closer to a potential invation from Europe—was relatively less affected.

The possibility of interning Italian aliens gradually disappeared as the government realized that sheer numbers made it an insurmountable administrative problem. In addition, it would hinder war production, disrupt the economy, and have political ramifications in the 1942 congressional elections. On October 12 (appropriately Columbus Day), 1942, the government lifted remaining travel and curfew provisions, implemented simplified procedures for naturalization of aliens, and abrogated the enemy classification of Italian aliens.

Treatment of Italian prisoners of war (POWs) was one of numerous wartime problems that had no simple or satisfactory answer. The first POWs came to the United States in 1943 as Britain virtually ran out of space and pleaded for help in maintaining the increasing number of enemy captives. Most were captured in North Africa, Sicily, and southern Italy. Eventually 375,000 German and fifty thousand Italian POWs went through processing centers to settle in camps across the country. At first, Italians went to southern and southwestern camps in Colorado, Missouri, Arizona, Utah, Georgia, Texas, and Tennessee. The U.S. government adhered to the 1929 Geneva Convention Relative to the Treatment of Prisoners of War that prohibited prisoners from engaging in war-related work. But there was no shortage of permissible work available for which prisoners volunteered to escape boredom and to earn extra pay. Farmers and ranchers near POW camps contracted for workers, picking them up at camp at 7:00 A.M. and returning them by 5:00 P.M. POWs supplied much needed farm labor helping to plant and harvest corn, cotton, peanuts, onions, potatoes, carrots, and sugar beets. In New Mexico a few prisoners became cowboys, roping and branding calves. When fields were some distance from the base camps, temporary branch camps formed using high school gymnasiums, National Guard armories, vacant warehouses, and dormitories provided by Great Western Sugar Company for housing. Townspeople greeted POWs with curiosity rather than fear and watched as they cheerfully sang on their way to work and played soccer with town teams for recreation.

When Italy became a cobelligerent in October 1943, the status of Italian POWs changed. Italy's new leader, Marshal Pietro Badoglio, declared that all POWs should help the Allied cause, but how this would be accomplished was a source of friction between Badoglio and General Dwight Eisenhower. No longer subject to the 1929 Geneva Convention, Italian prisoners could engage in any labor short of combat. As a way of channeling this new source of labor, the United States created Italian Service Units (ISUs) in early 1944 and recruited Italian prisoners to join. They agreed to help America in the war against Germany and to obey orders from American military of-

ficers. In return, "volunteers" received eight dollars of their twenty-four-dollar-a-month salary in cash and sixteen dollars in canteen coupons. They could have visits from relatives, expanded mail privileges, and the chance to leave base on weekends if accompanied by an American military escort. As of June 1944, 33,672 enlisted men and 1,090 officers out of 44,335 enlisted men and 3,278 officers in the POW camps signed up. The army identified approximately two thousand Italian prisoners as "Fascists" who were ineligible to become ISU members. Those who refused to volunteer were not being unpatriotic, but legitimately feared endangering family in northern Italy or compromising their standing in the Italian army.

German POWs quickly replaced Italians in agricultural areas as the Italians went to coastal and industrial sites for combat-related work. Some Italian POWs enrolled in special training programs and English classes. But so desperate was the need for manpower that many had to leave training and learn on the job. As a means of identification, ISU members wore surplus or used U.S. Army uniforms with all buttons and insignia removed. A green broussard with "Italy" in white letters was sewn on the left sleeve halfway between the elbow and shoulder. The front of the service hat bore a green and red circular cloth patch with "Italy" in white letters.

The government designated Fort Wadsworth, Staten Island, New York, as headquarters for the Italian Service Units and named Brigadier General John M. Eager as chief administrator. General Eager had served as military attaché at the American embassy in Rome, was fluent in Italian, and sensitive to discrimination visited upon the POWs from time to time. His office coordinated food, clothing, and housing for the two hundred ISUs. One of his least desirable jobs was to answer complaints by citizens who believed the prisoners received preferential treatment while American boys fought overseas.

Italian communities along the East Coast delighted in having the Italian POWs nearby. Churches, Italian organizations, and individual families hosted groups of Italians at banquets, dances, trips to the opera, and other social functions with local women. There was no shortage of invitations for Christmas and holidays when Italian women prepared sumptuous meals for the men. But many townspeople resented this special treatment and called it coddling. Newspaper editorials joined in the criticism. As a result, excursions to cities were curtailed and many POWs felt that they had been deceived by exaggerated promises when they joined the ISU.

Social mixing inevitably led to romance. All POWs had to return home, but this did not keep Italian American women from writing to President Franklin Roosevelt, Eleanor Roosevelt, and Secretary of War Henry Stimson pleading to exempt their fiancés who in some instances had fathered a child. Although marriages were forbidden, a few took place, which enabled husbands to return to the United States much more quickly than those who waited for their women to come to Italy to wed and then return to the States.

As the war drew to a close, General Eager asked that ISU men be repatriated quickly as a reward for their war contribution. They received a larger baggage allowance than non-ISU members and were permitted to take items purchased or given to them by friends—frequently rationed to the general public. Finally, a debate arose over whether ISU members should receive a certificate of service. A proposed certificate was drafted but apparently never implemented. On repatriation their ISU form was stamped VOID in red letters and given to them as a souvenir.

The war had placed Italian POWs in an ambivalent situation. Americans who had husbands, sons, or brothers fighting and dying overseas were understandably angered to see POWs enjoying themselves at social events. Yet those who worked closely with Italian volunteers knew how they had substantially contributed to the Allied victory. Fortunately at least some of the young men found friendship and understanding in the Italian communities that reached out to make the soldiers' lives away from home a little more tolerable. Their situation represented the complexity of war on the home front.

Janet E. Worrall
Rose D. Scherini

Bibliography

Diggins, John P. *Mussolini and Fascism, The View from America*. Princeton: Princeton University Press, 1972.

DiStasi, Lawrence, ed. *Una Storia Segreta: When Italian Americans Were Enemy Aliens*. Berkeley: American Italian Historical Association, Western Regional Chaper, 1994.

Dunn, Geoffrey. "Male Notte: Santa Cruz Italian Relocation and Restrictions During World War II." *Santa Cruz County History Journal* 1 (1994): 83–89.

Fox, Stephen. *The Unknown Internment: An Oral History of the Relocation of Italian Americans during World War II*. Boston: Twayne, 1990.

Keefer, Louis. "Italian POW's and the Italian American Community, 1943–1945: An Overview." In *Italian Americans and Their Public and Private Lives*, edited by Frank J. Cavaioli, Angela Danzi, and Salvatore J. LaGumina, 48–53. New York: American Italian Historical Association, 1987.

———. *Italian Prisoners of War in America 1942–1946, Captive or Allies?* New York: Praeger, 1992.

Lothrop, Gloria Ricci. "The Untold Story: The Effect of the Second World War on California Italians." *Journal of the West* 35, no. 1 (1996): 6–14.

Moore, John Hammond. "Italian POWs in America: War Is Not Always Hell." *Prologue* (fall 1976): 141–151.

Pozzetta, George E. "My Children Are My Jewels: Italian American Generations during World War II." In *Home-front War: World War II and American Society*, edited by Kenneth P. O'Brien and Lynn H. Parsons. Westport, CT: Greenwood, 1995.

Scherini, Rose D. "The Fascist/Anti-Fascist Struggle in San Francisco." In *New Explorations in Italian American Studies*, edited by Richard N. Juliani and Sandra P. Juliani, 63–71. New York: American Italian Historical Association, 1994.

Worrall, Janet E. "Italian Prisoners of War in the United States: 1943–45." In *Italian Americans in Transition*, edited by Joseph V. Scelsa, Salvatore J. LaGumina, and Lydio Tomasi, 253–261. New York: American Italian Historical Association, 1990.

———. "Reflections on Italian Prisoners of War: Fort Wadsworth, 1943–46." *Italian Americana* 10 (spring/summer 1992): 147–155.

See also FASCISM; WARTIME MILITARY AND HOME FRONT ACTIVITIES

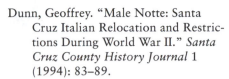

Z

Zambelli Family
See FIREWORKS INDUSTRY

Zappulla, Joseph (1901–1977)
A significant contributor to Italian American literary life, Joseph Zappulla was born in Sicily. With a limited education he migrated to the United States as a young man and became a self-taught man of letters.

He worked as a writer for several Italian American newspapers in various cities, wrote scripts for Italian American radio, and published his own Italian American newspaper and literary journals. His crowning achievement was his poetry, for which he received acclaim from noted critics. Linguist Mario Pei admired Zappulla's "purity of form," "the clarity of ideas," "his absolute mastery of the Italian language," "the exquisiteness of his feelings," ". . . a man who writes in the noble tradition of Alfieri and Fascolo, of Leopardi and Carducci, a man who doesn't give up the struggle and resign himself to obscure language."

His published books, *Voci nell'ombra* (1924), *Vette e abissi: Liriche e poemi* (1936), *Mette lontane* (1962), and *Poesi* (1965), were written and published in Italian. His writings capture the poignancy and pecu-liar fate of the immigrant; he used multi-faceted emotional strains, sadness, tenderness, and soul-searching motifs to capture his subject. Zappulla expressed these sentiments in a poem that recounts his return to Sicily after many years to see his dying mother:

> How sad returning to the ancient land
> Where time stagnates, Cold invades
> the old houses; lonely snowcapped
> hills give no leaf a welcome
> nor full moon smile to the returning
> guest. I do not find
> the good I left behind. Nothing is
>   changed
> yet one and all are strange and indifferent.
> The change lies in me. Time and distance
> have placed a cold barrier
> between my land and me. The gone years
> are dead, dead. Of the gay childhood
> only inutile regrets remain.

> *Salvatore J. LaGumina*

Bibliography
Alfonsi, Ferdinando. *Italo-American Poets.*
    Catanzaro, Italy: Antonio Carello, 1985.
*American Italian Historical Association
    Newsletter.* No. 2 (December 1977): 10.

See also POETRY

Index

Barbera, Joseph, 94–95
Barbuti, Raymond J., 54–55, 608, 614
Barelli, I., 75
Barelli, Joseph, 75
Barelli and Co., 75
Barili, Clotilda, 428
Barolini, Antonio, 55
Barolini, Helen, 45, 49, 55–56, 342, 343,
    345, 346, 694–695, 698, 699
Baroni, Geno C., 56–58, 115, 401
Barre, Raoul, 94
Barre, Vermont, 424, 425
Barriscale, Bessie, 388
Barsotti, Carlo, 76–77, 510
Bart, Anna, 346
Bartoletti, Efrem, 525
Barziza, Decimus et Ultimus, 670
Basile, Gloria Vitanza, 700
Basilone, John, 365–366
Bassani, Giorgio, 303
Basso, Hamilton, 408
Bavasi, Emil J., 81
Bayma, Joseph, 285
Beccherini, Francesco, 115
Beck, James, 101
Behar, Joy (Josephine Occhiuto), 135
Being Born, 109
Belfi, John, 97
Bella figura, 47–48
Bellanca, Augusto, 58, 326, 525
Bellanca, Frank Merlo, 450, 525, 528
Bellanca, Giuseppe Mario, 58–59, 450, 561
Bellanca Airplane School, 59, 450
Belleville, New Jersey, 43
Bellini, Carlo, 286, 305
Belluschi, Pietro, 286
Belmont, New York, 43
Belmont-Cragin community, Chicago, 108
Beltrami, Giacomo Constantino, 206
Benasutti, Marion, 344, 410
Benjamin, Dorothy Park, 100
Bennett, Michael (Michael Bennett Di
    Figlia), 59–60, 167–168
Bennett, Tony (Anthony Dominick
    Benedetto), 96, 239, 491, 627
Bensonhurst, New York, 43, 290–291, 298,
    320, 333
Bentivoglio, Mary Constance, 683
Bentivoglio, Mary Magdalen, 683
Berardinelli, Nicola, 294
Berio, Luciano, 286
Bernardi, Adria, 107
Bernardin, Joseph, 60–61, 109, 111, 115
Berra, Lawrence Peter "Yogi," 61–62, 288,
609, 610
Bertelli, Angelo, 612
Bertelli, Giuseppe, 326, 524, 525, 620
Bertelli, Riccardo, 36
Bertinelli, Valerie, 626
Bertody, Francis, 368, 370
Bertoglio, Dominic, 76
Bertoglio Mercantile Co., 76
Bertoia, Harry, 38
Better World John LaCorte Institute, 330
Bevilacqua, Alexander, 516
Bevilacqua, Anthony J., 62–63
Biaggi, Jackie, 403
Biaggi, Mario, 128
Biaggini, Benjamin F., 81
Bianca No. 2, 38
Bianchi, Al, 611
Bianchi Opera Co., 428
Bianco, Carla, 240
Biasone, Dan, 611
Biasotti, Roberto, 22
Biesta, Federico, 512
Biggio, Craig, 610
Bimboni, Alberto, 139
Biondi, Frank, 81
Birth of Aviation in the United States, The,
    35
Biscaccianti, Eliza (Ostinelli), 63, 428
Black Hand, 154
Black Madonna, 681
Blackshirts, 528, 529
Blasis, Carlo, 164
Blue Island, Chicago, 107
Boccafoglio family, 675
Bocce, 63–64
Bodie, Ping, 609
Boehm, Edward Marshall, 64
Boehm, Helen Franzolin, 64–65, 81, 82
Boehm Porcelain Studio, 64
Boiardi, Hector, 65–66
Boitano, Brian, 614
Bollettino dell'Emigrazione, 548
Bonacci, Frank, 66
Bonanni, Pietro, 34
Bonaparte, Charles Joseph, 66–67, 330, 334
Bonaparte, Jerome Napoleon, 66
Bonaparte, Susan May (Williams), 66
Bonavita, Rose, 67–68
Bonetti, Edward, 413
Bonfanti, Maria, 164
Bono, Mary Jo, 346
Bono, Sonny (Salvator Philip), 493
Borgatti, Anthony A., Jr., 68
Borgese, G. A., 362

Maraschi, Anthony, 113, 285
Marcantonio, Vito, 356–358, 483, 529
Marca-Relli, Corrado, 39
March, James, 481
Marchello, Maurice, 294
Marchetti, Gino, 613
Marchione, Margherita Frances, 358
Marchisio, Juvenal, 12, 13
Marciano, Rocky, 358–359, 608, 611, 612
Marcioni, Italo, 359–360
Marconi, Guglielmo, 101, 449–450, 583
Margaret Fuller, 55
Margiotti, Charles, 482
Mariani, John, 675
Marimò, Carolina, 102
Marimpietri, Anzuino, 326
Marinaro, Ed, 613
Marini, Nicola, 3
Marino, James, 322
Mariucci, John, 614
Marotta, Kenny, 347
Marra, Joseph M., 285
Martell, Dominic A., 329
Martin, Dean (Dino Paul Crocetti),
    360–361, 490, 591, 592, 627
Martini, Louis M., 676
Martini, John, 670
Martino, Al (Alfred Cini), 493
Martino, Donald, 141
Martino, Frank D., 329
Martirano, Salvatore, 142
Martorella, Millie, 614
Martorella, Rosanne, 403
Maruan, Joseph, 370
Marvel Comics Group, 96, 97
Maryland
    Little Italy, 51–52
    newspapers/periodicals in, 516
Maryland Pressed Steel Corp., 59
Mascagni, Pietro, 428, 429
Mascari, Frank, 297
Masnata, Aloysius, 285
Maso, Carole, 346, 347, 698, 699
Mason, Jimilu, 35
Massachusetts
    Boston, 69, 532–533
    newspapers/periodicals in, 514
Massagli, Mark Tully, 329
Massari, Vincent, 294
Massaro, Salvatore. *See* Lang, Eddie
Massimino, Rollie, 610–611
Mastroserio, Rocco, 96
Mastro-Valerio, Alessandro, 530
Matera, Lia, 414

Matteo (Matteo Vittucci), 170
Mature, Victor, 227
Maturo, Joseph, 37
Mauran, Joseph, 368
May, Martin, 52
Mazza, Bob, 675
Mazzaro, Jerome, 477
Mazzei, Philip (Filippo), 84, 358, 361–362,
    368, 480, 497, 669, 675
Mazzella, Camillus, 286
Mazzilli, Lee, 609
Mazzini Society, 40, 58, 362–363, 435, 512
Mazzitello, Joseph Anthony, 452
Mazzo, Kay, 166
Mazzocchi, Tony, 329
Mazzucchelli, David, 98
Mazzuchelli, Samuel, 112, 363–365
McBain, Ed (Salvatore Lombino), 414
McCarran-Walters Act, 296, 547
McCarthy, Joseph, 143
McCluskey, John, 114
McDonald, Michael Cassius, 153
McLande, Guy Richards, 188
Medal of Honor winners, 365–366
Medical ethics, 366–368
Medici, Cosmo, 32
Medicine
    clinical, 370–372
    hospitals, 369
    physicians, 368–369
Melaragno, Olendo, 119
Mele, Sam, 610
Melfi, Leonard, 469–470
Melillo, Oscar, 609
Melrose Park, Chicago, 107
Memoirs of a Beatnik, 49
Mennin, Peter, 140
Menotti, Gian Carlo, 139–140, 372–373,
    430
Mental health, 373–376
Mental Retardation Institute, 266, 371
Mercante, Arthur L., 376–377, 611
Mercer, Johnny, 142, 143, 144
Merlino, Francesco Saverio, 523
Merola, Gaetano, 429
Messina, Mary Grace. *See* King, Morgana
Metro-Goldwyn-Mayer (MGM), 95
Metropolitan Museum of Art, 38, 39, 106
Metropolitan Opera Co., 258, 259, 428,
    430
Meucci, Antonio, 330, 377–378, 449, 584
Mezzogiorno, 193
Miceli, Frank, 345, 410, 411
Michelina food entrees, 81, 455